Brill's
New Pauly

ANTIQUITY
VOLUME 3

CAT-CYP

Brill's New Pauly

Brill's

Encyclopaedia of the Ancient World

New Pauly

Edited by
Hubert Cancik and
Helmuth Schneider

English Edition:
Managing Editor *Christine F. Salazar*
Assistant Editors *Astrid Möller, Antonia Ruppel
and David Warburton*

ANTIQUITY
VOLUME 3

CAT-CYP

BRILL
LEIDEN - BOSTON
2003

Originally published in German as DER NEUE
PAULY. Enzyklopädie der Antike. Herausgegeben
von Hubert Cancik und Helmuth Schneider.
Copyright © J.B. Metzlersche Verlagsbuch-
handlung und Carl Ernst Poeschel Verlag
GmbH 1996ff./1999ff. Stuttgart/Weimar

Cover design: TopicA (Antoinette Hanekuyk)
Front: Delphi, temple area
Spine: Tabula Peutingeriana

Translation by protext TRANSLATIONS B.V.

Data structuring and typesetting:
pagina GmbH, Tübingen, Germany

The publication of this work was supported
by a grant from the GOETHE-INSTITUT INTER
NATIONES.

ISBN (volume) 90 04 12266 4
ISBN (set) 90 04 12259 1

This book is printed on acid-free paper.

PRINTED IN THE NETHERLANDS

Table of Contents

Notes to the User

Arrangement of Entries

The entries are arranged alphabetically and, if applicable, placed in chronological order. In the case of alternative forms or sub-entries, cross-references will lead to the respective main entry. Composite entries can be found in more than one place (e.g. *a commentariis* refers to *commentariis, a*).

Identical entries are differentiated by numbering. Identical Greek and Oriental names are arranged chronologically without consideration of people's nicknames. Roman names are ordered alphabetically, first according to the *gentilicium* or *nomen* (family name), then the *cognomen* (literally 'additional name' or nickname) and finally the *praenomen* or 'fore-name' (e.g. M. *Aemilius Scaurus* is found under *Aemilius*, not *Scaurus*).

However, well-known classical authors are lemmatized according to their conventional names in English; this group of persons is not found under the family name, but under their *cognomen* (e.g. Cicero, not Tullius). In large entries the Republic and the Imperial period are treated separately.

Spelling of Entries

Greek words and names are as a rule latinized, following the predominant practice of reference works in the English language, with the notable exception of technical terms. Institutions and places (cities, rivers, islands, countries etc.) often have their conventional English names (e.g. *Rome* not *Roma*). The latinized versions of Greek names and words are generally followed by the Greek and the literal transliteration in brackets, e.g. *Aeschylus* (Αἰσχύλος; *Aischýlos*).

Oriental proper names are usually spelled according to the 'Tübinger Atlas des Vorderen Orients' (TAVO), but again conventional names in English are also used. In the maps, the names of cities, rivers, islands, countries etc. follow ancient spelling and are transliterated fully to allow for differences in time, e.g. both Καππαδόκια and *Cappadocia* can be found. The transliteration of non-Latin scripts can be found in the 'List of Transliterations'.

Latin and transliterated Greek words are italicized in the article text. However, where Greek transliterations do not follow immediately upon a word written in Greek, they will generally appear in italics, but without accents or makra.

Abbreviations

All abbreviations can be found in the 'List of Abbreviations' in the first volume. Collections of inscriptions, coins and papyri are listed under their *sigla*.

Bibliographies

Most entries have bibliographies, consisting of numbered and/or alphabetically organized references. References within the text to the numbered bibliographic items are in square brackets (e.g. [1.5 n.23] refers to the first title of the bibliography, page 5, note 23). The abbreviations within the bibliographies follow the rules of the 'List of Abbreviations'.

Maps

Texts and maps are closely linked and complementary, but some maps also treat problems outside the text. The authors of the maps are listed in the 'List of Maps'.

Cross-references

Articles are linked through a system of cross-references with an arrow → before the entry that is being referred to.

Cross-references to related entries are given at the end of an article, generally before the bibliographic notes. If reference is made to a homonymous entry, the respective number is also added.

Cross-references to entries in the *Classical Tradition* volumes are added in small capitals.

It can occur that in a cross-reference a name is spelled differently from the surrounding text: e.g., a cross-reference to Mark Antony has to be to Marcus → Antonius, as his name will be found in a list of other names containing the component 'Antonius'.

List of Transliterations

Transliteration of ancient Greek

α	a	alpha
αι	ai	
αυ	au	
β	b	beta
γ	g	gamma; γ before γ, κ, ξ, χ: n
δ	d	delta
ε	e	epsilon
ει	ei	
ευ	eu	
ζ	z	z(d)eta
η	ē	eta
ηυ	ēu	
θ	th	theta
ι	i	iota
κ	k	kappa
λ	l	la(m)bda
μ	m	mu
ν	n	nu
ξ	x	xi
ο	o	omicron
οι	oi	
ου	ou	
π	p	pi
ϱ	r	rho
σ, ς	s	sigma
τ	t	tau
υ	y	upsilon
φ	ph	phi
χ	ch	chi
ψ	ps	psi
ω	ō	omega
‘	h	spiritus asper
ᾳ	ai	iota subscriptum (similarly ῃ, ῳ)

In transliterated Greek the accents are retained (acute ´, grave `, and circumflex ^). Long vowels with the circumflex accent have no separate indication of vowel length (makron).

Transliteration of Hebrew

א	a	alef
ב	b	bet
ג	g	gimel
ד	d	dalet
ה	h	he
ו	w	vav
ז	z	zayin
ח	ḥ	khet
ט	ṭ	tet
י	y	yod
כ	k	kaf
ל	l	lamed
מ	m	mem
נ	n	nun
ס	s	samek
ע	‘	ayin
פ	p/f	pe
צ	ṣ	tsade
ק	q	qof
ר	r	resh
שׂ	ś	sin
שׁ	š	shin
ת	t	tav

Pronunciation of Turkish

Turkish uses Latin script since 1928. Pronunciation and spelling generally follow the same rules as European languages. Phonology according to G. Lewis, Turkish Grammar, 2000.

A	a	French a in *avoir*
B	b	b
C	c	j in *jam*
Ç	ç	ch in *church*
D	d	d
E	e	French ê in *être*
F	f	f
G	g	g in *gate* or in *angular*
Ğ	ğ	lengthens preceding vowel
H	h	h in *have*
I	ı	i in *cousin*
İ	i	French i in *si*
J	j	French j
K	k	c in *cat* or in *cure*
L	l	l in *list* or in *wool*
M	m	m

N	n	n	
O	o	French o in *note*
Ö	ö	German ö
P	p	p
R	r	r
S	s	s in *sit*
Ş	ş	sh in *shape*
T	t	t
U	u	u in *put*
Ü	ü	German ü
V	v	v
Y	y	y in *yet*
Z	z	z

Transliteration of Arabic, Persian, and Ottoman Turkish

ء, ا	ʾ, ā	ʾ	ʾ	hamza, alif
ب	b	b	b	bāʾ
پ	–	p	p	pe
ت	t	t	t	tāʾ
ث	t̲	s̱	s̱	t̲āʾ
ج	ǧ	ǧ	ǧ	ǧīm
چ	–	č	č	čim
ح	ḥ	ḥ	ḥ	ḥāʾ
خ	ḫ	ḫ	ḫ	ḫāʾ
د	d	d	d	dāl
ذ	d̲	z̲	z̲	dāl
ر	r	r	r	rāʾ
ز	z	z	z	zāy
ژ	–	ž	ž	že
س	s	s	s	sīn
ش	š	š	š	šīn
ص	ṣ	ṣ	ṣ	ṣād
ض	ḍ	ḍ	ḍ	ḍād
ط	ṭ	ṭ	ṭ	ṭāʾ
ظ	ẓ	ẓ	ẓ	ẓāʾ
ع	ʿ	ʿ	ʿ	ʿain
غ	ġ	ġ	ġ	ġain
ف	f	f	f	fāʾ
ق	q	q	q, k	qāf
ك	k	k	k, g, ñ	kāf
گ	–	g	g, ñ	gāf
ل	l	l	l	lām
م	m	m	m	mīm
ن	n	n	n	nūn
ه	h	h	h	hāʾ
و	w, ū	v	v	wāw
ى	y, ī	y	y	yāʾ

Transliteration of other languages

Akkadian (Assyrian-Babylonian), Hittite and Sumerian are transliterated according to the rules of RLA and TAVO. For Egyptian the rules of the Lexikon der Ägyptologie are used. The transliteration of Indo-European follows RIX, HGG. The transliteration of Old Indian is after M. MAYRHOFER, Etymologisches Wörterbuch des Altindoarischen, 1992ff. Avestian is done according to K. HOFFMANN, B. FORSSMAN, Avestische Laut- und Flexionslehre, 1996. Old Persian follows R.G. KENT, Old Persian, ²1953 (additions from K. HOFFMANN, Aufsätze zur Indoiranistik vol. 2, 1976, 622ff.); other Iranian languages are after R. SCHMITT, Compendium linguarum Iranicarum, 1989, and after D.N. MACKENZIE, A Concise Pahlavi Dictionary, ³1990. For Armenian the rules of R. SCHMITT, Grammatik des Klassisch-Armenischen, 1981, and of the Revue des études arméniennes, apply. The languages of Asia Minor are transliterated according to HbdOr. For Mycenean, Cyprian see HEUBECK and MASSON; for Italic scripts and Etruscan see VETTER and ET.

List of Abbreviations

1. Special Characters

→	see (cross-reference)	i̯, u̯	consonantal i, u
<	originated from (ling.)	m̥, n̥	vocalized m, n
>	evolved into (ling.)	l̥, r̥	vocalized l, r
√	root	|	syllable end
*	born	#	word end
∞	married	⟨ ⟩	transliteration
*	reconstructed form (ling.)	/ /	phonemic representation
ă	short vowel	[ ]	apocryphal
ā	long vowel		

2. List of General Abbreviations

Common abbreviations (e.g., etc.) are not included in the list of general abbreviations.

A.	Aulus
a.u.c.	ab urbe condita
abl.	ablative
acc.	accusative
aed. cur.	aedilis curulis
aed. pl.	aedilis plebi
Ap(p).	Appius
Athens, AM	Athens, Acropolis Museum
Athens, BM	Athens, Benaki Museum
Athens, NM	Athens, National Museum
Athens, NUM	Athens, Numismatic Museum
b.	born
Baltimore, WAG	Baltimore, Walters Art Gallery
Basle, AM	Basle, Antikenmuseum
Berlin, PM	Berlin, Pergamonmuseum
Berlin, SM	Berlin, Staatliche Museen
bk(s).	book(s)
Bonn, RL	Bonn, Rheinisches Landesmuseum
Boston, MFA	Boston, Museum of Fine Arts
C.	Gaius
c.	circa
Cambridge, FM	Cambridge, Fitzwilliam Museum
carm.	carmen, carmina
cent.	century
ch.	chapter
Cn.	Gnaeus
conc.	acta concilii
col.	column
Cologne, RGM	Cologne, Römisch Germanisches Museum
comm.	commentary
contd.	continued
Copenhagen, NCG	Copenhagen, Ny Carlsberg Glyptothek
Copenhagen, NM	Copenhagen, National Museum
Copenhagen, TM	Copenhagen, Thorvaldsen Museum
cos.	consul
cos. des.	consul designatus
cos. ord.	consul ordinarius
cos. suff.	consul suffectus
cur.	curator
D., Dec.	Decimus
d.	died
dat.	dative
decret.	decretum, decreta
f.l.	falsa lectio
fem.	feminine
fig(s).	figure(s)
fla.	flamen
Florence, MA	Florence, Museo Archeologico
Florence, UF	Florence, Uffizi
fr.	fragment
Frankfurt, LH	Frankfurt, Liebighaus
gen.	genitive

Geneva, MAH	Geneva, Musée d'Art et d'Histoire	Palermo, MAN	Palermo, Museo Archeologico Nazionale
Ger.	German	Paris, BN	Paris, Bibliothèque Nationale
Gk.	Greek	Paris, CM	Paris, Cabinet des Médailles
Hamburg, MKG	Hamburg, Museum für Kunst und Ge-werbe	Paris, LV	Paris, Louvre
Hanover, KM	Hanover, Kestner-Museum	pl.	plate
		plur.	plural
Imp.	Imperator	pon. max.	pontifex maximus
inventory no.	inventory number	pr(aef).	praefatio
		praef.	praefectus
Istanbul, AM	Istanbul, Archaeological Museum	procos.	proconsul
		procur.	procurator
itin.	itineraria	propr.	propraetor
Kassel, SK	Kassel, Staatliche Kunstsammlungen	Ps.-	Pseudo
l.	lex	Q.	Quintus
l.	line	qu.	quaestor
L.	Lucius	r	recto
l.c.	loco citato	rev.	revised
Lat.	Latin	Rome, MC	Rome, Museo Capitolino
leg.	leges	Rome, MN	Rome, Museo Nazionale
lib.	liber, libri	Rome, VA	Rome, Villa Albani
ling.	linguistic(ally)	Rome, VG	Rome, Villa Giulia
loc.	locative	Rome, MV	Rome, Museo Vaticano
London, BM	London, British Museum	S.	Sextus
		s.v.	sub voce
M'.	Manius	SC	senatus consultum
M.	Marcus	sc.	scilicet
Madrid, PR	Madrid, Prado	schol.	scholion, scholia
Malibu, GM	Malibu, Getty Museum	Ser.	Servius
		serm.	sermo
masc.	masculinum, masculine	s(in)g.	singular
Moscow, PM	Moscow, Pushkin Museum	Sp.	Spurius
MS(S)	manuscript(s)	St.	Saint
Munich, GL	Munich, Glyptothek	St. Peters-burg, HR	St. Petersburg, Hermitage
Munich, SA	Munich, Staatliche Antikensammlung	T.	Titus
Munich, SM	Munich, Staatliche Münzsammlung	t.t.	terminus technicus
		The Hague, MK	The Hague, Muntenkabinet
Mus.	Museum, Musée, Museo		Thessaloniki, National Museum
N.	Numerius	Thessaloniki, NM	
n.d.	no date	Ti., Tib.	Tiberius
Naples, MN	Naples, Museo Nazionale	tit.	titulus
neutr.	neutrum, neuter, neutral	tr. mil.	tribunus militum
New York, MMA	New York, Metropolitan Museum of Arts	tr. pl.	tribunus plebis
		Univ.	Universität, University, Université, Uni-versità
no.	number		
nom.	nominative	v.	verse
NT	New Testament	v	verso
Op., Opp.	Opus, Opera	Vienna, KM	Vienna, Kunsthistorisches Museum
opt.	optative	vir clar.	vir clarissimus
OT	Old Testament	vir ill.	vir illustris
Oxford, AM	Oxford, Ashmolean Museum	vir spect.	vir spectabilis
		vol.	volume
p.	page		
P	Papyrus		
P.	Publius		

3. Abbreviations used in the Bibliographies

This list contains abbreviations of English, German, French, Italian and Latin words used in the bibliographies.

Abh.	Abhandlung
Acad.	Academia, Académie, Academy
Act.	acta, acts, actes
Akad.	Akademie
Akt.	Akten
Anz.	Anzeiger
app./App.	appendix, appendices/Appendizes
Arch.	Archäologie
Beih.	Beiheft
Beil.	Beilage
Beitr.	Beitrag
Ber.	Bericht
Bull.	Bulletin, Bullettino
Cat.	Catalogue, Catalogo
Cod.	Codex, Codices, Codizes
Coll.	Collectio
Congr.	Congress, Congrès, Congresso
Const.	Constitutio
Corp.	Corporation
Diss.	Dissertation
ed.	edidit, editio, editor, edited (by)
edd.	ediderunt
edn.	edition
Ergbd.	Ergänzungsband
Ergh.	Ergänzungsheft
ES	Einzelschrift
Ét.	Études
Etym.	Etymologie
exc.	excerpta
Festg.	Festgabe
FS	Festschrift
Geogr.	Geographie
Ges.	Gesellschaft
Gesch.	Geschichte
Gramm.	Grammatik
gloss.	glossaria
gr(iech).	griechisch
GS	Gedenkschrift
H.	Heft
Hab.	Habilitation
Hdb.	Handbuch

Hs.	Handschrift
HWB	Handwörterbuch
Inschr.	Inschrift
Inscr.	Inscriptiones
I(n)st(it).	Institut, Institute, Istituto
Jb.	Jahrbuch
Jbb.	Jahrbücher
Jh.	Jahrhundert
Journ.	Journal
Jt.	Jahrtausend
Kat.	Katalog
Komm.	Kommentar
Kongr.	Kongreß
KS	Kleine Schriften
Lex.	Lexicon, Lexikon
Mél.	Mélanges
Mitt.	Mitteilungen
Nachr.	Nachrichten
N.S.	Neue Serie, New Series, Nouvelle Série, Nuova Seria
Proc.	Proceedings
Prov.	Provinz
Rel.	Religion
Rev.	Review, Revue
Rhet.	Rhetorik
Riv.	Rivista
repr.	reprint
röm.	romisch
SB	Sitzungsbericht
Ser.	Serie, Series, Série, Seria
Soc.	Society, Societé, Società
Stud.	Studia, Studien, Studies, Studi
suppl./Suppl.	supplement/Supplement
suppl. vol(s)	supplementary volume(s)
Top.	Topographie
tract.	tractatus
Trag.	Tragödie, Tragiker
trans.	translation, translated (by)
Übers.	Übersetzung, übersetzt
Unt.	Untersuchung
Verh.	Verhandlung
WB	Wörterbuch
wiss.	wissenschaftlich
Zschr.	Zeitschrift

4. Bibliographic Abbreviations

A&A
Antike und Abendland
A&R
Atene e Roma
AA
Archäologischer Anzeiger
AAA
Annals of Archaeology and Anthropology
AAAlg
S. GSELL, Atlas archéologique de l'Algérie. Édition spéciale des cartes au 200.000 du Service Géographique de l' Armée, 1911, repr. 1973
AAHG
Anzeiger für die Altertumswissenschaften, publication of the Österreichische Humanistische Gesellschaft
AArch
Acta archeologica
AASO
The Annual of the American Schools of Oriental Research
AATun 050
E. BABELON, R. CAGNAT, S. REINACH (ed.), Atlas archéologique de la Tunisie (1 : 50.000), 1893
AATun 100
R. CAGNAT, A. MERLIN (ed.), Atlas archéologique de la Tunisie (1: 100.000), 1914
AAWG
Abhandlungen der Akademie der Wissenschaften in Göttingen. Philologisch-historische Klasse
AAWM
Abhandlungen der Akademie der Wissenschaften und Literatur in Mainz. Geistes- und sozialwissenschaftliche Klasse
AAWW
Anzeiger der Österreichischen Akademie der Wissenschaften in Wien. Philosophisch-historische Klasse
ABAW
Abhandlungen der Bayerischen Akademie der Wissenschaften. Philosophisch-historische Klasse
Abel
F.-M. ABEL, Géographie de la Palestine 2 vols., 1933 – 38
ABG,
Archiv für Begriffsgeschichte: Bausteine zu einem historischen Wörterbuch der Philosophie
ABr
P. ARNDT, F. BRUCKMANN (ed.), Griechische und römische Porträts, 1891 – 1912; E. LIPPOLD (ed.), Text vol., 1958
ABSA
Annual of the British School at Athens
AC
L'Antiquité Classique
Acta
Acta conventus neo-latini Lovaniensis, 1973

AD
Archaiologikon Deltion
ADAIK
Abhandlungen des Deutschen Archäologischen Instituts Kairo
Adam
J.P. ADAM, La construction romaine. Matériaux et techniques, 1984
ADAW
Abhandlungen der Deutschen Akademie der Wissenschaften zu Berlin. Klasse für Sprachen, Literatur und Kunst
ADB
Allgemeine Deutsche Biographie
AdI
Annali dell'Istituto di Corrispondenza Archeologica
AE
L'Année épigraphique
AEA
Archivo Espanol de Arqueología
AEM
Archäologisch-epigraphische Mitteilungen aus Österreich
AfO
Archiv für Orientforschung
AGD
Antike Gemmen in deutschen Sammlungen 4 vols., 1968–75
AGM
Archiv für Geschichte der Medizin
Agora
The Athenian Agora. Results of the Excavations by the American School of Classical Studies of Athens, 1953 ff.
AGPh
Archiv für Geschichte der Philosophie
AGR
Akten der Gesellschaft für griechische und hellenistische Rechtsgeschichte
AHAW
Abhandlungen der Heidelberger Akademie der Wissenschaften. Philosophisch-historische Klasse
AHES
Archive for History of Exact Sciences
AIHS
Archives internationales d'histoire des sciences
AION
Annali del Seminario di Studi del Mondo Classico, Sezione di Archeologia e Storia antica
AJ
The Archaeological Journal of the Royal Archaeological Institute of Great Britain and Ireland
AJA
American Journal of Archaeology
AJAH
American Journal of Ancient History

AJBA
   Australian Journal of Biblical Archaeology
AJN
   American Journal of Numismatics
AJPh
   American Journal of Philology
AK
   Antike Kunst
AKG
   Archiv für Kulturgeschichte
AKL
   G. MEISSNER (ed.), Allgemeines Künsterlexikon: Die
   bildenden Künstler aller Zeiten und Völker, ²1991
   ff.
AKM
   Abhandlungen für die Kunde des Morgenlandes
Albrecht
   M. v. ALBRECHT, Geschichte der römischen Litera-
   tur, ²1994
Alessio
   G. ALESSIO, Lexicon etymologicum. Supplemento ai
   Dizionari etimologici latini e romanzi, 1976
Alexander
   M.C. ALEXANDER, Trials in the Late Roman Repub-
   lic: 149 BC to 50 BC (Phoenix Suppl. Vol. 26), 1990
Alföldi
   A. ALFÖLDI, Die monarchische Repräsentation im
   römischen Kaiserreiche, 1970, repr. ³1980
Alföldy, FH
   G. ALFÖLDY, Fasti Hispanienses. Senatorische
   Reichsbeamte und Offiziere in den spanischen Pro-
   vinzen des römischen Reiches von Augustus bis Dio-
   kletian, 1969
Alföldy, Konsulat
   G. ALFÖLDY, Konsulat und Senatorenstand unter
   den Antoninen. Prosopographische Untersuchungen
   zur senatorischen Führungsschicht (Antiquitas 1,
   27), 1977
Alföldy, RG
   G. ALFÖLDY, Die römische Gesellschaft. Ausge-
   wählte Beiträge, 1986
Alföldy, RH
   G. ALFÖLDY, Römische Heeresgeschichte, 1987
Alföldy, RS
   G. ALFÖLDY, Römische Sozialgeschichte, ³1984
ALLG
   Archiv für lateinische Lexikographie und Gramma-
   tik
Altaner
   B. ALTANER, Patrologie. Leben, Schriften und Lehre
   der Kirchenväter, ⁹1980
AMI
   Archäologische Mitteilungen aus Iran
Amyx, Addenda
   C.W. NEEFT, Addenda et Corrigenda to D.A. Amyx,
   Corinthian Vase-Painting, 1991
Amyx, CVP
   D.A. AMYX, Corinthian Vase-Painting of the Ar-
   chaic Period 3 vols., 1988

Anadolu
   Anadolu (Anatolia)
Anatolica
   Anatolica
AncSoc
   Ancient Society
Anderson
   J.G. ANDERSON, A Journey of Exploration in Pontus
   (Studia pontica 1), 1903
Anderson Cumont/Grégoire
   J.G. ANDERSON, F. CUMONT, H. GRÉGOIRE, Recueil
   des inscriptions grecques et latines du Pont et de l'Ar-
   ménie (Studia pontica 3), 1910
André, botan.
   J. ANDRÉ, Lexique des termes de botanique en latin,
   1956
André, oiseaux
   J. ANDRÉ, Les noms d'oiseaux en latin, 1967
André, plantes
   J. ANDRÉ, Les noms de plantes dans la Rome an-
   tique, 1985
Andrews
   K. ANDREWS, The Castles of Morea, 1953
ANET
   J.B. PRITCHARD, Ancient Near Eastern Texts Relat-
   ing to the Old Testament, ³1969, repr. 1992
AnnSAAt
   Annuario della Scuola Archeologica di Atene
ANRW
   H. TEMPORINI, W. HAASE (ed.), Aufstieg und Nie-
   dergang der römischen Welt, 1972 ff.
ANSMusN
   Museum Notes. American Numismatic Society
AntAfr
   Antiquités africaines
AntChr
   Antike und Christentum
AntPl
   Antike Plastik
AO
   Der Alte Orient
AOAT
   Alter Orient und Altes Testament
APF
   Archiv für Papyrusforschung und verwandte Gebie-
   te
APh
   L'Année philologique
Arangio-Ruiz
   V. ARANGIO-RUIZ, Storia del diritto romano, ⁶1953
Arcadia
   Arcadia. Zeitschrift für vergleichende Literaturwis-
   senschaft
ArchCl
   Archeologia Classica
ArchE
   Archaiologike ephemeris
ArcheologijaSof
   Archeologija. Organ na Archeologiceskija institut i
   muzej pri B'lgarskata akademija na naukite

ArchHom
   Archaeologia Homerica, 1967ff.
ArtAntMod
   Arte antica e moderna
ARW
   Archiv für Religionswissenschaft
AS
   Anatolian Studies
ASAA
   Annuario della Scuola Archeologica di Atene e delle
   Missioni italiane in Oriente
ASL
   Archiv für das Studium der neueren Sprachen und
   Literaturen
ASNP
   Annali della Scuola Normale Superiore di Pisa, Clas-
   se di Lettere e Filosofia
ASpr
   Die Alten Sprachen
ASR
   B. ANDREAE (ed.), Die antiken Sarkophagreliefs,
   1952 ff.
Athenaeum
   Athenaeum
ATL
   B.D. MERITT, H.T. WADE-GERY, M.F. McGRECOR,
   Athenian Tribute Lists 4 vols., 1939–53
AU
   Der altsprachliche Unterricht
Aulock
   H. v. AULOCK, Münzen und Städte Pisidiens
   (MDAI(Ist) Suppl. 8) 2 vols., 1977–79
Austin
   C. AUSTIN (ed.), Comicorum graecorum fragmenta
   in papyris reperta, 1973
BA
   Bolletino d'Arte del Ministero della Publica Istruzi-
   one
BAB
   Bulletin de l'Académie Royale de Belgique. Classe
   des Lettres
BABesch
   Bulletin antieke beschaving. Annual Papers on Clas-
   sical Archaeology
Badian, Clientelae
   E. BADIAN, Foreign Clientelae, 1958
Badian, Imperialism
   E. BADIAN, Roman Imperialism in the Late Repub-
   lic, 1967
BaF
   Baghdader Forschungen
Bagnall
   R.S. BAGNALL ET AL., Consuls of the Later Roman
   Empire (Philological Monographs of the American
   Philological Association 36), 1987
BalkE
   Balkansko ezikoznanie
BalkSt
   Balkan Studies

BaM
   Baghdader Mitteilungen
Bardenhewer, GAL
   O. BARDENHEWER, Geschichte der altkirchlichen Li-
   teratur, Vols. 1–2, ²1913 f.; Vols. 3–5, 1912–32;
   repr. Vols. 1–5, 1962
Bardenhewer, Patr.
   O. BARDENHEWER, Patrologie, ³1910
Bardon
   H. BARDON, La littérature latine inconnue 2 vols.,
   1952 – 56
Baron
   W. BARON (ed.), Beiträge zur Methode der Wissen-
   schaftsgeschichte, 1967
BASO
   Bulletin of the American Schools of Oriental Rese-
   arch
Bauer/Aland
   W. BAUER, K. ALAND (ed.), Griechisch-deutsches
   Wörterbuch zu den Schriften des Neuen Testamen-
   tes und der frühchristlichen Literatur, ⁶1988
Baumann, LRRP
   R.A. BAUMAN, Lawyers in Roman Republican Poli-
   tics. A study of the Roman Jurists in their Political
   Setting, 316–82 BC (Münchener Beiträge zur Papy-
   rusforschung und antiken Rechtsgeschichte), 1983
Baumann, LRTP
   R.A. BAUMAN, Lawyers in Roman Transitional Poli-
   tics. A Study of the Roman Jurists in their Political
   Setting in the Late Republic and Triumvirate (Mün-
   chener Beiträge zur Papyrusforschung und antiken
   Rechtsgeschichte), 1985
BB
   Bezzenbergers Beiträge zur Kunde der indogerma-
   nischen Sprachen
BCAR
   Bollettino della Commissione Archeologica Comu-
   nale di Roma
BCH
   Bulletin de Correspondance Hellénique
BE
   Bulletin épigraphique
Beazley, ABV
   J.D. BEAZLEY, Attic Black-figure Vase-Painters,
   1956
Beazley, Addenda²
   TH.H. CARPENTER (ed.), Beazley Addenda, ²1989
Beazley, ARV²
   J.D. BEAZLEY, Attic Red-figure Vase-Painters,
   ²1963
BeazIey, EVP
   J.D. BEAZLEY, Etruscan Vase Painting, 1947
Beazley, Paralipomena
   J.D. BEAZLEY, Paralipomena. Additions to Attic
   Black-figure Vase-Painters and to Attic Red-figure
   Vase-Painters, ²1971
Bechtel, Dial.¹
   F. BECHTEL, Die griechischen Dialekte 3 vols.,
   1921–24

Bechtel, Dial.²
F. BECHTEL, Die griechischen Dialekte 3 vols.,
⁴1963
Bechtel, HPN
F. BECHTEL, Die historischen Personennamen des
Griechischen bis zur Kaiserzeit, 1917
Belke
K. BELKE, Galatien und Lykaonien (Denkschriften
der Österreichischen Akademie der Wissenschaften,
Philosophisch-Historische Klasse 172; TIB 4), 1984
Belke/Mersich
K. BELKE, N. MERSICH, Phrygien und Pisidien
(Denkschriften der Österreichischen Akademie der
Wissenschaften, Philosophisch-Historische Klasse
211; TIB 7), 1990
Bell
K.E. BELL, Place-Names in Classical Mythology,
Greece, 1989
Beloch, Bevölkerung
K.J. BELOCH, Die Bevölkerung der griechisch-römi-
schen Welt, 1886
Beloch, GG
K.J. BELOCH, Griechische Geschichte 4 vols.,
²1912–27, repr. 1967
Beloch, RG
K.J. BELOCH, Römische Geschichte bis zum Beginn
der Punischen Kriege, 1926
Bengtson
H. BENGTSON, Die Strategie in der hellenistischen
Zeit. Ein Beitrag zum antiken Staatsrecht (Münche-
ner Beiträge zur Papyrusforschung und antiken
Rechtsgeschichte 26, 32, 36) 3 vols., 1937–52, ed.
repr. 1964–67
Berger
E.H. BERGER, Geschichte der wissenschaftlichen
Erdkunde der Griechen, ²1903
Berve
II. BERVE, Das Alexanderreich auf prosopographi-
scher Grundlage, 1926
Beyen
H. G. BEYEN, Die pompejanische Wanddekoration
vom zweiten bis zum vierten Stil 2 vols., 1938–60
BFC
Bolletino di filologia classica
BGU
Ägyptische (Griechische) Urkunden aus den Kaiser-
lichen (from Vol. 6 on Staatlichen) Museen zu Berlin
13 vols., 1895–1976
BHM
Bulletin of the History of Medicine
BIAO
Bulletin de l'Institut français d'Archéologie Orien-
tale
BiblH&R
Bibliothèque d'Humanisme et Renaissance
BiblLing
Bibliographie linguistique / Linguistic Bibliography
BIBR
Bulletin de l'Institut Belge de Rome

Bickerman
E. BICKERMANN, Chronologie (Einleitung in die Al-
tertumswissenschaft III 5), 1933
BICS
Bulletin of the Institute of Classical Studies of the
University of London
BIES
The Bulletin of the Israel Exploration Society
BiogJahr
Biographisches Jahrbuch für Altertumskunde
Birley
A.R. BIRLEY, The Fasti of Roman Britain, 1981
BJ
Bonner Jahrbücher des Rheinischen Landesmuse-
ums in Bonn und des Vereins von Altertumsfreunden
im Rheinlande
BKT
Berliner Klassikertexte 8 vols., 1904–39
BKV
Bibliothek der Kirchenväter (Kempten ed.) 63 vols.,
²1911–31
Blänsdorf
J. BLÄNSDORF (ed.), Theater und Gesellschaft im Im-
perium Romanum, 1990
Blass
F. BLASS, Die attische Beredsamkeit, 3 vols.,
³1887–98, repr. 1979
Blass/Debrunner/Rehkopf
F. BLASS, A. DEBRUNNER, F. REHKOPF, Grammatik
des neutestamentlichen Griechisch, ¹⁵1979
Blümner, PrAlt.
H. BLÜMNER, Die römischen Privataltertümer
(HdbA IV 2, 2), ³1911
Blümner, Techn.
H. BLÜMNER, Technologie und Terminologie der
Gewerbe und Künste bei Griechen und Römern,
Vol. 1, ²1912; Vols. 2–4, 1875–87, repr. 1969
BMC, Gr
A Catalogue of the Greek Coins in the British Mu-
seum 29 vols., 1873–1965
BMCByz
W. WROTH (ed.), Catalogue of the Imperial Byzan-
tine Coins in the British Museum 2 vols., 1908, repr.
1966
BMCIR
Bryn Mawr Classical Review
BMCRE
H. MATTINGLY (ed.), Coins of the Roman Empire in
the British Museum 6 vols., 1962–76
BMCRR
H.A. GRUEBER (ed.), Coins of the Roman Republic
in the British Museum 3 vols., 1970
BN
Beiträge zur Namensforschung
Bolgar, Culture 1
R. BOLGAR, Classical Influences on European Cul-
ture A.D. 500 – 1500, 1971
Bolgar, Culture 2
R. BOLGAR, Classical Influences on European Cul-
ture A.D. 1500–1700, 1974

Bolgar, Thought
 R. BOLGAR, Classical Influences on Western Thought A.D. 1650–1870, 1977
Bon
 A. BON, La Morée franque 2 vols., 1969
Bonner
 S.F. BONNER, Education in Ancient Rome, 1977
Bopearachchi
 O. BOPEARACHCHI, Monnaies gréco-bactriennes et indo-grecques. Catalogue raisonné, 1991
Borinski
 K. BORINSKI, Die Antike in Poetik und Kunsttheorie vom Ausgang des klassischen Altertums bis auf Goethe und Wilhelm von Humboldt 2 vols., 1914–24, repr. 1965
Borza
 E.N. BORZA, In the shadow of Olympus. The emergence of Macedon, 1990
Bouché-Leclerq
 A. BOUCHÉ-LECLERQ, Histoire de la divination dans l'antiquité 3 vols., 1879–82, repr. 1978 in 4 vols.
BPhC
 Bibliotheca Philologica Classica
BrBr
 H. BRUNN, F. BRUCKMANN, Denkmäler griechischer und römischer Skulpturen, 1888–1947
BRGK
 Bericht der Römisch-Germanischen Kommission des Deutschen Archäologischen Instituts
Briggs/Calder
 W.W. BRIGGS, W.M. CALDER III, Classical Scholarship. A Biographical Encyclopedia, 1990
Bruchmann
 C.F.H. BRUCHMANN, Epitheta deorum quae apud poetas graecos leguntur, 1893
Brugmann/Delbrück
 K. BRUGMANN, B. DELBRÜCK, Grundriß der vergleichenden Grammatik der indogermanischen Sprachen, Vols. 1–2, 1897–1916; Vols. 3–5, 1893–1900
Brugmann /Thumb
 K. BRUGMANN, A. THUMB (ed.), Griechische Grammatik, ⁴1913
Brunhölzl
 F. BRUNHÖLZL, Geschichte der lateinischen Literatur des Mittelalters 2 vols., 1975–92
Brunt
 P.A. BRUNT, Italian Manpower 222 B. C. – A. D. 14, 1971
Bruun
 C. BRUUN, The Water Supply of Ancient Rome. A Study of Imperial Administration (Commentationes Humanarum Litterarum 93), 1991
Bryer/Winfield
 A. BRYER, D. WINFIELD, The Byzantine Monuments and Topography of Pontus (Dumbarton Oaks Studies 20) 2 vols., 1985
BSABR
 Bulletin de Liaison de la Société des Amis de la Bibliothèque Salomon Reinach

BSL
 Bulletin de la Société de Linguistique de Paris
BSO(A)S
 Bulletin of the School of Oriental (from Vol. 10 ff. and African) Studies
BTCGI
 G. NENCI (ed.), Bibliografia topografica della colonizzazione greca in Italia e nelle isole tirreniche, 1980 ff.
Buck
 A. BUCK (ed.), Die Rezeption der Antike, 1981
Burkert
 W. BURKERT, Griechische Religion der archaischen und klassischen Epoche, 1977
Busolt/Swoboda
 G. BUSOLT, H. SWOBODA, Griechische Staatskunde (HdbA IV 1, 1) 2 vols., ³1920–26, repr. 1972–79
BWG
 Berichte zur Wissenschaftsgeschichte
BWPr
 Winckelmanns-Programm der Archäologischen Gesellschaft zu Berlin
Byzantion
 Byzantion. Revue internationale des études byzantines
ByzF
 Byzantinische Forschungen. Internationale Zeitschrift für Byzantinistik
BYzZ
 Byzantinische Zeitschrift
Caballos
 A. CABALLOS, Los senadores hispanoromanos y la romanización de Hispania (Siglos I al III p.C.), Vol. 1: Prosopografia (Monografias del Departamento de Historia Antigua de la Universidad de Sevilla 5), 1990
CAF
 T. KOCK (ed.), Comicorum Atticorum Fragmenta, 3 vols., 1880–88
CAG
 Commentaria in Aristotelem Graeca 18 vols., 1885–1909
CAH
 The Cambridge Ancient History 12 text- and 5 ill. vols., 1924–39 (Vol. 1 as 2nd ed.), vols. 1–2, ³1970–75; vols. 3,1 and 3,3 ff., ²1982 ff.; vol. 3,2, ¹1991
Carney
 T.F. CARNEY, Bureaucracy in Traditional Society. Romano-Byzantine Bureaucracies Viewed from Within, 1971
Cartledge/Millett/Todd
 P. CARTLEDGE, P. MILLETT, S. TODD (ed.), Nomos, Essays in Athenian Law, Politics and Society, 1990
Cary
 M. CARY, The Geographical Background of Greek and Roman History, 1949
Casson, Ships
 L. CASSON, Ships and Seamanship in the Ancient World, 1971

Casson, Trade
  L. CASSON, Ancient Trade and Society, 1984
CAT
  Catalogus Tragicorum et Tragoediarum (in TrGF
  Vol. 1)
CatLitPap
  H.J.M. MILNE (ed.), Catalogue of the Literary Pa-
  pyri in the British Museum, 1927
CCAG
  F. CUMONT ET AL. (ed.), Catalogus Codicum As-
  trologorum Graecorum 12 vols. in 20 parts, 1898–
  1940
CCL
  Corpus Christianorum. Series Latina, 1954 ff.
CE
  Cronache Ercolanesi
CEG
  P.A. HANSEN (ed.), Carmina epigraphica Graeca
  (Texts and Commentary 12; 15), 1983 ff.
CeM
  Classica et Mediaevalia
CGF
  G. KAIBEL (ed.), Comicorum Graecorum Fragmen-
  ta, ²1958
CGL
  G. GÖTZ (ed.), Corpus glossariorum Latinorum, 7
  vols., 1888–1923, repr. 1965
Chantraine
  P. CHANTRAINE, Dictionnaire étymologique de la
  langue grecque 4 vols., 1968–80
CHCL-G
  E.J. KENNEY (ed.), The Cambridge History of Clas-
  sical Literature. Greek Literature, 1985 ff.
CHCL-L
  E.J. KENNEY (ed.), The Cambridge History of Clas-
  sical Literature. Latin Literature, 1982 ff.
Chiron
  Chiron. Mitteilungen der Kommission für alte Ge-
  schichte und Epigraphik des Deutschen Archäolo-
  gischen Instituts
Christ
  K. CHRIST, Geschichte der römischen Kaiserzeit von
  Augustus bis zu Konstantin, 1988
Christ, RGG
  K. CHRIST, Römische Geschichte und deutsche Ge-
  schichtswissenschaft, 1982
Christ, RGW
  K. CHRIST, Römische Geschichte und Wissen-
  schaftsgeschichte 3 vols., 1982–83
Christ/Momigliano
  K. CHRIST, A. MOMIGLIANO, Die Antike im 19.
  Jahrhundert in Italien und Deutschland, 1988
CIA
  A. KIRCHHOFF ET AL. (ed.), Corpus Inscriptionum
  Atticarum, 1873; Suppl.: 1877–91
CIC
  Corpus Iuris Canonici 2 vols., 1879–81, repr. 1959
CID
  Corpus des inscriptions de Delphes 3 vols., 1977–92

CIE
  C. PAULI (ed.), Corpus Inscriptionum Etruscarum,
  Vol. 1–2, 1893–1921; Vol. 3,1 ff., 1982 ff.
CIG
  Corpus Inscriptionum Graecarum 4 vols., 1828–77
CIL
  Corpus Inscriptionum Latinarum, 1863 ff.
CIL III Add.
  M. SASEL-KOS, Inscriptiones latinae in Graecia re-
  pertae. Additamenta ad CIL III (Epigrafia e antichità
  5), 1979
CIRB
  Corpus Inscriptionum regni Bosporani, 1965
CIS
  Corpus Inscriptionum Semiticarum 5 parts, 1881–
  1951
CJ
  Classical Journal
CL
  Cultura Neolatina
Clairmont
  C.W. CLAIRMONT, Attic Classical Tombstones 7
  vols., 1993
Clauss
  M. CLAUSS, Der magister officiorum in der Spätan-
  tike (4.–6. Jahrhundert). Das Amt und sein Einfluß
  auf die kaiserliche Politik (Vestigia 32), 1981
CLE
  F. BÜCHELER, E. LOMMATZSCH (ed.), Carmina La-
  tina Epigraphica (Anthologia latina 2) 3 vols.,
  1895–1926
CM
  Clio Medica. Acta Academiae historiae medicinae
CMA
  Cahiers de l'Institut du Moyen Age grec et latin
CMB
  W.M. CALDER III, D.J. KRAMER, An Introductory
  Bibliography to the History of Classical Scholarship,
  Chiefly in the XIXth and XXth Centuries, 1992
CMG
  Corpus Medicorum Graecorum, 1908 ff.
CMIK
  J. CHADWICK, Corpus of Mycenaean Inscriptions
  from Knossos (Incunabula Graeca 88), 1986 ff.
CML
  Corpus Medicorum Latinorum, 1915 ff.
CMS
  F. MATZ ET AL. (ed.), Corpus der minoischen und
  mykenischen Siegel, 1964 ff.
CodMan
  Codices manuscripti. Zeitschrift für Handschriften-
  kunde
Coing
  H. COING, Europäisches Privatrecht 2 vols., 1985–
  89
CollAlex
  I.U. POWELL (ed.), Collectanea Alexandrina, 1925
CollRau
  J. V. UNGERN-STERNBERG (ed.), Colloquia Raurica,
  1988 ff.

Conway/Johnson /Whatmough
R.S. CONWAY, S.E. JOHNSON, J. WHATMOUGH, The Prae-Italic dialects of Italy 3 vols., 1933, repr. 1968

Conze
A. CONZE, Die attischen Grabreliefs 4 vols., 1893–1922

Courtney
E. COURTNEY, The Fragmentary Latin Poets, 1993

CPF
F. ADORNO (ed.), Corpus dei Papiri Filosofici greci e latini, 1989 ff.

CPG
M. GEERARD (Vols. 1–5), F. GLORIE, (Vol. 5), Clavis patrum graecorum 5 vols., 1974–87

CPh
Classical Philology

CPL
E. DEKKERS, A. GAAR, Clavis patrum latinorum (CCL), ³1995

CQ
Classical Quarterly

CR
Classical Review

CRAI
Comptes rendus des séances de l'Académie des inscriptions et belles-lettres

CRF
O. RIBBECK (ed.), Comicorum Romanorum Fragmenta, 1871, repr. 1962

CSCT
Columbia Studies in the Classical Tradition

CSE
Corpus Speculorum Etruscorum, 1990 ff.

CSEL
Corpus Scriptorum ecclesiasticorum Latinorum, 1866 ff.

SCIR
Corpus Signorum Imperii Romani, 1963 ff.

Cumont, Pont
F. CUMONT, E. CUMONT, Voyage d'exploration archéologique dans le Pont et la Petite Arménie (Studia pontica 2), 1906

Cumont, Religions
F. CUMONT, Les Religions orientales dans le paganisme romain, ³1929, repr. 1981

Curtius
E.R. CURTIUS, Europäische Literatur und lateinisches Mittelalter, ¹¹1993

CVA
Corpus Vasorum Antiquorum, 1923 ff.

CW
The Classical World

D'Arms
J.H. D'ARMS, Commerce and Social Standing in Ancient Rome, 1981

D'Arms/Kopff
J.H. D'ARMS, E.C. KOPFF (ed.), The Seaborne Commerce of Ancient Rome: Studies in Archaeology and History (Memoirs of the American Academy in Rome 36), 1980

Dacia
Dacia. Revue d'archéologie et d'histoire ancienne

Davies
J.K. DAVIES, Athenian Propertied Families 600–300 BC, 1971

DB
F. VIGOUROUX (ed.), Dictionnaire de la Bible, 1881 ff.

DCPP
E. LIPIŃSKI ET AL. (ed.), Dictionnaire de la Civilisation Phénicienne et Punique, 1992

Degrassi, FCap.
A. DEGRASSI, Fasti Capitolini (Corpus scriptorum Latinorum Paravianum), 1954

Degrassi, FCIR
A. DEGRASSI, I Fasti consolari dell'Impero Romano, 1952

Deichgräber
K. DEICHGRÄBER, Die griechische Empirikerschule, 1930

Delmaire
R. DELMAIRE, Les responsables des finances impériales au Bas-Empire romain (IVᵉ-VIᵉ s). Études prosopographiques (Collection Latomus 203), 1989

Demandt
A. DEMANDT, Der Fall Roms: die Auflösung des römischen Reiches im Urteil der Nachwelt, 1984

Demougin
S. DEMOUGIN, Prosopographie des Chevaliers romains Julio-Claudiens (43 av.J -C.–70 ap.J.-C.) (Collection de l'École Française de Rome 153), 1992

Deubner
L. DEUBNER, Attische Feste, 1932

Develin
R. DEVELIN, Athenian Officials 684–321 B.C. 1949

Devijver
H. DEVIJVER, Prosopographia militiarum equestrium quae fuerunt ab Augusto ad Gallienum (Symbolae Facultatis Litterarum et Philosophiae Lovaniensis Ser. A 3) 3 vols., 1976–80; 2 Suppl. Vols.: 1987–93

DHA
Dialogues d'histoire ancienne

DHGE
A. BAUDRILLART, R. AUBERT (ed.), Dictionnaire d'Histoire et de Géographie Ecclésiastiques 1912 ff.

DID
Didascaliae Tragicae/Ludorum Tragicorum (in TrGF Vol. 1)

Diels, DG
H. DIELS, Doxographi Graeci, 1879

Diels/Kranz
H. DIELS, W. KRANZ (ed.), Fragmente der Vorsokratiker 3 vols., ⁹1951 f., repr. Vol.1, 1992; Vol. 2, 1985; Vol. 3, 1993

Dierauer
U. DIERAUER, Tier und Mensch im Denken der Antike, 1977

Dietz
K. DIETZ, Senatus contra principem. Untersuchungen zur senatorischen Opposition gegen Kaiser Maximinus Thrax (Vestigia 29), 1980

Dihle
A. DIHLE, Die griechische und lateinische Literatur der Kaiserzeit: von Augustus bis Justinian, 1989

DiskAB
Diskussionen zur archäologischen Bauforschung, 1974 ff.

Dixon
S. DIXON, The Roman Family, 1992

DJD
Discoveries in the Judaean Desert, 1955 ff.

DLZ
Deutsche Literaturzeitung für Kritik der internationalen Wissenschaft

DMA
J.R. STRAYER ET AL. (ed.), Dictionary of the Middle Ages 13 vols., 1982–89

Dmic
F. AURA JORRO, Diccionario Micénico, 1985

Dörrie/Baltes
H. DÖRRIE, M. BALTES (ed.), Der Platonismus in der Antike, 1987 ff.

Domaszewski
A.V. DOMASZEWSKI, Aufsätze zur römischen Heeresgeschichte, 1972

Domaszewski /Dobson
A.V. DOMASZEWSKI, B. DOBSON, Die Rangordnung des römischen Heeres, ²1967

Domergue
C. DOMERGUE, Les mines de la péninsule Iberique dans l'Antiquité Romaine, 1990

Drumann /Groebe
W. DRUMANN, P. GROEBE (ed.), Geschichte Roms in seinem Übergange von der republikanischen zur monarchischen Verfassung 6 vols., 1899–1929, repr. 1964

DS
C. DAREMBERG, E. SAGLIO (ed.), Dictionnaire des antiquités grecques et romaines d'après les textes et les monuments 6 vols., 1877–1919, repr. 1969

Dulckeit /Schwarz /Waldstein
G. DULCKEIT, F. SCHWARZ, W. WALDSTEIN, Römische Rechtsgeschichte. Ein Studienbuch (Juristische Kurz Lehrbücher), 1995

Dumézil
G. DUMÉZIL, La religion romaine archaïque, suivi d'un appendice sur la religion des Etrusques, 1974

Duncan-Jones, Economy
R. DUNCAN-JONES, The Economy of the Roman Empire. Quantitative Studies, 1974

Duncan-Jones, Structure
R. DUNCAN-JONES, Structure and Scale in the Roman Economy, 1990

DVjS
Deutsche Vierteljahrsschrift für Literaturwissenschaft und Geistesgeschichte

EA
Epigraphica Anatolica. Zeitschrift für Epigraphik und historische Geographie Anatoliens

EAA
R. BIANCHI BANDINELLI (ed.), Enciclopedia dell'arte antica classica e orientale, 1958 ff.

EB
G. CAMPS, Encyclopédie Berbère 1984 ff.

Ebert
F. EBERT, Fachausdrücke des griechischen Bauhandwerks, Vol. 1: Der Tempel, 1910

EC
Essays in Criticism

Eck
W. ECK, Die Statthalter der germanischen Provinzen vom 1.–3. Jahrhundert (Epigraphische Studien 14), 1985

Eckstein
F.A. ECKSTEIN, Nomenclator philologorum, 1871

Edelstein, AM
L. EDELSTEIN, Ancient medicine, 1967

Edelstein, Asclepius
E.J. and L. EDELSTEIN, Asclepius. A Collection and Interpretation of the Testimonies, 1945

Eder, Demokratie
W. EDER (ed.), Die athenische Demokratie im 4. Jahrhundert v. Chr. Vollendung oder Verfall einer Verfassungsform? Akten eines Symposiums, 3. – 7. August 1992, 1995

Eder, Staat
W. EDER (ed.), Staat und Staatlichkeit in der frühen römischen Republik: Akten eines Symposiums, 12. – 15. Juli 1988, 1990

EDM
K. RANKE, W. BREDNICH (ed.), Enzyklopädie des Märchens. Handwörterbuch zur historischen und vergleichenden Erzählforschung, 1977 ff.

EDRL
A. BERGER, Encyclopedic Dictionary of Roman Law (TAPhA N.S. 43,2), 1953, repr. 1968

EEpigr
Ephemeris Epigraphica

EI
Encyclopaedia of Islam, 1960 ff.

Eissfeldt
O. EISSFELDT (ed.), Handbuch zum Alten Testament, ³1964 ff.

Emerita
Emerita. Revista de linguistica y filologia clasica

EncIr
E. YARSHATER (ed.), Encyclopaedia Iranica, 1985

Entretiens
Entretiens sur l'antiquité classique (Fondation Hardt)

EOS
Atti del Colloquio Internazionale AIEGL su Epigrafia e Ordine Senatorio: Roma, 14–20 maggio 1981, 2 vols., 1982

EpGF
M. DAVIES, Epicorum graecorum fragmenta, 1988
EpGr
G. KAIBEL (ed.), Epigrammata Graeca ex lapidibus conlecta, 1878
Epicurea
H. USENER (ed.), Epicurea, 1887, repr. 1963
EPRO
Études préliminaires aux religions orientales dans l'Empire Romain, 1961 ff.
Eranos
Eranos. Acta Philologica Suecana
Er-Jb
Eranos-Jahrbuch
Erasmus
Erasmus. Speculum Scientiarum. Internationales Literaturblatt der Geisteswissenschaften
Eretz Israel
Eretz-Israel, Archaeological, Historical and Geographical Studies
Ernout/Meillet
A. ERNOUT, A. MEILLET, Dictionnaire étymologique de la langue latine, ⁴1959
Errington
R.M. ERRINGTON, Geschichte Makedoniens. Von den Anfängen bis zum Untergang des Königreiches, 1986
ESAR
T. FRANK (ed.), An Economic Survey of Ancient Rome 6 vols., 1933–40
Espérandieu, Inscr.
E. ESPÉRANDIEU, Inscriptions latines de Gaule 2 vols., 1929–36
Espérandieu, Rec.
E. ESPÉRANDIEU, Recueil généneral des bas-reliefs, statues et bustes de la Gaule Romaine 16 vols., 1907–81
ET
H. RIX (ed.), Etruskische Texte (ScriptOralia 23, 24, Reihe A 6,7) 2 vols., 1991
ETAM
Ergänzungsbände zu den Tituli Asiae minoris, 1966 ff.
Euph.
Euphorion
EV
F. DELLA CORTE ET AL. (ed.), Enciclopedia Virgiliana 5 vols. in 6 parts, 1984–91
Evans
D.E. EVANS, Gaulish Personal names. A study of some continental Celtic formations, 1967
F&F
Forschungen und Fortschritte
Farnell, Cults
L.R. FARNELL, The Cults of the Greek States 5 vols., 1896–1909
Farnell, GHC
L.R. FARNELL, Greek Hero Cults and Ideas of Immortality, 1921

FCG
A. MEINEKE (ed.), Fragmenta Comicorum Graecorum 5 vols., 1839–57, repr. 1970
FCS
Fifteenth-Century Studies
FdD
Fouilles de Delphes, 1902 ff.
FGE
D.L. PAGE, Further Greek Epigrams, 1981
FGrH
F. JACOBY, Die Fragmente der griechischen Historiker, 3 parts in 14 vols., 1923–58, Part 1: ²1957
FHG
C. MÜLLER (ed.), Fragmenta Historicorum Graecorum 5 vols., 1841–1970
Fick/Bechtel
A. FICK, F. BECHTEL, Die griechischen Personennamen, ²1894
FiE
Forschungen in Ephesos, 1906 ff.
Filologia
La Filologia Greca e Latina nel secolo XX, 1989
Finley, Ancient Economy
M.I. FINLEY, The Ancient Economy, ²1984
Finley, Ancient Slavery
M.I. FINLEY, Ancient Slavery and Modern Ideology, 1980
Finley, Economy
M.I. FINLEY, B.D. SHAW, R.P. SALLER (ed.), Economy and Society in Ancient Greece, 1981
Finley, Property
M.I. FINLEY (ed.), Studies in Roman Property, 1976
FIRA
S. RICCOBONO, J. BAVIERA (ed.), Fontes iuris Romani anteiustiniani 3 vols., ²1968
FIRBruns
K.G. BRUNS, TH. MOMMSEN, O. GRADENWITZ (ed.), Fontes iuris Romani antiqui, 1909, repr. 1969
Fittschen/Zanker
K. FITTSCHEN, P. ZANKER, Katalog der römischen Porträts in den capitolinischen Museen und den anderen kommunalen Museen der Stadt Rom, 1983 ff.
Flach
D. FLACH, Römische Agrargeschichte (HdbA III 9), 1990
Flashar
H. FLASHAR, Inszenierung der Antike. Das griechische Drama auf der Bühne der Neuzeit, 1991
Flashar, Medizin
H. FLASHAR (ed.), Antike Medizin, 1971
FMS
Frühmittelalterliche Studien, Jahrbuch des Instituts für Frühmittelalter-Forschung der Universität Münster
Fossey
J.M. FOSSEY, Topography and Population of Ancient Boiotia, Vol. 1, 1988
FOst
L. VIDMANN, Fasti Ostienses, 1982

Fowler
W.W. FOWLER, The Roman Festivals of the Period of the Republic. An Introduction to the Study of the Religion of the Romans, 1899
FPD
I. PISO, Fasti Provinciae Daciae, Vol. 1: Die senatorischen Amtsträger (Antiquitas 1,43), 1993
FPL
W. MOREL, C. BÜCHNER (ed.), Fragmenta Poetarum Latinorum epicorum et lyricorum, ²1982
FPR
A. BÄHRENS (ed.), Fragmenta Poetarum Romanorum, 1886
Frazer
J.G. FRAZER, The Golden Bough. A Study in Magic and Religion, 8 parts in 12 vols., Vols. 1–3, 5–9, ³1911–14; Vols. 4, 10–12, 1911–15
Frenzel
E. FRENZEL, Stoffe der Weltliteratur, ⁸1992
Friedländer
L. FRIEDLÄNDER, G. WISSOWA (ed.), Darstellungen aus der Sittengeschichte Roms 4 vols., ¹⁰1921–23
Frier, Landlords
B.W. FRIER, Landlords and Tenants in Imperial Rome, 1980
Frier, PontMax
B.W. FRIER, Libri annales pontificum maximorum. The origins of the Annalistic Tradition (Papers and Monographs of the American Academy in Rome 27), 1979
Frisk
H. FRISK, Griechisches etymologisches Wörterbuch (Indogermanische Bibliothek: Reihe 2) 3 vols., 1960–72
FRLANT
Forschungen zur Religion und Literatur des Alten und Neuen Testaments
Fuchs/Floren
W. FUCHS, J. FLOREN, Die Griechische Plastik, Vol. 1: Die geometrische und archaische Plastik, 1987
Furtwängler
A. FURTWÄNGLER, Die antiken Gemmen. Geschichte der Steinschneidekunst im klassischen Altertum 3 vols., 1900
Furtwängler/Reichhold
A. FURTWÄNGLER, K. REICHHOLD, Griechische Vasenmalerie 3 vols., 1904–32
Fushöller
D. FUSHÖLLER, Tunesien und Ostalgerien in der Römerzeit, 1979
G&R
Greece and Rome
GA
A.S.F. GOW, D.L. PAGE, The Greek Anthology, Vol. 1: Hellenistic Epigrams, 1965; Vol. 2: The Garland of Philip, 1968
Gardner
P. GARDNER, A History of Ancient Coinage, 700–300 B.C., 1918

Gardthausen
V. GARDTHAUSEN, Augustus und Seine Zeit, 2 parts in 6 vols., 1891–1904
Garnsey
P. GARNSEY, Famine and Food Supply in the Graeco-Roman World. Responses to Risk and Crisis, 1988
Garnsey/Hopkins/Whittaker
P. GARNSEY, K. HOPKINS, C.R. WHITTAKER (ed.), Trade in the Ancient Economy, 1983
Garnsey/Saller
P. GARNSEY, R. SALLER, The Roman Empire, Economy, Society and Culture, 1987
GCS
Die griechischen christlichen Schriftsteller der ersten Jahrhunderte, 1897 ff.
Gehrke
H.-J. GEHRKE, Jenseits von Athen und Sparta. Das Dritte Griechenland und seine Staatenwelt, 1986
Gentili/Prato
B. GENTILI, C. PRATO (ed.), Poetarum elegiacorum testimonia et fragmenta, Vol. 1, ²1988; Vol. 2, 1985
Georges
K.E. GEORGES, Ausführliches lateinisch-deutsches Handwörterbuch 2 vols., ⁸1912–18, repr. 1992
Gérard-Rousseau
M. GÉRARD-ROUSSEAU, Les mentions religieuses dans les tablettes mycéniennes, 1968
Germania
Germania. Anzeiger der Römisch-Germanischen Kommission des Deutschen Archäologischen Instituts
Gernet
L. GERNET, Droit et société dans la Grèce ancienne (Institut de droit romain, Publication 13), 1955, repr. 1964
Geus
K. GEUS, Prosopographie der literarisch bezeugten Karthager (Studia Phoenicia 13 Orientalia Lovaniensia analecta 59), 1994
GGA
Göttingische Gelehrte Anzeigen
GGM
C. MÜLLER (ed.), Geographi Graeci Minores 2 vols., Tabulae, 1855–61
GGPh¹
F. ÜBERWEG (ed.), Grundriß der Geschichte der Philosophie; K, PRÄCHTER, Teil 1: Die Philosophie des Altertums, ¹²1926, repr. 1953
GGPh²
W. OTTO, U. HAUSMANN (ed.), Grundriß der Geschichte der Philosophie; H. FLASHAR (ed.), vol. 3: Die Philosophie der Antike, 1983, vol. 4: Die hellenistische Philosophie, 1994
GHW 1
H. BENGTSON, V. MILOJCIC ET AL., Großer Historischer Weltatlas des Bayrischen Schulbuchverlages 1. Vorgeschichte und Altertum, ⁶1978
GHW 2
J. ENGEL, W. MACER, A. BIRKEN ET AL., Großer His-

torischer Weltatlas des Bayrischen Schulbuchverlages 2. Mittelalter, ²1979

GIBM
C.T. Newton et al. (ed.), The Collection of Ancient Greek Inscriptions in the British Museum 4 vols., 1874–1916

Gillispie
C.C. Gillispie (ed.), Dictionary of scientific biography 14 vols. and index, 1970–80, repr. 1981; 2 Suppl. Vols., 1978–90

GL
H. Keil (ed.), Grammatici Latini 7 vols., 1855–80

GLM
A. Riese (ed.), Geographi Latini Minores, 1878

Glotta
Glotta. Zeitschrift für griechische und lateinische Sprache

GMth
F. Zaminer (ed.), Geschichte der Musiktheorie, 1984 ff.

Gnomon
Gnomon. Kritische Zeitschrift für die gesamte klassische Altertumswissenschaft

Göbl
R. Göbl, Antike Numismatik 2 vols., 1978

Goleniševev
I.N. Goleniševev-Kutuzov, Il Rinascimento italiano e le letterature slave dei secoli XV e XVI, 1973

Gordon
A.E. Gordon, Album of Dated Latin Inscriptions 4 vols., 1958–65

Goulet
R. Goulet (ed.), Dictionnaire des philosophes antiques, 1989 ff.

Graf
F. Graf, Nordionische Kulte. Religionsgeschichtliche und epigraphische Untersuchungen zu den Kulten von Chios, Erythrai, Klazomenai und Phokaia, 1985

GRBS
Greek, Roman and Byzantine Studies

Grenier
A. Grenier, Manuel d'archéologie gallo-romaine 4 vols., 1931–60; vols. 1 and 2, repr. 1985

GRF
H. Funaioli (ed.), Grammaticae Romanae Fragmenta, 1907

GRF(add)
A. Mazzarino, Grammaticae Romanae Fragmenta aetatis Caesareae (accedunt volumini Funaioliano addenda), 1955

GRLMA
Grundriß der romanischen Literaturen des Mittelalters

Gruen, Last Gen.
E.S. Gruen, The Last Generation of the Roman Republic, 1974

Gruen, Rome
E.S. Gruen, The Hellenistic World and the Coming of Rome, 1984, repr. 1986

Gruppe
O. Gruppe, Geschichte der klassischen Mythologie und Religionsgeschichte während des Mittelalters im Abendland und während der Neuzeit, 1921

Gundel
W. and H-G. Gundel, Astrologumena. Die astrologische Literatur in der Antike und ihre Geschichte, 1966

Guthrie
W.K.C. Guthrie, A History of Greek Philosophy 6 vols., 1962–81

GVI
W. Peek (ed.), Griechische Vers-Inschriften, Vol. I, 1955

Gymnasium
Gymnasium. Zeitschrift für Kultur der Antike und humanistische Bildung

HABES
Heidelberger althistorische Beiträge und epigraphische Studien, 1986 ff.

Habicht
C. Habicht, Athen. Die Geschichte der Stadt in hellenistischer Zeit, 1995

Hakkert
A.M. Hakkert (ed.), Lexicon of Greek and Roman Cities and Place-Names in Antiquity c. 1500 B.C. – c. A.D. 500, 1990 ff.

Halfmann
H. Halfmann, Die Senatoren aus dem östlichen Teil des Imperium Romanum bis zum Ende des 2. Jahrhunderts n. Chr. (Hypomnemata 58), 1979

Hamburger
K. Hamburger, Von Sophokles zu Sartre. Griechische Dramenfiguren antik und modern, 1962

Hannestad
N. Hannestad, Roman Art and Imperial Policy, 1986

Hansen, Democracy
M.H. Hansen, The Athenian Democracy in the Age of Demosthenes. Structure, Principles and Ideology, 1991, repr. 1993

Harris
W.V. Harris, War and Imperialism in Republican Rome 327–70 B.C., 1979

Hasebroek
J. Hasebroek, Griechische Wirtschafts- und Gesellschaftsgeschichte bis zur Perserzeit, 1931

HbdOr
B. Spuler (ed.), Handbuch der Orientalistik, 1952 ff.

HbdrA
J. Marquardt, TH. Mommsen, Handbuch der römischen Alterthümer, vols. 1–3, ³1887 f.; vols. 4–7, ²1881–86

HBr
P. Herrmann, R. Herbig, (ed.), Denkmäler der Malerei des Altertums 2 vols., 1904–50

HDA
H. Bächtold-Stäubli et al. (ed.), Handwörter-

buch des deutschen Aberglaubens 10 vols., 1927–42, repr. 1987

HdArch

W. Otto, U. Hausmann (ed.), Handbuch der Archäologie. Im Rahmen des HdbA 7 vols., 1969–90

HdbA

I. v. Müller, H. Bengtson (ed.), Handbuch der Altertumswissenschaft, 1977 ff.

Heckel

W. Heckel, Marshals of Alexander's Empire, 1978

Heinemann

K. Heinemann, Die tragischen Gestalten der Griechen in der Weltliteratur, 1920

Helbig

W. Helbig, Führer durch die öffentlichen Sammlungen klassischer Altertümer in Rom 4 vols., ⁴1963–72

Hephaistos

Hephaistos. Kritische Zeitschrift zu Theorie und Praxis der Archäologie, Kunstwissenschaft und angrenzender Gebiete

Hermes

Hermes. Zeitschrift für klassische Philologie

Herrscherbild

Das römische Herrscherbild, 1939 ff.

Herzog, Staatsverfassung

E. v. Herzog, Geschichte und System der römischen Staatsverfassung 2 vols., 1884–91, repr. 1965

Hesperia

Hesperia. Journal of the American School of Classical Studies at Athens

Heubeck

A. Heubeck, Schrift (Archaeologia Homerica Chapter X Vol. 3), 1979

Heumann/Seckel

H.G. Heumann, E. Seckel (ed.), Handlexikon zu den Quellen des römischen Rechts, ¹¹1971

Highet

G. Highet, The Classical Tradition: Greek and Roman Influences on Western literature, ⁴1968, repr. 1985

Hild

F. Hild, Kilikien und Isaurien (Denkschriften der Österreichischen Akademie der Wissenschaften, Philosophisch-Historische Klasse 215; TIB 5) 2 vols., 1990

Hild/Restle

F. Hild, M. Restle, Kappadokien (Kappadokia, Charsianon, Sebasteia und Lykandos) (Denkschriften der Österreichischen Akademie der Wissenschaften: Philosophisch-Historische Klasse 149; TIB 2), 1981

Hirschfeld

O. Hirschfeld, Die kaiserlichen Verwaltungsbeamten bis auf Diocletian, ²1905

Historia

Historia. Zeitschrift für Alte Geschichte

HJb

Historisches Jahrbuch

HLav

Humanistica Lavanensia

HLL

R. Herzog, P.L. Schmidt (ed.), Handbuch der lateinischen Literatur der Antike, 1989 ff.

HM

A History of Macedonia, Vol. 1: N.G.L. Hammond, Historical geography and prehistory, 1972; Vol. 2: N.G.L. Hammond, G.T. Griffith, 550–336 BC, 1979; Vol. 3: N.G.L. Hammond, F.W. Walbank, 336–167 BC, 1988

HmT

H.H. Eggebrecht, Handwörterbuch der musikalischen Terminologie, 1972 ff.

HN

B.V. Head, Historia numorum. A manual of Greek numismatics, ²1911

Hodge

T.A. Hodge, Roman Aqueducts and Water Supply, 1992

Hölbl

G. Hölbl, Geschichte des Ptolemäerreiches. Politik, Ideologie und religiöse Kultur von Alexander den Großen bis zur römischen Eroberung, 1994

Hölkeskamp

K.-J. Hölkeskamp, Die Entstehung der Nobilität. Studien zur sozialen und politischen Geschichte der Römischen Republik im 4.Jh. v. Chr., 1987

Hoffmann

D. Hofmann, Das spätrömische Bewegungsheer und die Notitia dignitatum (Epigraphische Studien 7) 2 vols., 1969 f. = (Diss.), 1958

Holder

A. Holder, Alt-celtischer Sprachschatz 3 vols., 1896-1913, repr. 1961 f.

Honsell

H. Honsell, Römisches Recht (Springer-Lehrbuch), ³1994

Hopfner

T. Hopfner, Griechisch-ägyptischer Offenbarungszauber 2 vols. in 3 parts, 1921–24, repr. 1974–90

Hopkins, Conquerors

K. Hopkins, Conquerors and Slaves. Sociological Studies in Roman History, Vol. 1, 1978

Hopkins, Death

K. Hopkins, Death and Renewal. Sociological Studies in Roman History, Vol. 2, 1983

HR

History of Religions

HRR

H. Peter (ed.), Historicorum Romanorum Reliquiae, Vol. 1, 1914; Vol. 2, 1906, repr. 1967

HrwG

H. Cancik, B. Gladigow, M. Laubscher (from Vol. 2: K.-H. Kohl) (ed.), Handbuch religionswissenschaftlicher Grundbegriffe, 1988 ff.

HS

Historische Sprachforschung

HSM
Histoire des sciences médicales
HSPh
Harvard Studies in Classical Philology
Hülser
K. HÜLSER, Die Fragmente zur Dialektik der Stoiker.
Neue Sammlung der Texte mit deutscher Überset-
zung und Kommentaren 4 vols., 1987 f.
Humphrey
J.H. HUMPHREY, Roman Circuses. Arenas for
Chariot Racing, 1986
Hunger, Literatur
H. HUNGER, Die hochsprachlich profane Literatur
der Byzantiner (HdbA 12, 5) 2 vols., 1978
Hunger, Mythologie
H. HUNGER (ed.), Lexikon der griechischen und rö-
mischen Mythologie, ⁶1969
Huss
W. HUSS, Geschichte der Karthager (HdbA III 8),
1985
HWdPh
J. RITTER, K. GRÜNDER (ed.), Historisches Wörter-
buch der Philosophie, 1971 ff.
HWdR
G. UEDING (ed.), Historisches Wörterbuch der Rhe-
torik, 1992 ff.
HZ
Historische Zeitschrift
IA
Iranica Antiqua
IconRel
T.P. v. BAAREN (ed.), Iconography of Religions,
1970 ff.
ICUR
A. FERRUA, G.B. DE ROSSI, Inscriptiones christianae
urbis Romae, 1922ff.
IDélos
Inscriptions de Délos, 1926 ff.
IDidyma
A. REHM (ed.), Didyma, Vol. 2: Die Inschriften,
1958
IEG
M. L. WEST (ed.), Iambi et elegi Graeci ante Alexan-
drum cantati 2 vols., 1989–92
IEJ
Israel Exploration Journal
IER
Illustrierte Enzyklopädie der Renaissance
IEry
H. ENGELMANN (ed.), Die Inschriften von Erythrai
und Klazomenai 2 vols., 1972 f.
IF
Indogermanische Forschungen
IG
Inscriptiones Graecae, 1873 ff.
IGA
H. ROEHL (ed.), Inscriptiones Graecae antiquissi-
mae praeter Atticas in Attica repertas, 1882, repr.
1977

IGBulg
G. MIHAILOV (ed.), Inscriptiones Graecae in Bulga-
ria repertae 5 vols., 1956–1996
IGLS
Inscriptions grecques et latines de la Syrie, 1929 ff.
IGR
R. CAGNAT ET AL. (ed.), Inscriptiones Graecae ad res
Romanas pertinentes 4 vols., 1906–27
IGUR
L. MORETTI, Inscriptiones Graecae urbis Romae 4
vols., 1968–90
IJCT
International Journal of the Classical Tradition
IJsewijn
J. IJSEWIJN, Companion to Neo Latin Studies,
²1990 ff.
IK
Die Inschriften griechischer Städte aus Kleinasien,
1972 ff.
ILCV
E. DIEHL (ed.), Inscriptiones Latinae Christianae
Veteres orientis 3 vols., 1925–31, repr. 1961; J. MO-
REAU, H.I. MARROU (ed.), Suppl., 1967
ILLRP
A. DEGRASSI (ed.), Inscriptiones Latinae liberae rei
publicae 2 vols., 1957–63, repr. 1972
ILS
H. DESSAU (ed.), Inscriptiones Latinae Selectae 3
vols. in 5 parts, 1892–1916, repr. ⁴1974
IMagn.
O. KERN (ed.), Die Inschriften von Magnesia am
Mäander, 1900, repr. 1967
IMU
Italia medioevale e umanistica
Index
Index. Quaderni camerti di studi romanistici
InscrIt
A. DEGRASSI (ed.), Inscriptiones Italiae, 1931 ff.
IOSPE
V. LATYSCHEW (ed.), Inscriptiones antiquae orae
septentrionalis ponti Euxini Graecae et Latinae 3
vols., 1885–1901, repr. 1965
IPNB
M. MAYRHOFER, R. SCHMITT (ed.), Iranisches Per-
sonennamenbuch, 1979 ff.
IPQ
International Philosophical Quaterly
IPriene
F. HILLER VON GÄRTRINGEN, Inschriften von Priene,
1906
Irmscher
J. IRMSCHER (ed.), Renaissance und Humanismus in
Mittel- und Osteuropa, 1962
Isager/Skydsgaard
S. ISAGER, J.E. SKYDSGAARD, Ancient Greek Agricul-
ture, An Introduction, 1992
Isis
Isis

IstForsch
    Istanbuler Forschungen des Deutschen Archäologi-
    schen Instituts
Iura
    IURA, Rivista internazionale di diritto romano e an-
    tico
IvOl
    W. DITTENBERGER, K. PURGOLD, Inschriften von
    Olympia, 1896, repr. 1966
Jaffé
    P. JAFFÉ, Regesta pontificum Romanorum ab con-
    dita ecclesia ad annum 1198 2 vols., ²1985–88
JBAA
    The Journal of the British Archaeological Associa-
    tion
JbAC
    Jahrbuch für Antike und Christentum
JCS
    Journal of Cuneiform Studies
JDAI
    Jahrbuch des Deutschen Archäologischen Instituts
JEA
    The Journal of Egyptian Archaeology
Jenkyns, DaD
    R. JENKYNS, Dignity and Decadence: Classicism and
    the Victorians, 1992
Jenkyns, Legacy
    R. JENKYNS, The Legacy of Rome: A New Appraisal,
    1992
JHAS
    Journal for the History of Arabic Science
JHB
    Journal of the History of Biology
JHM
    Journal of the History of Medicine and Allied Sci-
    ences
JHPh
    Journal of the History of Philosophy
JHS
    Journal of Hellenic Studies
JLW
    Jahrbuch für Liturgiewissenschaft
JMRS
    Journal of Medieval and Renaissance Studies
JNES
    Journal of Near Eastern Studies
JNG
    Jahrbuch für Numismatik und Geldgeschichte
JÖAI
    Jahreshefte des Österreichischen Archäologischen
    Instituts
Jones, Cities
    A.H.M. JONES, The Cities of the Eastern Roman
    Provinces, ²1971
Jones, Economy
    A.H.M. JONES, The Roman Economy. Studies in
    Ancient Economic and Administrative History,
    1974

Jones, LRE
    A.H.M. JONES, The Later Roman Empire 284–602.
    A Social, Economic and Administrative Survey,
    1964
Jones, RGL
    A.H.M. JONES, Studies in Roman Government and
    Law, 1968
Jost
    M. JOST, Sanctuaires et cultes d'Arcadie, 1985
JPh
    Journal of Philosophy
JRGZ
    Jahrbuch des Römisch-Germanischen Zentralmu-
    seums
JRS
    Journal of Roman Studies
Justi
    F. JUSTI, Iranisches Namenbuch, 1895
JWG
    Jahrbuch für Wirtschaftsgeschichte
JWI
    Journal of the Warburg and Courtauld Institutes
Kadmos
    Kadmos. Zeitschrift für vor- und frühgriechische
    Epigraphik
KAI
    H. DONNER, W. RÖLLIG, Kanaanaeische und ara-
    maeische Inschriften 3 vols., ³1971–1976
Kajanto, Cognomina
    I. KAJANTO, The Latin Cognomina, 1965
Kajanto, Supernomina
    I. KAJANTO, Supernomina. A study in Latin epigra-
    phy (Commentationes humanarum litterarum 40,
    1), 1966
Kamptz
    H. V. KAMPTZ, Homerische Personennamen.
    Sprachwissenschaftliche und historische Klassifika-
    tion, 1982 = II. V. KAMPTZ, Sprachwissenschaftliche
    und historische Klassifikation der homerischen Per-
    sonennamen (Diss.), 1958
Karlowa
    O. KARLOWA, Römische Rechtsgeschichte 2 vols.,
    1885–1901
Kaser, AJ
    M. KASER, Das altrömische Jus. Studien zur Rechts-
    vorstellung und Rechtsgeschichte der Römer, 1949
Kaser, RPR
    M. KASER, Das römische Privatrecht (Rechtsge-
    schichte des Altertums Part 3, Vol. 3; HbdA 10, 3, 3)
    2 vols., ³1971–75
Kaser, RZ
    M. KASER, Das römische Zivilprozessrecht (Rechts-
    geschichte des Altertums Part 3, Vol. 4; HbdA 10, 3,
    4), 1966
Kearns
    E. KEARNS, The Heroes of Attica, 1989 (BICS Suppl.
    57)
Keller
    O. KELLER, Die antike Tierwelt 2 vols., 1909–20,
    repr. 1963

Kelnhofer
F. KELNHOFER, Die topographische Bezugsgrundlage der Tabula Imperii Byzantini (Denkschriften der Österreichischen Akademie der Wissenschaften: Philosophisch-Historische Klasse 125 Beih.; TIB 1, Beih.), 1976

Kienast
D. KIENAST, Römische Kaisertabelle. Grundzüge einer römischen Kaiserchronologie, 1990

Kindler
W. JENS (ed.), Kindlers Neues Literatur Lexikon 20 vols., 1988–92

Kinkel
G. KINKEL, (ed.), Epicorum Graecorum Fragmenta, 1877

Kirsten /Kraiker
E. KIRSTEN, W. KRAIKER, Griechenlandkunde. Ein Führer zu klassischen Stätten, ⁵1967

Kleberg
T. KLEBERG, Hôtels, restaurants et cabarets dans l'antiquité Romaine. Études historiques et philologiques, 1957

Klio
Klio. Beiträge zur Alten Geschichte

KlP
K. ZIEGLER (ed.), Der Kleine Pauly. Lexikon der Antike 5 vols., 1964–75, repr. 1979

Knobloch
J. KNOBLOCH ET AL. (ed.), Sprachwissenschaftliches Wörterbuch (Indogermanische Bibliothek 2), 1986 ff (1st installment 1961)

Koch/Sichtermann
G. KOCH, H. SICHTERMANN, Römische Sarkophage, 1982

Koder
J. KODER, Der Lebensraum der Byzantiner. Historisch-geographischer Abriß ihres mittelalterlichen Staates im östlichen Mittelmeerraum, 1984

Koder/Hild
J. KODER, F. HILD, Hellas und Thessalia (Denkschriften der Österreichischen Akademie der Wissenschaften, Philosophisch-Historische Klasse 125; TIB 1), 1976

Kraft
K. KRAFT, Gesammelte Aufsätze zur antiken Geschichte und Militärgeschichte, 1973

Kromayer/Veith
J. KROMAYER, G. VEITH, Heerwesen und Kriegführung der Griechen und Römer, 1928, repr. 1963

Krumbacher
K. KRUMBACHER, Geschichte der byzantinischen Litteratur von Justinian bis zum Ende des oströmischen Reiches (527–1453) (HdbA 9, 1), ²1897, repr. 1970

KSd
J. FRIEDRICH (ed.), Kleinasiatische Sprachdenkmäler (Kleine Texte für Vorlesungen und Übungen 163), 1932

KUB
Keilschrifturkunden von Boghazköi

Kühner/Blass
R. KÜHNER, F. BLASS, Ausführliche Grammatik der griechischen Sprache. Teil 1: Elementar- und Formenlehre 2 vols., ³1890–92

Kühner/Gerth
R. KÜHNER, B. GERTH, Ausführliche Grammatik der griechischen Sprache. Teil 2: Satzlehre 2 vols., ³1898–1904; W. M. CALDER III, Index locorum, 1965

Kühner/Holzweißig
R. KÜHNER, F. HOLZWEISSIG, Ausführliche Grammatik der lateinischen Sprache. Teil I: Elementar-, Formen- und Wortlehre, ²1912

Kühner/Stegmann
R. KÜHNER, C. STEGMANN, Ausführliche Grammatik der lateinischen Sprache. Teil 2: Satzlehre, 2 vols., ⁴1962 (revised by A. THIERFELDER); G.S. SCHWARZ, R. L. WERTIS, Index locorum, 1980

Kullmann/Atlhoff
W. KULLMANN, J. ALTHOFF (ed.), Vermittlung und Tradierung von Wissen in der griechischen Kultur, 1993

Kunkel
W. KUNKEL, Herkunft und soziale Stellung der römischen Juristen, ²1967

KWdH
H.H. SCHMITT (ed.), Kleines Wörterbuch des Hellenismus, ²1993

Lacey
W.K. LACEY, The Family in Classical Greece, 1968

LÄ
W. HELCK ET AL. (ed.), Lexikon der Ägyptologie 7 vols., 1975–92 (1st installment 1972)

LAK
H. BRUNNER, K. FLESSEL, F. HILLER ET AL. (ed.), Lexikon Alte Kulturen 3 vols., 1990–93

Lanciani
R. LANCIANI, Forma urbis Romae, 1893–1901

Lange
C.C.L. LANGE, Römische Altertümer, Vols. 1–2, ²1876–79; Vol. 3, 1876

Langosch
K. LANGOSCH, Mittellatein und Europa, 1990

Latomus
Latomus. Revue d'études latines

Latte
K. LATTE, Römische Religionsgeschichte (HdbA 5, 4), 1960, repr. 1992

Lauffer, BL
S. LAUFFER, Die Bergwerkssklaven von Laureion, ²1979

Lauffer, Griechenland
S. LAUFFER (ed.), Griechenland. Lexikon der historischen Stätten von den Anfängen bis zur Gegenwart, 1989

Lausberg
H. LAUSBERG, Handbuch der literarischen Rhetorik. Eine Grundlegung der Literaturwissenschaft, ³1990

LAW
C. ANDRESEN ET AL.(ed.), Lexikon der Alten Welt, 1965, repr. 1990
LCI
Lexikon der christlichen lkonographie
LdA
J. IRMSCHER (ed.), Lexikon der Antike, ¹⁰1990
Le Bohec
Y. LE BOHEC, L'armée romaine. Sous le Haut-Empire, 1989
Leitner
H. LEITNER, Zoologische Terminologie beim Älteren Plinius (Diss.), 1972
Leo
F. LEO, Geschichte der römischen Literatur. I. Die archaische Literatur, 1913, repr. 1958
Lesky
A. LESKY, Geschichte der griechischen Literatur, ³1971, repr. 1993
Leumann
M. LEUMANN, Lateinische Laut- und Formenlehre (HdbA II 2, 1), 1977
Leunissen
P.M.M. LEUNISSEN, Konsuln und Konsulare in der Zeit von Commodus bis zu Alexander Severus (180–235 n. Chr.) (Dutch Monographs in Ancient History and Archaeology 6), 1989
Lewis/Short
C.T. LEWIS, C. SHORT, A Latin Dictionary, ²1980
LFE
B. SNELL (ed.), Lexikon des frühgriechischen Epos, 1979 ff. (1st installment 1955)
LGPN
P.M. FRASER ET AL. (ed.), A Lexicon of Greek Personal Names, 1987 ff.
Liebenam
W. LIEBENAM, Städteverwaltung im römischen Kaiserreich, 1900
Lietzmann
H. LIETZMANN, Geschichte der Alten Kirche, ⁴/⁵1975
LIMC
J. BOARDMAN ET AL. (ed.), Lexicon Iconographicum Mythologiae Classicae, 1981 ff.
Lippold
G. LIPPOLD, Die griechische Plastik (HdArch III), 1950
Lipsius
J.H. LIPSIUS, Das attische Recht und Rechtsverfahren. Mit Benutzung des Attischen Processes 3 vols., 1905–15, repr. 1984
Lloyd-Jones
H. LLOYD-JONES, Blood for the Ghosts – Classical Influences in the Nineteenth and Twentieth Centuries, 1982
LMA
R.-H. BAUTIER, R. AUTY (ed.), Lexikon des Mittelalters 7 vols., 1980–93 (1st installment 1977), 3rd vol. repr. 1995

Lobel/Page
E. LOBEL, D. PAGE (ed.), Poetarum lesbiorum fragmenta, 1955, repr. 1968
Loewy
E. LOEWY (ed.), Inschriften griechischer Bildhauer, 1885, repr. 1965
LPh
T. SCHNEIDER, Lexikon der Pharaonen. Die altägyptischen Könige von der Frühzeit bis zur Römerherrschaft, 1994
LRKA
Friedrich Lübkers Reallexikon des Klassischen Altertums, ⁸1914
LSAG
L.H. JEFFERY, The Local Scripts of Archaic Greece. A Study of the Origin of the Greek Alphabet and its Development from the Eighth to the Fifth Centuries B.C., ²1990
LSAM
F. SOKOLOWSKI, Lois sacrées de l'Asie mineure, 1955
LSCG
F. SOKOLOWSKI, Lois sacrées des cités grecques, 1969
LSCG, Suppl
F. SOKOLOWSKI, Lois sacrées des cités grecques, Supplément, 1962
LSJ
H.G. LIDDELL, R. SCOTT, H.S. JONES ET AL. (ed.), A Greek-English Lexicon, ⁹1940; Suppl.: 1968, repr. 1992
LThK²
J. HÖFER, K. RAHNER (ed.), Lexikon für Theologie und Kirche 14 vols., ²1957–86
LThK¹
W. KASPER ET AL. (ed.), Lexikon für Theologie und Kirche, ¹1993 ff.
LTUR
E.M. STEINBY (ed.), Lexicon Topographicum Urbis Romae, 1993 ff.
LUA
Lunds Universitets Arsskrift / Acta Universitatis Lundensis
Lugli, Fontes
G. LUGLI (ed.), Fontes ad topographiam veteris urbis Romae pertinentes, 6 of 8 vols. partially appeared, 1952–62
Lugli, Monumenti
G. LUGLI, I Monumenti antichi di Roma e suburbio, 3 vols., 1930–38; Suppl.: 1940
Lustrum
Lustrum. Internationale Forschungsberichte aus dem Bereich des klassischen Altertums
M&H
Mediaevalia et Humanistica. Studies in Medieval and Renaissance Society
MacDonald
G. MACDONALD, Catalogue of Greek Coins in the Hunterian Collection, University of Glasgow 3 vols., 1899–1905

MacDowell
D. M. MACDOWELL, The law in Classical Athens (Aspects of Greek and Roman life), 1978
MAev.
Medium Aevum
Magie
D. MAGIE, Roman Rule in Asia Minor to the End of the Third Century after Christ, 1950, repr. 1975
MAII
Mosaici Antichi in Italia, 1967 ff
MAMA
Monumenta Asiae minoris Antiqua, 1927ff.
Manitius
M. MANITIUS, Geschichte der lateinischen Literatur des Mittelalters (HdbA 9, 2) 3 vols., 1911–31, repr. 1973–76
MarbWPr
Marburger-Winckelmann-Programm
Marganne
M.H. MARGANNE, Inventaire analytique des papyrus grecs de médecine, 1981
Marrou
H.-I. MARROU, Geschichte der Erziehung im klassischen Altertum (translation of Histoire de l'éducation dans l'antiquité), ²1977
Martinelli
M. MARTINELLI (ed.), La ceramica degli Etruschi, 1987
Martino, SCR
F. DE MARTINO, Storia della costituzione romana 5 vols., ²1972–75; Indici 1990
Martino, WG
F. DE MARTINO, Wirtschaftsgeschichte des alten Rom, ²1991
Masson
O. MASSON, Les inscriptions chypriotes syllabiques. Recueil critique et commenté (Études chypriotes 1), ²1983
Matz/Duhn
F. MATZ, F. v. DUHN (ed.), Antike Bildwerke in Rom mit Ausschluß der größeren Sammlungen 3 vols., 1881 f.
MAVORS
M.P. SPEIDEL (ed.), Roman Army Researches 1984 ff.
MDAI(A)
Mitteilungen des Deutschen Archäologischen Instituts, Athenische Abteilung
MDAI(Dam)
Damaszener Mitteilungen des Deutschen Archäologischen Instituts
MDAI(Ist)
Istanbuler Mitteilungen des Deutschen Archäologischen Instituts
MDAI(K)
Mitteilungen des Deutschen Archäologischen Instituts (Abteilung Kairo)
MDAI(R)
Mitteilungen des Deutschen Archäologischen Instituts, Römische Abteilung

MDOG
Mitteilungen der Deutschen Orient-Gesellschaft zu Berlin
MededRom
Mededelingen van het Nederlands Historisch Instituut te Rome
Mediaevalia
Mediaevalia
Mediaevistik
Mediaevistik. Internationale Zeitschrift für interdisziplinäre Mittelalterforschung
MEFRA
Mélanges d'Archéologie et d'Histoire de l'École Française de Rome. Antiquité
Meiggs
R. MEIGGS, Trees and Timber in the Ancient Mediterranean World, 1982
Merkelbach/West
R. MERKELBACH, M.L. WEST (ed.), Fragmenta Hesiodea, 1967
Mette
H.J. METTE, Urkunden dramatischer Aufführungen in Griechenland, 1977
MG
Monuments Grecs
MGG¹
F. BLUME (ed.), Die Musik in Geschichte und Gegenwart. Allgemeine Enzyklopädie der Musik 17 vols., 1949–86, repr. 1989
MGG²
L. FINSCHER (ed.), Die Musik in Geschichte und Gegenwart 20 vols., ²1994 ff.
MGH
Monumenta Germaniae Historica inde ab anno Christi quingentesimo usque ad annum millesimum et quingentesimum, 1826 ff.
MGH AA
Monumenta Germaniae Historica: Auctores Antiquissimi
MGH DD
Monumenta Germaniae Historica: Diplomata
MGH Epp
Monumenta Germaniae Historica: Epistulae
MGH PL
Monumenta Germaniae Historica: Poetae Latini medii aevi
MGH SS ·
Monumenta Germaniae Historica: Scriptores
MGrecs
Monuments Grecs publiés par l'Association pour l'Encouragement des Etudes grecques en France 2 vols., 1872–97
MH
Museum Helveticum
MiB
Musikgeschichte in Bildern
Millar, Emperor
F.G.B. MILLAR, The Emperor in the Roman World, 1977

Millar, Near East
  F.G.B. MILLAR, The Roman Near East, 1993
Miller
  K. MILLER, Itineraria Romana. Römische Reisewe-
  ge an der Hand der Tabula Peutingeriana, 1916,
  repr. 1988
Millett
  P. MILLETT, Lending and Borrowing in Ancient
  Athens, 1991
Minos
  Minos
MIO
  Mitteilungen des Instituts für Orientforschung
MIR
  Moneta Imperii Romani. Österreichische Akademie
  der Wissenschaften. Veröffentlichungen der Numis-
  matischen Kommission
Mitchell
  S. MITCHELL, Anatolia. Land, Men and Gods in Asia
  Minor 2 vols., 1993
Mitteis
  L. MITTEIS, Reichsrecht und Volksrecht in den öst-
  lichen Provinzen des römischen Kaiserreichs. Mit
  Beiträgen zur Kenntnis des griechischen Rechts und
  der spätrömischen Rechtsentwicklung, 1891, repr.
  1984
Mittcis/Wilcken
  L. MITTEIS, U. WILCKEN, Grundzüge und Chresto-
  mathie der Papyruskunde, 1912, repr. 1978
ML
  R. MEIGGS, D. LEWIS (ed.), A Selection of Greek
  Historical Inscriptions to the End of the Fifth Cen-
  tury B.C., ²1988
MLatJb
  Mittellateinisches Jahrbuch. Internationale Zeit-
  schrift für Mediävistik
Mnemosyne
  Mnemosyne. Bibliotheca Classica Batava
MNVP
  Mitteilungen und Nachrichten des Deutschen Paläs-
  tinavereins
MNW
  H. MEIER ET AL. (ed.), Kulturwissenschaftliche Bi-
  bliographie zum Nachleben der Antike 2 vols.,
  1931–38
Mollard-Besques
  S. MOLLARD-BESQUES, Musée National du Louvre.
  Catalogue raisonné des figurines et reliefs en terre-
  cuite grecs, étrusques et romains 4 vols., 1954–86
Momigliano
  A. MOMIGLIANO, Contributi alla storia degli studi
  classici, 1955 ff.
Mommsen, Schriften
  TH. MOMMSEN, Gesammelte Schriften 8 vols.,
  1904–13, repr. 1965
Mommsen, Staatsrecht
  TH. MOMMSEN, Römisches Staatsrecht 3 vols., Vol.
  1, ³1887; Vol. 2 f., 1887 f.

Mommsen Strafrecht
  TH. MOMMSEN, Römisches Strafrecht, 1899, repr.
  1955
Mon.Ant.ined.
  Monumenti Antichi inediti
Moos
  P. v. MOOS, Geschichte als Topik, 1988
Moraux
  P. MORAUX, Der Aristotelismus bei den Griechen
  von Andronikos bis Alexander von Aphrodisias (Pe-
  ripatoi 5 und 6) 2 vols., 1973–84
Moreau
  J. MOREAU, Dictionnaire de géographie historique
  de la Gaule et de la France, 1972; Suppl.: 1983
Moretti
  L. MORETTI (ed.), Iscrizioni storiche ellenistiche 2
  vols., 1967–76
MP
  Modern Philology
MPalerne
  Mémoires du Centre Jean Palerne
MRR
  T.R.S. BROUGHTON, The Magistrates of the Roman
  Republic 2 vols., 1951–52; Suppl.: 1986
MSG
  C. JAN (ed.), Musici scriptores Graeci, 1895; Suppl.:
  1899, repr. 1962
Müller
  D. MÜLLER, Topographischer Bildkommentar zu
  den Historien Herodots: Griechenland im Umfang
  des heutigen griechischen Staatsgebiets, 1987
Müller-Wiener
  W. MÜLLER-WIENER, Bildlexikon zur Topographie
  Istanbuls, 1977
Münzer¹
  F. MÜNZER, Römische Adelsparteien und Adelsfa-
  milien, 1920
Münzer²
  F. MÜNZER, Römische Adelsparteien und Adelsfa-
  milien, ²1963
Murray/Price
  O. MURRAY, S. PRICE (ed.), The Greek City: From
  Homer to Alexander, 1990
Muséon
  Muséon Revue d'Études Orientales
MVAG
  Mitteilungen der Vorderasiatischen (Ägyptischen)
  Gesellschaft
MVPhW
  Mitteilungen des Vereins klassischer Philologen in
  Wien
MythGr
  Mythographi Graeci 3 vols., 1894–1902; Vol. 1,
  ²1926
Nash
  E. NASH, Bildlexikon zur Topographie des antiken
  Rom, 1961 f.
NC
  Numismatic Chronicle

NClio
　La Nouvelle Clio
NDB
　Neue Deutsche Biographie, 1953 ff.; Vols. 1–6, repr.
　1971
NEAEHL
　E. STERN (ed.), The New Encyclopedia of Archaeo-
　logical Excavations in the Holy Land 4 vols., 1993
Neoph.
　Neophilologus
Newald
　R. NEWALD, Nachleben des antiken Geistes im
　Abendland bis zum Beginn des Humanismus, 1960
NGrove
　The New Grove Dictionary of Music and Musicians,
　⁶1980
NGroveInst
　The New Grove Dictionary of Musical Instruments,
　1994
NHCod
　Nag Hammadi Codex
NHS
　Nag Hammadi Studies
Nicolet
　C. NICOLET, L' Ordre équestre à l'époque républi-
　caine 312–43 av. J.-C. 2 vols., 1966–74
Nilsson, Feste
　M.P. NILSSON, Griechische Feste von religiöser Be-
　deutung mit Ausschluss der attischen, 1906
Nilsson, GGR,
　M.P. NILSSON, Geschichte der griechischen Religion
　(HdbA 5, 2), Vol. 1, ³1967, repr. 1992; Vol. 2, ⁴1988
Nilsson, MMR
　M.P. NILSSON, The Minoan-Mycenaean Religion
　and its Survival in Greek Religion, ²1950
Nissen
　H. NISSEN, Italische Landeskunde 2 vols., 1883–
　1902
Nock
　A.D. NOCK, Essays on Religion and the Ancient
　World, 1972
Noethlichs
　K.L. NOETHLICHS, Beamtentum und Dienstverge-
　hen. Zur Staatsverwaltung in der Spätantike, 1981
Norden, Kunstprosa
　E. NORDEN, Die antike Kunstprosa vom 6. Jh. v.
　Chr. bis in die Zeit der Renaissance, ⁶1961
Norden, Literatur
　E. NORDEN, Die römische Literatur, ⁶1961
NSA
　Notizie degli scavi di antichità
NTM
　Schriftenreihe für Geschichte der Naturwissenschaf-
　ten, Technik und Medizin
Nutton
　V. NUTTON, From Democedes to Harvey. Studies in
　the History of Medicine (Collected Studies Series
　277), 1988

NZ
　Numismatische Zeitschrift
OA
　J.G. BAITER, H. SAUPPE (ed.), Oratores Attici 3 vols.,
　1839–43
OBO
　Orbis Biblicus et Orientalis
OCD
　N.G. HAMMOND, H.H. SCULLARD (ed.), The Ox-
　ford Classical Dictionary, ²1970, ³1996
ODB
　A.P. KAZHDAN ET AL. (ed.), The Oxford Dictionary
　of Byzantium, 1991 ff.
OF
　O. KERN (ed.), Orphicorum Fragmenta, ³1972
OGIS
　W. DITTENBERGER (ed.), Orientis Graeci Inscripti-
　ones Selectae 2 vols., 1903–05, repr. 1960
OLD
　P.G.W. GLARE (ed.), Oxford Latin Dictionary, 1982
　(1st installment 1968)
OIF
　Olympische Forschungen, 1941 ff.
Oliver
　J.H. OLIVER, Greek Constitutions of Early Roman
　Emperors from Inscriptions and Papyri, 1989
Olivieri
　D. OLIVIERI, Dizionario di toponomastica lombar-
　da. Nomi di comuni, frazioni, casali, monti, corsi
　d'acqua, ecc. della regione lombarda, studiati in rap-
　porto alle loro origine, ²1961
Olshausen/Biller/Wagner
　E. OLSHAUSEN, J. BILLER, J. WAGNER, Historisch-
　geographische Aspekte der Geschichte des Ponti-
　schen und Armenischen Reiches. Untersuchungen
　Zur historischen Geographie von Pontos unter den
　Mithradatiden (TAVO 29), Vol. 1, 1984
OLZ
　Orientalistische Literaturzeitung
OpAth
　Opuscula Atheniensia, 1953 ff.
OpRom
　Opuscula Romana
ORF
　E. MALCOVATI, Oratorum Romanorum Fragmenta
　(Corpus scriptorum Latinorum Paravianum 56–58);
　vols., 1930
Orientalia
　Orientalia, Neue Folge
Osborne
　R. OSBORNE, Classical Landscape with Figures: The
　Ancient Greek City and its Countryside, 1987
Overbeck
　J. OVERBECK, Die antiken Schriftquellen zur Ge-
　schichte der bildenden Künste bei den Griechen,
　1868, repr. 1959
PA
　J. KIRCHNER, Prosopographia Attica 2 vols., 1901–
　03, repr. 1966

Pack
  R.A. PACK (ed.), The Greek and Latin Literary Texts
  from Greco-Roman Egypt, ²1965
Panofsky
  E. PANOFSKY, Renaissance und Renaissancen in
  Western Art, 1960
Pape/Benseler
  W. PAPE, G.E. BENSELER, Wörterbuch der griechi-
  schen Eigennamen 2 vols., 1863–1870
PAPhS
  Proceedings of the American Philosophical Society
Parke
  H.W. PARKE, Festivals of the Athenians, 1977
Parke/Wormell
  H.W. PARKE, D.E.W. WORMELL, The Delphic Ora-
  cle, 1956
PBSR
  Papers of the British School at Rome
PCA
  Proceedings of die Classical Association. London
PCG
  R. KASSEL, C. AUSTIN (ed.), Poetae comici graeci,
  1983 ff.
PCPhS
  Proceedings of the Cambridge Philological Society
PdP
  La Parola del Passato
PE
  R. STILLWELL ET AL. (ed.), The Princeton Encyclo-
  pedia of Classical Sites, 1976
Peacock
  D.P.S. PEACOCK, Pottery in the Roman World: An
  Ethnoarchaeological Approach, 1982
PEG I
  A. BERNABÉ (ed.), Poetae epici graeci. Testimonia et
  fragmenta. Pars I, 1987
Pfeiffer, KPI
  R. PFEIFFER, Geschichte der Klassischen Philologie.
  Von den Anfängen bis zum Ende des Hellenismus,
  1978
Pfeiffer KPII
  R. PFEIFFER, Die Klassische Philologie von Petrarca
  bis Mommsen, 1982
Pfiffig
  A.J. PFIFFIG, Religio Etrusca, 1975
Pflaum
  H.G.PFLAUM, Les carrières procuratoriennes
  équestres sous le Haut-Empire Romain 3 vols. and
  figs., 1960 f.; Suppl.: 1982
Pfuhl
  E. PFUHL, Malerei und Zeichnung der Griechen,
  1923
Pfuhl/Möbius
  E. PFUHL, H. MÖBIUS, Die ostgriechischen Grabre-
  liefs 2 vols., 1977–79
PG
  J.P. MIGNE (ed.), Patrologiae cursus completus, se-
  ries Graeca 161 vols., 1857–1866; Conspectus auc-
  torum: 1882; Indices 2 vols.: 1912–32

PGM
  K. PREISENDANZ, A. HENRICHS (ed.), Papyri Grae-
  cae Magicae. Die griechischen Zauberpapyri 2 vols.,
  ²1973 f. (1928–31)
Philippson /Kirsten
  A. PHILIPPSON, A. LEHMANN, E. KIRSTEN (ed.), Die
  griechischen Landschaften. Eine Landeskunde 4
  vols., 1950–59
Philologus
  Philologus. Zeitschrift für klassische Philologie
PhQ
  Philological Quarterly
Phronesis
  Phronesis
PhU
  Philologische Untersuchungen
PhW
  Berliner Philologische Wochenschrift
Picard
  CH. PICARD, Manuel d'archéologie grecque. La
  sculpture, 1935 ff.
Pickard-Cambridge/Gould/Lewis
  A.W. PICKARD-CAMBRIDGE, J. GOULD, D.M. LE-
  WIS, The Dramatic Festivals of Athens, ²1988
Pickard-Cambridge/Webster
  A.W. PICKARD-CAMBRIDGE, T.B.L. WEBSTER,
  Dithyramb, Tragedy and Comedy, ²1962
Pigler, I
  A. PIGLER, Barockthermen. Eine Auswahl von Ver-
  zeichnissen zur lkonographie des 17. Und 18. Jahr-
  hunderts. 2 vols., ²1974; Ill. Vol.: 1974
PIR
  Prosopographia imperii Romani saeculi, Vol. I-III,
  ²1933 ff.
PL
  J.P. MIGNI (ed.), Patrologiae cursus completus, se-
  ries Latina 221 vols., 1844–65 partly repr. 5 Suppl.
  Vols., 1958–74; Index: 1965
PLM
  AE. BAEHRENS (ed.), Poetae Latini Minores 5 vols.,
  1879–83
PLRE
  A.H.M. JONES, J.R. MARTINDALE, J. MORRIS (ed.),
  The Prosopography of the Later Roman Empire 3
  vols. in 4 parts, 1971–1992
PMG
  D.L. PAGE, Poetae melici graeci, 1962
PMGF
  M. DAVIES (ed.), Poetarum melicorum Graecorum
  fragmenta, 1991
PMGTr
  H.D. BETZ (ed.), The Greek Magical Papyri in
  Translation, Including the Demotic Spells, ²1992
Poccetti
  D. POCCETTI, Nuovi documenti italici a complemen-
  to del manuale di E. Vetter (Orientamenti linguistici
  8), 1979
Pökel
  W. PÖKEL, Philologisches Schriftstellerlexikon,
  1882, repr. ²1974

Poetica
  Poetica. Zeitschrift für Sprach- und Literaturwissenschaft
Pokorny
  J. POKORNY, Indogermanisches etymologisches Wörterbuch 2 vols., ²1989
Poulsen
  F. POULSEN, Catalogue of Ancient Sculpture in the Ny Carlsberg Glyptotek, 1951
PP
  W. PEREMANS (ed.), Prosopographia Ptolemaica (Studia hellenistica) 9 vols., 1950–81, repr. Vol. 1–3, 1977
PPM
  Pompei, Pitture e Mosaici, 1990 ff.
Praktika
  Πρακτικά της εν Αθήναις αρχαιολογικάς εταιρείας
Préaux
  C. PRÉAUX, L'économie royale des Lagides, 1939, repr. 1980
Preller/Robert
  L. PRELLER, C. ROBERT, Griechische Mythologie, ⁵1964 ff.
Pritchett
  K. PRITCHETT, Studies in Ancient Greek Topography (University of California Publications, Classical Studies) 8 vols., 1969–92
PropKg
  K. BITTEL ET AL. (ed.), Propyläen Kunstgeschichte 22 vols., 1966–80, repr. 1985
Prosdocimi
  A.L. PROSDOCIMI, M. CRISTOFANI, Lingue dialetti dell'Italia antica, 1978; A. MARINETTI, Aggiornamenti ed Indici, 1984
PrZ
  Prähistorische Zeitschrift
PSI
  G. VITELLI, M. NORSA, V. BARTOLETTI ET AL. (ed.), Papiri greci e latini (Pubblicazione della Soc. Italiana per la ricerca dei pap. greci e latini in Egitto), 1912 ff.
QSt
  Quellen und Studien zur Geschichte und Kultur des Altertums und des Mittelalters
Quasten
  J. QUASTEN, Patrology 2 vols., 1950–53
RA
  Revue Archéologique
RAC
  T. KLAUSER, E. DASSMANN (ed.), Reallexikon für Antike und Christentum. Sachwörterbuch zur Auseinandersetzung des Christentums mit der antiken Welt, 1950 ff. (1st installment 1941)
RACr
  Rivista di Archeologia Cristiana
Radermacher
  L. RADERMACHER, Artium Scriptores. Reste der voraristotelischen Rhetorik, 1951
Radke
  G. RADKE, Die Götter Altitaliens, ²1979

Raepsaet-Charlier
  M-T. RAEPSAET-CHARLIER, Prosopographie des femmes de l'ordre sénatorial (l. – II. siècles) (Fonds René Draguet 4) 2 vols., 1987
RÄRG
  H. BONNET, Reallexikon der ägyptischen Religionsgeschichte, ²1971
RAL
  Rendiconti della Classe di Scienze morali, storiche e filologiche dell'Academia dei Lincei
Ramsay
  W.M. RAMSAY, The Cities and Bishoprics of Phrygia 2 vols., 1895–97
RAssyr
  Revue d'assyriologie et d'archéologie orientale
Rawson, Culture
  E. RAWSON, Roman Culture and Society. Collected Papers, 1991
Rawson, Family
  B. RAWSON (ed.), The Family in Ancient Rome. New Perspectives, 1986
RB
  P. WIRTH (ed.), Reallexikon der Byzantinistik, 1968 ff.
RBA
  Revue Belge d'archéologie et d'histoire de l'art
RBi
  Revue biblique
RBK
  K. WESSEL, M. RESTLE (ed.), Reallexikon zur byzantinischen Kunst, 1966 ff. (1st installment 1963)
RBN
  Revue Belge de numismatique
RBPh
  Revue Belge de philologie et d'histoire
RDAC
  Report of the Department of Antiquities, Cyprus
RDK
  O. SCHMITT (ed.), Reallexikon zur deutschen Kunstgeschichte, 1937ff.
RE
  G. WISSOWA ET AL., (ed.), Paulys Real-Encyclopädie der classischen Altertumswissenschaft, Neue Bearbeitung, 1893–1980
REA
  Revue des études anciennes
REByz
  Revue des études byzantines
REG
  Revue des études grecques
Rehm
  W. REHM, Griechentum und Goethezeit, ³1952, ⁴1968
Reinach, RP
  S. REINACH, Répertoire de peintures grecques er romaines, 1922
Reinach, RR
  S. REINACH, Répertoire de reliefs grecs et romains 3 vols., 1909–12

Reinach RSt
> S. REINACH, Répertoire de la statuaire greque et ro-
> maine 6 vols., 1897–1930, repr. 1965–69

REL
> Revue des études latines

Rer.nat.scr.Gr.min
> O. KELLER (ed.), Rerum naturalium scriptores Gra-
> eci minores, 1877

Reynolds
> L.D. REYNOLDS (ed.), Texts and Transmission: A
> Survey of the Latin Classics, 1983

Reynolds/Wilson
> L.D. REYNOLDS, N.G. WILSON, Scribes and Schol-
> ars. A Guide to the Transmission of Greek and Latin
> Literature, ³1991

RFIC
> Rivista di filologia e di istruzione classica

RG
> W.H. WADDINGTON, E. BABELON, Recueil général
> des monnaies grecques d'Asie mineure (Subsidia epi-
> graphica 5) 2 vols., 1908–1925, repr. 1976

RGA
> H. BECK ET AL. (ed.), Reallexikon der germanischen
> Altertumskunde, ²1973 ff. (1st installment 1968);
> Suppl.: 1986 ff.

RGG
> K. GALLING (ed.), Die Religion in Geschichte und
> Gegenwart. Handwörterbuch für Theologie und Re-
> ligionswissenschaft 7 vols., ³1957–65, repr. 1980

RGRW
> Religion in the Graeco-Roman World

RGVV
> Religionsgeschichtliche Versuche und Vorarbeiten

RH
> Revue historique

RHA
> Revue hittite et asianique

RhM
> Rheinisches Museum für Philologie

Rhodes
> P.J. RHODES, A commentary on the Aristotelian
> Athenaion Politeia, ²1993

RHPhR
> Revue d'histoire et de philosophie religieuses

RHR
> Revue de l'histoire des religions

RHS
> Revue historique des Sciences et leurs applications

RIA
> Rivista dell'Istituto nazionale d'archeologia e storia
> dell'arte

RIC
> H. MATTINGLY, E.A. SYDENHAM, The Roman Im-
> perial Coinage 10 vols., 1923–94

Richardson
> L. RICHARDSON (Jr.), A New Topographical Dic-
> tionary of Ancient Rome, 1992

Richter, Furniture
> G.M.A. RICHTER, The Furniture of the Greeks,
> Etruscans and Romans, 1969

Richter, Korai
> G.M.A. RICHTER, Korai, Archaic Greek Maidens,
> 1968

Richter, Kouroi
> G.M.A. RICHTER, Kouroi, Archaic Greek Youths,
> ³1970

Richter, Portraits
> G.M.A. RICHTER, The Portraits of the Greeks 3 vols.
> and suppl., 1965–72

RIDA
> Revue internationale des droits de l'antiquité

RIG
> P-M. DUVAL (ed.), Recueil des inscriptions gauloi-
> ses, 1985 ff.

RIL
> Rendiconti dell'Istituto Lombardo, classe di lettere,
> scienze morali e storiche

Rivet
> A.L.F. RIVET, Gallia Narbonensis with a Chapter on
> Alpes Maritimae. Southern France in Roman Times,
> 1988

Rivet/Smith
> A.L.F. RIVET, C. SMITH, The Place-Names of Ro-
> man Britain, 1979

RLA
> E. EBELING ET AL. (ed.), Reallexikon der Assyriolo-
> gie und vorderasiatischen Archäologie, 1928 ff.

RLV
> M. EBERT (ed.), Reallexikon der Vorgeschichte 15
> vols., 1924–32

RMD
> M.M. ROXAN, Roman military diplomas (Occasion-
> al Publications of the Institute of Archaeology of the
> University of London 2 and 9), Vol. 1, (1954–77),
> 1978; Vol. 2, (1978–84), 1985; Vol. 3, (1985–94),
> 1994

RN
> Revue numismatique

Robert, OMS
> L. ROBERT, Opera minora selecta 7 vols., 1969–90

Robert, Villes
> L. ROBERT, Villes d'Asie Mineure. Etudes de géo-
> graphie ancienne, ²1902

Robertson
> A.S. ROBERTSON, Roman Imperial Coins in the
> Hunter Coin Cabinet, University of Glasgow 5 vols.,
> 1962–82

Rohde
> E. ROHDE, Psyche. Seelenkult und Unsterblichkeits-
> glaube der Griechen, ²1898, repr. 1991

Roscher
> W.H. ROSCHER, Ausführliches Lexikon der grie-
> chischen und römischen Mythologie 6 vols.,
> ³1884–1937, repr. 1992 f.; 4 Suppl. Vols.: 1893–
> 1921

Rostovtzeff, Hellenistic World
> M.I. ROSTOVTZEFF, The Social and Economic His-
> tory of the Hellenistic World, ²1953

Rostovtzeff, Roman Empire
M.I. ROSTOVTZEFF, The Social and Economic History of the Roman Empire, ²1957
Rotondi
G. ROTONDI, Leges publicae populi Romani. Elenco cronologico con una introduzione sull' attività legislativa dei comizi romani, 1912, repr. 1990
RPAA
Rendiconti della Pontificia Accademia di Archeologia
RPC
A. BURNETT, M. AMANDRY, P.P. RIPOLLÈS (ed.), Roman Provincial Coinage, 1992 ff.
RPh
Revue de philologie
RQ
Renaissance Quarterly
RQA
Römische Quartalsschrift für christliche Altertumskunde und für Kirchengeschichte
RRC
M. CRAWFORD, Roman Republican Coinage, 1974, repr. 1991
RSC
Rivista di Studi Classici
Rubin
B. RUBIN, Das Zeitalter Iustinians, 1960
Ruggiero
E. DE RUGGIERO, Dizionario epigrafico di antichità romana, 1895 ff., Vols. 1–3: repr. 1961 f.
Saeculum
Saeculum. Jahrbuch für Universalgeschichte
Saller
R. SALLER, Personal Patronage Under the Early Empire, 1982
Salomies
O. SALOMIES, Die römischen Vornamen. Studien zur römischen Namengebung (Commentationes humanarum litterarum 82), 1987
Samuel
A.E. SAMUEL, Greek and Roman Chronology. Calendars and Years in Classical Antiquity (HdbA I 7), 1972
Sandys
J.E. SANDYS, A History of Classical Scholarship 3 vols., ²1906–21, repr. 1964
SAWW
Sitzungsberichte der Österreichischen Akademie der Wissenschaften in Wien
SB
Sammelbuch griechischer Urkunden aus Ägypten (Inschriften und Papyri), Vols. 1–2: F. PREISIGKE (ed.), 1913–22; Vols. 3–5: F. BILABEL (ed.), 1926–34
SBAW
Sitzungsberichte der Bayerischen Akademie der Wissenschaften
SCCGF
J. DEMIAŃCZUK (ed.), Supplementum comicum comoediae Graecae fragmenta, 1912

Schachter
A. SCHACHTER, The Cults of Boiotia 4 vols., 1981–94
Schäfer
A. SCHÄFER, Demosthenes und seine Zeit 3 vols., ²1885–87, repr. 1967
Schanz/Hosius
M. SCHANZ, C. HOSIUS, G. KRÜGER, Geschichte der römischen Literatur bis zum Gesetzgebungswerk des Kaisers Justinian (HdbA 8), Vol. 1, ⁴1927, repr. 1979; Vol. 2, ⁴1935, repr. 1980; Vol. 3, ³1922, repr. 1969; Vol. 4,1, ²1914, repr. 1970; Vol. 4,2, 1920, repr. 1971
Scheid, Collège
J. SCHEID, Le collège des frères arvales. Étude prosopographique du recrutement (69 –304) (Saggi di storia antica 1), 1990
Scheid, Recrutement
J. SCHEID, Les frères arvales. Recrutement et origine sociale sous les empereurs julio-claudiens (Bibliothèque de l'École des Hautes Études, Section des Sciences Religieuses 77), 1975
Schlesier
R. SCHLESIER, Kulte, Mythen und Gelehrte – Anthropologie der Antike seit 1800, 1994
Schmid/Stählin I
W. SCHMID, O. STÄHLIN, Geschichte der griechischen Literatur. Erster Theil: Die klassische Periode der griechische Literatur VII 1) 5 vols., 1929–48, repr. 1961–80
Schmid/Stählin II
W. CHRIST, W. SCHMID, O. STÄHLIN, Geschichte der griechischen Litteratur bis auf die Zeit Justinians. Zweiter Theil: Die nachklassische Periode der griechischen Litteratur (HdbA VII 2) 2 vols., ⁶1920–24, repr. 1961–81
Schmidt
K.H. SCHMIDT, Die Komposition in gallischen Personennamen in: Zeitschrift für celtische Philologie 26, 1957, 33–301 = (Diss.), 1954
Schönfeld
M. SCHÖNFELD, Wörterbuch der altgermanischen Personen- und Völkernamen (Germanische Bibliothek Abt. 1, Reihe 4, 2), 1911, repr. ²1965)
Scholiall
H. ERBSE (ed.), Scholia Graeca in Homeri Iliadem (Scholia vetera) 7 vols., 1969–88
SChr
Sources Chrétiennes 300 vols., 1942 ff.
Schrötter
F. v. SCHRÖTTER (ed.), Wörterbuch der Münzkunde, ²1970
Schürer
E. SCHÜRER, G. VERMÈS, The history of the Jewish people in the age of Jesus Christ (175 B.C. – A.D. 135) 3 vols., 1973–87
Schulten, Landeskunde
A. SCHULTEN, Iberische Landeskunde. Geographie des antiken Spanien 2 vols., 1955–57 (translation of the Spanish edition of 1952)

Schulz
 F. SCHULZ, Geschichte der römischen Rechtswissen-
 schaft, 1961, repr. 1975
Schulze
 W. SCHULZE, Zur Geschichte lateinischer Eigenna-
 men, 1904
Schwyzer, Dial.
 E. SCHWYZER (ed.), Dialectorum Graecarum exem-
 pla epigraphica potiora, ³1923
Schwyzer, Gramm.
 E. SCHWYZER, Griechische Grammatik, Vol. 1: All-
 gemeiner Teil. Lautlehre Wortbildung, Flexion
 (HdbA II 1, 1), 1939
Schwyzer/Debrunner
 E. SCHWYZER, A. DEBRUNNER, Griechische Gram-
 matik, Vol. 2: Syntax und syntaktische Stilistik
 (HdbA II 1,2), 1950; D. J. GEORGACAS, Register zu
 beiden Bänden, 1953; F. RADT, S. RADT, Stellenre-
 gister, 1971
Scullard
 H. H. SCULLARD, Festivals and Ceremonies of the
 Roman Republic, 1981
SDAW
 Sitzungsberichte der Deutschen Akademie der Wis-
 senschaften zu Berlin
SDI II
 Studia et documenta historiae et iuris
SE
 Studi Etruschi
Seeck
 O. SEECK, Regesten der Kaiser und Päpste für die
 Jahre 311 bis 470 n. Chr. Vorarbeiten zu einer Pro-
 sopographie der christlichen Kaiserzeit, 1919, repr.
 1964
SEG
 Supplementum epigraphicum Graecum, 1923 ff.
Seltman
 C. SELTMAN, Greek Coins. A History of Metallic
 Currency and Coinage down to the Fall of the Hel-
 lenistic Kingdoms, ²1905
Sezgin
 F. SEZGIN, Geschichte des arabischen Schrifttums,
 Vol.3: Medizin, Pharmazie, Zoologie, Tierheilkunde
 bis ca. 430 H., 1970
SGAW
 Sitzungsberichte der Göttinger Akademie der Wis-
 senschaften
SGDI
 H. COLLITZ ET AL. (ed.), Sammlung der griechischen
 Dialekt-Inschriften 4 vols., 1884–1915
SGLG
 K. ALPERS, H. ERBSE, A. KLEINLOGEL (ed.), Samm-
 lung griechischer und lateinischer Grammatiker 7
 vols., 1974–88
SH
 H. LLOYD-JONES, P. PARSONS (ed.), Supplementum
 Hellenisticum, 1983
SHAW
 Sitzungsberichte der Heidelberger Akademie der
 Wissenschaften

Sherk
 R.K. SHERK, Roman Documents from the Greek
 East: Senatus Consulta and Epistulae to the Age of
 Augustus, 1969
SicA
 Sicilia archeologica
SIFC
 Studi italiani di filologia classica
SiH
 Studies in the Humanities
Simon, GG
 E. SIMON, Die Götter der Griechen, ⁴1992
Simon, GR
 E. SIMON, 1 Die Götter der Römer, 1990
SLG
 D. PAGE (ed.), Supplementum lyricis graecis, 1974
SM
 Schweizer Münzblatter
SMEA
 Studi Micenei ed Egeo-Anatolici
Smith
 W.D. SMITH, The Hippocratic tradition (Cornell pu-
 blications in the history of science), 1979
SMSR
 Studi e materiali di storia delle religioni
SMV
 Studi mediolatini e volgari
SNG
 Sylloge Nummorum Graecorum
SNR
 Schweizerische Numismatische Rundschau
Solin/Salomies
 H. SOLIN, O. SALOMIES, Repertorium nominum
 gentilium et cognominum Latinorum (Alpha –
 Omega: Reihe A 80), ²1994
Sommer
 F. SOMMER, Handbuch der lateinischen Laut- und
 Formenlehre. Eine Einführung in das sprachwissen-
 schaftliche Studium des Latein (Indogermanische
 Bibliothek 1, 1, 3, 1), ³1914
Soustal, Nikopolis
 P. SOUSTAL, Nikopolis und Kephallenia (Denk-
 schriften der Akademie der Wissenschaften, Philo-
 sophisch-Historische Klasse I 50; TIB 3), 1981
Soustal, Thrakien
 P. SOUSTAL, Thrakien. Thrake, Rodope und Hai-
 mimontos (Denkschriften der Österreichischen Aka-
 demie der Wissenschaften, Philosophisch-Histori-
 sche Klasse 221; TIB 6), 1991
Sovoronos
 J.N. SOVORONOS, Das Athener Nationalmuseum 3
 vols., 1908–37
Spec.
 Speculum
Spengel
 L. SPENGEL, (ed.), Rhetores Graeci 3 vols., 1853–56,
 repr. 1966
SPrAW
 Sitzungsberichte der Preußischen Akademie der
 Wissenschaften

SSAC
Studi storici per l'antichità classica
SSR
G. GIANNANTONI (ed.), Socratis et Socraticorum Reliquiae 4 vols., 1990
Staden
H. V. STADEN, Herophilus, The Art of Medicine in Early Alexandria, 1989
Stein, Präfekten
A. STEIN, Die Präfekten von Ägypten in der römischen Kaiserzeit (Dissertationes Bernenses Series 1, 1), 1950
Stein, Spätröm.R.
E. STEIN, Geschichte des spätrömischen Reiches, Vol. 1, 1928; French version, 1959; Vol. 2, French only, 1949
Stewart
A. STEWART, Greek sculpture. An exploration 2 vols., 1990
StM
Studi Medievali
Strong/Brown
D. STRONG, D. BROWN (ed.), Roman Crafts, 1976
Stv
Die Staatsverträge des Altertums, Vol. 2: H. BENGTSON, R. WERNER (ed.), Die Verträge der griechisch-römischen Welt von 700 bis 338, ²1975; Vol. 3: H.H. SCHMITT (ed.), Die Verträge der griechisch-römischen Welt 338 bis 200 v. Chr., 1969
SVF
J. V. ARNIM (ed.), Stoicorum veterum fragmenta 3 vols., 1903–05; Index: 1924, repr. 1964
Syll.²
W. DITTENBERGER, Sylloge inscriptionum Graecarum 3 vols., ²1898–1909
Syll.³
F. HILLER VON GAERTRINGEN ET AL. (ed.), Sylloge inscriptionum Graecarum 4 vols., ³1915–24, repr. 1960
Syme, AA
R. SYME, The Augustan Aristocracy, 1986
Syme, RP
E. BADIAN (Vols. 1,2), A.R. BIRLEY (Vols. 3–7) (ed.) R. SYME, Roman Papers 7 vols., 1979–91
Syme, RR
K. SYME, The Roman Revolution, 1939
Syme, Tacitus
R. SYME, Tacitus 2 vols., 1958
Symposion
Symposion, Akten der Gesellschaft für Griechische und Hellenistische Rechtsgeschichte
Syria
Syria. Revue d'art oriental et d'archéologie
TAM
Tituli Asiae minoris, 1901 ff.
TAPhA
Transactions and Proceedings of the American Philological Association

Taubenschlag
R. TAUBENSCHLAG, The law of Greco-Roman Egypt in the light of the Papyri: 332 B. C. – 640 A. D., ²1955
TAVO
H. BRUNNER, W. RÖLLIG (ed.), Tübinger Atlas des Vorderen Orients, Beihefte, Teil B: Geschichte, 1969 ff.
TeherF
Teheraner Forschungen
TGF
A. NAUCK (ed.), Tragicorum Graecorum Fragmenta, ²1889, 2nd repr. 1983
ThGL
H. STEPHANUS, C. B. HASE, W. UND L. DINDORF ET AL. (ed.), Thesaurus graecae linguae, 1831 ff., repr. 1954
ThlL
Thesaurus linguae Latinae, 1900 ff.
ThlL, Onom.
Thesaurus linguae Latinae, Supplementum onomasticon. Nomina propria Latina, Vol. 2 (C – Cyzistra), 1907–1913; Vol. 3 (D – Donusa), 1918–1923
ThLZ
Theologische Literaturzeitung Monatsschrift für das gesamte Gebiet der Theologie und Religionswissenschaft
Thomasson
B.E. THOMASSON, Laterculi Praesidum 3 vols. in 5 parts, 1972–1990
Thumb/Kieckers
A. THUMB, E. KIECKERS, Handbuch der griechischen Dialekte (Indogermanische Bibliothek 1, 1, 1), ²1932
Thumb/Scherer
A. THUMB, A. SCHERER, Handbuch der griechischen Dialekte (Indogermanische Bibliothek, 1, 1, 2), ²1959
ThWAT
G.J. BOTTERWECK, H.-J. FABRY (ed.), Theologisches Wörterbuch zum Alten Testament, 1973 ff.
ThWB
G. KITTEL, G. FRIEDRICH (ed.), Theologisches Wörterbuch zum Neuen Testament 11 vols., 1933–79, repr. 1990
TIB
H. HUNGER (ed.). Tabula Imperii Byzantini 7 vols., 1976–1990
Timm
S. TIMM, Das christlich-koptische Ägypten in arabischer Zeit. Eine Sammlung christlicher Stätten in Ägypten in arabischer Zeit, unter Ausschluß von Alexandria, Kairo, des Apa-Mena-Klosters (Der Abu Mina), des Sketis (Wadi n-Natrun) und der Sinai-Region (TAVO 41) 6 parts, 1984–92
TIR
Tabula Imperii Romani, 1934 ff.
TIR/IP
Y. TSAFRIR, L. DI SEGNI, J. GREEN, Tabula Imperii

Romani. Iudaea – Palaestina. Eretz Israel in the Hellenistic, Roman and Byzantine Periods, 1994

Tod
M.N. Tod (ed.), A Selection of Greek Historical Inscriptions to the End of the Fifth Century BC, Vol. 1: ²1951, repr. 1985; Vol. 2: ²1950

Tovar
A. Tovar, Iberische Landeskunde 2: Die Völker und Städte des antiken Hispanien, Vol. 1 Baetica, 1974; Vol. 2: Lusitanien, 1976; Vol. 3: Tarraconensis, 1989

Toynbee, Hannibal
A.J. Toynbee, Hannibal's legacy. The Hannibalic war's effects on Roman life 2 vols., 1965

Toynbee, Tierwelt
J.M.C. Toynbee, Tierwelt der Antike, 1983

TPhS
Transactions of the Philological Society Oxford

Traill, Attica
J. S. Traill, The Political Organization of Attica, 1975

Traill, PAA
J. S. Traill, Persons of Ancient Athens, 1994 ff.

Travlos, Athen
J. Travlos, Bildlexikon zur Topographie des antiken Athen, 1971

Travlos, Attika
J. Travlos, Bildlexikon zur Topographie des antiken Attika, 1988

TRE
G. Krause, G. Müller (ed.), Theologische Realenzyklopädie, 1977 ff. (1st installment 1976)

Treggiari
S. Treggiari, Roman Marriage. Iusti Coniuges from the Time of Cicero to the Time of Ulpian, 1991

Treitinger
O. Treitinger, Die Oströmische Kaiser- und Reichsidee nach ihrer Gestaltung im höfischen Zeremoniell, 1938, repr. 1969

Trendall, Lucania
A.D. Trendall, The Red-figured Vases of Lucania, Campania and Sicily, 1967

Trendall, Paestum
A.D. Trendall, The Red-figured Vases of Paestum, 1987

Trendall/Cambitoglou
A.D. Trendall, The Red-figured Vases of Apulia 2 vols., 1978–82

TRF
O. Ribbeck (ed.), Tragicorum Romanorum Fragmenta, ²1871, repr. 1962

TRG
Tijdschrift voor rechtsgeschiedenis

TrGF
B. Snell, R. Kannicht, S. Radt (ed.), Tragicorum graecorum fragmenta, Vol. 1, ²1986; Vols. 2–4, 1977–85

Trombley
F.R. Trombley, Hellenic Religion and Christianization c. 370–529 (Religions in the Graeco-Roman World 115) 2 vols., 1993 f.

TU
Texte und Untersuchungen zur Geschichte der altchristlichen Literatur

TUAT
O. Kaiser (ed.), Texte aus der Umwelt des Alten Testaments, 1985 ff. (1st installment 1982)

TürkAD
Türk arkeoloji dergisi

Ullmann
M. Ullmann, Die Medizin im Islam, 1970

UPZ
U. Wilcken (ed.), Urkunden der Ptolemäerzeit (Ältere Funde) 2 vols., 1927–57

v. Haehling
R. v. Haehling, Die Religionszugehörigkeit der hohen Amtsträger des Römischen Reiches seit Constantins I. Alleinherrschaft bis zum Ende der Theodosianischen Dynastie (324–450 bzw. 455 n. Chr.) (Antiquitas 3, 23), 1978

VDI
Vestnik Drevnej Istorii

Ventris/Chadwick
M. Ventris, J. Chadwick, Documents in Mycenean Greek, ²1973

Vetter
E. Vetter, Handbuch der italischen Dialekte, 1953

VIR
Vocabularium iurisprudentiae Romanae 5 vols., 1903–39

VisRel
Visible Religion

Vittinghoff
F. Vittinghoff (ed.), Europäische Wirtschafts- und Sozialgeschichte in der römischen Kaiserzeit, 1990

VL
W. Stammler, K. Langosch, K. Ruh et al. (ed.), Die deutsche Literatur des Mittelalters. Verfasserslexikon, ²1978 ff.

Vogel-Weidemann
U. Vogel-Weidemann, Die Statthalter von Africa und Asia in den Jahren 14–68 n.Chr. Eine Untersuchung zum Verhältnis von Princeps und Senat (Antiquitas 1, 31), 1982

VT
Vetus Testamentum. Quarterly Published by the International Organization of Old Testament Scholars

Wacher
R. Wacher (ed.), The Roman World 2 vols., 1987

Walde/Hofmann
A. Walde, J.B. Hofmann, Lateinisches etymologisches Wörterbuch 3 vols., ³1938–56

Walde/Pokorny
A. Walde, J. Pokorny (ed.), Vergleichendes Wörterbuch der indogermanischen Sprachen 3 vols., 1927–32, repr. 1973

Walz
C. Walz (ed.), Rhetores Graeci 9 vols., 1832–36, repr. 1968

WbMyth

H.W. HAUSSIG (ed.), Wörterbuch der Mythologie, Teil 1: Die alten Kulturvölker, 1965 ff.

Weber

W. WEBER, Biographisches Lexikon zur Geschichtswissenschaft in Deutschland, Österreich und der Schweiz, ²1987

Wehrli, Erbe

F. WEHRLI (ed.), Das Erbe der Antike, 1963

Wehrli, Schule

F. WEHRLI (ed.), Die Schule des Aristoteles 10 vols., 1967–69; 2 Suppl. Vols.: 1974–78

Welles

C.B. WELLES, Royal Correspondence in the Hellenistic Period: A Study in Greek Epigraphy, 1934

Wenger

L. WENGER, Die Quellen des römischen Rechts (Denkschriften der Österreichischen Akademie der Wissenschaften. Philosophisch-Historische Klasse 2), 1953

Wernicke

I. WERNICKE, Die Kelten in Italien. Die Einwanderung und die frühen Handelsbeziehungen zu den Etruskern (Diss.), 1989 = (Palingenesia), 1991

Whatmough

J. WHATMOUGH, The dialects of Ancient Gaul. Prolegomena and records of the dialects 5 vols., 1949–51, repr. in 1 vol., 1970

White, Farming

K.D. WHITE, Roman Farming, 1970

White, Technology

K.D. WHITE, Greek and Roman Technology, 1983, repr. 1986

Whitehead

D. WHITEHEAD, The demes of Attica, 1986

Whittaker

C.R. WHITTAKER (ed.), Pastoral Economies in Classical Antiquity, 1988

Wide

S. WIDE, Lakonische Kulte, 1893

Wieacker, PGN

F. WIEACKER, Privatrechtsgeschichte der Neuzeit, ²1967

Wieacker, RRG

F. WIEACKER, Römische Rechtsgeschichte, Vol. 1, 1988

Wilamowitz

U. v. WILAMOWITZ-MOELLENDORFF, Der Glaube der Hellenen 2 vols., ²1955, repr. 1994

Will

E. WILL, Histoire politique du monde hellénistique (323–30 av. J. C.) 2 vols., ²1979–82

Winter

R. KEKULÉ (ed.), Die antiken Terrakotten, III 1, 2: F. WINTER, Die Typen der figürlichen Terrakotten, 1903

WJA

Würzburger Jahrbücher für die Altertumswissenschaft

WMT

L.I. CONRAD ET AL., The Western medical tradition. 800 BC to A.D. 1800, 1995

WO

Die Welt des Orients. Wissenschaftliche Beiträge zur Kunde des Morgenlandes

Wolff

H.J. WOLFF, Das Recht der griechischen Papyri Ägyptens in der Zeit der Ptolemaeer und des Prinzipats (Rechtsgeschichte des Altertums Part 5; HbdA 10, 5), 1978

WS

Wiener Studien, Zeitschrift für klassische Philologie und Patristik

WUNT

Wissenschaftliche Untersuchungen zum Neuen Testament

WVDOG

Wissenschaftliche Veröffentlichungen der Deutschen Orient-Gesellschaft

WZKM

Wiener Zeitschrift für die Kunde des Morgenlandes

YCIS

Yale Classical Studies

ZA

Zeitschrift für Assyriologie und Vorderasiatische Archäologie

ZÄS

Zeitschrift für ägyptische Sprache und Altertumskunde

ZATW

Zeitschrift für die Alttestamentliche Wissenschaft

Zazoff, AG

P. ZAZOFF, Die antiken Gemmen, 1983

Zazoff, GuG

P. ZAZOFF, H. ZAZOFF, Gemmensammler und Gemmenforscher. Von einer noblen Passion zur Wissenschaft, 1983

ZDMG

Zeitschrift der Deutschen Morgenländischen Gesellschaft

ZDP

Zeitschrift für deutsche Philologie

Zeller

E. ZELLER, Die Philosophie der Griechen in ihrer geschichtlichen Entwicklung 4 vols., 1844–52, repr. 1963

Zeller/Mondolfo

E. ZELLER, R. MONDOLFO, La filosofia dei Greci nel suo sviluppo storico, Vol. 3, 1961

ZfN

Zeitschrift für Numismatik

Zgusta

L. ZGUSTA, Kleinasiatische Ortsnamen, 1984

Zimmer

G. ZIMMER, Römische Berufsdarstellungen, 1982

ZKG,

Zeitschrift für Kirchengeschichte

ZNTW

Zeitschrift für die Neutestamentfiche Wissenschaft und die Kunde der älteren Kirche

5. Ancient Authors and Titles of Works

Abd	Abdias	Anth. Gr.	Anthologia Graeca
Acc.	Accius	Anth. Lat.	Anthologia Latina (Riese
Ach.Tat.	Achilles Tatius		²1894/1906)
Act. Arv.	Acta fratrum Arvalium	Anth. Pal.	Anthologia Palatina
Act. lud. saec.	Acta ludorum saecularium	Anth. Plan.	Anthologia Planudea
Acts	Acts of the Apostles	Antiph.	Antiphon
Aet.	Aetius	Antisth.	Antisthenes
Aeth.	Aetheriae peregrinatio	Apc.	Apocalypse
Ael. Ep.	Aelianus, Epistulae	Apoll. Rhod.	Apollonius Rhodius
NA	De natura animalium	Apollod.	Apollodorus, Library
VH	Varia historia	App. B Civ.	Appianus, Bella civilia
Aen. Tact.	Aeneas Tacticus	Celt.	Celtica
Aesch. Ag.	Aeschylus, Agamemnon	Hann.	Hannibalica
Cho.	Choephoroi	Hisp.	Iberica
Eum.	Eumenides	Ill.	Illyrica
Pers.	Persae	It.	Italica
PV	Prometheus	Lib.	Libyca
Sept.	Septem adversus Thebas	Mac.	Macedonica
Supp.	Supplices	Mith.	Mithridatius
Aeschin. In Ctes.	Aeschines, In Ctesiphontem	Num.	Numidica
Leg.	De falsa legatione	Reg.	Regia
In Tim.	In Timarchum	Sam.	Samnitica
Aesop.	Aesopus	Sic.	Sicula
Alc.	Alcaeus	Syr.	Syriaca
Alc. Avit.	Alcimus Ecdicius Avitus	App. Verg.	Appendix Vergiliana
Alex. Aphr.	Alexander of Aphrodisias	Apul. Apol.	Apuleius, Apologia
Alci.	Alciphron	Flor.	Florida
Alcm.	Alcman	Met.	Metamorphoses
Alex. Polyh.	Alexander Polyhistor	Arat.	Aratus
Am	Amos	Archil.	Archilochus
Ambr. Epist.	Ambrosius, Epistulae	Archim.	Archimedes
Exc. Sat.	De excessu Fratris (Satyri)	Archyt.	Archytas
Obit. Theod.	De obitu Theodosii	Arist. Quint.	Aristides Quintilianus
Obit. Valent.	De obitu Valentiniani (iunioris)	Aristaen.	Aristaenetus
Off.	De officiis ministrorum	Aristid.	Aelius Aristides
Paenit.	De paenitentia	Aristob.	Aristoboulos
Amm. Marc.	Ammianus Marcellinus	Aristoph. Ach.	Aristophanes, Acharnenses
Anac.	Anacreon	Av.	Aves
Anaxag.	Anaxagoras	Eccl.	Ecclesiazusae
Anaximand.	Anaximander	Equ.	Equites
Anaximen.	Anaximenes	Lys.	Lysistrata
And.	Andocides	Nub.	Nubes
Anecd. Bekk.	Anecdota Graeca ed. I. Bekker	Pax	Pax
Anecd. Par.	Anecdota Graeca ed. J.A. Kramer	Plut.	Plutus
Anon. de rebus bell.	Anonymus de rebus bellicis (Ireland 1984)	Ran.	Ranae

Thesm.	Thesmophoriazusae	Epist.	Epistulae
Vesp.	Vespae	Retract.	Retractationes
Aristot. An.	Aristotle, De anima (Becker 1831– 70)	Serm.	Sermones
		Soliloq.	Soliloquia
		Trin.	De trinitate
An. post.	Analytica posteriora	Aur. Vict.	Aurelius Victor
An. pr.	Analytica priora	Auson. Mos.	Ausonius, Mosella (Peiper 1976)
Ath. Pol.	Athenaion Politeia	Urb.	Ordo nobilium urbium
Aud.	De audibilibus	Avell.	Collectio Avellana
Cael.	De caelo	Avien.	Avienus
Cat.	Categoriae	Babr.	Babrius
Col.	De coloribus	Bacchyl.	Bacchylides
Div.	De divinatione	Bar	Baruch
Eth. Eud.	Ethica Eudemia	Bas.	Basilicorum libri LX (Heimbach)
Eth. Nic.	Ethica Nicomachea	Basil.	Basilius
Gen. an.	De generatione animalium	Batr.	Batrachomyomachia
Gen. corr.	De generatione et corruptione	Bell. Afr.	Bellum Africum
Hist. an.	Historia animalium	Bell. Alex.	Bellum Alexandrinum
Mag. mor.	Magna moralia	Bell. Hisp.	Bellum Hispaniense
Metaph.	Metaphysica	Boeth.	Boethius
Mete.	Meteorologica	Caes. B Civ.	Caesar, De bello civili
Mir.	Mirabilia	B Gall.	De bello Gallico
Mot. an.	De motu animalium	Callim. Epigr.	Callimachus, Epigrammata
Mund.	De mundo	Fr.	Fragmentum (Pfeiffer)
Oec.	Oeconomica	H.	Hymni
Part. an.	De partibus animalium	Calp. Ecl.	Calpurnius Siculus, Eclogae
Phgn.	Physiognomica	Cass. Dio	Cassius Dio
Ph.	Physica	Cassian.	Iohannes Cassianus
Poet.	Poetica	Cassiod. Inst.	Cassiodorus, Institutiones
Pol.	Politica	Var.	Variae
Pr.	Problemata	Cato Agr.	Cato, De agri cultura
Rh.	Rhetorica	Orig.	Origines (HRR)
Rh. Al	Rhetorica ad Alexandrum	Catull.	Catullus, Carmina
Sens.	De sensu	Celsus, Med.	Cornelius Celsus, De medicina
Somn.	De somno et vigilia	Celsus, Dig.	Iuventius Celsus, Digesta
Soph. el.	Sophistici elenchi	Censorinus, DN	Censorinus, De die natali
Spir.	De spiritu	Chalcid.	Chalcidius
Top.	Topica	Charisius,	Charisius, Ars grammatica (Bar-
Aristox. Harm.	Aristoxenus, Harmonica	Gramm.	wick 1964)
Arnob.	Arnobius, Adversus nationes	1 Chr, 2 Chr	Chronicle
Arr. Anab.	Arrianus, Anabasis	Chron. pasch.	Chronicon paschale
Cyn.	Cynegeticus	Chron. min.	Chronica minora
Ind.	Indica	Cic. Acad. 1	Cicero, Academicorum posterio-
Peripl. p. eux.	Periplus ponti Euxini		rum liber 1
Succ.	Historia successorum Alexandri	Acad. 2	Lucullus sive Academicorum pri-
Tact.	Tactica		orum liber 2
Artem.	Artemidorus	Ad Q. Fr.	Epistulae ad Quintum fratrem
Ascon.	Asconius (Stangl Vol. 2, 1912)	Arat.	Aratea (Soubiran 1972)
Athan. ad Const	Athanasius, Apologia ad Constan-	Arch.	Pro Archia poeta
	tium	Att.	Epistulae ad Atticum
c. Ar.	Apologia contra Arianos	Balb.	Pro L. Balbo
Fuga	Apologia de fuga sua	Brut.	Brutus
Hist. Ar.	Historia Arianorum ad mona-	Caecin.	Pro A. Caecina
	chos	Cael.	Pro M. Caelio
Ath.	Athenaeus (Casaubon 1597) (List	Cat.	In Catilinam
	of books, pages, letters)	Cato	Cato maior de senectute
Aug. Civ.	Augustinus, De civitate dei	Clu.	Pro A. Cluentio
Conf.	Confessiones	De or.	De oratore
Doctr. christ.	De doctrina christiana		

Deiot.	Pro rege Deiotaro	Cod. Theod.	Codex Theodosianus
Div.	De divinatione	Col	Letter to the Colossians
Div. Caec.	Divinatio in Q. Caecilium	Coll.	Mosaicarum et Romanarum legum
Dom.	De domo sua		collatio
Fam.	Epistulae ad familiares	Columella	Columella
Fat.	De fato	Comm.	Commodianus
Fin.	De finibus bonorum et malorum	Cons.	Consultatio veteris cuiusdam iuris-
Flac.	Pro L. Valerio Flacco		consulti
Font.	Pro M. Fonteio	Const.	Constitutio Sirmondiana
Har. resp.	De haruspicum responso	1 Cor, 2 Cor	Letters to the Corinthians
Inv.	De inventione	Coripp.	Corippus
Lael.	Laelius de amicitia	Curt.	Curtius Rufus, Historiae Alexandri
Leg.	De legibus		Magni
Leg. agr.	De lege agraria	Cypr.	Cyprianus
Lig.	Pro Q. Ligario	Dan	Daniel
Leg. Man.	Pro lege Manilia (de imperio Cn.	Din.	Dinarchus
	Pompei)	Demad.	Demades
Marcell.	Pro M. Marcello	Democr.	Democritus
Mil.	Pro T. Annio Milone	Dem. Or.	Demosthenes, orationes
Mur.	Pro L. Murena	Dig.	Corpus Iuris Civilis, Digesta
Nat. D.	De natura deorum		(Mommsen 1905, author pres-
Off.	De officiis		ented where applicable)
Opt. Gen.	De optimo genere oratorum	Diod. Sic.	Diodorus Siculus
Orat.	Orator	Diog. Laert.	Diogenes Laertius
P. Red. Quir.	Oratio post reditum ad Quirites	Diom.	Diomedes, ars grammatica
P. Red. Sen.	Oratio post reditum in senatu	Dion. Chrys.	Dion Chrysostomos
Parad.	Paradoxa	Dion. Hal. Ant.	Dionysius Halicarnasseus, Antiqui-
Part. or.	Partitiones oratoriae	Rom.	tates Romanae
Phil.	In M. Antonium orationes Phi-	Comp.	De compositione verborum
	lippicae	Rhet.	Ars rhetorica
Philo.	Libri philosophici	Dionys. Per.	Dionysius Periegeta
Pis.	In L. Pisonem	Dion. Thrax	Dionysius Thrax
Planc.	Pro Cn. Plancio	DK	Diels / Kranz (preceded by fragment
Prov. cons.	De provinciis consularibus		number)
Q. Rosc.	Pro Q. Roscio comoedo	Donat.	Donatus grammaticus
Quinct.	Pro P. Quinctio	Drac.	Dracontius
Rab. perd.	Pro C. Rabirio perduellionis reo	Dt	Deuteronomy = 5. Moses
Rab. Post.	Pro C. Rabirio Postumo	Edict. praet. dig.	Edictum perpetuum in Dig.
Rep.	De re publica	Emp.	Empedocles
Rosc. Am.	Pro Sex. Roscio Amerino	Enn. Ann.	Ennius, Annales (Skutsch 1985)
Scaur.	Pro M. Aemilio Scauro	Sat.	Saturae (Vahlen ²1928)
Sest.	Pro P. Sestio	Scaen.	Fragmenta scaenica (Vahlen
Sull.	Pro P. Sulla		²1928)
Tim.	Timaeus	Ennod.	Ennodius
Top.	Topica	Eph	Letter to the Ephesians
Tull.	Pro M. Tullio	Ephor.	Ephoros of Cyme (FGrH 70)
Tusc.	Tusculanae disputationes	Epicurus	Epicurus
Vatin.	In P. Vatinium testem interroga-	Epict.	Epictetus
	tio	Eratosth.	Eratosthenes
Verr. 1, 2	In Verrem actio prima, secunda	Esr	Esra
Claud. Carm.	Claudius Claudianus, Carmina	Est	Esther
	(Hall 1985)	Et. Gen.	Etymologicum genuinum
Rapt. Pros.	De raptu Proserpinae	Et. Gud.	Etymologicum Gudianum
Clem. Al.	Clemens Alexandrinus	EM	Etymologicum magnum
Cod. Greg.	Codex Gregorianus	Euc.	Euclides elementa
Cod. Herm.	Codex Hermogenianus	Eunap. VS	Eunapius, Vitae sophistarum
Cod. Iust.	Corpus Iuris Civilis, Codex Iustini-	Eur. Alc.	Euripides, Alcestis
	anus (Krueger 1900)	Andr.	Andromacha

Bacch.	Bacchae	Mart.	De virtutibus Martini
Beller.	Bellerophon	Vit. patr.	De vita patrum
Cyc.	Cyclops	Hab	Habakuk
El.	Electra	Hagg	Haggai
Hec.	Hecuba	Harpocr.	Harpocrates
Hel.	Helena	Hdt.	Herodotus
Heracl.	Heraclidae	Hebr	Letter to the Hebrews
HF	Hercules	Hegesipp.	Hegesippus (= Flavius Josephus)
Hipp.	Hippolytus	Hecat.	Hecataeus
Hyps.	Hypsipyle	Hell. Oxy.	Hellennica Oxyrhynchia
Ion	Ion	Hen	Henoch
IA	Iphigenia Aulidensis	Heph.	Hephaestion grammaticus (Alexandrinus)
IT	Iphigenia Taurica		
Med.	Medea	Heracl.	Heraclitus
Or.	Orestes	Heraclid. Pont.	Heraclides Ponticus
Phoen.	Phoenissae	Herc. O.	Hercules Oetaeus
Rhes.	Rhesus	Herm.	Hermes Trismegistus
Supp.	Supplices	Herm. Mand.	Hermas, Mandata
Tro.	Troades	Sim.	Similitudines
Euseb. Dem. evang.	Eusebios, Demonstratio Evangelica	Vis.	Visiones
		Hermog.	Hermogenes
Hist. eccl.	Historia Ecclesiastica	Hdn.	Herodianus
On.	Onomastikon (Klostermann 1904)	Heron	Heron
		Hes. Cat.	Hesiodus, Catalogus feminarum (Merkelbach /West 1967)
Praep. evang.	Praeparatio Evangelica		
Eust.	Eustathius	Op.	Opera et dies
Eutr.	Eutropius	Sc.	Scutum (Merkelbach /West1967)
Ev. Ver.	Evangelium Veritatis		
Ex	Exodus = 2. Moses	Theog.	Theogonia
Ez	Ezechiel	Hsch.	Hesychius
Fast.	Fasti	Hil.	Hilarius
Fest.	Festus (Lindsay 1913)	Hippoc.	Hippocrates
Firm. Mat.	Firmicus Maternus	H. Hom.	Hymni Homerici
Flor. Epit.	Florus, Epitoma de Tito Livio	Hom. Il.	Homerus, Ilias
Florent.	Florentinus	Od.	Odyssea
Frontin. Aq.	Frontinus, De aquae ductu urbis Romae	Hor. Ars P.	Horatius, Ars poetica
		Carm.	Carmina
Str.	Strategemata	Carm. saec.	Carmen saeculare
Fulg.	Fulgentius Afer	Epist.	Epistulae
Fulg. Rusp.	Fulgentius Ruspensis	Epod.	Epodi
Gai. Inst.	Gaius, Institutiones	Sat.	Satirae (sermones)
Gal	Letter to the Galatians	Hos	Hosea
Gal.	Galenus	Hyg. Poet. Astr.	Hyginus, Astronomica (Le Bœuffle 1983)
Gell. NA	Gellius, Noctes Atticae		
Geogr. Rav	Geographus Ravennas (Schnetz 1940)	Fab.	Fabulae
		Hyp.	Hypereides
Gp.	Geoponica	Iambl. Myst.	Iamblichus, De mysteriis
Gn	Genesis = 1. Moses	Protr.	Protrepticus in philosophiam
Gorg.	Gorgias	VP	De vita Pythagorica
Greg. M. Dial.	Gregorius Magnus, Dialogi (de miraculis patrum Italicorum)	Iav.	Iavolenus Priscus
		Inst. Iust.	Corpus Juris Civilis, Institutiones (Krueger 1905)
Epist.	Epistulae		
Past.	Regula pastoralis	Ioh. Chrys. Epist.	Iohannes Chrysostomos, Epistulae
Greg. Naz. Epist.	Gregorius Nazianzenus, Epistulae	Hom. ...	Homiliae in ...
Or.	Orationes	Ioh. Mal.	Iohannes Malalas, Chronographia
Greg. Nyss.	Gregorius Nyssenus	Iord. Get.	Iordanes, De origine actibusque Getarum
Greg. Tur. Franc.	Gregorius of Tours, Historia Francorum		
		Iren.	Irenaeus (Rousseau/Doutreleau 1965–82)

Is.	Isaiah	Lex Visig.	Leges Visigothorum
Isid. Nat.	Isidorus, De natura rerum	Lex XII tab.	Lex duodecim tabularum
Orig.	Origines	Lib. Ep.	Libanius, Epistulae
Isoc. Or.	Isocrates, Orationes	Or.	Orationes
It. Ant.	Itinerarium, Antonini	Liv.	Livius, Ab urbe condita
Aug.	Augusti	Lc	Lucas (Luke)
Burd.	Burdigalense vel Hierosolymita-	Luc.	Lucanus, Bellum civile
	num	Lucil.	Lucilius, Saturae (Marx 1904)
Plac.	Placentini	Lucr.	Lucretius, De rerum natura
Iul. Vict. Rhet.	C. Iulius Victor, Ars rhetorica	Lucian, Alex.	Lucian, Alexander
Iuvenc.	Iuvencus, Evangelia (Huemer	Anach.	Anacharsis
	1891)	Cal.	Calumniae non temere creden-
Jac	Letter of Jacob		dum
Jdt	Judith	Catapl.	Cataplus
Jer	Jeremiah	Demon.	Demonax
Jer. Chron.	Jerome, Chronicon	Dial. D.	Dialogi deorum
Comm. in Ez.	Commentaria in Ezechielem (PL	Dial. meret.	Dialogi meretricium
	25)	Dial. mort.	Dialogi mortuorum
Ep.	Epistulae	Her.	Herodotus
On.	Onomastikon (Klostermann	Hermot.	Hermotimus
	1904)	Hist. conscr.	Quomodo historia conscribenda
Vir. ill.	De viris illustribus		sit
1 – 3 Jo	1st – 3rd letters of John	Ind.	Adversus indoctum
Jo	John	Iupp. trag.	Iuppiter tragoedus
Joël	Joël	Luct.	De luctu
Jon	Jona	Macr.	Macrobii
Jos. Ant. Iud.	Josephus, Antiquitates Iudaicae	Nigr.	Nigrinus
BI	Bellum Iudaicum	Philops.	Philopseudes
Ap.	Contra Apionem	Pseudol.	Pseudologista
Vit.	De sua vita	Salt.	De saltatione
Jos	Joshua	Somn.	Somnium
Jud	Letter of Judas	Symp.	Symposium
Julian. Ep.	Julianus, Epistulae	Syr. D.	De Syria dea
In Gal.	In Galilaeos	Trag.	Tragoedopodagra
Mis.	Misopogon	Ver. hist.	Verae historiae, 1, 2
Or.	Orationes	Vit. auct.	Vitarum auctio
Symp.	Symposium	Lv	Leviticus = 3. Moses
Just. Epit.	Justinus, Epitoma historiarum Phi-	LXX	Septuaginta
	lippicarum	Lydus, Mag.	Lydus, De magistratibus
Justin. Apol.	Justinus Martyr, Apologia	Mens.	De mensibus
Dial.	Dialogus cum Tryphone	Lycoph.	Lycophron
Juv.	Juvenalis, Saturae	Lycurg.	Lycurgus
1 Kg, 2 Kg	1, 2 Kings	Lys.	Lysias
KH	Khania (place where Linear B tables	M. Aur.	Marcus Aurelius Antoninus Augus-
	were discovered)		tus
KN	Knossos (place where Linear B ta-	Macrob. Sat.	Macrobius, Saturnalia
	bles were discovered)	In Somn.	Commentarii in Ciceronis som-
Lactant. Div.	Lactantius, Divinae institutiones		nium Scipionis
inst.		1 Macc, 2 Macc	Maccabees
Ira	De ira dei	Mal	Maleachi
De mort. pers.	De mortibus persecutorum	Manil.	Manilius, Astronomica (Goold
Opif.	De opificio dei		1985)
Lam.	Lamentations	Mar. Vict.	Marius Victorinus
Lex Irnit.	Lex Irnitana	Mart.	Martialis
Lex Malac.	Lex municipii Malacitani	Mart. Cap.	Martianus Capella
Lex Rubr.	Lex Rubria de Gallia cisalpina	Max. Tyr.	Maximus Tyrius (Trapp 1994)
Lex Salpens.	Lex municipii Salpensani	Mela	Pomponius Mela
Lex Urson.	Lex coloniae Iuliae Genetivae Ur-	Melanipp.	Melanippides
	sonensis		

Men. Dys.	Menander, Dyskolos	P Abinn.	Papyrus editions according to H.I.
Epit.	Epitrepontes		BELL ET AL. (ED.), The Abinnaeus
Fr.	Fragmentum (Körte)		Archive papers of a Roman offic-
Pk.	Perikeiromene		er in the reign of Constantius II,
Sam.	Samia		1962
Mi	Micha	P Bodmer	Papyrus editions according to V.
Mimn.	Mimnermus		MARTIN, R. KASSER ET AL. (ED.),
Min. Fel.	Minucius Felix, Octavius (Kytzler		Papyrus Bodmer 1954ff.
	1982,²1992)	P CZ	Papyrus editions according to C.C.
Mk	Mark		EDGAR (ED.), Zenon Papyri
Mod.	Herennius Modestinus		(Catalogue général des Antiqui-
Mosch.	Moschus		tés égyptiennes du Musée du Cai-
Mt	Matthew		re) 4 vols., 1925ff.
MY	Mycenae (place where Linear B ta-	P Hercul.	Papyrus editions according to Pa-
	bles were discovered)		pyri aus Herculaneum
Naev.	Naevius (carmina according to	P Lond.	Papyrus editions according to F.G.
	FPL)		KENYON ET AL. (ED.), Greek Pa-
Nah	Nahum		pyri in the British Museum 7
Neh	Nehemia		vols., 1893–1974
Nemes.	Nemesianus	P Mich	Papyrus editions according to C.C.
Nep. Att.	Cornelius Nepos, Atticus		EDGAR, A.E.R. BOAK, J.G. WIN-
Hann.	Hannibal		TER ET AL. (ED.), Papyri in the
Nic. Alex.	Nicander, Alexipharmaka		University of Michigan Collecti-
Ther.	Theriaka		on 13 vols., 1931–1977
Nicom.	Nicomachus	P Oxy.	Papyrus editions according to B.P.
Nm	Numbers = 4. Moses		GRENFELL, A.S. HUNT ET AL.
Non.	Nonius Marcellus (L. Mueller		(ED.), The Oxyrhynchus Papyri,
	1888)		1898 ff.
Nonnus, Dion.	Nonnus, Dionysiaca	Pall. Agric.	Palladius, Opus agriculturae
Not. Dign. Occ.	Notitia dignitatum occidentis	Laus.	Historia Lausiaca
Not. Dign. Or.	Notitia dignitatum orientis	Pan. Lat.	Panegyrici Latini
Not. Episc.	Notitia dignitatum et episcoporum	Papin.	Aemilius Papinianus
Nov.	Corpus Iuris Civilis, Leges Novellae	Paroemiogr.	Paroemiographi Graeci
	(Schoell/Kroll 1904)	Pass. mart.	Passiones martyrum
Obseq.	Julius Obsequens, Prodigia (Ross-	Paul Fest.	Paulus Diaconus, Epitoma Festi
	bach 1910)	Paul Nol.	Paulinus Nolanus
Opp. Hal.	Oppianus, Halieutica	Paulus, Sent.	Julius Paulus, Sententiae
Kyn.	Kynegetica	Paus.	Pausanias
Or. Sib.	Oracula Sibyllina	Pelag.	Pelagius
Orib.	Oribasius	Peripl. m. Eux.	Periplus maris Euxini
Orig.	Origenes	Peripl. m.m.	Periplus maris magni
OrMan	Oratio Manasse	Peripl. m.r.	Periplus maris rubri
Oros.	Orosius	Pers.	Persius, Saturae
Orph. A.	Orpheus, Argonautica	1 Petr, 2 Petr	Letters of Peter
Fr.	Fragmentum (Kern)	Petron. Sat.	Petronius, Satyrica (Müller 1961)
H.	Hymni	Phaedr.	Phaedrus, Fabulae (Guaglianone
Ov. Am.	Ovidius, Amores		1969)
Ars am.	Ars amatoria	Phil	Letter to the Philippians
Epist.	Epistulae (Heroides)	Phil.	Philo
Fast.	Fasti	Philarg. Verg. ecl.	Philargyrius grammaticus, Expla-
Ib.	Ibis		natio in eclogas Vergilii
Medic.	Medicamina faciei femineae	Philod.	Philodemus
Met.	Metamorphoses	Phlp.	Philoponus
Pont.	Epistulae ex Ponto	Philostr. VA	Philostratus, Vita Apollonii
Rem. am.	Remedia amoris	Imag.	Imagines
Tr.	Tristia	VS	Vitae sophistarum
P	Papyrus editions according to E.G.	Phm	Letter to Philemon
	TURNER, Greek Papyri. An Intro-	Phot.	Photius (Bekker 1824)
	duction, 159–178		

Phryn.	Phrynichus
Pind. Fr.	Pindar, Fragments (Snell/Maehler)
Isthm.	Isthmian Odes
Nem.	Nemean Odes
Ol.	Olympian Odes
Pae.	Paeanes
Pyth.	Pythian Odes
Pl. Alc. 1	Plato, Alcibiades 1 (Stephanus)
Alc. 2	Alcibiades 2
Ap.	Apologia
Ax.	Axiochus
Chrm.	Charmides
Def.	Definitiones
Demod.	Demodocus
Epin.	Epinomis
Ep.	Epistulae
Erast.	Erastae
Erx.	Eryxias
Euthd.	Euthydemus
Euthphr.	Euthyophron
Grg.	Gorgias
Hp. mai.	Hippias maior
Hp. mi.	Hippias minor
Hipparch.	Hipparchus
Ion	Ion
Cleit.	Cleitophon
Crat.	Cratylus
Crit.	Criton
Criti.	Critias
La.	Laches
Leg.	Leges
Ly.	Lysis
Men.	Menon
Min.	Minos
Menex.	Menexenus
Prm.	Parmenides
Phd.	Phaedon
Phdr.	Phaedrus
Phlb.	Philebos
Plt.	Politicus
Prt.	Protagoras
Resp.	De re publica
Sis.	Sisyphus
Soph.	Sophista
Symp.	Symposium
Thg.	Theages
Tht.	Theaetetus
Ti.	Timaeus
Plaut. Amph.	Plautus, Amphitruo (fr.according to Leo 1895 f.)
Asin.	Asinaria
Aul.	Aulularia
Bacch.	Bacchides
Capt.	Captivi
Cas.	Casina
Cist.	Cistellaria
Curc.	Curculio
Epid.	Epidicus

Men.	Menaechmi
Merc.	Mercator
Mil.	Miles gloriosus
Mostell.	Mostellaria
Poen.	Poenulus
Pseud.	Pseudolus
Rud.	Rudens
Stich.	Stichus
Trin.	Trinummus
Truc.	Truculentus
Vid.	Vidularia
Plin. HN	Plinius maior, Naturalis historia
Plin. Ep.	Plinius minor, Epistulae
Pan.	Panegyricus
Plot.	Plotinus
Plut.	Plutarchus, Vitae parallelae (with the respective name)
Amat.	Amatorius (chapter and page numbers)
De def. or.	De defectu oraculorum
De E	De E apud Delphos
De Pyth. or.	De Pythiae oraculis
Desera	De sera numinis vindicta
De Is. et Os.	De Iside et Osiride (with chapter and page numbers)
Mor.	moralia (apart from the separately mentioned works; with p. numbers)
Quaest. Graec.	Quaestiones Graecae (with chapter numbers)
Quaest. Rom.	Quaestiones Romanae (with ch. numbers)
Symp.	Quaestiones convivales (book, chapter, page number)
Pol.	Polybius
Pol. Silv.	Polemius Silvius
Poll.	Pollux
Polyaenus, Strat.	Polyaenus, Strategemata
Polyc.	Polycarpus, Letter
Pompon.	Sextus Pomponius
Pomp. Trog.	Pompeius Trogus
Porph.	Porphyrius
Porph. Hor. comm.	Porphyrio, Commentum in Horatii carmina
Posidon.	Posidonius
Priap.	Priapea
Prisc.	Priscianus
Prob.	Pseudo-Probian writings
Procop. Aed.	Procopius, De aedificiis
Goth.	Bellum Gothicum
Pers.	Bellum Persicum
Vand.	Bellum Vandalicum
Arc.	Historia arcana
Procl.	Proclus
Prop.	Propertius, Elegiae
Prosp.	Prosper Tiro
Prov.	Proverbs
Prudent.	Prudentius

Ps (Pss)	Psalm(s)	Med.	Medea
Ps.-Acro	Ps.-Acro in Horatium	Q Nat.	Naturales quaestiones
Ps.-Aristot. Lin. insec.	Pseudo-Aristotle, De lineis insecabilibus	Oed.	Oedipus
Mech.	Mechanica	Phaedr.	Phaedra
Ps.-Sall. In Tull.	Pseudo-Sallustius, In M.Tullium Ciceronem invectiva	Phoen.	Phoenissae
		Thy.	Thyestes
Rep.	Epistulae ad Caesarem senem de re publica	Tranq.	De tranquillitate animi
		Tro.	Troades
Ptol. Alm.	Ptolemy, Almagest	Serv. auct.	Servius auctus Danielis
Geog.	Geographia	Serv. Aen.	Servius, Commentarius in Vergilii Aeneida
Harm.	Harmonica	Ecl.	Commentarius in Vergilii eclogas
Tetr.	Tetrabiblos	Georg.	Commentarius in Vergilii georgica
PY	Pylos (place where Linear B tablets were discovered)		
4 Q Flor	Florilegium, Cave 4	SHA Ael.	Scriptores Historiae Augustae, Aelius
4 Q Patr	Patriarch's blessing, Cave 4		
1 Q pHab	Habakuk-Midrash, Cave 1	Alb.	Clodius Albinus
4 Q pNah	Nahum-Midrash, Cave 4	Alex. Sev.	Alexander Severus
4 Q test	Testimonia, Cave 4	Aur.	M. Aurelius
1 QH	Songs of Praise, Cave 1	Aurel.	Aurelianus
1 QM	War list, Cave 1	Avid. Cass.	Avidius Cassius
1 QS	Comunal rule, Cave 1	Car.	Carus et Carinus et Numerianus
1 QSa	Community rule, Cave 1	Carac.	Antoninus Caracalla
1 QSb	Blessings, Cave 1	Clod.	Claudius
Quint. Smyrn.	Quintus Smyrnaeus	Comm.	Commodus
Quint. Decl.	Quintilianus, Declamationes minores (Shackleton Bailey 1989)	Diad.	Diadumenus Antoninus
		Did. Iul.	Didius Iulianus
Inst.	Institutio oratoria	Gall.	Gallieni duo
R. Gest. div. Aug.	Res gestae divi Augusti	Gord.	Gordiani tres
Rhet. Her.	Rhetorica ad C. Herennium	Hadr.	Hadrianus
Rom	Letter to the Romans	Heliogab.	Heliogabalus
Rt	Ruth	Max. Balb.	Maximus et Balbus
Rufin.	Tyrannius Rufinus	Opil.	Opilius Macrinus
Rut. Namat.	Rutilius Claudius Namatianus, De reditu suo	Pert.	Helvius Pertinax
		Pesc. Nig.	Pescennius Niger
S. Sol.	Song of Solomon	Pius	Antoninus Pius
Sext. Emp.	Sextus Empiricus	Quadr. tyr.	quadraginta tyranni
Sach	Sacharia	Sev.	Severus
Sall. Catil.	Sallustius, De coniuratione Catilinae	Tac.	Tacitus
		Tyr. Trig.	triginta Tyranni
Hist.	Historiae	Valer.	Valeriani duo
Iug.	De bello Iugurthino	Sid. Apoll. Carm.	Apollinaris Sidonius, Carmina
Salv. Gub.	Salvianus, De gubernatione dei	Epist.	Epistulae
1 Sam 2 Sam	Samuel	Sil. Pun.	Silius Italicus, Punica
Schol. (before an author's name)	Scholia to the author in question	Simon.	Simonides
		Simpl.	Simplicius
		Sir	Jesus Sirach
Sedul.	Sedulius	Scyl.	Scylax, Periplus
Sen. Controv.	Seneca maior, Controversiae	Scymn.	Scymnus, Periegesis
Suas.	Suasoriae	Socr.	Socrates, Historia ecclesiastica
Sen. Ag.	Seneca minor, Agamemno	Sol.	Solon
Apocol.	Divi Claudii apocolocyntosis	Solin.	Solinus
Ben.	De beneficiis	Soph. Aj.	Sophocles, Ajax
Clem.	De clementia (Hosius ²1914)	Ant.	Antigone
Dial.	Dialogi	El.	Electra
Ep.	Epistulae morales ad Lucilium	Ichn.	Ichneutae
Herc. f.	Hercules furens	OC	Oedipus Coloneus
		OT	Oedipus Tyrannus

Phil.	Philoctetes		1 Thess, 2 Thess	Letters to the Thessalonians
Trach.	Trachiniae		Thgn.	Theognis
Sor. Gyn.	Soranus, Gynaecia		Thuc.	Thucydides
Sozom. Hist. eccl.	Sozomenus, Historia ecclesiastica		TI	Tiryns (place where Linear B tablets were discovered)
Stat. Achil.	Statius, Achilleis		Tib.	Tibullus, Elegiae
Silv.	Silvae		1 Tim, 2 Tim	Letters to Timothy
Theb.	Thebais		Tit	Letter to Titus
Steph. Byz.	Stephanus Byzantius		Tob	Tobit
Stesich.	Stesichorus		Tzetz. Anteh.	Tzetzes, Antehomerica
Stob.	Stobaeus		Chil.	Chiliades
Str.	Strabo (books, chapters)		Posth.	Posthomerica
Suda	Suda = Suidas		Ulp.	Ulpianus (Ulpiani regulae)
Suet. Aug.	Suetonius, Divus Augustus (Ihm 1907)		Val. Fl.	Valerius Flaccus, Argonautica
			Val. Max.	Valerius Maximus, Facta et dicta memorabilia
Calig.	Caligula			
Claud.	Divus Claudius		Varro, Ling.	Varro, De lingua Latina
Dom.	Domitianus		Rust.	Res rusticae
Gram.	De grammaticis (Kaster 1995)		Sat. Men.	Saturae Menippeae (Astbury 1985)
Iul.	Divus Iulius			
Tib.	Divus Tiberius		Vat.	Fragmenta Vaticana
Tit.	Divus Titus		Veg. Mil.	Vegetius, Epitoma rei militaris
Vesp.	Divus Vespasianus		Vell.	Pat. Velleius Paterculus, Historiae Romanae
Vit.	Vitellius			
Sulp. Sev.	Sulpicius Severus		Ven. Fort.	Venantius Fortunatus
Symmachus, Ep.	Symmachus, Epistulae		Verg. Aen.	Vergilius, Aeneis
Or.	Orationes		Catal.	Catalepton
Relat.	Relationes		Ecl.	Eclogae
Synes. epist.	Synesius, Epistulae		G.	Georgica
Sync.	Syncellus		Vir. ill.	De viris illustribus
Tab. Peut.	Tabula Peutingeriana		Vitr. De arch.	Vitruvius, De architectura
Tac. Agr.	Tacitus, Agricola		Vulg.	Vulgate
Ann.	Annales		Wisd.	Wisdom
Dial.	Dialogus de oratoribus		Xen. Ages.	Xenophon, Agesilaus
Germ.	Germania		An.	Anabasis
Hist.	Historiae		Ap.	Apologia
Ter. Maur.	Terentianus Maurus		Ath. pol.	Athenaion politeia
Ter. Ad.	Terentius, Adelphoe		Cyn.	Cynegeticus
An.	Andria		Cyr.	Cyropaedia
Eun.	Eunuchus		Eq.	De equitandi ratione
Haut.	H(e)autontimorumenos		Eq. mag.	De equitum magistro
Hec.	Hecyra		Hell.	Hellenica
Phorm.	Phormio		Hier.	Hieron
Tert. Apol.	Tertullianus, Apologeticum		Lac.	Respublica Lacedaemoniorum
Ad nat.	Ad nationes (Borleffs 1954)		Mem.	Memorabilia
TH	Thebes (place where Linear B tables were discovered)		Oec.	Oeconomicus
			Symp.	Dymposium
Them. Or.	Themistius, Orationes		Vect.	De vectigalibus
Theoc. Epigr.	Theocritus, Epigrammata		Xenoph.	Xenophanes
Id.	Idylls		Zen.	Zeno
Theod. Epist.	Theodoretus, Epistulae		Zenob.	Zenobius
Gr. aff. Cur.	Graecarum affectionum curatio		Zenod.	Zenodotus
Hist. eccl.	Historia ecclesiastica		Zeph	Zephania
Theopomp.	Theopompus		Zon.	Zonaras
Theophr. Caus. pl.	Theophrastus, De causis plantarum		Zos.	Zosimus
Char.	Characteres			
Hist. pl.	Historia plantarum			

List of Illustrations and Maps

Illustrations are found in the corresponding entries.
ND means redrawing following the instructions of the
author or after the listed materials.
RP means reproduction with minor changes.

Some of the maps serve to visualize the subject matter
and to complement the articles. In such cases, there will
be a reference to the corresponding entry. Only literature that was used exclusively for the maps is listed.

Lemma Title AUTHORS Bibliography

Catapult
ND according to: D. BAATZ, Bauten und Katapulte
des röm. Heeres, 1994
Gastraphetes according to Hero: BAATZ, 287, fig.
287, fig. 3.
Trigger mechanism of the *gastraphetes* according to
Hero: BAATZ, 287, fig. 4.
Catapult according to Vitruvius (10,10), top view
and side elevation: BAATZ, 179, fig. 7.
Torsion spring of a catapult (schematic respresen-
tation): BAATZ, 187, fig. 1.

Cavalry
Roman riding-harness; reconstruction (1st cent.
BC)
ND according to: M. KEMKES, J. SCHEUERBRANDT,
Zw. Patrouille und Parade. Die röm. Reiterei am
Limes, 1997, 39, fig. 35.

Celtic languages
Celtic languages (with scripts used)
ND: S. ZIEGLER

The Celts
[1] The Celts
ND: V. PINGEL (according to: L. Pauli (ed.), Die Kelten in Mitteleuropa, 1980, 31 with fig.)

[2] The Galatian tribal states in Asia Minor up to
their absorption into the Roman province of Galatia
(3rd cent. – 25 BC)
ND: K. STROBEL

Central-plan building
[1] Antiochia [1] on the Orontes: St. Babylas, AD
379/380 (ground-plan)
ND according to: B. BRENK, Spätant. und frühes
Christentum (PropKg Suppl. 1), 1985, 225, fig. 55.

[2] Spalatum (Split): Mausoleum of Diocletian,
early 4th cent. AD (ground-plan)
ND according to: J. AND T. MARASOVIĆ, Diokleci-
janova Palača, 1968, fig. 35.

[3] Ravenna: S. Vitale, consecrated AD 547
(ground-plan)
ND according to: G. MÜLLER, W. Vogel, dtv-Atlas
zur Baukunst 1, 1974, 268.

[4] Constantinopolis: Hagia Sophia, AD 532–537
and 558–563 (ground-plan)
ND according to: A.M. SCHNEIDER, Die Hagia Sophia zu Konstantinopel, 1939, 36, fig. 1.

Christianity
The spread of Christianity (1st – 4th cents. AD)
EDITORIAL TEAM TÜBINGEN
Bibliography: A.v. HARNACK, Die Mission und Aus-
breitung des Christentums in den ersten 3 Jh., [4]1924
(repr. 1966); F. VAN DER MEER, C. MOHRMANN,
Bildatlas der frühchristl. Welt, 1959, 16f.; W.
FREND, Martyrdom and Persecution in the Early
Church, 1965; H. JEDIN, K.S. LATOURETTE (ed.),
Atlas zur Kirchengesch., 1970, new edition 1987.

Chronographer
The November leaf in the Chronographer of AD
354 (Codex Romanus Ims, Barb. Lat. 2154, fol. 22)
represents an ingenious summarizing depiction of
the cult of Isis.
RP according to: M.R. SALZMAN, The Codex-Calendar of 354, 1990, fig. 22.

Clocks
[1] Sun dials
Pythagoreion (Samos). Arch. Museum, Inv. nos.
322/323 (2nd half of the 2nd cent. BC, Hellenistic-
late antique resp.)
ND according to: R. TÖLLE, Uhren auf Samos, in: P.
Zazoff (ed.), Opus Nobile. FS U. Jantzen, 1969,
166, fig. 10; 167, fig. 11.

[2] Water-clock of Ctesibius; hypothetical reconstruction (after Vitr. 9,8,2–7)
ND according to: R. TÖLLE, Uhren auf Samos, in: P.
Zazoff (ed.), Opus Nobile. FS U. Jantzen, 1969,
169, fig. 12.

Doric colonization (8th – c. 6th cent.BC)
ND: EDITORIAL TEAM TÜBINGEN

Column
[1] Doric column. Agrigento, Temple of the Dioscuri
(480 – 460 BC)
ND according to: D. MERTENS, Der Tempel von Segesta und die dor. Tempelbaukunst des griech. Wes-
tens in klass. Zeit, 1984, 121, fig. 68.

[2] Columns and bases
ND according to: W. MÜLLER-WIENER, Griech.
Bauwesen in der Ant., 1988, 122, fig. 69; B. WESEN-
BERG, Kapitelle und Basen, 1971, plate 160; J.M.
VON MAUCH (ed.), Die architektonischen Ordnun-
gen der Griechen und Römer, ⁷1875, plate 20.

[2] Corinthian capitals
ND according to: H. BAUER, Korinthische Kapitelle
des 4. und 3. Jh. v. Chr., 1973, appendix. /. 15;
EAA. Atlante dei complessi figurati 1, 1973, tab.
368; J. VON EGLE, Praktische Baustil- und Baufor-
menlehre auf gesch. Grundlage, n.d., part IV, plate
56, part V, plate 17; M.F. SQUARCIAPINO, Sculture
del Foro Severiano di Leptis Magna, 1974, plate 92.

[3] Openwork capital; Constantinople, Hagia Sophia, west conch (6th cent. AD)
ND according to: EAA. Atlante dei complessi figurati 1, 1973, plate 303.

[4] Tuscan half-column; Rome, Collosseum (AD 80)
ND according to: H. KÄHLER, Die Hagia Sophia,
1967, plate 75.

Constantinopolis
Byzantium-Constantinopolis: archaeological site
map with extant and reconstructed monuments (up
to the 8th cent. AD)
ND: EDITORIAL TEAM TÜBINGEN/E. OLSHAUSEN

Constantinus
Stemma of the family of Constantine the Great
ND: B. BLECKMANN

Construction technique
[1] Greek construction technique using ashlars:
quarrying (above) and transport of building material (below).

[2] Greek constructions technique using cut stone:
joggling (above) and clamping (below).

[3] Greek construction technique; various lifting de-
vices
RP according to: L. SCHNEIDER, CH. HÖCKER,
Griech. Festland, 1966, 92 fig. 1. 2; 93 fig. 3, 4, 6.

[4] Roman construction technique: construction of
a core made of *opus caementicium* (above), and various facings of tuffa (middle) and brick (below).
RP according to: F. RAKOB, Bautypen und Bautechnik, in: Hell. in Mittelitalien II Abh. der Akademie
der Wiss. in Göttingen, 1976, 371 figs. II a-c, 381
fig. 5.

Corduba
Colonia Patricia Corduba
ND: R. HIDALGO, J. F. MURILLO, A. VENTURA/EDI-
TORIAL TEAM TÜBINGEN A. VENTURA, J. M. BERMÚ-
DEZ, P. LEÓN, Análisis arqueológico de Córdoba
Romana, in: P. LEÓN ALONSO (ed.), Colonia Patri-
cia Corduba, Coloquio internacional, Córdoba
1993, 1996, 87–128, here: 111
A. IBÁÑEZ CASTRO, Córdoba hispano-romano,
1983.

Corinthus/Corinth
Corinthus (lower city)
ND according to: M.I. FINLEY, Atlas of Classical
Archaeology, 1977, 155.

Corinthian vases
Vessel shapes in Corinthian pottery
ND: M. HAASE/M. STEINHART

Cornelius
The Cornelii Scipiones and their family relations
(3rd/2nd cents. BC)
NZ: K.-L. ELVERS

Crete
[1] Hellenistic Crete, up to the Roman conquest (4th
– 1st cents. BC)
ND: EDITORIAL TEAM TÜBINGEN/H. SONNABEND/
E. OLSHAUSEN

[2] The double province of Creta et Cyrenae (96 BC
– c. AD 395)
ND: EDITORIAL TEAM TÜBINGEN/H. SONNABEND/
E. OLSHAUSEN

Crockery
Bronze vessels (depot find) from Augusta Rauri-
ca/Augst (Roman)
ND according to: W. DRACK, R. FELLMANN, Die
Römer in der Schweiz, 1988, 165, fig. 128.

Crypta, Cryptoporticus
Tivoli, Villa Hadriana. Crypta below the Temple of
Aphrodite
RP according to: R. FÖRTSCH, Arch. Komm. zu den
Villenbriefen des jüngeren Plinius, 1993, plate 67,1.

List of Authors

Albiani, Maria Grazia, Bologna	M.G.A.	Cobet, Justus, Essen	J.CO.
Alonso-Núñez, José Miguel, Madrid	J.M.A.-N.	Colpe, Carsten, Berlin	C.C.
Ambühl, Annemarie, Basle	A.A.	Corbier, Mireille, Paris	MI.CO.
Ameling, Walter, Jena	W.A.	Courtney, Edward, Charlottesville, VA	ED.C.
Andreau, Jean, Paris	J.A.	Cüppers, Heinz, Trier	H.C.
Apathy, Peter, Linz	P.A.	Daverio Rocchi, Giovanna, Milan	G.D.R.
Baatz, Dietwulf, Bad Homburg	D.BA.	de la Genière, Juliette, Nevilly-sur-Seine	J.d.G.
Bäbler, Balbina, Göttingen	B.BÄ.	de Souza, Philip, Twickenham	P.d.S.
Backhaus, Knut, Paderborn	KN.B.	Decker, Wolfgang, Cologne	W.D.
Badian, Ernst, Cambridge, MA	E.B.	Degani, Enzo, Bologna	E.D.
Baltes, Matthias, Münster	M.BA.	Deger-Jalkotzy, Sigrid, Salzburg	S.D.-J.
Baratte, François, Paris	F.BA.	Detel, Wolfgang, Frankfurt/Main	W.DE.
Barceló, Pedro, Potsdam	P.B.	Di Marco, Massimo, Fondi (Latina)	M.D.MA.
Baumhauer, Otto A., Bremen	O.B.	Dietz, Karlheinz, Würzburg	K.DI.
Beck, Hans, Cologne	HA.BE.	Dohrn-van Rossum, Gerhard, Chemnitz	G.D.-V.R.
Belke, Klaus, Vienna	K.BE.	Dorandi, Tiziano, Paris	T.D.
Berger, Albrecht, Berlin	AL.B.	Döring, Klaus, Bamberg	K.D.
Berlejung, Angelika, Heidelberg	A.BER.	Dörner, Friedrich Karl, Münster	F.K.D.
Berschin, Walter, Heidelberg	W.B.	Dräger, Paul, Trier	P.D.
Betegh, Gábor, Budapest	G.BE.	Drew-Bear, Thomas, Lyons	T.D.-B.
Bieberstein, Klaus, Fribourg	K.B.	Drexhage, Hans-Joachim, Marburg/Lahn	H.-J.D.
Bieg, Gebhard, Tübingen	GE.BI.	Dreyer, Boris, Göttingen	BO.D.
Binder, Gerhard, Bochum	G.BI.	Duridanov, Ludmil, Freiburg	L.D.
Binder, Vera, Gießen	V.BI.	Eck, Werner, Cologne	W.E.
Birley, A.R., Düsseldorf	A.B.	Eder, Walter, Bochum	W.ED.
Bleckmann, Bruno, Berne	B.BL.	Edzard, Dietz Otto, Munich	D.O.E.
Bloch, René, Princeton, NJ	R.B.	Ego, Beate, Osnabrück	B.E.
Bloedhorn, Hanswulf, Jerusalem	H.BL.	Elvers, Karl-Ludwig, Bochum	K.-L.E.
Bonfante, Larissa, New York	L.B.	Engelmann, Helmut, Cologne	HE.EN.
Bowie, Ewen, Oxford	E.BO.	Engels, Johannes, Cologne	J.E.
Brändle, Rudolf, Basle	R.BR.	Englund, Robert K., Berlin	R.K.E.
von Bredow, Iris, Stuttgart	I.v.B.	Erler, Michael, Würzburg	M.ER.
Brentjes, Burchard, Berlin	B.B.	Errington, Robert Malcolm, Marburg/Lahn	MA.ER.
Briese, Christoph, Randers	CH.B.	Euskirchen, Marion, Bonn	M.E.
Bringmann, Klaus, Frankfurt/Main	K.BR.	Falco, Giulia, Athens	GI.F.
Brizzi, Giovanni, Bologna	G.BR.	Fantuzzi, Marco, Florence	M.FA.
Brodersen, Kai, Newcastle and Mannheim	K.BRO.	Fell, Martin, Münster	M.FE.
Broggiato, Maria, London	MA.BR.	Fitschen, Klaus, Kiel	K.FI.
Brown, David, Berlin	DA.BR.	Fornaro, Sotera, Sassari	S.FO.
Buonocore, Marco, Rome	M.BU.	Förtsch, Reinhard, Cologne	R.F.
Burckhardt, Leonhard, Basle	LE.BU.	Franke, Thomas, Bochum	T.F.
Burford Cooper, Alison, Ann Arbor	A.B.-C.	Frateantonio, Christa, Gießen-Erfurt	C.F.
Burian, Jan, Prague	J.BU.	Frede, Michael, Oxford	M.FR.
Caduff, Gian Andrea, Zizers	G.A.C.	Freitag, Klaus, Münster	K.F.
Calboli, Gualtiero, Bologna	G.C.	Frey, Alexandra, Basle	AL.FR.
Calboli Montefusco, Lucia, Bologna	L.C.M.	Frezouls †, Edmond, Straßburg	E.FR.
Campbell, J. Brian, Belfast	J.CA.	Funke, Peter, Münster	P.F.
Cancik-Kirschbaum, Eva, Berlin	E.C.-K.	Furley, William D., Heidelberg	W.D.F.
Cataudella, Michele, Florence	M.CA.	Fürst, Alfons, Bamberg	A.FÜ.
Cavallo, Guglielmo, Rome	GU.C.	Fusillo, Massimo, L'Aquila	M.FU.
Christmann, Eckhard, Heidelberg	E.C.	Galli, Lucia, Florence	L.G.

Galsterer, Hartmut, Bonn	H. GA.	Kalcyk, Hansjörg, Petershausen	H. KAL.
Gamauf, Richard, Vienna	R. GA.	Kaletsch, Hans, Regensburg	H. KA.
Gärtner, Hans Armin, Heidelberg	H. A. G.	Karttunen, Klaus, Helsinki	K. K.
Gatti, Paolo, Triento	P. G.	Kaster, Robert A., Princeton	R. A. K.
Gerber, Simon, Berlin	S. GE.	Kearns, Emily, Oxford	E. K.
Geus, Klaus, Bamberg	KL. GE.	Kessler, Karlheinz, Emskirchen	K. KE.
Giaro, Tomasz, Frankfurt/Main	T. G.	Kienast, Dietmar, Neu-Esting	D. K.
Gizewski, Christian, Berlin	C. G.	Kierdorf, Wilhelm, Cologne	W. K.
Glassner, Jean-Jacques, Paris	J.-J. G.	King, Helen, Reading	H. K.
Glei, Reinhold F., Bochum	R. GL.	Kinzl, Konrad, Peterborough	K. KI.
Glock, Andreas, Jena	AN. GL.	Klodt, Claudia, Hamburg	CL. K.
Gordon, Richard L., Ilmmünster	R. GOR.	Klose, Dietrich, Munich	DI. K.
Gottschalk, Hans, Leeds	H. G.	Koch, Klaus, Hamburg	K. KO.
Goulet-Cazé, Marie-Odile, Antony	M. G.-C.	Köckert, Matthias, Berlin	M. K.
Graf, Fritz, Princeton, NJ	F. G.	Kolb, Anne, Zurich	A. K.
Graßhoff, Gerd, Berne	GE. G.	Krafft, Fritz, Marburg/Lahn	F. KR.
Graßl, Herbert, Salzburg	H. GR.	Kramolisch, Herwig, Eppelheim	HE. KR.
Grieshammer, Reinhard, Heidelberg	R. GR.	Krause, Jens-Uwe, Munich	J. K.
Groß-Albenhausen, Kirsten, Frankfurt/Main	K. G.-A.	Krebernik, Manfred, Munich	M. KR.
Gruber, Joachim, Erlangen	J. GR.	Kuchenbuch, Ludolf, Hagen	LU. KU.
Günther, Linda-Marie, Bochum	L.-M. G.	Kugelmeier, Christoph, Berlin	CHR. KU.
Gutsfeld, Andreas, Münster	A. G.	Kühne, Hartmut, Berlin	H. KÜ.
Haase, Mareile, Erfurt	M. HAA.	Kuhrt, Amélie, London	A. KU.
Hadot, Ilsetraut, Limours	I. H.	Kundert, Lukas, Basle	LUK. KU.
Hadot, Pierre, Limours	P. HA.	Kunst, Christiane, Potsdam	C. KU.
Hahn, Johannes, Münster	J. H.	Lafond, Yves, Bochum	Y. L.
Hailer, Ulf, Tübingen	U. HA.	Latacz, Joachim, Basle	J. L.
Harder, Ruth Elisabeth, Zurich	R. HA.	Lausberg, Marion, Augsburg	MA. L.
Hauser, Stefan R., Berlin	S. HA.	Le Bohec, Yann, Lyons	Y. L. B.
Heckel, Hartwig, Bochum	H. H.	Lefèvre, Eckhard, Freiburg	E. L.
Heimgartner, Martin, Basle	M. HE.	Leisten, Thomas, Princeton, NJ	T. L.
Heinze, Theodor, Geneva	T. H.	Leonhardt, Jürgen, Marburg/Lahn	J. LE.
Hengstl, Joachim, Marburg/Lahn	JO. HE.	Leppin, Hartmut, Frankfurt/Main	H. L.
Herz, Peter, Regensburg	P. H.	Ley, Anne, Xanten	A. L.
Herzhoff, Bernhard, Trier	B. HE.	Lezzi-Hafter, Adrienne, Kilchberg	A. L.-H.
Hidber, Thomas, Göttingen	T. HI.	Liebermann, Wolf-Lüder, Bielefeld	W.-L. L.
Hild, Friedrich, Vienna	F. H.	Linke, Bernhard, Dresden	B. LI.
Hintze, Almut, Cambridge	A. HI.	Lintott, A. W., Oxford	A. W. L.
Höcker, Christoph, Kissing	C. HÖ.	Lohmann, Hans, Bochum	H. LO.
Hoesch, Nicola, Munich	N. H.	Makris, Georgios, Bochum	G. MA.
Hoffmann, Philippe, Paris	PH. H.	Manganaro, Giacomo, Sant' Agata li Battiata	GI. MA.
Hofmann, Heinz, Tübingen	H. HO.	Manthe, Ulrich, Passau	U. M.
Högemann, Peter, Tübingen	PE. HÖ.	Marek, Christian, Zurich	C. MA.
Hölkeskamp, Karl-Joachim, Cologne	K.-J. H.	Marengo, Silvia Maria, Macerata	S. M. M.
Hollender, Elisabeth, Cologne	E. H.	Markschies, Christoph, Heidelberg	C. M.
Holzhausen, Jens, Berlin	J. HO.	Mastino, Attilio, Sassari	A. MA.
Hönle, Augusta, Rottweil	A. HÖ.	Maul, Stefan, Heidelberg	S. M.
Hübner, Wolfgang, Münster	W. H.	Mehl, Andreas, Halle/Saale	A. ME.
Hünemörder, Christian, Hamburg	C. HÜ.	Meier, Mischa, Bielefeld	M. MEI.
Hunger, Hermann, Vienna	H. HU.	Meissel, Franz-Stefan, Vienna	F. ME.
Hurschmann, Rolf, Hamburg	R. H.	Meister, Klaus, Berlin	K. MEI.
Huß, Werner, Munich	W. HU.	Mennella, Giovanni, Genoa	G. ME.
Inwood, Brad, Toronto, ON	B. I.	Meyer, Doris, Straßburg	DO. ME.
Jameson, Michael, Stanford	MI. JA.	Meyer †, Ernst, Zurich	E. MEY.
Jansen-Winkeln, Karl, Berlin	K. J.-W.	Michel, Raphael, Basle	RA. MI.
Job, Michael, Marburg/Lahn	M. J.	Michel, Simone, Hamburg	S. MI.
Jongman, Willem, Groningen	W. J.	Mlasowsky, Alexander, Hannover	A. M.
von Kaenel, Hans-Markus, Frankfurt/Main		Möller, Astrid, Freiburg	A. MÖ.
	H.-M. V. K.		

Mommsen, Heide, Stuttgart	H.M.	Schachter, Albert, Montreal	A.S.
Montanari, Franco, Pisa	F.M.	Schaffner, Brigitte, Basle	B.SCH.
Muggia, Anna, Pavia	A.MU.	Scheer, Tanja, Rome	T.S.
Müller, Stefan, Hagen	S.MÜ.	Scheibler, Ingeborg, Krefeld	I.S.
Müller, Walter W., Marburg/Lahn	W.W.M.	Scheid, John, Paris	J.S.
Nadig, Peter C., Duisburg	P.N.	Scherf, Johannes, Tübingen	JO.S.
Najock, Dietmar, Berlin	D.N.	Schiemann, Gottfried, Tübingen	G.S.
Neschke, Ada, Lausanne	A.NE.	Schlapbach, Karin, Zurich	K.SCHL.
Nesselrath, Heinz-Günther, Göttingen	H.-G.NE.	Schlesier, Renate, Paderborn	RE.S.
Neudecker, Richard, Rome	R.N.	Schmidt, Peter Lebrecht, Konstanz	P.L.S.
Neumann, Hans, Berlin	H.N.	Schmitt-Pantel, Pauline, Paris	P.S.-P.
Niehoff, Johannes, Freiburg	J.N.	Schmitz, Winfried, Bielefeld	W.S.
Nielsen, Inge, Hamburg	I.N.	Schmitzer, Ulrich, Erlangen	U.SCH.
Niemeyer, Hans Georg, Hamburg	H.G.N.	Scholz, Udo W., Würzburg	U.W.S.
Nissen, Hans Jörg, Berlin	H.J.N.	Schön, Franz, Regensburg	F.SCH.
Nünlist, René, Providence, RI	RE.N.	Schönig, Claus, Mainz	CL.SCH.
Nutton, Vivian, London	V.N.	Schottky, Martin, Pretzfeld	M.SCH.
Oelsner, Joachim, Leipzig	J.OE.	Schreiner, Peter, Cologne	P.S.
Olshausen, Eckart, Stuttgart	E.O.	Schwertheim, Elmar, Münster	E.SCH.
Osing, Jürgen, Berlin	J.OS.	Seidlmayer, Stephan Johannes, Berlin	S.S.
Pack, Edgar, Cologne	E.P.	Selzer, Christoph, Frankfurt/Main	C.S.
Padgett, J.Michael, Princeton	M.P.	Senff, Reinhard, Bochum	R.SE.
Pappalardo, Umberto, Naples	U.PA.	Sharples, Robert, London	R.S.
Parra, Maria Cecilia, Pisa	M.C.P.	Sievertsen, Uwe, Tübingen	U.S.
Patané, Rosario, Catania	RO.PA.	Simon, Dietrich, Jena	DI.S.
Patzek, Barbara, Essen	B.P.	Smolak, Kurt, Vienna	K.SM.
Paulus, Christoph Georg, Berlin	C.PA.	Sonnabend, Holger, Stuttgart	H.SO.
Pekridou-Gorecki, Anastasia, Frankfurt/Main	A.P.-G.	Spickermann, Wolfgang, Bochum	W.SP.
Peter, Ulrike, Berlin	U.P.	Spitzbart, Günter, Herscheid	G.SP.
Pingel, Volker, Bochum	V.P.	Stanzel, Karl-Heinz, Tübingen	K.-H.S.
Plontke-Lüning, Annegret, Jena	A.P.-L.	Starke, Frank, Tübingen	F.S.
Pongratz-Leisten, Beate, Bryn Mawr	B.P.-L.	Stegmann, Helena, Bonn	H.S.
Porod, Robert, Graz	RO.PO.	Steimer, Bruno, Freiburg	BR.ST.
Portmann, Werner, Berlin	W.P.	Stein-Hölkeskamp, Elke, Cologne	E.S.-H.
Prescendi, Francesca, Geneva	FR.P.	Steinbauer, Dieter, Regensburg	D.ST.
Pressler, Frank, Freiburg	F.P.	Steinhart, Matthias, Freiburg	M.ST.
Quack, Joachim, Berlin	JO.QU.	Stoevesandt, Magdalene, Basle	MA.ST.
Raepsaet, Georges, Brussels	G.R.	Stoffel, Eliane, Altkirch	EL.STO.
von Reden, Sitta, Bristol	S.v.R.	Strauch, Daniel, Berlin	D.S.
Reitz, Christiane, Rostock	CH.R.	Strobel, Karl, Klagenfurt	K.ST.
Renaud, François, Moncton, NB	F.R.	Stroh, Wilfried, Munich	W.STR.
Renger, Johannes, Berlin	J.RE.	Strothmann, Meret, Bochum	ME.STR.
Rhodes, Peter J., Durham	P.J.R.	Stumpf, Gerd, Munich	GE.S.
Richmond, John A., Blackrock, VA	J.A.R.	Takacs, Sarolta A., Cambridge, MA	S.TA.
Riederer, Josef, Berlin	JO.R.	Täuber, Hans, Vienna	H.TÄ.
Riedweg, Christoph, Zurich	C.RI.	Thür, Gerhard, Graz	G.T.
Riemer, Peter, Potsdam	P.RI.	Tinnefeld, Franz, Munich	F.T.
Rist, Josef, Würzburg	J.RI.	Todd, Malcolm, Exeter	M.TO.
Rix, Helmut, Freiburg	H.R.	Tokhtas'ev, Sergej R., St.Petersburg	S.R.T.
Robbins, Emmet, Toronto, ON	E.R.	Tomaschitz, Kurt, Vienna	K.T.
Rüpke, Jörg, Erfurt	J.R.	Toral-Niehoff, Isabel, Freiburg	I.T.-N.
Sallmann, Klaus, Mainz	KL.SA.	Touwaide, Alain, Madrid	A.TO.
Salzman, Michele Renée, Riverside, Ca	M.SA.	Treidler, Hans, Berlin	H.T.
Sancisi-Weerdenburg, Helen, Utrecht	H.S.-W.	Trombley, Frank R., Cardiff	F.R.T.
Sartori, Antonio, Milan	A.SA.	Uggeri, Giovanni, Florence	G.U.
Šašel Kos, Marjeta, Ljubljana	M.Š.K.	von Ungern-Sternberg, Jürgen, Basle	J.v.U.-S.
Sauer, Vera, Stuttgart	V.S.	van de Mieroop, Marc, New York	M.v.M.
Savvidis, Kyriakos, Bochum	K.SA.	Visser, Edzard, Basle	E.V.

Cat

I. Egypt and the Near East   II. Classical Antiquity

I. Egypt and the Near East

The cat was particularly significant in Egypt where there is evidence of it being kept as a pet from the beginning of the 2nd millennium BC at the latest; the period of its domestication, however, stretched far into the 1st millennium. The Egyptian cat used to be regarded as the precursor of the European domestic cat, but today it is assumed that the origin of the latter was the Near East: it was first mentioned in Mesopotamia [1] in the 17th cent. BC as a wild animal; for the 1st millennium, there is certainly evidence of domestic cats in that area. A literary text (1st millennium) mentions an 'Indian' cat (*šurān Meluḫḫa*). In the 1st millennium BC however, *Meluḫḫa* refers to Nubia, and so perhaps the Nubian pigmented cat is meant.

In Egypt there is good evidence of cats from the Middle Kingdom onwards, both pictorially and in inscriptions (also as a name); the high regard for them increased constantly, reaching its peak in the 1st millennium where they were extremely frequent as pets and as sacred animals, particularly of the goddess Bastet, and had special protection (cf. Diod. Sic. 1,83; Hdt. 2,66). From this period there are large animal cemeteries with cat mummies and numerous bronze figures of cats.

1 J. Malek, The Cat in Ancient Egypt, 1993   2 L. Störk, s.v. Katze, LÄ 3, 367–70.   K.J.-W.

II. Classical Antiquity

1) Wild cat (*Felis silvestris*): The first literary reports of the αἴλουρος/*aílouros* or αἰέλορος/*aiéloros* in the Greek world are Soph. Ichn. 269; Aristoph. Ach. 879; the animal only spread gradually from Africa (Egypt and Nubia) to Europe. Varro (Rust. 3,11,3 and 12,3; cf. Columella 8,3,6; 14,9 and 15,1; Babr. 17; Gp. 13,6) calls the *faelis* a predator detrimental to chicken farms and duck and hare breeding. Aristot. Hist. an. 8(9),6,612b 14f. calls it a 'bird-eater' (ὀρνιθοφάγος/*ornithophágos*) (cf. Sen. Ep. 121). Plin. HN 10,202 describes its hunting as lying in wait for birds and mice and explains that it covers its excrements with earth to hide the smell that would betray its presence. In fables (Aesop. 7; 16 and 81 Hausrath) it is considered crafty and cunning like the → fox, but often is not successful as a hunter. It lives for six years (Aristot. Hist. an. 6,35,580a 23f.; Plin. HN 10,179), has just as many young as dogs have, and the male, standing up, inseminates the female as she lies down (Aristot. Hist. an. 5,2,540a 10–13; cf. Plin. HN 10,174). At night, their eyes glow (Plin. HN 11,151). Their tongue is rough (Plin. HN 11,172).

2) The domestic cat (*Felis ocreata domestica*): It was believed to have been introduced to Europe from Egypt where it was venerated as sacred (Hdt. 2,66f.; Diod. Sic. 1,83; Cic. Tusc. 5,78; Ov. Met. 5,330; Plin. HN 6,178). Mart. 13,69 is the first Latin literary mention. Pall. Agric. 4,9,4 praises the *cattus* (cf. Anth. Lat. 181 and 375) as a mole hunter. This name entered the languages of Central Europe from the time of the peoples' migration onwards. As *murilegus* or *musio* (Isid. Orig. 12,2,38) its behaviour as a pet is described in detail e.g. in Thomas of Cantimpré 4,76 [1. 151f.].

1 H. Boese (ed.), Thomas Cantimpratensis, Liber de natura rerum, 1973.

V. Hehn, Kulturpflanzen und Haustiere (ed. O Schrader), [8]1911, repr. 1963, 463–476; Keller vol. 1, 64–81.   C.HÜ.

Catabathmus (Καταβαθμός; *Katabathmós*). In the Ptolemaic period, the fort of C. with its harbour — modern Sollum — was the border town from Egypt to the → Cyrenaea. C. retained is border town character throughout subsequent cents. Its strategic location was important. Source references: Sall. Iug. 19,3; Str. 17,1,5; 13; 3,1; 22; Mela 1,40; Plin. HN 5,38f.; It. Ant. 71,7; Stadiasmus maris magni 29f. (GGM I 437f.). The surroundings of the settlement are also occasionally referred to as *Katabathmós* — C. ('descent') *mégas*; cf. Pol. 31,18,9; Ptol. 4,5,4; Sol. 27,3; Oros. 1,2,88.

H. Kees, s.v. Katabathmus (2), RE 10, 2449f.   W.HU.

Catacecaumene (Κατακεκαυμένη; *Katakekauménē*, 'burnt earth').

[1] Volcanic zone, characterized by ash-like soil and black rocks, in western Asia Minor (Mysia and eastern Lydia: Xanthus FGrH 765 F 13; Str. 12,8,18f.), about 40×10 km in size (exaggerated in Str. 13,4,11) on the upper reaches of the Maeander, which flows through the C. (Str. 13,4,5); parallel to it in the south is a volcano-free crystalline schistose zone; separate from that the fault line of the Kogamus valley with Philadelphia (Alaşehir), very prone to earthquakes. Wine was grown on the treeless C. (Str. 13,4,11; 14,1,15; Plin. HN 14,75; Steph. Byz. s.v. Katakekaumene). The mythological fire-spitting monster Typhon (→ Typhoeus) was linked with the C. (Str. 12,8,19; 13,4,6 with Hom. Il. 2,782f.).

L. Bürchner, s.v. K., RE 10, 2462f.; K. Buresch, Aus Lydien, 1898, 99f.; Magie 2, 783; A. Philippson, Das Vulkangebiet von Kula, die Katakekaumene der Alten, in: Petermanns Mitteilungen 59, 1912/13, 237–241.   H.KA.

[2] (Κατακεκαυμένη, Peripl. M. Rubr. 20; Ptol. 6,7,44), Exusta (Plin. HN 6,175), 'burnt (island)'; identifiable with the Red Sea volcanic island of Ǧabal Ṭayr or Ǧabal

Ṭāʾir 'bird mountain' (15° 33′ north, 41° 50′ east), which rises up to a height of 245 m and serves as a landmark for seafarers.

L. CASSON, The Periplus Maris Erythraei, 1989, 147.
W.W.M.

Catacombs
A. FUNCTION, ARCHITECTURE, DEVELOPMENT
B. PAINTINGS IN CATACOMBS

A. FUNCTION, ARCHITECTURE, DEVELOPMENT

Derived from the ancient local name of the underground Christian burial complex S. Sebastiano (*coemeterium catacumbas* from Greek *katà kýmbas*, 'near the hollows') by the *via Appia* near Rome, the underground → necropoleis, rediscovered in Rome since the 16th cent., were also called catacombs instead of *coemeterium* or *crypta*. As differentiated from smaller, private → *hypogaea*, catacombs in modern research are understood to be larger community cemeteries using suitable geological layers (e.g. tuff) for burial in underground tunnel systems. Today, the associated aboveground burial districts have often disappeared. Apart from the *c.* 70 sites in Rome, there is further evidence of catacombs e.g. in Latium, Naples, on Sicily, Malta and Melos.

Beginning with A. BOSIO and then since G. B. DE ROSSI, mainly the catacombs of Rome were investigated in respect of their origins and periods of use: during the course of the 2nd cent. AD, the burial in urns, organized by funeral associations (*collegia funeraticia*; see → *collegium* [1]), became unfashionable. As of the end of the 2nd cent., more and more mausoleums characterized as private, pagan or usually non-Christian were extended by the addition of small underground burial sites. This cost-effective solution was taken up by Christians in particular who, consistent with their belief in corporal resurrection, preferred to be interred rather than cremated despite the extra cost. Furthermore, catacombs offered space for the burial of poorer members of the community, a requirement emanating from Christian *caritas*. Characteristic is the intensive utilization of space in grid-like systems of tunnels which could accommodate later extensions. Jews, too, and other communities used the catacombs for burials. But most of the sites and the largest ones amongst them were used as Christian community cemeteries. These can probably trace their origins back to endowments, as is indicated e.g. by the names *Domitilla* and *Priscilla*, or directly to a papal initiative, as is documented for *S. Callisto*. The most common type of grave was the simple *loculus* (flat wall grave) that was recessed into the corridor wall; furthermore, there were *formae* (floor graves) and more expensive *arcosolia* (arch graves) that could also be part of *cubicula* (chambers), spaces in the style of family tombs.

Almost all catacombs show two phases of construction: a moderate growth during the brief period of peace occurring between the Valentinianic, and Diocletian persecutions (AD 258–303) and a strong growth in the 4th cent. after the Constantinian reform (AD 312), during which time the conversion of the upper social strata is also reflected in more impressive *cubicula*. Pope → Damasus (366–384) intensively promoted the martyr cult by having the graves of those killed during the prosecutions located, remodelled in a monumental fashion and furnished with entries and exits for pilgrims to have easy access. A number of underground basilicas *ad corpus* and the heavy concentration of burials in grave areas *retro sanctos* (i.e. near the martyrs) are evidence of Church-inspired as well as private worship as of the last third of the 4th cent. The catacombs still remained places of pilgrimage in the 5th and 6th cents., but it is likely that burials became rare after the invasion by the Goths in AD 410. With the systematic translocation of relics into safe, inner-city churches during the 8th and 9th cents., this final purpose of the catacombs came to an end as well.

B. PAINTINGS IN CATACOMBS

Excavating the corridors, the burial itself, closing the graves with bricks or marble plates and attaching commemorative symbols such as glass containing leaf-gold or inscriptions was the task of *fossores* (grave diggers), who often probably also carried out the paintings found on graves.

Despite an often low artistic quality, paintings in catacombs are of great importance because, with more than 400 groups of paintings, they represent the largest, comprehensive quantity of paintings from late antiquity and, at the same time, document the emergence of a Christian art in the West. Initially with tentative and experimental attempts, symbolically reduced Christian scenes mainly of the OT appear in the 1st half of the 3rd cent. AD in systems of wall divisions known from residential buildings in Rome and Ostia. In the course of the century, a limited canon of images, mostly OT stories of salvation (e.g. Daniel amongst the lions, Noah in the ark, Jonah) emerges, which is increasingly added to, as of the 4th cent., by NT miracle and salvation episodes (e.g. worship of the Magi, multiplying of bread, wine miracle). The transformation of Endymion to Jonah or of the bucolic shepherd to Christ the good shepherd demonstrates the liberal treatment by painters of traditional imagery in order to make the new, Christian content of pictures accessible. In addition to the Roman catacombs, this trait is especially well documented in the Januarius catacombs in Naples. A surprisingly (for scholars) unproblematic juxtaposition of 'pagan' and 'Christian' myths was found in the private catacombs of the Via Latina. But also in the community catacombs there are paintings, alongside the schematic salvation pictures repeated in formulaic fashion, with original image combinations adapted to personal concepts of salvation. Finally, with the emergence of the → martyr cult, theologically well-thought-out image themes become more and more prominent such as, for

example, the dead being led into paradise or saints acclaiming Christ. Despite intensive research, many art-historic aspects and questions related to the interpretation of the images in a wider context remain under discussion.
→ Funerary architecture; → Grave paintings; → Necropoleis; → Wall paintings; ROME

A. BOSIO, Roma Sotterranea, 1632 (repr. 1998); H. BRANDENBURG, Überlegungen zu Ursprung und Entstehung der K. Roms, in: E. DASSMANN (ed.), Vivarium. FS T. Klauser, 1984, 11–49; J. G. DECKERS, H. R. SEELIGER, G. MIETKE, Die K. 'Santi Marcellino e Pietro', 1987; J. G. DECKERS, G. MIETKE, A. WEILAND, Die K. 'Anonima di Via Anapo', 1991; Id., Die K. 'Commodilla', 1994; G. B. DE ROSSI, La Roma sotterranea cristiana, vol. 1–3, 1864–77; J. ENGEMANN, Altes und Neues zu Beispielen heidnischer und christl. K.-Bilder im spätant. Rom, in: JbAC 26, 1983, 128–151; U. FASOLA, Le catacombe di San Gennaro a Capodimonte, 1975; A. FERRUA, K., Unbekannte Bilder des frühen Christentums an der Via Latina, 1991; V. FIOCCHI NICOLAI, s.v. Katakomben, RAC (in print); Id., F. BISCONTI, D. MAZZOLENI, Roms christl. K., 1998; A. NESTORI, Repertorio topografico delle pitture delle catacombe romane, ²1993; P. PERGOLA, Le catacombe romane, 1997; J. WILPERT, Die Malereien der K. Roms, 1903.   NO.ZI.

Catadupa Name of the first Nile cataract on the border between Egypt and Nubia near → Elephantine, first attested in Hdt. 2,17. The name alludes to the noisy roaring of the water (Cic. Rep. 6,19).

H. KEES, s.v. Katadupa, RE 10, 2458.   K.J.-W.

Catalauni A tribal group of Gallia Belgica, who probably originally settled in the area of the Remi, in the modern Champagne. Its name and its capital of the same name, modern Châlon-sur-Marne, are only mentioned by later authors (Amm. Marc. 15,11,10; 27,2,4; Eutr. 9,13; Jer. Chron. AD 274; Not. Gall. 6,4; *Duro catalauni*: It. Ant. 361). The → Catuvellauni, who migrated to southern Britannia, are probably part of the same tribal group.
→ Campi Catalauni   F. SCH.

Catalepton Surviving manuscripts under this name (→ Appendix Vergiliana) include 19 short poems: 3 Priapea and 16 mixed ones, obviously the result of confusion in earlier collections (*C. et Priapea et Epigrammata*: Donat. vita Verg. 56; *Priape a C. Epigrammata*: Servius, vita Verg. 15). The title (κατὰ λεπτόν; *katà leptón*) is Alexandrian and means 'small things' or 'smaller poems'. The collection is metrically very varied. The influence of Catullus and parallels with Virgil can be observed in these *Priapea*—which correspond with the → *Priapea* in the larger collection—and in the other 16 poems. The latter could consist of a core of six pairs (1–7, 2–10, 3–16, 4–11, 5–8, 6–12) and four poems added later. Several pieces are very clever, others are banal. Virgil's authorship is disputed. Dating varies between 43 and 19 BC (or even later).

EDITIONS: → Appendix Vergiliana.
COMMENTARY: R. E. H. WESTENDORP BOERMA, P. Vergili Maronis Catalepton, 2 vols., 1949–1963.   J.A.R.

Catalogue
A. DEFINITION   B. POETRY   C. PROSE

A. DEFINITION
A catalogue is a listing of similar terms in an homogenous context, which in its form is clearly delineated. Each of its components is an 'element of a continuous development' [4. 64]. There is no coherent ancient definition; one characteristic feature is numbering (cf. Hom. Od. 16,235), which also played an important part in the differentiated aesthetical evaluation by the ancient Homer philologists (cf. schol. on Hom. Il. 2,494ff. and frequent other examples). Aristotle sees the catalogue as an instrument for the creation of order (Aristot. Poet. 1459a 35). In the use of catalogues as creative elements, there is a strong cross-influence between literary genres.

B. POETRY
Probably the oldest extant catalogue is the Catalogue of Ships in Homer (Il. 2,484–877). Attempts to use it in order to deduct the Mycenaean sources of the poet of the *Iliad* or use it for dating purposes have not led to unambiguous results (cf. [10. 168–236]). GIOVANNINI [5] maintains as probable sources → *itineraria* or lists of envoys (*theoroi*) which were ordered according to geographical principles. For chronological reasons alone, connections with the literary periegesis (→ Periegetes) and → Peripl(o)us are of secondary importance. Because from the earliest origin of transmitted literature catalogues have been an essential element of epic narratives, they appear regularly in the epic literature, be it as listings of troop contingents, variously ordered or weighted according to geographical origins or characters of their leaders, or be it as lists of individual warriors, such as the suitors in the house of Odysseus (Hom. Od. 16,247–253) or the Argonauts (Apoll. Rhod. 1,23–233, more extensive than Homer's Catalogue of Ships). In the further development, catalogues, frequently introduced by an invocation to the muses, remained a set component of epic poetry.

There is some uncertainty regarding catalogues in early Roman epics; the naming of the 12 Olympic gods (fr. 62 V² = 239 SK. with commentary) in Ennius' 'Annals' is on a different level. Virgil works other narrative elements into the subtly organized catalogues of the *Aeneis* (7,641–817 and 10,120–145), such as an → *Ekphrasis* (7,812–817: [2]). At times he expands them into short scenes, hinting at the future fate of the characters in question, e.g. in Verg. Aen. 7,750–760 [9; 7]. This increasing tendency to soften the strict form of a catalogue becomes really obvious in the post-Virgilian epic, when for example Lucan entirely abandons listing personal names, concentrating instead on the collective deaths of the characters listed (as in 3,689–696).

The archaic period is also when we see the origin of the genealogical catalogues, examples of which are transmitted in the *corpus Hesiodeum* (→ Hesiodus). The fecundity of this genre becomes not only apparent in the related catalogues of the *Iliad* (Hom. Il. 6,151–211: Glaucon' s descent, 24,247–264 and schol. z.St.: the sons of Priamus), but particularly in the genre of the 'Ehoiaí', in which following the introductory formula of ἢ οἵη (*è hoíē*) the lovers of heroes and their descendants are listed (→ Hesiodus B. 2.). Information about the subsequently developed catalogue literature is only very sparse. Antimachus' 'Lyde', Nicaenetus' 'Catalogue of Women' (cf. Ath. 1,590b), Phanocles' 'Erotes' (καλοί), and especially Callimachus' 'Aetia' are cited as successful examples of this genre.

In → didactic poetry, chains of proofs are used as supporting evidence for the thesis in question (cf. below for rhetoric). → Lyric poetry continues with the attempts at expanding the possible topics; certain subjects such as catalogues of poets are part of the epigrammatic repertoire (→ epigram; cf. Anth. Pal. 4,1f.; 9,26) and later that of the Roman → elegy (e.g. Hor. Sat. 1,10,78–99; Prop. 2,34,61–66; Ov. Am. 1,15,9–30; Ov. Tr. 2,359–484; [1]). The influence of Alexandrian literary catalogues (*pínakes*) seems as yet unresolved. In his 'Metamorphoses', Ovid finally displays a masterful treatment of the catalogue genre, distancing himself from the epic tradition in imitation of the Hellenistic catalogue poetry. Alongside parodies of epics (Ov. Met. 3,206–225: the dogs of Actaeon), there are formal experiments (8,300–317: the enumeration of those participating in the hunt of the Calydonian boar is extended by narrative), which are even expanded beyond genre boundaries. Thus Ovid also refers to hymnic poetry as well as to the lists of examples in both didactic poetry and particularly rhetoric [8]. Naturally this had considerable influence on post-Ovidian epic poetry.

C. PROSE

Even though a catalogue of the opposing parties seems to be an indispensable element of → historiography, there are some significant differences. Whereas Herodotus (3,90–96: tributaries to the Persians; 7,61–99: contingents in the Persian War) endeavours to provide exact figures, Thucydides (7,57f.: ships off Sicily) after one global statement (52,1) foregoes any further mention of them. In his recapitulation of the Trojan War (1,10,4), however, he strives for a meticulous reconstruction of the figures provided by Homer. In rhetoric, the use of series of *paradeígmata* (*exempla*) as embellishment or proof is most closely related to catalogues. Starting from orations such as that in Hom. Il. 5,381–415 and 1,260–274, rhetorical theory has defined the functions of this stylistic element (Aristot. Rh. 1393a 28–1394a 23; Rhet. Her. 1,6,10; 2,29,46; Quint. Inst. 5,11,6) and commented on it in conjunction with the → priamel [1].

1 U. BERNHARDT, Die Funktion der Katalog in Ovids Exilpoesie, 1986   2 W. BOYD, Virgil's Camilla and the Tra-

ditions of Catalogue and Ecphrasis, in: AJPh 113, 1992, 213–234   3 E. COURTNEY, Vergil's Military Catalogues and Their Antecedents, in: Vergilius 34, 1988, 3–8   4 J. GASSNER, Katalog im röm. Epos, diss. Munich 1973   5 A. GIOVANNINI, Étude historique sur les origines du catalogue des vaisseaux, 1969   6 W. KÜHLMANN, Katalog und Erzählung, diss. Freiburg/Br. 1973   7 J. J. O'HARA, Messapus, Cycnus, and the Alphabetical Order of Vergil's Catalogue of Italian Heroes, in: Phoenix 43, 1989, 35–38   8 C. REITZ, Zur Funktion der Katalog in Ovids Metamorphosen, in: W. SCHUBERT, Ovid: Werk und Wirkung, FS für M.v. Albrecht, 1998, 359–372   9 C. F. SAYLOR, The Magnificent Fifteen: Vergil's Catalogues of the Latin and Etruscan Forces, in: CPh 69, 1974, 249–257   10 G. S. KIRK, The Iliad Commentary vol. 1, 1995.   CH.R.

Catane (Κατάνη; *Katánē*, Lat. *Catina*). City on the east coast of Sicily on the fertile plain south of the volcano Mount → Etna [1], modern Catania; it was founded in 729 BC by Chalcidians who had some years previously settled in Naxos. In the 2nd half of the 6th cent., the lawgiver → Charondas was active in C; the town was visited by → Ibycus and → Xenophanes; → Stesichorus died there. In the 1st half of the 5th cent., C. was under the rule of Syracuse; → Hieron [1] removed its inhabitants to Leontini, resettled the town with 10,000 new citizens and renamed it → Aetne [2]; Pind. Pyth. 1 and the Hyporchema fr. 108f. were meant for Hieron of Aetne, Aeschylus' tragedy *Aitnaioi* for the new town. After the overthrow of the → Deinomenids, the original inhabitants returned to C.; the inhabitants of Aetne moved to Inessa, now renamed Aetne.

In a volcanic eruption in 425 BC, C. was devastated by a lava flow (Thuc. 3,116,1). In 415 BC, C. served as the operational base of the Athenians against Syracuse, and later, after their catastrophic defeat, their survivors sought refuge there. The Carthaginian incursion saved C. from the revenge of the victorious Syracusans, but in 403 BC, it was captured by Dionysius [1], its inhabitants enslaved, and the town resettled with Campanian mercenaries (moved to Aetna/Inessa in 396 BC). In 353 BC, Callippus, who had murdered Dion [I 1], seized the town; in 344, it was ruled by Mamercus, who joined forces with Timoleon. In 278 BC, C. was one of the first towns in Sicily to open its gates to Pyrrhus, and in the First → Punic War, it was captured by the Romans in 263 BC. C. became a *civitas decumana* within the Roman province. The town was badly damaged in the First Slave War in 135 BC, and in 123 BC, it was once again destroyed by a volcanic eruption (cf. Diod. Sic. 11; 13f.; 16; 19; 22; 24). The wealthy inhabitants of the town suffered under → Verres (Cic. Verr. 2,3,103; 4,50; 99–102). C. was badly damaged in the war of the future Augustus against Sex. Pompeius; from the time of Augustus, C. was a Roman colony.

C. was located on grounds that had been inhabited from prehistoric times. The flourishing of the town in the imperial age is evident in its extensive ruins (walls, aqueducts, public baths, mosaics, two theatres within the town and an amphitheatre outside), that survived the frequent devastations by volcanic eruptions and earthquakes (documented particularly for 251, 1170, 1669, 1693) as well as the destruction by Henry VI in 1197. Extensive necropoleis around C. yielded rich archaeological results (also from earlier periods). Numerous inscriptions (IG XIV 448–566; CIL X 7014–7119; 8312), continuously increased by new finds. Some of the coins of C. are of particular beauty (HN 13–135).

BTCGI 5, 153–177; G. RIZZA, s.v. Catania, EAA 2. Suppl., 1994, 59–61; E. PROCELLI, Appunti per una topografia di Catania pregreca, in: Kokalos 38, 1992, 69–78; A. PATANÈ, Saggi di scavo all'intorno del Castello Ursino di Catania, in: Kokalos 39/40, 1993/94, II 1, 901–907; B. GENTILI (ed.), Catania Antica. Atti Convegno Catania 1992, 1997.　　　　　　　　　　　　GI.F. and K.Z.

Cataonia (Καταονία; *Kataonía*). Region and *strategia* in south-eastern Cappadocia between Taurus and Antitaurus, bordering on Cilicia, Commagene, and Melitene (Str. 11,12,2; 12,1,1–2,4), originally a Luwian-speaking region; in 301 BC, it fell to Seleucus I, probably as a dowry of Stratonice for Ariarathes III of Cappadocia; in AD 17, it became part of the province of Cappadocia, belonged to → Armenia Minor under Diocletian, to Armenia II in AD 386, and to Armenia III in AD 536.

W. RUGE, s.v. K., RE 10, 2478f.; HILD/RESTLE, 202.　　　　　　　　　　　　　　K. ST.

Catapult

A. THE INVENTION OF CATAPULTS　B. HELLENISTIC PERIOD　C. ROME　D. MECHANICAL HAND WEAPONS　E. USE AND EFFECT

A. THE INVENTION OF CATAPULTS

The ancient catapult was a long-range weapon of war which threw its projectiles by means of spring power. There probably is no other technical device from antiquity about which we have equally comprehensive information from illustrated technical treatises (Philo, Vitruvius, Heron), historiography (Ammianus Marcellinus), specialist military literature (Vegetius) and other illustrations. In recent times the number of archaeological finds which complement the literary evidence has also increased appreciably. The first catapults were built in around 400 BC in Syracuse for the struggle against Carthage (Diod. Sic. 14,41–43). The aim had been to develop a weapon with longer range and greater striking force than the hand-held bow (Heron, Belopoiika 71–81). The first step in its conception was the mechanization of the Mediterranean bow-grip; its transformation into a trigger mechanism of metal and wood resulted in the γαστραφέτης (*gastraphétēs*), a weapon similar to a crossbow, with the bow itself strengthened. This invention represented a turning-point in weapons technology, for projectile weapons now no longer depended on the strength of an individ-

ual. Large bow-catapults, supported on a carriage and tensioned with a windlass, were constructed as early as the first half of the 4th cent. BC. The heavy bow-catapults now required a specialized team of men to operate them. The bow-arms of the *gastraphétēs* and the early bow-catapults were of composite construction, of wood, strips of horn and sinew. There is a technical limit to the size of such spring elements (Heron, Belopoiika 81), which Greek technicians however overcame around the middle of the 4th cent. BC by replacing the sprung bow arms with springs made of twisted rope (torsion springs; rope made from hair or animal sinews). The new twin-armed torsion catapults were more compact, and could be made very large (Heron, Belopoiika 81–83).

B. HELLENISTIC PERIOD

In Athens, the torsion catapult (καταπάλτης/*katapáltēs*, later καταπέλτης/*katapéltēs*) is first attested in inscriptions of 326 BC at the latest (IG² II 1467 B, col. II 18–56) Presumably, the weapon had already been used by Alexander [4] the Great. Torsion catapults rapidly spread over the Hellenistic world as they were considered indispensable in attacking and defending cities. During the 3rd cent. BC Greek technicians, especially in Alexandria and Rhodes, competed with variant systems: the air-pressure catapult (ἀερότονον, *aerótonon*), the bronze-spring catapult (χαλκότονον, *chalkótonon*; both attributed to → Ctesibius of Alexandria; cf. Philo, Belopoiika 70–78) and a torsion catapult with repeater capability (καταπέλτης πολυβόλος, *katapéltēs polybólos*), said to have been constructed by Dionysius of Alexandria (Philo, Belopoiika 73–74). These weapons, although of technical interest, remained militarily insignificant. Experimentation and practical experience led to the formulation of construction principles, and thus to improvements in the torsion catapult, in the 3rd cent. BC. They were differentiated for the light arrow-throwing catapult (εὐθύτονον, *euthýtonon*) and the heavy stone-thrower (παλίντονον, *palíntonon*). The constructional rules, which were published in specialist works and included mathematical formulae and technical drawings (Philo, Belopoiika 51–56; Heron, Belopoiika 91–119), permitted catapults of various sizes to be built; the arrow-throwing catapults were referred to by the length of the arrow, the stone-throwers by the weight of the projectile. The carriages of these catapults were made of wood reinforced by metal fittings. The Hellenistic empires and important cities such as Rhodes, Massalia and Carthage had considerable stocks of such catapults: in 149 BC Carthage had to surrender some 2,000 catapults to Rome (App. Lib. 80).

C. ROME

It was during the Pyrrhic Wars (280–272 BC) that Rome first came into contact with catapults, which from the Punic Wars onwards were used especially in sieges. It however was not until around the end of the Roman Republic that torsion catapults (*tormenta*) be-

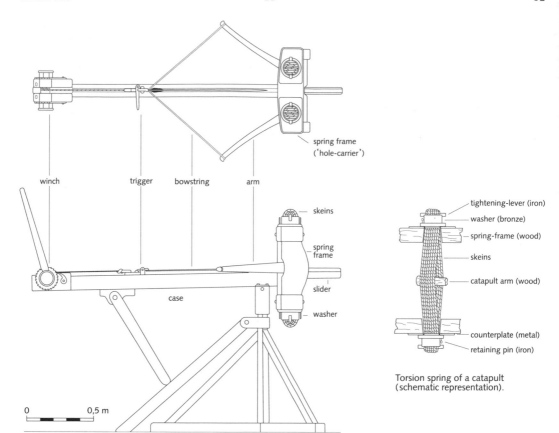

spring frame
('hole-carrier')

winch   trigger   bowstring   arm

skeins

spring
frame

case

slider

washer

tightening-lever (iron)
washer (bronze)
spring-frame (wood)
skeins
catapult arm (wood)
counterplate (metal)
retaining pin (iron)

Torsion spring of a catapult
(schematic representation).

0   0,5 m

Catapult according to Vitruvius (10, 10); top view and side elevation.

came part of the regular equipment of the legions. Specialist technicians were involved in the construction of *tormenta*, among them were Vitruvius (Vitr. De arch. 1 Praef. 2) and C. Vedennius Moderatus (ILS 2034 = CIL IV 2725). In his discussion of catapults, Vitruvius follows a slightly modified form of the Hellenistic construction rules (*catapulta, scorpio*: Vitr. De arch. 10,10; *ballista*: Vitr. De arch. 10,11). During the Principate, every *centuria* of a legion was assigned an arrow-throwing catapult (*scorpio*), every legionary cohort a stone-thrower (*ballista*); thus a legion had 10 stone-throwers and some 60 arrow-throwing catapults (Veg. Mil. 2,25). One-talent *ballistae* are attested as the heaviest legionary catapults (projectile weight *c*. 26 kg; Ios. Bell. Iud. 5,270).

In around AD 100 Roman weapon technologists freed themselves from the Hellenistic construction rules and developed a new type of arrow-throwing catapult with a broad iron frame (ill. on Trajan's Column). Arrow-throwing catapults were mounted on single-axle carriages, and in late antiquity, when arrow-throwing catapults were also referred to as *ballista*, were called *carroballista* (Veg. Mil. 3,24). Heavy, twin-armed torsion catapults were also given a newly designed, broad frame, which however was made of wood with metal fittings. Another stone-thrower (*onager*) is

attested from the 4th cent. AD; this was a heavy, single-armed catapult with a single, horizontally set torsion spring. Its construction was based on the mechanization of the staff sling (Amm. Marc. 23,4,4–7). With the fall of the western Roman Empire, construction and use of catapults ceased in the west; in Byzantium however catapults continued to be used (Procop. Goth. 1,21,14–19).

D. MECHANICAL HAND WEAPONS

From the 2nd cent. AD, a further crossbow is attested besides the *gastraphétēs;* it originally served as a hunting weapon. In late antiquity it becomes army issue under the name of *arcuballista* (Veg. Mil. 4,22). From the 1st cent. AD crossbow-like torsion weapons were also used in the Roman army, but only found more frequent application in late antiquity (*manuballista*; Veg. Mil. 2,15; 4,22).

E. USE AND EFFECT

Torsion catapults including stone throwers were normally used at short range with a flat trajectory. The most effective combat range lay between 50 and 170 m. No body armour or shield could withstand the striking force of an arrow-throwing catapult. In defending a fortress, the stone-throwing catapults were used against

Gastraphetes according to Hero.

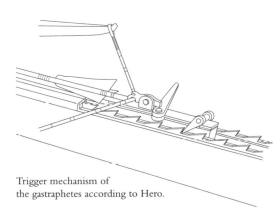

Trigger mechanism of
the gastraphetes according to Hero.

enemy defensives, siege engines and catapults. Although in attack on a defensive wall stone-throwing catapults could not make any breaches, they could destroy battlements and the upper parts of defensive towers. However, due to transportation problems, heavy stone-throwing catapults were seldom used in the field. Catapults thus rarely exerted a decisive influence on battle strategy (Tac. Hist. 3,23).
→ Siegecraft

1 D. BAATZ, Bauten und K. des röm. Heeres (Mavors 11), 1994   2 T. G. KOLIAS, Byz. Waffen, 1988, 240   3 E. W. MARSDEN, Greek and Roman Artillery, Vol. 1: Historical Development, 1969; Vol. 2: Technical Treatises, 1971   4 E. SCHRAMM, Die ant. Geschütze der Saalburg, 1918, repr. 1980   5 ZIMMER, catalogue no. 151.   D.BA.

Categories (κατηγορίαι; *katēgoríai*, Lat. *praedicamenta*).
A. DEFINITION   B. ARISTOTLE AND THE STOICS
C. PS.-ARCHYTAS   D. PLOTINUS, PORPHYRY AND NEOPLATONISM

A. DEFINITION
'Category' is a universal term: categories are conceived partly as 'classes' or genres of object, partly as concepts or meanings, and partly as universal 'predicates' (basic forms of statement; Greek κατηγορίαι).
→ Aristotle, the Stoics and → Neoplatonism (Plotinus and the commentators on Aristotle) developed various doctrines concerning categories, relating to various disciplines (grammar and logic, semantics and predication theory, physics and ontology, also psychology).

B. ARISTOTLE AND THE STOICS
Full lists of the ten Aristotelian categories exist only in two texts (Aristot. Cat. 4,1b 25–2a 4, and Top. 1,9,103b 20–39). They are associated with a doctrine of the homonymy of all that exists, and give expression to the manifold meaning of 'existence' (for Aristotle, 'existence' does not represent a genre). The term concerns '[syntactically] disjoint' expressions signifying: substance (οὐσία, τί ἐστι; *ousía, tí esti*), quantity (ποσόν; *posón*), quality (ποιόν; *poión*), relation (πρός τι; *prós ti*), place (πού; *poú*), time (ποτέ; *poté*), situation (κεῖσθαι; *keîsthai*), state (ἔχειν; *échein*), action (ποιεῖν; *poiein*) and being acted upon (πάσχειν; *páschein*). Incomplete listings of categories are to be found in other parts of the Corpus Aristotelicum (e.g. Aristot. Metaph. 5,7,1017a 24–30 and 28,1024b 12–15; 6,2,1026a 33–b 1; 7,1,1028a 10–b 7; 9,1,1045b 27–33; 11,12,1068a 8–14; Eth. Nic. 1,4(6),1096a 23–27ff.; Eth. Eud. 1,8,1217b 20–40, with a comparison of the homonymy of all that exists with the homonymy of the good). The competing approach of the Stoics, emphasizing the four categories of substantial (ὑποκείμενον; *hypokeímenon*), qualified (ποιὸν; *poiòn* or ποῖον; *poîon*), disposed (πὼς ἔχον; *pòs échon* or πῶς ἔχον; *pôs échon*) and relatively disposed (πρὸς τί πως ἔχον; *pròs tí pōs échon*) as a 'consecutive system of testing, to which all reality is to be subjected' [9], (cf. SVF 2, 369–375, and HÜLSER, 4.3.2, fr. 827–873), was never as successful as the Aristotelian approach.

C. PS.-ARCHYTAS
After Andronicus [4] of Rhodes had edited Aristotle's works, the success of the Aristotelian approach is attested by the pseudo-Pythagorean work Περὶ τῶν καθόλου λόγων ('On universal concepts') written between the middle of the 1st cent. BC and the 1st cent. AD under the name of Archytas [2] of Tarentum. The work comprises a version of Aristotle's system of categories in Dorian dialect together with some extracts from the 'Physics' (with elements of Stoic philosophy), containing variations which go back to more recent discussions of the doctrine of categories itself. In the sense of a congruence between Pythagoras, Plato and Aristotle, members of the Neoplatonic school from Iamblichus onwards (4th cent. AD) agreed that Ps.-Archytas was to be regarded as a source for Aristotle's 'Categories'.

D. PLOTINUS, PORPHYRY, AND NEOPLATONISM
→ Plotinus (3rd cent. AD) wrote his three essays 'On the genres of existence' (Enneads 6,1–3 = essays 42–44

in chronological order) against Aristotle, but also against the Stoics. He criticizes Aristotle's categories for lacking unity, and so not being real genres, and for being inadequately susceptible to application to the intelligible world. He reduces them to five genres (substance, quantity, quality, relation and motion), replacing the final five with the five 'greatest genres' (μέγιστα γένη; *mégista géne*) from Plato's 'Sophist' (254d 4–255a 2ff.), which he interprets ontologically as genres of the intelligible. → Porphyrius countered Plotinus' criticism of Aristotle's categories; during the 270s AD in Sicily he wrote commentaries on the 'Organon' and the 'Isagoge', as well as two commentaries on the 'Categories' (one short commentary in question and answer form, CAG 4,1, and a longer one 'To Gedalios', known to us via Dexippus and Simplicius). Porphyrius, falling back on the Peripatetic tradition of commentary (Boethus [4] of Sidon, Herminus, Alexander [26] of Aphrodisias i. a.), attempted to find a solution to the reservations of Plotinus and to reconcile him with Aristotle; he thus stood at the beginning of the process of interpreting the 'Categories' counter to Plotinus and with a view to harmonization, a tendency which was to be a feature of later Neoplatonism. In this perspective, Aristotle now provided a propaedeutic to the philosophy of Plato. The study of logic began with the 'Categories', yet preceded by the 'Isagoge' of Porphyry and together with 'De interpretatione', the 'Prior Analytics' and the 'Posterior Analytics' (as well as the 'Topics' with its appendix 'De Sophisticis Elenchis'), it became the instrument (ὄργανον; *órganon*) of science.

The categories are the primary terms which allow the formation of the affirmative proposition (ἀποφαντικὸς λόγος; *apophantikòs lógos*): the premise (πρότασις; *prótasis*), the syllogism and the apodictic syllogism. Aristotle's 'Categories', which were read with keen interest throughout the whole of antiquity (cf. the summary by Simpl. in Aristot. Cat. p. 1,3–3,17 KALBFLEISCH), occupied an extraordinarily important position in the curriculum of the Neoplatonic schools of Alexandria and Athens during the 5th and 6th cents. AD. Numerous Greek commentaries (published in the CAG) have survived in their entirety; Boethius' Latin commentary (PL 64, 159 A 1f.), written at the beginning of the 6th cent. AD, transmitted Neoplatonic teachings to the Middle Ages. These teachings had been developed by Porphyry and → Iamblichus [2], and were taught in all the schools during the 4th–6th cents. AD (Dexippus [4], Ammonius [12], Iohannes Philoponos, Simplicius, Olympiodorus [4] and David [2] or Elijah [2]). They were still fundamental to the thinking of the anonymous author of the Scholia of the Codex Vaticanus Urbinas Graecus 35, copied in around 900 by Arethas (ed. M. SHARE, 1994). In accordance with their *skopós* ('object, aim'), the 'categories' are the 'first' and simplest words, both within the framework of their meaning and in human speech (as uttered by the individual soul from its location within the body). These words signify the first, elementary objects (the most

universal, transcendental genres, τὰ γενικώτατα γένη; *tà genikótata géne*) through the medium of the soul's first, elementary concepts, in Neoplatonic linguistics corresponding to 'meanings' and representing universal concepts.

The triad comprising words, concepts and objects, as given at the beginning of Aristotle's 'De interpretatione' (16a 3–18) and transmitted to medieval philosophy by Boethius in his commentary, mirrors ontologically a transcendental union of objects and their respective concepts within the divine intellect (interpreting Aristotle, e.g. In Aristot. An. 3,4,430a 3–5; cf. Simpl., In Aristot. Cat. p. 12,13ff. KALBFLEISCH). A vocabulary comprising these first signifying words arises in the context of a linguistic 'first setting' (πρώτη θέσις; *prôte thésis*); this is followed by a 'second setting', which gives rise to all linguistic elements necessary for the formation of complex propositions (thus also for science), as well as metalinguistic terms (the parts of speech). By means of this doctrine, the Neoplatonists attempted to connect the Plato of the 'Cratylus' with the Aristotle of the 'De interpretatione'; the φύσει (*phýsei*; 'by nature') approach with the θέσει (*thései*; 'by determination') approach (Ammonius, In Aristot. De interpretatione p. 34,15–41,11 BUSSE).

1 [F.]A. TRENDELENBURG, Gesch. der Kategorienlehre. Zwei Abh., 1846 2 P. AUBENQUE, Le problème de l'être chez Aristote, ³1972 3 Id. (ed.), Concepts et catégories dans la pensée antique, 1980 4 TH. A. SZLEZÁK, Pseudo-Archytas über die Kategorien (Peripatoi 4), 1972 5 MORAUX 5–6, 1973–1984 6 CL. IMBERT, Pour une réinterpretation des catégories stoïciennes, in: H. JOLY (ed.), Philos. du langage et grammaire dans l' Antiquité, 1986, 263–285 7 CHR. EVANGELIOU, Aristotle's Categories and Porphyry (Philosophia antiqua 48), 1988 8 I. HADOT et al., Simplicius. Commentaire sur les »Catégories«, fasc. I et III (Philosophia antiqua 50–51), 1990 9 FR. ILDEFONSE, La naissance de la grammaire dans l' Antiquité grecque, 1997. PH.H.

Catenae

Catenae A genre of Biblical commentaries first appearing in the 6th cent. AD, of which there were many examples in the Middle Ages. In the exegesis of Biblical texts, excerpts of extant commentaries by Church Fathers were reworked into 'chain commentaries' or *catenae*. The existence of several writings by the Church Fathers is only known through these *catenae*. If the excerpts are written on the margins of the manuscripts around the Biblical text, they are described as margin *catenae*, and if the commentary follows on from the text, they are known as broad *catenae* → Florilegium; → Scholia

ALTANER, 21–24 (lit.), 460f.; 514–518; H. CHADWICK, s.v. Florilegium, RAC 7, 1151; R. DEVREESSE, Chaines exégétiques grecques: DictBibl Suppl. 1, 1928, 1084–1233; G. DORIVAL, Les chaines exégétiques grecques sur les Psaumes: contribution à l'étude d'une forme littéraire, 1986–1992; U. and D. HAGEDORN, Die älteren griech. Katenen zum Buch Hiob vol. 1 (Patristische Texte und Stud. 40), 1994. R.B.

Cathaei (Καθαῖοι; *Kathaîoi*). Indian people in the Punjab either east of the → Hydraotes or between → Hydaspes and → Acesines [2], subjugated by Alexander the Great (Arr. Anab. 5,22; Diod. Sic. 17,91,2; Curt. et al.); perhaps to be identified with Sanskrit *Kāthaka* (attested as a Vedic school, as also the Kambistholoi and Madyandinoi). Their customs (burning of widows, bride selection, wearing jewellery and high regard for physical beauty) were described by Onesicritus (fr. 34 in Str.) who also reports that there were many metals in their country, but that they did not know how to exploit them. They were neighbours of the king → Sopeithes. K.K.

Catilina L. Sergius C. came from a patrician gens that had been politically unsuccessful for a relatively long time. Born in 108 at the latest, he appears on 17. Nov. 89 BC in the *consilium* of the consul Pompeius Strabo as L. Sergi(us) L. f. Tro(mentina) [1. 160ff.]. At the end of the 80s he was legate to Sulla (Sall. Hist. 1,46) [2. 110ff.]. He probably did not murder his brother [3. 1688], but he probably killed M. Marius Gratidianus (Q. Cic. comm. pet. 10; Ascon. 84; 90C), the brother of his wife Gratidia (Schol. Bern. in Luc. 2,173; Sall. Hist. 1,45) [2. 105f.], and also Q. Caecilius, his sister's husband (Q. Cic. comm. pet. 9). In 73 he was unsuccessfully charged by Clodius with illicit sexual relations with the Vestal Fabia (Ascon. 91C) [4. 60f.]. After the praetorship of 68 he took over the province of Africa. Because of the threat of the *repetundae* case (Ascon. 85; 89 C) or his failure to make his application on time (Sall. Catil. 18,3), his candidature for the consulship was rejected in 65; it remains unclear whether it was for the proper elections [5. 44ff.] or the new elections after those initially elected were condemned [6. 226ff.]. The so-called 'First Catilinarian Conspiracy' at the end of 66 is generally doubted [7. 88ff.; 8. 338ff.]; In any case there were rumours in 65 of a murder plot against the consuls (Ascon. 92 C; Cic. Sull. 81) [9. 289ff.]. Although Cicero was convinced of C.'s guilt (Att. 1,10,1), he considered defending him at the *repetundae* case in the middle of 65 (Att. 1,2,1), but then refused to do so (Ascon. 85 C) (differently [10. 50f.]). The lax conduct of the trial on the part of the prosecutor Clodius (Ascon. 87 C), the evidence of the consuls (Cic. Sull. 81) and the acquittal show that C. still belonged to the establishment.

As consuls, the Optimates now, however, gave preference to the *homo novus* Cicero who vigorously attacked C. and C. Antonius in the election campaign in 64. Cicero and Antonius were elected. Again C. was charged with taking part in Sulla's proscriptions but with Caesar as the presiding judge he was acquitted (Ascon. 90/91C; Cass. Dio 37,10,3). Even in his last election campaign for the consulship in 62 C. still did not develop any revolutionary plans. His proposal of the *tabulae novae* amounted, in Cicero's polemical interpretation, only to a general redemption of debt (Catil. 2,18); indeed C. only demanded a reduction in interest and easier repayments in a liquidity crisis [11. 15ff.]. In any case there was considerable potential for social unrest amongst the populace (Cic. Cat. 2,17–24; Sall. Catil. 36–39) with whom C. sought closer ties after his defeat in the election. It is hard to decide whether he was driven by his own will [12. 221ff.] or Cicero's manoeuvring [13. 195ff.; 14. 240ff.] as it is Cicero's perspective that has shaped what has been passed down to us. In spite of the *senatus consultum ultimum* of 21 October (Sall. Catil. 29,2) and the *decretum tumultus* as a reaction to the revolt of C. Manlius in Etruria on 27 October (Sall. Catil. 59,5; Cass. Dio 37,31,1), and in spite too of an action of Aemilius Paullus based on the *lex Plautia de vi* (Sall. Catil. 31,4), C. remained in Rome [15. 87ff.]. Cicero's first Catilinarian speech on 7 or [16. 85f.] or 8 November [17. 141ff.] finally induced him to take over the leadership of the rebellion (Sall. Catil. 35) [18. 47ff.; 19. 211ff.]. In the middle of November he was declared a *hostis* (Sall. Catil. 36,2). The careless tactics of the conspirators who had stayed behind in Rome led to their downfall at the beginning of December [20; 21]. C. was defeated with the remainder of his army at the beginning of 62 by the legate Petreius (Sall. Catil. 59/60).

C. appears both in the works of Cicero and in those of Sallust as an unscrupulous criminal, and occasionally, when necessary, as having less malevolent traits (Cic. Cael. 12–14; Sall. Catil. 60,7). Both, however, acknowledge his energy and perseverance (Cic. Cat. 2,9; Sall. Catil. 5).

1 N. CRINITI, L'epigrafe di Asculum di Gn. Pompeo Strabone, 1970   2 P. McGUSHIN, Sallust, The Histories, 1, 1992   3 F. MÜNZER, s.v. Sergius 1, RE 2 A   4 E.S. GRUEN, Some Criminal Trials of the Late Republic, in: Athenaeum 49, 1971, 54–69   5 F.X. RYAN, The Consular Candidacy of Catiline in 66, in: MH 52, 1995, 45–48   6 F.V. SUMNER, The Consular Elections of 66 B.C., in: Phoenix 19, 1965, 226–231   7 R. SYME, Sallust, 1964   8 R. SEAGER, The First Catilinarian Conspiracy, in: Historia 13, 1964, 338–347   9 K. VRETSKA, C. Sallustius Crispus. De Catilinae Coniuratione, 2 vols., 1976   10 W. WILL, Der röm. Mob, 1991   11 A. GIOVANNINI, C. et le problème des dettes, in: Leaders and Masses in the Roman World, Studies in Honour of Zvi Yavetz, 1995, 15–32   12 H. SCHNEIDER, Wirtschaft und Politik, 1974   13 K.H. WATERS, Cicero, Sallust and Catiline, in: Historia 19, 1970, 195–216   14 R. SEAGER, Justa Catilinae, in: Historia 22, 1973, 240–248   15 J.v. UNGERN-STERNBERG, Unt. zum spätrepublikanischen Notstandsrecht, 1970   16 M. GELZER, Cicero. Ein biographischer Versuch, 1969   17 H. DREXLER, Die Catilinarische Verschwörung, 1976   18 J.v. UNGERN-STERNBERG, Ciceros erste Catilinarische Rede und Diodor XL 5a, in: Gymnasium 78, 1971, 47–54   19 W.W. BATSTONE, Cicero's Construction of Consular Ethos in the First Catilinarian, in: TAPhA 124, 1994, 211–266   20 A. DRUMMOND, Law, Politics and Power. Sallust and the Execution of the Catilinarian Conspirators, 1995   21 J.v. UNGERN-STERNBERG, Das Verfahren gegen die Catilinarier oder: Der vermiedene Prozeß, in: U. MANTHE, J.v. UNGERN-STERNBERG (ed.), Polit. Prozesse in Rom, 1997.

L. A. Burckhardt, Polit. Strategien der Optimaten in der
späten röm. Republik, 1988; M. Gelzer, s.v. Sergius 23,
RE 2 A, 1693–1711; Ch. Meier, Der Ernstfall im alten
Rom, in: R. Altmann, (ed.), Der Ernstfall, 1979, 40–73;
W. Nippel, Public Order in Ancient Rome, 1995; Z. Yavetz, The Failure of Catiline's Conspiracy, in: Historia
12, 1963, 485–489.   J.v.U.-S.

Catilius

[1] [Ca]tilius Longus. *Eques* from Apamea in Bithynia
who was accepted into the Senate by Vespasian (CIL III
335 = Eck, ZPE 42, 1981, 242ff. = AE 1982, 860).
[2] L.C. Severus. Descendant of C. [3]. as attested in
Frater Arvalis, 213 and 218; probably *procos. Asiae*
(IGR IV 1281) [1. 112f., 418f.].
[3] L.C.Severus Iulianus Claudius Reginus. Senator
from Bithynia, see C. [1] [2. 133ff.; 3. 127ff.]. Praetorian career with many offices, *cos. suff.* 110, consular
governor of Armenia and Cappadocia during Trajan's
Parthian War. 117 Legate of Syria, *cos. ord.* II 120,
procos. Africae c. 124/125, *praef. urbi* until 138. As he
declared himself against Antoninus Pius' adoption, he
was dismissed by Hadrian (SHA Hadr. 24,6–8). He was
one of the ancestors of Marcus Aurelius (SHA Aur.
1,3f.; PIR[2] C 558) [4. 232ff.].

> 1 Scheid, Collège   2 Halfmann, Senatoren   3 Cor-
> sten, in: EA 6, 1985   4 Birley, Marcus Aurelius, [2]1988.
>   W.E.

Catillus Mythical founder of Tibur (Hor. Carm.
1,18,2; Sil. 4,225; Stat. Silv. 1,3,100). According to
Cato (Orig. fr. 56 in Solin. 2,7) he was an Arcadian and
fleet commander of Euander. A certain Sextius considered him to be an Argive (Solin. 2,7). He was the son of
an Argive seer → Amphiaraus and upon the behest of
his grandfather he moved to Italy as → *ver sacrum*. His
three sons Tiburtus (Tibur/Tiburnus), Coras and C.
drove the Sicans out of their town and then called it
Tibur (Solin. ibid; Verg. Aen. 7,670 with Serv.; Hor.
Carm. 2,6,5; Plin. HN 16,237).   R.B.

Catinus

[1] Dish of clay or metal for meals (fish, meat, desserts).
Vessel for the kitchen and cooking, for sacrificial offerings and for melting metals; identified by graffiti probably as the vessel forms Dragendorff 31 and 32 (→ Clay
vessels). Bowls (→ *acetabulum*) were also called *catinus*.
→ Terra sigillata; → Clay vessels

> G. Hilgers, Lat. names of vessels, BJ 31. Supplement
> 1969, 48f., 142–144; F. Fless, Opferdiener und Kultmu-
> siker auf stadtröm. histor. Reliefs, 1995, 19f.   R.H.

[2] *Catinus* (*-um*) or *catillus* (*-um*). The melting crucible
made of clayey earth *tasconium* for receiving the melted
gold during smelting, according to Plin. HN 33,69.
[3] A pressure tank [1. 495] inside the bronze pump of
→ Ctesibius from Alexandria (Vitr. 10,7,1–3).

> 1 W. Schmidt (ed.), Heronis Alexandrini opera omnia,
> vol. 1, 1899.   C.HÜ.

Catius Plebeian surname (ThlL, Onom. 264f.).
I. Republican period   II. Imperial period

I. Republican period

[I 1] C., Q. In 210 BC plebeian *aedile*, in 207 legate of
the consul C. Claudius Nero. In 205 envoy to Delphi to
deliver the booty resulting from the defeat of Hasdrubal
(Liv. 28,45,12).
[I 2] C. Vestinus, C. Military tribune under Antonius 43
BC at Mutina, was taken prisoner by Plancus (Cic. Fam.
10,23,5).   K.-L.E.

II. Imperial period

[II 1] C. see → Caesius [II 4].
[II 2] L.C.Celer. Praetorian governor of Thrace, *cos.
suff. c.* 241, consular legate of Moesia superior 242 (AE
1952, 191) [1. 87f.]. It is uncertain whether he is the
same as the *praetor urbanus* of AE 1955, 166 [1. 88,
no. 6a; 2. 120ff.].
[II 3] C. Clemens. According to CIL III 6924 presumably he and not his brother C. [II 4] was the governor of
Cappadocia in 238 [3. 93, n. 4; 4. 199].
[II 4] Sex. C. Clementinus Priscillianus. Son of the suffect consul [Catius? Lepi]dus; as a boy took part in the
secular games of 204. *Cos. ord.* 230, already in 231
attested as governor of Upper Germania (PIR[2] C 564)
[3. 92f.].
[II 5] C.C.Marcellus. *Cos. suff.* in 153 (PIR[2] C 569)
[2. 121f.].
[II 6] P.C.Sabinus. Tribune in the *legio XIII Gemina*
(AE 1956, 204); *praetor urbanus*. He was probably a
praetorian governor in Noricum around 206/208
(Cass. Dio 76,9,2; CIL III 5727); *cos. suff.* between 208
and 210; *curator aedium sacrarum et operum publicorum* 210; *cos.* II 216 (PIR[2] C 571) [5. 250]. Because of
the extremely short interval between the 1st and 2nd
consulship [4. 113] he must have been one of the closest
supporters of Caracalla. C. [II 2] and [II 3] may have
been his sons.

> 1 W. Eck, RE Suppl. 14   2 Dietz   3 Eck, Statth.
> 4 Leunissen   5 A. Kolb, Die kaiserliche Bauverwaltung,
> 1993.   W.E.

Cato Roman cognomen perhaps of Etruscan origin
[1. 310, 315, 418], in conjunction with *catus* ('astute',
'crafty' [2; 3. 250]. In Republican times widespread in
the families of the Hostilii and Valerii, prominent
among the Porcii, according to whose model C. is used
now and again as a synonym for a conservative Roman;
quite rarely also as *gentilicium* [1. 303].
→ Porcius

> 1 Schulze   2 Walde/Hofmann, 1,183   3 Kajanto, Cog-
> nomina.   K.-L.E.

[1] Porcius C., M. (234–149 BC), 'Cato the Elder',
'Censorius', energetic politician and founder of Roman

prose literature, is the best known Roman of the pre-Ciceronian period. Apart from numerous testimonials about himself (in speeches) and reports by Livy there are biographies by Cornelius → Nepos and → Plutarchus; the image in Cicero's *Cato maior* is knowledgeable but idealized.

A. LIFE   B. WRITINGS

A. LIFE

Born in 234 in Tusculum of a family of *eques*, C. fought from 217/6 in the war against Hannibal, was *tribunus militum* in Sicily in 214, and took part in 207 in the battle of → Sena Gallica. With the support of the patrician L. → Valerius Flaccus he applied for Roman municipal offices, was *quaestor* (under P. Cornelius Scipio) in 204, in 199 plebeian *aedile*, in 198 *praetor* in Sardinia (actions against profiteers: Liv. 32,27,3–4), achieved the consulship in 195 (together with his patron Flaccus), took over command in Spain where he achieved great military successes north of the Ebro and rendered outstanding services organizing the Roman administration (Liv. 34,8–21, according to Cato's model [1. 302–7]); celebrated as a result a triumph in 194 (Fast. triumph.; Liv. 34,46,2). In 191 he took part (as *tribunus militum*: Pol. 20,10,10) in the war against → Antiochus [5] III in Greece where he acted as Roman envoy (among others in Athens: Liv. 35,50,4) as well as in the battle at Thermopylae; in 189 he was sent as Senate envoy to M. → Fulvius Nobilior in Aetolia (or. fr. 130 M.). As *censor* in 184 he distinguished himself through his severity at the *lectio senatus* and inspection of the *eques*, through ascetic measures in establishing the census (Liv. 39,44,2–3), his support for state revenue and construction of utilitarian buildings (extension of the sewerage system; → Basilica Porcia); in this way he earned for himself the cognomen 'Censorius' (cf. Sen. Ep. 87,9; Plin. HN, praef. 30 and *passim*.; Tac. Ann. 3,66,1). Until his death (autumn 149) the restless and self-willed man involved himself constantly in all political feuds and contentious matters, especially as a speaker in the people's assembly and Senate, frequently also in court (he was prosecuted 44 times in politically motivated lawsuits but he was always acquitted: Plin. HN 7,100). He fought for the → *mos maiorum*, for fair treatment of dependent communities and peoples, against the excesses of the nobility, outward luxuries and the immoderate influence of Greek culture; e.g. in 155 he made sure of the rapid departure of the Athenian delegation of philosophers. In the last years of his life he mainly devoted himself to the 3rd Punic War and the complete annihilation of Carthage.

From his first marriage to one Licinia, C. was the father of M. → Porcius C. Licinianus (died in 152), from his second marriage (in old age), he was the father of M. Porcius C. Salonianus (born *c.* 154).

B. WRITINGS

C. wrote in various fields for decades. Unifying elements are C.'s educational intentions, the marked tendency towards self-promotion and the natural talent for effective linguistic expression (*Romani generis disertissimus*, Sall. Hist. 1,4 M.).

a) Speeches: C. published many of the speeches he presented, obviously on the basis of fondly held concepts (or. fr. 173 M.); at least two (*Pro Rhodiensibus*; *In S. Sulpicium Galbam*) were incorporated in his historical works. Cicero knew more than 150 of these texts; remnants of *c.* 80 speeches from the time of his consulship in 195 until the year of his death in 149 are extant. The publication was documentary in nature and did not serve aesthetic goals but rather self-promotion and the pursuance of politics above and beyond the immediate time. In his speeches he also gives his opinion on questions of legislative policy [8].

b) Didactic writings: The *Libri ad filium* that belong to a relatively early period, contained the important established part of the education of a young Roman; it was more akin to a loose collection of *dicta* and *praecepta* [1. 332–340] than an early encyclopaedia on the topics of agriculture, medicine and rhetorics (see in this regard [2. 104] etc.). Apart from this there was certainly a monograph *De re militari* (evidence p. 80–82; more extensive suppositions in [3. 79–87]), perhaps a further supposition regarding questions of the *ius civile* (Cic. Cato 38; sole fr. in Fest. 144,18 L.). A collection of the *Carmen de moribus* (citations in Gell. NA 11,2) was also a collection of didactic statements. The book *De agricultura* has been preserved as a manuscript, it is a guide for the municipal property owner to profitable management of his estate, it uses Greek models but is mainly based on the author's own practical experience (→ Agrarian writers). Very significant from the point of view of legal history are the purchase and lease forms passed down to us [9]. The construction of the writing is unsatisfactory not just because the author lacked experience in creating larger connections but also because of later additions and insertions over the course of time (noticeable ch. 124; 133; 156/7: further suggestions, sometimes too far-reaching [4; 5]).

c) Historical writings: Between 170 and 149 C. wrote the *Origines* in 7 books, depicting Roman history from the early period until 149, for the first time in the Latin language. Contrary to widespread opinion, C. provided an outline of the whole of Roman history [6], but compensated for the dearth of material from the older period (book 1–3) by drawing strongly upon Italian regional and cultural knowledge, local traditions and especially legends regarding the foundation of Rome. Books 4 and 5 dealt in abbreviated form with the Punic Wars and the expansion in the east to Pydna, the last 2 books (apparently much broader) treated the events of the most recent past. The depiction alternated between concise presentation (e.g. fr. 84; 91 P.) and detailed narration of anecdotes (fr. 86/7) and exemplary individual scenes (fr. 83: also [7. 38–50]). From book

5 C. included several speeches. Magistrates and generals were not mentioned by name but rather their functions were described (Nep. 3,4; Plin. HN 8,11; Cato fr. 83; 86/87). The style with its powerful unconventionality links poetic and vernacular elements, is realistic, linguistically innovative and expressive (acknowledged in Cic. Brut. 66).

1 A.E. ASTIN, Cato the Censor, 1978   2 D. KIENAST, Cato der Zensor, 1954 (repr. 1979)   3 J.M. NAP, Ad Catonis librum de re militari, in: Mnemosyne 55, 1927, 79–87   4 A. MAZZARINO, Introduzione al De agri cultura di Catone, 1952   5 W. RICHTER, Gegenständliches Denken — archa. Ordnen, 1978   6 W. KIERDORF, Catos 'Origines' und die Anfänge der röm. Geschichtsschreibung, in: Chiron 10, 1980, 205–224   7 M. VON ALBRECHT, Meister röm. Prosa, ²1983   8 BAUMAN, LRRP, 170ff.   9 WIEACKER, RRG, 538f.

TEXTS: Fragments of speeches in ORF⁴, 12–97, with philological commentary by M.T. SBLENDORIO CUGUSI, 1982; De agricultura, ed. by A. MAZZARINO, 1962 (²1982), with a commentary by P. THIELSCHER, 1963, and R. GOUJARD, 1975; Origines, in: HRR 1, 55–97, with a commentary by M. CHASSIGNET, 1986; detailed commentary only vol. 1 (W.A. SCHRÖDER, 1971) and the Pro Rhodiensibus speech (G. CALBOLI, 1978); H. JORDAN, M. Catonis praeter librum de re rustica quae exstant, 1860 (repr. 1967); Complete Latin-German edition by O. SCHÖNBERGER, 1980.

BIBLIOGRAPHY: S. BOSCHERINI, Lingua e scienza greca nel De agri cultura di Catone, 1970; M. CHASSIGNET, Caton et l'impérialisme romain au IIᵉ siècle av. J.-C. d'après les Origines, in: Latomus 46, 1987, 285–300; F. DELLA CORTE, Catone Censore, ²1969; H. DOHR, Die ital. Gutshöfe nach den Schriften Catos und Varros, diss. 1965; FLACH; PL. FRACCARO, in: Opuscula 1, 1956, 115–256; 417–508; M. GELZER, R. HELM, s.v. Cato (9), RE 22, 108–165; C. LETTA, L''Italia dei mores Romani' nelle 'Origines' di Catone, in: Athenaeum 62, 1984, 3–30; 416–439; R. TILL, Die Sprache Catos, 1935 (revised by C. DE MEO, 1968).   W.K.

[2] **Porcius Cato, M.** (died 46 BC), 'Cato the Younger', see Porcius.

Catreus (Κατρεύς; *Katreús*). Son of → Minos and Pasiphae, eponym of the Cretan town Catre; he is killed by his son → Althaemenes, even though he fled to Rhodes to avoid his father who had been warned by an oracle (Apollod. 3,12–16); when his grandson → Menelaus takes part in his funeral, Paris kidnaps Helena (ibid. 3,3).   F.G.

Cattabaneis see → Qatabān

Cattigara (Καττίγαρα; *Kattígara*). Port in South-East Asia first mentioned by Ptol. (1,11,1; 17,4; 23) and Marcianus of Heraclia (1,46, GGM I, p. 538); a ὅρμος τῶν Σινῶν ('harbour of the Sinai'). The name of the Σῖναι (*Sînai*) points to C. being in the region of the Gulf of Tonking, of the ancient Μέγας κόλπος (*Mégas kólpos*) [1] or Σινῶν κόλπος (*Sinôn kólpos*) [2], as Marcianus himself and also Ptol. 7,3,3 call it. It formed the southern border of the *Sînai* and, according to ancient belief in around AD 200 it represented the eastern end of the → *Oikouménē*. In this area only modern Hanoi at the mouth of the Song-koi is possible as the ancient C. According to F. VON RICHTHOFEN it is identical with the ancient Kiau-tshi (called Kau-tsheh by Marco Polo; [3. 46f.]). According to later Chinese reports (7th–10th cents. AD) all the kings of the South Seas who came from the Han Period onward went via Kiau-tschi/Hanoi to show their respect to the emperor. Egyptian seafarers in the service of Rome advanced at the end of the 2nd cent. AD as far as C., which formed the centre of an extensive trade that was probably mainly conducted by the Sabaeans (→ Saba) of southern Arabia.

In spite of the late mention of C. in Graeco-Roman literature, it must have already been discovered much earlier as a result of the long journeys of the Arabs and the seafaring inhabitants of → Taprobane (Sri Lanka) to East Asia. According to his accounting Str. 15,693, → Nearchus first became acquainted with the silk fabrics through the sea route (→ Silk Road).

We cannot be certain that C. is the same as Hanoi. Further north, even though outside the *Mégas kólpos*, Canton (Kwang-tung) situated on the river Sikiang fulfils all the conditions for a good trading port; Arabs and Persians came there in the 3rd cent. AD at any rate, which is why it is occasionally claimed for C., especially given the fairly opaque topography of South-East and East Asia [4]. We must rule out locating C. at the mouth of the Mekong.

1 H. TREIDLER, s.v. Μέγας κόλπος, RE Suppl. 10, 385f.   2 A. HERRMANN, s.v. Sinai (1), RE 3A, 221   3 Id., s.v. Kattigara, RE 11, 46–51   4 OCD¹, 175.

A. FORBIGER, Hdb. der alten Geogr. 2, 1962, 479.
B.B./H.T.

Cattiterides (Καττιτερίδες; *Kattiterídes*, 'tin islands'). The C. were probably the regions and islands of the Atlantic coast of both Gaul and Britain; C. also generally referred to the south-west of Britain and the off-shore islands. Most ancient authors had but little specific knowledge of this region. Thus Pliny reports that the Greek Midacritus was the first to import tin from the island of *Cassiteris* (*Midacritus*, Plin. HN 7,197), without providing exact topographical details. Hdt. 3,115 doubted the very existence of these tin islands, probably because the Carthaginians kept their trade routes to the west absolutely secret. At the end of the 4th cent. BC, Pytheas visited the tin deposits of Belerion in the south-west of Britain and learned of the tine trade on the island of *Ictis*. The tin trade routes only became properly known through P. Licinius Crassus — probably the proconsul of Spain from 96 to 93 BC [1]. According to Str. (2,5,15; 2,5,30; 3,2,9; 3,5,11), there were 10 tin islands; he also describes the extraction of tin and the indigenous people working the mines. At the time that the Romans established a firm foothold in Britain, the name C. was no longer in common use.

Undoubtedly, it was the tin deposits in Devon and Cornwall which drew general attention to the tin islands, but not islands like the Isle of Wight or the Scilly Isles, where no tin was mined [2].
→ Tin

1 C.F. C. Hawkes, Pytheas, 1977   2 M.Todd, The South-West to AD 1000, 1987, 185–188.

M. Cary, E.H. Warmington, The Ancient Explorers, 1929; A.L. F. Rivet, C.Smith, The Place-Names of Roman Britain, 1979, 42f.   M.TO.

Cattle
I. General information   II. The Near East and Egypt   III. Greece   IV. Rome

I. General information
Cattle (*Bos taurus*) belong to the *bovine* family and are descended from the Eurasian big-horned aurochs (*Bos primigenius*). Longhorn wild cattle were most likely domesticated in Central Asia between 10,000 to 8,000 BC and in the Near East around 7,000 to 6,000 BC. In the 3rd millennium BC various breeds of domesticated cattle spread throughout Europe. Herds of wild cattle still existed in the forested regions of the eastern Mediterranean, such as Dardania and Thrace (Varro, Rust. 2,1,5), as well as in Central Europe (Caes. B Gall. 6,28).

In antiquity, cattle were not principally bred for meat, but rather as draught animals. Throughout history up to the Industrial Revolution, a harnessed yoke of oxen provided the power for any kind of heavy draught work, such as ploughing or transport. Cattle developed the strength to pull approximately 588.6 N (=60 kg weight) at a speed of 0.6/0.7 metres per second. Therefore, the strength of the bull was approximately a fourth to a fifth below that of the draught horse. The stamina of oxen even in the case of long hours of work was repeatedly emphasized. A yoke of oxen often worked uninterrupted for nine or even 10 hours.   G.R.

II. The Near East and Egypt
Sumerian *gud*, bull, ox, *áb*, cow, *amar*, calf; Akkadian *alpu* bull, ox [5]; Egyptian *jwз* and *ng(з)*, furthermore, various names according to gender, age, appearance, use, etc.

The Near East and Egypt lay within the area throughout which the aurochs (*Bos primigenius*) originally lived. The aurochs was evidently used to breed domestic cattle (*Bos taurus*) in various places. The earliest evidence of this comes from the southern Anatolian-Levantine region from the 7th millennium BC [1. 73]. Throughout history, cattle have made up a large portion of the animals kept by man. From the emergence of written records in Mesopotamia (end of the 4th millennium BC), cattle have often been mentioned [7]. Categorized according to gender, age, colour, and breed(?), long → lists were prepared that were included in school texts [6; 5. 368ff.]. In addition to

their significance as providers of meat, milk [5. 371f.], leather and manure (primarily as a fuel), cattle were particularly vital as draught animals [4. 267–279] for the → plough in Mesopotamian agriculture. For the brief duration of the Akkad dynasty (c. 2350–2150 BC), we have pictorial representations of the water buffalo (*Bubalus arnee*), indigenous to the Indus region and as such probably an exotic peculiarity [2]. The bull as an incarnation of sexual potency repeatedly appears as a divine epithet (e.g. Baʿal, Adad, Enlil [9. 165ff.]; → Bull cults).

Domestic cattle are known to have existed in Egypt from the Badari culture (beginning of the 4th millennium BC) onwards [8]. Numerous depictions provide evidence of various breeds: long-horned, short-horned, and hornless cattle as well as humpbacked cattle (Zebu). Particularly from the Old Empire we know of large cattle herds, but at the same time also of attempts to enlarge herds through trade, but also cattle raids. Wall paintings in tombs from the Old Empire onwards depict numerous scenes of cattle breeding and keeping and various manners of use.

In Egypt, too, cattle were important for the economy as suppliers of essential products such as milk, leather, manure and meat. Particularly important, however, they were as work animals. In addition, they were essential for the → sacrifice in numerous → rituals. The significance of cattle in everyday life is on the one hand reflected in the matriarchal deities who could take on the form of a cow (Hathor, Nut) and on the other in the sexual potency of the gods represented by the bull (e.g. Amun; see also → Apis [1], → Mnevis). The epithet 'Strong bull' for the ruler is also connected to this.

1 C. Becker, Early Domestication in the Southern Levant as Viewed from Late PPNB Basta, in: L. K. Horwitz et al., Animal Domestication in the Southern Levant, in: Paléorient 25, 1999, 63–80   2 R.M. Boehmer, Das Auftreten des Wasserbüffels in histor. Zeit und seine sumer. Bezeichnung, in: ZA 64, 1975, 1–19   3 J. Boessneck, Die Haustiere in Altäg., 1953   4 Bulletin on Sumerian Agriculture vol. 7–8 (Domestic Animals of Mesopotamia): 1993/1995   5 Chicago Assyrian Dictionary A/1, 1964, 364–372   6 R.K. Englund, H. J.Nissen, Die lexikalischen Listen der archa. Texte aus Uruk, 1993   7 M. W. Green, Animal Husbandry at Uruk in the Archaic Period, in: JNES 39, 1980, 1–35   8 L. Sörk, s. v. Rind, LÄ 5, 257–263   9 K. Tallqvist, Akkad. Götterepitheta, 1938   10 E. Vila, L'exploitation des animaux en Mésopotamie aux IVe et IIIe mill. avant J. C., 1998   11 F.E. Zeuner, Gesch. der Haustiere, 1967.   H. J.N. and J. RE.

III. Greece
Cattle (βοῦς/*boûs*) were the most important domesticated animals in the Greek world, both in economic terms as well as for religious practice and symbolism. The significance of cattle is already evident in the Homeric epics (Hom. Il. 13, 703–707; 15,630–636; 17,61–67; 17,657–664; 18,520–534; 18,573–586; Hom. Od. 14,100; 20,209–212); beef was eaten often (Hom. Il. 7,466; 23,26–56; Hom. Od. 3,421–463).

Furthermore, cattle served as a standard of value (Hom. Il. 6,236; 23,703; 23,705; Hom. Od. 1,431). Until the late archaic period Greece, due to a low population density, had more space for pastures, and the wealth of the → aristocracy also included cattle herds (cf. Megara: Aristot. Pol. 1305a). Nevertheless, it should not be assumed that a society of herdsmen was dominant in Greece up to the archaic period in Greece and that farming only played a minor role. It is unlikely that cattle herds ever formed the basis of Greek agriculture.

Cattle were primarily used for transporting heavy loads, for ploughing (→ Plough) and threshing; for the farmers, the strength of the ox was indispensable, as advice from Hesiod demonstrates: 'First obtain a house, a wife, and an ox for ploughing.' (Hes. Op. 405). On this verse, Aristotle comments: 'The ox is the poor man's substitute for slaves' (Aristot. Pol. 1252b). The importance of cattle as work animals is also emphasized by both Aeschylus and Plato (Aesch. PV 462–465; Pl. Resp. 370d-e). The horses of antiquity were not suitable for ploughing; they were too small and too light and had a difficult temper. Only the → mule, which is incapable of reproducing, represented an alternative (cf. Hom Il. 10,351–353), which however was clearly not as economical. The majority of male animals that were used as draught animals for farmers were castrated because uncastrated bulls could not be brought under control (→ Castration of animals).

The production of → milk and → cheese was not the primary goal of keeping cattle in ancient Greece; beef, on the other hand, was an important element of human → nutrition, the meat mostly being consumed in connection with a sacrificial ritual: cattle were considered the most noble of sacrificial animals offered to the gods by a city state or a ruler. Individual persons and small groups of citizens in classical Greece did make sacrifices, but usually of smaller animals that were not as expensive (→ Sheep; → Sacrifices I and III): the sacrificial calendar of the Athenian Demos of → Erchia from the 4th cent. BC for example does not mention oxen (LSCG 18). A sacrificial calendar of the same period, which applied to the cult group of the → Tetrapolis of Marathon, shows that a cow cost more than eight times as much as a mother sheep while providing five times as much meat.

A distinction was made between cattle to be used as work animals and those intended for sacrifice, with the exception of those few rituals in which the work animal was the central focus. The Athenian sacrificial ritual of Βουφόνια/→ Bouphónia focussed on the sin of killing a work ox; the ceremony ended with the conviction and condemnation of the axe (Paus. 1,24,4; 1,28,10; Porph. de abstinentia 2,28–30). The Bouphónia may not be seen, however, as a key to understanding sacrifices in general because the ritual used a work ox as the sacrificial animal. Although more exact information is unavailable, it is doubtful that it was generally a taboo to consume the meat of work animals. The meat of sacrificial animals could be purchased in the slaughterhou-

ses; that is why Paul warned the Christians of Corinth not to consume meat that had been purchased from the market (1 Kor 8).

Cowhide was valuable material for straps, belts, containers, clothing and armour (cf. Pl. Resp. 370e; → Leather). The skin from sacrificial animals could be given to priests — as in Athens — or sold by the city state (IG II² 1496). In spite of the large number of animal sacrifices, Athens imported large numbers of skins in the 4th cent. BC (Dem. Or. 34,10).

It only rarely occurred that a bull or cow would be selected for sacrifice and then raised particularly for that purpose (Magnesia on the Maeander: LSAM 32; Bargylia: SEG 45,1508). Sacrificial animals were mostly purchased from farmers. Athens officially employed people to acquire oxen (Dem. Or. 21,171; IG II² 334; 1496): the city had a large demand for sacrificial animals because during a single festival up to 300 heads of cattle could be sacrificed (Isoc. Or. 7,29); due to limited pasturelands in Attica, it was necessary to import cattle from other regions in Greece. As their names imply, Boeotia and Euboea provided good conditions for cattle breeding. In northern Greece, it was Thessaly (cf. Xen. Hell. 6,4,29) and Epirus with their well irrigated pastures that were famous for their cattle breeding (Aristot. Hist. an. 522b; 595b; cf. Varro, Rust. 2,5,10). The modern Greek landscape should not lead one to underestimate the opportunities for breeding cattle in ancient Greece; even Venetian sketches from the period around AD 1700 offer an impressive picture of cattle breeding in the Argolid.

Greek mythology often refers to herds belonging to individual deities; Homer for example describes the cattle herds of the sun god Helius (Hom. Od. 12,127–141; cf. also Hdt. 9,93), and one hymn describes how Hermes stole the cattle of Apollo (h. Hom. 4). The bull was an important symbol in Bronze Age Crete as the drawings of Minoan art demonstrate (→ Religion [VI]); in myth, Zeus takes the form of a bull to seduce → Europa, and Poseidon sends a bull from the sea to kill → Hippolytus (Eur. Hipp. 1213–1229). Cows, too, could possess a symbolic or religious function: in Hermion(e), four old women killed four cows with sickles and sacrificed them to → Demeter Chthonia (Paus. 2,35,4–10); in a jealous rage, Hera transformed → Io into a cow. The goddess → Hera herself bore the epithet βοῶπις/boôpis ('cow-eyed') as she probably had a close relationship to cattle. The cows on the frieze of the → Parthenon were probably sacrificial animals intended for → Athena. From the 8th to the 6th cent. BC, small figures of cattle made of bronze and clay were widespread → votive offerings.

→ Artemis (I. C.) Tauropolos; → Energy (B.2.); → Meat, consumption of; → Minotaur; → Sacrifices; → Bull cults; → Husbandry

1 A. BURFORD, Land and Labour in the Greek World, 1993, 144–156   2 W. BURKERT, Homo necans, 1972 (²1997)   3 H. GRASSL, Zur Gesch. des Viehhandels im klassischen Griechenland, in: MBAH 4, 1985, 77–87

4 S. HODKINSON, Animal Husbandry in the Greek Polis, in: WHITTAKER, 35–74   5 ISAGER/SKYDSGAARD, 89–91; 96–107   6 M. H. JAMESON, C. N. RUNNELS, Tj. VAN ANDEL, A Greek Countryside: The Southern Argolid from Prehistory to the Present Day, 1994, 285–287   7 M. H. JAMESON, Sacrifice and Animal Husbandry, in: WHITTAKER, 87–119   8 H. KRAEMER, s. v. Rind, RE Suppl. 7, 1155–1185   9 W. RICHTER, Die Landwirtschaft im Homerischen Zeitalter (ArchHom 2=H), 1968 10 V. ROSIVACH, The System of Public Sacrifice in Fourth-Century Athens, 1994   11 WHITE, Farming 12 K. ZEISSIG, Die Rinderzucht im alten Griechenland, Diss. Giessen, 1934.   MI.JA.

IV. ROME

Cattle were an important topic for Roman agronomists (→ Agrarian writers); the Latin language already had sophisticated terminology for cattle which distinguished according to age and gender: bos ('horned animal/cattle'), taurus ('bull'), vacca ('cow'), forda/horda ('pregnant cow'), iuvencus ('young bull') and vitulus/vitellus ('calf'; cf. Varro, Rust. 2,5,6). The agronomists dealt with all aspects of breeding and keeping of cattle, particularly the ox, the most important draught animal (Varro, Rust. 1,20; 2,5; Colum. 6,1–27; Plin. HN 8,176–186; 11 passim). → Columella, who like Varro stresses the pre-eminence of cattle in animal husbandry (Colum. 6 praef. 7: nec dubium ... ceteras pecudes bos honore superare debeat, praesertim in Italia; cf. Varro, Rust. 2,5,3), lists four breeds in Italy: Campanian cattle with a white coat, small, not very strong; the large Umbrian breed with a white and sometimes red coat; the enormous Etruscan breed which was very strong; as well as the breed of cattle from the Apennines, which was not as handsome, but strong and very robust. Since these breeds did not produce much milk, calves in Italy were sometimes given milk from the cevae from Altinum (Colum. 6,1,1 ff.; 6,24,5). Roman landowners were greatly interested in purchasing sturdy animals with strong necks and solid horns; there was detailed knowledge of the desirable characteristics of oxen to be used as work animals in → agriculture (Varro, Rust. 21,1; Colum. 6,1,3).

With good pasture lands, cows between the ages of three to 10 gave birth to one calf every year; when there were feed shortages, only one every other year. The calves, which suckled from their mothers for one year, were identified by a brand (Colum. 6,21; 6,24,4; Verg. G. 3,157 ff.). Cattle feed (bubus pabulum) — especially for the work animals — had to be of high quality (Cato Agr. 54; cf. Colum. 6,3), and the sheds (bubilia) were to be well protected (Varro, Rust. 1,13,1).

As in Greece, cattle in Italy were primarily used as work animals, while breeding cattle to produce meat only played a minor role. There was a clear distinction between the animals that were kept in the pastures and the work animals (Varro, Rust. 2 praef. 4). Columella ranked cattle exclusively among the work animals — along with mules, horses and donkeys (Colum. 6 praef. 6). For Virgil, there was a close correlation between horse and cattle breeding (Verg. G. 3,49–209); cattle served either as work animals, primarily for ploughing (→ Plough), but were also raised for sacrifice or selected for breeding (Verg. G. 3,157–161).

The yoke was either laid in front of the withers on the neck or tied in front of the horns. Both methods had advantages and disadvantages which were already discussed in antiquity (Colum. 2,2,22–24). According to → Cato [1] three yoke of oxen, three oxen drivers, and three donkeys were required for ploughing a 60 hectare olive tree grove; for a vineyard of 25 hectares, one yoke of oxen and one oxen driver were required (Cato Agr. 10,1–2; 11,1); → Saserna felt that two yoke of oxen were sufficient for a 50 hectare farm (Varro, Rust. 1,19,1). The training of oxen, which was supposed to begin around the age of three, is described in detail by Columella, as is the treatment of diseases (Colum. 6,2; 6,4–19; cf. 2,3). In Cato's opinion, nothing was more useful than handling oxen well (Cato Agr. 54,5: nihil est quod magis expediat quam boves bene curare). Cows, too, were used as work animals (Varro, Rust. 1,20,4; Colum. 6,24,4; Anth. Gr. 9,274; 10,101). In → land transport oxen were also used for pulling heavy loads, in which case several yokes of oxen could be harnessed behind one another or in the shape of a fan. In late antiquity, oxen pulled ships loaded with grain along the Tiber from Portus [1] upstream to Rome (Procop. Goth. 1,26,10–12).

Beef was a highly valued foodstuff in Roman society (Cic. Fam. 9,20,1; cf. Apicius 8,353–356; Gal. 15,879 K.). The price edict issued by Diocletian (→ Edictum [3] Diocletiani) set beef (carnis bubulae) and goat meat at the maximum price of eight denari per pound, and pork at a maximum of 12 denari per pound (Ed. Diocl. 4,1–3). → Leather could be used to manufacture shields, clothing, harnesses, helmets, saddles, kitchenware and belts. → Cheese made of cow's milk was not as widespread as sheep's cheese or goat's cheese; however, several sorts were known from Gades and Gaul (Str. 3,5,4; Plin. HN 11,240).

Bulls and oxen were mythological symbols of power, strength and wealth. All ancient religions integrated horned animals into their symbolic systems, their mythological designs and their rites and magical practices. The Egyptian → Apis cult was well known in Rome (Plin. HN 8,184–186). The → Suovetaurilia — the sacrifice of a bull, hog and ram, took place on different occasions, for example during the → lustratio (expiatory sacrifice for purification) of the army, of the → populus (Liv. 1,44,2; Varro, Rust. 2,1,10; cf. Tac. Ann. 6,37,2), of the fields (Cato. Agr. 141,1), and in → triumph. During the celebration of the Hordicalia a pregnant cow was sacrificed (Varro, Rust. 2,5,6). Cattle were used to create the furrows that established the borders of a property or a city (Ov. Fast. 4,819–826; Verg. Aen. 5,755). A rural sacrifice was made annually for the well-being of cattle (Cato Agr. 83; cf. 131 ff.).

Ancient works of art often included images of cattle, mostly of bulls, but also cows and calves. The → Andocides Painter for example depicted in large scale on a belly amphora a bull being led to sacrifice by Heracles (Boston MFA; BEAZLEY, ABV 255,6); yokes of oxen ploughing are depicted on a bowl by Nicosthenes (Berlin SM; BEAZLEY, ABV 223,66) and on a black-figured amphora (New York private collection; [2]). Similar depictions can be found on Roman mosaics from southern France and Africa (mosaic from Saint-Romain-en-Gal; mosaic from Caesarea/Cherchel in Algeria). Furthermore widely known in antiquity was a sculpture by → Myron [3] that depicted a cow supposed to have almost appeared alive (praised by poets in epigrams: Anth. Gr. 9,173–742; 9,793–798).

→ Agrarian writers; → Energy (B.2.); → Land transport; → Agriculture; → Horse; → Bull cults

1 N. BENECKE, Arch. Studien zur Entwicklung der Haustierhaltung, 1994   2 J. BOARDMAN (ed.), Gesch. der ant. Kunst, 1997, 80   3 J. CLUTTON-BROCK, A Natural History of Domesticated Mammals, 1987   4 FLACH 5 S. LEPETZ, L'amélioration des races à l'époque gallo-romaine: l'exemple du boeuf, in: Homme et animal dans l'antiquité gallo-romaine, 1995, 67–79   6 Id., L'animal dans la societé gallo-romaine de la France, 1996 7 WHITE, Farming   8 F. ZEUNER, The History of Domesticated Animals, 1964.   G.R.

Catualda Marcomannian noble who had fled from → Marbod to the Gothic Gutones. At the instigation of Drusus he invaded the kingdom of Marbod in *c.* AD 18 with the help of the Gutones who wanted to free themselves from Marcomanni subjugation and drove him into exile in Ravenna. Shortly afterwards he himself was driven out by the Hermundurian Vibilius and fled to Forum Iulii (Fréjus) (Tac. Ann. 2, 62–63).   W.ED.

Catugnatus (Κατούγνατος; *Katoúgnatos*). Celtic name compound 'for battle born, well acquainted with battle' [1. 168]. Leader of the → Allobroges who plundered Gallia Narbonensis in 61 BC. C. was able for a long time successfully to hold his ground against the Romans and also to save himself when they seized the town of Solonum which he was defending (Cass. Dio 47,1–48,2; Liv. per. 103).

1 SCHMIDT.   W.SP.

Catullus

[1] Valerius C., C. Roman poet of the 1st cent. BC born in Verona (*scriptor lyricus Veronae nascitur*, Jer. Chron. a. Abr. 1930). The *praenomen* is confirmed through Apul. Apol. 10, the *nomen gentile* by Suet. Iul. 73 and Porph. ad Hor. Sat. 1,10,18. The Valerii Catulli are known from the time of Augustus onwards as a senatorial family. In the later Republic they probably formed equestrian *domus nobiles* in the Transpadanic 'Latin colony' Verona [1. 335–348]. C. refers to himself as a *Transpadanus* (39,13) and describes Sirmio in the region of Verona as his home (31,9; cf. 67,34). His father regularly gave hospitality to Caesar during his

proconsulship in Gaul (Suet. Iul. 73). However C.'s literary and social career was centred on Rome (68,34f.). *Urbanus* was one of his expressions of the highest praise (22,2; 39,8).

Jerome (Chron. a. Abr. 1930, 1959) records his birth in 87/86 BC and his death at the age of 30 in 58/57 BC (Olympics 173,2 and 180,3). His age at death is based on from Suetonius, *De poetis* and is probably correct, however the dates are not. All externally datable references in C.'s poems (11,9–12; 29,11f.; 45,22; 49,7; 52,2f.; 53,2f.; 55,5; 84,7; 113,2) belong to the years 55–54 BC. If the poet's journey to Bithynia in the *cohors* of the proconsul Memmius (4; 10; 28; 31; 46: presumably C. Memmius *pr.* 58) took place when he had just turned 20, then the life dates 81–52, 80–51 or 79–50 are plausible, but these are of necessity hypothetical.

In spite of the jokes about 'cobwebs in his counting house' (13,8), C. was certainly not poor. He did not need any patron and he was certainly sufficiently socially secure to write satirically about Roman politicians (28; 47; 52; 54; 108) and aristocratic ladies (27), to address Cicero with unconcealed irony (49) and especially to attack Caesar and Pompey (29; 93) and their supporter Mamurra (29; 57; 94; 105; 114f.). Caesar admitted that the poems about Mamurra were *perpetua stigmata* but accepted C.'s apology and invited him to a meal (Suet. Iul. 73). Vituperative verse was one of the genres most frequently linked with C. (Quint. Inst. 10,1,96; Tac. Ann. 4,34,5; Diom. gramm. 1,485; Porph. Hor. comm. 1,16,24). But he also knew how to write splendid → occasional poetry like the *hymenaion* (wedding poem) for Manlius Torquatus (61) or the Callimachus translation for Hortensius Hortalus (65; 66).

His closest friends were writers: the orator and poet C. → Licinius Calvus, Q. → Cornificius, → Veranius [2. 266–269], C. → Asinius Pollio, Cornelius → Nepos and C. → Helvius Cinna.

→ Parthenius as a living example of the 'Alexandrian' tradition of Callimachus and Euphorion had a significant influence on the Roman poet [3]. C. and his friends admired the erudition and refinement of the Alexandrians and cultivated in particular the art of → epyllium; Cinna's *Zmyrna* was welcomed by C. as a masterpiece (95), and his own poem about the wedding of Peleus and Thetis (64) is written with self-assured literary mastery [4. 85–150]. C. attacked traditional genres as pompous and naive (15; 22; 36; 95); he and his friends probably belonged to the 'new poets' (→ Neoteric poets), to 'Euphorion's Singers' whom Cicero condemned because of their rejection of Ennius (Cic. Orat. 161; Tusc. 3,45; cf. Att. 7,2,1).

An additional common interest was in love poetry (Ov. Tr. 2,427–436, regarding C., Calvus, Cinna, Cornificius etc.). C.' s love poems for Lesbia immortalized both himself and her (Prop. 2,34,88). *Lesbia* was a pseudonym that alluded to Sappho whose metre C. used for two of the most powerfully effective poems about her (11; 51). The woman's real name was Clodia

(Apul. apol. 10), and C.'s allusion to her brother (79,1: *Lesbius est pulcher*) hints that she was a sister of P. → Clodius Pulcher (people's tribune 58 BC). She was married and the two had to meet in secret (68,67–69. 145f.; cf. 83,1); of greater significance is that she had other lovers and C. had to fight for her attention (37,13; 68,135–37). The poems create a moving drama of love and jealousy, desire and betrayal in which generations of readers have rediscovered a directness and authenticity of experience that none of C.'s many successors and imitators ever achieved.

Liber Catulli Veronensis [5] was probably published late in 54 or 53 BC. There is no reason at all to regard it as a posthumous collection. The poems are arranged carefully and in a considered manner [6. 1–31]. After the dedication a cycle of love poems is introduced by the *passer* ('sparrow') after whom the collection is named (Mart. 1,7,3; 4,14,13f.). Carm. 14b refers to a second, this time homosexual cycle. Carm. 27 introduces satire and (especially iambic) invective (36,5; 54,6). Complex alternation of themes and metres renders the 1st part of the collection (1–60) a coherent whole. A Callimachean allusion to the muse Urania (61,2) introduces the second part that consists of two wedding poems, a vivid galliambic hymn to Cybele and the epic about Peleus and Thetis (61–64). These greater works are, in every respect, of central significance for the *oeuvre*. Carm. 65 introduces the distichs of the collection with mourning for the death of C.'s brother (65,12: *carmina maesta*); again Callimachus and the Muses describe the transition. Four long elegiac poems culminate in an elaborate mythical meditation on the poet's own experience with regard to both his love for his girlfriend and his lamentation about his brother (68b). The short distichs and epigrams that follow next (69–116) again take up the thematic complexity of the first part. The collection ends in the future tense (116,7f.) with an apparent turning away from Callimachean poetry. The extremely controversial suggestion was made [2. 183–189] that C. then devoted himself to the stage and that the mimes attributed to a certain → Catullus Mimographus (Mart. 5,30,3; Juv. 8,186; 13,111; Tert. adversus Valentinianos 14) were the work of the last years of his life. Certainly he did, however, continue to write: Fragments from poems not contained in *liber* (e.g. Non. 193M), and also of prose works (Varro, Ling. 6,6; schol. Bern. comment. Luc. 1,544) are extant.

C. died young and famous (Ov. Am. 3,9,61). He had an enormous influence on → Vergilius and → Elegy, was highly regarded by Martial and Pliny as a writer of light verse and was still read at the time of Gellius and Apuleius (2nd cent. AD). Scholars from → Festus to → Isidorus demonstrate knowledge of his work, perhaps second-hand, but he never became a classic writer read in schools. In the Middle Ages he disappeared almost entirely. Only a single handwritten manuscript of the *Liber* escaped destruction when it was delivered to Verona 'from distant lands' about 1300. It is the archetype of all extant handwritten manuscripts [7. 1–23].

The *editio princeps* was printed in 1472 in Venice. Since that time there has never been any doubt about C.'s status as one of the greatest poets of antiquity.

1 T.P. WISEMAN, Roman Studies, 1987   2 Id., Catullus and his World, 1985   3 W.CLAUSEN, Callimachus and Latin Poetry, in: GRBS 5, 1964, 181–196   4 R.JENKYNS, Three Classical Poets, 1982   5 J.D. MINYARD, The source of the Catullus Veronensis liber, in: CW 81, 1988, 343–353   6 T.P. WISEMAN, Catullan Questions, 1969   7 J.H. GAISSER, Catullus and his Renaissance Readers, 1993.

EDITIONS: R.A. B. MYNORS, 1958; H.BARDON, 1973; D.F. S. THOMSON, 1978; W.EISENHUT, ⁸1979.
COMMENTARIES: E.BAEHRENS, 1885; R.ELLIS, ²1889; G.FRIEDRICH, 1908; M.LENCHANTIN DE GUBERNATIS, ²1947; W.KROLL, ³1958; C.J.FORDYCE, 1961; K.QUINN, 1970; H.-P.SYNDIKUS, 4 vols., 1984–90.
REFERENCES: H.HARRAUER, 1979; J.P. HOLOKA, 1985.
LIT.: A.L. WHEELER, Catullus and the Traditions of Ancient Poetry, 1934; M.SCHUSTER, s.v. Valerius Catullus 123), RE 7 A, 2353–2410; L.FERRERO, Interpretazione di Catullo, 1955; K.QUINN, The Catullan Revolution, 1959; E.SCHAFER, Das Verhältnis von Erlebnis und Kunstgestalt bei Catullus, 1966; J.GRANAROLO, L'œuvre de Catulle, 1967; K.QUINN, Catullus, 1973; J.GRANAROLO, Catullus, ce vivant, 1982; E. A. SCHMIDT, Catullus, 1985; P.FEDELI, Introduzione a Catullo, 1990. Collections: K.QUINN, Approaches to Catullus, 1972; R.HEINE (ed.), Catullus, 1975.   T.W.

[2] **C. Mimographus.** His life dates and circumstances are unknown. C. achieved fame as a result of the mime *Laureolus* — performed shortly before Caligula's murder — in which the escape, capture and crucifixion of the robber Laureolus were presented and the stage was awash with fake blood (Suet. Cal. 57,4); real blood flowed in AD 80 when a condemned criminal had to play Laureolus at the Amphitheatre (Mart. spect. 7). The mime *Phasma* was also the work of C. (Juv. 8,186), obviously a tumultuous ghost play (the addition of *clamosus* places it in the category of mime sound pieces). Martial calls C. *facundus* (5,30,3), Iuvenal *urbanus* (13,111). Tertullian still mentions C. (adversus Valentianos 14).

M.BONARIA, Romani mimi, 1965, 80, 133–135; SCHANZ-HOSIUS II⁴, 564–565, 823; D. F. SUTTON, Seneca on the Stage, 1986, 63–67.   L.BE.

Catulus Roman cognomen ('the Young Dog') in the family of the Lutatii (→ Lutatius).

KAJANTO, Cognomina 326.   K.-L.E.

[1] **Epigrammatist.** see → Lutatius Catulus, Q.

Catumelus (Catmelus). Celtic name compound 'ceaseless in battle' [1. 168]. Gallic prince who commanded a camp of relief troops on the Roman side in the campaign against the Histrians at Lake Timavus in 178 BC (Liv. 41,1,8).

1 SCHMIDT.   W.SP.

Catumerus (Actumerus). Celtic name — passed down in various forms — of a Chatti prince, grandfather of → Italicus (Tac. Ann. 11,16,1; 11,17,1). Strabo (7,1,4) calls him Οὐκρόμηρος (*Oukrómēros*).

E. KOESTERMANN, Cornelius Tacitus Annalen, 11–13 und 57–58, 1967; A. SCHERER, Die kelt.-german. Namengleichungen, in: Corolla Linguistica 1955, 199–210. W.SP.

Caturiges Gallic tribe, settling in the → Alpes Cottiae on the upper course of the Durance, mistakenly placed by Ptol. 3,1,35 in the Alpes Graiae, and by Str. 4,6,6 in the mountains above the Salassi. In Caes. B Gall. 1,10,4, the C. are named as a tribe hostile to Rome. Plin. HN 3,125 sees the C. as expelled → Insubres. They were conquered under Augustus (CIL V 7231; 7817 = Plin. HN 3,137). Their capitals were Caturigomagus (modern Chorges) and Eburodunum (modern Embrun). Since the time of Diocletian (AD 284–305), they belonged to the province of Alpes Maritimae.

G. BARRUOL, Les peuples préromains du sud-est de la Gaule, 1975, 340–344; J. PRIEUR, La province romaine des Alpes Cottiennes, 1968, 77f. H.GR.

Catuvellauni Powerful tribe in Britannia north of the lower Thames, who most likely had links with the Gallic Catualauni. Their most influential rulers were Tasciovanus and his son → Cunobellinus [1]. Following the conquest of Britannia by Claudius (Cass. Dio 60,20,2), the C. were organized as a *civitas* with → Verulamium as its centre (Tac. Ann. 14,33).

1 S. S. FRERE, Britannia, ³1987, 44f.

S. S. FRERE, Verulamium Excavations 1, 1972; R. E. M. and T. V. WHEELER, Verulamium, 1936; K. BRANIGAN, The C., 1985. M.TO.

Catuvolcus see → Ambiorix

Cauca Celtiberian town, modern Coca (province of Segovia). First mentioned in the context of the brutal war conducted by → Lucullus in 151 BC (App. Ib. 51f.). Scipio, too, laid the town to ruins in the course of his battle against Numantia (App. Ib. 89). In the imperial age, the town belonged to the *conventus* of → Clunia (Plin. HN 3,26), and gained fame as the birthplace of emperor → Theodosius I (Zos. 4,24,4).

TOVAR 3, 334; F. WATTEMBERG, La región vaccea, 1959. P.B.

Caucasa (Καύκασα; *Kaúkasa*). Port on the northern coast of Chios (Hdt. 5,33,1); its inhabitants are epigraphically referred to as *Kaukaseís* (SGDI 5654; SEG 19, 575; *Apollon Kaukaseus* and *Artemis Kaukasis* in Erythrae, Syll.³ 3, 1014a,19f.).

L. BÜRCHNER, s.v. K., RE 6, 2292. H.KAL.

Caucasia The country between the Black Sea and the Caspian Sea, with the Great → Caucasus, was settled from the 4th millennium BC onwards and until today is distinctively polyethnic. From the late 3rd millennium onwards, C. became a centre of → bronze metallurgy for the Near Easter; at the end of the 2nd millennium beginning of → iron metallurgy. In the 9th–6th cents. C. was affected by the expansion of the → Urarṭu empire; in northern C. lived → Scythian and → Sarmatian tribes. From the 6th cent. BC onwards, the Pontos coast was settled by Greeks (→ Colchis). In the Hellenistic period there was an uprising of the kingdoms of → Armenia and → Iberia [1]. With Pompey's oriental campaign in 66/65 BC the region came under the Roman sphere of influence — among other reasons because of its strategic position against the northern nomads — and until the end of antiquity remained a buffer zone between Iran and Rome; in northern C. migrations of peoples took place from the 3rd cent. AD onwards (→ Alani, → Goti, → Huns).

K. PLATT, Armenien, Wiederentdeckung einer Kulturlandschaft (exhibition catalogue), 1995; W. MARKOWIN, R. MUNTSCHAJEW, Kunst und Kultur im Nordkaukasus, 1988. A.P.-L.

Caucasiae Pylae (Καυκάσιαι Πύλαι; *Kaukásiai Pýlai*). Pass in the → Caucasus, only mentioned in Plin. HN 6,30; the same as what is now the Georgian military road, described in Ptol. 5,8,9 as Σαρματικαὶ Πύλαι (*Sarmatikaì Pýlai*). B.B.

Caucasian languages The languages of the Caucasus area (with the exception of → Georgian not attested until modern times) that do not belong to any of the neighbouring language families (Indo-Germanic, Turkic, Semitic) and are considered autochthonous. The assignment of today's Caucasian ethnic groups to the ethnonyms mentioned in the ancient sources (e.g. the Circassians — self-designation *Adəγe* — and the Κερκέται/*Kerkétai* of Hecataeus, the Abchasians and Abasinians — self-designation *Apswa* — and the Ἀψίλαι/*Apsílai* or Ἀβασκοί/*Abaskoí* of Arrian) remains uncertain in many respects.

Kinship ties are only evident within the three large groups [1. 398ff.] (southern Caucasus: Georgian, Lazic, Mingrelian and Svanic; western Caucasus: Abchasian-Circassian; eastern Caucasus: Chechen-Ingush and Daghestan languages) but more recent research tends to separate the northern Caucasian languages (CL) — because they are genetically closely related — from the southern Caucasian languages. Kinship ties with other languages (Basque, Dravidian, languages of Old Asia Minor) have to date not been proven.

Some CL are very heterogeneous as regards sound, morphology and syntax. But there are also common elements across the languages in the sound types and the morphosyntax: 1. Ejective (i.e. spoken with a glottal stop), uvular and (not everywhere) pharyngal conso-

nants; widespread phonological labialization and pha-
ryngalization of consonants; in northern Caucasian
also lateral fricatives and affricates; 2. Ergative
construction, i.e. the agent of the transitive verb is formally distinguished from the subject of intransitive
verbs, which is given exactly the same name as the direct
object of the transitive verb; the personal subject of
interjection verbs is in the dative in many CL. The
inflection morphology diverges sharply: absence of the
nominal case with the polypersonal verb (affixes for a
maximum of four actants) in western Caucasian
Abchasian as opposed to extended nominal inflection
(18 cases) in the apersonal verb in eastern Caucasian
Lezgi (the southern CL occupy an intermediate position). Signs of vowel gradations and infixations are
widespread. From a lexical point of view, the CL have
been influenced to varying degrees by borrowings particularly from Iranian, Arabic, Turkish and Russian.
The adoption into the CL of ancient borrowings from
Indo-Germanic languages [3] is disputed; likewise borrowings from the CL by Indo Germanic languages (e.g.
the Indo-Germanic words for 'horse' and 'flax, linen':
Latin *equus*, *linum*).

1 G.KLIMOV, Einführung in die kaukas. Sprachwiss.
(trans. from Russian by J.GIPPERT), 1994   2 Λ.C.
HARRIS et al. (ed.), The Indigenous Languages of the Caucasus, 1989ff.   3 G.KLIMOV, Some Thoughts on Indo-
European-Kartvelian Relations, in: Journal of Indo-European Studies 19, 1991, 325–341.   M.J.

Caucasus (Καυκάσιον ὄρος; *Kaukásion óros*,
Hdt. 3,97; Καύκασον ὄρος; *Kaúkason óros*, App. praef.
4, App. Mith. 103; καυκάσια ὄρη, Str. 11,2,1; *Caucasii/
Caucasei montes*, Plin. HN 5,98; 6,47; Mela 1,15; 1,19;
Geogr. Rav. 2,20). First mentioned at Aesch. PV 422;
719 (πόλισμα καυκάσου, καύκασον); the name has been
retained until today. High mountain range (1,100 km
long, up to 60 km wide) between the Black Sea and the
Caspian Sea that separated the world of the northern
steppe peoples (Scythians, Sarmatians, Alanians) from
the cultures of southern Caucasia and was at the same
time considered to be the border between Asia and
Europe; the most important transit routes were the
→ *Caucasiae Pylae* (crossing pass) and *Albaniai Pylai*
(road of Derbent). The C. and the numerous mountain
peoples are discussed in 11,2,14–19; 5,4–7.   A.P.-L.
In the Byzantine period, roads for the Byzantine silk
trade traversed the C.; with its partly Christian population (→ Armenia, → Armenians, → Georgia, Georgians) it was situated on the northern boundary of the
Sāssānid, later of the Arabic empire.
→ Albania [1]; → Iberia [1]; → Caucasia; → Colchis

G.OSTROGORSKY, Gesch. des byz. Staates, ³1963, 260f.;
A.Herrmann, s.v. Kaukasos (3), RE 11, 59–62.   G.MA.

Caucon (Καύκων; *Kaúkōn*). Eponymous hero of the
Peloponnesian people of the → Caucones [1]; his genealogy is dependent on the ancient localization of the
people first named in Hom. Od. 3. 366. His grave was
shown in Lepreum in Triphylia (Paus. 5,5,5; Str. 8,345),
and according to the Triphylian cult centre on Samicon,
he is seen as the son of Poseidon (Ael. NA 1,24). Yet as a
result of the Arcadian localization, C. is also the son of
Arcas (schol. Hom. Od. 3,366) or of Lycaon (Apollod.
3,97). Finally, C. is connected with Messenia and the
→ mysteries of the Great Gods of Andania: at the
founding of Megalopolis he receives a sacrifice (Paus.
4,27,6); as hierophant of the Andanian mysteries, he is
said to have appeared to Epaminondas and to the commander Epiteles who was allied with him before the
battle of Leuctra, and to have promised Epaminondas
fame and victory if he would give the Messenians their
homeland, as well as to have shown Epiteles the buried
holy book with the cult statutes of the mysteries (Paus.
4,26,6–8). Here C. is seen as the Athenian who brought
the mysteries from Eleusis to Andania, which reflects
the attempt to connect these local mysteries with those
of Eleusis (Paus. 4,1,5).   F.G.

Caucones (Καύκωνες; *Kaúkōnes*).
[1] Hom. Od. 3,366 prompted logographers and exege-
tes of Homer to place the settlement area of this tribe on
the Peloponnese. The results of these investigations are
recorded by Strabo (7,7,1f.; 8,3,11; 8,3,16f.). Accordingly, the C. settled chiefly in Triphylia (grave of
Caucon in → Lepreum), but also penetrated into Arcadia and Messenia. Antimachus even referred to the
western Achaean → Dyme [1] as Cauconian (schol.
Lycoph. 571), probably after a stream by the name of
Caucon. Hecataeus considered the C. to be non-Greek
(FGrH 1 F 119).

A.M. BIRASCHI, Strabone e Omero, in: Id. (ed.), Strabone
e la Grecia, 1994, 23–57.   Y.L.

[2] Tribe on the Parthenius, the border river between
→ Bithynia and → Paphlagonia, with Tieium as their
city (Str. 12,542). They were considered allies of the
Trojans (Hom. Il. 10,429); with them, Poseidon found
safety for Aeneas who was fighting against Achilles
(Hom. Il. 20,329).   RA.MI.

Caudex Cognomen ('the ship's plank') of Ap. Claudius
C., *cos.* 264 BC; the original legend was passed down
through Seneca (dial. 10,13,4).   K.-L.E.

Caudini Samnite tribe, capital → Caudium (Liv.
23,41,13; Plin. HN 3,105). Subjugated in 275 BC by L.
Cornelius Lentulus, whose family from then on bore the
cognomen of 'Caudinus'.   M.BU.

Caudium Capital of the Samnite → Caudini, modern
Montesarchio; *mansio* on the *via Appia* between
→ Capua and → Beneventum, possibly *municipium*.
Grave gifts, found in the necropolis near Montesarchio,
indicate habitation from the 8th to the 3rd cents. BC. C.
was twice enclosed by a walled circle; the later ring,
established in the south-east of the town, was possibly

built in conjunction with the *renormatio*, which Augustus undertook after 31 BC for the veterans of the *legio XXX*.

G. D'HENRY, EAA Suppl., 193–195; Structures agraires (Coll. Éc. Fr. Rom., 100), 1987, 164–167.   M.BU.

Caulonia (Καυλωνία; *Kaulōnía*, Lat. *Caulonia, Caulonea*).
Achaean colony on the eastern coast of Bruttium, founded by Typhon of Aegium (Paus. 6,3,12) at the end of the 8th cent. BC, near the modern Monasterace Marina [1]. C. came under the rule of → Croton, and was eventually considered a Crotoniate foundation (Ps.-Scymn. GGM 1, 318f.). Its initial autonomy is verified by the minting of coins from the 6th cent. BC onwards. Its economic mainstay was the timber trade (Thuc. 7,25,2). In 388 BC, C. was besieged by Dionysius I, and captured and destroyed in 387 BC, its *chóra* assigned to Locri Epizephyrii. C. was rebuilt by Dionysius II, and seized by Campanians from Rhegium in 280 BC. C. was finally deserted after its capture by the Romans in 205 BC in the course of the Second Punic War (Str. 6,1,10). Archaeological data: Greek pottery (late geometric); town structure with fortifications clearly discernible. In addition to a Doric temple (430–420 BC), several cult sites are documented by architectural terracottas on the hill of Passoliera, amongst them a large extra-mural sanctuary (cult as yet unidentified; 6th cent. BC).

1 P. ORSI, Caulonia, in: Monumenti Antichi dei Lincei 23, 1916, 685–944.

E. TOMASELLO, Monasterace Marina, in: NSA ser. VIII, 26, 1972, 685–944; H. TREZINY, Kaulonia 1, 1989; E. GRECO, Archeologia della Magna Grecia, 1992; BTCGI 10, 190–217.   A.MU.

Caunus (Καῦνος; *Kaûnos*).
[1] Eponym of the Carian town C. [2], who gains contours chiefly in connection with his twin sister → Byblis. The myths depict various constellations of their incestuous relationship (Parthenius 11).

S. JACKSON, Apollonius of Rhodes: the Cleite and Byblis Suicides, in: SIFC 14, 1997, 48–54.   C.W.

[2] Coastal town in the border areas between Caria and Lycia on the Kalbis (Str. 14,2,2; present-day Dalyan çayı), now inland, 3 km from the sea, ruins across from Dalyan. The Caunians were seen as autochthonous, though they themselves claimed Cretan origins (Hdt. 1,172; Str. 14,2,3); they had their own customs, but their language was similar to Carian; inscriptions are in an alphabet differing from Carian.

C. was conquered in 546 BC by Harpagus [1] (Hdt. 1,171; 176), took part in the Ionian uprising (Hdt. 5,103) and was a member in the → Delian League; after 387/6 upgraded to a Greek city (under → Hecatomnus, → Maussolus). The *Basileus Kaunios* (*Zeus Kaunios*) was the chief god of C. The city was occupied in 333 by

Ptolemy and Asander [1] (Arr. Anab. 2,5,7; Curt. 3,7,4), taken in 313 by Antigonus [1] and in 309 by Ptolemy (Diod. Sic. 19,75,5; 20,27,2); in 287/6 under Demetrius [2] (Plut. Demetrius 49), in 285 under Lysimachus, after that Ptolemaic Egypt purchased it from Rhodes in 197 or 195 for 200 talents. In 189–167 (or 185–165) it was under a Rhodian governor. In 167 C. seceded from Rhodes, but was again subjugated (Pol. 30,5,11; 5,13f.; Liv. 45,25,11ff.). In 166 the Roman Senate ordered the withdrawal of the Rhodian garrison from C. (Pol. 30,21,3; Str. 14,2,3); C. was free. Calynda, annexed by C. in 166, was lost to Rhodes in 163 (Pol. 31,4f.).

From 129 C. was *civitas libera* of the province Asia, in 88 on → Mithridates VI's side; it abided by the 'blood command of Ephesus' (App. Mith. 23) and therefore was again put under the control of Rhodes by the Senate in 81; before 51–50 it was again absorbed into the province of Asia (Cic. Fam. 13,56,3). In the imperial period *oppidum liberum* (Plin. HN 5,104); in AD 80 C. was again dependent on Rhodes (Dion. Chrys. 31,124f.).

C. lay in a fertile environment, though unhealthy, due to malaria (Dion. Chrys. 32. 92). The city exported slaves, salt fish, pine resin, figs (*cauneae*, also highly regarded in Italy: Cic. Div. 2,84; Plin. HN 15,83; Columella 10,414; Stat. Silv. 1,6,15) and sea salt, which was used to make eye salves and plasters (Plin. HN 31,99). In the cliff wall across from Dalyan, there are rock-cut tombs, in the upper row with Ionian temple façades (4th cent. BC). In the city area there are two acropolis hills, the eastern one rising precipitously (presumably the Imbros, Str. 14,2,3), on the city side with a medieval double wall, the western one lower; in antiquity the hills were connected by a wall. Above the city on the high plateau, the pronounced line of a wall (at the northern edge from the Hecatomnidian period, so from the Hellenistic period, west of the harbour from the late classical period), is potentially Heraclium, conquered in 309 BC by Ptolemy. A theatre, early Christian basilica and thermal springs are to be found; in the lower city the stoa, a small Dorian megaron for Zeus Kaunios, a → *tholos*, presumably a nymphaeum of the imperial period. At the harbour there is a rotunda and the remains of shipyards (Str. 14,2,3); at the agora north of the harbour there is a stoa (inscription of honour for L. Licinius Murena) and a pump room. Remains of the harbour bày are today Sülüklü gölü ('Leech Sea').

E. AKURGAL, Griech. und röm. Kunst in der Türkei, 1987, 428; G. E. BEAN, Notes and Inscriptions from Caunus, in: JHS 73, 1953, 10–35; 74, 1954, 85–110, especially 97ff. (on the customs inscription); Id., Kleinasien 3, 1974, 175–188; BENGTSON 3, 175; L. BÜRCHNER, s.v. K. (1), RE 11, 86–88; M. COLLIGNON, Ville de Kaune, in: BCH 1, 1877, 338–346; P. M. FRASER, G. E. BEAN, The Rhodian Peraea and Islands, 1954, 52f., 68ff., 118f.; MAGIE 2, 922, 926, 952, 958, 1111, 1123; H. METZGER et al., La stèle trilingue du Létôon, (Fouilles de Xanthos 6), 1979; L. ROBERT, À Caunos avec Quintus de Smyrne, in: BCH 108, 1984, 499–532; P. ROOS, Research at Caunus, in: OpAth 8, 1968, 149ff.; Id., Topographical and Other Notes on

Southern Caria, in: OpAth 9, 1969, 60ff.; Id., The Rock-Tombs of Caunus 1–2, 1972–74; Id., Survey of Rock-Cut Chamber-Tombs in Caria, 1: South-Eastern Caria and the Lyco-Carian Borderland, 1985; B. SCHMALTZ, K., 1988/9, Belleten 55, 1991, 121–177 (research report); H. H. SCHMITT, Rom und Rhodos, 1957, 77, 111f., 156ff.; J. WAGNER, Südtürkei, 1991, 35–41.   H.KA.

Caupona see → Inn

Caurus (Χῶρος; *Chôros*, Plin. HN 2,119). The turbulent north-west wind that blows from 30° from west to north. It is sometimes (as in Vitr. De arch. 1,6,10) distinguished from the *Corus*.
→ Winds

R. BÖKER, s.v. Winde, RE 8 A, 2294,45ff., 2352 (fig. 14), 2356,16 (*corus!*), 2373 (fig. 26: wind star of Vitruvius) and 2375 (fig. 27: wind-rose of Pliny).   C.HÜ.

Causa The term *causa* (cause, motive, purpose, legal grounds) is often used to describe the circumstance which explains or justifies a situation. Thus Cicero goes into the question of whether every event can be traced back to a *causa* (Fat., in particular 34), concerns himself with the *causa* of a killing (Rosc. Am. 61) and the *causa* for the receipt of money (Q. Rosc. 40). Typical usages in legal language [1] are:

The legal case itself is called *causa*, e.g. the famous *causa Curiana*, Q. Mucius → Scaevola (Cic. De or. 1,180) [4]. A dispute over money is a *causa pecuniaria*. The *causas dicere*, the address by a party to a trial, is undertaken by a → *causidicus*. The *praetor* does not allow a second trial for the same cause, *de eadem causa*. If he himself (and exceptionally not the *iudex*) examines the circumstances of a case, it is called a *causa cognitio*.

The legal position regarding an article of property is decided *inter alia* on the basis of the *causa* of its acquisition (*causa possessionis*). Acquisition of property by a *iusta causa* (*traditionis*), a circumstance justifying the transfer of ownership (e.g. purchase: *causa emptionis*), becomes ownership immediately upon transfer of the article. If the acquirer has received the article from a source other than the owner he can become its owner by → *usucapio* (usucaption), if, *inter alia*, a *causa usucapionis* is given. The enforceability of a → *stipulatio* can depend upon evidence of the *causa stipulationis* [5] (grounds for the obligation). From this use of the word *causa* comes the term 'causal' for a transaction whose potential effectiveness is based on recognized grounds. On the other hand, transactions that are effective merely by the observance of a formula, even in the absence of a *causa*, are termed 'abstract', e.g. the → *mancipatio*. For Julian, however, even in the case of *traditio*, mere agreement as to the transfer of ownership replaces the *causa* (Dig. 41,1,36 against the prevailing doctrine; e.g. Ulp. Dig. 12,1,18). In the case of *usucapio*, many jurists (e.g. Neratius Dig. 41,10,5) allow that pardonable belief in the existence of a *causa* is sufficient to establish legal ownership ('putative title')[2].

Even after effective acquisition of the article, the *causa* remains significant in determining whether the acquirer may retain the asset. → *Condictio* allows for reimbursement when a payment has been made in error without a *causa* (*condictio indebiti, condictio sine causa*), when the *causa* has unexpectedly failed to materialize (*condictio causa data causa non secuta*, e.g. a dowry when the marriage has failed to be concluded), or when the *causa* is impermissible by statute (*condictio ob turpem vel iniustam causam*, e.g. extortion).

In the law of succession (→ Succession, law of) *causa* provides the grounds for a claim on an asset from the inheritance: *causa testamenti, causa fideicommissi* etc.

In interpretation of the → *lex Aquilia, causam mortis praestare* (*praebere*) [3] describes an act that, although it led to the death of a slave or four-legged herd animal, does not correspond to the sense of the word *occidere* in the 1st chapter of the *lex*: the plaintiff in this case can pursue his claim only by an analogous action (→ *actio in factum*).

1 V. A. GEORGESCU, Le mot *causa* dans le Latin juridique, in: Études de philologie juridique et de droit romain, 1940, 129–239   2 TH. MAYER-MALY, Das Putativtitelproblem bei der usucapio, 1962   3 D. NÖRR, Causa mortis, 1986   4 J. W. TELLEGEN, Oratores, Iurisprudentes and the 'Causa Curiana', in: RIDA 30, 1983, 293–311   5 J. G. WOLF, Causa stipulationis, 1970.   R.WI.

Causality
A. CONCEPT   B. PRE-SOCRATICS   C. PLATO
D. ARISTOTLE   E. STOA

A. CONCEPT

The concept of causality does not begin to take shape until the Middle Ages (Lat. *causalitas*), and is not attested in ancient literature. But, from the beginning, the philosophers and scientists of antiquity reflected on the forms that can be taken by the chain of events (causality in its broadest sense). A particular topic of discussion was the extent to which events in the cosmos are causally linked (principle of causality).

B. PRE-SOCRATICS

In early Greek thought, material objects and things are primarily vehicles for forces and powers. Correspondingly, the principles of pre-Socratic natural philosophy (→ Pre-Socratics; e.g. earth, water or fire) are mainly defined under the aspect of their powers and qualities (Semonides fr. 7 DIEHL; Anaximen. fr. 13 B 1 DK; Heracl. fr. 22 B 76 DK; Parmenides fr. 28 B9 DK; Emp. fr. 31 B 21,1–9 DK; Anaxag. fr. 59 B 15–16 DK). From this perspective, causality has its origin in objects that actualize their kinetic and qualitative dispositions, bringing about an effect in other objects which, in their turn, exhibit dispositions appropriate to the effect to be brought about (Anaximand. fr. 12 B 1 DK; Xenoph. fr. 21 B 30 DK; Emp. fr. 31 B 65, B 67, B 71, B 81, B 98 DK; Anaxag. fr. 59 B 13, B 19 DK). But, at the same time, the pre-Socratic natural philosophers interpreted cosmic events in the light of all-embracing, abstract and sometimes cyclic regular systems. As a consequence of this conception, for an event (so-called αἰτιολογία, *aitiología*) to be declared it had to be classified within a regular cosmic system (Anaximen. fr. 13 B 1 DK; Heracl. fr. 22 B 8; B 51; B 67; B 90; B 126 DK; Emp. fr. 31 B 20; B 22; B 26 DK; Democr. fr. 68 A 135 DK; for *aitiología* Democr. fr. 68 B 118 DK).

Thus it was the pre-Socratic philosophers who developed those great models of causality that have substantially defined later western thinking, and whose interrelationship has always remained as contentious as it has been vital: the model based on agents, according to which an object brings about causal effects in other objects as a function of its dispositions, and the model based on regularity, according to which individual causes and their effects exemplify cosmic regularities. Some pre-Socratic systems (especially → Atomism) have additionally formulated an all-embracing principle of causality, according to which nothing in the cosmos happens without a cause (Leucippus fr. 67 B 2 DK; Aristot. Gen. 789b 2 on Democritus; Diog. Laert. 9,45).

C. Plato

On first sight, Plato appears to occupy an anomalous position in the history of the conception of causality in antiquity. In a famous passage from the 'Phaedon' he rigorously rejects the pre-Socratic conception of causality, and instead relies on the doctrine of forms as a model for the investigation of causes and causality, proposing the following formula: the cause (αἰτία, *aitía*) that an individual object *a* has property *F* is that *a* partakes in the form *F* (Pl. Phd. 96a–101e; although cf. Pl. Ti. 47e–48b). He thus outlines a formal ontological conception of causality: the cause for individual objects being structured and thus identifiable and existent is their relationship to Platonic forms. Upon closer examination, however, this formal model represents an important theoretical step in the history of the concept of causality. For the Platonic forms represent the realm of regularities (moral, mathematical and empirical), and Plato's formula for causality establishes an explicit connection between the dispositions of individual objects and their integration within regular systems: the former being dependent on the latter. This model consequently provides a basis for the unification of the two pre-Socratic models of causality: essentially, Plato proposes that the model based on agents derives from that based on regularity.

D. Aristotle

Aristotle's view is that the most important kinds of answer to questions *why* (*dia ti*) correspond to the most important forms of cause and causal relationship. Answers to questions *why* are statements having the character of demonstrations, i.e. valid syllogisms of the form (i) A applies to every B, (ii) B applies to (every) C → (iii) A applies to (every) C, such that (ii) may be classi-

fied as an Aristotelian cause (efficient or moving cause, final cause, material cause, formal cause) of (iii) (Aristot. Ph. 2,3; 2,7,198a 14–21; Metaph. 1,3,983a 25–32; An. post. 2,11; 1,14; 1,2,71b 9–16, 22–31; 1,13,78a 22–28; Metaph. 7,17). Thus causal relationships always subsist between facts, and essentially between facts having the aspect of actualizations of potentials, i.e. the realization of dispositions (*dynámeis*) belonging to things. The material cause (*hýlē*) explains why particular dispositions are present; the efficient cause explains why the realization of dispositions is set in motion, and the final cause (*télos*) explains the end-form of this process (this is the form of Aristotelian *aitiología*). Causality is therefore the transmission of force or motion (from the mover to the moved) or hypothetical necessity (of material or conditional properties in relation to the end-form of the process) or material necessity (dispositions following from material properties). Causality, however, always depends on regularities; cf. the major premise (i); but it does not necessarily comprise a strict chronology (Aristot. An. post. 2,12). To this extent, Aristotle follows Plato in providing a perfect and consistent unity between the model of causality dependent on regularity and that dependent on agents. But Aristotle is no determinist: not every fact is part of a causal chain. There are contingent facts, and there are contingent causes and effects (the sub-premise (ii) and consequently also the conclusion (iii) of demonstrations may describe contingent, singular facts that might also not have occurred).

E. Stoa

Stoic philosophy imposed rigorous restrictions on the concept of causality in antiquity. The concept of cause is confined to that of efficient physical cause: every cause is a body possessing a particular activity whose causal effect consists in the transference of a motion or kinetic force to another body by physical contact (if necessary via the mediation of the *pneúma*) (Sext. Emp. PH 3,14; SVF II 336, 338–341, 346, 351). An internal potential of the affected body is thereby actualized, and it is for the most part the combination of the external cause (*synaítion*) with the internal cause (*autotelès aítion*) that brings about an effect. So far, the Stoics again seem to be basing their conception on the model of causality dependent upon agents. But this impression is deceptive, for at the same time they tie causality to regularities which work without exception but with necessity. Under the same general conditions, particular causes necessarily bring about the same effects in all situations (the Stoics thus come close to the modern conception of the laws of nature). In the final analysis, this law of causality governs all events in the cosmos without exception, thus linking them in an uninterrupted causal chain (SVF I 89, II 917–925, 945–951, 959 (broadest formulation of the Stoic principle of causality), 1000). This cosmic structure allows inductively supported predictions; however, the Stoics were on the whole sceptical as regards possibilities for the investigation of causes (*aitiología*) (Str. 2,3,8; Gal., Placita Hippocratis et Platonis 348,16ff; 395,12ff.; 400,2ff. MUELLER). Most Stoics sought to avoid the disastrous moral and philosophical consequences of this strict determinism by stressing that the internal cause of an active object secures that object's responsibility for the effect (SVF II 974–1007, especially 974, 979, 984, 1002, 1004).

It is the Stoic conception of causality that had a decisive influence on the development of the concept of causality in modern physics: causality is the transference of an effect between bodies, subject to the natural laws of regularity and without exception determinative of natural events. However, the Stoics always based their thinking on proximate effects via direct physical contact. The most important contribution of late antiquity to the history of the concept of causality was the Neoplatonic assault on the principle of proximate effect. The possibility of remote effects was postulated against a background of mystic and religious experiences, and was to play a significant role in modern physics (Iambl. at Simpl. Cat. 302. 29).

J. BARNES, The Presocratic Philosophers, 2 vols., 1979; W. DETEL, Aristoteles, Analytica Posteriora, 2 vols., 1993; H. FRÄNKEL, Dichtung und Philos. des frühen Griechentums, 1962; M. FREDE, The Original Notion of Cause, in: M. SCHOFIELD, M. BURNYEAT, J. BARNES (ed.), Doubt and Dogmatism: Studies in Hellenistic Philosophy, 1980; M. HOSSENFELDER, Stoa, Epikureismus und Skepsis (Gesch. der Philos. 3), 1985; A. A. LONG, Hellenistic Philosophy, 1986; J. MORAVCSIK, What Makes Reality Intelligible? Reflections on Aristotle's Theory of Aitia, in: L. JUDSON (ed.), Aristotle's Physics: A Collection of Essays, 1991; K. REICHS, Der histor. Ursprung des Naturgesetzbegriffes, in: FS E. Kapp, 1958; S. SAMBURSKY, Das physikalische Weltbild der Ant., 1965; R. SORABIJ, Necessity, Cause and Blame, 1980; Id., Causation, Laws and Necessity, 1980; Id., Matter, Space and Motion: Theories in Ambiguity and Their Sequel, 1988; G. VLASTOS, Plato's Universe, 1975, ch. 1. W.DE.

Causidicus A court orator who appears in court as a champion of a party. Whilst Cic. De or. 1,202 uses the term in an obviously derogatory sense as being distinct from a true orator, and whilst a similar evaluation is evident in Gai. Dig. 1,2,1 (*causas dicentibus*), *causidicus* is later applied in inscriptions (CIL 5,5894) and constitutions as a neutral vocational title alongside (Cod. Iust. 2,6,6) or identical (Cod. Theod. 2,10,5) to → *advocatus*. As such, a *causidicus* belonged to the state controlled professional association (Cod. Iust. 2,7,11, 1) of orators appearing in court. The original disparagement was due to the alleged lack of oratorical skills attributed to the *causidicus* (Cic. Or. 30) and the dearth of legal knowledge (Sen. Apocol. 12). His main task was to plead a case for which he for his part quite often required legal assistance (Quint. Inst. 12,3,2). After the disappearance of the *ius respondendi* under Diocletian, the prestige and social standing of the *cau-*

sidicus rose, and this goes hand in hand with a better legal education — at least in the east.
→ Defensor

KASER, RZ, 454; F. WIEACKER, Recht und Ges. in der Spätant., 1964, 83ff. C.PA.

Cauterization Therapeutic intervention in human and veterinary medicine, consisting of the causing of a 'burn' on the surface of the body using two different techniques with their respective indications: a burn in the actual sense by means of an iron made red-hot on coals, then by means of a lamp-wick (*mýkēs*, e.g. Hippoc. De internis affectionibus 212,14 L.); it was used to make the tissue contract. In this way it was said that a mechanical repair of fractures was achieved [3. 164–165], or in the case of a poisonous bite or sting, the poison in the wound was destroyed (cf. [Dioscorides], Theriaca, praef.). Cauterization was however used particularly in surgery if haemostasis was indicated; after putting on a tourniquet towards the heart, it could be efficiently performed through the burning of the ends of the blood vessels (representations of cauteries in the Arabic manuscripts of Abul Qassim [4]; cauterization scenes in the Turkish manuscripts of Šaraf-ad-dīn ibn 'Alī [1. 182–183]). On the other hand, cauterization involved the use of caustic plasters at certain points on the body to treat internal diseases: the idea was to induce irritation and in this way hyperaemia, that was said to make a substance distributed in the organism rise up from the inside to the surface of the body and become concentrated in one place; this substance was — about up to the time of Plato (1st half of the 4th cent. BC, see below) — the pathogenic substance, then later one of the fluids of the physiological system. The caustic substances were irritant plants (mustard, squill, hellebore) or the *kantharis*, an epispastic insect that cannot be defined more precisely [2. 222–243].

Traces of this very ancient (from the Stone Age?) and not specifically Greek form of treatment that was often used in connection with cutting [2. 149–154], were then particularly likely to survive in treatises from the time of Hippocrates that are known to have a Cnidian orientation (→ Chrysippus [3]). It had to compete with the removal of the pathogenic substance by vomiting or purgation. Cauterization was limited from about the time of Plato (Pl. Resp. 3, 406d; 4, 426b; Phdr. 268b; see also [Aristot.] Probl. 1, 32, 34) to extreme cases ([Hippoc.] Aphorismi 7, 87); at the same time the mentality of the Greeks was such that they rejected cauterization by means of the iron, which they attributed to the Scythians ([Hippoc.] De aere, aquis, locis 20) and Libyans (Hdt. 4, 187). Cauterization was also practized in Roman times (Celsus 3,21,9) and continued in the surgical tradition of the Byzantines, Arabs and the Occident.

1 D. BRANDENBURG, Islamic Miniature Painting in Medical Manuscripts, 1982 2 G. LORENZ, Ant. Krankenbehandlung in histor.-vergleichender Sicht, 1990

3 G. MAJNO, The Healing Hand, 1975   4 M. S. SPINK, G. L. LEWIS, Albucasis, On Surgery and Instruments, 1973.

E. KIND, s.v. καυτήρ, RE 11, 93f.; Id., s.v. Kauterisation, RE 11, 94–99.   A.TO.

Cautes, Cautopates (Καύτης, Καυτοπάτης; *Kaútēs, Kautopátēs*). Antithetical pair of companions of → Mithras, associated with a large number of attributes, e.g. burning torches [1]. The etymology is disputed, the most plausible being the derivation from old Iranian **kaut* 'young' [2]. Already the earliest iconographic representation displays them as complementary opposites [3]. They are the 'twin brothers' who are nourished by Mithras' water miracle (Mithraeum of Santa Prisca, Rome). The only literary documentation (Porph. de antro Nympharum 24 with conjecture *Arethusa*, p. 24,14f.; cf. [4]) associates *Cautopates* with the north and with cold (death/*génesis*), *Cautes* with the south and with heat (life/*apogénesis*) [5]. However, on c. 50 reliefs, on which *Cautes* is pictured to the left, *Cautopates* to the right, *Cautes* points to the rising sun, while *Cautopates* points to the setting sun.

→ Mithras

1 J. R. HINNELLS, The Iconography of Cautes and Cautopates: the Data, in: Journal of Mithraic Studies 1, 1976, 36–67   2 M. SCHWARTZ, Cautes and Cautopates, the Mithraic Torchbearers, in: J. R. HINNELLS (ed.), Mithraic Studies 2, 1975, 406–423   3 M. J. VERMASEREN, Corpus Inscriptionum et Monumentorum Religionis Mithriacae, 1956–60, 2269 (c. AD 100)   4 L. SIMONINI, L'antro delle ninfe, 1986, 70, 2f.   5 R. HANNAH, The Image of Cautes and Cautopates in the Mithraic Tauroctony Icon, in: M. P. J. DILLON (ed.), Rel. in the Ancient World: New Themes and Approaches, 1996, 177–192.   R.GOR.

Cautio (from *cavere*). A conditional promise of payment in the form of a → *stipulatio*, to secure a right. If this promise is linked to a pledge (→ *pignus*) or a → surety, then it is also called a → *satisdatio*. For Roman legal praxis, *cautiones* were a tried and tested means to anticipate future problems.

By Roman procedural law, legal representatives could act only as independent parties to a case, so that the verdict was pronounced for or against them (Gai. Inst. 4,86). For this reason, if the defendant was represented, the plaintiff ensured by means of a *cautio iudicatum solvi* (Dig. 46,7) that the verdict would be enacted should it be in his favour; the defendant in his turn, if the plaintiff was represented, had recourse to a *cautio ratam rem (dominum) habiturum* (Dig. 46,8), to ensure that he would not be exposed to a further action. Surrender of the disputed article to whoever turned out the victor could be achieved by means of the so-called sponsion procedure (→ *rei vindicatio*) by *cautio pro praede litis et vindiciarum*. Should an action for surrender of an article not succeed because the defendant had without his fault lost the article, but it could be foreseen that it would return to him, he could be required to promise to surrender it then to the plaintiff (*cautio de restituendo*: Dig. 4,2,14,5). In the time of Justinian the defendant had to promise by *cautio iudicio sisti* (Inst.4,11,2) to be present during the entire proceedings.

A person who by → *emancipatio* had left the household, but nevertheless wished to share in the inheritance along with the → *sui heredes*, had to guarantee by *cautio* that he would bring his own assets into the sum to be divided. An heir could require from a legatee an undertaking to pay compensation should the heir otherwise not be left with at least one quarter of the inheritance (→ *beneficium legis Falcidiae*). Conversely, conditional or fixed-term legatees could require from the heir a delaying *cautio legatorum servandorum causa*. Should a person be bequeathed an asset on condition that he *not* do something (e.g. remarriage clause), it was often only by his death that it could be established whether he had a claim. This situation was remedied by the *cautio Muciana* (according to Q. → Mucius Scaevola, Dig. 35,1,7 pr.): the legatee's claim was immediately validated, but he had to promise to return the asset to the estate if he should ever act contrary to the bequest.

By the *cautio rei uxoriae* (Dig. 24,3,56) the bridegroom promised to return the dowry (→ *dos*) if the marriage should ever be dissolved. A guardian guaranteed his ward's indemnity by means of the *cautio rem pupilli salvam fore* (Dig. 46,6). Partners undertook the internal balancing of expenditure by *cautio* (Dig. 17,2,67 pr.).

If a property should present a danger, e.g. from a building in danger of collapse, the endangered neighbour could demand a *cautio damni infecti*, by which, should the danger come about, he could demand compensation without having to prove that the property owner was at fault. A usufructuary (→ *usus fructus*) had to guarantee by *cautio usufructuaria* (Dig. 7,9) to return the article undamaged to its owner.

The word *cautio* can also mean certificate, promissory note.

→ Stipulatio; → Satisdatio

R. KNÜTEL, Der mehrfache Verfall von Kautionen, in: ZRG 92, 1975, 130–161; J. M. RAINER, Bau- und nachbarrechtliche Bestimmungen im klass. röm. Recht, 1987, 97–151.   R.WI.

Cavades

[1] C.I. Sassanid king from AD 488, son of → Perozes. After he had first played individual powerful families off against each other, he supported the social-religious movement of → Mazdac in order to destroy the power of the aristocracy. This led in 496 to a conspiracy of the Zarathustrian clergy with the higher nobility, in the course of which C.'s brother Zamasphes was elevated to the throne whilst he himself disappeared in the 'castle of oblivion'. C. managed however to escape to the Hephthalites and with their help he won back sovereignty in 499. Financial obligations towards his allies drove him to a war against eastern Rome that ended in

505/06 with a limited peace. In the later years of his government a drastic change occurred with regard to the Mazdacites: Probably at the instigation of his third son Chosroes, C. authorized the annihilation of Mazdac and his followers around 528/29. C., who died in September 531, did not experience the end of the war with Byzantium that broke out shortly before this (PLRE 2, 273f.).

[2] **C. II. Scheroes.** Sassanid king, son of → Chosroes [I 6] II who in early 628 heeded the urgings of dissatisfied nobles to remove his father from office and murder him. He died after several months, presumably of the plague (PLRE 3A, 276f.).

A. LIPPOLD, s.v. Zamasphes, RE 9A, 2308f.; K. SCHIPP-MANN, Grundzüge der Gesch. des sasanidischen Reiches, 1990; E. YARSHATER, Mazdakism, in: CHI 3(2), 1983, 991–1024.   M.SCH.

Cavalcade Painter Main master of the 'Gorgoneion group' active around 580 BC, a group of painters involved in → Corinthian vase painting who mainly decorated bowls and kraters; they are named after a frequent motif of the pictures inside the bowls. The outside of bowls painted by the Cavalcade Painter (CP) mostly show friezes with horsemen (hence the name), battle scenes and animal friezes; one example showing the 'suicide of Ajax' rich with inscriptions of names (Basle, AM, BS 1404). The kraters show friezes with horsemen, battle scenes, rows of chariots and animal friezes. The nine works by the CP are regarded as amongst the best of his time. It has been ascertained that they were found in Aegina and Kameiros (Rhodes).

AMYX, CVP, 197f.; AMYX, Addenda, 57; B. KREUZER (ed.), Frühe Zeichner 1500—500 v.Chr., exhibition catalogue Freiburg, 1992, 31f., no. 21.   M.ST.

Cavalry
I. ANCIENT ORIENT   II. GREECE   III. ROME

I. ANCIENT ORIENT
A. HISTORY   B. EQUIPMENT, TACTICAL DEPLOYMENT

A. HISTORY
With the development of the skill of driving teams of horses in the 1st half of the 2nd millennium BC, the methodological foundations of riding also were in place (→ Horse III, → Horsemanship). Although there is definite evidence of mounted messengers and scouts from as early as the 14th/13th cents. BC onwards (Akkado-gram ^LÚPETHALLUM 'rider' in Hittite texts; Egyptian pictorial evidence [10]), the use of the cavalry as an armed force did not develop until during the 9th/8th cents. Decisive in this was the difficulty of fighting while riding: whereas the → war chariot made possible a division of duties between the driver and the archer, the mounted archer had to control his horse while at the same time → bow-shooting.

According to the evidence of Assyrian palace reliefs (cf. especially [1; 2]) the oldest phase of military riding, which is tangible through inscriptions from Tukultī-Ninurta II (891–884) and through images from Assur-naṣirpal II (884–859), is still characterized by a division of duties: following the model of war chariots, teams of two were formed as the smallest tactical unit in which the horse of the archer was guided by the accompanying rider, who was equipped with sword and shield and later with a spear. These teams of two were used together with war chariots; in the middle of the 9th cent. the ratio was 1 : 1, which by the 2nd half of the 8th cent. had shifted more and more in favour of the cavalry. The change from a team of two to two riders who, although still paired, are fighting independently of each other is first encountered under Tiglatpileser III (745–727); however, this developmental step obviously first required that the bow be dispensed with, as both riders only used the spear as their weapon of attack.

The transition to the independent mounted archer was ultimately made possible by a tassel strap that, particularly well visible on reliefs of Assurbanipal (669–631), but already introduced at the time of Sargon II (722–705), was attached to the reins as one would a martingale; the weight of the tassel strap maintained the horse's dependence on the snaffle bit (and in this way control over the horse) for as long as the rider had to manipulate the bow with both hands [5. 136]. Together with the greater mobility of the rider (especially in mountainous terrain), this innovation finally ensured the superiority of the cavalry over the light war chariot, the military use of which became obsolete at about the same time.

Although the sources illuminate particularly the Assyrian conditions, the relevant Assyrian and indigenous reports (Attic, hieroglyphic Luwian, Urartian) let us assume that in the contemporary states within Syria and Asia Minor, there was a parallel or sometimes even faster development of the cavalry. The latter applies particularly to → Urartu, the high mountain landscape of which was very unsuitable for the use of war chariots and thus favoured the military cavalry. According to the evidence of Urartian inscriptions, the number of war chariots taking part in campaigns was negligible already in 800 BC, while the cavalry contingent made up a good 40% of the total mobilized army [6. 458]. It is therefore probable that Urartu played a key role in the origin and development of the ancient Oriental cavalry.

The fact that, from an evolutionary point of view, the cavalry derives from the use of the war chariot refutes at the same time the earlier theory (e.g. [4. 218f.]) that the military cavalry was adopted from Iranian 'mounted peoples'. Furthermore, in view of the comparatively late appearance of the → Cimmerii and → Scythians in the Near East (from the end of the 8th and the 2nd half of the 7th cent. respectively) and of diverse ancient Oriental influences on Scythian culture, one ought to assume today that their military cavalry tradition did not develop until it came into contact with

Urarṭu and Assyria [8. 307–312]. The cavalry of the
→ Medes that, according to Hdt. 1,73,3, is said to have
learnt the art of archery (on horseback) from the Scythians, and that is succeeded by the Persian cavalry (cf.
Str. 11,13,9) obviously also stood in the ancient Oriental tradition (on the Persian cavalry see also [3. 300–
304]). The same certainly also applies to the cavalry of
the Lydians (→ Lydia) that was equal to the Persian cavalry (Hdt. 1,27; 1,79 f.) and probably linked up with the
cavalry of the Luwian states of Asia Minor (Tabal,
Tuwana, Adana; → Asia Minor III C.; cf. [11. 121²⁴⁵])
and the cavalry of the → Phrygians, on which there is
still insufficient information (but this is presumably
only because of the vagaries of transmission).

B. EQUIPMENT, TACTICAL DEPLOYMENT

The Assyrian cavalryman originally sat on the bare
back of his horse, barefoot and—apart from his helmet
—without special protective clothing. A horse blanket
and boots, occasionally observable amongst the Assyrians' enemies as early as the 9th cent., only gained general acceptance from the end of the 8th cent.
onwards. Use of coat of mail and knee protection is
attested from the 2nd half of the 8th cent. and the beginning of the 7th cent. respectively. The mounted archer
of the 7th cent. was additionally armed with a short
sword and a short spear [5. fig. 78].

As in the case of the war chariot, the most important
duties of the cavalry included enemy reconnaissance,
securing the rear and flanks of their own infantry and
particularly the pursuit of the defeated enemy. However, because of the unstable balance of the cavalryman,
who rode without stirrups, the cavalry was suitable neither for a frontal attack on a well-organized infantry
nor for close combat; this also applies to the Persian
cavalry of the 5th/4th cents. (Xen. Hell. 3,4,14; Xen.
An. 1,10,13; 3,2,18). The main elements of fighting tactics, which were likewise adopted from the war chariot,
were 'attack, turn and retreat' (Akkadian aṣû seḫru u
târu); they therefore also were an essential part of the
training of horse and rider [7. 84 f., l.173] (cf. in this
regard Xen. Eq. 7,17; 8,12). The particular purpose of
the hasty retreat was to entice the enemy cavalrymen
into the immediate proximity of one's own infantry (cf.
Hdt. 4,128,3). Depictions of mounted archers on Assyrian reliefs almost exclusively show the arrows being
shot forward; shooting backwards ('→ Parthian shot')
however, which Xen. An. 3,3,10 attests for the Persian
cavalry, is pictorially represented already at the time of
Assurnaṣirpal II (884–859) (cf. the figures [4. 220] and
generally [9]).

1 R.D. BARNETT, Assyr. Palastreliefs, 1960   2 Id.,
M. FALKNER, The Sculptures of Tiglath-Pileser III, 1962
3 P. HÖGEMANN, Das alte Vorderasien und die Achä-
meniden, 1992   4 K. JETTMAR, Die frühen Steppenvöl-
ker, 1965   5 M.A. LITTAUER, J.H. CROUWEL, Wheeled
Vehicles and Ridden Animals in the Ancient Near East,
1979   6 W. MAYER, Politik und Kriegskunst der Assyrer,
1995   7 Id., Sargons Feldzug gegen Urartu, in: MDOG
115, 1983, 65–132   8 R. ROLLE, Urartu und die Reiter-

nomaden, in: Saeculum 28, 1977, 291–336   9 M. RO-
STOVTZEFF, The Parthian Shot, in: AJA 47, 1943, 174–187
10 A.R. SCHULMAN, Egyptian Representations of Horsemen and Riding in the New Kingdom, in: JNES 16, 1957,
263–271   11 F. STARKE, Ausbildung und Training von
Streitwagenpferden, 1995.   F.S.

II. GREECE

In the time of Homer, horse-breeding was a luxury
which only the → aristocracy could afford; accordingly,
horses were a symbol of their social rank (→ Aristokratia). Unlike in the Oriental empires, especially
Assyria, horses in Greece were only used for transportation to the battlefield; the actual battle was fought on
foot. There are, however, unclear references to a greater
significance of the cavalry in pre- and protogeometric
times. The representations on vases from the early 7th
cent. BC confirm this finding for the archaic period
[3. 13]: as a rule, there was no actual cavalry (but see
[6. 21 ff.]). Of course, there also were regions already in
archaic times that provided favourable preconditions
for breeding and in which the use of horses for warfare
was widespread. Especially Thessaly and Macedonia,
but also Boeotia and western Greece, had famous cavalry troops even at that time, and also later; about their
size and organization however we know very little
[6. 29 ff.]. Athens and the city states on the Peloponnese
on the other hand had only a small cavalry, if any
[2. 1 ff.]. Terrain that often was unsuitable for horses,
their expensive upkeep, the rise of the phalanx and the
social development with this, as well as the high regard
for hoplites all put tight constraints on the use of a cavalry; to this we probably have to add that horses were
hard to control and inadequately protected during a
battle (Xen. Eq. 12,8 f.).

Between 480 and 430 BC Athens built up a cavalry
with a maximum authorized strength of 1,200 men,
200 of whom were → hippotoxótai [2. 39 ff.; 5. 9 ff.];
the cavalry was led by two hipparchs (Xen. Hipp. 1,2;
9,3; Aristot. Ath. Pol. 61,4 f.). It was armed with jave-
lins (Xen. Hipp. 1,21). Xenophon considered it necessary to select horses for the cavalry carefully, and to
intensively train cavalrymen and horses in preparation
for military deployment (Xen. Hipp. 1,3 f.; 1,13;
8,1 ff.). In the 4th cent. BC, Athens is said to have spent
40 talents a year on the pay for the cavalry (Xen. Hipp.
1,19). Because many of the cavalry's rich members took
sides in favour of the tyranny of the Thirty (→ Triakonta) its reputation deteriorated after 403 BC. In the
same period Boeotia had a cavalry of 1,100 men.

Even though the cavalry was very advantageous for
→ phalanx tactics (flank protection, flank attack, mobility in territorial defence, reconnaissance and pursuit), the military role it played in the 5th and early 4th
cent. BC generally was a secondary, but often not a
negligible one. Not until Philip II of Macedonia [4] and
Alexander [4] the Great did the cavalry develop into an
autonomous fighting force [6. 153 ff.; 4]. Between 359
and 336 BC Philip II [4] increased the size of the Mace-

donian cavalry from 600 to 1,800 or even 3,300 men (Diod. Sic. 16,4,3; 17,17,4 f.); recruits came from the Macedonian nobility and the landowners. It probably was already Philip, who for attack purposes arranged, the cavalry into a spearhead formation (Ael. Tact. 18,4; cf. Asclepiodotus 7,3; Arr. Tact. 16,6) that was very effective in the battle of Chaeronea in 338 BC (Diod. Sic. 16,86,3 f.). Under Alexander, as under the → Diadochi, the heavy cavalry was used as a weapon of attack, the strike power of which was often decisive in battle; the riders of this heavy cavalry were called → *hetaíroi*. The cavalrymen's weapons differed according to their tasks: the *hetairoi* normally wore a breastplate, helmet, cavalry sarissa (→ Sarissa) and a sword [6. 156].

→ Armies; → Hippeis; → Horse; → Prodromoi

1 J.K. Anderson, Ancient Greek Horsemanship, 1961 2 G.R. Bugh, The Horsemen of Athens, 1988 3 P.A.L. Greenhalgh, Early Greek Warfare, 1973 4 HM 2, 408 ff. 5 I.G. Spence, The Cavalry of Classical Greece, 1993 6 L.J. Worley, The Cavalry of Ancient Greece, 1994.   LE. BU.

III. Rome

According to Livy, the cavalry in early Rome is said to have consisted of 300 aristocrats who were able to stable a horse (Liv. 1,13,8); they made up the *ordo equester* (→ *equites Romani*, cf. Cic. Rep. 2,36). Later the cavalry was increased to 1,800 men (Liv. 1,43,8 f.) who were divided up into 18 *centuriae* and who received public support for the upkeep of their horses (*equites equo publico*). From the late 3rd cent. BC onwards, 300 cavalrymen belonged to each → legion (Pol. 2,2,4); the cavalry units, 10 → *turmae* with 30 cavalrymen, each were answerable to a → *decurio* (Pol. 6,25,1; cf. also Veg. Mil. 2,14; for pay and rations cf. Pol. 6,39).

As early as before the 2nd Punic War (end of the 3rd cent. BC) the → *socii*, the allied Italic cities and peoples, supplied relatively large contingents of cavalrymen. In addition the cavalry of allied rulers or peoples outside of Italy became increasingly important: at the battle of Zama in 202 BC Cornelius [I 71] Scipio Africanus used not just the Italian cavalry but also Numidian cavalrymen under → Massinissa (Liv. 30,33,2; 30,33,13; 30,35,1 f.); the final mention of cavalry of the Latin or Italic allies refers to the war against → Jugurtha (Sall. Iug. 95,1). The Numidian and Spanish cavalry were in particularly high regard; Caesar recruited Gallic and Germanic cavalrymen during the conquest of Gaul in 58–52 BC; in the battles for Alesia in 52 BC the Germanic cavalry made a decisive contribution to Caesar's victory (Caes. B Gall. 1,15,1; 6,4,6; 6,43,1, 7,13,1; 7,34,1; 7,65,4; 7,88). In 42 BC several thousand cavalry, particularly from Gaul, Spain, Thessaly and Thrace, belonged to the army of Junius [I 10] Brutus and Cassius [I 10] (App. B Civ. 4,88).

Augustus incorporated the troops from the provinces into the Roman army as → *auxilia*; the cavalry

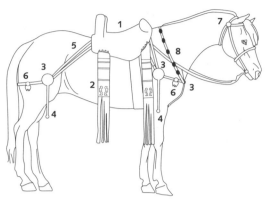

Roman riding-harness; reconstruction (1st cent. BC).

1. Saddle	5. Strap loops (haunch straps)
2. Girth fittings	6. Pendant
3. Strap junction	7. Simple ornamental mountings
4. Pendant strap fittings	8. Melon beads

units — the *alae* (→ *ala* [2]) — each consisted of 480–500 men whose commander was a *praefectus* from the *ordo equester*. The *alae miliariae* with a strength of 800–1,000 cavalrymen had probably been existing since Flavian times and developed into elite units of the cavalry. Other units, the *cohortes equitatae* (→ *cohors*), consisted simultaneously of infantry and cavalry that however probably operated independently of each other during a battle. In the legions too there were riders, who were recruited from the legionary soldiers and mainly served as messengers, scouts or escorts. According to Flavius Josephus [2], each legion of the army of Titus outside Jerusalem had 120 cavalrymen; it however is unclear whether this also applies to the other Roman legions (Ios. Bell. Iud. 3,120). Cavalry of the auxiliary troops could also be detached to serve as bodyguards for high-ranking officers in the provinces (*equites singulares*); the *princeps* himself had a mounted bodyguard (*equites singulares Augusti*).

In the first two cents. AD the cavalry would before a battle be lined up on the flanks; its tactical duty was to support the infantry and to cover the flanks of the legions. From the 3rd cent. onwards the cavalry took on a more strongly offensive role; Gallienus (253–268) appears to have created a special cavalry unit which had its own commander and which, at least part of the time, was stationed in Mediolanum (now Milan) (Zos. 1,40,1). Under Diocletian (284–305) the number of cavalrymen was increased; at the same time new units were created (*vexillationes*) that presumably had a strength of 500 men and were deployed both in the field forces (→ *comitatenses*) of Constantine and in the territorial troops (→ *limitanei*). In the late 3rd cent. *cunei* of cavalry (*cuneus*: literally 'spearhead') were also stationed along the Danube border.

During the principate, the equipment of Roman cavalrymen consisted of a → helmet, → armour, → shield, → sword and a lance or spear. In addition to the regular cavalry, units of mounted archers and camel riders (→ *dromedarii*) were set up; in late antiquity in particular, the military superiority of the Roman cavalry was based on the use of archers on horseback (Procop. Goth. 1,27,27–29). In the 2nd cent. the Romans also adopted the idea of armoured cavalry whose horses also wore armour (*catafractarii*, → *katáphraktoi*; *clibanarii*). The Roman cavalrymen did not use stirrups but sat on skilfully constructed saddles that were attached to the horse with several belts in such a way that they could not slip.

Hadrian, who in 128 stationed Roman troops in North Africa, gave an address in which he praised the manoeuvres of the cavalry units in great detail (ILS 2487; 9134). Arrian described the training exercises of the cavalry (Arr. Tact. 32,3–44).

Pictorial representations of Roman cavalry are to be found on countless tomb reliefs of members of the *alae* (Cologne, RGM: tombstones of Romanus and T. Flavius Bassus, CIL XIII 8305; CIL XIII 8308 = ILS 2512; Bonn, RL: tombstone of Vonatorix; Mainz, Landesmuseum: tombstone of C. Romanius, CIL XIII 7029; cavalryman with bow and arrow: tombstones of Flavius Proclus and of Maris).

→ Weapons; → Armies; → Horse

2   1 K. DIXON, P. SOUTHERN, The Roman Cavalry, 1992
2 A. HYLAND, Equus: The Horse in the Roman World, 1990   3 Id., Training in the Roman Cavalry, 1993
4 M. JUNKELMANN, Die Reiter Roms, 3 vols., 1990–1992
5 L. KEPPIE, The Making of the Roman Army, 1984.   J.CA.

Cavarillus Celtic name compound from *cavar* 'powerful, strong' [1. 331–332]. Noble Aeduan, as a successor of → Litaviccus in 52 BC commander of an infantry contingent of his tribe for Caesar. C. defected to Vercingetorix and was captured in battle together with Cotus and → Eporedorix (Caes. B Gall. 7,67,7).

1 EVANS.

H. BANNERT, s.v. C., RE Suppl. 15, 87–88.   W.SP.

Cavarinus Celtic name compound (see Cavarillus). King of the Senones, appointed by Caesar as a successor to his brother Moritasgus. In 54 BC, condemned to death by his own tribe, he had to flee. A year later he did, however, again lead a Senonian cavalry contingent on Caesar's side against → Ambiorix (Caes. B Gall. 5,54,2; 6,5,2).   W.SP.

Cavarus, Cauarus (Καύαρος; *Kaúaros*). Last king of the Celtic realm in East Thrace with capital in → Tyle in the late 3rd cent. BC (Pol. 4,46,4). Numerous finds of bronze coins, of which several nominals and types were issued, caused a renewed discussion of the location and nature of his kingdom in recent research [1. 7–15; 2]. C.'s silver coins were minted in → Cabyle [3]. Polybius praised C.'s achievements: he safeguarded merchant shipping in the Black Sea, supported Byzantium in 220

BC in a war against Rhodes and effected a peace (Pol. 4,52,1–2; 8,22).

1 L. LAZAROV, The Problem of the Celtic State in Thrace, in: Bulgarian Historical Review 21/2–3, 1993, 3–22
2 M. DOMARADZKI, La diffusion des monnaies de Cavaros au Nord-Est de la Thrace, in: Eirene 31, 1995, 120–128
3 D. DRAGANOV, The Minting of Silver Coins of Cabyle and of King Cavarus, in: Études Balkaniques 20/4, 1984, 94–109.

K. STROBEL, Die Galater, vol. 1, 1996, 233–236.   U.P.

Cavea ('hollow'). 1. Animal cage, beehive. 2. Grid rack placed by fullers over coal fires to dry materials. 3. Terrace-shaped rising seating area in the → amphitheatre, → odeum and → theatre, also common as a public meeting place (e.g. Athens, Pnyx). In larger facilities divided by ambulatories into *prima*, *media* and *summa cavea* that were allocated to various groups of people.

W. A. MCDONALD, The Political Meeting Places of the Greeks, 1943; J. A. HANSON, Roman Theatre-Temples, 1959; D. B. SMALL, Social Correlations to the Greek Cavea in the Roman Period, in: S. Macready, F.H. Thompson (ed.), Roman Architecture in the Greek World, 1987, 85–93; W. WURSTER, Die Architektur des griech. Theaters, in: Ant. Welt 24, 1993, 20–42.   C.HÖ.

Cave sanctuaries Cave sanctuaries existed in antiquity in two contexts in particular: firstly as 'sacred caves' of the Bronze Age and Neolithic cultures, as well as of the Minoan palace period in Crete, and secondly as 'initiation caves' in the archaic period and classical Greek periods, later also in the Roman West.

The caves of Minoan Crete in particular have been relatively well researched. Fifteen caves are definitely confirmed there (incl. the caves of Skotinó at Knossos, and the caves of Vernapheto and Kamares), whilst it is assumed that additional caves exist [1. 55ff.]. In the caves, votive offerings were found of clay vessels, grain remnants and animal bones. The best-known cave is probably the so-called 'cave of Zeus' on Cretan Ida. According to mythological traditions of antiquity, Zeus was supposed to have been brought up there by the → Curetes (Str. 10,4,8; Diod. Sic. 5,70,2 and 4; Paus. 5,7,6). A special feature of this cave is that it continued to be frequented in the post-Minoan period, and from the 8th cent. 'sacrificial festivals involving initiation' (male puberty rites) were performed [1. 91].

In the Roman Imperial Age the purpose of the cave sanctuaries of the cult of Mithras was undoubtedly initiation. According to Porph. 6, → Zoroaster, in honour of → Mithras reshaped a natural cave in the mountainous country of Persia so that it resembled an image of the cosmos. Later Roman Mithraic cultic sites were modelled on this — artificial subterranean caves were built or the cave was built into the ground floor of homes wherever soil conditions so dictated (details, [2. 133ff.]).

→ Grotto; → Sanctuary

1 BURKERT   2 R. MERKELBACH, Mithras, 1984.

B. RUTKOWSKI, K. NOWIKKI, The Psychro Cave and Other Grottoes in Crete, 1996.   C.F.

Caystru pedion

[1] (Καύστρου/Καύστριον πεδίον; *Kaÿstrou/Kaÿstrion pedion*). River plain of the → Caystrus [1] from the plain of Kilbis on the upper course of the river (Κιλβιανὸν πεδίον, Str. 13,4,13; Steph. Byz. s.v. Assos) to the west; on its middle or rather lower course was the Ἄσιος λειμών (*Ásios leimṓn*; 'Asian meadow') with flocks of wild geese, cranes, and swans (Hom. Il. 2,461; Cic. Orat. 163; Str. 14,1,45). Mount Tmolus afforded a view on the surrounding plains, including the Caystrou pedion (CP) (Str. 13,4,5); descending from the mountain, the CP was reached near Hypaipa (Str. 13,4,7f.), north of the modern Ödemiş.

L. BÜRCHNER, s.v. Καΰστριανὸν πεδίον, RE 11, 100; Id., s.v. Ephesos, RE 5, 2799–2802; D. KNIBBE, s.v. Ephesos, RE Suppl. 12, 270f.; H.-E. STIER, E. KIRSTEN, Westermann Atlas zur Weltgesch. 1, 19 V.   H.KA.

[2] (Καΰστρου πεδίον; *Kaÿstrou pedion*). 'Inhabited town' (Xen. An. 1,2,11; cf. Xen. Cyr. 2,1,5) in central Phrygia between → Ceramon agora and Thymbrium, undoubtedly in the river plain of the Akar Çay between Afyon and Eber Gölü.

W. RUGE, s.v. K., RE 11, 101.   T.D.-B.

Caystrus

[1] River in Lydia (Καΰστριος; *Kaÿstrios*: Hom. Il. 2,461; Hdt. 5,100; Κάΰστρος; *Káÿstros*: Str. 13,3,2; Arr. Anab. 5,6,4; Mela 1,88), modern Küçük Menderes ('Little Maeander'); it rises on the southern slopes of Mount Tmolus above Coloë (modern Keles near Kiraz); it flows through the plain of Kilbis, then through the → Caystrou pedion [1], absorbs from the right tributaries from Mount Tmolus, from the left those from the Mesogis mountains (modern Cevizli daği) (Plin. HN 5,115), and discharges into the sea north of Ephesus; even in antiquity, the C. filled its estuary with mud deposits (Str. 15,1,16; Plin. loc. cit.) and [1. 6ff.] increasingly cut off Ephesus from the sea (to about 10 km today).

1 F. HUEBER, Ephesos, 1997, with figs. 1, 39, 48, 59.

L. BÜRCHNER, s.v. K., RE 11, 100f.; W.-D. HÜTTEROTH, Türkei, 1982, 64f.; MILLER, 719; A. PHILIPPSON, Top. Karte des westl. Kleinasien, 1910; H.-E. STIER, E. KIRSTEN, Westermann Atlas zur Weltgesch. 1, 19 V.   H.KA.

[2] (Κάΰστρος; *Káÿstros*). River in central Phrygia, not documented in literature, whose name was deduced from the town of → Caystrou pedion (Xen. An. 1,2,11) and the river of the same name (modern Küçük Menderes) between Sardes and Ephesus. Modern Akar Çay, which flows from the Afyon region to Eber Gölü.

W. RUGE, s.v. Phrygia, RE 20, 835.   T.D.-B.

Cebenna mons Mountain range in Gallia (modern Cévennes), separating the Arverni from the Helvii (Caes. B Gall. 7,8; 56).   Y.L.

Cebes (Κέβης; *Kébēs*) from Thebes. Friend of Socrates (Pl. Crit. 45b; Xen. Mem. 1,2,48; 3,11,17); together with his companion Simmias → Socrates' main interlocutor in Plato's '*Phaedon*'. According to Pl. Phd. 61d-e, before coming to Athens C. met the Pythagorean → Philolaus in Thebes, but was himself not a Pythagorean [1]. In Diog. Laert. 2,125 three dialogues (not extant), with the titles *Pínax* ('Painting'), *Hebdómē* ('The Seventh Day') and *Phrýnichos*, are attributed to C.

The dialogue entitled *Pínax* and falsely attributed to C. was probably written during the 1st cent. AD; the first author to attest to it is Lucian (De Mercede Conductis 42; Rhetorum Praeceptor 6). In the dialogue, an anonymous speaker reports how in a sanctuary of Cronus a likewise anonymous old man explained to him a painting on display there, representing in allegorical form the false and the correct path in life. The text enjoyed considerable popularity during the 16th and 17th cents.

1 TH. EBERT, Sokrates als Pythagoreer und die Anamnesis in Platons Phaidon, AAWM 1994 no. 13, 8–10.

EDITIONS: K. PRAECHTER, Cebes, Pinax, 1893; D. PESCE, La tavola di Cebete, 1982.
BIBLIOGRAPHY: J.T. FITZGERALD, L.M. WHITE, The Tabula of Cebes, 1983; R. JOLY, Le Tableau de Cébès et la philos. religieuse, 1963; C.E. LUTZ, S. SIDER, Ps. Cebes, in: Cat. translationum et commentariorum VI, 1986, 1–14; VII, 1992, 299–300; R. SCHLEIER, Tabula Cebetis. Stud. zur Rezeption einer ant. Bildbeschreibung im 16. und 17. Jh., 1973.   K.D.

Cebren (Κέβρην; *Kébrēn*). Town in the Troad, located on two hills, Çal Daği and the Fuğla Tepesi near Akpınarköyü on the middle reaches of the Scamander. On the opposing bank of the river lay Scepsis with whom C. was in perpetual dispute. C. was the residence of one of Priam's illegitimate sons (Hom. Il. 16,738; Str. 13,1,33). It had been founded by Cyme (Ephor. FGrH 239 F 22); earliest pottery finds point to the 7th cent. BC [1. 333]. COOK, however, assumes a foundation from Mytilene [1. 337]. Previously a member of the → Delian League, C. found itself in around 400 BC under the rule of the female Persian *hyparchos* → Mania. In 399 BC, C. was captured by the Spartan Dercylidas (Xen. Hell. 3,1,17–20). In 360/359 BC, the Athenian *strategos* Charidemos occupied the town; however, he soon had to give way again to Persian pressure (Dem. Or. 23,154). Between 310 and 306 BC, → Antigonus [1] brought about a *synoikismós*, joining C. with Alexandria Troas. The continued existence of the settlement is questionable, even though the town was named in the 3rd cent. BC on an honorary decree from Assos (IK, Assos no. 4). ROBERT [2] even assumes a further *synoikismós* for 281 BC with Berytis (Βέρυτις) to the town of Antioch.

1 J. M. COOK, The Troad, 1973   2 L. ROBERT, Études de numismatique grecque, 1951.

W. ORTH, Die Diadochenzeit im Spiegel der histor. Geogr., 1993; W. JUDEICH, Bericht über eine Reise im nordwestl. Kleinasien. SB Berlin 1898, 531ff.; W. LEAF, Strabo on the Troad, 1923.   E. SCH.

Cebriones (Κεβριόνης; *Kebriónēs*). Bastard son of → Priamus, half-brother of → Hector, who makes him his chariot driver after Archeptolemus' death (Hom. Il. 8,318f.). C. participates in the storming of the Greeks' ship camp; the chariot is entrusted to a weaker fighter for this time period (ibid. 12,91ff.). Finally, Patroclus kills C. with the throw of a stone and ridicules him as he falls from the chariot by comparing him with a diver (ibid. 16,737–750).

P. WATHELET, Dictionnaire des Troyens de l'Iliade, Vol. 1, 1988, 677–679.   RE. N.

Cecropis (Κεκροπίς; *Kekropís*). After the phyle reforms of → Cleisthenes [2] the seventh of the 10 phyles of Attica (→ Attica with map); its eponymous hero: → Cecrops. At the time of the 10 phyles, C. comprised 11 (four *asty*, five *mesogeia*, and two *paralia*) demes. From 307/6 to 201/0 BC, Daedalidae, Melite and Xypete changed over to Demetrias. In line with the other Cleisthenian phyles, C. transferred one deme each to the phyles of Ptolemaïs (224/3 BC), Attalis (200 BC), and Hadrianis (AD 127/8). Instead of eight, only six demes appear in the list of prytanes IG II² 1782 of AD 177/8. → Attalus [4]

TRAILL, Attica, xvii, 11f., 20f., 23 no. 11, 28, 50f., 57, 71, 85, 102, 106, 133, table 7; J. S. TRAILL, Demos and Trittys, 1986, 1ff., 134ff.   H. LO.

Cecropius C. was the prefect of a cavalry division (the *ala Dalmatorum*) and participated in the conspiracy against emperor → Gallienus, whom he murdered in AD 268 near Milan (SHA Gall. 14,4; 7ff.; Zos. 1,40,2). PIR² C 595.   T. F.

Cecrops (Κέκροψ; *Kékrops*). Indigenous (Apollod. 3,177) Attic first king, who was revered cultically on the acropolis of → Athens, where his grave also lay (Antiochus-Pherecydes FGrH 333 F 1). The Cecropion (building inscription Erechtheion IG I³ 474,56. 56–63) is presumably identical with the structure at the southwest corner of the Erechtheion, which was taken into consideration during the construction of the temple, and can be dated before the → Persian Wars (Hecatompedon inscription IG I³ 4B, 10–11). An inscription of the Augustan period names a priest of C. from the lineage of the Amynandrides (IG III 1, 1276). At Apollod. 3,177 and in Marmor Parium (FGrH 239 A), C. is called the first king of Athens, and in the king-lists a later invented C. II is found as successor of → Erechtheus (Paus. 1,5,3; Apollod. 3,196 and 204). According

to Philochorus (FGrH 328 F 92 = Euseb. Praep. evang. 10,10,7) C.'s reign began in 1607 BC; he ruled for 50 years according to Philochorus (FGrH 328 F 93). His appearance is thought to have been double-natured (*diphyḗs*) the lower part of his body being in snake form (Eur. Ion 1163–1164; Apollod. 3,177; schol. Aristoph. Vesp. 438; as in Eupolis in the 'Kolakes' fr. 159 PCG V monsters of man and tuna), in the plastic arts C. is shown in purely human form when he is together with the other phyle heroes [2. 1089–1091]. Rationalistic explanations attempt to substantiate his biformity with his bilingualism (he came from the Egyptian Saïs: Philochorus FGrH 328 F 93, schol. Aristoph. Plut. 773) or a change in his being (Plut. Mor. 551ef).

As first king, C. is the founder of numerous civilizing achievements such as monogamy (schol. Aristoph. Plut. 773), funeral rites (Cic. Leg. 2. 63) or the alphabet (Tac. Ann. 11,14,2) and he led people out of the condition of savagery (schol. Aristoph. Plut. 773). In the cultic field C. is attributed with the institution of the worship of → Zeus Hypatus (Paus. 8,2,3) and Kronos (Philochorus FGrH 328 F 97 = Macrob. Sat. 1,10,22) as well as the first image of → Hermes (Paus. 1,27,1); in the political field he is attributed with the uniting of the 12 Attic cities into a community (Philochorus FGrH 328 F 94) and with the first census (Philochorus FGrH 328 F 95). Under his government the inhabitants of Attica were called Cecropides (Hdt. 8, 44), city and landscape Cecropia (Plin. HN 7, 194; Apollod. 3,177) and later too the name retained the lustre of the time-honoured and noble (Lucian. Timon 23; Anth. Pal. 11,319,5). C.'s wife appears as Aglaurus [1], as his daughters Aglaurus [2], Pandrosus and Herse (Paus. 1,2,6; Apollod. 3,180), as his son Erysichthon (Apollod. 3,180), who died during C.'s lifetime and therefore could not take over the rulership (Cranaus as successor, Paus. 1,2,6; at Isoc. Or. 12,126 Erichthonius).

C. plays a certain role in the argument between → Athena and → Poseidon for the Attic land, whether it be as referee (Callim. Fr. 194. 66–68), as witness to Athena's planting of the olive tree (for which the 12 gods decided in her favour, Apollod. 3. 178) or as organizer of the census commanded by an oracle, which owing to the greater number of women has a fortunate outcome for Athena (Varro in Aug. B Civ. 18. 9). Since the Cleisthenian reform (→ Cleisthenes), C. is one of 10 eponymous phyle heroes (Paus. 10,10,1); 11 demes can be attributed to the phyle Cecropis [1. 372]. Sporadic evidence points to other landscapes in Greece, e.g. to Megara (Hsch. s.v. ἐν δ' Αἴθυια), Euboea (Heroon as son of Pandium, Paus. 9,33,1) and to Thrace and Thessalonica (Steph. Byz. s.v. Κεκροπία). His astralization as Aquarius, documented nowhere else, is said in Hyg. Poet. astr. 2,29, to be due to the fact that at the time of C. wine had not yet been invented and water held sway.

1 WHITEHEAD   2 I. KASPER-BUTZ, B. KNITTLMAYER, I. KRAUSKOPF, s.v. K., LIMC 6.1, 1084–1091; fig.: LIMC 6.2, 721–723.   JO. S.

Cecryphalea (Κεκρυφάλεια; *Kekrypháleia*). Island in the Saronic Gulf, presumably the modern Angistri, mentioned in conjunction with the naval battle between Athens and Aegina in 458 BC (Thuc. 1,105; Diod. Sic. 11,78,2; Plin. HN 4,57; Steph. Byz. s.v. Kekryphaleia)

E. MEYER, s.v. Pityonesos, RE 20, 1880f.; PHILIPPSON/ KIRSTEN 3, 45.   H. KAL.

Cedalium (Κηδαλίων, κήδαλον, *Kēdalíōn, kédalon*, which probably describes a tool: 'poker'?). Comes from the island of Naxos, initiates → Hephaestus into the blacksmith's craft at the request of his mother → Hera (schol. Hom. Il. 14,296). On Lemnos, Hephaestus makes C. the leader of blinded → Orion. Sitting on his shoulders, C. leads Orion towards the sun, through whose rays Orion is healed of his blindness (Hes. fr. 148a M-W; Eratosth. Katasterismoi 32; Apollod. 1,4,3). Scarcely more than the title is known of Sophocles' satyr play 'C.'. (TrGF IV fr. 328–333).

R. VOLLKOMMER, s.v. K., LIMC 5.1, 978–979   RE.N

Cedi (Κηδοί; *Kēdoí*). Attic deme of the phyle Erechtheis, two → *bouleutaí*. Its location is uncertain, hardly near Kara (as in [3]), the finding place of the deme decree IG II² 1212, which apparently was released neither by C. nor by Themacus [4. 392]. Epitaphs point to a possible location east of the → Hymettus range, possibly near Koropi: [1. 100 no. 118, 103 no. 137; 2].

1 A. MILCHHOEFER, Antikenbericht aus Attika, in: MDAI(A) 12, 1887, 81–104   2 TRAILL, Attica, 7; 38; 69; 110 no. 61, table 1   3 J.S. TRAILL, Demos and Trittys, 1986, 125   4 WHITEHEAD, Index zur Inschr. IG II² 1212.   H. LO.

Cediae Town in the province of → Numidia, south-east of Mascula, modern Henchir Ounkif. From the time of Diocletian (AD 284–305) at the latest, the administration of the *res publica Cediensium* lay in the hands of *duumviri*. CIL VIII Suppl. 2, 17655. Inscriptions: CIL VIII 2, 10727–10732; Suppl. 2, 17655–17667, 17759.

AAAlg, sheet 39, no. 43; C. LEPELLEY, Les cités de l'Afrique romaine 2, 1981, 401.   W. HU.

Cedon (Κήδων; *Kédōn*).

[1] Athenian, possibly of the → Alcmaeonid family, attempted in vain before 514 BC to topple the tyrannis of the → Peisistratids. This glorious deed was later commemorated at symposia with a → scolion (Aristot. Ath. pol. 20,5).

RHODES, 248.   E. S.-H.

[2] Athenian, under Chabrias he commanded the left wing in the naval battle of Naxos (and Paros) in the autumn of 376 BC, during which he was killed (Ephoros in Diod. 15,34,3–6). However, according to Plutarch (Plut. Phocion 6) Phocion led the left wing, which

is impossible since Phocion, born in 401, was still too young for the office. PA 8281.   BO.D.

Cedreae (Κεδρέαι, also Κεδρεῖαι, Κεδρεαί; *Kedréai, Kedreîai, Kedreaí*). Town in Caria on the eastern end of the Ceramic Gulf, on the island of Şehir adası and on the mainland near Taşbükü. Originally, its population was purely Carian, later Carian-Greek (μιξοβάρβαροι, *mixobárbaroi*, Xen. Hell. 2,1,15). The inhabitants of C. spoke the dialect of Dorian Asia Minor (cf. inscriptions). At the end of the 6th cent. BC, Hecat. mentions C. as a town (FGrH 1 F 248); in the 5th cent., it was a member of the → Delian League (IG I³ 259,5,17). In 406 BC, it was captured by Lysander and its inhabitants enslaved (Xen. loc. cit.). In the Hellenistic period, C. was one of the most important settlements of the Rhodian Peraea in Caria, a *dámos* (→ Demos) within the Rhodian federation. In the 2nd cent. BC, athletic *agones* were held in C. In around AD 70, Vespasianus was honoured in C. [1. 554].

Ruins date from the late classical to Roman times: mighty quays in squared-stone masonry with towers, both on the mainland and the island; on the eastern part of the island the remains of an Apollo temple, a theatre, and dwellings; on its western part an agora (inscriptions); on the mainland a necropolis (chamber tombs, sarcophagi).

1 W. BLÜMEL, Die Inschr. der rhodischen Peraia (IK 38), 1991.

G.E. BEAN, Kleinasien 3, 1974, 165f.; L. BÜRCHNER, s.v. K., RE 11, 111f.; P.M. FRASER, G.E. BEAN, The Rhodian Peraea and Islands, 1954, 67, 69, 81, 96; MAGIE 2, 879, 952f., 1030; L. ROBERT, Ét. Anatoliennes, 1937, 476 fn. 1.   H. KA.

Cedrus (κέδρος, *kédros*, Cedar). This evergreen genus of conifer was common throughout the northern hemisphere during the Cretaceous and Tertiary, but largely died out during the second to last ice age. Only in the Himalayas (*C. deodara*), in Lebanon (only approximately 400 trees left) and Asia Minor (*C. libani = libanotica*, in the Taurus and the Antitaurus), on Cyprus (*C. brevifolia*) and in the Atlas (below 2,700 m, *C. atlantica*) do related species still grow. As early as *c.* 2750 BC, the aromatic and durable wood of the cedar was being exported to Egypt from the Taurus and from Lebanon. Examples of its use were in buildings and sarcophagi, as well as in the temples and palaces of David and Solomon. Its cones fall apart, unlike those of the genera *Pinus* and *Larix*. The resin was used for embalming. According to Hdt. 4,75, Scythian women used a paste containing imported cedar wood as a cosmetic. Dioscorides (1,77 [1. II.76–78] = 1,105 [2. 98ff.]) and Pliny (HN 24,17–20 and *passim*) mention a multitude of medicinal uses. Theophrastus (Hist. pl. 5,7,1–2 and 4) recommends the wood for → shipbuilding and housebuilding (→ Building trade). The Homeric κέδρος (Od. 5,60) is probably a species of juniper.

→ Timber

1 M. WELLMANN (ed.), Pedanii Dioscuridis de materia medica vol. 1, 1908, repr. 1958   2 J. BERENDES (ed.), Des Pedanios Dioskurides Arzneimittellehre übers. und mit Erl. versehen, 1902, repr. 1970.   C.HÜ.

Ceionia

[1] **C. Fabia.** Daughter of Ceionius [3], sister of L. Verus, betrothed to → Marcus Aurelius. The betrothal was dissolved (SHA Aur. 4,5; 6,2) after the death of Hadrian. She was married to Plautius Quintillus, *cos. ord.* 159. After the death of Faustina she tried in vain to marry Marcus Aurelius (SHA Aur. 29,10; PIR² C 612; [1; 2. 246]).

[2] **C. Plautia.** Sister of C. [1]; wife of Q. Servilius Pudens, *cos. ord.* 166 (PIR² C 614).

1 RAEPSAET-CHARLIER no. 205   2 BIRLEY, Marcus Aurelius, ²1988.   W.E.

Ceionius

[1] **C. Commodus, L.** A native of Etruria; senator from the time of Nero; *cos. ord.* 78; governor of Syria from AD 78/79; married to Appia Severa (PIR² C 603) [1. I 308; 2. 45 A. 22].

[2] **C. Commodus, L.** Son of [1]. *Cos. ord.* AD 106 (PIR² C 604). Married to one Plautia, their son being C. [3].

[3] **C. Commodus, L. = Aelius Caesar, L.** Son of [2]. His maternal half-brother was M. Vettulenus Civica Barbarus [3. 845]. Born on 13 January in about AD 103; of his pre-consular career only his praetorship is known (for the year [4. 246]). *Cos. ord.* 136. Adopted by Hadrian after 19 June 136. From then on he bore the name L. Aelius Caesar. He received the *tribunicia potestas*, perhaps from 10 December 136 (no recurrence is attested), and an *imperium proconsulare* (CIL III 4366 = ILS 319). The adoption went through in spite of his being ill (Cass. Dio 69,17,1). *Cos. ord.* II 137; sent to Pannonia in order to familiarize himself with the provinces and with the army; numerous missions came to him there (IG V 1,37; IGR IV 862; I. Magnesia 180). Coins bearing his name RIC II 391ff. 480ff. Returned to Rome owing to his illness; died on 1 January 138. Upon completion of the → Mausoleum Hadriani interred there in 139 (CIL VI 985 = ILS 329). C. was married to one Avidia (RAEPSAET-CHARLIER no. 128); his son was the future → Lucius Verus; his daughters Ceionia Fabia and Ceionia Plautia (PIR² C 605).

[4] **C. Commodus, L.** see → Verus

[5] **C. Silvanus, M.** *Cos. ord.* AD 156. Probably a grandchild of C. [2]; related to C. [3] (PIR² C 610).

1 THOMASSON, Lat.   2 HALFMANN, in: EA 8, 1986   3 ECK, RE Suppl. 14   4 BIRLEY, Marcus Aurelius, ²1988.   W.E.

[6] **C. Iulianus Camenius, M.** In AD 324 *consularis Campaniae;* between 326 and 331 *procos. Africae;* from 10 May 333 until 26 April 334 *praef. urbi* (PLRE 1, 476).

[7] **C. Rufius Albinus.** Son of C. [8]. Born on 14 or 15 March AD 303 (Firm. Mat. Math. 2,29,10); after exile *procos.* of Achaea and Asia; *cos.* (335) and *praef. urbi* (30.12.335 — 10.3.337). Praised as *philosophus* in a laudatory decree of the Senate (ILS 1222). Perhaps the author of a Roman history in verse (Prisc. 7,22, Gramm. Lat. 2,304 KEIL; PLRE 1, 37).

[8] **C. Rufius Volusianus, C.** For eight years from AD 281/283 *corrector Italiae* (ILS 1213 and CIL X 1655); c. 305 *procos. Africae.* Sent to Africa as *praef. praet.* under → Maxentius, in 309 or 310 with a small military force he ended the usurpation of Domitius Alexander (Aur. Vict. Caes. 40,18; Zos. 2,14,2). As a reward, he was *praef urbi* from 28 October 310 — 28 November 311, and in September 311 received the consulship. In spite of his links with Maxentius, after the victory of → Constantinus [1], who was concerned to win over the Senate, he became *comes* to the emperor, again *praef. urbi* (8.12.313 — 20.8.315), and in 314 consul with Petronius Annianus. As a heathen, C. belonged to the priestly colleges of the *XVviri sacris faciundis* and to the *VIIviri epulonum.* C. seems to have fallen out of favour during Constantine's visit to Rome in 315, and to have been sent into exile (PLRE 1, 976).

T.D. BARNES, Two Senators under Constantine, in: JRS 65, 1975, 40–49.   B.BL.

[9] **C. Rufius Volusianus, C.** (in Amm. Marc. and Zos.: Lampadius). In AD 355 *praef. praet. Galliarum* (Zos. 2,55,3). He was involved in the usurpation of → Silvanus (Amm. Marc. 15,5,4f. and 13). In 365 became *praef. urbis Romae* (Cod. Theod. 1,6,5 i.a.). He had his name affixed to many buildings, even when they were not erected by him (Amm. Marc. 27,3,7; CIL VI 1170–1174. 3866). His own construction activities led to uprisings (Amm. Marc. 27,3,8–9). He was a non-Christian (CIL VI 846). One of his sons, Lollianus, was executed for 'sorcery' (Amm. Marc. 28,1,26). A second son was C. [11]. PLRE 1,978–980 no. 5.

[10] **Publilius C. Iulianus.** possibly held the *cura statuarum* in c. AD 354 (CIL VI 1159). Before 370 he was *corrector Tusciae et Umbriae* (CIL XI 4118). He is not to be identified with Emperor Iulianus' uncle (Iulianus) (cf. self-correction in [1]). PLRE 1,476f. no. 27.

1 O. SEECK, Die Briefe des Libanius, 1906, 190.

[11] **Publilius C. Caecina Albinus.** Possibly son to C. [9]. Contemporary and friend of → Symmachus (Ep. 8,25), like whom he was a non-Christian and *pontifex* (if he is the individual referred to in Ep. 107,1 of Jerome). He is one of the main characters in the 'Saturnalia' of → Macrobius (1,2,15). In c. AD 365 he was *consularis Numidiae* (CIL VIII 2242, 2388 i.a.). His wife and his daughter → Laeta were possibly Christians (Jer. Ep. 107,1f.). His son was C. [14], his grandson C. [15]. PLRE 1,34f. no. 8.

[12] **Alfenius C. Iulianus.** (in the Cod. Theod.: Camenius), 343–385. Possibly grandson to [6]; non-Christian (ILS 1264). Perhaps to be identified with the Came-

nius mentioned in Amm. Marc. 28,1,27, prosecuted in *c.* 371 with his brother Tarracius Bassus for 'sorcery', but acquitted. *Consularis Numidiae* (before 381), *vicarius Africae* 381 (Cod. Theod.12,1,84). PLRE 1, 474f. no. 25.

[13] **C. Rufius Albinus.** possibly son to [9]; *praef. urbis Romae* 389–391 (Cod. Theod. 2,8,19; Cod. Iust. 6,1,8; ILS 789). Non-Christian; interlocutor in the 'Saturnalia' of Macrobius (1,2,16), where he is regarded as one of the most learned men of the age (6,1,1). He was still alive in 416 (Rut. Namat. 1,168). PLRE 1,37f. no. 15.

[14] **C. Caecina Decius Albinus.** Son of [11] (Macrob. Sat. 1,2,3). *Consularis Numidiae* (CIL VIII 7034), *procos. Campaniae* AD 398 (Symmachus, Ep. 7,40; 6,23). *Quaestor sacri palatii* or *mag. officiorum c.* 400 (Symmachus, Ep. 7,47.49); *praef. urbis Romae* 402 (Cod. Theod. 7,13,15). Recipient of letters from → Symmachus (Ep. 7,35–41). PLRE 1,35f. no. 10.

[15] **C. Caecina Decius Acinatius Albinus.** Possibly son to [14]. In AD 414 at a young age he was *praef. urbis Romae* (Rut. Namat. 1,466ff.; Cod. Theod. 13,5,38; CIL VI 1659). He asked the emperor for improved provisions of food for Rome (Olympiodor FHG fr. 25). He is probably to be identified with Flavius Albinus, in which case he would have been made *praef. urbis Romae* for a second time in 426 (Cod. Theod. 5,1,7). Fl. Albinus was *praef. praet. Italiae* in 443–449 (Nov. Val. 2,3 i.a.), in 444 *cos. posterior,* from 446 attested as *patricius* (Nov. Val. 21,1). PLRE 2,50f. no. 7.

[16] **C. Rufius Antonius Agrypnius Volusianus.** Son of [14] (Rut. Namat. 1,168). He was *procos. Africae* before AD 412 (ibid. 1,173f.). His Christian mother tried in vain to convert him (Aug. Epist. 123; 136). *Quaestor sacri palatii* (Rut. Namat. 1,171f.), *praef. urbis Romae* 417/8 (Rut. Namat. 1,167ff.; CIL VI 1194, 1661). A further, earlier city prefecture is improbable (PLRE 2,1185). In 428/9 he was *praef. praet. Italiae* (Cod. Theod. 1,10,8; Cod. Iust. 11,71,5). He died a Christian *c.* 437 (Gerontius, vita S. Melaniae, 53–55). PLRE 2, 1184f. no. 6.   W.P.

Ceiriadae (Κειριάδαι; *Keiriádai*). Attic *asty* deme of the phyle Hippothontis, two → *bouleutaí*. Its location outside the wall of Athens west of the Hill of the Nymphs and the Pnyx [2. 51] (today Ano Petralona) is verified by the Βάραθρον (*Bárathron*), a gorge in C., into which those condemned to death were thrown (Anecd. Bekk. 1,219,10) [1].
→ Athens

1 Th. THALHEIM, s.v. Βάραθρον, RE 2, 2853   2 TRAILL, Attica, 51; 69; 110 no. 62, table 8   3 WHITEHEAD, 26, 83.   H.LO.

Ceisus (Κεισός, Κίσσος; *Keisós, Kíssos*). Eldest son of the Heraclid → Temenus, king of Argus, and the brother of → Phalces, Cerynes, Agaius (different at Apollod. 2,179) and → Hyrnetho. When the king prefers Hyrnetho and her husband → Deiphontes over his sons as his

successors, they conspire under the leadership of C. against their father and have him murdered. They, however, are forced from the throne by the army in favour of the legitimate royal couple and are banished from the land (Nicolaus of Damascus FGrH 90 F 30; Diod. Sic. 7,13,1). According to another account, C. succeeds his father after the conspiracy (Paus. 2,19,1).   RA.MI.

Celadon (Κελάδων; *Keládōn*). Tributary of the → Alpheius between Pylos and Arcadia, rising on Mt. Lycaeum — its identification is a Homeric problem (Hom. Il. 7,133–135: Nestor's tale of the fight of the Pylians against the Arcadians 'by the rapid river C. under the walls of Pheia, and round about the waters of the river Iardanus'). Even ancient Homeric philologists tried in vain to determine the location of the C. in the coastal region (cf. Didymus, schol. Hom. Il. 7,135; Str. 8,3,21; cf. also Paus. 8,38,9: Κέλαδος/*Kélados*).   E.O.

Celadus Imperial freedman of the Augustan age (Suet. Aug. 67,1). In *c.* 7–4 BC he unmasked the alleged son of Herod, the false Alexander (Ios. Ant. Iud. 17,332; Bell. Iud. 2,106–110). Perhaps mentioned in CIL VI 23338 and XIV 3524.   D.K.

Celadussae Dalmatian archipelago (Plin. HN 3,152) opposite → Iader. Some of the islands (i.a. the modern Ugljan and Pašman) were included in the centuriation of that colony.

J.J. WILKES, Dalmatia, 1969, 208f.   D.S.

Celaenae (Κελαιναί; *Kelainaí*). Former main town of Phrygia (Liv. 38,13), later founded again as → Apamea [2] by → Antiochus [2] I (Str. 12,8,15); modern Dinar. In C. stood a palace of Xerxes (Xen. An. 1,2,9) with a → *parádeisos* ('game reserve') of Cyrus (Xen. An. 1,2,7); it is named after Celaenus, a son of Poseidon, venerated in C. because of frequent earthquakes (Str. 12,8,18; but the coins of C. depict Zeus and Dionysus Kelaineus). According to legend, Athena invented the flute near C.; the satyr → Marsyas picked it up and dared to challenge Apollo to a flute contest; in punishment, the god flayed him alive. Marsyas supposedly saved C. in 268 BC from being attacked by the Galatians (Paus. 10,30,9). Various authors mention for different periods the following rivers in conjunction with C.: → Menander, → Marsyas, Orgas, Catarrhectes, and Obrimas (the first three with the spring Therma on coins minted by C. during the rule of Gordianus III; for identification [1. 112–125]) as well as the sources Klaion and Gelon.

1 P. CHUVIN, Mythologie et géographie dionysiaques, 1992.

W. RUGE, s.v. K., RE 11, 133f.; MÜLLER, 129–148.
          T.D.-B.

Celaeno (Κελαινώ, *Kelainố*, of κελαινός/'dark').
[1] One of the → Pleiades (Hes. fr. 275,2 RZACH; Ov. Fast. 4,173), by Poseidon mother of Lycus (Apollod. 3,111; Eratosth. Katasterismoi 23) and of Nycteus (Hyg. Poet. Astr. 2,21).
[2] One of the → Harpies living with the Strophades, who predicts to the Aeneads that they would devour their tables before the founding of the city (Verg. Aen. 3,209–258; cf. Val. Fl. 4,453ff.).   C.W.

Celaetha (Κελαίθα; *Kelaítha*). Town, according to a list of *theorodokoi* from Delphi from the 2nd cent. BC, located near → Cierium and Metropolis in south-western Thessaly. Probably not identical with the *vicus Celathara* which the Aetolians seized and plundered in the course of their raid into Dolopia and southern Thessaly in 198 BC (Liv. 32,13,12f.). In contrast, *Kelaíthra* is documented as a Boeotian town 'near Arne' (presumably more likely Cierium in Thessaly) (Steph. Byz. s.v. Κελαίθρα).

> B. HELLY, Incursions chez les Dolopes, in: I. BLUM (ed.), Topographie antique et géographie historique en pays grec, 1992, 48–91, esp. 77ff., 85ff.; F. STÄHLIN, Das hellenische Thessalien, 1924, 133.   HE.KR.

Celeia Modern Célje (Cilli). Settlement in Noricum on the amber trade route near an originally Celtic-Illyrian settlement at the mouth of the Voglajna into the Savinja (Sann). C. owed its early and rapid development to its favourable location on one of the main access routes to the Illyro-Italian gateway. Under the emperor Claudius, it was probably a → *municipium* of the *tribus Claudia* (CIL III 5143; 5227; cf. CIL VI 2382) which, in the middle of the 2nd cent., supplied high-ranking imperial officials [1]. This town, which was surrounded with a wall in the 2nd cent. AD, has only partially been investigated underneath its modern building stock (the forum was probably in the north-west, the artisan quarter in the south-east). Floods in the second half of the 3rd cent. led to a reduction in its size and enclosure by a wall. As early as the 4th cent. AD, C. was a cathedral city; two cemeterial churches of the 5th/6th cents. [2]; south-west of C., on the road to Emona, the necropolis of Šempeter [2. 355–358; 3] and the military camp of Ločica, which the *legio II Italica* temporarily occupied during the wars against the → Marcomanni.

> 1 J. ŠAŠEL, Opera Selecta, 1993, 206–219
> 2 S. CIGLENECKI, in: Arh. Vestnik 44, 1993, 213–221 (on early Christianity)   3 V. KOLŠEK, Röm. Österreich 17/18, 1989–90, 143–146.
>
> J. ŠAŠEL, s.v. C., PE, 210; Id., s.v. C., RE Suppl. 12, 139–148; Id., Opera Selecta, 1993, 583–587 and Register.   K.DI.

Celenderis (Κελένδερις; *Kelénderis*). Town in → Cilicia Tracheia (Str. 14,5,3), founded by the Syrian Sandacus, colonized by Samos [1. 105]; the harbour with its ornate arcades is depicted on a mosaic (cf. also Tab. Peut.

10,3; [4]), modern Gilindire. Member of the → Delian League. Captured by the Sassanids in AD 260 (Res Gestae divi Saporis 30). Suffragan diocese of Seleucia/Calycadnus. Renamed as Palaiopolis in the Middle Ages.

> 1 E. BLUMENTHAL, Die altgriech. Siedlungskolonisation ..., 1963   2 W. RUGE, s.v. K. (2), RE 11, 138   3 HILD/HELLENKEMPER, 298   4 L. ZOROĞLU, K. 1, 1994.   F.H.

Celer Cognomen, the origin of which is given in a story by Plutarch (Coriolanus 11,4); also a nickname [1. 66,248].
[1] Military tribune who intervened in Judaea against internal Jewish disturbances. Sent for judgement to Rome, he was returned to Jerusalem by the emperor and there beheaded (Ios. Ant. Iud. 20,132–136; Bell. Iud. 2,244–246). PIR C 617.
[2] In AD 92 *legatus Augusti pro praetore Hispaniae cit.* or *legatus iuridicus* (Mart. 7,52,1–4). PIR C 620.
[3] Roman *eques*, put to death by → Domitianus on account of an accusation of a sexual relationship with the Vestal Cornelia (Plin. Ep. 4,11,10; Suet. Dom. 8,4). PIR C 621.

> 1 KAJANTO, Cognomina.   M.STR.

[4] Nero's architect; with Severus he designed the layout of the → *domus aurea*, as well as planning a canal from the Arvernian Lake to the Tiber (Tac. Ann. 15,42); he is possibly to be identified with the *architectus* C. in P. Ryl. 608 = CPL 248 [1. 28f.].

> 1 H. COTTON, Documentary Letters, 1981.   W.E.

[5] Close friend to → Hadrianus (M. Aur. 8,25); probably identical with the teacher of rhetoric to → Marcus Aurelius (SHA Marc. 2,4) and → Verus (SHA Verus 2,5). Aristides calls him γραμματεὺς βασιλικός (*grammateùs basilikós*) (Aristid. Or. 26,335 p.519 DINDORF). PIR C388.
[6] In AD 429 proconsul of Africa, *vir clarissimus* (Aug. Epist. 139). → Augustinus debated Christianity with C., who was a Donatist (Aug. Epist. 56; 57). PLRE 2, 275 (C. 1).

> F. F. MORGENSTERN, Die Briefpartner des Augustinus von Hippo, 1993, 74.   M.STR.

[7] **P.C.** Roman *eques*; see → P. Celerius.

Celerinus Prefect of Egypt. In AD 283 after the death of → Carus he turned down the imperial rank offered to him by his soldiers (Claudian. Epithal. Palladii et Celerinae 25,70–82). PIR² C 635.   A.B.

Celerius, P. (in editions of Tacitus erroneously P. Celer); patrimonial procurator in Asia to Claudius and Nero (I. Eph. 7,2,3043/44; SEG 39, 1172). At the end of 54, C. murdered Iunius Silanus, *procos. Asiae*, at the behest of → Agrippina; in 57 accused in the Senate by the Province of Asia; but the trial was dragged out until his death (Tac. Ann. 13,1,2. 33,1).

W. Eck, in: Splendissima Civitas, Études ... en hommage à
F. Jaques, 1996, 67ff.   W.E.

Celery The name given to umbellate plants from the
Araliaceae family that had large, shiny leaves and were
suitable for making wreaths, namely the → ivy (κισσός,
ἕλιξ, *hedera*), sacred to Dionysus/Bacchus, and several
umbelliferous plants. The following pot-herbs are
meant in particular:

1) Celery (*apium graveolens L.*), as σέλινον (*sélinon*)
mentioned already in Hom. Il. 2,776 and Od. 5,72; as
garden celery, σέλινον κηπαῖον (*sélinon kēpaîon*), celery
is referred to in Dioscorides for its cooling, pain-reliev-
ing and anti-inflammatory effect (3,64 [1. 75f.] and
3,67 [2. 305]); Pliny discusses the plant under the name
of *apium* (HN 19,124; 20,112–118, here also with
regard to the bisexual nature of celery, its use in cooking
and its exceptional healing powers).

2) Small horse celery, *smyrnium olusatrum*,
(σμύρνιον; *smýrnion*, Dioscorides 3,68 [1. 78f.] and
3,72 [2. 307f.]), which grew in dry wasteland and was
supposed to have warming powers, *olus atrum* in Plin.
HN 19,162.

3) Parsley *petroselinum hortense* (πετροσέλινον; *pe-
troselinon*, Dioscorides 3,66 [1. 77] and 3,70 [2. 306],
which was almost unknown in ancient times and not
cultivated until later; here with regard to its medicinal
significance) on steep slopes in Macedonia is *Atha-
mantha macedonica* according to Sprengel's opinion
on this passage.

1 Wellmann 2   2 Berendes.   C.HÜ.

Celetrum (*Celetrum*). Town in the Epirote or rather
upper Macedonian region of Orestis, only once mentioned in literature with this name (Liv. 31,40,2), but
because of the clearly described location identified as
the modern Kastoria. Probably founded anew under
Galerius at the beginning of the 4th cent. AD as Diokle-
tianopolis, afterwards deserted, rebuilt under Justinian
(Procop. Aed. 4,3). Bishop's seat in the 6th cent. AD
(Hierocles, Synekdemos 642,12).

F. Papazoglou, Les villes de Macédoine, 1988, 238f.
                                                         MA.ER.

Celeus (Κελεός; *Keleós*). An Eleusinian local hero, local
king and husband of → Metaneira, who upon the wish
of his four daughters hospitably receives → Demeter
who is wandering in search of her daughter, entrusts to
her the care of her newborn son → Demophon [1] and
finally builds her first temple after her epiphany (H.
Hom. Cer.; a slightly different version according to the
old poet Pamphus is given in Paus. 1,38,3); as a local
hero, C. receives cult worship at the Eleusinia (LSCG
10,72). Presumably due to his hospitality, the foundation of the public feeding in the Ath. Prytaneion (Plut.
symp. 4,4,1) is later attributed to him; however, he is
also seen as the instigator of an assassination attempt
on the Eleusinian hero Triptolemus (Hyg. Fab. 147).

N. J. Richardson, The Homeric Hymn to Demeter,
1974, 177–179.   F.G.

Celeutor (Κελεύτωρ; *Keleútōr*). C. and his brothers
snatch the rulership from their uncle → Oeneus, king of
Aetolia, and lock him up; they make their father
→ Agrius [1] king, until Diomedes frees his grandfather
Oeneus and kills all of Agrius' sons except for two who
are able to flee. Since Oeneus is too old, Diomedes
hands over the rulership to Oeneus' son-in-law → An-
draemon [1] (Apollod. 1,77f.; Paus. 2,25,2; Hyg. Fab.
175).   AL.FR.

Cella ('Chamber, room, cell, booth').
[1] Technical term coined by Vitruvius (4,1 and *passim*)
for the space enclosed by walls within an ancient
→ temple (Greek: σηκός, *sēkós*). The formal development of the Greek temple *cella* from early Greek domestic architecture (→ House), together with the related development of the peripteral temple (→ Peristasis), is still
a subject for debate. In monumental stone structures
from the 7th cent. BC onwards, the *cella* served for the
safe-keeping of the cult image or the image of the god,
and also as the temple or state treasury (→ Temple);
ritual activities took place here only on a few, exceptional occasions (→ Altar; → Cult image). The prestigious divine images made of precious materials that
were kept in the *cella* (e.g. the Zeus of Olympia and
→ Phidias' Athena Parthenos) were often not cult images, not having any cult function: they were accessible
to the visitor as showpieces, sometimes a gallery even
being provided from which they could be admired
(→ Parthenon).

The *cella* in early Greek temples was long, at first
consisting of a single room (sometimes with vestibule),
often divided into two naves by a central row of
columns (Samos, Eretria, Isthmia, Argos, Thermus).
The early 6th cent. sees the development of the three-
roomed *cella*, the typical sequence being: pronaos
(antechamber); main room; with the rearmost room
either as an opisthodomos (→ Temple), separated from
the main room (early: Olympia, temple of Hera; Corcyra, temple of Artemis) or as an adyton, accessible only
from the main room and inaccessible from the outside
(predominant in Western Greece, rare in Asia Minor
[e.g. Ephesus, archaic Artemison] and virtually non-existent in the Greek motherland [in dispute: some
temples to Artemis, e.g. at Aulis, Brauron]). At the same
time, there are anomalous two-roomed forms (6th cent.
BC, e.g. Samos, Metapontum; similarly in the 4th cent.
some 'short temples', e.g. Epidaurus), occasional four-
roomed (Corinth) and multi-roomed structures
(Athens, old temple of Athena). From the 6th cent., the
typical temple *cella* is subdivided into three naves by
two rows of tall columns (e.g. the Temple of Aphaia on
Aegina). In rare cases, motivated for the most part by
cult-related tradition or function, the σηκός (*sēkós*) remained unroofed (Didyma, temple to Apollo; the
Olympieum at Acragas; Selinunt G). In small temples

with antas, round temples and → treasuries, in both the Greek and Roman periods, the *cella* was predominantly a single room. Apart from a few examples (e.g. the → Parthenon in Athens, the temple to Athena on Delos), the *cella* was windowless, and in every case was closed by a massive door.

The form of the *cella* in Roman podium temples depends upon the dedication; the *cellae* of the Capitoline temples, modelled on the Etruscan temple, were usually rectilinear or virtually square in plan, and subdivided into three chambers of equal depth but unequal width to accommodate the Capitoline Triad: two narrower chambers at the sides (for Juno and Minerva); a broader central chamber (for Jupiter). In every other case the *cella* was oblong in form, and either single-roomed or provided with an antechamber/pronaos.

EBERT 3–5, 14–19; E. WILL, Art parthe et art grec. L'adyton dans le temple syrien de l'époque impériale, in: Études d'archéologie classique 2, 1959, 123–147; A. MALLWITZ, Cella und Adyton des Apollontempels in Bassai, in: MDAI(A) 77, 1962, 140–177; A. BOETHIUS, J. B. WARD-PERKINS, Etruscan and Roman Architecture, 1970, 29–56, 132–148; P. GROS, Aurea Templa, 1976, 101–151; T. KALPAXIS, Früharcha. Baukunst, 1976, 17–81; S.K. THALMANN, The Adyton in the Greek Temples of South Italy and Sicily, 1980; M. B. HOLLINSHEAD, Against Iphigeneia's Adyton in Three Mainland Temples, in: AJA 89, 1985, 419–440; W. MARTINI, Vom Herdhaus zum Peripteros, in: JDAI 101, 1986, 23–36; F. SEILER, Die griech. Tholos, 1986, 78–81, 96–98, 116–119; G. GRUBEN, Anfänge des Monumentalbaus auf Naxos, in: DiskAB 5, 1991, 63–71; D. METZLER, 'Abstandsbetonung'. Zur Entwicklung des Innenraums griech. Tempel, in: Hephaistos 13, 1995, 58–72 (with additional literature); B. FEHR, The Greek Temple in the Early Archaic Period, in: Hephaistos 14, 1996, 165–191; CH. HÖCKER, Architektur als Metapher, in: Hephaistos 14, 1996, 54–58 with note 36.

[2] In ancient architectural terminology also a small room, its function not more precisely defined; often a cellar space in a Roman → house or farmstead; see [1; 2].

1 GEORGES, 1, s.v. *cella* (references) 2 W. H. GROSS, s.v. *cella*, KlP 1, 1100f. C.HÖ.

Celmis (Κέλμις, *Kélmis*; older form evidently Σκέλμις in Callim. Fr. 100,1 PF. and Nonnus, Dion. 14,39; 37,164). One of the → Daktyloi Idaioi skilled in the blacksmith's craft. Proverbially, C. ἐν σιδήρῳ (Zenob. 4,80) according to a passage in the Sophoclean satyr play *Kōphoí* (TGF, fr. 337 N.²) is used to describe excessively power-conscious persons. C., who is the playmate of the boy Zeus in Ovid (Met. 4,281f.), is transformed into steel because he reviles Rhea. C.W.

Celones (Κέλωνες; *Kélōnes*). Tribe, only mentioned in Diod. Sic. 17,110,4, who during Xerxes' campaign were deported from Boeotia to Media, where Alexander the Great still found them in 326 BC. Probably a mix-up with the Euboean → Eretria [1] whose inhabi-

tants were deported by Datis and Artaphernes in 490 BC (Hdt. 6,119,1f.; Str. 16,1,25; Anth. Pal. 7,256; 259; cf. also the Gortuae, mentioned in Curt. 4,12,11, who supposedly followed the Persians from Euboea to Media). P.F.

Celossa (Κηλῶσσα; *Kēlôssa*, Str. 6,8,24; Κηλοῦσα; *Kēloûsa*, Xen. Hell. 4,7,7; Κηλούσσα; *Kēloûssa*, Paus. 2,12,4), modern Megalovouni. Mountain range between Phlius and Argos (1273 m), with an Artemis sanctuary [1].

1 M. TH. MITSOS, Inscriptions of the Eastern Peloponnesus, in: Hesperia 18, 1949, 75. E.MEY. and E.O.

Celsus (Κέλσος; *Kélsos*).

[I] Platonic writer, 2nd half of the 2nd cent. AD; author of 'The True Doctrine' (Ἀληθὴς λόγος, *Alēthēs lógos*), an anti-Christian text thoroughly refuted by the Christian → Origenes (at the request of his friend and patron Ambrosius), in his eight volume 'Against the Text of Celsus entitled: The True Doctrine' [1. 180–301]. Nothing is known about the ethical work announced by C. (8,76). Everything we do know about him and his work comes down to us via Origen, and even he was entirely dependent on the *Alēthēs lógos* for his conclusions regarding C.'s person, period, teaches and opinions. Although Origen acknowledges C.'s view of himself as a follower of Plato (4,83), he falsely identifies him with an Epicurean of the same name (1,8) [1. 27, 188, 196f.; 2. 5186f., 5191f.]. As Origen extensively quotes and refutes C.'s work section by section, large parts of the *Alēthēs lógos* can be recovered from his refutation. The work seems to have comprised only one book. Its structure and aims are matters of dispute, but may be reconstructed to some extent [1. 15–26, 38, 118–176].

According to C., 'many peoples are akin in following one and the same doctrine' (1,14a). In its essentials, this kinship has been passed down through the ages (ἀρχαῖος ἄνωθεν λόγος; *archaîos ánōthen lógos*), as the wisest and oldest peoples, (τὰ ἀρχαιότατα καὶ σοφώτατα γένη; *tà archaiótata kaì sophōtata génē*) as well as wise men in the past (ἄνδρες ἀρχαῖοι καὶ σοφοί; *ándres archaîoi kaì sophoî*), have made it their concern. Among these oldest and wisest peoples C. counts i. a. the Egyptians, the Arcadians, the Assyrians, the Athenians, the Chaldeans, the Eleusinians, the Indians, the Celts, the Persians and the Samothraceans; among the sages of antiquity i. a. Heraclitus, Hesiod, Homer, Musaeus, Orpheus, Pherecydes, Pythagoras, Zoroaster and also Plato (1,5; 14; 16; 4,36; 6,3; 12f.; 42; 80; 7,28; 53; 8,68); for even Plato's teaching was by no means new (6,10; 13), but an expression of this same, ancient 'true Logos', which in him manifests itself in a quite particular way (6,1; 3): in his metaphysics and theology [3; 4. 82–85, 329–332; 5. 79–83], but also in his demonology, his doctrine of the soul, his cosmology and his anthropology [2. 5203–5211; 5. 83f.]. The 'old' or 'true doctrine' receives its final form in Plato; in the Platonic thinkers its final interpretation.

C. accuses the Christians and the Jews of having broken with the common tradition of all ancient peoples, and therefore with the *alēthès lógos* (8,2); the Jews had fallen away from the Egyptians (3,5–8; 4,31), and the Christians from the Jews (2,4; 5,33). So the characteristic of both religions was not harmony (ὁμόνοια; *homónoia*, ὁμολογία; *homología*), but discord or the obsession for innovation (στάσις; *stásis*, καινοτομία; *kainotomía*, 3,5–14). Jews and Christians wanted to be special and were not (5,25; 34; 41): on the contrary, their doctrines had their source in the 'old doctrine' (*palaiòs lógos*) common to the ancient peoples, and where they strayed from this doctrine it was merely a case of failures in understanding (3,16; cf. 4,11).

One of the main sources for the Jewish and Christian religions was, of course, that of the Egyptians (6,42). The Jews had also taken doctrines from the Persians (6,22; 23), the Jews and Christians doctrines from the Greeks (6,12; 13), especially from the Cabiri on Samothrace (6,23), from Homer and from Plato (6,7; 21; 7,28; 31), but in a form that was in part misunderstood and distorted (6,7; 15; 16; 19; 47; 7,28; 32; 58). Because they had become distanced from traditional cults and from the Roman state they represented a danger to the continued existence of the Empire (8,68) [2. 5212f.].

C'.s influence on Christian and later anti-Christian writers is disputed; the latter question requires new research [1. 60–62]. But even more necessary is a new edition with commentary.

1 K. Pichler, Streit um das Christentum. Der Angriff des Kelsos und die Antwort des Origenes, 1980   2 M. Frede, Celsus philosophus Platonicus, in: ANRW II 36.7, 1994, 5183–5213   3 H. Dörrie, Die platonische Theologie des Kelsos in ihrer Auseinandersetzung mit der christl. Theologie (Nachr. der Akad. der Wiss. in Göttingen, philol.-histor. Kl.), 1967 (2), 19–55 = Id., Platonica minora, 1976, 229–262   4 Dörrie/Baltes IV, 1996   5 S. Lilla, Introduzione al Medio platonismo, 1992.

Editions: R. Bader, Der ἀληθὴς λόγος des Kelsos, 1940 (Tübinger Beitr. zur Altertumswiss. 33); M. Borret, Origène, Contre Celse I–IV, 1967–1969 (SChr 132, 136, 147, 150).
Translation: H. Chadwick, Origen: Contra Celsum, ²1965. P. Pilhofer, Presbyteron kreitton, 1990, 285–289.
Bibliography: L. Deitz, Bibliographie du platonisme impérial antérieur à Plotin: 1926–1986, in: ANRW II 36.1, 1987, 145–147.   M.BA.

[II] Commonly occurring cognomen (cf. PIR² 2, 145–147).

[1] C. Friend of Ovid and of Aurelius Cotta Maximus; Ovid consoles Cotta on the death of C. (Pont. 1,9) [1. 90].

[2] C. *Eques* from Alba Pompeia, admitted to the Senate by Trajan (CIL V 7153; PIR² C 647).

[3] C. Supposed conspirator against Antoninus Pius; fictitious letter in SHA Avid. Cass. 10,1. (PIR² C 644).

[4] C. Supposed usurper against Gallienus (PIR² C 646).

[5] C. Aelianus. Supposedly *cos. suff.* in AD 238; mentioned in a spurious letter SHA Max. Balb. 17,2 (PIR² C 649).

[6] C. Plancianus. *Cos. suff.* with Avidius Cassius (CIL XVI 124), probably in AD 166 [2. V 691ff.]. Re possible kinship [3. 320].

1 Syme, History in Ovid, 1978   2 Syme, RP, 5
3 Alföldy, Konsulat.   W.E.

[7] Cornelius C., A. An encyclopaedist of the time of Tiberius (14–37); in the tradition of the *disciplinae* of → Cato and → Varro he wrote *Artes* ('Arts'), comprising more than 26 volumes and covering the disciplines of agriculture, medicine, warfare, rhetoric, philosophy and jurisprudence. Of these, only the most extensive part survives, the eight-volume *De medicina*; so that, although to C. as to Varro the topic was a part of general culture, he comes down to us as a medical historian. The work begins with a concise historical outline down to → Themison, presents a division into dietetics (hygiene), drug-lore (pharmacology) and practical medicine (surgery), as well as distinguishing between the rational and the empirical schools of medicine; book one then covers dietetics, book two general pathology and therapeutics, book three diseases of the whole body, book four those of individual organs (with an introduction to anatomy), books five-six pharmacology, book seven surgery, book eight diseases of the skeleton. Earlier theories using only one source (Cassius [1]; Varro) gave way to a method of direct and undogmatic use of Greek textbooks, especially those relating to Alexandrian surgery. Reception is confined to → Plinius the Elder and → Marcellus Empiricus; since the 9th cent. the text has come down in only a few MSS.

Lost: *De agricultura* in five books (Columella 1,1,14; 2,2,15) is praised by → Columella for its meticulous style (9,2,1) and breadth of scope (a classification of its contents attempted [2]); Hyginus, Virgil, Iulius Atticus, the Sasernae and especially → Mago are established sources. The work was used by Columella, Pliny the Elder and Gargilius Martialis. The Rhetoric in seven books (according to Schol. Juv. 6,44), often quoted by → Quintilianus, followed practical, forensic lines (Quint. Inst. 2,15,32). Of the rest, *De re militari* is attested only in Veg. Mil. 1,8, *De iuris prudentia* only in Quint. Inst. 12,11,24. There is debate as to whether *De philosophia* is dogmatic-ethical in character, as Quint. Inst. 10,1,124 (*Sextios secutus*) has it, or of a doxographical nature, as suggested in Aug. Haeres. Prol. (*opiniones omnium philosophorum qui sectas varias condiderunt*) (always provided that each is referring to the same C.). Quintilian was more reserved in his judgment (*mediocri vir ingenio*, inst. 12,11,24), but admired C.' versatility (*ut eum scisse omnia illa credamus*). C.' influence nevertheless remained modest.

→ Artes liberales; → Education/Culture

1 M. WELLMANN, A. Cornelius Celsus, 1913   2 R. REI-
TZENSTEIN, De scriptorum rei rusticae ... libris deperditis,
diss. Berlin 1884.

EDITIONS: F. MARX, 1915 (CML 1); W.G. SPENCER, 3
vols. 1935–38; G. SERBAT, 1995; Praefatio: PH. MUDRY,
1982; B. and S. CONTINO, 1988.
INDEX: W.F. RICHARDSON, 1982.
BIBLIOGRAPHY: PH. MUDRY, ANRW II 37, 1993, 787–
799.
LITERATURE: K. BARWICK, Zu den Schriften des Cornelius Celsus und des alten Cato, in: WJA 3, 1948, 117–132;
W. KRENKEL, Zu den Artes des Cornelius Celsus, in: Philologus 103, 1959, 114–129; Medicine: L. LIMMER,
G. KRIEGLSTEIN, Augenheilkunde im Rom der frühen Kaiserzeit, 1992; G. SABBAH, P. MUDRY (ed.), La médecine de
Cornelius Celsus (Memorie Palerne 13), 1994; Philosophy: A. DYROFF, Der philosophische Teil der Encyclopä-
die des Cornelius Celsus, in: RhM 84, 1939, 7–16; On the
Toletanus text: H.D. JOCELYN, The new chapters of the
ninth book of Cornelius Celsus Artes, in: Papers of the
Liverpool Latin Seminar 5, 1986, 299–336.   KL.SA.

Celtianis The *castellum* to the north of Cirta belonged
to the region of Cirta, the modern El Meraba or Beni
Ouelbane. Under Marcus Aurelius (AD 161–180) the
res publica of C. had a *consilium decurionum*. CIL VIII
Suppl. 2, 19689f. Numerous inscriptions inform us
about everyday life in C.: CIL VIII Suppl. 2, 19688–
19847; Inscr. latines de l'Algérie 2,1, 2084–3398.

AAAlg, folio 8, no. 91; H.-G. PFLAUM, Remarques sur
l'onomastique de Castellum Celtianum, in: E. SWOBODA
(ed.), Carnuntina, 1956, 126–151.   W.HU.

Celtiberi It used to be the accepted view that C. were
'Iberian Celts', i.e. Celts who had migrated into Iberian
lands (first in Str. 3,4,5). A. SCHULTEN, by contrast, postulated that they were 'Celtic Iberians', i.e. Iberians who
had advanced from the east coast into Celtic areas. The
C. inhabited a large part of the central Spanish plateau
(Meseta). They never formed a political unit; of significance in this context is the fact that they had no collective name for referring to themselves. They were divided into several tribes, such as the → Arevaci, Lusones,
→ Belli, Titti and Pelendones. These tribes, too, did not
form a political federation, but were themselves divided
into independent families, clans and communities. Traditionally, they were seen as wild and uncivilized. They
had their own, rarely used script — cf. the bronze tablet
of Luzaga [1. 171]. Little is known of their religion
(lunar cult, human sacrifices?). Allegedly, they left the
bodies of those who had died in battle to be mauled by
vultures ([2. 196–199]; Sil. Pun. 3, 340–343; [3. 21]).
They extracted gold from rivers and operated silver and
iron mines [2. 173f.], as well as potteries [2. 192–93].
They were such masters at producing weapons that the
Romans adopted both sword (Pol. fr. 96) and *pilum*
[4. 1333] from them. Their belligerence was immense,
forcing Rome to wage costly wars against them from
181 to 133 BC. The fall of → Numantia destroyed their

power but, until 44 BC, there were still several uprisings. In 104 BC they beat back the invading → Cimbri
(Liv. per. 67).

1 E. HÜBNER, Monumenta Linguae Ibericae, 1893
2 A. SCHULTEN, Numantia 1, 1914   3 F. BLEICHING,
Span. Landes- und Volkskunde bei Sil. Italicus, 1928
4 A. SCHULTEN, s.v. Pilum, RE 20, 1333.

A. SCHULTEN, Fontes Hispaniae Antiquae, 1925ff., I–VI,
VIII, IX; HOLDER 1, 959ff.; Id. 3, 1194ff.; L. PERICOT, La
España primitiva, 1950; R. MARTIN VALLS, A. ESPARZA,
Génesis y evolución de la Cultura Celtibérica, in: M. AL-
MAGRO-GORBEA, G. RUIZ ZAPATERO(ed.), Paleoetnologia
de la Península Ibérica, 1992, 259–279.   P.B.

Celtiberic see → Hispania, languages; → Celtic languages

Celtic Archaeology
A. GENERAL B. SOURCES C. METHODS D. MAIN
FOCUS OF RESEARCH

A. GENERAL
Celtic archaeology (CA) investigates the material
legacy of groups of the population from the Iron Age,
mostly in southern and south-western Central Europe,
in addition to the → Germanic archaeology, which borders onto it to the north and north-east. This concerns
the → Hallstatt culture of the early and the → La Tène
culture of the late Iron Age. The equating of this archaeologically knowable cultures with the ethnicity of
the → Celts is not constantly and unambiguously possible; thus → Caesar's Gauls (→ Gallia) can definitely be
identified with the late La Tène culture in present-day
France, but the identification of → Herodotus' [1]
Κελτοί/*Keltoí* 'on the upper Danube' with the late Hallstatt culture of about the same era of the late 6th or
early 5th cents. BC in south-west Germany, Switzerland and eastern France is much more uncertain.
Whether the archaeological groups, which are found
there, of the early Hallstatt culture (late 8th-end
7th cents. BC) or actually from the late Bronze Age
→ Urn-field culture (12th–8th cents. BC) can also already be addressed as 'Celts' or 'proto-Celts', is even
more questionable.

B. SOURCES
The sources for the archaeological assessment of the
Celts are fairly fragmented and of limited usefulness as
evidence. The graves and sometimes immense burial
fields always play a particularly large part in this, whose
riches in burial gifts and arrangement yield information
on social structure, demographic aspects, religious
ideas, etc., of the respective population groups. First,
there are, mostly in the 6th/5th cents. BC, tumuli —
sometimes richly appointed (→ royal grave) — and
tumulus fields, in which a strongly differentiated social
population structure is delineated. From the middle of
the 5thcent., large burial grounds with flat graves containing body burials then prevail. This custom gradual-

ly changed to cremation in the 3rd/2nd cents., which predominated at the end of the Celtic La Tène culture in the last cent. BC, at least in some regions. In the course of this development, it appears that the stratification of the population, which is so clearly visible in the graves in the earlier period, recedes and the burials are much more uniformly structured and equipped. The picture of the settlements is for the older segment determined by open, village-like and also fortified (hill) settlements (e.g. the → Heuneburg). The peak is formed by the city-like large settlements of the → *oppida*, which can be found archaeologically well beyond the Gallic area — in the east up to the Carpathians and eastern Alps, in the North into the transalpine area. In addition, there are cult sites, sacrificial sites, such as, e.g., the → 'Viereck-schanzen' or certain lakes, moors or rivers (La Tène, etc.). An important group of sources is the discovered objects themselves, whose form, production, material, decoration, etc., make manifold indications possible as to the technical ability (i.e. → Crafts, → Metallurgy), commercial connections and routes (→ Etrusci, maps: Etruscan exports; → Royal grave with map), economy, religion, etc. A decorating style of vegetal and zoomor-phic elements, which in a characteristic manner have been transformed from their Mediterranean roots (Greek/Etruscan), is representative of a typically Celtic art style of the 5th–3rd cents. BC. The Celtic coins, which are present in abundance, give insight into eco-nomical connections and groupings which have been developed.

C. METHODS

At the forefront of the working method of CA are, of course, the traditional methods of excavation and sur-veys to gain access to the archaeological source ma-terial. Numerous settlements and whole burial fields have, in the meantime, been surveyed systematically like, e.g., → Heuneburg, → Glauberg, → Dürrnberg, → Hochdorf, → Manching, → Bibracte etc. Analysis of discoveries of individual pieces, working out of typical form elements (e.g., with → fibulae, other → jewellery, → clay vessels, → weapons), contemplating related finds, stylistic analyses of typical ornaments, etc., lead to archaeological phase structuring of the Celtic La Tène culture, but also to regional differentiations and connections with older or neighbouring cultures.

Increasingly, all kinds of different scientific methods are employed in order to record further areas of Celtic cultural history or to achieve more exact results. Through absolute dating, especially through dendro-chronology by means of tree-ring analyses of wood finds, single periods of Celtic cultural development of the late Hallstatt and La Tène cultures can be deter-mined quite precisely. Material analyses using physics and chemistry give detailed insight into the technology used for the different raw materials (ore, metal, → glass, ceramics, etc.), their origin and their preparation and processing techniques. Biological methods of palaeo-botany and palaeozoology disclose aspects of → agri-culture, such as, e.g., the plants cultivated, the animals kept, the methods of harvesting and slaughtering, stor-age, etc., with very interesting results; furthermore, the environmental conditions, their changes and extensive climatic variations can be reconstructed. Anthropology is finally especially employed to determine — e.g. through burial field analyses — demographic aspects, such as nutrition and health conditions, or the medical knowledge of the Celts. In addition, anthropology can demonstrate that in the Celtic cultural sphere, people were characterized extensively by fairly specific distinc-tive features, among which the skeletons of the late Hallstatt culture can also be included. This testifies to the development already mentioned (see A. and D.) of the Celts of this group.

D. MAIN FOCUS OF RESEARCH

CA first and foremost tries to investigate criteria in the archaeological findings, which enable identification of the material culture of the Celts and a separation from other peoples (e.g., → Germani, → Ligures, Iberi-ans (→ Hispania), → Daci etc.,) and cultures. The roots and originating areas of the development of the Celtic culture have already been an investigative objective of Celtic archaeology for a long time. It is, however, evi-dent that besides late Iron Age autochthonous elements, certainly the intensive stimuli from the Mediterranean area (Italy, Greece) are determining factors, but that ultimately the question remains open, since when and where and with which archaeological discoveries one can speak of 'Celts'. Closely linked to this is the ques-tion regarding the spread of Celtic culture during the various eras of the late Iron Age. From a central area during the late Hallstatt/early La Tène period in the 6th/5th cents. BC (see map), the area of the Celts or the La Tène culture, which could be defined archaeologi-cally from central France to Bohemia and from the Alps to the transalpine area, expanded from the Atlantic to Transylvania and from the British Isles to the Po valley by the last cent. BC.

The archaeological evidence for the historically tra-ditional migration of the Celts, especially to Italy and to south-eastern Europe, including Anatolia (→ Celts III in the east, with map; → Galatia) in the 4th/3rd cents. BC is scarce; it is mostly the inventory of individual graves and findings, such as, e.g., fibulae and other items, while there are no Celtic settlements or large burial fields on the lower Danube, in Anatolia or in central Italy. A more intensive Celtic acquisition of land or → colonization cannot be gleaned in this connection from archaeological sources. It is also difficult to iden-tify migration within the Celtic area of later times (the expansion of the → Cimbri and → Teutoni or the moves of the → Helvetii) in the general picture given by the findings. Contact between the Iberian world and the Celtic La Tène culture of central Europe leads to the development of Celtiberian cultural groups in Spain and Portugal in the 4th–3rd cents. BC (→ Celtiberi, → Pyrenean peninsula); these maintain or form, however, their own archaeological profile, in which only a few elements point to central Europe. The division of the Celtic world into tribes, known from many written sources, can hardly be determined from the archaeological findings; the regional structure of La Tène culture apparently mirrors other groupings within the Celtic culture.

A further research objective is the comparison of archaeological data about the cultural history of the Celts with the statements of the Greek and Roman written sources and also with linguistic and onomastic research. When critically examined, there are multiple additions, but also deviations and possible corrections: e.g., regarding the above-mentioned 'migrations', the role of the Celts on the → Iberian peninsula, the evaluation of the level of Celtic culture — with → coinage, → writing, technological skills, social structures, etc. –, the expansion of the 'oppidum civilization' (→ oppidum) in the area on the right of the Rhine. From the one-sided viewpoint of the Greek or Roman author, there certainly is some misinformation — for lack of a corresponding tradition from a Celtic angle. The continuation of the Celtic style and cultural elements — especially in the British Isles — into the Middle Ages, is also researched by CA.

→ Fortifications; → Funerary architecture; CELTIC-GERMANIC ARCHAEOLOGY

H. DANNHEIMER, R. GEBHARD, Das kelt. Jt., 1993; M. EGG, C. PARE, Die Metallzeiten in Europa und im Vorderen Orient: Die Abt. Vorgesch. im Röm.-German. Zentral-Mus. Mainz, 1995, 192–222; M. GREEN (ed.), The Celtic World, 1995; A. HAFFNER (ed.), Heiligtümer und Opferkulte der Kelten, 1995; P. JACOBSTHAL, Early Celtic Art, 1944; S. KLUG, Die Ethnogenese der Kelten aus der Sicht der Anthropologie, in: W. BERNHARD, A. KANDLER-PÁLSSON (ed.), Ethnogenese europ. Völker, 1986, 225–246; S. MOSCATI (ed.), I Celti, 1991; L. PAULI (ed.), Die Kelten in Mitteleuropa, 1980; S. PLOUIN and others (ed.), Trésors Celtes et Gaulois. Le Rhin supérieur entre 800 et 50 avant J.-C., 1996; K. SPINDLER, Die frühen Kelten, 1983.   V.P.

Celtic languages

The Celtic languages (CL) belong to the group of → Centum languages within the → Indo-European languages. The hypothesis that the preliminary phases of the Italic and the Celtic language branch form a unit was long disputed. For morphological reasons in particular (common innovations exclusive to Celtic and Italic), early Italic-Celtic language unity is, however, probable [1]. The CL are usually subdivided in two regards.

a) Purely geographical classification as 'mainland Celtic' and 'island Celtic' without reference to differences or common features in dialect. In the literature, some of it extensive, there is evidence of the island Celtic languages Cymric (Welsh), Cornish and Breton from c. the 7th/8th cent. AD and of Irish from as early as the 4th/5th cents. AD (→ Ogam). Irish, Welsh and Breton are still spoken even today. On the other hand, there is rather scant evidence of the mainland Celtic languages Gaulish, Celtiberian, → Lepontic, which died out at an early date (see below).

b) Classification according to linguistic features as 'p Celtic' — Indo-Germanic k^w becomes p in Gaulish (pinpetos 'fifth'), Lepontic, Welsh (pumed, pymed 'fifth'), Cornish, Breton — and as 'q Celtic' — Indo-Germanic k^w remains preserved in Celtiberian (necue 'and not') and the most ancient Irish (Ogam personal name Eqagni 'little horse') and later becomes k or ch (e.g. Old Irish nech 'and not').

Inscriptions in CL on the mainland are mainly found in four areas: a) the north and centre of Hispania: Celtiberian; b) area around Lake Lugano: Lepontic; c) Gallia Cisalpina and Transalpina: Gaulish with lesser dialects; d) lesser areas in Asia Minor: Galatia (see map).

Witnesses to these mainland Celtic languages in the languages themselves survive from the period of the 3rd cent. BC to the 4th cent. AD, particularly in votive inscriptions and inscriptions on household effects, e.g. the potter's manufacturing notes in La Graufesenque, several relatively long texts with magical, religious or judicial content, e.g. the bronze of Larzac, the inscriptions of Botorrita and several calendars, particularly the calendar of Coligny. Even if mainland Celtic languages were able to be preserved for a long time in several areas, they must, however, have been displaced by Latin by the 6th/7th cents. at the latest. The Celts, who did not become acquainted with the principle of 'writing' until they came into contact with Roman and Greek culture, did not create their own writing (exception: Ogam) but mainly used the Greek (Gaulish, Galatian) and Latin scripts (Gaulish, Celtiberian, island CL), and sometimes also the Etruscan (Lepontic) and Iberian scripts (Celtiberian). Celtic words and frequently personal names, national names and place names are often found in Latin contexts (particularly in Caesar), e.g. druides 'druids' (dru- 'oak', -uid- 'knowledgeable'), Aremorici (name of a people: are — cf. Old Irish ar-, 'to, at', mori-, Old Irish muir, 'sea'), Vercingetorix (personal name: uer- 'over', cingeto-, Old Irish cing, genitive cinged, 'hero', 'warrior', rīx, Old Irish rí, 'king'). Secondary transmission from Greek provided Celtic with, for example, κούρμι 'beer' (Dioscorides; cf. Old Irish cuirm 'beer'). The CL have often survived in place names, names of peoples and personal names; e.g. Lyon (< Gaulish Lug(u)dunum 'lookout fortress'), Kempten (< Cambiodunum 'fortress on the river bend'), Paris (< Parisii 'the Parisians'), York (< Eburacum with eburo- 'yew tree'). Celtic loan words have mainly been carried over into Latin (carrus, paraveredus, caballus, gladius) and from there into Ibero-Roman and Gallo-Roman (Spanish camino, French chemin 'way', cf. Celtiberian camanom 'way') [2; 3], as well as into Germanic, e.g. German Reich < Gaulish *rīgio- 'kingdom', re Gaulish rīk-s 'king'; Eisen, eisern, English iron, from *īsarno-.

After the conquest of Britain by the Romans, a great many Latin loan words entered Irish, Welsh and Breton

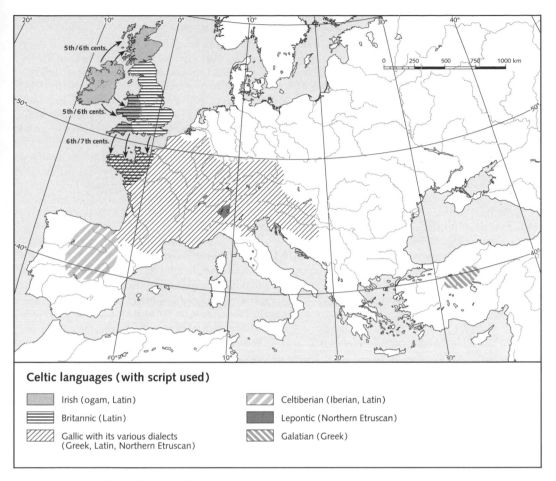

Celtic languages (with script used)

▨ Irish (ogam, Latin)		▨ Celtiberian (Iberian, Latin)	
▤ Britannic (Latin)		▦ Lepontic (Northern Etruscan)	
▨ Gallic with its various dialects (Greek, Latin, Northern Etruscan)		▨ Galatian (Greek)	

(Welsh *plant* 'crowd of children', Irish *clan* 'clan' < Latin *planta*; Welsh *ffenestr* 'window' < Latin *fenestra*) ([4] with bibliography).

→ Hispania, languages; → Indo-European languages; → Centum languages; → Lepontic; → Ogam

1 W. COWGILL, Italic and Celtic Superlatives and the Dialects of Indo-European, in: G. CARDONA et al. (ed.), Indo-European and Indo-Europeans, 1970, 113–153   2 M. L. PORZIO GERNIA, Gli elementi celtici del latino, in: E. CAMPANILE (ed.), I Celti d'Italia, 1981, 97–122   3 K. H. SCHMIDT, K. Wortgut im Lat., in: Glotta 44, 1967, 151–174   4 Id., Latin and Celtic: Genetic Relationship and Areal Contacts, in: Bull. of the Board of Celtic Studies 38, 1991, 1–19.

P.-H. BILLY, Thesaurus Linguae Gallicae, 1993; H. BIRKHAN, Die Kelten, 1997; Id., Germanen und Kelten bis zum Ausgang der Römerzeit, 1970; P.-M. DUVAL, Die Kelten, 1978; EVANS; HOLDER; K. H. JACKSON, Language and History in Early Britain, 1953; P.-Y. LAMBERT, La langue Gauloise, 1994; H. LEWIS, H. PEDERSEN, A Concise Comparative Celtic Grammar, 1937, Suppl. 1961; W. MEID, Celtiberian Inscriptions, 1994; Id., Die k.S. und Literaturen, 1997; Id., Gall. oder Lat.?, 1980; Id., Gaulish Inscriptions, 1992; H. PEDERSEN, Vergleichende Gramm. der k.S., 1909/1913; K. H. SCHMIDT, Galat. Sprachreste, in: E. SCHWERTHEIM (ed.), Forschungen in Galatien, 1994, 15–28; Id., Celtic Movements in the First Millenium B.C., in: Journal of Indo-European Studies 20, 1992, 145–178; SCHMIDT; R. THURNEYSEN, A Grammar of Old Irish, 1946; WHATMOUGH; S. ZIEGLER, s.v. Gallien. § 5 Sprachliches, RGA 10, 370–376.

MAPS: M. LEJEUNE, RIG II/1, 1988, 5 (Lepontic).   S.ZI.

Celts

I. NAME   II. CELTS IN THE WEST   III. CELTS IN THE EAST

I. NAME

The name C. is first used by the Greek authors of the 5th cent. BC (Hdt. 4,49: Κελτοί; *Keltoí*; Scyl. 18). Their settlement area was called *Keltikḗ* (Κελτική). In around 270 BC, the term 'Galatians' (Γαλάται; *Galátai*) is found in Timaeus, the name exclusively applied to the C. in the east. The Greeks clearly distinguished between C. and Galatians. Confusion arose from the translation of *Galli* as *Galatai* by the Romans (Caes. B Gall. 1,1,1). *Galatai* as an alternative term for C. is surely connected with a second wave of Celtic immigration into Gaul in around 390 BC (Pol. 1,6); for an opposing view to that discussed here see [2. 123ff.]. In line with the ancient differentiation, it is nowadays accepted custom to refer to the ancient inhabitants of Galatia as 'Galates', and to the Celtic population of Gaul and → Gallia Cisalpina as 'Gauls'; C. is used as the generic term and also includes related tribes outside the regions already mentioned.

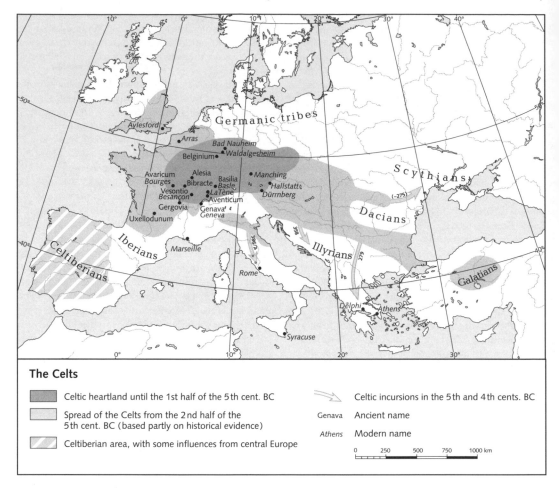

The Celts

▨ Celtic heartland until the 1st half of the 5th cent. BC

▨ Spread of the Celts from the 2nd half of the
    5th cent. BC (based partly on historical evidence)

▨ Celtiberian area, with some influences from central Europe

⇗ Celtic incursions in the 5th and 4th cents. BC

Genava Ancient name

Athens Modern name

0   250   500   750   1000 km

II. Celts in the West
A. Settlement area   B. Origins and
Hallstatt culture   C. La Tène culture
D. Further development

A. Settlement area

At the time of their greatest expansion, the C. occupied a vast area within Europe, extending in the west to the Atlantic from the Iberian peninsula to the British Isles, in the north to the great plains of Germany and Poland, in the east to the Carpathian arc, and in the south to the Mediterranean from the Catalan coast across the northern flank of the Apennine to the southern edge of the Danube basin. The preference of the early C. for elevated plains or hills dissected by river valleys is clearly discernible. Such an environment suits an economy in which agriculture was supplemented by livestock breeding. Conversely, the C. only showed little interest in the great plains, high mountains, or the coastal strips with their particular living conditions. The central area of the C. was in the region north of the Alps. Through this wide area flowed large rivers, communication routes from time immemorial. A key role was played by central Switzerland as the most important junction of the routes to the Danube valley, the Rhi-

neland, the Saône valley, northern Italy, and the Rhône valley. The rest of northern Gaul was linked to the core region by the elevated plain of the Champagne and by the Moselle valley, which joined the important point of intersection in the Rhineland between Mannheim and Koblenz. Apart from the Rhône and the rivers the Champagne region, both the Seine and the Loire were undoubtedly seen as the most important river routes, linking the Atlantic coast with the interior.

B. Origins and Hallstatt culture

Between 1800 and 1200 BC, settlement areas of a proto-Celtic culture developed, extending from southern Germany to parts of central and western Europe. Between 1200 and 750 BC, Celtic influence expanded into southern France and Spain. In around 725 BC, following the intrusion of the → Cimmerii into the Danube valley, a Celtic civilization of the first Iron Age (Hallstatt period) emerged in southern Germany, in modern Czechia and Slovakia, in Austria and France, which maintained good links with regional cultures and neighbouring tribes (Ligures, Iberi, Illyrii). From about 650 BC onwards, the expansion both of Greek colonization and of Etruscan trade along the southern coasts of France favoured an increasing contact between the C.

and the Mediterranean region. In addition, trade relations between Etruria and the Rhine valley intensified across the Alpine passes. → Massalia, founded in around 600 BC, increasingly dominated the exchange of goods between Greeks and C., which between 550 and 480 BC took place via the Rhône valley. During the first period the → Hallstatt culture (c. 850–600 BC), the population seems to have been widely scattered.

Social differences which have developed from the neolithic period onwards further intensify. Chieftains were buried with their chariots; warriors can be identified by their swords; the great majority of graves, however, contain just simple objects. A certain cultural uniformity across wide geographical areas is discernible, but the population was entirely split into small regional communities, ruled by local dynasties whose graves are found in *tumuli*. An important phenomenon is the development of fortifications in the Hallstatt area from the 9th cent. BC onwards. A further change took place from beginning of the 6th cent. BC regarding the development of trade relations with the Mediterranean region: a north-south axis gradually emerged. By contrast, the ancient east-west axis, which had been used for the transport of copper and tin — essential raw material for the production of bronze — gradually declined in importance. The *Keltiké* of the Hallstatt culture thus took over the advantageous role of intermediary in the exchange of goods between northern Europe and the Mediterranean region via the Rhône furrow and the Alpine passes. Archaeologically documented is the existence of a number of hill forts, of residences of Celtic rulers, and of → princely graves, as on the upper reaches of the Danube (the → Heuneburg at the crossing-point between north, south, west, and the Danube valley; and the Hohenasperg c. 100 km north of the Heuneburg) and in Burgundy (Vix).

C. La Tène culture

At the beginning of the 5th cent. BC, the principalities fell into rapid decline. Residences disappeared, at times under violent circumstances, burials lost in splendour, and imported luxury goods became rarer. However, in certain regions (Wetterau/Hesse, southern Thuringia, northern Bavaria, and Bohemia) important political and economic centres continued to exist into the 4th cent. BC, e.g. Ehrenbürg near Forchheim, Steinsburg (Thuringia; climax in the early La Tène, town-like centre) or Závist (Bohemia), smaller regional centres up to the beginning of the middle La Tène period (Eierberg, northern Lower Franconia, cf. [1. 110ff.; 2. 153f., 178f.]). Within the area of the German low mountain ranges, large refuge keeps developed in the later stages of the early La Tène period, indicating a new political association of larger tribal communities. The → Glauberg (Hesse) with its large hilltop fortifications and monumental graves (dynastic cult of the dead, life-size statues) reveals a supraregional centre of government of the early La Tène period with clear links to the Italian region [3]. Apparently at the same time, new powerful and prosperous centres develop in the north, especially in the Hunsrück/Eifel regions, on both sides of the Moselle, and in the Champagne. Typical of the onset of this period are the general use of → iron, and belligerent movements.

The graves of the Moselle and Marne regions are not as splendid as those of the Hallstatt princes, but they contain quite valuable implements, with important regional differences. Apart form objects imported from Greece and Etruria, local craft products are found, often imitations of the imported goods. The four-wheeled chariots of the princely graves are replaced by two-wheeled war-chariots (e.g. in the graves of Berru, La Gorge-Meillet, Sept-Saulx, Cuperly, Somme-Bionne, Waldalgesheim, and → Dürrnberg). Alongside the tombs of noblemen, there is a large number of warrior graves, furnished with some iron weaponry, a clear indication of the increased importance of this group. Some graves are linked with fortified hilltop settlements, used as residences or, more frequently, as refuges. Although the structure of theses societies was also predominantly hierarchical, there is no evidence either of the strongly centralized regions, typical for the principalities of the 6th cent. BC, nor of seignioralties. Rather, there seem to have been small autonomous communities, ruled by chieftains, whose power did not extend beyond their territories.

Most characteristic for the further restructuring of Celtic society is the *oppidum*: a town with simple fortifications on an important trade route or close to significant deposits of mineral resources. It is the economic centre of a region, which brought together craftsmen of various specialized trades, in which the main market was held, and which increasingly became a political and sometimes also a cultic centre (e.g. → Alesia, → Bibracte, Heidengraben, Kelheim or Závist).

The C. of the → La Tène culture were fearsome warriors, who made use of a remarkable → metallurgy, and who were frequently used as → mercenaries by the powers around the Mediterranean. Their southward migration soon became radical and massive. Between the 6th and 5th cents. BC, overpopulation as well as a shortage of cultivable land caused by a worsening of the climate prompted whole tribes (→ Senones, → Lingones, → Boii) or bellicose bands from the densely populated northern *Keltiké* and other regions (e.g. Bohemia), attracted by the promise of riches and frequently led by former mercenaries, to cross the Alps or to migrate along the well-known great trade routes. As early as the 5th cent. BC, they reached the south-east of Gaul, subjugated the → Ligures, and threatened Massalia, before they invaded into Italy at the beginning of the 4th cent. (Liv. 5,34; Pol. 2,17,3ff.). In 387 BC, the Romans suffered defeat at the → Allia. The Senones settled on a strip of land along the Adriatic coast — 60 km wide and 100 km long — between Pesaro and Macerata (*ager Gallicus*), a region of immense strategical importance, as it controlled the access to the Tiber valley and thus to central Italy and therefore constituted a permanent threat to the towns of Apulia and Campania. A renewed Celtic incursion across the Alps in 181 BC led to the foundation of the Roman colony of → Aquileia [1]. Internal displacement of Celtic tribes during the last three cents. BC resulted in the occupation of southern Britain by the → Belgae (Caes. B Gall. 5,12,2), and the Mediterranean coast by the → Volcae Tectosages and Volcae Arecomici, archaeologically traceable around → Narbo and in the Rhône delta. The last of these movements — the displacement and finally emigration of the → Helvetii — led to → Caesar's actions and thus the integration of Gaul into the Imperium Romanum.

D. Further development

Everywhere else within Celtic Europe, only complete and successful conquests are historically evident: with reference to Gaul in a wider sense (i.e. France, Belgium, and northern Switzerland), Str. 4,1,1 attests to a homogenous language; furthermore, there is a rather higher density of Celtic personal names in the peripheral areas than in the centre. In Gallia Cisalpina, the only areas to remain non-Celtic were Liguria, the Alpine valleys east of Lake Garda (Raeti), and Venetia. → Britannia was probably already Celtic prior to the invasion by the Belgae; Its religion (Caes. B Gall. 6,13,11f.) and language (Tac. Agr. 11) were similar to those of Gaul. In Bohemia, *oppida* (Hradiště near Prague) and other archaeological finds confirm the presence of Celtic Boii (Tac. Germ. 28; 70ff.; 127ff.). The limits of the Celtic expansion to the east are marked by Celtic tribal and personal names in Pannonia as well as ancient reports about Celtic → Iapodes and Scorisci in Illyricum (Str. 4,6,10; Pol. 1,6,4).

On the Iberian peninsula, there are no finds from the La Tène period nor an ancient tradition regarding immigration movements. Onomastics and inscriptions from the north and west show some Celtic characteristics, but differ significantly from those of Gaul. The names of the Celtici and → Celtiberi probably originated from Latin or Greek observers who had noticed similarities with the *Celtae* north of the Pyrenees. A particularly early Celtic penetration into Spain and Portugal is assumed. There is still uncertainty regarding many of the peripheral areas, especially the north-eastern border of Gaul; the existence of Germanic groups and also of other ethnic groups that were neither Celtic nor Germanic is presumed for Belgium and the middle and lower Rhine. Whether one should reckon with Celtic 'conquests' in all of these peripheral areas, or assume merely a cultural exchange across language barriers, remains generally unanswerable on the basis of the available sources.

The decline of Celtic culture, seen first of all as a loss of Celtic language area (→ Celtic languages), began in the east. The expansion of the Germanic tribes is detectable from the 2nd cent. BC (→ Cimbri, around 113 BC), at the time of Caesar, it was in full swing: the → Suebi under → Ariovistus; resettlement of the → Ubii to the left bank of the Rhine by → Agrippa [1] in 38 BC; the

decline of the power of the → Boii in Pannonia and Bohemia (Tac. Germ. 42; Plin. HN 3,146). In the other Celtic areas of the continent, Celtic language and autonomy increasingly fell victim to political and linguistic → Romanization. Both the duration and course of this process are disputed, also the extent to which remote areas such as Brittany or the coastal mountain ranges of Cantabria have been spared by it.

Celtic languages and social structures only survived within the British Isles; their area shrank with the onset of the Anglo-Saxon conquest in the 5th cent. AD, but survived to the early modern era in Cornwall, Wales, Scotland, and Ireland, and still today in Wales and remoter areas of Scotland and Ireland. In Brittany, immigrants from southern England reintroduced or revived Celtic folklore in the early Middle Ages.

1 S. Gerlach, Der Eierberg, 1995   2 K. Strobel, Die Galater 1, 1996   3 F.-R. Herrmann, O.-H. Frey, Ein frühkelt. Fürstengrabhügel am Glauberg, Wetteraukreis, Hessen, in: Germania 75, 1997, 459–550.

D. Allen, The Coins of the Ancient Celts, 1980; F. Audouze, O. Buchsenschutz, Villes, villages et campagnes de l'Europe celtique, 1989; G. Bergonzi, P. Piana Agostinetti, s.v. La Tène (Civiltà di), EAA², 272–284; P. Brun, Princes et princesses de la Celtique, 1987; Id., B. Chaume (ed.), Vix et les éphémères principautés celtiques, 1997; F. Burillo Mozota et al., Celtiberos, 1988; B. Cunliffe, The Ancient Celts, 1997; G. Dobesch, Die K. in Österreich nach den ältesten Ber. der Ant., 1980; P. Drda, A. Rybova, Les Celtes de Bohême, 1995; P. M. Duval, Les Celtes, 1977; Id., G. Pinault, Les calendriers (Coligny, Villards d'Héria), 1986; Id., V. Kruta (ed.), Les mouvements celtiques du Vᵉ au Iᵉʳ siècle avant notre ère, 1979; F. Fischer, Frühkelt. Fürstengräber in Mitteleuropa (Antike Welt 13), 1982; A. Furger-Gunti, Die Helvetier, 1984; V. Kruta, L'Europe des origines, 1992; Id. (ed.), Les Celtes au IIIᵉ siècle av. J.-C. (Études celtiques 28, 1991), 1993; Id., W. Forman, Les Celtes en Occident, 1985; V. Kruta, E. Lessing et al., Les Celtes, 1978; F. Le Roux, Chr. Guyonvarc'h, La société celtique, 1991; E. Lessing, Hallstatt, 1980; J. P. Mohen et al. (ed.), Les princes celtes et la Méditerranée, 1988; S. Moscati et al. (ed.), I Celti, 1991; B. Raftery, Pagan Celtic Ireland, 1994; H. D. Rankin, Celts and the Classical World, 1987 (repr. 1996); S. Rieckhoff, Süddeutschland im Spannungsfeld von Kelten, Germanen und Römern (TZ Beih. 19), 1995; D. and Y. Roman, Histoire de la Gaule, 1997; K. H. Schmidt (ed.), Gesch. und Kultur der K., 1986; K. Spindler, Die frühen K., 1983; M. Szabo, Les Celtes de l'Est, 1992.   Y. L.

III. Celts in the East

A. Celts in south-eastern Europe B. Celts in Asia Minor (Galatae) 1. Introduction 2. Terminology 3. History IV. The image of the Celts in antiquity V. Religion

A. Celts in south-eastern Europe

Around 400 BC or rather in the first decades of the 4th cent. BC, the early La Tène world saw a phase of migration [1. 33ff., 58ff., 153ff.]: new Celtic groups came to northern Italy; the central Danube and Carpathian regions were penetrated, and the eastern Celtic world reshaped by these movements. In the 2nd half of the 4th cent., an influential centre of La Tène civilization had developed in the central Danube basin. By 338 BC, Celts had already penetrated into northern Bosnia and northern Serbia; in 335 BC, they established diplomatic relations with Alexander the Great (treaty of friendship and *symmachia*).

In the 4th cent. BC, Celtic mercenaries are present in the Mediterranean region (Carthage, → Dionysius [1] I.). These movements across wide areas were made possible by a mobile society of aristocratic warriors and their followers. The political, religious and social change in the transition from the late Hallstatt to the early La Tène periods focussed on the figure of the solitary fighter of noble descent as the sword-wielding champion; the leader of the highest nobility drove into battle on his two-wheeled war chariot. Of decisive military importance were the cavalry of noblemen and the violent army of foot soldiers whose death-defying assault (development of a specific sword-belt) sought to decide the battle. Their way of life remained rural and sedentary. Their mobility took two basic forms: the military campaign, carried out by a band of warriors, or migration of several accumulated tribal groups with the conquest of land as its ultimate goal. Phases of migration alternate with those of territorialization, thus creating considerable social mobility. Each phase in the development of the historical peoples is linked with ethnogenetic processes.

After the death of → Lysimachus and the chaos of 281/0 BC, the Celtic tribes who had settled around the Drava, Sava and Danube mounted three campaigns in 280 BC, against Paeonia, Thrace, and Illyria [1. 214ff.]. The latter encountered Ptolemy Ceraunos; the Macedonian king and his army suffered comprehensive defeat, Macedonia was ransacked. From this traumatic event originated the outstanding military nimbus of the C. in the Hellenistic world. In 279 BC, → Brennus [2] mounted his major campaign through Macedonia into Greece. The defensive position of several Greek states at the → Thermopylae fell apart, after the Aetolians departed to repulse an attack by a Celtic detachment (massacre of Callion). The Celtic attack on → Delphi in the winter of 279/8 was repulsed, and the retreating C. incurred heavy losses. In 277 BC, → Antigonus [2] Gonatas defeated a Celtic army near Lysimachea; this first major victory in a battle against the C. brought him great prestige as saviour from the barbarian threat, and recognition as Macedonian king. In southern Pannonia and the northern part of Upper Moesia, the large tribal federation of the → Scordisci developed. Units moving to Thrace founded there the Celtic realm of → Tyle, a comparatively loosely structured formation, destroyed by → Thracians in 214/12 BC. In 218 BC, → Attalus [4] I enlisted as mercenaries the Aegosages in Thrace and later, despite a mutiny, settled them as agreed at the Hellespont; in 216 BC, → Prusias I annihilated them in the course of his policy of expansion (Pol. 5,77f.; 111).

B. CELTS IN ASIA MINOR (GALATAE)

1. INTRODUCTION

The establishment of the Galatae in Asia Minor and their maintenance of an independent state until 25 BC was a result of the politics of the Hellenistic powers and later of Rome: the Galatae quickly became an integral part of the Hellenistic power system; from that the ideological image of the Galatian 'Barbarian' must be differentiated.

2. TERMINOLOGY

[1. 123ff.]. The name *Galátai* (Γαλάται) and its related diminutive Latin form of *Galli* means 'brave and wild warriors'; it is the name by which the band of warrior referred to itself, the expression of the collective warrior identity of the arrière-ban. As a name used by outsiders, it becomes a generalised term, understood as referring to ethnicity. In Greek usage, the older collective ethnic term of *Keltoí* was still in common use in the 4th cent. BC; *Galátai* became synonymous as a generalized name. The same applies to the Latin nomenclature regarding the Gauls. In addition, for the Galatae of Asia Minor the Romans also developed the concept of *Gallograeci*, based on the Roman view of their outward appearance. The use of the term Galatians by Paul the Apostle corresponds with its Hellenistic understanding and has to be interpreted as referring to the historical-ethnic Galatae (Christian congregations in a rural Galatian environment) [1. 117ff.].

3. HISTORY

In 278/7 BC, migrating units of the → Tolistobogii and the → Trocmi, later also of the → Tectosages, were brought to Asia Minor on a contractual relationship as *sýmmachoi* of → Nicomedes' I and the other signatories to the anti-Seleucid alliance; they were successful in action from 277 to 275 BC. In reward, Nicomedes gave to them in c. 275/4 the eastern part of the newly conquered northern Phrygia as a settlement area, and from → Mithridates I they received a section of western Cappadocia in 274/272 in return for their support against a Ptolemaic landing (conflict with → Heraclea [7] Pontica about the town of Amastris). This became the territory of the Trocmi, whereas the Tolistobogii as the strongest group held the area west of Ancyra with the urban centre of → Gordium (see map). The comparatively small Celtic groups with strong demographical imbalances dominated socially the numerically far stronger rural population of this rich agricultural area, and shaped this newly developed historical region of → Galatia in its ethnic identity and language [1. 139ff.] into early Byzantine times. The large historical tribes are the result of ethnogenetic and culturalization processes in the course of the settlement (Galatization), in the course of which the Galatai also stimulated the → Hellenization of central Anatolia; however, everyday culture continued to be shaped by the earlier population.

The three large tribes were each divided into four politically independent sections with their own tradition of ethnic names; at their head was in each case a 'quarter leader' (*tetrárchēs* or *regulus*), furthermore a

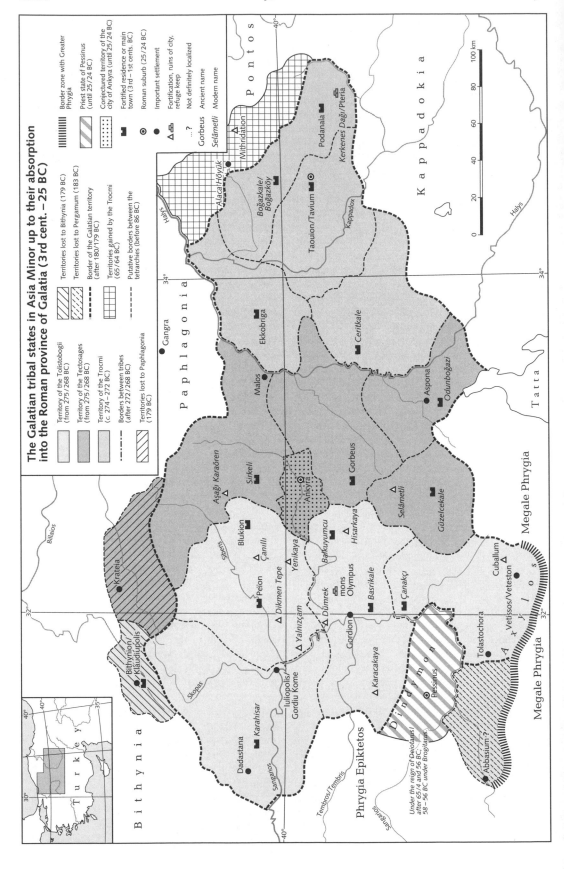

The Galatian tribal states in Asia Minor up to their absorption into the Roman province of Galatia (3rd cent. – 25 BC)

Territory of the Tolistobogii (from 275/268 BC)

Territory of the Tectosages (from 275/268 BC)

Territory of the Trocmi (c. 274–272 BC)

Borders between tribes (after 272/268 BC)

Territories lost to Paphlagonia (179 BC)

Border zone with Greater Phrygia

Priest state of Pessinus (until 25/24 BC)

Conjectured territory of the city of Ankyra (until 25/24 BC)

Territories lost to Bithynia (179 BC)

Territories lost to Pergamum (183 BC)

Border of the Galatian territory (after 180/179 BC)

Territories gained by the Trocmi (65/64 BC)

Putative borders between the tetrarchies (before 86 BC)

Fortified residence or main town (3rd–1st cents. BC)

Roman suburb (25/24 BC)

Important settlement

Fortification, ruins of city, refuge keep

Not definitely localized

Gorbeus   Ancient name
Selâmetli   Modern name

Under the reign of Deiotaros after 65/64 and 56 BC, 58–56 BC under Brogitarus.

judge and an armourer with two *hypostratophýlakes* (Str. 12,5,1). They descended from the leading families. Apart from the 12 'quarter' tribes, the Galatai were further subdivided into 183 clans, each with its own identity (*populi*, Plin. HN 5,146; clan structure). The 12 tetrarchies were joined in a federation with a federal sanctuary (Drynemeton, sacred oak grove) and a representative council (3 × 100 members); it exercised the judicial power over life and death and thus guaranteed the internal peace within the clan and tribal units. Only in exceptional circumstances and for a limited period of time was there a common leadership of individual tribes or one of all of the Galatae. Attempts to gain a royal position failed; for the duration of their independent statehood, the title of king could only be won with non-Galatian territories.

In 270/268 BC, the Galatae went to war against → Antiochus [2] I, who probably defeated them in 268 BC in the 'battle of the elephants' and made them pillars of Seleucid rule in Asia Minor. After that, the Galatae became involved in the internal conflicts of the Hellenistic states, e.g. in 253 or rather prior to 250 in the Bithynian war of succession and in from 240 to 238/7 in the fratricidal war between Seleucus II and Antiochus Hierax, whose main military support were the Galatae (this was the reason for the attack by Seleucus and his subsequent defeat in 238 BC by Hierax and the Galatae near Ancyra). Attalus I exploited the weakness in the position of the usurper Hierax for his fight for Pergamene supremacy; his first step was to break off all diplomatic relations to the Tolistobogii. In around 238/7, he defeated these at the Caicus springs, a feat which — stylized as the ideal victory over barbarians for the salvation of the Hellenes — legitimized his assumption of the royal title. This was followed by victories over Hierax and his Galatian allies—who seceded from him in 230 or at least before 228 BC — in the course of which his father-in-law Ziaëlas of Bithynia was killed. Peaceful and friendly relations between Pergamum and the Galatae developed. In 192/190, eleven of the tetrarchs were allied with → Antiochus [5] III against Pergamum and Rome.

In 189 BC, Cn. Manlius Vulso embarked on his campaign against the allies of Antiochus in Asia Minor, which ended with the victories over the Tolistobogii at Mount Olympus, and over the Tectosages, Trocmi, Morzius of Paphlagonia, and Ariarathes IV of Cappadocia at Mount Magaba. The celebrations of this victory by the towns of Asia Minor followed in the tradition of the Hellenistic victory against the Galatian barbarians. In the peace treaty of 188 BC, the Romans forbade the Galatai further military involvement outside their territories and thus prevented them from playing an active role in Roman-controlled Asia Minor. From 187 to 184/3, Prusias I and the Galatae fought a war against Pergamene preponderance: the victory of → Eumenes' [3] II secured Pergamene suzerainty over the Galatae. From 182 to 179, Pharnaces I went to war against Eumenes II and his allies, amongst them Prusias II and Morzius; several tetrarchs joined with Pharnaces. This resulted in the loss of territories of the Tolistobogii and Tectosages in the north (the Bolu basin to Bithynia; the Gerede basin, where Gaizatorix ruled, to Paphlagonia), and strictest Pergamene suzerainty over the Galatae. They rose in 168/166 as the core of an anti-Pergamum rebellion. In 166 BC, Eumenes II was victorious once again, but Rome restored Galatian independence and guaranteed it as a counterbalance to Pergamum.

In 89 BC, Galatian *socii* were part of the army mobilized against → Mithridates VI. After the Roman defeat, Galatia was not occupied immediately; the families of the tetrarchs were interned in Pergamum, where in 86 BC they failed in a conspiracy in their ranks. Mithridates VI had almost the entire tetrarchic nobility killed and ordered the occupation of Galatia. This was the decisive turning point in Galatian history. Three surviving tetrarchs, each at the head of one of the large tribes, led a movement of resistance, amongst them → Deiotarus I. Still in 86 BC, they succeeded in driving out the Pontic satraps and garrisons. In 73 BC, Deiotarus annihilated a Pontic army under the leadership of Eumachus. Galatian contingents fought in the armies of Lucullus and Pompey. In 65/4 BC, Pompey confirmed ruling tetrarchs in accordance with their dynastic (Str. 12,3,1) legitimization: Deiotarus from 86 BC as the sole tetrarch of the Tolistobogii, Brogitarus as that of the Trocmi, and Castor I Tarcondarius and Domnilausas tetrarchs of the Tectosages. Deiotarus was given the Gazelonitis, the eastern Pontic territory, and Armenia Minor, together with the regal title, and Brogitarus the Pontic border region including Mithridatium.

In 59 BC, the Senate formally awarded the regal title to Deiotarus, equally to Brogitarus. The latter was given control over Pessinus, but in 56 BC lost it to Deiotarus, who from 52 BC also ruled over the Trocmi after the death of Brogitarus. In 47 BC, Deiotarus was defeated by Pharnaces II at Nicopolis, and Armenia Minor and the territory of the Trocmi were seized by Caesar. From 47 to 46 BC, Mithradates of Pergamum, a nephew of Brogitarus, ruled as tetrarch of the Trocmi; his death was followed once again by an occupation by Deiotarus, who in 43/2 BC disposed of Castor I, the ruling tetrarch of the Tectosages. Until his death in 41/40 BC, Deiotarus remained the sole tetrarch of all Galatae. In 41/0 BC, Castor II, the son of Castor I and grandson of Deiotarus, became king of → Paphlagonia — succeeded there by his son Deiotarus Philadelphus (37/6–6/5 BC) — and tetrarch of all Galatae. → Amyntas [9], son of Dyitalus, a member of the tetrarchic nobility and former chancellor of Deiotarus, was in 39 BC awarded Pisidia and Phrygia Paroreios together with the regal title, followed by Lycaonia in 37/6, and became tetrarch of all Galatae. After 31/0 BC, he also received Cilicia Tracheia (→ Cilices), and conquered the territory of Antipater of Derbe. Amyntas, Rome's most powerful vassal in Asia Minor, died in 25 BC during the campaign against the Homonadenses. Augustus annexed his kingdom as the province of → Galatia.

IV. THE IMAGE OF THE CELTS IN ANTIQUITY

The image of the Celtic 'Barbarians' in the Hellenistic tradition and the Roman concept of the C. as the enemy — exploited in domestic policy, deliberately taking up the Greek topos, and particularly obvious in the Livian tradition (systematic negative portrayal and topos of Barbarian character) [1. 105ff.; 3] — continued to have an effect even on the academic historical literature (general image of their uncivilized, even hostile to civilization, non-sedentary nature) [1. 18ff., 54ff.; 2; 4]. The Greek type of the northern Celtic 'barbarian' was already formed in the 4th cent. BC, and by the 3rd cent., it had become a set ideologically functionalized typification: excessive in victory and defeat, without moderation or reason, displaying a negative trait with a suicidal or self-destructive tendency, bestial in nature, personifying the threatening stranger and the powers of chaos, offending against divine and human laws (archaic customs of war, human sacrifices, trespasses of sanctuaries). This is reflected in the iconography: bristling hair style (warrior style), coarse physiognomy, strange moustaches, excessive burning agitation, nudity when fighting, with typical shield and sword belt, even though in reality these were only the distinctive features of certain groups of elite warriors ('warrior order').

The pan-Hellenic defensive victory at Delphi against the first Barbarian invasion since 480 BC became a new focus of historical and political identity of the Greeks, and raised to the same level as the Persian Wars. In 278 BC, the Delphic → Soteria were instituted as the first pan-Hellenic victory celebration since the → Persian Wars. The defeat of the C./Galatae was seen as the ideal 'victory over the Barbarians' for the salvation of the Greeks and the repulse of the powers of chaos, and thus of importance for all of Greece; it legitimized the victorious general's claim to hegemonic power or respectively his monarchic position by proving his position as the charismatic victor. This is the way in which → Antigonus [2] Gonatas stylized his victory at Lysimachea, as did Pyrrhus his victory over the Celtic mercenaries of Antigonus in 274 BC, Ptolemy II the annihilation of his 4,000 mutinous mercenaries in 275 BC, Antiochus I his victory in the 'Elephant Battle', and Prusias I the extermination of the Aegosages. Under the Attalids (→ Attalus, with stemma), the ideology of the victory over the Galatae — from 278 BC an important element of Hellenistic political ideology — reached its climax with the monuments in Pergamum, Delphi, Delos and Athens. From 225/222 or respectively 189, Rome laid claim to being the true victor over the C. both in the west and in the east.

→ Celtic languages (with map); → Hallstatt culture; → La Tène culture; → Celtic archaeology; → Asia Minor (with map)

1 K. STROBEL, Die Galater 1, 1996   2 Id., Keltensieg und Galatersieger, in: E. SCHWERTHEIM (ed.), Forsch. in Galatien (Asia Minor Stud. 12), 1994, 67–96   3 B. KREMER, Das Bild der K. bis in augusteische Zeit, 1994   4 I. OPELT,

W. SPEYER, R. M. SCHNEIDER, s.v. Barbar, RAC Suppl. 1, 811–962   5 H.-J. SCHALLES, Unters. zur Kulturpolitik der pergamenischen Herrscher im 3. Jh., 1985.

H. BIRKHAN, Kelten, ²1997; H. DANNHEIMER, R. GEBHARD (ed.), Das kelt. Jt., 1993; W. HOBEN, Unters. zur Stellung kleinasiat. Dynasten in den Machtkämpfen der ausgehenden Republik, 1969; S. MITCHELL, Termessos, King Amyntas, and the War with the Sandaliôtai, in: D. FRENCH (ed.), Stud. in the History and Topography of Lycia and Pisidia, 1994, 95–105; G. NACHTERGAEL, Les Galates en Grèce et les Sôteria de Delphes, 1977; F. STÄHELIN, Gesch. der kleinasiat. Galater, ²1907; K. STROBEL, Die Galater im hell. Kleinasien, in: J. SEIBERT (ed.), Hell. Stud., Gedenkschr. H. Bengtson, 1991, 101–134; Id., Die Galater 1–2, 1996–1999; Id., Mithradates VI., in: Ktema 21, 1996, 55–94.   K. ST.

V. RELIGION

The Celtic tribes were not united in one nation. For that reason, it is not possible to talk of *one* Celtic religion. For the late Celtic period (1st cent. BC), literary, epigraphical, and archaeological sources all show clearly discernible common religious structures — at least as far as the mainland C. are concerned; in the final analysis, all of these stem from the common Indo-European origin.

A. DEITIES   B. CULT   1. HUMAN SACRIFICES   2. CULT SITES

A. DEITIES

Even though → *interpretatio Romana* enabled the Roman conquerors of Celtic settlement areas at least partially to equate Celtic deities with Graeco-Roman ones, there are distinct differences between the Celtic pantheon and its associated religious concepts and the Graeco-Roman deities with their rather narrowly defined functions.

Caesar (Caes. B. Gall. 6,17), reports of the Gallic tribes that 'Mercurius' ranked first in their worship, followed — without differences in rank — by 'Apollo' (curing diseases), 'Mars' (leading in war), 'Jupiter' (ruling the heavens), and 'Minerva' (teaching arts and crafts), and he names 'Dis Pater' as the divine ancestor of all Gauls. Caesar makes no mention of the native names of the deities on his list, and his *interpretatio* records only inadequately their nature which, according to other sources, was much more complex; this makes more difficult to assign those Celtic deities whose names are known. Of the (main) deities → Teutates, → Esus, and → Taranis as mentioned by Lucan (1,443ff.) in the 1st cent. AD, the more recent *adnotationes* and *commenta* to Lucan [1; 2] equate Teutates as well as Esus with Mars, Taranis with Jupiter as well as with Dis Pater. This shows that, in contrast with Roman deities, Celtic ones could possess widely differing qualities. The god Mars, for example, is epigraphically evident in Gaul with about 50 indigenous epithets. In these, the Celtic god of that name is not only the god of war, but a much more comprehensive god of — in the widest sense — fertility and healing.

If a multitude of deities with defined local, regional or tribal backgrounds can all be interpreted as being equivalent to the Roman god Mars, this does indicate that they were most likely variants of one and the same deity with its origins in pan-Celtic concepts. The supra-regional distribution of Celtic deities as preserved in a number of epigraphs and images from the Roman period also points to this. Apart from the deities already mentioned who were more clearly defined by *interpretatio Romana* and whose main functions were protection and healing, also included were those deities without counterpart in the Greco-Roman pantheon, such as: → Sucellus, the god of the mallet; the antlered god, depicted as sitting cross-legged and accompanied by snake, deer and bull, named → Cernunnos in the only surviving inscribed image on the altar of the Nautae Parisiaci, his image probably also shown on the Gundestrup cauldron; the three-headed and sometimes horned god whose name is not recorded; → Ogmius, the god who takes his armed followers with him on chains fastened to his tongue; Lugus, accompanied by ravens; the equestrian goddess → Epona as well as the fertile → Matres or Matronae. In all that, the depiction of Celtic deities from the Roman period display — alongside the Hellenistic-Roman typological repertoire — genuine Celtic elements in the combination of attributes: the use of indigenous dress and accessories (especially the → torques), the cross-legged way of sitting, the pairing of certain male and female deities.

The image of the tricephalic god as well as the triple or multiple representations of a deity are the Celtic expression of the totality and universality of that deity. The remarkable diversity of local and regional tutelary and healing goddesses, often linked with water, probably all stem from the original cult of a small number of or even only one mother goddess. Frequently, as noted in their names, Celtic deities are linked with animals: Epona with equids, Artio with the bear, the Matres with hound and hare, Arduina and Moccus with a hog or wild boar, Lugus and Nantosvelta with ravens, Cernunnos with deer and snake, the Gallic Mercury and Mars with rams or bulls, and Esus with bull or cranes. However, it would be wrong to infer from that the existence of original theriomorphic deities or rather totemism. By contrast, certain species of trees enjoyed cultic worship. Pliny the Elder (HN 16,45) reports that nothing was more sacred to the Celts than mistletoe and the oaks on which it grew. This fits in with epigraphical votives to Deus Robur and Deus Fagus and similar, dating from the Roman period in Gaul. The images of trees on the altars of the Matronae of the Rhine region also point to an original → tree cult. Significant natural features such as mountain ranges or individual peaks were also worshipped, as were various bodies of water. Springs were particularly venerable, as verified by the large numbers of deities worshipped there. Depots of votive offerings, at times with a continuity in finds dating back to the Bronze Age, indicate that even isolated rock formations were numinous locations.

B. CULT

The mythologies of the Celtic cultural sphere are largely unknown, as these — together with doctrines and cultic rites — were dominated by the druids (→ Druidae) and only passed on in oral tradition. Together with seers and bards, the druids formed the priestly caste which the latter dominated because of their religious influence, but also their influence on society in general. The collections of legends of the island Celts, which had been passed on orally until they were recorded in writing in the 11th or 12th cents. AD, probably under Christian influence, only provide a limited base for mythological research, because of their great distance in time as well as in space. The most important ancient sources (Posidonius, Caesar, Lucan) report of the great superstitiousness of the Gauls, of magic, of prophecy by inspecting the entrails of sacrificial animals or augury from the flight of birds, and of a belief in an afterlife and migration of the souls. The belief in an afterlife prompted the ancient authors to comparisons with Pythagorean teachings (→ Pythagoras); consequently, the druids were also referred to as philosophers.

1. HUMAN SACRIFICES

Reports about human sacrifices in ancient sources, traditionally considered tendentious, have increasingly gained in credibility through recent archaeological finds. Thus the large-scale depot with thousands of bones of adult men and hundreds of weapons, discovered in Ribemont-sur-Acre in the grounds of a La Tène cult site, brings to mind reports about the sacrifice of prisoners of war and captured weapons (Diod. Sic. 5,32,6); finds and evidence point to the reconstruction of tropaeum-like fixed headless bodies in battle armour and formation on a raised drying platform. The stone portico of Roquepertuse suggests the separate display of skulls at the entrance to the sacrificial site. Skeletons squeezed into narrow pits in front of the entrance to a cult building of the late La Tène settlement of Acy-Romaine (Reims) seem to confirm reports of the sacrifice of civilians (Caes. B Gall. 6.16). While the archaeological finds allow an at least rudimentary deduction of the cultic rites, they do not throw any light onto the identity of the deities in receipt of these sacrifices, as to date no cult image has been found *in situ* (iconographically, even the few surviving pre-Roman images of presumed cultic character, such as the two monumental wooden statues from Lake Geneva near Villeneuve, cannot be assigned to particular gods).

As early as the late Celtic period, at the very latest since the politically motivated ostracism and expulsion of the druids under emperor Claudius (mid 1st cent. AD), the usage and customs of sacrifices changed. The sacrificial object (weapons, tools, precious metals and similar) was largely turned into a symbolic sacrifice (wheel-shaped pendants, miniature tools, coins). In animal sacrifices — as evident on some votive reliefs — bulls and horses were replaced by goats, sheep, and pigs. There is no further evidence of human sacrifices.

2. CULT SITES

Architecturally conceived cult sites are distinguished by an enclosure of ramparts/palisades and ditches, as were funeral sites which were presumably used for the veneration of heroized ancestors (Glauberg, Vix). Nearly square enclosures surround post-build houses of equal shape that stood above the sacrificial pits serving as altars. In Gallic sanctuaries with a cultic tradition which survived into the Roman period, these basic ground-plans are found as predecessors of the distinctive Romano-Celtic temples. Not finally clarified is the role of the numerous *Viereckschanzen* (rectangular earthwork), predominantly found in southern central Europe, less so in France and there in a divergent function. Looking at all the examples of such earthworks in southern Germany which have been investigated in detail, presumably at least those dating from the late La Tène period should be seen predominantly as sanctuaries, but even with these, a monofunctional interpretation ought to be resisted.

1 H. USENER (ed.), M. Annaei Lucani Commenta Bernensia, 1869, 32f. 2 J. ZWICKER, Fontes religionis Celticae, vol. 1, 1934, 51,18; 52,19.

W. KRAUSE, Die Kelten. Religionsgesch. Lesebuch 13, 1929; J. MOREAU, Die Welt der K., 1958; J. DEVRIES, Kelt. Rel., in: Die Rel. der Menschheit 18, 1961; H. DANNHEIMER, R. GEBHARD (ed.), Das kelt. Jahrtausend, 1993; A. HAFFNER (ed.), Heiligtümer und Opferkulte der K., 1995 (bibliography); H. BIRKHAN, K., 1997. M.E.

Cemenelum Capital (*oppidum*) of the Vediantian Ligures, already inhabited in the Neolithic age, modern Cimiez near Nice. Under Augustus capital of the province of Alpes Maritimae (Diod. Sic. 29,28; Ptol. 3,1,43; Plin. HN 3,47), C. was a *municipium* of the *tribus Claudia* under the administration of *IIviri* on the *via Iulia Augusta;* under Diocletian, C. was assigned to Eburodunum in the Alpes Cottiae (It. Ant. 296; Not. Galliarum 17,7; Tab. Peut. 3,3). Bishop's seat (Hilarus Papa, ep. 4). Remains: residential quarters, aqueducts, baths, amphitheatre, necropoleis. Furthermore, an early Christian basilica and baptisterium.

Fontes Ligurum et Liguriae antiquae, 1976, s.v. C.; F. BENOIT, Cimiez, 1977; G. LAGUERRE, Inscriptions antiques de Nice-Cimiez, 1975. G.ME.

Cemetery see → Necropolis

Cempsi Only mentioned by Avien. 182ff. and by Dionys. Per. 338. They were probably a Celtic tribe (different in [1. 978]), who originally lived on the island of Cartare (probably in the → Baetis delta), later south of the Tagus and in the Anas valley. Possibly identical with the Celtici (cf. Str. 3,1,6).

1 Holder 1.

A. SCHULTEN, Fontes Hispaniae Antiquae 1, ²1955, 104ff.; TOVAR 2, 195f. P.B.

Cena The main daily meal of the Romans. Over the cents. it was largely influenced by Greek table culture: it shifted from midday to evening-time; while it was originally consumed sitting in the atrium or the kitchen, the upper classes at least later took it lying down in special, richly furnished dining rooms (→ *triclinium*); to the original sequence of main course (*mensa prima*) and dessert (*mensa secunda*) was added the starter course (*gustatio*). The duration and contents of the *cena* depended on the occasion, and above all on economic circumstances. The ordinary people ate modestly, in towns often only in snack bars, but frequently at public *cenae*, which fulfilled an important function especially in Italy. On the other hand, from the late Republic onwards the upper classes expended considerable sums on choice dishes accompanied by entertainments and followed by bouts of drinking (→ *comissatio*), which led more than once to the passing of laws against luxury. The upper class *cena* ideally brought together nine people who might be of various gender, age and status; in this respect, it appears to have been an occasion of social equality. However, absolute regard was given to the differing status of the participants: in formal circumstances the *locus consularis* was reserved as place of honour; the men, and from the end of the Republic also the women, lay on sofas; children and dependants, on the other hand, had to sit, sometimes at a separate table; even the quality of the food and drink sometimes varied for individual participants. The consistent practice of making offerings to the gods demonstrates the significant religious dimension of the *cena* (examples of the *cena*: Hor. Sat. 2,8,3; Petron. Sat. 28–78; Mart. 10,48; Juv. 11; Macrob. Sat. 3,13,12).

→ Meals

A. MAU, s.v. C. 2), RE 3, 1895–1897; J. MARQUARDT, Das Privatleben der Römer 1, ²1886; C. MOREL, E. SAGLIO, s.v. Coena, DS 1, 1269–1282. A.G.

Cenabum Capital of the → Carnutes on the Loire, more likely Orléans than Gien (Caes. B Gall. 7; 8), derived from Genabum/C.; Celtic root *gen*, 'mouth', 'river mouth'. C. was the starting point of the uprising of 52 BC under the command of → Vercingetorix; subsequently, Caesar ordered C. to be laid waste. Having suffered badly in the crises of the 3rd cent. AD, C. lost its name. From then on, it became capital of the *civitas Aurelianorum*. In AD 451, it was besieged by Attila.

J. DEBAL, Les Gaulois en Orléanais, ²1974; M. PROVOST, Le Val de Loire dans l'Antiquité, 1993. Y.L.

Cenaculum From Latin *ceno*; originally the dining room on the upper floor of the Roman → house. From time to time the term *cenaculum* includes the entire upper floor (Varro, Ling. 5,162; Fest. 54,6); the rooms described as *cenacula* were for accommodating guests of an inferior rank or slaves. They could also be the object of a lease; *cenaculum* became in this context synonymous with shabby housing.

GEORGES, 1, 1067, s.v. *c.* (sources); G.MATTHIAE, s.v. Cenacolo, EAA 2, 467 (bibliography).   C.HÖ.

Cena Cypriani Biblical parody in Latin by an unknown writer (not the → Heptateuch poet), attributed to → Cyprianus and presumably originating in the 4th/5th cents. as a reaction to edifying exegeses (Zeno Veronensis, tractatus 1,24): In 472 'maxims' in the manner of a catalogue with a framework of brief textual links, the 120 guests at a wedding in Cana (drawn from OT, NT, NT Apocrypha) are assigned seating, clothes, dishes etc. in often enigmatic accord with each character. The near-blasphemous treatment of Jesus and the proximity to pagan literature (→ Vespa, *Testamentum porcelli*, → cento and → symposium literature) are redolent more of comic/satirical than of didactic/mnemonic intent. The Cena Cypriani was popular in the Middle Ages (more than 50 MSS as well as four partly metric adaptations and one commentary); BACHTIN cited it as a paradigm of medieval 'comedic culture'.
→ Parody

W. AX, R. F. GLEI (ed.), Literaturparodie in Ant. und MA, 1993, 153–170; P. LEHMANN, Die Parodie im MA, ²1963 (1922), 12–16; C. MODESTO, Stud. zur Cena Cypriani und zu deren Rezeption, 1992 (ed., trans., comm.).   R.GL.

Cenaeum (Κήναιον, *Kénaion*; Lat. *Cenaeum*). The north-western foothills of → Euboea, modern Cape Lihada, a flat alluvial promontory of a Neocene coastal terrace, with a sanctuary of Zeus Kenaios (Scyl. 58). The sanctuary which was probably fortified in Hellenistic times did not have a temple. On C. were the towns of Athenae Diades and Dion. In 427/6 BC, an earthquake caused parts of the peninsula to disappear into the sea (Demetrius of Callatis, FGrH 85 F 6). Sources: H. Hom. 1,219; Thuc. 3,93,1; Str. 1,3,20; 9,4,4; 9,4,17; 9,5,13; 10,1,2; 10,1,5; 10,1,9; Ptol. 3,14,22; Liv. 36,20,5; Plin. HN 4,63; Mela 2,107; Solin. 11,24; IG XII 9, 188.

H. v. GEISAU, s.v. K., RE 11, 163f.; PHILIPPSON/KIRSTEN 1, 569ff.   H.KAL.

Cenchreae (Κεγχρεαί; *Kenchreaí*).
[1] Settlement en route from Argos to Tegea with graves of Argives fallen in the battle at the nearby Hysiae (according to Pausanias in 669/8 BC). C. was on the northern slope of Mount Ctenias opposite Hysiae on the southern side. Not exactly localizable, possibly near the modern Sta Nera, *c.* 3 km north-east of Achladokambos. The 'Pyramid of C.' at the exit of the valley further towards the north-east above the Argive plain presumably is the peel tower (*pýrgos*) of a farm. Sources: Str. 8,6,17; Paus. 2,24,7.

H. M. FRACCHIA, The Peloponnesian Pyramids Reconsidered, in: AJA 89, 1985, 683–689; PRITCHETT 3, 1980, 58–64; Id., Thucydides' Pentekontaetia and other Essays, 1995, 207–228.   Y.L.

[2] (Κεγχρεαί; *Kenchreaí* and several variations, Lat. *Cenchreae*). Port of → Corinth on the Saronic Gulf, about 7 km south-east. on the northern shore of a shallow bay near the modern Kehries, frequently mentioned in ancient literature (first in Thuc. 4,42,4; 44,4; 8,10,1; 20,4; 23,1; cf. esp. Apul. Met. 10,35). Prehistoric settlement on the hillside above the harbour. C. was extended on a large scale in Roman times and continued to exist throughout antiquity. Scyl. 55 describes C. as being fortified. C. is depicted on coins. Significant sections of the two breakwaters have been excavated, which protected the harbour to the north-east and the southwest, as well as buildings dating from the 1st and 2nd cents. AD. Paus. 2,2,3 mentions an Aphrodite temple, cults of Asclepius and → Isis (the Isis feast also in Apul. Met. 11,8–11; 16f.), and a bronze statue of Poseidon (cf. also Callim. H. 4,271). A Christian community is already mention in Paul's epistle to the Romans (16,1), the alleged diocese of C., however, is a legend. After C., the Saronic Gulf was also known as *Kenchreátēs* (Κεγχρεάτης) (Scymn. 508f.). Inscriptions: IG IV 206f.; SEG 11,50. Coins: [1. vol. 3].

1 R. SCRANTON et al., K., 5 vols., 1976–1981.

D. MUSTI, M. TORELLI, Pausania. Guida della Grecia, 2. La Corinzia e l'Argolide, 1986, 214–216.   Y.L.

Cenchreus (Κέγχρειος, Κέγχριος; *Kénchreios, Kénchrios, Cenchreus*). Stream south-west of Ephesus (Alexander Aetolus fr. 2 POWELL; Str. 14,1,20; Paus. 7,5,10; Tac. Ann. 3,61,1), modern Arvalia Çayı (not the Değirmen dere, but cf.[1]); it rises at Mount Solmissus (modern Agadağ), and before its sedimentation flowed into the bay of the Caystrus, nowadays from the left into the → Caystrus [1] itself. The C. ran through the Ortygia, the grove in which Leto allegedly gave birth to Apollo and Artemis (Str., Tac. loc. cit.); it was the location of a sanctuary of Opis-Artemis (→ Opis), where an annual feast took place. The river god C. is depicted on coins from the 1st half of the 2nd cent. AD [2].

1 J. KEIL, Ortygia, die Geburtsstätte der ephesischen Artemis, in: JÖAI 21/2, 1922/1924, 113–119   2 S. KARWIESE, s.v. Ephesos, RE Suppl. 12, 335f.

O. BENNDORF, in: FiE 1, 1906, 76–79; L. BÜRCHNER, s.v. Ephesos, RE 5, 2773 fig. 2, 2782; F. HUEBER, Ephesos, 1997, 30f. with fig. 2, 39; S. KARWIESE, Groß ist die Artemis von Ephesos, 1995, 79, 104 with fig. 79.   H.KA.

Cenomanni
[1] A people of southern Gaul, near Massilia (Plin. HN 3,130).

M. PY, Les Gaulois du midi, 1993.

[2] Tribe of the Aulerci in the region of modern Maine, between the Loire and the Seine. Their capital was *civitas Cenomanorum*, the modern Le Mans (Notitia Galliarum 3,2).   Y.L.

[3] (Cenomani). Tribe of the Gallic Aulerci, originally living in the Maine (probably the modern Le Mans: Not. Gall. 3,3, or Marseilles: Plin. HN 3,130); migrated to Italy before the 4th cent. (Pol. 2,17; Liv. 5,35,1; Str. 5,1,9). Originally of La Tène culture, they settled in the region of the Golasecca culture, between Oglio, Po and Adige, in close contact with Etruria Padana and the Veneti. They were centred on the future cities of Brixia and Verona (Liv. 5,35,1) or Cremona (Plin. HN 3,130), more questionably Bergomum, Mantua and Tridentum (Ptol. 3,1,31). Allied with the Romans against the Insubres and the Boii during the 2nd Punic War (Pol. 2,23f.; Liv. 2,55), they rose up against Rome under Punic leadership (200–197 BC), but were subjugated (Liv. 32,30f.; Diod. Sic. 29,14) and lost all social and cultural identity.

R. SCUDERI, I Cenomani, 1975, 117–155.   A.SA.

Censores Former consuls seem to have been chosen as officers of the census for the first time in 443 BC by a *lex de creandis censoribus*, the purpose being to free the consuls of this duty (Liv. 4,8,3; similarly Dion. Hal. Ant. Rom. 2,62). The tradition of the office being held in common by a patrician and a plebeian probably becomes the norm only after the *leges Liciniae Sextiae* of 367. Regular censuses every five years (*lustrum*) made a regular election of censors necessary from this time. But there were occasional departures from the prescribed interval; even, during the 2nd and 3rd cents. BC (Priscian 9,38 KEIL) for an extended period. After the *lex Aemilia Mamerca de censura minuenda* of 434 the period of office for the censorship is only one and a half years instead of five (Liv. 4,24,5; 9,24,7–9), regardless of the duration of a *lustrum*. The collegiate character of the office permits the → intercession of the one against the as yet untried official actions of the other. The range of duties belonging to the office, moreover, dictates that its holders always act in concert. From its beginnings as a subordinate function delegated by the consulate, although already entrusted with: a) official supervision of the public *scribae;* b) the administration of the official roll; c) the procedural arrangements for the assessment of capital holdings; d) the implementation of the popular count (Liv. 4,24,5), in the 3rd and 2nd cents. BC the office for a while acquires central importance in internal politics, especially under prominent censors such as M. Porcius → Cato Censorius. Even before this time, the censors' powers had gradually increased; thus the *lex Ovinia* of 312, transferring the *lectio senatus* to the censors. Event powers are as follows: e) in connection with the census itself, the assignment to, or removal of citizens from the roll of electors to the centuriate assemblies, including the *eques* (*classis equitum*), the *tribus*, the tribal assemblies, and the Senate; f) jurisdiction (*regimen morum*) over breaches of private and public morality (*mores*), of familial and religious duties, of standards of moderation and decency of lifestyle, of duties of patronage, duties of political and corporative

honour and example, and military discipline. All citizens entitled to the vote are subject to the supervision of the censors. The office therefore comprises neither mere jurisdiction over the standing of *eques* and senators nor in the real sense a juridical function, although the sanctions invoked can have serious implications: warnings (*admonitiones*), reprimands (*notae*) and removal of privileges, for example through removal from the Senate or demotion from the equestrian *classis* to a low-ranking electoral class or *tribus* (*senatu movere, equum demere, tribu movere*, Plut. Cato Mai. 5ff.; Val. Max. 2,9); g) the authority to oversee the administration of the public purse and to order measures for its employment, for example the leasing of public lands (*agri vectigales*), mines, monopolies, rights to collect customs duties or taxes, as well as the setting of rating guidelines for new taxes (Cic. Leg. 3,7; Liv. 45,15,4 and 8; Dig. 1,2,2,17). The effect of this proliferation of powers gave the office a high political profile; its insignia included, as for consuls, the *sella curulis* and the *toga praetexta*, but owing to the lack of *imperium* not the *fasces*. A frequent consequence is that the office is misused in a political and partisan manner — probably sufficient reason for its elimination by → Sulla, within whose extraordinary official powers it is swallowed up. After its reintroduction in AD 70, Caesar eliminates it once again, and in its place declares himself *praefectus morum*. Although the office is revived again under the Augustan restoration, and often during the 1st cent. AD even appears among the emperor's titles as a part of his formal functions, at least in important cases the prerogatives previously belonging to the censors are now entirely the emperor's, even when he does not himself formally occupy the office of censor. By the 2nd cent. at the latest, therefore, the office falls into disuse; its duties fall to the administrative strata serving the → census, the provincial and city administrations or the courts, insofar as the emperor does not take them upon himself (e.g. in overseeing the morals of prominent individuals). → Consul; → Censuales; → Mores

JONES, LRE 427ff. (finance), 970ff. (morals); MOMMSEN, Staatsrecht 2,2, 331–469; J. SUOLAHTI, The Roman Censors, 1963, 15–79.   C.G.

Censorinus

[1] Character invented by the author of → *Historia Augusta*; one of the so-called 30 tyrants, supposedly usurper under Claudius Gothicus, he was killed after seven days. For *vita*, SHA Tyr. Trig. 31,12; 32,8–33,6. PIR[2] C 656.

K.-P. JOHNE, Kaiserbiographie und Senatsaristokratie, 1976, 122–28.   A.B.

[2] **Caelius C., C.** High official of the time of → Constantinus the Great. He is known only from an inscription from Campania (ILS 1216), where the offices held by him are named. PLRE 1,196 no. 2.

[3] **Caelius C.** *Consularis Numidiae* between 375 and 378 (CIL VIII 2216), perhaps identical with the addressee of Symmachus, Ep. 8,27. PLRE 1,196 no. 1.

W.P.

[4] A grammarian living in the 1st half of the 3rd cent. AD (Cassiod. Inst. 2,1,1; Prisc. Gramm. 2,13,19); besides a lost work *De accentibus* (Prisc. Gramm. 3,27,24; 45,25; Cassiod. Inst. 2,5,10), which treated i.a. functional differences in the emphasis of prepositional adverbs, C. wrote the treatise *De die natali* (Sid. Apoll. Carm. 14, Epist. 3; Cassiod. Inst. 2,6,1; July/August of AD 238) for his patron Q. Caerellius. On the pattern of Varro's *Logistorici,* the 1st part (2–14) covers the genetic, astrological (→ astrology) and numerological aspects (heptad and ennead, → Number mysticism) of birthdays, after i.a. → Varro (*Tubero de origine humana*; *Atticus de numeris*); the 2nd part (16–24) compares the uses of chronography, after i.a. → Suetonius, *De anno Romanorum*, and Varro, *Antiquitates de temporibus*. On his own account, C. also incorporates the work of Greek specialists (perhaps acquired via doxographic handbooks). Of scientific note are the sections on procreation and embryology [1], planetary theory [2], musical method [3] and the dual schematic of secular games [4] (→ Ludi saeculares). C. is seldom cited, his text being based on the 7th-cent. Coloniensis 166 (with the → Fragmentum Censorini). The humanist J. J. SCALIGER valued this latter work as *liber aureolus* ('golden book') in the literary wasteland of the 3rd cent.

1 E. LESKY, Die Zeugungs- und Vererbungslehren der Ant. und ihr Nachwirken, AAWM 1950, 19; Id., Alkmaion bei Aetios und Caelius, in: Hermes 80, 1952, 249–255 2 C.v. JAN, Die Harmonie der Sphären, in: Philologus 52, 1893, 13–37 3 L. RICHTER, Griech. Tradition im Musikschrifttum der Römer, in: Archiv für Musikwiss. 22, 1965, 69–98 4 P. WEISS, Die 'Säkularspiele' der Republik, eine annalistische Fiktion?, in: MDAI(R) 80, 1973, 205–217 5 R. M. THOMSON, The reception of Caelius, in: Antichthon 14, 1980, 177–185.

EDITIONS: K. SALLMANN, 1983 (with bibliography); C. A. RAPISARDA, 1991 (with Italian translation); G. ROCCA-SERRA, 1980 (French); K. SALLMANN, 1988 (Ger.).
BIBLIOGRAPHY: K. SALLMANN, Caelius' De die natali, in: Hermes 111, 1983, 233–248; Id., HLL § 441.
SOURCES: F. FRANCESCHI, Caelius e Varrone, in: Aevum 28, 1954, 393–418. KL.SA.

Censorius Niger, C. Perhaps from Solva in Noricum [1. 80]; after AD 132 procurator in Mauretania Tingitana [2. 49 n. 79, 80]; after 135 procurator in Noricum (CIL III 5174; 5181). He was a close friend of → Fronto (Fronto, Ad Ant. Pium 3, p. 157 VAN DEN HOUT), and at first of the *praef. praetorio* Gavius Maximus, whom he then insulted in his will (Fronto, Ad Ant. Pium 4, p. 159). PIR² C 658.

1 G. ALFÖLDY, Noricum, 1974 (sources for C. 244) 2 G. WINKLER, Reichsbeamte von Noricum ..., 1969, no. 10.

PFLAUM 1, 226–229, no. 97 b, 201 Text 13. M.STR.

Censorship
I. DEFINITION II. JUDAISM III. GREECE
IV. ROME

I. DEFINITION
Censorship — from Lat. *censura* ('examination', Middle Latin 'supervision, reprimand') — describes the control (preventative or pre-censorship) and/or the suppression (repressive or post-censorship) of written records, esp. literary ones. In antiquity, censorship was unknown in the sense of a set institution, such as existed later in the age of Absolutism or, if more concealed, in the totalitarian systems of the modern age; however, at certain times and places, it was exercised for political or religious reasons or both. Linked with censorship were measures of varying harshness against authors (prohibition, forced exile, execution) and their works (removal from libraries, destruction).

II. JUDAISM
Sporadical references to protecting political and religious texts from textual alterations (sometimes by adding a curse formula) indicate a fear of distortion or destruction of such literature (a famous example: Moses' admonishment, Deut. 4,2 und 13,1). The incidents of censorship and book destruction in the Judaism of the Hellenistic period are part of the larger framework of the canonization of the Old Testament and the fight against heretic tendencies; for the period after AD 70, there are at times striking similarities with equivalent disputes within the Ancient Church (extensivcly in [11. 112–119]; ⟩ Heresy).

III. GREECE
The Old → Comedy enjoyed a certain freedom in respect of political criticism and polemics, but its curtailment was frequently attempted [11. 46 f.]. One form of censorship in Classical Greece is evident in the trials for → *asébeia* of → Protagoras [1] (probably shortly before 420 BC) and → Socrates [2] (399); in the case of Protagoras, the public burning of his works is reported (Cic. Nat. D. 1,63). We also know of measures taken against philosophers (esp. Epicureans) and other critical voices from the Hellenistic period [11. 48–50]; as later in Rome, the problem was frequently solved by expulsions (cf. S. Emp. Adv. math. 2,25: individual philosophers' schools; Ath. 4,184c: several occupational groups; Ath. 12,547a-b: Epicureans; Ath. 13,610e: all philosophers). In extreme cases, criticizing a Hellenistic → ruler could carry the death sentence: the 'protest poet' → Sotades [2] was allegedly drowned in the 1st half of the 3rd cent. BC after having attacked Ptolemy [3] II.; it is uncertain, however, whether in the case of the grammarian → Daphitas criticism of the ruler also played a role. A different form of censorship is represented by the literary criticism in → Plato's [1] 'Laws': A controlling committee was to be charged with censoring poetic works in respect of transgressions of the law (tragedies, but also the Homeric epics: e.g. Pl. Resp.

386c–387e; 607a; Pl. Leg. 801c-d; 817b-d, Greek terms: ἐξαιρέω/exhairéō i. a.).

IV. ROME
A. REPUBLIC B. FROM AUGUSTUS TO THE END OF THE 3RD CENT. AD C. 4TH. CENT. TO THE END OF ANTIQUITY

A. REPUBLIC

The *ludi Romani* (→ *ludi* III. G.) of 240 BC saw the first performance of a Greek drama in Latin language: It has to be presumed that in his selection of future subject matter, its author → Livius [III 1] Andronicus depended on the aediles in charge of these games, who much preferred Roman national over controversial Greek topics [9]. Roman comedy (→ Plautus, → Terentius [III 1]) was apolitical, with the possible exception of → Naevius: somewhat earlier in time, he came into conflict with the nobility (→ *nobiles*), who were apparently exercising censorship. A kind of freedom comparable with that of the Old (Attic) Comedy was enjoyed in the 2nd cent. by the satirist → Lucilius [6], whose polemics, targeted also at his living contemporaries, remained without successor (→ Horatius [7]; → Iuvenalis). From the Republic and the early Principate, occasional confiscations and destructions (such as *conquirere* and *comburere*) of prophetic-ritual works are reported [8. 160 f.; 268–270; 11. 51 f.]; there is also documentary evidence of the expulsions of philosophers (Suet. Gram. 25; Ath. 12,547a; Plut. Cato maior 22) and Chaldaeans (*mathematici*, 'astrologers': 139 BC, presumably in conjunction with the burning of books; [3. 58 and generally 233–248]); furthermore the censorship of Latin teachers of rhetoric (Suet. Gram. 25; → Plotius [I 1] Gallus).

B. FROM AUGUSTUS TO THE END OF THE 3RD CENT. AD

From as early as 33 and 28 BC as well as from the reign of Tiberius [1] (AD 14—37) further expulsions of Chaldaeans and magicians are known (→ Magic III. C.5.; [11. 54 f.; 64]); for the mistrust towards philosophers in the 1st cent. cf. [4. 253–255]. Expulsions from the country were carried out at the behest of → Vespasianus (Cass. Dio 65,13,2: probably AD 74) and → Domitianus [1] (Tac. Agr. 2,2; Plin. Ep. 3,11,2 f. in conjunction with the execution of → Arulenus [2] Rusticus: AD 93). In the world of literature, there were repeated attempts at censorship from the latter years of Augustan rule onwards → Augustus. At least according to his own statement, the banishment of → Ovidius Naso was in part the result of censorship; *de facto* however it was more likely the outcome of a scandal at the imperial court (allegedly, all of his works were removed from public libraries: Ov. Tr. 3,1). Censorship was particularly pitiless when dealing with historians, biographers, and orators who were suspected of republican convictions or links with opposition circles: still in the Augustan period T. → Labienus [4] (suicide after his

books were banned and destroyed) and Cassius [III 8] (prohibition of his works, relegation, deportation under Tiberius; → *relegatio*; *deportatio*), in the Tiberian period → Cremutius Cordus (confiscation and burning of his historical works, suicide by self-starvation [12; 2]), → Aemilius [II 14] Scaurus Mamercus (copies of his speeches were burnt, he committed suicide); during the reign of Domitian → Arulenus [2] Rusticus and → Herennius [II 11] Senecio (execution and burning of books in both instances: Tac. Agr. 2,1), furthermore an otherwise unknown Hermogenes of Tarsus (Suet. Dom. 10,1). Further material from the 1st cent. AD: [11. 65–74].

How much conditions had changed in comparison with the late Republic is demonstrated by the fact that then the invectives and satirical epigrams by Catullus [1] and Licinius [I 31] Macer Calvus against Caesar and Pompey [I 3] remained without consequences for them, whereas Aelius Saturninus and Sextius [II 8] Paconianus (AD 35) had to pay with their lives for publishing similar poetry (Cass. Dio 57,22,5; Tac. Ann. 6,39,1).

While in the 1st cent. AD censorship used the pretence of *laesa* → *maiestas* gratuitously, the 2nd cent. showed much greater tolerance, with authors and philosophers enjoying an astonishing degree of freedom of opinion. A new turn in censorship was heralded — in an extension of the widespread prohibition of magical books — by the destruction of the works of other religions (e.g. Torah rolls [11. 74]). The edicts of → Diocletianus resulted in the persecution of the Manichaeans (→ Mani) and Christians and the burning of the holy books of both of these communities [11. 76–79].

C. 4TH. CENT. TO THE END OF ANTIQUITY

The latter was repeated during the restoration of non-Christian cults under the rule of emperor → Iulianus [11]. From the recognition of Christianity by emperor → Constantinus [1] (AD 313) the new alliance of state and church then applied the same measures against those who were now referred to as 'heathens' (*gentes*), also against the 'heretics' (*haeretici*) within their own ranks. Criticism from within the Church was rare: censorship legitimized itself as the fight against false doctrine. Not only pagan religious texts, magic books, morally offensive literature and dramatic works were under threat, but also and esp. disturbing writings by the followers of → Novatianus, → Marcion, → Donatus [1], of → Montanism and the Manichaeans (→ Mani), to name but a few, as well as later the followers of → Pelagius [4], of → Semipelagianism, → Nestorianism and → Monophysitism ([1. 163–197; 11. 142–157]; rich in source material: [6]).

V. MIDDLE AGES AND EARLY MODERN PERIOD

A famous example of censorship, punishment of an author, and destruction of his books in the early 12th cent. was Petrus Abaelard, who was initially tortured and castrated because of his relationship with Heloise, later accused of heresy on account of his work *De uni-*

tate et trinitate and sentenced to eternal silence. From the 13th to 15th cents., a veritable campaign against the → Talmud took place, in which even outstanding scholars such as Albertus Magnus participated [10. 31–34]. In the early years of the 15th cent., the reform movement of the Wycliffites with its anti-papal and national roots spread across England; while it was suppressed in its place of origin, it soon spread to continental Europe: one of its pioneers in Prague was JOHN HUS, who in 1410 was banned and prohibited from preaching; his books were burned, and despite the assurance of free passage, HUS was condemned to death by fire during the Council of Constance in 1415 [7. 307–487]. In 1520, the papal nuntius ALEANDER ordered the public burning of LUTHER's three main reformatory treatises in Leuven; in December of that year LUTHER responded by burning the papal bull threatening his excommunication. During the Council of Trieste (1564) the Counterreformation assembled the *Index librorum prohibitorum* ('Index of forbidden Books'), thus providing the inquisition with a foundation in Church law, covering all variations of censorship from tolerance to persecution of an author and the destruction of his works (renounced only after the Second Vatican Council). A description comparable with that of ancient reports of book burnings is provided by Goethe in his 'Dichtung und Wahrheit' ('Poetry and Truth'; Part I, Book IV).
→ Heresy; → Literary activity; → Maiestas; → Polemics; → Propaganda; → Suicide; → Capital punishment; → Tolerance; → Exile; → Author; CENSORSHIP

1 W. BAUER, Rechtgläubigkeit und Ketzerei im älteren Christentum, ²1964   2 H. CANCIK, Zensur und Gedächtnis. Zu Tacitus Annales IV 32–36, in: AU 29, 1986, H. 4, 16–35   3 F. H. CRAMER, Astrology in Roman Law and Politics, 1954   4 FRIEDLÄNDER, vol. 3   5 L. GIL, Censura en el mundo antiguo, 1961   6 A. HILGENFELD, Die Ketzergeschichte des Urchristentums, 1884 (repr. 1963) 7 M. D. LAMBERT, Ketzerei im MA. Häresien von Bogumil bis Hus, 1981   8 LATTE   9 E. LEFÈVRE, Die polit.-aitiologische Ideologie der Tragödien des Livius Andronicus, in: Quaderni di Cultura e di Tradizione Classica 8, 1990, 9–20   10 H. J. SCHÜTZ, Verbotene Bücher, 1990 11 W. SPEYER, Büchervernichtung und Zensur des Geistes bei Heiden, Juden und Christen, 1981   12 W. SUERBAUM, Der Historiker und die Freiheit des Wortes, in: G. RADKE (ed.), Politik und lit. Kunst im Werk des Tacitus, 1971, 61–99.   G. Bl. and H. H.

Censuales Assessment of citizens for tax purposes (→ *census*) in republican Rome is carried out by subordinate officials of free status (*scribae*) and by bonded state servants (*servi publici a censu* or *censuales*), under the political responsibility of the → *censores* insofar as they are in office. But supervision of the administration of the tax registers (*libri censuales*) is carried out by a chief administrator, probably from early times called *magister census*. There are also *census* officials, occasionally termed *censuales,* in provincial administrations and in cities with their own constitution.

At first this remains the case under the Empire (Liv. 43,16, 13; CIL VI 2333–2335). But the uppermost tax authority becomes part of the central imperial government (*aerarium; fiscus Caesaris; sacrae largitiones*). In late antiquity, *censuales* means the same as *scribae, logographi* and *tabularii* (Cod. Iust. 10,71,1). Further officials with partly *census*-related duties (*numerarii, regerendarii, rationales, a scriniis canonum*) are located in the imperial palace, on the staff of the *praefecti praetorio* and the provincial governors, and in the *civitates* (Not. Dign. Or. 3,14,20; Cod. Iust. 10,71,3). A senatorial *censualis* in the Rome and Constantinople of late antiquity is the *magister census*, whose duties include *census* of the senators, moral supervision of students in the city, the publication of wills in official safekeeping, the emergency care of orphans and overall supervision of the staging of public games (Cod. Theod. 8,12,8; 14,9,1; 6,4,26f.; Cod. Iust. 1,3,31).

JONES, LRE 553, 592, 600; MOMMSEN, Staatsrecht 1, 329f., 370.   C.G.

Census From the general meaning of *censere* (etymologically from *centrum*) the following specialized uses of the term *census* are derived:

1. The *census* of citizens in the Republican period. According to Roman historical tradition (Liv. 1,42,5), it was first the kings and later the consuls who carried out censuses of the citizenry in order to establish obligations for military and other types of service, and liability for tax. From 443 BC (Liv. 4,8,2) two censors bear responsibility for the census over a term of office lasting five years (→ *lustrum*). They have to announce the principles of their administration in an edict, and (probably) complete their official business within a period of 18 months. This includes receiving the declaration all Roman citizens (*patres familias*) have to make concerning their family circumstances and their financial situation (*inter cives Romanos censum profiteri* — Ulp. 1,9); investigating the *vitia* (including those of moral nature) contained in those declarations or made known by other means; reviewing citizens' membership of one of the four urban and 31 rural *tribus* of Rome, of the eventual 193 (Cic. Rep. 2,22) *centuriae* of the *comitia centuriata*, of the class of → *equites* or of the Roman Senate (*lectio senatus*), and administering new membership allocations. In the area of moral jurisdiction (*regimen morum*), they may not only administer reprimands (*notae*), but also decree the reallocation of citizens to a less prestigious (i.e. urban) → *tribus* or *centuria* (*tribu amovere*), or their removal from the equestrian class or the Senate on the grounds of moral turpitude. It is also the function of the *census* to examine state assets and financial management by the magistrates, and if necessary undertake their reorganization. Upon the completion of the censors' office, an expiatory sacrifice is made, from which the five-year cycle of the census also takes its name.

2. In addition, during the Republic and later, the term *census* describes the entering into the tax registers of *subiecti* liable for tax under Roman jurisdiction — i.e. those who are not *cives Romani* — together with an estimation of their taxable assets (*caput*). This is primarily a responsibility of provincial administrations and associated city states, in late antiquity also of the praetorian prefectures (Dig. 50,15; Cod. Iust. 11,38,10).

3. The term *census* also describes the tax declaration made by the citizen himself; furthermore his taxable assets, his tax liability over the course of a tax period, and the land register associated with the collection of taxes (→ *libri censuales*, Medieval Latin *capitastra* — Dig. 10, 1,11; 36,1,17).

→ Censor; → Senatus; → Comitia (centuriata and tributa); → Time; → Capitatio

JONES, LRE, 453ff.; MOMMSEN, Staatsrecht 2, 331ff.; J.SUOLAHTI, The Roman Censors, 1963, 20ff., 47ff.
                 C.G.

Centaurs (Greek Κένταυρος, pl. Κένταυροι; Ἱπποκένταυροι; Κενταυρίδες; *Kéntauros*, pl. *Kéntauroi; Hippokéntauroi; Kentaurídes*).

I. MYTHOLOGY II. ICONOGRAPHY

I. MYTHOLOGY
A. DEFINITION B. DESCENT AND CENTAUROMACHIES C. CHARACTER AS MONSTERS

A. DEFINITION
Centaurs are four-legged → monsters consisting of man and horse, their homeland was seen as the Greek mainland, generally speaking the forested mountains of Thessaly, especially the Pholoe Range and Cape Malea. They often appear as an aggressive group of evil-doers, who cause offence especially by raping women. They challenge not only heroes (such as Heracles, Peleus, Atalante) but also humans (groups). All battles end with their defeat and expulsion. Individuals such as → Eurytion, Hasbolos, → Hylaeus and → Nessus for the most part share the characteristics of the group; exceptions who are friendly towards humans are → Chiron and → Pholus. Families and female centaurs, who let the tribe become the counter-picture of human society, are first documented in the 5th cent. BC and are probably an invention of the painter → Zeuxis, who was the first to portray a female centaur (Lucian. Zeuxis 3,4; centaur families: Philostr. Imag. 2,3; Ov. Met. 12,393–428; Vitr. De arch. 7,5,5).

B. DESCENT AND CENTAUROMACHIES
Their tribal father is → Centaurus, the son of → Ixion and the horse-shaped → Nephele (Pind. Pyth. 2,42–48). The written records vary as to whether the first descendant of the pairing with horses were human-horsebeings already, or only later descendants.

Diod. Sic. 4,69–70 compares the human-form centaurs with the hippocentaurs (Lucian. Zeuxis 3,4 however, applies the terms synonymously). Other genealogies are offered by schol. Il. 1,266 (the slave Dia is united in one night not only with Ixion but also with → Pegasus) and Nonnus, who names three classes of centaurs (Nonnus, Dion. 14,143ff.; 193ff.). The most important myth is the battle of → Lapiths and centaurs. The two of them are half-brothers at Diod. Sic. 4,70, who quarrel over their inheritance. According to Homer, this fight is the cause and anticipation of all later battles between humans and centaurs (Hom. Il. 2,741ff; Od. 21,295ff.). The most complete account is to be found in Ov. Met. 12,210–535. While in the early versions the cause of the argument is not given, later ones report that at the wedding of the Lapith → Peirithous, the centaurs attempt in a stupor to assault the women. Ares as the instigator of the fight appears only in the Roman authors: Verg. Aen. 7,304 and Serv. Aen.). The Lapiths decide the battle for themselves (Apollod. epit. 1,21f.). After being expelled from Thessaly, a few of the centaurs flee into the Pholoe range where they pillage the land and kill the inhabitants (Diod. Sic. 4,70). When → Heracles visits the centaur Pholus, by provocation of the centaurs a fight develops which despite the intervention of their mother Nephele ends with the defeat of the centaurs (Diod. Sic. 4,12).

C. CHARACTER AS MONSTERS
Homer already separates the centaurs from the humans (Hom. Od. 21,303), though he does not explicitly mention their animal form. Pindar (fr. 166 MAEHLER) describes them as animals despite their human components. The centaurs are animal-humans, in whom the aggressiveness of the animal is paired with the human mind. Their main characteristics are lechery and a craving for wine and are therefore connected with Dionysus like the → Sileni, who are different in character and appearance (also animal-shaped, but not a threat to culture) (Nonnus, Dion. 14,143ff.; Eur. IA 1058ff.; Plin. HN 33,155). As a sacrilegious anti-society that devours raw meat (Hes. Theog. 542) and is inevitably defeated by civilized man, they are a counterpart to the mythological people of the → Amazones.

C.ANGELINO, E.SALVANESCHI (Edd.): Il Centauro. Florilegio di testi letterari e figurativi, 1986; E.BETHE, s.v. K., RE 11, 172–179; P.DU BOIS, Centaur and Amazons: Women and the Pre-History of the Great Chain of Being, 1991; G.DUMÉZIL, Le problème des Centaures, 1929; M.O. HOWEY, The Horse in Magic and Myth, 1923; A.ISARD, Le centaure dans la légende et dans l'art, 1939.
                 C.W.

II. ICONOGRAPHY
Early depictions record centaurs in completely human form with the trunk and hind legs of a horse (clay statuette from Lefkandi, Eretria, Mus., late 10th cent. BC, late geometric vases, from 725–700 BC); the human front legs are only sporadically shown with

horse-hooves ('Campana'Dinus, Copenhagen, NM, 540/525 BC). Since the 2nd half of the 7th cent. BC, centaurs are formed as horses with human upper bodies, especially on Attic vases: François-Krater (Florence, MA, 570 BC), on which the Thessalian centauromachy is reliably depicted for the first time. In the architectural sculpture of the 5th and 4th cents. BC, the battle is again given form with the centaurs offending the (social) order: west gable of the Temple of Zeus in Olympia (in 460 BC), south metopes of the Parthenon (447–440 BC), west frieze of the Hephaisteion in Athens (in 440 BC), cella frieze of the Temple of Apollo in Bassae (late 5th cent. BC), south frieze of the Heroon of Gjölbasi-Trysa (380–370 BC), frieze of the mausoleum in Halicarnassus (middle of the 4th cent. BC) etc.

For weapons the centaurs carry at first only branches and uprooted trees; in the battle against the → Lapiths they also use vessels and other household equipment; beginning in the 5th cent. BC they are often given an animal fur as protection. Depictions of the hospitable centaur → Pholus are linked with the Pholoe adventure of Heracles; more common is his pursuit by the centaurs who are lured by the wine (Corinth. Scyphus, Paris, LV, 590/580 BC); not preserved are scenes on the same theme on the → Cypselus chest, mid–6th cent. BC (Paus. 5,19,9) and on the 'throne' of Apollo of Amyclae, late 6th cent. BC (Paus. 3,18,10–11). The Nessus scene is especially to be found on archaic vases (Amphora of the Nettos Painter, Athens, NM, in 620 BC). → Chiron, characterized as a friendly and wise centaur, appears for instance as the tutor of Achilles and advisor of Peleus (present at his wedding with Thetis: François-Krater; Amphora, Munich, SA, 510–500 BC). To emphasize their savagery, centaurs are often depicted with long hair, a straggly beard, a snub nose and horse ears. Attributes like drinking vessels, wreaths, musical instruments and similar objects in the classical period increasingly connect them with the Dionysian circle. In the Roman period the spectrum of Greek centaur iconography is mostly adopted unchanged, e.g. in wall paintings and mosaics, on the sarcophagi of the 2nd–3rd cent. AD, and in glyptics and toreutics (Achilles plate from the silver treasury of Castrum Rauracense, AD 330–345).
→ Chiron; → Nessus; → Pholus

D. CASTRIOTA, Myth, Ethos and Actuality. Official Art in Fifth-Century B.C. Athens, 1992, 34–43, 152–165; L. MARANGOU, M. LEVENTOPOULOU et al., s.v. Kentauroi et Kentaurides, LIMC 8.1, 671–721 (with further literature); R. OSBORNE, Framing the Centaur. Reading 5th-Century Architectural Sculpture, in: S. GOLDHILL, R. OSBORNE (ed.), Art and Text in Ancient Greek Culture, 1994, 52–84; C. WEBER-LEHMANN, s.v. Kentauroi (in Etruria), LIMC 8.1, Suppl., 721–727.   A.L.

Centaurus (Κένταυρος; *Kéntauros*).
[1] According to Pind. Pyth. 2,21ff. son of → Ixion and → Nephele (the supposed Hera). C. fathers the → centaurs with the mares of Pelion (Diod. Sic. 4,70).

[2] According to Virgil (Aen. 5,122; 10,195), name of a ship with the figure of a centaur.
[3] The constellation C., usually identified with → Chiron or → Pholus.   C.W.

Centenionalis Roman copper coin, following the AD 356 edict of Constantius II and Julian equated with the colloquially named *maiorina* (Cod. Theod. 9,23,1), and decreed by a law of AD 349 to be of copper and silver (Cod. Theod. 9,21,1). Minting of what was then known exclusively as the *centenionalis* ceased in the West by an edict of Honorius and Arcadius of AD 395 (Cod. Theod. 9,23,2), but it continues in the East until about AD 425. The three denominations introduced in the coinage reform of AD 348, of copper with a maximum of 3.0 per cent silver, weigh *c.* 5.25 g, 4.25 g and 2.5 g, but their nomenclature is uncertain. Generally speaking, the largest denomination is called *maiorina*, the middle one *centenionalis* and the smallest the half of the latter. The fast-ensuing reduction in weight of the largest denomination may have led to the *maiorina*'s being occasionally equated with the *centenionalis*.
→ Maiorina; → Coinage reforms

M. F. HENDY, Studies in the Byzantine Monetary Economy *c.* 300–1450, 1985, s.v. Centenionalis.; W. HAHN, Die Ostprägung des Röm. Reiches im 5.Jh. (408–491), 1989, especially 15ff.   A.M.

Centesima In one particular sense indicates → interest of one hundredth of the sum advanced per month, i.e. after Caesar's reform of the calendar 12 per cent per year. Towards the end of the Republic, this is the maximum rate allowed by law, applying in all cases where there is a justifiable obligation to pay interest, unless a lower rate is agreed (from 1 per cent = *uncia* to 11 per cent = *deunx* per *centesima* in each case; Cic. Ad Att. 5,21,11). It is not impossible that the *lex XII tab.* (8,18) in effect laid down the same maximum annual rate (*nam primo XII tabulis sanctum, ne quis unciario faenore amplius exerceret* — Tac. Ann. 6,16). As, for debtors in critical economic circumstances, an interest rate of 12 per cent *per annum* could be high, other measures for the statutory regulation of interest (*leges fenebres*) were continually being enacted under the Republic and the Empire, rates being set below the *centesima* and higher demands as a rule being punishable as usury (*faeneratio*) (Gai. Inst. 4,23). In late antiquity (Cod. Iust. 4,32,26,2), the normal maximum level of interest provided for by law is 8 per cent *per annum*.

G. BILLETER, Gesch. des Zinsfußes im griech.-röm. Alt., 1898; KASER, RPR 1, 497f.; T. FRANK, An Economic Survey on Ancient Rome 1, 1959, 13ff., 26ff., 205, 262ff., 347.   C.G.

Centho Roman cognomen (perhaps of Etruscan origin) in the Claudian family [1. 149]; probably linked to *cento* 'suit of rags' [2. 200].

1 Schulze   2 Walde/Hofmann I³.   K.-L.E.

Cento

A. Definition B. Greek C. Latin cento
poetry D. History of influence

A. Definition

Greek χέντρων (*kéntrōn*) and Latin *cento* — the linguistic historical relationship between the words is a
matter of contention [20. 11–13] — have in common,
even though their meanings do not quite cover the same
fields, the fact that they describe a quilt made of remnants of used material sewn together, and then in the
figurative sense a text that was assembled of disparate
verse parts (up to one and a half verses) from well-
known poets to form a new continuous meaningful
message; a 'patchwork poem'; this is the most detailed
and strictest ancient definition of the literary cento with
the metric rules for this *technopaignion* in Auson.
Cento nuptialis p. 160,21–32 Prete (cf. Tert., De praescriptione haereticorum 39; Isid. Orig. 1,39,25). Of fundamental significance for this type of reception is the
constant consciousness of the literary model and the
excitement produced by allusion [12. 209], with the
poet of the cento contrasting parodistically with the
model (Auson. Cento nuptialis p. 168/9) or taking its
dignity, as particularly in the case of the Christian *cen-
tonarii* (cf. Anth. Pal. 1,119,2f. on Patricius). The cento
should be assigned to → Classicism and represents an
extreme case of → intertextuality. This poses the fundamental problem associated with citation, reminiscence,
imitatio and *aemulatio* [15]; it should be expected that
cento poetry is interdependent. The retreat to the primary text that is fundamental to the cento demonstrates
a broad spectrum of functionalizations yet to be described that for their part would have to be placed in a
hierarchy, e.g.: neutralization and liberation for popular themes using diverse techniques [see in this regard 2;
13], (parodistic) alienation, allegorization; on the side
of the new text's author and public: taking possession
of authority, artistic pleasure, semantic enrichment
(contrast and analogy). The prerequisite for the public
is always precise knowledge of the wording of the texts
used, for example especially of the canonical authors
Homer and Virgil.   H.A.G. and W.-L.L.

B. Greek

[20. 18–60]: The technique of integrating equal
words, groups of words and whole verses was already
practised in oral poetry with the creative variation essentially predominant [16. XXIX–XXXV]; Eustathius
(on Hom. Il. 17,142–168, p. 1099,51) was even able to
compare the Glaucus speech with the later Homeric
centones. Distancing from the model is first seen in the
parody of Homer and others by Hipponax, Hegemon
of Thasos and the → Batrachomyomachia; however, it
does not form a continuum of Homeric parts. It is a
matter of contention whether Aristoph. Ran. 1264–68,
1285–95, 1309–22 and Pax 1089–93, 1270–74,
1282–3 and 1286–7, like other similar groups of verses
in other authors (e.g. Petron. Sat. 132), should be re-

garded as cento or as pasticcio [20. 21–22,31–32]. Centones clearly can be demonstrated from the 2nd cent.
AD onwards: e.g. in Lucian, Arius, Iren. 1,9,4 [4. 1931;
20. 22–24]. A special feature is the Euripides-cento, the
drama *Christus patiens* with 2610 iambic trimetres.
Further Greek centones: Anth. Pal. 9,361; 381f. H.A.G.

C. Latin cento poetry

There is evidence of Latin 'patchwork poems' from
the 2nd cent. AD (but perhaps as early as Ovid?, see
Quint. Inst. 6,3,96) onwards (Tert. De praescriptione
haereticorum 39), probably according to the Hellenistic
prototype [8. 19–55; 14]. Perhaps → Culex and
→ Ciris, in any case, however, Encolpius-Petronius (Petron. Sat. 132,11) should be considered preliminary
stages. The cento arises from *memoria* and in this way
to a large extent from school instruction (cf. Aug. Civ.
1,3); Virgil serves first and foremost as a model text.
The transitions to 'cento-like' poetry and to diverse
techniques of allusion are fluid. The *Cento nuptialis* of
→ Ausonius, a parodic Virgilian cento, is the peak of
pagan cento poetry (4th cent.), with special importance
attaching to the (obscene) *imminutio*. The marked parodic moment adds to this. The cento *De alea* (Anth.
Lat. 8) comes close to Ausonius in this regard. Especially worthy of emphasis is the *Medea* of → Hosidius Geta,
a Virgilian cento in tragic form (borrowing from
Seneca). Anth. Lat. 9–15 (comparable with the Homeric centones Anth. Pal. 9, 381f.) also deal with mythical
subjects (Narcissus, Judgement of Paris — passed down
as the work of Mavortius, cos. AD 527 –, Hippodamia,
Hercules and Antaeus, Progne, and Philomela, Europa,
Alcesta). The epic *Epithalamium* of → Luxurius in the
tradition of Stat. Silv. 1,2 on the wedding of the Vandal
Fridus for its part shows clear echoes of Ausonius. Further Latin centones are Anth. Lat. 1,1, p. 33–82; CSEL
16,1: Poetae Christiani minores, 1888, 513–627
(Schenkl).

The Christian centones have a special place in which
the pagan-classical and Christian culture are integrated.
The widespread low opinion of cento poetry increasingly requires new evaluation [10]. In this way, the oldest
and most important cento (probably from the sixties of
the 4th cent.), that of the aristocratic Roman woman
Faltonia Betitia → Proba (see Isid. Orig. 1,39,26; De
viris illustribus 5; pace [22] with late dating to 385–88
or Easter 387 and attributed to Anicia Faltonia Proba)
that in spite of expulsion from the church canon was
widely distributed and appreciated (also the Christian
Homeric cento of the Empress Eudocia was influenced
by it), in imitation of Minucius Felix and especially of
Lactantius [cf. however 1], is understood as a minimal
form of autonomous Christian poetry. Jer. Ep. 53,7 criticizes this way of teaching the Bible as arbitrary and
depraved. Three additional Christian Virgilian centones, passed down to us in one manuscript each, were
less widely distributed: the dialogue of about the same
time (?) — according to [21. 62⁴¹, 105ff.] estimated as
not until after 400 (?) — that has not been preserved

intact, between the shepherds Meliboeus and Tityrus (Anth. Lat. 719a) of Pomponius (Isid. Orig. 1,39,26), a transposition of theological instruction to the bucolic sphere; the cento Anth. Lat. 719 that is even more garbled, upon which the first editor E. MARTÈNE bestowed the title *De verbi incarnatione*; and finally *De ecclesia* (Anth. Lat. 16. 16a; [25]) that contains a sermon and was recited very successfully in public. When the author (identified as Mavortius on the basis of a corrupt passage — see above — which is, however, a matter of speculation) was praised as *Maro Junior* he rejected this emphatically in a cento improvisation (Anth. Lat. 16a; v. 11–116 SCHENKL). Both centones are not securely dated (5th/6th cents.). The material of the CE demonstrates the atrophying of the cento into imitation and borrowing, the papyrus PSI 2. 142 (late 5th cent. AD) provides a Virgilian cento paraphrase — probably as a school exercise. — Cf. generally → Biblical poetry and Christian pastoral poetry; *De lege Domini* and *De nativitate, vita, passione et resurrectione Domini* are a two-part cento (8th/9th cents.), essentially from the → *Carmen adversus Marcionitas*.   W.-L.L.

D. HISTORY OF INFLUENCE

Cento poetry continued to be fostered in the Middle Ages, the Renaissance and the Baroque period, the basis being the ancient prototypes, and the models chosen were not just Virgil and the Bible but also well-known contemporary authors [11]. In modern times, too, it is represented [23] (see Goethe's Hafis cento).   H.A.G.

1 V. BUCHHEIT, Vergildeutung im Cento Probae, in: Grazer Beiträge 15, 1988, 161–176   2 M.R. CACIOLI, Adattamenti semantici e sintattici nel Centone virgiliano di Proba, in: SIFC 41, 1969, 188–246   3 F.E. CONSOLINO, Da Osidio Geta ad Ausonio e Proba, in: A&R n.s. 28, 1983, 133–151   4 O. CRUSIUS, s.v. Cento, RE III 2, 1929–1932   5 D. DAUBE, The influence of interpretation on writing (1970), in: Collected Studies in Roman Law, vol. 2, 1991, 1245–1262, here 1256ff.   6 J.O. DELEPIERRE, Tableau de la littérature du centon chez les anciens et chez les modernes, 1874/75   7 M. DE NONNO, Per il testo e l'esegesi del centone *Hippodamia*, in: Studi latini e italiani 5, 1991, 33–44   8 F. ERMINI, Il centone di Proba e la poesia centonaria latina, 1909   9 H. HARRAUER, R. PINTAUDI, Virgilio ed il dimenticato 'recto' di PSI II 142, in: Tyche 6, 1991, 87–90   10 R. HERZOG, Die Bibelepik der lat. Spätantike, 1, 1975   11 C. HOCH, s.v. Cento II–IV, in: HWdR 2, 152–57   12 R. LAMACCHIA, Dall'arte allusiva al centone, in: n.s. 3, 1958, 193–216   13 Id.: Problemi di interpretazione semantica in un centone virgiliano, in: Maia n.s. 10, 1958, 161–188   14 Id.: s.v. Centoni, in: EV 1, 733–37   15 W.-L. LIEBERMANN, HLL S (1989) § 554 295–6 (C24), 303–4 lit. 36)   16 A. PARRY, The Making of Homeric verse, 1971   17 Z. PAVLOVSKIS, Proba and the Semiotics of the Narrative Virgilian Cento, in: Vergilius 35, 1989, 70–84   18 J.-M. POINSOTTE, Les Juifs dans les centons latins chrétiens, in: Recherches Augustiniennes 21, 1986, 85–116   19 G. POLARA, I centoni, in: Lo spazio letterario di Roma antica, vol. 3, 1990, 245–75 (bibliography)   20 G. SALANITRO, Osidio Geta, Medea, 1981   21 W. SCHMID, Tityrus Christianus (1953), in: K. GARBER (ed.), Europäische Bukolik und Georgik, 1976, 44–121   22 D. SHANZER, The Anonymous Carmen contra paganos and the Date and Identity of the Centonist Proba, in: Revue des Études Augustiniennes 32, 1986, 232–48 (see also Recherches Augustiniennes 27, 1994, 75–96)   23 TH. VERWEYEN, G. WITTING, The Cento, in: H.F. PLATT (ed.), Intertextuality, 1991, 165–78   24 J.L. VIDAL, La technique de composition du Centon virgilien *Versus ad gratiam Domini sive Tityrus*, in: Revue des Études Augustiniennes 29, 1983, 233–256   25 Id., Christiana Vergiliana I. Vergilius eucharistiae cantor, in: Studia Virgiliana, 1985, 207–216.
                                        H.A.G. and W.-L.L.

Centobriga Town mentioned only in the context of the anecdote about → Metellus' mild treatment of the besieged population of C. (142 BC; Val. Max. 5,1,5; Liv. POxy. 161–163). C. — the name is Celtic [1. 989] — was probably situated in the valley of the Jalón [3. 354].

1 HOLDER 1   2 A. SCHULTEN, Fontes Hispaniae Antiquae 4, 1937, 33f.   3 Id., Numantia 1, 1914   4 TOVAR 3, 369–370.
                                             P.B.

Central-plan building The term central-plan building (CB) describes an edifice — either detached or integrated into an architectural ensemble — with main axes of equal or nearly equal lengths, so that none is dominant. The basic shapes of a CB are a circle, a square, or a regular polygon, sometimes with an additional projection to set off the entrance. According to this definition, the Greek → tholos is a centralized building, as are various other examples of circular → funerary architecture (→ Tumulus; esp. the mausolea of Augustus and Hadrian in Rome with their influence on subsequent funeral architecture: → Mausoleum Augusti; → Mausoleum Hadriani). The CB — as an architectural phenomenon particularly widespread in Roman and early

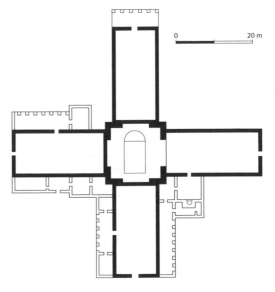

Antiochia [1] on the Orontes: St. Babylas, AD 379/380 (ground-plan)

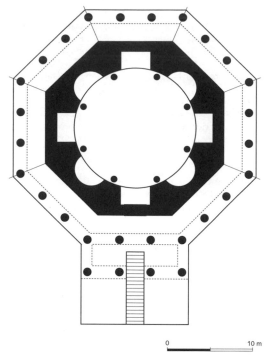

Spalatum (Split): Mausoleum of Diocletian, early 4th cent. AD (ground-plan)

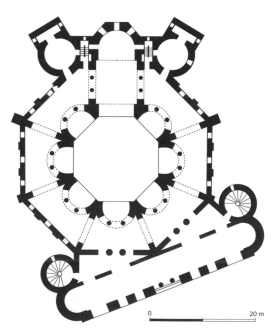

Ravenna: S. Vitale, consecrated AD 547 (ground-plan)

Christian architecture — is typologically the opposite of a longitudinal building, most prominently represented by → temple, → stoa [1]/colonnade and → basilica. The term CB is also used for the cross-shaped arrangement of two basilica structures within an imagi-

nary square with a prominent — and in Christian church architecture often domed — centre (quincunx/cross-in-square plan church, e.g. St. Babylas in Antioch [1], late 4th cent.; see illustr.).

The main characteristic of the CB is its lack of direction, making it impossible for the user to walk purposefully through the building. Thus it becomes an outstanding type of building, in a manner of speaking the 'ultimate destination' at the end of a journey. From this functional or rather use-orientated view, the circular temples and the funeral architecture of the early and middle imperial age — generally without public access — have to be excluded, as there the emphasis is on the visual appearance of the exterior view, not on fashioning the impression of the interior space. In respect of its appearance, the monumental, detached CB building has to be differentiated from the one that is integrated into a larger architectural complex. In Roman architecture from the 1st cent. AD onwards, the latter type can be found increasingly frequently in the context of various representative building complexes: in the architecture of thermal baths (from the point of view of heating engineering prudently located at the centre of the enfilade of rooms within the → thermal baths complex) as well as in → palaces and → villas (Piazza d'Oro of Hadrian's villa near → Tibur/Tivoli; the 'garden hall' of Licinius in Rome), the latter used as representational rooms. Early examples are the domed buildings of Baiae (→ Dome) and the CB within Nero's → *domus aurea* complex in Rome; the common feature of all of these is the prominent role they played in the original designated use of the building.

The paradigm of a free-standing CB is the → Pantheon [2] in Rome. From the 3rd cent. AD, the interior of the mausolea of rulers — i. a. the rotunda of Galerius in → Thessalonica [1], Diocletian's mausoleum within his palatial villa in → Spalatum/Split (cf. illustr.; → Palace with illustr.), Constantine's mausoleum [1] in Constantinople etc. — were as CB also fashioned in view of their three-dimensional effect; frequently, these mausolea were later turned into churches, thus making them immediately related to CB as free-standing churches (cf. here S. Stefano Rotondo in Rome; S. Vitale in → Ravenna, see illustr.). These building concepts could be expanded by a variety of architectural ensembles, framing or at times even obscuring the CB (→ Atrium; side chapels and further rooms; cf. e.g. the → Hagia Sophia in Constantinople, see illustr.). The ground plan — circular, octagonal or regular-polygonal — could be structured by a number of ambulatories, three-sided apses ('cloverleaf shape') and niches etc., and — in contrast with the cone-shaped roofs of the circular temples — the building was generally domed (→ Dome; → Roofing). From the late 4h cent. onwards, it became a common trend — though in complete contradiction of the original design concept — to introduce an axial orientation of entrance, altar, and → apse. Equally within the Christian context, a → baptisterium (free-standing or as part of a larger architectural com-

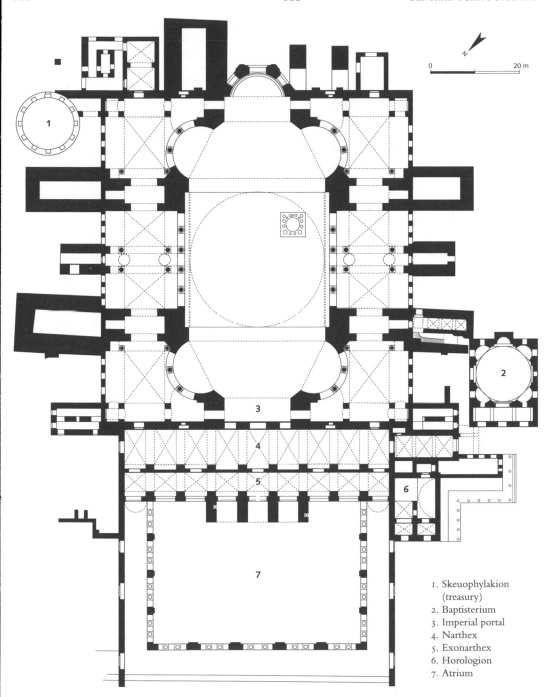

1. Skeuophylakion
   (treasury)
2. Baptisterium
3. Imperial portal
4. Narthex
5. Exonarthex
6. Horologion
7. Atrium

Constantinopolis: Hagia Sophia, AD 532-537 and 558-563 (ground-plan)

plex) was also commonly built as a CB, particularly in the West. In → Islam, too, CB are used in religious context. (→ Mosque).
→ Church I.

D. BONIVER, Der Zentralraum, 1937; F. W. DEICHMANN, Einführung in die christl. Arch., 1983, 82–84, 249 f., 261; F. FINK, Die Kuppel über dem Viereck, 1958; R. KRAUTHEIMER, Early Christian and Byzantine Architecture, ⁴1986; F. RAKOB, Die Rotunde in Palestrina, in: JDAI(R) 1990, 61–92; Id., Le cupole di Baia, in: M. GIGANTE (ed.), Civiltà dei Campi Flegrei, conf. Naples, 1992, 229–258; G. STANZL, Längsbau und Zentralbau als Grundthemen der frühchristl. Architektur, 1979; M. UNTERMANN, Der Zentralbau im MA, 1989, 7–13.   C. HÖ.

Centrites (Κεντρίτης, *Kentrítēs*, Xen. An. 4,3,1; Diod. Sic. 14,27,7); according to the route description in Xenophon, the same as the eastern confluent of the Tigris Bohtan Su (province of Siirt), Byzantine Zirmas, Arabic Zarm. Accordingly, the C. formed the boundary between the region of the → Carduchi and Armenia, or rather the Armenian satrapy of → Tiribazus. In the winter of 401/400 BC the Greeks crossed the C. at a widening of the valley with settlements on river terraces, possibly *c*. 15 km north of the confluence with the Tigris, near the mouth of the Zorova Su.

F.H. WEISSBACH, s.v. Kentrites, RE 11, 181. K.KE.

Centumcellae (Κεντουκέλλαι; *Kentoukéllai*). Port constructed in AD 106/07 under Trajan on the Tyrrhenian coast of Etruria (Plin. Ep. 6,31,1); the modern Civitavecchia. A detailed description is found in Plin. and Rut. Namat. 1,237ff. Identification of C. with the city of Τραιανὸς λιμήν (*Traianòs limén*) in Ptol. 3,1,4 (between Populonia and Telamon) seems implausible. As early as the 6th cent. AD, Procopius (BG 2,7,18; 3,13,12; 4,37; cf. Agathias 1,11) describes C. as an important, populous town. C. was destroyed by Saracens in AD 812.
→ Etruscans; → Etruria

S. BASTIANELLI, C., in: Italia Romana. Municipi e Colonia 1, 14. M.CA.

Centum languages The mnemonic Centum (from Latin *centum*) stands for those Indo-Germanic languages in which there is coincidence between the palatal series *k̂*, *ĝ*, *ĝ*ʰ and the unaccented *k*, *g*, *g*ʰ series of the Old Indo-Germanic tectals (→ Gutturals) and the unaccented series: Old Indo-Germanic **kreuh₂-* 'bloody flesh' > Latin *cruor*, Greek *kréas*, **k̂r̥d-* 'heart' > Latin *cor*, Greek *kardía*. Otherwise (in so-called → Satem languages) the palatals preserved as independent phonemes become sibilants. In Centum the labio-velars *k*ʷ, *g*ʷ, *g*ʷʰ (initially) remain preserved as phonemes, e.g. in ancient Greek and → Mycenean with little loss **k*ʷ > *k* as well as *u*. Earlier research evaluated the Centum-Satem separation as the oldest and most important isogloss of Indo-Germanic languages, which, from a geographical point of view should correspond to a west-east distribution. There are, however, reasons to assume that the relevant sound developments did not take place until the (pre)individual language period, i.e. that Centum like Latin (with the Italic languages) or Greek implemented the phoneme coincidence independently of each other. Aside from the classical languages, → Anatolian languages (some disputed), → Germanic languages, → Celtic languages and → Tocharic (mostly **k*ʷ > **k*) belong to the Centum languages.
→ Gutturals; → Indo-European languages; → Phonetics

W. COWGILL, M. MAYRHOFER, Idg. Gramm. I.1/2, 1986, 102–109; J. TISCHLER, Hundert Jahre *kentum-satem* Theorie, in: IF 95, 1990, 63–98. D.ST.

Centumviri The term *centumviri* ('hundred men') refers to a court whose existence, according to heavily disputed theory, probably goes back to the beginnings of the Republic; its proceedings are documented throughout the period, and it is only at its sittings that the ancient symbol of state sovereignty, the wooden lance (*hasta*, Dig. 1,2,2,29) was displayed, Gai. Inst. 4,16; Cic. De or. 1,57,242; Top. 17,65. The court's composition is suggested by its name: from each of the 35 → *tribus*, three men were chosen as members (giving 105 'men of the hundred'; see Fest. 47: ... *et, licet quinque amplius quam centum fuerint, tamen quo facilius nominarentur, centumviri sunt dicti* ('although five more than a hundred, for convenience they were called *centumviri*'). This imprecision must have pertained even before 241 BC, when there were only 33 or less *tribus*; it follows that the number of the court's members holds no negative implication as to its great age; see also Varro, Rust. 2,1,26: *sic numerus non est ut sit ad amussim, ut non est ... centumvirale esse iudicium Romae*. The court is still active at the beginning of the 2nd cent. AD (Plin. Ep. 6,12; Gai. Inst. 4,31), and is mentioned in Dig. 5,2,17 pr.; 34,3,30 even as late as the beginning of the 3rd cent., so that it seems to have survived the various stages of development in civil law (*legis actiones*, procedures by *formula* and by *cognitio*).

The individual judges were elected, during the Principate chosen by lot; under Trajan they numbered (briefly?) 180 (Plin. Ep. 6,33,3). The *centumviri* court was headed by a *praetor hastarius*; whether he ever led proceedings *in iure* is doubtful (Gai. Inst. 4,31). The court did not sit as a plenum, but in four chambers (*consilia, tribunalia*; Quint. Inst. 12,5,6), which by the Principate at the latest were led by a magistrate: the latter, after Augustus' dissolution of the court of *decemviri* (responsible for deciding questions of liberty), probably being one of the *decemviri stlitibus iudicandis* (Suet. Aug. 36). The *centumviri* essentially had jurisdiction over inheritance claims and probably claims concerning liberty, status and property (Dig. 42,1,38; 40,1,24 pr., also — as an illustrative list — Cic. De or. 1,38,173). However, as all these matters could also be heard by a judge sitting alone, the *iudex unus*, (Quint. Inst. 5,10,115), jurisdiction seems to have been dependent upon agreement between the parties (Plin. Ep. 5,1,7). Such agreement might occur in the case of disputes of interest to the public, especially those concerning questions of inheritance among the upper classes, above all the senatorial class. A celebrated example is the *causa Curiana* in 93 BC, a dispute over the naming of an alternative heir: the rhetor L. Licinius Crassus won, arguing for interpretation according to the intention of the testator, against the literal arguments of the lawyer Q. Mucius Scaevola; i. a. Cic. Brut. 39,144ff. The fame of the case derives from the greater openness of the proceedings. It was because of this factor that a hearing before the *centumviri* was more popular with the rhetors than one before the *iudex unus*, which took place at the home of the judge; Cic. De or. 1,38,173 (but see also Plin. Ep. 2,14,1). The → *querela inofficiosi testamenti* (action to declare a will null and void), with a claim of mental incapacity (*color insaniae*) of the testator, is typical of the rhetor's stock in trade (Plin. Ep. 6,12).

Despite Paulus, Sent. 5,9,1 (= 5,13,1 Liebs), access to the *centumviri* court did not generally depend upon an action being of a certain minimum value. Even when the formulary proceedings had been presented by a *l. Aebutia*, procedure was always in accordance with the formalities of the → *legis actio sacramento*; see Gai. Inst. 4,31,95; Gell. NA 16,10,8. Consequently, the *sponsio praeiudicialis*, a legal dispute about the object of contention (*sacramentum*, Gai. Inst. 4,16), was delivered during that part of the proceedings held before the magistrate (*in iure*), the arguments before the court concerning solely the sum, and only indirectly the real subject in dispute. The result was that the cumbersome procedure by *legis actio* was preferred to the *condemnatio pecuniaria* of the formulary procedure: should the losing party refuse to conform to the finding thus arrived at incidentally, and therefore without force of law, (a situation which, in view of the representative nature of the court and the publicity involved, may have been relatively rare), the use of force by the winning party was at least thereby declared legitimate. Of course, with the 'triumphant progress' of the procedure by *cognitio*, this 'natural enforcement effect' declined in significance, giving way to the new system's mode of natural enforcement.

W. Kunkel, Unt. zur Entwicklung des röm. Kriminalverfahrens, 1962, 115; Kaser, RZ, 37; O. Behrends, Der Zwölftafelprozeß, 1974; J. M. Kelly, Studies in the Civil Judicature, 1976, 1; Wieacker, RRG, 435.   C.PA.

Centuria In general signifies an amount measured by or divided into units of 100, and can therefore relate e.g. to plots of land as well as to people. Thus the relationship to the figure 100 can be lost, the word then referring merely to a mathematically exactly measured or divided amount.

A. Political   B. Military

A. Political

Centuria is particularly used in the constitution of the Roman Republic to denote the electorate for the → *comitia centuriata*. In this meaning, the term probably derives from the contingent of 100 foot soldiers that, according to the historical tradition of the Augustan era, each of the 30 *curiae* had to contribute annually to the *legio* of Rome under the kings. From here, the term may have been transferred to the total number of citizens of military age of a → *curia* appearing in a military muster on the → *Campus Martius*: originally organized *curiatim*, thus at the same time *centuriatim*. Thence, after the introduction of the *comitia centuriata* as a type of popular assembly in its own right, the term may have come to be applied to the electorates of the new assemblies. As the constitution develops, the *centuriae* of the centuriate assemblies come to include a very large global proportion of Rome's citizens. In Cicero's time, the numbers in the *centuriae* of the → *equites* and the *prima classis* are, however, far lower than in those *centuriae* that always took last place in the electoral process; e.g. *centuria velatorum adcensorum*, containing the large number of *proletarii*. The *c.* 215 BC reorganization of the 35 Roman → *tribus* (four 'urban/proletariate', 31 'rural/landowning'), produces a situation which, while clear cut, is not yet entirely resolved, especially as the census and military service are also organized via the *tribus*; this is indicated, for instance, by the figures of 70 for the *prima classis* (twice 35) and 210 (four times four) for other, low-ranking and populous *classes* (Cic. Rep. 2,22,39; Dion. Hal. Ant. Rom. 4,21; Liv. 1,43,12).
→ Census

F. F. Abbott, A History and Description of Roman Political Institutions, ³1963, 253ff.; Mommsen, Staatsrecht, 3, 245ff.; A. Rosenberg, Unt. zur röm. Zenturienverfassung, 1911.   C.G.

B. Military

Ancient authors, in depicting the early history of Rome, associated that epoch's military structure with the three → *tribus* of the regal period, each of them providing 1,000 soldiers, divided into units of 100. As the structure of the legion changed, so did the size of the *centuria*. Polybius' description of the Roman army probably derives from the period after the 2nd Punic War (after 200 BC), when the size of a legion varied between 4,200 and 5,000 men, soldiers being ordered in three ranks of battle, the *hastati* and the *principes* in the front two, the *triarii* in the third. Each of the front two ranks was subdivided into 10 maniples of 120 men, the third into 10 maniples of 60 men. As each maniple comprised two *centuriae*, a legion consisted of 60 *centuriae*. Some details are still unclear, but it is evident that the *centuria* was no longer a 100–strong troop of men.

C. → Marius (*cos.* 107 BC) is credited with having perfected the transformation of the legion, the cohort (→ *cohors*) now becoming the most important tactical unit. Some Roman authors believed that each *centuria* comprised 100 men, even after Marius; but this is improbable, as a *centuria* before Marius already held less than 100 men. A legion during the late Republic had 10 cohorts, each consisting of six *centuriae*; each *centuria* had 80 men, and was commanded by a → *centurio*.

During the Principate, the *centuria* remained the basic unit of the legion; by the time of the Flavians at the latest, a legion consisted of 59 *centuriae*; the first cohort comprised only five, these, however, being double the strength of the other *centuriae*. This is attested by the ground plan of the fort at Inchtuthil in Scotland (*c.* AD 84–86).

The *centuriae* were of extraordinary importance for the military organization and fighting morale of the army. Each *centuria* was subdivided into 10 squads, each of eight soldiers; they lived in the same barracks hut and shared the same tent on campaigns; these men trained, fought and ate together. The significance of the *centuriae* in the Roman army is indicated by the status and relatively high pay of the *centurio*, as well as by the frequent references to *centuriae* and *centuriones* in inscriptions and documents. A *centuria* could as a rule be recognized by the name of its *centurio*, as e.g. 'second *cohors, centuria* of Faustinus' (ILS 2304).

The *centuriae* were also of vital organizational importance for those units stationed in Rome: the Praetorians, the city cohorts and the *vigiles*. *Centuriae* in the → *auxilia* probably consisted of 80 men, while a *cohors quingenaria* comprised six *centuriae*, and a *cohors milliaria* 10. As for the fleet, the crew of a warship, regardless of its size, was likewise called a *centuria* and commanded by a *centurio*.

1 P. A. HOLDER, Studies in the Auxilia of the Roman Army from Augustus to Trajan, 1980   2 L. KEPPIE, The Making of the Roman Army, 1984   3 Y. LE BOHEC, L'armée romaine, 1989   4 M. REDDÉ, Mare nostrum. Les infrastructures, le dispositif et l'histoire de la marine militaire sous l'empire romain, 1986.   J.CA.

Centurio With the exception of the senators and the *equites,* the *centurio* was the most important officer in the Roman army. In the 1st cent. BC, a cohort (→ *cohors*) contained six *centuriones*, each commanding a → *centuria* of 80 men, and bearing titles reflecting the former mode of organization by maniples: *pilus prior, pilus posterior, princeps prior, princeps posterior, hastatus prior, hastatus posterior*. By the Flavian period at the latest, there were only five *centuriones* in the first cohort, which was, however, the highest ranking cohort in the legion (*primi ordines*). There were four levels of promotion below the highest ranking *centurio*, the *primus pilus*. It is not clear whether the *centuriones* in the remaining nine cohorts differed only by seniority of service, or whether their rank depended upon which cohort they belonged to.

During the Principate it was mainly long-serving soldiers of the legions or former Praetorians — often, however, members of the *ordo equester* — who were promoted to *centurio*. This is indicated by the high incomes enjoyed by the *centuriones*, who during the 1st cent. received roughly 15 times the salary of an ordinary soldier. There were also *centuriones* among the troops stationed in Rome and in the cohorts of the *auxilia*, but they did not bear the same titles as the legionary *centuriones*. The *centuriones* were responsible for the administration and discipline of their *centuria*; as they were very experienced soldiers, their advice was sought as a matter of course by senior officers. *Centuriones* could also take command of a limited number of troops for special duties. Promotion within the centurionate entailed social mobility, especially as a *primus pilus*, after serving for a year in this rank, could be accepted into the → *ordo equester*, thus attracting further opportunities for advancement. With their good pay and prospects, *centuriones* could be relied upon to show a high degree of loyalty to the princeps.

1 E. B. BIRLEY, Promotions and Transfers in the Roman Army II the Centurionate, in: Carnuntum Jb. 1965, 21–33   2 LE BOHEC   3 B. DOBSON, The Significance of the Centurion and Primipilaris in the Roman Army and Administration, ANRW II 1, 1974, 392–434   4 Id., Die Primipilares, 1978   5 DOMASZEWSKI/DOBSON   6 L. KEPPIE, The Making of the Roman Army, 1984.   J.CA.

Centuripae (Κεντόριπα; *Kentóripa,* Lat. *Centuripa(e), Centuripinum*). Siculan town 30 km south-west of the volcano Mt. → Aetne [1] (height 726 m) in a strategically important location between the plain of Catana and the interior. In 414–413 BC affiliation with Athens (Thuc. 6,94,3; 7,32). Involved in the events at the times of Dionysius, Timoleon, Agathocles, and Hieron II. In the First Punic War, C. signed a peace treaty with Rome in 263 BC (Diod. Sic. 23,4). Within the Roman province of Sicilia, C. was one of only a few *civitates liberae atque immunes* (Cic. Verr. 2,3,13; cf. 2,2,163; 4,50; 5,83). Archaeological evidence: late prehistoric paintings, Neolithic and Bronze Age settlements; necropoleis from the 8th cent. BC onwards; Hellenistic terracottas; bronze coins dating from Timoleon into the 2nd/1st cents. BC. Remains of buildings, sculptures from the Roman period.

G. MANGANARO, Una biblioteca storica nel ginnasio a Tauromenion nel II sec. a.C., in: PdP 29, 1974, 395ff.; Id., Iscrizioni, epitaffi ed epigrammi in greco della Sicilia centro-orientale di epoca romana, in: MEFRA, 106, 1994, 85f., 102f.; BTCGI 5, 235–243; R. CALCIATI, Corpus Nummorum Siculorum 3, 1987, 163–179; R. PATANÉ, Timoleonte a Centuripe e ad Agira, in: Cronache di Archeologia 31, 1992, 67–82; G. RIZZA, s.v. Centuripe, EAA 2. Suppl. 2, 1994, 100; W. ECK, Senatorische Familien der Kaiserzeit in der Prov. Sizilien, in: ZPE 113, 1996, 109–128.   RO.PA.

Centuripe vases Brightly painted ceramics of the 3rd/2nd cents. BC, named after the place of their discovery in Sicily. Vessel forms (→ Pottery, shapes and types of) are *pyxis, lekanis* and *lebes,* and infrequently other types such as *lekythos*. The painting, in tempera colours (white, pink, black, yellow, red, gold, with isolated instances of green and blue) on a ground of orange-coloured clay (friezes of acanthus, tendrils and architectonic forms, heads, busts) is executed only on one side of the vessel. The vessels are of considerable height (50 cm on average), individual parts being separately finished and fitted together. Figurative themes are limited to scenes of women with Eros and marriage scenes; figures of gods (Dionysus) and theatrical scenes are rarer.

U. WINTERMEYER, Die polychrome Reliefkeramik aus Centuripe, in: JDAI 90, 1975, 136–241; P. W. DEUSSEN, The Polychromatic Ceramics of Centuripe, 1988; E. SIMON, Vasi di Centuripe con scena della commedia nuova, in: Dioniso 59, 1989, 45–63.   R.H.

Ceos

[1] (Κέως; *Kéōs*). Northernmost of the western Cyclades (Xen. Hell. 5,4,61: Κέως; Hdt. 8,76; Bacchyl. 6,5; 16: Κέος; *Kéos*; Liv. 36,15: *Cia*), modern Kea. Twelve nautical miles off the southern tip of Attica, from which it is separated by the island of Makronisos. C. has an area of 131 km², is mountainous (Prophitis Elias 567 m), and predominantly consists of crystalline slate. Silver deposits at the Hagios Symeon, where copper slags have also been found [9. 88f.].

On the Kephala promontory at the north-western tip of the island was a late neolithic fishing settlement (4th millennium BC); south of it on the promontory of Hagia Irini are the remains of a Bronze Age settlement, which with its sanctuary dedicated to Dionysus shows continuos use even into the archaic period [1; 2]. At other locations, prehistoric finds have also been unearthed. Early Cycladic pottery (3rd millennium BC; [3. 14]) — according to tradition, the earliest inhabitants of C. were → Carians and → Leleges; of pre-Greek origin are the place names of Carthaea, Poeessia, Caressia as well as C. The Greek colonization supposedly started from Arcadia, Naupactus, and Athens.

In historical times, there were four cities on C.: Iulis (modern Kea, in the centre of the island), Carthaea (in the south-east near the modern Poles), Poeessa (modern Pisses, in the south-west), and Coressia (probably in the 3rd cent. BC also called Arsinoe: IG XII 5, 1061; IMagn. 50,78; [4. 144ff.], modern Korissia on the south-western coast). In Strabo's time, Coresia and Poeessa had been abandoned, their inhabitants resettled respectively in Iulis or Carthaea. Following a short period of dependence on Eretria, these four cities became independent at the end of the 6th cent. BC (Str. 10,1,10). C. took part in the Persian Wars, was a member of the → Delian League (ATL 1,306f.; 3,197f.), also of the Second → Athenian League (IG II² 404). In the Hellenistic period, C. belonged to the Nesiotic League. In around 220 BC, it joined the Aetolian Confederacy [7. 204, 215]. From about 200 BC, it was allied with Rhodes (Pol. 16,26,10; Liv. 31,15,8; SEG 14,544; [8. 159ff.]). Mark Antony presented the island as a gift to the Athenians(App. B Civ. 5,1,7).

From Iulis hailed → Simonides and his nephew → Bacchylides, from C. the logographer → Xenomedes (FGrH III B no. 442), → Erasistratus, the sophist → Prodicus, as well as → Ariston [3] [5. 27ff.]. C. owned a treasure house on Delos (Hdt. 4,35) [6. 54f.]. The *kouros* of C. (*c.* 530 BC) was found in a part of the city of Iulis, near the monumental rock sculpture of a resting lion (early 6th cent. BC).

1 J.L. CASKEY, Excavations in Keos, in: Hesperia 31, 1962, 263ff.; 33, 1964, 314ff. 2 G.DAUX, Chroniques des fouilles 1963, s.v. Céos, in: BCH 88, 1964, 821–829 3 D.FIMMEN, Die kret.-myk. Kultur, ²1924 4 L. ROBERT, Hellenica 11/12, 1944ff., 144ff. 5 WEHRLI, Schule 6 6 N.M. KONTOLEON, Guide to Delos, 1950 (Greek) 7 R.FLACELIÈRE, Les Aitoliens à Délphes, 1937 8 P.M. FRASER, G.E. BEAN, The Rhodian Peraea and Islands, 1954 9 H.W. CATLING, Archaeology in Greece 1988–

1989, s.v. Keos, in: Archaeological Reports 35, 1988/9, 88f.

L.BÜRCHNER, s.v. K. (2), RE 11, 182–190; J.TH. BENT, Aegean Islands, ²1966; J.E. COLEMAN, K. 1, 1977; CHR. DUNANT, J.THOMOPOULOS, Inscriptions de Céos, in: BCH 78, 1954, 316–348; P.GRAINDOR, Kykladika, in: Musée Belge 25, 1921, 78ff.; Id., Fouilles de Karthaia, in: BCH 29, 1905, 329–361; 30, 1906, 92–102, 433–452; H.KALETSCH, s.v. Kea, in: LAUFFER, Griechenland, 315–318; D.M. LEWIS, The Federal Constitution of Keos, in: ABSA 57, 1962, 1–4; PHILIPPSON/KIRSTEN 4, 66ff.; A. PRIDIK, De Cei insula rebus, 1892; L. ROSS, Reisen auf den Inseln des ägäischen Meeres 1, 1840, 110ff.; K. CH. STORCK, Die ältesten Sagen der Insel K., 1912, 192.

H.KAL. and E.MEY.

[2] (Κέος; *Kéos*). Settlement near Cape → Cynosura on Salamis, mentioned in Hdt. 8,76,1 in conjunction with the battle of 480 BC (Greeks against the Persians under Xerxes). Not localizable.

C.HIGNETT, Xerxes' Invasion of Greece, 1963, 218ff., 397ff.

H.KAL.

Cephalae (Κεφαλαί; *Kephalaí*).

Foothills (literally 'heads'), marking the western entrance to the Great Syrte, modern Cape Mesrâta or Râs Bou-Chaifa. Str. 17,3,19; Plut. Dion 25,8; Ptol. 4,3,13; Stadiasmus maris magni 92 (GGM I 460).

H.KEES, s.v. K., RE 11, 190.

W.HU.

Cephale (Κεφαλή; *Kephalé*).

Attic *paralia* deme of the phyle Acamantis, nine (12) → *bouleutaí*, modern Keratea [4. 47]. C.'s eponymous hero, Cephalus [1], was the ancestral hero of the Cephalids, the kings of → Thoricus. Early Mycenaean princely residence at an elevation of 220 m [2], in classical times presumably several settlement centres. Important necropolis (from the geometric period into the 4th cent. BC) in Rudseri [1]. Numerous cults [1. 491; 3], i.a. of Aphrodite [3. 36] and the → Dioscuri (Paus. 1,31,1).

1 H.G. BUCHHOLZ, Ein Friedhof im Gebiet des att. Demos Kephale, in: AA 1963, 455–498 2 H.LOHMANN, Atene, 1993, 65 with n. 468 3 S.SOLDERS, Die außerstädt. Kulte und die Einigung Attikas, 1931, Index s.v. K. 4 TRAILL, Attica, 47; 59; 67; 110 no. 63, table 5.

WHITEHEAD, Index s.v. K.

H.LO.

Cephalium (Κεφαλίων; *Kephalíōn*).

[1] Slave of Cicero, who, as letter messenger, attended to the correspondence with Atticus in 49 BC and with Q. Cicero in 47 (Cic. Att. 7,25; 9,19,4; 10,1,2; 2,1; 15,1; 11,12,1; 16,4).

P.N.

[2] Pseudonymous (?) Hadrianic historian and orator, whose *vita* in the Suda s.v. is confused with that of Cephalon; author of a work *Moúsai* or *Pantodapaì Históríai* ('Muses' or 'Medley stories', 9 bks) in the Ionian dialect, which encompassed the period from → Ninus and → Semiramis up to Alexander [4] the

Great. Based essentially on → Ctesias and → Castor [2] [1; 3], his universal history, despite a striking rationalism [2] and numerous source references is not a serious historical work; however, it was used by Eusebius [7] and the Byzantines (mostly indirectly). Other writings (i.a. *Melétai rhētorikaí*) can no longer be traced.

1 E. SCHWARTZ, Die Königslisten des Eratosthenes und Kastor, 1894   2 F. JACOBY, s.v. K. (4), RE 11,191f.   3 F. Jacoby, FGrH 93   4 R. DREWS, Assyria in Classical Universal Histories, in: Historia 14, 1965, 135–137.   KL.GE.

Cephallenia (Κεφαλληνία; *Kephallēnía*). The largest of the Ionian islands west of Greece, with an area of about 761 km², a length of 50 km with a north-south orientation and a maximum width of 25 km. Because of the contour of the island and the high limestone mountains (modern Enos, Efmorfia, Agia Dinati), several separate settlement areas existed which only in modern times were linked by roads. From the main body of the island to the north protrudes the Erisos peninsula, while in the west, the latter is linked by a 4 km narrow isthmus to the Paliki peninsula. Opposite Paliki, separated by the Gulf of Levadi, and east of the modern chief place of Argostoli are the fertile plain of Krania and the uplands of Livatho. In the south-eastern settlement area were the interior plain of Arakli (Agia Irini) as well as the coastal towns of Poros and Skala, in the east the harbour settlement of Sami with a fertile plain. Further settlement pockets were in the interior of the island (e.g. in the Pilaros valley). The prominent peak of Mount Aenus (today Enos), the highest mountain of the islands of the Ionian Sea (1628 m), is visible from 150 km, and is to this day covered with woodlands of the indigenous Cephalonian firs. No archaeological proof has been found of the sanctuary of Zeus Ainesios located there according to Str. 10,2,15.

Of the Mycenaean finds, the most important is the tholos tomb of Tsannata near Poros, first built in *c.* 1400 BC (LH II) and rebuilt about 100 years later (LH III A) [5]. From the Late Helladic III B-C, several cemeteries with chamber tombs are known in the districts of Argostoli and Paliki (e.g. Mazarakata, Metaxata, Lakkithra) [2; 8 with map; 9].

Homer describes the Cephallenians as subjects of Odysseus (Hom. Il. 2,631–7; Hom. Od. 20,210; 24,355; 378; 429), but only explicitly refers to an island of Samos. It is disputed whether this refers to all of C. (Str. 10,2,10) or only the environs of the later town of Same. Some academics recognize in the Homeric island of Doulichion the Paliki peninsula [11] or even identify the Ithaka of the 'Odyssey' with C. [12]. In historical times, C. only refers to the island with four independent cities (Thuc. 2,30,2): Same (modern Sami) on the coast opposite Ithaca, Pronni near the modern Poros, Crane south-east of the modern Argostoli, Pale north of the modern Lixuri on the Paliki peninsula.

The alleged participation of the Paleans in the battle of Plataeae in 479 BC (Hdt. 9,28,5; 31,4) is an erroneous confusion with that of the *Valeioi* (Elis). In 456

BC, → Tolmides led C. into union with Athens (Diod. Sic. 11,84,7), in 435 Pale supported Corinth (Thuc. 1,27,2); in 431 BC, all of C. was once more allied with Athens (Thuc. 2,30,2). In 375 BC, → Timotheus led Pronni to membership of the Second → Athenian League (IG II–III² 43; 96; [3. 14–47, 103–108]), and in 372 BC, Iphicrates prevailed upon the remaining cities (Xen. Hell. 6,2,31; 33; 38; StV 2, 267; [3. 74f.]). From about 226 BC, C. entertained close relations with the Aetolian Confederacy [4]; in 223/2 BC, an Aetolian colony was sent to Same (IG IX 1² 1, 2; SEG 37, 427 no. 165); in 218 BC, Philip V was unsuccessful in his attack on Pronni and Pale (Pol. 5,3,3f.). In 189 BC, Same was besieged by Fulvius [I 15] Nobilior and subsequently destroyed (Liv. 38,28,5–30,1). After 59 BC, the island belonged to C. Antonius [I 2] (Str. 10,2,13). Plin. HN 4,54 refers to C. as a *civitas libera*; on an inscription, Pale called itself free and autonomous (IG II–III² 3301). Hadrian gave C. as a gift to the Athenians (Cass. Dio 69,16,2). In the 2nd cent. AD, C. belonged to the province of Epirus (Ptol. 3,18,9). The port of Panormus (modern Phiskardo) in the north-east of the island is a new foundation of the late Hellenistic period (Artem. fr. 55 STIEHLE; Anth. Pal. 10,25; SEG 37, 790; Hierocles, Synekdemos 648,6); just as Same, it prospered in Roman times.

In the 4th cent. AD, C. is referred to as wealthy (Expositio totius orbis 64, as *Cephalonia*, from late antiquity the typical form of the name, cf. Procop. Goth. 3,40,14). In AD 550/1, C. served as a base for the Byzantine reconquest of Italy (Procop. Goth. loc. cit.). From AD 787, C. is documented as a diocese. Coins: [1; 7]; Inscriptions: IG IX 1, 610–652; SEG 3, 448–450; 17, 250f.; 23, 388–390; 25, 607; 27, 179; 30, 516f.; 34, 475; 39, 380 and 486; 40, 466; 41, 323; IGUR 1239; [6; 10].

1 BMC, Gr (Peloponnes) 77–93   2 S. BRODBECK-JUKER, Myk. Funde von K. im Arch. Mus. Neuchâtel, 1986   3 J. CARGILL, The Second Athenian League, 1981   4 R. FLACELIÈRE, Les Aitoliens à Delphes, 1937, 258, 284f.   5 L. KOLONAS, Tsannata Porou, in: AD 47 B1, 1992, 154–157   6 K. J. RIGSBY, Asylia, 1996, no. 85   7 RPC, 271f.   8 R. HOPE SIMPSON, Mycenean Greece, 1981, 156–158   9 CH. SOUYOUDZOGLOU-HAYWOOD, Mycenean Refugees and the Kefalonian Cemetries, in: Praktika tou E' Diethnous Panoniou Synedriou, 1991, 59–67   10 D. STRAUCH, Aus der Arbeit am Inschr.-Corpus der Ion. Inseln: IG IX 1², 4, in: Chiron 27, 1997, 217–226   11 E. VISSER, Homers Kat. der Schiffe, 1997, 574–598   12 H. WARNECKE, Die histor.-geogr. Lösung des Ithaka-Problems, in: Orbis Terrarum 3, 1997, 77–99.

Archaeological Reports 39, 1992/3, 25; K. BIEDERMANN, Die Insel K. im Alt., 1887; H. KALETSCH, s.v. K., in: LAUFFER, Griechenland, 319–321; G. KAVVADIAS, I palaiolithiki Kephalonia, 1984; J. PARTSCH, K. und Ithaka (Petermanns Mitt., supplement 98), 1890; PHILIPPSON/KIRSTEN 2, 503–527, 558–566, 600–604; SOUSTAL, Nikopolis, 149f., 154f., 175–177, 185, 187f., 220f., 234, 254; R. SPEICH, Korfu und die Ion. Inseln, 1982, 249–290.   D.S.

Cephaloedium

Cephaloedium (Κεφαλοίδιον, Κεφαλοιδίς; *Kephaloídion, Kephaloidís, Cephaloedium*). Town on a cape of the northern coast of Sicily, modern Cefalù, repeatedly mentioned in conjunction with → Dionysius [1] I and → Agathocles [2] (Diod. Sic. 14,56,2; 78,7; 20,56,3; 77,3), captured by the Romans in 254 BC during the First Punic War (Diod. Sic. 23,18,3), subsequently a *civitas decumana*. Plundered by Verres (Cic. Verr. 2,2,128; 3,103). Archaeology: Remains of archaic fortifications; on the acropolis a 'Temple of Diana' in pre-Greek layout. Copious coin collections [1. 97, 99], especially from Lipara in the Mus. Mandralisca. Inscriptions: IG XIV 349–351; CIL X 2, 7456f.; [2].

1 G.K. JENKLAS, in: Atti IV Conv. Studi Numismatici 1973, 1975   2 A.TULLIO, s.v. Cefalù, EAA², 90–93.
GI.MA. and K.Z.

Cephalus

Cephalus (Κέφαλος, *Képhalos*).
[1] Athenian hero, eponym of the Attic deme → Cephale (north-west of Thoricus) and founding father of the Cephalid lineage (Pherecydes, FGrH 3 F 34; Hsch. s.v. Κεφαλίδαι). C. is regarded a) as the son of the Athenian king → Pandarus (Pandium) or of → Hermes and Herse, the daughter of Cecrops; or b) as the son of the Phocian king Deion(eus) and Diomede, the daughter of Xuthus, whereby he becomes the brother of Aenetus, Phylacus, Actor and Asteropeia.

C. is an exceptional hunter with breathtaking beauty. When hunting on the slopes of Hymettus, he is pursued and abducted by the goddess → Eos. Children of this human-divine mésalliance, according to different traditions, are → Phaethon (Hes. Theog. 986f.), → Tithonus (Apollod. 3,14,3) and Hesperus (Hyg. Poet. Astr. 2,42,4). In later versions of the C. myth, the fate of → Procris is contaminated with the Eos story (Ov. Met. 7,655ff.; Hyg. Fab. 189; Antoninus Liberalis 41). She is the first human wife of C. (the second is the Boeotian Clymene [3], with whom he fathers Iphiclus. Hyg. Fab. 14,2; Hes. fr. 62 M.-W.). Like C. she is an excellent huntress, who receives her javelin that never misses its mark and the dog → Laelaps from Minos (Apollod. 3,15,1–3) or Artemis (Ov. Met. 7. 753ff.), and passes them on to C.

Their marriage is plagued by relationship crises — adultery, doubt as to fidelity, and quarrels. Jealous Eos persuades C. to test Procris' fidelity: C., disguised, has almost no trouble in moving her to adultery. And Procris' converse attempts are crowned by success when she dresses as a man to entice C. into a homosexual liaison. Although the mutual lack of fidelity leads to a reconciliation, Procris is no longer to be convinced of C.'s fidelity. When she follows him out of mistrust during his frequent hunting expeditions on the Hymettus, she listens in on his conversation with the heat-moderating aura, the air (or the cloud Nephele). C., who mistakes her for game hiding in the bushes, kills her by mistake (Pherecydes loc. cit.; Ov. Ars am. 685–746). The court at Areopagus condemns C. for this homicide

to lifelong exile from Attica (Apollod. 3. 15). After that, C. takes part in Thebes in the hunt for the Teumessian fox, after whom he sets the hound Laelaps; furthermore, he helps Amphitryon to successfully decide the war against the Taphians or Teleboae (Apollod. 2,4,7). C. then settles on the island → Cephallenia, named after him, where he marries Lysippe (Str. 10,2,14; Paus. 1,37,6). The four tribes/towns of the island are named after their four sons (EM 507. 26: Pronoi, Samaioi, Kraneioi, Paleis).

I.LAVIN, Cephalus and Procris. Transformations of an Ovidian Myth, in: JWI 17, 1954, 260ff.; CH. SEGAL, Ovid's Cephalus and Procris: Myth and Tragedy, in: Grazer Beitr. 7, 1978, 175–205; E.SIMANTONI-BOURNIA, s.v. K., LIMC 6.1, 1–6.   C.W.

[2] Syracusan, son of Lysanias and father of the rhetorician → Lysias, lived for 30 years in Athens as a metic (→ Metoikoi) and friend of Pericles (Lys. 30. 12,4), died before 404 BC. Allegedly (Plut. Mor. 835c), C. had to flee from the Syracusan tyrant Gelon [1]. Plato honours C. by letting him appear in the 1st book of *Politeía* as a conversation partner (Pl. Resp. 328b-c and *passim*) [1].
[3] Athenian from the deme Collytus (?), a potter by profession, after the end of the Peloponnesian War an active rhetorician, who consistently supported the reconstruction of democracy in 403 BC (Din. 1,76; Dem. Or. 18,219), defended the rhetorician → Andocides [1] in 399 in the mysteries trial (Andoc. 1,115f. and 150), proposed in 387/6 a probouleutic decree, by which Phanocritus of Paros was conferred with the proxeny (→ Proxenia) (IG II² 29,6), sealed as the envoy of Athens in 384–3 prepared an alliance with Chios that led the way for the later history of the Second → Delian League (IG II² 34,35ff.), and allegedly applied in 379–8 for Athenian support for the Thebans in the battle against the Spartans (Din. 1,38–39; Diod. Sic. 15,25f.; but cf. Xen. Hell. 5,4,19) [2; 3; 4;].

1 D.WHITEHEAD, The Ideology of the Athenian Metic, 1977, 16, 160   2 PA 8277   3 J.SUNDWALL, Nachträge zur Prosopographia Attica, 1910, 109   4 DEVELIN no. 1581.   J.E.

Cepheus

Cepheus (Κηφεύς; *Kēpheús*).
[1] Arcadian local hero, son of → Aleus [1], the founder of Tegea, and of Neaera, founding hero of the city of → Caphyae (whose name is derived from C.). His daughter Antinoe founded Mantinea. C. later takes over the rulership of Tegea from his father. When → Hercules, after the conquest of the Neleid kingdom, sets off on a punitive expedition against the Spartan king → Hippocoon, he invites C. and his twenty sons to take part; all of them are killed in this campaign. He is cited as a participant in the Argonauts' expedition in Apoll. Rhod. (1,161).

M. JOST, Sanctuaires et cultes d'Arcadie, 1985, 367f.

[2] Son of Belos (= Baal), father of → Andromeda and husband of → Cassiepea. The area under C.'s control is

pinpointed as the (south)east of the area of Greek cultural influence: according to Hdt. 7,61 in Persia, according to Hellanicus in Babylon (Steph. Byz. s.v. Χαλδαῖοι), according to Paus. 4,35,9 in Phoenician Joppa; in Euripides' *Andromeda* 'Ethiopia' is considered to be his territory. Because Cassiepea commits a crime against the Nereids, C. is compelled to offer his daughter to a sea monster, but Andromeda is saved by → Perseus (Apollod. 2,43f., Ov. Met. 4,668ff.). After their death, C. and his family are sent into the heavens as constellations (Eratosth. Katasterismoi 15). The connection of Perseus as progenitor of Grecian dynasties with an oriental ruler may reflect historical developments of the Mycenaean period.

F. BUBEL, Euripides, Andromeda, 1991, 24–44.   E.V.

[3] see → Constellations

Cephisia (Κηφισιά; *Kēphisiá*). Attic *mesogeia* deme of the phyle Erechtheis, six (eight) → *bouleutaí*, modern Kifissia [1. 38]. Location of the Attic *dodekapolis* (Philochorus in Str. 9,1,20; FGrH B Fr. 94). Suburb of → Athens with abundant springs and forests, west of the → Pentelicon (Harpocr. s.v. Κηφισιεύς; Diog. Laert. 3,41; Synes. Epist. 272) with a *villa* of Herodes [16] Atticus (Gell. NA 1,2,2; 18,10,2; Philostr. VS 2,1,12) [2. 197 fig. 251–254]. His family used to be attributed with a Roman tomb on the Plateia Platanou [2. 197f. fig. 255–257; 3]. A deme decree (2nd half of the 4th cent. BC) [4. 248; 382 no. 68] provides the earliest evidence of a → *palaistra* in a rural Attic deme.

1 TRAILL, Attica, 15; 38; 59; 63; 67; 110 no. 64, table 1
2 TRAVLOS, Attika, 197ff., fig. 250–257   3 A. TSCHIRA, Eine röm. Grabkammer in K., in: AA 1948/49, 83–97.
4 WHITEHEAD, Index s.v. K.   H.LO.

Cephisius (Κηφίσιος; *Kēphísios*). The Athenian C. was the main accuser of → Andocides [1] in the Trial of the Mysteries in 399 BC; C. levelled harsh reproaches against his political and religious violations, which must in part be ascribed to rhetorical slander (And. 1,92–93; Lys. 6,42).

A. MISSIOU, The Subversive Oratory of Andokides, 1992, 50.   J.E.

Cephisodorus (Κηφισόδωρος; *Kēphisódōros*).
[1] Poet of the Attic Old Comedy, for whom Lysias records a not further specified victory in 402 BC (Lys. or. 21,4) and whose name also appears on the list of winners at the Dionysia (after Nicophon and Theopompus) [1. test. 2; 3]. The titles of four pieces are transmitted (Ἀμαζόνες/'The Amazons', Ἀντιλαΐς/'Antilaïs', Τροφώνιος/'Trophonius', Ὗς/'Hys') as well as a total of 13 verses; the longest fragment of these contains five verses of a dialogue, in which an effeminate master orders his slave to buy perfume and ointments [1. fr. 3].

1 PCG IV, 1983, 63.   T.HI.

[2] Athenian from Marathon, commander of the cavalry in the battle of Mantinea in 362 BC, who died in a skirmish prior to the battle (Ephoros FGrH 70 F 85; cf. Xen. Hell. 7,5,15 [Diod. Sic. 15,85,3f.]), in which C. — alongside → Gryllus [2] — proved his excellence (Paus. 8,9,10; Harpocration s.v. Kephisodoros). PA 8376.
        BO.D.

[3] Bronze sculptor. Pliny refers with praise to C.'s statue of Athena and an altar to Zeus Soter in the Piraeus, for which location Pausanias describes a statue of Athena and one of Zeus without any reference to the artist. Identifications which had been suggested based on a document relief of 325–322 BC have become obsolete after a revised reading of the inscriptions; C.'s creative period remains unknown. A possible confusion with Cephisodotus [4] has been suspected.

OVERBECK no. 1141; LIPPOLD, 275; G. CARETTONI, EAA 4, 340 no. 1; M. MEYER, Die griech. Urkundenreliefs, 1989, 172f.   R.N.

[4] Athenian from Xypete, influential politician *c.* 226–196 BC: military treasurer (204/3) and treasurer of the grain fund (203/2), envoy to Rome in 200 (?) as well as in 198/97 (MORETTI 33; Pol. 18,10,11; Paus. 1,36,5f.). As an exponent of the anti-Macedonian faction in Athens, C. changed to a pro-Roman policy on the eve of the Second Macedonian War (200–197 BC), following the examples of Attalus I, the Rhodians and Aetolians (cf. Liv. 31,1,9) [1. 201–206]. C. died in the spring of 195 BC.

1 HABICHT.   L.-M.G.

It is possible that C. [5] and [7] or [6] and [7] are identical, but C. [5] and [6] are clearly distinguished by the reference to their respective origins:
[5] Athenian rhetor, a pupil of → Isocrates, 4th cent. BC. It is known from Dion. Hal. (De Isocrate 18,4) and Athenaeus (2,60de; 3,122bc; 8,354c) that he wrote a treatise in four vols in defence of his teacher against attacks by Aristotle, arguing that Isocrates' work as a logographer was of no great importance and that immoral aphorisms could also be found in the works of other authors, and also himself attacked Aristotle (among other things because of his interest in proverbs); with that he also criticized Plato in the wrong assumption that Aristotle had adopted Plato's philosophy without any changes (Dion. Hal. Epistula ad Pompeium 1,16; Numenius in Euseb. Praep. evang. 14,6,9f.). There are also references to C. as the author of a didactic work on rhetoric (Dion. Hal. Epistula ad Ammaeum 1,2).
[6] Theban, according to Ath. 12,548ef the author of a treatise on the Macedonian general Antipater.
[7] According to schol. Aristot. Eth. Nic. 3,11,46 (CAG 20,166,2 = FGrH 112) the author of a history of the Third → Sacred War.   M.W.

Cephisodotus (Κηφισόδωτος; *Kēphisódōtos*).

[1] Athenian *stratēgós*, killed in 405/4 BC in the battle of → Aigos Potami or executed afterwards with other Athenian prisoners of war (Xen. Hell. 2,1,16–32; Diod. Sic. 13,105f.; Plut. Alcibiades 36,4; Plut. Lysander 13,1) [1].

[2] Athenian *stratēgós* from the Acharnae deme; friend of → Charidemus [2], on whose request he was sent with a command to the Hellespont in 360/59 BC. Since Charidemus had switched to fight on → Cotys' [I 1] side, he and C. unexpectedly faced each other as enemies. A treaty negotiated by C. to end hostilities was rejected by Athens, C. was deposed, accused with an → *eisangelía* and sentenced to pay five talents. (Dem. Or. 19,180; 23,153–167; Aeschin. In Ctes. 51f. with schol.; Androtion FGrH 324 F 19). It is doubtful if C. is identical with the *árchōn* of 358/7 [2; 3].

[3] One of the Athenian envoys at the peace negotiations in Sparta in 372/1 BC (Xen. Hell. 6,3,2); in 369 he participated in the discussion before the → *ekklēsía* on the terms of the alliance with Sparta. On C.'s initiative the supreme command on land and at sea was to change every five days (Xen. Hell. 7,1,1; 7,1,12–14). In 367/6 he petitioned for a council decree against the Aetolian federation and the inhabitants of Trichoneum (TOD 137), in 364/3 for an honorary decree for Straton, the king of Sidon (TOD 139), in 358/7 for a → *psḗphisma* to support Euboea (Aristot. Rh. 1411a 6–11) [4].

→ Athens III; → Strategos

    1 PA 8312   2 PA 8313 = DEVELIN no. 1601 and possibly PA 8314 = DEVELIN no. 1599   3 M. H. HANSEN, Eisangelia, 1975, no. 96   4 PA 8331 = DEVELIN no. 1603.
                                                 J.E.

[4] Sculptor from Athens. C. was an in-law of Phocion and the founder of a sculptor family with his son (?) → Praxiteles and his grandsons → C. [5] and Timarchus. The period of his acme is considered to be 372–369 BC. His most famous bronze work, Eirene with the boy Plutus in the agora of Athens, was created about 377–371 BC and has been identified in copies from images on coins and prize amphoras (Munich, GL). A bronze Hermes with the Dionysus child and statues of philosophers, among them a *contionans manu elata* ('speaker with raised hand') are explicitly attributed to the elder C. by Pliny. The attribution of several statues of the Muses on the Helicon is disputed; C. probably participated in a group of nine Muses [4], since the others by → Strongylium and Olympiosthenes are from the late 5th cent.; another group of three Muses may be by C. [5]. A cult image group in Megalopolis is also disputed as being C. [4] or [5].

    OVERBECK no. 878; 1137–1140; 1143; G. RICHTER, The Sculpture and Sculptors of the Greeks, 1950, 257–259; LIPPOLD 223–225; J. MARCADÉ, Recueil des signatures de sculpteurs grecs, 1, 1953, 51; D. MUSTILLI, in: EAA 4, 342–344 no. 1; I. LINFERT-REICH, Musen- und Dichterinnenfiguren des 4. und frühen 3. Jh., typescript, diss. Freiburg 1971, 8f., 29f.; H. JUNG, Zur Eirene des Kephisodot, in: JDAI 91, 1976, 97–134; L. TODISCO, Scultura greca del IV secolo, 1993, 63–65.

[5] Sculptor from Athens. C. was a member of the Athenian wealthy class and a student and son of → Praxiteles, grandson (?) of → C. [4] and brother of Timarchus, with whom he worked. His acme according to tradition in 296–293 BC is too late since a base signature in Eleusis is already dated at about 344 BC. Further bases with signatures of the brothers are preserved in Athens, Delphi, Cos, Megara and Troezen. Several works by C. later found their way to Rome; a Leto stood in the Apollo temple on the Palatine, Asclepius and Artemis in the Juno temple of the Porticus Octaviae, an Aphrodite in the collection of Asinius Pollio. In Athens a statue of Enyo near the Ares temple in the agora and wooden statues of Lycurgus and his sons in the Erechtheion are attested. In Thebes C. and Timarchus created a Dionysus statue or an altar. A cult image group in Megalopolis — with Zeus, Artemis and Megalopolis — is usually attributed to C. [5] but could equally well be by C. [4] since the creative period of the co-worker → Xenophon is unknown. The attribution of two groups of Muses on the Helicon to C. [4] or C. [5] is disputed.

    Written sources praise C. as the perfecter of the art of Praxiteles and his realistic details, especially in a → *sýmplegma* ('interlacing') later kept in Pergamum. Its identification with erotic satyr and maenad groups that are extant in copies is uncertain since a group of wrestlers is also possible. Herondas praises a statue by the sons of Praxiteles in the Asclepieum of Cos as lifelike. Philosophers and the poetesses Myro and Anyte are named among his portraits. A portrait of Menander from the Dionysus theatre of Athens is known, of which Roman copies and its throne with inscription are preserved. Other identifications and attributions are hypothetical.

    OVERBECK no. 1160; 1331–1341; LIPPOLD, 299–301; J. MARCADÉ, Recueil des signatures de sculpteurs grecs, 1, 1953, 53–59; W. FUCHS, Die Vorbilder der neuattischen Reliefs, 1959, 71; D. MUSTILLI, EAA 4, 344f. no. 2; I. LINFERT-REICH, Musen- und Dichterinnenfiguren des 4. und frühen 3. Jh., typescript, diss. Freiburg 1971, 8–11; 29f.; 43–47; DAVIES, 286–290; H. P. MÜLLER, Praxiteles und Kephisodot der Jüngere. Zwei griech. Bildhauer aus hohen Ges.-Schichten?, in: Klio 70, 1988, 346–361; R. KABUS-PREISSHOFEN, Die hell. Plastik der Insel Kos, 1989, 52–63; 73; STEWART, 295–297; K. FITTSCHEN, Zur Rekonstruktion griech. Dichterstatuen, 1. Die Statue des Menander, in: MDAI(A) 106, 1991, 243–279; L. TODISCO, Scultura greca del IV secolo, 1993, 132–136; P. MORENO, Scultura ellenistica, 1994, 108f.; 175–177.
                                                 R.N.

Cephis(s)us

[1] (Κηφισ(σ)ός; *Kēphis(s)ós*). Main river of central Greece (Pind. Ol. 14,1; Pind. Pyth. 4,46). Its perennial main source is in → Lilaea (Phocis) at Mount Parnassus (Hom. Il. 2,523; Str. 9,2,19; Paus. 9,24,1; 10,33,4f.; Plin. HN 4,27; around the spring was an important sanctuary whose priests were eponymous for Lilaea: FdD 3,4,2, p. 206–209, no. 132–135); further non-permanent sources were in Doris. The C. passes through Phocis and Boeotia, and flows south-east of Orchome-

nus, together with other rivers, into Lake Copais, a lake without any surface outlet (therefore also called Kephisis, Hom. Il. 5,709), which is drained by katavothra into the Gulf of Euboea, into the bay of → Larymna (Locrian into Hellenistic times, then Boeotian) as well as the bay of Skroponeri.

Mythology: son of Oceanus and Thetys, no homogenous genealogy, often tied in with local myths; the nymph Lilaea is considered to be his daughter (documentary evidence in [1]).

1 R. LATTE, s.v. K. (12), RE 11, 250.

F. BÖLTE, s.v. K. (1), RE 11, 241–244; PHILIPPSON/KIRSTEN 1, 395; 419–431; 470ff.; 480f.; P. M. WALLACE, Strabo's Description of Boiotia, 1979, 79.   M.FE.

[2] (Κεφισ(σ)ός; *Kephis(s)ós*). Main river of the *pedion* (the plain) of Athens with tributaries from all the surrounding mountains. Its easternmost sources are on the southern slope of Mt. Parnes, strengthened by further sources further down, but not perennial (Str. 9,1,24), nowadays completely canalized. In antiquity (Str. 9,1,24), the main source was taken to be the strongest tributary rising from the western slope of Mount Pentelicon in Trinemea (modern Kokkinaras) east of Cephisia, which takes its name from the river. Used in the *pedion* for the irrigation of fields (Soph. OC 685ff.), the C. passes under the road to Piraeus and the Long Walls and discharges into the bay of Phalerum. It most important tributary is the Ilisus. A cult of the C. is evident for Phalerum in Eur. Ion 1261 and Ael. VH 2,33, furthermore in IG II² 4547f., for Oropus in Paus. 1,34,3. Documentary evidence: Str. 9,24,1; Paus. 1,37,3f.; Xen. Hell. 2,4,19.

F. BÖLTE, s.v. K. (3), RE 11, 244ff.; PHILIPPSON/KIRSTEN 1, 798f.

[3] (Κηφισ(σ)ός; *Kēphis(s)ós*). River on the eastern edge of the Thriasian plain in Attica (modern Sarantapotamos), rising as Kokkini at Mount Cithaeron above Vilia and joining with the Sarantapotamos before entering the Thriasia (Paus. 1,38,5). Regulatory work on the river during the Hadrianic period (AD 117–138) is documented in Eus. (Jer.) Chron. 166, a bridge of the 4th cent. BC in IG II² 1191; Syll.3 1048,15ff. For the Hadrianic bridge 1 km east of Eleusis, see [1].

1 TRAVLOS, Attika, 98, 178f., fig. 243–244.

F. BÖLTE, s.v. K. (4), RE 11, 248f.; PHILIPPSON/KIRSTEN 1, 861.   H.LO.

[4] (Κηφισ(σ)ός; *Kēphissós*). Right tributary of the → Inachus [2] in Argolis (Paus. 2,15,5; Str. 9,3,16), the stream of the modern Epano-Belesi. It traversed from north to south the agora in Argos, where a sanctuary was dedicated to it (Paus. 2,20,6f.), and was canalized latest from the 5th cent. BC.

CH. KRITZAS, Χρονικά, in: AD 27, 1972, B'1, 211; P. MARCHETTI, Recherches sur les mythes et la topographie d'Argos. 4: L'agora revisitée, in: BCH 119, 1995, 453–456.   Y.L.

Cepus (Κηπός, Κηποί; *Kēpós, Kēpoí*). Milesian foundation on the Asian shore of the Bosporus [2], north of Phanagorea, in the Sindice (Ps.-Scyl. 72, opposing view in Str. 11,2,10), possibly the modern Artjuhovskoe gorodište. Ancient settlement with rich *kurgans*, or tumuli. From the mid 6th cent. BC onwards up to the incursions by the Huns, C. was the starting point for the Hellenization of the interior of the country. When the sons of Paerisades I fought for the Bosporan throne (310 BC), Prytanis sought refuge in C. (Diod. Sic. 20,22–25). Gylon, the grandfather of Demosthenes, was given C. by a Bosporan king (Aeschin. In Ctes. 171).

V. F. GAIDUKEVIČ, Das Bosporanische Reich, 1971, 215f.   I.v.B.

Cera (κηρός; *kērós*). According to Plin. HN 11,11, (bees)wax was one of the most widely used materials. Among the properties of *cera* are conservation of shape, the capacity to seal and adhere (Hom. Od. 12,47–49 and passim), inflammability (→ Lighting), lustre; *cera* also aids the healing process (Dioscorides 2,83,3; Plin. HN 22,116). When warmed, *cera* is easy to work, but also becomes soft or fluid (→ Icarus). *Cera* was used in → sculpture; → painting; in bronze casting; in magic (for amulets and articulated dolls etc.); in funerary art (→ *imagines maiorum*); in the embalming process; in shipbuilding; with resin in the cooper's trade. According to myth, Apollo built the temple at Delphi of *cera* and feathers. Tableware was polished with *cera*; it was poured over fruit to give it lustre, or various objects and foodstuffs were imitated in *cera*. The special properties of *cera* made it particularly important as a writing material when applied to tablets of wood or ivory; it adhered readily to the writing base, its softness permitted impressions to be made and erased, and a text could be conserved as long as required.

→ Writing tablet; → Writing materials

R. BÜLL, E. MOSER, s.v. Wachs, RE Suppl. 13, 1347–1426; R. FUCHS, s.v. Wachs, LÄ 6, 1088–1094; E. LANGLOTZ, Beobachtungen über die ant. Ganosis, in: AA, 1968, 470–474.   R.H.

Ceraea (Κεραία; Κεραῖαι; *Keraía, Keraîai*). Town on Crete in the north-west of the island, of undetermined location between Lappa and Polyrrhenia (Steph. Byz. s.v. Βήνη). In the Lyttian War (220 v.Chr.), C. — together with other Cretan towns — seceded from Cnossus and Gortyn (Pol. 4,53,6). In 183 BC, it was one of the Cretan towns to enter an alliance with Eumenes II of Pergamum [1. 179].

1 M. GUARDUCCI (ed.), Inscriptiones Creticae IV, 1950.   H.SO.

Cerambus (Κέραμβος, *Kérambos*). Son of Euseirus (son of Poseidon) and the nymph Eidothea; a shepherd on the Othrys, he invents the panpipes and the lyre, and his playing sets the nymphs dancing. He does not follow Pan's advice to flee from the imminent, icy cold winter. C. and his flock freeze to death under the mass of snow. The nymphs transform him into a beetle with long feelers resembling a lyre (Antoninus Liberalis 22; Cerambyx: stag beetle; cf. Hsch. s.v. Κεράμβυξ). However Ovid in contrast reports (Met. 7,353-356) that the nymphs provide C. with wings, so that he can escape from the Deucalion flood.   C.W.

Cerameis (Κεραμεῖς; *Krameîs*). Attic *asty* deme of the phyle Acamantis, six → *bouleutaí*. Provenance from this deme is expressed by ἐκ Κεραμέων (*ek Kraméōn*). Sources [1. LXXf.] consistently refer to the place as → Kerameikos. This was called the most beautiful of Athenian suburbs (Thuc. 2,34,5; → Athens, map), and was located inside — and to the northwest outside — the Dipylon Gate between Sacred Way to Eleusis and the road to the Academy. The *hóroi Krameíkou* alongside the latter (IG II² 2617-2619) probably marked the deme border, contrary to [2. 167; 5. 300; 6. 29[109]; 7] (for deme borders [4]). C. was the starting point for the procession of the → Panathenaea; it contained the potters' quarter and the most noble necropolis with public and private graves [3; 5]. No public inscriptions; a → *démarchos* is attested in IG I³ 425 Z. 30 [2. 58], a cult of the eponymous hero Ceramus in Paus. (1,3,1), Philochorus (FGrH 328 F 25) and the Suda (s.v. Κεραμίς).

1 E. CURTIUS, Stadtgesch. von Athen, 1891   2 W. JUDEICH, Top. von Athen, ²1931   3 U. KNIGGE, Der Kerameikos von Athen, 1988   4 H. LOHMANN, Atene, 1993, 55ff.   5 TRAVLOS, Athen, 299-322 fig. 391-424   6 WHITEHEAD, Index s.v. K.   7 R. E. WYCHERLEY, Agora 3, 221-224.

TRAILL, Attica, 47, 63, 67, 110 no. 65, table 5.   H.LO.

Ceramon agora (Κεράμων ἀγορά; *Kerámōn agorá*). A 'populated town' between Peltae and → Caystrou pedion, 'the last town (in Phrygia) in the direction of Mysia', only mentioned in Xen. An. 1,2,11; localization impossible.

W. RUGE, s.v. K., RE 11, 254f.   T.D.-B.

Ceramus (Κέραμος; *Kéramos*). Town in south-western Caria on the northern coast of the gulf named after C. (Κεράμειος or Κεραμικὸς κόλπος; *Krámeios/Kramikòs kólpos, sinus Ceramicus*; modern Gökova körfezi), removed from the coast by the delta formation of the — in the end subterranean — Koca Çay (Str. 14,2,15), modern Kemerdere near Ören (Plin. HN 5,109; Ptol. 5,2,10; Paus. 6,13,3f.). Originally Carian, it was Hellenized from the 6th cent. BC (archaic kouros head, *c.* 540/530 [1]); in 454/3 BC, it was a member of the → Delian League (IG I³ 259,5,18), and in Hellenistic times belonged to the *koinon* of the Chrysoreis (Str. 14,2,25). In 189/8, C. was given by Rome to Rhodes, and declared free in 167 BC; C. soon returned to Rhodian control; in 81 BC, Sulla assigned C. to → Stratonicea (OGIS 441,51; [2. Test. 14]). Inscriptions are extant [2] and, starting with the 2nd cent. BC, coins [3]. Archaeological evidence: A section of the town walls (early Hellenistic) is extant on a slope, outside the gates are sarcophagi, Carian graves, remains probably of a temple of Zeus Chrysaoreus (the main god of C.), east of C. remains of a Corinthian temple (Kurşunlu Yapı) with a founder's inscription by the priest M. Aurelius Chrysantas.

1 E. AKURGAL, Die Kunst Anatoliens von Homer bis Alexander, 1961, 266f.   2 E. VARINLIOĞLU, Die Inschr. von K. (IK 30), 1986   3 HN, 613.

G. E. BEAN, Kleinasien 3, 1974, 53-58; L. BÜRCHNER, s.v. Keramos, RE 11, 255; P. M. FRASER, G. E. BEAN, The Rhodian Peraea and Islands, 1954, 110f.; ROBERT, Villes, 61, 167; H. H. SCHMITT, Rom und Rhodos, 1957, 176f.; M. SPANU, K. di Caria. Storia e monumenti, 1997.   H.KA.

Cerasus (Κερασοῦς; *Kerasoûs*). Harbour town on the river of the same name on the south coast of the Black Sea (→ Pontus Euxinus), a colony of Sinope, to be located three days' march west of Trapezus (Xen. An. 5,3,2; Diod. Sic. 14,30,5) and east of Vakfıkebir; to be differentiated from the C. west of Sinope (Scylax 89: Karaköy on the Karasu?), and also from the town which under Pharnaces I (185-160/54 BC) was joined in a *synoikismós* with Cotyora and renamed Pharnacaca (modern Giresun; Arr. Peripl. p. eux. 24; Anon. Peripl. p. eux. 34 with the island of Aretias or Areos Nesos, modern Giresun Adası; cf. Str. 12,3,17). From which of these towns Lucullus took the particularly delicious species of cherry to Rome (Ath. 2,35), cannot be determined.   E.O.

Cerata (Κέρατα; *Krata*). Peaks, named after their peculiar shape ('horns') (modern Trikeraton; Trikeri, 470 m), in the mountains on the border between Attica and Megaris east of Eleusis (Diod. Sic. 11,65,1; Plut. Themistocles 13,1; Str. 9,1,11).

F. BÖLTE, s.v. K., RE 11, 265f.   PHILIPPSON/KIRSTEN, vol. 1, 760; 973.   H.LO.

Ceraunian Mountains (Κεραύνια ὄρη; *Keraúnia órē*). The most northern of the coastal ranges of Epirus (Str. 7,5,8; 7,6,1; 7,7,5), modern Rëza e Kanalit (or Karaburun) in Albania. It starts in the south at the Çikë range (2045 m) and ends in the north in the far protruding Cape → Acroceraunia. The rugged limestone heights (up to 1593 m) are much feared because of their frequent thunderstorms, after which they were named 'Thunder Mountains'. Only in the south were ancient landings or settlements found: Kemara/Chimera (modern Himarë) [1. 679] and Palaeste (modern Palasë) [1. 125], where Caesar landed with his army in 48 BC. Sources: Scyl. 26f.; Plin. HN 3,97; 3,145; 4,1f.; 4,4; Mela 2,54; Ptol. 3,13,1f.; Dionys. Per. 389; Geogr. Rav. 5,13; Guido, Geographia 112.

1 N. G. L. HAMMOND, Epirus, 1967.   D.S.

Cerausium (Κεραύσιον; *Keraúsion*). The springs of the Neda rise on Mount C., a part of the → Lycaeum, (Paus. 8,41,3); it is therefore to be localized in the mountainous region between the modern Likeo and Tetrazio.

E. MEYER, s.v. K, in: RE Suppl. 9, 382. E.O.

Cerberus (Κέρβερος, *Kérberos*). A guard dog that belongs to the standard repertoire of the Graeco-Roman → Underworld who signals and prevents any unauthorized entry into, or departure from, the realm of the dead. He often appears at the side of → Hades and/or → Persephone. In the Hellenistic age C. in a changed form was also associated with the god → Sarapis (Macrob. Sat. 1,20,13–14).

C. is mentioned for the first time — although without a name or any more detailed description — in Homer in connection with the adventures of → Hercules in the Underworld (Hom. Il. 8,366ff.; cf. Od. 11, 623ff.). The first mention of a name and a genealogy is offered in Hes. Theog. 306–312: C.'s parents are the monsters → Typhon and → Echidna, his siblings Orthrus (→ Geryoneus), → Hydra [1] and → Chimaera, all of whom are characterized by multiple heads and a vestment of serpents. There are various opinions regarding C.'s appearance, especially the kind and number of heads: Hes. Theog. 769ff. describes him as having fifty heads, he is a hound from hell devouring raw flesh and with a piercing howl; Pind. Dithyramboi 2, fr. 249a even states that he has one hundred heads. Most literary sources describe him as having four legs with three dogs' heads and also bearing numerous serpents' heads at the neck and throat (e.g. Apollod. 2,5,12; Verg. Aen. 6,417ff.; Sen. Herc. f. 782ff.; exception: Hor. Carm. 3,11,17–20). In the myth C., like his siblings, is associated with Hercules, who pulls him to the Upperworld. C.'s spittle, dropping on to the earth, is the aetion for the poisonous foxglove (*Aconitum*). Those who interpret myths from a rationalist perspective place C. as either a poisonous snake or a wild dog (Hecataeus FGrH 1 F 27) (Plut. Thes. 31,4). See [4] with regard to the allegorical interpretation of C. in the Middle Ages and the Renaissance as the earth, avarice or death.

1 S. EITREM, s.v. K., RE 11, 271–282 2 B. LINCOLN, The Hellhound, in: Journal of Indo-European Studies 7, 1979, 273–286 3 M. SANADER, K. in der Ant., Diss. Innsbruck 1983 4 J. J. H. SAVAGE, The Medieval Trad. of Cerberus, in: Traditio 7, 1949–51, 405–410 5 H. THIRY, La diffusion du mythe de Cerbère (ca. 540–400), in: Živa Antika 22, 1972, 61–70 6 S. WOODFORD, J. SPIER, s.v. K, LIMC 6.1, 24–32. C.W.

Cercaphus (Κέρκαφος; *Kérkaphos*). One of the seven → Heliadae, of → Cydippe [3] father of the eponyms of the Rhodian towns of Lindus, Ialysus and Cameirus (Pind. Ol. 7,73 with schol. 7,131c-d; 132c; 135; Diod. Sic. 5,57,8; Str. 14,2,8). T.H.

Cercasorus (Κερκάσωρος, Κερκέσουρα; *Kerkásōros*, *Kerkésoura*). Town in Lower Egypt where, according to Hdt. 2,15; 2,17, the Nile divides into the branches of Pelusium and Canobus, according to Str. 17,806 situated on the west bank opposite Heliopolis, perhaps the Egyptian Ḥwt-šd-ȝbd.

F. GOMAÀ, s.v. Hutsched-abed, LÄ 3, 89–90. K.J.-W.

Cercetae (Κερκέται; *Kerkétai*). Tribe on the north-eastern coast of the → Pontus Euxinus on the slopes of the Caucasus. The name of what are today the Circassians was known to Greek geographers early on, but the details they provide about where the C. lived do not agree with each other (according to Str. 11,492; 496f. between the → Heniochi and the → Moschi).

W. KROLL, s.v. Kerketai, RE 11, 291f.; T. M. MINAJEVA, Archaeological Research in the Land of the Circassians (Russian), 1953, 34ff.; CH. DANOFF, s.v. Pontos Euxeinos, RE Suppl. 9, 1017ff. B.B. and CHR.D.

Cercidas (Κερκιδᾶς, Κερκίδας; *Kerkidâs*, *Kerkídas*).
[1] C., an Arcadian orator mentioned by → Demosthenes [2] (Dem. Or. 18,295) in his famous 'list of traitors' in the speech 'On the Crown' and supposedly acting in the political interest of → Philippus II (similar also Theopomp. FGrH 115 F 119; Pol. 18,14,1–2). The conclusiveness of the accusations by Demosthenes and Theopompus can no longer be verified. C. was descended from a rich family of Megalopolis in Arcadia and was related to the poet of the same name [1].
[2] A *damiorgós*, i.e. one of the probably 50 empowered members of the Arcadian League Council (→ Demiourgos [2]), who is mentioned in a list of victors in 308 BC (IG V 2, 550) [2].

1 H. WANKEL, Demosthenes. Rede für Ktesiphon über den Kranz, 1976, 1250f. 2 J. A. O. LARSEN, Greek Federal States, 1968, 187. J.E.

[3] C. of Megalopolis, famous as the author of the *Meliambi*, lived from about 290 BC to the last quarter of the 3rd cent. He served his hometown about 226 as a delegate of the Achaean League to the Macedonian king Antigonus [3] Doson (Pol. 2,48) and in 222 as the leader of a contingent of 1,000 Megalopolitans deployed by Antigonus against Sparta at Sellasia (Pol. 2,65). Other sources note his remarkable activity as the lawmaker of the Achaeans (Ptol. Hephaestion at Phot. Bibl. p. 151a 6–20 = 3,64 HENRY). Athenaeus (8,347d-e) mentions him as a Cynic; this is confirmed by the title 'The Meliambi of the Cynic Cercidas' (Κερκίδα Κυνὸς Μελίαμβοι: POxy. 1082 fr. 4, l. 15–17), and some passages in the *Meliambi*: fr. 6a-b mentions Zeno of Citium, fr. 60 praises Diogenes of Sinope as 'true descendant of Zeus and heavenly dog' (ἀλαθέως Διογένης Ζανὸς γόνος οὐράνιός τε κύων). The extant remains of the *Meliambi* also exhibit similarities in content to Cynic → diatribes: greed, carnal lust and pursuit of pleasure are castigated; a simple and honest life is presented as exemplary. Lo-

MIENTO sees no contradiction between the high position of C. in public life and his Cynical philosophy; in the age of C., Cynicism was not a 'proletarian philosophy', but had both poor and wealthy adherents [1. 26–31].

The term *meliambos* designates a poem whose content matches the genre of 'satirical poems' (= *iambos*) but is composed in a lyrical metre (= *melos*) [1. 31]. The publication of POxy 1082 revealed several larger fragments of his work: fr. 1 castigates — probably based on Aristophanes' *Plutus* — the gods for not distributing wealth more justly among people. Fr. 2 treats two different 'winds' of love brought by Aphrodite to people: a moderate, enjoyable breeze and a dangerous, unruly storm. In fr. 3 the poet addresses his own, aging self (θυμέ); here he appears to separate joys fit for youth from those suited to a grey-haired senior. The theme of the *Meliambi* — as suits the author's philosophical Cynicism — may be described as aphorisms. Of its poetical form it may be said, without being able to achieve certainty in → colometry, that C. places a dactylic metre (frequently a hemiepes) next to a partial iamb (e.g. ⏑⏑–⏑⏑–– + x –⏑⏑ x) and repeats this pattern *katà stíchon* [4]. It is questionable whether 'dactylo-epitritic' [7] is the correct term for this.

C.'s language is distinguished by astonishing creativity in the formation of new composita; this trait probably fits with the 'outraged' style of the diatribe, some of which may be derived from the humorous word creations of → Aristophanes [3]. Both the mixed genre of the *meliambos* and the extremely stilted expression of language appear Hellenistic in C.'s writings.

EDITIONS: 1 L. LOMIENTO (ed.), Cercidas. Testimonia et Fragmenta, 1993 (42–48 on metrics; extensive bibliography 57–73) 2 CollAlex p. 201–213 (219) 3 E. DIEHL (ed.), Anthologia Lyrica Graeca 3, ³1952, 141–152 4 P. MAAS, Cercidae cynici meliambi nuper inventi κωλομετρίᾳ instructi, in: Berliner Philol. Wochenschr. vol. 31, no. 32, 1911, 1011f. 5 A. HUNT, The Oxyrhynchus Papyri 8, 1911, 20–59.
LITERATURE: 6 E. LIVREA, Studi Cercidei, 1986 7 M. L. WEST, Greek Metre, 1982, 140. W.D.F.

Cercina (Κέρκιν(ν)α; *Kérkin(n)a*). Island, or rather twin islands (Gharbi and Chergui), in the Gulf of Gabès, 20 km from Sfax, modern Kerkenna. Sources: Hdt. 4,195 (Κύραυις); Ps.-Scyl. 110 (GGM 1, 87); Str. 17,3,16; Mela 2,105; Plin. HN 5,41; Ptol. 4,3,35; Agathemerus 21f. (GGM 2, 483); It. Ant. 518,3f.; Stadiasmus Maris Magni 112 (GGM 1, 468). C. was part of the Carthaginian empire and boasted excellent harbours (Diod. Sic. 5,12,4). In historical sources, C. is mentioned in the context of → Dion (Plut. Dion 25,7f.), and of the Second Punic War (Pol. 3,96,12; Liv. 22,31,1f.), in conjunction with Hannibal (Liv. 33,48,3), Marius (Plut. Mar. 40,14), and in connection with the African War by the followers of Caesar against the Pompeians (Bell. Afr. 8,3–5; 34). Following the fall of Carthage, C. became an *urbs libera* and in Caesarean times, Roman

(Bell. Afr. 8,3–5). Under Augustus, it was a place of exile (Tac. Ann. 1,53,4; 4,13,3).
→ Exilium

J. DESANGES, Pline l'Ancien. Histoire naturelle. Livre 5,1–46, 1980, 434–438; J. KOLENDO, Le rôle économique des îles Kerkena ..., in: BCTH N.F. 17 B (1981), 1984, 241–248, also 249. W. HU.

Cercine (Κερκίνη; *Kerkínē*). Uninhabited mountain chain forming the border between Sinti and Maedi in the south and Paeones in the north, through which in 429 BC → Sitalces marched to Doberus against the Macedonian King Perdiccas II. To that end, he himself had to have a path built through the mountains (Thuc. 2,98,1f.). The C. are equated with the mountain ridges of Belasica, Orbelos, or Kruša in the border region between Macedonia and Thrace. It is possible though that the name C. refers to a number of smaller mountain ranges — along the line from Kočani-Boboševo, Struma to Belasica — that were later known collectively as Orbelos.

A. FOL, T. SPIRIDONOV, Istoričeska geografija na trakijskite plemana, 1983, 118f. I.V.B.

Cercinitis (Κερκινῖτις; *Kerkinîtis*). Ionian foundation from the 6th cent. BC in the north-western part of the Crimea near the modern village of Evpatorija (Hellanicus FGrH 4 F 70; Str. 12,3,18; Arr. Peripl. p. eux. 19,5), from the middle of the 4th cent. BC in the possession of Chersonesus [3] [1. 352] and closely linked with it; second largest town with an important port, agriculture and crafts, also Doric inscriptions [1. 339]. From the 2nd to the 1st cents. BC, C. was on several occasions captured by the Scythians. Diophantus, Mithridates' VI general, recaptured C. and renamed it Eupatoria. C. continued to exist into the 2nd cent. AD.

1 IOSPE 1².

A. N. ŠČEGLOV, Severo-zapadnyj Krym v antičnuju epohu, 1, 1978; E. I. SOLOMIK, Graffiti c hory Hersonesa, 1984, no. 114–176; A. N. ZOGRAPH, Ancient Coinage, II, 1977, 254–256. I.V.B.

Cercopes (Κέρκωπες, *Kérkōpes*; regarding κέρκος, 'tail': 'those with tails'; used also as a swear word, cf. Diog. Laert. 9, 114). The number and names of these sons of → Theia and → Oceanus (Suda s.v. Κέρκωπες) vary; they usually appear as a pair (e.g. Olus and Eurybatus; Acmon/Aclemon and Passalus; Sillus and Tribalus). In Asia Minor their home is given as Ephesus, or on the Greek mainland as Thermopylae. The C. are elf-like proverbial scoundrels and good-for-nothings, who are very closely associated with the Hercules legend: → Hercules falls asleep exhausted, but is woken up by the C. who with constant malice also steal his weapons. After he has caught them and tied them upside down to a wooden pole, he releases them because of their amusing witticisms about the oracle of their mother, that they should be on their guard against the man with the black bottom, whom they identify as Hercules (Melampyges: Suda s.v. Μελαμπύγου τύχοις). Other versions report that he kills them or gives them to → Omphale or hands them over to → Eurystheus (Diod. Sic. 4,31,7). Later, Zeus, whom they also try to deceive, transforms them into stone (Pherecydes FGrH 3 F 77) or puts them on the 'Island of Monkeys' Pithecusa-Ischia (Xenagoras FGrH 240 F 28; Ov. Met. 14, 89ff.). The C. stories were depicted numerously and in a striking way, e.g., on the metope of the C.'s temple in Selinus around 550 BC.

S. WOODFORD, s.v. K., LIMC 6.1, 32–35.　　　C.W.

Cercyon (Κερκυών; Kerkyón).

[1] In Attic legend, a fiend living in Eleusis, son of Poseidon (Paus. 1,14,3; depicted differently in Hyg. Fab. 38, Apollod. epit. 1,3), accustomed to overpowering passers-by in a deadly wrestling game until defeated by → Theseus (Plut. Thes. 11; Paus. 1,39,3). The battle against C. is a fixed component of the cycle of Theseus' deeds, depicted pictorially from the late 6th cent. BC [1], and it is also attested to in literature since Aeschylus' satyr play 'C.' (TrGF F 102–107) and Bacchyl. 18,26 (cf. Isoc. Or. 10,29; Diod. Sic. 4,59,5; Ov. Met. 7,439) [2]. C. also appears as a cruel father of → Alope in tragedy.
[2] Arcadian, son of Agamedes, father of → Hippothous [4] (Paus. 8,5,4), later identified with C. [1], who is said to have fled from Arcadia to Eleusis (Callim. Fr. 49,8ff. HOLLIS [3]; Plut. Thes. 11,1; Charax FGrH 103 F 5).

1 J. NEILS, s.v. Theseus, LIMC 7.1, 925–929, 932f.
2 F. BROMMER, Theseus: Die Taten des griech. Helden in der ant. Kunst und Lit., 1982, 19–21　　3 Callimachus: Hecale, ed. A. S. HOLLIS, 1990, 88f., 200f.　　A.A.

Cerdo (Κερδώ, Kerdó, the 'purveyor of gain'). The wife of the Argival primordial man → Phoroneus; she has a tomb (and therefore a cult) on the agora of → Argos, next to the shrine of → Asclepius (Paus. 2,21,1).　　F.G.

Cerdylium (Κερδύλιον; Kerdýlion). Elevated settlement on the right bank of the Strymon within the territory of Argilus near → Amphipolis in Thrace. There Brasidas took up position against the Athenians in 422 BC (Thuc. 5,6,3ff.).　　I.v.B.

Cerea (Κέρεια; Kéreia). Island of the Cyclades (15 km², height of more than 200 m) between Naxos and Amorgos, modern Keros (Stadiasmus maris magni 282; Geogr. Rav. 5,21: Cerus). In 425/4, it was a member of the Delian League (tribute of 630 drachmas, [1. vol. 1, 231, 308f., 501; vol. 3, 198]). Excavations uncovered an important early Cycladic settlement. Idol finds in the National Museum in Athens.

1 ATL.

L. BÜRCHNER, s.v. K., RE 11, 253; PHILIPPSON/KIRSTEN vol. 4, 146f.; E. KARPODINI-DEMETRIADE, Die griech.

Inseln, 1987, 82; H. KALETSCH, s.v. Keros, in: LAUFFER, Griechenland, 328; IG XII 7 p. VII.　　H.KAL. and E.MEY.

Cerealius Unknown poet of epigrams, two of whose satirical poems survive: one pillories a poetaster (Anth. Pal. 11,129), the other is an interesting literary manifesto against the affectations of the Attic orators, regarded by C. as being as empty as they were abstruse (Anth. Pal. 11,144, cf. Lucillius, Anth. Pal. 11,142). At least chronologically plausible is his identification with Iulius Cerialis, the friend of Martial (Mart. Epigr. 11,52,1).　　E.D.

Cerebia (Κηρεβία; Kērebía). Wife of Poseidon, mother of → Dictys [1] and → Polydectes, who rules over the Cycladean island of Seriphus (schol. Lycoph. 838). But according to Hesiod (fr. 6 RZACH) and Apollodorus (1,88), Magnes and a Naead are the parents of both of them.　　AL.FR.

Ceremonial dress Wearing the ceremonial dress (CD) distinguished persons in society and identified them in their official roles. This holds true particularly for priestesses, state officials, but also for delegates (herald's staff) and others. In Greece, priests wore a white robe (Pl. Leg. 12,965a), the ungirded → chiton, which could also be red, or, less often, dyed with saffron or purple. Another characteristic was the → wreath (stephanophóroi, 'wearers of the wreath', was thus the name of priests in e.g. Miletus); less commonly, priests displayed the attributes of the respective deity (priestesses in Athens and Pallene). Priests wore an especially conspicuous official dress consisting of red robes and an iron sword during sacrificial ceremonies for the fallen soldiers of Plataiai. The Arrhephoroi in Athena's service wore a white robe with special gold jewellery. It is unknown whether the seer's netlike robe was a theatre dress or a CD (Poll. 4,116). State officials also wore a wreath to signify their office; also, evidence exists of a headband (FGrH 328 F 64 Philochorus, → diádēma); in Athens, the archon basileus was dressed in special shoes (βασιλίδες) and in a long, ungirded chiton (κρητικόν, eastern frieze of the → Parthenon).

CD was highly significant in Republican and Imperial Rome, as the colour scheme of the → toga indicated the political importance of the wearer and distinguished him from the simple citizen (togatus). Curulian officials wore a white toga praetexta with purple seams and a → tunica with purple stripes as a badge of honour (→ sella curulis). They kept the right to wear the toga praetexta on festive occasions even after resigning from office. Officials wore the entirely purple toga picta and the palm-embroidered tunica palmata only during triumph (vestis triumphalis) and when presiding over certain games (for example the ludi apollinares), with the exception of Caesar (Cass. Dio 44,4). Similarly, the emperors wore their triumphal robes only on special occasions (cf. however Cass. Dio 67,4 on Domitian), otherwise they wore the toga praetexta. On leaving the realm of *domi* and entering the realm of *militiae*, the commander dressed in armour with the purple or white → *paludamentum*, or in the tunica with *paludamentum* (Liv. 36,3,14; 37,4,3; 40,26,2 and passim; Tac. Hist. 2,89). Among priests, the double-layered *toga praetexta* (*toga duplex*, → *laena*) combined with a felt hat was worn by Flamines only in state sacrifices, except for the *flamen Dialis*, who always wore the *toga praetexta*. → Clavus; → Trabea; fig. see → Clothing

MOMMSEN, Staatsrecht 408–432; R. DELBRÜCK, Die Consulardiptychen und verwandte Denkmäler, 1929; A. ALF-ÖLDI, Insignien und Tracht der röm. Kaiser, in: MDAI(R) 50, 1935, 1–171; Id., Der frühröm. Reiteradel und seine Ehrenabzeichen, 1952; E. KÜNZL, Der röm. Triumph, 1988, 85–108; A. PEKRIDOU-GORECKI, Mode im ant. Griechenland, 1989, 125–132; TH. SCHÄFER, Imperii Insignia. Sella Curulis und Fasces. Zur Repräsentation röm. Magistrate, MDAI(R) 29. suppl., 1989; H. R. GOETTE, Studien zu röm. Togadarstellungen, 1990, 2–19; G. STEI-GERWALD, Das kaiserliche Purpurprivileg in spätröm. und frühbyz. Zeit, in: JbAC 33, 1990, 209–239.   R.H.

Ceremony

I. MESOPOTAMIA   II. EGYPT   III. IRAN

I. MESOPOTAMIA

In contrast with cultic → rituals, the secular ceremonies of Mesopotamia have up to now rarely been the subject of academic research. On the whole, it has to be assumed that individual and communal life in the societies of the Ancient Orient in general and that of the → ruler in particular were dominated by numerous rules, resulting in more or less standardized patterns of behaviour. The reconstruction of such non-cultic ceremonies is largely dependent on secondary references, esp. in letters but also in mythical and epic tales; pictorial evidence can be found on cylindrical → seals and on → reliefs in Neo-Assyrian palaces.

Thus it was customary, for example, for a royal emissary to stand when delivering his sovereign's message. In myths, the behaviour towards a guest is mentioned: no wish was to be denied to him (TUAT 3, 764, l. 95–102). Generally, anybody approaching the ruler had to prostrate himself (→ Proskynesis). Royal banquets were apparently strictly regulated: dressing the guests in dignified robes, exchange of presents, anointment with fragrant oils, seating order etc. Seal prints from the time of the 3rd dynasty of Ur (21st cent. BC) allow some inferences to the corresponding court protocol from the way in which a petitioner approached the deity.

In the judicial system, there were numerous symbolic and ceremonial acts that accompanied a legal deal or were imperative for its implementation. The social interaction of people was in many aspects governed by the principles of → reciprocity, apparent in ceremonially determined behaviour patterns.

→ Ruler I.; → Court titles A.

K. F. MÜLLER, Das assyr. Ritual, 1937.   E. C.-K.

II. EGYPT

Comparatively little is known about Egyptian ceremonies. Generally, it has to be assumed that strict rules existed governing the conduct at the royal court. Indirectly these are verified by a reference in the 'Book of the Temple' to the head teacher teaching the children of the → priests i.a. all rules of how to behave in the royal household [4]. Individual autobiographical phrases (such as 'he who enters the palace while the great remain outside', PKrall 8,23–10,1) show that only a few of the civil servants had the right of being received by the king in private audience. A list of courtly ranks indicated whether in the audience hall the bearer of a certain title was to stand to the left or right of the ruler [2. T. XIII]. This corresponds with Demotic tales describing regular court audiences with the king sitting on the throne and the courtiers standing to his left or right, only moving into the centre when it was their turn to speak. In the 'Duties of the Vizier' [1], dress code and seating order were clearly set out. The teachings of Ptahhotep (› Wisc sayings II.) dealt with the behaviour in the antechamber of an official [5. 146 f.]. Amongst the Greek authors, it is Diodorus in particular (Diod. Sic. 1,70–72) who transmitted how little an Egyptian king could determine his own life, how much it was governed by strict regulations [3]. Herodotus (2,173) by contrast depicts king → Amasis [2] as quite fond of his drink and rather less formal.

1 G. P. F. DEN BOORN, The Duties of the Vizier, 1988 2 F. LL. GRIFFITH, H. M. F. PETRIE, Two Hieroglyphic Papyri from Tanis, 1889   3 O. MURRAY, Hecataeus of Abdera and Pharaonic Kingship, in: JEA 56, 1970, 141–171   4 J. F. QUACK, Die Dienstanweisung des Oberlehrers aus dem Buch vom Tempel, in: H. BEINLICH (ed.), 5. Ägyptologische Tempeltagung Würzburg, 2002, 159–171 5 P. VERNUS, Le discours politique de l'enseignement de Ptahhotep, in: J. ASSMAN, E. BLUMENTHAL (ed.), Lit. und Politik im pharaonischen und ptolem. Äg., 1999, 139–152.   JO. QU.

III. IRAN

A. ACHAEMENIDS   1. DEATH OF A KING AND EN-THRONEMENT OF HIS SUCCESSOR   2. ENCOUNTERS WITH SUBJECTS   3. COURT PROTOCOL 4. PRAYERS AND CULTIC ROLE OF THE KING B. ARSACIDS   C. SĀSSĀNIDS

A. ACHAEMENIDS

All known information about ceremonies at the Achaemenid court (→ Achaemenids) stems almost entirely from the Greek tradition (not least the → Alexander historians), and thus is not free of outside interpretation and evaluation, and of topical features. They bring into focus two aspects of royal life in particular: a) the death of a ruler and the accession to the throne of his successor, and b) court etiquette when meeting or dining with the → Great King. Court and prayer ceremonies also feature on Achaemenid reliefs in the palaces (→ Persepolis) and on tomb facades as well as in objects of Achaemenid minor arts (gem cutting). The protocol at the court of the Great King also influenced that at the courts of → satraps and dynasts.

1. DEATH OF A KING AND ENTHRONEMENT OF HIS SUCCESSOR

Upon the death of a → ruler, the sacred fires were put out (Diod. Sic. 17,114,4 f.) and a general mourning decreed (Arr. Anab. 8,14,9; Curt. 10,5,18). It was the duty of the heir to the throne to take care of his predecessor's funeral; presumably from the time of → Cambyses [2] II., there were regular sacrifices for the dead kings (Ctesias FGrH 688 F 13). In an elaborate ceremony in and around the sanctuary of → Anāhitā in → Pasargadae, the new Great King was invested soon after in front of a small number of people (references in Plut. Artaxerxes 3,1–3); several symbolic acts or rites served to emphasize the sacral (investiture by the gods) and dynastic character of the Achaemenid monarchy (presence of priests/'magi' — presumably identical with the tutors of the prince; invocation of → Ahura Mazdā; donning of the robes of Cyrus [2] the Great). A kind of rite of passage is evident in the temporary resort to simple dishes (fig cake, pistachio nuts, soured milk). In a further phase of the investiture (of which Plut. claims not to have any knowledge), the ruler presumably received the insignia of his power (certain robes, upright tiara, sceptre, lotus blossom, lance, and bow), showed himself to this subjects, and confirmed privileges and positions (Diod. Sic. 11,71,2; Ios. ant. Iud. 11,185) [5].

2. ENCOUNTERS WITH SUBJECTS

The Achaemenid 'itinerant kingship' brought the → ruler in contact with his subjects on numerous occasions. Even though the idea of a → 'New Year's celebration' in Persepolis has to be abandoned, formal receptions were held in this and other royal residences as well as in towns and villages en route of the king's travels, which in accordance with local traditions followed a ceremonial protocol (cf. e.g. Alexander [4] the Great's entry into → Babylon, which presumably also accorded with Achaemenid customs: Curt. 5,1,17–23; cf. Arr. Anab. 3,16,3). Greek sources also describe the → reciprocity of exchanging presents (Ael. VH 1,31.33; Plut. Artaxerxes 4,5) and the personal contact between ruler and subjects as well as between Persians of equal or different ranks [4; 7; 6. 196–207; 14. 29–41, 257–260].

3. COURT PROTOCOL

Different settings of formal encounters and royal appearance (official dress, insignia etc.) at court (e.g. during audiences) are transmitted by Greek sources as well as Achaemenid reliefs (e.g. on → proskynesis and prostration [15]); it is impossible to say with certainty which tasks the numerous officials and dignitaries, answerable solely to the king and dependent on his favour (cf. Aristot. Mund. 398a), were charged with (or even whom exactly the reliefs depicted [6. 269–273]). The numerous and lavish banquets followed a strict protocol in order to underline the superior position of the ruler, to restrict access to the dinner, and to protect the Great King from assassination attempts [6. 274–279, 297–309; 11].

4. PRAYERS AND CULTIC ROLE OF THE KING

Reliefs, inscriptions, seal prints and Greek sources provide a wealth of information about the role of the king in cultic ceremonies. With the help of certain — at times ritual — prayers, prayer positions and cultic or sacrificial acts, the Great King underlined in war as in peace the dependance of his rulership and his 'welfare' (*farnah*) on the favour of the gods [6. 252–265].

B. ARSACIDS

A lot less is known about the court protocol of the → Parthians. As part of their Hellenistic-Seleucid heritage, they had adopted the notion of the ruler's 'divinity' [15]; they were familiar with → proskynesis [15] as well as with the Hellenistic system of courtly titles (OGIS 430). Their rulers, too, wore special ceremonial robes and carried special regnal insignia [13]. When compared with Achaemenid conditions, the Parthian aristocracy played a noticeably stronger role at the coronation ceremony of an Arsacid ruler (the right to confirm the synhedrion: Just. Epit. 42,4,1; the right of the head of the Surenas clan to crown the ruler: Plut. Crassus 21; Tac. Ann. 6,42). During feasts and banquets at the royal court, but also at the courts of aristocrats, it was both customary and popular to enjoy — at times musical — performances of material drawn from myths and legends [2].

C. SĀSSĀNIDS

Prominent amongst records of the Sāssānid monarchy and its court protocol (compilation without determination of source value in [1]; cf. [14]) are the inscriptions of King Narseh (→ Narses [1]) of → Paikuli (NPi; AD 293, see below [9]) alongside the late-Sāssānid/middle-Persian works pertaining to wisdom (*andarz*) and court literature [8. 171–205]. The inscriptions record *verbatim* the letters between Narseh and the nobles and dignitaries of his empire exchanged prior to his accession to the throne, as well as the speeches held at his acclamation, so that there would be no doubt regarding the legality of his succession (NPi §§ 68; 73; 75, see [9]). The literary works, on the other hand, — such as *Husraw ud Rğdak* ('Chosroes and his Page') — provide information about courtly virtues and the aims of courtly education, but also about the intricacies of the royal household of that period [8. 178–181]. Other texts, such as the 'Ardaxšīr novel' ([8. 192–200]; → Ardashir [1]), are taken also as descriptions of life at the court of the last of the → Sāssānids (c. 6th/7th cents. AD); the genre of the 'royal testaments' [8. 189 f.] preserves idealized speeches from the throne. In addition, some bardic poetry has also survived [8. 200–202]. Even though the 'Book of Lords' (*Xvadāy-nāmag*) focusses on the ideal type of ruler and subject in the stories of the lives of kings, heroes, and legends and is only extant in post-Sāssānid adaptations, it provides a great deal of information about Sāssānid court protocol. [1]. However, the extent to which the best-known of these adaptations, Firdausī's *Šāhnameh* and the texts

of Arabo-Persian historiography, can also be used as source material for the late-Sāssānid royal household still needs to be investigated in detail. In contrast, the report of the deeds of Šābuhr I (→ Sapor [1] I) [10] and the Manichaean tradition with its references to the numerous courtly offices and ranks permit the conclusion that the protocol at the Sāssānid court was very elaborate even as early as the 3rd cent. Images of the ruler on reliefs, silver bowls, seals, bulls, and coins illustrate particularly the outer appearance of the king (robes, head dress, weapons, throne etc.), tokens and gestures of reverence, as well as scenes of royal life (investiture, hunt etc.) [1]. Information about Sāssānid royal titles and forms of diplomatic relations, but also about the conduct of the 'king at war' is provided by the Roman-Byzantine literature [12]. Epigraphically preserved endowments of fire temples alongside endowments or rather sacrifices for the salvation of the souls of the living and the dead allow the assumption of corresponding rites and ceremonies as well as prayers to Zoroastrian deities (→ Zoroastrianism); equally, the Neo-Persian 'Letter of Tansar' [3; 8. 189 f.] can be taken as pointing to a set procedure for the investiture and coronation of a Sāssānid ruler.

→ Religion V.

1 M. ABKAʿI-KHAVARI, Das Bild des Königs in der Sāsānidenzeit, 2000   2 M. BOYCE, The Parthian gōsān and the Iranian Minstrel Trad., in: Journ. of the Royal Asiatic Society 1957, 10–45   3 Id., The Letter of Tansar, 1968   4 P. BRIANT, Hérodote et la société perse, in: G. NENCI, O. REVERDIN (ed.), Hérodote et les peuples non grecs, 1990, 69–104   5 Id., Le roi est mort: vive le roi! Remarques sur les rites et rituels de succession chez les Achéménides, in: J. KELLENS (ed.), La Religion iranienne à l'époque achéménide, 1991, 1–11   6 Id., Histoire de l'empire perse, 1996   7 P. CALMEYER, Zur Darstellung von Standesunterschieden in Persepolis, in: AMI N. F. 24, 1991, 35–51   8 C. G. CERETI, La letteratura pahlavi, 2001   9 H. HUMBACH, P. O. SKJÆRVØ, The Sassanian Inscription of Paikuli, 1978–1983   10 PH. HUYSE, Die dreisprachige Inschr. Šābuhrs I. an der Kaʿba-i Zardušt (ŠKZ), 1999   11 H. SANCISI-WEERDENBURG, Persian Food. Stereotypes and Political Identity, in: J. WITKIN et al. (ed.), Food in Antiquity, 1995, 286–302   12 M. WHITBY, The Persian King at War, in: E. DABROWA (ed.), The Roman and Byzantine Army in the East, 1994, 227–263   13 J. WIESEHÖFER, 'King of Kings' and 'Philhellên': Kingship in Arsacid Iran, in: P. BILDE et al. (ed.), Aspects of Hellenistic Kingship, 1996, 55–66   14 Id., Ancient Persia, ²2001   15 Id., 'Denn ihr huldigt nicht einem Menschen als eurem Herrscher, sondern nur den Göttern'. Bemerkungen zur Proskynese in Iran, in: M. MAGGI et al. (ed.), Religious Themes and Texts of Pre-Islamic Iran and Central Asia, FS Gh. Gnoli, (2002).   J. W.

IV. CLASSICAL ANTIQUITY
A. GENERAL   B. HELLENISM   C. ROME
1. PRINCIPATE   2. LATE ANTIQUITY   3. EVALUATION   V. BYZANTIUM

A. GENERAL

Ceremonies as a form of symbolic communication, attributing set meanings to the actions of those participating and thus providing a figurative expression of the social, political, and cultural order, have been studied by scholars of Ancient History predominantly in conjunction with → court and monarchy (→ monarchía) during the Hellenistic and the Roman imperial period. [2. 31 f.; 12. 43–46; 1; 5. 38–46]. The analysis of ceremonial manifestations of political and social inequalities at the time of the Greek polis and the Roman Republic in urban life (reverence towards officials, seating orders in theatres) and in domestic life (morning reception, placement of visitors at an evening feast) has only just begun to attract the interest of scholars [6. vol. 2, 59–81].

B. HELLENISM

The very sparse sources regarding the protocol at Hellenistic courts indicate rules of behaviour and interaction governing royal audiences and public appearances of the royal court. Alexander [4] the Great's attempt to turn the personal contact with the king into a medium of ceremonial demonstration of rank through the introduction of → proskýnēsis, was not copied by the later Hellenistic kings with regard to their Greek-Macedonian 'friends' (phíloi → Court titles). A change is only indicated by the introduction of a differentiated system of court titles from the beginning of the 2nd cent. BC. With these, the aristocracy of the Hellenistic empires was bound by an order of priority graded in its proximity to each king, which seems to indicate some kind of display of social hierarchy in court protocol.

C. ROME
1. PRINCIPATE

At the Roman imperial court of the first two cents. AD, aristocratic interaction at the → salutatio and at → banquets followed the traditional patterns; the ceremonial manifestation of status continued to correspond to the political-social ranking of the elite according to ordines and various senatorial offices. Attempts by the emperors → Caligula, → Nero, → Domitianus and → Commodus to enforce proskýnēsis or their being addressed as dominus et deus ('Lord and God') have to be seen as deliberate degradations of the aristocracy and remained only temporary. In the long run, those forms of communication prevailed which by mutual signs of respect (e.g. embrace and → kiss at the salutatio) signalled the equality of the emperor and his senatorial peers; sources refer with praise to this 'civil' behaviour (civilitas) by the emperors [11. 33]. New forms of ceremonies developed mainly outside of the palace in the urban context, e.g. the → adventus ceremonies on visits of the → emperor to provincial cities or on his return to Rome. The urban population, ordered according to rank, would meet him at a set distance from the city and ceremoniously escort him back into it.

2. LATE ANTIQUITY

After the imperial court in the course of the 3rd cent. AD had distanced itself more and more from Rome and its Senate (→ Soldier emperors), → Diocletianus set out new rules governing the court protocol which expressed the hierarchical order of the elite in formalized interaction with the emperor at the imperial court. They centred around the admission (→ *admissio*) in order of rank to the → *adoratio*, the veneration of the emperor involving prostration and kissing the imperial purple robe. In a similar manner, the imperial council (→ *consistorium*) became a medium for the presentation of rank order with the arrangement of its participants in spatially discrete echelons.

3. EVALUATION

From the 4th cent. BC into late antiquity, contemporary sources criticized the ancient court protocol as a manifestation of 'barbarian', esp. Persian servitude (e.g. Xen. An. 3,2,13; Sen. Benef. 2,12,2; Eutr. 9,26). Modern research, for a long time influenced by the history of ideas [1; 10], has tried to explain its development as the influence of Oriental examples, without, however, questioning why such protocol always only prevailed after a considerable time delay, despite the existence of a royal court, monarchical rule, and readily accessible models in each case. The reason may lie in the continued influence of a specific political integration within the ancient societies of the classical Greek and Roman periods, i.e. in the close link between the social manifestation of rank and the exercising of political functions within the context of urban communities which continued even under monarchical rule and ran counter to any hierarchical integration of the elite in court protocol [13.105 f.].

→ Aristocracy; → Ruler; → Court; → Court titles; → Ruler cult; → Ritual

1 A. ALFÖLDI, Die monarchische Repräsentation im röm. Kaiserreiche, 1970 2 E. BIKERMAN, Institutions des Séleucides, 1938 3 D. CANNADINE, S. PRICE (ed.), Rituals of Royalty, 1987 4 H. GABELMANN, Ant. Audienz- und Tribunalszenen, 1984 5 F. KOLB, Herrscherideologie in der Spätant., 2001 6 W. KROLL, Die Kultur der ciceronischen Zeit, 2 vols., 1933 7 J. LEHNEN, Adventus principis, 1997 8 H. LÖHKEN, Ordines dignitatum, 1982 9 J. PROCOPÉ, s. v. Höflichkeit, RAC 15, 1991, 930–986 10 TREITINGER 11 A. WALLACE-HADILL, Civilis princeps, in: JRS 72, 1982, 32–48 12 G. WEBER, Der Königshof im Hell., in: A. WINTERLING (ed.), Ant. Höfe im Vergleich, 1997, 27–71 13 A. WINTERLING, Hof ohne 'Staat', in: Id. (ed.), Ant. Höfe im Vergleich, 1997, 91–112 14 Id., Aula Caesaris, 1999 15 Id. (ed.), Comitatus, 1998. A. WI.

V. BYZANTIUM
A. GENERAL B. SOURCES C. STATE OF RESEARCH

A. GENERAL

Court protocol at the Byzantine imperial court is ascertainable in its basic outlines as well as in some detail, thanks to a good number of extant sources. Especially the 'Book of Ceremonies' (see [1]), compiled in Constantinople towards the end of the 10th cent. at the orders of emperor Constantine VII Porphyrogenitus (→ Constantinus [9]), but only finally edited after the emperor's death at the instigation of his chief chamberlain Basileios, provides valuable material. Like the texts from the Book of Ceremonies, those of other relevant sources originate from a wide range of periods and were written for very different purposes. There is no doubt that court protocol underwent significant changes from late antiquity to the late Byzantine period (4th to 15th cents.) [9. 1–3], which cannot be continuously reconstructed, but which to some degree can be demonstrated for single aspects, such as e.g. the triumphs of victorious emperors [10] or receptions of foreign envoys [15].

B. SOURCES

Written source material for the Byzantine court protocol can be divided up into descriptive (reports and minutes) and prescriptive texts (most of them containing the introductory formula: 'What needs to be observed when ...') [9. 3–8]. However, the division between the two is fluid, because even a source describing minutely a certain ceremonial procedure can lead to a prescriptive text. It should be made clear that there is no documentary basis pertaining to all epochs of Byzantine rule and all aspects of Byzantine court protocol. Many details were assumed to be commonly known, and thus were not recorded in any of the sources, whereas other aspects were repeated almost *ad nauseam*. Concerning pictorial representations, the narrative ones should be treated with caution as far as the procedural sequence of a ceremony is concerned, and the purely symbolic ones should not be used at all for that purpose; however, they convey an impression of the visual appearance of insignia [11].

The best-documented ceremony of the late antique/early Byzantine period (4th to 6th cents.) is that of the emperor's coronation [12; 13. 10–30], namely by texts from the Book of Ceremonies [1] (bk. 1, ch. 84–95, by Petrus Patricius, 6th cent.) and by a poetic description (Corippus) of the succession of → Iustinus [4] II to emperor → Iustinianus [1] I [5; 6].

Most ceremonies described in the Book of Ceremonies ([1]; list of contents: [8]) refer to the middle-Byzantine period (7th to 10th cents.). The greater part of Book 1 is subdivided into two larger sections of prescriptive material: religious ceremonies during the course of the Church year (ch. 1–37 REISKE; [19. 1–12]) and secular ones (ch. 38–83; here ch. 52–53: the → *Klētorológion*, a handbook for the organization of imperial banquets, written by Philotheos in 899; [3]). This is followed by minutes of late antique coronations (ch. 84–95 REISKE) and, in ch. 96 f., by additions dating from 963, after that in ed. [1] an appendix about the protocol concerning imperial travels (now: [4]). Book 2 contains a wide mix of all sorts of material without any discernible order.

Pseudo-Kodinos (see [7]), written in around 1350, focusses predominantly on the hierarchy of offices and titles at the imperial court, but also contains material on late Byzantine ceremonies (ceremonies within the Church year, coronation of the emperor, award of courtly honours, promotion to → patriarch, reception of a foreign bride) and on ceremonial dress [18; 19. 39–52].

C. STATE OF RESEARCH

A new critical edition of the entire Book of Ceremonies is urgently needed. A new commentary, however still based on the old edition by REISKE, is in preparation. Only after the publication of these two preparatory works would it make sense to attempt a comprehensive analysis of Byzantine ceremonies as a whole, which would also need to take into account individual bits of information on ceremonies in historiography, poetry, and other sources. As far as possible, it should also duly consider the changes in protocol in the different epochs of Byzantine history, and basically take into account five different ceremonial dimensions [9. 10–19]: temporal (ceremonies that are regularly repeated in the course of the day or year [16. 135–139] as well as those that take place irregularly on certain occasions); spatial (the connection between location and meaning of a ceremonial procedure); social (the role of the various social strata in ceremonies; [19. 167–198]); institutional (courtly officials as servants of protocol); ritual (symbolic acts; objects, e.g. purple robes and porphyry [14; 17], the organ [20] or insignia [11]).
→ Court; → Court titles (D.); → Emperor (II.), → Administration (IX.)

EDITIONS: 1 I. I. REISKE, Das sog. 'Zeremonienbuch': Constantini Porphyrogeniti De c(a)erimoniis aulae Byzantinae, 2. vols., 1829/30 (text and comm.) 2 A. VOGT, Constantin VII Porphyrogennète, Le livre des cérémonies 2 vols., 1935/40 (partial ed. with French trans. and comm.) 3 N. OIKONOMIDÉS, Les listes de préséance byzantines, 1972, 65–235 (partial ed. with French trans. and comm.) 4 J. HALDON, Constantinus Porphyrogenitus, Three Treatises on Imperial Military Expeditions, 1990 (partial ed. with Engl. trans.) 5 A. CAMERON, Corippus, In laudem Iustini imperatoris, 1976 6 U. J. STACHE, Corippus, In laudem Iustini Augusti minoris, 1976 (comm.) 7 J. VERPEAUX, Pseudo-Kodinos, Traité des offices, 1966.

BIBLIOGRAPHY: 8 M. McCORMICK, s. v. De Ceremoniis, ODB 1, 595–597 9 Id., Analysing Imperial Ceremonies, in: Jahrbuch der öst. Byzantinistik 35, 1985, 1–20 10 ID., Eternal Victory, 1986 11 K. WESSEL et al., s. v. Insignien, Reallex. der byz. Kunst 3, 369–408 12 R.-J. LILIE, s. v. Krönung, Reallexicon d. byz. Kunst 5, 439–454 13 R.-J. LILIE, Byzanz — Kaiser und Reich,

1994 14 G. STEIGERWALD, Das kaiserliche Purpurprivileg, in: JbAC 33, 1990, 209–239 15 F. TINNEFELD, Ceremonies for Foreign Ambassadors, in: ByzF 19, 1993, 193–213 16 Id., Saisonales Zeremoniell und Brauchtum in Byzanz, in: P. DILG et al. (ed.), Rhythmus und Saisonalität, 1995, 135–141 17 G. DAGRON, Nés dans la pourpre, in: Travaux et Mémoires 12, 1994, 105–142 18 E. PILTZ, Le costume officiel des dignitaires byzantins à l'époque Paléologue, 1994 19 H. MAGUIRE (ed.), Byzantine Court Culture, 1997 20 N. MALIARAS, Die Orgel im byz. Hofzeremoniell des 9. und 10. Jh., 1991. F. T.

Cereres see → Ceres

Ceres

A. CULT IN EARLY ITALY   B. ROME   1. STATE CULT
2. PRIVATE CULT   C. PROVINCES   D. CONTINUED
INFLUENCE

A. CULT IN EARLY ITALY

Italian goddess who was connected especially with grain, as well as with the realm of the dead and who was equated early in Roman history with the Greek Demeter. Numerous inscriptions prove the cult's existence in central and southern Italy from the late 7th cent. BC onwards. Wherever it is possible to ascertain details, she is especially associated with grain (Faliscan inscription from the period about 600 [1. 241; 2. 43], Paelignian inscription from Corfinium [1. 204; 3], Oscan tablet from Agnone c. 250 BC [1. 147; 4], bust from Aricia with a garland of wheat [2. 49 fig. 57]), but she is also connected with the lives of women and motherhood (tablet from Agnone; link with Venus among the Paelignians [5]) and probably with the Underworld (defixio of Capua [1. 6]). The forms of the name make the connection with *crescere* and *creare* (**cer-* 'to grow') probable; this was already posited by ancient interpreters. She is also associated with the shadowy *Cerus manus* of the song of the Salians, whom Fest. interprets (p. 109,4, cf. Varro, Ling. 7,26) as *creator bonus* [6. 23].

B. ROME

In Rome C. is associated with → Liber and → Libera, forming a triad of deities; from the point of view of worship, she is also closely linked on many occasions with → Tellus; Varro also interprets her simply as Terra (rer. div. fr. 270 CARDAUNS, cf. Ling. 5,64: C. is derived from *gerere fruges*).

1. STATE CULT

In the sphere of the state, she is a goddess with whose temple and cult the plebeians were closely connected; in the public and private cult she has connections with a diet of grain, and with women and the dead. In iconography [7], literature and worship, she is frequently understood as a Greek goddess. Images and texts take up the Greek myths about Demeter and Kore; like the name Demeter in Greek, C. was generally used metonymically from the time of Naevius (com. 121) and Lucil. (200 M.) for bread or food; her cult is regarded as part of the *sacra peregrina* (Fest. p. 268) and derived from Greece by the ancient interpreters.

In a similar manner, the opinions of researchers are very divided as to what extent the old Italian C. can still be reconstructed in Rome. More recent research is more sceptical than earlier research; so the matter of the extent to which the list of the 12 *Sondergötter* invoked by the *flamen Cerialis* together with C. and Tellus indicates ancient tradition or a later sacerdotal systematization (Serv. Auct. georg. 1,21; → Indigitamenta) [6. 68–77; 8] has for instance not yet been clarified. The great age and the old roots of the cult are in any case proven by the existence of a Flamen Cerialis (CIL IX 5028), perhaps also through the *mundus Cereris* (see below); more difficult to date is the connection of C. with divorce (see below), which is attributed to a law of Romulus. Clearly perceptible is firstly the development of the cult in the first years of the Republic through the construction of the main temple for the trio of deities, C., Liber and Libera. The triad is said to represent the Eleusinian one of → Demeter, → Kore and → Iacchus [9], however, this is problematical in itself; in any case the Greek origin was clear to the Romans. The temple was situated on the Aventine near the Circus Maximus. It is unlikely that the poros foundations under the church of S. Maria in Cosmedin are part of it (they are more likely to belong to the Ara Maxima). Its positioning on the western slopes of the Aventine above the Circus [10. 80] is more probable; this is compatible with the usual placement of Greek temples to Demeter [11], and in any event, the temple lay outside the Pomerium. On the occasion of a crisis in basic supplies through crop failure and import difficulties, the dictator A. Postumius in the year 496 (Dion. Hal. Ant. Rom. 6,17,3–4), basing his decision on the Sibylline Books, vowed the construction of the temple and it was consecrated by Spurius Cassius, the sole patrician bearer of this name, during his second consulate in 493 (Ant. 6,94,3). The temple retained its archaic appearance (Vitruvius 3,3,5) given to it by its architects — the Greeks Damophilus and Gorgasus are mentioned (Plin. HN 35,154) as coroplasts and artists; however, during the restoration undertaken by Augustus, the clay gable figures were lost (Tac. Ann. 2,49; Plin. ibid.). The temple kept records of the Senate decisions under the supervision of the plebeian aediles (Liv. 3,55,13); it received assets seized by the plebeian magistrates for offences against the protective laws (*leges sacratae*; Dion. Hal. Ant. Rom. 6,89,3; Liv. 3,55,7); here many votive offerings from fines were set up (Liv. 2,41,10: Spurius Cassius; 10,23,13; 27,6,19; 27,36,9; 33,25,3). Priestesses were brought in from a Greek town in southern Italy (Naples or Elea); they had charge of the cult in its Greek form but were given Roman citizenship (Cic. Balb. 55); during their time in office they had to maintain sexual abstinence, as was also the case elsewhere (Tert. Monogam. 17) [3]. At least in 133 BC, Rome regarded Sicilian Henna as the actual home of the goddess, and at the behest of the Sibylline Books, sent a delegation there (Cic. Verr. 2,4,108).

The main festival of C. were the *ludi Ceriales* from 12–19 April (Liv. 30,39,8; Ov. Fast. 4,393f.; 679–712). It was organized by the plebeian aediles; the festival was primarily a plebeian one in contrast to the *ludi Megalenses*, the festival of the patricians from 4–10 April (Gell. NA 18,2,11). The principal day was 19th April, the old feast day of the Cerialia and the day of the founding of the temple; on this day there were horse races, and foxes were let loose in the Circus with burning torches attached to their tails (Ov. Fast. 4,681–712). The significance of the ritual is controversial, the connection to the cultivation of grain is usually assumed because of Ovid's aition [12. 36f.]. Also the calendar connection with the *Fordicidia* of 13th April, at which a pregnant cow was sacrificed to Tellus, links C. more closely with this sphere, and the subsequent festivals of the → Parilia (19th April), Vinalia (23th April) and Robigalia (25 April) had similar associations.

The *feriae Sementivae* in January during a break in sowing were dedicated exclusively to agriculture; during these festivities a pregnant sow was sacrificed to C. and Tellus jointly (Ov. Fast. 1,671–674) [9]. In August each year the women celebrated the *sacrum anniversarium Cereris*, which supposedly also came from Greece, but which already existed at the time of the battle of Cannae (Varro at Non. p. 44; Liv. 22,56,4; Fest. s.v. Graeca sacra, p. 86,7; Val. Max. 1,1,15; Arnob. 2,73). The main features are the wearing of white clothes (as in the *ludi Ceriales*, Ov. Fast. 4,619) and perhaps a prohibition on wine (Dion. Hal. Ant. Rom. 1,33,1), abstinence from sex (Ov. Am. 3,10,1) and a taboo on names (Serv. Aen. 4,58). The festival had similarities with the Greek → Thesmophoria and was connected to the myth of the abduction of Kore (Serv. Georg. 1,344); perhaps Cicero's legislation regarding the night-time celebrations of women relates to this (Leg. 2,21; 37). In any event, the festival had the character of Mysteries (*initia*). Not all details of the ritual associated with the *anniversarium Cereris* can be neatly attributed to this; some may also belong to the *ieiunium Cereris*, celebrated on 4th September; which was introduced at the behest of the Sibylline Books in 191 BC (Liv. 36,37,4).

On 13th December, the day when the temple of Tellus in Carina was founded, a → *lectisternium* was regularly arranged for C. (Arnob. 7,32, cf. CIL I² p. 336f.); in exceptional *lectisternia* in 217 BC she is named for the first time as one of the 12 deities (Liv. 22,10,9). On 21 December a pregnant sow, bread and mead were sacrificed to her and Hercules, (Macrob. Sat. 3,11,10); the sacrificing of a pregnant animal like that in the *Fordicidia* was part of the eerie realm of the earth goddess (Macrob. Sat. 1,12,20). The existence of a *mundus Cereris*, which was held three times a year and thereby signalled a strange, exceptional period of time (Fest. p. 126,4), extended this further in the direction of a link between C. and the subterranean depths of the realm of the dead. Other authors link the *mundus* with the Manes (Cato in Fest. p. 144,18) and with Dis and Proserpina (Macrob. Sat. 1,16,16). In times of crisis, the women performed ritual supplicatory walks (*supplicationes*) to C. and her daughter (Liv. 41,28,2; Tac. Ann. 15,44) and gathered gifts for them (Obsequ. 43; 46; 53).

The associations with Tellus in the state cult emphasize the agrarian side of C. This is also evident from the resolution of the XII Tables to the effect that whoever damaged someone else's seeds became the property of C. and was hanged (Plin. HN 18,13), and also from the fact that the temple of C. gave bread to those seeking asylum (Varro ap. Non. p. 63 L.). Even if this had therefore already always been part of the general process of supplying food (her temple had been founded during a supply crisis), in the course of the late Republic she generally became more and more closely associated with grain supplies; Caesar created the *aediles plebei Ceriales* to safeguard the annona (→ Cura annonae). When Augustus finally consecrated an altar to C. and Ops Augusta on 10 August 7 BC, this aspect was emphasized once again (CIL I² p. 324).

2. PRIVATE CULT

Her agrarian significance is also obvious in private worship: Roman farmers and landowners made sacrifices to her before the harvest (Cato, Agr. 134, cf. Gell. NA 4,6,8) and presented to her the first fruits of the crop (Fest. p. 423,1). Furthermore, the private cult emphasized the connection of the goddess with marriage and the dead. The wedding torch was carried before her (Fest. p. 77,21), and according to a law of Romulus, the assets of a man who illegally disowned his wife were forfeited to C. (Plut. Romulus 22,3). A sow was also sacrificed to her after a death in order to regain ritual purity (Veranius in Fest. p. 296,37; cf. Varro in Non. p. 240 L.; Gell. NA 4,6,8). Like → Demeter, she also has connections with the realm of the dead which are clear from the *mundus Cereris*.

C. PROVINCES

In the Imperial Age, C., as the goddess of grain and bestower of prosperity, became increasingly significant; from the late Republic onwards, her image appeared on coins together with Annona, and from the time of Livia, numerous empresses were associated with her in imperial ideology [12. 169–181]. Especially well attested is her cult in the grain-growing belt of North Africa where dedications to C. were the prevailing custom; the plural is usually explained as referring to C. and Proserpina, but other interpretations are conceivable [13].

D. CONTINUED INFLUENCE

From late Christian antiquity onwards, numerous saints adopted her role of protector of cereal crops [14]. In the Middle Ages and the early modern period, C. continued to be influential, primarily because of the euhemeristic and allegorical interpretation of the mythology of → Demeter, as Ovid or Claudian told it, and on which Lucretius and especially Isidore (8,11,59–68) based their interpretation [15].

1 VETTER 1   2 E. SIMON, Die Götter der Römer, 1990 3 E. PERUZZI, La sacerdotessa di Corfinio, in: PdP 50, 1995, 5–15   4 G. DEVOTO, Il panteon di Agnone, in: SE 35, 1967, 179–197   5 G. COLONNA, Sul sacerdozio peligno di Cerere e Venere, in: ArchCl 8, 1953, 216–217 6 H. LE BONNIEC, Le culte de Cérès à Rome des origines à la fin de la République, 1958   7 S. DE ANGELI, LIMC 4.1, 893–908   8 J. BAYET, Les *feriae sementivae* et les indigitations dans le culte de Cérès et de Tellus, in: RHR 137, 1950, 172–206 = Croyances et rites dans la Rome antique, 1971, 177–205   9 F. ALTHEIM, Terra Mater, 1931 10 L. RICHARDSON, A New Topographic Dictionary of Ancient Rome, 1992   11 GRAF, 273   12 B. S. SPAETH, The Roman Goddess C., 1996   13 G. PUGLIESE-CARRATELLI, Cereres, in: PdP 36, 1981, 367–382 = Tra Cadmo e Orfeo, 1990, 295–299   14 P. BERGER, The Goddess Obscured. Transformations of the Grain Protectress from Goddess to Saint, 1985   15 J. SEZNEC, La survivance des dieux antiques, 1940.   F.G.

Ceressus (Κερησσός; *Kerēssós*). Fortress in Boeotia near Thespiae, its localization disputed [1]. According to tradition, the citizens of Thespiae retreated twice to C.: in the 6th cent. BC prior to the battle of C. in the Thessalian-Boeotian war [2], and again in 371 BC in the war between the secessionist citizens of Thespiae and the Boeotians [3]. Source references: Plut. Camillus 19,138a; Plut. Mor. 866f; Paus. 9,14,1–4.

1 R. J. BUCK, The Site of Ceressus, in: Teiresias, Suppl. 1, 1972, 31–40   2 M. SORDI, La battaglia di Ceresso e la secessione di Tespie, in: J. FOSSEY (ed.), Boeotia antiqua 3, 1993, 25–32   3 C. TUPLIN, The Fate of Thespiae during the Theban Hegemony, in: Athenaeum 64, 1986, 333f.   K.F.

Cerethrius (Κερέθριος; *Keréthrios*). Leader of one of the three parts of the Galatian army who plundered Thrace in 280 BC (Paus. 10,19,7).
→ Belgius; → Brennus [2]   W.SP.

Cerfennia *Statio* on the *via Valeria* (It. Ant. 309,4), starting-point of the *via Claudia Valeria* (CIL IX 5973); modern S. Felicità in Cerfenna near Collarmele.

NISSEN, 2, 455.   U.PA.

Cerialis Roman cognomen (also Caerialis, Caerealis) of Latin origin, derived from the adjectival *Cerealis* ('belonging to Ceres'); current from the Julian-Claudian era onwards (SCHULZE, 486f.; ThlL, Onom. 2,344f.).   M.MEI.

[1] Brother of → Iustina, the wife of → Valentinianus I (Amm. Marc. 28,2,10). *Tribunus stabuli* (Amm. Marc. 30,5,19). In AD 375 he helped his nephew → Valentinianus II to the throne (Amm. Marc. 30,10,5). PLRE 1,197.   W.P.

[2] In AD 405 *dux Libyarum*. Described by → Synesius (epist. 130) as corrupt and negligent; supposed not to have opposed the invasion of the African Maketai. PLRE 2, 280f.   H.L.

[3] Bishop of Castellum Ripense in Mauretania Caesariensis. Wrote a *Libellus contra Maximinum Arianum* (Gennadius, vir. ill. 93; PL 58,757–768).

BARDENHEWER, GAL 4,548f. R.B.

Cerinthus (Κήρινθος; *Kérinthos*).
[1] Town on the eastern coast of → Euboea (Hom. Il. 2,538; Str. 10,1,3; 5), localized near the modern Mandudion. The origins of C. date back into the Neolithic. In historical times, C. probably belonged to → Histiaea. Inscriptions: IG XII 9, 1184f.

E. FREUND, s.v. K., in: LAUFFER, Griechenland, 323.
H. KAL.

[2] Jewish-Christian → Gnostic, contemporary with the Apostles (1st/ early 2nd cents. AD). According to the main witness → Irenaeus [2] (Iren. Adversus haereses 1,26,1), he denied, while teaching in Asia Minor, the creation of the world by the supreme God. With that he combined a 'Christology of division and incorporation' [2. 37]. He dismissed the virgin birth and saw Jesus solely as the natural son of Joseph and Mary, upon whom at his baptism Christ descended, only to leave him again before the Passion. According to Irenaeus (Iren. Adversus haereses 3,11,1), the apostle John directed his gospel against C. and his teachings — according to Polycarpus of Smyrna, he had even met C. in person (ibid. 3,3,4). Later authors complete the reports by Irenaeus, but also contradict them at times. Thus Hippolytus knows of C.'s training in Egyptian sciences (probably a genuine tradition independent of Irenaeus:[4]). As an opponent of Paul, whose views supposedly were chiliastic, who insisted on circumcision and who was the alleged author of the Apocalypse, he is opposed by the Roman Gaius (i.a. Euseb. Hist. eccl. 3,28,2). → Epiphanius [1] of Salamis sees C. predominantly as a Judaist. He also reports on the followers of C., commonly known as Cerinthians, and names Galatia as their main sphere of activity (Epiphanius, Adversus haereses 28,1,1; 28,6,4; 28,8,1f.). It remains open whether the people mentioned in 1 Joh 2,19 ought to be identified as the disciples of C. According to Epiphanius, the Cerinthians used a truncated version of the gospel of Matthew, wrongly described as the gospel of C.

1 G. BARDY, Cérinthe, in: RBi 30, 1921, 344–373 2 H.-J. KLAUCK, Der erste Johannesbrief, 1991, 34–42 3 A.F. J. KLIJN, G.J. REININK, Patristic Evidence for Jewish-Christian Sects, 1973, 3–19 4 B.G. WRIGHT III, Cerinthus *Apud* Hippolytus, in: The Second Century 4, 1984, 103–115. J.RI.

Cernunnos Celtic god with deer's antlers, who is often portrayed seated with crossed legs accompanied by snakes, deer and bulls. The *interpretatio Romana* does not apply to him; however, through the addition of the snakes, the purse or the coins running out of a sack, there is evidence of allusions to the Gallo-Roman god

Mercury. With the latter and with Apollo he appears in the relief in Reims [1. V 3653]. Overall the graphic depictions indicate the fertile character of C., he is certainly not a god of the dead. For the numerous portrayals from imperial times that probably began in the time of Tiberius and that are predominantly found in eastern Gaul, the designation C. is confirmed by the inscription and representation on the altar in Paris [1. IV 3133]. DE VRIES assumed that C.' origin was pre-Gallic.

1 ESPÉRANDIEU, Inscr.

P. B. BOBER, in: AJA 55, 1951, 13ff.; J. DE VRIES, Kelt. Religion, 1961, 104ff.; P. PETRU, in: Situla 4, 1961, 46ff.; G. BAUCHHENSS, s.v. Apollo und C., LIMC 2.1, 464; H. VERTET, in: Bull. Soc. Nat. Ant. France, 1985, 163ff.; S. SANIE, in: Germania 65, 1987, 215ff. M.E.

Cerretani Iberian tribe of the southern Pyrenees, province of Cerona (Str. 3,4,11). Earliest mention in Avien. Or. mar. 550 (*Ceretes*). Steph. Byz. knows of a city called Brachyle in the land of the C. They were famous for the quality of their ham (Mart. 13,54). In the imperial age, the tribe divided into Iuliani and Augustani (Plin. HN 3,23).

TOVAR 3, 44f., 447. P.B.

Cerrinius Roman gentilicium (also Cerinius) of Oscan origin, derived from *Ceres*; frequently attested in Pompeii and the surrounding area [1. 467f.].
[1] According to Liv. 39,13,9, Minnius and Herennius Cerrinii were the first men to be initiated into the Bacchic mysteries, by their mother, a priestess of Dionysus. After the Senate, seeing the cult as a conspiracy, had banned the so-called → Bacchanalia in 186 BC (CIL I² 581), Minnius, as its leading figure, was arrested in Ardea (Liv. 39,17,6; 19,2).

1 SCHULZE. M.MEI.

Cersobleptes (Cersebleptes). Thracian king known to ancient authors as Κερσοβλέπτης (*Kersobléptēs*, in inscriptions (e.g. Syll.³ 195 = FdD III 1, 392) and on a vessel of the hoard find of Rogozen [1. 197 no. 15] Κερσεβλέπτης (*Kersebléptēs*). His small bronze coins bear the legend KEP (*KER*).

C. followed his father → Cotys [I 1] I, to power in 360 BC (Dem. Or. 23,163). He attempted to maintain Odrysian power on the → Chersonesus and, therefore, engaged in a permanent conflict with Athens that was marked by varying success. C. received active support from his brother-in-law, the Greek mercenary leader → Charidemus [2] (Dem. Or. 23,129). In 358 C. ruled the entire Chersonese (Dem. Or. 23,171; 176–178). However, the struggle against the pretenders to his throne, → Berisades and → Amadocus [2], led in 357 to a division of the realm that was sealed in a treaty with Athens. C. retained the eastern part. He was forced to recognize the power of Athens on the Chersonese and could only hold Cardia (Dem. Or. 23,170; 173; 181–183; Diod. Sic. 16,34,4; IG II/III² 126; ToD 151; ATL II 104, T 78d; StV 303). In the following years Thrace was conquered piecemeal by Philip II. C. had to accept Macedonian sovereignty in 351 and send his son to Philip II as a hostage (Aeschin. Leg. 81–83; StV 319). In 346 Philip II took C.'s main fortress, Hieron Oros, and in 342/1 C. was permanently deprived of the throne (Dem. Or. 12,8; 10; Diod. Sic. 16,71,1).

1 SEG 37, 1987 (1990), no. 618.

E. BADIAN, Philip II and Thrace, in: Pulpudeva 4, 1980 (1983), 51–71; U. PETER, Die Mz. der thrak. Dynasten (5.–3. Jh.v.Chr.), 1997, 125–132. U.P.

Cerynea (Κερύνεια; Kerýneia).

[1] (Arcadian Καρύνεια; Karýneia). Inland town in Achaea (Peloponnese), not originally listed amongst the 12 cities of the Achaean Confederacy in Hdt. 1,145 and Str. 8,7,4. According to Str. 8,7,5, C.'s location was high up in the mountains between Bura and the sea. For a long time, C. was identified with remains found above the village of Rizomylo and the coastal road near the modern Keryneia. Following on from WILHELM, MEYER suggested to localize the town to the north of the modern Mamousia between the gorges of Kerynitis and Bouraïkos in a place formerly identified as Bura [1. 130–132]. The ruins above Rizomylo are attributed to the ancient town of Callistae, which is only known from inscriptions and coins [1. 142; 2. 87f]. Ancient remains have been found in Marmousia: geometric vessels, graves from the 4th/3rd cent. BC, a heroon, and building remains from the Hellenistic period. C. was inhabited from Mycenaean into Roman times [3; 4. 36; 5]. In around 460 BC [6], the town opened its gates to those citizens of Mycenae who had been driven out (Paus. 7,25,5f.). Originally C. was presumably only a small citadel in the mountains for the defence of the inhabitants of → Helice [1], but later it gained independence and became a member of the Achaean Confederacy, taking the place of Aegae, a town deserted by its inhabitants. The river Κερυνίτης (Kerynítēs), passing the town to the east, took its name from C.; nowadays the river Vouphousia or Kalavryta. Source references: Pol. 2,41,8; 14f.; 43,2. Coins: HN 417.

1 E. MEYER, Peloponnesische Wanderungen, 1939 2 Id., Neue Peloponnesische Wanderungen, 1957 3 J.K. ANDERSON, Excavations near Mamousia, in: ABSA 48, 1953, 154–171 4 TH. J. PAPADOPOULOS, Mycenaean Achaea 1 (Studies in Mediterranean Archaeology 55), 1979 5 I. DEKOULAKOU, Ἀνασκαφὴ Μαμουσίας, in: Praktika 1981, 1983, 183 6 M. PIÉRART, Deux notes sur l'histoire de Mycènes, in: Serta Leodiensia secunda, 1992, 377–382. Y.L.

[2] Harbour town on the northern coast of Cyprus, modern Kyrenia. The independent principality was dissolved in 312 BC by Ptolemy I and placed under the control of → Nicocreon of Salamis. In late antiquity, C. was a bishop's seat. Very few ancient remains are known, with the exception of a few graves in a necropolis west of the town. A Greek shipwreck was found off the coast.

MASSON, 268f.; E. OBERHUMMER, s.v. K., RE 11, 344–347; H.W. SWINY, M.L. KATZEV, The Kyrenia Shipwreck, in: D.J. BLACKMAN (ed.), Marine Archaeology, 1973, 339–355. R.SE.

Ceryx (Κῆρυξ; Kêryx).

Progenitor of the priestly lineage of Ceryces officiating in Eleusis, according to whom he was the son of Hermes and one of the three daughters of Cecrops, → Aglaurus [2], → Herse or → Pandrosus; according to another genealogy, he was the son of Eumolpus (schol. Soph. OC 1053). RA.MI.

Cesnola Painter

Named after his geometric krater, formerly in the Cesnola collection (h. 114.9 cm with lid, from Kourion/Cyprus, now in New York, MMA, Inv. 74. 51. 965; → Geometric pottery). The work of the anonymous vase painter combines motifs from the Middle East with those from mainland Greece and the Greek islands. In the past, both the unusual form of the eponymous krater and the combination of decorative motifs led to discussion as to its date and origin, but these are now confirmed by analysis of the clay used in the Cesnola Krater and the finds on Euboea (Euboean LG I). His work, mainly kraters and jugs, has been found i.a. on → Delos, in → Al Mina, → Lefkandi, → Eretria and → Samos.

J.N. COLDSTREAM, The Cesnola Painter, in: BICS 18, 1971, 1 — 15; P.P. KAHANE, Ikonologische Unt. zur griech.- geom. Kunst: Der Cesnola-Krater aus Kourion, in: AK 16, 1973, 114–138; D.v. BOTHMER i.a., Greek Art of the Aegean Islands. Exhibition catalogue. New York, 1979, 112f. no. 63; J. BOARDMAN, in: R.E. JONES (ed.), Greek and Cypriot Pottery. A Review of Scientific Studies, 1986, 659f. pl. 8, 10. R.H.

Cessetani

Iberian tribe [2. 1032]. Within its territory was the town of Cissa, which is mentioned for 218 BC (Pol. 3,76,5; Liv. 21,60,7 [1. 57, 60]; appearing as Ces(s)e on many Iberian coins [3. 83f. cf. 65–78]). Its most likely site was north of the Iberus near Tarraco. Undoubtedly, the C. gave their name to the regio Cessetania (Plin. HN 3,21; for comment on the variation of Kossetanio: Ptol. 2,6,17); [4. 1995].

1 A. SCHULTEN, Fontes Hispaniae Antiquae 3, 1935 2 HOLDER 1 3 A. VIVES, La Moneda Hispánica 2, 1924 4 E. HÜBNER, s.v. C., RE 3, 1995.

TOVAR 3, 35. P.B.

Cessio

Transfer, in the legal sense the cession of a right. Distinction is to be made between a) the cession of a claim, b) the cession of all one's property by way of bankruptcy (cessio bonorum) and c) cession of ownership before the praetor (→ in iure cessio).

a) The modern jurist understands by cession an agreement to transfer a claim, with the effect that, in place of the former creditor (cessor), claim against the debtor (*debitor cessus*) falls to a new creditor (cessee). The idea of such a transfer without the agreement of the debtor is foreign to the Romans. They see the → *obligatio* as a *vinculum iuris*, tied to the persons of → *creditor* and → *debitor*, and whose personal nature is even expressed by the term *nomen*. Transfer of a claim can therefore be effected only by a → *novatio* of the claim (Gai. Inst. 2,38), requiring the co-operation of the debtor and implying the extinction of all guarantees (e.g. pledge, security).

The creditor may, without the agreement of the debtor, appoint another person by *mandatum ad agendum* as his representative in court to pursue the *actio* against the debtor. If, at the same time, it is agreed that the other person is to receive the proceeds as → *procurator in rem suam* (e.g. because the claim has been sold to him), then financially speaking this amounts to a cession of claim. In this connection, Roman sources sometimes speak of *cessio actionum*.

As mere representative in court, the mandatory asserts an assumed right; up until the → *litis contestatio* the mandator retains his prerogative as creditor to dispose of his claim (e.g. by deferment or remission), or to recall the mandate. The position of the *procurator in rem suam* is strengthened by imperial fiats which, for example, grant the procurator an *actio utilis* (analogous suit) should his pursuance of the case be curtailed by the death of the creditor (Cod. Iust. 4,10,1). Antoninus Pius grants it to the purchaser of an estate against debtors to the estate; the debtors may have recourse to an *exceptio doli* against the seller (defence of malice, Ulp. Dig. 2,14,16 pr.). The same principle seems soon to have been extended to the sale of individual claims (cf. Cod. Iust. 4,10,2; 4,39,8), giving medieval jurists the basis for the development of a doctrine of transfer which is valid, up to the present day.

b) On the basis of a *lex Iulia* probably going back to Augustus, an insolvent debtor could escape impending execution of the debt (Cod. Iust. 7,71,1) as well as → *infamia* (Cod. Iust. 2,11,11) by relinquishing his assets (*cessio bonorum*). Thereupon, the *praetor* assigned the property to the creditors (*missio in bona*) so that, by liquidating it, they could satisfy their claims (cf. Gai. Inst. 3,78). The *cessio bonorum* requires, of course, that no *fraus* (malice, also → *dolus*) can be imputed to the debtor. The debtor is judged only on the basis of *id quod facere potest* (according to his means) (Ulp. Dig. 46,3,4 pr.); he is left the minimum necessary for subsistence (since the Middle Ages the so-called *beneficium competentiae*).

→ Mandate; → Beneficium

TRANSFER OF CLAIM: W.-D. GEHRICH, Kognitur und Prokuratur in rem suam als Zessionsformen des röm. Rechts, 1963; K. LUIG, Zur Gesch. der Zessionslehre, 1963, 2–9; W. ROZWADOWSKI, Studi sul trasferimento dei crediti in diritto romano, in: Bullettino dell' Ist. di Diritto Romano 76, 1973, 11–170.
RELINQUISHING OF ASSETS: W. PAKTER, The Mystery of 'cessio bonorum', in: Index 22, 1994, 323–342. F.ME.

Cestius Plebeian family name, attested since the 1st cent. BC; also occurred in Praeneste (ThlL, Onom. 354f); the family is politically insignificant [2].

I. REPUBLICAN PERIOD II. IMPERIAL PERIOD

I. REPUBLICAN PERIOD

[I 1] **C.** Architect of the *pons Cestius* between the right bank of the Tiber and Tiber Island, probably during the late republican period; otherwise unknown.

[I 2] **C., C.** Praetor (?) 44 BC; probably proscribed by Antonius in 43.

[I 3] **C., L.** Praetor and mint master 43 BC (minting of gold coins RRC 491; MRR 3, 53).

[I 4] **C. Epulo, C.** Known from his tomb monument, the so-called pyramid of C. at the Porta Ostiensis in Rome [1. 353f]. He was people's tribune, praetor and *VIIvir epulonum* (CIL VI 1374) in the late republican or early Augustan period, one of his heirs being M. Agrippa [1]; died 12 BC (CIL VI 1375). PIR² C 686.

[I 5] **C. Macedonicus.** Perusian who assumed the cognomen as a participant in the Macedonian wars. After the fall of his home town in AD 40, as *princeps* of Perusia he set fire to his house, thereby causing the destruction by fire of the entire town; he subsequently killed himself (Vell. Pat. 2,74).

1 RICHARDSON 2 T.P. WISEMAN, New men in the Roman Senate, 1971, 224. K.-L.E.

II. IMPERIAL PERIOD

[II 1] **C., N.** In AD 55 *cos. suff.* in place of Nero (CIL IV 5513). PIR C 689.

[II 2] **C. Gallus, C.** *Cos.* AD 35 (IGRR 1, 495; CIL VI 33950; Cass. Dio 58,2,5,2). In AD 21 C. prosecuted Annia Rufilla for deception (Tac. Ann. 3,36,2); in 32 he took over the prosecution in the *maiestas* case against Q. Servaeus and Minucius Thermus (Tac. Ann. 6,7,2). PIR C 690.

[II 3] **C.** Son of C. [II 2], *cos. suff.* AD 42 (CIL VI 2015); in 63 was *legatus Aug. pro praetore* in Syria (Ios. Bell. Iud. 2,280; Tac. Ann. 15,25,3). In 66 in Judea he fought the procurator Gessius Florus (Ios. Bell. Iud. 2,333–335; 499–538; Tac. Hist. 5,10), who was removed the following year by Vespasian after C.' death (Suet. Vesp. 4,5). PIR C 691. M.STR.

[II 4] **C. Pius, L.** Greek from Smyrna, active in Rome at the time of Augustus (*floruit* 13 BC, Jer. Chron. from section 2004; Suet. Rhet. fr. 91 REIFFERSCHEID), but never appeared as a public or courtroom orator. In → Seneca the Elder he is quoted almost as often as Arellius → Fuscus; younger commentators preferred C. even to Cicero (see Sen. Controv. 3, pr. 14). C., *nullius ingeni nisi sui amator* (Suas. 7,12) and *mordacissimus* (Controv. 7, pr. 8), reproached Quintilius Varus' son for the downfall of his father (1,3,10); for his contempt for Cicero received a hiding from the latter's son in the province of Asia (Suas. 7,13). His style, though impoverished in vocabulary because of his imperfect mastery of Latin, was rich in thoughts (Controv. 7,1,27); he was a follower of the Asianic style, and made overabundant use of tropes, metaphor and paradox.

F.G. LINDNER, De Cestio Pio, Progr. Züllichau 1858; J.BRZOSKA, s.v. C. no. 13, RE 3, 2008–2011; PIR ²C 694; S.F. BONNER, Roman Declamation, 1969; L.A. SUSSMAN, Arellius Fuscus and the Unity of the Elder Seneca's Suasoriae, in: RhM 120, 1977, 310–317; R.A. KASTER, Suetonius, De gramm. et rhet., 1995, 327–329 (problematic)
G.C.

Cestri (Κέστροι; *Késtroi*). Town in Cilicia Tracheia (Hierocles, Synekdemos 709,5; in Ptol. 5,7,5 corrupted Κάϋστρος), modern Macar Kalesi, 6 km south-east of Selinus [1. 155f. (with sketch plan); 2].

1 G.E. BEAN, T.B. MITFORD, Journeys in Rough Cilicia 1964–1968, 1970 2 HILD/HELLENKEMPER 1, 301.
K.T.

Cestrine (Κεστρίνη; *Kestrínē*). Region in Epirus opposite Corcyra north of the Thyamis, nowadays in the Albanian-Greek border region. According to Hecataeus (in Thuc. 1,46,4; [3. 446f.]) belonging to the → Chaones, from the 4th cent. BC (?) to the territory of the Thesproti. A coastal settlement by the name of *Cestria* is mentioned in Plin. HN 4,4; [2. 111f.; 3. 677f.]. C. was famous for its cattle (Hsch. s.v. Κεστρινικοὶ βόες). Inscriptions: [1. 126, 137, 586].

1 P.CABANES, L' Épire, 1976 2 S.I. DAKARIS, Thesprotia, 1972 3 N.G.L. HAMMOND, Epirus, 1967. D.S.

Cestrinus (Κεστρῖνος; *Kestrînos*). Eponym of the Greek region of → Cestrine, previously Cammania, in southern Thesprotia opposite the island of Cercyra (Steph. Byz. s.v. Καμμανία). C. is the son of → Helenus [1] and → Andromache; after the death of Helenus, Molossus, the son of Neoptolemus and Andromache, took power in Thesprotia, as a result of which C. emigrated to Cammania; as the new ruler he gave it its name (Paus. 1,11,1f.; 2,23,6). E.V.

Ceteii (Κήτειοι; *Kéteioi*). Warriors of → Eurypylus [2] (Hom. Od. 11,521; Str. 13,1,69f.), whose origin is in Mysian Theutrania in western Asia Minor (schol. Hom. loc. cit.). The name C. is interpreted variously: either as 'the Great ones' or as derived from the river Ceteius (Hsch. s.v. K.; Str. loc. cit.). AL.FR.

Ceteus (Κητεύς; *Kēteús*). Mythical king in Arcadia, son of → Lycaon; according to Pherecydes in Apollod. 3,7,2 also the father of → Callisto. C.W.

Cethegus Roman cognomen of a branch of the patrician → Cornelii (ThlL, Onom. 356–59). Attested from the 3rd cent. BC onwards; also Cetegus (Cic. Or. 160); Greek Κέθηγος (*Kéthēgos*), supposedly because the family refused to wear the *tunica* (Porph. Hor. Ars P. 50). Also attested in inscriptions as a family name

[1. 293]. There is perhaps no connection between the imperial and republican bearers of the name.

1 SCHULZE. K.-L.E.

[1] Rufius Petronius Nicomachus C. *Cos.* AD 504, *patricius* from c. 512, *mag. officiorum, princeps senatus*. During the siege of Rome by → Totila in 545 C. was accused of treachery and retired to Constantinople (*Liber pontificalis vita Vigilii* 7; Procop. Goth. 7,13). In 552/53 he held negotiations with Pope Vigilius on behalf of Justinian. Under Pope Pelagius I (556–561) he was back in Italy. PLRE 2,281f. M.MEI.

Cetium Today St. Pölten. A town in → Noricum, situated at the intersection of ancient roads frequented from early times; etymologically probably linked to Celtic *keto* — 'wood, forest' (cf. → *Cetius mons*). The *municipium Aelium Cetensium* of the time of Hadrian (CIL III 5630; 5652; 11799) was destroyed in the wars against the → Marcomanni, but soon recovered [1]. Since 1949 significant excavations on the site of the ancient town, which has been built up in modern times. Some slight evidence of Christianity in what little remains of the late Roman settlement area; St. Florian lived here [2].

1 P.SCHERRER, in: H.FRIESINGER, J.TEJRAL, A.STUPPNER (ed.), Markomannenkriege, 1995, 447–455 2 R.HARREITHER, Der hl. Florian, in: R.BRATOŽ (ed.), West-Illyr. und Nordost-It. in der spätröm. Zeit, 1996, 235–262, especially 239f.

TIR M 33, 34; G.WINKLER, s.v. C., RE Suppl. 14, 90–95; H.UBL, CSIR I 6, 1979; P.SCHERRER, Landeshauptstadt St. Pölten — Arch. Bausteine I, II, 1991, 1994. K.DI.

Cetius Faventinus, M. C.' *liber artis architectonicae* (name and title not ascertained until 1871/1879): a vulgarized, individual adaptation of Vitruvius on domestic architecture, survives in MSS of Vitruvius. If it came down via → Gargilius Martialis [1], then it belongs in the middle or [2] at the end of the 3rd cent. AD; C. is quoted in → Palladius and in → Isidorus of Seville.

EDITION: F.KROHN, Vitruv, 1912, 262–283.
BIBLIOGRAPHY: 1 M.WELLMANN, Palladius und Gargilius Martialis, in: Hermes 43, 1908, 1–31 2 H.PLOMMER, Vitruvius and later Roman building manuals, 1973, 39–85 (with translation) 3 K.SALLMANN, HLL § 450
KL.SA.

Ceto (Κητώ; *Kētố*). Daughter of Pontus and Gaia. By her brother → Phorcys, she gives birth to the → Graeae, the Gorgons (→ Gorgo), and → Echidna and the serpent who guards the golden apples of the → Hesperides (Hes. Theog. 238; 270–336; Apollod. 1,10; 2,37); according to a later version the → Hesperides are also her daughters (schol. Apoll. Rhod. 4,1399). RA.MI.

Cetriporis (Κετρίπορις; *Ketríporis*). Thracian king, who followed his father → Berisades together with his brothers as rulers of western Thrace. They were supported by the Greek mercenary leader → Athenodorus [1] (Dem. Or. 23,10) and in 356 BC concluded— together with Lyppeus of Paeonia and Grabus of Illyria —an alliance with Athens against → Philippus II (IG II/ III² 127; Syll.³ 1, 196; StV 309; TOD 157) [1. 27]. However, the coalition was unsuccessful and C. became a vassal of the Macedonian king (Diod. Sic. 16,22,3). C. issued very beautiful bronze coins in several nominal values.

1 C.L. LAWTON, Attic Document Reliefs, 1995.

E. BADIAN, Philip II and Thrace, in: Pulpudeva 4, 1980 (1983), 51–71; U. PETER, Die Mz. der thrak. Dynasten (5.– 3. Jh.v.Chr.), 1997, 144–146.   U.P.

Cetrius C. Severus C., tribune of the praetorians; in AD 69, together with Subrius Dexter and Pompeius Longinus, he came out in support of → Galba to oppose the incipient rise of → Otho (Tac. Hist. 1,31). He is probably the *beneficiarius* from ILS 2073. PIR C 703.
                                                            M.STR.

Cettus (Κηττός; *Kēttós*). Attic *asty* [2] or *mesogeia* deme [3] of the phyle Leontis, three (four) *bouleutaí*. Inscriptions confirm neither the location near Daphni [2] nor the one in the region north-east of Menidi [3. 174f.].

1 TRAILL, Attica, 18, 43, 62, 68, 110 no. 66, table 4 2 J.S. TRAILL, Demos and Trittys, 1986, 81 fn. 7, 130 3 E. VANDERPOOL, The Acharnanian Aqueduct, in: Χαριστήριον εἰς Ἀναστάσιον Κ. Ὀρλάνδον 1, 1965, 166– 175.   H.LO.

Cetus see → Constellations

Ceutrones
[1] Small tribe in Flanders, *clientes* of the Nervii (Caes. B Gall. 5,39,1).

C. GOUDINEAU, César et la Gaule, 1990; E.M. WIGHTMAN, Gallia Belgica, 1985.   Y.L.

[2] Celtic people in the → Alpes Graiae, in the valley of the Isère (Caes. B Gall. 1,10,4; Str. 4,4,6; Ptol. 3,1,33); known for copper mining (Plin. HN 34,3) and cheesemaking (Plin. HN 11,240). Granted → *ius Latii*, probably under Claudius (Plin. HN 3,135). Main centres were Axima (Aime) and Darantasia (Moutiers).

G. BARRUOL, Les peuples préromains du sud-est de la Gaule, 1975, 313–316; G. WALSER, Via per Alpes Graias, 1986, 78–80.   H.GR.

Ceylon see → Toprobane

Ceyx (Κήϋξ; *Kéyx*). Son of Hesperus and Philonis (Apollod. 1,7,4), king of → Trachis. C. grants asylum to Hercules in his flight from Calydon, who went from there to his death on the Oeta, and to his spouse Deianira (Apollod. 2,7,6; Diod. Sic. 4,57,1). C. later also

receives the Heraclides, whom he must however send on their way (Hecataeus FGrH 1 F 30). C.'s life is marked by blows of fate: his son Hippasus participates in Hercules' campaign against Oechalia and loses his life (Apollod. 2,7,7). C. likewise loses his wayward brother Daedalion and the latter's daughter (Ov. Met. 11,270; Hyg. Fab. 244) and his son-in-law → Cycnus. There are two versions regarding the end of C. and his wife Alcyone [2], a daughter of Aeolus: the two hybristically call themselves Zeus and Hera and as punishment are turned into kingfishers (Apollod. loc.cit.). The better-known version is reported by Ovid (Ov. Met. 11, 410ff; Hyg. Fab. 65; Lucian Halcyon 1ff.). It is one of the most touching love stories of antiquity: C. who after the death of his brother wants to consult the oracle of → Apollo at Clarus, loses his life in a huge storm at sea. Alcyone is informed of this in a dream, given to her by Juno. When she finds the corpse of C. on the beach, both are transformed into kingfishers, during the breeding period of which there is calm.

A.H.F. Griffin, The Ceyx Legend in Ovid's Metamorphoses Book 11, in: CQ 33, 1981, 147–154.   C.W.

Chabakta (Χάβακτα; *Chábakta* on coins, HN 498; Χάβακα; *Chábaka* Str. 12,3,16). Pontic fortress, whose name appears on pseudo-autonomous coins of → Mithridates VI; likely fortress structures identified near Kaleköy/Ünye on the coast of northern Turkey (tomb and two staircases cut into the rock).

OLSHAUSEN/BILLER/WAGNER, 120; W.H. WADDINGTON, E. BABELON, TH. REINACH, Recueil général des monnaies grecques d'Asie Mineure 1,1, ²1925, 104f.   E.O.

Chaberis (Χαβηρὶς ἐμπόριον; *Chabērìs empórion*). Harbour town of the Soringoi at the mouth of the Chaberos (Kāveri) in southern India, in Ptol. 7,1,13. Old Indian (Tamil) Kāveripattinam or Pumpuhar; port of the Chola Empire. A Greek settlement is mentioned in classic Tamil poetry.   K.K.

Chabon (Χάβον; *Chábon*). Scythian fortress 'in the middle of the land of the Scythians' (IOSPE 1², 352,13; 29), built by Scilurus and his sons (Str. 7,4,3); served as a base against Mithridates VI; one of his generals, Diophantus, forced the Scythians to surrender C. (Str. 7,4,4).

V.F. GAJDUKEVIČ, Das Bosporanische Reich, 1971, 309.
                                                     I.v.B. and S.R.T.

Chabrias (Χαβρίας; *Chabrías*). Important Athenian general and mercenary leader. Taking part in → Thrasybulus' campaigns in Thrace during the Corinthian War, at the beginning of 389 BC he succeeded → Iphicrates as general in the Peloponnese. In 388 he set off for Cyprus with Athenian forces to support King Evagoras against Persia. On the way there, victory against the

Spartans on Aegina (Xen. Hell. 5,1,10–13). When the King's Peace (386) made it impossible for him to remain in Cyprus, C. entered the service of the Egyptian pharaoh → Acoris. C. was successful in defending the Nile delta against Persian attempts to regain Egypt as a satrapy. In 380 as a result of Persian pressure recalled to Athens. As *strategos* in the years 379/8–376/5 he barred the Spartan King Cleombrotus' way through Eleutherae on his march against Thebes; in 378 employed the fixed phalanx tactic against Agesilaus II of Sparta; in 377 led a fleet campaign against Histiaea; and in the autumn of 376 defeated Sparta's fleet in the great sea battle of Naxos, thereby bringing many islands into the 2nd Athenian League. For this he was honoured with a statue on the Agora (Xen. Hell. 5,4,61; Dem. Or. 20,75ff.; Diod. Sic. 15, 29–35). With successes against the Triballi in 375 he won further cities in the northern Aegean for the League (Diod. Sic. 15,36,4). From 373/2 frequent additional terms as *strategos*. Not always successful in the Peloponnese against the Thebans, in 366 he was accused of treachery, but acquitted (Dem. Or. 21,64). In 363/2 he forced the island of Ceos back into union with Athens (IG II² 404 and 111). C. 360 he entered the service of the Egyptian pharaoh → Tachos; together with Agesilaus II he prepared the Pharaoh's campaign against the king of the Persians. After the overthrow of Tachos, in 359 C. returned to Athens. He was a trierarch when killed during the storming of the rebellious island of Chios in 357.

J. BUCKLER, A second look at the monument of Chabrias, in: Hesperia 41, 1972, 466–474 pl. 115f.; J. CARGILL, The Second Athenian League, 1981; DAVIES, 560f.; M. DREHER, Hegemon und Symmachoi, 1995; W. K. PRITCHETT, The Greek State at War 2, 1974, 72–77   W.S.

Chaereas (Χαιρέας; *Chairéas*).

[1] Son of Archestratus (Lycomide?) of Athens. In 411/10 BC co-*strategos* in Samos, sent to Athens on the → Paralus, but was able to return (Thuc. 8,74,1–3; 86,3). In 410 *strategos* at Cyzicus (Diod. Sic. 13,49,6; 50,7; 51,3). PA 15093.

DAVIES, 9238; FRASER/MATTHEWS, GPN 2, 1994, 469, no. 3; A. W. GOMME et al., Historical Commentary on Thucydides, 5, 1981, 266–268.   K.KI.

[2] Nauarch of Ptolemy IX; perhaps *strategos* of Cyprus; 88 BC defeats Ptolemy X in Cyprus.

I. MICHAELIDOU-NICOLAOU, Prosopography of Ptolemaic Cyprus, 1976, 126 no. 1.   W.A.

[3] Historian of Hannibal, of unknown origin; probably a contemporary of Hannibal and a member of his entourage. Polybius (3,20,5) characterizes his work (similarly that of Sosylus of Lacedaemon) as 'gossip from the barber's shop and the street corner.' Motive for this dismissive verdict was probably the work's tendency to be highly favourable to Hannibal. FGrH 177 (with commentary).

K. MEISTER, Histor. Kritik bei Polybios,1975,167ff.
                    K.MEI.

[4] Sculptor in bronze; mentioned in Pliny's catalogue of portraitists. Various suggestions as to the identification of the likenesses he made of Philip and Alexander are not universally accepted.

L. GUERRINI, s.v. Chaireas 1, EAA 2, 531.   R.N.

Chaeredemus (Χαιρέδημος; *Chairédēmos*).

One of the three brothers of → Epicurus, who, like him, devoted themselves to philosophy (Diog. Laert. 10,3). He predeceased Epicurus, who bestowed funerary gifts in his memory (Diog. Laert. 10,18) and dedicated a book to him (Diog. Laert. 10,27 and Plut. An recte dictum sit latenter esse vivendum 1129a).   T.D.

Chaeremon (Χαιρήμων; *Chairḗmōn*).

[1] Tragedian; mentioned by the comedy writers Eubulus (Ath. 2,43c) and Ephippus (Juv. fr. 9 KOCK in Ath. 11,482b), which locates him in the middle of the 4th cent. BC. Performed again 276–19 at the Naïa in Dodona (DID B 11,13); titles: *Alphesiboea*, 'Achilles killer of Thersites' (Apulian vase, Boston 03.804 [1. 166]), *Dionysus, Thyestes, Io, The Centaur, The Minyae, Odysseus, Oeneus* and more than 40 fragments.) counts him among those writers whose plays are fully effective only when read (→ Anagnostikoi; cf. fr. 14b Acrostichon) [2. 188–90].

1 T. B. L. WEBSTER, Monuments illustrating Tragedy and Satyr Play, ²1967   2 G. A. SEECK, Chaeremon, in: Id. (ed.), Das griech. Drama, 1979

METTE, 198; B. GAULY et al. (ed.), Musa Tragica, 1991, 71; TrGF 71.   F.P.

[2] From Alexandria; Stoic philosopher, → grammarian and Hellenized Egyptian priest in Alexandria (1st cent. AD). He was appointed tutor to the young Nero. C. was a professor of grammar in Alexandria and probably took part in the Alexandrian delegation to Rome under Emperor Claudius (AD 40). He wrote a 'History of Egypt', which probably contained his explanations of the hieroglyphs and the Egyptian priesthood. He also wrote on comets and grammar. His work exhibited theological allegory in the Stoic manner.
→ Nero

1 P. W. VAN DER HORST, Chaeremon: Egyptian Priest and Stoic Philosopher, 1984   2 FGrH 618   3 M. FREDE, 'Ch.', ANRW II 36.3, 1989, 2067–2103.   B.I.

[3] Epigrammatic poet of the 'Garland' of Meleager (Anth. Pal. 4,1,51); probably lived from the 4th to the 3rd cent. BC [2]; author of three epitaphs. One is probably an actual inscription (Anth. Pal. 7,469 = GVI 998; verse 2 = CEG 724,4); the other two hark back to the old struggle (*c.* 547 BC) between Argos and Sparta over ownership of Thyrea (loc. cit. 7,720f., cf. Hdt. 1,82).

1 GA I 1, 75f.; 2, 220–222   2 M. G. ALBIANI, CEG 724, Hansen: un ignorato plagio (AP VII 468,9s. [Mel.] e 469,2 [Chaerem.]), in: Eikasmós 5, 1994, 237–242.   E.D.

Chaerephon (Χαιρεφῶν; *Chairephón*). From the Attic deme of Sphettus; from early youth a passionate follower of → Socrates. In Aristophanes' *Clouds*, *Wasps* and *Birds* C. is lampooned as an especially zealous and ascetic pupil of Socrates. As a committed democrat, he lived in exile during the tyranny of the → Thirty (404–403 BC) (Pl. Ap. 21a). C. was already dead by the time of Socrates' trial (399 BC). Plato () and Xenophon (Apol. 14) report that C. once asked the oracle at Delphi whether anyone was wiser than Socrates, and received a negative answer. It is not entirely impossible that this story is a myth invented by the Socratics [1]. C. is a participant in the Platonic dialogues *Charmides* and *Gorgias*.

1 K. DÖRING, Sokrates, in: GGPh 2.1, 1997, 155.

EDITION: SSR VI B 11–21. K.D.

Chaerestratus Son of Chaeredemus; Attic sculptor from → Rhamnus. On a prosopographical basis, his creative period has been deduced to have been in the early 3rd cent. BC, but by some to *c.* 320 BC. This is significant for the chronology of early Hellenistic developments in style, as the statue of Themis in the sanctuary of Nemesis at Rhamnus (Athens, AM) is signed by C. Further works are attributed to him by way of style.

J. MARCADÉ, Recueil des signatures des sculpteurs grecs, 1, 1953, no. 11–12; P. MORENO, Scultura ellenistica, 1994, 168–172 fig.; B. S. RIDGWAY, Hellenistic Sculpture, 1, 1990, 55–57 fig. R.N.

Chaerion Writer of comedies, attested only epigraphically; he evidently once won first prize at the Attic Dionysia [1. test. *2], and also in 154 BC second place at the Great Dionysia with the play 'The false self-accuser' [1. test. 1].

1 PCG IV, 1983, 69. H.-G.NE.

Chaeris (Χαῖρις; *Chaîris*). Greek grammarian of the school of Aristarchus of Samothrace; father of a grammarian called Apollonius [7] (ὁ τοῦ Χαίριδος; *ho toû Chaíridos*). It is not clear whether he lived directly after Aristarchus. His work was used by Tryphon, Didymus and Herodianus. We are better informed about his exegesis on Homer: about 10 fragments are known from the *scholiae*, and Schol. Hom. Od. 7,80 mentions the title Διορθωτικά (*Diorthōtiká*; 'Improvements'). C. is also quoted about 10 times in the Pindar *scholiae*, almost exclusively at P. 4. There are also a few quotations in the Aristophanes *scholiae*. His name being perhaps often confused with that of → Chares [6] (Χάρης; *Chárēs*), the attribution of one piece Περὶ γραμματικῆς (*Perì grammatikês*; 'On grammar') is uncertain (Sext. Emp. Adversus Mathematicos 1,76).

→ Apollonius [7]; → Chares; → Didymus; → Herodianus; → Sextus Empiricus; → Tryphon

EDITION: R. BERNDT, De Charete, Chaeride, Alexione grammaticis eorumque reliquiis I, 1902, 3–18, 31–50.

BIBLIOGRAPHY: A. BLAU, De Aristarchi discipulis, 1883, 56–67; L. COHN, s.v. Chairis, RE 3, 2031; A. LUDWICH, Aristarchs Homer. Textkritik I, 1884–85, 50; F. SUSEMIHL, Gesch. der griech. Lit. in der Alexandrinerzeit II, 1891–1892, 166–167. F.M.

Chaeron (Χαίρων; *Chaírōn*).
[1] Mythical son of Apollo and Thero (in Plut. Sulla 17: Thuro); founder of the city named after him, → Chaeronea (Hes. Cat. fr. 252 M-W = Paus. 9,40,5f.; Hellanicus FGrH 379 F3). Plutarch names a son dead in childhood after him (Consolatio ad uxorem 5 p. 609d). R.B.

[2] Spartan polemarch who died in 403 BC in → Pausanias' assault on Piraeus. He was buried on the Cerameicus (Xen. Hell. 2,4,33; Lys. epit. 63). His grave has been positively identified from an inscription [1].

1 G. KARO, Arch. Funde aus dem Jahre 1929 und der ersten Hälfte von 1930, in: AA 45, 1930, 88–167, especially 90–92. M.MEI.

[3] Spartan politician, who as leader of the Spartans banished in 188 BC by the Achaeans appealed to the Roman Senate in 184/83 and obtained their return (Pol. 22,3,1; 23,4). After the formal reacceptance of Sparta into the Achaean League, C. was sent to Rome in 182 (Pol. 23,18). Following the reforms of → Nabis, in 181/80 he began to distribute the property of exiles to impoverished citizens; when envoys of the Achaean League wanted to investigate his handling of public funds, C. murdered their leader. The Achaean *strategos* finally put an end to his activities by taking C. prisoner and probably having him executed (Pol. 24,7).
→ Pausanias

P. CARTLEDGE, A. SPAWFORTH, Hellenistic and Roman Sparta, 1989; GRUEN, Rome, 2. M.MEI.

[4] Of Pallene. He studied philosophy under Plato and Xenocrates, then distinguished himself as a wrestler and before 331 BC was appointed tyrant of Pallene by → Antipater [1]. He held on to power by means of social revolution and terror, with the support of Macedonian troops. The duration of his rule is unknown, but it certainly lasted until after the death of → Agis [3].

BERVE 2, no. 818. E.B.

Chaeronea (Χαιρώνεια, Χηρώνια; *Chairṓneia*, *Chērṓnia*). Westernmost town of → Boeotia on the border to Phocis, located in the northern foothills of the Thurion range in the Cephissus valley near the modern C. (formerly Kapraina). Sources: Paus. 9,40,5–41,7; Str. 9,2,37. A prehistoric settlement has been found to the north-east on the banks of the Cephissus [2. 382f.], a Mycenaean chamber tomb close to the modern C., a Hellenistic-Roman theatre at the foot of the castle hill, which still bears the remains of the acropolis fortifications [4].

According to tradition, C. was the first place where the immigrant Boeotians settled (Plut. Cimon 1,478e). C. is first mentioned in historical sources in connection with its capture by the Athenian → Tolmides in 447 BC (Thuc. 1,113,1, also Diod. Sic. 12,6,1). Up to and beyond 424 BC a dependency of → Orchomenus [6], C. then, until 387/6 BC, constituted — together with Acraephia and Copae — one of the 11 districts of the Boeotian League, and took turns with them in supplying a → boiotarchēs (Hell. Oxy. 19,3,394–396). Following a short period of independence, from 371 to 338 BC C. was a member (possibly as a restored federal district) of the Boeotian League, which had been renewed under Theban control. When the league was reconstituted yet again in 335 BC, C. became an independent member and remained as such up to the league's dissolution in 146 BC; it continued to exist in Roman times [3. 578ff.], until an earthquake destroyed the town in AD 551 (Procop. Goth. 4,25,16f.). Several insights regarding C.'s history and monuments can be found in the works of Plutarch who hailed from C. [1. 480iff.].

Because of its strategically advantageous location on the important north-south route through the Cephissus valley, C. was repeatedly the site of decisive battles: in 338 BC, the Macedonians under the command of Philip II triumphed over the anti-Macedonian alliance of Greek states (Diod. Sic. 16,85,5–86,6); a stone lion, adorning the tomb of the Theban war dead (Paus. 9,40,10) with 252 bodies and two cremated remains, is found east of C. In 245 BC, a victory over the Boeotian League at C. (Pol. 20,4f.; Plut. Aratus 16) enabled the Aetolians to strengthen their dominant position in central Greece. In 86 BC, Sulla destroyed the army of Mithridates VI at C. (App. Mith. 42–45; Plut. Sulla 16–19; SEG 41,448). Inscriptions: IG VII 3287–3465; SEG III, 367–369; 17,226; 28,44–452; 29,440f.; 36,415; 38,380; cf. also [5. 496ff.].

1 J. BUCKLER, Plutarch and Autopsy, ANRW II 33.6, 4788–4830 2 FOSSEY, 375–385 3 J.M. FOSSEY, The Cities of the Copais in the Roman Period, ANRW II 7.1, 549–591 4 Id., Les fortifications de l'acropole de Cheronée, in: Id., Papers in Boiotian Topography and History, 1990, 100–121 5 D. KNOEPFLER, Sept années de recherches sur l'épigraphie de la Béotie, in: Chiron 22, 1992, 411–503 6 J.A. O. LARSEN, Orchomenos and the Formation of the Boeotian Confederacy in 447 B. C., in: CPh 50, 1960, 9–18.

J. KODER, Chaironeia, TIB 1, 138; N.D. PAPACHATZIS, Παυσανίου Ελλάδος Περιήγησις, 5, ²1981, 260–266; P. W. WALLACE, Strabo's Description of Boiotia, 1979, 146–148.   P.F.

Chair see → Seat

Chairekrates see → Socratics

Chalastra (Χαλάστρα; *Chalástra*).
[1] City at the mouth of the Axius (Str. 7 fr. 20; 23; cf. Hdt. 7,123), identified by Hecataeus as belonging to Thrace (Steph. Byz. s.v.). The population was recruited for the foundation of Thessalonica (Str. 7 fr. 21). Not located.

F. PAPAZOGLOU, Les villes de Macédoine, 1988, 199.
                                                                                MA.ER.

[2] Natron-bearing lake, probably near the town of the same name (Steph. Byz. s.v.; Plin. HN 31,107; Suda s.v.).   MA.ER.

Chalce (Χάλκη; *Chálkē*). Island off the north coast of Rhodes (29 km²). The polis of C. (remains of acropolis, temple to Apollo, necropolis) belonged to Rhodian Camirus. During the 5th cent. BC a member of the Delian League.

P.M. FRASER, G.E. BEAN, The Rhodian Peraea and Islands, 1954, 144f.   H.SO.

Chalcedonense Definition of faith of the Council of → Chalcedon (AD 451; → *Sýnodos* II. D.): Christ is completely God and man, of one substance with God the father (→ Nicaenum) and with humanity. When Christ became man, both natures united into one indivisible person (πρόσωπον/*prósōpon*, ὑπόστασις/*hypóstasis*; against → Nestorius), but remained distinct in their duality (against → Cyrillus [2]). The teaching of the two natures in Christ, rejected by → Monophysitism, was contested in the Greek Church until 518 (→ Henotikon). The councils of 553 and 680/1 established the future interpretation of Christ.
→ Eutyches [3]; → Hypostasis [2]; → Leo [3]; → Synodos II.; → Theodoretus [1]; → Trinity

EDITION: E. SCHWARTZ, Acta conciliorum oecumenicorum II,1,2, 129 f.
BIBLIOGRAPHY: K. BEYSCHLAG, Grundriß der Dogmengeschichte II.1, 1991; A. GRILLMEIER, H. BACHT (ed.), Das Konzil von Chalkedon 1–3, 1951–1954.   S. GE.

Chalcidian vase painting Important type of 6th-cent. BC black-figured vase, named for the appended mythological names in the Chalcidian alphabet; none of the painters or potters is known [1. 2f.; 2. 181ff.]. RUMPF and others placed Chalcidian vase painting (CVP) on Euboea, whereas today Rhegium is favoured [1; 2. 15ff.; 3. *passim*]. The question must, however, remain open, especially as some of the Chalcidian vases bear trademarks otherwise found only on vases not manufactured in Italy [1. 53]. The genre begins *c.* 560 BC with no discernible precursors, and already comes to an end *c.* 510 BC. During these 50 years, 15 painters or groups of painters can be distinguished, and about 600 vases survive (some of them unattributable to any one painter). The CVP distinguishes itself by its outstanding potter's craft; the glaze is for the most part fired a deep black; red and white are used extensively, as are scratched marks. As regards shape (→ Pottery, shapes and types of), the neck amphora with variations is preferred (about a quarter of all vases), then eye-bowls, oinochoai and hydriae; kraters, *skyphoi* and *pyxides* occur more rarely, and exceptionally *lekanis* and cups (after Etruscan models). Especially notable among the particular features of these always strict and concise vase forms is the Chalcidian vase-foot, often imitated in Attic black-figure and red-figure bowls (e.g. in the form of a trochilus) [2. 284ff.]. The main master of the early CVP is the so-called Inscription Painter, of the younger generation of Phineus painters, with his productive workshop (more than 170 surviving vases). Highly decorative and splendidly effective images such as animal friezes, riders, heraldic images or combinations of men, women and youths, without narrative content, are preferred; often, a large, cruciform lotus leaf is included. A whole series of painters confines itself entirely to this range of motifs. Mythological images are rare but outstanding, almost half of them attributed to the Inscription Painter. While the mythology of the gods hardly figures (the two versions of the 'Return of Hephaestus' remain exceptions), the deeds of Heracles, the Trojan cycle and the saga of the Argonauts are especially popular. Silenus with nymphs and the running Gorgo occur frequently [2. 84ff.]. The effect of the figures is always lithe and vivid. Especially favoured ornaments are chains of buds and rosettes. CVP is influenced by Athens, Corinth and especially Ionia, and are succeeded by Pseudo-Chalcidian vase painting. Chalcidian vases have been found mostly in Italy (Caere, Vulci, Rhegium); but mention must also be made of Ampurias, Izmir, Marseilles and Scyros [1. 279 no. 27; 2. 26ff.].

1 A. RUMPF, Chalkidische Vasen, 1927   2 J. KECK, Studien zur Rezeption fremder Einflüsse in der chalkidischen Keramik, 1988   3 M. IOZZO, Ceramica 'calcidese'. Atti e Memorie della Soc. Magna Graecia, ser. 3, II, 1994.

M. IOZZO, in: ArchCl 42, 1990, 507–515 (review of 2); E. SIMON, Die griech. Vasen, ²1981, pl. XVIIIf., 39f.   M.ST.

Chalcidice (Χαλκιδική; *Chalkidikḗ*). The name C., used today for the entire peninsula with its three extended fingers, in antiquity referred only to the area occupied by the Chalcidians on Sithonia and its hinterland, which they probably settled before the great period of Greek colonization (middle of the 8th cent. BC). The coastal towns are first mentioned by name at the time of Xerxes' march, and later, together with inland towns, as members of the Athenian League. In 432 the majority seceded from Athens, abandoning the coastal towns of Mecyberna, Singus and Gale and combining in a state around Olynthus. Some of the population of the abandoned towns moved to Olynthus, some to → Apollonia [3], the region south of the Bolbe. The newly formed Chalcidian state minted coins bearing the inscription

ΧΑΛΚΙΔΕΩΝ (*Chalkideōn*), and in the Peloponnesian War was active militarily and diplomatically on the side opposing Athens, even when after the successes of Cleon it was restricted to the close environs of Olynthus, and destined by the conditions of the peace of Nikias to be once and for all dissolved into its original component parts. The population of Olynthus, enlarged from 432, maintained its claim to represent the Chalcidian state. From the beginning of the 4th cent. at the latest, Olynthus initiated a union with its neighbouring towns to form a Chalcidian League, which soon went beyond its ethnic limits and finally even threatened the Macedonian state. The Macedonian king and the towns of Acanthus and Apollonia turned for help to the Spartans, who in a three-year war (382–379) compelled the League to dissolve; but there continued to be a (western) Chalcidian state centred on Olynthus. C. 375 it became a member of the 2nd Athenian League, then became stronger and in the 360s went on to reconstitute the League, which in 357/6 allied itself with Philip II against Athens, receiving Anthemus and Potidaea from the king. It was at this time that the League attained its greatest historical extent. However, the unilateral peace concluded with Athens (352) marred relations with Philip, and the war that broke out in 349 ended with the destruction of Olynthus and the annexation of the whole of C. A major part of C. was later joined to the polis territory of newly founded Cassandreia.

M. B. HATZOPOULOS, Actes de vente de la Chalcidique centrale, 1988; D. KNOEPFLER, 1989, 23–58; M. MOGGI, 11, 1974, 1–11; A. PANAYOTOU, in: ΠΟΙΚΙΛΑ, 1990, 191–226; F. PAPAZOGLOU, Les villes de Macédoine à l'époque romaine, 1988, 424–431; U. WESTERMARK, The Coinage of the Chalcidian League Reconsidered, in: Studies in Ancient History and Numismatics Presented to Rudi Thomsen, 1988, 91–103; M. ZAHRNT, Olynth und die Chalkidier, 1971.   M.Z.

In the Byzantine period, C. came under the control of the *thema* and metropolis of Thessalonica. From the 11th/12th cents. the monasteries on Athos extended their landownership there to create great estates.

Archives de l'Athos, 1937ff.; J. LEFORT, Villages de Macédoine, I. La Chalcidique occidentale, 1982.   G.MA.

Chalciope (Χαλκιόπη; *Chalkiópē*).
[1] Daughter of Chalcodon (king of the Abantes: Hom. Il. 2,541) or of Rhexenor; second wife of Aegeus before Medea (Apollod. 3,207; Schol. Eur. Med. 673).
[2] Daughter of Aeetes and Idyia; sister of Medea, wife of Phrixus, mother of Argos, Mela, Phrontis and Kytis(s)orus (Apollod. 1,83; Herodor FGrH F 39; Apoll. Rhod. 2,1148ff.); in Pherecydes (FGrH F 25) she is called Euenia (also C. and Iophossa; cf. Hes. fr. 255 M-W; Acusilaus FGrH F 38); probably Apoll. Rhod. (3,248ff.) makes C. mediator between the Argonauts and Aeetes, or between Jason and Medea.

[3] Daughter of King Eurypylus of Cos; mother by Heracles of Thessalus (Pherecydes FGrH F 78; Apollod. 2,166).

→ Aeetes; → Aegeus; → Argonauts; → Argos; → Euenia; → Eurypylus; → Heracles; → Jason; → Iophossa; → Medea; → Melas; → Phrixus; → Phrontis; → Rhexenor; → Thessalus   P.D.

Chalcis (Χαλκίς; *Chalkís*).

[1] In Euboea on the Euripus; by its especially strategic position the most important town on the island. It remains uncertain whether the name C. derives from the ore deposits around C.; these deposits were already exhausted in the Hellenistic period. The region around C. with the → Arethusa [2] spring was already settled in the sub-Neolithic period; Mycenaean burials have also been confirmed. The Homeric catalogue of ships names the → Abantes, migrants from the mainland, as inhabitants of the town; there was still an Abantis phyle during the Roman imperial period. In historical times the population was entirely Ionic. During the 8th cent. BC C. was a flourishing mercantile town, allied to Corinth. C. together with Eretria founded many colonies in Chalcidice, Italy and Sicily: i.a. → Cyme, → Rhegium and Zancle (→ Messana). The Chalcidian-Corinthian standard of coinage was widespread, as was the Chalcidian alphabet. C. emerged victorious from the struggle with Eretria over the Lelantine plain (→ Lelantion pedion) in the first half of the 7th cent. BC.

The attempt to suppress embryonic democratic movements in Athens ended in catastrophic defeat. Four thousand Attic cleruchs settled the Lelantine plain. In 490 BC the advancing Persians spared C.; 10 years later Athens had to give the Chalcidians 20 ships to man as their contribution to the struggle against the Persians. After the victory over the Persians C. joined the → Delian League, having to pay an annual tribute of 30,000 drachmas. Incipient independence movements were suppressed by Athens. C. substantially lost its sovereignty in matters of taxation and law, and eventually even its coinage rights. In 411 BC C. was linked for the first time to the mainland by a dam and a wooden bridge. In 377 BC C. joined the second → Athenian League, but came increasingly under the control of Thebes. The Chalcidians fought against Philip II at Chaeronea. In the age of the Diadochi, C. with the mainland bridgehead at Canethus was a heavily fortified Macedonian naval base. Under Philip V it was one of the 'three fetters of Greece', along with Acrocorinth and → Demetrias.

After the battle of Cynoscephalae (197 BC), C. fell to the Romans for the first time. Before the beginning of the war against Perseus the Romans again occupied C., but in 146 BC arbitrary actions by Roman officials caused C. to join the war of the Achaean League against Rome. As punishment, the walls of the fortress were razed.

Only under Justinian were the fortifications and the bridge over the Euripus restored. Gradually, *Euripus* in its popular form *Egripos* took over from the name C. The Venetians, from 1366 masters of all Euboea, reconstituted C. as a powerful fortress; the Byzantine basilica of Hag. Paraskevi was converted into a Gothic church, and an aqueduct built across the Lelantine plain. On 12 July 1470 C. was stormed by the Turks under Mehmed II, concluding the Turkish conquest of Greece. From 1832 C. again belonged to Greece. In 1892 the Venetian town walls and the Turkish bridge-castle Kara Baba, built around 1686 on the mainland shore on the site of ancient Canethus, were demolished in the course of the widening of the Euripus.

> S. C. Bakhuizen, Studies in the topography of Chalcis on Euboea, 1985; D. Knoepfler, Contributions a l'épigraphie de Chalcis, in: BCH 114, 1990, 473–498; E. Freund, s.v. Chalkis, in: Lauffer, Griechenland, 164–166; S. Lauffer, Chalkis 1, 1943.   H.KAL.

[2] Port town on the Aetolian coast east of the mountain of the same name (Str. 10,2,21, the modern Varassova) near Kato Vasiliki. Described in Hom. Il. 2,640 and Alcm. 11 fr. 35,2 as Aetolian, according to Thuc. 1,108 a Corinthian colony. C. is not the fortified complex on the eastern slope of the hill (refuge? [1]), but the settlement mound 300 m east of Vasiliki: Mycenaean and especially classical-Hellenistic pottery, temple remains [2] and an early Christian basilica [3; 4].

> 1 S. Bommeljé, Aetolia, 1987, 112   2 C. Antonetti, Les Étoliens, 1990, 283f.   3 Soustal, Nikopolis, 121f.   4 A. Paliuras, Κάτω Βασιλικὴ Αιτωλίας, in: Ergon, 1989, 40–43.   D.S.

Chaldaea
Used in the strictest sense, C. is the Greek, or respectively, Latin name for the extreme south of Mesopotamia and also the region around the Persian Gulf (also Χαλδαῖα χώρα; *Chaldaîa chóra*, 'Chaldaean land'); its extent — at least partially — coincides with the coastal land mentioned in early old oriental sources. The name is derived from the Semitic tribal group of the Chaldaeans — probably to be distinguished from the Arameans — who have been evident in the south of Mesopotamia from the early 1st millennium BC. Accad. *māt Kaldi* was used by Assyrians and Babylonians, but never as a name for their own tribe by the Chaldaeans themselves; Hebrew ['*aeraeṣ*] *Kaśdīm*; the biblical Aramaic *Kaśdaja* is used in the OT as a synonym for 'Babylonian', 'Babylonians' (transmutation of sound from *l* to *s*). In ancient authors, C. is practically not encountered as a political entity. A strict differentiation between C. and → Babylonia is only partially supported by traditional sources. On the one hand, C. is seen as a region of Babylonia (Str. 16,739; Ptol. Geogr. 5,20), and on the other as a region in the south of Mesopotamia, separate from Babylonia (Str. loc. cit.), or as a neighbouring region of Babylonia (Amm. Marc. 23,6). It is likely that C. and Babylonia were used synonymously (Plin. HN 5,90; Steph. Byz. s.v. C.; the work of → Berossos is traditionally both referred to as *Babyloniaká* and as *Chaldaiká*). The expansion of the term to

encompass the entire south of Mesopotamia (= Babylonia) is an indication of the influence which rulers of Chaldaean descent have at times wielded, and which is also the backdrop to Hdt. 1,181 and 183, where he describes the priests of → Babylon as → Chaldaei. There is also documentary evidence of C. itself expanding into Assyria to its north (Hsch. s.v. ἡ Χαλδαική; according to Ath. 12, 529f., Chaldaiká and Assýria grámmata — i.e. their → cuneiform script — are identical). Plin. HN 6,130, also 134, refers to the lakes and marshes of the Tigris delta as chaldaicus lacus. J.OE.

Chaldaei (Chaldaeans). Originally the term describing a tribe of western Semitic origin, attested from the early 1st millennium BC in Babylonia. The most important tribes — named after their ancestral heros eponymos as 'house (bīt) of [personal name]' — lived in far-flung settlements in the extreme south of Mesopotamia (Bīt Amukani, Bīt Jakīn) and south of → Borsipa (Bīt Dakkuri). Babylonia's resistance to Assyrian overlordship essentially originated with the C. The final Babylonian dynasty, which under → Nebuchadnezzar II founded the Neo-Babylonian empire, was probably of Chaldaean origin. Māt Kaldu ('C.-Land') in late cuneiform texts as well as Kaśdîm in the OT and C. in classical sources are used as a synonym for 'Babylonians'. The Armenian C. mentioned by Xenophon have nothing to do with the C. of Babylonia. In biblical (Deut. 1.4; 2.2,4) as well as classical tradition (e.g. Diod. Sic. 2,29–31; Diog. Laert. 1,1,6; Hdt. 1,181,183), after the fall of the Babylonian Empire the term C. was transferred to the Babylonian astrologers, sorcerers (→ Magic), seers and scholars much esteemed in Rome and Greece. This demonstrates the extent to which → astrology and → divination were felt to be characteristic of Babylonian culture.

J. A. BRINKMAN, Prelude to Empire, 1984; Id., OrNS 46, 1977, 304–325; D.O. EDZARD, RLA 5, 1976–80, 291–297. S.M.

Chalia (Χαλία; Chalía). Town on the east coast of Boeotia, to be localized either north-west of Chalcis near the modern Drosia (into the 20th cent. known as τὰ Χαλία) [1. 78], or in the vicinity of Aulis [2. 215]. Involved in a territorial dispute with Chalcis: Theopompus, FGrH 115 F 211f.; dating uncertain.

1 FOSSEY, 77–78. 2 C. BURSIAN, Geogr. von Griechenland 1, 1862. P.F.

Chalitani Town in Sicily (ILS 1188; 2nd cent. AD); identified either with Chalae/Chalis (in Gela, It. Ant. 95,6) [1] or with a vicus near Halicyae [2].

1 G. ALFÖLDY, Die Legionslegaten röm. Rheinarmeen, 1967, 61f. 2 G. MANGANARO, La Sicilia da Sesto Pompeo a Diocleziano, ANRW II 1.1, 78 n. 429 R.J.A. WILSON, Sicily under the Roman Empire, 1990, 385 no. 141. GI.MA.

Chalk This dyeing, fine-textured earthy limestone was formed in the sea in the Cretaceous period from foraminifera and coccolites. Greek: γύψος, λευκὴ γή (gýpsos, leukḗ gḗ. The Latin name creta is derived perhaps from cerno 'sieved (earth)'[1]. In antiquity, chalk was needed to make paints and coloured pencils. Plin. HN 35,44 knew of both silver chalk (creta argentaria) and chalk mixed with → purple paint (purpurissimum) as a by-product of the dyeing of cloth. Seven colours, including white lead (cerussa), bond, according to Plin. HN 35,49, with dry, but not with moist chalk. The way in which chalk was used differed depending on its origin, e.g. creta Eretria (Plin. HN. 35,38) as material for the painters → Nicomachus and → Parrhasius, and as a medicine for headaches and for locating suppurative foci. The creta Selinusia (Plin. HN 35,46) was used for make-up and whitewashing walls and — mixed with woad (vitrum) — as a substitute for indigo (indicum; Vitr. De arch. 7,14,2). By creta Columella 2,15,4 means alumina.

1 WALDE/HOFMANN.

O. LAGERCRANTZ, s.v. K., RE 11, 1701ff. C.HÜ.

Chalkos (χαλκοῦς; chalkoûs). In Pollux (4,175; 9,65f. 81) generally described as a bronze coin, the chalkous was the smallest fraction of a coin in Greek poleis. In Athens one obolos makes 8 [1. 47], in Delphi and Epidaurus 12 [1.56ff.], in Priene 16 chalkoi [1. 61f.]. The weight of the chalkos varied; the bronze coins from Seleucia/Tigris having an X (= Chalkos) under Antiochus IV weigh c. 2.8–5 g [2. 271f.]; a Neronian coin with the value marking ΧΑΛΚΟΥΣ in Antiochia/ Orontes weighs c. 2.5 g [3].
→ Obolos

1 M.N. TOD, Epigraphical Notes on Greek Coinage II. CHALKOUS, in: NC 6.6, 1946, 47–62 2 E.T. NEWELL, The Coinage of the Eastern Seleucid Mints from Seleucus I to Antiochus III, 1978 3 RPC, 1, 1992, 623. 629 no. 4302 pl. 163.

RPC, 1, 1992, 370ff. A.M.

Chalybes (Χάλυβες; Χάλυβοι; Chálybes, Chályboi, Hecat. FGrH 1 F 203). A people famous for their skill in ironwork; they were even credited with the invention of iron; indeed the extraction and working of gold and silver were associated with the C. Sometimes located on the north shore of the Black Sea (original homeland? Aesch. PV 714f.), but generally in the northern Anatolian mountains west of the → Halys (Hdt. 1,28), extending in the east as far as → Pharnacaea and → Trapezus (Str. 12,3,19ff.), in the south to the territory of the Armenians.

W. J. HAMILTON, Researches in Asia Minor, Pontus and Armenia 1, 1842, 271ff.; H. WEIMERT, Wirtschaft als landschaftsgebundenes Phänomen, 1984, 88, 97ff. E.O.

Chamaeleon

[1] From Heraclea Pontica. Peripatetic of the 2nd half of the 4th cent. BC. He wrote works of a popular/ethical nature and a long series of anecdotal monographs on poets from Homer to → Anaxandrides. His ethical views were conventional, and his entire body of work conditioned by the popularizing tradition of his school. → Aristotelianism

WEHRLI, Schule ²1969, 49–88; F. WEHRLI, in: GGPh 3, 555–7.   H.G.

[2] (χαμαιλέων; *chamailéōn*). A reptile found in India and Egypt (Plin. HN 11,188). Its shape, its timidity and the turning movement of its eyes were known, but it was assumed that it lived only on air. The ability of the slim (Aristot. Part. an. 4,11,692a20–24) animal to change its colour was a matter of controversy and discussion in ancient times: Aristotle attributed it to fear and anaemia, Theophrastus (?, in Plut. Soll. an. 27,978e-f) only to fear and (in Phot. bibl. 278; like Plin. HN 8,120–122) adaptation to the environment. Sen. Q Nat. 1,5,7 considered agitation and the angle of incidence of light. The detailed description in Aristot. Hist. an. 2,11,503a15–b28 is an outside interpolation. People are compared to it (Aristot. Eth. Nic. 1,11,1100b6; Plut. Alcibiades 23; De adulatore et amico 9). Plin. HN 28,117 uses the gall for eye diseases. Gell. NA 10,12,1ff. and Plin. HN 28,112–118 reluctantly cite a great deal of superstitious and organotherapeutical matters from a special book of Ps.-Democritus. › Artemidorus [6] interprets its appearance in dreams as an omen of ill fortune (oneirokritica 2,13).

KELLER 2, 281–284.   C.HÜ.

Chamaimelon

(χαμαίμηλον; *chamaímēlon, chamo-milla*, camomile). Certainly the composite *Matricaria chamomilla* L. that was cultivated as a medicinal plant from Neolithic times onwards. Plin. HN 22,53 knew not just its name, → anthemis, but also the nomenclature allegedly based on its apple smell (*quod odorem mali habeat*, but in reality probably the result of its hemispherical thalamus), and emphasized its anti-inflammatory healing power (Plin. HN 22,53; Dioscorides 3,137 [1. II.145ff.] = 3,144 [2. 352ff.]).

1 M. WELLMANN (ed.), Pedanii Dioscuridis de materia medica, Vol. 2, 1906, repr. 1958   2 J. BERENDES (ed.), Des Pedanios Dioskurides Arzneimittellehre übers. und mit Erl. versehen, 1902, repr. 1970.   C.HÜ.

Chamavi

Germanic tribe (of uncertain etymology); they preceded the Tubantes and Usipetes as inhabitants of land on the lower Rhine, which was later to become Roman military land (Tac. Ann. 13,55,2); before 12 BC they lived east of the Tencteri, west of the → Bructeri and north of the Marsi (cf. the early medieval district of 'Hamaland' around Deventer between IJssel and Rhine). After the defeat of the Bructeri in AD 98, the C. from the west began to settle in the Bructeri's former territory (Tac. Germ. 33,1; 34,1; TIR M 33,34). Battled by Rome in AD 294/5 and in around 310, and forced to accept peace in AD 358, the C. settled in the land of the → Francs (Tab. Peut. 2,1–3). C. who were taken prisoner were transplanted to Gallia as → *laeti*, others pressed into military service (Not. Dign. or. 31,61).

G. NEUMANN (et al.), s.v. Chamaver, RGA 4, 368–370; W. WILL, Roms 'Klientel-Randstaaten' am Rhein? Survey in: BJ 187, 1987, 1–61, especially 21.   K.DI.

Chamber pot

The terms ἀμίς/*amís*, λάσανα/*lásana*, Lat. *matella, matellio, matula* described vessels made of various materials used in agriculture (Cato Agr. 10,2; 11,3) as well as vessels for water and washing in the household; but they were particularly used to designate chamber pots (Aristoph. Plut. 816f.) that were set up in the latrine or were portable (Anth. Pal. 11,74,7; Hor. Sat. 1,6,109; Petron. Sat. 27). Ath. 1,519e attributed to the Sybarites (→ Sybaris) the first use of chamber pots; from there, the chamber pot was brought to Athens. During the symposium, a special slave (*lasanophóros*), whose service was considered very lowly, administered the chamber pot (in Martial upon a snap of his master's fingers: 1,37; 3,82; 6,89; 14,119). The chamber pot for women was called *skáphion*, Lat. *scaphium* (Juv. 6,264). Other vessels functioning as chamber pots are also mentioned: *trulla* (Iuv. 3,108) or Greek *stamníon*. *Matella* and *lasanum* were also used as swearwords (Anth. Lat. 205,13; Petron. Sat. 45,8).

W. HILGERS, Lat. Gefäßnamen (31. Beih. BJ), 1969, 217–219; K. SCHAUENBURG, Σειληνός οὖρον, in: MDAI(R) 81, 1974, 313–316; R. NEUDECKER, Die Pracht der Latrine, 1994, s.v. Nachttopf and *passim*.   R.H.

Chamois

(*rubicapra*). Like the → mountain goat (*ibex*) the chamois, which belongs to the bovine family, lives in the Alps (Plin. HN 8,214). Its horns are bent backwards (*cornua in dorsum adunca*) in contrast to those of the *dammae* (→ Gazelles) that are directed forwards; Plin. HN 11,124, perhaps from his own experience. For the supposed healing of consumption through chamois fat mixed in equal proportions with milk, Plin. HN 28,231 refers, however, to an author who possibly confused chamois with wild goats. This confusion is to be found in many authors, such as Homer (Od. 9,118), Cato in Varro, Rust. 2,3,3 (but see [1.vol. 1,299]) and Verg. Aen. 4,152 [2. 49].

1 KELLER   2 O. KELLER, Thiere des class. Alterthums, 1887.   C.HÜ.

Chancellery

Chancellery, Modern High German 'Kanzlei' (from Lat. *cancelli* via OHG *canceli, cancli*), in abstract terms signifies a functional area in which documents are prepared, issued, transferred and safeguarded for legal dealings. Since antiquity this was particularly the activity of courts and officialdom. In the Roman Imperial period several names for chancellery

— *officium, cancelli* (*cancer* = grid), *scrinium* (= receptacle for scrolls or shrine) and *burellum* (late Latin = screen, office) — and differing organizational forms existed. In provincial civil and military administrations they were small offices (*officia*) with a staff of a few dozen (cf. e.g. Cod. Iust. 1,27,2,20ff. and Nov. 24-27, respective salary lists). At the imperial court or the seat of a *praefectus praetorio* (Cod. Iust. 1,27,1,21ff.) a staff of several hundred was distributed over several *scrinia* and *scolae*, among them the *scrinia ab epistulis, a memoria, a libellis* and *a dispositionibus* of the palace who were bearers of rich traditions (→ *scrinium*). Professional record-making was handled, for example, by → *notarii* (of the palace: Cod. Iust. 12,7) and → *exceptores* (Cod. Iust. 12,23,7,2). In the praefect's administration the following *scrinia* might be found: *primum, commentariensis, ab actis, exceptorum* and *libellorum*. As in the palace, there were also services for the organization of audiences (*nomenclatores*), forwarding and public proclamation (*singularii, cursores, mittendarii, praecones*), cashiers (*arcarii*), enforcement (*draconarii*) and archiving (*chartularii*). Generally, the chancellery is subject to an official who holds central responsibility: e.g. in the palace the *magister officiorum*, for the *praefectus praetorio* a → *cancellarius*, in provincial civil and regional military administrations an *assessor* (Cod. Iust. 1,27,21; 1,31; 1,51).

→ Bureaucracy III; → Administration

HIRSCHFELD, 318-342; JONES, LRE, 367-369, 427f., 459f.; H. C. TEITLER, Notarii and exceptores, 1985. C.G.

Channe (χάννη, χάννα; *chánnē, chánna*). A fish of the perch family, perhaps the comber (*Serranus cabrilla*), according to Aristot. Hist. an. 8,13,598a 13 a saltwater fish that, according to 8,2,591a 10, was carnivorous. Ath. 7,327f emphasizes its large mouth, the black and red stripes as well as, in 8,355c, its tender flesh. As no males were known — the *channe* indeed is a hermaphrodite — it was thought that the female fertilized itself (Aristot. Hist. an. 4,11,538a 19; Plin. HN 9,56 and 32,153, according to Ov. Halieutica 108).

LEITNER, 82f. C.HÜ.

Chaones, Chaonia (Χάονες, Χαονία; *Cháones, Chaonía*). Important people to the north of Epirus, between the Aous and the Acroceraunia, opposite Corcyra (Str. 7,7,5; Ptol. 3,14,7). Although originally based on village settlements (Scyl. 28), in the 6th cent. BC C. contained the cities of → Buthrotum, → Onchesmus and → Phoenice (main centre), and later Chimera and → Antigonea [4]. Mentioned in connection with the Peloponnesian and Macedonian Wars: Thuc. 2,80f.; Liv. 32,5; 43,23. Inscriptions: SEG 15, 397; 24, 448; 38, 468; 38, 470; IG IV² 95 l. 29; IG IX 1², 2, 243.

F. PRENDI, La Chaonie préhistorique et ses rapports avec les régions de l'Illyrie du Sud, in: P. CABANES (ed.), L'Illyrie méridionale et l'Épire dans l'antiquité 2, 1993, 17-28; N. G. L. HAMMOND, Epirus, 1967. D.S.

Chaos (Χάος; *Cháos*). It is with chaos, presumably a derivative of χαίνω/χάσκω (*chaínō/cháskō*; 'to gape'), with the meaning 'hole', 'gaping fissure' (Aristot. Ph. 208b 25ff.: 'empty space'), as that which is no further reducible but nevertheless exists, that Hes. Theog. 116 and 123 ushers in the creation of the world. Chaos is the abyss, to be closed by heaven and earth [1. 12], and replaces the dualism contained in the Akkadian concept of the original state (sea not yet separated from ground water) and in Philo's reworking of a Phoenician cosmogony (FGrH 790 F2: a dark firmament and dim chaos) [2. 391-7]. From it emerge Nyx and Erebus, personifications of the dark, together with their offspring, differentiated by Hesiod from those of Gaia, who arises independently of chaos. Chaos subsists beyond the term of its cosmogonic function (Theog. 700; 814), and then denotes a region difficult to define [3. 34-43]. According to the Orphics, chaos and → Aether arise together out of → Chronos [3. 26-8]. A material conception in part links chaos with χέω (*chéō*; 'to pour') in the following interpretations: a) air-filled space (Bacchyl. 5,27, Schol. Hes. Theog. 116), b) water (Pherecydes fr. 1a DIELS/KRANZ vol. 2 (1985), vol. 3 (1993); Zen. fr. 679 HÜLSER) and c) *rudis indigestaque moles* (Ov. Met. 1,7), whence is formed our modern conception of chaos [4. 132-4].

1 W. BURKERT, in: M. MÜNZEL (ed.), Ursprung, 1987 2 U. HÖLSCHER, Anaximander, H 81, 1953 3 G. S. KIRK, J. E. RAVEN, M. SCHOFIELD, The Presocratic Philosophers, ²1983 4 G. MAURACH, Ovids Kosmogonie, in: Gymnasium 86, 1979, 131-148.

L.A. Cordo, ΧΑΟΣ,1989. G.A.C.

Characene Term derived from the city of Charax (→ Charax Spasinou), and describing the territory at the confluence of the Euphrates and the Tigris and on the northern margin of the Persian Gulf (Plin. HN 6,136, on → Susiana; Ptol. Geogr. 6,3,3, on → Elymaeis); as a geographical term roughly corresponding to → Mesene (original form in oriental sources: *Maišan*), although the exact relationship between the two terms is unknown. Once power had passed from the Seleucids to the Parthians (141 BC), the local rulers were able to establish and assert themselves as vassal kings on the Parthians' behalf. Founder of the dynasty was Hyspaosines, of Iranian origin judging by his name, and at first appointed administrator of the Seleucid eparchy on the Red Sea by Antiochus IV (166/165 BC). He was briefly able to extend his rule as far as Babylon (127 BC attested as ruler in cuneiform texts from there). Twenty-three rulers can be identified up to the end of the Parthian period (mostly with Iranian or Babylonian/ Aramaic names); the last of them, Abinergaos III, falling in AD 222 to the Sassanid → Ardashir [1] I. The most important source is the various mintings of coins, which had wide currency, having also been found outside the territory (e.g. in Susa). In disputes between the Parthians and Rome C. repeatedly came down on the side of Rome. The wealth of the region rested on its maritime position, affording the port of Charax Spasinou a key trading position between the Middle East and the Orient (India). The most famous individual from C. is the geographical writer → Isidorus of Charax (late 1st cent. AD).

→ Bilingual inscriptions; → Charax Spasinou; → Mesene

S. A. NODELMAN, A Preliminary History of Characene, in: Berytus 13, 1959/60, 83–123; G. LE RIDER, Mémoires de Mission Archéologique en Iran 38, 1965. J.OE.

Characteres see → Magic

Charadra (χαράδρα; *charádra*). Generic Greek term for non-perennial streams or rivers, or deeply eroded valleys and gorges (Italian *torrente*, Modern Greek *rhevma*) [1]. Attic inscriptions of the → Poletai, especially mining leases, mention many *charadrai* [2].
[1] Major river in northern Attica, springing from the north-eastern foot of the Parnes and flowing into the plain of Marathon; also called the Marathon stream or the Oenoe [3; 4]. Proverbial in referring to troubles brought upon oneself, as a large-scale plan to tame the stream came to nothing: Suda, Hsch., Phot. s.v. Οἰναῖοι (Οἰνόη) τὴν χαράδραν.

1 Agora 19, 1991, 245, index s.v. Charadra   2 LSJ, s.v. Charadra, 1976   3 A. MILCHHOEFER, explanatory text, in: E. CURTIUS, J. A. KAUPERT (ed.), Karten von Attika 9, 1990, Index s.v. Charadra   4 PHILIPPSON/KIRSTEN 1, 784f., 787. II.LO.

[2] City on the summit of a hill in eastern Phocis, *c.* 20 stadia from Lilaea (Paus. 10,33,6); named after the Charadrus, a tributary of the Cephissus, which flows *c.* 4 km to the north of C. C. was one of the Phocian cities pillaged by the Persians (480 BC) and later (346 BC) destroyed by Philip II (Hdt. 8,33; Paus. 10,3,3). Its exact location is still a subject for debate — between Mariolata [2. 4], Ano-Suvala [1. 3] and Erochos [5]. Remains of walls (5th–4th cents. BC).
→ Phocis; → Lilaea

1 C. BURSIAN, Geogr. von Griechenland 1, 1892, 161   2 J. G. FRAZER, Pausanias' Description of Greece, ²5, 1913, 415–418   3 W. M. LEAKE, Travels in Northern Greece 2, 1835, 69, 71, 86   4 MÜLLER, 460   5 L. B. TILLARD, The Fortifications of Phokis, in: ABSA 17, 1910, 54–75.

BUCKLER, s.v. Charadra., RE 3, 2114; MÜLLER, 460; PAPACHATZIS 5, 428–429; A. PHILIPPSON, s.v. Erochos, RE 6, 482–483; F. SCHOBER, Phokis, 1924, 26; TIB I 137 (s.v. Boion). G.D.R.

[3] Town on the east coast of the gulf of Messenia, near Thalamae (Str. 8,4,4); not located. Y.L.

Charadrios (χαραδριός; *charadriós*). A water bird, perhaps a shearwater, nesting in holes in the ground and in cliffs, and seldom seen by day (Aristoph. Av. 266). It was held to be gluttonous (Aristoph. Av. 1140f.), of ugly colour and cry (Ps.-Aristot. Hist. An. 9,11, 615a1–3), and said to be white (9,3,593b 17; Pl. Grg. 494 b). Sight of it was supposed to heal jaundice, and accordingly it was sold covered (Ael. NA 17,13; Plut. Symp. 5,7,2; Heliodor 3,8 i.a.). In Plin. HN 30,94 it is called *avis icterus* or *galgulus*, owing to its yellow colour. In the Greek Physiologus (c. 3) and in Latin and colloquial versions of it, the gaze of the charadrius, when shown to an invalid, indicates whether or not the patient will recover. It is in this way that the *caladrius*, thought by many to be the plover, found its way into medieval encyclopaedias of natural history (e.g. Thomas of Cantimpré, 5,24).
→ Birds

KELLER 2, 179f.   F. MCCULLOCH, Mediaeval Latin and French Bestiaries, 1960, 99ff.   Thomas Cantimpratensis, Liber de natura rerum, ed. H. BOESE, 1973. C.HÜ.

Charadrus (Χάραδρος; *Cháradros*).
A. TOWNS   B. RIVERS

A. TOWNS
[1] Town in southern Epirus, from 167 BC independent of the Epirote *koinon*. By means of a border agreement (SEG 35, 665; *c.* 160 BC) located to the north-west of → Ambracia, near the modern Palaia-Philippias; Pol. 4,63; 21,26.

BCH 112, 1988, 359–373; V. KARATZENI, Τὸ ἱερὸν ὄρος, in: FS Dakaris, 1995, 289–299. D.S.

[2] Port and river (FGrH 1 Hecat. fr. 265) in Cilicia Tracheia, the modern Yakacık (previously Kalediran), 25 km to the west of Anemourion. A polis in the 4th cent. BC (Scyl. 102); during the 2nd half of the 3rd cent. BC a Ptolemaic garrison under a *hegemon* (inscription: [3]); later insignificant (Str. 14,5,3: ἔρυμα (*éryma*); stadiasmus maris magni 199: χωρίον (*chōríon*); IGR 3, 838: ἐ[πί]ν(ε)ιον Λαμωτῶν (*e[pí]n(e)ion Lamōtôn*). Mid–5th cent. diocese [2]. No remains worthy of mention.

1 G. BEAN, T. B. MITFORD, Journeys in Rough Cilicia 1962 and 1963, 1965, 42f.   2 H. HELLENKEMPER, F. HILD, Kilikien und Isaurien (TIB 5), 1990, s.v. C.   3 AJA 1961, 135 no. 35. K.T.

B. RIVERS
Generic see → Charadra.
[3] Coastal river of Achaea, north of Patrae (Paus. 7,22,11). [1; 2].
[4] Stream in northern Messenia; tributary of the Amphitus near Andania (Paus. 4,33,5).
[5] Stream in eastern Phocis below → Charadra [2] (Paus. 10,33,6).
[6] *Rhevma* in Argive Cynuria (Stat. Theb. 4,46).
[7] *Rhevma* in the plain of Argos, skirting to the north around Argos; the modern Xerias (Thuc. 5,60; Paus. 2,25,2).

1 L. BÜRCHNER, s.v. Charadros 2, RE 3,2, 2115
2 Παυσανίου Ἑλλάδος Περιήγησις. Βιβλία 7 καὶ 8. Ἀχαϊκὰ
καὶ Ἀρκαδικά, 1980, 136 n. 3   3 L. BÜRCHNER, s.v. Charadros 3, RE 3,2, 2116   4 O. KERN, s.v. Charadros 3, RE
Suppl. 3, 243   5 Παυσανίου Ἑλλάδος Περιήγησις. Βιβλία
4, 5 καὶ 6. Μεσσηνικὰ καὶ Ἡλιακά, 1979, 146 note 3
6 L. BÜRCHNER, s.v. Charadros 1, RE 3,1, 2116   7 Id.,
s.v. Charadros 4, RE 3,1, 2116   8 Id., s.v. Charadros 5,
RE 3,1, 2116   9 Παυσανίου Ἑλλάδος Περιήγησις. Βιβλία
2 καὶ 3. Κορινθιακὰ καὶ Λακωνικά, 1976, 185 note 2.

H.LO.

Charax (Χάραξ; *Chárax*). A. Claudius C. from Pergamum; Greek historian. He lived during the 2nd cent.
AD under Hadrian, Antoninus Pius and Marcus Aurelius, was a priest and in AD 147 consul. C. wrote a
universal history in 40 books, covering especially Greek
and — from book 12 — Roman history up to the period
of 'Nero and his successors' (Suda s.v. = T 1). The work
was later summarized and used by Stephanus of Byzantium under the title *Chroniká*. The fragments relate
mostly to mythological times, as it was mainly for his
euhemeristic and allegorical interpretation of the myths
that the Byzantines drew on C. FGrH 103 (comm. and
add. to 2 AB in 3 B, 741f.). (PIR 2, 189).

J. and L. ROBERT, Bulletin épigraphique, REG 74, 1961,
215f.   K.MEI.

Charax Spasin(o)u Important mercantile centre in
southernmost Mesopotamia, and capital of → Characene; now convincingly located near Ğabal Ḫayabir,
between Qurna and Forat [1]. Charax Spasinou (CS) is
regarded as a re-foundation of → Alexandria [4], a city
established on the Persian Gulf by Alexander the Great
(cf. [2. 1390–1395]), renovated by Antiochus IV in
166/165 and renamed Antioch [3. 2445]. The source of
the name is the Aramaic *karkā* 'fortified settlement'; the
epithet Spasinou derives from the first ruler of the local
dynasty, Hyspaosines (from c. 140 BC, died between?
... and 109/8). CS fulfilled an important function as an
entrepôt in the eastern trade and probably also a centre
for the pearl trade. As attested by inscriptions, even the
Palmyrenes had a permanent settlement there. A *Karh
Maisan*, said to have been founded by the Sassanid
Ardashir I, is mentioned in an Arabian inscription (safely to be identified with CS).

1 J. HANSMAN, in: IA 7, 1967, 21–58   2 F.C. ANDREAS,
s.v. Alexandreia 13), RE 1, 1390–1395   3 S. FRAENKEL,
s.v. Antiocheia 10), RE 1, 2445.   J.OE.

Charcoal Alongside → wood, charcoal (ἄνθραξ; *án-
thrax, carbo*) was the most commonly used fuel in antiquity; already known in Egypt and Mesopotamia, it
was produced from selected woods (Theophr. Hist. pl.
5,9,1ff.: oak, walnut, pine, spruce) by a controlled
reduction process (wood: 50 % carbon; charcoal: 80–
90 %), resulting in an appreciable increase in calorific
value (29,000 in contrast to 16,500 kJ/kg in wood).

Charcoal was produced in kilns (κάμινος; *káminos,
calyx*) constructed from straight, tightly packed timber
taken from the trunk of the tree, which was then covered with an airtight layer of earth (Theophr. Hist. pl.
5,9,4; 9,3,1f.; Plin. HN 16,23) so as to prevent the kiln
itself from burning away. The production of tar by setting spruce trunks to smoulder was technically very
similar to this (Plin. HN 16,52f.). The carbonization
process led to a clear reduction in weight, thus facilitating the transport of the charcoal. Several distinct
types of charcoal were known of in antiquity, whose
varying degrees of quality depended on the wood used.
The best charcoal came from trees of dense and solid
wood, which were still in full sap when felled. Old trees
were regarded as unsuitable for the production of charcoal. Charcoal made from walnut was preferred for the
working of → iron, spruce for that of silver (Theophr.
Hist. pl. 5,9,1ff.).

Charcoal was indispensable for many technological
purposes, as for example the production and processing
of metal (→ Metallurgy); but also in coin production.
To a lesser extent it was used for heating (charcoal bra-
ziers) and cult purposes: as an offertory flame going out
would have been of ominous significance, charcoal for
this purpose was carefully selected (Plin. HN 16,24).
For Delos there survives data regarding the purchase of
charcoal for cult ceremonies (IDélos 287; 338; 372;
442); some 100 drachma were spent for this purpose
every year.

In late antiquity the transport of charcoal was a
high-priority task, imposed on landowners as a *munus*
(lesser public obligation) (Cod. Theod. 11,16,15;
11,16,18; from AD 382 and 390 respectively). In the
case of charcoal intended for coinage purposes or weapon production, no excuse (*excusatio*) from this duty
was allowed (Cod. Theod. 11,16,18: *carbonis ab eo
inlatio non cogetur nisi vel monetalis cusio vel antiquo
more necessaria fabricatio poscit armorum*; i.e. provision of charcoal should not be enforced, unless that was
required for the minting of coins or the necessary manufacture of weapons). It is not certain whether this charcoal was provided as taxation in kind or produced by
direct public contract.

→ Fuels

1 BLÜMNER, Techn. 2, 347–356   2 MEIGGS, 451ff.
P.H.

Chares (Χάρης; *Chárēs*).
[1] Athenian *strategos* of the 4th cent. BC. In 367/6 he
supported Phleius when it was hard-pressed by Argos
and Sicyon. The aid he gave to the oligarchs on Corcyra
led to that island's leaving the 2nd Athenian League,
and brought Athens discredit among its confederates.
Not re-elected as *strategos* until 357/6. The treaty between Athens and the Thracian kings → Berisades,
Amadocus I and Cersobleptes under C. in 357 both
confirmed the division of Thracian rule and established
Athenian possession of the Chersonesus. During the

Social War in 357, C. fought unsuccessfully before Chios, but in 356/5 was again elected *strategos*, and with the *strategoi* Iphicrates, Menestheus and Timotheus relieved Samos, which was being besieged by Chians, Rhodians and Byzantines. On his own authority he joined battle at Embata against the disaffected confederates, was beaten, and blamed his fellow generals, who were ordered home and prosecuted on the strength of C.' report. In order to pay his troops, C. allied himself with the rebellious satrap → Artabazus. As an Athenian *strategos*, in 354/3 C. defeated a Macedonian mercenary army, and in 353/2 regained Sestus. In response to Demosthenes' repeated warnings, in 348 an Athenian citizen army under C.' command was sent to Olynthus, but was too late to prevent Philip II from taking the town. Between 347/6 and 339/8 C. frequently fought as *strategos* in the northern Aegean against Philip II, and in 338 was defeated at Amphissa. In 337 as *strategos* he took part in the battle of Chaeronea. After the conquest of Thebes (335) he fled from Athens before Alexander the Great, and surrendered to him at Ilium in 333; he then entered Persian service, but in 332 in Mytilene capitulated before the Macedonians in return for free passage. He seems to have died around 324.

J. CARGILL, The Second Athenian League, 1981, 172–176; 181; DAVIES, 568f.; R.A. MOYSEY, Chares and Athenian Foreign Policy, in: CJ 80, 1984, 221–227; R.W. PARKER, Chares Angelethen. Biography of a Fourth-Century Athenian Strategos, 1986; J.T. ROBERTS, Chares, Lysicles and the Battle of Chaeronea, in: Klio 64, 1982, 367–371; W.K. PRITCHETT, The Greek State at War, 2, 1974, 77–85. W.S.

[2] From Mytilene; at least from 327 BC under → Alexander [4] he was entrusted after the Persian manner with the conduct of audiences, and after Alexander's death wrote a book entitled 'Stories of Alexander', in which he recounted anecdotes from life at court and also on campaign, as e.g. the → *proskynesis* dispute, the marriages at Susa, the death of → Calanus. He usually emphasizes luxury, feasts and drinking, but the extracts in → Athenaeus [3] also offer items of natural history. Some interesting incidents in his stories may be unrestrained inventions (e.g. the single combat between Alexander and → Darius at the battle of Issus: F 6). He is to be regarded as an anecdotalist, not a historian (FGrH 2B, no. 125).

BERVE 2, no. 820; L. PEARSON, The Lost Histories of Alexander the Great, 1960, 50–61. E.B.

[3] Late 4th or early 5th cent. BC; wrote aphorisms in iambic trimeters of two to four verses in length, showing the influence of Euripides and of 4th cent. philosophy. Fifty lines in an early Ptolemaic papyrus [1] can be identified by means of corresponding extracts in Stobaeus (3,17,3 or TGF 826; further examples 3,33,4 and 3,38,3) and in Lydus (Mens. 4,113).

1 G.A. GERHARD, in: SHAW 1912,13 (ed.)

EDITIONS: Pap. Heidelberg 434 (early Ptolemaic); J.U. POWELL, CollAlex 223.
BIBLIOGRAPHY: U.v. WILAMOWITZ, Lesefrüchte, in: Hermes 34, 1899, 608–9; R.PHILIPPSON, in: PhW 34, 1914,801–2; O. HENSE, Chares und Verwandtes, in: RhM 72, 1917/18, 14–24. E.BO.

[4] Sculptor in bronze from Lindos; pupil of → Lysippus; in 304–293 BC created the 'Colossus of Rhodes', a 32-m-high bronze statue of Helios, regarded as one of the → Wonders of the World. It was destroyed in 228 BC by an earthquake. A Byzantine account of its re-erection by Hadrian is implausible, and its reconstruction astride the harbour as an access for ships is incorrect. An Apollo/Helios statue from Civitavecchia gives some impression of the statue. In 57 BC a colossal bronze head by C. was displayed on the Capitol in Rome.

P.MORENO, Scultura ellenistica, 1994, 126–148 fig.; OVERBECK, nos.1516, 1539, 1556 (sources); L. TODISCO, Scultura greca del IV secolo, 1993, 141f. R.N.

[5] Late Corinthian vase painter from around 560/550 BC. His modest pyxis, showing a horseback fight between Greeks and Trojans (names given) and one of the three painters' signatures from Corinth, is in the Louvre: χάρες μ'ἔγραψε (*Cháres m'égrapse*).

AMYX, CVP 255f. 569f.; AMYX, Addenda 76. LIMC 6, 451, s.v. Memnon no. 10a. M.ST.

[6] Greek grammarian; school of Apollonius [2] of Rhodes, therefore probably lived between the 3rd and 2nd cents. BC. A book entitled Περὶ ἱστοριῶν τοῦ Ἀπολλωνίου 'On Stories of Apollonius') is attributed to him in the Schol. Apoll. Rhod. 2,1053 (cf. also Schol. Apoll. Rhod. 4,1470). It is uncertain whether the C. mentioned in Photius, Suda (η 100 ADLER) and EM (416,36 s.v. ἦ δ' ὅς) can be identified with him. In the sources he may be confused with → Chaeris (Χαῖρις), so attribution of a Περὶ γραμματικῆς is uncertain (Sext. Emp. Adversus Mathematicos 1,76).

→ Apollonius [2] Rhodius; → Chaeris; → Sextus Empiricus

EDITIONS: R.BERNDT, De Charete, Chaeride, Alexione grammaticis eorumque reliquiis, 1902, I 3–18, 18–31
BIBLIOGRAPHY: A.BLAU, De Aristarchi discipulis, 1883, 65–67; L. COHN, s.v. Chares, RE 3, 2130; A.LUDWICH, Die Formel ἦ δ' ὅς, in: RhM 41, 1886, 437–453. F.M.

Chariboea see → Porcis

Charicles (Χαρικλῆς; *Chariklês*).
[1] Athenian from the phyle of Oeneis; son of Apollodorus. As a democrat in 415 BC he investigated the Mutilation of the Herms with Peisander (Andoc. 1,36), and in 414/13 was *strategos* in the Peloponnesian campaign (Thuc. 7,20;26; Diod. Sic. 13,9,2). However, in 411 he followed Peisander over to the 'Four hundred' (Lys. 13,73f.). In 404 played a significant role in the oligarchy of the 'Thirty' (Xen. Hell. 2,3,2; Mem.

1,2,31; Andoc. 1,101; Aristot. Pol. 1305b26); exiled in 403, later to return (Isoc. Or. 16,42; PA 15407).

DAVIES, 13479; P. M. FRASER, E. MATTHEWS, A Lexicon of Greek personal names, vol. 2, 1994, 475, no. 5; A. W. GOMME, Historical Commentary on Thucydides 4, 1983, 396; P. KRENTZ, The thirty at Athens, 1982. K. KI.

[2] Athenian; son-in-law of → Phocion. In 324 BC accused of accepting bribes in the Harpalus affair (Plut. Phocion 21f.). In 319, shortly after fleeing Athens, sentenced to death in his absence together with Phocion (ibid. 34f.).

A. TRITLE, Phocion the Good, 1988, 119, 121. W.S.

Chariclides Writer of comedies in the 3rd cent. BC (cf. the not entirely compelling epigraphical evidence [1. test.]), of which the sole surviving fragment consists of a — textually uncertain — invocation of Hecate in *versus paroemiaci* (from *Halysis*, 'The Chain', 'The Magical Bond'?).

1 PCG IV, 1983, 70f. H.-G.NE.

Chariclo (Χαρικλώ; *Chariklṓ*).
[1] Naiad; wife of → Chiron; daughter of Apollo, Perseus or Oceanus; mother of Carystus (Hes. Cat. fr. 42; Schol. Pind. Pyth. 4,182 DRACHMANN). Always depicted near to Chiron, also i.a. as a member of Peleus' and Thetis' marriage procession.
[2] Nymph; wife of Eueres. According to Pherecydes, being a favourite of Athena she obtains for her son → Teiresias, blinded by Athena, a staff and the gift of understanding the songs of birds (Apollod. 3,70; Callim. H. 5,59).

U. FINSTER-HOTZ, s.v. Chariklo I, LIMC 3.1, 189–191; F. CANCIANI, s.v. Chariklo II, LIMC 3.1, 191. R.B.

Charidemus (Χαρίδημος; *Charídēmos*).
[1] Member of an Athenian delegation which in 359 BC requested the help of Philip II in taking Amphipolis (Theopomp. FGrH 115 F 30a). W.S.
[2] Mercenary leader from Oreos. Main source Dem. Or. 23, especially 144ff. In 360 C. entered the service of the Thracian King → Cotys I, whose daughter he married. After Cotys' death he endeavoured to establish the minor → Cersobleptes as ruler of Thrace. Upon the intervention of Athens in 357, however, Cersobleptes was obliged to allow the Odrysian realm to be divided, and the Chersonesus ceded to Athens (IG II² 126; StV 303). In return, C. was granted Athenian citizenship and other honours. In 353/2 C. had an application made to the Athenians to elect him as *strategos*. Euthycles petitioned against his request for conferment of special protective rights (Dem. Or. 23). In 351 C. operated as an Athenian *strategos* in the Chersonesus against Philip of Macedonia. He was elected *strategos* after the battle of Chaeronea (338), but in 335 Alex-

ander demanded his extradition. C. fled to Darius III, who had him executed for excessively candid criticism.

DAVIES, 570–572; D. H. KELLY, Charidemos' citizenship, in: ZPE 83, 1990, 96–109; M. J. OSBORNE, Naturalization in Athens, 3, 1983, 56–58 W.S.

Charillus (Χάριλλος; *Chárillos*, in Hdt. 8,131 Χαρίλαος; *Charílaos*). Historically uncertain Spartan king, Eurypontid; according to Sosibius (FGrH 595 F 2), ruled 874–811 BC and with King Archelaus conquered the perioikic city of Aegys (Paus. 3,2,5), but defeated by the Tegeans (Paus. 8,5,9). This data arises from constructions based on legend. K.-W.W.

Charinus (Χαρῖνος; *Charînos*).
[1] In 433/32 BC, in accordance with the wishes of Pericles, proposed a statute of eternal hatred and active enmity towards Megara, owing to the murder of a herald (Plut. Pericles 30,3; Mor. 812C-D; PA 15434).

DEVELIN 101; P. M. FRASER, E. MATTHEWS, A Lexicon of Greek personal names, vol. 2, 1994, 475, no. 4.

[2] Athenian friendly towards Macedonia, c. 340 BC (Dem. Or. 58,37f.; Din. 1,63; PA 15437).

P. M. FRASER, E. MATTHEWS, A Lexicon of Greek personal names, vol. 2, 1994, 475, no. 9 (?=53); I. WORTHINGTON, Historical commentary on Dinarchus, 1992. K. KI.

[3] A choliambic poem by C. is quoted by Ptolemaeus Chennus (in Phot. Bibl. Cod. 190, p. 71/72, 5–13 HENRY). Apparently C., enamoured of Eros, cup-bearer to (Mithridates) Eupator, sought relief by throwing himself from the Leucadian rock [1]. Mortally wounded, he uttered four choliambs abusing the Leucadian rock as a deceiver and cursing Eupator himself. The story is dubious, and nothing excludes a late-Hellenic origin for the verses.

1 K.-H. TOMBERG, Die Kaine Historia des Ptolemaios Chennos, 1968, 147–151.

A. D. KNOX, Cercidas and the Choliambic Poets, in: J. RUSTEN, J. C. CUNNINGHAM, A. D. KNOX (ed.), Theophrastus: Characters. Herod. Mimes. Cercidas ... (Loeb Classical Library 225), 1993, 490f.; SH fr. 313. W.D.F.

Charisius (Χαρίσιος; *Charísios*).
[I] Attic orator at the end of the 4th cent. BC; contemporary of Demetrius of Phalerum, Demochares and Menander. He was active as a → logographer, and imitated → Lysias (Cic. Brut. 286). Speeches by him were still extant at the time of Quintilian, at that time being ascribed by many to → Menander (Quint. Inst. 10,1,70). Only three passages have survived, in Latin translation in Rutilius Lupus (1,10; 2,6; 2,16).

BLASS, 3,2, 351f. M.W.

[II]

[1] C., Aurelius Arcadius. Jurist, probably of eastern origin; *magister libellorum* under Diocletian [2. 69ff.]; wrote 'monographs' on process law (*De testibus*) and administrative law (*De officio praefecti praetorio*, *De muneris civilibus*; on both works [1]). PLRE I, 200f.

1 F. GRELLE, Arcadio Carisio, in: Index 15, 1987, 63–77
2 D. LIEBS, Recht und Rechtslit., in: HLL V.   T.G.

[2] Presbyter and *diákonos* in Philadelphia (Lydia). At the ecumenical council in Ephesus in 431 he reports on a creed of Nestorian stamp originating in Constantinople, and in contrasting it with his own effectively rejects it.

C. J. v. HEFELE, Conciliengesch., ²1873, 2, 206f.   R.B.

[3] C., Flavius Sosipater. Latin grammarian who in *c.* 362 in Constantinople wrote an *Ars grammatica*, which has not survived in its entirety. Its contents can be reconstructed on the basis of the index (p. 1–3 BARWICK). Book 1: basic concepts and inflection of nouns; book 2: amplification of basic concepts and parts of speech; book 3: conjugations; book 4 (largely lost): style and metre; book 5: idioms (lists of forms, combinations of words, sentence structures, compared with the Greek). The *Synonyma Ciceronis* (p. 412–449 BARWICK) and the *Differentiae* (p. 387–403 BARWICK) at least cannot be directly attributed to C. (counter-argument in [1]). The work is on the whole unoriginal: there are passages taken straight from → Cominianus, → Remmius Palaemon and → Iulius Romanus (possibly also → Flavius Caper i.a.). The text of *Ars* in MS Neapolitanus 4.A.8 (followed in [1]) represents an abridged version. It may have influenced → Diomedes, → Rufinus and → Priscianus, and was presumably used by compilers of bilingual glossaries such as Ps.-Philoxenus and Ps.-Cyrillus.

Another version under the name of Cominianus (or Flavianus) developed from the 5th cent.; it is to be located in the Anglo-Saxon world, whence it directly influenced many collections: Malsacanus, Anonymus ad Cuimnanum, Ars Ambrosiana, Clemens Scotus i.a. An abridged edition of this *Cominianus* is used by Bonifatius; traces of it may also be found in continental Europe: in the Hofbibliothek, Aachen, and also in southern Italy.

EDITIONS: 1 K. BARWICK, 1925 (²1964) GL 1,1–296.
BIBLIOGRAPHY: HLL § 523,2.   P.G.

Charites (Graces) (Χάριτες; *Chárites*). Group of goddesses who embody beauty, happiness and abundance. They appear for the first time in Homer, where their number, like that of the Muses is ambiguous; it is however clear that more than one existed and that not all were of the same age. Hera promises Hypnos that she will give him as his wife Pasithee, one of the younger Charites, whom he desires (Hom. Il. 14,267–276). In Il. 18,382f. one Charis is also the wife of Hephaestus, who is actually married to Aphrodite in the Odyssey. Remarkably, Hera is obviously not jealous of these illegitimate children of her husband, indeed she even agrees that one of them should marry her own son; according to Hes. Theog. 945f. (although it is uncertain to whom this passage should be attributed) this is Aglaea, the youngest of the Charites. Hesiod (Theog. 907–909) gives them a genealogy as with the Muses: they are daughters of Zeus and the daughter of Oceanus, Eurynome; they are called Aglaea, Euphrosyne and Thalia (also called ἱερατεινή/*hierateinḗ*). They live with Himerus on Olympus beside the Muses (Hes. Theog. 64) and they assisted with the creation of → Pandora (Hes. Op. 73).

The Charites became proverbial models of feminine grace, talent and beauty: praiseworthy maidens possess Χαρίτων ἀμαρύγματα (*Charítōn amarýgmata*) or κάλλος (*kállos*) [1]. The names of the Charites are abstract qualities in contrast to those of the Muses, so it is harder to view the Charites as individuals. But whilst the Muses make no secret of their contempt for humans (Hes. Theog. 26), the Charites (even if Theog. 910f. are not authentic) are benevolent. The Charites also belong to a younger generation; whilst the Muses are the daughters of a Titaness, the Charites are granddaughters of a Titan. Modern researchers associate the Charites with the Horae that represent natural forces, but the Charites represent the effects of the human spirit (e.g., [2]).

In the practice of the cult, the Charites of Orchomenus are the best known (Hes. fr. 71 MW; Pind. Ol. 14); possibly their triune nature arose in this region as people connected the name with a triad of local goddesses [3. 141]. According to Paus. 9.38,1, these Charites were worshipped in the form of meteorites. It is difficult to ascertain the age of this custom. The inhabitants of Orchomenus celebrated the Charitesia in honour of the Charites. Evidence of this exists only from the 1st and possibly the 2nd cent. BC. They were primarily musical and dramatic, and direct evidence of this can be seen from three lists of victors (IG VII 3195–3197); there was however also an athletic element to their nature (IG II/III 3160). The agon was very probably organized in imitation of and in competition with the much better-known Museia of Thespiae ([3. 142–144]; cf. also the tradition which located Hesiod's grave in Orchomenus [4]).

Charites — but clearly without a link with those of Orchomenus — were also venerated in other places. The Spartans and Athenians each venerated two: Clete and Phaenna in Sparta (Paus. 9,35,1), Auxo and Hegemone in Athens (Paus. 9,35,2). Elsewhere they appeared as a group, without specific names (e.g., LSCG, Suppl. 10A81; 25E45; LSAM 20,11; LSCG 1A13f.; 4,3; 114B1; 151D5, cf. [5]). It is impossible to define their exact role as goddesses in these places.

1 M. L. WEST, ed. & comm., Hesiod, Works and Days, 1978, 73   2 E. B. HARRISON, LIMC 3.1, 191–203   3 SCHACHTER   4 R. SCODEL, Hesiod redivivus, in: GRBS 21, 1980, 301–320   5 FARNELL, Cults, Bd. 5, 462–464.

M. ROCCHI, Contributi allo studio delle Ch. I, in: Studii Classice 18, 1979, 5–16; II, 19, 1980, 19–28   A.S.

Chariton (Χαρίτων; *Charítōn*).
A. LIFE   B. THE NOVEL   C. RECEPTION

A. LIFE

We have no direct information about the author of the earliest complete surviving novel, beyond that given by him at the beginning of the book; there he presents himself as secretary to the orator Athenagoras, originating from Aphrodisias in Caria. It has been conjectured that all these details, including the name Chariton, were invented in order to establish a symbolic link to the theme of love and to the setting (on the Syracusan Athenagoras cf. Thuc. 6,35); but both personal names are epigraphically attested in Aphrodisias. ROHDE, who regarded the simplicity of style as a rhetorical effect, dated C. to the 5th cent. AD [1]; newly discovered papyri caused the date to be put back at least five cents.; a still earlier date, in the 1st cent. BC, has been suggested on linguistic grounds [2]. Perhaps the not overly kind reference in Persius (*post prandia Callirhoen do*,) represents the *terminus ante quem*: *Callirhoe* being the original title of the work, as this explicitly confirms; but from the Byzantine period the title 'Chaireas and Callirhoe' predominated.

B. THE NOVEL

Beginning with his *incipit* in imitation of Thucydides, C. endeavours to give the impression of an historiographical work; as with the Parthenope novel (which, along with the → Chione novel, is perhaps to be attributed to the same C.) the action is placed in the 5th cent. BC; historical figures appear, such as the Syracusan *strategos* Hermocrates, famous for his victory over the Athenians, and the Persian King Artaxerxes II Mnemon; the lengthy account of the Egyptian uprising, keeping closely to the actual uprising of 389–387 BC led by the Athenian Chabrias (Chaereas is perhaps a play on his name), and the summaries at the beginning of the book, reminiscent of Xenophon's *Anabasis*, also lend the work a pseudo-historical air. But, as is shown by various anachronisms, (especially the discrepancy between the life of Hermocrates and the reign of Artaxerxes), the historical element serves only as background, lending a lofty air to a work of private and sentimental character. *Callirhoe* and *Parthenope* in effect correspond to the historical novel à la Walter Scott [3]. The story begins with the 'Romeo and Juliet' motif (the children of two rival families fall in love with each other); the impediment is, however, immediately set aside because of a plebiscite, and, as in Xenophon of Ephesus, the marriage of the two protagonists takes place at the very beginning of the book. The action is set in motion by the apparent death of Callirhoe, caused by a kick from the jealous Chaereas; after being abducted by brigands and sold in Miletus, Callirhoe eventually consents to marriage with the noble Dionysius, but only

for the sake of the child she is expecting by Chaereas (I–III). The story then turns to the parallel adventures of Chaereas, who is searching for his wife in Miletus and the whole of Caria, where he is the slave of the satrap Mithridates, himself also in love with Callirhoe (III–V). Midway through the novel the action moves to Babylon, where the lengthy process of the dramatic 'resurrection' of Chaereas takes place (VI); this is at first interrupted by the king's falling in love (VII); then a war prevents its continuation (VII), and finally leads to the couple's reunion and their return to Syracuse (VIII).

Like Xenophon of Ephesus, C., too, makes use of a narrator who, while external and all-knowing, frequently identifies with the subjective viewpoint of the characters (for example when Callirhoe rises from the grave [4]), and often comments on the story in the first person: as when, interestingly, he addresses himself to the reader (8,1,4) and anticipates the happy ending in Aristotelian terms [5]. From a thematic point of view too, 'Chaereas and Callirhoe' is distinguished by rich psychological character portrayal, e.g. that of the female protagonist and the rival lover Dionysius, with whom the text displays distinct if suppressed sympathy (cf. the letter in 8,4,5). In the portrayal of his characters C. uses many dramatic techniques; the part played by direct speech, set pieces and monologues is considerable (noteworthy is the way internal conflict is expressed in Callirhoe's monologues before her marriage to Dionysius). Among writers of romantic novels, C. comes closest to the Menippean *prosimetrum* technique of a → Lucianus or a → Petronius; his story is scattered with a great number of Homeric quotations, reinforcing the intertextual dialogue with the epic model [6].

C. RECEPTION

Like Xenophon of Ephesus, for cents. C. came down in only one MS; the *editio princeps* of 1750 by J. D'ORVILLE and the Latin translation by REISKE did not appear until after the great baroque renaissance of the Greek novel. However, C. GESNER has accepted the thesis of direct influence on a novella by Matteo Bandello via a reading of the Laurentian MS [7. 64–70].

→ Chione novel; → Novel; → Parthenope novel; → Xenophon of Ephesus; NOVEL

1 E. ROHDE, Der griech. Roman und seine Vorläufer, 1876   2 A.D. PAPANIKOLAU, Ch.-Studien, 1973   3 T. HÄGG, Callirhoe and Parthenope: The Beginnings of the Historical Novel, in: Classical Antiquity 6, 1987, 184–204   4 B.P. REARDON, Theme, Structure, and Narrative in Chariton, in: YClS 27, 1982, 1–27   5 A. RIJKSBARON, Ch. 8,1,4 und Arist. Poet. 1449b28, in: Philologus 128, 1984, 306–7   6 M. FUSILLO, Il testo nel testo. La citazione nel romanzo greco, in: Materiali e Discussioni per l'analisi dei testi classici 25, 1990, 27–48   7 C. GESNER, Shakespeare and the Greek Romance, 1970.

C.W. MÜLLER, Chariton von Aphrodisias und die Theorie des Romans in der Ant., in: A&A 22, 1976, 115–136;
B.E. PERRY, Chariton and His Romance from a Literary-Historical Point of View, in: AJPh 51, 1930, 93–134;
C. RUIZ MONTERO, Chariton von Aphrodisias. Ein Über-

blick, ANRW II 34.2, 1994, 1006–1054; G. SCHMELING, Chariton, 1974.   M.FU.

Charixenus (Χαρίξενος; *Charíxenos*).
[1] C. from Trichonium (Aetolia). In 288/7 BC, 281/0 and 270/69 *strategos* of the Aetolian League (IG IX² 5, 14, 54) [1. 267 note 4].
[2] Aetolian; son of Cydrion. In 260 BC hipparch (IG IX² 18,18); 255/4, 246/5, 241/0 and 234/3 *strategos* of the Aetolian League (IG IX² 3 B). In the latter role, in 246/5 he invited Greek cities to celebrate the newly organized festival of the → Soteria in Delphi [2. 435–447 no. 21–27]. In 241/0 he led an Aetolian campaign against the Achaeans and the Spartans (Pol. 4,34,9). He dedicated an equestrian statue in Delphi (IG IX² 181) and was honoured in Athens [1. 234f., 242f., 267; 2. 282, 330–334].
[3] *Archon* in Delphi 277/6 (SEG 15,337) [2. 263].
[4] Son of Proxenos; an Aetolian from Trichonium; *agōnothétēs* of the *soteria c.* 220 BC [2. 280, 479f. no. 64]. For C.' dates [1]–[4] [3. 215f.].

1 R. FLACELIÈRE, Les Aitoliens à Delphes, 1937
2 G. NACHTERGAEL, Les Galates en Grèce et les Sotéria de Delphes, 1977   3 W.B. DINSMOOR, The Archons of Athens in the Hellenistic Age, 1931.   W.S.

Charmadas (Χαρμάδας; *Charmádas* or Χαρμίδας; *Charmídas*). Lived *c.* 165– 91 BC (cf. Cic. De or. 2,360). Apollod. Chronica 119–130 DORANDI (= FGrH 244 F 59; subsequently Philod. Ind. Acad. 31,35–32,10) very probably relates to him: a pupil of Carneades, after founding his own school he returned to the Academy. In Sext. Emp. Pyrrhōneioi hypotypóseis 1,220 and Euseb. Praep. evang. 14,4,16 mentioned with Philo as founder of a 'Fourth Academy'. Probably most important as a teacher of rhetoric (cf. Cic. De or. 1,82–92) who nevertheless emphasized the pre-eminence of philosophy (Sext. Emp. Adversus mathematicos 2,20).
→ Academy; › Philo

W. GÖRLER, in: GGPh² 4.2, 1995, 906–908.   K.-H.S.

Charmides (Χαρμίδης; *Charmídēs*).
[1] Son of Glaucon, from an old Athenian noble family; brother of → Periktione the mother of Plato, and cousin of → Critias. C. was one of the committee of the 'Ten' appointed by the 'Thirty' and officiating in Piraeus during the despotic rule of the 'Thirty' (→ Triakonta; 404–403 BC); its powers are not precisely known (Plat. Ep. 7,324c5. Aristot. Ath. Pol. 35,1). He was killed in 403 during the fighting that accompanied the fall of the 'Thirty' (Xen. Hell. 2,4,19). During his youth C. belonged to the circle around Socrates. Plato's *Charmides* is named after him.
EDITION: SSR VI B 22–28.   K.D.

[2] Epicurean philosopher; friend of Arcesilaus (Cic. Fin. 5,94). The suggestion in [1. 151f.] that the name should be inserted into a passage in the book *De libertate dicendi* by Philodemus () should be rejected.

1 H. USENER, Epicurea, 1887.   T.D.

Charmion (Χάρμιον; *Chármion*). Maid to → Cleopatra VII; ascribed decisive political influence by the propaganda of Octavian; she died with the queen. PP 6, 14736.   W.A.

Charmis (Χάρμις; *Chármis*) Greek physician from Massilia, who went to Rome *c.* AD 55. Thanks to his cold-water cures he soon made a name there, and gained many wealthy patients (Plin. HN 29,10). For one treatment he invoiced a patient from the provinces for HS 200,000 (Plin. HN 29, 22), and demanded a similarly exorbitant price of 1,000 Attic drachmas for a single dose of an antidote (Gal. 14,114,127). During his lifetime C. invested IIS 20 million in public construction projects in Massilia, and at his death left a similarly large sum. His interests may also have extended to ornithology, as Ael. VH 5,38 quotes him in connection with a description of the behaviour of the nightingale.   V.N.

Charon (Χάρων; *Chárōn*).
[1] Poetic coining from χαροπός (*charopós*) 'dark-gazing' [1. 309]; probably originally a euphemistic term for death [2. 229f.; 3. 32f.], and personified in epic poetry during the 6th cent. at the earliest (Orpheus: Serv. Aen. 6,392; Minyas) [1. 305,1; 2. 229]; not mentioned in Homer; earliest attested in the Minyas epic (PEG I: beginning 5th cent.?); thereafter popular as a burlesque figure, especially in Athenian dramatic poetry (Eur. HF, Alc.; Aristoph. Ran.) and in Lucianus (Dial. Mort. 22, Ch.), but also in funerary epigrams. C., as πορθμεύς (*porthmeús*; Minyas EpGF fr. 1) or *portitor* ('customs agent', Verg. Aen. 6,298 [4. 221]), transports the dead, brought to him by Hermes, across a reed-lined underworld lake for burial, in a boat with oars and pole (fig. on Attic *lekythoi* [12]); C. may transport living people only in return for the 'Golden Bough' (Verg. Aen. 6,137; 406ff.); for ferrying Heracles he spent a year in chains (Serv. Aen. 6,392). A small coin (obol), frequently found in graves in the mouths of the dead, was later explained as payment for the ferryman (Charon's penny; first literary mention: Aristoph. Ran. 140), which must be tendered even if one helps with the rowing; but was originally in token of possessions left behind [1. 305; 5. 25, 306f.; 6. 296]. The original sense of C. as the god of death probably returned to the fore during the imperial age (*deus*: Cic. Nat. 3,43; Verg. Aen. 6,304; CIL VIII 8992); also in modern Greek folklore, especially as Χάρος (*Cháros*) or Χάροντας (*Chárontas*) [2. 229ff.; 4. 222; 7. 222ff.; 8. 85ff.]. Ekphrasis of appearance: Verg. Aen. 6,299ff.

Charu(n) the Etruscan spirit of death, armed with a symbolic hammer and often depicted with greenish-blue skin, figured from the end of the 5th cent. on burial frescos and urns [8; 12], primarily as a companion of the dead and guardian of graves; in the arena, as *Ditis pater* or *Iovis frater* with *malle(ol)us*, to drag away the dead gladiators (Tert. Apol. 15, 5; Nat. 1,10,47). As there is also a ferryman of the dead in Sumer and Egypt [6. 303,21], these are all independently arising folk myths; derivation of the Greek C. from the Egyptian (Diod. Sic. 1,92,2; 96,8) should be dismissed.

→ Lesche; → Obolos; → Orpheus; → Orphic poetry; → Polygnotus; → Portitor; → Underworld

1 WILAMOWITZ I, 1931   2 Id., Lesefrüchte, in: Hermes 34, 1899, 227–230 (38, re WASER)   3 H. SCHOLZ, Der Hund in der griech.-röm. Magie und Religion, 1937   4 E. NORDEN, P. Vergilius Maro Aeneis Buch VI, ⁴1957   5 ROHDE   6 BURKERT   7 B. SCHMIDT, Das Volksleben der Neugriechen und das hellenische Alterthum I, 1871   8 O. WASER, Charon, Charun, Charos, 1878   9 F. DE RUYT, Charun, démon étrusque de la mort, 1934   10 S. CLES-REDEN, Das versunkene Volk, 1948   11 A. J. PFIFFIG, Einführung in die Etruskologie, ⁴1991   12 CHANTRAINE, s.v. Charon, in: FRISK   13 E. MAVLEEV, s.v. Charon, LIMC 3.2, 225–236   14 C. SOURVINOU-IN-WOOD, Reading Greek Death, 1995, 303–361.
ILLUSTRATIONS: ROSCHER 1, 885ff.   R. HERBIG, Götter und Dämonen der Etrusker, 1965, pl. 30,2, 34, 36, 39   S. CLES-REDEN, Das versunkene Volk, 1948, pl. 64, 69.
P.D.

[2] Master builder (τέκτων; *tékton*), *persona loquens* in Archil. fr. 19 WEST (Aristot. Rh. 3,148b30).

K. J. DOVER, in: Entretiens 10, 1963, 206ff.   M.D.MA.

[3] From Lampsacus. He is described by several ancient authors (Plut. Mor. 859b; Tert. Anim. 40; Dion. Hal. Thuc. 5; Pompon. 3,7) as a precursor of → Herodotus. According to the Suda (s.v. = T 1) he was 'born under Darius' (521–486 BC) and was author of the following works: *Aithiopika*, *Persika* (two books), *Hellenika* (four books), 'On Lampsacus' (two books), 'Chronicle of Lampsacus' (*Hóroi Lampsakēnôn*, four books), 'Prytaneis of the Lacedaemonians' (a → chronicle), 'Foundations of cities' (two books), *Kretika* (three books) and a → Periplus of the regions beyond the 'Pillars of Hercules'.

This most copious canon of work, scarcely conceivable for such an early period, induced JACOBY to move C.'s date to the end of the 5th cent., placing him chronologically and thematically close to Hellanicus of Lesbos, whose writings he would have augmented by means of more extensive coverage of regional geographies and city foundations. Those who, on the other hand, accept the earlier chronology, such as, more recently, PICCIRILLI and MOGGI, allow that, of the works named, only *Persika* and the 'Chronicle of Lampsacus' are genuine, and regard C. as an important precursor and source to Herodotus. Accordingly, these latter researchers have an essentially higher regard for C.'s innovative contribution to Greek historiography than proponents of the later date, who see him (much as they see Hellanicus) as above all else an 'overly prolific writer'.

Unfortunately, the meagre fragments available do not permit a definitive resolution of the dating question. Fragment 1 from the 'Chronicle of Lampsacus', come down to us verbatim in Athenaeus (12, p. 520 D-F), is revealing as to C.'s literary style. It indicates that this did not merely consist of facts and events strung together, but contained highly amusing passages of a novelistic nature. FGrH 262 (with commentary).

K. VON FRITZ, Die griech. Geschichtsschreibung, vol. 1, 1967, 518ff.; F. JACOBY, Charon von Lampsakos, in: SIFC 15, 1938, 207–242 (= treatise on Greek historiography, 1956, 178–206); A. HEPPERLE, Charon von Lampsakos, FS O. Regenbogen, 1956, 67–76; O. LENDLE, Einführung in die griech. Geschichtsschreibung, 1992, 71ff.; K. MEISTER, Die griech. Geschichtsschreibung, 1990, 24; M. MOGGI, Autori grechi di Persiká 2: Carone di Lampsaco, in: ASNP 7, 1977, 1–26; L. PICCIRILLI, Charone di Lampsaco e Erodoto, in: ASNP 5, 1975, 1239–54.
K.MEI.

[4] From Naucratis; Hellenistic period (?). Wrote a chronicle of the priests of Alexandria and other works on Egypt (Suda s.v. = T 1). Modern researchers frequently attribute to him works that are attested for → C. [3] of Lampsacus. FGrH 612.   K.MEI.

Charondas (Χαρώνδας; *Charṓndas*). From Catana; was regarded with → Zaleucus as the greatest lawgiver of the western Greek colonies, and compared to → Lycurgus and → Solon (Pl. Resp. 599d-e; Cic. Leg. 1,57). His dates cannot be exactly determined (mid-7th cent. to end of the 6th cent. BC). There is also no authentic documentation on C. as a person; like many lawgivers he is surrounded in legend [1].

C.'s laws, which were introduced in → Catana, → Rhegium and the other Chalcidian cities of lower Italy and Sicily (Aristot. Pol. 1274a 23ff.; Heracl. Lemb. fr. 55 DILTS), cannot be reconstructed in detail. Aristotle praises the precision of these νόμοι (*nómoi*), but picks out only one concrete law on court procedures against false witness statements, designating all the rest unoriginal (Pol. 1274b 6–8). Like Zaleucus, C., too, was said to have established differentiated sentences for different offences (Herodas, Mim. 2,46–56); laws setting graduated fines for non-attendance of court hearings, as well as others on property transactions were also attributed to him (Aristot. Pol. 1297a 21–24; Theophr. fr. 97,5 WIMMER) [2]. The laws mentioned in Diodorus are for the most part not historical (12,11,3–19,2).

Whether those ancient laws, belonging to the 6th cent., go back to a unified *nomothesia* of C. is doubtful. The historical C. was no 'constitutional father', but the author of isolated measures relating to particular situations. No general 'aristocratic-oligarchic' tendency can be postulated.

1 A. SZEGEDY-MASZAK, Legends of the Greek Lawgivers, in: GRBS 19, 1978, 199–209   2 M. GAGARIN, Early Greek Law, 1986, 64–67, 70–75.

M. Mühl, Die Gesetze des Zaleukos und Ch., in: Klio 22, 1929, 105–124, 432–463; G. Vallet, Rhégion et Zancle, 1958, 313–320.   K.-J.H.

Charon's fare Reward to the ferryman Charon for the journey across the river of the underworld (ναῦλον, πορθμήϊον; *naûlon, porthmḗïon*). A coin was placed under the tongue of the corpse or between its teeth [1. 349; 2; 3. 193f., 249f.]. The coin is often old, in bad condition or foreign; antique fakes or coin-like discs were also used, as in Greek graves of the 4th–2nd cents. BC [3. 250].
→ Charon [1]; → Dead, cult of the

1 J. Marquart, Das Privatleben der Römer, ²1886 2 Schrötter, 100, s.v. Charonsfährgeld 3 D. C. Kurtz, J. Boardman, Thanatos. Tod und Jenseits bei den Griechen, 1985.

P. Sartori, Die Totenmünze, in: ARW 1899, 205–225; Caronte. Un obolo per l'aldilà, Atti Salerno 1995 (= PdP 50, 1995), especially 165–354.   A.M.

Charops (Χάροψ; *Chárops*).
[1] Epithet by which Heracles was worshipped in Boeotia near the sanctuary of Zeus on Mount Laphystion. It was there that, in Boeotian tradition, he fetched Cerberus from the underworld (Paus. 9,34,5).
[2] Thracian; father of Oeagrus, grandfather of Orpheus. After the death of the Thracian King → Lycurgus, Dionysus appointed C. as one of his followers and initiated him into the Bacchic rites; C. then told the god of the assault planned by Lycurgus against Dionysus and the Maenads (Diod. Sic. 3,65,4–6).

L. Brisson, Orphée et l'Orphisme dans l'Antiquité gréco-romaine, 1995, IV 2873.

[3] Ruler on Syme; father of → Nireus (Hom. Il. 2,672; Hyg. Fab. 97, 270).
[4] Trojan, son of Hippasus, was killed by Odysseus before Troy (Hom. Il. 11,426; Ov. Met. 13,260). On a Chalcidian amphora from the 6th cent. C. is killed by Diomedes [1].

1 J. Boardman, s.v. Diomedes 1), LIMC 3.1, 400 no. 19.   R.B.

Chartophylax High ecclesiastical office, one of the five or six deacons responsible for the administration of the patriarchate of Constantinople. As an archivist and librarian, the C. was as a rule highly cultured; he had access to forbidden writings and administrated the library of the patriarchate, which was probably the most important collection of ancient Greek writings during the high Middle Ages. Georgios → Choiroboskos — besides other 8th–10th cent. incumbents — rendered outstanding services to the conservation of the cultural heritage of the ancient world.

J. Darrouzès, Recherches sur les ΟΦΦΙΚΙΑ de l'église byzantine, 1970, 334–353, 508–525.   G.MA.

Charybdis (Χάρυβδις; *Chárybdis*). Cliff with a dangerous whirlpool, which together with Scylla, situated opposite it, originally formed a rocky portal, that was part of the route of the Argonauts on their return journey between Sirens and Planctae (on which Thrinacia follows), and which the → Argo successfully passes (Apollod. 1,136; Apoll. Rhod. 4,922f.; cf. Ov. Met. 7,62ff.; Orph. A. 1253ff., where the Argo comes through the Pillars of Hercules and C. is already located in Sicily, whilst Scylla is missing). Homer focussed the adventure, according to a plan, around Thrinacia (Hom. Od. 12.73ff.): warned by Circe, Odysseus, coming from the Sirens, avoids C. with exaggerated caution (which cost the lives of six companions who died because of Scylla: Hom. Od. 12.234ff.); three times a day C. sucks in everything, (Od. 12.104: etymological pun Χάρυβδις ἀναρρυβδεῖ, *C. anarrhybdeî*, yet etymologically unexplained) and spits it all out again. After the theft of the cattle and the shipwreck, as he again enters the strait, Odysseus swings from the keel and mast to the fig tree on the C. that is not very high; after C. disgorges the planks, he jumps down again (Hom. Od. 12.428ff.; Apollod. epit. 7.20ff.) [1. 91f.]. Thuc. 4,24,5 and Schol. Apoll. Rhod. 4,825–31 first attested that the location of this was the Strait of Messina. Aeneas avoids Scylla and C. (daughter of Neptune and Terra in Serv. Aen. 3,420) by circumnavigating Sicily (Verg. Aen. 3,420ff; 3,555ff.). Other abysses are also called C., e.g. the Orontes between Apamea and Antioch (Str. 6,2,9). Proverb: *Incidis (incidit) in Scyllam cupiens (qui vult) vitare Charybdin* (W. of Châtillon Alex. 5,301, following Apostol. 16,49).
→ Aeneas; → Argo; → Argonauts; → Homer (Odyssee); → Circe; → Odysseus; → Planctae; → Sirens; → Scylla; → Thrinacia

1 K. Reinhardt, Die Abenteuer der Odyssee, in: Id., Tradition und Geist, 1960, 47–124.

O. Waser, Skylla und Ch. in der Lit. und Kunst der Griechen und Römer, 1894.   P.D.

Chasuarii Germanic people; 'people of the Hase' (easterly tributary of the Ems); neighbours of the Chamavi (Tac. Germ. 34,1), living south of the Suebi and west of the Chatti (Ptol. 2,11,11), they left their home country (possibly as early as *c*. AD 98) and under Gallienus took possession of Roman territory east of Mainz (Laterculus Veronensis 15,6).

G. Neumann et al., s.v. Chasuarier, RGA 4, 375f.   K.DI.

Chatti Germanic tribe (first mentioned in Str. 7,1,3f.; etymology uncertain), renowned for their martial discipline; settled by Rome in the region around the mouth of the Main, they later occupied particularly the basins of the Hessian depression south of the Cherusci and east of the Usipetes. Classed with the → Hermiones in Plin. HN 4,100, they lost the battle for a saline river to the Hermunduri in AD 58, but inflicted a devastating defeat on the Cherusci. In constant opposition to Rome, they raided Roman territory well into the 3rd cent. AD, each raid answered by punitive action (especially 39/40, 50, 162, 170/1, probably AD 213). Germanicus triumphed over the C., Domitian waged war on them from AD 83 to 85 [1], and possibly Saturninus in 89, after they had assisted Antonius [II 15] [2. 203ff.]. Because of that, they lost the fertile region of the Wetterau. By the 4th cent. AD, they still managed to keep their independence between Franci and Burgundiones (laterculus Veronensis 13). Whether they actually joined the tribal league of the Franci is contentious, but in AD 392 they were their allies against → Arbogastes. From the 6th cent. AD, the Hassii, Hessi, Hessones appear by name within the territory of the C., the modern Hessen.

1 K. STROBEL, Der Chattenkrieg Domitians, in: Germania 65, 1987, 423–452   2 Id., Der Aufstand des L. Antonius Saturninus und der sog. zweite Chattenkrieg Domitians, in: Tyche 1, 1986, 203–220.

G. NEUMANN et. al., s.v. Chatten, RGA 4, 377–391.
K.DI.

Chattuarii Germanic people; on the basis of etymology inhabitants of a former Chattian territory; possibly to be identified with the → Chasuarii. As neighbours of the Bructeri and the Cherusci counted as the 'weaker' inland peoples (Str. 7,1,3f.; Vell. Pat. 2,105,1); possibly to be identified with the Attuarii, who show up in the 4th cent. as part of a Frankish confederacy (Amm. Marc. 20,10,2); during the Middle Ages the C. are settled from the lower Ruhr and Lippe to the left bank of the Rhine.

→ Chatti; → Francs

G. NEUMANN et al., s.v. Chattwarier, RGA 4, 391–393; J. KUNOW, Das Limesvorland der südl. Germania inferior, in: BJ 187, 1987, 63–77, especially 70f.   K.DI.

Chauci Warlike Germanic seafaring tribe (etymologically related to the Gothic *háuhs*, Old High German *hôh-* 'high'; Str. 7,1,3; idealized in Tac. Germ. 35). The C. lived north of the Angrivarii on the North Sea coast, on both banks of the lower Weser, and were divided into the 'lesser' and the 'greater' C. (Tac. Ann. 11,19,2; Ptol. 2,11,7; 9; Plin. HN 16,2–5). They were fought by Drusus and subjected to Roman rule in AD 5; despite a Roman occupational force and the fact that they had to supply auxiliary forces, they still managed to create further problems: by fighting against Quinctilius → Varus (avenged by Gabinius 'Chaucius' in AD 41), by marauding the coasts of Gallia, and by participating in the → Batavian revolt. They expanded southward at the expense of the Cherusci and in AD 400 were settling east of the Rhine (Claud. Carm. 18,379; 21,225).

G. NEUMANN et al., s.v. Chauken, RGA 4, 393–413; W. WILL, Roms 'Klientel-Randstaaten' am Rhein?, in: BJ 187, 1987, 1–61, especially 31–38.   K.DI.

Chazars The C. (Turkish, roughly 'vagabonds') belong to the group of Turkish-Altaic peoples and are attested from the 3rd/4th cents. AD. Originally nomadic, in the 7th cent. they founded an autonomous empire reaching from the Black Sea to the Don. Their king (Qağan) was political and religious leader. Although they did not develop their own written language they left behind loan words in Arabic, Greek, Armenian, Georgian, Hebrew and Persian i.a. Their campaigns of conquest reached as far as the → Chersonesus and what is now Bulgaria. During the first Arabian-C. war on the borders of the → Caucasus they were first allies, then enemies of the Byzantine empire. In 737 their empire was conquered by the Arabs. However, until *c.* 965 they represented an insuperable obstacle for the Rus, who advanced as far as the Caspian Sea. C. 740 numerous members of the ruling elite converted to Judaism.

D. M. DUNLOP, The History of the Jewish Khazars, (Princeton oriental studies 16), 1954 (repr. 1967); P. B. GOLDEN, Khazar studies: An historico-philological inquiry into the origins of the Khazars, Kiadó Academy, Budapest. Bibliotheca orientalis Hungarica, 25/1,2, 1980; N. GOLF, O. PRITSAK, Khazarian Hebrew Documents of the Tenth Century, 1982.   K.SA.

Cheese
I. ANCIENT ORIENT   II. GRAECO-ROMAN ANTIQUITY

I. ANCIENT ORIENT
Cheese, together with grain and fish, was one of the most important foods for the people of the ancient Orient. After the oil in the butter (Sumer. ì.nun, Akkad. *ḫimētu*) had been completely removed, the buttermilk was processed into a fat-free cheese that therefore kept well for a long time; it is similar to the hard cheese called *kašk* in the modern Middle East. Cheese was also mixed with various ingredients (grain, dates, wine and numerous spices) and then brought as an offering to the gods, often, as is to be expected, together with butter oil. Cheese is seldom mentioned in Babylonian literature.

K. BUTZ, Konzentrationen wirtschaftl. Macht im Königreich Larsa, in: WZKM 65–66, 1973/74, 37–45; M. STOL, s.v. Milchprodukte, RLA 8, 189–201; R. ENGLUND, Regulating Dairy Productivity in the Ur III Period, in: Orientalia 64, 1995, 377–429; T. JACOBSEN, Lad in the Desert, in: Journal of the American Oriental Society 103, 1983, 193–200.   R.K.E.

II. GRAECO-ROMAN ANTIQUITY
Since earliest times milk, which goes off easily (Hom. Od. 9,246–249), was further processed into cheese (Greek τυρός; *tyrós*, Latin *caseus*) — in the Mediterranean it was primarily sheep and goat's milk, in the north of the ancient world mainly cow's milk (cf. Aristot. Hist. an. 3,20,521b–522b). Soft or fresh cheese (*caseus mollis* or *recens*) meant for immediate consumption was dried for a short time and then salted (Varro, Rust. 2,11,3); the production of hard cheese (*caseus aridus* or

vetus) that could be stored required stronger salting and longer drying, the cheese often also being flavoured with → spices like thyme, pepper or pine nuts (Columella De re rustica 7,8,6–7). A Roman speciality seems to have been cheese smoked over wood (Plin. HN 11,241). Highly regarded everywhere in Greece was cheese from Ceos (Ael. NA 16,32) and Sicily (Ath. 14,658a), in Italy varieties from the Vestine country, the Alps and the Apennines (Plin. HN 11,241). Local fresh and dry cheese was relatively inexpensive (Diog. Laert. 6,36; cf. also the Edictum Diocletiani 5,11; 6,96 LAUFFER) and therefore, also because of its pleasant taste, a food that was popular in all parts of society. It was mostly eaten for breakfast (Mart. 13,31) and lunch together with bread (Apul. Met. 1,18,8) or vegetables (Ath. 12,542f) but not as part of the main evening meal (→ *deípnon* or → *cena*). Only during luxurious meals was cheese, especially in its dry variety served as an hors d'oeuvre, or more commonly as a dessert (Ath. 11,462e) that would whet again the thirst for wine. In gastronomy a lot of grated cheese was used to make cakes and sweet dishes (Aristoph. Ach. 1125; Celsus. artes 2,18), pastes (*polenta caseata*; Apul. Met. 1,4,1) and savoury creams (App. Vergiliana, Moretum). Cheese was also an important ingredient in bread (Anth. Pal. 6,155), fish stew (*tyrotarichum*; Apicius 4,2,17), and even in → beverages (*kykeṓn*: a mixed drink made of wine, cheese and flour; Hom. Il. 11,639–640). Doctors warned against cheese as being hard to digest (Hippoc. Perí diaítēs 51; Celsus, artes 2,25) but utilized its therapeutic effect for internal and external applications (Plin. HN 28,205–207).

J. ANDRÉ, L'alimentation et la cuisine à Rome, ²1981; E. COUGNY, s.v. Caseus, DS 1, 931–935; A. DALBY, Siren Feasts. A History of Food and Gastronomy in Greece, 1996; W. KROLL, s.v. Käse, RE 10, 1489–1496.   A.G.

Chefren (Egyptian *Ḥʿj.f-Rʿ*, possibly *Rʿ-ḫʿj.f*; Hdt. 2,127 Χεφρήν (*Chephrén*), Diod. Sic. 1,64 Κεφρήν (*Kephrén*), Manetho in allusion to Cheops Σοῦφις (*Soûphis*), Ps.-Eratosth. fr. 17 Σαῶφις (*Saôphis*). Fourth ruler of the 4th dynasty; according to the Turin royal papyrus reigned 26 years (*c.* 2500 BC). Nothing is known of political events during his reign. After the death of his brother Djedefre C. erected his own monument at the necropolis of his father → Cheops in → Giza, building the second largest pyramid. Mortuary and valley temple are well preserved, with rich statuary. The great → Sphinx with its temple also forms part of this ensemble. Herodotus characterizes C. in the same negative image as his father.

J. v. BECKERATH, s.v. C., LÄ 1, 933.   S.S.

Cheirographon (χειρόγραφον; *cheirógraphon*), literally 'handwriting' (handwritten note). Along with the → *syngraphe* the most common form of private document in the Egyptian papyri. Entering the Roman world from the 3rd/2nd cents. BC onwards, the *cheirogra-*

phon tends towards the style of the private letter, and is not restricted to any particular type of transaction. Witnesses were a customary feature. The *cheirographon* would usually be in the hands of the person authorized by it. In the Roman period, the *cheirographon* could by δημοσίωσις (*dēmosíōsis*: incorporation in an official archive) attain equal standing as legal evidence with notaries' certificates written by the → *agoranómos*.

WOLFF, 106ff.   G.T.

Cheiromanteia see → Divination

Cheirotonia (χειροτονία; *cheirotonía*, 'raising the hand'). Method of voting in popular assemblies and other Greek committees. In large assemblies votes thus given were probably not counted: the chairman would have to decide where the majority voice lay. Distinct from *cheirotonía* is voting by *psēphophoría* ('throwing-in of ballot stones'), which made possible the precise counting of votes in a secret ballot. Notwithstanding the method actually used, the tendency in Athens and generally was to use the term *cheirotonein* in the case of elections and the term *psēphízesthai* in the case of decisions on public affairs: in the Athenian popular assembly *cheirotonía* was used in elections as well as in other votes (so long as a quorum of 6,000 was not required); courts of law used *psēphophoría* exclusively.

M. H. HANSEN, How did the Athenian Ecclesia vote?, in: GRBS 18, 1977, 123–37 (= The Athenian Ecclesia, 1983, 103–21).   P.J.R.

Chelcias (Χελκίας; *Chelkías*). Son of Onias IV; brother of Ananias (died 103). From 105–103 BC commander of the army of → Cleopatra III.

PP 2, 2183; 8, 342a.   W.A.

Chelone *Chelonai* (χελώνη; *chelónē*, 'tortoise') were for the most part movable, wooden protective devices used by besieging armies. In the form of χ. χωστρίδες (*chelónai chōstrídes*) they protected sappers as they i.a. levelled the ground by raising dykes; in the form of χ. ὀρυκτρίδες, *oryktrídes* (Lat. *musculi*) as they penetrated or undermined walls. 'Ram tortoises' protected battering rams. Used in Greece probably since the 5th cent., they were especially widely used during the Hellenistic and Roman periods.

→ Fortifications; → Siegecraft

O. LENDLE, Schildkröten. Ant. Kriegsmaschinen in poliorketischen Texten, 1975.   L.B.

Chemmis

[1] In Diod. Sic. 1,63 name of the builder of the largest of the three pyramids of → Giza (→ Cheops).
[2] In ancient authors the name of an important town in Upper Egypt, the modern Achmim, 200 km north of

Luxor on the right bank of the Nile; capital of the 9th district of Upper Egypt (Panopolites). Diod. Sic. 1,18 uses the form *Chemmo*. Besides *Ipw* the names *w n Mnw* and *Ḫntj Mnw* have come down in ancient Egyptian, indicating the local deity Min, normally equated with → Pan (Panopolis). Hdt. 2,91 identifies the Egyptian god with → Perseus, and the 'climb for Min' ritual, performed at Min's festival, with gymnastic games. Plin. HN 5,11,2 describes C. as the most important city in Egypt. Arab writers of the Middle Ages also counted the city's temples among the most important in Egypt. Owing to subsequent levels of construction and demolition virtually no remains have been preserved. In antiquity C. was famed for its weavers and stonemasons (Str. 17,1,41–43). In AD 447 → Nestorius died in C. [1].

[3] According to Hdt. 2,156 and Hecat. fr. 284 (in Steph. Byz. s.v.) the name of a floating island in a lake near the temple of → Buto on the western delta; Egyptian *ḫ-bjt*, 'papyrus thicket of the king of Lower Egypt'. A myth of the birth of Horus by Isis was already established here during the Old Kingdom. According to a later tradition (Ebers Pap. 958, New Kingdom) Isis gave birth here to Shu and Tefnut, who were equated with → Apollo and → Artemis [2].

1 J. KARIG, s.v. C., LÄ 1, 54–55   2 H. ALTENMÜLLER, s.v. C., LÄ 1, 921–922.   R.GR.

Cheops (Egyptian *Nmw-ḫwj.f-wj*; Hdt. Χέοψ (*Chéops*), Manetho Σοῦφις (*Soûphis*), Ps.-Eratosth. fr. 17 Σαῶφις (*Saôphis*); in Diod. Sic. 1,63 also → Chemmis/Χέμμις). Second ruler of the 4th dynasty; according to the Turin Papyrus of Kings reigned 23 years (*c.* 2550 BC). Nothing is known of political events during his reign. C. inaugurated the necropolis at → Giza, where with the construction of his pyramid (the largest) and establishment of a cemetery for members of the elite he realized the concept of a unified royal residence necropolis, expressing the centralized structure of the 4th dynasty state apparatus around the person of the king. Stone inscriptions of C. are known from Nubia and Sinai; the sole three-dimensional representation of the king is an ivory statuette from → Abydus [2]. Hdt. 2,124ff. depicts C. as a ruthless tyrant who subordinated everything to the construction of his monument. Whether this negative view is rooted in Egyptian tradition (Westcar Papyrus) remains contentious.

J. v. BECKERATH, s.v. C., LÄ 1, 932f.   S.S.

Cherry Tree (κέρασος; *kérasos*, Latin *cerasus* with unclarified etymology, as the name of the town → Cerasus, contrary to explanations in Isid. Orig. 17,7,16, is derived from the cherry tree; the cherries are called κεράσια; *kerásia*, Latin *cerasia*). The wild cherry existed in Europe at least from the Middle Stone Age onwards [1. 112]. The grafted sweet cherry was introduced to Italy from the Black Sea in 74 BC by → Licinius Lucul-

lus (Plin. HN 15,102ff.). It quickly spread all the way to Britannia. Pliny already knew several varieties that today however are hardly identifiable any more (Plin. HN 15,102ff., cf. 16,123 and 125; 17,234). Ath. 2,51a-b maintains, with a quotation from → Diphilus [6] of Siphnus (around 300 BC) with regard to its dietary qualities, that it had already been previously known in Greece for a long time. Theophr. Hist. pl. 3,13,1–3 appears to refer to the bird cherry (*Prunus avium* subspecies *silvestris*). From the time of Varro (Rust. 1,39,2) it is mentioned for its astringent effect. cf. e.g. Galen (De alimentorum facultatibus 2,12). For Italy Columella recommends that grafting be done as early as the end of December (11,2,96) or mid-January (11,2,11); Pall. Agric. 11,12,4–8 describes in detail its demands on the soil and its cultivation.

1 K. und F. BERTSCH, Gesch. unserer Kulturpflanzen, 1949.

V. HEHN, Kulturpflanzen und Haustiere (ed. O. SCHRADER), ⁸1911, repr. 1963, 404–410; F. OLCK, s.v. Kirschbaum, RE 11, 509–515.   C.HÜ.

Chersias (Χερσίας; *Chersías*). From Orchomenus; Plutarch in his 'Banquet of the Seven Sages' has C. taking part in the conversations as a poet (Mor. 156f), contemporary and close friend of → Periander, tyrant of Corinth (end of the 7th/beginning 6th cent. BC). Two hexameters by the poet (Paus. 9,38,9), in which the city's hero Aspledon is described as the son of Poseidon and Midea, are supposed to attest to the accuracy of local tradition in the Boeotian city of the same name. Pausanias' explicit comment that in his time the poetry of C. was no longer known (9,38,10), together with reference to a dubious source, the Corinthian historian → Callippus, gives rise to doubts as to the authenticity of the quotation. Pausanias further reports that the inhabitants of Orchomenus ascribe the epigram on Hesiod's grave to C.   C.S.

Chersicrates (Χερσικράτης; *Chersikrátēs*). Corinthian; descendant of the Bacchiads (Timaeus FGrH 566 F 80). According to Str. 6,2,4 C. was left behind by → Archias, founder of Syracuse, on the way to Sicily, and settled Corcyra. The credibility of these inherently contradictory statements must be doubted.   M.MEI.

Chersiphron (Χερσίφρων; *Chersíphrōn*) from Cnossus. Father of → Metagenes; these two being the → architects of the archaic → dipteros of Artemis at Ephesus (2nd half of the 6th cent. BC), as recorded in Strabo (14,640), Vitruvius (3,2,7) and Pliny (HN 7,125; 36,95). Both of them wrote about this temple in a work which was evidently still known to Vitruvius (Vitr. De arch. 7,1,12), and is one of the earliest formulations of ancient architectural theory (→ Architecture, theory of); through his development of a device based on rollers, for the transport of large and/or heavy components over difficult terrain from the → quarry to the construction site (Vitr. De arch. 10,2,11), C. was also regarded as a pioneer of ancient engineering (→ Construction technique).

H. BRUNN, Gesch. der griech. Künstler, 2, ²1889, 232–233 (Sources); L. GUERRINI, s.v. Chersiphron (literature), EAA 2; W. SCHABER, Die archa. Tempel der Artemis von Ephesos, 1982; H. SVENSON-EVERS, Die griech. Architekten archa. und klass. Zeit, 1996, 67–100; B. WESENBERG, Zu den Schriften der griech. Architekten, in: DiasAB 4, 1983, 39–48.   C.HÖ.

Cherson see → Chersonesus [3]

Chersonesus (Χερσόνησος; *Chersónēsos*).
[1] The peninsula nowadays called Gallipoli (more than 900 km²); traces of prehistoric settlement, a strategically favourable position, and fertile. First mentioned in Hom. Il. 2,844f., as homeland of the Thracians Acamas and Peirous. Aeolian colonization in the 7th cent. BC (Alopekonnesos, Madytus, Sestus); Ionian (Cardia, Limnae by Miletus and Clazomenae, Elaeus by Teos) somewhat later. The powerful Thracian tribes (Apsinthi, Dolonci) long remained hostile. In order to protect the C., → Miltiades the Elder, who with the assent of the Dolonci ruled as tyrant over the C., had the Bulair isthmus fortified with a wall from Cardia to Pactya (Hdt. 6,36). After the war with Lampsacus, → Miltiades the Younger was despatched from Athens to the C. After the invasion of the Scythians in 496, in 493 he ceded the C. to Darius. Sestus was a Persian satrapy. Pericles had the wall restored and sent settlers to Sestus and Callipolis. From 466, the whole of the C. was a member of the → Delian League. Athens fought for the C. until 387, because of its importance for imports of wheat. At this time, the whole of the C. was probably exclusively settled by Greeks. From 405 to 386 the C. was temporarily under Spartan rule. In 398 the Spartan Dercylidas renovated the wall. Owing to the expansion of the Odrysae, until its capture by Philip II (338 BC) the C. was under Thracian rule, forcing Athens into numerous diplomatic initiatives in face of rulers such as Cotys I, Amadocus and Cersobleptes. In 280/79 Celts moved through the C.; Antigonus [2] Gonatas defeated them decisively in 277. The C. was alternately under Seleucids, Ptolemies, Antigonids and (from 189) Attalids. At the time of Attalus II an invasion by Thracians under Dielylis, king of the Caeni. In 133 the C. came under Roman rule as a legacy of Attalus III, and from 12 BC part of it was an imperial domain.

In the 1st half of the 2nd cent. a *prov. Chersonesus* was created, with procuratorial seat in Koila/Coela. In the time of Justinian (6th cent. AD), who had the wall rebuilt, there were sporadic raids by Huns and Slavs.

U. KAHRSTEDT, Beitr. zur Gesch. der Thrak. Chersonesos, 1954; B. ISAAC, The Greek Settlement in Thrace until the Macedonian Conquest, 1986, 159–197.   I.v.B.

[2] Peninsula between Maeotis in the east and the Pontus Euxinus in the west, joined to the mainland by a long isthmus; the southerly continuation of the south Russian steppe; often called the Tauric C., less frequently the Scythian C. (Hdt. 4,17–31; 99–101; Str. 7,4; Scylax 68); the modern Crimea. Str. 7,4,2 distinguishes the greater C. (the entire peninsula) from the smaller C. (the part jutting out into the Black Sea); Hdt. 4,99 calls the eastern part τρηχέη (*trēchéē*; 'rough'); mild climate, fertile soil. From the 7th cent. BC colonized by Greeks, who continually had to contend with the tribes living there (Tauri in the mountains, Scythae further to the north). The city of C. controlled the west, the Bosporan kingdom the east. Goti and Heruli settled during the 3rd cent. AD (Sync. 717), then from the 70s of the 4th cent. retreated to the south-west, under pressure from the Hunni and other Turkic peoples and later also the Slavs (Procop. Goth. 4,5). During the 5th cent. Hunni and Chazars also settled on the C., from the 6th cent. under the control of Constantinople.

A. N. ŠČEGLOV, Severo-zapadnyi Krym v antičnuju epohy, 1978; D. B. ŠELOV, Der nördl. Schwarzmeerraum in der Ant., in: H. HEINEN (ed.), Die Gesch. des Alt. im Spiegel der sowjetischen Forsch., 1980.   I.v.B.

[3]
A. GREEK AND ROMAN PERIODS   B. BYZANTINE PERIOD

A. GREEK AND ROMAN PERIODS
Dorian colony in the south-western Crimea, founded during the 2nd half of the 5th cent. BC by Heraclea, according to Ps.-Scymn. 850 with the participation of citizens of Delos. Gained extensive territory early on (Cercinitis, *Kalòs limén*). Coins minted from the 4th cent. BC. At the end of the 2nd cent. BC Mithridates VI prevented C. from being captured by the Scythae (Str. 7,4,3ff.; IOSPE 1², 352); but C. lost its outlying possessions. Shortly afterwards alliance with the Sarmatae against the Scythae (Polyaenus, Strat. 8,56). Incorporated by Asander into the Bosporan kingdom. After a siege by the Scythae in AD 60/61, Roman troops and a naval squadron were stationed in C. on the orders of the emperor Nero (Ios. Bell. Iud. 2,16,4). Owing to the continual threat from the Scythae, Cotys II was installed as ruler by Hadrian (Phlegon of Tralleis, Olympiades 15, fr. 20, FGrR 257). Through the mediation of Heraclea, under Antoninus Pius C. won back its independence (IOSPE 1², 361). During the incursions of the Goti in the 4th cent., C. remained free and an ally of Rome; it suffered severely under the assaults of the Hunni.

V. E. GAIDUKEVIČ, Das Bosporanische Reich, 1971; J. VINOGRADOV, M. ZOLOTAREV, Le Chersonèse de la fin de l'archaisme, in: Le Pont-Euxin vu par les grecs, 1990, 85–119.   I.v.B. and S.R.T.

B. BYZANTINE PERIOD
→ Iustinianus I (527–565) initiated defensive works. When, in the 9th cent., the cities and the fortified settlements called *klímata* were brought together in a → *théma*, the city became the seat of the *strategos*; it

played a significant role in the transit trade [1] and in the Christianization of the Russians. The city survived until the end of the 15th cent., retaining its Greek character. Today ruins near modern Sebastopol.

1 G. MORAVCSIK (ed.), Constantinus Porphyrogenitus, De administrando imperio, ²1967, 286.

SOURCES: A. PERTUSI (ed.), Costantino Porfirogenito, De thematibus, 1952, 182f.
BIBLIOGRAPHY: D. OBOLENSKY, The Crimea and the North before 1204, in: Id., The Byzantine Inheritance of Eastern Europe, 1982; I. SOKOLOVA, Монеты и печати византийского Херсона (= Coins and Seals of Byzantine Chersonesus), 1983.   G.MA.

Cherusci Germanic tribe (first mentioned in Caes. B Gall. 6,10,5; etymology uncertain, possibly connected with *herut, German 'Hirsch' [deer]?). They settled south of the Angrivarii and west of the Langobardi, between Weser and Elbe, and north of the Harz mountains. In a state of permanent internal dispute, they were subjugated by Claudius Drusus (in 12 and 9 BC), and by Tiberius (AD 4). However, in AD 9, → Arminius, who was in Roman service, led a successful uprising against Quinctilius → Varus by parts of the C., whose political influence at times extended far beyond their settlement area. The C. also succeeded in their resistance against Maroboduus, but only one member of the Cheruscan royal house survived the internal feuds of AD 47. Despite being related by marriage to the C., the Chatti waged war against them, because they were seen as friends of Rome, leading to the final annihilation of the C. before AD 100 (Tac. Germ. 36,1, cf. modern commentaries).

TIR M 33, 34; G. NEUMANN et al., s.v. Cherusker, RGA 4, 430–435; W. WILL, Roms 'Klientel-Randstaaten' am Rhein?, in: BJ 187, 1987, 1–61, especially 44–55; R. WIEGELS, W. WOESLER (ed.), Arminius und die Varusschlacht, 1995.   K.DI.

Cheslimus Jos. Ant. Jud. 1,6,2 (§ 137 N.) calls Cheslimus (Χέσλοιμος; *Chésloimos*) the eponym of a tribe descended from the Egyptians, which in his model is called *kasluhīm* (Gen. 10.14 and 1 Chr. 1.12; LXX Χασλ- and Χασμωνι[ε]ιμ, Vulg. C(h)asluim). In Josephus their kindred people are the → Philistines, whilst in his model these had previously inhabited the land of the *kasluhīm*. If the commentary which states this does not belong to the *kaptōrīm* (cf. Jer 47,4 and Am 9,7), then the *kaptōrīm* must have settled in the coastal areas of Egypt, which were attacked in the 12th cent. BC by the Sea Peoples (→ Sea Peoples, migrations of), from directly across the sea or who had made their way through the Palestinian coastal region. Whether the C. or the *kasluhīm* were also ethnically related to these people cannot be confirmed. Of the proposed identities of the C. (evidence in the Heb. dictionary and [1. 614f.]), the most worthy of discussion, from a geographical viewpoint, are therefore those which point to the inhabitants of Casiotis or the Libyan Νασαμῶνες

→ Nasamones (Hdt. 2,32; 4,172, 182, 190; people living as nomads around the oasis of Amon).

1 Dictionnaire de la Bible 1.   C.C.

Chestnut The sweet chestnut (*Castanea sativa Mill.*) already grew in southern Europe in early historic times. Theophrastus calls the fruit εὐβοϊκή (*euboiké* sc. *karýa*) and describes it in Hist. pl. 1,11,3 as enveloped in a leather-like skin. According to Hist. pl. 4,5,4, the tree was very common on Euboea and in the area around Magnesia. Its wood, that was by nature resistant to rotting (5,4,2, according to 5,4,4 even in water), is recommended as especially suitable for carpentry work exposed to the weather and the soil (5,7,7). Before chestnut beams break, they warn those standing under them with a noise (5,6,1). Charcoal (ἄνθραξ) from their soft wood was used to smelt iron (7,9,2). In contrast to the dark bast around the lotus root, Theophr. Hist. pl. 4,8,11 calls its fruit — that otherwise as καρύα/*karýa* or βάλανος/*bálanos* was hardly distinguished from other nuts — κασταναϊκὸν κάρυον/*kastanaikòn káryon*. Plin. HN 15,92–94 describes the *nuces castaneas* (so called also in Verg. Ecl. 2,52) very precisely and names several varieties that are partly produced through grafting. The smoothest fruits were used as food, although this was partly controversial (Ath. 2,54c-d), and the rougher ones for fattening pigs. Columella 4,33,1–5 gives exact instructions for laying out a chestnut forest (*castanetum*) that would profitably produce supporting posts for the vineyards. Pall. Agric. 12,7,17–22 describes their sowing (particularly in November/December) and grafting, even on the willow tree (*salix*). Through the Romans the chestnut was introduced to southern Germany. Dioscorides 1,106,3 WELLMANN = 1,145 BERENDES calls it astringent and prescribes the flesh of the fruit as an antidote for poisoning. The horse chestnut (*Aesculus hippocastanum L.*), that constitutes its own family, only came from the northern Balkans to southern Europe in the 16th cent. [1. 399f.].

1 V. HEHN, Kulturpflanzen und Haustiere (ed. O. SCHRADER), ⁸1911, repr. 1963.

H. STADLER, s.v. Kastanie, RE 10, 2338–2342.   C.HÜ.

Chests (ζύγαστρον/*zýgastron*, κιβωτός/*kibōtós*, κιβώτιον/*kibótion*, λάρναξ/*lárnax*, χηλός/*chēlós*; Latin *arca, cista*). Chests made of wood, bronze or other materials were used in the household for storing and transporting clothes, household goods, book rolls (→ *scrinium*), equipment, provisions, etc. Chests could be simple and undecorated, or decorated with ornamental or figurative reliefs on their sides (→ Praenestine cistae). Wooden chests often had metal fittings, which were also decorated, for reinforcing edges and corners. Apart from rectangular chests, there also were cylindrical and polygonal ones (the Casket of the Muses of the Esquiline treasure [1. 75–78 Pl. 12–16]); they stood on feet or sat flat on the floor.

Chests played a significant role in myths of → child exposure (cf., e.g., → Danac, → Dionysus, → Telephus [1], → Rhoeo, → Tennes [1], → Thoas [1]) and rescue (e.g., → Deucalion [2]). Chests were also dedicated in sanctuaries; of these the → Cypselus Chest in Olympia is the best known [2]. The appearance and technical furnishings of ancient chests are known from clay and stone sculptures, images on vases and other art forms. Remains of chests are known from the Mycaenean and later periods but complete specimens made of bronze or precious metal also are preserved (e.g., the Projecta casket from the Esquiline treasure [1. 72–75 Taf. 1–6]). → Arca; → Cista; → Muses (with Fig..)

1 K. SHELTON, The Esquiline Treasure, 1981
2 R. SPLITTER, Die »Kypseloslade« in Olympia. Form, Funktion und Bildschmuck: eine arch. Rekonstruktion, 2000.

RICHTER, Furniture, 71–78; 95 f.; 114; E. BR, Griech. Truhenbehälter, in: JDAI 100, 1985, 1–168; L. A. SCHNEIDER, Die Domäne als Weltbild, 1983, 4–38; M. KEMKES, Brn. Truhenbeschläge aus der röm. Villa von Eckartsbrunn, in: Fundber. aus Baden-W 16, 1991, 299–387.
R.H.

Chiasmus see → Parallelism

Chicago Painter Attic red-figured vase painter, active c. 455–450 BC, named for a *stamnos* in Chicago. Regarded as 'successor' to the Villa Giulia Painter, whose style he 'continued in a softer and more elegant manner' (BEAZLEY). He painted mainly *stamnoi*, *pelikai* and *hydriae* as well as various types of *krater*. His figures are tall and slender with expressive facial features, even the smaller pieces being distinguished by a richness of detail. 'Warrior's farewell' is his preferred motif, mythological scenes being rare. His *stamnoi* with Maenads in dignified procession or tranquil groups refer to the Lenaea vases of the Villa Giulia painter.

BEAZLEY, ARV², 628–632, 1662; G. SCHWARZ, Der Abschied des Amphiaraos, in: JÖAI 57, 1988/89, 39–54; M. ROBERTSON, The Art of Vase-Painting, 1992, 191–194.
M.P.

Chicken (Rooster) The domestic chicken, that was originally bred in southern Asia from several wild species of chicken, particularly the Bankiva chicken of the Sunda Islands and India, was introduced to China around 1400 BC and to Bactria and Iran before 1200 (hence Cratinus' name 'Persian bird' in Ath. 9,374d and Aristoph. Av. 485; 707; also 'Median bird' Aristoph. Av. 276), and from there to Mesopotamia and Asia Minor. There the Greeks encountered it and brought it to their motherland, also to Sicily and Lower Italy in the 6th cent. The large number of names mirrors how widespread it was: ἀλέκτωρ (aléktōr), 'the one who makes sleepless' (Batr. 192; Pind. Ol. 12,14; Aesch. Ag. 1671 and Eum. 861, always only poetic), ἀλεκτρυών (alektryón; since Theognis 864; since Aristoph. Nub. 662 also fem.), ἡ ἀλεκτορίς (hē alektorís; Hippoc. Int. 27

and Nat. Puer. 29; Epicharmus 152,172; Hecat. 58); as common poultry from the time of the tragic writers: ὁ ἐνοίκιος ὄρνις (ho enoíkios órnis; Aesch. Eum. 866; Soph. El. 18) and ἡ ὄρνις (θήλεια) (hē órnis (théleia); Soph.). This date of its naturalization is also confirmed by rooster illustrations on coins (Himera [1. pl. 5,40–42], early 5th cent.; Phaestus and Dardanus [1. pl. 5,38 and 43], middle of the 5th cent.). Magnificent roosters adorn mosaics from late antiquity [8. 250f. and pl. 131].

Fighting cocks — on whose victories people bet in public places — were bred in different locations, e.g. on Rhodes and in Tanagra (Plin. HN 10,48). The cock fights that Themistocles supposedly introduced — perhaps based on those in Asia Minor (Ael. VH 2,28, cf. Plin. HN 10,50) — were popular as public entertainment (cf. Aristoph. Av. 759; Lucil. 300f. M.) and criticized by Plato (Leg. 7,880) and, among others, Aeschines (Tim. 53). A silver stater from Leucas [1. pl. 5,46] depicts a rooster in fighting position, cameos also show actual fighting scenes (e.g. [1. pl. 21,33 and 35]; cf. [2]). Support for the rooster's frequently praised courage in battle (Pind. Ol. 12,14; Aesch. Eum. 813; Plin. HN 10,47; Ael. NA 4,29) was provided through appropriate feeding with garlic (σκόροδον) and onions (κρόμμυον; Xen. Symp. 4,9; Schol. Aristoph. Equ. 494). Friends also liked to give each other a rooster (with erotic connotations; cf. the representations of roosters and Eros on cameos [1. pl. 16,31; 21,47–50; 21,54]), its constant willingness to mate: Aristot. Hist. an. 1,1,488b 4, likewise for the rock partridge: Hist. an. 8(9),8,613b 25f.).

As a bird of the deity of light, its crowing announcing the coming of the morning (Theognis 863f.; Plin. HN 10,46), the rooster was, following Persian custom, an attribute of Hermes, Helios-Apollo, Eos and Mithras, and was supposed to keep away demons such as the basilisks (Ael. NA 3,31). With this apotropaic quality, it often adorns tombstones, urns, weapons etc. The lion's fear of it (Aesop. 84 and 292 HAUSRATH; Ael. NA 3,31 and 5,50; Plin. HN. 8,52 and 10,47; Lucr. 4,710–17), or rather: its crowing is perhaps also of religious origin. Roosters were sacrificed to Asclepius and Hercules (Pl. Phd. 118; Ael. NA 17,46; Artem. 255,24; Plut. Symp. 4,10,1). As a bird of the light, it also was an attribute of Christ for Christians (Prud. Liber cathemerinon 1).

As a supplier of eggs and meat, the chicken played a lesser role in Greece than in Rome from the 1st cent. BC onwards, though the breeding and fattening of chickens is said to have been important on Delos (Varro, Rust. 3,9,2; Columella 8,2,4; Plin. HN 10,139). Chicken meat was considered by Galen (De bonis malisque sucis 3,1; De alim. fac. 3,18,3) to be easily digestible and nutritious. According to 3,21,1, fresh eggs, only briefly boiled, were also to be recommended. In Italy hybridizations gave rise to a brownish breed that is still called 'Italian' and lays a great number of eggs. In Germany, Gaul and Britain there had also already been domesticated chickens from presumably the late Hallstatt and early La Tène period onwards (Caes. B Gall. 5,12; cf. [3. 69ff.; 4. 6ff.]). Only from the 1st cent. AD onwards is there evidence (bone finds) of the larger Roman breeds in those areas. Aristotle conducted a very precise biological investigation of the reproduction of chickens and the development of the young in the egg (main passages: Hist. an. 5,13,544a 31–33 and 6,1,558b 10–22 regarding reproduction and ovogenesis; Hist. an. 6,3,561a 6–562a 20 regarding the development of the young; Hist. an. 4,9,536a 30–32 regarding the behaviour of a rooster after its victory over rivals; 8(9),49,631b 8–18 regarding sexual behavioural disorders of both the male and the female, etc.). The crystalline gastroliths *alectoriae* are said to have made the athlete Milon of Croton invincible (Plin. HN 37,144). Details about breeding are to be found in Columella 8,2,2–15 to 7,5 and Pallad. 1,27.

Pliny (HN 10,48ff.) examines the role of the sacred chickens (*pulli*), the so-called *auspicium ex tripudiis*, i.e. the investigating of the will of the gods through the eating behaviour of the animals which formed a part of Roman cult prior to state ventures (→ Divination). The first evidence of this is for 325 BC (Liv. 8,30). Cicero (Div. 1,28; 2,72; Nat. D. 2,7) shows through his ironic report that this procedure was often manipulated [5. 1,82ff.; 6. 532; 7] and also not taken seriously any more.

→ Cockfighting

1 F. Imhoof-Blumer, O. Keller, Tier- und Pflanzenbilder, 1889, repr. 1972 2 K. Schneider, s.v. Hahnenkämpfe, RE 7, 2210 3 O. F. Gandert, Zur Abstammungsund Kulturgesch. des Hausgeflügels, insbes. des Haushuhns, in: Beitr. zur Frühgesch. der Landwirtschaft 1, 1953 4 W. Schweizer, Zur Frühgesch. des Haushuhns in Mitteleuropa, diss. München 1961 5 Mommsen, Staatsrecht 6 G. Wissowa, Religion und Kultus der Römer, ²1912 7 Marbach, s.v. Tripudium, RE 7 A, 230ff. 8 Toynbee, Tierwelt.

B. Lorentz, Kulturgesch. Beitr. zur Tierkunde des Alt. Die Hühnervögel, 1904, III–XIV (Jb. Kgl. Gymn. Wurzen). C.HÜ.

Chicory (χιχόριον, χιχόρη, χίχορα; *kichórion, kichórē, kíchora* in Theophr. Hist. pl. 1,10,7; 7,7,3 and passim; *cichorium, cichoreum, cichora* in Plin. HN 21,88, and ἐντύβιον, ἔντυβον, *intybus* or *intubus* Columella 11,3,27; Plin. HN 19,129). The endive, the name for two related composite species native to the Mediterranean Sea: 1) the mainly perennial wild succory (*Cicorium intybus* L.) with its hirsute shoot that are more than one metre high; it has many names in common with the plantain (*plantago*) that grows in the same location and was likewise made into syrup and distillate, as well as with the sunflower (*helianthus*) and the heliotrope (*heliotropium, solsequium*), as they turn their flowers towards the sun. 2) The endive *Cichoria endivia* L. that is almost bare and lives for one to two years; its ligulate flowers are usually azure or white.

According to Plin. HN 21,88 the endive was first cultivated in Egypt. As its leaves were eaten as winter salad, its name has been derived from Egyptian *tubi* (= January). The leaves of both species were used as vegetables and for salad; together with the roots, a juice was made that was used against inflammation, constipation, but also warts and worms (cf. Plin. HN 20,73f.). In modern times a coffee substitute was made from the burnt roots of a cultivated strain of *C. intybus*; this was also used to make coffee go further. C.HÜ.

→ Salad

Chidibbia Town in Africa proconsularis in the valley of Medjerda, modern Slouguia. Initially C. was a simple *civitas*, but at the latest at the end of the 2nd cent. AD, it was under the administration of *undecimprimi* (CIL VIII 1, 1327; Suppl. I, 14875) and in the 3rd cent., rose to the status of → *municipium*. Inscriptions: CIL VIII 1, 1326–1352; VIII 2, 10614; Suppl. I, 14870–14879; BCTH 1932/33, 198f.

C. Lepelley, Les cités de l'Afrique romaine 2, 1981, 105. W.HU.

Chigi Painter Late proto-Corinthian vase painter from c. 640 BC, named for the exceptional vase in Rome (VG, formerly Chigi collection; the term Chigi Painter (CP) has displaced 'Macmillan Painter' in archaeological terminology). The Chigi Vase is the earliest and most richly painted Corinthian *olpe*, with a volute handle. Separated by black bands picked out in light colours (decorative motifs, a hare hunt), three polychrome friezes follow one below the other: a battle, with the oldest representation of a hoplite phalanx; then adjacent to each other a judgment of Paris (accompanied by non-Corinthian names), riders and vehicles, a double sphinx and a lion hunt; lowermost a shallower frieze with hare and fox hunts. Also, on the *aryballoi* with lion head spouts in Berlin and London ('Macmillan *aryballos*'), miniature hoplites, riders and hunting scenes; on the Aegina *olpe* fragment a hunt.

All the pieces are distinguished by excellent painting in polychrome (black slip, brown, yellow, purple, white), rich scratch-work and lively images. The CP, who did not come from Corinth, is joined by other painters, some of them of high quality, to form the so-called Chigi group, who paint mainly *aryballoi* and *olpai* with animal friezes, mythological scenes, or *olpai* in various colours with tongues of foliage.

Amyx, CVP 31–33, 301, 334, 369f. 557 no. 2; Amyx, Addenda 15; E. Simon, Die griech. Vasen², 1981 pl. 25, VII; M. Akurgal, Eine protokorinthische Oinochoe aus Erythrai, in: MDAI(I) 42, 1992, 83–89. M.ST.

Child, Childhood
A. THE CONCEPTION OF CHILDHOOD AND ATTITUDE TOWARDS THE CHILD   B. BIRTH AND ACCEPTANCE OF THE CHILD   C. EARLY CHILDHOOD AND CARERS   D. SICKNESS AND DEATH   E. SLAVE CHILDREN

A. THE CONCEPTION OF CHILDHOOD AND ATTITUDE TOWARDS THE CHILD

In antiquity, numerous terms for the child (in literature, legal language etc.) distinguish stages of childhood (βρέφος/*bréphos*, παιδίον/*paidíon*, παῖς/*paîs*; Lat. *infans*, *puer*), stress the different significance of the child to each of its parents (*pais/téknon*) or the child's unfitness to be held guilty or responsible before the law (*infans*, *impuber*); some of these terms possess a broad spectrum of meaning [6. 12–22].

In the dichotomy of childhood and adulthood as observed in both Greece and Rome, childhood in itself as a phase of life possessed no worth; it was described as a phase of incomplete human existence [6. 1–22; 12. 17–25]. This attitude, which could always be accompanied by empathy with the daily existence and fate of the child, had not yet disappeared in the Hellenistic period; still there already was a more intensive and close relationship to the child, which was now observed and represented in images and poetry for its own sake. Pleasure was taken in its unfeigned naturalness and its integrity; its distinctive physical and emotional nature was already being acknowledged. From the 1st cent. BC, Roman literature (cf. Cic. Att. 1,10,6; 7,2,4) and art also took children and childhood as themes, emphasized the specific characteristics of the child as opposed to the adult, and also discovered an emotive language (pet names) and iconography [3. 102f.]. There furthermore is praise for the *puer senex*, the gifted child acting like an adult. In late antiquity, Augustine (Aug. Conf. 1) described childhood succinctly, taking the behaviour of children as a basis for postulating the infant's sinfulness, and approving the use of force in the upbringing of children.

B. BIRTH AND ACCEPTANCE OF THE CHILD

Literary, philosophical, legal and medical texts that express the desire people in antiquity felt for children, or rather: that cite the begetting of children as the true purpose of marriage and the duty of a good citizen (cf. e.g. Plin. Ep. 4,15,3 and the legal formula *liberorum quaerendorum causa*), display knowledge of the risks to the health of child and mother at the time of birth and infancy [9. 93f., 103ff.], but also of the significance of the marriage bond and with it of the child's legal status. The purification of the house after a → birth, and the acceptance of the child by the κύριος (→ *Kyrios*) or → *pater familias* are placatory signs to the gods; the delayed acceptance ceremony (ἀμφιδρόμια/*amphidrómia*; → *lustratio*) and the even later naming and registration, while recording legal recognition of the child, at the same time attest to awareness of the dangers to its

physical well-being (Pl. Tht. 160e–161a; Aristot. Hist. an. 588a; Macrob. Sat. 1,16,36) [5. 51–56; 2. 284–287; 4. 323–327]. Examinations of the child's physical constitution were recommended by doctors, and indeed put into practice in Sparta.

C. EARLY CHILDHOOD AND CARERS

In addition to mother and siblings, there also were other people who maintained close contact with the children of a household during the phases of their infancy and early childhood: in rich households, for example, → wet-nurses (most of them were slaves), *paedagogi* and other servants; in poorer families relations and neighbours or their children (on the father cf. Aristoph. Nub. 1380–1385). Doctors and philosophers wrote not only on the selection of and the physical and personal suitability for this circle of people (Plut. Mor. 4b–5a), but also about the child's early upbringing and character formation [1. 13–36, 37–75]. At this age, provided that economic circumstances did not already necessitate enlisting them for work [1. 103–124], the children had leisure for imitative and free play (with hoops, yo-yos, balls, nuts etc.); ancient theories of education endeavoured to put even this play phase to the service of → education (Pl. Leg. 643b-d; Aristot. Pol. 1336a; cf. for the Christian era Jer. Ep. 107,4). This first phase of life, where there even were specific festivals for small children (e.g. in Athens the χόες/*chóes*), ended with the beginning of schooling outside the home, or the ἀγωγή (→ *Agoge*), for boys, and with training both within and (especially in the Hellenistic period and Rome) outside the home for girls from about seven years of age.

D. SICKNESS AND DEATH

Given the high perinatal and childhood mortality, there has been a tendency to suggest that parents in antiquity were indifferent to the deaths of their children (lit. in [5. 48–51]), or that they developed strategies for emotional self-protection (cf. Cic. Tusc. 1,93); in recent times, researchers have occasionally even gone so far as to postulate child abuse and infanticide as veritable hallmarks of ancient society. Even though, however, the tradition may well contain testimony of parental cruelty and inadequate care, there equally exists evidence of parental affection, love and mourning [5]. When e.g. small children are under-represented in funerary inscriptions, remained unmentioned in acts of public remembrance or were granted only restricted rites and periods of mourning (Vat. 321), this probably was due to the fact that they were not yet recognized as full members of the family, and that their early death precluded them from ever being considered for bearing family traditions, caring for their parents, keeping the cult of ancestors, contributing their labour, or being heirs. One also has to consider that the ancient customs of remembrance and dedication were strongly dependent on literary and social conventions; it will hardly be possible to equate the attitude of a mother towards her child — effected by the pains and fears of pregnancy, birth and childcare, and mostly without voice in the tradition — to that of fathers, doctors, jurists, politicians or moralists. Infant death in antiquity — as in developing countries today — was closely related to parental poverty, malnourishment and childhood diseases. When children had survived the first years of their lives, especially critical in this respect, *mors immatura* affected the parents all the more strongly [5].

E. SLAVE CHILDREN

Unfree birth played a significant role in the perpetuation of slavery in Greece, Graeco-Roman Egypt and the western part of the Roman Empire. The life of 'houseborn slaves' (οἰκογενεῖς/*oikogeneîs*, Lat. *vernae*: training, concubinage, sale or manumission) depended upon the social status and plans of their master. In Roman literature, slave children are depicted as impudent and badly brought up (Sen. De Providentia 1,6; Hor. Sat. 2,6,66; Mart. 10,3,1); still, slave owners seem to have positively valued such *vernae* (Sen. Ep. 12,3) [7].
→ Education; → Family planning; → Family; → Birth; → Youth; → Children's games; → Child exposure

1 K. BRADLEY, Discovering the Roman Family, 1991 2 M. DEISSMANN-MERTEN, Zur Sozialgesch. des Kindes im ant. Griechenland, in: [8], 267–316 3 S. DIXON, The Roman Family, 1992, 98–132 4 E. EYBEN, Sozialgesch. des Kindes im Röm. Altertum, in: [8], 317–363 5 P. GARNSEY, Child-Rearing in Ancient Italy, in: D. I. KERTZER, R. P. SALLER (eds.), The Family in Italy from Antiquity to the Present, 1991, 48–65 6 M. GOLDEN, Children and Childhood in Classical Athens, 1990 7 E. HERRMANN, Ex ancilla natus, 1994 8 J. MARTIN, A. NITSCHKE (eds.), Zur Sozialgesch. der Kindheit, 1986 9 T. G. PARKIN, Demography and Roman Society, 1992 10 B. RAWSON, Adult-Child Relationships in Roman Society, in: Id. (ed.), Marriage, Divorce and Children in Ancient Rome, 1991, 7–30 11 Id., The Iconography of Roman Childhood, in: Id., P. WEAVER (ed.), The Roman Family in Italy, 1997, 205–232 (commentary by J. HUDKINSON, 233–238) 12 TH. WIEDEMANN, Adults and Children in the Roman Empire, 1989.   J.W.

Child emperors see → Emperors, child

Childeric I Frankish king (*c.* 436–482), son of the *hếrōs epốnymos* Meroveus and father of → Clovis I. (Chlodovechus). C. ruled the Frankish province of Tournai from *c.* 463, and was frequently victorious as an ally of Rome fighting in northern Gallia against the West Goths and the Saxons. He was probably also entrusted with administrating the province of *Belgica II* (Greg. Tur. Franc. 2,9–27; Fredegar 3,11–12 MGH SRM 2). A legend relates that he interrupted his reign with eight years' exile in Thuringia (Greg. Tur. Franc. 2,12).

U. NONN, s.v. Childeric I., LMA 2, 1817f.; J. WERNER, Childeric Gesch. und Arch., in: AW 14, 1983, 28–35; S. FAMING, s.v. Childeric I., Medieval France. An Encyclopedia, 1995, 217.
PLAY : P. ERNST, Childeric Ein Trauerspiel, 1959.   W.SP.

C.'s tomb was discovered in 1653 at his capital Tournai, and identified by the inscription on a signet ring. Only a part of the extensive grave goods survives (Paris, LV). They and the entire tomb complex reflect C.'s status as a Germanic warrior king who was at the same time a high-ranking Roman officer (signet ring, late Roman gold onion head fibula and coins).
→ Clovis I; → Francs; → Funerary architecture

RGA 4, s.v. C., 441–460; P. PÉRIN, M. KAZANSKI, Das Grab Ch. I., in: Die Franken — Wegbereiter Europas. Exhibition catalogue Reiss-Museum Mannheim, 1996, 173–182.   V.P.

Child exposure Exposure of children (Greek ἔκθεσις/ *ékthesis*; Lat. *expositio/oblatio*), which must be clearly distinguished from infanticide, is to be seen as a method of ancient family planning. The decision whether to expose an infant lay with the head of the family: in Greece — with the exception of Sparta, where the phyle elders (τῶν φυλετῶν οἱ πρεσβύτατοι) examined newly born infants either to order or to forbid that they be raised — this was the κύριος/→ *kýrios*; in Rome the *pater familias*. Demographic theories regarding the frequency of infant exposure are not unproblematic as both the attractiveness of the theme, as for instance in the ancient → novel, and the imprecise terminology do not allow for certainty as regards the evidence. The exposure of children, however, is well attested also outside fictional texts (cf. P Oxy. 744). The exposure or killing of children with physical defects is said to have been especially common (Plut. Lycurgus 16; Pl. Resp. 460c; Aristot. Pol. 1335b; Sor. 2,6), but, in view of the genetic defects attested in the Hippocratic texts and elsewhere, we ought to be careful in this matter. The literature cites several old Roman laws and customs concerning the killing or exposure of 'deformed children' (Lex XII tab. 4,1; Dion. Hal. Ant. Rom. 2,15,2; Cic. Leg. 3,19; Sen. De Ira 1,15,2; Liv. 27,37,5f.); these however refer primarily not to a generalized practice, but to the conception of the child born defective as a *portentum* (evil omen). Illegitimate children, too, were subjected to exposure, although there are many examples of νόθοι/*nóthoi*, Lat. *spurii* (→ Nothos, *spurius*), who were not exposed.

It is generally assumed that female infants were more often exposed than males; in view of the anthropologically attested preference for male births in traditional societies this may be so; but an appreciably higher rate of exposure of girls would necessarily have had clearly evident repercussions on the number of marriageable women. As reasons for the exposure of children we primarily have to assume economic and social hardship, birth out of wedlock or as a result of adultery, and perhaps also fear of 'dangerous' progeny. Depending on the circumstances, new-born children will probably have been looked at in many different ways: as additional mouths to feed, potential heirs or bearers of dowries, or as a future labour force. Polybius supposedly alludes to a conscious policy of population control in

Greece (Pol. 36,17); the limited demographic understanding we find in antiquity however makes this unlikely.

The choice of sites for exposure (dung-heaps, shrines, populated places) and the use of γνωρίσματα/ *gnōrísmata*, Lat. *crepundia* (recognition marks) indicates the parents' desire that their children should survive and later be identified. Those who did survive might meet a harsh fate (slavery, begging, prostitution). In Athens and Rome the foundling seems to have nominally remained under the κυριεία/*kyrieía*, Lat. *patria potestas* of the biological father or the → *pater familias*. Sources from the time of Constantine oppose a *de iure* enslavement of foundlings; *de facto* however many free children probably became unfree. From AD 331 the finder specified the standing of the child taken in (Cod. Theod. 5,9,1f.); from AD 529 the *expositus* (exposed infant) was always accorded freeborn status (Cod. Iust. 1,4,24). By AD 374 at the latest (Cod. Theod. 9,14,1; cf. Cod. Iust. 8,51,2; 9,16,7), the exposure of infants became a capital crime.

The first open condemnation of the practice can be found in Philo (Phil. De Specialibus Legibus 3,110–119), whose position was later shared by many Christian authors such as Tertullian (Tert. Apol. 9,6f.; Tert. Ad nat. 1,15).

→ Abandonment myths; → Family planning; → Birth; → Ruler, birth of the

1 D. ENGELS, The Problem of Female Infanticide in the Greco-Roman World, in: CPh 75, 1980, 112–120 2 E. EYBEN, Family Planning in Antiquity, in: AncSoc 11–12, 1980/81, 5–82 3 M. GOLDEN, Demography and the Exposure of Girls at Athens, in: Phoenix 35, 1981, 316–331 4 F. KUDLIEN, Wie erkannte der ant. Ehemann einen Bankert?, in: RhM 132, 1989, 204–214 5 H. S. NIELSEN, Alumnus: A Term of Relation Denoting Quasi-Adoption, in: Classica et Mediaevalia 38, 1987, 141–188 6 R. OLDENZIEL, The Historiography of Infanticide in Antiquity, in: J. BLOK, P. MASON (eds.), Sexual Asymmetry, 1987, 87–107 7 C. PATTERSON, 'Not Worth the Rearing'. The Causes of Infant Exposure in Ancient Greece, in: TAPhA 115, 1985, 103–123 8 S. TREGGIARI, Roman Marriage, 1991.   J.W.

Children's Games The educational value of children's games was already known in antiquity; thus Plato (Pl. Leg. 643b-c; cf. Aristot. Pol. 7,17,1336a) saw in games imitating the activities of adults a preparation for later life. Quintilian (Quint. Inst. 1,1,20; 1,1,26; 1,3,11) fostered guessing games, games with ivory letters and learning in games in order to promote the child's mental capacities; for this purpose, the *ostomáchion* game (*loculus Archimedius*) — in which 14 variously shaped geometric figures had to be placed into a square or objects, people or animals — was particularly suited.

The children of antiquity had a large range of toys and games, the literary evidence of which is now rather incomplete and to a large extent based on Poll. 9,94–129; for example, Suetonius' work 'On the games of the Greeks' (cf. p. 322–331 REIFFERSCHEID) and Crates'

Paidiaí (cf. Ath. 11,478f.) have been lost. Many of the games were more a pastime, like catching fruit and similar things with one's mouth (Suet. Claud. 27,1), running howling after passers-by or pulling philosophers' beards (Hor. Sat. 1,3,133–135; Hor. Ars P. 455f.); other games arose out of the occasion, like walking on ice (Anth. Pal. 7,542; 9,56; cf. also Petron. Sat. 64,12). Small children had fun with rattles, rattling toys, little bells or toy animals made of clay, wax or bronze. Later there were → tops, yo-yos, swings, seesaws, hobby-horse riding, little carts, hoop rolling, for boys among others the game with soldiers, for girls with miniature furniture or devices, as well as dolls (with partially moveable limbs). Also worthy of mention are marionettes (νευρόσπαστα, *neuróspasta*, cf. Hor. Sat. 2,7,82; → puppet shows) that were, however, mostly performed by professional puppeteers (cf. Petron. Sat. 34,8–10; Vitr. De arch. 10,7,4 for moveable and sound-producing dolls); there do not appear to have been any doll's houses. Toys were kept in little boxes. Ancient art frequently depicts children with toys or at play (→ Choe), and finds of ancient toys are fairly common.

Children also built sandcastles for themselves, made figures out of clay and even produced their own toys (e.g. Aristoph. Nub. 877–881). Children in ancient times also played with animals. Birds (doves), hares and dogs are the main animals worthy of mention here; in this way, for example, mice were made to pull a little cart (Hor. Sat. 2,3,247f.), and strings were also tied around the legs of birds or beetles and they were made to fly (Aristoph. Nub. 764); several statues, however, show children torturing animals, for example, letting a cat reach for a bird which they were holding by the wings, or a tortoise tied by one leg hanging over a dog. For boys and girls there were various group games to pass the time, including → ball games, → Games of dexterity, → running and catching games or → riddles. Many games imitated the actions of adults; in the → *basilínda* game the 'king' who was determined by lot had to be obeyed by the other children, the 'soldiers' (Poll. 9,110). Court scenes (*ludus ad iudices*), gladiator and soldier games were also played. → Astragalos [2] and nuts in particular were also very popular as toys (→ Games of dexterity) — thus Pers. 1,10 describes growing up as *nuces relinquere* ('leaving the nuts'). Toys were consecrated in sanctuaries when children became adults (e.g. Pers. 2,70; Anth. Pal. 6,280; 282; 309; → Wedding customs; → Tops), and were put into the graves of children who had died.

R. AMEDICK, Die Sarkophage mit Darstellungen aus dem Menschenleben 4. Vita Privata, 1991, 97–104; L. DEUBNER, Spiele und Spielzeug der Griechen, in: Die Antike 6, 1930, 162–177; G. V. HOORN, Choes and Anthesteria, 1951; A. RIECHE, Röm. Kinder- und Gesellschaftsspiele (Limesmuseum Aalen 34), 1984; H. RÜHFEL, Kinderleben im klassischen Athen, 1984; Id., Das Kind in der griech. Kunst, 1984; K. SCHAUENBURG, Erotenspiele, 1 and 2, in: Antike Welt 7, 1976, H. 3, 39–52; H. 4, 28–35; E. SCHMIDT, Spielzeug und Spiele der Kinder im klassischen Altertum, 1971; C. WEISS, A. BUHL, Votivgaben aus Ton. Jojo oder Fadenspule, in: AA 1990, 494–505.   R.H.

Chiliarchos Commander of a 1,000–man contingent in the Macedonian and Ptolemaic armies (e.g. Arr. Anab. 1,22,7). At the same time, the term serves as a Greek translation for the commander of the royal guard in Persia, the 1,000 μηλοφόροι (*mēlophóroi*) (Aesch. Pers. 304). After the conquest of Persia the expression came to apply to the most important office in the new imperial order after Alexander's death (Diod. Sic. 18,48,4). The military and political powers attached to it are unclear. With the emergence of the kingdoms of the Diadochi this sense of the term became obsolete.

L.B.

Chilon (Χίλων; *Chílōn*).
[1] From Sparta; son of Damagetus; owing to his leading role in the politics of Sparta (ephor *c.* 556 BC), in the middle of the 6th cent. he became first ephor (Sosicrates FHG IV 502 [1]); also ascribed to him was the strengthening of the ephorate in relation to the kings (Diog. Laert. 1,68). Owing to his elegiac poetry and his wisdom he was counted among the 'Seven Sages' of archaic Greece (Pl. Prt. 343a; Diog. Laert. 1,68–73). Rylands papyrus 18 (= FGrH 105 F 1) names him along with Anaxandridas II as an opponent of tyrants such as Aeschines in Sicyon [2; 3]; this legend was probably extant as early as the 5th cent. Collections of his famous sayings (τὰ Χίλωνος παραγγέλματα; *tà Chílōnos parangélmata*), whose laconic nature became proverbial (ὁ Χιλώνειος τρόπος; *ho Chilōneios trópos*) Diog. Laert. 1,72), survive in Diogenes Laertius, Plutarch ('Banquet of the Seven Sages') and Stobaeus. Nothing has survived of his elegies; a lyric fragment (BERGK III 199) refers with Solonic values to gold as the touchstone of human character. A letter to Periander, tersely written in Doric (Diog. Laert. 1,73), has an authentic air. That his was the greatest role in the development of what is called the Lycurgan order [5. 243ff.] is a modern thesis which cannot be substantiated by reference to Sparta's superiority over its rivals from the middle of the 6th cent. The strengthening of the → ephorate ascribed to him, is the outcome of a longer process of development [6. 75–84]. There is no evidence as to the particular powers enjoyed by C. as ephor [7. 21]. According to Paus. 3,16,4 a *heroon* was dedicated to him in Sparta. Among influences are two epigrams (Anth. Pal. 7,88 and 9,596), as well as a mosaic portrait in the Römisch-Germanisches Museum, Cologne.

1 V. EHRENBERG, Neugründer des Staates, 1925, 5ff., especially 46ff.   2 D.M. LEAHY, Chilon and Aeschines, in: Bulletin of the John Rylands Library 38, 1956, 406–435   3 Id., Chilon and Aeschines again, in: Phoenix 13, 1959, 31–37.   4 R. BERNHARDT, Die Entstehung der Legende von der tyrannenfeindlichen Außenpolitik Spartas im 6. und 5. Jh. v. Chr., in: Historia 36, 1987, 257–289   5 F. KIECHLE, Lakonien und Sparta, 1963   6 L. THOMMEN, Lakedaimonion Politeia, 1996   7 C.M. STIBBE, Chilon of Sparta, in: Medelingen van het Nederlands Instituut te Rome 46, 1985, 7–24.

W. G. FORREST, A History of Sparta 950–192 B.C., 1968, 76ff.

K.-W.W. and W.D.F.

[2] Spartiate from a royal house, probably Eurypontid; 219 BC failed in an attempted putsch with supporters of → Cleomenes III. He promised radical reforms, but did not find wide support (Pol. 4,81).

K.-W.W.

Chilonis (Χιλωνίς; *Chilōnís*).
[1] Legendary figure, said to be the wife of king → Theopompus, whom she is supposed to have freed from imprisonment by Messenians (Polyaenus, Strat. 8,34; Quint. Inst. 2,17,20; Plut. Lycurgus 7,2; Mor. 779e).
[2] Wife of → Cleonymus, son of Cleomenes II; she committed adultery with Acrotatus, later to be king; after the death of Cleonymus, who had left Sparta because of her, and joined Pyrrhus, she apparently married Acrotatus (Syll.³ 430; Plut. Pyrrhus 26,17–24; 27,10; 28,5f.).
[3] Daughter of Leonidas II, whom she followed into exile in 242 BC; after his return in 241, however, she went into exile with her husband Cleombrotus, who had taken part in the putsch against his father-in-law and usurped the royal title (Plut. Agis 17,1–18,3).

K.-W.W.

Chilperic
[1] C. I, Burgundian king; died *c.* 480. Co-ruler from 457, after the death of his brother Gundic in *c.* 472 he replaced the latter as *magister militum Galliarum* (Sid. Apoll. Epist. 5,6,2). First having fought against the West Goths, he eventually went over to their side and dissolved the treaty of federation with the Western Roman Empire.
→ Magister militum

J. RICHARD, s.v. Chilperic I., LMA 2, 1824f.; A. DEMANDT, s.v. Chilperic, RE Suppl. 12, 1588.

W.SP.

[2] Merovingian king, born *c.* 537 youngest son of Chlotar I, after whose death in 561 the kingdom was divided between his four sons. At first C. ruled only the region of Soissons, but in 567 after the death of his brother Charibert was able to add large parts of northern and southern Gaul. He then fought in various alliances against his brothers Gunthram and Sigbert, and eventually after 575 (Sigbert died) ruled over the largest Merovingian kingdom (Greg. Tur. Franc. 4, 22–6,46; Edict. Chilperici MGH chapter 1 no. 4). C. was active as a writer and interested in theology; one poem survives (MGH PP 4,455). While Venantius Fortunatus (Carm. 9,1–3 MGH AA 4,1) sings his praises as a strong and cultured king, Gregory of Tours judges him as 'Nero' and 'Herod' of his time (Franc. 6,46).

U. NONN, s.v. Chilperich I., LMA 2, 1825; S. FAMING, s.v. Chilperic I., Medieval France. An Encyclopedia, 1995, 217–218.

W.SP.

Chimaera (χίμαιρα; *chímaira*). C., 'goat', is the Lycian monster, 'lion in front, snake behind, and she-goat in the middle' (Hom. Il. 6,181 = Lucr. 5,905), slain by

→ Bellerophon. It is the child of → Typhon by Echidna, mother of the → Sphinx (Phix: Hes. Theog. 319–326); a different tradition says it was reared by the Lycian Amisodarus (Hom. Il. 16,328). A firm component of the myth, since Homer, is that it breathes fire: according to Ov. Met. 9,647 and Apollod. 2,31 from the eponymous goat's head (otherwise see [1]) so often portrayed in pictures [2; 3]. In Virgil's 'Underworld' it lives in company with other monsters (Aen. 6,288, likewise Lucian Dial. Mort. 30,1).

In natural allegorical interpretations C. has been understood as a volcanic mountain (Plin. HN 2,236; 5,100; Isid. Etym. 11,3,36 i.a.), from an ethical standpoint as an image for the ages of man (Isid. Etym. 1,40,4). In post-antiquity C. became a metaphor for unfounded notions and fantasies.

1 H. USENER, KS 4, 1913, 302f.   2 A. JACQUEMIN, s.v. Chimaira, LIMC 3.1, 249–259   M.L. SCHMITT, Bellerophon and the Chimaira in archaic Greek art, in: AJA 70, 1966, 341–347.   F.G.

China (Σῖνα; *Sîna*). C. comprises within its modern borders several ancient cultural zones, with various traditions and tics looking to the west and the south. The steppe zone in the north was in continuous contact with western Siberia and eastern Europe from at least the 2nd millennium BC, always under the influence of the central Chinese cultures of the Yellow River region and the coastal zone. Southern China was orientated towards the south and south-east. Traffic along the 'silk roads' is attested since the Achaemenid period, and C. seems to have been accessible by sea since the 2nd–3rd cents. AD. C. and the Chinese became known to the ancient world in two ways: on the one hand it was known as the land of the → Seres silk producers; on the other, contact with C. by sea made it known as Θῖναι (*Thînai*) or Σῖναι ἢ Θῖναι (*Sînai è Thînai*) (Ptol. 7,3,6), probably derived from the name of the Qin dynasty: corresponding to *ai Cīnasthāna* in Cosmas Indikopleustes, 2,45ff. (*c*. AD 550) as Τζίνιστα (*Tsínista*). The *Periplus Maris Erythraei* provides the most exact rendering of the Old Chinese *Ts'in*, with the form Θῖν (*Thîn*). A perhaps apocryphal embassy from An-tun (M. Aurelius Antoninus) is mentioned in the Han annals (→ Seres). The west provided metalware, glass, slaves and precious metals; exports were iron, cushions and → silk (Tac. Ann. 2,33; Suet. Cal. 52; Marinus of Tyrene; Ptol. 1,11,3–6, 13–1). Tendencies from the ancient West in 2nd–3rd cents. AD Buddhist wall paintings from Miran could go back to Roman contacts as well as to the Graeco-Bactrian traditions of the Kushans. Greek traditions in the form of fables, as well as Syrian/Manichaean and Christian/Nestorian motifs, occur among the Turfan texts (→ Turfan).

→ CHINA

A. DIHLE, Antike und Orient, 1984.   B.B.

Chiomara (Χιομάρα; *Chiomára*). Celtic name of the wife of the Tolistobogian king → Ortiagon [1. 156]. In 189 BC, after the victory of Cn. → Manlius Vulso over the Galatians at Olympus, C. came into the hands of a *centurio*. When he first sexually assaulted her and then wanted to set her free in return for a high ransom, she had him killed at the handover. She delivered his head to her husband. Polybius is supposed to have met her personally in Sardis, evidently when she was interned there after the fall of Ortiagon in 183 BC. Plutarch cites her as an exemplary heroine (Plut. Mor. 258E-F; cf. Pol. 21,38; Liv. 38,24).

1 L. WEISGERBER, Galatische Sprachreste, in: Natalicium. FS J. Geffken, 1931, 151–175.

H. RANKIN, Celts and the Classical World, 1987, 247–248; F. W. WALBANK, A Historical Commentary on Polybios, vol. 3, 1979, 151–152.   W.SP.

Chion (Χίων; *Chíōn*). From Heraclea; pupil of Plato; in 353/352 BC he killed Clearchus, tyrant of Heraclea. A collection of 17 letters in his name has come down to us; they reflect C.'s life from the time he moves to Athens to visit Plato's school to the moment when, having received news of Clearchus' seizure of power, he returns to Heraclea to carry out the assassination. Although the authenticity of these letters has found defenders [1], they are in all probability spurious; they were probably written in the 1st cent. AD, and perhaps originated within Heraclea, where the life and deeds of the historic C. were perpetuated by indigenous historians [2]. The economy of the narrative structure justifies the description of epistolary novel.

→ Epistolary novel; → Heraclea

1 Q. CATAUDELLA, Sull'autenticità delle lettere di Chione di Eraclea, in: Memorie dell'Accademia nazionale di Lincei Ser. VIII, 24, 1980, 649–751   2 B. ZUCCHELLI, A proposito dell' epistolario di Chione d'Eraclea, in: Paideia 41, 1986, 13–24.

I. DÜRING, Chion of Heraclea, A novel in letters. ed. with introduction and commentary, 1951; D. KONSTAN, P. MITSIS, Chion of Heraclea: a philosophical novel in letters, in: Apeiron 23, 1990, 257–279.   M.FU. and L.G.

Chione (Χιόνη; *Chiónē*).
[1] Daughter of Boreas and Oreithyia; mother of → Eumolpus by Poseidon. To avoid discovery she threw her child into the sea, but it was rescued by Poseidon (Eur. Erechtheus fr. 349 TGF; Apollod. 3,199–201). The name C., from χιών (*chión*) 'snow', is fitting for a daughter of the north wind; another C., daughter of Arcturus, was said to have been abducted by Boreas and given birth by him to the three Hyperborean priests of Apollo (Hecat. FGrH 264 F 12; Ps-Plut. Fluv. 5,3).
[2] Daughter of Daedalion; mother of Autolycus by Hermes, and of Philammon by Apollo (Ov. Met. 11,291–309; Hyg. Fab. 200–1). Probably for this reason the name is generic for a prostitute (e.g. Mart. 3,30,4; Juv. 1,3,136). In other sources this figure is called → Philonis.   E.K.

Chione novel (Χιόνη; *Chiónē*). A Greek novel, usually thus named after the putative female protagonist; three fragments survive, known to us only from WILCKEN's summary transcription of a Coptic palimpsest, the so-called *Codex Thebanus*, which was subsequently lost. The meagre fragments are difficult to interpret, but seem to show Chione as protagonist, courted by many suitors and then forced into marriage against her will; with her lover, she considers how she can end her life. Clear similarities to the → Chariton novel (also contained in the *Cod. Thebanus*) lead to the supposition that the two texts are contemporary with one another, perhaps that both are by Chariton. It is very doubtful whether two further fragments surviving on papyrus are related to the Chione novel [1].

→ Chariton; → Novel

1 M. GRONEWALD, Ein neues Fragment zu einem Roman (P. Berl. 10535 = PACK² 2631 + P. Berl. 21234 uned.), in: ZPE 35, 1979, 15–20; C. LUCKE, Bemerkungen zu zwei Romanfragmenten (P. Berl. 10535 = PACK² 2631 and P. Berl. 21234), in: ZPE 54, 1984, 41–47.

U. WILCKEN, Eine neue Roman-Hs., in: Archiv für Papyrusforschung 1, 1901, 227–272; S. STEPHENS, J. J. WINKLER (ed.), Ancient Greek novels: The fragments, 1993; N. MARINI, Osservazioni sul 'romanzo di Chione', in: Athenaeum 81, 1993, 587–600.   M.FU. and L.G.

Chionides (Χιωνίδης; *Chiōnídēs*). Earliest Attic comedy-writer known by name. As πρωταγωνιστής, *prōtagōnistés* (the sense of the term as used here is disputed [2. 132]) of the Old → Comedy, C. is said to have had a play performed as early as 'eight years before the Persian wars' (i.e. 486 BC counting inclusively) [1. test. 1]; this date is usually regarded as the beginning of the state-organized comedic *agones* at the Great Dionysia [2. 82]. Aristotle, too, places C., along with → Magnes, at the beginnings of Attic Comedy [1. test. 2]. Three titles of plays by C. have survived ('The Heroes', 'The Persians or the Assyrians', 'The Beggars'); half of the eight surviving fragments (which do not say much) are assigned to 'The Beggars', C.'s authorship of which is, however, cast in doubt by two source witnesses (fr. 4; 7). Whether the two other titles and the fragments pertaining to them are authentic must probably likewise remain uncertain [3. 240].

1 PCG IV, 1983, 72–76   2 A. W. PICKARD-CAMBRIDGE, The dramatic festivals of Athens, ²1968   3 F. STOESSL, Die Anfänge der Theatergesch. Athens, in: Grazer Beiträge 2, 1974, 239f.; 8, 1979, 58.   H.-G.NE.

Chionnes (Χιόννης; *Chiónnēs*). Writer of comedies, from 1st cent. BC Thebes; known only from inscriptions; he was victor at the Amphiareia and the Rhomaea in Oropus [1. test.].

1 PCG IV, 1983, 77.   H.-G.NE.

Chios (Χίος; *Chíos*).
A. INTRODUCTION   B. GRAECO-ROMAN PERIOD
C. BYZANTINE PERIOD

A. INTRODUCTION
Large (856 km²) island, *c.* 8 km from the mainland. The ancient settlements were on the east coast, where the main city of the same name is today (few traces, an earthquake in 1881 having destroyed nearly all buildings on the island). Highest point is the Pelinaion (1297 m). The east and south-east of C. is very fertile. In antiquity C. was also called Makre or Pityussa, 'Land of fir trees', its inhabitants being regarded as the 'richest of the Greeks' (Thuc. 8,45,4). Main products of note are wine and the resin of the mastic tree (*pistacia lentiscus*). Settlement occurred as early as the Neolithic (finds at Emporio in the south — continuity of settlement here up to the late Roman period — and in the limestone cave at Hag. Gala). C. 1000 BC settled by Ionian people with some Aeolian elements (preserved in the dialect of C.; cf. the language of the Homeric epics).

B. GRAECO-ROMAN PERIOD
During the 5th cent. C. was a member of the → Delian League; it seceded in 412 BC, and in spite of the defeat at Delphinium (near Langada on the northeast coast) resisted Athens successfully. C. was the first member of the 2nd → Athenian League, but again left it in 357 BC. Subsequently C. entered into alliance with Cos, Byzantium and Rhodes, under the protectorate of Mausolus. Restoration of democracy under Alexander.
From 190 BC C. sided with Rome, and under Sulla became → *civitas libera*. Christianity took hold in C. as early as the 3rd cent. AD, early churches appearing at Emporio and at Phanai on the site of a temple to Apollo.

M. BALLANCE, J. BOARDMAN, S. CORBETT et al., Excavations in Chios, 1952–1955; Byzantine Emporio, 1989; J. BOARDMAN (ed.), Chios. A conference at the Homereion in C. 1984, 1986; E. B. FRENCH, Archaeology in Greece 1993–94, 66; H. KALETSCH, s.v. Chios, in: LAUFFER, Griechenland, 170–174; A. N. TSARAVOPOULOS, Η αρχαια πολη της Χίου, in: Horos 4, 1986, 124–144.   H.KAL.

C. BYZANTINE PERIOD
After sustained construction activity during the 6th cent. [1. 423f.], radical changes are evident in the 7th, possibly related to Arab incursions; thus *c.* 660 the fortress of Emporio is destroyed by fire. After a lengthy gap in the records, at the beginning of the 9th cent. C. belongs to the → *thema* Aigaion Pelagos under an archon [1]. Subsequently, sovereignty alternates between Byzantines, Turks and Genoese.

T. E. GREGORY, s.v. C., ODB.   J.N.

Chirisophus (Χειρίσοφος; *Cheirísophos*).
[1] Spartiate; on the instructions of his polis, at Issus in 401 BC he joined the army of the younger → Cyrus with 700 hoplites (Xen. An. 1,4,3; Diod. Sic. 14,19,4f.); after

Cyrus' death at Cunaxa C. was sent by → Clearchus to Ariaeus, to offer him the Persian throne (Xen. An. 2,1,4f.). After Clearchus had been imprisoned and put to death, C. received supreme command of the entire remaining army (Diod. Sic. 14,27,1), and led the retreat to Trebizond: a fact Xenophon sought to play down for the increase of his own fame. After failing in 400 to receive sufficient ships from → Anaxibius, the Spartan nauarch in Byzantium, to continue by sea, he rejoined the army at Sinope (Xen. An. 6,1,15f.; Diod. Sic. 14,31,3), and led it to Heraclea; deposed in a mutiny, he moved from there to Calpe, where he died soon afterwards of a fever (Xen. An. 6,2,1–10; 6,4,11).   M.MEI.

[2] Silversmith of the Augustan period; he signed two silver cups decorated with Homeric scenes, found in Hoby (Denmark) and once in the possession of Silius Caecina (consul in AD 13). Surviving antique clay copies attest to their fame.
→ Toreutics

C.W. MÜLLER, Das Bildprogramm der Silberbecher von Hoby, in: JDAI 109, 1994, 231–352; V.H. POULSEN, Die Silberbecher von Hoby, in: AntPl 8, 1968, 69–74.   R.N.

Chirius Fortunatianus, C. see → Consultus Fortunatianus, C.

Chiron (Χίρων; *Chírōn* or Χείρων; *Cheírōn*). Centaur; son of the nymph Philyra and → Kronos; for the seduction of Philyra Cronus changed himself into a horse, which explains C.'s likeness to that animal (Apollod. 1,9; Verg. G. 3,92); his poetic name, after his mother, is Phil(l)yrides or Philyreios. Of his daughters, born to him by the nymph Chariclio, Ocyroe is an ecstatic seer (Ov. Met. 2,635–639); Endeis too, wife of → Aeacus and mother of Peleus, is held to be either his daughter (Hyg. Fab. 14,8) or that of → Sciron (Apollod. 3,158). He lives in a cave on the → Pelion, and his civilized ways distinguish him from the other centaurs, who are characterized as brutish [1]; Homer calls him 'the most righteous of the centaurs' (Il. 11,832, quoted in Ov. Fast. 1,413), Pindar 'lover of humanity' (P. 3,5). He has particular links with → Peleus, to whom he gives the ash spear (Hom. Il. 16,143 = 19,390), and whom he advises on how to win → Thetis; for this reason he figures in portrayals of the marriage of Peleus and Thetis [2]. He has healing powers (Hom. Il. 4,199; 1,832) and trains many heroes in the arts of hunting and warfare, healing and music: e.g. Peleus' son → Achilles (Hom. Il. 11,832; Hes. frg. 204,87), → Jason (Hes. Theog. 1001, frg. 40), → Asclepius (Pind. Pyth. 3,5–7; Nem. 3,54f.), → Actaeon (Apollod. 3,30); in the post-archaic period his expertise is extended to include astronomy, law and the rules regarding sacrifice. He is immortal ('a god' since Aesch. PV 1027; Soph. Trach. 714f.) until in the struggle with the attackers of → Pholus → Heracles hits him with a poisoned arrow, giving him a wound that cannot be healed, and he exchanges his life for that of Prometheus (Apollod. 2,84f.). Celestial legend transports him

to the heavens as Centaur (*centaurus*) or Sagittarius (*sagittarius*), attributing his death to a mishap unwanted by Heracles (Eratosth. Katasterismoi 40; Hyg. Poet. Astr. 2,38) or Achilles (Ov. Fast. 5,379–414).

In the history of religion, C. appears as a superhuman mentor, who, although living in a state of nature, initiates young heroes in their cultural tradition: which in the case of archaic Greece means especially hunting (as a preparation for war) and music [3]. Later mythologizers make him the human discoverer of veterinary medicine (Isid. Etym. 4,9,12); more originally, MACCHIAVELLI interprets the myth of Achilles' upbringing by C. as implying that the prince must use brute force as well as the law (Principe, ch. 18, p. 85 FIRPO).

1 G.S. KIRK, Myth, 1972, 152–162   2 M. GISLER-HUWILER, LIMC 3.1, 237–248   3 P. VIDAL-NAQUET, Le chasseur noir, 1981.   F.G.

Chiton (χιτών; *chitón*). Greek undergarment, originally of linen, then wool; probably of Semitic origin (→ Clothing). Frequent occurrences in Homer (e.g. Il. 2,42; 262; 416; 3,359; Od. 14,72; 19,242), show that the chiton was already a part of Greek costume in early times, and a favoured garment for men. The chiton came into fashion for women during the 1st half of the 6th cent. BC, and later replaced the → peplos (vase paintings, sculptures). The chiton consists of two rectangular lengths of material (*ptéryges*, wings), 150–180 cm wide and of varying length, sewn together lengthwise at their selvages. The cloth tube thus obtained was sewn together at two points at the shoulders, so as to provide at the upper end three openings for the head and the two arms (called a 'wide' chiton). If the tube was small, the armholes were left at the sides rather than at the upper edge ('tight' chiton). When made with more material, the chiton can be held together at the shoulders by means of pins or buttons instead of being sewn; in this way, depending on the fullness of the fabric, false sleeves can be created. A variation on the original look was produced by tubular sleeves reaching to the wrist, but it remains unclear how they were attached to the chiton; called a *chitòn cheiridōtós*, worn above all by serving women, people from the east, actors, participants in the Dionysian festival procession and musicians. The chiton is frequently worn with one or two belts; some of the material could be pulled up behind the belt so as to hang down in a bulge. The chiton was often of a length to reach the feet (*chitòn podérēs*) or even to form a train (*chitòn syrtós*).

While during the 5th cent. BC the long chiton predominates in women's dress, already in the late archaic period the short chiton (*chitōnískos*) was replacing the long chiton in men's clothing. From then on the long chiton served to characterize worthy old men, figures from myth (kings) and gods (Dionysus). The long chiton was worn by younger males only as formal dress or on cult occasions. The short chiton, on the other hand, became part of everyday costume; it was worn above all by men whose occupation demanded freedom of movement, i.e. soldiers under arms or foot travellers. Women did not wear this short form of the chiton, unless, for example, they were huntresses like → Atalanta and → Artemis. Besides the type that was closed at both shoulders (*chitòn amphimáschalos*) there was the *chitòn heteromáschalos*, closed at the left shoulder and leaving the right shoulder and right side of the body uncovered. This garment, called an → exomis, was worn by farmers, slaves and workers; in mythology and art, the *exomis* is the garment most favoured by → Hephaestus. The headgear associated with it was the → pilos.

M. BIEBER, Entwicklungsgesch. der griech. Tracht, 1967; Id., Charakter und Unterschiede der griech. und röm. Kleidung, in: AA 1973, 431–434; A. PEKRIDOU-GORECKI, Mode im ant. Griechenland, 1989, 71–77; 85–87; 134f.

R.H.

Chlaina (χλαῖνα; *chlaîna*, from χλαίνω; *chliaínō*, 'to warm'). Already mentioned in Homer (Il. 16,224; Od. 4,50 and *passim*) as a warm coat for men made out of sheep's wool to protect against cold and rain. The *chlaina* could be laid over the shoulders unfolded (ἁπλοῖς; *haploís*) or double-folded (δίπλαξ; *díplax*) and be held together with a pin; it could be red or purple in colour and decorated with patterns or figures (Hom.Il. 10,133; 22,441). The *chlaina* was, according to Poll. 7,46, worn as a cape over the → chiton and was part of the dress of farmers and shepherds as well as aristocrats of both sexes. Since the early archaic period (Melian amphora in Athens [1]) there is evidence of the *chlaina* especially in vase paintings (→ François Vase) in which it is worn by divine figures, heroes and heroines. In late archaeological art and from the 5th cent. BC onwards, there is only evidence of it amongst the philosophers (→ Tribon), *kitharoidoi* and on statues of divinities; otherwise, however, it is rarely represented or mentioned. At the beginning of the 5th cent. BC it was replaced by the → chlamys. A → blanket, too, could be called *chlaina* (Hom.Il. 24,646; Od. 3,349f.; Soph.Trach. 540). The comment in the literature that the *chlaina* was a winner's prize for competitions in Pallene is noteworthy (Str. 8,386; Poll. 7,67).
→ Himation; → Clothing

1 P. ARIAS, M. HIRMER, Griech. Vasen, 1964, pl. 22–23.

H. ÖHLER, Unt. zu den männlichen röm. Mantelstatuen 1, 1961; K. POLASCHEK, Unt. zu griech. Mantelstatuen, 1969.

R.H.

Chlamys (χλαμύς; *chlamýs*). Shoulder-coat made of wool for travellers, warriors and hunters. The many-coloured and embroidered *chlamys* appeared in the 6th cent. BC and originally came from Thessaly (Poll. 7,46; 10,124; Philostr. Heroïkos 674) where it was also awarded as a winner's prize after athletic contests (Eust. in Hom. Il. 2,732), or Macedonia (Aristot. fr. 500

ROSE). Typically it was worn as follows: the cloth of the ovally or rectangularly tailored coat was folded vertically, laid around the left side of the body, fed to the right shoulder from front and back and joined together with a → fibula. In this way the left arm was covered but the right one had complete freedom of movement. The *chlamys* could also be attached above the chest so that both arms could move freely. Because of the coat tails hanging down, the authors called the *chlamys* θεσσαλικαὶ πτέρυγες (*thessalikaì ptéryges*). In classical Greece the *chlamys* was generally widespread; in Athens it belonged with the → petasos to the dress of the → ephebes. In Greek art there is evidence of it amongst riders (Parthenon frieze), mythical hunters (→ Meleager), and especially Hermes (Hermes Ludovisi), Apollo (Apollo of Belvedere), and Eros (cf. Sappho 56D); often — especially on vase paintings — it is very difficult to differentiate from the → chlaina. In Plautus (e.g. Mil. 1423; Pseud. 1184) there is various evidence of it as a soldier's coat; it was also worn by Roman emperors (Hdn. 3,7,2; 7,5,3) and was part of the dress of aristocratic dignitaries at the Byzantine court.
→ Clothing; → Paludamentum

A. PEKRIDOU-GORECKI, Mode im antiken Griechenland, 1989, 88, 135 (with references).

R.H.

Chloe (Χλόη; *Chlóē*). 'Greening'; epiclesis of → Demeter (Ath. 14,618d/e). She had a shrine close to the Acropolis, where a ram was sacrificed to her (Paus. 1,22,3; Aristoph. Lys. 835; FGrH 328 F 6; Eupolis PCG V fr.196). She is also attested in Eleusis (IG II2 949,7), on Myconus (LSCG 96,11) and in the Tetrapolis (LSCG 20 B 49). An exuberant festival, the Chloia, placed by late antique theology at around springtime, was celebrated in her name (Cornutus, Theol. 28).

A. B. CHANDOR, The Attic Festivals of Demeter and their Relation to the Agricultural Year, diss. 1976, 132–136; GRAF, 273; NILSSON, Feste 328f.

R.B.

Chloris (Χλωρίς, Χλῶρις; *Chlōrís, Chlôris*).
[1] According to Ovid (Fast. 5,195ff.) the goddess → Flora was originally called C.; Zephyrus took her as his wife and made her goddess of flowers. This juxtaposition is an invention of Ovid. It was taken up by Lactantius (1,20,8) and by the *Anthologia Latina* (747R.).
[2] Daughter of → Amphion [1] and → Niobe. She was the only one of the daughters of Niobe to be spared by Artemis, because she prayed to Leto. Her image stood next to that of the goddess in the temple to Leto in Argus (Paus. 2,21,9; Hyg. Fab. 9f.; Apollod. 3,46).
[3] Daughter of Orchomenus; wife of → Ampyx. Mother of the seer Mopsus (Hyginus. Fab. 14,5; Paus. 5,17,10).
[4] Wife of the Pylian → Neleus; daughter of → Amphion [2] by Orchomenus (Hom. Od. 11,281–284; Hes. fr. 33a 6 M.-W.; Paus. 9,36,8). She was depicted in

Polygnotus' painting of the underworld in Delphi (Paus. 10,29,5).   R.B.

Chnubis (Χνοῦβις; *Chnoûbis*, also Χνοῦμις; *Chnoûmis* and Χνοῦφηις; *Chnoûphēis*, Str. 17,817).
[1] Greek form of the Egyptian Chnum, a ram-god, *ovis longipes palaeoaegyptiacus*, who appears early on as a human with a ram's head. → Elephantine, Esna, Hypselis and Antinoe are regarded as his cult centres. C. functions as a creator-god. In Elephantine he is lord of the cataract region, and along with the goddesses Satet and Anuket is considered to be protector of the sources of the Nile and dispenser of fertility. In Antinoe he is associated with Heqet the goddess of birth, a frog-goddess; both are revered as assistants at childbirth. He creates human beings on the potter's wheel. In the Graeco-Roman period association of C. with → Agathos Daimon is attested [1; 2].
[2] Town in Upper Egypt (Ptol. Geogr. 4,5,73).

1 R. REITZENSTEIN, Das iranische Erlösungsmysterium, 1921, 192   2 TH. HOPFNER, in: Archiv Orientalni 3, 1931, 150.

E. OTTO, s.v. Chnum, LÄ 1, 950–954.   R.GR.

Chnum see → Chnubis

Choaspes
[1] River in → Susiana, famed for the high quality of its water. The Persian king drank only (boiled) water from the Choaspes, carried for him on campaigns and journeys in silver jugs. Partially identified with the → Eulaeus, nowadays with the Karkhe or the Kârûn.
                                                            A.KU. and H.S.-W.
[2] River of the southern Hindu Kush, named only in the context of Alexander's campaign (Aristot. Mete. 1,13,16; Aristobulus in Str. 15,1,26); in Arr. Anab. 4,23,2 and Suda IV p. 812 under the name Χόης (today Kunaṛ), northerly tributary of the Κώφην (today Kābul), which it joins near Πλημούριον (*Plēmoúrion*) (Str. ibid.; Eustath. Comm. Dionys. Per. 1140; GGM II 402); Hsch. p. 1559 describes it as a river in India.

R. SCHMITT, Choaspes, in: EncIr.; P. BRIANT, L'eau du Grand Roi, in: L. MILANO (ed.), Drinking in Ancient Societies, 1994, 45–65; Atlas of the World II, 1959, Pl. 31 (Pakistan, Kashmir, Afghanistan).   B.B. and H.T.

Choba (Coba, Χωβάθ; *Chōbáth*, Χωβάτ; *Chōbát*).
Town in Mauretania Caesariensis, 50 km east of Saldae; the modern Ziama. (Sources: Ptol. 4,2,9; It. Ant. 18,2; Tab. Peut. 2,5; Geogr. Rav. 40,22). *Municipium* under Hadrian (AD 117–138): CIL VIII 2, 8375 [1. 495–497] (additional inscription: CIL VIII 2, 8374–8378; Suppl. 3, 20214).

1 L. LESCHI, in: BCTH 1946–1949, appeared 1953.

J.-P. LAPORTE, s.v. Choba, EB, 1933–1935.   W.HU.

Choerilus (Χοιρίλος; *Choirílos*).
[1] **from Samos.** Poet of the 5th cent. BC. Earliest known author of historically based epic poetry; died at the court of the Macedonian king Archelaus (413–399 BC) (Suda: SH 315 = PEG I, T 1). As late as 404 he is attested as participating in an *agon* of encomiastic poetry in honour of Lysander on Samos (Plut.: PEG I, T 3). These two dates derive from two separate and probably independent sources. The divergent chronologies in the Suda (C. as a contemporary of the epic poet Panyassis; a youth at the time of the second Persian War during the 75th Olympiad, 480/477) are either inventions or very rough estimates. The love affair reported in the Suda between C. and Herodotus also appears to be an invention, in all probability fed by the thematic correspondence between Herodotus' and C.' work (which was known in antiquity).

The subject of C.' epic was certainly the second Persian War, and possibly included the first Persian War as well as other events involving 'barbarians': the Suda summarizes its theme as 'the victory of the Athenians over Xerxes' (κατὰ Ξέρξου; *katà Xérxou*); the title was Περσικά/Περσηίς (*Persiká/ Persēís*) according to SH 318f. and 323 = PEG I, 3; 5; 10. The subtitle Χοιρίλου ποιήματα βαρβαρικά· μηδικά· περσικά SH 314 = PEG I, 6 can in any case be understood either as a) 'Barbarian Wars', b) 'The 1st Persian War', c) 'The 2nd Persian War' or 'a, that is b and c' [1]: a background similar to that which introduces the narrative climax of the second Persian War in Herodotus? The work's success with the Athenians, who resolved on a public performance as they did for the works of Homer, leads us to suppose that its character was more or less celebratory.

That C. functioned to some degree as a professional encomiast is shown by his participation in the *agon* of 404 in honour of Lysander (it is impossible to establish whether C. actually contributed a work dedicated to Lysander). This can perhaps be interpreted in the very light of this new kind of poetry established on the basis of the *epinikion* and the encomium. Its heyday falls in the lifetime of C. and the period shortly before. The boldness and autonomy of the choral metaphors may be related to the meagre expressive potential of the παραβολαί (*parabolaí*), ascribed by Aristotle to C. (Top. 157a 14; SH 327 = PEG I, T 7; Eust. 176, 34; identification with the tragedian Choerilus cannot be ruled out [2], but Aristot. Rh. 1415a 11 certainly refers to C. the epic poet). Besides, this C. expresses his impatience with the traditional restrictions imposed by the genre he has espoused: in a fragmentary *prooimion* (SH 317) C. poses the problems he faces in trying to be innovative as an epic poet as opposed to the simplicity of Homer's time, when the 'field' (i.e. probably themes and literary forms) was still untouched, whereas C. as 'last in the race', finds everything already 'staked out' and the *téchnai* (τέχναι; i.e. probably the literary genres) subjected to strict 'limits'.

Whether the title Ἀπορήματα Ἀρχιλόχου Εὐριπίδου Χοιρίλου in the catalogue of Aristotle's works by

Andronicus [4] of Rhodes (PEG I, T 14) relates to this or another C. is uncertain. It is, however, known that Aristotle (according to two fragments) and Praxiphanes (PEG I, T 5) took notice of C. Callim. Fr. 1,13–16 (PEG I, T 11) has been taken as a polemical allusion to C. According to Crates (the philosopher from Mallus?; Anth. Pal. 11,218 (PEG I, T 11)), Euphorion favoured C. over Antimachus [3] from Colophon: Crates, however, holds to his opposite opinion that Antimachus is better. Euphorion's opinion did not prevail; not one of the known canons gives consideration to C. (unlike Antimachus). Callimachus' pupil Ister (FGrH 334 F 61 = PEG I T 6) ascribed corrupt practices to C. at the court of Archelaus; similar rumours dogged the Hellenistic composers of encomia (→ Choerilus [3]). It is not possible to attest the survival of any particular text beyond the end of the imperial age; but C.'s historical epic was still being read in Oxyrhynchus during the 2nd/3rd cents. AD (the period of the papyrus with the subtitle, SH 314 = PEG I, T 6). On the Λαμαχά (Lamiaká) see → Choerilus [3].

1 SCHMID/STÄHLIN, I 2, 543   2 TrGF 2 T 9.

EDITIONS : P. RADICI COLACE, 1979 (with commentary); SH 1983; PEG I, 1987.
BIBLIOGRAPHY: A. BARIGAZZI, Mimnermo e Filita, Antimaco e Cerilo nel proemio degli Aitia di Callimaco, in: Hermes 84, 1956, 162–182; R. HÄUSSLER, Das histor. Epos I, 1976, 70–78; G. HUXLEY, Choerilus of Samos, in: GRBS 10, 1969, 12–29.   M.FA.

[2] from Athens. Tragedian; according to Suda χ 594 took part in his first competitions in 523/520 BC; he supposedly wrote 160 plays and celebrated 13 victories. In 499/496 he competed with Aeschylus and Pratinas (Suda π 2230). A model verse in 'Choerilian' metre survives. He is supposed to have made innovations in masks and costumes (?). One title is known: Alope.

METTE, 84; B. GAULY et al. (ed.), Musa Tragica, 1991, 2; TrGF 2.   F.P.

[3] from Iasus. Epic poet; travelled with Alexander the Great on his Asiatic expedition. Apart from verdicts given in antiquity regarding his output as a composer of encomiastic epic verse in the (paid) service of the ruler, nothing is known about him (Philod. Poem. I 25, 7ff., p. 87 SBORDONE; Hor. Epist. 2,1,232–234 and Ars 357; Curt. 8,5,8; Auson. Epist. 10, praef. 11; Ps.-Acro. on Hor. Epist. 2,1,233 and Ars 357; Porph. Hor. comm. on Ars 357). The judgments expressed are all more or less severe; they denigrate C., mostly by comparison with Homer. The juxtaposition of C. and Homer was presumably an almost commonplace device to characterize the unsuccessful encomiastic epic: perhaps unsuccessful because encomiastic? This attitude, condemning C. in advance, was obviously liable to belittle any good qualities C. might possess (most severe in their condemnation of C. are Horace and his commentators; their negative aesthetic estimation goes together with their contempt for the commercial motivation of his work).

Other contributory factors could be a dismissive attitude towards the explicit decision to flatter, fundamental to encomiastic verse, general antipathy towards commercial poetry (criticism of the greed of choral lyricists like Simonides is a commonplace), and the cult of Callimachus that flourished during the 1st cent. BC. Known references to C. date from this period. The Suda, with clear anachronism, attributes Λαμιαχά (Lamiaká), a piece about the Lamian War (332 BC), to C. [1]. The mistake arises from confusion between the two C.s (already present in the lemma: Χ. Σάμιος, τινὲς δὲ Ἰασέα). Λαμαχά has also been emended to Σαμαχά, a much more plausible title for C. [1] (SH 322 = PEG I, F 8). Attribution of fragments SH 329–332 to C. [3] or [1] presents similar difficulties.

1 F. MICHELAZZO, in: Prometheus 8, 1982, 31–42.
EDITION: SH.
BIBLIOGRAPHY: K. ZIEGLER, Das hell. Epos, ²1966 A. CAMERON, Callimachus in his World, 1995.   M.FA.

Choes see → Anthesteria

Choes pitchers [CP] Type three wine pitchers (→ Pottery, shapes and types of; → Chuos), used in Athens in drinking competitions on the day of Choes during the → Anthesteria. Not firmly identified with clay pitchers of similar size painted with freely chosen motifs. More easily differentiated are the small CP (5–15 cm high) produced in great numbers c. 400 BC. These bore images of children, pointing to sources that suggest the Choes as marking an important transition point in children's lives (IG II/III² 13139, 1368 l. 127–131). Some feast scenes, moreover, point to rites involving children on the day of Choes. Small CP were probably given as gifts to children at the festival of Choes; also generally as presents and as grave gifts.

H. HAMILTON, Choes and Anthesteria, 1992 (rev. by T. H. CARPENTER, in: CPh 89, 1994, 372–375); G. VAN HOORN, Choes and Anthesteria, 1951; H. RÜHFEL, Kinderleben im klass. Griechenland, 1984, 125–174.   I.S.

Choiak Name of the fourth month of the flood season in the Coptic calendar; from the Egyptian k3-ḥr-k3, originally the name of a festival [1]. The month begins on 27 November, shifted by the Gregorian calendar reform (October 1582).

1 F. DAUMAS, s.v. Choiak, LÄ 1, 958–960.   R.GR.

Choinix (χοῖνιξ; choînix). Greek term for a dry measure, especially for grain. Depending on the region, a choinix amounted to 1.01 l (Attica), 1.1 l (Aegina) or 1.52 l (Boeotia, Laconia). Under the Ptolemies, a choinix was equivalent to 0.82 l. The measure was based on the idea of the daily ration for a man. As a rule four kotylai (in late Egypt three) amounted to one choinix, whilst eight choinikes made a hekteus and 48 choinikes one medimnos (= 48.48 l or a maximum 72.96 l). According to VIEDEBANTT the choinix amounted to

0.906 l. NISSEN gives the Attic *choinix* in the time of Solon with 1.08 l, later it came to 1.228 l.

→ Hecteus; → Measure of volume; → Kotyle; → Medimnos

F. HULTSCH, Griech. und röm. Metrologie, ²1882; H. NISSEN, HbdA ²1, 1886, 8f.; F. HULTSCH, s.v. Choinix, RE III 2, 2356–2358; O. VIEDEBANTT, Forschungen zur Metrologie des Altertums, in: Abh. der königlich sächsischen Ges. der Wiss. 34.3, 1917; J. SHELTON, Artabs and Choenices, in: ZPE 24, 1977, 55–67; O. A. W. DILKE, Mathematik, Maße und Gewichte in der Antike, 1991.
A.M.

Choiroboskos Georgios (Χοιροβοσκός; *Choiroboskós*). Byzantine grammarian. His dates were for a long time problematic, but he has now been firmly placed in the 9th cent.: *terminus post quem* is his quotation (in the epimerismi) of authors in the 1st half of the 9th cent.; *terminus ante quem* use of his work in the *Etymologicum genuinum* (2nd half of the 9th cent.). He is ascribed the official title of οἰκουμενικὸς διδάσκαλος (*oikoumenikòs didáskalos*), which is attested for the 1st half of the 9th cent. Thus he fits well into the cultural milieu of the 9th-cent. renaissance (the time of Photius and Arethas), and the vogue for philological/grammatical writings which is characteristic of the period. The following works are known to us: 1. Preserved in its entirety, a thoroughgoing commentary on the grammatical *Canones* of Theodosius of Alexandria (used by *Etymologicum genuinum* and Eustathius); 2. Some *Excerpta*, come down to us under the name of a grammarian Heliodorus, a commentator on the Τέχνη γραμματική (*Téchnē grammatikḗ*) attributed to Dionysius Thrax; attached to this is a commentary on the treatise Περὶ προσῳδιῶν (*Perì prosōidiôn*), surviving as an appendix to the Τέχνη (*Téchnē*); 3. Περὶ ποσότητος (*Perì posótētos*), as part of Περὶ ὀρθογραφίας (*Perì orthographías*), a treatise (often quoted in Byzantine lexicons) which has not survived in its entirety; based on the analogous work by Herodianus; 4. Epimerismi on the Psalms; 5. A commentary on Hephaestion, transmitted anonymously; 6. A short treatise Περὶ τρόπων ποιητικῶν (*Perì trópōn poiētikôn*) (attribution is not quite certain). In the commentary on Theodosius, C. frequently refers to his lectures on Apollonius Dyscolus and Herodianus, which have not survived. Much has come down to us in the form of σχόλια ἀπὸ φωνῆς (*schólia apò phōnês*), thus as extracts from the classes he gave at the School of Constantinople.

→ Apollonius [11] Dyscolus; → Dionysius Thrax; → Epimerismi; → Etymologicum genuinum; → Eustathius; → Herodianus; → Hephaestion; → Scholia; → Theodosius

EDITIONS: A. HILGARD, Grammatici Graeci 4, 1, 1889, 101–371 (on 1); A. HILGARD, Grammatici Graeci 1, 3, 1901, 67–106 (on 2); I. BEKKER, Περὶ προσῳδιῶν, Anecdota Graeca, 675–708 (on 2); J. A. CRAMER, Anecdota Graeca II, 167–281; R. SCHNEIDER, Bodleiana, 1887, 20–33 (on 3); TH. GAISFORD, G. Choerobosci Dictata, 1842, III, 1–192 (on 4); M. CONSBRUCH, Hephaestionis Enchi-

ridion cum commentariis veteribus, 1906, 175–254 (on 5); SPENGEL, III 244–256 (on 6).

BIBLIOGRAPHY: L. COHN, s.v. Choiroboskos RE 3, 2363–2367; A. DICK, Epimerismi Homerici I, SGLG 5/1, 1983, 5–7; A. HILGARD, Grammatici Graeci 1, 3, XIV–XVIII and 4, LXI–CXXIII; HUNGER, Literatur II, 14, 19, 23, 50; W. J. W. KOSTER, De accentibus excerpta ex Choerobosco, Aetherio, Philopono, aliis, in: Mnemosyne 59, 1932, 132–164; KRUMBACHER, 583–85; B. A. MÜLLER, Zu Stephanos Byzantios, in: Hermes 53, 1918, 345–355; M. RICHARD, ΑΠΟ ΦΩΝΗΣ, in: Byzantion 20, 1950, 202–204; SCHMID/STÄHLIN II, 1079–80; CHR. THEODORIDIS, Der Hymnograph Klemens terminus post quem für Choiroboskos, in: ByzZ 73, 1980, 341–45.
F.M.

Cholargus (Χολαργός; *Cholargós*). Attic *asty* deme (→ Asty) of the Acamantis phyle; four (six) *bouleutai*. Its exact location is uncertain, presumably to the west or north-west of Athens, towards Phyle (Men. Dys. 33), the presumed location of the estate of Pericles, who hailed from C. (Thuc. 2,13; Plut. Pericles 3). Epitaphs for inhabitants of C. originate from Chaïdari (IG II² 7768). C. is one of those six or seven demes where the holding of → Thesmophoria is verified (IG II² 1184; LSCG no. 124); it also boasted a Python (ibid. l. 23), as well as a circular temenos of Heracles (IG II² 1248).

TRAILL, Attica, 47, 59, 68, 109 (no. 28), table 5; WHITEHEAD, Index s.v. C.
H.LO.

Choliambs see → Metre

Chollidae Listed amongst the *asty* demes of the Leontis phyle epigraphically [2. 99f.], but not in IG II² 2362 (200 BC); with four (?) *bouleutai*. Location debatable, probably neighbouring Acharnae, see Aristoph. Ach. 406. Archedemus, who had decorated the grotto of the Nymphs near Vari (→ Anagyrus), was naturalized in C.

1 TRAILL, 18ff., 109 (no. 29), table 4   2 Id., Diakris, the inland trittys of Leontis, in: Hesperia 47, 1978, 89–109   3 WHITEHEAD, 332 with fn. 35, 425.
H.LO.

Chomer see → Measure of volume

Chondros (χόνδρος; *chóndros, alica*). Groats of grain or spelt. The exact species cannot be established. Galen (Facult. nat. 1,6) relates it to wheat and describes the production of gruel (ῥόφημα) for people with stomach and gall bladder diseases (cf. Dioscorides 2,96 [1. I.73] = 2,118 [2.203f.] and Plin. HN. 18,112–113). Ps.-Hippoc. περὶ παθῶν (*perì pathôn*, 6,250 LITTRÉ) mentions it together with πτισάνη (*ptisánē*), κέγχρος (*kénchros*) and ἄλητον (*áleton*).

→ Special diet

1 M. WELLMANN (ed.), Pedanii Dioscuridis de materia medica, vol. 1, 1908, repr. 1958   2 J. BERENDES (ed.), Des Pedanios Dioskurides Arzneimittellehre, trans. and with explanations, 1902, repr. 1970.
C.HÜ.

Chora see → Territorium

Choragium see → Theatre

Choragos see → Choregos

Choral lyrics see → Lyric poetry, → Metre

Chorāsān Middle Persian xwarsārān, '[Land of the] Sunrise, the East'. Nowadays denotes the north-eastern part of Iran, with Mašhad as its administrative centre. In the pre-Islamic and early Islamic period C. included parts of Central Asia and western Afghanistan. It was under the Sassanids that C. first formed one of the four great provincial satrapies; it was ruled by a Spāhpat with his seat in Merv, having jurisdiction over the following districts (Yaʾqūbī, Taʾrīḫ I, 201): Nīšāpūr, Harāt, Marw, Marw ar-Rūd, Fāryāb, Ṭālaqān, Balḫ, Buḫārā, Bādḡīs, Abīward, Ḡarǧistān, Ṭūs, Saraḫs and Ǧurǧān. Muslim occupation of C. radiated from Baṣra, and began with the conquest of Nīšāpūr in 651/52, ending only after a protracted process of pacification. During the early Umayyad period C. was ruled by the governors of Baṣra (also Sīstān), enlisting the aid of members of northern Arabian tribes. The ʿAbbāsid revolution, which led to the fall of the ʿUmayyāds of Damascus, began in Merv and was carried out for the most part by Chorāsānians (Iranians and Arabs). In the mid 9th cent. AD Chorāsānian soldiers and officials formed the backbone of the ʿAbbāsid state. This process was still further reinforced when al-Maʾmūn, formerly governor of Merv, won the caliphate with the support of eastern Iran against his brother Amīn (813). It was only in the course of the 9th cent. that Nīšāpūr achieved the status of capital of Chorāsān.

W. BARTHOLD, An Historical Geography of Iran, 1984, 87–111; EI V, 55–59, s.v. Chorasan; E. HERZFELD, Khorasan, in: Islam 11, 1921, 107–174.   T.L.

Chorat Name of a stream east of the Jordan; not located (forms: Hebr. kᵉrît; LXX Χορράθ (Chorráth); Vulg. Carith; Eus. On. 174,16 Χορρά (Chorrá); Jer. On. 175,16 Ch.; Peregrinatio Aetheriae, CSEL 39, 58f. Corra). ABEL [1. 484f.], GLUECK [2] i.a. [3], arguing on the basis of the prophet Elias' having hidden there (1 Kg 17,3,5), identify C. with the Wadi el-Jubis in northern Gilead, which joins the Jordan to the south of Pella.

1 F.-M. ABEL, Géographie de la Palestine 2 vols., 1933–38 2 N. GLUECK, AASO 25–28, 1951, 219 3 J. DÖLLER, Geogr. und ethnographische Stud. zum III. und IV. Buch der Könige, 1904, 224ff.   M.K.

Choregia (ἡ χορηγία; hē chorēgía). Office of the choregos; from c. 500 BC a special form of → leitourgia in Athens. The choregia was imposed on prosperous citizens by the appropriate archon, and young notables were glad to use this kind of leiturgia in order to win political esteem (in 472 Pericles was choregos for Aeschylus' 'Persians'; cf. also Thuc. 6,16,3 on Alcibiades). The political significance of the choregia becomes especially clear in the dithyrambic agon, where it is not the poet but the choregos who is named in the inscription (→ Didaskaliai). Towards the end of the Peloponnesian War it was difficult to find enough prosperous citizens for the choregia, so that at the Great Dionysia of each of the years 406/405 BC the financial burdens were taken on by two citizens. In around 315 BC under Demetrius of Phalerum the choregia was replaced by the office of the → agonothetes, chosen by the people to look after the organization of events; the requisite expenses were borne by the people.
→ Choregos

A. BRINCK, Inscr. Graecae ad choregiam pertinentes, 1885; C. BOTTIN, Etude sur la chorégie dithyrambique en Attique jusqu'à l'époque de Démetrius de Phalère, in: RBPh 9, 1930, 749–782; 10, 1931, 5–32, 463–493; A. W. PICKARD-CAMBRIDGE, The Dramatic Festivals of Athens, ²1968 (1988), 75–77, 86–93.   B.Z.

Choregos (χορηγός; chorēgós). Literally 'chorus leader' (in lyric texts); in Athens the 'sponsor' of a lyric or dramatic chorus. The choregoi themselves were responsible for assembling their chorus of citizens, looking after their upkeep during the month of rehearsals, seeing to the smooth running of rehearsals, which were led by the poet or by a professional chorodidaskalos, and above all for meeting the costs. (In Plautus the choregos became a lender of costumes; in Plaut. Curc. 462–486 he makes a metatheatrical appearance.) Many ancillary services (parachoregema) were called for: extras, props, a subsidiary chorus; the choreutes expected lavish entertainment in connection with the performance (Aristoph. Ach. 1154). In return, the choregos was given prominence during the festival: he was granted the tripod as prize for the winning dithyramb (→ Lysicrates monument), and his name appeared before that of the poet in the official victory inscription [1. 5].
→ Chorus; → Choregia

1 H. J. METTE, Urkunden dramatischer Aufführungen in Griechenland, 1977 2 O. TAPLIN, Comic Angels, 1993

H.-D. BLUME, Einführung in das ant. Theaterwesen, ³1991; A. W. PICKARD-CAMBRIDGE, The Dramatic Festivals of Athens, ²1968   H.BL.

Chorezmia (Χορασμίη; Chorasmíē, Arabic Ḫwārizm). River-valley oasis on the lower Āmū-daryā. Settled by farmers since the 5th–4th millennia BC. In the Avesta (→ Avesta script) as xwarizm; mentioned in the → Bisutun inscription. The Chorezmians together with the Aryans formed a satrapy (Hdt. III,93,173 Hecat. fr.). Abū Raiḥān al-Bīrūnī gives the year 980 before the era of Alexander (1292 BC) as the beginning of the Chorezmian era. When in 329/328 Alexander wintered in → Maracanda he was visited by → Pharasmanes, king of the Chorezmians (Arr. Anab. 4,15,4); his capital was

→ Toprakkale. Džanbas-Kala performed a similar function. The coinage followed Graeco-Bactrian models. Burial place of the dynasty was the round castle at Koj Krylgan Kala. Partially subjugated by the Kushans, who secured the land with fortresses like Giaur Kaia. An extensive irrigation system expanded the area under cultivation and permitted the establishment of sites such as the Berkut Kala oasis with fortified estates. The irrigation system virtually drained the Aral Sea, and in the 6th cent. finally collapsed. During the 11th–12th cents. C. was in the possession of the Qıptčaqen, who reorganized the irrigation system and made it the centre of the Islamic empire of the Ḥwārizm Šāhs, around the city of Ūrgang, which in 1220/21 was destroyed along with the empire in the Mongol assault. It subsequently became the eastern trading centre of the Golden Horde. It was destroyed again by Tamerlane, along with other cities of C. Since that time C. has been a relatively isolated oasis, from the early 16th cent. under Uzbekh rule. Until its seizure by the Russians C. was an independent khanate.

→ Irrigation

A. MANKOVSKAJA, V. BULATOVA, Pamjatniki zod cestva Chorezma, 197X; S.P. TOLSTOV, Po drevnim del'tam Oksa i Jaksarta, 1962.   B.B.

Chorhe (Persian *Ḫurḫēh*). Ruins on a tributary of the Qom Rud south-west of Qom, partially excavated by A. HAKIMI in 1956 (unpublished); restored by H. RAH-BAR. HERZFELD interpreted the parts still visible as the remains of a Hellenistic temple ([1, 2], doubts in [3]). The excavation leaves no doubt that these are parts of a palace: a stoa of eight columns between projecting walls, probably part of a great court, with storerooms behind [7]. The forms of capitals and bases [4] are 'decadent Ionic' [6], certainly later than the Ionic capitals of the tomb facade at Qizqapan, probably later than the quadrifrons of Qal'eh Zohak [4]. The close positioning of the slender columns is reminiscent of the imperial period. Settlement continued into the Islamic period.

1 E. HERZFELD, Am Tor von Asien, 1920, 32 pl. XVIII 2 Id., Iran in the Ancient East, 1941, 283f., fig. 382ff., pl. 88f.   3 K. SCHIPPMANN, Die iran. Feuerheiligtümer, 1971, 424f.   4 W. KLEISS, in: AMI 6, 1973, 173f. fig. 9f., 180–182 fig. 18f.   5 Id., in: AMI 14, 1981, 65–67 6 D. HUFF, in: AMI 17, 1984, 244   7 W. KLEISS, in: AMI 18, 1985, 173–180.   PE.CA.

Choricius Sophist and rhetorician from the school of Gaza in the 1st half of the 6th cent.; pupil and successor of Procopius of Gaza. Two *enkōmia* to bishop Marcianus (Or. 1 and 2 FOERSTER/RICHTSTEIG) incorporate *ekphráseis* of two churches inaugurated by the bishop, together with their paintings. Thus C. is first to apply the tools of pagan rhetoric to Christian objects. He made two further eulogies to prominent individuals, *dux* Aratios and the *archon* Stephanus (Or. 3) as well as

general Summos (Or. 4); two wedding addresses to his pupil Zacharias (Or. 5) as well as to Procopius, Johannes and Elijah on the occasion of their triple marriage (Or. 6); two funeral orations to Maria, mother of Marcianus (Or. 7), and to his teacher Procopius (Or. 8). He wrote a speech on the occasion of the *brumalia* of Emperor Justinian I (Or. 13). In addition, 12 practice speeches (μελέται; *melétai, declamationes*) and 25 introductory speeches (διαλέξεις; *dialékseis*) survive i.a. A speech in the form of a mime's apologia (Or 23) is regarded as a last literary reference to the stage [1]. Bible references occur only in the *ekphráseis*, otherwise only occasional references to Christianity. C. was an expert classicist, and as an Attic specialist employed a wealth of quotations and allusions [2. 121–123]. The 9th-cent. patriarch → Photius of Constantinople reviews him in his *Bibliothékē* [3].

1 I. STEPHANES (ed.), Χορικίου σοφιστοῦ Γάζης Συνηγορία μίμων, 1986   2 R. HENRY, Photius. Bibliothèque II, 1960 (Cod. 160)   3 K. MALCHIN, De Choricii Gazaei veterum Graecorum scriptorum studiis, 1884.

EDITIONS: IO. FR. BOISSONADE (ed.), Choricii Gazaei Orationes, Declamationes, Fragmenta, 1846; R. FOERSTER, E. RICHTSTEIG (ed.), Choricii Gazaei Opera, 1929. BIBLIOGRAPHY: W. SCHMID, s.v. C., RE 3, 2424–2431; K. GERTH, s.v. Zweite Sophistik, RE Suppl. 8, 1956, 743; H. HUNGER, Die hochsprachliche profane Lit. der Byzantiner I, 1978, 121, 150; H. MAGUIRE, The halfcone vault of St. Stephen at Gasa, in: Dumbarton Oaks Papers 32, 1978, 319–325; C. MANGO, The Art of the Byzantine Empire 312–1453, 1972, 60–72.   G.MA.

Chorizontes (χωρίζοντες; *chōrízontes*). Collective name (from χωρίζειν; *chōrízein*, 'to separate') used in the Homer scholia to describe grammarians who, on the grounds of conscientious observation of linguistic and stylistic differences and contradictions in the '*Iliad*' and the '*Odyssey*', as well as their content, hold to the thesis that the '*Odyssey*' is not by Homer. The Alexandrian → grammarians, who held to the 'orthodox' position (established by Aristotle), saw Homer as author of both *Iliad* and *Odyssey*; in consequence, → Aristarchus [4] of Samothrace and his school maintained an energetic polemic against the *chorizontes*. Two grammarians, Xenon and Hellanicus, are known from Proclus' *Vita Homeri* (p. 102.3 ALLEN) as representatives of this tendency.

→ Aristarchus of Samothrace; → Hellanicus (grammarian); → Homer; → Xenon

EDITION: J. W. KOHL, De Chorizontibus, 1917. BIBLIOGRAPHY: L. COHN, s.v. C., RE 3, 2439; M. FUHRMANN, s.v. Xenon (15), RE 9 A, 1540; A. GUDEMAN, s.v. Hellanikos (7), RE 8, 153–55; J. W. KOHL, Die homer. Frage der Chorizonten, in: Neue Jbb. für klass. Alt. 1921, 198–214; F. MONTANARI, Hellanikos, SGLG 7, 1988, 45–73, 119–121; Id., Studi di filologia omerica antica II, 1995, 13–19; PFEIFFER, KPI, 261–2, 282, n. 126.   F.M.

Chorsiae (Χορσίαι, Χορσία; *Chorsíai, Chorsía*). Isolated Boeotian town on the Gulf of Corinth, above the bay of Hagios Sarandi. At first a dependency of Thespiae; independent in the 4th cent. BC. Phocians occupied C. in 347/346 BC, using it as a base for incursions into Boeotia. In 346 BC Philip II gave C. back to the Boeotians, after levelling its walls (sources: Dem. Or. 19,141; Scyl. 38; Diod. Sic. 16,58,1; Plin. HN 4,8; StV 3,565; SEG 22,410).

FOSSEY, 187–196.   K.F.

Chorus
A. CONCEPT   B. MANIFESTATIONS, GENRES
C. ATTIC DRAMA   D. CHRISTIANITY   E. STARS

A. CONCEPT
Χορός (*Chorós*), 'Ring dance, troupe of dancers, dance floor, chorus of singers' ('original meaning not ascertainable with any certainty' FRISK). Ring or group dance associated with singing; in the narrower sense the chorus trained for the performance of choral lyrics and songs in Attic drama. Surviving evidence (texts of choral lyrics, pictorial representations, descriptions) provides scarcely more than sketchy impressions of the lively whole. The loss of song meant that the union of word, movement, gesture and dance created by it also disappeared. It seems possible, though, that the metre may still provide access to the → rhythm.

B. MANIFESTATIONS, GENRES
Cult-associated group dances occurred widely in the ancient orient, in Egypt and in Israel (→ Dance). The particular course of development among the Greeks, which must have been set in train long before the emergence of the written tradition, presupposes that cult and festival were not confined to theurgical song. Among the earliest evidence are the verses of Homer and depictions of ring dances on vases of the geometric period. The choral lyric discernible since the 7th cent. BC blossomed in ever new creative guises during the 6th and down to the middle of the 5th cent., enjoying a discrete late flowering in the choral song of Attic drama. The union of poetry, music and dance required the intervention of the professional 'impresario' (ποιητής; *poiētḗs*) and the specialist chorus. A clear demarcation from other forms of song and dance often seems difficult or impossible to surmise today, as for example when Homer has Demodocus sing a comic song in epic hexameters while a group of dancers treads the θεῖος χορός (*theîos chorós*; 'divine round') (Od. 8,264). The division between choral and solo lyrics (cf. χορῳδία μονῳδία; *chorōidía monōidía* in Pl. Leg. 764 d-e) says little either about the intrinsic distinction between the two genres. And the assignment of names to dances and vice versa frequently seems to remain hypothetical. In myth it is the Muses who dance and sing the divine χορός (*chorós*) to Apollo's lyre (Hes. Theog. 7; → Terpsichore), similar to the circle of nymphs around Artemis

(Hom. Il. 16,182f.). Then Cretans also sing and dance the paean to Apollo's lyre (H. Hom. Apollon. 514ff.). Attic vases and reliefs show dancing nymphs led by Hermes. In day to day life choral songs and dances belonged to the cult and the festival (festivals of gods and heroes, cult of the dead, marriage, sporting and musical competitions, feasts, the grape harvest). There are many examples of cult-linked dances, e.g. to Apollo on Delos (Thuc. 3,104), at Delphi (Alc. p. 22 TREU; Paus. 4,4,1) and Sparta/Amyclae (Ath. 4,139 e), to Aphrodite on Delos (γέρανος; *géranos*, Plut. Thes. 21,1f.), to Hera at Argos. Names of choral songs are already given in Homer: Linos (Il. 18,570), → paean (Hom. Il. 1,473), → threnos (Hom. Il. 24,721), → hymenaios (Hom. Il. 18,493) and others (Il. 18,590; Od. 6,101; Hom. Od. 23,133f.). For the Gymnopaedia in Sparta c. 665 BC, Thaletas instituted group dances (Ath. 15,678 C) such as → hyporchema; others were → *embaterion* and *hormos* for mixed dances (Lucian Salt. 11). → *Hymnoi* too, are attested early on (Pind. N. 8, 50; cf. Hdt. 4,35), as are → *prosodion* (Paus. 4,4,1) and → dithyramb (Archil. fr. 77 D). Texts of choral lyrics (→ Lyric poetry) survive from the time of Alcman; a → Partheneion sung by 11 girls at the feast of Artemis (fr. 1 PMG) displays a monostrophic structure (two-part form attested by Heph. 74,18). Stesichorus (fr. S 7–87 SLG) and Ibycus (fr. 1 PMG) wrote songs in triad form with strophe, antistrophe and epode; foremost among later exponents were Pindar and Bacchylides (→ Epinikion). The poet himself or the chorus leader or teacher (Pl. Leg. 812e) rehearsed the chorus in their singing. The number of *choreutai* varied (preferred: 7, 9, 10, 12). The dithyramb was performed as a κύκλιος χορός (*kýklios chorós*) by 50 *choreutai*. Accompanying instruments were sometimes the *kithara*, sometimes the *aulos*, often both (Pind. N. 9,8). In spite of good pictorial representations, gestures, steps, figures and formations are difficult to reconstruct. Choral *agones* for men or youths are attested, first for Athens (Dionysia, Panathenaea i.a.) and increasingly elsewhere. The theme of the *agon* was evidently the dithyramb, a special favourite in the 5th and 4th cents. Underpinned by *technitai* and in the shadow of ancient models choral poetry survived into the Hellenistic age, in encomia, paeans, hymns; examples survive in inscriptions, i.a. at Delphi (→ Philodamus, → Aristonous), some accompanied by musical notation.

C. ATTIC DRAMA
In Attic drama, with its genres of → tragedy, → satyr play and → comedy originating in the chorus, each with its own (nowadays disputed) developmental history, the art of the choral song developed independently. The musical component of the drama, vital to its festive character, fell to the chorus (later also to the → monody), its status as an element distinct from the 'recitative' character of the actors accentuated by use of the Doric dialect. The repeated individual strophe or triad was replaced by a series of ever new pairs of strophes,

melded rhythmically and musically to each moment of the action. The choral component comprised → *parodos*, → *stasimon* and → *exodos*, in ancient comedy the seven-part → *parabasis*. There was also verbal interchange between chorus/chorus leader and actors, as well as shared laments (→ Kommoi). *Emméleia* has come down as the name of the choral dance in tragedy, *kórdax* in comedy, *síkinnis* in the satyr play (Ath. 1,20e). The place in the theatre where the chorus danced was the *orchestra*. Still to the fore in Aeschylus, in the plays of his successors the chorus declined in significance. In the beginning 12 *choreutai* took part, in Sophocles 15, in the comedy 24. They moved in a rectangular formation: in the tragedy five rows each of three *choreutai*, in the comedy six rows of four (Poll. 4,108f.). The chorus seldom left the stage (Aesch. Eum. before 244; Soph. Aj. before 866). The variety of metre and form of the strophe suggests an analogous musical structure. Every year, the *archon* chose three *choregoi* from among the richer citizens, to be responsible for the three stage choruses (selection of members, financing of the production up to the moment of performance). As, in the form's heyday, a piece would be performed only once, everything must have depended on clarity of speech, sustained by music, dance and movement. Repeated performances began after 386 BC, especially outside of Athens. In the Hellenistic theatre there was promotion of actors, virtuoso singers and instrumentalists; the age of the dramatic chorus was past. In Rome from the 1st cent. BC, *chorus* entered language and literature as a loan-word (revival of the chorus in the tragedies of Seneca).

D. CHRISTIANITY

A new order was emerging in the Hellenistic world. The Septuagint translates the Hebrew *mahôl* with χορός (*chorós*) in the sense of round dance (Pss 149,3; 150,4; Ex 32,19). The same word then came to denote the Christian flock or community (Ignatius Ant. ad Rom. 2,2). Clement of Alexandria called the Church a holy chorus of the soul (str. 7,14 = § 87,3); the Gnostic became one with the divine chorus through sacrifice, prayer etc. (7,7, = § 49,4), and, spiritually speaking, lived in the chorus of the saints (§ 80,2), always surrounded by the chorus of the angels (7,12 = § 78,6). The Jewish conceptions, of the ἄγγελος (*ángelos*) as messenger of God (OT) and of accompanying χοροί (*choroí*) (Ios. Ant. Iud. 7,85), underwent reinterpretation under Christianity (NT, individualized forms, patron saints, archangels, hierarchy). The mystic concept, influenced by Neoplatonism, of ascent towards god via the three times three hierarchy of the angelic chorus reached the Latin world of the Middle Ages via Ps.-Dionysius Areopagites. The Christian demand that the community sing as it were with one voice (Ignatius ad Ephes. 4,2) found expression in the singing of the liturgy in choral unison (cf. Marcus Diaconus Vita Porph. 20). And finally, from the 7th cent., the place in the church occupied by the clerical chorus was called the *chorus* (choir) (Johan-

nes Moschus, Pratum spirit. 126 MIGNE, PG 87,2988 B).

E. STARS

In a metaphorical sense, the stars or the planets were described as a chorus. The image of the αἰθέριοι χοροί (*aithérioi choroí* 'celestial round') of the stars (Eur. El. 467), which may have corresponded to an age-old conception, occurs repeatedly in Greek and Roman literature, as in Pl. Ti. 40c, Mesomedes (2,17 HEITSCH), Philo (De opificio mundi 115), Horace (Carm. 4,14,21) and in Christian writers (1 Clem. Rom. ad Cor. 20,3; Ignatius ad Ephes. 19,2).

REISCH s.v. Ch., Χορηγία, Χορηγός, Χορικοὶ ἀγῶνες, Χοροδιδάσκαλος, Χοροστάτης, RE 3, 2374ff.; F. WEEGE, Der Tanz in der Ant., 1926; A. W. PICKARD-CAMBRIDGE, Dithyramb, tragedy and comedy, ²1962; R. HAMMERSTEIN, Die Musik der Engel, 1962; R. COWHURST, Representations of performances of choral lyric on Greek monuments, 1963 (unpublished); R. TÖLLE, Frühgriech. Reigentänze (diss.), 1964; L. B. LAWLER, The dance of the ancient Greek theatre, 1964; G. PRUDHOMMEAU, La danse grecque antique, 1965; G. MÜLLER, Chor und Handlung bei den griech. Tragikern, in: H. DILLER (ed.), Sophokles, 1967, 212–238; T. B. L. WEBSTER, The Greek chorus, 1970; J. RODE, Das Chor-Lied, in: W. JENS (ed.), Die Bauformen der griech. Tragödie, 1971, 85–115; A. LESKY, Die tragische Dichtung der Hellenen, ³1972; R. W. B. BURTON, The chorus in Sophocles' tragedies, 1980; W. MULLEN, Choreia: Pindar and dance, 1982; M. HOSE, Studien zum Chor bei Euripides 2 vols., 1990f.; B. ZIMMERMANN, Unt. zur Form und dramatischen Technik der Aristophanischen Komödien, 3 vols., 1984(²1985)–1987; Dithyrambos, 1992. F.Z.

Chorzene (Procop. Aed. 3,3; *Chorzianene*, Procop. Pers. 2,24; Armenian: Xorjean/Xorjayn). Region in Armenia, south of the upper course of the Euphrates on the river Gayl, modern Perisuyu, with Koloberd the capital. Modern Kiği in the centre of the Karagöl Dağları south-west of Theodosiopolis (Erzurum), eastern Turkey.

R. H. HEWSEN (ed.), The Geography of Ananias of Širak, 1991, 19, 154f. A.P.-L.

Chosroes

[1] Parthian king; see → Osroes.

[2] C. was most probably the name of the Arsacid king of Armenia who took part in the Parthian war of Septimius Severus, and in 214 or 216 was captured by Caracalla. His name was not given in the Greek sources, but mention of an 'Armenian C.' in an inscription at Egyptian Thebes (CIG 4821) may relate to him. The thesis of Armenian writers, frequently taken up by researchers, making one 'Khosrow' contemporary to the fall of the Parthian empire, is false: the Persian invasion did not come until the time of C.' son Tiridates II.

[3] C. II. of Armenia; son and successor of Tiridates 'the Great'; ruled c. 330–338. It is only in Armenian histo-

riography that he is referred to as 'Khosrow Kotak' ('C. the Lesser'). Whether he moved the provincial capital from Artaxata to Dvin is disputed (PLRE 1, 202).

[4] C. III. of Armenia. The division of the country between Rome and Persia, agreed in 384/389, falls within his period. C. ruled as a shadow king in Persian Armenia from 384 to 389, when he was dethroned by the Sassanid → Wahram IV and replaced by his brother → Wramshapuh. Restored as king at the wish of the Armenian nobility after the death of Wramshapuh, after a short reign he died in 417.

M.-L. CHAUMONT, s.v. Armenia and Iran II, EncIr. 2, 418–438; R. H. HEWSEN, The Successors of Tiridates the Great, in: REArm 13, 1978–1979, 99–126; E. KETTENHOFEN, Tirdâd und die Inschr. von Paikuli, 1995; Id., s.v. Dvin, EncIr. 7, 616–619; M. SCHOTTKY, Dunkle Punkte in der armen. Königsliste, in: AMI 27, 1994, 223–235; J. STURM, s.v. Persamenia, RE 19, 932–938; C. TOUMANOFF, The Third-Century Armenian Arsacids, in: REArm 6, 1969, 233–281; Id., s.v. Arsacids VII, EncIr. 2, 543–546.   M.SCH.

[5] C. I Anushirvan. ('immortal soul of'); the most important Sassanid king, born *c.* 496, ruled from September 531. The son of → Cavades I, he exploited the weakness of the high aristocracy, brought about by the Mazdakite disturbances, to push through social, economic and military reforms. An important component of the latter was the introduction of a fixed tax on property in place of a variable tax on yield. He additionally created a court aristocracy owing loyalty only to him, and supported the small aristocratic landowners. His foreign policy is especially characterized by conflicts with East Rome: the war he inherited from his father was ended in 532 by an 'eternal peace', but broke out again in 540 and continued, interrupted by frequent truces, until 562. A 50–year peace was then agreed, bringing C. increased tribute payments. Two years before, with the help of the West Turks, he had been able to destroy the kingdom of the Hephthalites. In 571 C. brought about the conquest of the Yemen and the expulsion of the Aksumites (Ethiopians), who were allies of Byzantium. During his last years there were renewed disputes with East Rome: in 572 → Iustinus II attacked Nisibis, but one year later at Dara a Byzantine army had to capitulate. C. died in February/March 579 without seeing the end of hostilities (PLRE 3A, 303–306).

[6] C. II Abarvez. ('the victorious'), nephew of C. I. He came to the throne in 590 in connection with a revolt against his father → Hormisdas IV by the army commander Wahram Tshobin, but in the same year, 590, fled to Byzantium. Military help from Emperor → Mauricius led in 591 to his restoration and the ousting of Wahram Tshobin. Peacefully inclined towards Mauricius, after the latter's removal by → Phocas C. began a lengthy war against Byzantium. In the course of these campaigns, which C. on the whole left to his commanders, Jerusalem was conquered in 614 and Alexandria in 619; in 626 Constantinople had to endure a siege by the Avars and Persians. Reorganization of the Byzantine

forces by → Heraclius led to a decisive victory over the Persians at Niniveh. C. was deposed and at the beginning of 628 murdered. His relationship with his favourite wife Shirin is a special theme in Persian poetry (PLRE 3A, 306–308).

[7] The name C. appears many more times in the kinglist during the final phase of the Sassanid empire. Thus C. III, a nephew of Hormisdas IV, sought to win the throne from a base in Chorasan, probably contemporaneously with Sharwaraz and → Boran, but he was soon murdered (PLRE 3A, 308). C. IV appears to have ruled (directly?) before Yazdgird III. Many researchers cite a (probably unhistorical) C. V.

F. ALTHEIM, R. STIEHL, Ein asiatischer Staat, vol. 1, 1954; Id., Finanzgesch. der Spätant., 1957; R. N. FRYE, The Political History of Iran under the Sasanians, in: CHI 3 (1), 1983, 153ff.; F. GOUBERT, Les rapports de Khosrau II avec l'empereur Maurice, in: Byzantion 19, 1949, 79–98; M. GRIGNASCHI, La riforma tributaria di Ḥosrô I e il feudalismo Sassanide, in: La Persia nel Medioevo, 1971, 87–131; K. GÜTERBOCK, Byzanz und Persien in ihren diplomatischen und völkerrechtlichen Beziehungen im Zeitalter Justinians, 1906; M. HIGGINS, The Persian War of Emperor Maurice, 1939; E. KETTENHOFEN, s.v. Deportations II, EncIr. 7, 297–308; K. SCHIPPMANN, Grundzüge der Gesch. des sasanidischen Reiches, 1990; J. WIESEHÖFER, Das ant. Persien, 1994.   M.SCH.

Chous (χοῦς, χοεύς; *choûs, choeús*).

[1] Jug or decanter (height a little over 20 cm); used on the second day of the → Anthesteria during the wine-drinking competition. Probably used as a measure of volume for the prescribed quantity of wine. On Choes Day the three-year-old children receive a small choes decanter (H 6–8 cm) as a symbol of their entry into life. [2, 50f.; 1, 96ff.].

As a measure of volume for liquids the *chous* is divided into 12 *kotylai* and 72 *kyathoi* and amounts to 1/12 of the *metretes*. Depending on the region, the *chous* contained 4.56 l (Laconia), 3.04 l (Aegina) or 3.24 l (Solonic), later 3.28 l (Attica). In Ptolemaic Egypt the Attic *chous* was used and was supplemented in the Roman period by a *chous* of 4.92 l. According to VIEDEBANTT and OXÉ the *chous* contained 2.718 l. The Attic *chous* was considered equal to the Roman *congius*.

→ Anthesteria; → Congius; → Measure of volume; → Kotyle; → Kyathos; → Metretes

1 L. DEUBNER, Att. Feste, 1932   2 I. SCHEIBLER, Griech. Töpferkunst, 1983.

F. HULTSCH, Griech. und röm. Metrologie, ²1882; O. VIEDEBANTT, Forsch. zur Metrologie des Alt., in: Abh. der königl. sächs. Ges. d. Wiss. 34.3, 1917; G. VAN HOORN, Choes and Anthesteria, 1951; J. R. GREEN, Choes of the Later Fifth Century, in: ABSA 66, 1971, 189–228; E. M. STERN, in: TH. LORENZ (ed.), Thiasos, 1978, 27–37; O. A. W. DILKE, Mathematik, Maße und Gewichte in der Ant., 1991.   A.M.

[2] Χούς (*Choús*), (LXX; Jos. ant. Iud. 1,131 Χουσαῖος; *Chousaîos*) for Hebrew Kūš, Egyptian since the Middle Kingdom *kẖš* = Kaši (in the → Amarna letters), Old Persian kūšā; according to the Table of the Nations (Gen. 10,6–8; 1 Chr. 1,8–19; also FGH 4, 541 fr. 4,1) the name of the son of → Ham. As the name of country and people for the neighbouring Egypt (→ Nubia) south of the 2nd Cataract (e.g. Ez 29,10; 30,4, 9; Jes 11,11; 20;3–5) the word however is translated as Αἰθιοπία/ Αἰθίοψ (*Aithiopía, Aithíops*).   S.S.

Chreia The term *chreia* originated in a philosophical context and that is also the area in which it is applied. It refers to the transmission of a saying (χρεία λογική; *chreía logiké*: Hermog. 6,9f. RABE) or an action (χρεία πρακτική; *chreía praktiké*: Hermog. 6,11f. RABE), attributed to a certain person, but it could also appear in a mixed form (χρεία μικτή; *chreía mikté*: Hermog. 6,13f. RABE). As its appellation spells out, the *chreia* was seen as useful in different situations of everyday life, and in order to make their use easier, there were collections for learning by heart, in a way similar to → *apophthegmata*, → *gnomai* and *apomnemoneumata*, from which, however, it differed in several aspects. In contrast with the γνώμη (*gnómē*) — with which the *chreia* is most frequently compared and which always takes the form of an anonymous and universal maxim — the *chreia* was tied to certain circumstances and always attributed to a certain person. The *chreia* could also take the form of a question and answer, or finally it could be used merely for the sake of enjoyment (Theon, Rhet. Graeci II 96,24ff. SPENGEL), while the γνώμη (*gnóme*) serves the purpose of exhortation exclusively. Within the framework of teaching, the *chreia* always appears among the first exercises in the texts of → *progymnasmata*.

L. CALBOLI MONTEFUSCO, Die progymnasmatische γνώμη in der griech.-röm. Rhet., in: Papers on Rhetoric I,1993,25–33; M. FAUSER, Die Chreia, in. Euph. 81, 1987, 414–425; R. HOCK/E. O'NEIL, The Chreia in Ancient Rhetoric, 1986; H. R. HOLLERBACH, Zur Bed. des Wortes Chreia, 1964.   L.C.M.

Chrematistai (Χρηματισταί; *Chrēmatistaí*). In the Egypt of the Ptolemies, judges delegated by the king to try fiscal and civil cases for all sectors of the population. They were probably introduced in the 2nd cent. BC. The courts had jurisdiction over an individual nome, or several in combination. In the provinces the *chrematistai* courts lapsed during the early part of the Roman Empire; in Alexandria they are attested into the 3rd cent. AD, with a somewhat modified range of functions.

H. J. WOLFF, Das Justizwesen der Ptolemäer, ²1970; H. A. RUPPRECHT, Einführung in die Papyruskunde, 1994, 143.   G.T.

Chrematistike The term χρηματιστική (*chrēmatistiké*, sc. *téchnē*) is generally translated by 'the art of acquiring money', but should be understood in a wider sense as the practice of acquiring exchange goods (χρήματα, *chrémata*). It is attested only in the political philosophy of the 4th cent. BC (Pl. Grg. 477e; Euthyd. 307a; Aristot. Pol. 1256a1ff.). Aristoteles compares *chrematistike* with οἰκονομική (*oikonomiké*, sc. *téchnē*, art of housekeeping), and distinguishes it from κτητική (*ktētiké*, art of acquisition). He first describes κτητική as a component of οἰκονομική, in as far as an → *oikos* (household) survives not only by means of things provided directly by nature, but needs additional goods. This acquisitive practice is in accordance with nature, as it is subject to the limit of satiety (1256b 26–39). *Chrematistike*, on the other hand, is characterized by the fact that its object is to increase wealth that is not confined to an *oikos*; it is against nature, as it serves no purpose apart from that of its own increase, which is subject to no limit (cf. 1257b 25). Aristotle's critique of *chrematistike* is closely connected with his critique of money and trade. (1256b 40f.1258a 19). His conception of *chrematistike* had a vital influence, via Thomas Aquinas, on the development of the Christian theory of money.

1 S. MEIKLE, Aristotle's Economic Thought, 1995 2 S.v. REDEN, Exchange in Ancient Greece, 1995, 182–87.   S.v.R.

Chremonidean War The Chremonidean War is named after → Chremonides, son of Eteocles from the Aethalidae deme [1]. It was at his behest that Athens entered an alliance with Sparta and other states during the archonship of Peithidemos [2]. The official purpose of this new alliance of the Hellenes supported by → Ptolemaeus II was to protect the freedom of the Hellenes, their → autonomy and the constitutions of the allies. Its political and soon military opponent was → Antigonus Gonatas. The dates of the beginning of the war in the archonship of Peithidemos (268/267 BC), of the death of King Areus of Sparta (265/264) and of the end of the war in the archonship of Antipater (263/262) are disputed [3].

When Athens was besieged by the Macedonians, attempts by her allies to relieve the siege by means of an advance past Corinth and landings by Ptolemy's forces met with failure. Antigonus won the land war (Diod. Sic. 20,29,1; Plut. Agis 3,7; Paus. 1,1,1; 1,7,3; 3,6,4–6; Just. Epit. 26,2,1–12; Frontin. Str. 3,4,1–2; Str. 9,1,21; Ath. 6,250f.) [4] in a battle near Corinth, in which Areus fell. The date of Antigonus' sea victory over Ptolemy's fleet off Cos in 262/261 and how that victory was connected with the war are uncertain [5]. As a consequence of his victory Antigonus became ruler of Athens. Macedonian occupying forces remained in the city of Athens until 255 BC, and in Piraeus until 229. Although the democratic organs of the polis resumed their functions in the very year after the capitulation, new voices held sway in Athens, and they spoke in favour of co-operation with Macedonia. From 262 to 255 BC Antigonus probably entrusted Demetrius son of Phanostratus from Phalerum with 'oversight' over Athenian politics [6]. PA 15572.

→ Athens; → Glaucus

1 W.S. FERGUSON, Hellenistic Athens, 1911 (repr. 1974), 176–185   2 R. ETIENNE, M. PIÉRART, Un décret du Koinon des Héllènes à Platées en l'honneur de Glaucon, fils d'Etéoclès, d'Athènes, in: BCH 99, 1975, 51–75   3 CH. HABICHT, Aristeides, Sohn des Mnesitheos, aus Lamptrai, in: Chiron 6, 1976, 7–10, now in: Id., Athen in hell. Zeit, 1994, 340–343   4 H. HEINEN, Unt. zur hell. Gesch. des 3.Jh. v.Chr., 1972, 102–117   5 J.J. GABBERT, The Anarchic Dating of the Chremonidean War, in: CJ 82, 1986/87, 230–235   6 T. DORANDI, Ricerche sulla cronologia dei filosofi ellenistici, 1991, 26–27   7 G. REGER, The Date of the Battle of Kos, in: AJAH 10, 1985 [1993], 155–177   8 K. BURASELIS, Das hell. Makedonien und die Ägäis, 1982, 146–151   9 CH. HABICHT, Studien zur Gesch. Athens in hell. Zeit, 1982.   J.E.

Chremonides (Χρεμωνίδης; *Chremōnídēs*). Son of Eteocles; Athenian politician of the 3rd cent. BC, from the Aethalidae deme. In the summer of 268 BC he proposed the resolution that the Athenian people ally themselves with Sparta and other Greek states; their decision led to the Chremonidean War (cf. IG II² 686–687 = StV 476), at the end of which C. fled to Ptolemy II in Alexandria with his brother Glaucon (cf. Teles, περὶ φυγῆς p. 23 HENSE). There he became a counsellor and adviser (σύμβουλος; *sýmboulos* and πάρεδρος; *páredros*, Teles p. 23 H.). It was as a nauarch of Ptolemy that he was defeated by the Rhodians before Ephesus in the 250s (Polyaenus, Strat. 5,18). PA 15572.

→ Athens; → Chremonidean War

W.S. FERGUSON, Hellenistic Athens, 1911 (repr. 1974), 176–185; HABICHT 147–153ff.   J.E.

Chresis (χρῆσις; *chrêsis*). Literally 'make use (of)', but also 'place (something) at (somebody's) disposal', embracing the modern senses of loan (the meaning 'oracle' can be disregarded here). For loan transactions, already in Athens *chresis* alternates with the narrower, technical term → *dáneion* (Dem. Or. 49,6; 7; 17; 21; 44; 48).
CHRESIS

H.-A. RUPPRECHT, Unt. zum Darlehen im Recht der graeco-ägypt. Papyri der Ptolemäerzeit 1967, 6ff.; Id., Einführung in die Papyruskunde, 1994, 118.   G.T.

Chrestus (Χρηστός; *Chrēstós*) from Byzantium. Sophist; pupil and emulator of → Herodes Atticus; taught in Athens. He had 100 pupils, among them many of significance; an alcoholic; he declined the attempt of the Athenians shortly after 180 to appoint him as successor to Hadrianus as professor of rhetoric in Athens. He died at *c.* 50 years of age (Philostr. VS 2,11).

I. AVOTINS, The Holders of the Chairs of Rhetoric at Athens, in: HSPh 79, 1975, 320–1.   E.BO.

Christian archaeology see → Byzantium III; → Late antiquity, archaeology of

Christianity
A. DEFINITION   B.1 CULTURAL ADAPTATION   B.2 CULT   C. CULT OFFICIALS   D. EXPANSION   E. LANGUAGE   E.1 JESUS AND THE BIBLE   E.2 THE LITURGY, THE LANGUAGE OF WORSHIP   E.3 CHURCH FATHERS AND CHRISTIAN LITERATURE   E.4 THE CHRISTIAN ORIENT

A. DEFINITION
Christianity (Χριστιανισμός, *Christianismós*) was a monotheistic religious system (→ Monotheism) which emerged from Judaism in the procuratorial province of Judaea during the 1st cent. AD. At Christianity's centre were the life and mission of Jesus of Nazareth, whose adherents regarded him as the 'Messiah', or God's 'anointed' (Χριστός, *Christós*), and as his son, wholly participating in the nature of God.

B.1 CULTURAL ADAPTATION
The word 'Christian' (χριστιανός, *christianós*) arose after *c.* 36 in Antioch in Syria, when Hellenistic adherents of Christ were driven out of Jerusalem (Acts 11,26). The term Christianity is first attested in the letters of Ignatius of Antioch (*c.* 110); here, Christianity is compared to Jewish faith and customs (Mag. 10; Philad. 6,1) and acknowledged to be a detested cult (Rom. 3,3). In the middle of the 2nd cent. some Christian leaders described Christianity as an orally taught philosophical doctrine (λόγος, *lógos*) (Martyr. Polyc. 10,1). The fact that Celsus attacked Christianity in a work entitled 'True Doctrine' (ἀληθὴς λόγος, *alēthès lógos*), reflects the situation that resulted from contact between Christianity and the Hellenistic world. The geographical expansion of these contacts and their cultural context between *c.* 30–60 were taken up in the Christian book → Acts of the Apostles, where e.g. it is said that → Paul introduced Christianity on the Areopagus in Athens to an audience of Stoics and Epicureans, who were expecting a new teaching (καινὴ διδαχή, *kainè didachḗ*) concerning strange gods (ξένα δαιμόνια, *xéna daimónia*). Paul is supposed to have used in support of his argument an altar dedicated to 'the unknown god(s)' (→ agnostòs theós). The apostle proceeded to identify the latter with Christ by means of a verse from the pre-Socratic philosopher Epimenides, which mentions the rising of the Cretan Zeus from the grave (Acts 17,28). When men schooled in rhetoric, philosophy and the Greek *paideia* espoused Christianity, the mode of instruction became more structured. This is demonstrated in the two *Apologiae* of the martyr Justin and in the works of other authors from the Apologetic movement, such as Athenagoras of Athens, and reaches its zenith in *c.* 248 in → Origen's *Contra Celsum*. This body of work replaced the earlier epistolographic, apocalyptic and didactic literature of the so-called → Apostolic Fathers, whose teachings were based on a

synthesis of oral tradition and a not yet entirely defined canon of holy writings, comprising the gospels, the Acts of the Apostles, the letters of Paul, other writings from various sources, and, of course, the → Septuagint.

The synthesis of Greek Christianity and philosophy took place in the late 2nd and 3rd cent. with the foundation and growth of the catechetical school in Alexandria under the leadership of → Pantaenus and his successors → Clemens (of Alexandria) and Origen. Clement, in works such as the *Stromateis*, the *Paedagogus* and the *Protrepticus*, mostly drew his conclusions from literary examples. His successor Origen, on the other hand, a pupil of the philosopher Ammonius Sakkas, developed in his *De Principiis* (περὶ ἀρχῶν, *perì archôn*) a Middle Platonic theology that, until its condemnation by the fifth ecumenical council in 553, was dominant in Greek Christianity. In commentaries on the gospels of Matthew and John, Origen took the allegorical method of interpreting religious texts, as taught in the Alexandrian schools on the basis of Homer, and applied it to Christian biblical exegesis. This and Origen's logos-based theology had a profound influence on Alexandrian religious thought. His ideas represented a substrate of Arian theology, condemned in the councils of Nicaea in 325 and Constantinople in 389; they even influenced to some degree the preoccupation with Cyril of Alexandria's logos 'as God's unique being become flesh', which later developed into Monophysitism, rejected at the council of Chalcedon in 451. Origen also compiled the *Hexapla*, a work in six columns comprising the Hebrew holy scriptures, their transcription into Greek characters, and the four most important translations then in use, including the *Septuagint* (→ Bible translations). Origen had appropriated the methods of textual criticism used in Alexandrian schools. The *Hexapla* became a polemical tool in debates with the Jews. Origen's move to Caesarea made that city an important centre of Christian learning. → Eusebius of Caesarea, ecclesiastical historian and exegetist, and → Gregorius Thaumaturgos were Origen's principal champions. The latter, as bishop of Neocaesarea in Pontus, laid the foundation for the Cappadocian Church Fathers → Basilius, → Gregorius of Nyssa and → Gregorius of Nazianzus in the 4th cent., whose Platonism and Christianization of the Greek *paideía* were determining factors in the nascent Christian sophism of the 5th–6th cents.

In the Latin west, Platonism became important only in the later 4th cent., via → Ambrosius bishop of Milan and → Augustinus of Hippo; it endured throughout the Carolingian renaissance, from → Boethius down to the time of Johannes Scotus Eriugena (*c.* 810–875), who acquired and translated Greek Neoplatonic texts by authors such as Ps.-Dionysius the Areopagite. From the time of → Tertullianus (flourished *c.* 200), western Christianity accepted the rhetorical tradition of Latin literature, while rejecting the *mores* of Roman society, the political and religious traditions of the Roman state and Ciceronean Platonism. Hence Tertullian's *dictum*: 'An end to all plans for a Stoic, Platonic or Dialectic Christianity!' (Praescr. 7). Later on, Augustine linked Christianity with Plotinus' Neoplatonism and used literary examples from Virgil's poetry for his *De civitate Dei* (413–425).

B.2 CULT

Christianity was monotheistic, recognized no other gods but the Christian Trinity, and excluded the claims of all other religious cults (θρησκεία, *thrēskeía*), (1 Cor. 8, 4–6; Euseb. Hist. eccl. 7,11,7–9). The expression 'one god alone' (εἷς θεὸς μόνος, *heis theòs mónos*) occurs frequently in Christian inscriptions of the 4th–5th cents. [1. 313–315]. The expression 'one god' derives in part from a pagan henotheism of the late 3rd cent., which endeavoured to express the great power of one sole god. A person was initiated into Christianity by being baptized, i.e. sprinkled with or submersed in water while the formulae of the Trinity were recited. The earliest Christian rites were carried out in house churches like that of → Dura Europus, unaccompanied by any requirement of ritual purity (abstinence from meat, from contact with the dead and from sexual relations) on the part of the priest. There was also no *temenos*, or any sanctified area set aside for the sacrifice. The earliest ritual comprised the recital of the formulae of the Eucharist, readings from holy scripture and the collection of → alms (Mk 14, 22–26; Didache 9,3; Just. Apol. 1, 61–67). The development of complex liturgical ceremonial is indicated *c.* 215 in the 'Apostolic Tradition' of Hippolytus of Rome, but there are few indications of the existence of large churches at this time. These are first referred to in 260 in Emperor Gallienus' edict of restitution to the bishops of Egypt (Euseb. Hist. eccl. 7,13). → Constantinus, the first Christian emperor, granted funds to the bishop of Rome for the construction and running of churches. From then onwards, the Roman → basilica became the principal type of church [2]. The round, rectangular or octagonal *martyria* or martyrs' chapels occur from the early 5th cent., e.g. St. Laurentius in Milan, St. Sergius and St. Bacchus in Constantinople and San Vitale in Ravenna. Pilgrimages to Palestine and to regional shrines became an important characteristic of Christianity. Constantine had a great cupola built over the Holy Sepulchre in Jerusalem, and established a basilica over the *martyrium* of St Peter in Rome. A related phenomenon was the cult of martyrs' relics. It developed in the African provinces, in part out of the pre-Christian feast of the dead at the graves of family members (ILCV 1570), a custom which was subsequently Christianized (ILCV 1571; 3710–3726). Ambrosius of Milan suggested to Augustine's mother Monica that she avoid as *superstitio* such feasts at martyrs' shrines (Aug. Conf. 6,2). Elsewhere, the cult of martyrs was institutionalized by episcopal sanction and met with approval amongst the people. This is attested by many small chapels in proconsular Africa and Numidia (CIL VIII 1, 5664; 5665), the eastern shrines of St. Theodore in Euchaita in Helenopontus, St. Sergius (patron of Christian Arabs) in Resapha and St. John in Ephesus (Ioh. Mosch. Prat. Spir. 180), and especially the widespread cult of St. Anastasius (→ Anastasius [4] Monachus), the Persian, whose relics arrived in Jerusalem and 8th cent. Rome [3]. In the Roman east the monasteries of celebrated monks became places of pilgrimage; among them Qal'at Sim'ān, that of the → stylite St Symeon the Elder, surrounded by a cathedral, basilicas and a pilgrims' hostel [1. 163–173; 184–199; 253f.]. It remained an important shrine until the dead and living → martyrs, → bishops and → monks of the 10th cent. assumed the typically Roman status of the *patronus* [4] as regards their social obligations. Martyrs' shrines, especially those possessing the right of asylum (→ Asylia), kept up the pre-Christian concept of a holy sanctuary (SEG 4,720) [5].

C. Cult officials

The earliest attested Christian cult officials are *presbýteroi*, *diákonoi*, *epískopoi*, *prophḗtai* and *apóstoloi*. Many early texts are imprecise as to the offices of apostolic authority, but others associate this clearly with the office of bishop or 'overseer' (ἐπίσκοπος, *epískopos*) (I. Clem. 42; Ign. Sm. 8). By the end of the 3rd cent., most cities enjoying the right of Roman citizenship had bishops, and by the 5th cent. and later this became the rule (Cod. Iust. 1,3,35). By the middle of the 3rd cent. some local churches had gained higher jurisdictional status, analogous to that of a capital city. Thus Rome had jurisdiction over the bishoprics of suburbicarian Italy, Carthage over proconsular Africa and Numidia, Ephesus over the province of Asia, Alexandria over Egypt and Antioch over Syria and Cilicia. These higher bishoprics (apart from Carthage and Ephesus) became patriarchates, together with the new Christian capital of Byzantium, between 381 and 451 renamed New Rome or Constantinople, and Jerusalem (451) [6]. Especially after Diocletian's subdivision of the provinces, bishops in provincial capitals exerted similar rights over their colleagues within the provincial territories. During the latter part of the 3rd cent. a system of provincial synods became typical; these met under the chairmanship of the metropolitan, as for example those held in Africa under Cyprian of Carthage. The system of general or ecumenical councils, called in order to clarify vital points of doctrine and to issue canons, was built up under the authority of the Christian emperors from the time of Constantine the Great. The emperor, or more often the imperial legate, chaired the sittings, and the imperial postal service (*cursus publicus*) was used to summon bishops to the sittings and to publish decrees. This system was established by the seventh ecumenical council at Nicaea in 787 [7]. The clergy below the level of bishop, citing the example of Rome during the episcopate of Cornelius in c. 250 (Euseb. Hist. eccl. 6,43,11), consisted of priests (leaders of churches), deacons, deputy deacons, acolytes (altar-servers), exorcists and doorkeepers. The priests conducted the liturgy in the *tituli* or churches, while the deacons oversaw the collection, the cemeteries and the church buildings. In the Greek east the lower spiritual offices were subsumed in the subdiaconate. In the larger churches, an archdeacon presided over the college of deacons, and was often regarded as the legitimate heir to the bishopric, as e.g. Athanasius of Alexandria. In regions with few towns, such as Asia Minor, special rural bishops (χωρεπίσκοποι, *chōrepískopoi*) made circuits through the village communities, but could not ordain priests or deacons: the *chorepiskopos* filled this function at the time of the council of Nicaea in 325, but during the later 4th cent. he was replaced in Asia Minor and Syria by the rural priest (περιοδευτής, *periodeutḗs*). The latter are frequently attested in Syria and Arabia, where they served the bishop as supervisors in the *territorium* of the city, and played an important role in the Christianization process [1. 282–381 passim]. A law of 530 laid severe administrative burdens on the bishops, prescribing the inspection of public buildings, baths, aqueducts, harbours, wells, towers, bridges and streets and the oversight of major payments and receipts (Cod. Iust. 1,4,26). A result of this overburdening of the bishops was that the people turned to the monks at times of moral and material crisis. The monastic movement originated in Egypt, in the early part of Antonius' reign (not later than c. 270), and by the 4th cent. became a dominant feature of Christianity. Two basic types of monastic life developed: the solitary, enclosed or anchorite order and the communal or coenobitic. The first was common in Egypt, Syria and post-Roman Wales, where the monk had a cell in an uninhabited area and kept to a strict routine (ἄσκησις, *áskēsis*) of fasting and reciting psalms. → Pachomius, a former Roman soldier, conducted a coenobitic monastic style in Egypt on the model of a Roman military camp. The monks lived in cells grouped around a central church, practised → ascesis, met regularly for the liturgy and pursued craft-based trades. This system spread as far as Asia Minor, where Basil of Caesarea provided it with an official set of rules, adding instruction in theology and philosophy to the daily routine. In around 420, Iohannes → Cassianus brought the system to the Latin West, to Lérins near Marseilles. Benedict's analogous monastic rule, developed during the 6th cent. in central Italy, was influential in the medieval West. There were also important monastic centres in Rome, where many Syrian and Greek monks lived, in the Judaean desert at the monastery of St Sabas, and in the 6th cent. even on Mount Sinai. At the same time, Celtic monasticism was developing on Iona. At the end of the 8th cent. Studion in Constantinople had become the leading Byzantine monastery.

D. Expansion

No conclusive studies on this theme as yet exist, and many points are controversial. Christianity originally took hold in the Greek coastal cities of the eastern Mediterranean, such as Ephesus, Corinth and Thessalonica. Missionaries like Paul first went into the synagogues, but when their efforts bore no fruit they

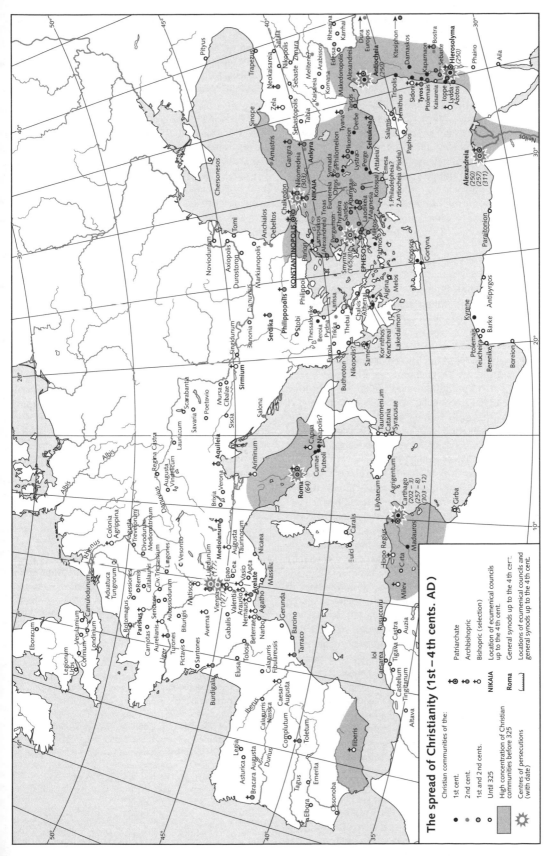

The spread of Christianity (1st–4th cents. AD)

Christian communities of the:

- 1st cent.
- 2nd cent.
- 1st and 2nd cents.
- Until 325

High concentration of Christian communities before 325

Centres of persecutions (with date)

Patriarchate

Archbishopric

Bishopric (selection)

NIKAIA   Location of ecumenical councils up to the 4th cent.

Roma   General synods up to the 4th cent.

Locations of ecumenical councils and general synods up to the 4th cent.

turned to the non-Jewish population. Christianity also took hold within Rome's large foreign population. Parables in Hermas' 'Shepherd' point to the acceptance of Christianity by craft workers employed on urban construction projects under Trajan and Hadrian (Vis. 3,2, 5–7; Simon. 9, 2–5), as well as bronze-founders (Vis. 3,9, 3), many slaves and freedpersons (Vis. 3,6, 7), suburban peasants (Vis. 3,1, 2) and the urban poor (Vis. 3,9, 3). The Christian population of Rome in c. 175 is estimated at about 10,000, and in c. 254 at about 30,000–50,000. Greek was the predominant language of literature and liturgy at the time of → Hippolytus. The first Latin-speaking bishop was Victor (189–199). Funerary inscriptions from the period between c. 166–234 indicate a process of Latinization and Christianization amongst men of equestrian rank (ILCV 276), veterans (ILCV 277; 427), slaves and freedpersons from the imperial household (ILCV 349; 705A; 3872), among them at the time of Commodus even the influential M. Aurelius Prosnetes (ILCV 3332). A tradition from the time of bishop Damasus (366–84) identified M. Vibius Liberis, consul suffectus in 166, as a Christian martyr (ILCV 56). A wife of Postumus Quietus (cos. 272) is said to have been a Christian (CIL VI 31749a). This trend can also be detected in the Octavius of Minucius Felix, who seems to suggest a Stoic Christianity. The quasi-Constantinian XP (Chi-Rho) was already in use in the Rome of c. 279 (ILCV 3315). In Italy in c. 250 there were about 60 bishops; but Christian inscriptions in the provinces are rare, only Clusium in Tuscia (ILCV 3032; 3915 etc.) and Asisium (?) (CIL II 2, 5458) yielding examples.

The main cause of the rapid expansion of Christianity after 312 was the privileged status it had received from (Fl. Valerius) Constantine, the first Christian emperor. He gave subsidies in money and in kind, donated land from the res privata, promulgated laws favouring Christian mores and the cult, and associated Christianity with his bona fortuna [8]. At this time Christianity was the favoured cult of the princeps, a situation that changed slowly up to c. 384–392, when the laws of Gratianus and Theodosius I made Christianity more or less the 'official' imperial religion [9]. This process persisted under later Christian emperors down to the publication of the second edition of the Cod. Iust. in 534. A law revived from Zeno's reign (481–84) required the baptism of all Roman citizens (Cod. Iust. 1,11,10,1). The synodal list of the council of Nicaea shows that in 325 there were already bishops in most cities of the empire [10]. But this is a bad demographic indicator. The territoria of cities in most of the provinces, with the partial exception of Phrygia, where Christian inscriptions clearly occur in c. 250, were not intensively Christianized until the early/mid 5th cent. [11]. Antioch and Alexandria already had a large Christian population at an early period, as did some provincial cities such as Edessa in Osrhoene, where in 201 King Abgar IX permitted a form of Christianity. On the eve, so to speak, of the great persecutions (303–312), provincial cities and

capitals such as Eumeneia and Orcistus in Phrygia and Maiuma in Palaestina were predominantly Christian. Bostra in the province of Arabia was approximately half Christian in c. 362 (Julian Ep. 41 WRIGHT). Other towns such as Harran/Carrhae in Osrhoene, Baalbek/Heliopolis and Emesa in Phoenice Libanensis had a pagan majority and were even hostile to Christianity [12]. Parts of Phoenicia and Arabia seem never to have been Christianized (IGLS 2962). In some parts of Egypt, despite the optimistic comments of Christian authors like Eusebius and the apparent proofs afforded by papyri, Christianity spread only slowly; as evidence the Greek and demotic Egyptian inscriptions in Philae and Deir al-Bahai (SEG 41, 1612–1615). In the west, the Loire valley around Tours was not Christianized until the later 4th and the 5th cent. [13]. The situation in Britannia and Cisalpine Gaul was similar [14]. The process is, moreover, obscured by the 'Christianization of rites': Christian forms given to ancient peasant rites, thus perhaps concealing the survival of polytheism in the countryside. Ireland provides numerous examples of Christian monks and bishops imitating druidic rites. Arab pastoralists crossing the limes in order to visit important shrines, such as the cell of Eutychius in the Judaean desert and the shrine of St Sergius in Resapha, took Christianity beyond the borders of the empire. In the 4th cent. Christianity reached Nubia, as can be seen from the inscription of King Silko of Dongola in Talmis, where the king celebrates his victory over the Blemmyes in a quasi-Constantinian triumphal formula: (καὶ ὁ θεὸς ἔδωκέν μοι τὸ νίκημα, 'God gave me victory') [15]. Later Nubian Christianity is illustrated in the inscriptions and frescos of Faras.

1 F. TROMBLEY, Hellenic Religion and Christianization ²1994   2 R. KRAUTHEIMER, Three Christian Capitals, 1983, 12–31   3 H. USENER, Acta M. Anastasii Persae, 1894, 12–27   4 P. BROWN, The Cult of the Saints, 1981, 55–68   5 A. DAIN, G. ROUILLARD, Une inscription relative au droit d' asile, in: Byzantion 5, 1930, 315–326 6 E. HONIGMANN, s.v. Juvenal of Jerusalem, Dumbarton Oaks Papers, 1950, 209–279   7 M. ANASTOS, Iconoclasm and Imperial Rule 717–842, in: Cambridge Medieval History 4/1, 1966, 84–87   8 T. BARNES, Constantine and Eusebius, 1981, 245–260   9 J. MATTHEWS, Western Aristocracies and Imperial Court AD 364–425, 1975, 183–222   10 A. VON HARNACK, The Expansion of Christianity in the First Three Centuries ²1905, 240–446 11 W. CALDER, s.v. Philadelphia and Montanism, in: Bulletin of the John Rylands Library 7, 1922–1923, 336–349 12 F. TROMBLEY, Religious Transition in Sixth Century Syria, in: Byz. Forsch. 20, 1994, 170–172   13 C. STANCLIFFE, From Town to Country: The Christianisation of the Tourraine 370–600, in: D. BAKER (ed.), The Church in Town and Countryside, 1979, 43–59   14 R. LIZZI, Ambrose's Contemporaries and the Christianization of Northern Italy, in: JRS 80, 1990, 156–173   15 R. LEPSIUS, Die griech. Inschr. des nubischen Königs Silko, in: Hermes 10, 1876, 129–144.

A. ARMSTRONG, The Cambridge History of Later Greek and Early Medieval Philosophy, 1967; T. BARNES, Constantine and Eusebius, 1981; Id., From Eusebius to Augustine, 1994; P.Brown, Augustine of Hippo, 1967; H.Chadwick, Early Christian Thought and Classical Tradition, 1966; F.Deichmann, s.v. Christianisierung II (Monumente), RAC 2, 1228–1241; H.Delehaye, Les origines du culte des martyrs, 1933; W.Frend, The Rise of Christianity, 1984; C.R. Galvao-Sobrino, Funerary epigraphy and the spread of Christianity, in: Athenaeum 83, 1995, 431–462; M.Haren, Medieval Thought ²1992; A.v. Harnack, Die Mission und Ausbreitung des Ch. in den ersten Jh., ⁴1924; W.Jaeger, Early Christianity and Greek Paideia, 1961; B.Kötting, s.v. Ch. I (Ausbreitung), RAC 2, 1138–1159; R.Krautheimer, Early Christian and Byzantine Architecture, 1965; K.Latourette, A History of the Expansion of Christianity, 1937–47; R.Markus, The End of Ancient Christianity, 1990; J.Pelikan, Christianity and Classical Culture, 1993; C.Thomas, Christianity in Roman Britain to AD 500, 1981; G.Vikan, Byzantine Pilgrimage Art, 1982.　　F.R.T.

Maps: A.v. Harnack, Die Mission und Ausbreitung des Chr. in den ersten drei Jh., ⁴1924, repr. 1966; F. van der Meer, C.Mohrmann, Bildatlas der frühchristl. Welt, 1959, 16f.; W.Frend, Martyrdom and Persecution in the Early Church, 1965; H.Jedin, K.S. Latourette (ed.), Atlas zur Kirchengeschichte, 1970 (New edition 1987).

E. Language

E.1 Jesus and the Bible

Palestine at the time of Jesus is a multi-ethnic society, characterized by the large number of languages represented there. While Hebrew, reserved for services in the synagogue and for the reading of the scriptures, was increasingly becoming the liturgical language, Aramaic was the predominant language of the countryside. Jesus too, in instructing his disciples and in his preaching, would probably have used the western Aramaic dialect of his hometown in Galilee. In the urban environment, however, and especially in Jerusalem, the strongly Hellenized population spoke → Koiné (ἡ κοινὴ διάλεκτος = the general, common language), the form of Greek that was the universal language of the civilized Hellenistic world, even in the Jewish diaspora. It was in this popular *lingua franca* that the story of Jesus was written down in the NT. Thus Greek became the main language of the Christian mission. In order to make the scriptures available to a wider public, the first translations of the Bible into national languages were already being made from the 2nd/3rd cents. (cf. Vetus Latina, early Syriac and Coptic translations of the Bible).

E.2 The liturgy, the language of worship

Owing to the course taken by the early Christian mission, Greek, the language of high culture, became the main language of the Church, even in the western part of the Roman Empire. Thus the local community in Rome first celebrated their liturgy in Greek; in North Africa too, its use in ecclesiastical contexts was very common, even outside the liturgy (cf. *Passio Perpetuae et Felicitatis*). Bilingualism, moreover, was a widespread phenomenon in the ancient Church (cf. Peregrinatio Egeriae 47,3f.; Jer. Ep. 108,29). While the languages of the western nations played no part in the liturgy, Latin steadily increased in importance, and from the 3rd cent. replaced Greek in the west as the main language of the Church. The first beginnings of more intensive use of Latin in the Roman Church (i.a. inscriptions in the papal crypt of San Callisto) can be detected in the middle of the 3rd cent. But it was only under the Roman bishop Damasus (366–384) that Greek was relinquished as the language of the liturgy in Rome, and the use of Latin made binding c. 380. In the East, on the other hand, Greek remained the dominant language in Church and society.

E.3 Church Fathers and Christian literature

Christians strove from early times to enter into dialogue on an equal footing with the cultured strata of ancient society. Taking over standard Greek, rooted as it was in the traditional cultural canon, offered an opportunity to achieve this end. The language of Christian literature thus shares the pagan literary classicism of the imperial period, while comprising many elements alien to that tradition. Among these elements are neologisms formed in the course of the formulation of dogma, as well as powerful echoes of the language of the → Bible. Relatively rare in early cents., in the 4th cent. the use of standard Greek becomes the norm, which only a few authors (i.a. → Epiphanius) manage to resist. Fundamental to this radical alteration was the changed social standing of the Church as a consequence of the Edict of Milan (313), and especially the marked influx of educated people into the episcopacy [2. 198]. Christian authors meanwhile adapted traditional literary forms and genres to correspond to their needs. A similar development took place in the realm of Latin Christian literature. Thus one can hardly speak of Christian Latin as the language of a special grouping within society, even though numerous distinctive coinings can be detected in vocabulary and syntax, especially in the areas of the liturgy and theological terminology [4.78].

E.4 The Christian Orient

Early on, the needs of missionaries and preachers led to the translation of immanent Christian traditions into other languages, the eastern Roman world proving itself to be a particularly fertile field in this respect. The process was favoured by the large number of peoples and languages represented in the region, as well as by widespread bilingualism, particularly in the Syrian-Palestinian sector and in Egypt. Thus, with the Christianization of the various peoples, Armenian, Georgian and later Arabic attained the status of Church languages. Similarly, Coptic, a late form of the Egyptian language, became a literary language by way of Christianity. Owing to an impressive wealth of indigenous Christian literature (→ Ephraem), Syriac, derived from the Aramaic of Osrhoëne, acquires a particular status. → Bible translations; → Christian Palestinian language and literature; → Damasus; → Latin

1 G. BARDY, La question des langues dans l'Église ancienne I, 1948   2 C. FABRICIUS, Der sprachliche Klassizismus der griech. Kirchenväter, in: JbAC 10, 1967, 187–199   3 TH. KLAUSER, Der Übergang der röm. Kirche von der griech. zur lat. Liturgiesprache. In: Miscellanea Giovanni Mercati I, 1946, 472–482   4 G. KRETSCHMAR, S.V. Kirchensprache, TRE 19, 1990, 74–92   5 CHR. MOHRMANN, Études sur le latin des chrétiens. 4 Vol., 1957–1977   6 G. NEUMANN, J. UNTERMANN (ed.), Die Sprachen im röm. Reich der Kaiserzeit, 1980 (Beihefte der Bonner Jahrbücher 40)   7 H. PETERSMANN, De vetustissimis christianorum libris in linguam latinam versis, in: Augustinianum 42, 1993, 305–324.   J.RI.

Christian Palestinian language and literature
A. LANGUAGE   B. LITERATURE

A. LANGUAGE

Christian Palestinian is a dialect of → Aramaic, more precisely of Western Aramaic, to which belong Nabataean, Palmyrenian, Judaeo-Aramaic, Samaritan and the still extant New Western Aramaic (Maʿalūla linguistic enclave near Damascus, Syria). As it uses one of the older Syriac- (i.e. Estrangelō, in reality στρογγύλη; *stroggylē*) related scripts, in the non-German language area it tends to be called Syro-Palestinian, although it lies closer to the Judaeo-Palestinian Aramaic of some *targumim* than to classical Syriac. It was evidently used in originally Aramaic-speaking Christian communities who later joined the Chalcedonian arm of the imperial Church (→ Melchites); by no means, however, did it remain confined to Palestine in the narrower geographical sense, but was also widespread in East Jordan (e.g. in Ǧeraš) and as far as Egypt: the biblical texts come from the monastery of St Catherine in Sinai, the Geniza in Cairo and the monastery of Castellion in the Judaean desert (Hyrcania/Khirbet Mird: [15. 526]). Perhaps when the pilgrim Egeria (Peregrinatio Egeriae 47,3) and Jerome (Ep. 108,29) refer to a trilingual liturgy in Palestine ('Greek-Latin-Syriac') it is of this dialect that they are speaking. It has occasionally been suggested that this literature was a creation of 6th-cent. Jewish converts [1]. It is true that the first instance so far known, an inscription from Evron, dates from 415 [2]; other inscriptions are mainly in smaller and more remote locations.

B. LITERATURE

Christian Palestinian literature consists in its entirety of translations from the Greek (complete list of editions up to 1903 in [19. VII–XVI] and up to 1963 in [3. 510⁸]). The major part is made up of biblical texts: the OT is attested in handwritten form in missals and other liturgical texts of the 6th–13th cents. [4; 5]. A fragmentary text of Jos 22,6–7, 9–19 was found in the Castellion monastery; M. BLACK published a *Euchologion* and a *Horologion* with biblical texts. The NT is attested for the most part in a missal contained in three MSS from the 11th/12th cents. The first instances originate possibly in the 6th cent., and it has been surmised

that these represent the writing down a cent. later of an oral tradition from the 4th cent. The textual character is described as 'for the most part normal koine, with occasional Alexandrian readings' [6. 206]. The fragmentary missals belong partly to the tradition of Antioch, partly (after the Byzantine re-conquest of Syria in the 11th cent.) to that of Constantinople.

1 F. ROSENTHAL, Die aramäistische Forsch. seit Th. Nöldekes Veröffentlichungen, 1939   2 V. TZAFERIS, in: Eretz-Israel 19, 1986, 36–51   3 C. PERROT, Un fragment christo-palestinien découvert à Khirbet Mird, in: RBi 70, 1963, 506–555   4 A. BAUMSTARK, Das Problem des christl.-palästin. Pentateuchtextes, in: Oriens Christianus 32, 1935, 201–223   5 L. DELEKAT, Die syropalästin. Jesaja-Übers., in: ZATW 71, 1959, 165–201   6 K. ALAND, B. ALAND, Der Text des NT, ²1989.   7 M. BLACK, Rituale Melchitarum, ²1938   8 Id., A Christian Palestinian Horologion, Texts and Studies. New Series 1, 1954   9 H. DUENSING, Christl. palästinisch-aram. Texte und Fragmente nebst einer Abh. über den Wert der palästin. LXX, 1906   10 M. H. GOSHEN-GOTTSTEIN, H. SHIRUN, The Bible in the Syropalestinian Version, Vol. 1, 1973   11 A. S. LEWIS, A Palestinian Syriac Lectionary containing Lessons from Pentateuch, Job, Prophets, Acts and Epistles, in: Studia Sinaitica 6, 1897   12 Id., M. D. GIBSON, The Palestinian Syriac Lectionary of the Gospels, 1899   13 A. S. LEWIS, Codex Climaci Rescriptus, in: Horae Semiticae 8, 1908   14 M. J. LAGRANGE, L'origine de la version syro-palestinienne des Evangiles, in: RBi 34 1925, 481–504   15 J. T. MILIK, Une inscription et une lettre en Araméen Christo-Palestinien, in: RBi 60, 1953, 526–539   16 C. MÜLLER-KESSLER, Gramm. des Christl.- Palästin.-Aramäischen I, 1991   17 TH. NÖLDEKE, Ueber den christl. palästin. Dialect, in: ZDMG 22, 1868, 443–527   18 F. SCHULTESS, Gramm. des christl.-palästin. Aramäisch, 1924   19 Id., Lexicon Syro-Palestinum, 1903   20 FR. SCHWALLY, Idioticon des christl.-palästin. Aramäisch, 1893 (review: F. Praetorius, in: ZDMG 48, 1894, 361–367).   C.M.

Christians, persecutions of see → Tolerance

Christodorus (Χριστόδωρος; *Christódōros*) from Coptus. Son of Paniscus; lived at the time of Anastasius I (491–518). Author of Πάτρια (*Pátria*), i.e. poems about the early histories of different cities (Thessalonica, Nakle, Miletus, Tralles, Aphrodisias and Constantinople). As well as Λυδιακά (*Lydiaká*), C. wrote an epic Ἰσαυρικά (*Isauriká*) about Anastasius' Isaurian wars. Extant is his ἔκφρασις (→ Ekphrasis) of the 80 statues in the baths of Zeuxippus in Constantinople, destroyed by fire during the Nika revolt of AD 532 (Anth. Pal. 2,1–416). He wrote two epigrams (Anth. Pal. 7,697 and 698) on the death of Iohannes of Epidamnus, *cos.* AD 467. Iohannes Lydus (De magistratibus populi Romani, 3,26) quotes a verse from C.' poem on the pupils of Proclus. The fragmentary poems surviving in Pap. Graec. Vindob. 29788B-C can perhaps also be attributed to C. The Suda mentions another C. from Thebes, perhaps identical with our C. Language and style as well as metrics betray the influence of Nonnus of Pan-

opolis, although C.' handling of metre does not achieve
the discipline of Nonnus, who lived some 50 years before him.

F. BAUMGARTEN, De Christodoro Poeta Thebano, 1881;
A. CAMERON, Wandering Poets. A Literary Movement in
Byzantine Egypt, in: Historia 14, 1965, 489; A. CAME-
RON, Claudian, 1970, 478–482; P. FRIEDLÄNDER, Johan-
nes von Gaza und Paulus Silentiarius, 1912, 94f.; R. C.
MCCAIL, P. Gr. Vindob. 29788C, Hexameter Encomium
on an unnamed Emperor, in: JHS 98, 1978, 38–63;
R. STUPPERICH, Das Statuenprogramm in den Zeuxip-
pos-Thermen, in: MDAI (Ist) 32, 1982, 210–235; T. VIL-
JAMAA, Studies in Greek Encomiastic Poetry of the Early
Byzantine Period, 1968, 29–31, 56–59; M. L. WEST,
Greek Metre, 1982, 177–180.   C.S.

Christos Paschon (Χριστὸς Πάσχων; *Christòs Pá-
schōn*; Lat. *Christus Patiens*). Christian drama on the
story of the Passion, in the form of a → cento. Abbreviated to *Ch. P.* by A. BLADUS (Ed. princeps, Rome
1542); a play of 2,632 lines, in the majority of MSS (mid
13th to beginning 16th cents.) entitled: 'From the hand
of our holy father Gregory the theologian, a dramatic
presentation (→ *Hypóthesis*) after Euripides, comprising the incarnation for our sakes of our Saviour Jesus
Christ and his world-redeeming passion'. The paraphrase, offering more synopsis than action, depicts the
Passion (1–847), death (848–1133), entombment
(1134–1905) and resurrection of Christ (1906–2531),
based on canonic and apocryphal models, together with
a prologue from the mouth of the writer (*1–*30) and a
prayer to Christ and Mary (2532–2602). The most
striking formal poetic features are the execution in 12-
syllable iambic trimeters (1461–1463: anapaestic dime-
ters!) and incorporation of verses from → Euripides [3],
cherished in Christian tradition, as well as → Aeschylus
and → Lycophron [4]. The authorship of → Gregorius
[3] of Nazianzus, unanimously recorded by the MSS,
has been debated since the Renaissance on the basis of
prosody, metre, lexicon and theological problems, but
[4; 12; 13] defend it against datings as late as the
12th cent. (the latest of these e.g. [10]) (Romanos Melo-
dos as *terminus ante quem*: [11]).

In contrast with the familiar → cento technique, as in
the *Homerokentra* of → Eudocia [1] i.a. [1; 2] (Homeric
verse and vocabulary also in the *Ch. P*), only about a
third of the text is 'stitched together'. Typically for the
genre, it includes scenic and thematic allusions to the
reference texts. In these allusions the prologue's characterization of the *Ch. P.* (*1–*3) as a hermeneutic
model for Christian reception of a prefiguratively
understood antique (tragic) work, as well as an example
of a Christian poetic, is realized. The drama continues
to excite interest in both these respects, especially in the
Renaissance and the Baroque ([9]: translated by a pupil
of Pietro VETTORI: [6]; H. GROTIUS, *Tragoedia Christus
patiens*, 1608; D. HEINSIUS, *De Tragoediae constitu-
tione*, ²1643, 1611, ch. XVII; J. MILTON, *Preface to
Samson Agonistes*, 1671), but on the other hand hardly
at all in the Byzantine theatre.

1 M. D. USHER (ed.), Eudociae Homerocentones, 1999
2 A.-L. REY (ed.), Patricius, Eudocie, Optimus, Côme de
Jérusalem, Centons Homériques, 1998   3 H. FUNKE,
Euripides, in: JbAC 8/9, 1965/6, 233–279.

EDITIONS AND TRANSLATIONS: 4 A. TUILIER, Grégoire
de Nazianze, La Passion du Christ. Tragédie, 1969 (edn.
and French trans.)   5 F. TRISOGLIO, Gregorio Nazian-
zeno, La Passione di Cristo, 1979 (It. trans.)   6 L. CACIO-
LLI (ed.), Giovanni da Falgano, Ippolito, Ecuba, Christus
patiens, 1995 (It. trans.).
BIBLIOGRAPHY: 7 E. FOLLIERI, Ancora una nota sul
Christos Paschon, in: ByzZ 84, 1991, 343–346
8 A. P. KAZHDAN, s. v. Christos Paschon, ODB 1, 442 f.
9 J. A. PARENTE JR., The Development of Religious Tragedy: The Humanist Reception of the Christos Paschon in
the Renaissance, in: The Sixteenth Century Journal 16,
1985, 351–368   10 K. POLLMANN, Jesus Christus und
Dionysos. Überlegungen zu dem Euripides-Cento Christus patiens, in: Jb. der Öst. Byzantinistik 47, 1987, 87–106
11 G. SWART, The Christos Paschon and Romanos the
Melodist, in: Acta Classica 33, 1990, 53–64   12 F. TRI-
SOGLIO, San Gregorio di Nazianzo e il Christos Paschon,
1996   13 A. TUILIER, Grégoire de Nazianze et le Christos
Paschon, in: REG 110, 1997, 632–647.   T. H.

Christus Patiens see → Christos Paschon

Chromis (Χρόμις; *Chrómis*).
[1] Son of Arsinous (Apollod. Epit. 3,35); ally of the
Trojans. With Ennomus leader of the Mysians (Hom. Il.
2,858; 17,218; 494; 534; Dictys 2,35). C. is then either
'forgotten' in the portrayal of the river battle (Hom. Il.
21) or replaced by Asteropaeus [1]. At a later time he is
regarded as *propator* of the Mysian Abbaetae [2].

1 W. KULLMANN, Die Quellen der Ilias, 1960, 175.
2 P. WEISS, s.v. C., LIMC 3.1, 275 no. 1.

K. JACHMANN, Der homer. Schiffskatalog und die Ilias,
1958, 144–146.

[2] Satyr in Virgil (Ecl. 6,13), in Ovid a companion of
Phineus (Met. 5,103) and a centaur (Met. 12,333)
killed by Peirithous.   R.B.

Chromius (Χρομίος; *Chromíos*).
[1] Son of Neleus and Chloris; brother of Nestor (Hom.
Od. 11,286).
[2] Companion at arms of Nestor (Hom. Il. 4,295).
[3] Son of Priam; killed by Diomedes (Hom. Il. 5,160;
Apollod. 3,152).
[4] Trojan; killed by Teucer (Hom. Il. 8,275).
[5] Lycian; killed by Odysseus (Hom. Il. 5,677).
[6] Son of Arsinous; see → Chromis [1].   R.B.

Chronica minora The Middle Greek counterparts of
the *chronica minora* of late antiquity offer hardly any
possibility of distinguishing between an original *breviarium*, a summary of a more substantial historical work
(*epitomé*) and a short chronicle (e.g. [1]). No → annals
in the strict sense of the word have come down to us
from the Greek world. From the late Byzantine and

post-Byzantine periods in particular, however, we have sequences of concise, precisely dated entries, the so-called Byzantine short chronicles. They contain information about the empire, the emperor, regions and cities, as well as the Turkish conquest, are full of colloquial colour and often sympathetically written.

→ Chronicle

1 C. MANGO (ed.), Nikephoros Patriarch of Constantinople, Short History, 1990.

K. TREU, Griech. Schreibernotizen als Quelle für polit., soziale und kulturelle Verhältnisse ihrer Zeit, in: Byzantinobulgarica 2, 1966, 127–143; P. SCHREINER, Die byz. Kleinchroniken I–III, 1975–1979; G. WEISS, Quellenkunde zur Gesch. von Byzanz, 2 vols., 1982, I 65–68, II 521. G.MA.

Chronicles

A. GENERAL B. THE ANCIENT ORIENT C. GREEK
D. ROMAN E. CHRISTIAN

A. GENERAL

Αἱ χρονικαὶ, τὰ χρονικά; *Hai chronikai, tà chroniká, chronicon*; Latin according to Isid. Orig. 5,37 *series temporum*. No antique or medieval description of the genre [1; 2]. Chronicles are written histories structured on a yearly basis. They vary from mere lists of dates to miniature narratives for individual years: it is then, as → annals — retrospective in the Roman period, ongoing and contemporaneous in the Carolingian — that they enter the realm of real → historiography. This progression may occur within one work, especially with more expansive treatment of the recent past. Because of the lack of comprehensive narrative structures we should speak of 'proto-history' [3. 178]. Typical characteristics are a) a concentration on local history (→ Atthis), the scope being widened only for particular historical motives (general Hellenistic cultural history; eponymy of Roman names in Italian chronicles; Christian universal chronicles), b) taking as a starting-point significant dates in the history of a society/institution (often beginning the work with a founding history), c) chronological commitment, and claims for the completeness of the author's own dates, leading at times to invention on a massive scale when it comes to early history.

Chronicles serve to bolster and/or legitimate the identity of a group; according to the particular context, they may be published in costly inscriptions or remain *de facto* unpublished as the autograph of a specialist author, thus setting themselves apart from other historiographic formats with claims to instruct or entertain (→ Breviarium, → Epitome). Their non-narrative form and official character often lead to overestimation of their historical reliability.

1 B. GUENÉE, Histoires, annales, chroniques, in: Annales ESC 28, 1973, 977–1016 2 H. HOFMANN, Artikulationsformen histor. Wissens in der lat. Historiographie des hohen und späten MA, in: La litterature historiographique des origines à 1500, vol. 2 (GRLM 11/2), 1987 3 J. RÜSEN, Zeit und Sinn, 1990. J.-J.G.

B. THE ANCIENT ORIENT

Texts in various literary formats from Mesopotamia are usually embraced within the term 'chronicle'. Common features of their content are noteworthy events and actions connected with Mesopotamian dynastic rulers or important shrines, presented in chronological sequence: reign by reign, year by year and sometimes month by month or even day by day. They are written in the third person, in a highly concise prose style, and lay particular emphasis on the chronological sequence of facts.

Five types of chronicle are distinguished. 1. Chronicles which present in list form the names of Mesopotamian rulers and the dates of their reigns (→ Kings' lists). They served to legitimize rule at the time of their compilation and on each occasion when they were updated. They form the foundation for the chronological reconstruction of Mesopotamian history. 2. The Assyrian chronicles: official texts serving administrative (→ Eponym lists) or ideological (i.a. the production of royal inscriptions) purposes. 3. Chronicles concerning the pious devotion of rulers to local shrines. They, too, had a legitimizing function. 4. Chronicles relating to the period from 748 BC to the Seleucids. They were produced in scholarly Babylonian circles, seemingly without reference to officialdom. 5. Chronicle-like compilations from the Neo-Babylonian era, relating to rulers from the dim and distant past up to the 8th cent. BC.

Recollection of past events varies according to each epoch: the chroniclers of the 3rd and 2nd millennia impart an archetypal view of history; those of the 1st millennium, on the other hand, use their more exact knowledge and a detailed classification of events to offer a paradigm of subliminal threats bearing down on the universe.

J. J. GLASSNER, Chroniques mésopotamiennes, 1993.

C. GREEK

Two kinds of chronicle existed in Greece; the first represented by significant authors even in the 5th cent., while the second did not blossom until Hellenistic times. Local annual chronicles, their dating based on indigenous eponym data, dealt with local events in a sometimes lively manner. General chronicles or chronographical works, with a universal historical orientation, listing events from political and military history, but also including cultural and literary developments (e.g. information about the lives and works of poets, historians and philosophers); revealing a plethora of dating systems based on synoptic eponym lists (e.g. Olympic champions, Athenian archons, Spartan ephors).

The main exponents of the first genre of chronicle in the 5th cent. BC were → Hellanicus of Lesbos ('Priestesses of Hera at Argos', 'Atthis', 'Karneonikai' [1. 323a; 2. 41f.]) and Charon of Lampsacus ('Annals of Samos', [1. 262; 2.24]; for timetables see [1. 239–261]); but local chronicles were much in vogue even in the 4th cent. and the Hellenistic period (FGrH III B:

'Gesch. von Städten und Völkern. Horographie und Ethnographie', no. 297–607; with commentary and notes).

The most significant representatives of the second genre were → Timaeus of Tauromenium (*Olympioni-kai*, FGrH 241), → Apollodorus [7] of Athens (*Chronika*, FGrH 244) and → Castor of Rhodes (*Chronikon Epitome*, FGrH 250). In addition there are stone chronicles, exceptional examples of which are the → Marmor Parium (FGrH 239) and the → Lindian Chronicle. The 'Priestesses of Hera at Argos' of Hellanicus represents a kind of transition between the two forms, as here 'the almost unbelievable attempt was made to apply a system of annual classification not merely to the history of one city, but to that of the whole of Greece' [3. 70]: this derives i.a. from fragments 79a and b, 84, as well as Thuc. 1,97,2 and 2,2,1: both Thucydides references relate to Hellanicus.

The thesis suggested by WILAMOWITZ [4], that the genesis of Greek historiography is analogous to that of the Roman annual chronicle, which emerged from the *annales maximi*, was received sceptically from the beginning, and is today generally regarded as defunct.

1 FGrH   2 K. MEISTER, Die griech. Geschichtsschreibung, 1990   3 O. LENDLE, Einführung in die griech. Geschichtsschreibung, 1992, 63–73, 277–81   4 U.VON WILAMOWITZ, Aristoteles und Athen, vol. 1, 1893.
J.-J.G.

D. ROMAN

The earliest Latin chronicles take second place to official records (→ *commentarii*) and the increasingly annal-like beginnings of historiography [1]. These early chronicles appear as bureaucratic lists containing events of military or constitutional import (→ *fasti*); dating by eponyms is frequently augmented by → chronography *ab urbe condita*, or by reference to → eras. In the form of *consularia*, they are assured a wide circulation in late antiquity [2; 3]. With the → Chronographer of 354 and the Latin translation of Eusebius' world chronicle by → Hieronymus (AD 381), the tradition of the *fasti* is joined by a Christian and, especially before → Beda, often eschatological approach to history and its reconstruction, at first consisting of mere parallel comparison or synopsis, but proceeding in the chronicles of the 5th/6th cents. to a fully integrated approach (→ Sulpicius Severus, *Chronica Gallica*, → Hydatius, → Marcellinus Comes, → Prosper Tiro and successors, → Cassiodorus [4; 5]). Augmenting the few canonic models with local contemporary history, chronicles together with → biography characterize the historiography of late antiquity and the early Middle Ages.

1 J.RÜPKE, Fasti, in: Klio 77, 1995, 184–202   2 Id., Geschichtsschreibung in Listenform, in: Philologus 141, 1997   3 R.W. BURGESS, The Chronicle of Hydatius and the Consularia Constantinopolitana, 1993   4 A.-D. VON DEN BRINCKEN, Studien zur lat. Weltchronistik …, 1957   5 S.MUHLBERGER, The 5th-Century Chroniclers, 1990.
J.-J.G.

E. CHRISTIAN

The Christian chronicle, based on antique models, forms a separate sub-genre in the literature of late antiquity, to continue in a broader form in the Middle Ages. Emerging from the chronographies of the 2nd/3rd cents. AD and from a background of anti-pagan propaganda, it owes its origins to desires, fed by theological concerns (apocalyptic expectations, catechesis), for a chronology of the whole of world history from a Christian point of view. Brevity and simplicity of expression become its distinguishing characteristics. It is accompanied by specifically Christian methods of calculating time, corresponding to the chronicle's eschatological aspect: Christ's coming at the end of time is taken as the end of history (doctrines of world time; → Eras).

After 221 Sextus Iulius Africanus was the first to write a chronography designed to calculate the end of the world on the basis of biblical data. Hippolytus follows with his chronicle of c. 234/5. After these chronological outlines, worked out primarily on the basis of the Bible and borrowings from Graeco-Roman history, Eusebius of Caesarea (died 339) is first to write a world chronicle in the real sense, appending to his work synchronous summaries of the historical dates of all known lands (Χρονικοὶ κανόνες; *chronikoi kanónes*) in a correlation of world and salvationist history. With the translation and adaptation by Jerome — he brings Eusebius' work forward to 378 — a work that lays the basis for chronicle writing in the west was produced.

Later generations find the models for their chronicles in Eusebius and Jerome (i.a. *Chronica Gallica*, Marcellinus Comes), while local chronicles also make an early appearance (Ravenna). In the Christian Orient too, chronicles form part of the established canons of the various national literatures (i.a. Chronicle of Edessa, John of Nikiou).

→ Chronica minora; → Chronicon paschale; → Eusebius of Caesarea; → Historiography; → Hieronymus; → Hippolytus

1 A.-D. VON DEN BRINCKEN, Stud. zur lat. Weltchronistik bis in das Zeitalter Ottos von Freising, 1957   2 B. CROKE, The Origins of the Christian World Chronicle, in: B.CROKE, A.EMMETT (ed.), History and Historians in Late Antiquity, 1983, 116–131   3 A.A. MOSSHAMMER, The Chronicle of Eusebius and Greek Chronographic Tradition, 1979   4 ST. MUHLBERGER, The fifth-century chroniclers, 1990, 8–23.
J.RI.

Chronicon paschale (Ἐπιτομὴ χρόνων; *Epitomè chrónōn*). The *chronicon paschale* (also *chronicon Alexandrinum*, *chronicon Constantinopolitanum*, *Fasti Siculi*, according to where the particular codex was discovered) was written by a cleric between 631 and 641 at the instigation of the patriarch → Sergius. In its introduction, the 'Easter Chronicle' contains explanations of the Easter cycle. The chronology originally went from Adam to the year 629, but the record breaks off after 628. The chronicler is an eyewitness to events after the reign of → Mauricius (602). The fact that the chronicle is augmented by historical notes and documentary evidence makes this, alongside the work of → Eusebius, one of the most significant works of Greek-Christian historiography. The birth of Christ is set at world-year 5501. The reference to the creation of the world fixed at 21 March 5509 is the first reference to the Proto-Byzantine era.

→ Eras

E. SCHWARZ, Griech. Geschichtsschreiber, 1957, 291–316; J. BEAUCAMP et al., Temps et Histoire. I. Le prologue de la Chronique pascale, Travaux et mémoires 7, 1979, 223–301.   K.SA.

Chronographer of 354 Name of a codex containing the → *fasti* of the city of Rome for the year AD 354. The codex was prepared for a rich Christian aristocrat by the name of Valentinus. The calligraphy itself was the work of Furius Dionysius Filocalus, and of extraordinary quality. The illustrations accompanying the Chronographus are the earliest whole-page illustrations in the history of western art, and may also be the work of Filocalus.

The calendar text and the description of the corresponding month were on opposing pages. The scenes portrayed were seasonal or popular motifs or religious feasts (cf. fig. Chronographus). Being the only surviving complete 4th cent. Roman → calendar, the Chronographus provides unique information on Roman religion and society. Of historical interest is the distinct emphasis given by the Chronographus to the cult of the emperor and the person of Emperor Constantius II, whose portrait decorates the codex.

But the calendar was only the central part of a much bigger 'almanach'. It contained [3. 24f.; later insertions are marked *] I: Dedication to Valentinus II: Depictions of the state *fortuna* (*Tyche*) of the cities of Rome, Constantinople, Trier and Alexandria III: Imperial dedication, list of the *natales Caesarum* IV: The planets and their legends V: *effectus XII signorum*. Text and signs of the Zodiac VI: Illustrated calendar text, distichs on the months [*quatrains on the months] VII: Portraits of the consuls, with emperor Constantius II and the Caesar Julian identified VIII: List of the Roman consuls IX: Calculations for the Easter festival X: List of the city prefects of Rome XI: Dates of death and burial places of the bishops of Rome XII: Dates of death and burial places of martyrs XIII: List of the bishops of Rome [*XIV: Districts of the city of Rome (*notitia*)] [*XV: World chronicle (*liber generationis*)] XVI: Chronicle of the city of Rome (*chronica urbis Romae*).

Some of the sections were illustrated. Illustrations of the Zodiac and the planets reflect contemporary interest in astrology. Some sections without illustrations contained extensive chronological and historical material. Thus, e.g., X and XVI emphasize the Roman origin of the codex, as do XI–XIII. The Christian data clearly addressed the dedicatee. The Chronographus shows us a society in transition, in which pagan culture

The November leaf in the Chronographer of AD 354 (Codex Romanus Ims, Barb. Lat. 2154, fol. 22) represents an ingenious summarizing depiction of the cult of Isis.

and literary traditions were being assimilated in a Christian aristocratic milieu [3]. The survival of the Chronographus suggests that it was a treasured object long after its use by Valentinus in Rome. → Polemius Silvius presumably consulted it when he wrote his own annotated calendar for the year 449. An illustrated copy (the Luxemburgensis) of the original was made in the Carolingian period. Several copies of the latter were produced in the 16th and 17th cents. The best of them (Romanus) was carried out under the careful supervision of the scholar NICHOLAS-CLAUDE FABRI DE PEIRESC, and is now in the Vatican library. The Luxemburgensis was unfortunately damaged, and some pages lost, before the Renaissance copies were made. Today it is entirely lost, only PEIRESC's detailed description remaining [3. 249–268].

EDITION: 1 T. MOMMSEN, Chronographus Anni CCCLIIII, MGH AA 9,1, 1892 (repr. 1981), 13–148.
BIBLIOGRAPHY: 2 H. STERN, Le Calendrier de 354, 1953   3 M. SALZMAN, On Roman Time: The Codex-Calendar of 354 and the Rhythms of Urban Life in Late Antiquity, 1990.   M.SA.

Chronography

I. General II. Mesopotamia III. Egypt
IV. Judaism V. Classical Antiquity
VI. Islam

I. General
A. Notions of measuring time B. Historiographic concepts and eras C. Calendar and
clocks D. Reception

A. Notions of measuring time

Most cultures have some method of measuring time, frequently based on periodical changes within nature or the stars. The oldest of these is the *pars-pro-toto* method, in which it is not a certain period of time as a whole that is connected, but a regularly recurring phenomenon within that time [1. 9 f.] (e.g. lunar phases). Metaphors of time or the measuring thereof play no great role in antiquity, with the exception of the field of → metrics. Usually, the focus was not on the precise measurement of time, but on the utilization of conventional time units such as generations or governments' terms of office. Accounts of time periods were often rounded, as in the explanation that three generations equalled 100 years (Hdt. 2,142); equally, certain points in time, defined as intervals from the present tense of the speaker, were given as rounded figures (Hdt. 2,145); age references on gravestones were also frequently stated as rounded figures (cf. Varro, Rust. 1,40,3: a calculation in days). Even without defining a starting-point in the past to indicate the beginning of an era (→ Eras), such time intervals could also be precisely counted in years backwards from a present date (e.g. → *Marmor Parium*) or alternatively stated in relative intervals (Eratosthenes FGrH 241 F 1a). The measuring of time does not necessarily imply numerical calculations: in line with the custom of naming years after significant events (Babylonia, see II below), officials or priests (Greece, Roman Republic, see V below), or the rule of an emperor (Rome), this, too, was seen as 'counting' (Sen. Dial. 5,31,2).

B. Historiographic concepts and eras

The measuring of time in antiquity is characterized by a coexistence of very diverse systems that have completely different scopes (see below). Most of these are only locally recognized and closely interlinked with other pragmatic considerations, and dominated by them. This is particularly true for → eponyms in chronology and the calculation in → eras with their expression of political responsibilities, or rather: dynastic continuity. It applies even more to further-reaching 'calculations' in multiples of years: the widely differing generation lengths found in ancient sources (between 23 and 40 years) and the resulting rounded figures or periodicities are historiographically more important than their empirical content, i.e. the assumed duration of a generation (cf. → Genealogy); genealogies themselves were incidentally not the only early chronogra-

phical element; frequently they are not even primarily used in that context.

Precise figures gain particular interest whenever they support any claims to an outstanding value of someone's own time. This kind of endowment with meaning can be observed in the secular system (→ *saeculum*) of the early Roman imperial period as well as in the Judaeo-Christian → apocalypses: a change of world-historical impact is either immediately impending or being realized. In all of this, it remains a feature of the European sense of time, compared with e.g. the Indian one, that well into the 19th cent. only a comparatively short time span is assumed for the chronology (the term itself is post-antique) of world history, which maybe is due to the limited needs of city states for global historical legitimization; based on Egyptian calculations, the range of — merely — 6,000 years for the entire of world history only became firmly established with the Christian chronology of → Sextus [2] Iulius Africanus.

Christian apologetics (→ apologists) led to new developments in the measuring of time, as the value of Christianity was to be emphasized by the greater age of it compared to other traditions. In around AD 300, → Eusebius [7] of Caesarea established in his Chronicle a chronology which remained valid into the early modern period; in the Middle Ages, it was known in the Latin translation by Jerome (→ Hieronymus). There are no parallels in antiquity to the early modern world chronology of Joseph J. Scaliger (1540–1609) [2], which expresses the entire prehistory as well as the future in an absolute number of days. It is true that the European eras in common modern use have their origins in antiquity or late antiquity (see below IV on Judaism and VI on Islam): the Christian era was established by → Dionysius [55] Exiguus in the first half of the 6th cent. AD and applied by → Beda Venerabilis (*c.* 673–735) [3]. However, these European eras have only found acceptance in post-antiquity, which is true also of the calculation *ante/post Christum natum*, attributed to Dionysius Petavius (1627), and to the Jewish world era (see below).

C. Calendar and clocks

Calendric dates play a very insignificant role in historiography, unless considered under aspects of → hemerology, or for the creation of synchronisms (e.g. Hdt. 7,166; 8,15; 9,100 f.) or significant periodicities (e.g. Tac. Ann. 15,41: historical town fires). In the daily life of ancient societies, calendric questions beyond establishing the rhythms of daily life (e.g. of festivals or market or court days, see → Fasti; → Nundinae) became of particular importance, whenever the empirical establishment of the length of a month or the alignment of lunar phases and solar years led to problems of intercalation (→ Calendar) or when various qualifications of time (→ Hemerology; → Astrology) conflicted. The wealth of datings in administrative texts and documents of the Ancient Orient as well as pre-Roman Italy and Hellenistic Egypt is evidence of the interest in precisely timed coordination and documentation. Hourly times are of only minor significance in the literary tradition, but usable sundials and water clocks (→ Clocks) had been developed both in Egypt and in the Graeco-Roman world: thus the Greek papyrus P Hib. I 110ᵛ, recording the daily register of a postal station complete with hour of the day, provides evidence of the use of hourly times by the administration beyond the proceedings of courts and committees. This fits in well with Suetonius' statement that Augustus added the time of day onto written documents (Suet. Aug. 50).

D. Reception

Subsequent European systems of measuring time were decisively influenced by Christian chronography (→ Historiography IV) together with the Roman calendar as modified by the Christians; both in turn had absorbed the technical knowledge of the Egyptian and Babylonian cultures. The fact that this calendar and this chronography were subsequently perceived as specifically Christian determined the future success as well as the limitations of their reception (Islam, French revolutionary calendar).

→ Eras; → Astrology; → Genealogy; → Historiography; → Calendar; → Clocks; → Time, concepts of; CHRONOGRAPHY

1 M. P. Nilsson, Primitive Time-Reckoning, 1920 2 A. Grafton, Joseph Scaliger: A Study in the History of Classical Scholarship, 2 vols., 1983/1993 3 F. Wallis (ed.), Bede, The Reckoning of Time, 1999 (Beda Venerabilis; with translation and commentary).

F. K. Ginzel, Hdb. der mathematischen und technischen Chronologie: Das Zeitrechnungswesen der Völker, 3 vols., 1906–1914; O. Leuze, Röm. Jahrzählung, 1909; V. Grumel, La chronologie, 1958 (Byzantine period); A. E. Samuel, Greek and Roman Chronology, 1972; R. Wendorff, Zeit und Kultur, 1980; H. Lietzmann, Zeitrechnung der röm. Kaiserzeit, des MA und der Neuzeit für die Jahre 1–2000 n. Chr., ⁴1984; H. Zemanek, Kalender und Chronologie, ⁵1990; A. Borst, Computus. Zeit und Zahl in der Gesch. Europas, 1990. J. R.

II. Mesopotamia

For the approximate description of longer periods of time, the number of generations was calculated (→ Family). This 'anthropomorphous' way of measuring time is also evident in orally transmitted and written → genealogies. Details regarding the typical duration of a generation are not transmitted. The reconstruction of genealogies results in uncertain or overly long periods of time.

Natural phenomena as regular and generally observable events formed the basis of Mesopotamian chronography: The rhythm of the celestial bodies (day/night, lunar phases, solstices, equinoxes), the → seasons with their related activities (→ Agriculture) or rather their associated natural phenomena and corresponding festivals (→ Feasts; e.g. → New Year's celebrations) helped to calculate and structure short time ranges.

The linear counting of years transposed the natural rhythm into a anthropogenous standardized measurement of time. As a rule, the basic year comprised 12 (lunar) months of 29 or 30 days respectively, with the addition, if required, of (lunisolar) intercalary months (→ Calendar). The month itself was structured by the lunar phases; groups of five or 10 days formed an administrative unit. Up to the middle of the 2nd millennium BC, the beginning of a year was with regional variations, linked to the autumn or spring equinoxes. Even the oldest texts (end of the 4th millennium, → Uruk) document the use of a standard year of 360 days for administrative purposes. The 360–day year also formed the foundation for the astronomical theories and calculations of the 2nd and 1st millennia BC (→ Astronomy). The equation and alignment of the calendric, the cultic, and the administrative year remains largely unclear.

In order to differentiate between individual years, year-names were used, documented in northern Syria (→ Ebla) from as early as the mid 3rd millennium, in Mesopotamia from c. 2300 BC. They refer to central political or cultic events of the previous year (e.g. 'the year in which the town of X was destroyed'). There is also evidence of the use for subsequent years (e.g. 'the year after the town of X was destroyed') as well as of naming a current year. Around the middle of the 2nd millennium, it became increasingly prevalent to measure time after the years of an individual regency, thus emphasizing a chronological range. In Babylonia, the formula 'year n of king X' became the official standard dating practice. The continuous count started afresh with each new ruler. In Assyria, the Old Assyrian custom of counting years by eponyms (→ Eponyms in chronology) was upheld to the very end of the Assyrian state; in the 15th cent., years were named after the royal rulers. The numbering of years by the duration of an individual ruler's reign was only used in annalistic texts (royal inscriptions).

Ordering time was a royal prerogative; thus changes in the political power of Mesopotamia manifested themselves in changes to the chronography, dual dating systems, and mixed forms in the format of dates. In the 3rd and early 2nd millennium, numerous local and regional systems for measuring annual dates coexisted. How time was measured was decreed by the political ruler at the time. The same applied to the subsequent period, when both Assyria and Babylonia formed large territorial states.

→ Lists were the most important organizational aid for measuring time: lists of year-names or eponyms alongside lists of → kings with the names of rulers and the duration of their regency. Chronography and history of events further interlink in the → chronicles, which basically represent little more than an extension of the ancient year-names.

An increasingly complex economic administration primarily necessitated the development of a chronography which permitted calculations over longer periods of time. Here as in jurisdiction (→ Cuneiform legal texts), exact datings were of great importance. Measuring time by the years of a regency resulted in year names combining events and distance information. The organizational complexity of measuring time becomes apparent in the necessity of keeping continuous lists of dates as reference material. There was no development of an 'absolute' measurement of time, i.e. one with an obligatory single point of reference independent of people or institutions. First steps towards such a system under → Nabonassar(us) are contentious. The Deluge (→ Deluge, legend of the) only operated as the fixed point of a mythological-historical chronography ('before/after the Flood').

Back to the middle of the 2nd millennium, it is possible to transpose the timekeeping of Mesopotamia — esp. by synchronisms with the Hellenistic one — into an absolute chronology. Chronologies of older historical periods are as yet only available in relative form.

From 311 BC, cuneiform documents in Mesopotamia as well as Aramaic documents in Ḥatra were dated in accordance with the Seleucid era, under Parthian rule according to the Arsacid era which began in 247 BC (occasional double dating according to Seleucid and Arsacid era [2] on the same document; → Eras). → Astronomy; → Historiography; → Calendar; → Months, names of the

1 R. K. ENGLUND, Administrative Timekeeping in Ancient Mesopotamia, in: Journ. of the Economic and Social History of the Orient 31, 1988, 121–185   2 J. RENGER, Vorstellungen von Zeit und Zeitmessung ... in der Überl. des alten Mesopot., in: H. FALK (ed.), Vom Herrscher zur Dynastie (2002).   E. C.-K.

III. EGYPT

From the onset of written records, the solar year had been the basis of Egyptian time reckoning, while the lunar calendar was restricted to cultic activities. The calculatory basis was a year of 365 days; there however were no leap years. In accordance with the natural conditions in Egypt, there were three seasons of 4 months each, i.e. 'Flood', 'Appearance (of the Seeds)', and 'Harvest'. Each month had 30 days, subdivided into units of 10 days. Outside of the normal course of time were the five additional 'epagomene' days at the end of the year, which were linked with the birthdays of the gods → Osiris, → Isis, → Horus, → Seth, and → Nephthys.

The numbering of years started afresh whenever a new → ruler ascended to the throne. In most of the epochs of Egyptian history, the first year of a ruler was counted from his accession to the throne to the following New Year's Day in order to ensure a continued alignment of natural year and regnal year. However, during the time of the New Kingdom, the regional years were numbered independent of the new year to the next anniversary of the accession to the throne. From the very earliest period (from c. 1300 BC), there were annals which recorded a ruler's most important deeds during a year. Such accounts of longer epochs were also published as engravings in stone (e.g. the 'Palermo Stone', [1]). On similar records were based the works of the Egyptian priest → Manetho [1] — who wrote in Greek –, whose list of → kings has survived in fragments and epitomes. The intercalation-free Egyptian year was used by the Greek mathematician Claudius → Ptolemaeus [65], and in his wake was later until the early modern period used by astronomers for calculations because of its straightforward simplicity. In his calendar reforms, → Caesar was strongly influenced by the Egyptian year, which thus became one of the roots of modern time reckoning.
→ Calendar

1 J. F. QUACK, Zw. Sonne und Mond. Z. im Alten Äg., in: H. FALK (ed.), Vom Herrscher zur Dynastie (2002) 2 K. SETHE, Die Zeitrechnung der alten Ägypter im Verhältnis zu der der anderen Völker, in: Nachr. der königlichen Ges. der Wiss. Göttingen, Philos.-histor. Klasse 1919, 287–320; 1920, 28–55 and 97–141.   JO. QU.

IV. JUDAISM

For the chronological ordering of events (biblical, historical, contemporary), thought to be of salvatory importance, Rabbinic Judaism counted in generations or referred to → eras of 1,000 years (cf. Psalm 90,4), each of which was reckoned to equal one day within a week of world time. The biblically set unit of 49 years (Jobel), still used in Qumran (→ Dead Sea) and some of the apocrypha (→ Apocryphal literature A.; 'Henoch', → *Liber Iubilaeorum*/'Book of Jubilees'), was later replaced by 19–year cycles which were founded in the lunisolar year. Traditionally, this system of time reckoning is attributed to Hillel II (AD 365); however, it was only hinted at by Hai Gaon (who died in AD 1038) and unequivocally documented for Abraham ben Chijja (1122). Such a cycle comprised 7 leap years (years 3, 6, 8, 11, 14, 17, 19), with an additional month (Adar 1, 30 days) intercalated. A year consisted of 12 (or 13) months of 29 or 30 days, counted from the new moon. Festive days were connected with lunar phases. The new year began in autumn, even though the liturgical calendar began in spring.

The most important unit of Jewish time measurement is the week consisting of 7 days. The day begins and ends with the evening, to be identified by the appearance of three visible stars. Times set for the adherence to certain religious commands were linked to sunrise, sunset, visibility of stars etc., in order separate the observance of religious commandments from any authorized system of time reckoning.

Whereas in the Bible and the apocrypha time is frequently reckoned according to the regnal years of the respective kings, a method also accepted in → Rabbinical literature as a way to measure biblical chronology, Jewish legal documents in antiquity and the MA followed the Seleucid calendar (from 312 BC; cf. → Eras C.1.). Alongside that, a method of time reckoning which began with the creation of the world (AD 240 = year 4000 after creation) was used for religious purposes; from the 9th/10th cents. AD, it also replaced the Seleucid calendar in everyday life. From late antiquity, the 19–year-cycles were also used in an eschatological context for the reckoning of time, with the figures read as words. Figures that — written in letters — make up words with a positive meaning (e.g. 255 = *rināh*) thus indicate salutary cycles.

E. MAHLER, Handbuch der jüd. Chronologie, 1916 (repr. 1967). E. H.

V. CLASSICAL ANTIQUITY

It is a characteristic of Graeco-Roman antiquity (esp. the Hellenistic period) that, in parallel with the increasing perception of first Greece and then the entire Hellenistic Mediterranean as a unit, a kind of universal → historiography developed, and with it the need of being able to align and compare various locally significant methods of 'counting' years. In order to localize events and people, not only synchronous dates were needed, but also a system for the co-ordination of synchronous and diachronous dates [vol. 1, 2.2, 446 f.]. As orally transmitted events were passed on without a chronological identification, ancient scholars, too, were faced with the task of fixing them chronographically [2; 3. 84 f.]. At the end of the 5th cent. BC, → Hellanicus [1] of Mytilene took the priestesses of Hera at Argos as the chronographical foundation of his universal history. After Thucydides (2,2) had defined the beginning of the → Peloponnesian War through the synchronization of various local dates, it was → Timaeus [2] of Tauromenium — his main work dealt with the Greek West, including Rome — who in *c.* 300 BC extended the synchronistic framework of Greek chronography through the addition of the Olympic victors (FGrH 566 T 10).

Not much later, → Eratosthenes [2] of Cyrene used the beginning of the Olympic games to define set periods (FGrH 241 F 1a), thus tracing the 1st Olympiad back to 776 BC (cf. → Olympia IV.). The earliest evidence for the assumption that historical time began with the first Olympiad, however, is only found in → Censorinus [4] (Censorinus, DN 21), who cites M. Terentius → Varro [2]. The counting of Olympiads became the reference point for all historiography, but never prevailed in public documents; its earliest appearances can be observed in the Olympic Chronicle (IG II/III² 2326: probably 276 BC; [4]) and in Q. → Fabius [I 35] Pictor, who employed the Olympiad era for the period of Rome's foundation [6. 1 F 8, commentary], but for his contemporary history used eponymous dating with reference to the consuls of each year.

For administrative datings in inscriptions, local eponymous officials (e.g. the → *árchontes* in Athens) were used, or — in the richly documented imperial age — local eras or the emperor's *tribunicia* → *potestas*, which equated to the years of his rule as Augustus. In the Hellenistic East, local eponyms were frequently recorded in → lists, thus impressively documenting the

tradition of the individual institution and with it that of the → polis (e.g. [5. no. 122–128]), although these chronographical attempts were never used in historiography. Within these various methods of dating which were all rooted in their respective environments, synchronisms did not increase the precision of the dating process, but by linking different spheres of activity and traditions they created a context-specific significance (e.g. in the synchronisms of the acts of Christian martyrs such as the Martyrium Pioni 23). In Hellenistic Egypt, correspondence was set by the regnal year and the months of the Macedonian and/or the Egyptian calendar. The different starting-points of the New Year presented a problem for the transposition of Hellenistic-Egyptian dates onto the Gregorian calendar: The regnal year varied dependent on the date of accession to the throne, the financial year began with the Egyptian month of Mecheir, and the Egyptian year, which furthermore operated without leap days (see above III.), started with the first day of the month of Thoth.

→ Eras; → Chronicle; → Eponyms in chronology; → Fasti; → Calendar; → Time, concepts of; CALENDAR; CHRONOGRAPHY

1 S. MAZZARINO, Il pensiero storico classico, vol. 1–2, 1965–66 2 D. HENIGE, The Chronology of Oral Tradition, 1974 3 A. A. MOSSHAMMER, The Chronicle of Eusebius and Greek Chronographic Tradition, 1979 4 J. EBERT, Die 'Olympische Chronik' IG II/III² 2326, in: Id., Agonismata, 1997, 237–252 5 TH. WIEGAND et al., Milet vol. 1.3, 1914 6 H. BECK, U. WALTER (ed.), Die frühen röm. Historiker, 2001. J. R.

A. MÖ.

VI. ISLAM

The Islamic calendar, which to this day is in common use throughout the entire Islamic world in the religious as well as the secular context, is a pure 12–month lunar calendar. The names of the months are predominantly of Old Arabic origin: 1. Muharram, 2. Ṣafar, 3. Rabīʿal-Awwal, 4. Rabīʿ al-Āḫir, 5. Ǧumādā al-Ūlā, 6. Ǧumādā al-Āḫira, 7. Raǧab, 8. Šaʿbān, 9. Ramaḍān, 10. Šawwāl 11. Dū-l-Qaʿda 12. Dū-l-Ḥiǧǧa. The empirical determination of the beginning of a new month based on the first nocturnal appearance of the waxing moon's crescent was rooted in Middle Eastern tradition; even though adverse weather conditions could occasionally affect the accuracy of this method, the astronomical calculation, though known, never fully prevailed.

Islamic time-reckoning begins with the Hiǧra (→ Mohammed's flight to Medina/→ Yatrib, July AD 622); this → era was allegedly introduced by Caliph ʿUmar 638 (= 17 Hiǧra). As the Islamic lunar year only comprises 354 days and does not correlate with the seasons, the solar calendar was also used in general practice. The Eastern Christian calendar, based on the Julian → calendar, was used for orientation; in the Middle East, the months retained their old Babylonian names, in North Africa and Spain, variations of the Roman names of the → months. In common use in some parts was the Seleucid Era (also wrongly named the Alexander Era, from 312 BC; → Eras C.1.), in others the Byzantine Era, and elsewhere the Byzantine indiction cycle (esp. in Egypt and North Africa; → *indictio*), in medieval Spain, the Spanish Era (from January 1, 38 BC) was still used. The official Muslim calendar of Iran is to this day based on the solar year (similar to the Egyptian year, but with the months bearing Iranian names), starting at the Hiğra.

F. C. DE BLOIS, s. v. Ta'rīḫ, EI², CD-ROM 1999; F. WÜSTENFELD et al., Vergleichungstabellen der muslimischen und christlichen Zeitrechnung, ³1961.　　　　I. T.-N.

Chronos (Χρόνος, 'Time'). Personification of Time, which appears in Greek religious thought as one of the primary powers and often as an allegorical reinterpretation of the primal deity → Kronos; cf. e.g. Pherecydes of Soros (DIELS, Vorsokr. 7 vol. 1), where C. appears next to the primal pair Zas and Chtonia as a primal deity [2; 3]. He is particularly important in the Orphic theogonies and cosmogonies from their beginnings on; instead of the Hesiodic → Chaos, he appears as the father of Eros (Orph. Fr. 37, cf. Orph. A. 13), as a winged snake with a lion's or bull's head that also bears the name → Hercules in the (Hellenistic) theogony of Jerome and Hellanicus (Orph. Fr. 54), and as 'Ageless Time', father of Aether, in the so-called Rhapsodic Theogony (Orph. Fr. 60; 66; 70), which combines older elements. Oriental ideas — Egyptian, Phoenician and especially Iranian — sometimes underlie these concepts [3]. Of particular importance is the Zoroastrian Zurvān akarana ('Infinite Time') [4].

Separated from this speculative poetry, in which time is understood as a fundamental given, are less defined personifications as in Solon (fr. 36,3) who speaks of Chronos' court of law, Pindar (Ol. 2,19) who calls him 'Father of All' and Sophocles (El. 179) who describes him as 'the god bringing relief' (εὐμαρὴς θεός) that sees and hears all, brings it to light and then hides it again. This provides the basis for threadbare genealogies, such as 'Day' as the daughter of Night and C. (Bacchyl. 7,1) or 'Right' and 'Truth' as the daughters of C. (Eur. fr. 223). The identification with Kronos (Plut. De Is. et Os. 32,363 D) led to an allegorical interpretation of the Roman rites of Saturn (Plut. Quaest. Rom. 11,266 D-E, cf. 12,266 F; Gell. NA 12,11,7). An established iconography did not exist [5]. Mediated by the Stoic allegoresis of the Kronos myth in Cic. Nat. 2,64 (SVF 2,1091), the interpretation of Kronos/Saturnus as 'Father Time', and especially the idea that Time devours its children (SVF 2,1087), in numerous ways continued its influence to the present via medieval (e.g. Ovid moralisé) and early modern treatises and images [6; 7]. → Claudianus

1 G. S. KIRK, J. E. RAVEN, M. SCHOFIELD, The Presocratic Philosophers, ²1982, 87　2 H. S. SCHIBLI, Pherekydes of Soros, 1990　3 M. L. WEST, The Orphic Poems, 1983, especially 190–194　4 Id., Early Greek Philosophy and

the East, 1971, 30–33　5 M. B. GALÁN, s.v. Ch., LIMC 3.1, 276–278　6 J. SEZNEC, La survivance des dieux antiques, 1940, passim.　7 M. CIAVOLELLA, A. A. IANUCCI (ed.), Saturn. From Antiquity to the Renaissance, 1992.
　　　　F.G.

Chrysanthius Neoplatonic (4th cent. AD), pupil of Iamblichus' pupil → Aedesius [1] in Pergamum. He taught the future emperor Julian, at first in Pergamum with Eusebius of Myndus, then in Ephesus with the Neoplatonic philosopher Maximus. C. was also the teacher of Eunapius, who, in his *Vitae philosophorum et sophistarum* (ch. 23 p. 90,21–101,16 GIANGRANDE), sketches a most vivid portrait of him.

R. GOULET, in: Id. 2, 1994, 320–323.　　　　P.HA.

Chrysaor(i)us (Χρυσάωρ; *Chrysáōr*). 'He with the golden sword' (Hes. Theog. 283).
[1] Attribute of Zeus in Stratoniceia (Caria), whose temple was the federal sanctuary of the Carian towns (Str. 14,660; CIG 2720f.).
[2] Eponymous hero of Caria, which was also called Χρυσαορίς (Paus. 5,21,10). He was the son of the Sisyphid Glaucus (Steph. Byz. 461 MEINEKE).
[3] Epithet of various gods: Apollo (Hom. Il. 5,509; 15,256 etc.), Artemis (oracle: Hdt. 8,77), Demeter (Hom. h. 2,4) and Orpheus (Pind. Fr. 128c,12 MAEHLER).
[4] When Perseus struck off Medusa's head, C. and Pegasus sprang forth as the fruit of her love affair with Poseidon. C. fathered Geryoneus with the Oceanid Callirhoe (Hes. Theog. 278–288; 979–983; Apollod. 2,41; Hyg. Fab. 30; 151; Paus. 1,35,7).

I. KRAUSKOPF, s.v. Gorgo/Gorgones, LIMC 4.1, 311–314 no. 289; 307–311.　　　　R.B.

Chrysaphius (Χρυσάφιος; *Chrysáphios*). *Chrysaphius qui et Ztummas*, eunuch. Under → Theodosius II he was *praepositus sacri cubiculi* as first eunuch also called *spatharius*. After → Cyrus was overthrown, he supposedly had decisive influence on the emperor, repelling all rivals by unethical means. In AD 449 C. planned to assassinate → Attila. This was uncovered, but he had enough influence to avoid being surrendered to the Huns. In the Nestorian controversy he supported his godfather → Eutyches against the Orthodox party and probably prepared the 'Robber Synod' of 449. At the instigation of → Pulcheria he was executed under → Marcianus (PLRE 2, 295–297, cf. [1. 122]).

1 A. LANIADO, Some Addenda to the PLRE, Vol. II, in: Historia 44, 1995, 121–128.　　　　H.L.

Chrysas Sicilian river close to the road to Morgantina in the territory of Agyrion (Diod. Sic. 14,95,2), modern Dittaino.

L. ROCCHETTI, EAA 2, 1959, 570; C. VITANZA, Arch. St. Sic. or., 12, 1915, 163–180.　　　　GI.MA.

Chryse (Χρυσῆ χερρόνησος; *Chrysê cherrónesos*). South-west Asian Peninsula (Peripl. m. r. 63; Ptol. 7,2,5, etc.), Lat. Promunturium Chryse (Plin. HN 6,20,55), probably on the modern Malacca Peninsula; cf. Sanskrit Suvarṇabhūmi 'Land of Gold' and Suvarṇadvīpa 'Island of Gold' in south-west Asia.

P. WHEATLEY, The Golden Khersonese. Studies in the historical geography of the Malay Peninsula before A.D. 1500, 1961.   K.K.

Chryse, Chrysa (Χρῦσα, Χρύση; *Chrýsa, Chrýsē*). Name of various islands and towns, among them a) an island near Lemnos, which sank in the time of Pausanias (8,33,4); b) in the time of Strabo a deserted port in the plain of Thebes on the Gulf of Adramyttium in southern Aeolis (ἡ Κιλίκιος X., Str. 13,1,48; 63), one of the residences of the Apollo priest Chryses (Hom. Il. 1,37); c) in the time of Strabo (13,1,47f.), a village located on a cliff above the sea near the Lecton promontory (Baba burnu?) with a temple of Apollo Smintheus, generally located on Göz Tepe.

J. M. COOK, The Troad, 1937, 232f.; L. BUFFO, I re ellenistici e i centri religiosi dell' Asia Minore, 1985, 28off.
                                                          H.KAL.

Chryseis (Χρυσηίς; *Chrysēís*). Etymology 'girl from → Chryse' or 'daughter of Chryses'. The daughter of the Apollo priest Chryses who was captured by → Achilles in Thebes and allotted to Agamemnon as a slave. When Chryses pleaded with Agamemnon to have C. returned, he was refused. On Chryses' prayer Apollo forced the return of C. by sending a plague. Agamemnon then demanded Achilles' captive → Briseis as a substitute and, thus, incurred his anger (Hom. Il. 1). According to schol. Il. 1,392 C. was originally called Astynome. According to a later legend, C. became pregnant with Agamemnon's child Chryses (Hyg. Fab. 21; Soph. TrGF IV 726–730).

I. KRAUSKOPF, s.v. Ch. I, LIMC 3.1, 281f.   R.B.

Chryselephantine technique see → Gold-ivory technique

Chrysermus of Alexandria (IDélos 1525). C. lived in about 150–120 BC; administrative official, 'relative of king Ptolemy', exegete (i.e. head of the civil service in Alexandria), director of the museum and ἐπὶ τῶν ἰατρῶν, a title that is often understood to mean the person responsible for all Egyptian doctors, which in turn led to the conclusion that there was a state organization of doctors. KUDLIEN is of the opinion that the title refers to the person responsible for the person in charge of the 'tax on doctors' [1]. Neither of these interpretations proves that C. himself was a doctor. A later C., about 50 BC, was a Herophilean [2] and interested in the science of the pulse.

1 F. KUDLIEN, Der griech. Arzt, in: AAMz, 1979, 32–40
2 v. STADEN, Herophilus, 523–528.   V.N.

Chrysippe (Χρυσίππη; *Chrysíppē*). Danaid who killed her spouse Chrysippus, son of Aegyptus (Apollod. 2,18; Hyg. Fab. 170).   R.B.

Chrysippus (Χρύσιππος; *Chrýsippos*).

[1] Favourite son of → Pelops from his first marriage with the nymph Axioche (schol. Pind. Ol. 1,89, schol. Eur. Or. 4) or Danais (Plut. Mor. 313E). Two tales are associated with him: Zeus (Praxilla 3,6 EDMONDS = Ath. 13 p. 603a) or → Laeus, C.'s teacher in chariot driving (thus presumably in the 'C.' of Euripides, TGF fr. 839–844, possibly already in the *Laios* of Aeschylus), became infatuated with the extraordinarily beautiful youth and abducted him either from his father's house or the Nemean games to Thebes (Hyg. Fab. 85). The wrath of Hera struck the Thebans, who did not punish this case of paedophilia, in the form of the sphinx (Peisander FGrH 16 F 10). After the violated C. had killed himself, his father Pelops cursed the house of Laius. — Or, C.'s brothers returned him by force to Pisa. The second C. episode may be linked to this latter version (Hyg. Fab. 85): as Pelops preferred C. to his other sons, Hippodamia feared that the children might not succeed to the throne and instigated her sons → Atreus and Thyestes to commit murder. The two then drowned C. in a well or hid his corpse there. The father's curse struck the perpetrators: Hippodamia, the brothers and their descendants (Hellanic. FGrH 4 F 157; Thuc. 1,9; schol. Eur. Or. 5). The murderers fled with Hippodamia (who, according to Hyg. Fab. 85; 243 committed suicide) to Midea (Paus. 6,20,7) or Mycenae.

E. BETHE, s.v. C. 1, RE 3, 2498–2500; H. LAMER, s.v. Laios, RE 12, 474–481; H. LLOYD-JONES, The Justice of Zeus, ²1983, 120f.; K. SCHEFOLD, s.v. C. 1, LIMC 3.1, 286–289; H. W. STOLL, s.v. C., Roscher 1, 902–905.   T.S.

[2]

A. LIFE   B. HISTORICAL SIGNIFICANCE
C. WORKS   D. PHILOSOPHICAL THOUGHT

A. LIFE
Stoic philosopher and third head of the school. Information on his biography mainly comes from Diog. Laert. (7,179–189). Son of a certain Apollonius (or Apollonides: Suda s.v.; Philod. [4] col. 37 knows both names) of Tarsus in Asia Minor. C. himself was born in Soli and eventually became an Athenian citizen (Plut. St. Rep. 1034a). The connection of Soli to the Athenian Stoa began with the poet Aratus [1] and was expanded by C. He took two of his nephews, Aristocreon and Philocrates, from Soli to Athens and saw to their philosophical education there (Diog. Laert. 7,185). He probably did the same for Hyllus of Soli ([1] col. 46). C.'s dates of birth and death are uncertain: the Suda places his death in the 143rd Olympiad (208–204 BC.). If he died at age 73, he was born between 281 and 277; oth-

ers however (Ps.-Lucian. Makrobii 20; Val. Max. 8,7 ext. 10) state that he died at the age of 80 or 81, which would date his birth back to 289.

Cleanthes (the second head of the school) was his most important Stoic teacher. C. put much store into not visiting the popular lectures of Cleanthes' rival Ariston [7] of Chios. He declared: 'If I had paid attention to what most people do, I would not have become a philosopher!' For a brief period C. may have studied with the school's founder Zeno before he died in 262 (Diog. Laert. 7,179). For a while he also studied in the Academy with Arcesilaus and Lacydes (Diog. Laert. 7,183f.). C. was at pains to remain politically neutral (unlike other Stoics) and did so with considerable success. He did not actively participate in Athenian politics and rejected royal support; his treatises contain no dedications to kings and he declined moving to king Ptolemy's court (when Cleanthes was asked to come or send someone in his place and C. refused, Sphaerus went instead: Diog. Laert. 7,185). Hecaton reports that C. turned to professional philosophical activity after his inheritance was confiscated for the 'royal treasury' (Diog. Laert. 7,181). This probably happened during the Syrio-Egyptian war of the 240s — but it remains unclear which side confiscated his property.

C. appears to have charged fees for his teaching (cf. Plut. St. Rep. 1043e–1044a regarding his opinions) and to have been a conscientious lecturer (Philod. [1] col. 38). He led a modest life and possessed only one slave (Diog. Laert. 7,185, she appears in anecdotes 7,181 and 183). C. was of slender stature (Diog. Laert. 7,182), which suited his former training as a long-distance runner (7,179), while Cleanthes was a boxer and labourer (Diog. Laert. 7,168). His slenderness is discussed in tales about his famous statue on the Cerameicus (Diog. Laert. 7,182). He was known for his hard work: during his career he produced 500 lines a day, and a total of 700 books (papyrus rolls), a catalogue of which is partially preserved in Diogenes Laertius (see below). His philosophical writings were criticized for their terse style, and he was also accused of bloating his works with long-winded quotes (Diog. Laert. 7,180–181). We know little about his private life; one anecdote however emphasizes his ability to drink a lot (a comment by his slave: 'only his legs get drunk', Diog. Laert. 7,183). In another anecdote his death is attributed to imprudent drinking at a bout hosted by one of his students. According to a different anecdote (Diog. Laert. 7,184f.) he died from laughing too hard at one of his own jokes.

B. HISTORICAL SIGNIFICANCE

As a sharp-minded and flexible thinker, he often spoke against the views of his teacher → Cleanthes and even → Zeno (but mostly he expounded what he thought were Zeno's true views). At the beginning of his teaching activity (probably already before Cleanthes' death, Diog. Laert. 7,179) he read in the Odeum and under the open sky in the Lyceum. His succession as head of the Stoa was by no means certain but once he was head of the school he promoted unity by speaking in favour of (accordingly interpreted) opinions of Zeno and against what he thought were erroneous teachings in the works of Aristo [7] of Chios, Cleanthes and others. The book title 'That Zeno used terms correctly' (Diog. Laert. 7,122) probably reflects this goal, as does his well-known interpretation of the meaning of Zeno's *phantasia* (Sext. Emp. M 2,227–231), in which Zeno rejected Cleanthes' view as 'absurd'. His treatise on Zeno's 'Republic' should perhaps be seen in the same light. C. had numerous students (many of whom are listed in Philod. [1] col. 47; many of his books are dedicated to them: [1] on this passage). That his students → Zeno of Tarsus and → Diogenes of Babylon became heads of the school and that → Antipater [10] of Tarsus, the student of Diogenes, succeeded him, reflects his influence. Therefore, it is unsurprising that his version of the Stoa became canonical and his views and methods dominated the school over generations. His significance is encapsulated in the exclamation: 'If C. had not existed, there would be no Stoa!' (Diog. Laert. 7,183). → Carneades, the great Academic philosopher of the next generation, gave C. the following tribute: 'If C. had not been, there would be no Carneades!' (Diog. Laert. 4,62). C.'s mastery of dialectics was already famous in antiquity and is reflected in the opinion that 'if the gods had a dialectic, it would surely be that of C.' (Diog. Laert. 7,180). This ability was often employed against sceptical challenges from the Academy and is referred to in the line written by → Aristocreon on the bronze statue erected for him in Athens, which claims that he is the 'Cutter of the Academic Knots' (Plut. St. Rep. 1033e). His involvement with Megarean dialectics (e.g. Diog. Laert. 7,186f.; Plut. St. Rep. 1036ef) and his positive interest in the theory of logic are remarkable. His intellectual pride was famous: to the question 'To whom shall I send my son for studies?' he answered: 'To me — for if I believed that there was someone better than me, I would be studying with him myself!' (Diog. Laert. 7,183). His intellectual independence and argumentative ability, which he demonstrated throughout his career, are summarized in the habitual self-praise 'I only need to be taught the principles, I can find the proof myself'. Diog. Laert. (7,179) relates his final rupture with Cleanthes to this. His arrogance and his personal loyalty to Cleanthes are combined in the exclamation directed at a dialectician who pressed Cleanthes with Sophist disputations: 'Stop distracting an old man from important matters and direct these disputes to us younger people' (Diog. Laert. 7,182).

C. WORKS

C.'s Vita in Diog. Laert. 7 ends with a book catalogue of the 1st cent. BC which, according to the standard Stoic classification of philosophy, is divided into three parts (*topoi*). Even though it is incomplete because of damage to the transmitted MSS, it is nevertheless a valuable source for his philosophical activities, especially as concerns his works on logic (that form the beginning of the catalogue). GOULET [2. 336] counted 119 titles and over 300 book rolls in the section on logic; the ethical part contains 43 titles and 122 book rolls, the section on physics is completely lost. Apart from the 162 titles preserved in Diog. Laert. (and discussed by P. HADOT [2. 336–356]; see also [3; 4]), another 55 titles, or a total of 217, are known. This suggests that the preserved titles refer to about 80 % of the almost 700 papyrus rolls that were ascribed to C. in antiquity. Therefore, they provide an adequate impression of his philosophical interests.

D. PHILOSOPHICAL THOUGHT

C.'s version of the Stoa was canonical for much of the school's history, and his work was considered to be systematic and definitive (→ Stoa). Like Zeno, C. taught that philosophical discourse was divided into three parts dealing with rational discourse (logic), the natural world (physics) and human fulfilment within it (ethics), but also that these aspects could not be sharply separated from each other neither *per se* nor in their transmission. Two different presentational sequences are associated with C.: on the one hand: logic, physics, ethics (Diog. Laert. 7,39f., quote from C.'s work 'Regarding rational discourse'), on the other logic, ethics, physics, which culminates in theology (Plut. St. Rep. 1035a). The relationship of theological and cosmological teachings to ethics and logic is complex, but BRUNSCHWIG [4] demonstrated that C. used a 'methodological dualism' that employed both the dialectic and demonstrative methods in the presentation of ethics. C.'s use of philosophical polemic both within and outside his school was supplemented by an interest in the thought of earlier philosophers (whom he often called 'the ancients'), especially Plato and the early Academics. He frequently presented himself as the defender of a sensible middle ground in a series of problematic earlier views, as the mediator between extreme philosophical choices (Cicero notes that he considered himself as the *arbiter honorarius* on the question of moral responsibility and predestination; Cic. Fat. 39). Apart from his concerns over method and the position of → dialectics in philosophy, C. occupied himself with a number of other topics in → logic. His comprehensive analysis of the *prágmata* (or *lektá*), the basic units of meaning, provided a framework for a comprehensive understanding of discourse phenomena at the boundaries between linguistics/grammar and logic/ philosophy of language. Complete and incomplete *lektá* were differentiated; the categorization included statements, claims, disjunctions, negations, privatives and differently modified claims, different forms of questions, commands etc. (→ Language, theory and philosophy). His studies of the relationship between sound and meaning, as well as of the 'cases' led to a special interest in peculiarities of language, solecisms and plurality of meaning [5. 28–30]. Perhaps his most enduring contribution to logic was his penetrating treatment of proof

and conclusion, which was more strongly based on the relationship of statements than on terminology. Inspired by Megarean dialecticians, he had a strong systematic interest in fallacies, false conclusions and logical paradoxes, especially such famous riddles as the Liar, the Nobody, the Heap (*sorites*), the Hooded Man and the Master Argument (κυριεύων λόγος), which was made famous by → Diodorus Cronus. He dedicated a small booklet to an attack on the philosophical technique of → Arcesilaus and developed arguments for and against the utility of general convictions in philosophy. These dialectical techniques were intended as part of the defence of the 'positive' teaching against Megarean and Academic attacks (Plut. St. Rep. 10).

In the area of physics C. strengthened and expanded the school's theories on teleology and providence by strongly emphasizing cosmic unity and rational divine planning. An etymological and allegorical argumentation linked Stoic theory to poetic and cultural traditions (→ Allegoresis). In physics and ethics C. endeavoured to claim Homer, Euripides and others (even works of art such as a painting in the temple of Hera on Samos: Diog. Laert. 7,187; Orig. c. Celsum 4,48) for Stoic theory. As a supplement to works on fundamental physical concepts (the elements, change, emptiness etc.) he elaborated the deterministic and cyclical theory of cosmic development that would climax in a complete fiery consumption of the world. The internal cohesion of the cosmos was secured by extensive use of *pneuma* (a composite of fire and air) as the structuring principle of the cosmos as a whole, for every physical object and especially for the human soul. C. defended determinism in providence and inserted the latter into a clever causal theory that made responsible human action compatible with an endless chain of fateful causes. C.'s interest in the logic of parts and the whole led him to his cosmology and considerations on the relationship of man and cosmos. C. also wrote on divination, including dream interpretation and oracles. His treatise 'On the soul' was significant for both ethics and physics.

Naturally, his epistemology above all concerned logic, but also influenced ethics. Rashness and hasty judgement in matters of serious importance were the worst mistakes a man could commit. In C.'s presentation the Stoic sage would never consent to a wrong opinion. This epistemological purism was central to his concept of a good character and a successful human life. Overall, C.'s ethical thought was a continuation of the thought of Zeno and Cleanthes. The constitution of the goal of life (to live in accordance with nature) and the duality of moral values (good and evil, virtue and vice) and other natural values (the so-called adiaphora) remained fundamental for his ethical thought. His particular interest in ethics contained the constitution of the virtues as physical qualities, οἰκείωσις (→ *oikeíōsis*, the naturalistic basis for human striving towards virtue), human action, the passions and their healing. (C.'s influential work 'On the passions' is well known through extensive quotes and discussions in Galen's

'On the teachings of Plato and Hippocrates'; → affects). Cosmological and political views entered his works on → law and on correct explanation (ὀρθὸς λόγος). His influence on the metaphorics of natural law is considerable [6. 70–84]. An anti-hedonistic polemic frequently surfaces in his works, and treatises on the topic of → justice include attacks on the views of Plato and Aristotle. The pragmatic side of ethics was not neglected. In addition to his examination of morally correct actions, C. wrote 'On appropriate action', 'On good deeds','On life styles' and (most remarkably) 'How to behave towards parents' (PMilVogliano [7. 112]), i.e. on the type of topic generally considered characteristic of later Stoicism. The breadth of his ethical work is demonstrated in his interest in → friendship, protreptic works, the question of how poetry must be read in the interest of moral development, and erotic love.

→ Stoa; → Zeno of Citium; → Cleanthes; → Carneades

1 T. DORANDI (ed.), Filodemo Storia dei filosofi: La stoà da Zenone a Panezio, 1994   2 R. GOULET et al., s.v. Chrysippe de Soles, in: Goulet 2, 1994, 329 365 3 J. BARNES, The Catalogue of Chrysippus' Logical Works, in: K.A. ALGRA et al. (ed.), Polyhistor, 1996, 169–84   4 J. BRUNSCHWIG, Sur un titre d'ouvrage de Chrysippe, in: Etudes sur les philosophies hellénistiques, 1995, 233–250   5 C. ATHERTON, The Stoics on Ambiguity, 1993   6 M. SCHOFIELD, The Stoic Idea of the City, 1991   7 Corpus dei papiri filosofici I 1.1, 1989.

H. VON ARNIM, s.v. Ch., RE 3, 2502–2509; SVF 2–3; K. HÜLSER, Die Frr. zur Dialektik der Stoiker, 1987–88; E. BREHIER, Chrysippe et l'ancien stoïcisme, 1951; H. DOERRIE, RE Suppl. 12, 148–55; M. FREDE, Die stoische Logik, 1974; J. GOULD, The Philosophy of Chrysippus, 1970; M. POHLENZ, Zenon und Chrysipp, in: NGWG 1938, 173–210.   B.I.

[3] of Cnidus. Doctor active in about 300 BC, teacher of Erasistratus (Diog. Laert. 7,186; Gal. 11,171). According to Pliny (HN 29,5), he was a gifted author who knew how to decisively change Hippocratic doctrine by rejecting bloodletting and highly effective purgatives as the pillars of every therapy (Gal. 11,230; 245) and understanding fever to be the consequence of the movement of arteries or the blood contained in them (Gal. 17A,873). Galen (CMG V 10,1,208) reported a treatment in which C. included the patient's irrational fears in his calculation. Galen appears to have only known C.'s writings through Erasistratus (11,221) so that mention of his name in a list of significant anatomists (15,136) may rest on pure speculation. Another C., who was active between 400 and 350 BC, accompanied Eudoxus to Egypt and left interesting observations (Diog. Laert. 8,89) may have been related to C. [1; 2], but — contrary to FRASER [8] — was by no means identical. Galen's apparent ignorance of the younger C.'s works suggests that the elder C. is the author of a treatise on vegetables (schol. Nic. Ther. 845; Pliny HN 1,20–30; 22; 83, in which he carefully described their medical use, ibid. 20,113). An independent treatise (Pliny HN 20,78) describes the healing powers of cabbage in

detail. Other formulae for soothing salves (Celsus, Artes 5,18,30) and a plaster against kidney pains (Rufus 6 DAREMBERG) may be attributable to our or an even later C. who was active about 275 BC and was a contemporary, possibly even a student, of Erasistratus (Diog. Laert. 7,186; schol. Theoc. 17,128).

→ Erasistratus; → Eudoxus

1 M. WELLMANN, s.v. Ch. 15, 16, RE 3, 2509–2511 2 I. GAROFALO, Erasistrati fragmenta, 1988, 21–22 3 P.M. FRASER, The career of Erasistratus of Ceos, in: Rev. Arch. 1, 1969, 518–537.   V.N.

[4] Inscriptionally attested Comic poet who performed a play on Delos in 259 BC [1. test.]; whether he is identical with the author of two trochaic tetrameters cited by later lexicographers (s.v. κοροι-, κορθυάλη) remains uncertain.

1 PCG IV, 1983, 78.   H.-G.NE.

[5] Greek grammarian, Pindar commentator, formerly [1] confused with the philosopher C. According to the Schol. Pind. Nem. 1,49c he lived after → Chaeris and before → Didymus (he might be identical with Cicero's learned freedman of the same name: cf. [4]). Apparently he explained the → critical signs of a predecessor, probably Aristarchus of Samothrace (Schol. Pind. Isthm. 3. 47c). The Scholia on Pindar restored another 20 fragments of his commentary, especially on the 'Isthmia'.

→ Pindarus; → Pindarus Scholia

1 A. BOECKH, Pindari Opera II 1, 1821, praef. XII 2 A. KÖRTE, Der Pindarcommentator Ch., in: RhM 55, 1900, 131–138   3 Id., s.v. Ch. (14a), RE Suppl. 1, 298–9. 4 F. MÜNZER, s.v. Ch. (10), RE 3, 2501.   F.M.

Chrysogonus Influential freedman of Sulla (therefore his full name L. Cornelius C.), who enriched himself significantly during the Proscriptions. He had Sex. Roscius retroactively placed on the Proscription list for the purpose of acquiring his property for little money. According to Cicero that is why he backed the patricide trial of the victim's son, Sex. → Roscius in 80 BC (Cic. Rosc. Am. *passim*).   K.-L.E.

Chrysolith see → Precious stones

Chrysophrys (χρυσόφρυς or χρυσωπός; *chrysóphrys, chrysōpós* in Plut. Soll. anim. 26,977f), *aurata*, sea bream, the genuine dorado. The popular edible fish that is up to 60 cm in size is often mentioned in comedies (Ath. 7,328a-b) and frequently portrayed (KELLER II, fig. 120,124 and 147). According to Aristotle, it lives in the sea close to land (hist. an. 8,13,598a10), spawns in rivers, maintains a prolonged sleep throughout the summer (Plin. HN 9,58: 60 days), eats flesh and is harpooned with a trident or caught in its sleep. The Romans kept it in breeding pools on the coast (Columella 8,16,8), as for example → Sergius Orata (cf. Varro, Rust. 3,3,10) in his → oyster breeding areas. → Archestratus [2] of Gela describes its preparation as

food (Ath. 7,328a-b; the length of 10 ells (about 20 feet) is exaggerated). Plin. HN 32,43 recommends it as an antidote for poisoned honey.
→ Fish

KELLER II, 369f.   C.HÜ.

Chrysorrhoas (Χρυσορρόας; *Chrysorrhóas*). River near Troezen that did not dry up even during protracted drought (Paus. 2,31,10). Identical with the modern Gephyraion to the west of the town.

G. WELTER, Troizen und Kalaureia, 1941, 15.   Y.L.

Chrysothemis (Χρυσόθεμις; *Chrysóthemis*).
[1] Beloved of Apollo. From their union Parthenus was born, but died as a child and was transformed into a constellation by Apollo (Hyg. Poet. Astr. 2,25). According to Diodorus (5,62,1f.) she was the wife of Staphylus and mother of Molpadia, Parthenus and Rhoeo. The latter bore Appollo's son → Anius.
[2] Daughter of Agamemnon and Clytaemnestra, sister of Laodice and Iphianassa (Hom. Il. 9,145.287), in Soph. El. 157 of Electra and Iphianassa, in Eur. Or. 23 of Elektra and Iphigenia (so also in Apollod. epit. 2,16).
[3] Cretan expiation priest. → Apollo was expiated by him (Pind. Pyth. Schol. hypothesis) or his father → Carmanor (Paus. 2,7,7; 30,3) after slaying the Pythian dragon. He emerged as the victor from the first Pythian hymnal competition (Paus. 10,7,2).

N. ICARD-GIANOLIO, s.v. Ch. I, LIMC 3.1, 292–293; NILSSON, GGR 1, 618.   R.B.

Chthonic deities (Χθόνιοι θεοί; *Chthónioi theoí*).
I. ANCIENT NEAR EAST II. GREECE

I. ANCIENT NEAR EAST
The Earth and the Heavens that fertilized her with rain were central to the world view of Ancient Oriental agrarian cultures. Their separation marks the beginning of creation (Sumerian 'Creation of the Hoe', 6,51ff.; Hittite Kumarbi Myth (→ Kumarbi), → Ullikummi, Song of) but a link holds them together (Geštinanna, 'the Heavenly Vine'). The disc of the Earth floats in the freshwater ocean → Apsû that is governed by → Enki, who in turn lives above the Underworld (→ Afterlife, concepts of) and has created the rivers Euphrates and Tigris in a sexual act ('Enki and the World Order', TUAT 3,402–420). Agriculture is directly linked to the origin of culture (the gods Ninazu and Ninmada take grain to Sumer, TUAT 3,360–63) and irrigation; many resulting products (grain, flax) and their divine representatives, as well as tools (hoe, plough [1. with bibliography]) are part of the creation myths (→ World, creation of the) and disputations TUAT 3,357–360 [1; 2]. Working the earth was seen as the analogue of the sexual act and led to a concept of the Earth as a mother and of mother deities whose positive aspect became mani-

fest in town and country goddesses as well as deities of birth and midwifery, their negative aspect in goddesses of the Underworld (Ereškigal, Allatum, Hurrite Allani, Lelwani) [4. 156].
Several vegetation deities arise from the encounter of Enki and Ninḫursanga (TUAT 3,363–386). Times of need that were not part of the regular cycle of seasons—drought, famine and earthquakes—are reflected in distress myths around the gods → Tammuz (god of herdsmen), Innana/Ištar, Enmešarra (god of grain and harvest), Telipinu (Hittite weather god) and Baal, the sun god (Ugaritic Baal cycle), that generally imply descent into the Underworld (TUAT 3,812ff.; [4]).
In Egypt, a strong link between Underworld and fertility is attested in the form of the god → Osiris who after his dismemberment rises again as a barley grain. As examples of harvest ceremonies we have attested the thanksgiving sacrifices to the god Renutet and the festivity for the fertility god → Min [3].
→ Aphrodite; → Demeter; → Defixio; → Dionysus; → Erinys; → Gaia; → Hades; → Hecate; → Hermes; → Hero cult; → Meilichius; → Moira; → Nephalia; → Nymphs; → Sacrifices; → Persephone; → Theology; → Titans; → Dead, cult of the; → Magic papyri; → Zeus

1 J. BOTTÉRO, La 'tenson' et la réflexion sur les choses, in: G. J. REINEK, H. L. J. VANSTIPHOUT (ed.), Dispute Poems and Dialogues, 1991, 7–22   2 Kindler, 19, 604–606 3 E. BRUNNER-TRAUT, s.v. Minfest, LÄ 4, 1982, 1414–144 4 V. HAAS, Gesch. der hethit. Rel., 1994   5 W. HELCK, s.v. Getreide, LÄ 2, 1977, 586–589   6 M. HUTTER, Altoriental. Vorstellungen von der Unterwelt, 1985   7 S. N. KRAMER, Sumerian Mythology, 1944.   B.P.-L.

II. GREECE
A. 1. GENERAL TERMINOLOGY 2. GENEALOGICAL DESIGNATION, USE AS PROPER NAME B. *Chthónioi* (Χθόνιοι/χθόνιοι) AS DEITIES AND DWELLERS OF THE UNDERWORLD 1. GROUPS OF GODS 2. THE DEAD AND HEROES 3. INDIVIDUAL DEITIES AS *chthónios* (χθόνιος) OR *chthonía* (χθονία) C. PHILOSOPHICAL THEOLOGY D. LITERATURE AND CULT E. HISTORY OF RESEARCH

A. χθόνιος (*chthónios*)
1. GENERAL TERMINOLOGY
The adjective *chthónios* is derived from the noun *chthṓn* (χθών) (CHANTRAINE s.v.), Earth (as the surface of the Underworld or depth of the Earth) and is used almost exclusively within poetic texts in religious contexts relating to the Underworld (Alcm. fr. 146 PMG; Anac. fr. 60 PMG; fr. 71,2 PMG; Pind. Pyth. 4,43; Pyth. 5,101; fr. 33d,6; in tragedy *passim*; Aristoph. Av. 1745; 1750; Ran. 1148), rarely in the meaning of αὐτόχθων (*autóchthōn*), 'indigenous' (fr. adesp. 274 TGF: Inachids; cf., with an Underworld connotation, Soph. OC 948: the Areopagus).
2. GENEALOGICAL DESIGNATION, USE AS PROPER NAME
On occasion the term is used to emphasize descent

from the Earth (Aeschyl. fr. 488: Chthonios, a Spartan from Thebes, cf. Paus. 9,5,3; Soph. Aj. 202: the descendants of Erechtheus; Eur. Bacch. 538: the *chthónion génos* of Pentheus; ibid. 541: Echion as *chthónios*). As proper names of non-divine mythical figures we find Chthonios and Chthonia in mythographers, scholiasts, lexicographers etc. particularly since Hellenistic times (e.g. Chthonia, an Argive woman in Hermione: Paus. 2,35,4).

B. *Chthónioi* (Χθόνιοι/χθόνιοι) AS DEITIES AND DWELLERS OF THE UNDERWORLD

In the literary tradition (especially in the tragedies with the plural used only in lyrical parts, usually in prayers and invocations) both communities of gods and the totality of the dead may be called *chthónioi*. In several cases (especially Aesch. Cho. 399; 476; Pers. 641; Eur. fr. 912,8; cf. Pind. Pyth. 4,159) anonymity and context do not permit differentiation between Underworld gods and the dead as forces of the Underworld.

1. GROUPS OF GODS

In Hesiod (Theog. 697) the Titans are characterized as *chthónioi* in the Battle of the Gods. *Chthónioi theoí* or *daímones* as collective designations for Underworld gods appear in tragedy either without names (in invocations: Eur. Hec. 79; fr. 868,1; as *chthónioi týrannoi*: Aesch. Cho. 359; in a series of anonymous groups of gods: Aesch. Ag. 89; cf. also *chthónioi* as forces of the Earth, differentiated from the forces of the sea and the air: Eur. fr. 27,4), or are specified in ritual prayer by naming individual deities (Ge, Hermes, and the king of the Underworld dwellers: Aesch. Pers. 628f.; cf. SEG 29,931–933, from Sicily). In the cult of the dead, dedications to the *theoì katachthónioi*, more rarely to the *theoí chthónioi*, are frequent on grave inscriptions, particularly in the Roman Imperial Period throughout the entire Mediterranean (Gytheium in Laconia: IG V 1, 1192, 1; for other regions cf. SEG *passim*). Roughly the same applies to curse tablets and *defixiones*. Groups of anonymous goddesses as *chthóniai theaí* include Demeter and her daughter Persephone as ruler of the Underworld (cult on Paros and in Sicilian Gela: the identity of the goddesses can be derived from the context in Hdt. 6,134,1 and 7,153,2; cf. Aristoph. Thesm. 101) and the Eumenids/Erinyes (in prayer: Soph. OC 1568; cf. Aesch. Eum. 115: *katà chthonòs theaí*). The characterization of the Moirae as goddesses of both the Heavens and the Earth (*ourániai chthóniaí te daímones*) in a lyrical fragment (fr. adesp. 100[b],3f. PMG: from a lost tragedy by Euripides?) and of the nymphs as *chthóniai theaí* in the intention of attributing them to a particular region are isolated cases (Apoll. Rhod. 4,1322; cf. 2,504).

2. THE DEAD AND HEROES

In Aeschylus the powerful dead dwelling in the Earth may be invoked as *chthónioi* without any link to groups of gods (Aesch. Supp. 25: the grave-dwelling *chthónioi* invoked together with the gods above, *hýpatoi theoí*).

3. INDIVIDUAL DEITIES AS *chthónios* (χθόνιος) OR *chthonía* (χθονία)

Hades is the *chthónios theós par excellence* (*chthónios theós*: Hes. Theog. 767; Eur. Phoen. 1321; *chthónios Háidēs*: Eur. Alc. 237; Andr. 544). As a complementary god to Olympian Zeus and spouse of Persephone he was already called Zeus *katachthónios* in a passage of Homer (Il. 9,457). Zeus *chthónios*, attested in the literary tradition since Hesiod (Erg. 465, together with Demeter, in the context of agriculture; Aeschyl. fr. 273a,9; Soph. OC 1606) was worshipped in a cult on Mykonos (together with Ge Chthonia: LSCG 96,25), in Corinth (Paus. 2,2,8) and Olympia (Paus. 5,14,8). It is uncertain whether this was a cultic synonym of Hades or an epiclesis of Zeus. In invocations Hermes may also be found as a *chthónios* in tragedy (Aesch. Cho. 124; 727; fr. 273a,8; Soph. Aj. 832; El. 111; Eur. Alc. 743), with traits of parody and a presumed citation of the opening of Aeschylus' *Choephoroi* in Aristophanes (Ran. 1126; 1138; 1145) as well as in the cult of the dead (Attica: IG III, Add. 101, and especially in Thessaly: SEG 34, 509 and *passim*). In the case of Ge/Gaia an epiclesis *chthonía* would be particularly natural, we however find her worshipped with this attribute only Mykonos (LSCG 96). Rather, it is almost exclusively Demeter (in close association with her daughter Persephone) who is the *chthonía theá* in worship (Hermione: e.g. IG IV 683; Paus. 2,35,5–10; Sparta, taken over from Hermione: Paus. 3,14,5; also in Asine and Sicilian Hermione: Syll.³ 1051 = IG IV 679) as well as in literature (Eur. HF 615: her grove in Hermione; cf. Apoll. Rhod. 4,987: Deo; 4,148: lady of the dead). From the 5th cent. onwards we also find increasingly frequent attestations of Hecate Chthonia (adesp. fr. 375,2 TrGF 2; Aristoph. fr. 515,1 PCG; Theoc. 2,12; also since the 2nd cent. BC in defixiones and magic papyri; cf. Plut. Mor. 290d3: dog sacrifices). Compared to these individual deities designated as Chtonios or Chtonia — Hades, Zeus, Hermes, Ge, Demeter/Persephone and Hecate — others are negligible (Typhon as *chthónios daímōn*: Aesch. Sept. 522; *chthonía* Phama: Soph. El. 1066; *chthonía* Gorgo: Eur. Ion 1054; *chthonía* Brimo: Apoll. Rhod. 3,862; *chthónios* Dionysus as son of Persephone: only since Harpocration, Orph. h. and Nonnus).

C. PHILOSOPHICAL THEOLOGY

A clear and distinct delimitation between the *chthónioi* and the *olýmpioi* (or *ouránioi*) was first propagated by Plato (Leg. 717a7; 828c6). It was particularly Plutarch (Mor. 269f8; Numa 14,3,6) as well as Iamblichus and Porphyrius who followed his lead. Within the theologizing philosophical tradition the tendency increasingly prevailed to characterize the chthonic deities collectively in purely negative fashion and to attribute to them certain altar types (or sacrificial pits: the most important passage for this in terms of the history of reception is Porph. *De antro nympharum* 6,19f.) and exclusively wineless (*nēphália*) and bloodless sacrifices

(Pl. Leg. 959d1). Furthermore, certain individual deities achieved particular significance as *chthónios* or *chthonía*: Kronos and Anubis, who are labelled with the epithet *chthónios* in Plutarch, as well as Hestia and Isis (both with the epiclesis *chthonía* in Porphyrius) stand out. The most important individual deities described as *chthonía* or *chthónios* in the philosophical-theological tradition are Ge, who is called *Chthoniē* by Pherecydes (cf. Emp. fr. 122,7 D.-K.) and who appears in Solon (in Aristot. Ath. Pol. 12,4) as the 'Greatest Mother of the Olympian Gods', Zeus (e.g. Aristot. Mund. 401a 25: as God of the Firmaments, also *ouranios* etc.) and Hermes (outside of poetry since Theopompus), whom Posidonius characterizes as *ouránios* at the same time (fr. 398,13 THEILER). In Plutarch both Aphrodite and Hecate have such a double name (*chthonía* and *ouranía* Aphrodite: Mor. 764d3; *chthonía* and *ouranía* Hecate: De def. or. 416e4f.).

D. LITERATURE AND CULT

Neither the poetic tradition nor the evidence of the cults permit a definitive and specific designation of the *chthónioi*, as a group or as individual deities, to purely negative characteristics, euphemistic names, or anonymity, or specific cult types. Rather, the same applies to them as to Greek deities in general: that they cause both bad and good and that cultic acts dedicated to them cannot be marshalled into a consistent, let alone dualistic system, but vary strongly in regional and heortological terms. Within Ancient Greek religion the *chthónioi* have no fundamentally special status.

E. HISTORY OF RESEARCH

Since KARL OTFRIED MÜLLER (who followed ancient attempts at a philosophical-theological systematization), a tendency prevailed among religious historians and classical philologists to grant the feature of duality or ambivalence exclusively to the 'Chthonians', but in contrast to describe the Olympian gods as unambivalent (see especially ERWIN ROHDE and JANE ELLEN HARRISON; the most important recent proponents of a fundamental difference between Chthonic and Olympic: KARL MEULI, W.K. C. GUTHRIE, WALTER BURKERT, ALBERT HENRICHS, cf. SCOTT SCULLION). The possibility of assigning certain symbolic animals (the snake), cult acts (e.g. purification and reconciliation rites), types of sacrifice (such as meatless and wineless sacrifices, *holokaustómata*, *enagísmata*, black sacrificial animals, appeasing libations of milk and honey) only to the *chthónioi* and, therefore, to identify certain deities or epicleses (such as Zeus Meilichius) as specifically chthonic has been doubted since ARTHUR FAIRBANKS (also by WILAMOWITZ, A. D. NOCK, JEAN RUDHARDT). FRITZ GRAF takes an intermediate position on this question. More recent research on local cults of the great gods and cults of the dead and heroes has ever more clearly demonstrated the inapplicability of concepts of 'chthonic religion', 'chthonic cult' and 'chthonic sacrifice', which are therefore now only rarely used.

→ Aphrodite; → Demeter; → Defixio; → Dionysus; → Erinys; → Gaia; → Hades; → Hecate; → Hermes; → Hero cult; → Meilichius; → Moira; → Nephalia; → Nymphs; → Sacrifices; → Persephone; → Theology; → Titans; → Dead, cult of the; → Magic papyri; → Zeus

BURKERT, 306–312; A. FAIRBANKS, The Chthonic Gods of Greek Religion, in: AJPh 21, 1900, 241–259; F. GRAF, Milch, Honig und Wein. Zum Verständnis der Libation im griech. Ritual, in: Perennitas. Studi in onore di Angelo Brelich, 1980, 209–221; A. HENRICHS, Namenlosigkeit und Euphemismus: Zur Ambivalenz der chthonischen Mächte im att. Drama, in: A. HARDER, H. HOFMANN (ed.), Fragmenta Dramatica, 1991, 161–201; R. SCHLESIER, Olympian versus Chthonian Religion, in: Scripta Classica Israelica 11, 1991/92, 38–51; Id., Olympische Religion und chthonische Religion, in: U. BIANCHI (ed.), The Notion of 'Religion' in Comparative Research. Selected Proceedings of the XVI JAHR Congress, 1994, 301–310; S. SCULLION, Olympian and Chthonian, in: Classical Antiquity 13, 1994, 75–119. RE.S.

Chullu (Κούλλου; *Koúllou*). Coastal town in the province of Numidia, modern Collo. (Sources: Ptol. 4,3,3; It. Ant. 19,1; Tab. Peut. 3,2; Iulius Honorius, Cosmographia 44,29; Geogr. Rav. 40,21; Guido 132,32). Mentioned by Solin. (26,1) because of its purple dye works, C. was possibly a Phoenician or Punic foundation, and in any case, under strong Punic influence [1. 343–368]. Under the governorship of P. Sittius it became a *colonia Minervia*, and later constituted one of the *quattuor coloniae Cirtenses* (inscriptions: CIL VIII 1, 6711; 8193–8196; Suppl. 2, 19916; Inscr. latines de l'Algérie 2,1, 419–426).

1 HÉLO, Notice ..., in: BCTH 1895.

E. BERNUS, s.v. Collo, EB, 2048–2050; S. LANCEL, E. LIPIŃSKI, s.v. C., DCPP, 108; C. LEPELLEY, Les cités de l'Afrique romaine 2, 1981, 282–285. W.HU.

Church (in early Christianity and late antiquity).
A. CONCEPT B. JESUS AND EARLY CHRISTIANITY C. THE OLD CHURCH AND WORLD AWARENESS D. MONARCHIC EPISCOPACY E. A NEW PEOPLE F. CHURCH UNITY G. TRANSCENDENCE AND LOCALITY H. METAPHYSICS AND POLITICS I. CHURCH BUILDINGS

A. CONCEPT

The Church means the community of both the Christians at a specific place, as well as all of Christianity. The latter meaning of the Church is a reality which transcends space and time, which is the subject of the early Christian creed (the creed of Constantinople, known as the Nicene Creed of the year 381: *Credo ... unam sanctam catholicam et apostolicam ecclesiam*: 'I believe in one sacred, catholic and apostolic Church') [1]. The English 'Church' is derived from the Greek κυριακόν/ *kyriakón* ('House of the Lord'). The Romance languages, through the connection with Latin, go back to the → *ekklēsía* (ἐκκλησία, Lat. *ecclesia*), which was used in the NT (for the Church as a whole, as well as for the individual communities). Its (secular) Greek use for the → people's assembly which met at any one time, is not unusual in the linguistic usage of early Christianity (Acts 19,32 and 39f.). However, originally, ἐκκλησία (τοῦ θεοῦ) /ekklēsía (toû theoû), 'Church/community (of God)', is the translation borrowed from the Septuagint of the Hebrew qᵉhal (Jahweh). As this meant the community (assembly) of Israel by name as religious group, subsequently as (chosen) people of God, then correspondingly the ekklēsía of the NT describes the new, final people of God.

B. JESUS AND EARLY CHRISTIANITY

Did → Jesus of Nazareth want to found a Church in this sense? His message, which expanded the eschatological level of expectation of Judaism into the unreachable sphere, was that the rule of God was nigh (Mk 1,15). Whether he himself envisaged gathering 'the Twelve' as representatives of the new Israel around him, and whether he had in mind building his (final) ekklēsía on Peter (the 'rock') (Mt 16,18), remains disputed. It must be regarded as certain that the followers of Jesus (presumably under the leadership of Peter) gathered themselves as a 'Church', as soon as a few of them, after Jesus' death at the cross, experienced the manifestations of the risen Christ, which awakened belief (the oldest traditional material still free from legendary embellishments: 1 Cor 15,3–5). This belief was known as a mission and a calling. The missionary energy, which was released, has driven the Church forward ever since.

On the historical terrain of early Christianity, which is difficult to grasp, several fundamental figures of the 'Church' appear clearer. The early Christian community of Jerusalem led by Peter, then by Jacob, brother of Jesus, practised a Judaism which had been modified by the faith in the Son of Man/Judge, who had been elevated to God. The 'Hellenists', i.e., Greek speaking Jewish Christians, who were more liberal with respect to Jewish law, proselytized, after their expulsion from Jerusalem (Acts 6 analyzed critically), under the followers of the pagan religions. The term 'Christian' first appeared in Syrian Antioch (Acts 11,26). Aware of a worldwide sacred event initiated by the elevation of the → Kyrios Jesus Christ (and in this respect in imitation of the great prophets) → Paul, the Hellenistic Judaeo-Christian, who came from sophisticated Tarsus, crossed the boundaries of the Jewish national religiosity in grand style and established Christianity among pagans, which was 'unbound by law', during his missionary journeys to the West. The communities of John are difficult to classify in the history of religion: the 'gnosticizing' language of the fourth → Gospel interprets the OT as evidence for the comprehensive work of the Son, Who is One with the Father (Jo 10,30).

C. THE OLD CHURCH AND WORLD AWARENESS

The oldest document of the Church (in the larger sense) from Greeks and Romans, the first letter of Clement, which was probably addressed from Rome to Corinth in the year 96, is also the first evidence for the thesis 'the old Church is the old world, which has grasped its Christian hour' (U. WICKERT). The stable, basic structure of the popular philosophically conceived cosmos is permeated by the God of Israel from this point on (ch. 20). The will of the biblical Creator founded this cosmos (ch. 33). Man is the superior creature (ibid.), and God starts the interpretation of history stressing God's saving grace with this Man (ch. 17f.), which leads to the incarnation of those who pre-existed, to the expiatory suffering of Jesus Christ (ch. 16,7). The parousia of the risen Christ is based on a world of which it is known that it temporarily rests on the Creator-will of God (ch. 50). Therefore, a balance between the creation and dissolution of the cosmos, which achieved in merging the Hellenistic synagogue with early Christian traditions, does not reveal any traces of the 'crisis', which the absence of the parousia is supposed to have brought on the early Church. That the Church succeeded is shown by the fiction of the 'presbyter succession': the Apostles had foreseen, that the leaders of the communities would follow one another according to rules (a Stoic-Roman pattern) (ch. 44). Thus the continuity of the Church, which would endure in history, became safeguarded.

D. MONARCHIC EPISCOPACY

It is certain that Bishop → Ignatius [1] of Antioch, who first understood the Church to be καθολική/katholikḗ ('Catholic'), i.e. universally referring to Christ (the letter to the Church in Smyrna 8,2), probably led a monepiscopacy around 110. The formal monarchic episcopacy develops in the West in the 2nd cent. Its most important witness is a Greek from Asia Minor → Irenaeus [2], bishop of Lyons since 177/78. His world awareness can be defined strictly Christologically: recapitulating Christ had the All combined in Himself and anticipated the eschatological future. By participating, the Church is stabilized by the succession of the Apostles, which safeguards it in its struggle against gnosis. The bishop, who takes up in the succession of the Apostles by laying on of hands, stands vice apostoli, in the place of the Apostle. Armed with the 'charisma of the truth', he attests to the apostolic doctrine (Iren. Adversus haereses 4,26,2)

E. A NEW PEOPLE

The letter to Diognetus, which was probably contemporaneous with Irenaeus, describes the historical-political awareness of the Church: Christendom is the new people (ch. 1,1: καινὸν γένος/kainòn génos; equivalents by other fathers: τρίτον γένος/tríton génos, Lat. tertium genus, 'third gender/people'). Against the background of texts, such as Gal 3,28, Eph 2,11ff., Jo 4,21f. the Church knows it is destined to take up Jews and others unto itself and to lead mankind to unity with the belief in Christ. In this sense, → Tertullianus the first Lat. Church writer, of around 200, describes the Christians as *gentes totius orbis*, 'people of the whole world' (Tert. Apol. 37,4).

F. CHURCH UNITY

→ Cyprianus [2] (died 258), the martyr bishop of Carthage, places the 'one' Church against the schisms of the 3rd cent. The Church is brought together in the 'sacral-juridical and sacral-political' (H. v. CAMPEN-HAUSEN) developing collegium of Bishops. *Ecclesia in episcopo*, the Church is in the bishop (Cypr. Epist. 66,8): this means, however, that through the actions of the bishops the heavenly Church, which has been brought to earth by Christ (Cypr. De unitate ecclesiae 7) becomes present in the secret (*sacramentum* according to Eph 5,32 = μυστήριον/*mystérion*, ibid. 4). The 2nd letter of Clement (14,1) and 'Shepherd of → Hermas' (8,1), both probably written around the middle of the 2nd cent. in Rome, recognize the Church from before the creation of the world as the first, fundamental creation. The idea may have jumped from Rome over to North Africa. Cyprian's episcopal, non-episcopal ecclesiology implies, that by preference the task of safeguarding the mystery of the unity devolves upon the Roman bishop. He is regarded as the successor of Peter, who was bestowed the power of the keys according to Mt 16,19 since the 3rd cent.: this was understood to mean the investiture of the first elected Apostle as (the first) bishop. Stephen I of Rome (254–257) continued Cyprian's thoughts in the so-called heretic feud, faded out the mystery, kept the *cathedra* ('bishop's throne') of *Petrus* in the centre and desired obedience from the entire Church: the moment of the birth of the papacy.

G. TRANSCENDENCE AND LOCALITY

With → Augustinus (354–430), Bishop of Hippo, D. WYRWA recognized two 'unblended and disparate' ecclesiastical conceptions: the *civitas dei* ('City of God') accomplishes the gradual progression of the divine people moving from the origins to eschatological perfection; its essential feature is the transcendental foundation. By contrast, in *totus Christi*, the 'whole Christ', Christ's own body graciously occupies the Church in present form. Both Stephen I and Pope → Leo [3] the Great (440–461) took a selection of Augustine's thoughts and placed the institution of the papacy at the centre, at the cost of the transcendental (vestiges of the *civitas*-teaching were absorbed by *totus Christus*). The primacy of Peter, rooted in his profound communion with Christ, is exercised by his deputy, the Bishop of Rome.

H. METAPHYSICS AND POLITICS

The great Alexandrian → Origenes (died 254) integrated the Church into his conceptual cosmic drama whereby the fallen Creation should be returned to its sound origin, in a cycle like that of Heraclitus. → Euse-

bius [7] of Caesarea (died 339) was a second-generation student of Origen and 'Father of Church History' who transformed the story of salvation into history, perceiving that through Constantine I a decisive step was made towards the unification of mankind in the true worship of God (Vita Constantini; cf. E. above). This reflected the power of the Emperor of the Eastern Empire within the Church from the 4th cent., from which the popes were only able to free themselves when they no longer recognized, but rather crowned, the Emperors of the West.

→ Christianity; → Hierarchy; → Church History; → Church Fathers; CHURCH

1 R. STAATS, Das Glaubensbekenntnis von Nizäa-Konstantinopel, 1996, 19–21.

K. BERGER, Theologiegesch. des Urchristentums ²1995; C. ANDRESEN, Die Kirchen der alten Christenheit (Die Rel. der Menschheit 29, 1/2), 1971; Id., A. M. RITTER, E. MÜHLENBERG et. al, Die Lehrentwicklung im Rahmen der Katholizität, in: C. ANDRESEN (ed.), Hdb. der Dogmen- und Theologiegesch., vol. 1, ²1999; H. v. CAMPENHAUSEN, Kirchliches Amt und geistliche Vollmacht in den ersten drei Jh. (Beitr. zur histor. Theologie 14), ²1963; U. WICKERT, Sacramentum Unitatis. Ein Beitr. zum Verständnis der Kirche bei Cyprian (Beih. zur Zschr. für die nt. Wiss. 41), 1971; D. WYRWA, Christus praesens. Ekklesiologische Studien zu Augustin und Leo d. Gr. Typescript Habilitation. Berlin, 1987. U.WI.

I. CHURCH BUILDINGS
see → Sacred architecture.

Church Fathers Recourse to the 'Fathers' (*patres*) as authoritative witnesses of Church doctrine developed in the context of the historically oriented theology early in Church history (→ Irenaeus [2] of Lyons, → Basilius [1] the Great, → Augustinus, → Cyrillius [2] of Alexandria) in order to secure the doctrine, and to demarcate an apologetic position with regard to other traditions. In the Middle Ages (and even already in the *Decretum Gelasianum*, early 6th cent.), ancient theology and the early Church were awarded authoritative validity. Many 'Fathers' were included, insofar as they were viewed as orthodox and generally belonging to the ranks of the 'patriarchal age', but in practice, certain 'Fathers' were given preference (above all → Ambrosius, → Hieronymus, → Augustinus, → Gregorius [3] the Great; → Athanasius, → Basilius the Great, Gregorius [3] of Nazianzus, Iohannes [4] Chrysostomos; (Ps.)→ Dionysius [54] Areopagites).

The use of the arguments in the Reformation and Counterreformation—based upon the scholasticism of the 'Fathers' — and the dogmatic orientation of the confessional dispute transformed the role of the 'Fathers' into a theological discipline, the *Theologia patristica* (J.F. BUDDEUS, 1727). Humanism and, more so, the Enlightenment opened up the 'Study of the Fathers' ('*Patrologia*' first used as the title of a book: J. GERHARD, posthumous, 1653) and the scientific study of the 'Texts of the Fathers' (editions, sources, methods and issues of authenticity), which has been dominated by a decidedly historical-critical perspective since the 19th cent. The formal definition of the former popular term 'Church Fathers' is obsolete today as the characteristics of orthodoxy (*doctrina orthodoxa*), personal integrity (*sanctus vitae*), acceptance by the Church (*approbatio ecclesiae*), and membership in the ancient Church (*antiquitas*) are now appreciated as being too stereotyped, preventing a coherent selection from the early Christian traditions. Modern patristics using trans- and interdisciplinary historical and literary methods is dedicated to the exploration of the whole of early Christian literature and theology, using all varieties of texts up to → Isidorus [9] of Seville (died 636) in the Latin West and → Iohannes [33] of Damascus (died c. 750) in the Greek East, treating the Christian texts as the first phase of the history of Christianity as well as part of the literary, religious, philosophical, social and cultural history of Graeco-Roman Late Antiquity.

Classical Lat. 'Patrology': Jerome, De viris illustribus (392 according to the prototype of Suetonius'), continued by Gennadius of Marseilles (around 480), Isidore of Seville (615/16), Ildefonso of Toledo (died 667). Greek: Photius, *Bibliothékē* (around 850).

→ Patristic Theology

> Editions and translations: Corpus Christianorum Series Apocryphorum; CCG; CCL; Corpus Christianorum Continuatio Mediaevalis; CSCO; CSEL; Fontes Christiani; GCS; MGH AA; PG; PL (with suppl. vols.); Patrologia Orientalis; Patrologia Syriaca; SChr.; BKV[1,2].
> Overviews: CPG; CPL.
> Manuals: B. Altaner, A. Stuiber, Patrologie. Leben, Schriften und Lehre der Kirchenväter, [9]1980, repr. 1993; S. Döpp, W. Geerlings (ed.), Lex. der ant. christl. Lit., [2]1999.
> Bibliography: 1 N. Brox, Zur Berufung auf 'Väter' des Glaubens, in: Th. Michels (ed.), Heuresis. Festschrift A. Rohracher, 1969, 42–67   2 Id., Patrologie, in: P. Eicher (ed.), New manual Theologischer Grundbegriffe, vol. 4, 1991, 184–192   3 E. Mühlenberg, s.v. Patristik, TRE 26, 97–106 (with literature).   A.FÜ.

Church History
A. Historical thinking in the Church
B. Ecclesiastical historiography

A. Historical thinking in the Church
The Christian → Church has always been conscious of history, even its own history, and even asserting a proprietary role, already reflected in the NT → canon (as in Luke's double work, → Acts of the Apostles, cf. [8]). History became a subject of theological reflection in the proofs of the apologists (→ Apologia; cf. [6]). They faced the task of placing a new religion at the centre of debate in the context of religious culture where tradition was the norm and a new religion like Christianity was viewed sceptically. The debate about heretics (→ Heresy) among Christians rapidly contributed to the need of establishing and demonstrating their

own orthodox by establishing an uninterrupted chain of succession from the Apostles (beginnings in the Pastoral letters, clearly formulated by → Irenaeus [2] of Lyons). This motif would appear to have been initially used by → Hegesippus [5] at the end of the 2nd cent. (five books *Hypomnémata*, not preserved). Chronography was developed as an independent genre in the 3rd cent. (cf. [4] and → Chronicle); → Sextus Iulius Africanus and → Hippolytus [2] were the most important representatives. In a unique fashion, their works combine a scientific-theoretical interest in universal history with eschatological theological calculations (or the contradiction of such). The tradition was continued by the chronicles of → Eusebius [7] of Caesarea and → Hieronymus, which had significant influence into the Middle Ages. The attempts at a theological division of history played a major role (seven days of Creation, or 70–week schemes, doctrine of world empires).

In his 'Church History', Eusebius linked the apologetic and anti-heretical traditions of historical thinking (see B. below). In the East, when the Church had become state religion, the genres justified in this fashion represented the principal witness for Christian historical thinking. Events in the West produced → Augustinus' *De Civitas Dei*, a major work which explicitly reflected historical theology (cf. [5]), where the conquest of Rome by the West Goths in 410 and the resulting reproach that the defeat could be traced back to the neglect of the traditional pagan religions was the concrete historical background — but not the sole key to understanding. Augustine's conceptual history of salvation was a broad arch linking two polities, the *civitas terrena* ('earthly state') and *civitas Dei* ('divine state') which invariably appear blended together in reality, but must ultimately be distinguished. A universal order of peace can thus only be anticipated in the eschatological horizon. The pessimistic view of concrete political realities (including the *Imperium Romanum*) is thus opposed to an optimistic view of (linearly conceived) universal history. However, for very good reasons, Augustine does not offer any concrete historiographical transformation of this conception. This was left to his disciple → Orosius, who took Augustine's hints and described these in a concrete historical work, the *Historia adversus paganos*, covering the period from the Creation until 418 (cf. [2]).

A series of additional genres reflects the historical thinking of the Church, such as, in particular hagiography (→ Acta Sanctorum) and → biography.

B. Ecclesiastical historiography
Eusebius [7] of Caesarea raises the claim to represent a completely new genre (HE 1,1,3) in the prooemium of his famous 'Church History' (*Ekklēsiastikè historía*). This claim, which the world that followed him did not dispute, is founded on a new combination of professions of classical historiography with theological matters concerning Christian historical thinking: the 'Church History' starts with Jesus Christ, who is then

described, following → Origenes as pre-existing Divine → Logos and is then traced in his Works as Incarnated into historical substantiation. The *diadochaí* (literally 'the successor') of the holy Apostles are programmatically named right at the beginning as the principle of representation (HE 1,1,1). This means, on the one hand, proof of the unbroken apostolic succession for the most important diocesan towns; on the other hand, in more general terms, it concerns the uninterrupted continuity of the doctrine, from Jesus Christ until the present-day Church — propelled in a strongly anti-Jewish and anti-heretic direction. Eusebios formally follows, in as much as the ancient historiographical tradition is concerned, new avenues, by abandoning fictive orations and expansive digressions and, instead of these, bases his account on verbally cited documents and sources. A marked literary and theological-historical interest is also noticeable (bibliographies of important authors, biography of Origen in book 6). The carefully and broadly prepared archival studies which Eusebius carried out for this received recognition from the start and make the work irreplaceable as a source up to the present.

It is of interest for the tradition of history and important for comprehensive understanding that Eusebius revised the 'Church History' many times (pioneering [7. 1402–1406]); the various stages of writing have left traces in manuscript records. The first edition goes back to before 303 (cf. [14. 189], or at least until then [1. 482–486]). In this respect, the 'Church History' is in any case 'not the historiographical confrontation of Diocletian's persecution and Constantinian change' [9. 175]. In the following period Eusebios updated and expanded his work several times, up to and including the victory of Constantinus [1] over Licinius in 324. The pleasure in the triumph of Christianity is clearly expressed, but plays a rather subordinate role as part of the political sphere of the work.

Although the 'Church History' of Eusebius was translated into Latin by → Rufinus at the beginning of the 5th cent. and had great influence in the West into the Middle Ages, only in the Greek East did the literary prototype prompt independent continuations. The Latin 'Church History' of Rufinus covered the period to 395, but in both books, which go beyond Eusebius' books, Rufinus based these extensively on the Greek 'Church History' (preserved only in French) of → Gelasius [1], who succeeded Eusebios as Bishop of Caesarea (cf. [11]). During the first half of the 5th cent., several works of similar size and conception were developed, which continued the 'Church History' of Eusebius into their own times: those of → Philostorgius, → Socrates, → Sozomenus, → Theodoretus. Basically they maintain the concept of their predecessors, but modify it, where the changed conditions of the times demand. This is particularly relevant with regard to the state. After the ambivalent experiences of the 4th cent. — the empire, which was Christian on the one hand, but not always orthodox on the other hand — a differentiated assessment was needed (cf. [3]). All the authors mentioned apply the imperial religious politics to their representation and even structure their work according to the reigns of the emperors. Socrates (5, pr. as well as 1,1,2) also considers the connections explicitly, and in a critical discussion with Eusebios.

The image also becomes more differentiated with reference to → heresy. The triumph of orthodoxy over deviating doctrines is, in any case, still a fundamental motif of ecclesiastical writing with Theodoretus. The Novatian Socrates (cf. [10. 235–257]) and the Anomoean Philostorgius had heterodox backgrounds themselves and could, therefore, not write 'Church History' as an unnuanced success story. While Philostorgius, in sharp delimitation against the Great Church, takes on the part of the unjustly persecuted, Socrates solicits reconciliation and presents argument and heresy as unavoidable, but improper motifs of 'Church History'. This attitude secured him a place in orthodox tradition, while the work of Philostorgius is preserved only in fragments (mostly by → Photius).

The similarity of the three 'Synoptics' Socrates, Sozomenus and Theodoretus led to the desire to produce a so-called 'canonical' Eusebius-continuation of the three works. Based on this work, → Theodorus Anagnostes created an *historia tripartita* at the beginning of the 6th cent., which he continued into his own time (only preserved in an epitome). Then, → Cassiodorus drew up a similar *historia tripartita* in Latin, with the aide of the monk Epiphanius, which again was disseminated widely, but without literary emulation.

Another independent ecclesiastical work was developed at the end of the 6th cent.: → Evagrius [3] Scholastikos describes the times of the Christological quarrels (from the council of Ephesus in 431 until the year 594). In addition to this main theme, the reporting about the state-political sphere obtains much coverage. Perhaps one of the reasons for the extinction of ecclesiastical writing in the Byzantine region can be found in the fact that the proprium of the genre could not be recognized clearly enough (while, on the contrary, important matters of ecclesiastical writing were entered into profane historiography). Nicephorus Callistus Xanthopoulos (14th cent.) can be described as an interesting, although singular latecomer.

The Greek ecclesiastical works had important effects on the (non-Chalcedonian) Armenian and Syrian literature, although the genre as such did not find autonomous representatives (exception: Iohannes [26] of Ephesus). The Armenians used mostly general historiography and the Syrians mostly chronistics as their tradition of ecclesiastical writing.

Further Greek authors of less importance, or whose works are only preserved in small fragments, are: Philippus of Side, Gelasius of Cyzicus, Iohannes [14] Diakrinomenos, Hesychius of Jerusalem, Zacharias Scholastikos, Basilius Cilix (details in [12. 207f.]).

→ Historiography; CHURCH HISTORY

1 R. W. BURGESS, The Dates and Editions of Eusebios' Chronici Canones and Historia ecclesiastica, in: Journal of Theological Studies 48, 1997, 471–504 2 H.-W. GOETZ, Die Geschichtstheologie des Orosius (Impulse der Forsch. 32), 1980 3 H. LEPPIN, Von Constantin dem Großen zu Theodosius II. Das christl. Kaisertum bei den Kirchenhistorikern Socrates, Sozomenus und Theodoret (Hypomnemata 110), 1996 4 A. A. MOSSHAMMER, The Chronicle of Eusebios and Greek Chronographic Tradition, 1979 5 G. J. P. O'DALY, s. v. De ciuitate dei, Augustinus-Lexikon, vol. 1, 1986–94, 969–1010 6 P. PILHOFER, Presbyteron kreitton. Der Altersbeweis der jüd. und christl. Apologeten und seine Vorgesch. (WUNT II 39), 1990 7 E. SCHWARTZ, s. v. Eusebios, Re 6, 1370–1439 8 G. E. STERLING, Historiography and Self-Definition. Josephus, Luke-Acts and Apologetic Historiography, 1992 9 D. TIMPE, Was ist Kirchengeschichte? Zum Gattungscharakter der Historia Ecclesiastica des Eusebios, in: W. DAHLHEIM et al. (ed.), FS R. Werner, 1989, 171–204 10 M. WALLRAFF, Der Kirchenhistoriker Sokrates. Unt. zu Geschichtsdarstellung, Methode und Person (Forsch. zur Kirchen- und Dogmengesch. 68), 1997 (literature) 11 F. WINKELMANN, Unt. zur K. des Gelasios von Kaisareia (SDAW, Klasse für Sprachen, Lit. und Kunst, 1965 H. 3), 1966 12 Id., Kirchengeschichtswerke, in: Ids., W. BRANDES (ed.), Quellen zur Gesch. des frühen Byzanz (4.–9. Jh.), Berliner byz. Arbeiten, 1990, 202–212 and 365f. 13 Id., s. v. Historiographie, RAC 15, 724–765 14 Id., Euseb von Kaisareia. Der Vater der Kirchengeschichte, 1991. M.WA.

Church property Originally, Christian communities met the costs for the Eucharist and their charitable activities through the voluntary gifts from their members (καρποφορίαι/*karpophoríai*); these donations continued to represent one of the most important sources of income for the early Church. By the 3rd cent. AD at the latest, the communities had their own property, which might consist of liturgical objects and robes, buildings for holding services, and cemeteries (Euseb. Hist. eccl. 7,13); the legal basis for ownership remains unclear. It was perhaps in this latter connection that Licinius' Edict of Restitution spoke of *ius corporis ... ecclesiarum* (Lactant. De mort. pers. 48,9). With Constantine I the situation regarding Church property changed fundamentally; in 321 he granted the Church the right of succession (Cod. Theod. 16,2,4), and made large-scale endowments of church buildings, estates and material assets. Rome alone received six great basilicas, supplied with liturgical equipment to the amount of 500 kg of gold and nearly 6 t of silver, together with a yearly income of 28,800 *solidi* (Lib. Pontificalis 34f.). Voluntary donations, gifts, bequests and yields on capital continued to form the basis of church finances; tithes, as based on the Old Testament, only appear in Merovingian Gaul at the end of the 6th cent. Devout members of the old elites transferred considerable fortunes to the Church, contributing to the accumulation of large-scale ecclesiastical holdings (e.g. → Melania: Vita Melaniae 21; › Olympias: Vita Olympiadis Diaconissae Diac. 5). It is possible that temple lands were regularly annexed

to the Church during the 4th cent. Fiscal privileges favoured church ownership of land (Cod. Theod. 11,1,1; 16,2,15; 16,2,40; 11,16,21; 11,16,22). From 434 the possessions of clergy who died without heir went to the Church (Cod. Theod. 5,3,1); bishops were expected to make an adequate will (Cod. Can. Eccl. Afr. 81 for AD 409) and did do so (Greg. Naz.: PG 37, 389–396; Caesarius [4] of Arelate: SChr 345, 380–397). Lay people, too, were supposed to remember the Church in their will (Salv., MGH AA I 120f.; Aug. Serm. 355,4: PL 39, 1572 i. a.), but there soon arose laws preventing dependants from being disadvantaged and clergy from legacy-hunting among rich widows and orphans (Cod. Theod. 16,2,20; cf. Jer. Ep. 52,6; Amm. Marc. 27,3,14; Cod. Theod. 16,2,27f.; [1]). From the time of Constantine the Church also received subsidies (*annona*; → *cura annonae*) for the support of widows, orphans and clergy (Theod. Hist. eccl. 1,11; 4,4; Sozom. Hist. eccl. 5,5; Cod. Iust. 1,2,12); by the mid 3rd cent. the Roman Church had, from its own resources, already supported more than 1,500 widows and poor people (› Alms). Emperor Iulianus [11] cancelled the *annona;* Jovian reintroduced it at a lower rate. The bishop, often with the support of a qualified member of the clergy (in the east: *oikonómos*), was responsible for church property and finances. From early times, the rule was that all income should in specific proportions be spent on the various functions of the Church (Cypr. Epist. 7); thus in Rome from the end of the 5th cent. the bishop, the clergy (more than 150 individuals; Euseb. Hist. eccl. 6,43,11) and the poor each received one quarter; a further quarter was set aside for the lighting and upkeep of church buildings (Simpl. Epist. 1; Gelasius Epist. 14,27); but there also were other methods for apportioning income. The economic situations of individual dioceses and communities varied a great deal, with information on the time before the 5th/6th cents. however hard to come by. In *c.* 280 the Church of Alexandria was active in the grain trade and in banking (P Amhurst I,3a), and in *c.* 315 already had eight churches (Antioch having only two until 380); the Arian bishop Georgius (357–361) succeeded in monopolizing the production of saltpetre, papyrus, reeds and salt, and in extracting a considerable income from control of the funeral trade (Epiphanius, Panarion 76, 1,5ff.); bishop Cyrillus (412–444) spent more than 2,500 pounds of gold on bribes to the imperial court (Acta Conciliorum Oecumenicorum I 4,222ff. SCHWARTZ). Under Justinian, the annual income of a bishop could vary between two and considerably more than 30 pounds of gold (Just. Epit. Nov. 123,3), which corresponded approximately to the pay of high secular officials. The ordinary clergy, especially in the countryside, led a far more meagre existence. A particular problem was posed by the potential for bishops to misuse church property to the advantage of their relatives or for exerting personal influence; the sale of lucrative ecclesiastical offices that carried with them the prospect of immunity (→ Simony) is also to be seen in this light. The statutory (and also synodical) restrictions that had been introduced from 470 onwards, culminated in Justinian's general ban on the disposal of church property (Cod. Iust. 1,2,24; cf. Just. Epit. Nov. 7 pr.; Cod. Iust. 1,2,14); exemptions to these rules however were soon to follow (Just. Epit. Nov. 64; 120 i.a.). Growing wealth also permitted an increase in charitable activities on behalf of the poor, the sick, → widows, → orphans, the old, foreigners and prisoners of war; *xenodochia* (→ *Xenodochion*; → Hospital), places of refuge and orphanages appeared. From the 4th cent., benevolent institutions as well as monasteries often also were endowed by laymen or emperors; they were provided with lands and were to some extent independently administered, but from 451 usually supervised by the local bishop (Council of Chalcedon, canon 8; Cod. Iust. 1,3,7; 34; Just. Epit. Nov. 120,6). The monasteries in particular often were considerable landowners and productive managers of their wealth, providing charitable services on an enormous scale: in about 450 the 'White Monastery' at → Panopolis in Upper Egypt (owning perhaps about 30 square miles of land) supported 20,000 refugees for a period of three months. The economic resources of the Church also allowed bishops to take over various public functions in the cities (improvements to the infrastructure, collection of taxes), as happened for example in Gaul. In the course of this development, bishops became city governors. The endowment of churches by individuals (Cod. Theod. 16,5,14 of 388 speaks of *ecclesiae publicae vel privatae*), in combination with the *patrocinium* of late antiquity, led to the phenomenon of private churches.

→ Church property

1 E. F. BRUCK, Kirchenväter und soziales Erbrecht, 1956
2 R. DELMAIRE, Largesses sacrées et res privata, 1989, 641–645 3 J. DURLIAT, Les finances publiques de Dioclétien aux Carolingiens (284–889), 1990, 58–63; 143–151 4 J. GAUDEMET, L'Église dans l'Empire romain (IVᵉ — Vᵉ siècles), 1958, 288–305 5 M. HEINZELMANN, Bischof und Herrschaft vom spätant. Gallien bis zu den karolingischen Hausmeiern, in: F. PRINZ (ed.), Herrschaft und Kirche, 1988, 23–82 (especially 37–57) 6 JONES, LRE II, 894–910 7 C. PIETRI, Roma Christiana I, 1976, 77–96; 558–573. J.H.

Church regulations
A. DEFINITION B. OVERVIEW C. CHARACTERISTICS OF THE GENRE D. QUESTION REGARDING AUTHORS E. CONTENT

A. DEFINITION
In the field of early Christianity, church regulations (CR) means a genre of early ecclesiastical texts which have as their subject explanations of the ecclesiastical constitution (position in the community), the worship (liturgy in the community) and discipline (ethical standards in the community). To this genre belong texts, which were developed over a period from the 2nd until the 5th cent. AD and which are intertwined with each other in a complicated framework of relationships of literary interdependence. Original texts are, as a rule, not available, but merely later (mostly oriental) versions of an original (mostly Greek) one, which must be reconstructed.

B. OVERVIEW
Twelve separate writings are described as CR, which can be divided into three groups of four texts each (collective editions do not exist): 1. The first and most important group contains four writings, which present themselves as literary units, independent of each other: the → Didache (*didachè tôn dódeka apostólōn*, developed probably at the end of the 1st cent. in Syria), the so-called *Traditio apostolica* (at the beginning of the 3rd cent. in Rome, attributed to → Hippolytus [2] of Rome), the *Didascalia* (*didaskalía tôn apostólōn*, around the middle of the 3rd cent. in Syria), the 'Apostolic Church Regulations' (*kanónes ekklēsiastikoì tôn hagíōn apostólōn*, Lat. *Canones ecclesiastici apostolorum*, at the end of the 3rd cent. in Egypt). 2. Three separate forms are literarily dependent on the *Traditio apostolica*: the *Canones Hippolyti* (developed during the 1st half of the 4th cent. in Egypt), the *Epitome Constitutionum apostolorum VIII* (beginning of the 5th cent.) as well as the *Testamentum Domini Nostri Iesu Christi* (beginning of the 5th cent.). The 'Apostolic Canons' (2nd half of the 4th cent.) have been added to these. 3. Those CR are described as collective works, in which writings of the first and/or second group are united; it is assumed that four of these collective works exist autonomously in literary form: the *Fragmentum Veronense LV* (developed in the 2nd half of the 4th cent.), the 'Apostolic Constitutions' (*diatagaì tôn hagíōn apostólōn*, Lat. *Constitutiones apostolorum*, around 375) — appended hereto are the above-mentioned 'Apostolic Canons' (8,47), of the further 'Alexandrine Sinodos' (middle of the 5th cent.) and as the latest collective work the *Oktateuchus Clementinus* (late 5th cent.).

C. CHARACTERISTICS OF THE GENRE
Characteristics of the genre are: the use of appellatives (catalogical paraenesis, exhorting speech, exhorting quotation) and prescriptive forms (apodictic decree with casuistic expansion and ensuing justification); use of categorical commonplaces; conceptual and (less often) material associations as formal emotional elements. As far as the structure of the communication of the CR is concerned, the speech to the addressees varies considerably, as it embraces appellative and prescriptive genres. The pseudo-apostolic stylization of the CR is not the fundamental aspect of the genre, as it serves merely as a literary means of expression to justify a specific traditional and standard understanding of the legitimate structure belonging to the genre, and in any case it does not apply to two of the four literary units (sc. *Didache, Traditio apostolica*).

D. Question regarding authors

The authors and/or compilers of the texts only claimed 'legislative competence' (*sc.* to formulate community 'law') when they could accomplish this while addressing a given community, and thus the validity of the various regulations applies only to that community. This does not, however, contradict the assertion of the universal validity of the genre (expressed, *i.a.* via pseudo-apostolic authority); the alleged addressee serves only as a pragmatic pretext for universal application. The actual compass of the regulations must be understood in the same fashion, as they tend towards comprehensively touching all aspects of community life while specifically denying any comprehensive character. Since the regulations are not conservatively directed towards the preservation and anchoring of existing relations they actually incorporate innovative potential, which found different means of expression: harmonizing divergent traditions (*Didache*), programmatically leaving preserved traditions open for possible additions (*Traditio apostolica*), and even the pursuit of specific goals (*Didascalia*). The written form of the regulations aimed at the legal composition of an existing or intended practice in the community. The very process of fixing and copying the regulations in writing allowed them to claim unlimited temporal validity.

E. Content

The essential content of the regulations lay in the Christian initiation (baptism), the Christian ritual meal (*agape*, Eucharist), and the official hierarchy, which crystallize Christian existence and guarantee the unity and stability of the community. In the ritual meal symbolizing unity, the dispersed community of the Diaspora is constituted (*Didache*); this communal meal is later justified as a 'sacrament' (*Traditio apostolica*, *Didascalia*). The communities appointed officials (initially so that they could preside over the ritual meal) and assigned specific responsibilities to different groups of servants (*Didache*). The holders of Church offices developed a consciousness of their role and their own official ethics, which led to the fundamental separation of the community into → clergy and laity, as part of the hierarchical division of offices in the *Traditio apostolica*, whereas the *Didascalia* proposed only the monarchical episcopacy (→ Episkopos), remaining unique in this narrow interpretation. The gradual loss of constitutional reality, the competition of the synodic legal order (→ Collectiones canonum) since the 4th cent., and the use of pseudo-epigraphy, increasingly suspect to its (official) recipients, by which the texts became more and more obviously situated in the realm of pseudo-reality, collectively contributed to the disappearance of this genre of theological production from the 5th cent.

1 P.F. Bradshaw, s.v. Kirchenordnungen, I. Altkirchliche, TRE 18, 662–670   2 R.H. Connolly, The So-Called Egyptian Church-Order and Derived Documents, 1916   3 G. Dix, H. Chadwick, The Treatise on the Apostolic Tradition, ²1968   4 A. Faivre, Naissance d'une hiérarchie, 1977   5 E. Hauler, Didascalia Apostolorum fragmenta Veronensia latina, 1900   6 C.N. Jefford (ed.), The Didache in Context. Essays, 1998   7 J. Magne, Tradition apostolique sur les charismes et Diataxeis des saints apôtres, 1975   8 G. Schöllgen, Die Didache als Kirchenordnung, in: JbAC 29, 1986, 5–26   9 Id., Die lit. Gattung der syrischen Didaskalie, in: Orientalia Christiana analecta 229, 1987, 149–159   10 Id., W. Geerlings (ed.), Fontes christiani, vol. 1, 1991 (Edition von Didache und Traditio apostolica)   11 Id., Der Abfassungszweck der frühchristl. Kirchenordnungen, in: JbAC 40, 1997, 55–77   12 E. Schwartz, Über die pseudapostolischen Kirchenordnungen, in: Id., Gesammelte Schriften, vol. 5, 1963, 193–273 = 1910   13 B. Steimer, Vertex traditionis, 1992.   BR.ST.

Church Slavonic is the normative written form of common Slavonic (językъ slověnьskъi). In its oldest form (Old Church Slavonic), it was used in liturgical practice because of the translations and missionary work of Constantine (› Cyrillus [5]) and Methodius (Vita Methodii 15). The conflict between Methodius (*archepiscopus Pannoniensis ecclesiae*) and the Roman Curia was not caused by his apostolic teachings, but by his reading of the liturgy of the *sacra missarum solemnia* in Slavonic language. Church Slavonic (CS) was elevated to the state of a liturgical language when Pope Hadrian II sanctified the Slavonic liturgical books during the reception of the two brothers and when he held the entire liturgy in Slavonic language in St Peter's Cathedral in Rome (Vita Constantini 17).

Recently, it has been argued that one must differentiate between Old CS as the language of the Church since 863/4 in the missionary areas of Constantine/Cyrillus and Methodius, i.e. the principalities ruled by Rastislav, Svętopulk and Kocel, and Old Bulgarian as the language of Church and Empire since AD 893 [4]. The difficulty of proving this claim lies in the fact that no MSS have survived from the time of the two Slavonic teachers. The language used in Moravia can only be reconstructed from later copies in various 'editions', since the autographs were lost either in the persecution of Methodius' students (since AD 885), or during the invasion of the Hungarians [7; 2; 5].

The problems surrounding the origin and the identification of CS can already be seen in the *Skazanie o pismenech* by Konstantin Kostenečki (*c.* 1380–1431) [3]. These problems became a bone of contention in Slavonic Studies in the 19th cent: inspired by Romanticism, several linguists attempted to view Old CS in the light of the national languages that developed later (Dobrovsky 1806, Kalaidović 1822, Kopitar 1838). The following are considered as regional variants ('editions') of CS after the collapse of the 'Great Moravian Kingdom' (906): Bulgarian (-Macedonian); East Slavonic-Kievian (later Russian), which was the only one to exist continuously beyond the High Middle Ages while vernacular influences replaced the traditional forms of CS in other countries; Serbian-Bosnian

(Shtokavian); Croatian (Chakavian), which probably was a direct derivation from the Old CS in Moravia or Bulgaria (→ Bulgaria; Bulgari); Bohemian and Polish [1]. Four 'centres of development' stand out for Old CS: prior to AD 863, the region surrounding Thessaloniki; from AD 863 to 885, Moravia and Bosnia-Slavonia; until AD 883, Pannonia (Western Hungary); from AD 885 to 893, Eastern and Western Bulgaria (Preslav, Ochrid). Furthermore, there are attempts at interpreting the difference between western-Slavonic Moravian and southern-Slavonic Old CS as → 'diglossia' [6. 284].

1 D. BOGDAN, La vie et l'œuvre des frères Constantine-Cyrille et Méthode, in: I. ANASTASIOU (ed.), Kyrillo kai Methodio, 1966, 31–82 2 A. DOSTÁL, La tradition cyril-lo-méthodienne en Moravie, in: I. ANASTASIOU (ed.), Kyrillo kai Methodio, 1966, 153–182 3 H. GOLDBLATT, Orthography and Orthodoxy: Constantin Kostenecki's Treatise on the Letters, 1977 4 R. PICCHIO, Pravoslav-noto slavjanstvo i starobălgarskata kulturna tradicija, 1993 5 R. VEČERKA, Zur Periodisierung des Alt-Kir-chenslavischen, in: Ann. Instituti Slavici 9, 1976, 92–121 6 Id., Das Alt-K. als Schriftsprache Großmährens, in: Wiener Slawistischer Almanach 6, 1980, 279–297 7 N. v. WIJK, Gesch. der alt-kirchenslavischen Sprache, 1931.   L.D.

Chvasak (*Hvasak* or *Husaksak*). Satrap of Susa at the time of 'the Great King Artabanus, son of Vologases' ([1; 2]; = Ardawan IV/V) in the Arsacid year 462=215 BC. From that year we have a grave or rather honorary stele from Susa that depicts both holding a ring [3]. Its inscription makes it the only exactly dated work of the late Arsacid period. Its tendency towards frontality of the ruler images and extreme linearity is typical [4]. It is improbable that the same satrap is depicted on a relief in Tang-i Sarvak [2].

1 R. GHIRSHMAN, Monument Piot 44, 1950, 97–107 2 F. ALTHEIM, R. STIEHL, Asien und Rom, 1952, 34 3 W. B. HENNING, Asia Major 2, 1952, 151–178 4 H. E. MATHIESEN, Sculpture in the Parthian Empire, vol. 2, 1992, 168f. fig. 29 and *passim*.

R. GHIRSHMAN, Parthians and Sassanians, 1962, 56f. fig. 70; L. VAN DEN BERGHE, Archéologie de l'Iran Ancien, 1959, 82, pl. 106c.   PE.CA.

Chytroi see → Anthesteria

Cibalae Important road junction in Pannonia inferior, modern Vinkovci (Croatia). *Municipium* since the time of Hadrian (CIL III 3267), *colonia Aurelia* from the 3rd cent. AD (CIL VI 2833). Monuments: remains of buildings, water pipes, thermal baths, graves, inscriptions, small finds. In AD 314 Licinius was defeated in a battle near C. by Constantine the Great (Eutr. 10,5; Zos. 2,18,4, also describing the location of C.).

TIR L 34 Budapest, 1968, 46f.   J. BU.

Cibyra (Κίβυρα; *Kíbyra*).
[1] Important town in southern Phrygia (modern Göl-hisar, formerly Horzum) on the border with Lycia. C. belonged to a tetrapolis with Bubon, Balbura, and Oenoanda, in which it had two votes, the other three member only one vote each; the tetrapolis was dissolved in 84 BC by L. → Licinius Murena, and C. incorporated into the Roman province of Asia (Str. 13,4,17); from about 56 to 49 BC, it was part of the province of → Cilicia. From the time of Diocletian, C. belonged to the province of Caria. C. was a member of the Panhellenium. Legend has it that C. was founded by Sparta [1. 497]; however, Str. (loc. cit.) notes that the town was founded by Lydians and subsequently settled by Pisidians, whose languages were spoken alongside Greek. With the new foundation of the town by Tiberius after an earthquake in AD 23 (Tac. Ann. 4,13) an era of local importance began. It was the centre of a legal district (*conventus*); Suffragan diocese of Stauro-polis (→ Aphrodisias [1]) in Caria. Extensive ruins: several theatres and temples, aqueduct, necropolis.

1 OGIS.

W. RUGE, s.v. K., RE 11, 374–377; Id., s.v. Phrygia, RE 20, 836; W. LESCHHORN, Ant. Ären (Historia Einzelschr. 81), 1993, 352–367.   T.D.-B.

[2] see → Pamphylia

Cicada (*Cicada plebeia*). The cicada (Greek; τέττιξ/ *téttix*, Gen. -ιγος or -ικος; Lat. *cicada*) was and is one of the best-known and most characteristic insects of the Mediterranean. Its typical song or noise (ἠχεῖν/*ēcheîn*, Hes. Op. 583; Sappho Fr. 89 D.; Anth. Pal. 7,196 and 201), produced by rubbing the wings against the opercula (cf. Aristot. Hist. an. 4,9,535b 7–9), is often the only sound on a hot summer day when all other animals are silent (e.g., Hes. Sc. 396; Aristoph. Av. 1095; Theoc. 5,110 and 7,139; Verg. Ecl. 2,13; G. 3,328). Sometimes this sound was considered pleasant, sometimes annoying (Mart. 10,58,3: *inhumanae cicadae*) and garrulous (cf. Hom. Il. 3,151f.; Pl. Phdr. 258e). Cicadas are an attribute of the Muses (Pl. Phdr. 262d; Anth. Pal. 10,16); in Callimachus (Aitia Fr. 1,30 PFEIFFER) the chirping becomes the symbol of higher poetry and the cicada a symbol of the poet (Anth. Pal. 12,98), the Muse as the poet's helper (Timon FGrH 566 F 43) or his subject (Anac. 32 B.).

The cicada was much observed in zoological terms: Aristotle describes it as an insect (Hist. an. 4,7,532b 10–17: two species, only the male of the larger species sings; Part. an. 4,5,682a 18–26: nutrition), it lives in dry and warm places especially on olive trees and multiplies by mating (Aristot. ibid. 5,30,556a 14–b 20, Aristot. Gen. an. 1,16,721a 2–4; cf. Plin. HN 11,92–95). Their colour is black or dark (Theoc. 7,138) and they have large, net-like wings. It was believed that these plant-juice-sucking insects fed on dew only (Hes. Sc. 393; Anth. Pal. 9,92; Verg. Ecl. 5,77), which is why they supposedly did not defecate. Mass occurrences were an omen of an unhealthy year (Theophr. De signis tempe-statum 54).

As a familiar animal, cicadas were often depicted, e.g., on a lance of Athena (Anth. Pal. 6,120), on coins [1.Plate 7,32–36] and gems [1.Plate 23,38]. According to Plin. HN 34,57, the sculptor → Myron [5] supposed-ly made a bronze of a cicada and a → grass-hopper. According to Hellanicus (FGrH 4 F 140), → Tithonus turned into a cicada

1 F.IMHOOF-BLUMER, O.KELLER, Tier- und Pflanzenbil-der auf Mz. und Gemmen des klass. Alt., 1889 (repr. 1972).

KELLER 2, 401–406. C.HÜ.

Cicereius Rare Roman family name.

C., C. Initially the scribe of Scipio Africanus Maior, in 173 BC after a prior, voluntarily withdrawn applica-tion he became praetor with Sardinia as his province. After the victory over the Corsicans he triumphed in 172 in monte Albano against the will of the Senate; in 168 he dedicated a temple to Juno Moneta. In 167 a member of the commission for the reorganization of Illyria. (MRR 1,408; 435).

E.BADIAN, The scribae of the Roman Republic, in: Klio 71, 1989, 584. K.-L.E.

Cicero
I. HISTORIC II. CICERO AS ORATOR AND WRITER

I. HISTORIC

M. Tullius C., born on 3 January 106 BC in → Arpi-num. The Tullii Cicerones maintained manifold rela-tions with the Roman urban aristocracy. They enabled C. to prepare for a public career in close association with the most important speakers of his time, L. Lici-nius Crassus (cos. 95) and M. Antony (cos. 99), as well as the leading authorities in civil and sacred law, Mucius Scaevola Augur and Mucius Scaevola Pontifex. The Social Wars and the subsequent civil war turmoil kept C. away from the forum. He was initiated into court in 81 under Sulla's dictatorship in the civil matter of P. Quinctius and in 80 in the public proceeding against Sex. Roscius of Ameria, the background of which was the terror of Sulla's proscriptions. The acquittal of Roscius from a malicious patricide charge that was achieved by C. was all the more remarkable because one of → Sulla's favourites, his freedman Chry-sogonus, had made common cause with the murderers and retroactively placed the victim on the proscription list for the purpose of acquiring the family estate togeth-er with the murderers. The case made C. a much sought-after attorney, and after two years of studies in Athens and Rhodes he resumed his legal activities in court. This gave him the connections a → novus homo required to rise into the ruling class through election to public of-fices (→ cursus honorum). In 75 he was subordinate to the governor of Sicily as quaestor and after the end of

his term entered the → Senate. In 70 he was elected aedi-lis, and as the patron of the Sicilians obtained the sen-tencing of the corrupt governor C. → Verres in spite of influential nobiles, but without incurring the hostility of the nobility. In 66 C. was praetor and gave his first major political speech in which he supported the pro-posed law of the people's tribune C. → Manilius to transfer the supreme command against Mithridates to → Pompeius. C. made himself vulnerable through a proposal popular with the people and the → publicani, and committed himself to Pompeius — again without breaking with the nobility.

Thus, in 64 the ground was prepared for an appli-cation to the consulate (→ consul). His strongest com-petitors L. Sergius Catilina and C. Antonius [I 2] were controversial and thus C. came first in the election. He brought down the agrarian law of the popular tribune P. Servilius Rullus — the backers of the application were → Caesar and M. Licinius → Crassus — and thus prevented Rullus from acquiring great power that would last over the next five years.

C.'s greatest success, the suppression of the 'Catiline conspiracy', was also the seed of the break in his career. → Catilina planned a violent overthrow after his repeat-ed application for a consulate had failed. It was mainly the debt problems burdening all levels of society that drove supporters into his arms — which gave the planned coup a dimension of social revolution. On 21 October 63, the Senate reacted to the recruitment of private army with the senatus consultum ultimum (→ Emergency, state of). In November Catiline was declared an enemy of the state. C. exposed Catiline's fellow conspirators in the city on 3 December and on the 9th he effected, against Caesar's vote, a Senate reso-lution advocating the execution of the immediate sus-pects. C. had them executed and thus violated the law, which prohibited the execution of a citizen without a sentence (the argument C. used in his defence, that the Catilinarians were public enemies, was irrelevant as those concerned had not been hostes, nor had they been found with weapon in hand).

In the political confrontation over provisioning Pompey's veterans and the ratification of the regula-tions introduced by him in the East, C. rapidly lost the leading role he had claimed. The formation of the First → Triumvirate that united Pompey, Crassus and Cae-sar, and Caesar's consulate sidelined him as a powerless critic of the situation. In response to his refusal to join the triple alliance, the associates smoothed the path of P. → Clodius [I 4], one of C.'s personal enemies, to the popular tribunate. In 58 Clodius effected the introduc-tion of a law that anyone who had a Roman citizen killed without a court sentence was to be shunned. C. left Rome before the vote and spent 15 months in exile. Upon his return C. disappointed the → Optimates, supported Pompey, who wanted an extraordinary im-perium to secure Rome's grain supply, and exposed himself with remarks against P. → Vatinius, the origina-tor of the extraordinary commands for Caesar, and through violation of one of Caesar's → agrarian laws. The renewal of the Triumvirate (in April 56) thwarted C.'s efforts. Against his convictions he became a helper of those in power: C. foiled the efforts of like-minded Optimates to end Caesar's Gallic command in the spring of 55, and in 56–54 defended supporters of the three rulers in court, among them P. Vatinius and A. Gabinius.

Only the trials that followed in 52 upon the killing of P. Clodius by T. → Annius [I 14] Milo permitted C. to once again demonstrate independence towards Pompey, then *consul sine collega*. He defended Milo and achieved the sentencing of T. → Munatius [I 5] Plancus, a supporter of P. Clodius. On 1 May 51 C. left Rome to take on the governorship of → Cilicia, where he obtained a victory in the Amanus mountains and was proclaimed → *Imperator*. The stay in Cilicia and his late return to Italy (in November 50) made him a mere spectator of the dramatic events that led to the civil war between Caesar and the Senate. His efforts to achieve a peaceful resolution to the conflict failed early in 49. C. evaded Caesar's overtures and joined Pompey in his army camp. After Pompey's defeat he returned to Italy and had to wait a year in Brundisium for Caesar's pardon.

Caesar's politics of reconciliation made C. hope that the return of the Optimates might be followed by the restoration of the old *res publica*. In the autumn of 46 he expressed this hope when he thanked Caesar for pardoning M. → Marcellus. The hope had dissipated when he supported a pardon for Q. → Ligarius and defended the Galatian king → Deiotarus against the accusation of having planned an attempt on Caesar's life and supported the revolt of Q. → Caecilius [I 5] Bassus in Syria. His praise for the younger M. → Porcius [I 7] Cato, who as a determined republican had declined Caesar's pardon and taken his life after the battle of Thapsus, was an implicit critique of Caesar and caused the latter to confront C.'s image of Cato in his *Anticato*.

C. was not privy to the conspiracy against Caesar. However, he welcomed it without reservation and only found fault with the fact that M. → Iunius Brutus and C. → Cassius [I 10] Longinus had not also eliminated the consul M. → Antonius [I 9]. He attempted again to take on a leading role. He mediated the compromise of 17 March 44, which declared the dictator's commands legal but granted his murderers an amnesty. This of course made the dictator's murder a crime, and the outbreak of popular anger at Caesar's funeral provided Antony with the opportunity of keeping the murderers away from political influence. C. was alarmed, especially since Antony with his *lex de permutatione provinciarum* (June 44), which granted him the Gallic provinces for five years, gave the impression that he would repeat Caesar's route to autocracy. Hopes for a political turnaround were shattered. On 2 September 44, C. gave a speech that disapproved of Antony's conduct of policy. In the Senate Antony cancelled his friendship with C., who in turn answered with the invective known as the Second Philippic Speech.

C. once again acquired a leading role when the conflict between the consul and Octavian (→ Augustus), Caesar's grand-nephew and heir, threatened to escalate into an armed confrontation. Not without misgivings, C. entered into an alliance with Octavian, who had assembled a private army from Caesar's veterans and enticed some of the consul's troops to join his side. This highly treasonable act required legalization by the Senate, which C. attempted to mediate. On 20 December 44 he obtained a resolution that explicitly approved of Octavian's actions and the resistance of D. → Iunius Brutus, the governor of → Gallia Cisalpina, at the time when the consul had wanted to take possession of his province. This political direction caused C.'s friends → Atticus and M. Brutus great apprehension. It amounted to a breach of the constitution and privileged a young traitor who was inextricably linked to Caesar's cause. But C. believed himself to be in control of the game. In the Senate on 1 January 43 he effected that Octavian, among other privileges, be granted an extraordinary command, and won the two consuls and former Caesarians A. → Hirtius and C. → Pansa over to his course. With inexhaustible energy C. attempted to mobilize all forces for a victory over Antony, the negotiations offered by whom he sabotaged. In the spring of 43 he came within reach of victory. Brutus and Cassius had taken over the provinces of Macedonia and Syria with the help of the troops stationed there, and C. saw to it that the Senate provided them with a comprehensive extraordinary command. At the end of April the armies led by the consuls and Octavian defeated Antony in two battles, and C. had him declared a public enemy.

The tide turned quickly. Antony had escaped to Gaul, where he won over the western governors and their troops, while Octavian changed direction. He was not willing to be used for the liquidation of the Caesarian 'party'. He demanded a consulate, and when his demand was rejected he occupied the city in July 43. After an irregular election he took up the consulate together with his kinsman Q. → Pedius. A *lex Pedia* outlawed Caesar's murderers, another law rehabilitated Antony. On Antony's demand C. was killed on 7 December 43 as one of the first victims of the new ruler's private → proscription agreements.

Any evaluation of the politician C. is dependent on that of his opponent Caesar, and will vary accordingly. The fact that his rich legacy of literature and letters reveals C. as a personality tending towards praise and overestimation of himself and fluctuating between timid depression and jubilant euphoria has had a negative effect on his evaluation. As a social climber he adapted to the conventions of the aristocratic republic, and as a person educated in history and philosophy he developed a strongly idealized and theoretical image of the traditional → *res publica*. Without a strong power base he had to qualify through outstanding achievements; these were made possible by his incomparable oratory talent, which he first used as an instrument for social ascent and then employed in political leadership. It was mainly due to the political circumstances that he never in his life, apart from its final act acquired true leadership. C. was obsessed with domestic order based on a consensus of the governing class and the people — this being the essence of his 'programme' of a *concordia omnium bonorum* ('the agreement of all good men') — in which the authority of arguments and merit was decisive in guiding the *res publica*. He did not have the means of power decisive in his time, money and troops, and it was the tragedy of his life that his great talents were largely anachronistic in a world in which huge treasuries extracted from the provinces and the Republican armies were used to make the consensus-based system of government collapse. He was not lacking in tactical skill and unyielding ruthlessness. As his political direction during the Catiline affair and importantly also in the struggle against Antony demonstrated, he was indeed willing to break laws and violate the constitutional order. But this did not happen because of the ambition of a politician striving for autocracy. In C.'s subjective perception the constitution was only ever violated to save the state. For the sake of this goal he in the end risked the very existence of the *res publica* and his life. That the Republic was perhaps already dying when for its salvation the very principles upon which it was based were sacrificed apparently never occurred to him.

M. FUHRMANN, C. und die röm. Republik, 1989; M. GELZER, C., 1969; CH. HABICHT, C. der Politiker, 1990; E. RAWSON, C., 1975; R.E. SMITH, C. the Statesman, 1966; D. STOCKTON, C., 1971   K.BR.

II. CICERO AS ORATOR AND WRITER
A. GENERAL   B. SPEECHES   C. LETTERS
D. THEORETICAL WRITINGS   E. OTHER WORKS
F. INFLUENCE

A. GENERAL
Apart from → Varro, C. is the only universal author in Roman antiquity; he composed speeches, letters, rhetorical and philosophical writings (with no clear-cut boundary between the two genres) as well as poetry. Of no other non-Christian author of Latin antiquity do we have more text. While speeches and letters are distributed over many years (speeches extant from 81–43, letters from 68–43), most theoretical writings were created in two shorter periods of his life (55–51, 46–44) during which he was forced into political inactivity.

B. SPEECHES
Fifty-eight speeches are preserved, partly with gaps; titles or fragments of about another 100 are known [1; 2]. C.'s speeches are the apex of Roman rhetoric; at the same time they are the only preserved examples from the classical period. Unlike the Greek orators he therefore cannot be compared to contemporaries. Speeches as a defender in court (hereinafter: A) and political speeches before the Senate or people (B) are roughly

equal in number. The former often have a political background; purely private legal cases are only found in the early years. C. only appeared as the prosecutor in the extortion trial (→ *repetundarum crimen*) against Verres. Speeches preceding his consulate: *Pro P. Quinctio* (81 BC, A), *Pro Sex. Roscio Amerino* (80, A), *Pro Q. Roscio Comoedo* (around 77 or 66?, A), *Pro Tullio* (72/71, A), *Divinatio in Caecilium* (preliminary proceeding regarding take-over of the prosecution in the Verres trial, 70), *In Verrem actio* I, II, 1–5 (these five speeches were not delivered but only worked out and published), *Pro M. Fonteio* (69, A), *Pro A. Caecina* (69 or around 71, A), *De imperio Cn. Pompei* (*De lege Manilia*, 66, B), *Pro A. Cluentio Habito* (66, A). Speeches of the consular year 63: *De lege agraria* (= *Contra Rullum*) 1–3 (B), *Pro C. Rabirio perduellionis reo* (A), *In Catilinam* 1–4 (B), *Pro Murena* (A). Speeches up to the proconsulate: *Pro P. Cornelio Sulla* (62, A), *Pro Archia* (62, A), *Pro L. Valerio Flacco* (59, A), *Oratio, cum senatui gratias egit*, *Oratio, cum populo gratias egit*, *De domo sua ad pontifices* (before the pontifical college) and *De haruspicum responso* (all in 57, B), *Pro P. Sestio* (56, A), and belonging to it *In P. Vatinium* (during the interrogation of the witnesses), *Pro M. Caelio* (56, A), *De provinciis consularibus* (56, B), *Pro L. Cornelio Balbo* (56, A), *In L. Calpurnium Pisonem* (55, B), *Pro Cn. Plancio* (54, A), *Pro Aemilio Scauro* (54, A), *Pro Rabirio Postumo* (54/3 or 53/2, A), *Pro T. Annio Milone* (52, A). The three speeches delivered during Caesar's autocracy are addressed directly to him: *Pro M. Marcello* (46, B), *Pro Q. Ligario* (46, A), *Pro rege Deiotaro* (45, A). Speeches after Caesar's murder: *Philippicae* 1–14 (44/43, B). C. published most of the speeches himself, and in spite of his reworking them, the original content was preserved in most cases [43. 31ff.; 26. 3ff.]. 12 speeches of the consular year 63 and the *Philippicae* 3–12 were collected as corpora after the model of the Φιλιππικοὶ λόγοι (*Philippikoì lógoi*) of › Demosthenes [44]. Reproductions of individual passages from Demosthenes and other Greek orators are frequent [45]. C.'s oratorical success depended not only on his elegant phrasing but also on a skilful tactical procedure [43; 26]; as they were each calculated to achieve a certain effect, the speeches do not necessarily reflect C.'s own opinion ([35]; the 'excursus on the Optimates', Sest. 99ff. probably represents an exception; relevant research history in [25]). Clear stylistic differences are noticeable depending on the occasion [20. 1241ff., 1300ff.]; the abundance of rhetorical means used at times was criticized in the 40s by adherents of strict → Atticism but vigorously defended by C. himself in the *Brutus* and the *Orator*.

C. LETTERS
C.'s → letters are the only collection of genuine utility letters preserved from antiquity (→ Epistle), i.e. they were originally only intended for the addressees. Preserved are the 16 vols. of the *Ad familiares* (not the original title), 16 vols. *Ad Atticum*, 3 vols. *Ad Q.*

fratrem (with 1,1 being a treatise on provincial administration), 2 vols. *Ad M. Brutum*, in total about 900 letters, among them about 100 letters of other persons to C. Other collections of letters are lost [28. 1199ff.]; a letter to Octavian is a forgery. C. himself seems to have planned a publication of letters in 44 (Att. 16,5,5); they however were not published until after his death; the Atticus letters (which do not include letters by Atticus himself) were only published in the 1st cent. AD. C.'s letters permit insight into his biography, his thoughts and feelings on a level impossible for any other person in antiquity; they are also important sources for the history of their time. The years 59–52 are relatively well, the years 49 and 46–43 very densely documented; only isolated letters are preserved from the period before 59. They range from short notes (Fam. 14,20) to very personal confessions (Fam. 14,4), exchanges on various topics (Att. 12,40), analyses of the political situation (Att. 10,8) and official letters for political purposes (Fam. 10,12); the 13th vol. of the Fam. contains only letters of recommendation. The writing style changes with the addressees; the letters to Atticus for example contain numerous Greek words. Generally, the syntax and choice of words are freer in the letters than in works intended directly for publication [20. 1272ff.].

D. THEORETICAL WRITINGS

(documentation and bibliography in [27]).

1. *De inventione* Two-volume textbook in the tradition of scholastic oratory (→ Rhetoric), written in about 80, perhaps even before the → *Rhetorica ad Herennium*, which is related in content. In the prooemia C. already exhibits philosophical interests.

2. The three great dialogues of the 50s, *De oratore* (55), *De re publica* (54–52) and *De legibus* (about 52?) clearly constitute a group of their own due to the style of the dialogue and the reminiscences of Platonic dialogues. In 3 vols. *De oratore* develops the knowledge of the ideal orator far beyond scholastic rhetoric. C.'s ideal concept, mainly represented by the dialogue speaker *Crassus*, is the combination of philosophical and rhetorical ability ('excursus on philosophers' 3,54–143). Despite inspirations from Greek philosophy the formulation of this ideal is C.'s own achievement. Of the six vols. of *De re publica* a quarter of the text is contained in a palimpsest found in 1819; only the conclusion, the *Somnium Scipionis*, was directly transmitted because → Macrobius commentated on it. In this work, C. masterfully uses Greek political theory to prove that the traditional Roman constitution is the ideal one [36]; that he wanted to see a leader with almost monarchical powers at its head is no longer assumed. Apart from *De oratore*, *De re publica* also is C.'s most perfect literary work. In *De legibus* C. expounds the laws of the ideal state described in *De re publica*. There is no information on the genesis of this work; internal criteria definitely indicate the 50s [40]. Three of at least five vols. are extant; whether the text was ever completed is uncertain. The smaller writings

Partitiones oratoriae (54?) and *De optimo genere oratorum* (regarding their authenticity [27. 1070]) were probably also created in the 50s.

3. Late works. Under Caesar's autocratic rule C. wrote two rhetorical writings, *Brutus* (early 46; a history of Roman rhetoric) and the *Orator* (a sketch of the ideal orator), both in response to the Atticistic critique of his rhetorical style; furthermore the *Paradoxa Stoicorum* (before May 46) and a tract in praise of the younger Cato (→ Porcius; not extant). Since the winter of 46/45 C. had planned a survey of Greek philosophy (a *volumen prooemiorum*, Att. 16,6,4 attesting to this); after the sudden death of his daughter Tullia in February 45 a *Consolatio* to himself was inserted [23. 91f.] (lost). Up to the summer of 45 we find in close succession the dialogues *Hortensius* (defense of philosophy in style of the Aristotelian Protreptikos; only fragments preserved), *Catulus* and *Lucullus* (epistemology; only the *Lucullus* is preserved), reworked as *Academici libri* in four vols. (only the beginning extant), the five vols. *De finibus bonorum et malorum* (teaching of the greatest good), five vols. *Tusculanae disputationes* (basic requirements for human happiness) and three vols. *De natura deorum*; another dialogue on physics which was probably intended to include the preserved translation from Plato's *Timaios*, was planned. At the time of Caesar's murder *De divinatione* (two vols.) was in progress; at about the same time the *Cato maior de senectute* was being written. Despite his return to politics C. still wrote *De fato* (spring of 44?), *Topica* (topics for orators; July 44), *Laelius de amicitia* (summer of 44) and *De officiis* (3 vols.; final edition is missing; work on it continuing up to November 44); lost are *De gloria* and the work *De virtutibus*. To what extent plans (that were never realized) for a *Symbouleutikon* to Caesar, a Σύλλογος πολιτικός (*Sýllogos politikós*) and a → dialogue in the style of → Heraclides (on Caesar's murder) are linked in content to the philosophical writings remains unclear. In writings of this period C. appears as a follower of the Sceptical → Academy that rejected certain knowledge but permitted finding an opinion probable (*probabile*); this had probably been his essential epistemological position ever since his acquaintance with Philon of Larissa in 88 ([24; 27. 1084ff.] rightly against [30]). The method of working out what is probable (in *Lucullus*, Fin., Nat. D., Div.; originally also envisioned for Fat.; the Tusc. are a special case) is the *disputatio in utramque partem*, which is implemented in the staging of the dialogues as the juxtaposition of speech (exposition of a philosophical viewpoint) and counter-speech (counterargument on a Sceptical basis). What C. himself considers *probabile* is usually not explicitly stated in these works, but made clear implicitly [32]; in *De officiis* he explicitly presents a Stoic position as the one appearing *probabile* in this case. C. uses Greek sources for topics in all of his works; their intellectual processing and arrangement however are his own, significant achievement; even in Off. 1/2, where he attaches himself directly to Panaetius' Περὶ τοῦ καθή-

κοντος (*Perì toû kathékontos*) he is still working very freely. Details of how dialogues were phrased and the choice of persons involved may be understood as open siding against Caesar [42].

E. OTHER WORKS

Prose works (all lost): a *hypomnema* on his consulate as the basis for poetic glorification (60), a kind of secret history (ἀνέκδοτα, *anékdota*, title probably *De consiliis suis*; mentioned in letters of 59 and 44); mourning speech for the sister of M. Cato (*Laus Porciae*); the writings *De auguriis* and *De iure civili in artem redigendo*; a geographical work; a translation of Xenophon's *Oikonomikos* and Plato's *Protagoras*. His poetry, which was little appreciated even in antiquity (see Tac. Dial. 21) stands linguistically and metrically between Ennius and Virgil. Directly transmitted are parts of the translation of → Aratus' *Phaenomena* (an early work like the poems *Glaukos, Alcyones* etc.); other titles: *Marius* (date unknown), *De consulatu suo* (60), *De temporibus suis* (3 vols., 55/54), a poem on Caesar's British campaign (54). Numerous, in part extensive metrical translations of Greek poets are interspersed among C.'s works (edition: [10]).

F. INFLUENCE

Consistent with the universal character of C.'s work, its influence is divided into several streams that have little to do with each other (bibliography in [27. 1156ff.]; surveys: [21] (late antiquity); [38] (Middle Ages); *varia* in [18, vols. 6–8; 12; 14]). C. had the broadest effect as a shaper of the Latin language and as a stylistic model; already in antiquity he became the 'Classic' of Latin literature. In his times as well as in the 1st and 2nd cent. AD there also were deviating stylistic ideals (→ Atticism and → Archaism respectively); but in Quintilian and in the teaching of oratory in late antiquity C. became the model of perfect eloquence; not even Christian authors could escape this influence (→ Lactantius becomes the *Cicero Christianus*, Jerome (→ Hieronymus) hears God's reproach in a dream [Epist. 22,30]: *Ciceronianus es, non Christianus*). In the Middle Ages direct linguistic imitation declined. In the Renaissance (especially the 16th cent.) C.'s language was elevated by many as the only guiding model; Erasmus opposed the excesses of this Ciceronianism in his *Ciceronianus*. The content of individual writings was received in very different ways; a survey differentiating according to works is lacking. C.'s indirect influence, e.g. through the writings of the Church Fathers, is also important in many places. Of individual works, *De inventione* probably had the greatest influence in the Middle Ages and the Renaissance as a basic textbook of rhetoric (together with the '*Herennius rhetoric*', which was for a long time attributed to C.). In comparison, the other rhetorical writings have had less of an impact. From late antiquity down to the modern period, his philosophical writings have been among the most-read philosophical works of the whole of antiquity. Overall,

works classifiable as practical ethics had the greatest influence — *De officiis* (model e.g. for → Ambrosius' *De officiis ministrorum*), also *Cato, Laelius*, the '*Tusculans*'; other works, e.g. *De natura deorum*, have found increased interest in certain phases of intellectual history. The *Hortensius* set → Augustinus on the road to conversion (Aug. Conf. 3,4). Down to the early modern period, the speeches were above all read and analyzed as linguistic and rhetorical patterns. Historical interest is still attested in the 1st cent. AD in Q. → Asconius Pedianus' commentaries, but then faded into the background until it sporadically re-emerged in the Renaissance. In the Middle Ages C. was considered the teacher *par excellence* of rhetoric and philosophy. The statesman and the person — and, therefore, the letters — only came into focus again in the Renaissance through (→ Petrarch). On the whole, those works of C. that today are considered his most individual achievements, especially the great speeches and *De oratore*, were less read in previous centuries. There was little appreciation of C. in the 19th and early 20th cents., especially in Germany; his theoretical works were merely considered poor reworkings of Greek originals. By contrast, the most recent research has again begun to appreciate C.'s intellectual significance.

RELIGION, CRITIQUE OF; REPUBLIC; RHETORIC, TEACHING OF

EDITIONS: 1 JANE W. CRAWFORD, M.T.C., The Lost and Unpublished Orations, 1984   2 Id., M.T.C., The Fragmentary Speeches, 1994   3 M. FUHRMANN, C., Reden, 7 vols., 1970–1982 (translation with introduction)   4 R. Y. TYRRELL, L. C. PURSER, The Correspondence of M.T.C., 7 vols., ³1904 (repr. 1969)   5 D. R. SHACKLETON-BAILEY, C.'s Letters to Atticus, 7 vols., 1965–1970; Epistulae ad familiares, 2 vols., 1977   6 C. F. W. MUELLER, Scripta omnia 4,3: Librorum deperditorum fragmenta, 1879, 231–414   7 I. GARBARINO, Fragmenta ex libris philosophicis, ex aliis libris deperditis, 1984   8 K. WEYSSENHOFF, Epistularum fragmenta, 1970   9 J. SOUBIRAN, Aratea. Fragments poétiques, 1972   10 FPL¹, 144–181   11 COURTNEY, 149–181.

COLLECTIONS: 12 K. BÜCHNER (ed.), Das neue Ciceronbild, 1971   13 W. W. FORTENBAUGH, P. STEINMETZ (ed.), C.'s Knowledge of the Peripatos, 1989   14 B. KYTZLER (ed.), C.s lit. Leistung, 1973   15 W. LUDWIG (ed.), Éloquence et rhétorique chez Cicéron, 1982   16 J. G. F. POWELL (ed.), C. the Philosopher, 1995   17 R. RADKE (ed.), C., 1968.

JOURNAL: 18 Ciceroniana, N.S., 1973ff.

BIBLIOGRAPHY: 19 G. ACHARD, Pratique rhétorique et idéologie politique dans les discours 'optimates' de C., 1981   20 M. v. ALBRECHT, s.v. T. C., M., Sprache und Stil, RE Suppl. 13,1237–1347   21 C. BECKER, s.v. C., RAC 3, 86–127   22 J. BOES, La philosophie et l'action dans la correspondance de C., 1990   23 K. BRINGMANN, Unt. zum späten C., 1971   24 W. BURKERT, C. als Platoniker und Skeptiker, in: Gymnasium 72, 1965, 175–200   25 J. CHRISTES, Cum dignitate otium (Cic. Sest. 98), in: Gymnasium 95, 1988, 303–315   26 C. J. CLASSEN, Recht, Rhet., Politik, 1985   27 G. GAWLICK, W. GÖRLER, C., in: GGPh², vol. 4,2, 991–1168   28 M. GELZER et al., s.v. T. C., M., RE 7A, 827–1274 (cf. [20])   29 K. M. GIRARDET, Die Ordnung der Welt, 1983 (on Leg.)

30 J. GLUCKER, C.'s philosophical affiliations, in: M. DILLON, A. A. LONG (ed.), The Question of 'Eclecticism', 1988, 34–69   31 W. GÖRLER, Unt. zu C.s Philos., 1974   32 J. LEONHARDT, C.s Kritik der Philosophenschulen, 1999   33 C. LÉVY, C. Academicus, 1992   34 P. MACKENDRICK, The Philosophical Books of C., 1989   35 CHR. NEUMEISTER, Grundsätze der forensischen Rhet., gezeigt an Gerichtsreden C.s, 1964   36 V. PÖSCHL, Röm. Staat und griech. Staatsdenken bei C., 1936 (repr. 1976)   37 A. PRIMMER, C. numerosus. Studien zum ant. Prosarhythmus, 1968   38 W. RÜEGG et al., s.v. C., LMA 2, 2063–2077   39 SCHANZ/HOSIUS 1, 400–550   40 P. L. SCHMIDT, Die Abfassungszeit von C.s Schrift über die Gesetze, 1969   41 Id., Die Überlieferung von C.s Schrift De legibus in MA und Renaissance, 1974   42 H. STRASBURGER, C.s philos. Spätwerk als Aufruf gegen die Herrschaft Caesars, 1990   43 W. STROH, Taxis und Taktik, 1975 (on the court speeches)   44 Id., C.s demosthenische Redezyklen, in: MH 40, 1983, 35–50   45 A. WEISCHE, C.s Nachahmung der att. Redner, 1972   46 TH. ZIELINSKI, C. im Wandel der Jahrhunderte, ³1912.   J.LE.

Cicones (Κίκονες; *Kíkones*). Tribal group on the northern Aegean coast between Nestus and Hebrus, the later settlement area of the Bistones and Sapaei, in the Homeric epics named as allies of the Trojans (Hom. Il. 2,846f.; 17,72f.). Homer distinguishes between the coastal C. and those in the northern mountains. Ismarus is described as a wealthy city of the C., and herds of sheep and cattle along with viticulture are also mentioned (Hom. Od. 9,39–59). It is doubtful whether the C. belonged to the Thracians. Their name became part of the mythological-Homeric onomastics of ancient literature.

V. VELKOV, Thraker und Phryger nach den Epen Homers, in: Studia Balcanica 5, 1971, 279–285.   I.v.B.

Cicynna (Κίκυννα; *Kíkynna*). Attic *mesogeia* deme of the phyle → Acamantis, two (three) *bouleutai*. Only one deme of C. is verifiable [1. 83; 3. 20]. Its location is uncertain (Chalidou? [1. 48; 2]).

1 TRAILL, Attica, 19, 48, 59, 68, 83, 110 no. 67, table 5   2 J. S. TRAILL, Demos and Trittys, 1986, 132   3 WHITEHEAD, Index s.v. K.   H.LO.

Cidame (*Cidamus* or *Cydamus*). Chief settlement of the Phazanii at the intersection of the borders of Libya, Tunisia, and Algeria, modern Gadames. According to Plin. HN 5,35f., the Phazanii have to be differentiated from the → Garamantes. Between the territories of both of these tribes was Mons Ater, modern Hamada el-Homra. C. — like → Garama — was captured in 20 BC by L. Cornelius [I 7] Balbus, *proconsul Africae*. A *vexillatio* of the *legio III Augusta* was stationed in the town [1]. C. played an important role in the Sahara trade. Under Justinian, the inhabitants of the town converted to Christianity (Procop. Aed. 6,3,9).

1 J. M. REYNOLDS, J. B. WARD PERKINS (ed.), The Inscriptions of Roman Tripolitana, 1952, 907–912.

P. TROUSSET, s.v. Cidamus, EB 13, 1953f.   W.HU.

Cidenas (Κιδήνας; *Kidénas*, Babylonian *Kidinnu*), Chaldean astronomer, at the latest in the 2nd cent. BC, mentioned by Strabo as well as Sudines and Naburianus, discoverer of the equation 251 synodic months = 269 anomalistic months, originator of system B of the Babylonian moon calendar. His observations were probably used by → Critodemus (CCAG 5,2,128,15), → Hipparchus [6] and → Ptolemaeus.

→ Astronomy

SOURCES: P. SCHNABEL, Berossos und die babylon.-hell. Lit., 1923, 121–130; O. NEUGEBAUER, Astronomical Cuneiform Texts, 1955, 22f.
LITERATURE: B. L. VAN DER WAERDEN, Das Alter der babylon. Mondrechnung, in: Archiv für Orientforschung 20, 1963, 97–102; F. H. WEISSBACH, W. KROLL, s.v. Kidenas, RE 11, 379.   W.H.

Cierium (Κιέριον; *Kiérion*). City in the Thessalian *tetras* Thessaliotis in the valley of the Cuarius (modern Sophaditikos or Onochonos), founded by invading Thessalians as their main town, north-east of the Boeotian founded town of → Arne [2]; in the following period, they drove the Boeotians back south to their historical seats (Thuc. 1,12,3; Str. 9,5,14). Arne is equated with Makria-Magoula, C. with the ruins on a nearby hill near the modern Pyrgos Kieriou. Near C. was the Thessalian tribal sanctuary of Athena Itonia (→ Iton). In 198 BC, C. surrendered to Flamininus (Liv. 32,15,3), was captured by Philip V in 191 BC (36,10,2), and shortly after handed over to the Romans (36,14,6). The settlement of a border conflict with Metropolis at the time of Tiberius is epigraphically documented in the temple of Hercules (IG IX 2, 261). Coins (HN 292).

B. HELLY, Incursions chez les Dolopes, in: I. BLUM (ed.), Topographie antique et géographie historique en pays grec, 1992, 48–91; V. MILOJČIĆ, in: AA 70, 1955, 229ff.; 75, 1960, 168; D. THEOCHARIS, The Tumulus of Exolophos and the Thessalian Invasion, in: AAA 1, 1968, 268ff.; F. STÄHLIN, Das hellenische Thessalien, 1924, 130f.   HE.KR.

Cietis (Κιῆτις, Κῆτις; *Kiêtis*, *Kêtis*). Region of → Cilicia Tracheia (comprising Cennatis, Lacanitis, Lalassis), which extended along the coast from → Anemurium to the mouth of the Calycadnus, and in the interior into the headwater region of the Calycadnus (Ptol. 5,7,3; 6). Its inhabitants were the *Cietae*, who in AD 52 laid siege to Anemurium (Tac. Ann. 6,41; 12,55). The minting of coins by → Antiochus [18] IV and several individual towns of the C. is evident. Cf. the *vita* of St. → Thecla [1. 276]; → Hagia Thekla.

1 G. DAGRON, Vie et miracles de Sainte Thècle, 1978.

W. RUGE, s.v. K(i)etis, RE 11, 380f.; HILD/HELLENKEMPER, 301.   F.H.

Cilices, Cilicia (Κίλικες, Κιλικία; *Kílikes, Kilikía*).
I. Cilices II. Cilicia III. History

I. Cilices

a) Tribe mentioned in Homer (Hom. Il. 6,397; 415; cf. Str. 13,1,7; 60), who settled in the southern Troad. b) The inhabitants of the region of Cilicia. The relationship between the two is not clear.

II. Cilicia

The name first appears around 858 BC in Assyrian sources as Ḫilakku; however, in these it only refers to the mountainous part of the region, where the Greeks first visited. An eponymous hero named Cilix appears in the mythological literature (e.g. Apollod. 3,1,1); supposedly, he settled in C. after originally coming from Phoenicia. The historical region of C. (Str. 14,5,1; Plin. HN 5,91–93) on the southern coast of Asia Minor stretched to → Coracesium or rather to the river Melas in the west, and in the east to the → Amanus mountains; its northern border is formed by the Taurus, passable in only a few places (→ Cilician Gates / Ciliciae Pylae [1]). The western mountainous regions is called 'Rugged, or Rough, C.' (Κιλικία τραχεῖα/*Kilikía tracheîa*, Lat. *Cilicia aspera*), the eastern one, dominated by the alluvial plains of the rivers → Cydnus, → Sarus, and → Pyramus, is known as 'Plain, or Flat, C.' (Κιλικία πεδιάς/*Kilikía pediás*, Lat. *Cilicia campestris*).

III. History
A. Pre-Greek period B. Greek and Roman period C. Byzantine period

A. Pre-Greek period

In pre-Greek history known as → Kizzuwatna. In the late Hittite period (9th/8th cents. BC), various local principalities developed within C., e.g. in → Karatepe (under Azitawadda), where a bilingual Luwian-Phoenician inscription refers to the 'house of' (Luwian) 'Muksas' or respectively (Phoenician) 'Mpš'; he is sometimes identified with the Greek seer → Mopsus, who supposedly also founded Mopsouhestia and Mallus. Furthermore, C. was an important exporter of silver to Egypt (Middle Kingdom) and Assyria (1st millennium BC).

B. Greek and Roman period

The settlement of Greek traders and colonists during the 8th and 7th cents. BC (e.g. in the Samian colonies of Nagidus and Celenderis, the Lindian Soli as well as Anchiale and Tarsus) is frequently also archaeologically evident. The collapse of Assyrian rule was followed by the rise of the Cilician kingdom of the Syennesis dynasty, who in Persian times still resided in Tarsus as vassals of the Persian king (Xen. An. 1,2,23). With the battle of → Issus (333 BC), C. became part of the empire of Alexander the Great, and subsequently of the Seleucid kingdom, who (most of all → Antiochus [6] IV) pressed on with the Hellenization of the country by founding or reconstituting numerous *póleis* (Seleucia on the Calycadnus, Antioch on the Cydnus = Tarsus, Seleucia on the Pyramus = Mopsouhestia, Hierapolis → Castabala, Epiphaneia). During the 3rd cent. BC, an intermittent Ptolemaic presence can be observed in 'Rugged C.' (→ Arsinoe [III 3]). The increasing weakness of the Seleucid kingdom towards the end of the 2nd cent. BC favoured the spread of piracy; to fight these pirates, the Romans first set up a praetorian *provincia* → Cilicia in 102 BC.

Between 78 and 74 BC, P. Servilius Vatia (later called Isauricus) subjugated the inhabitants of 'Rugged C'. 'Plain C.' had fallen to → Tigranes in 83 BC; only in 69 BC were those Cilicians whom he had deported to Tigranocerta returned to their former homeland by Lucullus (Plut. Lucullus 26; 29). Pompey who had been given the *imperium proconsulare maius* achieved a decisive victory against the pirates in 67 BC; he arranged for the settlement of his defeated opponents in Pompeiopolis (the former Soli) and other depopulated Cilician towns (Plut. Pompey 28; App. Mith. 96; → Piracy). In 51/0 BC, Cicero as *proconsul* led a successful campaign in Cilicia against the Eleutherokilikes in the Amanus mountains. The large province of Cilicia was dissolved by 43 BC, with the major part of 'Rugged C.' initially falling to → Amyntas [9] of Galatia, then to → Archelaus [7] of Cappadocia. Alongside other smaller client states (→ Olba), Tarcondimotus I (*topárchēs*, 'town commander', from c. 40 BC *basileús Philantónios*, 'king who loves Antonius'; coins) established a kingdom in 'Plain C.', which in both civil wars fought on the losing side (naval support for Pompey and Antony, Cass. Dio 41,63,1; 50,14,2; died at → Actium). Consequently, his son Tarcondimotus II Philopator lost his rulership in 30 BC (Cass. Dio 51,2,2), but was allowed to rule again between 20 BC and AD 17.

Caligula gave parts of C. to → Antiochus [18] IV of Commagene (Cass. Dio 59,8,2; foundation of Antiochia [3] on the Cragus, Iotape), the remainder was incorporated into the province of Syria. A separate province of Cilicia with Tarsus as its capital city was only created once again in AD 72 by Vespasian. In AD 194, Septimius Severus defeated his rival Pescennius Niger at the → Cilician Gates / Ciliciae Pylae [2]; in AD 260 Šapur I laid waste large tracts of C. Diocletian instituted 'Rugged C.' as a province in its own right, then called Isauria, with Seleucia as its capital.

→ Cilicia (Roman province); → Isauria; → Asia Minor, Hittite successor states (with map)

P. Desideri, A. M. Jasink, Cilicia — Dall'età di Kizzuwatna alla conquista macedone, 1990; C. Mutafian, La Cilicie au carrefour des empires, 1988; T. B. Mitford, Roman Rough Cilicia, in: ANRW II 7.2, 1230–1261; Hild/Hellenkemper; G. Dagron, D. Feissel, Inscriptions de Cilicie, 1987; SNG Schweiz 1/Levante, 1986; R. Ziegler, Kaiser, Heer und städtisches Geld, 1993; S. Hagel, K. Tomaschitz, Repertorium der westkilikischen Inschr., 1998.   H. Tä.

C. Byzantine period

In AD 400, 'Plain C.' was divided into two provinces with the respective capitals of → Tarsus (*Cilicia* sc. *Prima*) and → Anazarbus (*Cilicia Secunda*) (Not. Dign. or. 1,62; 94). The Church came under the patriarchy of → Antioch [1]. C. enjoyed a long period of prosperity, resulting in extensive — mainly ecclesiastical — building activities; from the mid 7th cent., it got ever closer to the borders of the caliphate and was largely depopulated. In around AD 700, C. was conquered by the Arabs and only returned to the Byzantine empire in AD 965. In the course of the resettlement, a large number of Armenians came to C. who after 1071 established there the kingdom of Lesser Armenia (until 1375).

HILD/HELLENKEMPER.   AL.B.

Cilicia First established in 102 BC as the → *provincia* of a Roman praetor (M. Antony) for the purpose of fighting piracy. The command was repeatedly renewed (e.g. 100 BC: IK 41,31) [1. 266] but the subjugation of the inhabitants of C. Tracheia by P. Servilius Vatia Isauricus (78–74) made a permanent Roman presence possible and was solidified by the victory of → Pompeius over the pirates (67) and Cicero's campaign against the Eleutherokilikes (51/50). After Caesar's death C. was ceded to native vassal rulers (→ Tarcondimotus) or administered as a part of Syria. In AD 72 Vespasian re-established the province of C. with → Tarsus as its capital. Under the Severi (late 2nd/early 3rd cent. AD) rivalries arose with → Anazarbus, which had been elevated to a metropolis (and was made capital of the province C. Secunda in the East by Theodosius I).
→ Cilices, Cilicia II

1 P. FREEMAN, The Province of C. and its Origins, in: Id., D. KENNEDY, The Defence of the Roman and Byzantine East, 1986, 253–275   2 T. B. MITFORD, Roman Rough C., ANRW II 7.2, 1980, 1230–1261   3 H. TAEUBER, Die syr.-kilikische Grenze während der Prinzipatszeit, in: Tyche 6, 1991, 201–210   4 HILD, Einleitung.   H.TÄ.

Cilician Gates / Ciliciae Pylae (Πύλαι Κιλίκιαι; *Pýlai Kilíkiai*).
[1] Narrow passage through the → Taurus at a height of 1,050 m, these day deeply buried underneath the motorway, modern Gülek Boğazı, through which passed the road from Tyana/Cappadocia to Tarsus/Cilicia (Str. 12,2,7); this pass played an important role i.a. in Xenophon's *Anabasis* (Xen. An. 1,4,4; 401 BC), during Alexander the Great's campaign (cf. Arr. Anab. 2,4,3; 333 BC), and in the fight of Septimius Severus against Pescennius Niger (Cass. Dio 74,7,1; AD193/4). A building inscription at the northern entrance to the Cilician Gates (CG) (from the time of Caracalla) refers to the *hóroi Kilíkōn* (ὅροι Κιλίκων, IGR III 892), the It. Burd. 578,5–579,1 to the *mutatio Pilas, fines Cappadociae et Ciliciae*. The road itself, a large part of which is preserved further south near Sağlıklı (formerly Bayramlı), with the ancient paved surface and an arch, was called *via Tauri* [1]. In the Middle Ages, the CG were known as Darb as-Salāma ('Pass of Salvation'), Porta Iuda, Kuklak kapan or Porta de Ferre [2. 263f.; 3. 213, 387].

1 R.P. HARPER, in: AS 20, 1970, 149–152   2 HILD/RESTLE   3 HILD/HELLENKEMPER.

W. RUGE, s.v. Κιλίκιαι Πύλαι, RE 11, 389f.; H. TREIDLER, s.v. Πύλαι Κιλίκιαι, RE Suppl. 9, 1352–1366; D. FRENCH, Roman Roads and Milestones of Asia Minor, Fasc. 1, 1981, 122f.   F.H.

[2] Pass *c.*10 km north von → Alexandria [3] between the Amanus range and the Mediterranean, known also as the 'Syrian Gates' (Xen. An. 1,4,4), to distinguish them from the CG [1]. Between AD 72 and about 300, it marked the border between the Roman provinces of → Cilicia and Syria [1]. The decisive battle between Septimius Severus and Pescennius Niger was fought in AD 194 in its immediate vicinity, near → Issus, after the latter had already suffered an earlier defeat at the Cilician Gates (Cass. Dio 74,7); in commemoration of this battle, a triumphal arch (Bab Yunus) was built and agones instituted.

1 H. TAEUBER, Die syr.-kilik. Grenze während der Prinzipatszeit, in: Tyche 6, 1991, 201–210   2 HILD/HELLENKEMPER, s.v. Kilikiai Pylai, 302.   H.TÄ.

Cilix (Κίλιξ; *Kílix*). Son of Telephassa and → Agenor [1], who sent him, with his brothers on the (futile) search for the kidnapped → Europa [2]. C. becomes the founder and eponym of Cilicia (Hyg. Fab. 178). C. also gains a part of Lycia, by helping Sarpedon in time of war (Apollod. 3,2ff.; Hdt. 7,91). In a later version Sarpedon, searching for his sister, is killed by his uncle C. who does not recognize him (vita Theclae PG 85, 478ff.; cf. the Song of Hildebrand). Schol. Apoll. Rhod. 2,178, citing various sources, calls C. the son of Phoenix and uncle of Agenor.   C.W.

Cilla
[1] (Κίλλα; *Kílla*, Lat. *Cilla*). There seem to have been at least two settlements of this name. One is mentioned in Hdt. 1,149; it was one of the eleven Aeolian cities, and, according to [1. 216f.], was not located in the Troad. The other is mentioned in the 'Iliad' (Hom. Il. 1,38; 452) and was supposedly located near Chryse and Thebe — probably north-west of the bay of Adramytteum; an exact localization has not been possible as yet. Different from that was perhaps also the town of C. that, according to Dictys (2,13), had been destroyed by the Greeks under Achilles' leadership; this should be localized in the vicinity of Neandria and Colonae. It remains uncertain with which of the latter two C. the famous sanctuary of Apollo Killaios (Str. 13,1,62) was associated.

1 W. LEAF, Troy, 1912   2 E. SCHWERTHEIM, Neandria, in: Id. (ed.), Neue Forsch. zu Neandria und Alexandria Troas, 1994, 21–37   3 J. STAUBER, Die Bucht von Adramytteion 1 (IK 50), 1996.   E.SCH.

[2] (Κίλλα; *Kílla*). Daughter of → Laomedon [1]. When the seer Aesacus prophecied with a view to → Hecuba who was pregnant with → Paris that mother and son had to die in order to avert disaster from Troy, due to a misinterpretation it was C. who was killed together with her son who had been born on the same day as Paris (Tzetz. on Lycoph. 224).   RE.N.

Cillactor see → Callicter

Cillae (Κέλλαι; *Kéllai*). *Mansio* on the road from Philippopolis to Hadrianopolis, modern Černa gora (Bulgaria). Honorary decrees and dedications from the imperial period (IGBulg 1515ff.); It. Ant. 136; Tab. Peut. 568.   I.v.B.

Cillas (Κίλλας; *Kíllas*, also *Kíllos*, Κίλλος). C., who according to the Troezenian legend is called Sphaerus, is the charioteer of → Pelops (Paus. 5,10,7; schol. Eur. Or. 990). On the way to a chariot race with Oenomaus, Cillas falls into the sea at Lesbos and drowns. Pelops erects a memorial to him, a temple of Apollo Killaios and founds the town of Cilla (Theopompus 339 FHG 1).   AL.FR.

Cilles (Κίλλης; *Kíllēs*). Macedonian, *phílos* and *stratēgós* of Ptolemy I, C. was able to drive Demetrius [2] from Syria after the battle of Gaza in 311 BC but was captured by him and sent back to Ptolemy. PP II/VIII 2164.   W.A.

Cilnius Name of an important family in Arretium (SCHULZE, 149); involved in a dispute with the town's citizens in 302 BC (Liv. 10,3,2 i.a.). Augustus called → Maecenas a Cilnian, which presumably only referred to his maternal ancestors (Macrob. Sat. 2,4,12).   K.-L.E.
[1] **C. Proculus, C.** From Arretium. *Cos. suff.* in AD 87 (AE 1949, 23). Father of C. [2].
[2] **C. Proculus, C.** Senator from Arretium (CIL XI 1833 and AE 1926, 123 belong together: [1. 239ff.] = AE 1985, 392). Praetorian (?) governor of Dalmatia in about AD 96/97(?), *cos. suff.* 100, consular legate of Moesia superior in AD 100 (CIL XVI 46); probably distinguished with fourfold → *dona militaria* during the Dacian wars. Probably a *comes* of Hadrian.

1 HALFMANN, in: ZPE 61, 1985.   W.E.

Cilurnum Roman camp on the western bank of the North Tyne, where Hadrian's wall crosses the river, modern Chesters; built in around AD 125 as a replacement for tower 27a [1. 89–91]. Garrison of the *ala II Asturum* in the 3rd cent. AD (CIL VII 585); prior to that, the camp may have accommodated cavalry (including Sarmatae). The camp gates are extant, as are *principia, praetorium,* two soldiers' quarters, extramural thermal baths, and the foundations of a bridge. South of the camp was an extended *vicus* [2].
→ Limes

1 D.J. BREEZE, The Northern Frontiers of Roman Britain, 1982   2 P. SALWAY, The Frontier People of Roman Britain, 1965   3 E.B. BIRLEY, Research on Hadrian's Wall, 1961, 172–174.   M.TO.

Cimberius Celtic (?) name of a leader of the Suebi who commanded a large tribal army together with his brother → Nasua in 58 BC [1. 438–440]. The attempt to cross the Middle Rhine and to aid → Ariovistus against Caesar failed because Ariovist was defeated in Alsace and subsequently fled across the Rhine (Caes. B Gall. 1,37,3; 1,54,1).

1 EVANS.

H. BANNERT, s.v. C., RE Suppl. 15, 88–89; G. WALSER, Caesar und die Germanen, 1956, 49.   W.SP.

Cimbri Germanic tribe, who apparently suddenly descended upon Gaul and Italy, but whose origins and itinerary remained a mystery to the Romans (Plut. Marius 11,4; sources in [1], cf. [3. 23–28]). Jutland is assumed to be their homeland, on the basis of a modern hypothesis; that they were driven out by the slow encroachment of the sea, is probably no more than an ancient presumption (Posidon. in Str. 2,3,6; 7,2,1f.). It is a contentious question whether the C. changed their way of life, resorted to robbery, and finally turned their attention to Italy [2], or whether they tried, under political leadership, to secure for themselves land and a nomadic existence as robbers by establishing themselves as clients or mercenaries within the fluctuating Celtic settlement area [3. 50]. The Cimbric migration, presumably, has to be seen as part of the differentiated migration movement of the final centuries BC, which can also be observed in the → Bastarnae, Sciri, and → Vandals, and for which there is evidence in both literary (Cimbric commander Lugus, Oros. 5,16,20) and archaeological sources [3. 50]. The 'repulse' of the Boii at the *silva Hercynia*, but also the march to the Scordisci and Taurisci on the Danube, the turning towards the → Helvetii (crossing of the Rhine in 111 BC: Vell. Pat. 2,8,3), as well as the affiliation of → Ambrones, Helvetian → Tigurini and → Teutoni: all have to be seen in the context of deliberate co-operation with tribes or parts of tribes. The armed conflict with the Romans, however, was less a sign of deliberate Cimbric aggression than the consequence of the Roman expansion into the Celtic arc north of Italy during the 2nd cent. BC. As it was the ultimate aim of both Rome and the C. to weaken the ancient *Keltike*, conflict became inevitable, whenever the C. encroached on the Roman sphere of interest; for example, when they utterly defeated Papirius near Noreia, who tried to block their further advance in 113 BC (Liv. Epit. 63). In Gaul, they operated as allied mercenaries of the Sequani against the Haedui (Aedui) and in 109 BC, triumphed in southern Gaul over Iunius Silanus (Liv. epit. 65), who quite likely provoked this war. In 107 BC Tigurini, who had penetrated into the territory of the → Allobroges, were successful against consul Cassius Longinus (Caes. B Gall. 1,7,4; 12,4–6; 30,2; Liv. Epit. 65), and in 105 BC, — after the C. had offered to negotiate — the Roman armies under the command of consul Mallius and proconsul Servilius Caepio were utterly defeated in the battle of → Arausio (modern Orange). When → Marius after his victory over Jugurtha prepared to ward off the Germans, the C., in a surprise move, turned to northern Spain, but driven back by the Celtiberi soon returned to Gaul, joined up with the Teutoni (in the lands of the Velio- casses, probably near Rouen), and set out to maraud all of Gaul, opposed only by the Belgae (Caes. B Gall. 2,4,2). Leaving behind 6,000 men (the core of the → Aduatuci: Caes. B Gall. 2,29,4) in the land of the Eburones, they set out on their march south, either immediately splitting up into two columns (Plut. Mar. 15,6), or forming three columns only after Marius' re- fusal to engage in battle at the confluence of the Isère and the Rhône (Oros. 5,16,9). While Teutoni and Ambrones were destroyed by Marius near → Aquae Sextiae (modern Aix-en-Provence) (Liv. Epit. 68), C. and Tigurini managed to advance to the Po (102 BC) *via* Noricum (Plut. Marius 15,5), across wintery Alpine passes, and through the barriers which consul Lutatius had put up in the Etsch valley. In the battle against the by now united Roman armies, the C., in their fight 'for the possession of the land' (ibid. 25,4), were wiped out on the *campi Raudii* near → Vercellae. In spite of the 'Cimbric trauma' [2], the empire was never in any real danger.

1 H.-W. GOETZ, K.-W. WELWEI (ed.), Altes Germanien I, 1995, 202–271 2 CH. TRZASKA-RICHTER, Furor Teu- tonicus, 1991 3 D. TIMPE, Kimberntradition und Kim- bernmythos, in: B. and P. SCARDIGLI (ed.), Germani in Ita- lia, 1994, 23–60. K.DI.

Cimissa (Κμίσσα; *Kimíssa*). Town in Sicily, known from two silver coins (*lítra*; *hēmídrachmon*) from the time of → Timoleon (mid 4th cent. BC); obverse: nymph's head, decorated with earrings, necklace and crown, bearing the legend OMONOIA, reverse: altar with burning sacrificial fire and the legend ΚΙΜΙΣΣΑΙΩΝ (finding-place: Raffe di Mussomeli Agri- gento); that is also the probably location of C.

G. MANGANARO, Homonoia dei Kimissaioi, Eunomia dei Geloi e la ninfa (termitana) Sardó, in: U. FELLMETH, H. SONNABEND (ed.), Alte Geschichte. FS E. Olshausen, 1998, 131–142. GI.MA.

Cimmerii (Κιμμέριοι; *Kimmérioi*, Lat. *Cimmerii*). No- madic tribe probably of Iranian descent, attested for the 8th/7th cents. BC. The Assyrian and Babylonian forms of the name were *Ga-mir, Gi-mir-a-a* and similar; in the OT they were referred to as *gmr*, in the Masora *Gòmär*. According to a document from the time of Sargon II [1. no. 30–32], the Urartian King Rusa I invaded the land of *Gami(ra)* (between 720 and 714 BC) and was defeated there. A further document from the same period attests to a Cimmerian intrusion into → Urartu

from the region south of Lake Urmia [2. no. 2,1]. The Transcaucasian region may thus have been the start- ing-point of Cimmerian aggression. In 679 BC, Teušpa, the king of the C., was defeated by the Assyrians at the town of Ḫubušnu. In the following years, there is evi- dence of the C. in the region west of Lake Van, in Parsua west of Media, and possibly in Ellipi between → Media and → Elam. At the time of the Median revolt (674–672 BC), they were allies of the Medes.

According to Str. 1,3,21, the C. penetrated into → Asia Minor after the death of the Phrygian king → Midas (about 700 to 675 BC). According to Assyrian sources, they attacked the Lydian kingdom in around 665 BC, but → Gyges, his successor, was able to repulse them with the help of → Assurbanipal. At the same time, there were C. in → Cappadocia, from where they also controlled parts of Syria. In 644 BC, they defeated the Lydians and captured their capital city of → Sardis. It is possible that the C. were allied with the Lycians and the Treres, who took Sardis once again by storm in 637 BC. From about 640 or 630 BC onwards, the C. — under the leadership of their king → Lygdamis (Akkad. *Dugdammē*) and in alliance with the Treres — began their attacks on the Aeolian and eastern Ionian Greek cities (Hdt. 1,6; Callim. H. 3,253ff.; Str. 1,3,21; 3,2,12; 11,2,5). They also invaded → Paphlagonia (Str. 1,3,21), the territory of → Sinope, → Heraclea [7] Pontica, and → Bithynia (Arr. FGrH 156 F 60; 76). In around 640 BC, they tried to enter into an alliance with the kingdom of Tabal, and twice mounted an attack against the Assyrians. Lygdamis died soon after the second attack. He was succeeded by his son Sa-an-dak-KUR-ru. After the Treres had been defeated by the Scythian king Madyes (Str. 1,3,21), the Lydian king → Alyattes suc- ceeded in crushing the C. towards the end of the 7th or beginning of the 6th cent. BC (Hdt. 1,16; Polyaenus, Strat. 7,2,1). With that, the C. disappear from historical records.

In Greek literature, Homer was the first to mention the C. in Hom. Od. 11,14, where they are described as inhabiting the territory beyond the → Oceanus, the al- leged location of the entrance to the Hades. The western Greeks localized this place very early on at the → *lacus Avernus* (Ephor. FGrH 70 F 134; Str. 5,4,5). The C. were also identified with the Celts (Posidon. FGrH 87 F 31). Almost all of the ancient literary authors of the Hellenistic and Roman times viewed the C. from the perspective of the 'Odyssey'. According to classical ancient historiography, however, the ancestral seats of the C. lay in the steppes of southern Russia to the north of the northern shores of the Black Sea. The first docu- mentary evidence for that is found in the *Arimáspeia* of Aristeas of Proconnesus (about 550 BC), according to which the → Scythians had driven the C. out of their ancestral land. According to Hdt. 4,11–13, Cimmerian aristocrats had killed each other so as not to give in to the demands of the people who — faced with Scythian supremacy — wanted to emigrate. Allegedly, after the kings were buried in barrows near the → Tyras, the C.

set out along the Causasian Black Sea coast towards Sinope.

At the Cimmerian → Bosporus [2], many toponyms point to the C.; this historical view originates with the early colonists along the Tyras and the Bosporus, and were accepted by the most of modern historians. Consequently, most of the pre-Scythian finds, such as those of the Černaja gora and Novočerkask cultures are attributed to the C. However, there are weighty arguments against that view: from the 10th cent. BC until the arrival of the Scythians, the lands on both sides of the Cimmerian Bosporus were largely uninhabited; Old Oriental sources provide other verifiable localizations; there are no analogies to the Novočerkask culture in the Transcaucasus, in Anatolia or the Middle East. It was probably only Greek colonists who first linked the remains of Bronze Age settlement and graves with the C., who in for them not so distant times had attacked the eastern coast of the → Pontus Euxinus and whose aggression had quite likely from very early on become legendary. In line with that, the colonists then created 'Cimmerian' toponomy along the Bosporus. According to archaeological finds, there is no distinction between the C. and the Scythians, which is why they are both thought to be Iranian.

1 S. PARPOLA, State Archives of Assyria 1. The Correspondence of Sargon II, 1987 2 K. DELLER, Ausgewählte neuassyr. Briefe betreffend Urartu zur Zeit Sargons II, in: P. E. PECORELLA et al., Tra lo Zagros e l'Urmia, 1984, 97-104.

A. I. TERENOŽKIN, Kimmerijcy, 1976; M. A. DANDAMAEV, Data of the Babylonian Documents from the 6th to the 5th Century B.C. on the Sakas, in: J. HARMATTA (ed.), Prolegomena to the Sources on the History of Preislamic Central Asia, 1970, 95-109; I. M. D'JAKONOV, The Cimmerians, in: Monumentum Georg Morgenstierne 1 (Acta Iranica 21), 1981, 103-140; A. I. IVANCIK, Les Cimmériens au Proche-Orient, 1993; S. R. TOKHTAS'EV, Die Kimmerier in der ant. Überl., in: Hyperboreus 2, fasc. 1, 1996, 1-46.   I.V.B.

Cimolos (Κίμωλος; *Kímolōs*). Island of the Cyclades (35 km²) north-east of Melos, mountainous (Palaiokastro 398 m), composed of the same volcanic tuff as Melos. 'Cimolian earth' (cimolite), a grease-dissolving soapy clay, was used for washing and for the production of porcelain. Another Cimolian export article were figs. The ancient town was situated in the south-west near the modern Hellenika. Some graves in the necropolis even date back to pre-Mycenaean times; finds range from the 2nd millennium BC into the Hellenistic period. Another ancient settlement was near the modern Palaiokastro, where the remains of a town wall and a round tower are extant. In 425/4 BC, C. was a member of the → Delian League with a tribute of 1,000 drachmas (ATL 1,312f.; 2,81; 3,24; 198). Sources: Aristoph. Ran. 712 with schol.; Str. 10,5,1; 3; Ptol. 3,15,8; Plin. HN 4,70. Inscriptions: IG XII 3, 1259f. and p. 336; SEG XII 367; HN 484.

L. BÜRCHNER, s.v. K., RE 11, 435f.; CH. MUSTAKAS, K., in: MDAI(A) 69/70, 1954/5, 153ff.; H. KALETSCH, s.v. K., in: LAUFFER, Griechenland, 328f.; PHILIPPSON/KIRSTEN 4, 186, 194f.   H.KAL.

Cimon (Κίμων; *Kímōn*).

[1] C., known as *Koálemos* ('the Stupid'), son of Stesagoras of Athens, born about 585 BC, had to leave Athens during the tyranny of → Peisistratus. During his exile he achieved two Olympic victories with the four-horse chariot (536 and 532 BC). Since C. had the 2nd victory proclaimed for Peisistratus, he was permitted to return. C.'s high prestige after his third Olympic victory (528) resulted in a conflict between him and the tyrant's successors. In any case Hippias [1] instigated his murder. As successors of his stepbrother → Militiades, C.'s sons Stesagoras and → Militiades became tyrants on the Chersonese (Hdt. 6,34; 38; 103).

DAVIES 8429 VII; M. STAHL, Aristokraten und Tyrannen im archa. Athen, 1987, 116ff.

[2] Son of → Militiades and the Thracian princess Hegesipyle, born about 510 BC, most important army commander and politician of Athens in the 70s and 60s of the 5th cent. After 478, C. was repeatedly elected as *stratēgós* and commanded the armed forces of the → Delian League during the all important operations between 476 and 463: he was responsible, for example, for the conquest of Eion [1] on the Strymon; the conquest of the island of Scyros and the expulsion of the Dolopians living there; the forceful incorporation of the town of Carystus on Euboea into the League; the military strike against → Naxos, which intended to leave the League; the campaign in Asia Minor, which culminated in the double battle at the Eurymedon, and finally in the siege of the renegade League member → Thasos (Thuc. 1,98-101). C. was acquitted of a charge of bribery levelled by domestic opponents in 463 ([Aristot.] Ath. pol. 27,1; Plut. Cimon 14,3-15,1).

In 462 the Athenians decided upon his suggestion to support Sparta in putting down the → helot uprising. However, when the Spartans sent the Athenian auxiliary corps back because its 'daring style' was feared and it was suspected of revolutionary tendencies, C. as the initiator was discredited (Thuc. 1,102; Plut. Cimon 16,8-17,2). During his absence the Areopagus had been disempowered in Athens on the initiative of → Ephialtes [2]. C.'s attempt to oppose this decision and to reverse the reform resulted in his ostracism (→ Ostrakismos) and the end of his political career (Pl. Grg. 516d; Plut. Cimon 15,3; 17,3). Supposedly, C. appeared in 458 on the battlefield of Tanagra to participate in the fight against the Spartans. However, he was not trusted and sent away. Whether he really managed to persuade his pro-Spartan friends to loyally engage on Athens' side and was rewarded with an early recall cannot be determined because of the state of the source material (And. 3,3; Theopomp. FGrH 115 F 88; Plut. Cimon 17,4-9; Plut. Pericles 10,1-5). When C. returned to

Athens he mediated a peace agreement with Sparta, participated in the campaign to recapture Cyprus and died there in an epidemic (And. 3,3; Aeschin. Leg. 172; Thuc. 1,112,4).

For a long time C. was considered the prototype of the 'conservative' aristocrat and representative of a pro-Spartan, anti-democratic policy. More recent research shows that his official status as a → *próxenos* and his personal contacts with Sparta did not influence his actions as a *stratēgós*: these aimed at an uncompromising expansion of the Delian League and the Athenian sphere of influence to the entire Aegaean. Even C.'s activities on the political stage in Athens do not present him as the 'leader of the party of the rich and noble', who 'struggled with the leaders of the people for power', as he was portrayed by the *Athēnaíōn Politeía* ([Aristot.] Ath. pol. 26,1). The generosity with which C. supported his fellow deme members with meals, clothing and alms, the public buildings he built and the spectacular return of the bones of the mythical king → Theseus, show that C. controlled the means to influence the public as tools with which an ambitious aristocrat could gain political influence even in democratic Athens (Plut. Cimon 4,5; 10,1–9; 13,6f.). C.'s career can be seen as an example that the interpretation of Athenian history in the 5th cent. through the Aristotelian matrix of an eternal conflict between aristocrats and democrats is misleading.

M. Steinbrecher, Der delisch-att. Seebund und die athen.-spartan. Beziehungen in der kimon. Ära, 1985; E. Stein-Hölkeskamp, Adelskultur und Polisgesellschaft, 1989, 218ff.

[3] Athenian, possibly a descendant of Cimon [2], was in 346 BC a member of a peace delegation to Philip II (Aeschin. Leg. 21; Dem. Or. 19, Hyp. 2 §4). Davies 8429 XV.   E.S.-H.

[4] Greek painter from Cleonae on Chalcidice, worked in the final years before 500 BC and the following decade. Apart from belonging to the group of monochrome painters, his innovations in painting technique, the κατάγραφα (*katágrapha*), were praised. This was important progress, especially with respect to the development of the body perspective from changing angles (→ Perspective). C. was able to depict heads and facial traits as well as complicated postures of figures with more variety than ever before by means of artful shortenings in angular and other perspectives. Individual body parts were also shown in more differentiated form by a more faithful representation of organic details, likewise the textile qualities of clothes (Plin. HN 35,56). All of these criteria can be seen on several red-figured Attic vase images of the so-called pioneer group, whose manufacturers were contemporaries of C. (→ Vase painters).

N. Hoesch, Bilder apulischer Vasen und ihr Zeugniswert für die Entwicklung der griech. Malerei, 1983, 98ff.; N. Koch, De Picturae Initiis, 1996, 28f.; G. Lippold, s.v. Kimon (10), RE 11, 454; I. Scheibler, Griech. Malerei der Ant., 1994.   N.H.

Cinadon (Κινάδων; *Kinádōn*). In 398 BC, C. a *hypomeion* ('Inferior'), thus presumably the son of Spartan parents but without full citizens' rights, sought widespread support for a revolt to overthrow the ruling class of the Spartiatae, by approaching → Helots, Neodamodes, *hypomeiones* and → Perioikoi. No details about his planned reforms are known. C. was betrayed, lured into a trap and killed after naming his fellow conspirators under torture. In Xenophon's version (Hell. 3,3,4–11), C. generalizes, exaggerating the tensions within Sparta.

P. Cartledge, Sparta and Lakonia, 1979, 312f.; M. Whitley, Two Shadows, in: A. Powell, St. Hodkinson (ed.), The Shadow of Sparta, 1994, 87–126, esp. 102f.   K.-W.WEL.

Cinadus (Κίναδος, *Kínados*, 'Fox'). One of the helmsmen of → Menelaus. His tomb is said to have existed on the Laconian foothills of the Onugnathus ('Donkey chin') opposite the island of → Cythera, not far from a shrine to Athena, supposedly built by Agamemnon (Paus. 3,22,10). In the 'Odyssey' (Hom. Od. 3,282) he is called → Phrontis; however, this person was buried on Cape Sunium.   RA.MI.

Cinaethon (Κιναίθων; *Kinaíthōn*). Epic poet from Sparta, thought to have lived in the 7th or 6th cent. BC. Nothing of his works survives in the original, but testimonia indicate that their basic characteristic was the representation of genealogies. A reference in the *Tabulae Iliacae* names C. as the author of an *Oedipodea*. Jer. Chron. 4,2, names him also as the author of a *Telegonia*, but traditionally this epic poem is associated with Eugammon. It is uncertain whether C. also wrote an epic on Heracles; an even more dubious claim, found in a scholion to Eur. Tro. 821, concerns C.'s authorship of the *Ilias Mikra* (→ Epic cycle).

Editions: PEG I 115–117; EpGF 92f., 142. Bibliography: U.v. Wilamowitz, Homer. Untersuchungen, 1884, 348f.; A. Rzach, s.v. Kinaithon, RE 11, 462f.   E.V.

Cincinnatus Roman cognomen ('curlyhead') of Cn. → Manlius C. (*cos.* in 480 BC) and especially occurring in the Gens Quinctia; attested between around 460 and 360 BC, originally used to differentiate the brothers L. → Quinctius C. (*dictator* in 458 BC) and T. Quinctius Capitolinus Barbatus, then apparently passed down in the family. There must have been a patrician bearer of the name as late as the 1st cent. AD (Suet. Cal. 35,1).

Kajanto, Cognomina, 223.   K.-L.E.

Cincius Name of a plebeian family that gained prominence during the Second Punic War (Schulze, 266).
K.-L.E.

[1] C., L. Antiquarian author probably of the late Republican period (1st cent. BC; since [6] differentiated from the historian L.C.Alimentus). Seven works of

grammarian, antiquarian and legal content are known from quotes in Festus, Gellius and others (fragments: [1. 1,252ff.; 2. 71ff.]): *De verbis priscis, De fastis, De comitiis, De consulum potestate, De officio iurisconsulti* (at least two vols.), *De re militari* (6 vols.: Gell. NA 16,4,6), *Mystagogicon libri* (at least two vols.; maybe a periegesis of the City of Rome). Livy's reference (7,3,7) to the *clavus annalis* probably pertained to this last work (HRR 1, p. CIX; [3; 4. 247] but see [5. 320]).

1 F.P. BREMER, Iurisprudentia antehadriana, 1896 (repr. 1985)   2 GRF   3 J.HEURGON, L. Cincius et la loi du *clavus annalis*, in: Athenaeum 42, 1964, 432–37   4 E.RAWSON, Intellectual Life in the Roman Republic, 1985, 247f.   5 G.P. VERBRUGGHE, L. Cincius Alimentus, in: Philologus 126, 1982, 316–323   6 M.HERTZ, De Luciis Cinciis, 1842.

SCHANZ/HOSIUS 1, 174ff.   W.K.

[2] C. Alimentus, L. Roman senator and historian. In 210 BC as *praet.* in Sicily (Liv. 26,28,3; [11]), there also employed as promagistrate in 209 to protect recently acquired Syracuse (Liv. 27,7,12; 27,8,16). In 208 unsuccessfully besieged Locri in South Italy, which had been occupied by the Carthaginians (Liv. 27,28,13–17) and shortly afterwards was part of a Senate delegation to the consul T. Quinctius Crispinus (Liv. 27,29,4). He was captured by the Carthaginians (probably towards the end of the Second Punic War) and there, according to his own statements, had conversations with → Hannibal (Liv. 21,38,3–5). After the end of the war (?) he composed a history of Rome in Greek that probably covered the period from the city's beginnings to the end of the war with Hannibal. Despite closely following his predecessor → Fabius [I 35] Pictor (HRR fr. 3; 5) he used his own approaches in several questions (e.g. dating the founding of Rome to 729/8 BC; tale of Sp. Maelius). Fragments: HRR 1, 40–43 (too restrictive) and FGrH 810.

B.W. FRIER, Libri Annales Pontificum Maximorum, 1979, 238f.; SCHANZ/HOSIUS 1, 174f.; G.P. VERBRUGGHE, L.C. Alimentus, in: Philologus 126, 1982, 316–323.   W.K.

[3] C. Alimentus, C. Probably a brother of C. [2], went to P. Scipio in Sicily with a Senate commission as a people's tribune in 204 BC; he was the originator of the *lex Cincia de donis et muneribus* (Cic. Cato 10 etc.) supported by Fabius Cunctator, which prohibited honoraria for *advocati* and also restricted extraordinary gifts (Roman Statutes 2, 1996, no. 47). In 193 he was battling the Ligurians as a *praefectus* (Liv. 34,56,1).   K.-L.E.

[4] C. Faliscus. Roman actor from Falerii (probably 2nd half of the 2nd cent. BC), who according to Don. de comoedia 6,3 introduced masks to Roman comedy. Diverging information in [1].

1 C.SAUNDERS, The introduction of masks on the Roman stage, in: AJPh 32, 1911, 58–73.

H.LEPPIN, Histrionen, 1992.   H.BL.

Cineas (Κινέας; *Kinéas*).

[1] C. of Konde, king (*basileús*) of the Thessalians, in 511 BC offered military help in the form of 1,000 Thessalian horsemen to the Athenian tyrant → Hippias [1] when he was threatened by the Spartans, and defeated them at Phalerum (Hdt. 5,63f.; [Aristot.] Ath. pol. 19,5).   B.P.

[2] The Thessalian C. (about 350–277 BC), diplomat of king → Pyrrhus, supposedly conquered more cities by the word than he — Pyrrhus — conquered by the sword (Plut. Pyrrhus 14,3). As an Epicurean he supposedly advised Pyrrhus against a war of conquest in Italy and apparently demonstrated the senselessness of an unlimited desire for conquest (ibid. 14,4–14). C. was sent ahead to Italy to prepare disembarkation in Tarent (ibid. 15,1; 16,1). Many ancient, usually pro-Roman, sources report his unsuccessful negotiations with the Romans after Pyrrhus' victories at Heraclea and Ausculum. C. was considered an expert on the Roman aristocracy; already after a day in Rome he greeted senators and equestrians by name (ibid. 18,4–7; Plin. HN 7,88) and allegedly called the Roman Senate a '→ synhedrion of kings' (ibid. 19,6; App. Samn. 10,2–3; Eutr. 2,13,2–3). In 278 C. negotiated with the towns of Sicily (Plut. Pyrrhus 22,4–5).

C., a student of → Demosthenes [2], also distinguished himself as the epitomator of the military treatises of Aeneas [2] Tacticus and as the author of a history of Thessaly (FGrH 603 T 1–3 and F 1–2).

P.E. GAROUFALIAS, Pyrrhus, King of Epirus, 1979; P. LÉVÊQUE, Pyrrhos, 1957.   J.E.

[3] Son of Dositheus [4] (PP I/VIII 249 etc.), father of Berenice (PP III 5060)? In 177/6–170/69 BC priest of the royal cult in Ptolemais; in 173 documented as an eponymous officer. C. played an important role in 169 in the → *synhédrion* of Ptolemy VI. PP II/VIII 1926?; III/IX 5169; VI 14610.

F.WALBANK, A Historical Commentary on Polybius 3, 1979, 353f.   W.A.

Cinerary Urn see → Urn

Cinesias (Κινησίας; *Kinēsías*). Athenian dithyrambic poet, whose creative period ranged from *c.* 425 to 390 BC. His father Meles (Pl. Grg. 501e–502a) is referred to in Pherecrates' *Ágrioi* (PCG VII 6, cf. Aristoph. Av. 766) as the worst kitharode imaginable. IG II² 3028 of the early 4th cent. BC preserves fragments of a dedication by a victorious *choregos* of a choir under C.'s direction. In 394/3 BC, in his function as → *bouleutés*, C. succeeded in his proposition to the people's assembly (IG II² 18) of honouring Dionysius I of Syracuse. Lysias (Ath. 551d–552f) attacked him in his speech in defence of Phanias, against whom C. had filed a charge of unlawfulness (*graphè paranómōn*).

C. was a favourite target for mockery by comic poets. Pherecrates in his *Cheírōn* has Music accusing him as one amongst others responsible for the decline of the → dithyrambus (PCG VII 155; cf. Pl. Grg. 501e–502a); Strattis wrote an entire comedy on C. (PCG VII 14–22), and Aristophanes, too, has him appear as a character in Av. 1372–1409, who wants to gather 'air-whisked preludes in the clouds' (→ Anabole), while delivering an example of his art. C. was also pilloried because of his sickliness and gauntness. In the *Gērytádēs*, Aristophanes numbers him amongst those emaciated people who had been sent by the poets into the underworld for a visit to Hades (PCG III.2 156); the same emaciation also seems ideal for flying (Aristoph. Ran. 1437; cf. Aristoph. Av. 1378). In Aristoph. Eccl. 328–330 it is mentioned that C. in an attack of diarrhoea tainted another man's tunic yellow. Ran. 366 (cf. schol.) is also a possible allusion to this incontinence, with C.'s reputation of godlessness enabling Aristophanes to portray this physical weakness as a deliberate act of sacrilege. In *Lysistrátē*, C. has to lend his name to Myrrhine's ridiculous husband. No fragments of C. himself have survived, but it is reported that Asclepius in a dithyramb of the same name restores Hippolytus to life and for this deed is killed by Zeus' thunderbolt (PMG 774–776).   E.R.

Cingetorix Celtic composite name, 'Warrior King' [1. 73–74; 2. 172].
[1] A pro-Roman chief of the → Treveri, who fought for the tribal leadership against his father-in-law → Indutiomarus. Despite initial successes of C. and his followers, Indutiomarus was able to have him declared a public enemy in 54 BC and to confiscate his estates. After the Treveri's defeat and Indutiomarus' death in 53 BC, Caesar rewarded C. for his loyalty by granting him the highest rank in the tribe (Caes. B Gall. 5,3,2–5; 5,4,3; 5,6,3; 5,57,2; 6,8,9).

1 EVANS 2 SCHMIDT.

H. HEINEN, Trier und das Trevererland in röm. Zeit, 1985, 23–25.

[2] One of four kings of Cantium (Kent) who, by order of → Cassivellaunus, attacked the Roman naval camp in their territory in the summer of 54 BC. The failure of this combined attack led to the stop of British resistance to Caesar's expeditionary force (Caes. B Gall. 5,22).

S. FRERE, Britannia, ²1978, 52–53.   W.SP.

Cinginnia Lusitanian settlement of unknown location. Val. Max. 6,4,1 reports an incident when, during his campaign of 136 BC, D. Iunius Brutus offered a large amount of gold to the besieged inhabitants of C., if they capitulated.

TOVAR 3, 270.   P.B.

Cingius Severus, C. *Cos. suff.* before 183, as he probably is identical to the *curator aedium sacrarum* in CIL VI 36874 (in 183 BC). If his proconsulate in Africa

(Tert. Scap. 4,3) fell into the year 190/191 (ILAfr. 265 [1. 864ff.]), he was already *suff.* in about 175. After → Commodus' death, he as *pontifex* demanded the destruction of all his statues (SHA Comm. 20,3ff.). Executed by Septimius Severus (SHA Sev. 13,9; PIR² C 735).

1 C. LETTA, in: Latomus 54, 1995.   W.E.

Cingonius Varro Senator. After the murder of the *praef. urbi* Pedanius Secundus in AD 61 he applied to have P.'s freedmen only banned from Italy (Tac. Ann. 14,45,2). He composed a speech to the praetorians for Nymphidius Sabinus; executed by Galba (Plut. Galba 14f.; Tac. Hist. 1,6,1.37,3; PIR² C 736). According to [1. 382] he may have been from the Transpadana.

1 SYME, RP 4.   W.E.

Cingulum
[1] Town in the → Picenum on the river Fiumicello (Musone). *Municipium* of the *tribus Velina* (Plin. HN 3,111); T. Labienus, who was from C., richly endowed the city with buildings at his own expense (Caes. B Civ. 1,15,2). Monuments: remains on the terrace of Borgo San Lorenzo under the modern Cingoli (Macerata); *opus reticulatum* walls, remains of a temple in the church; aqueduct (restored by Hadrian). The territory of C. extended to the mountain of the same name (Str. 5,2,10; possibly the modern Monte Cingulo).

P. L. DALL'AGLIO, Considerazioni storicotopografiche, in: C. dalle origini al sec. XVI. Atti XIX Conv. Studi Maceratesi, 1983, 1986, 55–73; N. ALFIERI, Labieno, C. e l'inizio della guerra civile, in: Id., 111–130.   G.U.

[2] see → Belt

Cinna
[1] (Κίννα, also Κίνα; *Kínna, Kína*). Town in the province of Galatia, modern Karahamzalı; in Antonine times (2nd cent. AD), the district of Proseilemmene was organized as a municipality (→ Proseilemmenitai); attested as a diocese of Galatia I possibly as early as AD 325, then into the 12th cent. AD.

BELKE, 198; MITCHELL 1, 96; K. STROBEL, Galatien und seine Grenzregionen, in: E. SCHWERTHEIM (ed.), Forsch. in Galatien (Asia Minor Stud. 12), 1994, 59.   K.ST.

[2] Cognomen (meaning uncertain) in the families of the → Cornelii and the → Helvii. On the poet C. see Helvius.

KAJANTO 106.   K.-L.E.

Cinnabar (κιννάβαρι/*kinnábari*, Lat. *minium*) is a mineral of red to brownish-red colour (mercury sulphide, HgS), mostly found in sedimental stone in the vicinity of volcanic activity. → Theophrastus, who provides a detailed description of cinnabar, distinguishes between natural and man-made cinnabar and cites Spain and Colchis as places of origin (Theophr. De lapidibus 58–60 EICHHOLZ).

According to → Plinius [1], who refers to Theophrastus, it was Callias [5] who supposedly discovered cinnabar in the → Laurium district towards the end of the 5th cent. BC; Pliny also mentions other cinnabar deposits in Spain, Colchis, and Ephesus (Plin. HN 33,113 f.). The Romans relocated the workshops from Ephesus to Rome, also processing there cinnabar from Spain. The cinnabar processing workshop in Rome was supposedly located near the temples of Flora and Quirinus (Vitr. De arch. 7,9,4). In one year, about 2,000 Roman pounds (c. 655 kg) were mined near Sisapo (cf. Str. 3,2,3) in the Baetica and subsequently taken to Rome. The price was fixed at 70 HS per pound; cinnabar extraction lay in the hands of a societas, accused by Pliny of adulterating the mineral with admixtures in order to maximize its profits (Plin. HN 33,118–120).

In Greece, cinnabar was used as a pigment for white-ground lekythoi (› lēkythos [1]), in early Rome to paint the statue of Jupiter on holidays and to colour the face of a triumphant military commander (→ Triumph); Pliny compares these traditions, which appear old-fashioned to him, with the customs of the Ethiopian peoples (Plin. HN 33,111–112). When cinnabar was used in → wall paintings, it had to be protected with a wax coating to prevent discolouration (Vitr. De arch. 7,9,2 f.).

→ Mining; → Metallurgy

1 F. BENTLEY, Poisons, Pigments and Metallurgy, in: Antiquity 45, 1971, 138–140   2 BLÜMNER, Techn. 4, 488–495   3 C. DOMERGUE, Les mines de la péninsule ibérique dans l'antiquité romaine, 1990   4 J. F. HEALY, Mining and Metallurgy in the Greek and Roman World, 1978, 190–192.   J. M. A.-N.

Cinnamon (κιννάμωμον/kinnámōmon, κασσία/kassía; Lat. cinnamomum, -a, cinnamum, cas(s)ia). In antiquity as now, the aromatic bark of various varieties of the cinnamon bush (esp. C. zeylanicum Br., C. cassis Br., C. Burmanni Bl.) was dried and sold in the form of rolled sticks. The → Phoenicians passed the knowledge (Hdt. 3,111) on to the Greeks, but the spice's real origin from south or south-eastern Asia (→ India II.) remained unknown. Thus it was generally assumed that cinnamon grew in the south-west of the Arabian peninsula and the opposing shores of eastern Africa (→ kinnamōmophóros chóra). Fabulous accounts took the place of authentic descriptions of the appearance of the bush (Hdt. 3,110 f.; Plin. HN 12,89–94; Arr. Anab. 7,20, even Theophr. Hist. pl. 9,5,1 f.). This was further aided by the name cas(s)ia which applied to a number of different plants. Dioscorides (1,13 WELLMANN = 1,12 BERENDES) was the first to provide an accurate and detailed description of eight different kinds of cassia bark. Cinnamon was used to aromatize sacrificial fires and smoke (Ov. Fast. 3,731), as an addition to perfumes and ointments, but predominantly in medicine as an

astringent and laxative. For that, bark, leaves, and fruits were used in various medicinal preparations for humans as well as animals. With the exception of wine (Theophr. De odoribus 32; Plin. HN 14, 107), cinnamon was not used for the flavouring of food in antiquity.

→ Spices

F. OLCK, s. v. Zimt, RE 3, 1638–1650.   C. HÜ.

Cinolis (Κίνωλις, also Κίναλις, Κιμωλίς; Kínōlis, Kínalis, Kimōlís). Small reloading point (empórion) on the Paphlagonian Black Sea coast between → Abonutichus and → Sinope, a more exact location according to the periploi (Arr. Peripl. p. eux. 14; Peripl. m. eux. 21) and Ptol. 5,4,2; possibly the modern Ginolu.

W. RUGE, s.v. Kimolis, RE 11, 435.   C.MA.

Cinyps River, discharging into the sea 18 km southeast of → Leptis Magna, modern Oued Caam. Source references: Hdt. 4,175; 198; Verg. G. 3,311–313; Mela 1,37; Plin. HN 5,27; Ptol. 4,3,13; 20 (probably not 4,6,11); Tab. Peut. 7,3f.; Vibius Sequester, Geographica 147 RIESE; Geogr. Rav. 38f.; Thgn. 2,98 CRAMER; Suda s.v. Κινύφειος. Probably towards the end of the 6th cent., → Dorieus [1], son of the Spartan king Anaxandridas, founded an → apoikía at the mouth of the C. However, its citizens could only hold on to their position for two years, when they were forced by the Lybian Macae and their allies, the Carthaginians, to return to Sparta (Hdt. 5,42). In consequence, this defeat of the Spartans brought to a halt any further Greek expansion on African soil. The ruins of the Spartan apoikía were still visible in the 4th cent. BC (Ps.-Scyl. 109, GGM I 85).

J. DESANGES, Catalogue des tribus africaines ..., 1962, 87; HUSS, 73f.; H. KEES, s.v. K., RE 11, 483f.; P. TROUSSET, s.v. Cinyps, EB 13, 1961f.   W.HU.

Cinyras (Κινύρας, Kinýras). Mythic founder of the temple of → Aphrodite of Paphus, and progenitor of the priestly family of the Cinyradae, who shared the leadership of the cult together with the Tamiradae family (whose ancestor, the Cilician seer Tamiras, C. had introduced), but later presided alone over the worship and oracle (Tac. Hist. 2,3). C. is connected with → Apollo (Pind. Pyth. 2,15), which indicates the role of singers in the cult. He is often regarded as a son of Apollo; but it is also said that he had emigrated from Assyria, and married Metharme, the daughter of Pygmalion (Apollod. 3,181). He is the father of a number of daughters, who came into conflict with Aphrodite; the best known is the incestuous love relationship between Smyrna and her father, out of which → Adonis was born (Ov. Met. 10,270–502, cf. Antoninus Liberalis 34); however, Adonis can also be considered to be the legitimate son (Apollod. 3,182). He lost his life through suicide on account of the incest (Hyg. Fab. 242) or because he challenged Apollo to a competition in the arts (Eust. 776,10; 827,34).

C. is already named in Hom. Il. 22,20f. as a Cypriot, who gave a splendid suit of armour to → Agamemnon [1]; later authors embellished this into a meeting, or even into a war between Agamemnon and C. In ancient poetry he is one of the rich oriental kings (Tyrtaeus 12,6, cf. Pind. Pyth. 2,15). His ties with Cyprus and similarly the interaction with Greece are old; later his connection with the Orient is emphasized, by making him an Assyrian and deriving his name from a Semitic root (schol. Hom. Il. 11,20). The story that C. sent Agamemnon clay ships probably reflects the significance of the large-scale Cyprian terracotta sculpture (Eust. re Hom. Il. 11,20; [2]).

1 M. L. WEST, The East Face of Helicon, 1997, 628f.
2 A. T. REYES, Archaic Cyprus. A Study of the Textual and Archaeological Evidence, 1994, 32. F.G.

Cippus As a stone monument with or without inscription, the cippus was used in particular for territorial delineation. Made as a free-standing sculpture, it marked burial sites and was linked as reference to the dead to magical ideas and should not be confused with steles. The basic form was phallic, 30–50 cm high and it was represented in diverse ways especially in Etruria (→ Etruscan Archaeology). Mostly onions, spheres or eggs top a pillar or cylinder. Special regional types in the 6th cent. BC are warrior heads (Orvieto) and cubes in relief with buds above them (Chiusi). In the 4th–3rd cents. BC women's burials were provided with a house-shaped cippus (Caere), and the first stylized portraits appeared (Arnth Paipnas in Tarquinia) and vegetable cippi with inscriptions (Perugia). From the 3rd cent. BC, in large numbers in the 1st cent. BC/1st cent. AD, the decoration showed Greek influence in all cippi along the Adriatic coast and in the rest of Italy. The rich house-shaped types of the Middle Italian cippus borrow from urns; pine cones, foliate plants or eggs top pillars with bucrania (Palaestrina). The so-called 'Liburnian cippus' on the Adriatic coast are cylindrical in shape with a scaled spherical top. Special forms are disc-shaped *cippi* with faceless heads (Campania) and *cupa*, lying barrels (Sardinia, North Africa, Hispania).

M. BLUMHOFER, Etruskische Cippi, 1993; S. DIEBNER, Cippi carsulani, in: ArchCl 38/40, 1986/88, 35–66; H. VON HESBERG, P. ZANKER (ed.), Röm. Gräberstraßen. Kolloquium München 1985, 1987; P. PENSABENE, Sulla tipologia e il simbolismo dei cippi funerari a pigna con corona di foglie d'acanto di Palestrina, in: ArchCl 34, 1982, 38–97; O. W. v. VACANO, s.v. *cippus*, LAW, 634f.
R.N.

Circe (Κίρκη, *Kírkē*, Lat. Circe, Circa). Immortal (Hom. Od. 12,302) goddess, with the gift of language (ibid. 10,136) and a nymph (ibid. 10,543), daughter of Helios and of the → Oceanid Perse(is), sister of → Aeetes (ibid. 10,135ff.; Hes. Theog. 956f.; Apollod. 1,83), of → Perses (Apollod. 1,147) and → Pasiphae (Apollod. 3,7), by Odysseus, she is the mother of → Agrius and Latinus (Hes. Theog. 1011ff.) as well as → Cassiphone (Lycoph. 808 with schol.). According to Diodorus (4,45,3ff.), C. is the daughter of Aeetes and → Hecate, sister of → Medea, wife of the king of the Sarmates; she poisons him and flees to Italy. In the myth of the → Argonauts, C. originally came from the west; she purifies → Jason and → Medea following the murder of → Apsyrtus ([1. 116]; Apollod. 1,134; Apoll. Rhod. 4,659ff. [2. 429]), which rules out a liaison between Jason and C. (and C. as a guide and parallel to Phineus: [3. 97ff., 112ff.]) [5. 3f.].

Homer places C. in the east because her niece Medea had been abducted a generation earlier by the Argonauts, and gives her the island of Aeaea (Hom. Od. 12,3f.), which he shapes from → Aea [5. 236, 247], in conformity with Medea. Here C. dwells in a fairy-tale countryside appropriate to the plot of the epic [6. 107ff.; 7. 134ff.] with serving women (Hom. Od. 10,348ff.) in a castle surrounded by a forest; with her magic she transforms the party of → Odysseus' companions led by → Eurylochus, through a poisoned drink and a blow from a staff, into swine, though they retain their human intelligence. When her magical arts fail to work on Odysseus, who was warned by Hermes and had defended himself with the magical herb moly, she realizes that he is the person who according to Hermes will conquer her; she invites him into her bed, but Odysseus only gets into it after she swears an oath not to harm him. Nevertheless, before he touches any of her food, [8] he demands the release of his companions from the magical spell. After one year's stay, the fighters demand to be released, which C. grants without dissent (Hom. Od. 10,133–574; Ov. Met. 14,243–309). Prior to this, at C.'s behest, Odysseus visits → Hades, in order to obtain advice from → Teiresias about the next stage of the journey (Hom. Od. 11), about which C. herself then gives more detailed information prior to releasing Odysseus with a favourable wind (Hom. Od. 12,1–150). In Hesiod (Theog. 1011ff.) C. is already living in the west again, where the sons of C. and Odysseus rule over the Tyrsenians, (Italy, → Circeii, Verg. Aen. 7,10ff. [2. 428ff.]; Ov. Met. 14,348). According to Nostoi fr. dub. 16 BERNABÉ or Telegonie F fr. 2 EpGF → Telemachus marries C.; → Telegonus, her son by Odysseus, who had unknowingly killed his father, however, marries → Penelope (cf. Apollod. epit. 7,36f.) [9]. According to Lycophron (808ff.), the dying Odysseus foresees the death of C. through Telemachus, as well as the latter's death through Cassiphone, Odysseus' and C.'s daughter. C. transforms her admirer → Calchus into a pig (Parthenius 12 MythGr), and out of jealousy she transforms the beloved of → Glaucus [1] — → Scylla — into a sea-monster (Ov. Met. 13,904ff.; 14,1ff.) and → Picus, who spurned her, into a woodpecker (Ov. Met. 14,313ff. [2. 436ff.]).

Behind the C. figure of the 'Odyssey' (and previously of the 'Argonautica') is a sorceress or witch from popular belief [10. 4ff.; 11. 49ff.; 12. 31ff.; 13], with parallels in other cultural groups (Near East: Ištar, Nergal/Ereškigal [12. 61ff.]) and connections with → Persephone [12. 127ff.; 2. 428]. A reflection of her originally elemental nature is the striking emphasis on her linguistic talents (Hom. Od. 10,136 [14. 80f.]). On the difference between C. (fantastic, legend) and → Calypso (epic, Homer's invention) cf. [1. 115ff.; 15. 77ff.]; on her further life and the history of the motif [16]; C. in art [17; 18].

1 U. v. WILAMOWITZ-MOELLENDORFF, Homer. Unt., 1884   2 C. SEGAL, Circean Temptations, in: TAPhA 99, 1968, 419–442   3 K. MEULI, Odyssee und Argonautika, 1921, repr. 1974   4 G. BECK, Beobachtungen zur K.-Episode in der Odyssee, in: Philologus 109, 1965, 1–29   5 U. v. WILAMOWITZ-MOELLENDORFF, Hell. Dichtung 2, 1924, ²1962   6 M. TREU, Von Homer zur Lyrik, 1955, ²1968   7 W. ELLIGER, Die Darstellung der Landschaft in der griech. Dichtung, 1975   8 A. DYCK, The Witch's Bed But Not Her Breakfast, in: RhM 124, 1981, 196–198   9 B. MADER, s.v. K., LFE 2,1425f.   10 L. RADERMACHER, Die Erzählungen der Odyssee, SAWW, 1915, 178.1   11 D.L. PAGE, Folktales in Homer's Odyssey, 1973   12 G. CRANE, Calypso, 1988   13 A. HEUBECK, A. HOEKSTRA, A Comm. on Homer's Odyssey 2, 1989, 50ff.   14 F. DIRLMEIER, Die 'schreckliche' Kalypso, 1967, in: Id., Ausgewählte Schriften zu Dichtung und Philos. der Griechen, 1970, 79–84   15 K. REINHARDT, Die Abenteuer der Odyssee, 1942/1948, in: Id., Trad. und Geist, 1960, 47–124   16 E. KAISER, Odyssee-Szenen als Topoi 2. Der Zauber K.s und Kalypsos, in: MH 21, 1964, 197–213   17 F. CANCIANI, s.v. K., LIMC 6.1, 48–59   18 M. LE GLAY, s.v. Circe, LIMC 6.1, 59f.   P.D.

Circeii Town (possibly Volscian) on the *mare Tyrrhenum* below the *mons Circeius*, on the southern border of Latium, modern San Felice C. (Latina province). → Tarquinius Superbus supposedly founded C. and Signia as a colony but the *coloni* were expelled by → Coriolanus (Liv. 1,56,3; 2,39). In 393 BC C. was a *colonia Latina*. After an uprising C. joined the → Latin League (338 BC). The town declined after the Second Punic War; after 89 BC it was a *municipium* (Cic. Fin. 4,7) of the *tribus Pomptina*. Its oysters were famous (Hor. Sat. 2,4,33) and Lepidus was exiled here. Archaeological monuments: villas of Tiberius and Domitian; remains on the Monte della Citadella: *opus polygonale* walls (cf. Signia), buildings in *opus reticulatum*; amphitheatre. Inscriptional attestations: CIL X, 6422–34.

G. LUGLI, C., 1928; S. AURIGEMMA, A. AURIGEMMA, C., 1957; M. FORA, Testimonianze epigrafiche, in: Miscellanea greca e romana 16, 1991, 191–216.   G.U.

Circius This name corresponds to the north-north-westerly wind Κιρίας blowing from Cape Circe to Cumae and interfering with the Phocians' navigation from Sicily to Massalia. As an originally local wind of Gallia narbonensis (Plin. HN 2,121) that reached all the way to Ostia, it was later included in the wind rose (not yet in Vitruvius).
→ Winds

W. BÖKER, s.v. Winde, RE 8 A, 2306ff.   C.HÜ.

Circles, literary When referring to antiquity, the modern term 'literary circle' describes the Maecenatic patronage of contemporary literature and the encouragement of young poets; however, generalizations and exaggerations (in the sense of the middle-class reading circles of the 19th cent.) have to be avoided (cf. gen. → Literary activity II.). Initially, these circles signify an acculturative boost following the conquest of Greece in the early 2nd cent. BC. → *Nobiles* such as M. → Fulvius [I 15] Nobilior [1. 536 f.] and L. → Aemilius [I 32] Paullus [1. 480–483] demonstrated their interest in (Greek) culture when, following the tradition of Hellenistic → rulers, they adorned themselves with the company of poets (→ Ennius [1]) or looted artefacts which they had transferred — even entire → libraries –, or when they could expect panegyric › *praetextae* performed at their funeral games (→ Dead, cult of the) (e.g. Ennius' *Ambracia* for Fulvius, Pacuvius' *Paulus* for Aemilius; at the funeral games of the latter, Terentius' [III 1] *Hecyra* and *Adelphoi* were performed once again). The term 'circle' is used in modern research (mediating between idealization and scepticism [1. 87 f., 483–487]) in the case of → Cornelius [I 70] Scipio the Younger (→ Scipionic circle), inspired by the (anachronistically depicted) interlocutors in Cicero's *De re publica*. In this instance, however, the focus is on education and interest in Greek philosophy and historiography, not specifically on poetry. Terence (see above) belonged to the generation of Scipio's father; the anti-optimate gossip in Suetonius' biography of him is altogether unbelievable [2] (cf. [1. 490]).

Thus it signifies a pivotal turning-point when Roman *nobiles* such as Q. → Lutatius [3] Catulus [1. 447–453] maintained friendly relations with both Greek and Latin poets and even wrote poetry themselves. In the case of Catulus, the term 'circle' may thus be justified (against exaggeration [1. 451–453]). Alongside these private circles there existed during the Republican period the → *collegium* [2] *poetarum*, which (probably from 179 BC) met in the *Templum Herculis Musarum* in Rome; it provided an (also public) platform or trial for the self-confidence of poets, e.g. in the erection of a monumental statue (of Accius) and the selection of plays for the → *ludi* and not least in 'open' poetry competitions (Hor. Epist. 2,2,92–105) (→ Competitions, artistic II. B.).

The activity of the literary circle repeatedly mentioned by Horatius [7] (e.g. Hor. Sat. 1,4,23–25 and 71–76; Hor. Epist. 1,19,37 f.) is symptomatic for the cultural peak of the Augustan age, in which competition with Greek literature resulted in a new poetological and poetic self-consciousness. Thus quite a sizeable public audience assembled to listen to → recitals of poems and the historical opus of → Asinius [I 4] Pollio (Sen. Controv. 4, pr. 2). In the entourage of M. → Valerius [II 16] Messalla Corvinus, one finds poets such as his niece → Sulpicia [2] or → Tibullus, → Ovidius, → Valgius [2] Rufus and → Aemilius [II 10] Macer, and finally the authors of → Catalepton 9 and the → Panegyricus Messallae (cf. [2. 1677–1680]). The focus of the central figure on the personal, on love poetry, is noticeable; this is reminiscent of Lutatius Catulus. Valgius also appears on the list (Hor. Sat. 1,10,81–84, set apart from Pollio and Messalla) of the Maecenatic circle (cf. → Maecenas [2] C.; [3. 70–83]), unmistakable as the potential author of an epic on Augustus, whereas in the circle on the whole representatives of high poetry (→ Varius [I 2] Rufus, → Vergilius [4], → Horatius [7]) prevail. In general, Horace paints a multifaceted picture of this circle as a fellowship of friends of different ranks, and also as the cradle of Augustan literature.

Finally, in the Imperial period, the emperors' interest in the political importance of the → ludi (e.g. the Capitoline agon of → Domitianus [1]) or in their self-presentation (in its literal meaning; e.g. the → Neronia) stifled the inclination to individual patronage within smaller circles (cf. → Competitions, artistic II. B.). An exception may have been Emperor Hadrian, whose wide cultural interest focussed primarily on philosophers and grammarians, but without excluding poets (SHA Hadr. 16). In the case of → Plinius [2] the Younger, the term 'cercle littéraire' has been used with some justification; this circle is evident in his letters, and, concluding from e.g. the scenarios of Gellius' [6] Noctes Atticae, certainly also met in his villas (e.g. Gell. NA 1,2,1; 19,5).
→ Literary activity; → Competitions, artistic II. B.

1 W. SUERBAUM, Q. Lutatius Catulus, in: HLL 1, 2002, 447–553   2 A. VALVO, Messalla Corvino negli studi più recenti, in: ANRW II 30.3, 1983, 1663–1680
3 E. FANTHAM, Roman Literary Culture from Cicero to Apuleius (1996)   4 A.-M. GUILLEMIN, Pline et la vie littéraire de son temps, 1929.

J.-L. FERRARY, Philhellénisme et impérialisme, 1988; B. K. GOLD (ed.), Literary and Artistic Patronage in Ancient Rome, 1982; K. QUINN, The Poet and His Audience in the Augustan Age, in: ANRW II 30.1, 1982, 75–180.
P. L. S.

Circulus lacteus see → Constellations

Circumcelliones The rebellious movement of the Circumcelliones (according to Augustine, from circum cellas vagare) spread in Numidia around AD 340 in the region of the Donatist Church [1]. The Circumcelliones, about whom reports first appeared around 320, were poor field workers, mainly day labourers, who had given up their work and who were initially also joined by small landowners ruined by debt. Apart from financial problems around 340, the main reason for the

movement's existence from 345 onwards was the prohibition of the Donatist Church by Emperor Constans. The Circumcelliones were incited by the Donatist bishops to perpetrate acts of terrorism against the Catholics.

It is known that there were two significant revolts of the Circumcelliones. About 340 the bands of Axido and Fasir attacked the farms of the large landowners and burnt their registers of debtors; the revolt, which went out of control, was suppressed — at the request of the Donatist bishops — by the comes Africae Taurinus. The second revolt was put down in 345/47 by the comes Silvester. The custom of seeking martyrdom through suicide then spread amongst the Circumcelliones. About 390 the Circumcelliones were exploited by the Donatist bishop Optatius of Timgad for acts of terrorism [2]. A final wave of suicides in about 411 is attested.
→ Martyrs

1 C. LEPELLEY, Les cités de l'Afrique romaine au Bas-Empire I, 1979, 91–98   2 LEPELLEY II, 472–474

E. TENGSTRÖM, Donatisten und Katholiken, 1964; C. LEPELLEY, Iuvenes et circoncelliones: les derniers sacrifices humains de l'Afrique romaine, in: AntAfr 15, 1980, 261–271
J.S.

Circumcisio Circumcision (Hebrew mûla, mîla; Greek περιτομή; peritomé; Latin circumcisio), the removal of the foreskin of the male member, was originally an apotropaic rite widespread amongst western Semitic peoples that was performed at the onset of puberty or prior to the wedding (cf. Exodus 4,26 Is. 9,24f; Jos. 5,4–9; Hdt. 2,104,1–3). As this custom was not known in Mesopotamia, circumcision became a distinguishing feature between the exiled people and the Babylonians during the time of Babylonian exile (597–538 BC); it counteracted assimilation and in a religious sense could be interpreted as a sign of the union between God and the descendants of → Abraham (cf. Gen. 17). While Gen. 34,24 and Jos. 5,6f tell of the circumcision of adults, the circumcision of male infants on the 8th day after birth became generally accepted during this period (cf. Lev. 12,4; Gen. 17,12 etc.; rabbinic evidence: bShab 132b; 135b; bPes 4a; bYom 28b and passim).

In the Hellenistic-Roman period, circumcision was considered as the nota Iudaica (sign of Jewishness) par exellence (cf. Tac. Hist. 5,1,5: ut diversitate noscantur). In contrast to the conservative religious circles, for whom circumcision was a sign of faithfulness to the God of Israel and his law, and who were even prepared for a martyr's death, the Jews who belonged to reform groups tried to reverse it surgically (epispasmós, cf. 1 Macc. 1,15f.). According to Aelius Spartianus (SHA Hadr. 14) the emperor's ban on circumcision even triggered the 2nd Jewish revolt (132–135); the short note according to which many in this period became recircumcized (tShab 15 [16],9), demonstrates the plurality of Palestinian Judaism in late antiquity in regard to circumcision. In anti-Jewish polemics, circumcision was frequently the butt of mockery of the Jews' 'inhuman customs' (cf. among others Str. 16,2,37; Petron. Sat. 68, 7b–8a; 102, 13; Salustius, De deis et mundo 9,5; Rut. Namat. 1,387–392).

O. BETZ, Beschneidung II. AT, Frühjudentum und NT, TRE 5, 716–722; M. STERN, Greek and Latin Authors on Jews and Judaism. Ed. with Introductions, Translations and Commentary, 3 vols., 1974, 1980 and 1984, Index s.v. C.   B.E.

Circus
I. ARCHITECTURE   II. GAMES

I. ARCHITECTURE
A. DEFINITION   B. ORIGIN   1. THE GREEK HIPPODROME   2. ETRUSCAN RACING TRACKS C. THE CIRCUS MAXIMUS AND OTHER CIRCUS BUILDINGS IN ROME   D. ITALY AND THE PROVINCES

A. DEFINITION
The circus was the biggest of all Roman places of leisure and was initially and mainly used for races with chariots drawn by teams of four or two (*quadrigae* or *bigae*). The canonical circus consisted of a long, comparatively narrow racetrack (*c.* 450 × 80 m; *arena*, from *harena*-, 'sand'), on both ends of which three cones (*metae*) on a platform served as markers for turning. The track led round a barrier that marked the central axis (*euripus*, Greek εὖριπος (*eúripos*), 'water ditch'; later also *spina*-, 'backbone, spine') and that was decorated with various monuments (including small shrines, altars, obelisks) and with the eggs and dolphins indicating the seven race rounds. On the two parallel long sides and the semicircular narrow side, the arena was surrounded by rows of seats for the audience. The audience area was built in the same manner as in the → theatres and → amphitheatres (i.e. with substructures, where necessary) and consisted of several circles which were possibly topped by a gallery. The other narrow side with the (usually 12) starting-gates (→ *carceres*) had a flat, asymmetrical arch shape so as to facilitate a staggered start. There were entrances both on the two narrow sides and on the long sides. Above the *carceres* were the boxes of the magistrates who organized the games. Close to the finishing line were the seats for the prize judges although they were also posted along the racetrack (especially at the 'critical' points, i.e. at the starting line and at the turning points). This canonical type was first developed in Rome, perhaps while reconstructing the Circus Maximus by Trajan. A well-preserved example of this type is the circus in → Leptis Magna built a little later.

B. ORIGIN
Two prototypes are usually mentioned with regard to the Roman circus, particularly for the earliest circus of all, the Circus Maximus: the Greek Hippodrome and Etruscan racing tracks.

1. THE GREEK HIPPODROME
The name comes from ἵππος (*híppos*, 'horse') and δρόμος (*drómos*, 'racing track'). There is already evidence in the 'Iliad' of horse races, for instance on the occasion of the funeral games of Patroclus. This type of sport was a fixed component of the four main athletic festivals in Greece (→ Olympia, → Delphi, → Isthmia, → Nemea) and also at many other venues. The hippodromes were, however, not permanent buildings but were erected on flat land where needed; for this purpose only one or two turning-markers (καμπτῆρες, *kamptêres*) and slopes as seating areas for the audience were necessary. Only in Olympia, where quadriga races were introduced in 680 BC, horse races in 648 and *biga* races in 408, there was a permanent hippodrome that is, however, only known through the description in Pausanias (6,20,10–21,1); the complicated starting-system (ὕσπληξ or ὕσπληγξ, *hýsplē(n)x*) is described in detail. There were no constantly available circles and protective facilities for the audience or set seats for the prize judges. In the case of hippodromes from the Hellenistic period too — likewise only known from written sources — there were no fixed buildings. The deviations from the canonical Roman circus are obvious: the Greek hippodromes were never turned into fixed architectural structures, there was no barrier in the middle, and the shape and size could vary greatly from place to place, which was also the reason why no Greek hippodromes were remodelled into standardized Roman circuses.

2. ETRUSCAN RACING TRACKS
The other precursor of the Roman circus was to be found in the Etruscan culture, the Etruscans having had horse races as early as the 6th cent. BC (see below). There had been a racing track in → Veii since the 6th cent. BC at the latest (Plut. Poblicola 13,4; Plin. HN 8,161), and this agrees very much with information in Livius that the Circus Maximus was built by the Etruscan kings Tarquinius Priscus (*c.* 600 BC; Liv. 1,35,8) and Tarquinius Superbus (late 6th cent. BC; Liv. 1,56,2). The Etruscan arenas are still less well known than the Greek hippodromes; as they were not fixed buildings, no example has been preserved. Some information can, however, be gleaned from pictorial sources. Rows of seats made of wood to provide places for the audience can be seen in paintings from the 6th cent. BC in the Tomba delle Bighe, Tarquinia (→ Necropoleis). A platform with the seats of the magistrates and prize judges (*sellae*) is represented on a → *cippus* of the 5th cent. BC from Chiusi (Palermo, MAN). These seats were probably called *fori* in Rome and put up in the Circus Maximus by the Etruscan kings (Liv. 1,35,8). Perhaps the starting- and finishing-lines were marked by a Doric column; the turning-markers were made of wood in Greece and Etruria alike.

C. THE CIRCUS MAXIMUS AND OTHER CIRCUS BUILDINGS IN ROME
The Circus Maximus was the model-shaping prototype for all further circuses and the biggest circus of all.

It existed as early as the regal period and was probably already erected by the first Etruscan king Tarquinius Priscus in conjunction with the draining of the valley between Palatine and Aventine. Further building took place throughout the entire Republican period. The *carceres* were built of wood in 329 BC (Liv. 8,20,2). Although it is frequently assumed that the barrier was built at the same time, it is only certain that it was built by the early imperial period; according to visual evidence it was not built in stone until the time of Trajan. An honorary arch (*fornix*) was built by Lucius Stertinius in 196 BC (Liv. 33,27,3–4); it may perhaps have stood at the same place on which a *fornix* in honour of Titus was built in AD 80–81 (in the *apex* of the semicircle). The eggs for counting the rounds were added when renovation was carried out later in 174 BC (Liv. 41,27,6). The monumentalization of the construction was begun by Caesar, continued by Agrippa (including the dolphins counting the rounds) and finished by Augustus. This building phase is mainly known through the description of Dionysius of Halicarnassus (Ant. Rom. 3,68,1–4) as findings from this period are lacking. Of the seats that were now put up on the two long sides and in the semicircle, two thirds continued to be of wood. A drainage ditch (*euripus*) surrounded the arena, on the one hand so as to drain the swampy land, on the other hand to protect the audience from wild animals together with a wall (*podium*) — because the circus was also used for → *munera* and → *venationes* (see below). Augustus had the first obelisk erected on the barrier (probably wooden and temporary), also a monumental *pulvinar* (R. Gest. div. Aug. 19), i.e. a shrine and a tribunal (stage) for the statues of the gods that were brought into the area as a sign of divine protection. From the *pulvinar* the emperor watched the competitions.

Parts of the complete alterations with the stucco wall and bricks undertaken under Trajan (after the Roman fire in AD 64 and a further fire shortly afterwards) are still preserved today. The Trajan circus is also represented on a fragment of the → *Forma Urbis Romae*. All circles, three in total, were now made of stone and the visitors sat in them according to their social status: the more important the person, the closer he was to the arena. Above was a gallery; the outside was divided by arcades that were topped with an attica, comparable with the → Colosseum. At least from this time onwards the building stood isolated; it was surrounded by a wide road in order to facilitate access through the vaulted entrances. The accesses led to steps and staircases as well as to shops housed on the ground floor. The Trajanic circus measured *c.* 620 × 140 m, the arena 580 × 79 m. The *spina* (*c.* 335 × 7–11 m) was finally remodelled into a fixed part, consisting of a *euripus* with several pools and fountains (perhaps above an older ditch from the regal period). The already existing statues were also supplemented by additional monuments, e.g. by a statue of Cybele on the lion. The estimate that there was seating for an audience of *c.*

150,000 is today considered more realistic than the high figures indicated in ancient sources. The Trajanic building phase of the Circus Maximus is also shown in most pictorial representations (e.g. on mosaics and coins) and influenced the circus buildings in the provinces. In the period that followed, various smaller alterations and restorations were undertaken including the erection of a further, even higher obelisk in AD 357. It was probably not until late antiquity that the towers were added beside the *carceres*. Such towers also existed at the circus of → Maxentius on the *via Appia* that was strongly influenced by the Circus Maximus. The Maxentius Circus, built together with the palace, is the only other preserved circus in Rome. The other circus buildings at Rome (the Circus Flaminius, erected in AD 220 on the southern Campus Martius, and the Circus Vaticanus or Circus Gai et Neronis, partially built over by St. Peter's Square and Cathedral, and the Circus Varianus, built by → Elagabalalus at his Villa Sessorianum) have been completely destroyed.

D. ITALY AND THE PROVINCES

In Italy there are only a few circuses outside Rome; mostly they were built at the initiative of the emperors: the circus of → Bovillae was built under Augustus and Tiberius, that of → Antium under Nero, and that of → Larium under Antoninus Pius. In North Africa and Spain the situation was comparably favourable; as horse-breeding was widespread there, relatively large numbers of circuses were built (mostly close to fairly big towns or the provincial capitals). In Spain circuses had already been built since the 1st cent. AD (in Merida and Tarragona); they were modelled on the Circus Maximus from the time of Caesar and Augustus. On the other hand, all the preserved circuses in North Africa are from the 2nd cent. AD and even later (the earliest in → Carthage and → Leptis Magna) and are based on the Trajanic Circus Maximus. In addition there were smaller circuses in the less important towns that were used intensively right through to late antiquity. In Gallia, Germania and Britannia circuses were, however, not very popular so only a few circuses are known. Apparently circuses and games were more significant in areas with pronounced Romanization. Large, monumental circuses were mostly not built there until late antiquity, frequently in conjunction with other buildings of the tetrarchs in the new residential towns (Trier and Milan), where the palace and the circus formed a unit, as in the case of the Maxentius buildings in Rome. This building pattern is also to be found in the east (e.g. → Thessaloniki, → Nicomedia, → Antioch).

Before these late circuses were built, there was another building type in the eastern provinces, as here, as opposed to in the west of the empire, chariot and horse races in the Greek style were common. Whilst the western circus kept closely to the dimensions and structures of the Circus Maximus (even if the arenas were shorter from time to time), the eastern facilities were wider in outlay, probably because of their multiple usage: they were probably also used for athletic competitions and gladiatorial games (→ Amphitheatre). Many circuses have been found in the Orient (e.g. Antioch, → Caesarea, → Gerasa, → Bostra, → Tyrus), but apart from → Gortyn on Crete, none have been discovered in Greece and Asia Minor. The eastern circuses are mostly from the 2nd and 3rd cents. AD when chariot races were experiencing a renaissance, the intensity of which increased even more in late antiquity (documented in the anonymous *Expositio Totius Mundi*). The most important circus in this part of the empire was the circus in Constantinople, probably begun under Septimius Severus and not completed until the reign of Constantine after he had elevated the town to the site of his new residence and the circus became part of the palace. This famous hippodrome continued to exist until the end of the Byzantine empire.

S. CERUTTI, The seven eggs of the Circus Maximus, in: Nikephoros 6, 1993, 167–176; F. COARELLI, Roma, Guide archeologiche Laterza 6, 1980, 327–331; HUMPHREY; Y. PORATH, Herod's 'amphitheater' at Caesarea: a multipurpose entertainment building, in: The Roman and Byzantine Near East, JRA, 14. Suppl., 1995, 15–27; J. ROUGÉ, Expositio Totius Mundi et Gentium, Sources Chrétiennes 124, 1966; T. P. WISEMAN, The Circus Flaminius, PBSR 42, 1974, 2–26.   I.N.

II. GAMES
A. SIGNIFICANCE AND DEFINITION B. ORIGIN
C. COURSE OF EVENTS D. ORIGIN, PROGRAMME
AND DEVELOPMENT E. STARS F. FACTIONES AND
FINANCING G. AUDIENCE

A. SIGNIFICANCE AND DEFINITION
Circus games have been and still are synonymous with state directed mass entertainment — according to Juvenal's expression, *panem et circenses* were the only thing the people of Rome wanted (Juv. 10,81). The circus games were considered the main attraction of Rome for the → *plebs* in Imperial times. They were despised by the intellectuals (Plin. Ep. 9,6), reviled by the Christian teachers (Tert. de spectaculis 7), but sponsored by almost all the emperors [1] and beloved of millions and copied by almost the entire Imperium Romanum [2]. For more than a millennium, circus games were held in the Circus Maximus, for the last time in January AD 550. The circus games were an integral part of the Roman state religion. They took place within the context of the *ludi publici*, the organization of which was the duty of the magistrates, initially of the aediles, and from the time of Augustus of the praetors.

In the cents. of the Roman Republic, a firm canon of annual festivals had developed that applied right into the 4th cent. AD: 1. The oldest and most revered *ludi publici* were the *ludi Romani magni* in honour of Jupiter Capitolinus. There is certainly evidence of them for the year 366 BC; they were held at the cost of the state under the leadership of two curule aediles. There is no evidence until 322 BC of them being constant annual

festivals celebrated from 4 to 19 September; the last five days were reserved for the circus games. 2. Following the model of the *ludi Romani*, the *ludi plebeii* were likewise organized in honour of Jupiter Capitolinus; there is evidence of them from 220 BC as an annual festival (festival programme: 4–17 November; the last three days were for circus games). 3. The *ludi Apollinares* were celebrated for the first time in 212 BC, and it was not until 208 BC that they were finally designated an annual festival (6–13 July, circus games only on the last day). 4. The *ludi ceriales* from 202 BC onwards as an annual festival for Ceres, Liber and Libera (12–19 April, circus games on the last day). 5. The *ludi megalenses* were celebrated from 194 BC onwards as an annual festival in honour of the mother of the gods Cybele (4–10 April, circus games on the first and last day). 6. The *ludi florales* were held from 173 BC onwards as an annual festival in honour of Flora (28 April to 3 May, circus games on the last day). However, these circus games did not consist of chariot races but still during Imperial times of *venationes* (animal hunting) and performances by animals in the Circus Maximus. Within the context of the set state worship, it was therefore guaranteed that there would be circus games on 13 days. The official festival calendar was constantly expanded by Sulla through the *ludi votivi*, so that a victory, a temple dedication, emperors' birthdays or government jubilees were celebrated (cf. Tert. De spectaculis 6). Days were always set down for circus games so that according to the calendar of Philocalus in AD 354, circus games were held on 64 out of a total of 175 → *feriae*.

B. ORIGIN
According to the thinking of the ancient world, the first duty of a founder of a political community was to correctly order the relationship with the gods. The Roman authors have therefore dated back the beginnings of the Roman festival calendar to the early monarchic period. According to Cicero (Rep. 2,12), Romulus held annual games in the circus in honour of the god → Consus. The arrangement of the festival calendar is attributed to Numa Pompilius (Cic. Rep. 2,27). The chronology of the early period was created so as to elevate the later state to mythic heights [3]. The great age of many cults that were later almost forgotten was confirmed by religious historical research: in the 3rd cent. AD, on 7 July, sacrifices were still being made to Consus on his subterranean *ad primas metas* altar (cf. Tert. De spectaculis 5). It is *communis opinio* that Consus, as can be seen from the name (derived from *condere*), was the god to whom offerings were made for the 'gathered in' earth [4]. For games and competitions at harvest festivals, the wide hollow of the valley between Palatine and Aventine was a highly suitable place. The *ludi* at the festival of Consus were, however, only a preliminary stage in the celebration of the *ludi Romani*, and their establishment in the Roman tradition is attributed to Tarquinius Superbus (Cic. Rep. 2,36,14–18). The *ludi*

Romani were the model of all later *ludi publici*. Actually the order of the circus games that was kept precise for cents. and that always constituted part of the *ludi publici* so clearly demonstrates Etruscan elements — *pompa circensis* and chariot races — that the origin of the circus games in the period of Etruscan rule is undoubted [5]. It remains uncertain at what intervals of time the *ludi Romani*, i.e. the first *ludi publici*, were held from their foundation in the 6th cent. BC to their reorganization in the 4th cent. BC.

C. COURSE OF EVENTS

The term circus encompasses the *pompa circensis* and the subsequent competitions in the Circus Maximus (→ Circus I). The *pompa circensis* raises the circus to the honourable status of a sacred act. It began on the Capitol at the Temple of Jupiter Capitolinus and went via the Forum to the Circus Maximus (Dion. Hal. Ant. Rom. 7,72), taking therefore exactly the opposite route of the triumphal marches that went via the Circus Maximus to the Forum [6]. The first circus games were probably celebrated after a triumph. Even in its later course of events, the *pompa circensis* copied the triumphal march; at its head the praetor drove the triumphal carriage (from the time of Augustus onwards, see above); he was dressed in the *tunica Iovis* like a triumphant leader (Juv. 11,193–196; 10,36–40). Over it he wore a richly draped *toga picta* [7]; on his head, supported by a slave, was the heavy *corona aurea*, and this, too, was an Etruscan relic that originally had a sacred meaning (Plin. HN 21,4; Tert. De spectaculis 7). The position of praetor was filled by the emperor or a consul when *ludi votivi* were also offered (Suet. Aug. 43,5; Juv. 10,41). In the description by Dion. Hal., Roman young people in military formation (riding and on foot) were at the head of the procession behind the Praetor's carriage. Young men followed, equipped for the weapon dance and accompanied by music; the contestants in the hippic contests with their horses and chariots and the athletes joined on. Dancers dressed as sileni and satyrs in shaggy sheepskins followed: to the sound of the flute and cithara, they performed their boisterous dances for the gods, the images of which (statues) — enthroned in richly decorated litters and carriages and surrounded by fragrant clouds of incense — formed the end and highlight of the procession. In a similar manner, groups of figures of Christ and saints, are still today, e.g. in Andalusia during the 'Semana santa', presented to the spectators in a long procession. The procession of the gods in Rome grew even longer through the cult of the emperor: Caesar's statue, even in his lifetime, was accorded a place among the gods (Suet. Iul. 76,1,9: *tensam et ferculum circensi pompa*); later this honour — posthumously only — was bestowed upon the members of the emperor's family, even women. Claudius, for example, had Livia's image presented on a carriage drawn by elephants (Suet. Claud. 11,2,3–5). The uniform ritual, repeated several times each year, bored the spectators, according to e.g. Seneca

(Controv. 1. prooem. 24,6f.); however, it was not dispensed with, for as long as polytheistic cults were practised in Rome. The procession marched the entire length of the Circus Maximus and went round the *metae* (goal or turning pillars) exactly like the races. The name of the show at the Circus Maximus was derived from this *circum metas* course of events (Varro, Ling. 5,153,3).

D. ORIGIN, PROGRAMME AND DEVELOPMENT

For Juvenal and the younger Pliny, circuses were synonymous with chariot races and the rapturous participation of the spectators in the success of charioteers, horses and party colours (see below). The programme of the circus games in the Republic and still under Augustus was more differentiated; it provided, after the *pompa*, for hippic contests of the most varied kinds, as well as athletic competitions: → footraces, → fist-fighting and → wrestling (Cic. Leg. 2,38; Dion. Hal. Ant. Rom. 7,73); several emperors (Augustus, Claudius) also allowed the presentation during the circus games of *ludi votivi* of the *lusus Troiae*, a paramilitary riders' game by young people from the most aristocratic families. Prior to the commencement of the athletic contests, women (from the beginning of the 1st cent. AD) had to leave the circus; this had been ordered by Augustus following Greek or Roman custom (Suet. Aug. 44,2,4–3,7). Tiberius was no friend of folk festivals and offered the Romans nothing beyond the statutory portion set down by the cult. He did not intervene in the traditional course of the circus games, but his successor, Emperor Caligula, who was considered a hippophile, probably did. In the four years of his reign, it is said that during the circus games horses and racing chariots dominated the circus from morning to evening, at most a *venatio* with African animals or a 'Troy game' was put in. Caligula had the athletic contests held at other open venues in Rome. They were of such little interest to him that he often did not watch them at all (Suet. Calig. 18). Claudius' preference were the gladiatorial fights; he put on various extravagant → *munera*. He did not intervene in the course of the circus games, i.e. he could not or did not want to revoke the predominance of the racing chariots in the circus. In the 14 years of his reign, a group of successful chariot drivers claimed the customary right that probably originated under Caligula (*inveterata licentia*) of annoying the populace with jokes and tricks (cf. Suet. Nero 16). This custom was forbidden by law in the first years of Nero's rule. This is not inconsistent with the fact that under Nero the chariot races were a decisive part of the circus games. In this form they fascinated contemporaries and posterity so much that they have even been made into films, e.g. in 'Ben Hur'.

Nero created a new field for the athletic contests: the → Neronia; according to the Greek model they were only to be celebrated every four years (Suet. Nero 12,3). Domitian brought this festival back to life as *certamen* (competition) in honour of Jupiter Capitolinus. The place for it was the gymnasium built by Nero, later probably the *stadium Domitiani*, today's Piazza Navona (cf. Suet. Dom. 4). From the 2nd cent. BC onwards, *venationes* took place in the circus, fights with beasts of prey of mostly African origin [8]. They were added on to the circus games on the occasion of great triumphs; the five-day *venatio* that ended Caesar's triumph in 46 BC at the Circus Maximus is famous. Augustus too gave *venationes in circo aut in foro aut in amphitheatris* (R. Gest. div. Aug. 22). Caligula added animal hunting to the programme of additional circus games. Actually, though, dangerous fights with wild animals were not part of the programme of the *ludi publici*. They were generally carried out by gladiators especially trained for them — the *bestiarii* — and this was part of the programme of a *munus*. In the towns of Campania *venationes* took place in the amphitheatre, as ultimately in Rome after the Flavian emperors had built the → Colosseum [9]. It should be noted in particular that the burning and crucifixion of Christians did not take place in the circus but in Nero's gardens (Tac. Ann. 15,44).

E. STARS

Since horse races dominated the circus, chariot drivers and horses were frequently topics of daily conversation for the Romans. Scorpus, the most successful chariot driver of the Flavian period, was praised and envied by Martial receiving everything Martial could possibly wish for: recognition, money, honorary statues all over the city, even undying fame through Martial's verse. (*clamosi gloria circi*, Mart. 10,53). Scorpus died at the age of 27 after 2,048 victories. In this way, he was the first who belonged to the top class of *miliarii*, i.e. chariot drivers with 1,000 or more victories.

There were stars of such kind in every generation; their successes have been passed down to us in well-documented form. Even in his lifetime, Publius Aelius Gutta Calpurnianus had built for himself, about the middle of the 2nd cent. [10], a monument on which were represented statues of his favourite horses with their names. In a detailed inscription (CIL VI 10047) the victories are listed: there are 1,127, divided into all four parties (see below). With Victor, a chestnut horse, Gutta was victorious 429 times for the green party. Only one horse is named the winner, the lead horse (*equus funalis*) on the left-hand side of the racing chariot, upon whose adroitness in the bend around the *metae* depended the success of a round. Obviously not every victory was considered equal. Gutta names various criteria: victory in the race *a pompa*, i.e. with horses that were still very nervous; victory *equorum anagonum*, i.e. with horses that had never before run a race. Another qualification is the (varying) number of chariots starting at the same time (4, 8, 12 or 16). Gutta once won a competition with 16 teams of horses and he won a competition with 12 teams 134 times. Some years after Gutta, Diocles was the star of the circus. His friends built a statue to him. As reported in the inscriptions on this monument (CIL XIV 2884; VI 10048), Diocles

began his career at the age of 18 and retired from the racetrack at 42. In these 24 years he took part in 4,257 races and won 1,462 times. The high number of races run in Rome in particular proves that exceptional chariot drivers took part in more than one race per day. Diocles, for example, participated in *c.* 170 races per year but there were a maximum 64 days of circus games in Rome (see above). Diocles therefore had three or four race starts per racing day. This was possible as it was set down that drivers could have up to 30 starts per day, under Domitian even 48 — although they were shorter races. This also explains the high number of Scorpus' victories, especially as a chariot driver could begin his career even as a boy.

F. FACTIONES AND FINANCING

Very little is known of the organization of the *ludi publici* in the Republican period. And yet even then athletes, horses, chariots and chariot drivers had to be obtained and paid. The attitude of the Romans to spectator competitions was quite different from that of the Greeks. Noble young Romans trained on the Campus Martius and also learned the difficult art of steering a chariot. But the *dignitas* of the nobility usually prevented them from entertaining a mixed festival audience; there were paid men of a low background for such things. In this way, specialists trained to cover the requirements of the circus games. The increase in chariot racing competitions raised the standards, fostered competition and boosted the quality of horses and chariot drivers. The racing sport became a professional matter for financially strong companies, the four → *factiones* ('parties'), the trademarks and the colours of which ultimately dominated the circus in Rome. The chariot driver wore the short *tunica* in the colour of the party for which he was driving at that time: a white (*albata*), red (*russata*), bluish (*veneta*) or green one (*prasina*). It was common to change the faction. The companies had to invest huge sums of money to procure suitable horses. The best racing horses were from Sicily, Calabria, Apulia, North Africa and Spain. For the care of the horses and for the preparation of the races each 'stable' had a string of specialists (cf. CIL VI 10074–10076: *aurigae, conditores, succonditores, sellarii, sutores, sarcinatores, medici, magistri, doctores, viatores, vilici, tentores, sparsores, hortatores*). The stars amongst the chariot drivers were, of course, also expensive. Scorpus (see above) earned 15 *sacci* of gold (Mart. 10,74) per hour, probably for one race. Diocles earned through his victories a fortune of *c.* 36,000,000 sesterces; at a time when a simple legionary earned about 1,400 sesterces a year. Despite this wealth the chariot drivers were among the *personae inhonesti* (Cod. Theod. 15,7,2). The *factiones* were a 'service business' for circus games. They operated on a high profit margin depending on the risk. The holder of the games had to pay the entire expenses; for the *ludi publici* in Rome this was still the praetor in the 4th cent. AD [11], the emperor paid for additional games [12]. The spectators were entertained free of charge.

G. Audience

For the circus games, one should not imagine the exclusive elegance of Ascot and even less the casualness of today's stadiums. Augustus ensured through a series of decrees that even in the circus the dignity of the *gens togata* was upheld: special seats were provided for senators, knights and youth in the *toga praetexta*. The *toga* without a coat was prescribed dress for men. Anyone who did not have light-coloured clothes was banned to the top rows (Suet. Aug. 44,2; Calp. Ecl. 7). The seats for women, as opposed to those in the *munera*, were not isolated: even in the time of Juvenal it was considered really charming to sit beside a *culta puella* (Juv. 11,202). Great comfort was not expected: the seats were narrow, *vela* ('sails') for protection from the sun could not be used at the Circus Maximus [13].

→ Aediles; → Chronographus

1 J. REGNER, s.v. Ludi circenses, RE Suppl. 7, 1626–1664 2 HUMPHREY, 149, 388, 433, 442 (maps)   3 LATTE, 9–17 4 E. SIMON, Die Götter der Römer, 1990, 95f.   5 HUMPHREY, 11–17   6 E. KÜNZL, Der röm. Triumph, 1988, 104–108   7 H. R. GOETTE, Studien zur röm. Togadarstellung, 1990, 6   8 ThlL, s.v. *africanae* (synonym for *venationes*), 126f.   9 F. COARELLI, Guida archeologica di Roma, 1974, 166–174   10 E. SIMON, in: HELBIG, vol. 2, no. 1796   11 O. SEECK, s.v. Symmachus, RE IV A 1, 1151 12 P. VEYNE, Zum 'Euergetismus' der Kaiser, in: Id., Brot und Spiele, 1988, 586–590   13 R. GRAEFE, Vela erunt I, 1979, 126f., 170.

A. CAMERON, Circus Factiones — Blues and Greens at Rome and Byzantium, 1976; CHRIST; DEMANDT; FRIEDLÄNDER; E. HABEL, s.v. *ludi publici*, RE Suppl. 5, 608–630; C. HEUCKE, Circus und Hippodrom als politischer Raum, 1994; A. HÖNLE, A. HENZE, Röm. Amphitheater und Stadien, 1981; S. MÜLLER, Das Volk der Athleten, 1995; K.-W. WEEBER, Panem et circenses, 1994.   A. HÖ.

Circus Flaminius see → Circus

Circus Maximus see → Circus

Cirik-Rabat-Kala Oval city site east of Lake Aral (800 × 600 m), with a citadel and six funerary buildings of the 4th–2nd cents. BC. Interpreted as the capital city of the → Apasiaci, abandoned in the late 2nd cent. BC. In the 3rd (?) cent. AD a rectangular fortification of the Khorezm state was built on the city site.

S. P. TOLSTOV, Po drevnim del'tam Oksa i Jaksarta, 1962.
                                                                      B.B.

Ciris Latin epic in 541 hexameters about → Scylla betraying her native city Megara to the Cretan king Minos and being transformed into a bird. The plot assumes knowledge of the mythical tradition and neglects narrative continuity and logic for the sake of individual scenes and profiling the heroine's emotions. This is characteristic of the epyllium in the elegiac tradition. Contrary to an ascription from late antiquity, Virgil (cf. Donat. Vita Verg. 17) has been ruled out as the author.

Agreement with entire verses of Virgil (e.g., especially F. LEO) can only be explained by the Ciris poet imitating Virgil [2. 36ff.]. Therefore, it is a product of the neoteric tradition, which required a Hellenic model (Parthenius?), but in textual terms it is entirely dependent on the — largely lost — Roman poetry of the late Republican/Augustan period. It was probably not created before Ovid or in the 2nd cent. AD (but so [2. 48ff.]), but in the Tiberian period (1st half of the 1st cent. AD). Transmission in the context of the → Appendix Vergiliana is based on two medieval manuscripts and a humanist branch [3].

EDITIONS: 1 F. R. D. GOODYEAR, in: App. Verg., 1966, 97–125   2 R. O. A. M. LYNE, 1978 (with commentary). BIBLIOGRAPHY: 3 M. D. REEVE, in: REYNOLDS, 437–440   4 F. R. D. GOODYEAR, s.v. C., EV 1, 798–800 5 F. MUNARI, Studi sulla C., 1944   6 C. CONTI, Rassegna di studi sull' App. Verg. (1955–1972), in: BSL 4, 1974, 248–259   7 J. RICHMOND, in: ANRW II 31.2, 1981, 1137–1141.   P.L.S.

Cirphis (Κίρφις; *Kírphis*). Mountain ridge south of Arachova in Boeotia, extending from the plain of Cirrha in the west to the Schiste in the east (Str. 9,3,3; FdD 3, 4, 280 c 24), where its highest peak rises (Xerovouni, 1503 m: cf. Pind. Hyporchemata d 5,4; b 3,11) and together with Mount Parnassus divides east and west Locris (Str. 9,3,1). It is uncertain if these references indicate the existence of an inhabited centre of the same name, whose location should be assumed near the modern village Desphina on the slopes of a hill at the southern edge of the Cirphis where traces of an ancient settlement were found. Cf. Steph. Byz. s.v. Σκίρφαι.

F. BÖLTE, s.v. K., RE 11, 507f.; F. SCHOBER, Phokis, 1924, 32; N. D. PAPACHATZIS, Παυσανίου Ελλάδος Περιήγησις 5, 1981, 284.   G.D.R.

Cirta (Cirta Regia, Punic *Krtn*). Numidian foundation on the other side of the Ampsaga river [1. 72 n. 141], modern Constantine. C. came under Punic influence no later than the 3rd cent. BC [2; 3]. It was first the chief city of Gaia, then of → Syphax and finally of → Massinissa and his successors (Liv. 29,32,14; 30,12,3–22; Str. 17,3,7; 13; Mela 1,30; App. Lib. 27,111f.; Oros. 4,18,21; Zon. 9,13).   W.HU.

After the fall of → Carthage, C. apparently received refugees from there who afterwards formed a strong Punic component in the cultural profile. Preservation of traditions can be seen in the presence of the sanctuary (Tophet?) of El Hofra on the settlement mound of C., which was dedicated to the god Ba'al Hamon. More than 800 votive steles (!) with the familiar iconography of Carthage's Tophet were found.   H.G.N.

Caesar, who appointed the mercenary leader P. → Sittius as lord of C. (App. B Civ. 4,54) [1. 549 n. 5], elevated the town to the rank of a *colonia Latina* and his successor Augustus raised it to a *colonia Romana*. Early in the 2nd cent. AD, C. became a provincial capital as the centre of the *res publica quattuor coloniarum Cirtensium* (with Milev, → Chullu and → Rusicade). C. was destroyed in AD 310 or 311 (Aur. Vict. 40,28) during the confrontation of the *praef. praetorio* of Maxentius, Ceionius, with the insurgent *vicarius* of the *dioecesis* Africa, L. Domitius Alexander. Constantine rebuilt C. and gave it the name Constantina. The *Numidia militaris* lost its autonomy at that time and C. became capital of the entire province of → Numidia. (Epigraphy: CIL VIII 1, 6939–7924; 2, 10866–10875; Suppl. 2, 19415–19671; Inscr. latines de l'Algérie 2,1, 468–1941; AE 1987, 1080 = CIL VIII 1, 4191 = Suppl. 2, 18489; 1989, 852; 875; 879–881; 884; 886; 893).

1 W. HUSS, Gesch. der Karthager, 1985   2 A. BERTHIER, R. CHARLIER, Le Sanctuaire punique d'El-Hofra à Constantine, 2 vol., 1952–1955   3 F. BERTRANDY, M. SZNYCER, Les stèles puniques de Constantine, 1987.

F. BERTRANDY, s.v. Constantine, DCPP, 117f.; Id., s.v. C., EB, 1964–1977; M.R. CATAUDELLA, Civitas castellum in area cirtense?, in: A. MASTINO, P. RUGGERI (ed.), L'Africa romana. Atti del X convegno di studio 1, 1994, 321–329; J. GASCOU, Pagus et castellum dans la Confédération Cirtéenne, in: AntAfr 19, 1983, 175–207; C. LEPELLEY, Les cités de l'Afrique romaine 2, 1981, 383–399.   W.HU.

Cisium see → Cart

Cispius Plebeian family name, historically first attested in the 1st cent. BC (ThlL, Onom. 460). According to later invention, a C. Laevius gave his name to the *Cispius mons* in the time of King Tullus Hostilius (Varro in Fest. p. 476).
C., M. as people's tribune, called for Cicero's reappointment in 57 BC (Cic. Red. Sen. 21; Sest. 76). In 56 (?) he was accused of *ambitus*, defended by Cicero without success (Cic. Planc. 75f.) and went into exile. Perhaps he was a praetor under Caesar (ILLRP 383; MRR 2, 463).   K.-L.E.

Cissa Also Gissa, Kissa (Plin. HN 3,140; 151). North Dalmatian island (modern Pag, Croatia) of the → Mentores (Scyl. 21). Ancient settlement near modern Časka, relationship with the Roman Calpurnii family.

J.J. WILKES, Dalmatia, 1969, 199; Id., The Illyrians, 1992.   D.S.

Cisseus (Κισσεύς; *Kisseús*, from Greek κισσός, 'ivy', the holy plant of → Dionysus; Latin *Cisseus*). Name of several mythical kings associated with Thrace and Macedonia (Dionysus' supposed native land) — the fabrication of these figures is evident. The father of → Hecabe (Eur. Hec. 3 with schol.), the guest of Anchises (Verg. Aen. 5,536f.), whom Serv. z.St. identifies with the former, the father of the Trojan priestess of Athena → Theano (Str. 7,330 fr. 24) are Thracian kings. The treacherous Macedonian king who receives the mythical Archelaus, the eponymous ancestor of Euripides' host, in Euripides' lost 'Archelaus' and intends to betray

him but is killed by Archelaus (Hyg. Fab. 219) is a character distinct from the familiar narrative scheme. Verg. Aen. 10,320 attributes the name in a learned construct to a Rutulian, who as son of the seer → Melampus, the founder of the Greek Dionysus cult (Hdt. 2,48f.), is also associated with Dionysus.
→ Archelaus [1], → Ivy   F.G.

Cissus (Κισσός; *Kissós*, 'ivy'). Dionysus C. was worshipped in Acharnae because ivy was supposedly created there (Paus. 1,31,6). C. participates in the *Dionysiaká* in the procession of Dionysus. Nonnus (Dion. 10,401ff.) tells that he raced Dionysus' favourite Ampelus and lost. When the dead Ampelus turned into a vine, C. turned into the ivy that grows around the vineyard (ibid. 12,97ff. and 188ff.)

H. BAUMANN, Griech. Pflanzenwelt in Mythos, Kunst und Lit., 1982, 85; A. KOSSATZ-DEISSMANN, s.v. K., LIMC 6.1, 61.   EL.STO.

Cista (κίστη, *kiste*). A round basket woven out of willow branches or tree bark, with a lid that often has the same height as the lower part and can be placed over it; also with a flapping lid or a disc-shaped lid. The *cista* is illustrated on numerous monuments, e.g., Attic and Lower Italian vases, funerary reliefs and Locrian clay tablets. Figurines have also been found. In marriage scenes they function as a gift to the woman. They apparently represent the female sphere since numerous household objects are visible when opened. On funerary reliefs and → naiskos scenes they are offered to or held by both men and women, presumably as a container for the funerary meal. Because the *cista* has been attested in Dionysian imagery, a relationship to the Bacchian mysteries has been sought. On Pergamenian and Roman coins with the *cista mystica*: → cistophori [1]. The *cista mystica* is also a component of cultic festivities, especially the Eleusian → mysteries (Aristoph. Thesm. 284f.). In the processions the *cista* was carried by a specially appointed κιστοφόρος (*kistophóros*). *Cistas* are also mentioned in myths (e.g., → Erichthonius).
→ Praenestine cistae

1 K. MATZ, Die dionysischen Sarkophage 1, 1968, 59–60.

E. BRÜMMER, Griech. Truhenbehälter, in: JDAI 100, 1985, 16–22.   R.H.

Cistern
I. GENERAL   II. ANCIENT ORIENT
III. PHOENICIAN-PUNIC REGION   IV. CLASSICAL ANTIQUITY

I. GENERAL
Cisterns as storage for rain water or as reservoirs for spring and well water were customary and necessary for a regulated and sufficient → water supply in the climati-

cally unfavourable regions of the southern and eastern Mediterranean, both as small systems for individual houses and farms and as communal systems for settlements. C.HÖ.

II. ANCIENT ORIENT
s. → Water supply I. D.

III. PHOENICIAN-PUNIC REGION
Systems for securing the water supply by collecting rainwater in cisterns were vital construction duties especially in urban communities in the arid and semi-arid zones of the eastern Mediterranean region and at the margins of Mesopotamia. Initially, they consisted of natural cavities (which could be extended in a bottle or pot shape) in impervious rock. The rock cistern of the Bronze Age mountain fortress of Fuente Alamo (province of Almería, SE Spain; El Argar culture, early 2nd millennium BC), which was extended upwards by masonry, was able to hold about 90 m³ [1]. The invention (as early as the 2nd millennium BC) and development of hydraulic mortar (with the addition of volcanic ash or Pozzoulan earth) permitted the building of masonry cisterns in loose soil. Carthaginian engineers were apparently leading in this technology since the 5th cent., in the 4th/3rd cents. almost every house in the densely populated metropolis possessed at least one subterranean cistern with predominantly flask-shaped outline, usually in the yard. The oldest known of these private cisterns, which was built about 400 BC, was able to hold 11.5 m³ [2].

1 H. SCHUBART, in: TH. ULBERT (ed.), Hispania antiqua. Denkmäler der Frühzeit, 2001, 550, Plate 91   2 H. G. NIEMEYER u.a., Die Grabung unter dem Decumanus Maximus von Karthago, in: MDAI(R) 102, 1995, 475–490.

V. FRITZ, Die Stadt im alten Israel, 1990, 124–131; W. MÜLLER-WIENER, Griech. Bauwesen in der Ant., 1988, 174; A. WILSON, Water Supply in Ancient Carthage, in: Carthage Papers (Journ. of Roman Archaeology, Suppl. 28), 1998, 65–68.   H. G. N.

IV. CLASSICAL ANTIQUITY
s. → Water supply II. D.

Cistophori Silver coins minted with the reduced Chian-Rhodian or Ptolemaic weight standard of 12.75 g that Eumenes II issued as local currency between about 175–160 BC to substitute for Seleucid coins and the Philhetairos tetradrachmes [3. 62; 4. 10ff.; 5. 45ff.]. Borrowed from the mystery cult in Pergamum, the name refers to the obverse motif of the Dionysian *cista mystica* consisting of an ivy reef from which a snake appears. The reverse side shows a goryt with two snakes. Cistophori were minted at various times by the more important towns of Asia Minor such as Ephesus, Pergamum, Sardeis and Smyrna, as well as in Bithynian Nicomedia [1. 166; 6. 130ff.]. Adopted by Roman governors such as Cicero, the cistophori were

minted by emperors Augustus (11.71 g), Claudius and Vespasian through to Hadrian (10.8–9.95 g) and finally under Septimius Severus and Caracalla as equivalents to three denarii [1. 151ff.; 2. 12ff.]. The motif of the *cista mystica* was already replaced under Augustus by the emperor's image and Roman personifications.
→ Cista mystica; → denarius; → didrachm; → drachm; → Coinage, standards of; → tetradrachm

1 A. M. WOODWARD, The Cistophoric Series and its Place in the Roman Coinage, in: R. A. G. CARSON, C. H. V. SUTHERLAND (ed.), Essays in Roman Coinage Presented to Harold Mattingly, 1956, 149–173   2 C. H. V. SUTHERLAND, The Cistophori of Augustus, 1970   3 TH. FISCHER, Tetradrachmen und Kistophor, in: H. A. CAHN, G. LE RIDER (ed.), Actes du 8ème congrès international de numismatique, New York-Washington 1973, 1976, 45–70   4 F. S. KLEINER, S. P. NOE, The Early Cistophoric Coinage, 1977   5 F. S. KLEINER, Further Reflections on the Early Cistophoric Coinage, in: ANSMusN 25, 1980, 45–52   6 W. E. METCALF, The Cistophori of Hadrian, 1980.

W. SZAIVERT, Stephanophoren und Kistophoren: Die mittelhell. Großsilberprägung und die röm. Ostpolit. in der Ägäis, in: Litterae Numism. Vindobonensis 2, 1988, 29–55.   A.M.

Citations, laws governing see → Volume 4, Addenda

Cithaeron (Κιθαιρών; *Kithairón*, Latin *Cithaeron*). A mountain range that is still forested (1407 m, Hagios Elias) to the north of the → Isthmus of Corinth and separating Boeotia on the north from the Megaris in the south-west and Attica in the south-east; the Pastra mountains (1025 m), the Skurta plateau (between 540 and 570 m) and the Parnes adjoin the C. in the east. Important connecting routes from and to Boeotia led over passes that were secured by fortifications and watch-towers (Hdt. 9,38f.; Thuc. 3,24; Xen. Hell. 5,4,37; 47; 6,4,5;), for example, the route over the 'Oak Heads' (Δρυὸς Κεφαλαί) or 'Three Heads' pass (585 m) (Τρεῖς Κεφαλαί) north of Eleutherae. Numerous cults (Dionysus, Zeus and Hera, Nymphs, Pan) and myths (Pentheus, Actaeon, Antiope, Oedipus, Niobe, Alcathous, Hercules, Teiresias) are associated with the C.

PHILIPPSON/KIRSTEN 1, 522ff.   E.O.

Citium (Κίτιον; *Kítion*). Important port city on the south coast of → Cyprus, modern Larnaca. Fortified Mycenaean town with temples and necropoleis [1], destroyed in the 11th cent. BC. On a stele from C., Sargon II claims Assyrian suzerainty in 709 BC. → Colonization emanating from Tyre in the 9th cent. BC established an increasing Phoenician presence, which peaked in usurpation by a Phoenician dynasty after C.'s unsuccessful participation in the → Ionian Revolt. The kings of the 5th and 4th cents. BC are known from coins and epigraphy. C. is the main provenance of Phoenician inscriptions on Cyprus (CIS 1,1, 35ff. no. 10–87). The

Phoenician name was at first *Qart-ḥadašt*, 'New Town', then *Ktj*, locally *ket-ti*, Greek *Kítion*, Latin *Citium*. In the 2nd half of the 5th cent BC, C.'s rule extended to neighbouring → Idalium and in the middle of the 4th cent. temporarily even to Tamassus. The strongly fortified town was besieged in vain by → Cimon [2] in 449 BC, conquered in 312 by Ptolemy I who executed Pumiathon, the last Phoenician king. Under the Ptolemies C. was garrisoned, in late antiquity it became a bishopric. → Zeno, the founder of the Stoa, and the doctors → Apollonius [16], Apollodorus and Artemidorus, all came from C.

Remains of sanctuaries from the archaic to late classical period are preserved on the 'Bamboula' hill [2; 3]. At the foot of the hill lie the remains of a once important harbour (Str. 14,6,3). Also, a large temple, possibly of Astarte, from the late 9th cent. BC on Mycenaean predecessor buildings with neighbouring metal workshops, destroyed by Ptolemy I; other sanctuaries in the town area. A theatre, gymnasium, stadium and hippodrome are attested from inscriptions. Extensive necropolis with monumental chamber graves and sarcophagi.

1 V. KARAGEORGHIS, Excavations at K. 1, 1974
2 E. GJERSTADT, K., in: The Swedish Cyprus Expedition 3, 1937, 1–75 3 J. F. SALLES et al., K. — Bamboula 4, Les niveaux hellénistiques, 1993.

Y. CALVET, K., in: M. YON (ed.), Kinyras (Traveaux de la maison de l'Orient 22), 1993, 107–138; E. GJERSTADT et al., s.v. K. in: The Swedish Cyprus Expedition 3, 1937; 4,2, 1948, 543; V. KARAGEORGHIS, K., 1976; MASSON, 272–274, no. 256–259; K. NICOLAOU, The Historical Topography of Kition, (Stud. in Mediterranean Archaeology 43), 1976; E. OBERHUMMER, s.v. K., RE 11, 535–545. R.SE.

Citizenship In Graeco-Roman antiquity terms comparable to the modern term citizenship, → *politeía* (πολιτεία) and → *civitas*, originally not only designated individual rights but also the totality of citizens, the political organization of citizens in the sense of a constitution and an autonomous community. Citizenship was usually attained by being born to parents with citizenship (→ *conubium*) or granted by resolution of the community or an authorized person, in Rome also through private manumission from slavery (→ *manumissio*). Admission to citizenship was very restrictive in Greece but relatively generous in Rome. Being a citizen secured general legal protection but did not provide the same rights for all citizens. Full use of citizenship was only open to adult males but still restricted by age and wealth, occupation and origin. Ancient citizenship was an essential, but not a sufficient condition for equal political participation by all holders of citizenship. Citizenship was lost with death, withdrawal because of political or criminal acts (→ *capitis deminutio*) or acceptance of another citizenship if there was no agreement between the respective communities (→ *isopoliteia*; *sympoliteia*).

Regarding the content of citizenship and its historical development, see also → civitas; → coloniae; → Latin Law; → origo; → quirites; → polis, polites.
CITIZENS

> W. EDER, Who Rules? Power and Participation in Athens and Rom, in: A. MOLHO, K. RAAFLAUB, J. EMLEN (ed.), City States in Classical Antiquity, 1991, 169–196; D. WHITEHEAD, Norms of Citizenship in Ancient Greece, ibid., 135–154. W.ED.

Citrus (χίτρος, cedar). This genus of Rutaceae consists of about 20, or rather a narrower spectrum of seven to eight species of evergreen trees and shrubs from subtropical and tropical Asia. The name *citrus* (χίτρος, χίτριον; *kítros, kítrion*) originally referred to conifers with aromatic wood, such as *Callitris articulata*. However, after Alexander's campaigns it was transferred to the species *Citrus medica,* which had been cultivated in Media and Persia for some time (μῆλον μηδικόν; *mêlon mēdikón,* χίτριον in Theophr. Hist. pl. 4,4,2; κεδρόμηλα (*kedrómela*) in Dioscurides 1,115 [1. 109] = 1,166 [2. 137f.]). This highly fragrant tree was introduced as a container plant into Italy and used to ward off moths and as an antidote against poison. The subspecies with edible fruit *C. limonum,* the lemon, was probably brought to southern Europe by the Arabs in the early Middle Ages. The 'Apples of the Hesperids' (μῆλα ἑσπερικά; *mêla hesperiká*), mistakenly considered as oranges, were probably apples or quince. Bitter oranges (*C. aurantium amara,* Pers. *nareng,* Arab. *narang,* Byz. νεράντζιον; *nerántzion, aurantium,* pomerance) were only imported in the 10th cent. by the Arabs from India to North Africa and Spain, the sweet variety (*C. aurantium sinensis* or *dulcis*) only in about 1550 by the Portuguese from China. In the 19th cent. the grapefruit (*C. decumana*) and the tangerine (*C. deliciosa = nobilis*) arrived and were often bred into new varieties.
→ Agrumen; → citrus fruit

> 1 M. WELLMANN (ed.), Pedanii Dioscuridis de materia med., vol. 1, 1908, repr. 1958 2 J. BERENDES (ed.), Des Pedanios Dioskurides Arzneimittellehre übers. und mit Erl. versehen, 1902, repr. 1970. C.HÜ.

City deity see → Volume 4, Addenda

Cius

[1] (Κίος; *Kíos*). Port town in the eastern part of the Gulf of → Propontis (which is named after it) on the river of the same name, modern Gemlik. C. was the starting-point of the roads to → Nicaea and → Prusa. According to Apoll. Rhod. 4,1470, a foundation of the Argonauts (→ Argonautae, map), coins show Hercules as the founder of the city (HN 512–514); according to Plin. HN 5,144 founded by Milesians. C. participated in the → Ionian Revolt (Hdt. 5,122) and was, as the only town in east Propontis, a member of the → Delian League from the beginning (ATL 3, 204 note 49; 4, 64). Philip V destroyed C. (Pol. 15,21ff.; 18,3,12; 4,7). Because it was rebuilt by Prusias I (*c.* 230–182 BC), C. was

temporarily called 'Prusias on the Sea'. In the Roman period C. was once more autonomous (Str. 12,4,3). In the Christian period an episcopal see.

T. CORSTEN, Die Inschr. von K. (IK 29), 1985.

H.KAL. and F.K.D.

[2] Roman fortification and *statio* on the road along the Danube from Carsium to Beroe and Troesmis in Moesia Inferior, modern Gîrliciu/Constanţa in Rumania (It. Ant. 224: *Cio*; Not. Dign. Or. 39,6,14: *Cii*). A Roman garrison may already be assumed in the 2nd and 3rd cents. AD, in the 4th cent. C. was the base of a *cuneus* (division) *equitum stablesianorum*. In 369 Emperor Valens defeated the Gothic king Athanaric there (CIL III 7494). Last fortification work in the Valentinian period. Archaeological finds: ruins, inscriptions, hoard find of the 4th cent.; civilian settlement in a nearby *vicus* (*Ramidava?*).

TIR L 35 Bukarest, 1969, 33, 78.   J.BU.

Civil law
I. ANCIENT ORIENT   II. PHARAONIC EGYPT

I. ANCIENT ORIENT
A. GENERAL   B. LEGAL RESPONSIBILITY   C. CONTINUATION OF THE FAMILY

A. GENERAL
The term civil law (CL), which is derived from Roman law, covers the legal position of individuals in legal transactions and with respect to family and society. Depending on the definition, family and inheritance law are part of CL. → Legal texts in cuneiform — as opposed to mature Roman law — as a pre-scientific legal system are legal institutions derived from practice — the modern categories used here are anachronistic. Sources and preliminary work on the legal systems of various regions of the Ancient Orient are available to different degrees. CL in → Nuzi (cf. [7]) and Neo-Assyrian CL (1st half of the 1st millennium BC; [15]) have similar traits to Jewish CL (see III. below).

B. LEGAL RESPONSIBILITY
'Individual' is a modern term. The individual in the Ancient Orient was characterized by his status in family and society as well as his name (sometimes with filiation) while women were characterized by their husband's name.

Entry into legal responsibility defined by age was unknown, as were customs of paternal power, guardianship and care (on name and age categories: Neo-Sumerian/Old Babylonian, 21st/17th cent., cf. [22. 215–219, 301f.], Neo-Assyrian [15. 125–134]; on parental powers [23. 155f.]). Family status and gender did not affect legal responsibility. The position of → women changed — in fact or law — in the specifics; it must not be considered universally low and was not associated in the first place with virginity (e.g., [10]).

Women as heads of households are attested from the Fara period (26th cent. BC). A 'legal person' did not exist; persons associated for business were only linked by contract (e.g., [14]; also → professional associations I).

Society consisted of free persons and slaves. Sources of → slavery were especially war captivity, offences, sale of relatives or oneself (e.g., Neo-Sumerian [6. 82–90]). Status as a slave did not necessarily mean incapacity to conduct business (e.g., Neo-Assyrian [15. 220–222]). Social position did not affect legal status (→ Aristocracy [1]) but legally significant dependencies also existed (e.g., [16. 307; 4. 115]). 'Citizenship' was unknown; foreigners (*aḫûm*; → aliens, position of), especially nomads, were simply considered 'foreign'.

C. CONTINUATION OF THE FAMILY
The role of the → family and its continuation had biological, religious and economic aspects. Legally, in particular → marriage, → adoption, arrogation and the law of → succession are relevant. Also, liability generally extended to family members. The economic significance is reflected in the term 'house' (Sumerian É/Akkadian *bītum*): it already denoted in Old Akkadian the family's economic association and in Old Assyrian the '(family) corporation'. Evidence from the Neo-Sumerian and Old-Babylonian period indicates communities of impartible inheritance. There were narrowly defined limits to leaving the family according to its importance. Passing on wealth served to protect the paternal generation's maintenance [17–21]. A modern perspective hides that inheritance was mostly transacted among the living — possibly effective at the time of death: either the lacking heir was replaced by adoption or the shares of family members were determined in a quasi-testamentary procedure; a testament in the true meaning and the arbitrary installation of non-familiar heirs did not exist. The width of variation in 'inheritance law' agreements was large; it seems to have covered almost every conceivable interest.

As elsewhere, the house-born children probably inherited directly in the Ancient Orient. Already in the early Dynastic period (25th/24th cents.) considerable private property is documented [16. 272–280] that could have resulted in arbitrary bequeathing of inheritance. However, it is not directly attested in the Old Babylonian period (more, e.g., Middle Assyrian). Natural heirs in Old Babylon were the sons, possibly even those with a slave woman (Codex Hammurapi §§ 170f.), as substitutes also a brother or father's brother. A wife was not a natural heir but could receive donations *inter vivos* or at the time of death together with the sons. Daughters had the right to inherit but were often paid off with a → dowry. At the time of death it was often given to the children or returned to the wife's family. Occasionally the eldest son received a preferential share (e.g., local Old Babylonian [12. 27–33]) or wealth was due to the children of the first marriage when the woman remarried (e.g., Middle Assyrian

[3]). Other special rights and goods cannot be determined. Acceptance in a child's place (Sumerian NAM.DUMU/Akkadian *mārâtum*) is already attested in the 3rd millennium [17. 53–55; 6. 110]. If there was a daughter, it was possible to continue the family by adopting her husband (Neo-Sumerian [11]). Receiving parties were also single women, slaves were adopted, (especially?) orphans and girls; also adults (Old Babylonian/Old Assyrian/Neo-Assyrian) and married couples (Old Assyrian). The contracts frequently contain duties of maintenance (also Middle Babylonian; [17–20]). Sale into adoption or marriage is documented in Neo-Assyrian records [15. 134–144]. In → Nuzi the so-called 'real-estate adoption' founded a relationship of maintenance or protection [4. 117f.; 16. 305]. Disinheriting was fundamentally impossible in the Ancient Orient (cf. e.g., [6. 110f.]).

1 F.R. KRAUS, Vom altmesopotamischen Erbrecht, in: J. BRUGMAN et al. (ed.), Essays on Oriental Laws of Succession, 1969, 1–17   2 Id., Erbrechtliche Terminologie im alten Mesopotamien, in: cf. [1], 18–57   3 M. DAVID, Ein Beitrag zum mittelassyr. Erbrecht, in: cf. [1], 78–81   4 G. DOSCH, Zur Struktur der Ges. des Königreichs Arraphe, 1993   5 E. EBELING, s.v. Erbe, Erbrecht, Enterbung, RLA 2, 458–462   6 A. FALKENSTEIN, Die neusumer. Gerichtsurkunden, vol. 1, 1956, 81–116   7 C.H. GORDON, Parallèles nouziennes aux lois et coutumes de l'ancien testament, in: Rev. Biblique 44, 1935, 34–41   8 S. GREENGUS, Legal and Social Institutions of Ancient Mesopotamia, in: J.M. SASSON (ed.), Civilizations of the Ancient Near East, vol. 1, 1995, 469–484   9 R. HAASE, Einführung in das Studium keilschriftlicher Rechtsquellen, 1965, 49–78   10 J. HENGSTL, 'Liebe' im Spiegel der sumer.-altbabylon. Codices, in: Ant. Welt 17, 1985, 56–58   11 Id., Die neusumer. Eintrittsehe, in: ZRG 109, 1992, 31–50   12 J. KLIMA, Unt. zum altbabylon. Erbrecht, 1940   13 V. KOROŠEC, Keilschriftrecht, in: HbdOr, Suppl. III, 1964, 49–219   14 H. LANZ, Die neubabylon. ḫarrānu-Geschäftsunternehmen, 1976   15 K. RADNER, Die neuassyr. Privatrechtsurkunden, 1997   16 J. RENGER, Institutional, Communal, and Individual Ownership or Possession of Arable Land in Ancient Mesopotamia ..., in: Chicago-Kent Law Review 71, 1995, 269–319   17 C. WILCKE, Care of the Elderly in Mesopotamia in the Third Millennium B.C., in: M. STOL, S. P. VLEEMING (ed.), The Care of the Elderly in the Ancient Near East, 1998, 23–57   18 M. STOL, Care of the Elderly in Mesopotamia in the Old Babylonian Period, in: see [17], 59–117   19 K. R. VEENHOF, Old Assyrian and Ancient Anatolian Evidence for the Care of the Elderly, in: see [17], 119–160   20 G. VAN DRIEL, Care of the Elderly: The Neo-Babylonian Period, in: see [17], 161–197   21 R. WESTBROOK, Legal Aspects of Care of the Elderly in the Ancient Near East, in: see [17], 241–250   22 C. WILCKE, Familiengründung im alten Babylonien, in: E. W. MÜLLER (ed.), Geschlechtsreife und Legitimation zur Zeugung, 1985, 213–317   23 R. YARON, The Laws of Eshnunna, 1988.

JO.HE.

II. PHARAONIC EGYPT

A. LEGAL SUBJECTS B. CONTINUATION OF THE FAMILY C. SACRIFICIAL DONATIONS III. JUDAIC LAW

A. LEGAL SUBJECTS

The striking imagery of Egyptian art reveals an image of the individual that has no parallel in written sources. In the Old Kingdom the sources indicate a tripartite history. It consisted of an → aristocracy (princes and officials: $p^*.t$), their subjects and dependents ($mr.t$, collectively $rḫy.t$) and the priesthood ($ḫnmm.t$; → priests). A slave-like layer of unfree persons with diminished rights ($ḥm$) developed towards the end of the Old Kingdom from Nubian and Asian → prisoners of war. In the following cents. it was augmented by impoverished Egyptians and their families as well as penal prisoners ($ḏ.t$ i.a.). They could all be traded (unlike — mostly in the Middle Kingdom — servants belonging to the house (b^*k)) through selling, rental or inheritance. Status was inherited but did not fundamentally preclude education, ability to conduct business and active and passive ability to participate in legal processes [16. 42–46]. From the New Kingdom on, manumission ($nmḥy.w$) of slaves for marriage and adoption is securely documented [1]. Despite the significant foreign component in the population [7], among it Jews[12], and Persian rule (after 525 BC), conclusions on the legal status of foreigners are almost impossible. Family status and gender did not affect legal responsibility (on the position of → women see [13]). The equal rank of man and woman in private law is particularly reflected in the law of marital property, which provided, e.g., a division of goods if the man remarried [9. 288–315].

When legal responsibility arrived while growing up is uncertain, possibly the father's or mother's brother assumed guardianship if it was not settled in a last will [5. 173–179]. The family was co-liable towards private creditors and the state [5. 201–208]. A still unelucidated relict of CL from the Persian period (6th–4th cents. BC) is the designation 'Persian descendant' (Πέρσης/ Περσίνη τῆς ἐπιγονῆς) in papyri of the Graeco-Roman period with which debtors submitted to enforcement [8. 312–315]. 'Judicial persons' did not exist, but trusts or foundations of sorts played a role.

B. CONTINUATION OF THE FAMILY

As elsewhere, the continuation of the family — if necessary by adoption — served to pass on wealth and maintain family members [10; 14]. Normally, the eldest son was the sole heir or received a preferred share; from what he received he had to pay funeral costs (possibly including the funerary sacrifice). Collateral relatives did not have to be explicitly excluded to not inherit. The willed inheritance primarily divided the estate. Wives had no right of inheritance, but they were compensated by marriage property agreements or transfers *inter vivos*. In the New Kingdom relatives were able to acquire a claim by participating in the funerary costs.

Adoption served both willed inheritance and succession to the (priestly) office [1; 4]. Egyptian law knew a unilateral, last will and revocable disposition of wealth but not a testament in the true meaning [17; 18]. There are indications of a fratrilinear succession [2].

C. Sacrificial donations

→ Sacrificial donations performed important functions in the area of family and family continuation. Material provision of a deceased (*jm*ḫw*) was a central concern of the everyday cult of the → dead. According to perceptions of the Other World, it secured the survival of the deceased after death. Initially reserved for deceased kings and officials, it increasingly extended to lower social layers since the Old Kingdom. To secure the cult of the dead independently of the continuation of the family, private donations with contractual obligations of funerary services and explicit appointment of a priest of the dead were instituted. A sacrificial foundation could also be appointed as the guardian of a community of inheritors. From the New Kingdom on there were donations for the image of → Pharaoh. The donor was instituted as the priest of Pharaoh's image; he was freed of maintenance for his family members and secured his old-age support.

→ Egyptian law; → Demotic law; → Family

1 S. Allam, Papyrus Turin 2021: Another Adoption Extraordinary, in: Ch. Cannuyer, J.-M. Kruchten (ed.), Individu, soc. et spiritualité dans l'Égypte pharaonique et copte. FS A. Théodoridès, 1993, 23–28   2 C. Bennett, The Structure of the Seventeenth Dynasty, in: Göttinger Miszellen 149, 1995, 25–32   3 W. Boochs, Altäg. Zivilrecht, 1999, 18–67   4 C. J. Eyre, The Adoption Papyrus in Its Social Context, in: JEA 78, 1992, 207–222   5 E. Feucht, Das Kind im Alten Äg., 1995   6 Id., Die Stellung der Frau im Alten Äg., in: J. Martin, R. Zoepffel (ed.), Aufgaben, Rollen und Räume von Mann und Frau, vol. 1, 1989, 239–306   7 R. Gundlach, Die Zwangsumsiedlung auswärtiger Bevölkerung als Mittel äg. Politik bis zum Ende des MR, 1994   8 Ph. Huyse, Die Perser in Äg. Ein onomastischer Beitrag zu ihrer Erforschung, in: AchHist vol. 6, 1991, 312–320   9 E. Lüddekens, Äg. Eheverträge, 1960   10 A. McDowell, Legal Aspects of Care of the Elderly in Egypt to the End of the New Kingdom, in: M. Stol, S. P. Vleeming (ed.), The Care of the Elderly in the Ancient Near East, 1998, 199–221   11 D. Meeks, Les donations aux temples dans l'Égypte du 1er millénaire avant J.-C, in: E. Lipiński (ed.), State and Temple Economy in the Ancient Near East, 1979, 605–687   12 J. Mélèze-Modrzejewski, Les Juifs d'Égypte. De Ramsès II à Hadrien, 1991   13 B. Menu, La condition de la femme dans l'Égypte pharaonique, in: Rev. Historique de Droit Français et Étranger 67, 1989, 3–25   14 P. W. Pestman, The Law of Succession in Ancient Egypt, in: J. Brugman et al. (ed.), Essays on Oriental Laws of Succession, 1969, 58–77   15 E. Seidl, Äg. Rechtsgesch. der Saiten- und Perserzeit, ²1956, 52–56, 71–83   16 Id., Einführung in die äg. Rechtsgesch. bis zum Ende des NR, vol. 1, ²1957, 42–46, 55–59   17 A. Théodoridès, L'acte à cause de mort dans l'Égypte pharaonique (Recueils de la Soc. Jean Bodin 59: Actes à cause de mort, vol. 1: Antiquité), 1992, 9–27   18 Id., Du rapport entre un con-

trat et un acte de disposition appelé *imyt-per* en égyptien, in: RIDA 3e sér. 40, 1993, 77–105.   Jo.He. and O.Wi.

III. Judaic law
A. General   B. Family   C. Continuation of the family   IV. Classical antiquity

A. General
The provisions of the Torah (→ Pentateuch) regarding CL belong to entirely different periods (→ Judaic law A.) and strongly deviate from the legal documents, which are only partially characterized by Judaic law (e.g., [10; 2. 21–27, 22⁷²/⁷³]). Development and details cannot be sufficiently represented here.

B. Family
According to the Torah, the legal responsibility of a person depended on family status and gender. Only an adult male had full legal standing and acquired the ability to conduct business at age 20. (Num 1,3: selected documentation). The head of a family had absolute powers of decision over his family (Gen 38,11). The wife — whose engagement was binding for marriage (Deut. 22,23–29) — was subject to the man (Gen 3,16) and only had few rights (e.g., [1]). As a widow she was in practice without protection. Family organization was patriarchal and possibly included the wives of sons and servants (Gen. 7,7). The family was liable and could be sold by a creditor (2 Kgs 4,1). Debt slavery was dissolved in the Sabbath (=7th; Ex 21,2) year, later in the Jubilee (=50th) year (Lv 25,54) [4. 36–57]. Sources of → slavery were captivity in war (Num 31,26), selling oneself (Lv 25,39–41), purchase (Lv 25,44) and house-born slaves (Gen. 17,12). Slave women were equal in sexual relationships or marriage to the son of a concubine or a daughter (Ex 21,7–11). Marriage and family were regulated by a multitude of rules [1; 12. 240–243].

Foreigners had some rights and legal protection in the post-prophetic period. Judaism was always closely surrounded by foreigners for religious, historical and geographical reasons; this is frequently reflected in the Torah [7. 309–314]. Hostility towards Jews can already be detected in Pharaonic Egypt ([11] cf. [3]). Legal documents of the Jewish communities do not reflect this just as they do not reflect the internal Jewish conflicts between Orthodox and assimilated Jews (e.g., [4. 2f.]).

C. Continuation of the family
Originally only sons inherited, including those of concubines; the eldest son had a revocable preferential right (Deut. 21,17). The duty of maintaining male relatives was linked to the estate. Preservation of the core property (*nahălā*), consisting of real estate and movables, was an important concern (Num 16,14); the right of inheritance originally assumed that landed property was tied to the tribe (Num. 36,9). Originally the closest male relative of the testator was the replacement heir with obligation to enter a levirate marriage (regarding

this: Deut. 25,5–10; [15. 69–89]; → marriage IV); later also daughters, possibly together with sons (Job 42,15; cf. Num. 36,1–12). The widow originally had no right of inheritance from her husband (Num. 27,8–11; [14]) but the documents attest maintenance arrangements [4. 71–76]. The right of inheritance was strictly oriented towards transfer of the estate among blood relatives (of the man). This prohibited the adoption of strangers; only members of the household could be adopted in place of a child (Gen. 15,3; [12. 243³⁹]). The estate was fundamentally only distributed *inter vivos* or on the deathbed (cf. 2 Sam. 17,23).

1 F. ALVAREZ-PÉREYRE, F. HEYMANN, Ein Streben nach Transzendenz. Das hebräische Muster der Familie und die jüd. Praxis, in: A. BURGUIÈRE et al. (ed.), Gesch. der Familie, vol. 1, 1996, 196–235   2 L. J. ARCHER, Her Price Is Beyond Rubies: The Jewish Woman in Graeco-Roman Palestine, 1990   3 E. BALTRUSCH, Bewunderung, Duldung, Ablehnung: Das Urteil über die Juden in der griech.-röm. Lit., in: Klio 80, 1998, 403–421 (with ibid. 81, 1999, 218)   4 J. COWEY, K. MARESCH, Urkunden aus dem *politeuma* der Juden von Herakleopolis (2001)   5 Z. W. FALK, Hebrew Law in Biblical Times. An Introduction, 1964, 111–170   6 Id., Introduction to Jewish Law of the Second Commonwealth, vol. 2, 1978, 248–349   7 E. FASCHER, s.v. Fremder, RAC 8, 306–347   8 R. WESTBROOK, Biblical Law, in: N.S. HECHT et al. (ed.), An Introduction to the History and Sources of Jewish Law, 1996   9 D. PIATELLI, Jewish Law During the Second Temple Period, in: s. [8], 1–17   10 J. MODRZEJEWSKI, Jewish Law and Hellenistic Legal Practice in the Light of Greek Papyri from Egypt, in: see [8], 75–99   11 H. HEINEN, Äg. Grundlagen des ant. Antijudaismus, in: Trierer Theologische Zschr. 101, 1992, 124–149   12 S. E. LOEWENSTAMM, Law, in: B. MAZAR (ed.), The World History of the Jewish People, vol. 3, 1971, 231–267   13 E. OTTO, Biblische Altersversorgung im altoriental. Rechtsvergleich, in: Zschr. für altorientalisches und biblisches Recht 1, 1995, 83–110   14 J. A. WAGENAAR, 'Give in the Hand of Your Maidservant the Property...' Some Remarks to the Second Ostracon from the Collection of Sh. Moussieff, in: Zschr. für altorientalisches und biblisches Recht 5, 1999, 15–27 (cf. A. LEMAIRE, ibid. 1–14)   15 R. WESTBROOK, Property and the Family in Biblical Law, 1991   16 R. YARON, Acts of Last Will in Jewish Law (Recueils de la Soc. Jean Bodin 59: Actes à cause de mort, vol. 1: Antiquité), 1992, 29–45   17 Id., Introduction to the Law of the Aramaic Papyri, 1961, 111–170.

REFERENCE WORKS: G. HERLITZ, B. KIRSCHNER (ed.), Jüd. Lexikon, 1927 (repr. 1982); M. GÖRG, B. LANG (ed.), Neues Bibel-Lex., 1988ff.; RGG, ⁴1998ff.   JO.HE.

IV. CLASSICAL ANTIQUITY
Characteristic of the structure of private CL both in Greece and Rome was the position of the individual in the → family. The modern concept of CL as the legal development of the individual does not do justice to classical antiquity. Personal freedom to develop is not characteristic but rather the situation in private power relationships either as power-holder or as subject. In Athens and Rome in particular, only few had private

dominion (cf. → *kyrieía*; → *manus*; → *patria potestas*): the paterfamilias and slave-owners (→ *kýrios* II.; → *dominus*, → *pater familias*). However, even those without rights are 'persons' in the parlance of Roman jurists (slaves and children of the house, → *persona*). The central category of CL, status, e.g., paterfamilias, → freedperson or house-born child, is derived from membership in a private dominion or lack thereof. The special terms of status changes in CL are derived from this, e.g., → manumission or discharge from the family association (→ *emancipatio*) as well as acceptance into a new one (→ adoption, *eispoíēsis*). The law of → succession is linked to CL because it serves the continuation of family dominion and the family association (→ *oíkos*; → Family IV.B.). Therefore, the law of succession belongs according to its function more to CL than pure pecuniary law (material and contract law). The CL of classical antiquity developed the law of private corporations (→ Professional associations II; → *collegium* I.; → *sýnodos*; → Association) as 'legal persons' only to a minor extent. The closest to such concepts are the ecclesiastical regulations of the Byzantine period, especially regarding pious donations (*piae causae*).

A. R. W. HARRISON, The Law of Athens, vol. 1, 1968, 61–205; KASER, RPR 1, 56–71, 270– 310; 2, 151–158.   G.S.

Civil war see → Volume 4, Addenda

Civitas
A. COMMUNITY B. CITIZENSHIP

A. COMMUNITY
Civitas is the totality of the *cives*, just as *societas* is that of the *socii*. Its meaning is largely synonymous with → *populus*, but it was rarely used by the Romans for their own state (instead: *populus Romanus*) but instead was the official expression for all non-Roman communities, tribes and Greek *poleis* with republican constitutions. A people of the state is the characteristic of a *civis*, almost always a defined territory with a certain → autonomy (*suis legibus uti*) and mostly an urban centre.

Classification was according to the legal basis of the relationship of the *civitas* with Rome as *civitas foederata* (community tied to Rome in a contract, usually in Italy, with *foedus aequum* or *iniquum*) or as a *civitas sine foedere* (community without contract, usually in the provinces, → *foedus*), or according to financial obligations that resulted from a contract: *stipendiaria* (taxed), *libera* (with its own administration), *immunis* (tax-free).

B. CITIZENSHIP
Membership in a Roman → tribus and — at least originally — a name of Roman type were characteristic. → Citizenship was acquired by birth from (free) parents possessing → *conubium*, by manumission by a Roman

citizen or by award, individually or collectively with the native community. It ends with death, sentencing to certain types of punishment (*capitis deminutio media*) or emigration and acceptance of another citizenship (*c. d. minima*, Gai. Inst. 1,162). It concerns actual political rights and duties such as elections and electibility, service in citizens' troops, summons (*provocatio*) before the people or the emperor, freedom from certain taxes and *munera* (LINK), the use of the *ius civile* and the toga.

Roman citizenship was probably never equal for all citizens. It depended on gender, age, income, origin and occupation. The *civitas sine suffragio* (without vote) is probably a late Republican term for the merely military integration of foreign communities such as Caere and Capua who maintained their internal order. In the early imperial period the *civitas optimo iure*, a 'citizenship with tax liberties' (LINK) arose. Latin law also developed into a lesser citizenship (→ Latin law).

Originally Roman citizenship could not be combined with other citizenships (*duarum civitatum civis noster esse iure civili nemo potest*, Cic. Balb. 28,1). This principle was only softened in the final years of the Republic but in the imperial period a combination of citizenship in the Roman Empire and local municipal citizenship was uncontested, although the question of the binding force of the legal systems associated with the respective citizenships was never clarified [1]. Citizenship was awarded in Rome from the earliest times and it was always less problematic than, for example, in Athens. This was related to the far lower degree of democratization in Rome, which did not let the pure number of citizens or new citizens become a problem for some time. Larger pushes in granting the *civitas Romana* to entire groups of the population occurred after the → Social War, then in the civil wars of the 1st cent. BC; Latin law was granted in the 1st cent. AD to the communities of Noricum and in Hispania. Caracalla finally gave Roman citizenship with the → *Constitutio Antoniniana* to almost all imperial inhabitants who did not already possess it in AD 212. Afterwards there were still individual grants, e.g., to all discharged soldiers of the auxiliary forces and to deserving provincials (→ Military certificates). Thus, Rome became the *communis patria* of all imperial residents (Dig. 50,1,33).

CITIZENS

1 MITTEIS.

H. GALSTERER, Herrschaft und Verwaltung im republikanischen It., 1976; E. OBERHUMMER, s.v. Coloniae, RE 4, 510–88.; S. LINK, Ut optimo iure optimaque lege cives Romani sint, in: ZRG 112, 1995, 370–384; A. N. SHERWIN-WHITE, The Roman Citizenship, 1973; F. VITTINGHOFF, Röm. Kolonisation und Bürgerrechtspolitik unter Caesar und Augustus, 1950; H. WOLFF, Die constitutio Antoniniana und Papyrus Gissensis 40 1, Diss. 1976.

H.GA.

Clanis Right tributary of the Tiber in Etruria, modern Chiana (Str. 5,3,7; App. B Civ. 1,89), flows south of Arezzo (Plin. HN. 3,54) and joins the Paglia near Orvieto. In AD 15 → Florentia objected to the plan of uniting the Clanis with the Arno to prevent flooding of the Tiber even though it was endangered by Arno floods (Tac. Ann. 1,76; 1,79; Cass. Dio 57,14).

A. FATUCCHI, in: Atti e memorie dell'Accademia Patavina 43, 1973/74, 332ff.

M.CA.

Clanius River in Campania (Lycophr. 718; Γλάνις; *Glánis*, Dion. Hal. Ant. Rom. 7,3), that in antiquity probably flowed into the *mare Tyrrhenum* near Liternum. Its floods endangered Acerrae (Verg. G. 2,225 with Serv.). Two Neolithic settlements (4th/3rd millennia BC) only 4 km from the river near Gricigliano and Orta di Atella suggest a considerable population density in the Campanian plain since the 4th millennium.

NISSEN, 2, 713.

U.PA.

Clarenna *Statio* between Ad Lunam and Grinario (Tab. Peut. 4,1), possibly the late Flavian garrison Donnstetten-Römerstein, which continued after about 150 into the 3rd cent. as a civilian settlement.

J. HEILIGMANN, Der 'Alb-Limes', 1990, 80–87.

K.DI.

Clarissimus see → Vir clarissimus

Clarus

[1] (Κλᾶρος; *Klâros*). Ionian sanctuary of → Apollo Klarios (since the protogeometric period, 10th cent. BC) with oracle (flowering 2nd cent. AD) in the territory of → Colophon, on the coastal plain of Ahmetbeyli. Well attested in literature and epigraphy (cf. h. Hom. ad Apollinem 1,40; h. Hom. ad Dianam 5; Thuc. 3,33; Str. 14,1,27; Paus. 7,3; Iambl. Myst. 3,11; Aristid. 3,317 JEBB; Tac. Ann. 2,54,2f.: Germanicus in C. in AD 18). Archaeological remains: round altar (2nd half of the 7th cent. BC), propylaea; archaic, early Hellenistic (4th cent. BC) Doric Apollo temple (restored by Emperor Hadrian), built over. Temple of Artemis Klaria; exedra (Roman period). Penteteric games are documented from inscriptions.

J. DE LA GENIÈRE, Claros, in: REA 100, 1998, 235–256; H. W. PARKE, The Oracles of Apollo in Asia Minor, 1985; J. und L. ROBERT, Claros I. Décrets hellénistiques, 1989; L. ROBERT, s.v. Claros, PE, 226.

J.D.G. and E.O.

Classical Period see → Periods, division into; → Classicism

Classicism
I. LITERARY HISTORY   II. LEGAL HISTORY

I. LITERARY HISTORY
A. GENERAL   B. GREEK CLASSICISM   C. ROMAN CLASSICISM

A. GENERAL
Classicism, a term formed early in the 19th cent. analogous and antithetically to 'Romanticism', initially means the same as the later neologism 'classical period': 'highest perfection', which was first attested in 1887 [1. 154] and in both English and French is still recognizable in the remaining ambivalence of the term classicism, especially in the contrast of 'classicism/neoclassicism' or 'classicisme/néoclassicisme' [2. 3, 5f.]. However, in the typological meaning preferred by WILAMOWITZ [3. 272], classicism is a periodization term meaning deliberate artistic and literary attachment to a model-like → canon, which is close to the ancient understanding of classicism: only a *classicus adsiduusque scriptor* ('exemplary and recognized writer') of the *cohors antiquior* ('older group') of orators and poets can guarantee the correctness of a term according to Fronto (in Gell. NA 19,8,15). Therefore, the period recognized as exemplary is elevated through imitation to the 'Classical'. The return to classical patterns (Latin *classici* = Greek ἐγκριθέντες/*enkrithéntes* or πραττόμενοι/*prattómenoi*) is usually preceded by an intermediate period with mostly baroque traits that is then despaired of by classicists so that a three-layered periodicity results (already a complaint by Dion. Hal. De antiquis rhetoribus 1 regarding Greek literature), which is visible in the classicism of the Italian Renaissance. The immediately preceding Latin Middle Ages were in part criticized, in part ignored by humanists of the Quattrocento, whereas antiquity was elevated to the classical standard.

B. GREEK CLASSICISM
In the Augustan period → Caecilius [III 5] of Cale Acte (with a preference for → Lysias) and → Dionysius [18] of Halicarnassus (declaring, e.g., → Demosthenes [2] and → Thucydides as models) mark a 'turn towards classicism' [4. 171] with a radical literary critique that rejects Hellenism and its programmes and praises the advantages of Greek literature of the 5th and 4th. cents. BC. The Greek period declared as classical from about 480 (victory over the Persians at Salamis) to 323 BC (death of Alexander the Great) refers in particular to the phenomenon of → Atticism. This was conceptualized according to Dion. Hal. Rhet. 3,1 in Rome (ἀρχὴ τῆς τοσαύτης μεταβολῆς ἐγένετο ἡ πάντων κρατοῦσα Ῥώμη, 'Omnipotent Rome was the starting-point of this great revolution'). With his writings *Brutus* and *Orator*, which express the Attic/Asianist controversy regarding simple or elaborate oratory style, Cicero signalled a contemporary (the mid 40s of the 1st cent. BC) interest in classicistic issues. Bearers of the Atticistic movement were M. → Iunius [I 10] Brutus, T. → Pomponius Atticus and C. Iulius → Caesar.

The required *mímēsis* (Latin *imitatio*) aimed at equality with the models or even surpassing them. The author of *Perì Hýpsous* (Περὶ Ὕψους, (Ps.-) → Longinus) discusses in the 1st (?) cent. AD the ideals of the Augustan classicists (especially Caecilius [III 5] of Cale Acte) with great emphasis on the poetic *phýsis* ('nature/disposition'). → Plutarch is rather more receptive as a classicist [6. 96]. *Kanónes* (Κανόνες, → canon) of classics were taken from the Alexandrian tradition [6. 84]. Dramatists, epic poets, historiographers, lyricists, philosophers and orators were arranged in groups. This was imitated on the Roman side at an early time by → Volcacius Sedigitus (2nd cent. BC), who analogous to the 10 Attic orators compiles a list of the best *palliata* poets (→ palliata) (De poetis fr. 1 MOREL).

Even within the era elevated as the Greek 'classical period', certain authors were already canonized, for example, the three tragedians → Aeschylus [1], → Euripides [1] and → Sophocles in 405 BC by the comedian → Aristophanes [3] (Ran. 72: οἱ μὲν γὰρ οὐκέτ' εἰσίν, οἱ δ' ὄντες κακοί, 'for these [i.e. the three] no longer are, and the others, the living, are bad') and then confirmed by literary criticism in the 4th cent. (cf. Heraclides [16] Ponticus fr. 179 WEHRLI). → Aristotle [6] indicates Sophocles as the terminal point in the development of tragedy in the first book of the 'Poetics' and considers the Sophoclean 'Oedipus Tyrannus' a model of the genres. Alexandrian philology is so familiar with the threesome of poets that the learned drama introductions (→ Hypothesis) of → Aristophanes [4] of Byzantium always only speak of παρ' οὐδετέρῳ ('in neither of the other two'), etc. The triad of comedy writers is only attested from the classicistic period (Hor. Sat. 1,4,1: *Eupolis atque Cratinus Aristophanesque poetae*).

Drama stood at the centre of classical Greek literature of the 5th cent. BC with the → epic playing a rather subordinate role. However, the Homeric poems are an exception: their paradigmatic effect extends over Greek and Roman antiquity, reaching a pronounced climax in Virgil's *Aeneid*. This is one reason why Greek classical literature is today considered as a period extending 'from Homer to the philosophers of the 4th cent. BC' [5. 192] in which various genres gradually attain perfection.

C. ROMAN CLASSICISM
The phenomenon of classicism in Roman literature can only be defined with difficulties because of its complexity. Already in the 3rd and 2nd cents. BC, the early poets → Livius Andronicus, → Naevius and → Ennius confronted Greek models with imitation while → Plautus even shows signs of an *aemulatio* (an innovative competition concerned with independence). The Roman classic of the 1st cent. BC would be inconceivable without Greek examples. Horace advises young poets to have them at hand day and night: *vos exemplaria Graeca/nocturna versate manu, versate diurna*

(Hor. Ars P. 268f.). With the exception of the prose writer Cato, Horace rejects all writers of the Roman pre-classic. However, the Hellenistic poets that were rejected by the Greeks were included among the models. Typical of the Roman recourse to Greek works is a diachronous → eclecticism that used everything available but that showed classicistic traits by rigourously absorbing only the best: → Virgil refers equally to both Homer and Apollonius Rhodius, Hesiod and Theocritus; → Horace [7] fancies himself a Roman Archilochus (Hor. Epist. 1,19,23ff.) but did not ignore Pindaric (cf. part of Carm. 4,2, also 4,4 and 4,14) and Callimachean poetry (cf. Carm. 4,15,1ff.); → Cicero as a transmitter of Greek philosophy was guided by the Academic, Peripatetic and Stoic thought of various periods (with a slight preference for Plato), as an orator also by Demosthenes and the contemporary Rhodian school of Apollonius → Molon). The greatest authors of Augustan → literature were soon considered classics because their works and style were imitated in the imperial period. Cicero and Virgil ruled the rhetorical school, supplanting the archaic Roman patterns, among them Ennius, and were considered equal to the Greeks. Even → Augustine attests to the parallelism of Homer and Virgil in education (Aug. Conf. 1,13f.).

The → archaism arising in the 1st cent. AD, which was subjected to a strict critique by the Atticist Quintilian (Inst. 2,5,21 and 8,3,60), incorporated the language of Ennius and → Sallust into classicism. Contrary to Greek classicism, Roman classicism differentiated between literary and political models: 'from the early imperial period to the present', 'specifically Roman values ... are sought in the early period of the Roman Republic' [7. 59].

→ Archaism; → Atticism; → Literature; CLASSICISM

1 TH. GELZER, Klassik und K., in: Gymnasium 82, 1975, 147–173   2 Id., Klassizismus, Attizismus und Asianismus, in: Id. (ed.), Le Classicisme à Rome (Entretiens 25), 1979, 1–55   3 U.v. WILAMOWITZ-MOELLENDORFF, Asianismus und Attizismus, in: KS III, 1969, 223–273   4 R. KASSEL, Die Abgrenzung des Hell. in der griech. Literaturgesch., in: Id., KS, 1991, 154–73   5 M. FUHRMANN, Dichtungstheorie der Ant., ²1992   6 H. FLASHAR, Die klassizistische Theorie der Mimesis, in: TH. GELZER (ed.), Le Classicisme à Rome (Entretiens 25), 1979, 79–111   7 DIHLE, ²1991.

K. BAUCH, Klassik-Klassizität-K., 1939/40, 429–440; A. DIHLE, Der Beginn des Attizismus, in: A* 23, 1977, 162–177; Id., Der griech. K., in: Heidelberger Jbb. 34, 1990, 147–156; M. GREENHALGH, Was ist K.?, 1990; W. VOSSKAMP (ed.), Klassik im Vergleich, 1993; TH. HIDBER, Das klassizistische Manifest des Dionys von Halikarnaß, 1996. P.RI.

II. LEGAL HISTORY
In 1790 Gustav HUGO [1] described the ancient jurists included in the → Digesta as the 'classical jurists'. Since then it has become customary — even internationally — to describe the Roman jurists from Antistius [II 3] Labeo (about the time of Christ's birth) to Mode-

stinus (died c. AD 235) as the legal classics. If one thinks of this term describing a cultural climax, this periodization appears arbitrary because the most important achievements of Roman law are older, in the period of the 'Ancients' (veteres) of the 2nd and 1st cent. BC, in which Q. → Mucius Scaevola, C. → Aquilius [I 12] Gallus and Cicero's friend Servius → Sulpicius Rufus lived, wrote and significantly influenced the edicts of the praetors with their suggestions (→ ius). However, the highest quality of Roman legal literature is accessible in the writings of the 2nd and early 3rd cents. AD, for example, in → Iuventius [II 2] Celsus, Salvius → Iulianus [1] and → Papinianus. Their intellectual achievements were in particular considered models of judicial-literary culture in pandect studies of the 19th cent. Even today, the presence of Roman law studies in legal faculties throughout Europe derives its legitimization in the first place from the high quality of 'classical' Roman legal literature. That this has been preserved at all to a significant degree (about 5 per cent) in the medium of the Digesta is based on the classicism of antiquity, ini- tially in the legal schools of eastern Rome (especially in Berytus), then in the 6th cent. because of Justinian and his legal minister → Tribonianus.

PANDECTISTIC; TEXT TRANSMISSION RESEARCH

1 G. HUGO, Lehrbuch und Chrestomathie des classischen Pandektenrechts zu exegetischen Vorlesungen, in: Beyträge zur civilistischen Bücherkunde I, 1790, 209   2 F. WIEACKER, Über das Klass. in der röm. Jurisprudenz, in: Id.., Vom röm. Recht, ²1961, 161–186   3 K.-H. SCHINDLER, Justinians Haltung zur Klassik, 1966. G.S.

Classicum see → Signals

Clastidium Main settlement of the Celtic-Ligurian Anares (Pol. 2,34) in the south of Ticinum, modern Casteggio. Traffic node. In 222 BC the Romans defeated the Gauls near C. (Pol. 2,69; Plut. Marcellus 6; topic of the praetexta of same name by Naevius [1. 30f.]). Relay point on the via Postumia, vicus of Placentia (CIL V 7357).

1 R. CHEVALLIER, La romanisation de la Celtique du Pô, 1979.

M. BARATTA, C., 1931. A.SA.

Claudia
I. REPUBLICAN PERIOD   II. IMPERIAL PERIOD

I. REPUBLICAN PERIOD
[I 1] A daughter of Ap. Claudius Caecus. Her wish, which she loudly expressed in a crowd, that her brother P. Claudius Pulcher (cos. 249 BC) should live and lose another battle at sea so that the mob would be decreased, was heavily fined (Ateius Capito in Gell. NA 10,6; Liv. per. 19; Suet. Tib. 2,3).

R. A. BAUMAN, Women and Politics in Ancient Rome, 1992, 19–20. ME.SCH.

[I 2] Daughter of Ap. Claudius Pulcher, *cos.* 143 BC, married Tiberius Gracchus (Plut. Tiberius Gracchus 4,1–4; App. B Civ. 1,55; Liv. per. 58).

[I 3] **C. Quinta.** Probably a daughter of P. Claudius Pulcher. In 204 BC when the ship carrying the sacred stone of the Magna Mater was stranded in the Tiber, she allegedly freed it by invoking her chastity (Liv. 29,14,11f.; Ov. Fast. 4,305–22; Plin. HN. 7,120; Suet. Tib. 2,3). Regarding honorary inscriptions and images cf. CIL VI 492–94; Val. Max. 1,8,11; Tac. Ann. 4,64,3 and CUMONT, Religions, pl. 1,5.

R.A. BAUMAN, Women and Politics in Ancient Rome, 1992, 28–29, 214.   ME.STR.

[I 4] Daughter of P. Clodius Pulcher and Fulvia, therefore the step-daughter of Mark Antony. Married upon demand of the soldiers in 43 BC as a 10-year old to Octavian (→ Augustus). The latter dissolved the marriage in 41 BC for political reasons (Suet. Aug. 62,1; Cass. Dio 46,56,3; 48,5,3; PIR² C 1057).

II. IMPERIAL PERIOD

[II 1] Daughter of the later emperor Claudius and Plautia Urgulanilla, born five months before their divorce. Claudius did not recognize her (Suet. Claud. 27,1).

[II 2] **C. Augusta.** Daughter of Nero and Poppaea, who immediately received the name Augusta at her birth on AD 21 January 63. Died at four months and deified (PIR² C 1061) [1. 100].

[II 3] The wife of the poet Statius. Her daughter was from a previous marriage. Statius addressed Silv. 3,5 to her for the purpose of persuading her to return with him to Naples (PIR² C 1062).

[II 4] **C. Acte.** Imperial slave, originally from Asia, later freed. Nero left his wife Octavia because of his passion for her. Fought by Agrippina (Tac. Ann. 13,12f. 14,2.63; Suet. Nero 28,1; Cass. Dio 61,7,1). Many of her slaves are known, also property at Puteoli and Velitrae (PIR² C 1067). In 68 she interred Nero's remains (Suet. Nero 50).

[II 5] **C. Basilo.** Senator's wife of consular rank, married to A. Iulius Proculus, *cos. suff.,* under Antoninus Pius. Originally from Synnada in Asia. Probably forced by Commodus to commit suicide together with her husband (SHA Comm. 7,7; RAEPSAET-CHARLIER no. 227) [2. 457ff.].

[II 6] **C. Caninia Severa.** Woman of senatorial rank, daughter of the first consul from Ephesus, Ti. Claudius Severus; she held several offices in her home town in the 1st half of the 3rd cent. (I. Eph. III 639. 648. 892) [3. 103, no. 412].

[II 7] **C. Capitolina.** Daughter of Claudius Balbillus. Married to C. Iulius Antiochus Philopappus, the son of the last king of Commagene, later to Iunius Rufus, *praef.* Aegypti 94–98 (PIR² C 1086; [4. 132] puts the marriages into the wrong sequence).

[II 8] **C. Marcella maior.** Daughter of C. Claudius Marcellus, *cos.* 50 BC, and Octavia, the sister of Octavian. Born about 43 BC, married to Agrippa until 21 BC,

when Augustus caused him to seek a divorce so he could marry Augustus' daughter Iulia. Marcella received Iullus Antonius, *cos. ord.* in 10 BC, as husband. There were children in both marriages (PIR² C 1102; RAEPSAET-CHARLIERno. 242) [5. 143ff.].

[II 9] **C. Marcella minor.** Sister of C. [II 8] Born in 39 BC after the death of her father [5. 147]. Perhaps married to an *ignotus,* then with M. Valerius Messalla Appianus, *cos. ord.,* in 12 BC, then with Paullus Aemilius Lepidus, probably the *cos. suff.,* in 34 BC. Her children are Valerius Messalla Barbatus, Claudia Pulchra and Paullus Aemilius Regillus, her grandchild Valeria Messalina, the wife of Claudius (PIR² C 1103) [5. 147ff.; 6. 226ff.]. Regarding the inscriptions of her slaves and *liberti* CIL VI 4414ff.; cf. [6. 230f.].

[II 10] **C. Octavia.** Daughter of Claudius [III 1], see → Octavia.

[II 11] **C. Pulchra.** Daughter of C. [II 9] and M. Valerius Messalla Appianus; born no later than 12 BC. Related to Agrippina (Tac. Ann. 4,52,1); married to P. Quinctilius Varus, her son is Quinctilius Varus. In 26 she was accused of → *maiestas* and *impudicitia* and sentenced (Tac. Ann. 4,52; 66,1) [5. 147ff].

1 KIENAST   2 MÜLLER, in: Chiron 10, 1980   3 W. ECK, RE Suppl. 14   4 HALFMANN   5 SYME, AA   6 U. FUSCO, G.L. GREGORI, in: ZPE 112, 1996, 226ff.   W.E.

Claudia fossa see → Fossa Claudia

Claudianus

[1] [...]us C. s. M. → Arruntius Claudianus

[2] **Claudius C.** Graeco-Latin poet (about AD 400) from Alexandria. C. first wrote Greek poetry of which the opening of a 'gigantomachy' is preserved, whose *praefatio* in elegiac distichs indicates recitation in Alexandria. Of the seven epigrams in the → *Anthologia Palatina* attributed to a Klaudianos (see Claudius → Claudianus [3]), four were written by this C. (5,86,, 9,140. 753f.). He may also be the writer of (lost) epic poems praising cities in Palestine and Asia Minor [3. 7–12]. C. was one of those 'wandering poets' [4], who earned their living by composing and reciting such epics and made a career in the service of various employers. Via Constantinople, where the Anth. Pal. 9,140 attests to a recitation in the library, he arrived in Rome in 393/4, where he recited his first Latin poem in early 395, a panegyric → epic on the consulate of the brothers Olybrius and Probinus of the *gens Anicia,* who were still boys. This performance secured him the favour of the Milanese court where, after the death of → Theodosius (395), the *magister militum* → Stilicho was regent for his son → Honorius (*384). In January 396 C. recited in Milan the festive poem for the 3rd consulate of Honorius and gained Stilicho's trust because in a fictive scene of this epic (142–162) he presented how the dying Theodosius appointed Stilicho *alone* as the guardian of *both* sons, Honorius in the West and → Arcadius (*about 377) in the East and installed him

as regent in *both* halves of the empire. C. defended this claim in all poems that he wrote as court poet, for which he received the office of *tribunus et notarius* and was honoured in 400 with a bronze statue in the Forum of Trajan in Rome whose inscription was preserved (CIL 6,1710 = ILS 2949).

C. composed panegyric epics on further consulates of Honorius (*cos. IV* 398, *cos. VI* 404), the Christian Neoplatonic philosopher Mallius Theodorus (399) and Stilicho (400, three books) on the occasion of successful wars against the African rebel Gildo (*Bellum Gildonicum*, 397, unfinished) and Alaric's Goths (*Bellum Geticum*, 402). On the other hand he mercilessly attacked the power holders in the East, who had rejected Stilicho's claim to rule, with → invective: in 396/7 the *magister militum* → Rufinus (two bks), in 399 the consul → Eutropius (two bks). Likewise, → fescennines and an epithalamium (→ Hymenaus) on the marriage of 13–year-old Honorius to Stilicho's 12–year-old daughter Maria (398) praised Stilicho [8. 126–132]. The only longer mythological poem, on the abduction of Proserpina (*De raptu Proserpinae*, 3 bks), remained unfinished and is difficult to date. The same genera are also represented in the collection of the 52 *Carmina minora*: laudatory poems (30 *Laus Serenae*, about 404), invectives (43f.; 50), epithalamia (25), letters (19; 31; 40f.), mythological poems (27 *Phoenix*; 53 *Gigantomachia*), also some → epigrams and → ekphraseis on towns, rivers, works of art, animals and natural objects. Cause for speculation on C.'s attitude to Christianity, of which there is no trace in the poetry (Aug. Civ. 5,26 calls him *a Christi nomine alienus*, 'removed from the name of Christ', Oros. 7,35,21 even a *paganus pervicacissimus*, 'a most stubborn pagan'), was provided by Carm. min. 32 *De Salvatore*, which as a commissioned work does not have to be a personal creed [5]. That no work can be dated after 404 and C. does not celebrate Stilicho's 2nd consulate in 405 was taken together with the incomplete state of *De Raptu*, *Laus Serenae* and the Latin *Gigantomachia*, as proof of C.'s death in 404; but it cannot be ruled out that the 'wandering poet' C. was searching for new patrons in 404 with nothing being preserved of this activity.

C. shaped the historical-political epic of late antiquity for centuries and developed the genera of the panegyric epic, which was composed for presentation at institutionalized events (consulate, victory celebrations) before a precisely defined audience (*concilium principis*, court, Senate) [14; cf. 8; 15; 20]. In his dual function as *laudator* and *narrator* the panegyric poet subjects the historical events to the structures of prose panegyric (→ Panegyric) by subordinating the aesthetic claim to the panegyric function and giving the audience affirmative instructions for reception in commentaries, reflections, interpretative models and offers of identification. Therefore, epic continuity is overshadowed by 'isolated images' [16. 106ff.], e.g., broad descriptions of individual scenes, which as profane 'reflective images' invite sympathy and identification. A specific

expression of this new function are the → praefationes, whose fixed scheme of introductory image, central allegoresis and concluding development of the theme is a prelude to the recital situation of the presentation [13. 119ff.].

C.'s relationship to the late antique Greek epic is unclear because of fragmentary transmission. His knowledge of the Augustan and Flavian Latin epic (1st cent. AD) and its creative reception are all the more evident. C. boldly uses all traditional linguistic and epic creative means: gods, demons and personifications initiate the epic plot and carry it forward [9], people mouth Stilicho's policies in long speeches, ekphrasis implicitly relates ideology and philosophical discourses justify historical meaning. He successfully paints grand images and scenes (council of hell: Ruf. 1,25ff., palace [2] and sea voyage of Venus: Epith. 49ff., *Spelunca Aevi*: Stil. 2,424ff., hunt: Stil. 3,237ff., flower-picking Proserpina: Rapt. 2,36ff.). Invoking Rome's great past, C. defends for his patrons the belief in eternal Rome (6. Cons. 361ff.; *Laudes Romae*: Stil. 3,130ff.), symbolized by the rejuvenation of an aged Roma (Gild. 17ff.) [3. 349ff.; 18. 133ff.].

C.'s form of the panegyric epic was used by his successors until the 6th cent. (→ Corippus, → Venantius Fortunatus) but his relationship to Prudentius remains unclear. The thesis of Stilicho commissioning a posthumous edition of epics relating to him [1] was recently questioned [11; 21]. Apparently four separate codices (Rapt. Pros., Carm. min., invectives/victory epics [*In Rufinum; In Eutropium; Bellum Geticum; In Gildonem*], festive poems) reached the Middle Ages, where they appear in library catalogues from the 8th cent. (Charlemagne's court library, Bobbio, Reichenau, St.Gall). The oldest MSS (8th/9th cents.) only contain parts of the *Carmina minora*; in the 11th cent. MSS of the *Carmina maiora* appear, in the 12th cent. *De Raptu* [10;11]: it was the actual *aetas Claudianea*, which was reflected in the sudden increase of MSS (over 300), the rise of *De Raptu* ('C. minor') as a school text [10. 69ff.], in commentaries [6] and also a productive reception (Alain de Lille, *Anticlaudianus*, c. 1183) [17]. The above scenes have a particularly strong effect in Chaucer, Boccaccio, Petrarca, Poliziano, Petrus Martyr [12], Vida, Tasso, Milton etc. [7]. C. is still the authoritative model for praising rulers in the 17th cent. [19], Theodosius' admonitions of Honorius (4. Cons. 214ff.), which are reminiscent of mirrors of princes, are often used; the mythical images, personifications and sentences affect literature (Montaigne, Montesquieu, Coleridge) and painting (Botticelli, Poussin) until the 18th cent. and even the 20th cent. [22; 9a; 3. 419ff.]. C. only served historicism as a historical source. The disinterest of the 20th cent. gave way to a shift in paradigms during the 60s and an increased turn towards late antiquity. Today, C.'s rank as one of the great poets of Latin literature is undisputed.

ED. PRINC.: B.CELSANUS, 1482.
EDITIONS: J.B. HALL, 1985; J.-L.CHARLET, 1991ff.

BIBLIOGRAPHY: 1 T. BIRT, Claudiani Claudii Carmina, 1892 (MGH AA 10) 2 G. BRADEN, C. and his influence, in: Arethusa 12, 1979, 203–231 3 A. CAMERON, C., 1970 4 Id., Wandering Poets, in: Historia 14, 1965, 470–509 5 J.-L. CHARLET, Théologie, politique et rhétorique ... d'après ... C., in: La poesia tardoantica, 1984, 259–287 6 A. K. CLARKE, P. M. GILES, The Comm. of Geoffrey of Vitry on C., De raptu Pros., 1973 7 S. DÖPP, C. und die lat. Epik zwischen 1300 und 1600, in: Res Publica Litterarum 12, 1989, 39–50 8 Id., Zeitgesch. in Dichtungen C., 1980 9 C. GNILKA, Götter und Dämonen in den Gedichten C.s, in: A 18, 1973, 144–160 9a H. HAASSE, Een nieuwer testament, 1966 10 J.B. HALL (ed.), C., De Raptu Proserpinae, 1969 11 Id., Prolegomena to C., 1986 12 U. HECHT, Der Pluto furens des Petrus Martyr Anglerius, 1992 13 R. HERZOG, Die allegorische Dichtkunst des Prudentius, 1966 14 H. HOFMANN, Überlegungen zu einer Theorie der nichtchristl. Epik der lat. Spätant., in: Philologus 132, 1988, 101–159 15 W. KIRSCH, Die lat. Versepik des 4.Jh., 1989 16 F. MEHMEL, Virgil und Apollonios Rhodios, 1940 17 P. OCHSENBEIN, Studien zum Anticlaudianus des Alanus ab Insulis, 1975 18 F. PASCHOUD, Roma Aeterna, 1967 19 P. L. SCHMIDT, Balde und C., in: Jacob Balde und seine Zeit, 1986, 157–184 20 Id., Politik und Dichtung in der Panegyrik C.s, 1976 21 Id., Die Überlieferungsgesch. von C.' Carmina maiora, in: Illinois Classical Studies 14, 1989, 391–415 22 Id., Zur niederen und höheren Kritik von C.' carmina minora, in: De Tertullien aux Mozarabes (Mélanges J. Fontaine) vol.1, 1992, 643–660 22 H. SUDERMANN, Die Lobgesänge des C., 1914. H.HO.

[3] (Claudius C.) Poet of the 5th cent AD (was with Cyrus of Panopolis at the court of Theodosius II, cf. Evagrius Hist. Eccl. 1,19). Apart from a lost Πάτρια (*Pátria*), he wrote on Tarsus, Anazarbus, Berytus (Beirut) and Nicaea (schol. Anth. Pal. 1,19). These were probably used by Nonnus (cf. Nonnus, Dion. 41,155), seven epigrams (Anth. Pal. 1,19f.; 5,86; 9,139f.; 753f.), of which a few show the influence of the Nonnian hexameter technique (especially 1,19 and 9,139). It cannot be entirely precluded that the poems 9,753f. were composed by the famous Claudius → Claudianus [2] who composed, for example, a Γιγαντομαχία (*Gigantomachía*) (they show some similarities to his Latin epigrams, cf. Carm. min. 34,1–6).

PANEGYRICS

A. WIFSTRAND, Von Kallimachos zu Nonnos, 1933, 159f.; A. CAMERON, Claudian. Poetry and Propaganda at the Court of Honorius, 1970, 6–14. E.D.

[4] C. Mamertus. Presbyter in Vienne (Gaul), knowledgeable in Greek and Roman poetry, a friend of → Sidonius Apollinaris, whose Epist. 4,3 and 4,11 allow some inferences regarding the life of C. His *De statu animae*, dedicated in AD 470 to Sidonius, is a disputation against bishop Faustus of Reii (who propounded the corporality of the soul). C. used Neoplatonic sources for the incorporeality of the soul (especially → Porphyrius). His treatise was popular in the Middle Ages.

EDITION: CSEL II, 1885
BIBLIOGRAPHY: W. SCHMID, s.v. C. Mamertus, RAC, 3, 1957, 169–179; P. COURCELLE, Les Lettres Grecques en Occident, ²1948, 223–235; E. L. FORTIN, Christianisme et culture philosophique au Vᵉ siècle. La querelle de l'âme humaine en Occident, 1959. P.HA.

Claudioupolis (Κλαυδιούπολις; *Klaudioúpolis*).
[1] Old settlement in the Salo region (Abant Gölü, Bolu basin and surrounding alpine pastures), today known as Bolu (Str. 12,4,7). It was a suburb of the free → Mariandyni, conquered by → Zipoetes in 281/0 BC, and Galatian from *c.* 275/4 to 179 (the residential fortress of the north-western Tolistobogian tetrarchy is located south of Bolu at the spa of Karacasu, already ancient at that time). Newly founded as the polis of Bythnion by Prusias II, it became a part of Bithynian Mesogaia, later of the province called → Bithynia et Pontus. Under Emperor Claudius (AD 41–54), it was renamed as C., and, as Antinous' [2] hometown, it received the name of Bithynion Hadriana in *c.* 130 (when the festivals of Hadrianeia Antinoeia were introduced). During the Tetrarchy (3rd/4th cent. AD), it served as a military garrison, and after 388 (dissenting: [1]), it became the metropolis of the province of Honoria. Known to be a bishop's seat since the Tetrarchy.

1 K. BELKE, Paphlagonien und Honorias, 1996, 66, 235–237, 270.

F. BECKER-BERTAU, Klaudiupolis (IK 31), 1986; K. STROBEL, Galatien und seine Grenzregionen, in: E. SCHWERTHEIM (ed.), Forsch. in Galatien (Asia Minor Stud. 12), 1994, 29–65; Id., Die Galater 1, 1996; BEDRI YALMAN, Bolu Hisartepe, in: IX. Türk Tarih Kongresi 1, 1986, 435–450, fig. 191–205. K.ST.

[2] (also: Κλαυδιόπολις). City in Isauria (Ptol. 5,6,22; Amm. 14,8,2; Hierocles, Synecdemus 709,10), located 53 km north-west of Seleucea on the Calycadnus, today known as Mut. C. can be identified (contrary to Ptol. 5,7,6) with *Colonia Iulia Augusta Felix Ninica* since the two formed a double community after being raised to municipal status under Claudius [2. 426ff.]; records show that it was a diocese since the Council of Nicaea (AD 325) [1]. Little remains of the settlement; a necropolis in the south-east [1].

1 HILD/HELLENKEMPER 1, 307f. 2 S. MITCHELL, Iconium and Ninica, in: Historia 28, 1979, 409–438. K.T.

Claudius Name of a Roman lineage (Sabine *Clausus*, with the vernacular variant of → *Clodius*, esp. in the 1st cent. BC). The Claudii supposedly immigrated to Rome from the Sabine city of Regillum at the beginning of the republic in 504 BC under their ancestor Att(i)us Clausus (→ Appius) and were immediately accepted into the circle of patrician families (Liv. 2,16,4–6), which explains why the early members received the invented epithets of *Inregillensis* C. [I 5–6] and *Sabinus* C. [I 31–32], [1. 155f.]. The praenomen *Appius* came to signify the family. Named after them was the Tribus Claudia north of Rome beyond the Anio, the 20th tribus to be established, probably in 495, although the gentile members of the family later belonged to other tribus as well [2]. Even late in the imperial period, the Claudians were remarkable for their unusual pride in their noble lineage (Tac. Ann. 1,4,3 *vetere atque insita Claudiae familiae superbia*). As a result, in the formation of the traditions of early Roman History the early Claudians, esp. the Decemvir C. [I 5] were stereotyped as typical representatives of a policy hostile to the people [3]. In the history of the *gens* (synopsis in Suet. Tib. 1,1ff.; cf. Tac. Ann. 12,25,2), the patrician branch is particularly important in *c.* 300 especially in the person of the censor Ap. C. [I 2] Caecus. He is the ancestor of the most important families of later times: the Pulchri [I 20–29] who played a significant role in the political life of the 1st cent. BC, the Centhones [I 4], and the Nerones [I 16–19] (C. [I 19] became the progenitor of the Julian-Claudian house of emperors through his marriage to Livia). Parallel to them and originally related to the patrician branch (Cic. De or. 1,176) was the plebeian branch of the family, whose main lineage were the Marcelli [I 7–15]. They are recognizable in political life since the *cos.* 331 C. [I 10], and owe their high status to C. [I 11], the commander of the 2nd Punic War, disappearing from view soon after the civil war with M. Marcellus, the nephew and presumptive successor of Augustus (C. [II 42]). The historian C. [I 30] does not belong to the great families. Due to awards of citizenship by the emperors C. and Nero, the name was very common during the imperial period (often abbreviated as *Cl.*), even in the Greek east.

1 B. LINKE, Von der Verwandtschaft zum Staat, 1995 2 L. R. TAYLOR, The Voting Districts of the Roman Republic, 1960, 36; 283–286   3 T. P. WISEMAN, Clio's Cosmetics, 1979, 57–139.
FAMILY TREES: MÜNZER, s.v. C., RE 3, 2666; 2731 DRUMANN/GROEBE 2, 140f. SYME, AA, Stemma VI and VII.

I. REPUBLICAN PERIOD   II. IMPERIAL PERIOD
III. EMPEROR   IV. PHYSICIANS, SCULPTORS, LAWYERS

I. REPUBLICAN PERIOD

[I 1] C., Q. As tribune of the people and supported by C. → Flaminius, he introduced a law in 218 according to which senators and sons of senators were not allowed to own ships which could hold more than 300 amphorae (Liv. 21,63,3), resulting in the withdrawal of senators from purely commercial enterprise (→ *equites Romani*).

[I 2] C. Caecus, Ap. Most important member of his family *c.* 300 BC; he received his cognomen due to his blindness in old age. His unusual career, known to us only through the Augustan Elogium (InscrIt. 13,3, no. 79), led him through various offices, began directly with the position of censor in 312, in which he institu-

ted major reforms (Diod. Sic. 20, 36, 1–6, *i.a.*; MRR 1, 160): the construction of the Aqua Appia and the → Via Appia; the transfer of the cult of Hercules at the Ara maxima from the family of the Potitii to state slaves (Cic. Cael. 34f., *i.a.*); the prohibition of the collegium of *tibicines* to hold their banquet at the temple of Jupiter (Liv. 9,30,5); the acceptance of non land-owning citizens into all tribus (in 304, it was limited again to the four urban tribus), and the admission of sons of freedpersons into the Senate (Liv. 9,46,10f.). Consul I in 307 (in Rome); in 304, he commissioned his freedperson and secretary Cn. → Flavius with the publication of a calendar of trial dates and of the legal formulas previously kept by the pontiffs (*ius Flavianum*, Liv. 9,46; Gell. NA 7,9,2ff.). He fought in Samnium as consul II in 296 and as praetor in 295, and, after the war, he erected a temple to Bellona on the Circus Flaminius. Advanced in years, he spoke against Pyrrhus' peace proposals in 280 after the defeat of the Romans at Heraclea (Plut. Pyrrh. 19; first Roman speech to be preserved in writing: Cic. Brut. 61; Sen. epist. 19,5,13; Tac. Dial. 18). Furthermore, he authored a collection of sententiae in Saturnia (*fabrum esse suae quemque fortunae*, Ps.-Sall. Rep. 1,1,2) and a legal treatise.

E. FERENCZY, From the Patrician to the Plebeian State, 1976; HÖLKESKAMP; J. SUOLAHTI, The Roman Censores, 1963.

[I 3] C. Caudex, Ap. In 264 BC, as consul, he was assigned to support the Mamertini against Hieron II and the Carthaginians. He ordered his military tribune C.C. to occupy the city of Messana and then crossed over to Sicily. These actions led to the start of the 1st Punic War (Enn. Ann. 223 VAHLEN; Pol. 1,10–12; 15, i.a.).

[I 4] C. Centho, Ap. Curulic aedil in 179 BC, praetor in the year of 175 in Hispania citerior where he remained in 174 in a proconsular imperium and defeated the Celtiberians (MRR 1, 404); later, a legate on numerous occasions.

[I 5] C. Crassus Inregillensis Sabinus, Ap. The Decemvir. Fictitious official career: consul I in 471 BC, consul II (?) In 451, leader of the collegium of the → *Decemviri* for the purpose of recording the Law of Twelve Tablets 451–449 (→ Tabulae Duodecimae). In annalistic tradition (Liv. 3,33ff.; Dion. Hal. Ant. Rom. 10,56; 11,24ff.; MRR 1, 45–48), he is the leader of the patricians in the fight against the plebeians. Originally, in the first decemvirate in 451, he was regarded as friendly to the plebeians, but in the second decemvirate, he develops into a tyrant hostile to plebeians, orders the murder of L. Siccius and trapped Verginia. Finally, these crimes result in the fall of the decemvirate.

[I 6] C. Crassus Inregillensis, Ap. Grandson of the Decemvir C. [I 5]. In 367 BC, he supposedly opposed the Licinian-Sextian Laws and thereby the admission of plebeians to the consul's office (Liv. 6,40–42). In 362, as dictator, he defeated the Hernici (Liv. 7,7–8). He died in 349 while in office as consul.

[I 7] **C. Marcellus.** Praetor in 80 BC, proconsul in Sicilia, augur until 44. Father of C. [I 8].   K.-L.E.

[I 8] **C. Marcellus, C.** Aedil in 56 (MRR 3, 54), praetor in 53 (?), consul in 50, cousin of the consuls of 49, → Claudius [I 9], and of 51, → Claudius [I 15]. During his year in office of 50, he acted as a determined enemy of Caesar's and instigated the latter's recall from Gallia (MRR 2, 247). After the start of the civil war, Caesar's early success in the spring of 49 prompted him to change sides (Cic. Att. 10,15,2). He died in early 40, having lost all political importance (App. B Civ. 5,273).

[I 9] **C. Marcellus, C.** Cousin of the last, praetor in 52 BC at the latest, consul in 49 (MRR 2, 256). In the civil war, he was a commanding officer in the fleet of Pompey (Caes. B Civ. 3,5,3). Not mentioned after 48.
    W.W.

[I 10] **C. Marcellus, M.** Consul in 331 BC, dictator (for the holding of elections) in 327, the first plebeian Claudian to rise to the office of consul.

[I 11] **C. Marcellus, M.** Conquerer of Syracuse. He had already fought in the 1st Punic War. As consul I in 222 BC, he defeated the Celts near Clastidium (which is the topic of → Naevius' tragedy by the same name). Their leader Viridomarus died by C.'s hand; the latter thereby won the *spolia opima* (Pol. 2,34–35; triumph *de Insubribus* InscrIt. 13,1 79; vow of temple for Honos and Virtus Liv. 27,25,7). During the 2nd Punic War he was first in Campania, as praetor II in 216 and in a proconsular imperium in 215 (MRR 1, 255). In 214, he was consul III after his election in 215 had been revoked for religious reasons (MRR 1, 254). Together with his colleague Q. → Fabius Maximus Verrucosus he conquered Casilinum and crossed over to Sicily, where he first conquered the Leontini. As proconsul in 213, he began the siege of Syracuse, which he took in 212 despite strong resistance (Liv. 25,23–31; death of → Archimedes). The city was plundered and its treasures were brought to Rome, where they promoted an interest in Greek art. C. is also the reason why the Marcelli were interested in Sicily. After standing against Hannibal in Lower Italy as consul IV in 210 and as proconsul in 209, he fell in an ambush near Venusia as consul for the 5th time in 208 (Pol. 10,32; Liv. 27,26–27).

[I 12] **C. Marcellus, M.** Son of C. [I 11], for whom he gave the funeral oration (Liv. 27,27,13). He had served as military tribune under his father, was tribune of the people in 204, aedil in 200, praetor in 198 in Sicilia, consul in 196 (triumph over Celts), censor in 189, pontifex 196–177.

[I 13] **C. Marcellus, M.** Tribune of the people in 171 BC, praetor and propraetor 169/168 in Spain, consul I in 166, consul II in 155 (battles against Celts), consul III and proconsul 152/151 in Spain. His peace efforts were not approved by the Senate.

[I 14] **C. Marcellus, M.** Distinguished himself in 102 BC at Aquae Sextia (Frontin. strat. 2,6,4), was legate in the Social War of 90 and praetor before 73 (?, cf. MRR 3, 55).

[I 15] **C. Marcellus, M.** Praetor in 54 BC at the latest. As consul in 51, he attempted to deprive Caesar of the governorship of Gaul. He went to Pharsalus in exile in Mytilene and did not take advantage of Caesar's mercy before Cicero's recommendation in 46 (*Pro Marcello*), but was murdered in Piraeus in 45 on his return trip to Italy and buried in Athens. Honoured in Cic. Fam. 11,12.

[I 16] **C. Nero, Ap.** In 197/196 BC, legate of T. Quinctius Flamininus in Greece, in 195, praetor in Hispania ulterior.

[I 17] **C. Nero, C.** In 214 BC, he served as legatus under C. [I 11] Marcellus, took part in the siege of Capua as praetor in 212 and as propraetor in 211, then took control of the situation in Spain in 211/210 following the deaths of the Scipios. As consul in 207, he beat Hasdrubal on the Metaurus (Liv. 27,43–51).

[I 18] **C. Nero, Ti.** Consul in 202 BC (MRR 1, 315).

[I 19] **C. Nero, Ti.** Husband of Livia and, with that, father of future Emperor Tiberius and of Drusus. First in Caesar's service (quaestor in 48 BC, proquaestor in 47, settlement of veterans in Gallia in 46–45), he became praetor in 42 and fought against Octavian (Suet. Tib. 4) in the Perusian War in 41, reprieved in 39. In 38, he had to get divorced from Liva according to Octavian's wish. He was pontifex from *c.* 46 until his death in 33.

[I 20] **C. Pulcher, Ap.** Son of C. [I 29], took part in the battle at Cannae in 216 BC, was praetor in 215, propraetor (?) in 214–213 in Sicily. As consul, he besieged Capua in 212 and died as proconsul in 211 after the fall of the city.

[I 21] **C. Pulcher, Ap.** Served in Greece numerous times (195–194 BC under T. Quinctius Flamininus, 184/83 and 174–93 as legate), consul in 185.

GRUEN, Rome.

[I 22] **C. Pulcher, Ap.** Consul in 143 BC, censor (and *princeps senatus*) in 136. He was an influential adversary of the younger Scipio and supported the reforms of his son-in-law Ti. Sempronius Gracchus (*IIIvir agris dividendis* 133–130: ILLRP 472f.; Plut. Ti. Gracchus 4; 9; 13).

[I 23] **C. Pulcher, Ap.** Son of C. [I 22], quaestor in 99, aedil in 91 (?), praetor in 89, as a follower of Sulla, consul in 79, interrex in 77, proconsul in Macedonia in 77–76 where he died (MRR 2, 82; 89).   K.-L.E.

[I 24] **C. Pulcher, Ap.** Son of the last, brother of Clodius [I 4], father-in-law of Caesar's murderer Iunius Brutus. In 72–70 BC, he was the legate of Lucullus (Plut. Luc. 19; 21; 23). As praetor of the year 57, he did not support Cicero's recall (Cic. Att. 4,1,6). In 56, he went to Sardinia as promagistrate (Plut. Caes. 21). He was consul in 54 and as such became involved in the largest bribery scandal of the late republic (Cic. Att. 4,17,2f.). From 53–51, he resided in Cilicia as proconsul. During this time, he plundered his province on a scale otherwise known only of Verres [1. 113]. His successor Cicero talked about a 'forever ruined and completely devastated province' upon his arrival there (Cic. Att. 5,16,2). In his office of censor in the year of 50, C. excluded Sallust *et al.* from the Senate because of immoral behaviour (Cass. Dio 40,63,4). In the civil war, he sided with Pompey (proconsul in Greece 49 or 48). He died before August of 48 (MRR 2, 261, 276).

1 E. BADIAN, Publicans and sinners, ²1976, 113–115.
W.W.

[I 25] C. Pulcher, Ap. Cicero repeatedly mentioned and commended him (cf. fam. 11,22). Consul in 38 BC. Proconsul in Spain (triumph in 32). He erected the theatre in Herculaneum (CIL X 1423f.). PIR I² C 982. K.-L.E.

[I 26] C. Pulcher, Ap. Nephew of Clodius [I 4]. He and his brother C. [I 25]) jointly prosecuted → Annius [I 14] Milo (Ascon. 34 Z. 9; 38 Z. 21; 54 Z. 9C). W.W.

[I 27] C. Pulcher, C. Important politician and commander; praetor in 180. As consul in 177 and as proconsul in 176 he fought in Northern Italy and Liguria (triumph). Censor in 169 with Ti. Sempronius Gracchus (conflict with taxed leaseholders). Member of the commission for the reorganization of Macedonia in 167. Augur from 195 until his death in 167.

[I 28] C. Pulcher, C. Mint master in 110 or 109 BC (RRC 300), quaestor in *c.* 105, aedil in 99, praetor in 95, consul in 92 (MRR 3, 57f.; Elogium: InscrIt 13,1, no. 70).

[I 29] C. Pulcher, P. Son of C. [I 2], aedil in 253 (milestone on the Via Appia ILLRP 448). As consul in 249, he suffered a major defeat with his fleet near Drepana (Pol. 1,49–51), supposedly because he had ignored the auspices and had thrown the sacred chickens into the water 'in order to at least make them drink if they do not want to eat' (Cic. Nat. 2,7 i.a.). When he was to appoint a dictator, he chose M.C. Glicia, his *scriba*, who then was removed from office immediately (Liv. per. 19; Suet. Tib. 2,2). He died soon after being convicted of high treason. K.-L.E.

[I 30] C. Quadrigarius, Q. (Livy refers to him only as C.). Important historian of the Sullan period (Vell. Pat. 2,9,6), possibly identical to the Clodius mentioned in Plutarch (Numa 1,2), author of a *élenchos chrónōn* [1. 273; 2. 104 n. 18]. Nothing is known about his origin or his status (the submissive statement in 79 suggests a dependent position). C. wrote *Annales* in at least 23 bks., beginning with the Gauls' attack on Rome (*c.* 390 BC) and reaching into the time of Sulla (fr. 84: 82 BC). The contemporary history was described in great detail (about 10 bks. covering the last 20 years) and apparently presented an optimatic point of view (fr. 79; 83). C. worked relatively freely within the annalistic pattern, he composed large narrative units and shaped individual scenes by using anecdotes, (fictitious) letters, and speeches. His descriptions of battle scenes are literary creations. Along with → Valerius Antias, the work was a major source for Livy (beginning with bk. 6) and was very popular among the archaists of the 2nd cent. AD due to its pleasant archaic style (analyzed in [3. 88ff.; 4. 20]). Fragments: HRR 1, 205–237; fr. 10b

allows stylistic comparisons with Livy (esp. [5. 110–126]).
→ Annalists

1 A. KLOTZ, Der Annalist Q. Claudius Quadrigarius, in: RhM 91, 1942, 268–285 2 D. TIMPE, Erwägungen zur jüngeren Annalistik, in: * 25, 1979, 97–119 3 M. ZIMMERER, Der Annalist Qu. Claud. Quadrigarius, 1937 4 E. BADIAN, The Early Historians, in: T. A. DOREY (ed.) Latin Historians, 1966, 1–38 5 M. v. ALBRECHT, Meister röm. Prosa, ²1983.

SCHANZ/HOSIUS, 1, 316ff. W.K.

[I 31] C. Sabinus Inregillensis, C. Consul 495 BC. Elogium InscrIt 13,3, no. 67; Liv 2,21,–27.

[I 32] C. Sabinus Inregillensis, C. Son of C. [I 31], consul in 460 BC; probably the brother of C., the Decemvir. [I 5]. As in C. [I 31], the details are annalistic inventions.
K.-L.E.

II. IMPERIAL PERIOD

[II 1] Father of Claudius [II 29] Etruscus. His name is Ti.
→ Iulius

[II 2] C. Acilius Cleobulus. Senator from Ephesus, son of C. [II 20], probably the father of Acilius Cleobulus, governor of Syria Palaestina 276–282 (CIL IX 2334 = ILS 1134).

W. ECK, in: ZPE 37, 1980, 68–113; Id., in: ZPE 113, 1996, 141ff.

[II 3] Ti. C. Agrippinus. Originally from Patara in Lycia, his father was Lyciarch. Regarding senatorial offices, he is known only as suffect consul (under Antoninus Pius, after 151). Furthermore, records indicate that he was *frater Arvalis* in 155 [1; 2]; possibly identical or related to the *procurator* in Asia of the year AD 119 [3].

1 HALFMANN 164f. 2 SCHEID, Collège 77f. 3 J. REYNOLDS, Aphrodisias and Rome, 1982, 116, 118.

[II 4] Ti. C.M.Appius Atilius Bradua Regillus Atticus. Son of C. [II 11]. He was admitted into patrician rank by Antoninus Pius; *cos. ord.* in 185; *proconsul Asiae* (IRT 517 = AE 1981, 863 does not refer to him). Despised by his father. He lived at least until the year 209/210, if IG II² 1077 Z. 89f. refers to him [1]. PIR² C 785.

1 W. AMELING, Herodes Atticus, vol. 2, 1983, 16ff.

[II 5] Ti. C. Aristion. Citizen of Ephesus, who, in his homeland, held the offices of prytanis, gymnasiarch, and grammateus of the people. In addition, he was → *archiereus* three times. All of his offices fall into the period of Domitian and Trajan. In Ephesus, he erected several public buildings (I. Eph. 2, 234f., 237, 239, 241, 424–25a, 461, 508; 3, 638; 5, 1498; 7, 3217, 4105, 5101, 5113). Pliny calls him *princeps Ephesiorum* in epist. 6,31,3. Internal enemies in Ephesus tried unsuccessfully to accuse him in front of Trajan (PIR² C 788) [1].

1 C.SCHULTE, Die Grammateis von Ephesos, 1994, 103f., 158f.

[II 6] **C. Attalus.** Proconsul of Crete-Cyrenae, unknown time period (AE 1960, 262).

[II 7] **C. Attalus.** Euergetes from Pergamum, perhaps father or brother of C. [II 8].

[II 8] **Ti. C. Attalus Paterculianus.** From Pergamum. Praetorian governor of Thracia under Commodus, removed from the Senate by Septimius Severus. According to Cass. Dio (80,3,5; 4,3), he was readmitted to the Senate through Caracalla. In 217/218, at the age of 65 at least, he was proconsul of Cyprus (AE 1910, 104 = 1950, 9). Murdered on Elagabalus' orders (PIR² C 795). Father or grandfather of C. [II 9].

[II 9] **Ti. C. Attalus Paterc(u)lianus.** Consular governor of Bithynia in 244, son or grandson of C. [II 8] [1]. The odds are that he is identical to the legate of Bythnia by the same name mentioned in ILS 8836. It is unclear, however, who is meant in IGR 4, 415; 416 (cf. PIR² C 800).

1 P.WEISS, in: E fontibus haurire. FS H. Chantraine, 1994, 362ff.

[II 10] **Ti. C. Atticus Herodes.** Son of C. [II 35], father of C. [II 11], Athenian. Under Nerva, he supposedly found a treasure in his house. It turned out to be a part of his father's fortune that had been hidden from confiscation (Philostr. VS 2,1,2). In Athens and Sparta, where he also worked as an euergetus, he took on municipal offices; he promoted Corinth as well. In 132, he apparently acted as the priest of Zeus in the inauguration of the Olympieion in Athens. Perhaps under Trajan, he received the *ornamenta praetoria* (AE 1919,8) from the Senate. He was accepted into the Senate under Hadrian, possibly not until the latter's 2nd stay in Athens. He was *cos. suff.* probably in 132 or in 133 (RMD 3, 159; CIL XVI 174). It is impossible that he was consul for a second time, an assumption that was made based on Philostr. VS 2,1,1. PIR² C 801, [1; 2; 3].

1 HALFMANN 121ff.   2 W.AMELING, Herodes Atticus, vol.1, 1983, 21ff.   3 A.BIRLEY, in: ZPE 117, 1997, 229f.

[II 11] **L. Vibullius Hipparchus Ti. C. Atticus Herod.** → Herodes Atticus

[II 12] **M. Aurelius C. Gothicus.** → Aurelius [II 33]

[II 13] **M. Aurelius C. Quintillus.** → Aurelius [II 9]

[II 14] **T.C. Aurelius Aristobulus.** → Aurelius [II 3]

[II 15] **Ti. C. Balbillus.** According to IEph. 7,3041/2, his hometown must be Ephesus. Equestrian career, honoured in the Britannic triumph by Emperor Claudius [III 1]. He was responsible for welcoming legations and for phrasing answers. Under Claudius, he was responsible for the administration of temples and of the → Mouseion in Egypt. From 55 until at least 59, he was praefect of Egypt; follower of Agrippina (Tac. Ann. 13,22,1). On his origins and career: [1; 2]. His daughter was Claudia Capitolina. He is probably not identical to

the astrologer Balbillus in Sueton (Nero 36,1), (PIR² C 813).

1 PFLAUM 1, 34ff.   2 DEMOUGIN 447ff.   W.E.

[II 16] **Ti. C. Caesar Britannicus.** → Britannicus.

[II 17] **Ti. C. Candidus.** After an equestrian career in which he reached the position of a lower procurator, he became senator. In AD 193, he was assigned to a special unit against Niger by → Septimius Severus and won the battle at Nicaea-Cius (Cass. Dio 74,6,6). In 195, he was one of the three Roman commanders in Severus' 1st Parthian war (Cass. Dio 75,2,3). In the meantime, he had removed Severus' adversaries in the province of Asia. Apparently on the way to the next civil war — against Albinus, he took on a similar task against adherents of the anti-emperor in Noricum. Finally in 197, he participated in the battle of Lugdunum and, meanwhile having been appointed to the office of *cos. suff*, he became governor of the province of Hispania Tarraconensis. There, he was forced to fight *adversus rebelles hh.pp.* for the third time (ILS 1140 and add.; also, the entire *cursus honorum*). PIR² C 823.

ALFÖLDY, FH, 43ff.   A.B.

[II 18] **A. C. Charax.** Pergamene, admitted to the Senate probably through Hadrian. His career is preserved in AE 1961, 320. Legate of Cilicia, suffect consul in 147 [1]. Philosopher according to Marcus Aurelius (8,25,2), euergetes of Pergamum [2].

1 VIDMAN, FO² 51   2 HALFMANN, 161f.   W.E.

[II 19] **Ti. C. Claudianus.** Originally from Numidia, ILS 1146–7 (Rusicade). C. was *candidatus Aug.* as praetor, legate of the two Dacian legions (in 195, of the *legio V Macedonia*, CIL III 905), commander of a Dacian expedition corps, probably in the civil war against D. → Clodius [II 1] Albinus, then governor of Pannonia inferior (CIL III 3745 from the year 198 on). *Cos. suff.* and governor of Pannonia superior, not before 201 [1]. PIR² C 834.

1 THOMASSON, 1, 106f., cf. 115.   A.B.

[II 20] **Ti. C. Cleobulus.** *Cos. suff.* probably under Caracalla, from an Ephesic family, married to Acilia Fristana (CIL IX 2334 = ILS 1134; I.Eph. 3, 636) [1]; cf. C. [II 2].

1 W.ECK, in: ZPE 37, 1980, 66ff.

[II 21] **C. Diognetus.** *Procurator usiacus* in Egypt, *praef. classis Ravennatis* in 206, *praef. classis Misenensis* in 209 (PIR² C 852; RMD 1, 73; 3, 189).

G.M. PARÁSSOGLOU, in: Chronique d'Égypte 62, 1987, 210f., 212f.

[II 22] **C. Dionysius.** *Praef. classis Misenensis* in 214 (RMD 2, 131). Perhaps identical to Dionysius, *procurator Asiae* in 211 (AE 1993, 1505).

[II 23] **C. Drusus.** Son of future Emperor Claudius [III 1] and of Plautia Urgulanilla. Engaged to a daughter of

Seianus in the year 20, died shortly thereafter (PIR² C 856).
W.E.

[II 24] Nero C. Drusus. (= Drusus maior), originally named Decimus C. Drusus, son of Ti. C. Nero and Livia Drusilla (who married Octavian three months before the birth of C.), stepson of → Augustus, younger brother of Tiberius (Suet. Claud. 1,1). Born on 11 April(?) 38 BC (not 14 January, as claimed in Suet. Claud. 11,3, cf. [1. 47ff.; 2. 91ff.]). C. was first brought to his father, but after his death in 34/32, C. came under Octavian's tutelage (Cass. Dio 48,44,4f.) and was raised in his home. In 19 BC, Augustus pushed the Senate to permit C. to begin the *cursus honorum* five years earlier than normal (Cass. Dio 54,10,4; cf. Tac. Ann. 3,19,1). Quaestor in the year 18. In 16, after his brother Tiberius left for Gaul, he carried on his brother's praetorian office activities (Cass. Dio 54,19,5f.). In the year 15, he fought against the Raeti as *legatus Augusti pro praetore*. He moved through the valleys of the Etsch and the Eisach and defeated the Raeti together with Tiberius. For this, he received the *ornamenta praetoria* (Vell. Pat. 2,95,1–2; Cass. Dio 54,22; Hor. Carm. 4,4,1–28; 4,14,8–24; cf. [3]). In 13, C. was appointed to the office of governor of the Tres Galliae. There, he held a census (Cass. Dio 54,25,1; ILS 212, 2,53ff.) and officially opened the *ara Romae et Augusti* on 1 August 12 at Lugdunum (Lyon), (Suet. Claud. 2,1). He repulsed attacks by the Germani, and, after establishing the *fossa Drusiana* (Rhine-North Sea, Tac. Ann. 2,8,1), advanced into the region of the Usipetes, Friesians, Bructeri, and Chauci (Cass. Dio 54,32,2; Tac. Ann. 4,72,1; Germ. 34). He returned to Rome in late 12. As *praetor urbanus* in the year 11 (Cass. Dio 54,34,1), he marched in the spring against the Usipetes, Sugambri, Cherusci, Tencteri, and Chatti (Liv. per. 140; Plin. HN 11,55; Tac. Ann. 1,56,1). He received the *ornamenta triumphalia* and the *ovatio* as well as the *imperium proconsulare*. C. gave the funeral oration for Octavia minor (Cass. Dio 54,35,4f.).

He spent the year 10 fighting the Chatti, then returned to Rome with Augustus and Tiberius (Cass. Dio 54,36,3f.); *cos. ord.* in 9 BC. (CIL V 3109; Vell. Pat. 2,97,3); augur (CIL IX 2443; AE 1926, 42). C. again marched to Germania, defeated the Chatti, Suebi, Marcomanni, devastated the region of the Cherusci up to the river Elbe, and secured the area by placing military units along the rivers Maas, Weser, and Elbe. He protected the shore of the Rhine with an embankment and 'more than 50 forts'. With bridges he linked Gesoriacum (Boulogne-sur-mer) and Bonn and expanded them into naval bases (Flor. 2,30; Tac. Ann. 13,53,2; Cass. Dio 55,1,2ff.). On his return from the Elbe between the rivers Saale and Rhine (Str. 7,1,3), he broke his lower leg as a result of falling from a horse and died 30 days later, late in the year of 9 BC (Liv. per. 142). Tiberius, sent by Augustus, found C. still alive, later took his body to Ticinum (Pavia), and from there, he and Augustus took it to Rome, where he was cremated and buried in the Mausoleum Augusti. The emperor and Tiberius gave the funeral orations (Cass. Dio 55,1,2ff.; Tac. Ann. 3,5,1; Suet. Claud. 1,5). Augustus authored *elogia* in verses and in prose (InscrIt 13,3 p. 15 no. 9, in reference to this: [4]). A → Consolatio *ad Liviam* handed down under Ovid's name is dedicated to C. He was deeply mourned by the people (Suet. Claud. 1,4; Tac. Ann. 1,33,2). C. and his descendants received the cognomen Germanicus, a triumphal arch on the Via Appia [5. 71ff.], and a cenotaph *apud Mogontiacum in ripa Rheni* (on the shore of the Rhine near Mainz), where the Rhine army as well as representatives of the Gaulic and Cisrhenanian *civitates* of Germania held a yearly memorial ceremony (Suet. Claud. 1,3; Cass. Dio 55,2,3; Eutr. 7,13,1; Tab. Siar. 1,26–34, in reference to this: [6]). His wife → Antonia minor, the daughter of Marcus Antonius, had given C. three children: → Germanicus, Livilla (→ Livia), and → Claudius [III 1], the future emperor.

1 S. PRIULI, Tituli 2, 1980   2 G. RADKE, Fasti Romani, 1990   3 K. KRAFT, KS 2, 1978, 321ff.   4 A. VASSILEIOU, Drusus imperator appellatus in Germania, in: ZPE 51, 1983, 213–214   5 W. D. LEBEK, Ehrenbogen und Prinzentod 9 v.Chr.- 23 n.Chr., in: ZPE 86, 1991, 47–78   6 Id., Die Mainzer Ehrungen für Germanicus, den älteren Drusus und Domitian, in: ZPE 78, 1989, 45–82

D. KIENAST, Augustus, 1982, 105, 206, 295, 299f., 345, 357.
COINS: RIC 1², 124ff.; 127ff.; 132; RPC 1, 1031; 2500; 3628.
PORTRAITS: Z. KISS, L'iconographie des princeps Julio-Claudiens, 1975, 86ff.; K. FITTSCHEN, P. ZANKER, Kat. der röm. Porträts in Kapitolinischen Mus. 1, 1985, 27ff. no. 22
D.K.

[II 25] C. Drusus. → Drusus [1].

[II 26] Ti. C. Nero. → Tiberius.

[II 27] Nero C. Drusus Germanicus. → Nero.

[II 28] Ti. C. Dryantianus Antoninus. Son of C. [II 3], senator. Married to Alexandria, the daughter of Avidius Cassius. Although he took part in the latter's revolt, he was spared by Marcus Aurelius, but his fortune was confiscated (Cod. Just. 9,8,6 pr.; PIR² C 859).

[II 29] C. Etruscus. Son of the imperial freedperson Ti. Iulius. At his father's death in the year 92, Statius addressed the poem silv. 3,3 to him. Of equestrian rank, related to senatorial families. He induced Domitian to end his father's exile. His bath is described by Statius silv. 1,5 and Mart. 6,42.

[II 30] C.C. Firmus. After a long procuratorian career, C. became financial procurator of Galatia (IGR 3,181 = MITCHELL, AS 27, 1977, 67ff.). Probably identical to the *praef. Aegypti* of the year 264 and perhaps also identical to the *corrector Aegypti* of 274 (MITCHELL ibid.; [1]).

1 G. BASTIANINI, in: ZPE 38, 1980, 88.

[II 31] M.C. Fronto. Probably from Pergamum; senatorial career, legate of the *legio I Minervia* (Bonn), which he led into the Parthian War in 162. *Cos. suff.* in 165, then entrusted with various assignments in the war of the Danube region, such as legate of Moesia superior and of Tres Daciae. He fell in battle against the Germani and Iazyges. A statue was erected in his honour on the Forum Traiani (CIL VI 1377 = 31640 = ILS 1098, possibly interpolated; CIL III 7505 = ILS 2311). PISO 94ff.

[II 32] C. Gallus. Praetorian governor of Numidia in 202/203, cos. suff. in 203?, consular governor of Dacia c. 207 (AE 1957, 123) [1; 2].

1 PISO 162ff.   2 B. E. THOMASSON, Fasti Africani, 1996.

[II 33] Ti. C. Gordianus. Senator from Tyana in Cappadocia. Via a proconsulate in Macedonia, he achieved command over the legio III Augusta in Numidia in 188, then became praef. aerarii Saturni and was designated as consul (AE 1954, 138f.) [1].

1 W. ECK, RE Suppl. 14, 100f.

[II 34] C. Hieronymianus. Legate of the legio VI Victrix in Britannia. Suffect consul, governor of Cappadocia before 212. Enraged that his wife had become a Christian, he moved savagely against the Christians (Tert. Scap. 3). Papinian gave him legal advice (Dig. 33,7,12,40f.) [1].

1 LEUNISSEN, Konsuln 159, 234.

[II 35] Ti. C. Hipparchus. Athenian, father of C. [II 10]. His fortune was confiscated under Domitian (Philostr. VS 2,1,2). PIR² C 889.

[II 36] C. Iulianus. Praefect of the fleet of Misenum under Nero. Perhaps procurator ludi magni in Rome (Plin. HN 37,45). He attempted to bring the fleet of Misenum over to Vespasian against Vitellius' orders. He was executed during Vitellius' conquest of Terracina (Tac. Hist. 3,57; 76f.). PIR² C 893.

[II 37] C. Iulianus. Praef. annonae with the rank title of perfectissimus vir in 201, praef. Aegypti between 203 and 205/6

H. PAVIS D' ESCURAC, Préfecture de l'annone, 1976, 354; G. BASTIANINI, in: ZPE 17, 1975, 305.   W.E.

[II 38] Appius C. Iulianus. Cos. suff., procos. Africae (CIL VIII 4845), cos. II ord. in AD 224. Probably praef. urbi at the same time (Dig. 31,87,3). PIR² C 901.   A.B.

[II 39] Ti. C. Iulianus. The suffect consul Iulianus of c. 130 could be identical to the senator of I.Eph. 7,2,5106/7, the grandson of Ti. Iulius Celsus Polemaeanus [1]. Probably father of C. [II 40].

1 HALFMANN 147f.

[II 40] Ti. C. Iulianus. Suffect consul in 154 (RMD 3, 169). Governor of Germania inferior in 160 [1]. Fronto addressed Ad amicos 1,5 and 1,20 to him. Probably the son of C. [II 39].

1 ECK, Statthalter, 175f.

[II 41] Ti. Iulius Aquilinus Castricius Saturninus C. Livianus. Equestrian, originally from Lycia (PIR² C 913; [1]). He was sent to Decebalus during the war

against the Dacians (Cass. Dio 68,9,2f.). Perhaps praef. praetorio already at that time, but definitely in the year 108 according to records (AE 1980, 647). During the Parthian war, he had friendly relations with Hadrian.

1 SYME, RP 3, 1276ff.

[II 42] M.C. Marcellus. Son of the consul of the same name in 50 BC and of → Octavia, the younger sister of Octavian-Augustus. Born in 42, in 39 already engaged to the daughter of Sex. Pompey (Cass. Dio 48,38,3). In the Actian triumph of 29, he rode on the right horse of the triumphal team (Suet. Tib. 6,4). During the Cantabrian war, he was in the entourage of Augustus. In 25, he was married to → Iulia, Augustus' daughter, in Rome. In 24, he was designated as aedil without having held any prior office. He was granted permission to apply for the consulate 10 years before the legally determined time. As aedil, he held magnificent games in 23, financed by Augustus. It appears that a serious disagreement arose between Marcellus and Agrippa, because Augustus supposedly designated his nephew as successor. It is indisputable that he would have played a decisive role in the exercise of sovereignty in any case, even if Augustus had not openly referred to him as his 'successor'. He died in September of 23 BC in Baiae. Augustus gave the funeral oration during the funus censorium. Marcellus was the first to be buried in Augustus' mausoleum (AE 1928, 88 = [1]). Virgil authored Aen. 6,860–886 to Marcellus (Prop. 3,18). As a memorial to him (→ memoria), Augustus built the theatrum Marcelli (R. Gest. div. Aug. 21); PIR² C 925.

1 H. v. HESBERG, S. PANCIERA, Das Mausoleum des Augustus, 1994, 88ff.

H. BRANDT, in: Chiron 25, 1995, 1ff.; SYME, RR 340ff.   W.E.

[II 43] M.C. Marcellus. Perhaps cos. suff. in 11 BC, although this is uncertain. PIR² C 928.

M.MEI. and ME. STR.

[II 44] M.C. Marcellus Aeserninus. Quaestor of Q. Cassius Longinus in Hispania Ulterior in 48 BC (Bell. Alex. 57,4–64,1). Exiled by Caesar, later again respected (Cass. Dio 42,15–16,2). Cos. ord. II in 22 BC (InscrIt 13,1 p. 273ff. Cass. Dio ind. 54). Magister of the XVviri sacris faciundis during the saecular games in 17 BC. (InscrIt 13,1 p. 63).

[II 45] M.C. Aeserninus. Grandson of C. [II 44], maternal grandson of Asinius Polli (Sen. Controv. 4 praef. 3f.). As a boy, he broke his leg during a game about Troy (Suet. Aug. 43,2). In AD 16, curator riparum et alvei Tiberis (CIL VI 31544a-c). Praetor peregrinus in 19 (InscrIt 13,1 p. 298). In 20, he refused to take on the defense of → Piso (Tac. Ann. 3,11,2). Famous orator (Sen. Suas. 2,9 and passim).   D.K.

[II 46] Ti. C. Marinus Pacatianus. Probably senator. Supreme commander of the Pannonian and Moesian provinces, was proclaimed emperor in AD 248 (Zos. 1,20,2; Zon. 12,19) but was murdered by soldiers (Zos.

1,21,2) after only a brief reign (RIC 4,3 104f.). PIR² C 930.

KIENAST, ²1996, 201 A.B.

[II 47] C. Maximus. Governor of Pannonia superior, the period from 150 to 154 is documented [1. 236]. Proconsul of Africa probably in 158/159. → Apuleius defended himself in before him (PIR² C 933). He is possibly identical to the [---] Maximus of CIL III 10336 = ILS 1062 (with *cursus honorum* up to *cura aed. sacr.*). This would also make him praetorian governor of Pannonia inferior *c.* 137–141, *cos. suff. c.* 142 [1. 143; 2. 483ff.]. He is identical to the philosopher by the name of C. Maximus mentioned by Marcus Aurelius [3].

1 ALFÖLDY, Konsulat Pannoniens, vol. 2, 1993 ²1987, 96f.
2 J. FITZ, Die Verwaltung Pannoniens, vol. 2, 1993
3 A. BIRLEY, Marcus Aurelius, ²1987, 96f.

[II 48] C. Modestus. Governor of Arabia *c.* 167/9 (AE 1977, 834; on the consulate [1]). Probably son of C. [II 49].

1 G. CAMODECA, in: ZPE 43, 1981, 207ff.

[II 49] L.C. Modestus. *Frater Arvalis*, documented for the period between 150 and 155 [1]. Probably father of C. [II 48].

1 SCHEID, Collège 78, 403.

[II 50] Ti. C. Nero Germanicus. Emperor → Claudius [III 1].

[II 51] Ti. C. Parthenius. Imperial slave, freed by Nero (cf. CIL VI 8761 = ILS 1736; CIL XV 7897; Mart. 4,45; 5,6). *Cubicularius* of Domitianus, on whom he exerted great influence. Supporter of the poet → Martial, who also names Parthenius' son Burrus. In 96, he took part in the conspiracy against Domitian. Party to proclamation of Nerva as emperor. He was murdered probably in 97 by the praetorians, against Nerva's will (PIR² 2, p. XXIf.).

[II 52] Ti. C. Pollio. Friend of → Pliny the younger. Equestrian procurator; at the end of his career, he was in charge of inheritance tax (Plin. Ep. 7,31; CIL VI 31032 = ILS 1418, [1]).

1 PFLAUM, 1, 124. W.E.

[II 53] Ti. C. Pompeianus. Tribune of the *legio I Minervia*, who apparently consecrated an altar for the well-being of Severus (ILS 4794) in Lugdunum/Lyon (probably in AD 197). It is more likely that he was an equestrian officer than the son of C. [II 54] and of Lucilla Augusta, who bore the name of Aurellius (*sic*) Commodus Pompeianus (RMD 1, 73) in his office of *cos. ord.* in 209 L. The latter was killed by Caracalla after 212 (Hdn. 4,6,3; SHA Carac. 3,8). PIR² C 974. A.B.

[II 54] Ti. C. Pompeianus. Originally from Antioch in Syria, his father was still of equestrian rank. Praetorian governor of Pannonia inferior in 167 (CIL XVI 123; RMD 3, 181). Suffect consul. After the death of Verus,

Marcus Aurelius married his widow to C. against her will, C. thus became the emperor's son-in-law. Several children were born from this marriage. He was *Cos. II ord.* in 173 together with Cn. Claudius Severus. He played a leading role in the wars along the Danube under Marcus Aurelius, and is often depicted next to the emperor on the reliefs of the Marcus column. According to Hdn. 1,6,4–7, he apparently tried in vain to encourage Commodus to continue fighting the war against the Germani in 180. He clearly did not participate in the conspiracy against Commodus in 182, which is why he survived (Cass. Dio 72,4,2). Pertinax and Didius Iulianus encouraged him to become emperor, but he declined (Cass. Dio 73,3,2f.). C. [II 52] was his son. PIR² C 972.

H.-G. PFLAUM, in: Journal des Savants 1961, 31ff.; HALFMANN 181f.; A. BIRLEY, Marcus Aurelius, ²1987.

[II 55] C. Pompeianus (Commodus) *Cos. ord.* in 231; unpublished military diploma. Son of C. [II 53]. PIR² C 972.

O. SALOMIES, in: Ktema 18, 1993, 104.

[II 56] C. Pompeianus Quintianus. Most likely the nephew of C. [II 54]. He married a daughter of Lucilla and L. → Verus, but reputedly also had intimate relations with Lucilla (Cass. Dio 72,4,4). He took part in the conspiracy against Commodus with whom, as a relative, he was outwardly close. Executed in 182. PIR² C 975. His son was Ti. C. Aurelius Quintianus, *cos.* in 235.

[II 57] Ti. C. Quartinus. An equestrian who may have stemmed from Puteoli. After his admission to the Senate, he had a long career, was governor of Lugdunensis and suffect consul in 130. Consular legate of Germania superior (CIL XVI 80), then perhaps in Britannia [1]. Possibly proconsul of Asia [2].

1 BIRLEY, 110ff. 2 ECK, Statthalter 56f.

[II 58] C. Restitutus. Senator, involved in the trial against Caecilius Classicus. Lawyer for the defendant (Plin. Ep. 3,9,16). PIR² C 996.

SYME, RP 3, 994f.

[II 59] Ti. C. Sacerdos Iulianus. *Frater Arvalis*, suffect consul in AD 100.

HALFMANN, 116f.

[II 60] Ti. C. Saturninus. Praetorian legate of Belgica, suffect consul, consular legate of Moesia inferior between 144/5 and 147 (PIR² C 1012; AE 1987, 867; RMD 3, 165).

[II 61] C.C. Severus. If AE 1968, 525 can be attributed to him, he was admitted to the Senate by Domitian, Nerva, or Trajan. First governor of the new province of Arabia from 106 until at least 115. Suffect consul in 112. Originally from Pompeiopolis in Paphlagonia. His son was C. [II 64]. PIR² C 1023.

HALFMANN, 135f.

[II 62] Cn. C. Severus. Son of C. [II 64]. Originally from Pompeiopolis in Paphlagonia. Suffect consul, perhaps in 167 [1], *cos. II ord.* in 173. Before 173, he married Annia Galeria Aurelia Faustina, the second daughter of Marcus Aurelius. Honoured as the emperor's son-in-law (ILS 8832; IGR 3, 1448; SEG 36, 1174). He accompanied Marcus Aurelius on his campaigns. On his and Galeria's descendants: PIR² C 1024 (cf. [2; 3]). Father of C. [II 65].

1 ALFÖLDY, Konsulat 182f. 2 H.-G. PFLAUM, in: Journal des Savants 1961, 29ff. 3 A. BIRLEY, Marcus Aurelius, ²1987, 247.

[II 63] Ti. C. Severus. First consul from Ephesus, probably towards the end of the 2nd cent. (I. Eph. 3,648). Married to Caninia Gargonilla, Claudia Caninia Severa was his daughter (I. Eph. 3, 892; 639; EOS 2, 628; [1]).

1 W. ECK, RE Suppl. 14, 102.

[II 64] Cn. C. Severus Arabianus. Son of C. [II 61]. Perhaps born during his father's governorship in Arabia. *Cos. ord.* in 146. He was one of → Marcus Aurelius' partners in philosophical discussions, apparently a peripatetic [1]. Fronto wrote to him *ad amicos* 1,1. Father of C. [II 62].

1 A. BIRLEY, Marcus Aurelius, ²1987, 95f.

[II 65] Ti. C. Severus Proculus. Son of C. [II 62], Marcus Aurelius' grandson. *Cos. ord.* 200. PIR² C 1028.

[II 66] Ti. C. Telemachus. Senator from Xanthus in Lycia, *cos. suff.*; *procos. Africae* in the early 3rd cent. PIR² C 1037.

[II 67] Ti. C. Telemachus. Related to C. [II 66]. Via a proconsulate of Cyprus and the command of a legion, he reached the position of suffect consul, probably early in the 3rd cent. (AE 1993, 1550).

M. CHRISTOL, TH. DREW-BEAR, in: Journal des Savants 1991, 195ff. W.E.

III. EMPEROR

[III 1] Emperor from AD 41 to 54. Youngest son of C. [II 24] and → Antonia minor, brother of Germanicus, nephew of → Tiberius, and uncle of Caligula. Born 1 August 10 BC in Lugdunum (Lyon). Supposedly, his name was Ti. Claudius Drusus at first, but after Tiberius' adoption of his brother Germanicus, it was changed to Ti. C. Nero Germanicus (Suet. Claud. 2,1). As a child, C. was sickly; his speech and gait were impaired so that he was hardly deemed capable of fulfilling a public role, which otherwise was taken for granted for a member of the *domus Augusta*. The letters of Augustus cited by Suetonius are telling in this regard (Suet. Claud. 4). He was raised in the house of his mother and grandmother Livia, cared for primarily by freedpersons. From an early age, he studied literature, in particular historiography, and published several essays (Suet. Claud. 3,1), among them a history of Rome in 41 bks. up to the year AD 14, a history of the Etruscans in

20 bks. and a history of Carthage in 8 bks., the two latter works in Greek (Suet. Claud. 41f.; [1; 2]). Public tasks were assigned him only rarely. Augustus bestowed the augurate upon him, but C. did not enter the Senate. Instead, he remained a member of the equestrian class, which repeatedly elected him as its representative (Suet. Claud. 6,1). Following Augustus' death, C. became *sodalis Augustalis*. Records also indicate that he was a member of the *sodales Titii*. Despite having been held back, C. enjoyed a special status simply by virtue of belonging to the *domus Augusta*. This is evident, for instance, in the fact that he was initially forgotten in the letter of thanks to the ruling family in December of 20 after the conclusion of the Piso trial, but was then added as a result of Nonius Asprenas' intervention (Tac. Ann. 3,18,2, cf. [3]). Also in the year 20, his son (C. [II 23]) from his first wife Plautia Urgulanilla was engaged to a daughter of → Seianus (Tac. Ann. 3,29,5).

As soon as → Caligula became emperor in March of 37, he designated C. as co-consul in July or August of that year. But C. was soon humiliated by him as well (Suet. Claud. 9,2). Since 39/40, C. was married to Valeria Messalina, who probably gave birth to the daughter Octavia in the year 40 and to the son Britannicus in early 41. C. presumably knew about the conspiracy that resulted in Caligula's removal on 24 January 41, but it is impossible to determine his precise role [4]. Herodes Agrippa, whose role was overemphasized by Josephus (Ant. Iud. 19,162ff.; 212ff.), was not the only one to support him. C. was elected to *imperator* by praetorian acclamation; their role was given prominence on coins as well. On 25 January, the Senate also agreed to C.'s accession to power, although there were opposing interests. An amnesty excluding only Caligula's actual murderers created the basis for an easing of the tensions. Nevertheless, C.'s relationship to the Senate always remained problematic. C. immediately received the usual privileges of a princeps: *tribunicia potestas, imperium proconsulare* (C. is the first emperor to be called *proconsul* occasionally), supreme pontifex. He assumed the title of *pater patriae* in early 42. He became consul altogether four times (*cos. V* in 51). He accepted a total of 27 imperial acclamations, a sign that he had a strong compensatory need. This may in part also be the reason for his expansion of the Roman Empire through the creation of many new provinces.

Two new provinces were established in Mauretania following Suetonius Paulinus' and Hosidius Geta's suppression of several revolts: Mauretania Caesariensis and Mauretania Tingitana, both governed by equestrian procurators. In 43, the region of the Lycian *koinón* in southern Asia Minor was taken by military force from Q. Veranius and turned into a praetorian imperial province. Shortly thereafter, between 44 and 47, the kingdom of Thrace was transformed into a procuratorian province — C. deemed direct rule superior to constant interventions by the Moesian governor. In contrast, C. did not undertake any further military actions along the eastern border against Armenia and Parthia, although Roman influence had seriously weakened there. Similarly, he did not allow Domitius Corbulo, the commander of the Lower Germanic army, to use stronger force against the Germanic tribes on the right bank of the Rhine, nor to station troops there [5]. The kingdom of Noricum, which had long been part of the Roman realm of influence, was also transformed into a procuratorian province in 46.

C. achieved lasting glory through the conquest of Britannia, which had not been attempted since Caesar's failure. Internal conflicts between Britannic kings provided the opportunity. A. Plautius, *cos. suff.* in 29, received the command over the invading troops of *c.* 40,000 men. Shortly before he reached the river Thames, he stopped to wait for C., who was to take supreme command himself in the victory over the enemies. After 16 days on the island and after the conquest of Camulodunum, C. left the new province and returned to Rome via Upper Italy and the Adriatic Sea, his absence having lasted about six months. The triumph was celebrated in 44; C. declined the victorious title of 'Britannicus' for himself and gave it to his son instead. The legionary legates of the campaign received triumphal insignia; and in 47 AD Plautius was permitted to march into Rome in an *ovatio*. Under the rule of Plautius' successors, the borders of the provinces were pushed further to the west and to the north. The king of the Silures, → Caratacus, was captured and presented in Rome by C. as in a triumph (Tac. Ann. 12,36ff.). In the year of 50, Camulodunum became a Roman colony, just as *oppidum Ubiorum* (modern Cologne) in Lower Germania. Agrippina was born there and, of course, her wish played the decisive role (Tac. Ann. 12,27,1; 32,2).

Although C. was personally acquainted with only few provinces from his trip to Britannia, his provincial policy was in general rational and oriented towards the needs of the subjects. Even though he refused to grant the Alexandrian citizenship to the Jewish population of Alexandria, he protected them from transgressions by Alexandrians and confirmed certain privileges for all Jewish communities (Jos. Ant. Iud. 19,279ff.; P Lond. 1912 = OLIVER no. 19; cf. [6]). He granted Latin law to a few tribes in the Alpes Graiae and Poeninae, and to cities in Noricum. Volubilis in Mauretania Tingitana received the rank of a *municipium civium Romanorum* (FIRA 1² no. 70); Caesarea in Mauretania Caesariensis became a Roman colony. He also confirmed the dubious citizenship of the Alpine tribes of the Anauni, Tulliasses, and Sinduni (ILS 206).

C. initiated road construction in many provinces, especially in Gaul and in Italy, where the connection to Raetia was expanded (ILS 208; CIL V 8003) and the *Via Claudia* was projected towards the Adriatic coast (ILS 209; [7]). In order to improve the Roman supply of grain, C. initiated the construction of a man-made harbour in → Ostia [8]. He also ordered the (not entirely succcesful) draining of Lake Fucina in an effort to support Italian agriculture.

C. granted Roman citizenship to men from the provinces on a large scale. Evidence for this can be found not so much in Seneca's statement (Apocol. 3,3) but more so in the fact that numerous individuals bear the name of Ti. Claudius, in the west and in the east. In granting citizenship, C. consciously recalled the example of Augustus and Tiberius, but was more generous by far. In a similar fashion, C. finally pushed through the granting of citizenship to auxiliary soldiers after 25 years of service. The first military certificates documenting the granting of the *civitas Romana* stem from the year of 52 (CIL XVI 1–3).

Although the Senate had first declared C. an enemy of the state following his acclamation by the Praetorians, and although the senator Furius Camillus Scribonianus had unsuccessfully revolted against C. as governor of Dalmatia in 42, C. was willing to make concessions to senators in order to improve cooperation. For this end, he used polite manners and established numerous suffect consulates as well as a second consulate for particularly important senators. L. Vitellius, who had been censor together with C. in. 47/48, even became *cos. III*. C. also honoured many senators with *ornamenta triumphalia*. C. brought many issues to the Senate that he could have decided on his own and encouraged objective discussion, not simply adulatory or cowardly agreement (FIRA 1² no. 44 III Z. 10ff.). For instance, he had the Senate confirm the authority of procurators in the administration of justice, probably including patrimonial and freedperson procurators (Tac. Ann. 12,60; [9]). Also, he complied with the desire of a few Gaule aristocrats to gain admission to the Senate by arguing their case, and succeeded in obtaining an affirmative decision of the Senate (Tac. Ann. 11,23–25,1; CIL XIII 1668 = ILS 212; [10]). He even had the Senate decide on the *ornamenta praetoria* for his freedman Pallas (Plin. Ep. 7,29,2; Tac. Ann. 12,53,2f.). These actions bespeak C.'s impartiality, but they also increased the tensions that had always existed in the Senate. For this reason, C. never entered the Senate without a group of body guards. Many senators were executed for various reasons, some because of conspiracies, others due to intrigues and fights in the entourage of the emperor. The hatred of many senators found expression in → Seneca's *Apocolocyntosis*.

One characteristic trait of C.'s government is the influence he granted to freedpersons in his entourage. The names that stand out the most are the following: Pallas, who occupied the function of *a rationibus* and thereby was in control of the emperor's entire finances; Narcissus, *ab epistulis*; Callistus, *a libellis*; Polybius, *a studiis*. Their power, however, resulted not from their 'official' positions, but from the influence they exerted due to their proximity to the ruler. In fact, they did not achieve any significant progress in the organization of the administration [11]. It is debatable, whether C. indeed was as dependent upon them as the traditional view holds. C. was greatly influenced by his wives: Valeria → Messalina caused the execution of many of her enemies through C., until she herself was executed in an informal trial following her formal marriage to C. Silius in 48. C. clearly took the situation very seriously, as is evident in his temporary subordination of the praetorians to the command of Narcissus, the freedperson (Tac. Ann. 11,26–38). Shortly thereafter, C. followed Pallas' advice and married his niece → Agrippina the younger. C. granted her civil rights and a real power never before enjoyed by the wife of a princeps. Already in the year of 50, C. adopted her son Domitius Ahenobarbus, the future emperor → Nero, who was clearly designated as C.'s successor through the political privileges awarded to him, and he married him to his daughter Octavia. Agrippina received the name of Augusta, her portrait appeared on Roman imperial coins. When C. made efforts to counteract the complete political isolation suffered by his son Britannicus, Agrippina had C. poisoned, supposedly with a mushroom dish, after successfully outmanoeuvring C.'s protector Narcissus (Tac. Ann. 12,66–69; Suet. Claud. 44f.). C. died on 13 October 54. He was consecrated as *divus* by decision of the Senate, a temple on Caelius Mons was decided upon, and Agrippina was nominated as priestess of the *divus*.

1 P.L. SCHMIDT, in: STROCKA (see bibliography below), 119ff.   2 J. MALITZ, in: STROCKA (see bibliography below), 133ff.   3 W. ECK, A. CABALLOS, F. FERNÁNDEZ, Das s.c. de Cn. Pisone patre, 1996, 245ff.   4 B. LEVICK, Claudius, 1990, 29ff.   5 ECK, Statthalter 118f.   6 H. BOTERMAN, Das Judenedikt des Kaisers C., 1996   7 W. ECK, Die staatliche Organisation It., 1979, 30   8 R. MEIGGS, Roman Ostia, ²1973, 54ff.   9 M. T. GRIFFIN, C. in Tacitus, in: CQ 40, 1990, 482ff.   10 F. VITTINGHOFF, Civitas Romana, 1994, 299ff.   11 W. ECK, in: STROCKA (see bibliography below), 23ff.

H.M. v. KAENEL, Münzprägung und Münzbildnis des Claudius, 1986; B. LEVICK, C., 1990; A. MOMIGLIANO, C., ²1961; V.M. SARAMUZZA, The Emperor C., 1940; V.M. STROCKA (ed.), Die Regierungszeit des C. (41–54 n.Chr.), 1994
COINS: RIC I², 114ff.
PORTRAIT: A.-K. MASSNER, Das röm. Herrscherbild 4, 1982, 126ff.   W.E.

[III 2] C. Gothicus. Imperator Caesar M. Aurelius Valerius Claudius Augustus. Born 10 May (Fasti Philocali I² 255; 264), c. AD 214 (Chron. pasch. 508). Of Dalmatian or Dardanic origin (SHA Clod. 11,9; cf. 14,2 *Illyricianae gentis vir*), although this information was probably invented by the author of the Historia Augusta. Similarly suspicious is the information that he was the son of a Gordianus (Aur. Vict. epit. Caes. 34,1) and that Probus was a relative of C.'s (SHA Prob. 3,2–4). Finally, we must regard the supposed connection to Constantius Chlorus as an invention, since it was not made public until the panegyric of the year 310 (Pan. Lat. 8,2; cf. Euseb. Hist. eccl. 10,8,4; SHA Clod. 13,2). The fictitious kinship with the second Flavian dynasty must have been the reason why he was named Flavius in the Historia Augusta (SHA Clod. 7,8; cf. 3,6; no other

records, s. [1. 63ff.] who deems possible his descent from Dacia Ripensis with a reference to Iulian's Mis. 367C and 350D). At the time of Gallienus' death in 268, A. stayed in Ticinum as tribune (Aur. Vict. Caes. 33,28; as cavalry leader in Zon. 12,26). Further details in the Historia Augusta about his career are fictitious (SHA Clod. 14–16). According to Zosimus, he took part in the murder of Gallienus (1,40,2). He was presumably proclaimed emperor in the early fall. Soon thereafter, he defeated the Alamanni on Lake Garda (Germanicus max., ILS 569). *Cos.* in 269. In that year, he also defeated the Goths and Heruli at Naissus (Zos. 1,42ff.) and called himself Gothicus maximus (ILS 571). He died of the plague in September of 270 (SHA Clod. 12,2; Zos. 1,46,2). PIR² A 1626; PLRE 1, 209.

1 R. SYME, Historia Augusta Papers, 1983.

RIC 5,1, 201–237; KIENAST, ²1996, 231–32; R. SYME, Emperors and Biography, 1971, 208ff.   A.B.

[III 3] Imperator Caesar M.C. Tacitus Augustus. → Tacitus

IV. PHYSICIANS, SCULPTORS, LAWYERS
[IV 1] C. Agathemerus. Greek physician in Rome (IG 14,1750 = IGUR 1247), whose tombstone is decorated with a very nice relief portrait representing him and his wife Myrtale. The clothing depicted in the portrait suggests a date of *c.* AD 110, and the skilful stonemasonry indicates that the client enjoyed considerable wealth. He was often confused with Claudius Agathurnus of Lacedaemon, a philosopher, physician, and friend of Aelius Cornutus and of the poet Persius (Suet. Vit. Persi). Although the emendation of Agathemerus is tempting, the simple fact alone that this physician is said to have reached a high age already in the 50's contradicts the identification often made in the past.
→ Persius

[IV 2] Ti. C. Menecrates. Active *c.* AD 50, Greek, the emperor's personal physician (perhaps of Tiberius, Gaius, and Claudius) and founder of his own medical system, a system that was clearly structured and logically thought through, developed in 156 bks. (IG 14,1759 = IGUR 686). He was supposed to have been awarded with honorary decrees from 'famous' cities. He is possibly identical to Menecrates, the author of a book of medicines entitled 'the Ruler' occasionally cited by → Galen (12,846; 896; 13,502; 937; 995; 14,306 K.). It is highly improbable, however, that he can be identified with the scholarly physician Menecrates of Sosandra, who was honoured by his homeland for his loyal services and also for his role as asiarch (IGRom. 4, 1359, cf. ZPE 1976, 93–96), because the honorary inscription does not contain any mention of a relationship to the imperial court, nor any activities outside of Asia Minor.
                                                                 V.N

[IV 3] C. Pollio Frugianus. Sculptor of Greek origin. His signature includes 'ἀπὸ μουσείου' on the bottom of the base of a copy of the so called 'Diomedes' by → Cresilas, a product of the 2nd cent. AD.

C. LANDWEHR, Juba II. als Diomedes, in: JDAI 107, 1992, 103–124; A. MAIURI, Il Diomede di Cuma, 1930.　R.N.

[IV 4] C. Saturninus. Possibly identical to the author of *Liber singularis de poenis paganorum* (Dig. 48,19,16; the *Index Florentinus* wrongly attributed it to → Venuleius Saturninus), a 3rd cent. AD commentator on wreaths (Tert. De corona 7,6) and PIR² C 1011.

D. LIEBS, Röm. Jurisprudenz in Africa, 1993, 23f.　T.G.

Claustra Alpium Iuliarum A system of late Roman fortifications in the frontier and trade zone between the towns of Emona, Forum Iulii, Tergeste and Tarsatica at the northeastern entrance of Italy (Illyro-Italian gate), supported in part by the natural barriers of the mountainous Karst landscape. It was mentioned repeatedly by ancient authors from Herodianus to Prosper Tiro and parts have been archaeologically explored. Literary evidence: Amm. Marc. 31,11,3.

B. SARIA, s.v. Nauportus (1), RE 16,2, 2011f.; J. ŠAŠEL, P. PETRU (ed.), Claustra Alpium Iuliarum, 1971.　M.Š.K.

Clausulae see → Prose rhythm

Clavus 'Nail', in the context of → clothing: 'stripes'. The decoration of a → tunic with purple *clavi* extending from the shoulder to the lower seam at the front and back, served to denote rank in Rome. Senators, their sons (since Augustus) and officials wore a tunic with broad stripes (*lati clavi*), equestrians one with small stripes (*angusti clavi*). The *clavi* could be woven in or sewn on, cf. → Dalmatica.

H. R. GOETTE, Studien zu röm. Togadarstellungen, 1990, 8–9; J. BERGEMANN, Röm. Reiterstatuen, 1990, 23–24; B. LEVICK, A Note on the latus clavus, in: Athenaeum 79, 1991, 239–244; A. STAUFFER, Textilien aus Ägypten, Kat. der Ausstellung Fribourg 1991/92, Nr. 43, 63, 74 u.ö.　R.H.

Clazomenae (Κλαζομεναί; *Klazomenaí*). Ionian town in Lydia on the south shore of the Gulf of Smyrna, near modern Urla, founded by → Colophon, assaulted by → Alyattes (Hdt. 1,16). For fear of the Persians, it relocated to the offshore island, which Alexander the Great later linked to the mainland by a causeway (Paus. 7,3,8f.). Clazomenae had a treasury in Delphi, was a member of the → Delian League, after leaving in 412 BC it was recovered (Thuc. 8,14; 22f.; 31). In the King's Peace of 386 Clazomenae became Persian. Home of → Anaxagoras [2], → Scopelianus and the rhetor → Zopyrus. Archaeology: painted ('Clazomenian') pottery sarcophagi, pottery of the 6th/5th cent. BC.

L. BÜRCHNER, s.v. K., RE 11, 554f.; PFUHL, 165ff.; R. M. COOK, A List of Clazomenian Pottery, in: ABSA 47, 1952, 123ff.; H. ENGELMANN, R. MERKELBACH, Die Inschr. von

Erythrai und K. (IK 2), 1973; R.v. BEEK, J. BEELEN, Excavations on Karantina Island in Klazomenai, in: Anatolica 17, 1991, 31–57; E. ISIK, Elektronstatere aus K. (Saarbrücker Stud. zur Arch. und Alten Gesch. 5), 1992.　K.Z. and HE.EN.

Cleaenete (Κλεαινέτη; *Kleinainétē*). The daughter of → Numenius, sister of Agathoclea [3]. in 166/5 BC priestess of Arsinoë [II 4] Philopator.

CHR. HABICHT, Athen in hell. Zeit, 1994, 109.　W.A.

Cleaenetus (Κλεαίνετος; *Kleaínetos*). Tragedian (TrGF I 84), won the 3rd place at the Lenaeans in 363 BC; mocked by → Alexis as not exacting (Fr. 268 PCG), by → Philodemus (84 T 3 TrGF I) as a worse poet than Euripides. 'Hypsipyle' is attested as a title.　B.Z.

Cleander (Κλέανδρος; *Kléandros*).
[1] C. of Gela. Son of Pantares. C. founded *c.* 505 BC the tyrannis in → Gela and was assassinated after governing for seven years. C. created the preconditions for the rise of Gela under his brother and successor Hippocrates [4] (Hdt. 7,154; Aristot. Pol. 1316a 37f.).

D. ASHERI, in: CAH 4², 1988, 758; H. BERVE, Die Tyrannis bei den Griechen, 1967, 137.　K.MEI.

[2] Spartan commander (*harmostḗs*) in Byzantium. After the Greek mercenary leaders had led the 'March of the Ten Thousand' to Calpe on the Black Sea, they were received with suspicion by C. in Byzantium in October 400 BC. But when the soldiers offered C. the supreme command, he was hospitable to → Xenophon. In Byzantium Xenophon negotiated the departure of the mercenaries towards Thrace with C. and through forceful action prevented a sacking of the town as the soldies grew restless (Xen. An. 6,6–7,1).　W.S.
[3] Son of Polemocrates, brother of → Cleitus [7], officer in the army of → Alexander [4]. In 332 BC he delivered to the latter 4,000 Greek mercenaries (Arr. Anab. 2,20,5; Curt. 4,3,11). At Gaugamela he commanded the 'original mercenaries' (Arr. Anab. 3,12,2). In 330 C. remained as deputy commander in Ecbatana with → Parmenion, the father of his sister-in-law. Late in 330, after the execution of → Philotas, he murdered Parmenion on Alexander's orders and assumed his command. After Alexander's return from India, C. and three of his officers were ordered to the court and then executed — allegedly because of the mistreatment of subjects.

BERVE 2, No. 422; HECKEL, 340.　E.B.

Cleandridas (Κλεανδρίδας; *Kleandrías*). Spartan; allegedly fought in 470 BC against Tegea (Polyaenus, Strat. 2,10,3) and in 446 as advisor of king → Pleistoanax he was bribed by Pericles on a campaign to Attica. Sentenced to death, C. fled (Diod. Sic. 13,106,10; Plut. Pericles 22f.) and became a citizen of

Thurii, where he functioned as general after 443 (Polyaenus, Strat. 2,10). The embellishment of the bribery affair probably only occurred after his son → Gylippus was convicted of embezzlement [1. 145].

1 K.L. NOETHLICHS, Bestechung, in: Historia 36, 1987, 129–170.   K.-W.WEL.

Cleanthes (Κλεάνθης; Kleánthēs).

[1] One of the earliest painters from Corinth, mentioned in Plin. HN 35,15f.; his name stands for the origin of the genera (prima pictura). C. was considered the inventor of line art, creating his work from outlines and filling them in. Stylistic comparisons with vase painting of the early 7th cent. date his work to the same period. Also only known from the literature (Str. 8,343; Athen. 8,346 BC) are his tableaus in a sanctuary near Olympia: the fall of Troy, the birth of Athena, also Poseidon handing Zeus a tuna.

N.J. KOCH, De Picturae Initiis, 1996, 23–25; I. SCHEIBLER, Griech. Malerei der Ant., 1994, 55f.; Id., Rezension zu KOCH, in: Gymnasium 105, 1998, 308f.   N.H.

[2] C. of Assus. Stoic philosopher and second head of the school. Biographical information is derived from Diogenes Laertios (7,168–176) and Philodemus' History of Stoicism (Coll. 18–29). C. was born in 331/0 BC in Assus, went in 281/0 to Athens; he had been a boxer before. His poverty forced him to take up crafts to finance his studies with → Zeno of Citium; he was known for his frugality and hard work. C. had the reputation of being a slow thinker, but after Zenon's death in 262/1 he was elected head of the school — keeping this position for 32 years until his death in 230/29 BC (Diog. Laert. 7,176). As head of the school he defended his concept of proper stoic theory against his fellow student → Ariston [7] of Chios and the academician → Arcesilaus [5] of Pitane. Like Ariston, C.'s own student → Chrysippus [2] of Soli left his school and began teaching independently; he later returned and became head of the Stoic school.

    C. wrote on a multitude of topics. Diog. Laert. 7,174f. listed 50 titles, all of them covering an area of philosophy with an inclination for ethics. C. also wrote philosophical poetry (e.g., the 'Hymns to Zeus'; SVF I 527, 537), and 'Interpretations of Heraclitus' (Τῶν Ἡρακλείτου ἐξηγήσεις, 4 B.). In physics he expounded the topic of a final convulsion of the earth by fire (ἐκπύρωσις, ekpýrōsis; SVF I 497) as well as the meaning of → fire. He also developed proofs for the existence of the gods. C. answered the 'Master Argument' of → Diodorus [4] Cronus (SVF I 489) by refuting the claim that everything past and real was necessary. He emphasized the cosmological basis of ethics by exclusively deriving Zenon's formula of 'life according to nature', from cosmic nature (Diog. Laert. 7,89), and he resisted Ariston's attempt to remove the role of the universal principle from ethical theory (Sen. Epist. 94–95).

FRAGMENTS: SVF I, 103–139.
BIBLIOGRAPHY: T. DORANDI (ed.), Filodemo, Storia dei filosofi: La stoà da Zenone a Panezio, 1994; C. GUÉRARD, Cléanthe d'Assos, in: GOULET 2, 1994, 406–415.   B.I.

[3] Physician freed by the younger Cato (→ Porcius Cato) in 46 BC (Plut. Cato Minor 70,1,4) and in vain attempted to suture the abdominal wound his benefactor had inflicted upon himself when commiting suicide.

                              V.N

Clearchus (Κλέαρχος; Kléarchos).

[1] Bronze sculptor from Rhegion. Because of his statue of Zeus Hypatus in Sparta, a → sphyrelaton according to the description, C. was wrongly considered the inventor of bronze statues by Pausanias. According to tradition he was a student of → Dipoenus and Scyllis or of → Daedalus as well as the teacher of → Pythagoras and, therefore, was active in the 2nd half of the 6th cent. BC.

OVERBECK No. 332f., 491; P.ROMANELLI, in: EAA 4, 365f.; J. PAPADOPOULOS, Xoana e sphyrelata, 1980, 82; FUCHS/FLOREN 428.   R.N.

[2] Spartan, son of Ramphias. When the naúarchos (commander of the fleet) Astyochus sent him in 411 BC from Miletus to the Hellespont with 40 triremes, C. lost the bulk of his fleet in a storm and arrived at his goal by land (Thuc. 8,39,2; 80). In the spring of 410 on the initiative of Agis [2] II he was given the assignment of protecting the Byzantines, who had broken with Athens and whose → próxenos he was (Xen. Hell. 1,1,36). The polis was taken by treason when C. wanted to obtain subsidies from Pharnabazus (Xen. Hell. 1,3,15–22). In 403, when unrest and Thracian attacks threatened Byzantium, C. again became harmostḗs (→ harmostai) but was cast out by Spartan troops because of his draconic rule. Sentenced to death, he fled to → Cyrus [3] the Younger, whom he served as mercenary leader against the Thracians and in 401, with apparent Spartan approval, as leader of the Greek mercenaries in his campaign against Artaxerxes [2] (Diod. Sic. 14,12,2–9; Xen. An. 1,1,9; Polyaenus, Strat. 2,2,6–10; Plut. Artaxerxes 6). Despite his success as the commander of the right wing at Cunaxa, C. was unable to prevent the defeat and death of Cyrus (Plut. Artaxerxes 8). As the recognized leader of the Greek mercenaries after the battle, C. was lured into a trap by Tissaphernes and killed on the orders of Artaxerxes (Xen. An. 1,2,9–2,6,1). C. was a seasoned leader of troops (Xen. An. 2,6,2–15), but fell prey to the temptations of power when Sparta acquired political responsibility in the Greek sphere after its victory in the → Peloponnesian War in 404.   K.-W.WEL.

[3] C. of → Heraclea [7], on the Pontus, attended lectures by Plato in Athens and was a student of → Isocrates. He received Athenian citizenship because of military achievements in the army of Timotheus. Despite being banned from his native town, as mercenary

commander in the service of the Persian dynast Mithridates he was named in 364 BC by the oligarchic council of Heraclea as the arbitrator to pacify internal unrest between property-owning nobles and the masses during a difficult period in foreign relations. However, C. seized power in the town with his mercenaries, drove out or killed the oligarchs and had extraordinary powers conferred upon himself. The formal existence of the institutions was maintained.

After an unsuccessful attempt to conquer Astacus [1], C. had the citizens of Heraclea disarmed. C. was the first ruler to establish a public library. After 12 years in power he was murdered in 353/52 in a palace revolt. C.'s son → Timotheus continued the dynasty.

K. TRAMPEDACH, Platon, die Akademie und die zeitgenöss. Politik, 1994, 79–87. W.S.

[4] Son of → Amastris [3] and → Dionysius [5]. He succeeded them in 306/5 BC under his mother's regency as king of → Heraclea [7]. When she married → Lysimachus in 302, C. assumed power and continued to exercise it (later together with his brother Oxathres) after her divorce and return. In 292 C. was taken prisoner with Lysimachus during the latter's campaign against the → Getae. He was soon released, supported Lysimachus in other campaigns but quarrelled with his mother. After her death (284) the sons received Lysimachus as a friend but he had them executed as matricides and annexed Heraclea.

S. M. BURSTEIN, Outpost of Hellenism, 1976, 47–65. E.B.

[5] Poet of the Middle or New Comedy. On an epigraphical list of victors at the Lenaeans, C. appears in the 1st place after Dionysius [31] and the 6th before Menander, i.e. his active period fell into the 2nd half of the 4th cent. BC. Traces of C.'s literary activity are only found in Athenaeus, who merely preserves three titles of plays (Κιθαρῳδός/'The Citharode', Κορίνθιοι/'The Corinthians', Πάνδροσος/'Pandrosus') and five short quotations of a total of 17 verses, among them one with the noteworthy thought that no one would drink if the headache came before enjoying the wine [1. fr. 3].

1 PCG IV, 1983, 79–81. T.HI.

[6] Peripatetic. As a student of Aristotle [6] he must have been born before 340 BC. If the title of his dialogue 'Arcesilaus' refers to the head of the Academy of the same name, he was still active in the 2nd quarter of the 3rd cent. but it may refer to another person.

Most of his writings deal with familiar areas of peripatetic popular philosophy: ethics, among them the Erōtiká (Fr. 21–35) and a large work 'On life forms' (Fr. 37–62); natural history (Fr. 96–110) and a treatise on proverbs and riddles (Fr. 63–95). Others exhibit a strong interest in Platonism: 'In praise of Plato' (Fr. 2), an explanation of the mathematical parts of Plato's 'State' (Fr. 3–4) and a dialogue 'On sleep', in which Aristotle appears as a discussion partner and tells of an experiment in hypnosis that was supposed to prove the independence of the soul from the body (Fr. 5–8). The deliberations in natural history are paradoxographically transformed, those on ethics into anecdotes. Crimes and dissolute lifestyles are described with relish only to be condemned with petty strictness (e.g., Fr. 48). There is no trace of a consideration of principles. Plutarch's judgment still applies: 'C. distorted much peripatetic thought'. (C., Fr. 97).

→ Aristotelianism

WEHRLI, Schule 3; Id., in GGPh 3, 1983, 547–51. H.G.

[7] High official of the 2nd half of the 4th cent. AD, of Thesprotic origin (Eun. Vit. soph. 7,5,2). He was educated in Constantinople by the grammarian Nicocles (Lib. Ep. 1265f.). Although C. was not a Christian (Lib. Ep. 1179), he held high offices under Constantius [2] II, Valens and Theodosius I (which cannot be determined in detail before 361: cf. Lib. Ep. 52, 90). As vicarius Asiae in 363–366 (Cod. Theod. 1,28,2) he supported Valens against the usurper Procopius (Eun. Vit. soph. 7,5,2f.). In 366–367 he was proconsul Asiae (Eun. Vit. soph. 7,5,5). He helped the pagan philosopher → Maximus and effected the dismissal of the praef. praet. Orientis Saturninius Secundus Salutius (Eun. Vit. soph. 7,5,9). He was twice praefectus urbis Constantinopolitanae (372–373 and 382–384, cf. Cod. Theod. 6,4,20; 15,2,3). C. had an aqueduct built in Constantinople (Jer. Chron. 247b HELM). In 384 he was consul together with Richomer. PLRE 1,211f. (Clearchus 1). W.P.

[8] Probably comes Orientis in AD 386, perhaps identical with the city prefect of Constantinople, who is attested in 400 (or 401 [2. 222])–402, and the praetorian prefect of Illyria during the reign of Arcadius (Cod. Iust. 12,57,9).

1 PLRE 1,213 2 AL. CAMERON, J. LONG, Barbarians and Politics at the Court of Arcadius, 1993. H.L.

Clearidas (Κλεαρίδας; Klearídas). Spartan, son of Cleonymus. Appointed by → Brasidas in 423 BC as commander at Amphipolis, C. proved himself after Brasidas' death in 422. After the peace of → Nicias he did not surrender the polis entrusted to him to the Athenians so its inhabitants would not be exposed to retaliation (Thuc. 5,21; 34). Unimpressed by the instructions of the leading committees in Sparta he instigated considerable new tensions between Sparta and Athens.

→ Peloponnesian War K.-W.WEL.

Cledonius Latin grammarian, compiled a commentary on the grammar of → Donatus at Constantinople in the 5th cent. He has been preserved in a very disorderly state, which in part reveals how the text, which originated in marginalia and scholastic notes on Donatus, was compiled in a later period.

EDITIONS: GL 5, 9–79.
BIBLIOGRAPHY: G. GOETZ, s.v. C., RE 4, 10; SCHANZ/HOSIUS 4,2, 207f.; V. DE ANGELIS, s.v. C., EV 1, 818f. P.G.

Cleidemus (Κλείδημος; *Kleídēmos*, also Cleitodemus, Κλειτόδημος; *Kleitódēmos*). From Athens, according to Pausanias (10,15,5 = FGrH 323 T 1) the earliest Atthidographer (→ *Atthis*). C. wrote *c.* 350 BC an *Atthís* in at least 4 books, which is also quoted in the *Protogonía* ('History of the First-Born People') and was distinguished by dramatic vividness according to Plutarch (Mor. 345E). It extended from the mythological creation of the world to the → Peloponnesian war: the last event recorded was in 415 BC (F 10). C., himself an *exēgētés* ('interpreter') of sacred law, also wrote an *Exēgētikón* (F 14).

EDITIONS: FGrH 323 with commentary.
BIBLIOGRAPHY: O. LENDLE, Einführung in die griech. Geschichtsschreibung, 1992, 146; K. MEISTER, Die griech. Geschichtsschreibung, 1990, 76.   K. MEI.

Cleinias (Κλεινίας; *Kleinías*).
[1] One of → Solon's friends, who heard of the → *seisáchtheia* in advance and, therefore, was able to unjustly enrich himself (Plut. Solon 15,6–9; cf. [Aristot.] Ath. Pol. 6,2). The story was probably invented in the late 5th cent. BC to discredit the descendants of these men (e.g., Alcibiades [3]).

DAVIES, 600 III; RHODES, 128f.; TRAILL, PAA 575270.

[2] Born *c.* 510 BC, son of Alcibiades [1], personally equipped and supplied a ship of 200 men for the war against Xerxes and distinguished himself at the battle of → Artemisium [1] (Hdt. 8,17; Plut. Alkibiades 1). C. is depicted on a bowl by the Ambrosius painter [1. 173, No. 5].

1 BEAZLEY, ARV² 2 DAVIES, 600 V TRAILL, PAA 575370.

[3] Born *c.* 480 BC, son of Alcibiades [2], father of Alcibiades [3], probably was the author of the Cleinias decree that in 448 regulated the mode of tribute payments in the → Delian League. C. was killed in battle in 446 at Coronea (Isoc. Or. 16,28; Pl. Alc. 1,112c; Plut. Alkibidades 1; ML 46).

DAVIES, 600 V; D. M. LEWIS, in: CAH V ²1992, 127ff.; TRAILL, PAA 575375.

[4] Born *c.* 447 BC. After the death of his father C. [3], he grew up with his brother Alcibiades [3] in the house of Pericles (Pl. Alc. 1,118e; Plat. Prt. 320a).

DAVIES, 600 VII; TRAILL, PAA 575390.

[5] Son of → Axiochus, was part of the circle around → Socrates. C. appears as a protagonist in Socratic dialogues (Plat. Euthd. 271b; 275a-b; Xen. Symp. 4,12f.; 23).

DAVIES, 600 VI; TRAILL, PAA 575385.   E.S.-H.

[6] Pythagorean from Tarent, contemporary of → Plato. When Plato wanted to burn all the books of Democritus within reach, Amyclas and C. deterred him by noting that they were already widely distributed (Aristox. Fr.

131 WEHRLI = Diog. Laert. 9,40). Other anecdotes present C. as the embodiment of Pythagorean virtues (loyalty to friends: C. helps a Pythagorean in financial need who was unknown to him: Diod. Sic. 10,4,1; Iambl. VP. 239; soothing anger with music: Chamaileon Fr. 4 WEHRLI = Ath. 624a, cf. Aristox. Fr. 30 WEHRLI = Iambl. VP. 197 etc.; rejection of the pleasure of love: Plut. Symp. 654b). Fragments of the Neopythagorean Pseudepigrapha in [1].
→ Pythagorean School

1 H. THESLEFF, The Pythagorean Texts of the Hellenistic Period, 1965, 108.   C. RI.

Cleinis (Κλεῖνις; *Kleînis*) was a rich Babylonian much beloved by → Apollo and → Artemis. Among the Hyperboreans he learnt that Apollo was honoured with a donkey sacrifice and wished to transfer this custom to Babylon. However, he encountered the misgivings of Apollo, who only appreciated the donkey sacrifice in the land of the Hyperboreans. C. stopped the sacrifice but his sons continued it. Thereupon, Apollo drove the donkeys mad. They ate C. and his sons who were then transformed into birds (Antoninus Liberalis 20).
→ Donkey cult; → Hyperborei   FR.P.

Cleinomachus (Κλεινόμαχος; *Kleinómachos*) of Thurii, student of → Euclides [2] of Megara, → Megarian School. According to Diog. Laert. 2,112, C. was the first to write 'on statements and predicates and such matters' (περὶ ἀξιωμάτων καὶ κατηγορημάτων καὶ τῶν τοιούτων). This comment hints at contributions to the development of dialectics that are greater than we can presently perceive. In any case, after C. some ancient historians of philosophy called the Megarian School the → 'Dialectics' (Diog. Laert. 1,19). → Speusippus made C. the title figure of one of his dialogues (Diog. Laert. 4,4).
→ Megarian School

SSR II I.   K.D.

Cleio (Greek Κλείω; *Kleíō*, Latin *Clio*; on the etymology from κλεός, 'fame' cf. Diod. Sic. 4,19; Plut. Symp. 9,14; Cornutus 14). One of the Muses (→ Muses; Hes. Theog. 77); as a nymph of the springs (Plut. De Pyth. or. 17,402c-d) or an → Oceanid (Verg. G. 4,341), C. is also a goddess of the waters, which is frequently associated with poetic inspiration [1]. Since Pindar (e.g., Pind. Nem. 3, 1–2; Pind. Ep. 3,3; 12,1–29; Pind. Ol. 2,1–2; cf. Hor. Carm. 1,12,2) and Bacchyl. (3,1–3; 12,1–3; 13,9,229), C. has been the patroness of works that describe noteworthy deeds of persons and towns in social history (as opposed to 'warlike' → Calliope). She appears in Callimachos as the narrator (Kall. Aitia 1,4; 1,6; 2,43 PF.). C. is considered the mother of the Thracian king → Rhesus (Schol. [Eur.] Rhes. 346), of → Hymenaeus [1] (ibid.) and → Hyacinthus (Apollod. 1,3,3).

1 M. T. CAMILLONI, Le Muse, 1997.

BIBLIOGRAPHY: see → Muses.   C.W.

Cleisonymus (Κλεισώνυμος; *Kleisōnymos*, 'Noted with Praise'; also Cleitonymus: Apollod. 3,176). Son of → Amphidamas [2] from Opus in Locria. He was accidentally slain by the young → Patroclus in a dispute during an → astragalos game, whereupon Patroclus was taken to safety with Peleus (Hom. Il. 23,84–90; Schol. Hom. Il. 12,1).   RA.MI.

Cleisthenes (Κλεισθένης; *Kleisthénōs*).
[1] Tyrant of Sicyon (*c.* 600–570 BC), son of Aristonymus, from the family of Orthagoras, whose tyranny lasted about 100 years (*c.* 665–565 BC.; Aristot. Pol. 1315b 11ff.; cf. Nicolaus of Damascus FGrH 90 F 61). During the war with Argus C. pursued an anti-Argive domestic ideology, including prohibition of the presentation of the Homeric epics because they favoured Argos. The Argive hero → Adrastus [1] was replaced by the Theban hero → Melanippus (Hdt. 5,67) against Delphi's advice. According to legend the three Doric phyles present in both Sicyon and Argos were given derogatory names, but C. called his own phyle *Archélaoi*, 'the leaders' (Hdt. 5,68). As commander during the First → Sacred War he gained prestige and the funds (Schol. Pind. Nem. 9,2; Paus. 10,37,6) with which he financed the stoa in Sicyon (Paus. 2,9,6) and buildings in Delphi, among them the first treasury of the Sicyonians. After a review of aristocratic suitors from Italy to Ionia came, he gave his daughter → Agariste [1], the later mother of the Athenian Cleisthenes [2], in marriage to the Alcmaeonid Megacles (→ Alcmaeonids) (Hdt. 6,126–130).

> H. BERVE, Die Tyrannis bei den Griechen, 1967, 27ff., 532ff.; A. GRIFFITH, Sikyon, 1982; L. DE LIBERO, Die archa. Tyrannis, 1996, 188ff.   B.P.

[2] Athenian. Politician of the late 6th cent. BC, son of the Alcmaeonid Megacles and Agariste, daughter of Cleisthenes [1]. Although the → Alcmaeonids went into exile after → Peisistratus' definitive seizure of power, C. returned to Athens and in 525/4 held office as archon (ML 6, fr. c). After Delphi exerted pressure on Sparta at the instigation of the Alcmaeonidae and in 511/10 with its help had driven Hippias [1], the son of Peisistratus, from Athens, C. and → Isagoras [1] quarrelled over pre-eminence in Athens. When Isagoras gained the upper hand and was appointed archon in 508/7, C. proposed a reform program, to outdo Isagoras in popularity. The latter turned to king Cleomenes [3] I of Sparta, who invoked the curse on the Alcmaeonid family (→ Cylon [1]) to drive C. and his followers from Athens. But the Athenians conspired against Isagoras and, thus, enabled C. to return and implement his plans for reform.
   The core of C.'s reforms was the reorganization of the citizenry (for which there were models in other poleis) focussing on the local level (→ Attica with a map of the phyle order): ten new 'tribes' (*phylaí*; → *phylē*) were created, each consisting of three parts (→ *trittýes*), with one part each being located or at least centered in one of the three regions (town, coast or inland, *ásty, paralía, mesógeios*) (differently in [3] and [4]). Each *trittýs* comprised one or more of the 139 demes (*démoi*; → *démos* [2]), i.e., the local municipalities (Hdt. 5,66–73; [Aristot.] Ath. Pol. 20f.; [5]). The demes were natural units but at least some of the *trittýes* were not. Therefore, it appears possible that C. attempted behind a facade of 'impartiality' (*isótēs*) and under the pretext 'of interspersing the people' to gain advantages for his family and to disadvantage other leading families [1]. The new organization became the foundation of public life: every Athenian had to belong to a demos and also one of the larger units to which his demos belonged. Each unit had its own assemblies and officials; in the polis as a whole the army, council and many public offices were divided according to these units. This organization demanded and promoted a high degree of participation by the average citizen and was the foundation for establishing classical democracy. The introduction of → ostracism is also attributed to C. ([Aristot.] Ath. Pol, 22,1; 3; cf. Androtion FGrH 324 F 6). According to the sources it was supposed to safeguard against potential tyrants but in fact it was probably meant to resolve disputes like those between C. and Isagoras.
   Attempts by Sparta to remove the new order were unsuccessful (→ Cleomenes [3] I.). Nothing else is known of C. Presumably he died shortly after. In the 5th cent. C. was considered the founder of → *dēmokratía*.

> 1 D. M. LEWIS, Cleisthenes and Attica, in: Historia 12, 1963, 22–40   2 M. OSTWALD, in: CAH ²IV, 1988, 303–346   3 P. SIEWERT, Die Trittyen Attikas und die Heeresreform des K., 1982   4 G. R. STANTON, The Trittyes of K., in: Chiron 24, 1994, 161–207   5 J. S. TRAILL, The Political Organization of Attica, 1975   6 J. MARTIN, Von K. zu Ephialtes, in: Chiron 4, 1974, 5–42   7 CHR. MEIER, K., in: Id., Die Entstehung des Politischen bei den Griechen, 1980.
>
> DAVIES, 375f.; LGPN II, s.v. Κλεισθένης (1); PA 8526.   P.J.R.

Cleitarchus (Κλείταρχος; *Kleítarchos*).
[1] Tyrant of Eretria. Even as a banned exile C. unsuccessfully attempted in 349/8 BC to seize Eretria, e.g., with the help of Philip II against an Athenian army under Phocion (Aeschin. In Ctes. 86–88 with Schol. [1. 318, n. 2]). Philip's intervention in Euboea in 343 and 342 [1. 502f., 545–549] brought C. to power (Dem. Or. 8,36; 9,57f.; 18,71; 19,87). Phocion expelled him in 341 (Philochorus FGrH 328 F 160; Diod. Sic. 16,74,1).
→ Tyrannis

> 1 N. G. L. HAMMOND, G. T. GRIFFITH, History of Macedonia, 1979.
>
> H. BERVE, Die Tyrannis bei den Griechen, 1967, 301f., 675.   J.CO.

[2] Son of → Dinon, → Alexander historian. The exact dates of his life are uncertain but according to Pliny

(HN 3,57f.) he met a Roman delegation in Babylon in 324/3 BC while with → Alexander [4] the Great, whom he probably only came to know there. C. may have later lived in → Alexandria [1] (FGrH 137 T 12). If C. collected his materials in Babylon, he probably published his history soon after Alexander's death. Only a few fragments remain (summary: [2. 215f.]), but the 'Vulgata' — the foundation of the histories of Alexander by → Curtius [II 8] Rufus, → Diodorus [18] Siculus, → Iustinus [5] and, in part, → Plutarch — appears to be based on C. C. probably used the earlier Alexander historians, but his material mostly consisted of the recollections of participants in the campaigns, among them squadron officers and soldiers. He described the fabulous encounter of Alexander with the Amazon queen and expanded on massacres, feasts and the wonders of India. Whether he was Curtius' source for the description of court intrigues is unknown. This rhetorically enhanced work remained the most widely read history of Alexander for a considerable time. Text: FGrH 137.

1 F. JACOBY, s.v. K. (2), RE 11, 622–654   2 L. PEARSON, The Lost Histories of Alexander the Great, 1960, 212ff.
E.B.

[3] Greek grammarian and lexicographer from Aegina, 1st or the turn of 2nd/1st cent BC, mentioned by Epaphroditus [3] (EM 221,33 s.v. γάργαρος), Pamphilus (Ath. 2,69d, cf. 11,475d) and perhaps Didymus [1] (if Schol. Hom. Il. 23,81a Κλέαρχος must be corrected Κλείταρχος). His glossographic work (at least 7 books) is quoted by Athenaeus with the title 'Glosses' (Γλῶσσαι, in another location Περὶ Γλωττῶν πραγματεία) and treats the lexicographic peculiarities of various dialects, some of which are not Greek, and sociolects such as nautical language.
→ Epaphroditus [3]; → Pamphilus; → Didymus [1]

EDITIONS: M. SCHMIDT, Clitarchi reliquiae, 1842.
BIBLIOGRAPHY: W. KROLL, s.v. K. (4), RE 11, 654–655; K. LATTE, Glossographika, in: Philologus 80, 1925, 169–171 (= Id., KS, 1968, 631–633); A. LUDWICH, Aristarchs homer. Textkritik, 1884–85, Vol. 1, 44; 51; 483.   F.M.

Cleite (Κλείτη; *Kleítē*, 'The Famous One'). The daughter of → Merops, newly wed wife of Cyzicus, king of the Doliones, who was killed by his guest → Jason [1] in a fatal night-time duel whereupon C. hung herself because of her grief (Apoll. Rhod. 1,974ff., 1063ff.; Parthenius 28 MythGr 2). The waters of spring came from C.'s tears (Orph. A. 594ff.; Schol. Apoll. Rhod. 1,1065f. [1]) or those of the nymphs of the grove crying around her (Apoll. Rhod. 1,1067ff. [2]).

1 H. FRÄNKEL, Noten zu den Argonautika des Apollonios, 1968, 130f.   2 S. JACKSON, Apollonius of Rhodes: The Cleite and Byblis Suicides, in: SIFC 15, 1997, 48–54.
A.A.

Cleitomachus (Κλειτόμαχος; *Kleitómachos*).
[1] Academic philosopher, probably born in 187/6 BC in Carthage, died in 110/109. Original name Hasdrubal (Philod. Academicorum Index 25.1–2). Presumably came to Athens in 163/2 (information in Diog. Laert. 4,67 is wrong). He entered the Academy in 159/8 After an elementary education of sorts with → Carneades [1], and studies in the Peripatos and the Stoa. Occasionally, his participation in the philosophers' delegation in 155 to Rome is doubted. In 140/139 the founding of his own school in the Palladion, after 129/8 probably back at the Academy again, initially without being prominent, from 127/6 to his death officially as the scholarch (reconstruction of events [1. 900f.]). Of the exceedingly numerous writings (Diog. Laert. 4,67: more than 400) only five are identifiable: his essential scepticism is evident in 'On restraint' (Περὶ ἐποχῆς), he also deals with problems in cognitive theory in a treatise dedicated to the satiricist Lucilius, a consolation is addressed to the citizens of his native town after its destruction (more in [1. 902f.]). A specific teaching of C. is not tangible; he reradicalized the sceptical position by vehemently turning against the probability theory of his teacher Carneades.

1 W. GÖRLER, K., GGPh² 4.2, 899–904.   K.-H.S.

[2] of Thebes. Outstanding athlete at the end of the 3rd cent. BC. According to Paus. 6,15,3 C. won at → Isthmian games in wrestling, boxing and the → pancratium on a single day (cf. also Anth. Pal. 9,588; his father Hermocrates donated the honorary statue) [1. No. 67]. Also, C. won three times in the pancratium in Delphi and was successful once each in the pancratium (Ol. 141 = 216 BC) and boxing (Ol. 142 = 212 v.Chr.) in Olympia [2. No. 584, 589; 3. No. 589]; the spectator psychology is remarkably well described at the latter event (Pol. 27,9,7–13) [4. 51f.; 5. 127f.].

1 J. EBERT, Epigramme auf Sieger an gymnischen und hippischen Agonen, 1972   2 L. MORETTI, Olympionikai, 1957   3 Id., Nuovo supplemento al catalogo degli olympionikai, in: Miscellanea greca e romana 12, 1987, 67–91   4 I. WEILER, Zum Verhalten der Zuschauer bei Wettkämpfen in der Alten Welt, in: E. KORNEXL (ed.), Spektrum der Sportwiss., 1987, 43–59   5 W. DECKER, Sport in der griech. Ant., 1995.   W.D.

Cleiton A sculptor of athlete statues mentioned in Xen. Mem. 3,10,6–8. He is not attested elsewhere and may be fictive.   DI.WI.

Cleitophon (Κλειτοφῶν; *Kleitophôn*). Athenian, a disciple of → Socrates (Pl. Resp. 1,328b; 340a-b). Plato's dialogue C. is named after him. C. proposed to consider Cleisthenes' constitution for the planned changes in 411 BC. In 404 he represented the *pátrios politeía* viewpoint together with → Theramenes and others ([Aristot.] Ath. Pol. 29,3; 34,3).

PA 8546; M. CHAMBERS, Aristoteles. Staat der Athener, 1990, 277; RHODES 375–377.   W.S.

Cleitor (Κλείτωρ, Arcad. Κλήτωρ). North Arcadian town in a small plain surrounded by mountains near modern Carnesi with a river of the same name, *c.* 3 km west of Kato-Klitoria, 11 km from the sources of the Ladon (→ Ladon [2]), with few remains (IG V 2, 367). An important transit area between the eastern plateau and the western mountain regions. C. had no acropolis, the settlement was located in a flat area with only two slightly higher areas. It was, nevertheless, one of the most important towns in Arcadia, in the history of which C. repeatedly played an important role. In the 3rd cent. AD C. still minted coins. The Koriasia games at the sanctuary of Athena (Artemis?) Koria north of the town (Paus. 8,21,4) are often named in inscriptions of winners; cf. also Pind. N. 86, Schol. Pind. Ol. 7,153 (Κώρεια). Sources: Str. 8,8,2; Paus. 8,21,1–4; Ptol. 3,16,19. Epigraphy: IG V 2, 367–410. Coins: HN, 446f.

JOST, 38–41; L. LACROIX, Helios, les Azanes et les origines de Cleitor en Arcadie, in: BAB 54, 1968, 318–327; E. MEYER, Peloponnesische Wanderungen, 1939, 109f.; Id., s.v. Kleitor, RE Suppl. 9, 383f.; Id., s.v. Kleitor, RE Suppl. 12, 513; G. PAPANDREOU, Ερευναι εν Καλαβρύτοις, in: Praktika 1920, 96–114; K. TAUSEND, Ein ant. Weg über den Chelmos, in: Österr. Jahreshefte 63, 1994, Beibl., 41–52; F. E. WINTER, Arcadian Notes, in: Échos du monde classique 8, 1989, 189–200.   Y.L.

Cleitus (Κλειτός, Κλεῖτος, Κλῖτος; *Kleitós, Kleîtos, Klîtos,* 'The Famous One').

[1] Nephew of the famous seer → Melampus, son of Mantius, father of Coeranus. He was abducted by Eos because of his beauty (Hom. Od. 15,249f.; Pherecydes FGrH 3 F 115a).

[2] Great nephew of C. [1], son of Polyidus and Eurydameia. He and his brother Euchenor marched with the Epigones (→ Epigoni [2]) against Thebes and then joined Agamemnon (Pherecydes ibid.).

[3] Trojan, son of Peisenor, companion of → Polydamas. He was killed by Teucer (Hom. Il. 15,445ff.).

[4] Lover of → Pallene, the daughter of king → Sithon. With her help he defeated his rival Dryas in a competition, married her and became her father's successor (Conon FGrH 26 F 10; Parthenius 6).

[5] King of the Thracian → Sithones. He married his daughter Chrysonoe to → Proteus who later assisted him in the war against the Bisaltes (Conon FGrH 26 F 32; Tabula Iliaca IG XIV 1284).   RA.MI.

[6] C. 'the Black' Son of Dropidas and brother of → Alexander's [4] nurse. At → Granicus in 334 BC C. saved the king's life. At → Gaugamela he commanded the 'royal squadron'. In 330 he took Macedonian troops from Ecbatana to Alexander in → Parthia. After the execution of → Philotas C. became commander of half of the → *hetairoi*. In 328 he was appointed satrap of the important frontier province → Bactria-Sogdiana but insulted the king at a feast and was slain by him. When Alexander claimed he wished to kill himself be-

cause of his regret, the army comforted him by condemning the dead man for treason (Curt. 8,1,19–2,12).

BERVE 2, No. 427; HECKEL 34–37.

[7] C. 'the White' Fought in → Alexander's [4] Indian campaign as taxiarch, then as hipparch. He was discharged in Opis in 324 BC with the troops under → Craterus [1], but after Alexander's death he became commander of the fleet at the Hellespont, where he defeated an Athenian fleet in 323/2 at Amorgus and then called himself Poseidon. In the agreement of → Triparadeisos of 320 he received the satrapy of Lydia but soon fled from → Antigonus [1] to → Polyperchon in Macedonia. In his service he surrendered → Phocion to the Athenians to be executed, defeated → Nicanor in a naval battle but in another his fleet was destroyed. He escaped by land but was captured by → Lysimachus and executed (Diod. Sic. 18,72).

BERVE 2, No. 428; HECKEL 185–187.

[8] Illyrian prince, son of Bardylis, was defeated together with → Glaucias [2] by Alexander [4] in 335 BC. C. fled to Glaucias and there disappeared from history (Arr. Anab. 1,5f.).

BERVE 2, No. 426.   E.B.

[9] (Κλεῖτος). Tragedian of the 2nd cent. BC (129 T 1 TrGF I), son of Callisthenes; a funerary inscription was found on the island of Teos (CIG II 3105).   B.Z.

Clematius

[1] C. of Alexandria was the *consularis Palaestinae* (Lib. Ep. 693) in *c.* AD 352/3. In the winter of 353/4 he became the victim of an intrigue in Antioch [1] and was executed without trial (Amm. Marc. 14,1,3). PLRE 1,213 (Clematius 1).

[2] C. held a high office in Antioch [1] at the time of the caesar Gallus (→ Constantius [5]), probably as an *agens in rebus* (Lib. Ep. 405, 435); in AD 357–358 *consularis Palaestinae* (Lib. Ep. 317). He was in close contact with → Libanius (cf. Ep. 312, 315, 317). PLRE 1,213f. (Clematius 2).

[3] C. of Palestine was a close friend of Libanius (Lib. Ep. 1283, 1458) and is only known from his letters. As a non-Christian C. was appointed as the high priest of Palestine by Iulianus [11] (Lib. epist. 1307); after the emperor's death (363) he was accused because of his actions against Christians (ibid. 1504) but not convicted (ibid. 1526). The mss. use 'Lem(m)atios' (cf., e.g., the apparatus of FÖRSTER regarding Ep. 1504, Z. 21). 'Clematius' is an amendment by WOLF and SEECK.   W.P.

Clemens

[1] of Rome. Since → Irenaeus (Haer. 3,3,3) recorded as the third bishop of Rome in the list of Roman bishops although the Roman congregation was probably led by a college of presbyters and not a bishop alone in the late 1st cent. All information on C. comes from later centu-

ries and documents the historical development of an image of C. but not the historical person. Dionysius of Corinth (Eus. HE, 4,23,11) considered C. the author of a letter of the Roman congregation to its brothers in the faith in Corinth. In the light of the dispute within the Corinthian community this first epistle of C. [1; 2. 1–107; 3. 77–151; 4] demands submission to the leaders installed by the Apostles or their successors. It is among the first Christian writings outside the NT (to which it belongs in the Syrian church) and is a central text with respect to the development of the official priesthood [17; 18]. In the manuscript transmission it is followed by the second epistle of C. [5; 3. 152–175; 6. 203–280], an admonishing address to the Christian community, probably composed in the East. It is dated before or in the middle of the 2nd cent. and is considered the oldest preserved Christian sermon. Apart from two letters *ad virgines* (3rd cent., Syria) [7], the tradition also associates the first Christian → 'novel' with C.: the Ps.-Clementines, whose reconstructed oldest version, the Basic Writings, probably was composed in Syria *c.* 230. The Greek version derived from them, the ὁμιλίαι (*Homiliai*) [8; 9], and → Rufinus' Latin translation, the *Recognitiones* [10; 11], which is preceded in Greek by a letter each from Peter and C. to the Lord's brother James, but in Latin only by the letter of C. to James (*epistula Clementis = epCl*). C. entered the → *collectiones canonum* of late Antiquity and the early Middle Ages with the *epCl* and also with another letter addressed to James (*Quoniam sicut a beato Petro*) [12]. The dissemination of church rules was also attributed to C., especially the *canones apostolorum*, which → Dionysius Exiguus translated into Latin [13].

Because C. was considered a student of → Peter from the outset and as the successor appointed by him, the hagiographic tradition had a special interest in him, whether as the pivotal point in the Roman list of succession (since the 2nd cent.), as martyr (attested since the 4th cent., and as a legend fixed in writing no later than the 6th cent. [14]). In the 6th cent. the *titulus Clementis* is associated with C. (for the history of this church in Rome [15]), to which the relics of C. were transferred by Cyril and Method from Cherson (Crimea), the Apostles of the Slavs, in 867 [16]. His memorial day is 23 November.

1 CPG 1001   2 J. A. FISCHER, Schriften des Urchristentums 1, [10]1993, (Greek/German)   3 A. LINDEMANN, H. PAULSEN (ed.), Die Apostolischen Väter, 1992 (Greek/German)   4 Fontes Christiani 15, 1994 (Greek/Latin/German)   5 CPG 1003   6 K. WENGST, Schriften des Urchristentums, 1984   7 CPG 1004   8 CPG 1015   9 B. REHM, G. STRECKER, GCS 42, [3]1992   10 H. J. FREDE, Kirchenschriftsteller. Verzeichnis und Sigel, [4]1995, 734 (FREDE)   11 B. REHM, F. PASCHKE, GCS 51, 1965   12 F. MAASSEN, Gesch. der Quellen und Lit. des canonischen Rechts im Abendlande, 1870, § 536 (= CPG 1007f.)   13 Id., § 534   14 SOCII BOLLANDINI (ed.), Bibliotheca Hagiographica Latina antiquae et mediae aetatis, 2 vols., 1898–1901, Suppl. editio altera, 1911 (BHL), 1848 (= CPL 2177, also FREDE, 57f.)   15 San Clemente miscellany I–IV, 2, 1977–1992   16 BHL 2073   17 J. MARTIN,

Die Genese des Amtspriestertums in der frühen Kirche, 1972   18 H. VON CAMPENHAUSEN, Kirchliches Amt und geistige Vollmacht in den ersten drei Jahrhunderten, 1953.

A. LINDEMANN, Die Clemensbriefe, 1992; LMA 2, 2138; LThK[3] 2, 1227–1231; RAC 3, 188–206; TRE 8, 113–123.
                                                                    E.W.

[2] Slave of → Agrippa Postumus (1st cent. AD), who wanted to take his master from Planasia to the German armies after the death of Augustus. However, after Agrippa's death he claimed to be the latter, but was caught and killed (Tac. Ann. 2,39–40; Suet. Tib. 25,1; Cass. Dio 57,16,3f.).   D.K.

[3] **T. Flavius Clemens** (Clement of Alexandria)
A. LIFE   B. THE MOST IMPORTANT WORKS
C. SIGNIFICANCE

A. LIFE
Died before AD 215/221, Christian philosopher and founder of the theological literature based on Greek education. A few of his own reports, but especially Eus. Hist eccl. 5,11 and 6,6 inform about C.'s life. Born in Alexandria or Athens (thus Epiphanius, Haereseum epitome 31,3). The search for a Christian teacher led C. via Syria, Palestine and Italy to Pantaenus in → Alexandria [1] in AD 180 (Clem. Al. stromateis 1,11,2), where he eventually taught Christian philosophy. That C. became the head of an (episcopal?) school (Eus. HE 6,6) is unlikely in this period. Persecutions in Alexandria (Eus. HE 6,1), possibly also the hostility of the bishop, caused C. to go to Alexander, the bishop of an unknown town in Cappadocia, where he taught (as a presbyter?) and wrote treatises. About 211 C. took a letter by Alexander to → Antioch [1]; in a letter of 215/216 (or 221?) Alexander speaks of C. as deceased.

B. THE MOST IMPORTANT WORKS
1) Προτρεπτικὸς πρὸς Ἕλληνας (*Protreptikòs pròs Héllēnas, Protr.*): apologetic admonition to the 'pagans' with the objective of converting them to the true *lógos* that is contrasted with the unreason and immorality of pagan religion (especially their mysteries).
2) Παιδαγωγός (*Paidagōgós, Paid.*, 3 books): continuation of the *Protr.* as a paraenesis, book 1 on the *lógos* as educator, book 2 and 3 with practical rules for life, at the end an anapaestic hymn to Christ as *lógos paidagōgós*.
3) Στρωματεῖς, Latin *Stromata* (*Strom.*, 7 books): 'patchwork', → poikilography with the central themes a) Greek philosophy and the Faith (books 1–2), b) asceticism and perfection (book 3–4), c) allegory and figure (Book 5) and d) the true gnostic (Book 6–7). Book 8, which follows in the manuscripts, contains sketches on logic, probably as preliminaries to the *Strom.* or other works.
4) Τίς ὁ σωζόμενος πλούσιος: homily (?) on Mk 10, 17–31.
5) *Excerpta ex Theodoto* against the Valentinian gnostics.

6) Exegetical writing: *Eclogae propheticae* and fragments of 8 books Ὑποτυπώσεις (*Hypotypóseis*, 'shadow figures'), e.g., on the origins of the Gospel of Mark.

7) Epistle fragment with apocryphal Gospel of Mark (first published in 1973; now GCS 39, 17f.).

C. SIGNIFICANCE

C. attempted the first synthesis combining Greek philosophy (→ Platonism; Stoicism) and Christian-Jewish revelation, founded on education and rhetoric but taut with tension. The target group was the wealthy upper class of Greek towns. The basic ontological and epistemological structure of C.'s philosophy is the originally Platonic three-stage conversion (taken from the initiation mysteries) via moral teachings to the spiritual view (ἐποπτεία, *epopteía*) through revelation of the divine *lógos*. Cognition occurs in the adaptation of the observer to the observed who then becomes a true (as opposed to a heretical) gnostic. This same three-step sequence would have been equivalent to the trilogy *Protreptikós-Paidagōgós-Didaskal(ik)ós*, which C. had originally planned. However, C. did not include the explanation of religious teachings, which were also deliberately hidden in the holy scriptures. The duty of the knowing is the allegorical-symbolic exegesis according to the method of → Philo. The influence of C. is particularly evident in → Origenes. Only → Photius' accusation of heterodoxy harmed C.'s reputation until he was rediscovered as an open-minded thinker and recorder of otherwise lost literature (quotations from *c.* 360 authors!).

→ Gnosticism; GNOSTICISM; → Gnostics; → Allegory; → Church Fathers

EDITIONS: CPG 1, 1983, 135–140; O. STÄHLIN, L. FRÜCHTEL, U. TREU, GCS 12, 15, 17, 39, 1905–1936 (4 vols.: vol.1, ³1972; vol. 2, ⁴1985; vol. 3, ²1970; vol. 4 ²1980, in part new); C. MONDÉSERT, H. I. MARROU et al., SChr 2, 23, 30, 38, 70, 108, 158, 278/79 (7 vols., Greek-French), 1948–1981; M. MARCOVICH, 1995 (Protr.); C. NARDI, 1985 (Ecl. Proph.); O. STÄHLIN, BKV² 7, 8, 17, 19, 20 (German); W. WILSON, Ante-Nicene Christian Library 4, 12, 22, 24 1882–1884 (English); G. PINI, 1985 (Strom.; Italian).
BIBLIOGRAPHY: O. STÄHLIN, HdA 7,2,2, 1924, 1310–1317; M. POHLENZ, in: Nachrichten der Ges. der Wiss. zu Göttingen (philosophical historical class), 1943, 103–180; ALTANER/STUIBER, ⁹1978, 188–197; A. MÉHAT, TRE 8, 101–113; D. WYWRA, Christl. Platonaneignung, 1983; C. RIEDWEG, Mysterienterminologie, 1987, 116ff.; A. VAN DEN HOEK, C. of A. and his use of Philo, 1988; DIHLE, 338–340; E. F. OSBORN, The emergence of Christian Theology, 1993; E. PROCTER, Christian Controversy, 1995. DO.ME.

Clementia Personification of clemency (ThlL, Onom. II, 487). Pliny (HN 2,14) names C. in a series of deified abstractions. The C. of Caesar [1; 2] was famous: the senate had a joint temple built for the Divus Iulius and the deified C. in which Caesar and the goddess were depicted extending their hands to each other (Plut.

Caes. 57,4; App. B Civ. 2,106; Cass. Dio 44,6,4). On the golden shield of Augustus C. is one of the four virtues attributed to him (R. Gest. div. Aug. 34). C. is the central theme in Seneca's *speculum regum* (De clementia).

1 M. TREU, Zur C. Caesars, in: MH 5, 1948, 197–217
2 S. WEINSTOCK, Divus Julius, 1971, 234–240.

T. HÖLSCHER, s.v. C., LIMC 3.1, 295–299. R.B.

Clementines see → Novel

Clement of Alexandria see → Clemens [3] of Alexandria

Cleobis and Biton (Κλέοβις; *Kleóbis*, Latin *Cleobis*; Βίτων; *Bítōn*). The story of the Argive brothers, told by Solon to Croesus as the example of greatest happiness (Hdt. 1,31), is assumed to be well-known by Cicero (Tusc. 1,113). The mother of C. and B., a priestess of Hera named Cydippe (Anth. Pal. 3,18), had to go to the Hera temple of Argus for a ritual activity. When her draught animals were not brought on time, C. and B. had themselves hitched before the wagon and pulled her 45 stadia to the temple. There the mother pleaded with the Gods for the best that could be bestowed upon humans for the *pietas* ('fear of god') of her sons, whereupon C. and B. died. In their memory the Argives donated statues to Delphi. It was thought that they were the archaic Kouroi (→ statues; → sculpture) of Delphi; according to a more recent interpretation these may, however, represent the → Dioscuri [1]. The purpose of the tale is to portray death as the release from the uncertainties of life that should be joyfully accepted.

1 P. E. ARIAS, s.v. B. et K., LIMC 1.1, 119f., No. 10. B.SCH.

Cleoboea (Κλεόβοια; *Kleóboia*).
[1] A virgin who supposedly brought the mysteries of → Demeter from Paros to Thasos. In the famous painting of → Polygnotus in Delphi she was depicted with a *cista mystica* — in iconography a symbol of keeping secrets (Paus. 10,28,3).
[2] Wife of Phobius, king of Miletus. She fell in love with Antheus, who was staying at court as a hostage, but sought revenge because he rejected her. She chased a tame partridge into a deep well and asked him to retrieve it. She thereby killed him first and then in desperation took her own life shortly after (Parthenius 14). RA.MI.

Cleobule (Κλεοβούλη; *Kleoboúlē*). Born *c.* 408 BC, died after 363, the daughter of Gylon, wife of the elder Demosthenes from Paeania, mother of the famous orator → Demosthenes [2] and a daughter (Dem. Or. 27 hypoth. § 1; Dem. Or. 28,1–3; Aeschin. In Ctes. 171f.; Plut. Demosthenes 4,2; Plut. Mor. 844A). Her marriage to Demosthenes can probably be dated to 386/5 or slightly earlier, his death probably to 376/5 BC. C., who still lived in 363 (Dem. Or. 28,20), accused Aphobus and the other guardians of her children of mismanagement and embezzlement.

Davies 3597 VII; PA 8556.   J.E.

Cleobuline (Κλεοβουλίνη). (Probably fictive) daughter of → Cleobulus [1] of Lindus, to whom riddles in an elegiac distichon (Fr. 1–2 West) or a single hexameter (Fr. 3 W.) have been attributed since the late 5th cent. BC (Dissoi logoi 3,10 = Fr. 2 W.).   E.BO.

Cleobulus (Κλεόβουλος; *Kleóboulos*).
[1] Tyrant of Lindus (Rhodes), flourished in the 7th–6th cent. BC, considered to be one of the → seven wise men [1]. He composed 'songs and riddles in about 3,000 verses' (Diog. Laert. 1,89). Apart from 20 sayings (I[6] p. 63, 1–12 DK), a short letter to Solon (Epist. p. 207 Hercher), a fragment of a scolion in a moralizing tone (SH 526). Preserved is only a funerary epigram in hexameter for king → Midas (Anth. Pal. 7,153 = GVI 1171a), quoted by Plato (Phaedr. 264d) and targeted by the satire of Simonides (PMG 581). A short poetic riddle in hexameters (Anth. Pal. 14,101) has been attributed to C., but also to his daughter → Cleobuline, a famous author of riddles.

    1 H. Berve, Die Tyrannis bei den Griechen, 1967, 119.   M.G.A.

[2] Athenian, son of Glaucus of Acharnae, uncle of the rhetor → Aeschines [2]; as *stratēgós* in the → Corinthian War the victor in a naval battle in 396/5 or 388/7 BC against the Spartan nauarch Chilon (Aeschin. Leg. 78). C. was also considered a respected soothsayer (SEG 16,193).

    PA 8558; Davies 14625 II, S. 544; Develin 1645; LGPN 2, s.v. Kleobulos (3).   J.E.

[3] Spartan, as ephor (→ Ephoroi) in 421/0 BC, C. rejected the → Nicias peace and attempted with → Xenares and other 'friends' to bring about an anti-Athenian alliance with the Argives, Corinthians and Boeotians through intrigues but failed because of the resistance of the four sections of the Boeotian council (Thuc. 5,36–39).   K.-W.WEL.
[4] Son of Ptolemy (PP VI 14945) of Alexandria, in 188/7 BC with relatives a delegate of Ptolemy V to Delphi, there as → *próxenos*.

    E. Olshausen, Prosopographie der hell. Königsgesandten 1, 1974, 54, No. 32.   W.A.

Cleochares (Κλεοχάρης; *Kleocháres*). Greek rhetor from Myrlea/Bithynia (Str. 12,4,9 = 566). According to Diog. Laert. 4,41 a lover of Arcesilaus, Demochares and Pythocles living therefore in the 3rd cent. BC, probably mostly in Athens. Apart from speeches, he wrote treatises in literary criticism; three works have been

transmitted: in a comparison of Isocrates and Demosthenes he used the famous image of an athlete's body for the style of the former and of a soldier's for that of the latter (Phot. 121b 9–16). His great respect for Demosthenes is also evident in the polyptoton with the name of Demosthenes quoted by Herodian (Spengel 3,97); another polyptoton, probably from a speech, is preserved in Latin by Rutilius Lupus (1,10).

    M.J. Lossau, Unt. zur ant. Demosthenes-Exegese, 1964, 52–65.   M.W.

Cleodamus (Κλεόδαμος; *Kleódamos*). C. of Byzantium, commissioned by → Gallienus with strengthening the fortifications of the cities near the mouth of the Danube against the → Heruli in AD 267 (SHA Gall. 13,6). In the same year (not later under Claudius II) C. drove the Heruli from Athens, which they had conquered (Zon. 12,26, p. 151 Dindorf III). PIR[2] C 1144.   K.G.-A.

Cleomachus (Κλεόμαχος; *Kleómachos*). *Kinaidographos*, born in Magnesia, dates uncertain. According to Str. 14,1,41 he was a boxer who after falling in love with a *kínaidos* and a prostitute, whom he supported, began to write in the obscene language of the *kínaidoi*. Heph. Enchiridion 11,2 (= Consbruch 392,10–15) states that the Ionian acatalectic dimeter *a maiore* was called the *Kleomacheion* and that this verse form contained Molossian metre and choriambs. Hephaestion cites (as does Trichas ad loc. Consbruch 395,10) an example but neither is definitely by C. The Dictaean Hymn to the Curetes (CollAlex 160f.; 4th or 3rd cent. BC) is composed in Cleomacheans with a iambo-aeolic refrain.

    SH 341–342; M.L. West, Greek Metre, 1982, 143–144.   E.R.

Cleombrotus (Κλεόμβροτος; *Kleómbrotos*).
[1] Agiad (→ Agiads), brother of Leonidas I who died at Thermopylae in 480 BC and guardian of the latter's son Pleistarchus. As commander of the Peloponnesian forces, C. directed the fortification of the Isthmus of Corinth before the battle of Salamis, but died late that year or in the winter of 480/79 (Hdt. 5,41; 7,205,1; 8,71; 9,10; Paus. 3,3,9).
[2] C. I. Agiad, after the banishment of his father Pausanias in 394 BC under the guardianship of Aristodemus; Spartan king in 380–371 BC (Diod. Sic. 15,23,2). C. operated in 378 without success against Thebes, where the Spartan garrison had been forced to withdraw (Xen. Hell. 5,4,14ff.), and failed in 376 at the Cithaeron pass (Xen. Hell. 5,4,59). However, in 372 he forced the retreat of the Thebans from Phocis (Xen. Hell. 6,1,1). In 371 again in Phocis, he received instructions to reenter Boeotia. C. was killed in 371 during the battle of Leuctra (Xen. Hell. 6,4,2–15; Diod. Sic. 15,54,6–55,5) [1. 82, 87–89, 90, 113f.].

[3] C. II. Spartan from a cadet branch of the → Agiads. C. became king in 242 BC after his father-in-law was overthrown, but had to go in exile after his return in 241 (Plut. Agis 11,7–9; 16,4–18,4; Paus. 3,6,7f.).

[4] Rich and much-travelled Spartan friend of → Plutarch, in whose work 'On the Cessation of the Oracles' he appears as a dialogue partner (Mor. 409E ff.). C. expounds scurrilous theses on the oil consumption of the eternal light and the longevity of demons [2. 178–180].

1 R. J. Buck, Boiotia and the Boiotian League, 432–371 B.C., 1994   2 P. Cartledge, A. Spawforth, Hellenistic and Roman Sparta, 1989.   K.-W.WEL.

[5] s. → Socratics

Cleomedes Author of an astronomical teaching manual, who lived between → Poseidonius and → Ptolemy (whom he does not quote). The textbook consisted of two parts designated scholia ('lectures', 'exercises'). The title Κυκλικῆς Θεωρίας μετεώρων α'/β' (*Kyklikês theorías meteôrōn a'/b'* was preserved in the manuscript. Books 1 and 2 probably unite two versions of a theory of the motional of celestial objects; Todd favoured Μετέωρα (*Metéōra*). C. does not present any original research, but compiled the thought of philosophers, mostly stoic (*sympátheia*; *ekpýrōsis*, 'world fire'; the earth as a minute *kéntron*, 'centre', in the middle of the huge spherical cosmos): → Crates of Mallus, → Aratus [4] and especially (even though only indirectly) → Poseidonius (agreement with → Geminus [1], → Plutarch, Achilleus and Plin. HN). He also quoted Homer, Heraclitus and → Hipparchus [6] (exact juxtaposition of Aldebaran and Antares, → constellations). He takes a polemical position against → Epicurus (2,1). C. is important as a source and because of his definitions. The final sentence (τὰ πολλὰ δὲ τῶν εἰρημένων ἐκ τῶν Ποσειδωνίου ἔκλαπται, 'the greater part of what was said was taken from the writings of Poseidonius ') was once suspected of being a scholion but is now considered authentic.

Book 1 treats cosmology, the zones of the earth, times of day and the seasons, planetary movements (especially the anomaly of the sun) and the size of the → Ecliptic; Book 2 the diameters of the sun, moon and fixed stars (the circumference of the earth was given by C. according to the *Arenarius* of → Archimedes [1] as 1:10000 of the sun's path), also moon theory (distance moon — earth 5,000,000 stadia), phases of the moon, → eclipses (the conical shape of the Earth's shadow), lateral and longitudinal motions of the → planets.

The 'Hymn to the Sun' (2,154–156) influenced Basil *Homiliae in Hexaëmeron*. A strong influence is evident in many medieval manuscripts; many humanists also took an early note of C.: Ed. princeps Brixen 1497, then Venice 1498, Latin commentary of Balfour (1605).

Editions: B. R. Todd, 1990 (Bibliography XXII–XXV). Bibliography: A. Rehm, s.v. Kleomedes (3), RE 11, 679–694; W. Schumacher, Unt. zur Datier. des Astro-

nomen Kleomedes, 1975; R. B. Todd, The Title of Cleomedes' Treatise, in: Philologus 129, 1985, 250–261; H. Weinhold, Die Astronomie in der ant. Schule, München 1912.   W.H.

Cleomenes (Κλεομένης; *Kleoménēs*).

[1] Athenian who rejected the Spartan terms of peace in the popular assembly in 404 BC (Plut. Lysandros 14).

[2] Spartan, member of a Spartan court of arbitration that allegedly awarded the island of → Salamis to the Athenians at the end of the 7th cent. BC (Plut. Solon 10).

[3] C. I. Spartan king, Agiad (→ Agiads), son of Anaxandridas [2] by his second wife, most important representative of the Spartan leadership about 500 BC with great personal authority. C. probably established his claim to kingship (probably *c.* 520) against his stepbrother → Dorieus [1] (Hdt. 5,42). It is not certain if he was already militarily active in 519 at Plataeae (Hdt. 6,108; Thuc. 3,68). He rejected a plea for help by the Samian Maeandrius *c.* 516 (Hdt. 3,148) and in *c.* 514 had close contact with Scythian delegates (Hdt. 6,84). His intervention in Athens in 510, which led to the toppling of the → Peisistratids, was significant (Hdt. 5,64f.). However, C.'s plan to support his Athenian friend → Isagoras [1] in 508/7 with a small force approved by Sparta against the reformer → Cleisthenes [2] failed (Hdt. 5,70–72). C.'s third campaign against Attica in 507/6 was probably a venture of the polis of Sparta because his co-regent → Damaratus and Spartan allies accompanied his army. The resistance of Damaratus, the Corinthians and other allies prevented Sparta from introducing a compliant regime in Athens. The quarrel led to legal restrictions of the powers to act of Spartan kings, who were no longer permitted to jointly lead armies (Hdt. 5,74f.). Still, C. was able to strengthen his position and in 499 to scuttle a petition for help from Aristagoras of Miletus by influencing the ephores (Hdt. 5,49; → Ionian Revolt). About 494 C. defeated the Argives at Sepeia but declined to continue the conflict and was charged for that reason (Hdt. 6,82) even though the military means were hardly sufficient for a siege of Argus. It remains uncertain if the suit originated with the ephorate or the followers of Damaratus. C. was acquitted and remained the most influential person in Sparta. As the Persian menace grew, in the attempt to preserve Spartan hegemony in Hellas and to protect the Athenians against a collaboration of the Aeginians with the Persians, C. demanded hostages from Aegina and achieved this against Damaratus, whom he had deposed by bribing the Delphic Oracle and then replaced with → Leotychidas (Hdt. 6,48–50; 65f.; 73).

When his intrigues became known, C. left Sparta and attempted to stir up leading Arcadians against his polis. Allegedly in fear of his machinations, he was recalled and reinstalled as king. Shortly thereafter, he allegedly committed suicide in a fit of insanity (Hdt. 6,74f.), a claim that may have been an attempt to cover up murder. The broad powers of Spartan kings of this age are evident in C.'s actions but the dangers threatening the *kósmos* Sparta because of the kings' struggles for power are equally evident. Certainly, the ephorate was strengthened as an institution. The initiative to eliminate C. originated with the king's relatives.

P. CARLIER, La vie politique à Sparte sous le règne de Cléomène Ier, in: Ktema 2, 1977, 65–84; ST. C. KLEIN, Cleomenes, 1973; M. MEIER, K. I. und Damaratos, in: Historische Anthropologie (in preparation); L. THOMMEN, Lakedaimonion Politeia, 1996, 67ff., 87ff., 99ff.

[4] Spartan, son of the 'regent' → Pausanias. As guardian of the later king Pausanias, C. led the raid in 427 BC into Attica (Thuc. 3,26; 5,16).

[5] C. II. Agiad (→ Agiads), son of Cleombrotus [2] I., (Paus. 1,13,4; 3,6,2; Plut. Agis 3), Spartan king in 370–309/8 BC as successor of his brother Agesipolis [2] II (Diod. Sic. 20,29,1).

[6] C. III. Son of Leonidas II, Spartan king in 235–222 and 219 BC; C. temporarily eliminated the ephorate and *de facto* the dual monarchy in 227 through a coup (→ Ephoroi) (Plut. Cleomenes 6–11) and, therefore, was considered a tyrant by his enemies in Sparta and the leadership of the Achaean Confederacy (Pol. 2,47,3; Plut. Aratos 38). C.'s objective was to regain Spartan hegemony in the Peloponnese and create the foundations for a new Spartan policy based on power in the style of the Hellenistic monarchs. C. sought to continue the reforms of Agis [4] IV by redistributing land and increasing the number of Spartans to 4,000 by granting full citizenship to select → *perioíkoi* (and probably also to *hypomeíones*, 'impoverished citizens') to whom he assigned new *klároi* (→ Kleros). After significant successes in fighting the Achaean Confederacy led by → Aratus [2] of Sicyon, C. was defeated at Sellasia in 223 by the Macedonian king Antigonus [3], against whom he also mobilized the → Helotes though without eliminating the institution of Helotism (Pol. 2,65; Plut. Cleomenes 23) [1. 64]. C. fled to the court of Ptolemy, where he was not given the hoped for support, and in 219, after a hopeless attempt to escape confinement, he committed suicide or had himself killed by his faithful followers (Pol. 5,34,11–39,6; Plut. Kleomenes 33–37).

1 J. DUCAT, Les Hilotes, 1990.

P. CARTLEDGE, A. SPAWFORTH, Hellenistic and Roman Sparta, 199249ff.; E. S. GRUEN, Aratus and the Achaean Alliance with Macedon, in: Historia 21, 1972, 609–625; B. SHIMRON, Late Sparta, 1972, 37ff.   K.-W.WEL.

[7] C. of Naucratis, was assigned by → Alexander [4] in Egypt with the administration of the border district east of the Nile delta, the construction of → Alexandria and supervision over the finances of all Egypt. Even before 323 BC there was an administrative reform in which C. replaced the nomarchs (→ Nomarches) responsible for civil administration with → satraps. He regulated the grain exports during the great famine in Greece, which stabilized the Egyptian situation and treasury but affected the memory of C. among the Greeks in a persis-

tently negative way. Doubts about his loyalty to Alexander, who assigned him the construction of two temples for Hephaestion [1] as late as in 323, are unfounded. When, after Alexander's death, → Ptolemy was made the new satrap of Egypt, C. became his hyparch (→ Hyparchia) without difficulty. The reason for his (probably early) execution by Ptolemy is unknown.

BERVE, No. 431; HÖLBL, 282 A. 12.   W.A.

[8] respected Syracusan, entrusted in 72 BC by → Verres with the supreme command of the fleet against the pirates. Verres did not punish him (unlike the ship captains subordinate to C.) despite his failures (Cic. Verr. 2,5,82–94; 133–135 *et passim*). C.'s wife Nike was allegedly the lover of Verres.   K.MEI.

[9] The name used by several Greek sculptors. Attribution of preserved works and others mentioned in sources to members of a family of artists is disputed. According to a signature not preserved in the original, C., the son of Apollodorus of Athens, created the Medici Venus (Florence, UF), a copy of the 1st cent. BC after a variant of the Cnidian Aphrodite. C., the son of Cleomenes, signed the statue of the so-called Germanicus (Paris, LV), which combines a classical Hermes type (Ludovisi) with an early Augustan portrait; he may have been the son of the older C. The assignment of other works is uncertain: the fragment of a colossal statue of Apollo in Piacenza with C.'s signature and an altar with the Iphigenia myth (Florence, UF) with the signature of a C. perhaps date from the 2nd half of the 1st cent. BC. The collection of Asinius Pollio in Rome contained statues of the muses by a C., who may be identical to the Athenian C. known from a signature in Thespiae.

OVERBECK No. 2226; LOEWY No. 344; 380; 513; G. LIPPOLD, Kopien und Umbildungen griech. Statuen, 1923, 180; A. PLASSART, Inscriptions de Thespies, in: BCH 50, 1926, 456; W. FUCHS, Die Vorbilder der neuattischen Reliefs, 1959, 134 (Altar); G. MANSUELLI, EAA 4, 369–371; A. STEWART, Attika, 1979, 85–86; 168; H. FRONING, Marmor-Schmuckreliefs mit griech. Mythen im 1. Jh.v.Chr., 1981, 132–140 (Altar); W. NEUMER-PFAU, Stud. zur Ikonographie und gesellschaftlichen Funktion hell. Aphrodite-Statuen, 1982, 183–191 (Aphrodite); C. MADERNA, Iuppiter, Diomedes und Merkur als Vorbilder für röm. Bildnisstatuen, 1988, 223–225 (Germanicus); B. S. RIDGWAY, Hellenistic Sculpture, 1, 1990, 354; P. MORENO, Scultura ellenistica, 1994, 733; F. REBECCHI, Sculture di tradizione colta nella Cisalpina repubblicana, in: Optima via, 1998, 189–206.   R.N.

Cleon (Κλέων; Kléōn).

[1] The most influential politician in Athens after 430 BC, as the operator of a tannery was the first important demagogue from the circle of tradesmen who were rising to political leadership. Sources paint a picture of a man who put his loyalty to the people (*démos*) before that to his friends, who cleverly exploited the moods prevalent among the people and procured a following for himself by promising material gains. C. opposed

→ Pericles at the beginning of the Peloponnesian War (Plut. Pericles 33,8; 35,5), in 427 after the suppression of the revolt of → Mytilene declared himself in favour of the killing or enslavement of all the inhabitants (Thuc. 3,36-40; Diod. Sic. 12,55,8ff.) and then acted as the fiercest opponent of → Nicias' peace policy. C. thwarted the truce negotiations in 425 after the occupation of Pylos and had himself fêted as the victor of Sphacteria (Thuc. 4,21ff.; 27-39). His attempt to have the knights (híppeis) more heavily taxed financially led in 426 to a charge of bribery (probolé); C. was sentenced to a fine of 5 talents. He brought about a significant increase in the tributes of the confederates (from 460 to 1460 talents) and increased the fees of jurymen from two to three oboli. In 423 C. put forward a motion for Scione, which had fallen away from Athens, to be destroyed and its citizens executed (Thuc. 4,122,6). As stratēgós he captured Torone in 422 (Thuc. 5,2ff.), but was killed in the same year at Amphipolis in the battle against → Brasidas. The death of the two generals made possible the peace of Nicias (Thuc. 5,6-10; 5,16,1; Diod. Sic. 12,74). In the comedies, especially Aristophanes' 'Knights', C. is caricatured as a flatterer and seducer of the people. Thucydides' depiction is also one-sided, possibly because he may have held C. responsible for his exile.

→ Peloponnesian War

F. BOURRIOT, La famille et le milieu social de Cléon, in: Historia 31, 1982, 404-435; E.M. CARAWAN, The Five Talents Cleon Coughed up, in: CQ 40, 1990, 137-147; W.R. CONNOR, The New Politicians of Fifth-Century Athens, 1971 (Review: J.K. DAVIES, in: Gnomon 47, 1975, 374-378); B. SMARCZYK, Unt. zur Rel.-Politik und polit. Propaganda Athens im Delisch-Att. Seebund, 1990. W.S.

[2] Bronze sculptor from Sicyon, pupil of Antiphanes. According to Pausanias, C. created a statue of Aphrodite in Olympia and also two of the earliest zánes, bronze statues of Zeus, from the fines of the athletes. One of the bases of these is extant from 388 BC with his signature. On the evidence of six further extant bases, C. made victors' statues in Delphi and Olympia which can be dated to the middle of the 4th cent. BC. Pliny calls C. a third-generation pupil of Polycletus. Of C.'s work only the stance of his statues is known. Pliny ascribes to him statues of philosophers.

OVERBECK no. 985; 1007-1013; J. MARCADÉ, Recueil des signatures de sculpteurs grecs, 1, 1953, 60f.; D. ARNOLD, Die Polykletnachfolge, 1969, 204-206. R.N.

[3] Attested from c. 262-249 BC by about 50 papyri [1] as a royal architect for the Arsinoite nome and adjacent areas. C. was responsible for all the state buildings, but in particular for the sewerage and irrigation works after the lowering of Lake Moeris. C. was at first high in the royal favour, but after a royal visit to the Arsinoite nome left office in disgrace.

1 J.P. MAHAFFY, J.G. SMYLY (ed.), The Flinders Petrie Papyri, 1905.

N. LEWIS, The Greeks in Ptolemaic Egypt, 1986, 37ff.; B. MERTENS, A Letter to the Architecton Kleon: PPetrie II 4,1+4,9, in: ZPE 59, 1985, 61-66. W.A.

[4] From Cicilia, was enslaved together with his brother → Comanus [3] and sold into Sicily. There in 136 BC C. gathered together a band of slaves and captured Acragas. He then joined → Eunus and was killed in 132 outside Enna in the 1st Sicilian Slave War against the Romans (Diod. Sic. 34,2.17; 20ff.; 43; Liv. Epit. 56).

K.MEI.

[5] Mysian, who in 41 BC first supported Antony [I 9] against the Parthians under Q. → Labienus [I 2], then (before 31 BC) the young Caesar (→ Augustus) against Antony. In this way C. first earned himself the temple state of Zeus of → Abrettene, then the even wealthier one of Mâ of → Comana Pontica. He renamed his home village of Gordiou Kome → Iuliupolis out of gratitude to the young Caesar (Str. 12,8,8ff.). Identification of C. with Medeius (Cass. Dio 51,2,3) is conceivable (lastly [1. 53 n. 372]).

1 C. MAREK, Stadt, Ära und Territorium in Pontus-Bithynía und Nord-Galatia, 1993. L. BOFFO, I re ellenistici e i centri religiosi dell' Asia Minore, 1985, 47f. E.O.

[6] C. from Curium (Cyprus). Author of Argonautiká (but cf. [4]) in several bks., probably in verses, which are quoted in three scholia to the first bk. of → Apollonius [2] Rhodius. Possibly identical to the elegiac poet, whose two verses are quoted by the EM 389,25-28. A comparison (sýnkrisis) between the Argonautiká of Apollonius and a work on the same subject together with mythographical comments and literary criticism (on the economy of the narrative) in a papyrus of the 2nd cent. BC (PMichigan inv. 1316ᵛ = SH 339 A; ed. princeps and comm. [2]) could also relate to C..

1 SH 339; 339 A   2 J.S. RUSTEN, Dionysius Scytobrachion, 1982, 53-64   3 W. WEINBERGER, s.v. Klima (9), RE 11, 719   4 U. v. WILAMOWITZ-MOELLENDORFF, Hell. Dichtung, 1924, 189, 231. S.FO.

[7] Gem cutter known from two signatures (→ Gem cutting) of the Imperial period (pupil of → Solon?): sardonyx fragment with Amazon's head (Wiesbaden) and gem with Apollo (material and current location unknown).

ZAZOFF, AG, 320, n. 91, pl. 93.8,9. S.MI.

Cleonae (Κλεωναί; Kleōnaí).

[1] City in the mountainous area south-west of → Corinth at the intersection of the roads from Corinth south towards the Peloponnese. City wall and minimal remains of buildings on a hill 4 km north-west of Hagios Vasilios. In the south outside C. is a small Doric temple, probably of Hercules (Diod. Sic. 4,33.3). C. is already mentioned in Hom. Il. 2,570. Part of the population is said to have migrated to → Clazomenae during the Doric Migration (Paus. 7,3.9). → Nemea was part

of C. and so it was responsible for organizing the Nemeian Games (Pind. Nem. 10,79; Plut. Aratus 28,3). At the beginning of the 5th cent. BC, C. was on the side of Argus and therefore also not involved in the Persian Wars. After the destruction of Mycenae soon after 479, C. received part of the territory and the population of this city (Str. 8,6,19; Paus. 7,25,6), but soon afterwards was dependent on Argus. Aratus [2] joined C. to the Achaean Confederacy (Plut. Aratus 28). In the 3rd cent. AD C. was once again minting its own coins and was therefore independent. Evidence: Pind. Ol. 10,37 with schol.; Plin. HN 4,12,20; 36,14; Paus. 2,15,1; Ptol. 3,16,20. Inscriptions: IG IV 489–491. Coins: HN 418, 440ff.

C. BLEGEN, Zygouries, 1928; P. N. DOUKELLIS, L. G. MENDONI (ed.), Structures rurales et sociétés antiques, 1994, 351–358; G. ROUX, Pausanias en Corinthie, 1958, 171f.; M. SAKELLARIOU, N. PHARAKLAS, Κορινθία καὶ Κλεωναία (Ancient Greek Cities 3), 1971. Y.L.

[2] East Phocian settlement, 4 km north of → Hyampolis, scene of the Phocian battle for independence under Daiphantus against the Thessalian infantry and cavalry shortly before the Persian Wars (end of 6th cent. BC), remembered as the 'Phocian Despair' (Φωκικὴ ἀπόνοια) (cf. Plut. Mulierum virtutes 244b-d; Pol. 16,32,1–4; Hdt. 8,27f.; Paus. 10,1,6ff.)

F. BÖLTE s.v. K. (3), RE 11, 728; P. ELLINGER, La légende nationale phocidienne, 1993; F. SCHOBER, Phokis, 1924, 33. G.D.R.

Cleonides (Κλεονείδης; *Kleoneídēs*). Presumably the author of an Εἰσαγωγὴ ἁρμονική/*Eisagōgè harmoniké* ('Introduction to Harmonics') in Aristoxenian tradition (→ Aristoxenus [1]), perhaps 2nd cent. AD. The subject matter of harmonics — notes, intervals, scale, system, key (τόνος/*tónos*), metabole, melopoeia — is clearly presented in subdivisions, definitions and examples, the note names (3f.) are in circuitous lists. Intervals (5) are differentiated by five categories, tone systems (8) by seven; in addition, there are complete lists of the types of fourths, fifths and octaves, the latter using the key names 'of the ancients'. C. mentions in addition to the usual tonic systems those with gaps in the scale or more than one *mésē* (a 'central note') (10f.). Under *tónos* he lists the 13 transposition scales of Aristoxenus (12), though without referring to the octave-species of the same names. The final chapters contain valuable details on metabole (13) and melopoeia (14). An important addition to the Aristoxenus texts.

MSG, 167–207; M. FUHRMANN, Das systematische Lehrbuch, 1960, 34–40. D.N.

Cleonymus (Κλεώνυμος; Kleónymos).
[1] Athenian politician; in the year 426/5 BC he put forward two important proposals: one concerned → Methone in Thrace, the other the collection of tri-

butes from the → Delian League (IG I³ 61,32–56; 68). C. was probably a member of the council in that year. In 415 he was one of the most enthusiastic supporters of an investigation into the religious scandals (→ Herms, mutilation of the; And. 1.27). Aristophanes derided him as a glutton, a liar and a coward (Equ. 1293; 1372; Nub. 353; 674; Vesp. 20; 592; 822).

LGPN II, s.v. Κλεώνυμος (2); PA 8680. P.J.R.

[2] Spartiate; by the agencies of his lover Archidamus, son of Agesilaus [2], obtained the acquittal of his father Sphodrias after his failed attack on Piraeus in 378 BC; was killed at Leuctra in 371 (Xen. Hell. 5,4,25–32).
[3] Agiad (→ Agiadae), son of Cleomenes [5] II. Passed over in the succession to the throne, in 303 BC as a mercenary leader with the approval of the Spartan leadership supported Tarentum against the Lucans, whom he forced into peace, subjugated Metapontum and conquered Corcyra, but after failures in Italy had to return to Greece (Diod. Sic. 20,104f.; Liv. 10,2,1–14). In *c.* 293, C. fought on the side of the Boeotians against Demetrius [2] Poliorcetes and withdrew after initial successes (Plut. Demetrius 39); 279 he conquered Troezen (Polyaenus, Strat. 2,29) and took part in operations against Messene and Zarax (Paus. 4.28.3; 3,24,1ff.). After misdemeanours by his wife Chilonis, C. left Sparta and joined → Pyrrhus (Plut. Pyrrhus 26,14–27,10). C. was an efficient troop commander, but was reputed to be despotic [1. 30, 32–34, 44].

2   1 P. CARTLEDGE, A. SPAWFORTH, Hellenistic Sparta, 1989. K.-W.WEL.

[4] Tyrant of Phleius. With the tyrants of Argus and Hermione he renounced rulership in 229/8 BC on the urging of Aratus [2] (Plut. Aratus 34ff.) and joined his city to the Achaean Confederacy (Pol. 2.44.6).
→ Tyrannis

H. BERVE, Die Tyrannis bei den Griechen, 1967, 400, 712. J.CO.

Cleopatra (Κλεοπάτρα; *Kleopátra*, Lat. Cleopatra).
I. MYTHOLOGY   II. HISTORICAL CHARACTERS

I. MYTHOLOGY
[I 1] Daughter of → Boreas and → Oreithyia, first wife of → Phineus. C. was rejected in favour of → Idaea [3], whom Phineus married as his second wife; her sons were blinded (Apollod. 3.200; Hyg. Fab. 18).
[I 2] Daughter of → Idas and → Marpessa, wife of → Meleager. After her abduction by Apollo she was also called 'Alcyone' after her mother's lament (Hom. Il. 9.556ff.) [1; 2]. In the Meleager episode, in which she persuaded him to put aside his anger and re-enter the battle, she fulfilled the same function as Patroclus in the story of Achilles. After Meleager's death she committed suicide (Apollod. 1.8.3; Hyg. Fab. 174.7).
[I 3] Daughter of King → Tros, who gave his name to the district of Troy, and → Callirhoe [3]. Her brothers were

→ Ilus [1], Assaracus and → Ganymede [1] (Apollod. 3.140).

[I 4] C. and Periboea were the first human 'sacrifices' chosen by lot whom the Locrians had to send to Troy each year to appease Athena for the crime of → Ajax [2]. There they lived in a temple as servants (Apollod. Epit. 6,20).

1 M.M. WILLOCK, The Iliad of Homer, 1978, 282
2 J. GRIFFIN, Homer. Iliad 9, 1995, 138.   FR.P.

II. HISTORICAL CHARACTERS
The last queen of Egypt see C. [II 12]

[II 1] Wife of → Perdiccas and from 413 BC of his successor Archelaus [1], who allegedly murdered C.'s son from her first marriage (Pl. Grg. 471c). She bore him a son, Orestes, who became his successor as a minor in 399, and probably two daughters (Aristot. Pol. 5,1311b).

[II 2] Niece of Attalus [1], married by → Philippus II for love (according to Satyrus in Ath. 13,557d, FGH III 161; cf. Plut. Alexander 9). At the wedding feast a fight broke out between Attalus and the crown-prince, Alexander [4], resulting in a radical change at Philip II's court: the king cast out → Olympias, who fled to her brother Alexander [6], exiled the prince and apparently turned more towards his nephew Amyntas [4]. Recalled on the advice of Demaratus [4], Alexander now felt threatened, leading to the → Pixodarus affair and the banishment of his friends. After Philip's murder in 336 BC, Olympias returned, killed C'.s new-born daughter and forced C. to commit suicide. Alexander, who officially regretted this (Plut. Alexander 10,7), exterminated her family (Just. Epit. 11.5.1).

BERVE 2, no. 434.

[II 3] Daughter of → Philippus II and → Olympias; younger sister of Alexander [4], with whom she remained in contact until his death. After Olympias' flight to Alexander [6] C. stayed with her father, who married her in 336 BC to this Alexander [6], in order to undermine Olympias' influence on him. C. bore him a daughter and a son, Neoptolemus, for whom she ruled during Alexander's [6] Italian campaign. After his death (331/30), C. was driven out by Olympias and lived as a widow with her children in Pella. After the death of her brother Alexander [4] (323), C. allegedly offered → Leonnatus her hand (Plut. Eumenes 3.5), but he was killed in 322 at Lamia (→ Lamian War). C. then went to Sardeis, hoping to be able to marry → Perdiccas. He, however, preferred a liaison with → Antipater [1] through his daughter → Nicaea. When Antipater became allied against him with → Antigonus [1], who blackened Perdiccas' name with him, Perdiccas asked for C.'s hand after all (Arr. fr. FGrH 156 F 9. 26). After his murder (320), C. supported Eumenes [1], but soon became reconciled with Antipater (Arr. ibid., F 10.8.40). C. continued to live in Sardeis, wooed by several of the → Diadochi, but interned by Antigonus. When she tried in

308 to flee to → Ptolemaeus, she was brought back to Sardeis and murdered. To avoid—probably justified—suspicion, Antigonus punished the female perpetrators and granted C. a royal burial (Diod. Sic. 20.37).

BERVE 2, no. 433; J. SEIBERT, Histor. Beiträge zu den dynast. Verbindungen in hell. Zeit, 1967, pp. 11–24.   E.B.

[II 4] C. I. Born c. 204 BC, daughter of Antiochus [5] III and Laodice [II 6], wife of Ptolemy V. The betrothal was decided in the summer of 196 (Pol. 18,51,10) and was sealed at the peace of 195; the marriage took place in the winter of 194/193 in → Raphia (Liv. 35,13,4; App. Syr. 5,18; Zon. 9,18). Nothing is known of any dowry, it is not expected that Antiochus [5] made any territorial concessions, even though Ptolemaic propaganda later derived from this marriage a claim on → Coele Syria (Pol. 28.20.6–10; Jos. Ant. Iud. 12.154ff.). In Alexandria C. was called hē Sýra ('the Syrian woman', App. Syr. 5.18), disparagingly rather than affectionately. Her children, Ptolemy (VI), C. [II 5] II and Ptolemy (VIII), were born after 186. The Memphis synod of priests conferred on C. in 185/184 the honours already decided upon in 196 for Ptolemy V [1. 198ff.]; Ptolemy and C. were worshipped as theoì epiphaneís (→ epiphanés). After the death of Ptolemy V (shortly after May 180) C. ruled as guardian of her son Ptolemy VI. Preparations for a Syrian war were abandoned. She was the first queen to have minting rights and is named in documents before her son. In 178/177 a priesthood of C. and her son was established in → Ptolemais. C. died between 8. 4. and 17. 5. 176; in 165/164 a priestess Kleopátras tês mētròs theâs epiphanoús was appointed in Ptolemais (from autumn 139 as priestess of 'Cleopatra, the mother', Kleopátras tês mētròs). PP VI 14515.

→ Egypt; → Ptolemies

1 K. SETHE (ed.), Hieroglyphische Urkunden der griech.-röm. Zeit, vol. 2, 1904.

PP VI 14515; M. HOLLEAUX, Études d'épigraphie et d'histoire grecque, 3, 1968, 339ff.; W. OTTO, Zur Gesch. der Zeit des 6. Ptolemäers, in: SBAW 11, 1934, 1ff.; G. RICHTER/R. SMITH, The Portraits of the Greeks, 1984, 234; F. WALBANK, A Historical Commentary on Polybius, vol. 2, 1967, 623; vol. 3, 1979, 17; 356; J. WHITEHORNE, Cleopatras, 1994, 80ff.

[II 5] C. II. Born soon after 190 BC as daughter of Ptolemy V and C. [II 4] I, on the death of her mother she was already given the title of basílissa ('queen') (IPhilae 11) and before 15. 4. 175 married her brother Ptolemy VI; both were worshipped as theoì philométores (→ philométōr). C. was the mother of Ptolemy Eupator (born 15. 10. 165?), C. [II 14] Thea, C. [II 6] III and a further Ptolemy (according to [1], Ptolemy [IX] Soter II was her son born c. 142, but see [2]). From Sept. 170 Ptolemy VIII was also officially involved in the rulership. The joint rulership did not end until between Oct. and Dec. 164 (the uprisings of → Dionysius [6] Petosarapis had been overcome); in 164/163 Ptolemy VIII ruled alone, however from Aug. 163 C. and Ptolemy VI were again worshipped as *theoì epiphaneís* (→ *epiphanēs*) and named together in the datings ([3. 160]: 'official joint rule'). Ptolemy VI died in July 145 and by 13. 8. 145 Ptolemy VIII was ruling, C. still being named beside him in the datings; both were worshipped as *theoì euergétai* (→ *euergétēs*). In 144 her son Ptolemy Memphites was born.; C. was now *theà euergétis*, but seems in the eyes of her brother to have posed a danger: he married C. [II 6] III between May 141 and Jan. 140. After initial problems, relationships became clear in the titulature at the beginning of 139: C. was *adelphḗ* ('sister'), C. III *gynḗ* ('wife').

At the beginning of Nov. 132 (PLond. 10384) the civil war between C. and Ptolemy VIII began; the cause is unclear. At the end of 131 Ptolemy VIII was driven out to → Cyprus and C. proclaimed herself *theà philométor sōteíra* ('saviour') and began counting the years of her reign from 'year 1', an unusual practise for a woman. Ptolemy VIII returned in the spring of 130; C. fled as soon as 129 to her son-in-law Demetrius [8] II in Syria. In 124, for unknown reasons, the co-rulership was reinstated, but Egypt was not under control again until after 118/117. After the death of Ptolemy VIII on 28. 6. 116, C. perhaps carried through Ptolemy IX's participation in the rulership. Co-rulership of Ptolemy IX and C. [II 6] III is mentioned on 29(?). 10. 116 (PRyl. 3, 20). (She supposedly shared the throne with Ptolemy IX from 116 to 107 [1]; but see [4. 19]).

1 S. CAUVILLE, D. DEVAUCHELLE, in: Revue d'Égyptologie 35, 1984, 31ff.   2 L. MOOREN, The Wives and Children of Ptolemy VIII Euergetes II, in: Proc. XVIII Congr. of Papyrology, vol. 2, 1988, 435–444   3 HÖLBL, 128ff.; 157ff.   4 E. VAN'T DACK et al., The Judaean-Syrian-Egyptian Conflict of 103–101 B.C., 1989   5 W. OTTO, H. BENGTSON, Zur Gesch. des Niedergangs des Ptolemäerreiches, in: SBAW 17, 1938   6 J. WHITEHORNE, Cleopatras, 1994   7 E. BRUNELLE, Die Bildnisse der Ptolemäerinnen, 1976, 63ff.; 75ff.

[II 6] C. III. Born *c.* 160 BC as daughter of Ptolemy VI and C. [II 5] II. (on events up to 116 see C. [II 5]), C. became a priestess in Ptolemais before 15. 12. 146; between May 141 and Jan. 140 Ptolemy VIII married her, because he saw in her a dynastic alternative to C. II. C. was mother of Ptolemy IX (born 140/139), Ptolemy X, C. [II 15] Tryphaeana, C. [II 7] IV and C. [II 8] V Selene (born 140/135). From 138/137 she was *theà euergétis* in place of her mother, in the civil war situation of 131 she was exalted by a priest (!) bearing the title *hieròs pólos Ísidos megálēs mētròs theṓn* ('holy priest of great Isis, the mother of gods'), which was supposed to recommend her to her Egyptian subjects. C. probably remained in Cyprus until 127.

After the death of Ptolemy VIII C. was allegedly allowed to choose with which son she wanted to rule; but by 116 the Alexandrians had already forced her against her will to rule with Ptolemy IX Soter II and not with Ptolemy X Alexander. From 116 onwards C. was named before her sons in all titulatures. The religious super-elevation was continued: in 116 there was a new cult with *stephanēphóros*, *phōsphóros* and a priestess: C. was compared to → Isis and made claim to an ability to triumph equal to that of a pharaoh: she was *theà philométor sóteira Nikēphóros* ('bringer of victory') *Dikaiosýnē* ('justice'). There were many internal disputes: Ptolemy IX was briefly ousted from the eponymous priest's office as early as 112 (OGIS 739), and in Oct. 110 (justified by a new cult) and March 108 (SEG 9.5) Ptolemy IX was briefly ousted by Ptolemy X. From Oct. 107 onwards C. ultimately ruled with Ptolemy X, whereas Ptolemy IX had fled to Cyprus. In 105/104 C. ousted Ptolemy X and became priestess of the Alexander cult [1]; she had filled the other eponymous priesthoods with her own followers; once again she was equated with → Maat, justice and order.

In the early summer of 103, Ptolemy IX tried to exploit a Jewish-Seleucid conflict in Palestine for his own purposes and to return to Egypt by the land route. C. pre-empted him with an invasion of Palestine, which, though bringing no territorial gains, kept Ptolemy IX away from Egypt. C. was killed by Ptolemy X between 14. and 26. 10. 101.

1 B. KRAMER, R. HÜBNER (ed.), Kölner Papyri, 1976, vol. 2, 81.

E. BRUNELLE, Die Bildnisse der Ptolemäerinnen, 1976, 66f., 75ff.; E. VAN'T DACK et al., The Judaean-Syrian-Egyptian Conflict of 103–101 B.C., 1989; HÖLBL, 172ff., 260ff.; W. OTTO, H. BENGTSON, Zur Gesch. des Niedergangs des Ptolemäerreiches, in: SBAW 17, 1938; J. WHITEHORNE, Cleopatras, 1994; Id., A Reassessment of Cleopatra III's Syrian Campaign, in: Chronique d'Égypte 70, 1995, 197–205.

[II 7] C. IV. Born *c.* 140/135 BC as daughter of Ptolemy VIII and C. [II 6] III, wife of Ptolemy IX, mother of C. [II 9] Berenice III. C. probably went with Ptolemy IX to Cyprus, where she stayed in the summer of 116 when her husband returned to Alexandria. C. was rejected by her husband on the command of her mother before March 115. She gathered an army in Cyprus and set out for Syria. There she offered her army to Antiochus [11] IX, with whom she was married from 115 to 112. After a defeat she was killed by Antiochus [10] VIII in 112 by command of her sister C. [II 15] Tryphaeana . PP VI 14519.

PP VI 14519; T. B. MITFORD, Helenos, in: JHS 79, 1959, 115ff.; W. OTTO, H. BENGTSON, Zur Gesch. des Niedergangs des Ptolemäerreiches, in: SBAW 17, 1938, 146ff.

[II 8] C. V. Selene. C. was born *c.* 140/135 BC as Selene and was a daughter of Ptolemy VIII and C. [II 6] III. She was married before April 115 by her mother to her brother Ptolemy IX, after he had had to repudiate C.[II 7] IV. After the wedding she assumed the name C.; there were at least two children. C. received the royal honours and was admitted to the cult of the *theoì philométores sotéres* (→ *philométōr*; → *sotḗr*), but was involved in the rulership only during the brief phase of

Ptolemy IX's expulsion to Cyrene (at the latest April 108). After his return she took second place to C. III, as before. When Ptolemy IX was forced by C. III to flee to Cyprus in the autumn of 107, C. remained in Alexandria.

Because C. III sought the support of Antiochus [10] VIII against Ptolemy IX, she married C. to the Seleucid in 103 . When he died in 96, C. became the wife of Antiochus [11] IX, for whom she represented legitimization against Seleucus VI; for the same reason from 95 to 92 (or 83) she became the wife of her stepson, Antiochus [12] X and became mother of Antiochus [14] XIII and a further son. After the death of Antiochus X she lived in Cilicia and Syrian Ptolemais and after Ptolemy XII came to power formulated claims to the Egyptian throne for her (Seleucid) sons; in 69 she was taken prisoner and killed by the Armenian king → Tigranes. PP VI 14520.

> PP VI 14520; W. OTTO, H. BENGTSON, Zur Gesch. des Niedergangs des Ptolemäerreiches, in: SBAW 17, 1938, 174ff.; J. WHITEHORN, Cleopatras, 1994, 164ff.

[II 9] C. Berenice III. Born c. 120 BC, daughter of Ptolemy IX and C. [II 7] IV, wife of Ptolemy X (beginning of Oct. 101– summer 88), as which she will have assumed the name C.; both were worshipped as *theoi philométores sotêres*. There was one daughter (FGrH 260 F 2.8). After her husband was driven out, in 88–81 C. was co-regent with her father, who married her because of her popularity with the Alexandrians. After his death (c. Dec. 81) she was sole ruler for six months as *theà → philopátōr*, but then in 80, under pressure from the Alexandrians and arranged by Sulla, married her (step-?)son Ptolemy XI, who murdered her after a few days (June 80).

> A. BERNAND, Une inscription de Cléopâtre Bérénice III, in: ZPE 89, 1991, 145f.; E. BLOEDOW, Beiträge zur Gesch. Ptolemaios' XII., diss. Würzburg 1963, 11ff.; E. VAN'T DACK et al., The Judaean-Syrian-Egyptian Conflict of 103–101 B.C., 1989, 152ff.; J. WHITEHORNE, Cleopatras, 1994, 174ff.

[II 10] C. VI Tryphaeana. Born c. 95 BC as daughter of Ptolemy IX, from 80/79 wife of her brother Ptolemy XII; both were worshipped as *theoi philopátores philádelphoi* (→ *philádelphos*). Mother of Berenice [7] (C. [II 11] as her daughter is probably unhistorical). Between Aug. 69 and Feb. 68 she disappears from datings (owing to brother's new marriage?). After Ptolemy XII was cast out in 58, she ruled for a short time jointly with Berenice or was named ruler to legitimize her (BGU VIII 1762). The 'joint rulership' ended before July 57 (BGU VIII 1757; cf. POxy. 3777), and C. now either supported the return of Ptolemy XII or was named by him for the sake of legitimization (in Edfu in Dec. 57 long before the return of the king, then in particular Medinet Habu Graff. 43 from 4. 1. 55). She must have died before Ptolemy XII.

> E. BRUNELLE, Die Bildnisse der Ptolemäerinnen, 1976, 67f.; L. M. RICKETTS, A Dual Queenship in the Reign of Berenice IV, in: Bulletin of the American Society of Papyrology 27, 1990, 49–60; J. WHITEHORNE, The Supposed Co-Regency of Cleopatra Tryphaena and Berenice IV (58–55 B.C.), in: B. KRAMER u.a. (ed.), Akten des 21. Internationalen Papyrologenkongresses Berlin 1995 (APF supplement 3), 1997, 109ff.

[II 11] C. Tryphaeana. according to FGrH 260 F 2.14 was a daughter of Ptolemy XII and C. [II 10] VI, who is supposed to have reigned in 58 BC, after her father was expelled, with her sister Berenice [7] and to have died in 57. This is probably a confusion with C. [II 10], so this C. is unhistorical.

> W. HUSS, Die Herkunft der Kleopatra Philopator, in: Aegyptus 70, 1990, 191–203; J. WHITEHORNE, in: APF, supplement 3, 1997, 109ff.

[II 12] C. VII, the last Ptolemaic queen, was born in Dec. 70/Jan. 69 BC as daughter of Ptolemy XII and a woman who was perhaps related to the high priests of Memphis. For reasons of dynastic continuity she had already been appointed co-regent by her father by 52; after his death she ruled alone as *theà → philopátōr* [1. 13]; joint rulership with her brother Ptolemy XIII is attested from at the latest 27. 10. 50 [2. 73], though there had been no testamentary provision for this. In the summer of 49 Ptolemy XIII is named alone. C. was forced out of Alexandria and withdrew to the Thebaid; her second brother, Ptolemy XIV, was already briefly named as joint-king [3. 57], while Rome recognized Ptolemy XII. as sole king. C. was driven out of Egypt at the beginning of 48 and gathered Arabian troops.

In 48 in Alexandria → Caesar invited both parties to dismiss their troops, which the weaker C. did at once: Caesar wanted the unachievable return to joint rulership. In the following battles Ptolemy XIII was killed and in the spring of 47 Caesar made C. sole queen; on 23. 6. 47 their (allegedly) mutual son Ptolemy XV Kaisar (known as 'Kaisarion'/'Caesarion') was born. Not until 46–44 was Ptolemy XIV named in the titulatures next to her (he had been installed in 48 by Caesar with Arsinoe [II 6] IV as king of Cyprus). The two ruled as *theoi philopátores philádelphoi* (→ *philopátōr*; → *philádelphos*), and C. stressed her proximity to → Isis—though there were by now Roman legions in the country. In mid 46 C. arrived in Rome to negotiate an alliance: the kings became *reges socii et amici* ('allied kings and friends'). It was not until shortly after the murder of Caesar that the pair returned to Egypt, where Ptolemy XIV was soon murdered. From mid 44 Ptolemy XV Kaisar was co-regent, but C. is named before her son in all the titulatures; from mid 43 C. also controlled Cyprus and tried to help the Caesarians with a fleet.

In 41, because of her stance in the Roman Civil War, C. was invited to Tarsus, where the famous association with M. → Antonius [I 9] began. Antony needed Egypt against the Parthians and made great territorial concessions to C.: at the latest in 38 she received parts of Cilicia, in 37/36 the principality of Chalcis, then Phoenicia, parts of Judaea and Arabia, and also land in Crete and Cyrene. On the part of the Romans this was a continuation of client state policies, a mutual fusion of Roman administration and Ptolemaic rule, while C. saw it as nominal rulership and secure income. With her increase in power C. began a new era in 37/36. When in 34 Antony celebrated his victory over Armenia, a great oriental kingdom was heralded (without actual consequences). C. became the 'queen of kings' and 'new Isis', while Ptolemy XV and C.'s children by Antony (the twins Alexander [19] Helios and C. [II 13] Selene, born in 39, and Ptolemy Philadelphus, born at the end of 36) received other titles. C. paid for a large part of the army with which Antony fought against Octavian (→ Augustus); after the battle of → Actium on 2 September 31, she fled to Alexandria, began to amass temple assets and tried in negotiations to save the rulership for her children, in other words to preserve the continuity of the Ptolemaic kingdom. Her suicide on 12.8.30 brought the end of the Ptolemaic dynasty and the last of the great Diadochi kingdoms, which now became the Roman province of Egypt. The necessity of concentrating on foreign policy had forced C. to neglect the internal administration of the kingdom: from 44 onwards there was a series of poor harvests and plagues — the independence of the civil servants increased without any effective countermeasures being declared.

The image of C. in Latin literature is marked by poets who were to a greater or lesser extent closely associated with → Octavianus, the victor of Actium (e.g. Hor. Carm. 1,37; Verg. Aen. 8, 675ff.; Prop. 3,11): they had no interest in allowing credence to C.'s attempt to operate even semi-independent policies, but only in depicting the Augustan side. C. thus becomes a symbol of the east, of softness, of the un-Roman — if a war was thought of as directed against her, there was no need in Rome to depict the clash with Antony as a civil war. — On the literary afterlife of the C. figure see [4] and [5].

1 R.MOND, O.H. MYERS (ed.), The Bucheum, vol. 2, 1934   2 M.-TH. LENGER, Corpus des ordonnances des Ptolémées, ²1980   3 L.M. RICKETTS, A Dual Queenship in the Reign of Berenice IV, in: Bulletin of the American Society of Papyrology 27, 1990, 49–60   4 L.HUGHES-HALLETT, Cleopatra, 1990   5 M.HAMER, Signs of Cleopatra, 1993.

E.BRUNELLE, Die Bildnisse der Ptolemäerinnen, 1976, 98ff.; M.CLAUSS, Kleopatra, 1995; L.CRISCUOLO, La successione a Tolemeo Aulete ed i pretesi matrimoni die Cleopatra VII con i fratelli, in: Id., G. GERACI (ed.), Egitto e storia antica, 1989, 325ff.; H.HEINEN, Rom und Äg. 51–47 v.Chr., 1966; HÖLBL, 205ff.; 264ff.; TH. SCHRAPEL, Das Reich der Kleopatra, 1996; H. VOLKMANN, Kleopatra, 1953.   W.A.

[II 13] C. Selene. Daughter of M. → Antonius [I 9] and → C. [II 12] VII, born c. 40 BC with her twin brother Alexander [19] Helios (Plut. Antonius 36,5). In 34 C. received Cyrene from Antony (Cass. Dio 49,41,3).

After Octavian's victory over Antony she, like her brother, was placed under close watch and in 29 BC paraded in Octavian's triumphal procession (Cass. Dio 51,21,8), but then brought up in the house of → Octavia with other children of Antony (Plut. Antonius 87.1f.; Suet. Aug. 17,5). In 20 Augustus married C. to → Juba [2] II of Mauretania (Plut. Antonius 87,2; Cass. Dio 51,15,6; Anth. Pal. 9.235), with whom she had a son, Ptolemy (Suet. Calig. 26,1; Cass. Dio 59,25,1). There probably was no daughter called Drusilla (Tac. Hist. 5,9,3) [1. 225–227]. On coins C. frequently appears as Isis and is designated as *basilissa* [2. 199–201]. The date of C.'s death is unknown [1. 227f.].

1 G.H. MACURDY, Hellenistic Queens, 1932   2 J.WHITEHORNE, Cleopatras, 1994.   H.S.

[II 14] C. Thea. C. was married in 150 BC by her father Ptolemy VI, during his interventions into the disputes over the Seleucid throne, to Alexander [13] Balas and in 146 to Demetrius [8] II. After Demetrius was taken prisoner by the Parthians, in 138 C. married his brother Antiochus [9] VII and ruled alone after his death in the Parthian War in 129 and from 125 jointly with her and Demetrius' son Antiochus [10] VIII. He forced her to commit suicide in 121 (1 Macc. 10,51–58; Jos. Ant. Iud. 13,80–82; 109–115; 221f.; App. Syr. 68,360–69,363) [1].

1 A.HOUGHTON, The Double Portrait Coins of Alexander Balas and Cleopatra Thea, in: SNR 67, 1988, 85–95.

[II 15] C. Tryphaeana. Daughter of Ptolemy VIII and C. [II 6] III. She was married from 124 BC to Antiochus [10] VIII. In 112 she killed her sister C. [II 7] IV, wife of Antiochus [11] IX and was murdered by him in 111 (Just. Epit. 39,2,3; 3,5ff.).

E.BEVAN, The House of Seleucus, 1902; G.H. MACURDY, Hellenistic Queens, 1932; WILL 2, 365; 374ff.   A.ME.

[II 16] Daughter of Mithridates VI of Pontus, from c. 95 BC wife of Tigranes VI of Armenia In the 3rd Mithridatic War, C. tried without much success to persuade her husband to lend aid against → Licinius Lucullus. After returning to her father she was threatened in 64 by an uprising in Phanagorea, but rescued by ships sent by Mithridates (Just. Epit. 38,3,2; Memnon FGrH 434,29,6; App. Mith. 104; 108).

J.SEIBERT, Histor. Beiträge zu den dynast. Verbindungen in der hell. Zeit, 1967.   M.SCH.

[II 17] Originating from Jerusalem, wife of → Herod [1] the Great, mother of the tetrarch → Philippus and → Herod [5] (Jos. Bell. Iud. 1.562; Ant. Iud. 17.21).   K.BR.

Cleopatra Selene → Cleopatra

Cleophantus (Κλεόφαντος; *Kleóphantos*).
[1] Son of → Themistocles and Archippe (Plut. Themistocles 32; Pl. Men. 93d-e), was honoured with civic rights in Lampsacus (ATL III,111-3). DAVIES 6669,VI.
    HA.BE.

[2] Greek doctor, active *c.* 270–250 BC, brother of → Erasistratus, pupil of → Chrysippus [3] of Cnidus and founder of a medical school (Gal., 17A 603 K.). He wrote a paper on the medical prescription of wine, which provided the model for a similar paper by → Asclepiades [6] of Bithynia (Celsus, De medicina 3.14) and was also used intensively by Pliny in bks. 20–27 of his *Historia naturalis*. C.'s treatise on gynaecological illnesses comprised at least eleven bks. (Sor. 2,17,53), even though, in the opinion of Soranus his elucidations on dystocia (difficult births) were incomplete. Like his teacher and his brother, C. believed an unnaturally rapid pulse signified fever (Erasistratus, fr. 193 GAROFALO).

[3] Greek doctor, active in 1st cent. BC or early 1st cent. AD; → Andromachus [4] the Elder quotes him with his prescriptions for dropsy (Gal. 13,262 = 985 C.) and his ointment preparation for the anal region (13,310 C.). Besides Antipater, who was active *c.* 30 BC, C. is cited as the source of a differing description of the famous antidote of → Mithridates Eupator. It is unproved whether C. can be identified with the well-to-do, distinguished Roman doctor of the same name of A. Cluentius Habitus from the year 74 BC (Cic. Clu. 47), who helped to reveal an attempt to poison the latter.   V.N.

Cleophon (Κλεοφῶν; *Kleophôn*).

[1] Athenian demagogue in the period after 411 BC, lyre-maker, apparently not very wealthy (Lys. 19.48). In 410 C. introduced the → *diobelía*, a maintenance payment to needy citizens ([Aristot.] Ath. Pol. 28,3). According to Diodorus (13,53,2) he brought about in 410/409, according to [Aristot.] Ath. Pol. 34,1 in 406/5, the rejection of peace negotiations with Sparta, though these could have been duplicates of his measures in 405/4, when he threatened everyone advising peace in blockaded Athens with a capital lawsuit (Lys. 13,8; Aeschin. Leg. 76; Tim. 150; Xen. Hell. 2,2,15). He is frequently mentioned in both tragedy and comedy, in Aristophanes (Ran. 1532) as a warmonger. In 404 he was charged on the pretext of infringement of military duty and condemned to death in illegitimate proceedings (Lys. 13,12; 30,9–14).
→ Peloponnesian War

RHODES, 354f., 424f.   W.S.

[2] C. of Athens, 4th cent. BC.; Suda χ 1730 names ten titles of tragedies (77 T 1 TrGF I), six of which also appear among the works of → Iophon [2] (22 T 1). No testimony reliably proves that C. wrote tragedies. Aristotle (Poet. 22,1458a 18; Rh. 3,7,1408a 10) speaks only in general of C.'s poetry and his style.   B.Z.

Cleophon Painter Attic red-figured vase painter (*c.* 435–415 BC). He is a younger member of the → Polygnotus [2] — group and named after a → *kalos* inscription on a stamnos in St. Petersburg. He painted primarily larger → pottery such as loutrophoroi, stamnoi, pelikai, hydriai and kraters, but also a few smaller vessels.

He was a talented draftsman and his best works are reminiscent of the classical earnestness of the → Parthenon friezes, the direct influence of which can be seen in a procession in honour of Apollo on a voluted krater in Ferrara [1]. His physically emphasized figures have large heads and characteristic eyes with heavy lids. Frequent themes of the CP are roaming revellers, musical presentations, sacrificial scenes and groups of women, on the reverse often accompanied by uniform types of cloaked men. Some scenes, especially warriors taking leave of a woman with eyes cast down, are repeated. Themes from mythology are rare: e.g. Apollo and Marsyas, the return of Hephaestus and four Amazonomachies. His pupil, the → Dinus Painter, continued his style in a 'gentler manner' (BEAZLEY).

> 1 J. BOARDMAN, Rf. Vasen aus Athen. Die klass. Zeit, 1989, fig. 171. BEAZLEY, ARV², 1143–1151, 1684, 1703, 1707 G. GUALANDI, Le ceramiche del Pittore di Kleophon rinvenute a Spina, in: ArtAntMod 19, 1962, 227–260; ArtAntMod 20, 1962, 341–383 M. HALM-TISSERANT, Le Peintre de Cléophon, 1984 S. MATHESON, Polygnotos, 1995, 135–147, 406–430.   M.P.

Cleophrades Painter Attic vase painter (*c.* 510–475 BC), who together with his contemporary, the → Berlin Painter, is seen as one of the best painters of large vessels of the late Archaic period. He was named by BEAZLEY [3] after the potter Cleophrades, whose signature was found on an early cup (Paris, CM 535, 699). The Cleophrades Painter (CP) learned his trade in the workshop of the red-figure 'Pioneers', apparently as a pupil of → Euthymides. His actual name is not known, the signature *Epiktetos* on a Berlin pelike is a forgery. The CP worked predominantly in the red-figure technique, but also produced some black-figured neck amphoras and → Panathenaic amphoras. He decorated a variety of vessels including bowls, but showed a definite preference for large vessels such as kraters, amphoras, hydrias, and stamnoi (→ Pottery, shapes and types of, with illustr.).

He decorated 20 chalice-shaped kraters, several of them with figure frieze encircling the body of the vessel, as in two representations of the return of → Hephaestus (Cambridge, MA, Harvard Univ., and Paris, LV). Some of the vessels are decorated on both sides, with the two images relating to each other — an attempt at narrative homogeneity, which was exceptional within his contemporary context. Among his most notable works are a pointed amphora in Munich, SA, showing → Dionysus and Maenads, a hydria in Naples, MN, depicting the → Ilioupersis, and a volute krater in Malibu, GM, a red-rimmed vessel with images of Heracles' deeds on the neck. On the numerous pelikai of his later period, the CP prefers simple generic subjects.

The precision of his lines and clarity of his compositions is the result of a careful developmental work, based on extensive draft sketches. His figures are large and lifelike, and show reason and will. Lips are frequently boldly outlined, nostrils are hooked or

S-shaped. Early figures show deeply hooked clavicles, later ones are straight. Hair is depicted in contour outlines; however, long after his contemporaries had abandoned that technique, the CP still used incision lines. In images of individual figures, hair is depicted by back dots in relief. Drapery is stylized in heavy folds; his himatia with their broad borders left in red are distinctive.

The influence of the CP is noticeable in the works of two of his contemporaries: the Boot Painter, a bowl painter who continued in the style of his later works, and the Troilos Painter, who worked in the same workshop decorating closed vessels.

→ Vase painters

1 BEAZLEY, ARV², 181–195, 1631–1633   2 BEAZLEY, ABV, 404f.   3 J. BEAZLEY, Der K.-M., 1933   4 G. RICHTER, The Kleophrades Painter, in: AJA 40, 1936, 100–115   5 A. GREIFENHAGEN, Neue Fragmente des K.-M., 1972   6 E. KUNZE-G, Der K.-M. unter Malern sf. Amphoren, 1992.   M.P.

Cleopompus (Κλεόπομπος; *Kleópompos*). Son of Cleinias, Athenian, as *stratēgós* in 431/0 BC led a fleet of 30 triremes against Opuntian Locris and conquered Thronium (Thuc. 2.26; Diod. Sic. 12.44.1). In the following year, jointly with → Hagnon [1] he commanded the second expeditionary corps to win back Potidaea (Thuc. 2.58.1f.).

→ Peloponnesian War

DEVELIN 1676; C. W. FORNARA, The Athenian Board of Generals from 501 to 404, 1971, 54f.   HA.BE.

Cleora (Κλεόρα; *Kleóra*). Spartan, wife of Agesilaus [2] II, mother of Archidamus [2] III (Xen. Hell. 3,4,29; 5,4,25; Plut. Agesilaus 19).   K.-W.WEL.

Cleostratus (Κλεόστρατος; *Kleóstratos*) of Tenedus, astronomer, probably at the end of the 6th cent. BC, according to Theophr. De signis 4, he made his observations from the Ida mountain range. His work, of which two hexameters have been handed down, is called in the *Vita Arati* (Commentariorum in Aratum reliquiae 324.10 MAASS) Φαινόμενα (*Phainómena*) — but there is no account in the differing catalogue of Achilleus (ibid. 79.2–6) —, in Ath. 7.278b Ἀστρολογία (*Astrología*; handed down as *gastrologia*). According to Plin. HN 2.31, C. was the first to name the zodiacal signs of Aries and Sagittarius and according to Hyg. Poet. Astr. 2,13 l. 499 VIRÉ, the first to name the extrazodiacal *Haedi* ('little goats'). He further commented on the early setting of Scorpio and created the first version of an *oktaeteris* (→ Calendar A. 3.). The majority of the fragments were handed down by the grammarian → Parmeniscus.

FRAGMENTS: DIELS/KRANZ I, 41f. (also: Theophr. De signis 4).
BIBLIOGRAPHY: F. BOLL, Sphaera, 1903, 192f.; Id., Ant. Beobachtungen farbiger Sterne, 1916, 70f.; J. K. FOTHE-

RINGHAM, Cleostratus, in: JHS 39, 1919, 164–184 and 45, 1925, 78–83; W. KROLL, s.v. K., RE suppl. 4,912f.   W.H.

Clepsydra (Κλεψύδρα; *Klepsýdra*).
[1] Spring from which the well named after Arsinoe, the mother of Asclepius, in the *agora* in Messene was fed (Paus. 4,31,6; 33,1), possibly corresponds to the village spring in Mavromati or a spring below Ithome peak (→ Ithome [1]).

E. MEYER, s.v. Messene, RE Suppl. 15, 142ff.; D. MUSTI, M. TORELLI, Pausania. Guida della Grecia 4, 1991, 252ff.   E.O.

[2] Since the Neolithic period the most important spring of the Acropolis of Athens on its north-west slope below the north wing of the Propylaea, its kerb was refashioned several times. Evidence: Paus. 1,28,4; Aristoph. Lys. 913 with schol.; Plut. Antonius 34,1; Hsch. s.v. K.; Phot. s.v. K.; Suda s.v. K.

W. JUDEICH, Die Top. von Athen, ²1931, 191ff.; TRAVLOS, Athen 323ff., fig. 425–434; R. E. WYCHERLEY, The Stones of Athens, 1978, 177.   H.LO.

[3] see → Clocks

Clerus The term *klêros* (κλῆρος; *klêros*, Lat. *clerus*; originally meaning '→ lot', 'share') as a collective name for Christian officials is based on Acts 1,16–26, where Matthias was chosen by casting lots to succeed Judas [2] as the twelfth disciple. In 1 Petr 5,3, the plural *klêroi* refers to the 'part', the 'shepherds' are entrusted with, i.e. the congregation. → Tertullianus [2] was the first to use the Latin term *clerus* in the modern sense (Tert. De monogamia 11–12; Tert. De fuga 11). Ever since → Cyprianus [2] († 258), *clerus* refers to the group of presbyters (→ Priests VI.), deacons (→ *diákonos*), the bishop (→ *epískopos* [2]), and other officials such as lectors, subdeacons, and exorcists. After the Constantine Reforms, the Christian *clerus* benefited from state privileges.

→ Church regulations; → Lot, election by II.C.   R.BR.

Clesonymus see → Kleisonymos

Cleuas (Κλεύας; *Kleúas*). Macedonian officer of → Perseus; as garrison commander of → Phanote (Epeirus) in the year 169 BC equally successful against Ap. → Claudius [I 4] Centho as subsequently at → Antigonea [4], where C. jointly with the Epirote general Philostratus forced the Romans back to Illyria (Liv. 43,21,5; 23,1–5).   L.-M.G.

Cliens, clientes Lat. name for free dependants of powerful Roman citizens of higher social status. Although this kind of dependancy was a widespread phenomenon in antiquity (Dion. Hal. Ant. Rom. 2,9 mentions the *pelátai* of Athens and the *penéstai* of Thessaly), Rome can be regarded as a special case in that here rights and duties of the *cliens* were precisely defined and his status in respect of his *patronus* was protected in Twelve Tables law (8.21). The *cliens* was in a relationship of allegiance (*in fide*) to his *patronus*, or, put another way, under his protection. There is no indication of a particular formal procedure by which a dependancy relationship of this kind was created. A freed slave and his descendants were expected to be *clientes* of their former master, but a freeborn man could also become a *cliens* by asking for protection. In return for protection and advice, according to Dion. Hal. Ant. Rom. 2.10, *clientes* were obliged to support the *patronus* financially by contributing to the dowry of his daughters or to ransom payments if the *patronus* or his sons were taken prisoner, to pay his fines and furthermore to take on the expenses arising from execution of his public offices. Gifts of *clientes* at the → Saturnalia, based on the *lex Publicia* (Macrob. Sat. 1,7,33; perhaps a law of C. Publicius Bibulus, *trib. plebis* 209 BC), were confined to wax lights (*cerei*); other gifts by *clientes* were forbidden by the *lex Cincia de donis* (probably 204 BC; MRR I 307). *Cliens* and *patronus* were not allowed to bring a lawsuit against one another or make statements as witnesses against one another in court (Dion. Hal. ibid.); this is confirmed by the *lex repetundarum* from the time of the Gracchi (CIL I², 583.10; 33). It was also expected that the *cliens* would show his *patronus* respect and grant him protection by his presence by turning up at his house for the morning greeting (*salutatio*) (Sen. Ben. 6,33–34) or accompanying him to the Forum (Liv. 38,51,6).

The *cliens* was originally advised by his *patronus* in legal matters and represented by him in court. In the late Republic, when litigation was becoming increasingly demanding both juristically and rhetorically, litigating parties turned to professional lawyers from the upper classes, so the terminology of the connection between *patronus* and *cliens* took on a special meaning. At this time the relationship between *cliens* and *patronus* also became more relaxed; it is difficult to estimate to what extent in the Republic a *patronus* could control the voting behaviour of his *clientes*. Election bribery (*ambitus*), which was on the increase in the 2nd cent. BC, was an indication of a weakening of the bond between *patronus* and *cliens*; this process was further accelerated by the legislation on voting which was introduced in 139 BC with the *lex Gabinia*.

With the expansion of the Imperium Romanum the *clientelae* also extended to the Italian cities and to peoples and rulers outside Italy. The terminology of the connection between *cliens* and *patronus* is already attested for the period soon after 88 BC (REYNOLDS, document 3,49ff.). In some *regiones*, such as Spain or Gallia, a link could be made to the native tradition of hospitality (*hospitium*) and relationships of dependancy. The connection between Rome and its allies was linguistically recorded partly with the aid of the terminology of the relationship between *patronus* and *cliens*, though it must be emphasized that this is a metaphor that overvalues the dependancy and also the moral duties. Although *clientela* connections between individual Romans and foreign communities multiplied in the late Republic, in the same period the influence of the great power politicians became overpowering.

The Principate saw the rise of in one single *patronus* who monopolized all politically important *clientela* connections. This was the *princeps*, among whose *clientes* were his own freedmen, the municipal *plebs*, soldiers of the army and the fleet and people belonging to the provincial upper classes. Romans of the imperial ruling class were, on the other hand, designated as *amici*, even if they still behaved as *clientes*. Other *clientelae* did not disappear completely, however. Foreign communities were still *clientes* of Roman senators. According to Tacitus, the important families at the time of the Julio-Claudian *principes* were still interested in increasing their prestige through their *clientelae* (Tac. Ann. 3,55,2; Hist. 1,4). Although the depictions of *clientelae* in Juvenal (1,95ff.) and Martial (6,88) as a ruthless battle for *sportulae* and the more valuable gifts as well as a connection without *fides* should not be overvalued, this institution did eventually lose its significance for the prestige of the powerful and likewise for the protection of the socially weak. In the Principate, *anteambulones* were mentioned, men who accompanied their masters in public (Suet. Vesp. 2.2; Mart. 2.18; 3.46). It is unclear whether these were always free *clientes* or could also be slaves of the master.

→ Patronus

1 BADIAN, Clientelae 2 P. A. BRUNT, The Fall of the Roman Republic, 1988, 382–422 3 M. GELZER, Die Nobilität der röm. Republik, 1912 (=KS 1, 68–75) 4 J. M. REYNOLDS, Aphrodisias and Rome, 1982, 49ff.

A.W.L.

Clientage, Clients see → *Cliens*

Clientela, military see → Military clientela

Climate, Environmental change

I. GENERAL POINTS II. ANCIENT TERM; METHODS II. LATIN

I. GENERAL POINTS

Climate is the sum of the weather phenomena occurring in a given region over longer periods of time. In combination with the nature of the soil, the water resources and other natural conditions it determines the possibility of human existence. Natural irregularities lead to differences in the energy radiation on to the earth's surface, the circulation of air masses and therefore the distribution of moisture. Changes affect in particular those areas on the limits of adequate natural water supply. Communities relying on a hunter-gatherer economy react differently to this from migratory herdsmen and these differently again from farming peoples, as the latter can cope with shorter climate setbacks more easily owing to their storage economy; more far-reaching changes in the water situation can force even agrarian populations to migrate.

The development and spread of agriculture were followed in rapid succession by interventions of man into the naturally formed systems of the environment. Overpasturing (removal of the vegetation cover) and irrigation (change in hydrographic conditions) etc. have changed regional climate and water resources and as a result of desertification, erosion and salination have left behind anthropogenic → deserts — a process which continues to the present day.   B.B.

II. ANCIENT TERM; METHODS

Klíma (χλίμα, Lat. *clima*, 'inclination') was the name given in antiquity since → Hipparchus [6] — possibly following → Eudoxus [1] and → Aratus [4] — to every circle on the earth's surface parallel to the equator which is characterized in that the sun's rays have the same angle of inclination towards the horizon at each of its points, in other words are located on the same geographical latitude. These *klímata* were then used as the basis for dividing the earth into → zones; from this in turn today's term climate developed.

Climate has hardly changed — seen on a large scale and over longish periods of time — since *c.* 3000 BC. Regionally, however, short-term fluctuations in climate have continually changed living conditions, especially in areas which, — as far as water balance or air temperature are concerned — were on the margin of agricultural practicability in any case. In research into climate development today, apart from the evaluation of literary sources and archaeological discoveries, among other things methods of glacier research and processes of dendrochronology, pollen analysis and sedimentology are applied. Admittedly it is still not possible to reconstruct the climatic conditions of every period for every location and to state the results with certainty in every case. Moreover, it is possible to determine only to a limited extent whether an anomaly really indicates a climate change or should be viewed as a, to some extent, regular deviation from the normal state. This is particularly difficult to decide in the Mediterranean, as the climate here is characterized by enormous variations in the course of the weather (temperature, precipitation) throughout the year. A further problem is posed by the attempt to record correctly the interactions of climate and historical events. Even though it is indisputable that climate changes have an effect on people's lives, it is nevertheless difficult to prove in individual cases a causal connection between climate (or else just weather) and historical events and to separate them from factors which lie, e.g. in social or economic development.

Climate changes were probably — at any rate in antiquity and the Middle Ages — primarily based on natural events, even though anthropogenic causes have played a part regionally (e.g. influencing the hydrographic balance by clearing vegetation). Finally, it needs to be considered that climate change and reshaping of the landscape can be chronologically so far apart that cause and effect cannot be directly related to one another either by those affected or by today's ob-

server. For instance, in late antiquity in large parts of north Africa a decline in agriculture, at least partly caused by lack of water, is evident, without it being possible to establish a simultaneous change in climate. This must have happened millennia earlier; during its heyday in the Carthaginian-Roman period north Africa lived off ground water reserves which had been laid in previously at a time of great rainfalls and which only gradually became exhausted in late antiquity owing to intensive farming.   V.S.

→ Meteorology; → Zone

K. W. BUTZER, Environmental Change in the Near East and Human Impact on the Land, in: J. M. SASSON (ed.), Civilizations of the Ancient Near East 1, 1995, 123–151; L. HEMPEL, s.v. K., Klimakunde, in: H. SONNABEND (ed.), Mensch und Landschaft in der Ant. 1999; J.-C. MISKOVKY et al (ed.), Géologie de la préhistoire: méthodes, techniques, applications, 1987; H. J. NISSEN, Grundriß einer Gesch. der Frühzeit des Vorderen Orients, 1995; E. OLSHAUSEN, Einführung in die histor. Geogr. der alten Welt, 1991, 202–204 n. 246, 248 (bibliography); W. STORKEBAUM (ed.), Wiss. Länderkunden, vols. 1ff., 1967ff. (with various new editions).   V.S. and B.B.

Climax (Κλῖμαξ; *Klîmax*).

[1] Wide pass provided with steps, which led out of the Inachus Valley of the Argolis near Melangea (possibly modern Pikerni) into the high plain of Mantinea (Paus. 8,6,4; cf. 2,25,3), modern Portes.   E.O.

[2] see → Pamphylia

Clipeus

[1] (*clipeata imago*). The bust on a round shield, in antiquity usually designated as *clipeus et imago* or εἰχὼν ἐν ὅπλῳ, is to be distinguished from relief medallions in the art of miniatures. *Clipei* painted on terracotta come from tombs (Centuripe); the earliest marble *clipei* attached to buildings come from Delos (Mithridates monument, *c.* 100 BC). The *clipeus* became widespread from the 1st cent. BC in Rome. Written sources on their invention suggest an origin in ancestor worship and military honours, though reports on Punic *clipei* of Hasdrubal are dubious. The first public display took place on the Temple of Bellona and the → Basilica Aemilia in Rome in 79/78 BC, probably transferred from the → atrium. Suspended *clipei* made of metal are reproduced in wall paintings. Small-format *clipei* on *signa* and the scabbards of swords attest the significance of gold, non-extant *clipei* in ruler worship. In the 1st cent. AD the spread of marble *clipei* began as a honorific form of → portraiture, which reached its high point in the 2nd cent.; bronze *clipei* are rare (Ankara). From then on they were also used for galleries of the gods (Chiragan), for historical portraits and portraits of intellectuals (Aphrodisias). From as early as the 1st cent. AD *clipei* appear on gravestones and from there are transferred to sarcophagi, where they are carried by representations of Eros or Nike.

→ Bust; → Portraiture; → Toreutics

G. BECATTI, s.v. clipeate immagini, EAA 2, 718–721; R. WINKES, *Clipeata imago*, 1969.   R.N.

[2] see → Shield

Cliternia

[1] City of the Aequiculi in the valley of the Salto, modern Capradosso; *municipium* of the *tribus Claudia*, connected to the Aquae Cutiliae; later in the *regio IV Augustea* (Plin. HN 3,107; Ptol. 3,1,56). CIL IX, p. 394, 4166–76.

NISSEN 2, 462.

[2] City in the extreme north of Apulia near Larinum on the Tifernus, *regio II* (Plin. HN 3,103; Mela 2,65: Claternia). Location uncertain, probably near Nuova C. (province of Compobasso).

NISSEN 2, 784.

Clitias (Κλιτίας; *Klitías*). Attic black-figured vase painter of the high Archaic period, *c.* 570–560 BC, master of the 'François Vase', which bears his signature twice and moreover that of the potter → Ergotimus. Both masters also signed a stand and two or three 'Gordium bowls', which, however, have little or no figurative painting. Moreover, several fragments with scenes from mythology have been attributed to C.

The 'François Vase', named after the archaeologist who found it, a monumental voluted krater (Florence, MA), with its lively mythological images is one of the most important masterworks of Greek vase painting. The entire body of the vessel is divided into frieze zones as in the style of animal friezes, though only the bottom frieze with its animal fights is reminiscent of these. In all the other friezes myths are narrated, most of the figures, and sometimes also objects, being epigraphically named. In spite of the delicate and precise style of the drawing, the method of narrative is powerful and uninhibited, sometimes even humorous. In the main frieze the ceremonial procession of the gods to the wedding of Peleus and Thetis is portrayed. The fate of their son Achilles is the subject of two further friezes (the Troilus episode and funeral games for Patroclus) and two handle pictures (in each case Ajax with the body of Achilles). Among the adventures of Peleus is the Calydonian boar hunt and perhaps also the centauromachy, while the return of Hephaestus can be linked to Thetis. Not part of this cycle of legends are the round dances of the Athenian children after Theseus has tamed the Minotaur, the two fleeing gorgons and the mistresses of the animals on the handles and finally the burlesque fight between pygmies and cranes on the foot of the vessel. The carefully thought-out connections relating to composition and content between the subjects have continually raised the question of a uniform agenda, which has been answered in a great variety of ways. The influence of pictorial (→ Sophilus) or literary models (Homer, Stesichorus) and of contemporary interests is also judged in different ways. The miniature style introduced by C. lives on, above all, in → little-master cups.

BEAZLEY, ABV, 66–79; BEAZLEY, Addenda², 21f.; E. SIMON, Die griech. Vasen, ²1981, pl. 51–57; C. ISLER-KERÉNYI, Der François-Krater zw. Athen und Chiusi, in: J. OAKLEY et al. (ed.), Athenian Potters and Painters, 1997, 523–539.   H.M.

Clitumnus Small river in Umbria, tributary of the Tiberis, modern Timia. The sources of the C. (between Spoletium and Fulginiae below Trebia) were made famous by Plin. Ep. 8,8; Caligula and Honorius visited them; they were surrounded by chapels for the god of the same name and other oracle deities, taken care of by the citizens of Hispellum; *sacraria* of a *statio* of the *via Flaminia* (It. Burd. 613); *villae* in the surrounding area. In S. Salvatore de Piscina (6th cent. AD) reused stones and inscriptions have been used in buildings (CIL II 4963).

H. HOLTZINGER, Der C.-Tempel bei Trevi, in: Zschr. für Bildende Kunst 16, 1881, 313–318; W. HOPPENSTADT, Die Basilica San Salvatore, 1912; A. P. FRUTAZ, Il tempietto del C., in: RACr 17, 1941, 245–264; F. W. DEICHMANN, Die Entstehung von Salvatorkirche und C.-Tempel bei Spoleto, in: MDAI(R) 58, 1943, 106–148; C. A. MASTRELLI, in: C. SANTORO (ed.), Studi storico-linguistici, 1978, 105–115; G. BENAZZI, A. BENAZZI, I dipinti murali e l'edicola marmorea del tempietto sul C., 1985.   G.U.

Clivus Capitolinus Road from the → Forum Romanum to the → Capitolium in Rome (Dion. Hal. 1,34,4; 6,1,4); began near the Carcer (Cic. Verr. 2,5,77). The Clivus Capitolinus (CC) was paved by the censors of the year 174 BC (Liv. 21,27,7) and adorned with a *porticus* near the Temple of Saturn (Liv. 41,27,7), possibly on the site of the Flavian *porticus* of the *dei consentes*. As public plots of land were sold on the outskirts of the Capitol as building land after 88 BC, it was possible to erect private houses on the CC. In the late Republican civil wars this was often the scene of battle (Cic. Rab. perd. 31; Ascon. 45 c; Cic. Att. 2,1,7; S. 28; Phil. 2,16; Mil. 64). The lower parts of the CC issuing from the area between the Temple of Saturn and the *porticus* of the *dei consentes* remained preserved; the continuation of this section at mid level can still be seen today. The upper part, which extended from a narrow bend (Dig. 9,2,52,2) as far as the entrance to the Capitol (Tac. Hist. 3,71,2) has not been preserved; this is where the arches of Scipio Africanus (Liv. 37,3,7) and Calpurnius (Vell. Pat. 2,3,2; App. B Civ. 1,16,70; Oros. Hist. 5,9,2) must have stood.

T. WISEMAN, in: LTUR 1, 280–281; RICHARDSON, 89.

Clivus Publicius The first road capable of being driven on on the predominantly plebeian Aventine in Rome, laid out by the plebeian aediles L. and M. Poblicius Malleolus (Varro, Ling. 5,158; Ov. Fast. 5,275) between 241 BC and 238 BC (Vell. Pat. 1,14,8; Plin. HN 18,286) from fines for embezzlement (Fest. 276 L.). The CP ran from the Porta Trigemina of the Forum Boarium along modern Via di Santa Prisca or modern Clivo dei Publicii (Liv. 26,10,5; 27,37,15; Frontin. Aq. 5).

F. COARELLI, in: LTUR 1, 284; RICHARDSON, 90.

Cloaca maxima The invention of the *cloacae* (Str. 5,8; Plin. HN 36,24) is stressed in ancient literature as one of the greatest achievements of civilization; Pliny (HN 36,105) ascribes it to → Tarquinius Priscus, others (Liv. 1,38,6; 1,56,2; Dion. Hal. 3,67,5; 4,44,1) to → Tarquinius Superbus. The edifice designated in Roman literature as Cloaca maxima (CM) (Liv. 1,56,2; Varro, Ling. 5,157) has not been located with certainty, but is generally identified which the largest sewage canal in Rome, preserved in various stages of construction, running from the Subura under the later Forum of Nerva towards the centre of the → Basilica Aemilia. In the first section the walls are made watertight by *opus signinum*, under the basilica the canal consists of travertine and Aniene tuff. A secondary diversion, which was carried out at the time of construction of the Forum of Nerva in large peperino blocks, circumvents the Basilica Aemilia, probably because of the unsafe building land and only touches it again with a canal connection in the western corner. The canal runs out into the *via Sacra* near the Temple of Venus Cloacina. After that remains of the oldest stage, in which a false vault had been formed with small tuff blocks, were used to build the late Republican version (→ Vaults and arches, construction of). Under the → Basilica Iulia the CM is designed as a barrel vault; near the → Pons Aemilius it runs out into the Tiber in an arch-shaped opening.

H. BAUER, in: LTUR 1, 288–290; RICHARDSON, 91–92.
                                                                              R.F.

Cloatius Verus Roman lexicographer with antiquarian interests, perhaps from the early Augustan period. He wrote about the meaning of Greek words (at least four *ordinatorum Graecorum libri*) and on Greek loanwords in Lat. (apparently also at least four bks. *Verba a Graecis tracta*). C. is quoted as a source by → Gellius (16,12) and → Macrobius (Sat. 3,6,2; 3,20,1). He is quite certainly the same Cloatius, whom → Pompeius Festus (→ Verrius Flaccus) cites as a specialist in sacred language, together with L. → Aelius, probably C.'s source.

GRF 467–473; HLL § 283   R.A.K.

Clocks
I. ANCIENT ORIENT AND EGYPT   II. CLASSICAL ANTIQUITY

I. ANCIENT ORIENT AND EGYPT
A. WATER CLOCKS   B. SUNDIALS   C. STARDIALS

A. WATER CLOCKS
Instrument for measuring time based on water flowing from a container have been found in Egypt, the oldest one being from the period of Amenophis [3]

(1392–1355 BC) [2. plate 18; 5. fig. III.25]. These instruments were normally shaped like flat-bottomed vases with a hole in the base, an outflow of 2 to 4 cm length and calibration marks on the inside. Time was measured by the water quantity by which the water level dropped in the vessel. According to [2.15] the narrowing was to secure that the same water level difference measured the same time (problems with this interpretation [9]). The name the *mḥ.s-pns.s*, 'one fills it, one empties it' was suggested for water clocks [6.178]. A water clock with inflowing water that presumably measured time relative to the rise of the water level was found at → Edfu [2; 12; 5. n. 81, figs. III.21a–III.36].

No devices of this type are preserved from Mesopotamia. An undecorated bowl from Nimrud with a hole in the bottom [3.119] may have been a 'sinking' water clock, which — set on the water surface — began to sink as soon as enough water had entered and measured a uniform time interval that way. The Akkadian term was probably *mašqu*; this implement supposedly also measured the duration of the moon's visibility. Another term from cuneiform writings for the water clock was Sumerian ^{giš}dib.dib/Akkadian *dibdibbu*, which onomatopoietically reflected the dripping of clocks. An Old Babylonian mathematical text describes a ^{giš}dib.dib that held between 32 and 135 l of water and measured time intervals by means of the lowering water level. This suggests that at that time a water clock with an almost constant water level was used. In a device of this type the speed at which the water level drops remains more or less the same. A device called *maštaqtum/maltaqtu* was plausibly interpreted as a water clock (rather less likely as a sand clock [4]). Based on BORCHARDT [2.15f.], NEUGEBAUER [11] suggested that the *maltaqtu* or *dibdibbu* should be understood as a device that emptied itself. The fact that the outflow is slower with a lower water level explains according to [11] the inexact ratio between the longest and the shortest duration of the night in many texts. However, this is not the case because [4] textual sources state that periods of equal duration were measured by equal weights of water. The model suggested by [2] was too simple [9].

B. SUNDIALS
Egyptian clocks for measuring shadow lengths have been documented from the time of Thutmosis [3] III. (1479–1425 BC), shadow direction clocks (vertically hanging sundials) from the times of Merenptah (1224–1214 BC) to the Roman period. The cross bar of the shadow clock, which was always oriented east/west, was called *mrḫyt*. In later periods (beginning in *c.* 320 BC) a shadow clock with a slant was used that was directly oriented towards the sun [5. fig. III.39–III.57].

No shadow clocks are preserved from Mesopotamia, but the ratio of shadow length and time was described in a somewhat confused manner in the text MUL.APIN II ii 21–42 [10]. Measurements along the

Sun dials

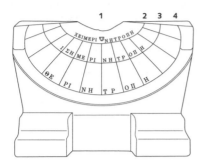

1 Hole for the metal
  pointer *(gnomon)*
2 Winter solstice
  (cheimerine trope)
3 Equinox
  (isemerine trope)
4 Sommer solstice
  (therine trope)

Pythagoreion (Samos). Arch. Museum,
Inv. no. 322 (2nd half of the 2nd cent. BC).

0   20 cm

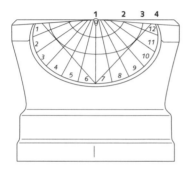

1 Hole for the metal
  pointer *(gnomon)*
2 Position of the sun in winter
3 Equinox
4 Position of the sun in summer
1-12 Hour segments

Pythagoreion (Samos). Arch. Museum,
Inv. no. 323 (Hellenistic-late antique).

0   20 cm

horizon and a relationship to the astronomical book of Enoch appear possible [8]. Unpublished texts describe the construction of a device that is either a sundial that divides the day into 12 temporal hours (*simanu*) [13.162–165] or a device for locating the → zodiac (in the summer towards the northeast of the rod, in the winter towards the southeast). Herodotus (2,109) was of the opinion that the Greeks took over the *pólos* ('concave sundial') and the *gnṓmōn* ('sundial rod') from Babylonia (s. below II.). It is doubtful that water and shadow clock technology was transferred from the Near East to India [7].

C. STARDIALS

A star clock that indicated the hours of the night by the crossing of the meridian by the decan stars (→ Astronomy B.2.) was already found in the Egyptian Old Kingdom (2nd half of the 3rd millennium BC) [5.56f.]. In Mesopotamia time measurement during the night using the *ziqpu* or culminating stars was known since at least the 1st half of the 1st millennium BC [3.111–113]. → Chronology

1 L. BRACK-BERNSEN, H. HUNGER, The Babylonian Zodiac, in: Centaurus 41, 1999, 280–292 2 L. BORCHARDT, Die Altäg. Zeitmessung, in: E. VON BASSERMAN-JORDAN (ed.), Die Gesch. der Zeitmessung und der Uhren, vol. 1,

1920 3 D. BROWN, The Cuneiform Conception of Celestial Space and Time, in: Cambridge Archaeological Journ. 10, 2000, 103–121 4 Id. et al., The Water Clock in Mesopotamia, in: AfO 46/47, 1999/2000, 130–148 5 M. CLAGETT, Ancient Egyptian Science. A Source Book, vol. 2: Calendars, Clocks, and Astronomy, 1995 6 J. J. CLÈRE, Review of M. F. L. MACADAM, The Temples of Kawa I (1949), in: Bibliotheca Orientalis 8, 1951, 174–180 7 H. FALK, Measuring Time in Mesopotamia and Ancient India, in: ZDMG 150, 2000, 107–132 8 U. GLESSMER, Horizontal Measuring in the Babylonian Astronomical Compendium Mul.Apin, in: Henoch 18, 1996, 259–282 9 J. HOYRUP, Note on Water-Clocks and on the Authority of Texts, in: AfO 44/45, 1997/98, 192–194 10 H. HUNGER, D. PINGREE, Mul.Apin — An Astronomical Compendium in Cuneiform (AfO Beih. 24), 1989 11 O. NEUGEBAUER, Stud. in Ancient Astronomy VIII. The Water Clock in Babylonian Astronomy, in: Isis 37, 1947, 37–43 12 A. POGO, Egyptian Water Clocks, in: Isis 25, 1936, 403–425 13 F. ROCHBERG-HALTON, Babylonian Seasonal Hours, in: Centaurus 32, 1989, 146–170.   DA.BR.

II. CLASSICAL ANTIQUITY

As devices for measuring and dividing the full day or day and night, clocks and the division into hours were considered in classical antiquity to be borrowings from the Ancient Civilizations within known history. Their distribution and development is closely associated with the calculation of hours.

A. Sundials   B. Water clocks   C. Special
clock constructions   D. Later Reception

A. Sundials

According to Herodotus' account (2,109,3) the Greeks received the sundial and its rod(πόλος/*pólos* and γνώμων/*gnómōn*) together with the division of day and night into twelve hours — of unequal length depending on the season — from the Babylonians. However, this transfer may also have come via Egypt. Primitive sundials and the use of uneven hours are attested there since the 2nd millennium BC. Diogenes [17] Laertius (2,1) attributes the invention of the *gnómōn* or a 'shadow catcher' (σκιόθηρον/*skióthēron*) and its introduction to Sparta in the 6th cent. BC to → Anaximander. The devices were also called 'hour indicators' = clocks (ὡρο-σκοπεῖον/ *hōro-skopeîon* or ωρο-λόγιον/*hōro-lógion*). However, the routine determination of the time of day was performed, according to Attic comedy, by means of shadow length, which was expressed in feet. (e.g., Aristoph. Eccl. 652).

During the 4th and 3rd cents. BC, astronomers and mathematicians developed sundials into reliable observation instruments that were able to incorporate or determine the angle of the → ecliptic and latitude (→ Climate II.), while theoretical gnomonics were refined. Hellenistic astronomers also used hours of equal length or equinoctial hours, but no sundials were constructed to reflect this fact. The preserved examples had level, partially spherical or spherical (σκάφη/*skáphē*), conical and cylindrical shapes [1]. The most detailed account of the various sundial types, their actual or presumed inventors and the methods for their construction is found in Vitruvius (9,7 and 9,8,1, → *análemma*). Apart from stationary sundials, Vitruvius also describes portable ones, the hanging travel clocks (*viatoria pensilia*), which could to some extent be used in all latitudes (*pros pan clima*). He attributes their invention to Theodosius [1] of Bithynia (1st cent. BC) [2].

Apart from dedications to gods or rulers, and the names of the donors, the rather rare inscriptions on sundials (cf. fig.) consist of numbers or letters for the hours of the day, the names of months and → zodiac symbols as well as occasionally stating a relationship to another donated object such as the furnishings of arenas, fountains, temples, schools or municipal scales (→ Donations). Pliny's account of the introduction of hourly division to Rome in the 3rd cent. BC notes mockingly that in 263 BC the Romans brought a sundial captured in Catania (→ Catana) to Rome and did not notice for 99 years that it showed the wrong time for their latitude. Cornelius [183] Scipio Nasica finally made possible the measurement of day and night hours in 159 BC in Rome by donating a water clock (*primus aqua divisit horas*) in a building (Plin. HN 7,212–215).

B. Water clocks

From the 6th cent. BC the κλεψύδρα/*kleps(h)ýdra* ('water thief'), which is named after a suction lifting device for liquids similar to a large pipette, has been recorded in Greece, initially when explaining physical phenomena. From the 5th cent. this simple device with a narrow outlet is repeatedly mentioned in the context

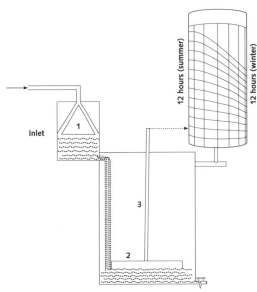

→ Water inlet
1 Regulator (regulates the influx of water, keeping the hydraulic pressure in the inlet receptacle constant)
2 Float
3 Column (indicates hours on the scale)

Water-clock of Ctesibius; hypothetical reconstruction (after Vitr. 9,8,2-7).

of limiting court speeches (first in Aristoph. Ach. 693). A water quantity usually measured in → *chous* [1] was allotted to each party as the time period (Aristot. Ath. Pol. 67,2), which was suspended for hearing witnesses and reading out documents. The plaintiff received more, the defence less time; in civil cases the disputed value was also considered. According to an inscription from Iasos [5] of the early 3rd cent. BC, the clepsydra was used as a check on punctuality by municipal committees: it was opened at sunrise; whoever arrived after it was empty, received no money for the day [4]. Speech limitations 'according to water' (πρὸς ὕδωρ) remained part of trial procedure until late antiquity. In the Byzantine period they fell out of use (Lydus, Mag. 2,16). The clepsydra became a clock (*hōrológion*) through a mathematical association of the daily hours with the liquid measure; later these measures were replaced by indicating the hours (Cass. Dio 40,52). Aeneas [2] Tacticus (22,24–25) addressed the problem of calibrating the run-off opening made necessary by the uneven water pressure when discussing the even allotment of military night watches. As a military night clock the clepsydra is often mentioned until the early Middle Ages.

Simple water clocks were often used to regulate distribution in irrigation systems in the southern Mediterranean region. Allotment by hours and half-hours is attested in inscriptions from → Lamasba and a papyrus of AD 113 from the Egyptian-Roman metropolis Ptolemaïs [3] Euergetis in which a ὑδρολόγιον/*hydrológion* is mentioned in accounts of the municipal water pipeline system [5]. The general use of this hourly water allocation is also evident in Italian inscriptions and Roman law (e.g., Dig. 43,20,5).

In the Hellenistic period improved water clocks (*hydrológia*) were used for astronomical observations, supposedly for measuring the diameters of the sun and moon, and for taking the pulse by Herophilus [1] (Marcellinus, De pulsibus 262 ff.). As motors or components of elaborate → automata, water clocks became a subject of Hellenistic → mechanics.

C. SPECIAL CLOCK CONSTRUCTIONS

Vitruvius (9,8,2 ff.) describes the clock constructions of → Ctesibius [1] (cf. fig.), in detail though not always clearly in technical terms. They had calibrated run-off openings, waves moved by floaters with counter-weights, indicator systems, 'faces' with hour and calendar markings for the entire year as well as moving figures and acoustic signals. These entertaining accessories are also found on the automata of → Hero of Alexandria. His relevant treatise Περὶ ὑδρίων ὡροσκοπείων/*Perí hydríōn hōroskopeíōn* ('On water clocks') is lost. The 2nd-cent. AD fragment of a disk with astronomical markings found near Salzburg is part of a clock with a moving face [6].

The multitude of sundials set up in important public places was supplemented in large cities by public indication of time and calendar by means of water clocks. In the Imperial period Rome's abundance of clocks was mocked just as much as the urban lifestyle that was regulated by hours and contrary to the normal course of the day. Little is known of the technical details of the water clocks in the agoras of Athens and Samos, the Amphiareion near Oropus, the Pergamum sanctuary and the theatre of Priene [7; 8]. To regulate the differing times for men and women, → baths and → thermal baths were often equipped with clocks. The octagonal 'Tower of the Winds' constructed in Athens in the 1st cent. BC by Andronicus of Cyrrhus combined a water clock with eight sundials and indication of wind direction by means of a rotating triton figure on its roof [9; 10].

Little is known about the development of gears for representing astronomical movements in clocks. (+50) The calendar mechanism of the 1st cent. BC found in 1961 near the island of Antikythera (→ Aegila) with epicyclical gears probably had no drive, and neither did the simpler 5th-cent. AD sundial from London [11; 12].

D. LATER RECEPTION

Ancient clock technology was transmitted to the European Middle Ages only in the simplest forms, the

clepsydra and primitive sundials. Cassiodorus reported in 507 sending a sundial and a water clock into the apparently backward Burgundian kingdom (Cassiod. Var. 1,45 f.) and later recommended in his manual for monastic life the *horologium aquatile* as a useful alarm for the 'soldiers of Christ' (Cassiod. Inst. 30,4 f.). The monastic alarm clock, which was important for a monastic routine conforming to the rules and especially the early morning offices, only became technically elaborate devices in the High Middle Ages and were developed into mechanical clocks in the late Middle Ages. The more exacting ancient clock technology was continued only in Byzantium even though the text of Vitruvius was well known in western monasteries. Procopius [2] of Gaza reported in detail before 529 on an elaborate public automaton clock in his town with an hourly gong and figures moving mechanically day and night [13]. These elaborate automaton clocks were developed further in the Islamic sphere by resorting to Hellenistic mechanics, e.g., Pseudo-Archimedes, and were occasionally sent as much-admired diplomatic gifts into the Latin West.

→ Astronomy; → Calendar; → Mechanics; → Time, concept of

1 S.L. GIBBS, Greek and Roman Sundials, 1976 2 E. BUCHNER, Ant. Reise-U., in: Chiron 1, 1971, 457–481 3 G. LANGMANN et al., Die ägypt. Wasserauslaufuhr aus Ephesos, in: JÖAI, Beiblatt 1, 1984, 1–67 4 S. YOUNG, An Athenian Clepsydra, in: Hesperia 8, 1939, 274–284 5 W. HABERMANN, Zur Wasserversorgung einer Metropole im kaiserzeitlichen Ägypten (Vestigia 53), 2000 6 O. BENNDORF et al., in: JÖAI 6, 1903, 32 ff. 7 R. TÖLLE, U. auf Samos, in: P. ZAZOFF (ed.), Opus nobile. FS U. Jantzen, 1969, 164–171 8 J.E. ARMSTRONG, J.M. CAMP, Notes on a Water Clock in the Athenian Agora, in: Hesperia 46, 1977, 147–161 9 J.V. NOBLE, D.J. DE SOLLA PRICE, The Water Clock in the Tower of the Winds, in: AJA 72, 1968, 345–355 with pls. 111–118 10 J. VON FREEDEN, Oikia Kyrrestu. Stud. zum sog. Turm der Winde in Athen, 1983 11 D. PRICE, Gears from the Greeks. The Antikythera Mechanism, in: TAPhA 64.7, 1974, 1–70 12 M.T. WRIGHT, The London Sundial-Calendar and the Early History of Geared Mechanisms, in: History of Technology 12, 1990, 65–102 13 H. DIELS, Über die von Prokop beschriebene Kunstuhr von Gaza: Ed. und Übers. von 'Ekphrasis Horologiou' (Abh. der preußischen Akademie der Wiss., Philos.-Histor. Kl. 1917.7).

G. BILFINGER, Die Zeitmesser der ant. Völker, 1886; A. REHM, s.v. Horologium, RE 8, 2416–2433; M.C.P. SCHMIDT, Die Entstehung der ant. W., 1912.   G.D.-v.R.

Clodia

[1] Born c. 94 BC, daughter of Ap. Claudius [I 23], sister of P. → Clodius [I 4] Pulcher, married to Q. Caecilius [I 22] Metellus Celer. In the opinion of most of the ancients (Plut. Cic. 29,2,–4; Quint. 6,3,25; 8,6,53; schol. Bob. 135–6 STANGL) and modern authors [1. 53–56] C. is an attractive, but 'immoral' courtesan, originating from a well-to-do family [2], which is sometimes based on the plausible identification of C. with Lesbia, the

mistress of the poet Catullus (c. 5; 7; 43; 51; 58; 72; 75 i.a.; [3, 273–275]); Cicero was mainly responsible for C.'s bad reputation with a speech which he made in 56 BC, in the trial initiated partly by C., for the defendant M. → Caelius [I 4] Rufus. C. became the butt of contemporary clichés and topoi of moral defamation (prostitution, incest with her brother; Cic. Cael. 30–38; 47–50; 62; 78). Even the sudden death of her husband in 59 BC became poisoning by C.(Cael. 60) [5. 106–151]. The reason for these attacks may lie in C.'s way of life, as she shed the standards traditionally applying to Roman → matrons and entered into public as well as intense relationships with several men, which were not always erotic, however, but motivated by literature and politics [4. 72–73]. Whether C., traces of whom disappear after 56, was ever in 'normal' contact with Cicero again in the 40s must remain doubtful [3. 277–287; 5. 111–114].

1 D. BALSDON, Roman Women, 1962   2 T.P. WISEMAN, C., in: Arion 2, 1975, 96–115   3 M. SKINNER, C. Metelli, in: TAPhA 113, 1983, 273–287   4 R. BAUMAN, Women and Politics in Ancient Rome, 1992   5 B. KRECK, Unt. zur polit. und sozialen Rolle der Frau in der späten röm. Republik, 1975.

[2] Daughter of Ap. Claudius [I 23] and younger sister of Clodia [1], wife of L. → Licinius Lucullus. On the occasion of the conflicts surrounding her brother Clodius [I 4], to whom C. was close politically, her husband separated from her in 62 BC on the pretext of her infidelity (Plut. Lucullus 38) and accused her 61 in court, typically, of incest with her brother.

DRUMANN-GROEBE 2, 319.

[3] Elder sister of Clodia [1] and Clodia [2], married to Q. Marcius Rex. She too was defamed by the accusation of incest with her brother (Cic. Fam. 1,9,15).   H.S.

Clodius In the 1st cent. BC, vernacular form of the *gentilicium* → Claudius (C. [I 4] and → Clodia), since late Republican period also an independent family name.
I. REPUBLICAN PERIOD   II. IMPERIAL PERIOD
III. WRITERS AND ORATORS

I. REPUBLICAN PERIOD

[I 1] C., C. In 43/42 BC follower and prefect of M. Brutus; he murdered C. Antonius [I 3].
[I 2] C., Sex. Henchman of P. Clodius [I 4] Pulcher, Sex. → Cloelius [2].
[I 3] C. Aesopus. Tragic actor in the late Republican period (→ Aesopus, C.); his son M.C. Aesopus was the first to bear the *gentilicium* in the early Imperial period (SCHANZ/HOSIUS 1, 149).   K.-L.E.
[I 4] C. Pulcher, P. Brother of the infamous consul Ap. → Claudius [I 24], was born *c.* 93 BC. In 68 he took part (as legate?) in the war against Mithridates and then in a mutiny of the army against the Roman commander, his brother-in-law Lucullus (Cass. Dio 36,2,1; Plut. Lucul-

lus 20,5). After a stay in Cilicia and Syria, having been captured by pirates in the meantime, in 65 C. returned to Rome. There he brought an unsuccessful case against Catiline, who was probably defended by Cicero (Fenestella HRR 2, fr. 20), based on the *lex repetundarum* [1. 48–52]. In 64 C. was military tribune (?) in Gallia Transalpina and in 61 *quaestor* in Sicily (MRR 2, 164, 180). The event which made him famous took place on the night of 4 December 62, when he crept in disguise into the Bona Dea cult celebrations being held at Caesar's house and which only women were allowed to attend. He was accused of crime against religion (*religio Clodiana*), but acquitted after a financial consideration by Crassus and protests from the → *plebs urbana* [1. 51ff.]. C.'s action has been explained in research as having solely private motives (relationship with Caesar's wife Pompeia); in fact, though, the altercation had no less of a political dimension and was clearly also staged as a provocation to Cicero: 5 December 62 was the anniversary of the execution of the Catilinarians, felt not only among the *plebs* to have been unlawful, for the carrying out of which the then consul Cicero had also used alleged omens from the Bona Dea (Plut. Cic. 20 [1. 52–58]). In 59, by curiate law and with Caesar's help [2. 58–62], C. had himself adopted by a plebeian, as he could not have stood for the people's tribunate as a patrician (probably also at this time relinquished the aristocratic family name Claudius and adopted the plebeian form Clodius). Active as people's tribune from 10.12.59, with a series of laws C. influenced political circumstances in Rome way beyond his one-year tenure of office. A law on the re-admittance of the old and founding of new → *collegia* and a *lex frumentaria* (free distribution of grain), which naturally secured its originator great popularity, was instrumental in increasing the political worth and social protection of the poorer city population. With a *lex de auspiciis* (on the application of the → *obnuntiatio*) and a *lex de censoribus* C. tried to control the arbitrariness of the higher-ranking magistrates. The law on the consular provinces promised him the support of the consuls A. → Gabinius and L. → Calpurnius [I 19] Piso for a further goal, the removal of his (and Caesar's) opponents Cicero and Cato from Rome. A *lex de capite civis Romani* (threat of *relegatio* in the event of the killing of a Roman citizen without legal verdict) restored not only an ancient right of freedom (→ *provocatio*), but was aimed in particular at Cicero, who in his consulate (63) had had the Catilinarians executed *indemnati*; with a *lex de exilio Ciceronis* (*c.* 24.4.58)) exile of the ex-consul was finally carried through. Cato had to leave Rome, as he was given by plebiscite the honourable as well as thankless task (*imperium extraordinarium*) of annexing the island of Cyprus and confiscating the crown treasures of King Ptolemy (on the laws [3. 46–71; 2. 70–82]).

Apart from his reputation as the scion of an influential *gens* and his good relations with the *populares* and also with some *optimates*, the status won in his tribunate year served C. above all as a backup for future attempts at independent policies. Manoeuvring between triumvirs and *optimates*, equally committed to personal career prospects and the interests of his clientele, the *plebs urbana*, which, due to their organization in *collegia* he could quickly mobilize, in spite of his occasional co-operation with Caesar, C. was largely an independent factor in Roman politics.

From 57, when Caesar's successes in Gallia made Pompey look for a power equivalent, Rome's political structure was heading for a crisis. The situation did admittedly relax with the agreements of Luca (1st → triumvirate), but finally escalated in 53, when after the death of Crassus and Iulia the power struggle between Pompey and Caesar was now unavoidable. With trials, → demonstrations and street riots the opponents fought with alternating coalitions on confused fronts. At the start of the year 52 no magistrates had been elected. Pompey, in particular, speculated on open confusion in the state and intended to present himself to the Senate as its saviour. C. applied (after his office as aedile in 56) for the praetorship and his long-term antagonist → Annius [I 14] Milo, friend of Cicero and Pompey, for the consulate. On 18 Jan. 52 Milo attacked C. with a troop of gladiators on the *via Appia* near Bovillae. In the doubtlessly planned murder the only thing to remain unclear is whether Pompey knew about it or whether Milo simply hoped for his subsequent approval. In Rome serious disturbances broke out and the Senate building in which the *plebs* had laid C.'s body in state, was burned down. Pompey, who distanced himself from Milo, received on 25.2 the extraordinary powers he had striven for and he became *consul sine collega*; after a sensational trial (dramatic depiction in Ascon. 30ff. C) Milo was banished for murder [3. 93–111].

The image later periods have of Clodius is marked by Cicero. It is that of an amoral demagogue, who, 'driven by hate, anger and short-sighted self-interest', terrorized the streets of Rome with his gangs and therefore 'greatly contributed to the fall of the Republic' [4. 647]; but cf. [5. 108f.]. The invectives in Cicero's orations consist only of an accumulation of all the commonplaces which he generally meted out to his opponents (even more, e.g. Calpurnius Piso or A.Gabinius). They have no credibility and neither are they in harmony with the depictions from Cicero's private letters (cf. Cic. Att. 14,13b,4). Clodius' violence turns out to be Ciceronian rhetoric; less blood flowed on the passing of the *leges Clodiae* than on Caesar's *leges Iuliae*. A differentiated evaluation of C., which also takes account of his more far-reaching intentions, is required.

1 Ph. Moreau, Clodiana religio, 1982   2 W.Will, Der röm. Mob, 1991 (sources)   3 H. Benner, Die Politik des P.C. Pulcher, 1987   4 Ch. Meier, s.v. C. Pulcher, LAW, 647   5 W.Nippel, Aufruhr und 'Polizei' in der röm. Republik, 1988.   w.w.

[I 5] **C. of Ancona.** Travelling drug-seller, who *c.* 85 BC visited Larinum on his sales journeys (Cic. Clu. 14.40); on a comparable travelling healer see CIL XI 5836). C.

sold to Statius Oppianicus the Elder for HS 2000 a medicine that the latter was to use to poison his mother-in-law Dinaea. After this transaction C. promptly left the city.   V.N.

[I 6] **C. Scriba.** Quoted in Servius auctus (Aen. 1,176; 2,229; cf. 1,52) as a glossographer. The *agnomen* is probably corrupt; identification customary since [1] with Ser. → Clodius [III 1] is doubtful [2. 70], because the *fomentum* (instead of *fomes*) glossarized in the meaning to be attached is late. This could of course be a mistake by a later compiler.

1 GRF 96   2 R. A. Kaster, C. Suetonius Tranquillus De grammaticis et rhetoribus 1995   an.gl.

II. Imperial period

[II 1] **D. C. Albinus.** = Imperator Caesar D.C. Septimius Albinus, of African origin, from Hadrumetum (SHA Alb. 1.3; 4.1); this detail, like many other things in the *vita*, is sometimes thought to be fictional (cf. [1] already), but could be defended on account of C.'s unusual gold coin with the *saeculum Frugiferum* (the *colonia* Hadrumetum had the epithet *frugifera*) (cf. [2] with reference to [3]). Under → Commodus he fought *c.* 182/84 in Dacia (Cass. Dio 72,8,1), probably as legionary legate (FPD 1, 267ff.). His *curriculum vitae* in the → Historia Augusta is invented (cf. [1; 2]); *cos. suff.* and, probably before the death of Commodus, governor of Britain (Cass. Dio 73,14,3; Hdn. 2,15,1, cf. SHA Alb. 13,4; 6). C. accepted from → Septimius Severus at the time of his coup in the year 193 the title of Caesar, but remained in his province. Coins were minted for him as Caesar (Hdn. 2,15,5); as the colleague of Severus he became *cos. II ord.* in 194. After the victory over Niger, Severus' attitude changed (Hdn. 3,5,2–6,1). At the end of 195 C. sought sole rule and named himself Augustus: on his coins he also retains the name Sep(timius), which he probably first assumed in 193. Declared *hostis* in Dec. 195 (Cass. Dio 75,4.1ff. mentions a circus demonstration against the new civil war in Rome), he transferred with his three legions to Gallia and defeated the Severan commander Virius Lupus (Cass. Dio 75,6,2), but on 19 February 197 Severus beat C.'s troops at Lugdunum. He himself was killed while escaping (Cass. Dio 75,5–7; Hdn. 3,7). PIR² C 1186.

1 J.Hasebroek, Die Fälschung der Vita Nigri und Vita Albini, 1916   2 Birley, 147   3 P. Cintas, in: Rev. Afr. 91, 1947, 1ff.

RIC 4,1, 40–53; A. R. Birley, The African Emperor Septimius Severus, ²1988; Kienast, ²1996, 160–161.   a.b.

[II 2] **Fabius C. Agrippianus Celsinus.** Consular governor of Caria et Phrygia between 249 and 251 (AE 1991, 1508; 1509a; 1511; 1513; cf. PIR² C 1161/2); on kinship cf. [1].

[II 3] **C.C. Crispinus.** *Cos. ord.* in 113; identical to Crispinus, the younger son of Vettius Bolanus, *suff.* 66; his mother tried to poison him *c.* 93 (Stat. Silv. 5,2,75ff.).

He may have obtained his *nomen gentile* by adoption (PIR² C 1164) [2. v 470, 644].

[II 4] P.C. Laetus Macrinus. Senator, praetorian governor of Lusitania probably in 261 (AE 1993, 914).

[II 5] T.C. Eprius Marcellus. → Eprius.

[II 6] C.C. Licinus. Suffect consul in AD 4, interested in literature and friendly with Hyginus and Ovid; wrote a Roman history in at least 21 bks.; only a few fragments extant (HRR II 77f.) [3. 112f.]. PIR² C 1167.

[II 7] L.C. Macer. Legate of the *legio III Augusta* in Africa in 69. Shortly before Nero's death he broke away from him, but did not join Galba. He minted coins on which he called himself *pro pr(aetore) Africae*, using the *libertas*. He set up a further legion with the epithet *Macriana*, which was disbanded again by Galba. Calvia Crispinilla had challenged him to rebel (Tac. Hist. 1,73). Galba had him killed by the procurator Trebonius Garutianus (PIR² C 1170).

[II 8] C.C. Nummus. Senator, who died in Ephesus during his quaesture (CIL III 429 = I.Eph. III 654).

[II 9] C.C. Nummus. *Cos. suff.* in 114 [4. 34]. The polyonymus of CIL X 1468 and III 429 = I.Eph. III 654 can perhaps be identified with him; in that case son of C. [II 6] ([5. 38f.]).

[II 10] M.C. Pupienus Maximus. → Pupienus

[II 11] L. Acilius Strabo C. Nummus. Perhaps legate of the *legio III Augusta* in Africa in 116 or consular special legate (ILAlg I 2829. 2939 to 2989); in the former case related to C. [II 7], in the latter identical to him [6].

[II 12] C. Pompeianus. *Curator aedium sacrarum* in 244; probably identical to the consul of 241 [7. 262f.].

[II 13] Q.C. Rufinus. Legate of Numidia in 191 or 192. In 193 present in Rome. Executed by Septimius Severus in 197 because of his association with Clodius Albinus (HA Sev. 13,5; PIR² C 1182).

[II 14] T.C. Saturninus Fidus. Governor of Thrace not before 236, suffect consul; probably under Gordianus consular legate of Cappadocia (PIR² C 1185); on possible kinship with Clodius Pupienus [8. 49ff.].

[II 15] P.C. Thrasea Paetus. Came from Patavium; married to Arria minor, the daughter of Caecina [II 5], who had taken part in the conspiracy of Arruntius Scribonianus in 42. After the latter's death in 42 he assumed the cognomen Paetus. In 56 suffect consul, member of the *XVviri sacris faciundis*. His involvement in the Stoically influenced political faction soon made itself felt. He accused Cossutianus Capito in 57 of crimes of *repetundae*. In 59 he left the Senate, when it passed resolutions on the occasion of the murder of Agrippina (Tac. Ann. 14,12,1). In 62 he opposed the death penalty of the praetor Antistius and the Senate followed him, even though Nero did not agree (Ann. 14,48f.). Without speaking out against the Principate, Thrasea continually showed where the limits were drawn, even for the *princeps*. Eventually Nero excluded him from his entourage; for instance, Thrasea was not allowed to come with the other senators to offer congratulations to Nero on the birth of his daughter (Ann. 15,23). At this he withdrew from the Senate, even at times of important decisions like the deification of Poppaea (Ann. 16,21,2). Ultimately he was incriminated by Cossutianus Capito, who had regained his seat in the Senate, and Eprius Marcellus and condemned by the Senate, but he was free to choose the method of death; he died by slitting the arteries in his wrists (Ann. 16,21; 22; 24–29; 33–35). His daughter Fannia married Helvidius Priscus, who was exiled in 66 (Tac. Hist. 4,5–8). A memorial to Thrasea was written by Arulenus Rusticus (Tac. Agr. 2; Suet. Dom. 10,3). He was later regarded as the prototype of the philosophically motivated critic of tyrannical rulership (cf. e.g. M.Aur. 1,14,2; PIR² C 1187 [9. 176f.; 10]).

1 M.Corbier, in: EOS II 719   2 Syme, RP   3 Syme, History in Ovid, 1978   4 Degrassi, FC   5 Salomies, Nomenclature, 1992   6 B.E. Thomasson, Fasti Africani, 1996   7 A.Kolb, Bauverwaltung, 1993   8 W.Eck, in: ZPE 37, 1980   9 M.Griffin, Nero, 1984   10 V.Rudich, Political Dissidence under Nero, 1993.
W.E.

III. Writers and Orators

[III 1] C., Ser. (also Claudius), *c.* 120–60, knight and philologist, related by marriage to L. → Aelius Stilo, but was driven out for plagiarizing him. He left Rome and died in a state of infirmity. Attested for C. are an *index* of genuine Plautines and a *commentarius*; only glossaries are extant [1]. Identity with C. [I 6] Scriba [1. 96; 2. 70] is controversial. His ranking as a scholar is unclear (cf. the plagiarism): Cicero's high regard (Att. 1,20,7; 2,1,12; Fam. 9,16,4) applies equally to C.'s kinsman L. → Papirius Paetus; Sueton (Gramm. 3.1) praises C. too sweepingly. As a scientist in Rome he was definitely a 'man at the forefront'.

1 GFR 95–98   2 R.A. Kaster, C. Suetonius Tranquillus De grammaticis et rhetoribus 1995, 70–73. 78–80
AN.GL.

[III 2] C., Sex. Rhetor of the 1st cent. BC from Sicily, teacher of the triumvir Mark Antony, with whom he was popular for his eloquence and wit; known for his habit of declaiming in two languages (Lat. and Greek) (Suet. Gram. 29; Sen. Controv. 9,3,13f.). Cic. Phil. 2,8; 43; 101 comments derogatorily on him.

J.Brzoska, s.v. C. (13), RE 4, 66f.   CHR.KU.

[III 3] C. Sabinus. Rhetor of Augustan period who was able to declaim elaborately in both Greek and Latin on the same day. This eccentric practise brought him mockery and criticism from his orator colleagues → Haterius, → Maecenas and → Cassius [III 3] Severus (Sen. Controv. 9,3,13f.).
→ Declamationes

[III 4] C. Tuscus. Latin author, quoted by Lydus *De ostentis* 59–70 in a corrupt Greek version, of a factual poem on weather signs in the course of the year. C. is perhaps identical to the Augustan poet C. Tuscus mentioned in Gell. NA 5,20,2, perhaps, though, invented by → Iohannes Lydus.

EDITION: C.WACHSMUTH, Lydus, de ostentis, 1897, 117–158.
BIBLIOGRAPHY: G.WISSOWA, s.v. C. (61), RE 4, 104
C.W.

Cloelia

[1] Young woman who was hostage of the Etruscan king → Porsenna (508 BC). She escaped, swam across the Tiber (or rode across it on horseback) and reached Rome safely with a group of young girls; she had to be returned to the king but, in recognition of her bravery, he released her and a number of the hostages. After the peace treaty the Romans honoured her with a statue on horseback at the Velia on the Sacra Via (Liv. 2,13,6–11; Flor. Epit. 1,4,7). She remained one of the most widespread examples of female bravery (Boccaccio, De claris mulieribus).

J.GAGÉ, Les otages de Porsenna, in: Hommages à H. Le Bonniec, in: Latomus 201, 1988, 236–245. R.B.

[2] Sulla's third wife (Plut. Sulla 6,20f.). K.-L.E.

Cloelius Name of a Roman patrician clan (also Clou-lius, RRC 260, 332 and Cluilius) that was reputed to have moved to Rome (Liv. 1,30,2) after the destruction, by King Tullus Hostilius, of Alba Longa, of which a C.C. had sovereignty (Liv. 1,22,3f.). According to later tradition, the clan was descended from a companion of Aeneas (Fest. p. 48) and was accorded particular respect in the earliest Republic. The connection between this family and the bearers of this name in the later Republic is unclear.
[1] Commander of the Volscians in 443 BC, defeated at Ardea and paraded in triumph (Liv. 4,9,12).
[2] C., Sex. (The form of the name is disputed), notorious henchman (dux operarum) of the plebeian tribune P. Clodius [I 4] Pulcher, who most notably orchestrated street riots on the latter's behalf in 58 BC and later (destruction of Cicero's house, Cic. Cael. 78). After Clodius' murder in 52 he arranged the funeral service amidst a great uproar that led to the burning of the Curia (Cic. Mil. 33; 90). He was condemned and did not return from exile until 44 after being pardoned by Mark Antony.

H.BENNER, Die Politik des P. Clodius Pulcher, 1987, 156–158; C.DAMON, Sex. Cloelius, Scriba, in: HSPh 94, 1992, 227–250.

[3] C., Tullus. In 438 BC an emissary to the Veian king Lars Tolumnius, who killed him and his three colleagues (Liv. 4,17,2). A famous group of statues of the four emissaries stood on the rostra until the late Republican period (Cic. Phil 9,4–5; there as Cluvius).
[4] C. Siculus, P. Consular tribune in 378 (MRR 1, 107).
[5] C. Siculus, Q. Consul in 498 BC together with T. Larcius Flavus, whom he is said to have appointed as the first dictator (MRR 1,11f.).

[6] C. Siculus, Q. Censor in 378 BC (Liv. 6,31,2).
[7] C. Siculus, T. Consular tribune in 444 BC, started a colony in Ardea in 442 (Liv. 4,11,5–7). K.-L.E.

Clonas (Κλονᾶς; Klonâs). Poet and musician who is claimed to be from both Tegea and Thebes; possibly early 7th cent. BC, as he is classified between → Terpander and → Archilochus (Ps.-Plut. De musica 1133a). Heraclides Ponticus (fr. 157 WEHRLI = Ps.-Plut. ibid. 1131f–1132c, cf. Poll. 4,79) credits him with elegiac poems and hexameters as well as with having introduced nómoi for vocal music (αὐλῴδια/aulṓidia) accompanied on the aulós, and processional songs (προσόδια/prosódia).

M.L. WEST, Ancient Greek Music, 1992, 333–334.
E.BO.

Clonius (Κλονίος; Kloníos).
[1] commanded, with four other leaders, the Boeotian contingent at Troy (Hom. Il. 2,495); died in a sea battle at the hand of → Agenor [5] (ibid. 15,340).
[2] Aeneas [1] had with him two Clonii, who fell in battle against Turnus and Messapus respectively (Verg. Aen. 9,574; 10,749). One of Aeneas' companions with the name of Clonius is said to have founded the gens Cloelia (Paul. Fest. 48,16 L.). RE.N.

Clothing

A. GENERAL 1. RAW MATERIALS 2. SOCIO-CULTURAL SIGNIFICANCE 3. STORAGE AND CARE 4. ARCHAEOLOGICAL FINDS B. CULTURALLY SPECIFIC CLOTHING 1. MINOAN CRETE 2. PHOENICIA 3. GREECE 4. ROME

A. GENERAL
1. RAW MATERIALS
Attested in early monuments from the Minoan and Mycenaean period, hides and leather, as well as wool, sheepskins and goatskins, are amongst the oldest materials used for clothing. The use of → linen or flax to make garments developed thanks to the agency of the Phoenicians; Alexander [4] the Great's wars of conquest introduced → silk into Greece. The Romans used the same materials for clothing as the Greeks; → cotton came into use as well in the 2nd cent. BC; silk did not reach Italy until the time of → Augustus. The hides and fur from beavers, camels and hares came to be used as well. Clothing was traditionally produced in the home; myth and art portray domestic weaving activity by women, of whom → Penelope and → Arachne are amongst the best known (→ Textile art, → Weaving, craft of weaving); poems occasionally celebrate the skills of weavers (e.g. Anth. Pal. 6,136). Many finished garments were well known and commanded high prices (e.g. Ath. 12,541a). In Imperial Egypt domestic production of clothing for the Roman legions took on a manufacturing dimension.

2. SOCIO-CULTURAL SIGNIFICANCE

Clothing was included with → jewellery and household equipment in a bride's dowry, was also regarded as suitable for → gifts (e.g. Paus. 8,24,8) and as a burial gift ended up in the graves of the dead (e.g. Hdt. 5,92, [1]). For the Greeks and Romans, clean clothing, appropriate to one's station (cf. e.g. App. B Civ. 4,186, Dion. Hal. Ant. Rom. 47,10,3) and its careful manner of draping were part and parcel of one's external image and caused them to regard races and people with other styles of dressing as peculiar. Thus, the Macrones, Melanchlaeni (Hdt. 4,107), Orthocorybantii, Pterophori, Satarchae (Mela 2,10), Scythians, Thyni and even mythical or historical individuals, such as Abrote or Melissa (Ath. 13,589f), Pythermus (Hdt. 1,152) and → Alcibiades [3] appeared especially odd. Clothing plays an important part in some myths; thus, → Philomela, for example, embroiders her fate on a garment, for → Themisto the false colour of clothing leads to a tragic misunderstanding cf. the miracle tale in Prop. 4,11,53–54. If it was open to the Greeks to select coloured or monocoloured — usually white — clothing from their own wardrobe, according to their own individual taste, the Romans had to observe a strict dress code in public; only Roman citizens were permitted to wear the → toga. The width and colour (e.g. purple), of the edging provided information about the social standing of the wearer (→ Clavus; → Tunica; → Toga); much the same was also true of footwear (→ Calceus; → Shoes). The role of clothing in cults also comes under this heading — such as putting new clothing on a → cult image (e.g. that of Apollo of Amyclae, of Athena Pallas in Athens, Hera at Olympia), or in cult games, e.g. in the Ludi Capitolini.

3. STORAGE AND CARE

Clothing was kept in storage chests (→ Furniture), as evidenced first in Homer (Hom. Il. 16,220; 24,328 and *passim*) and then in later writers (e.g. Theoc. 15,33); in Greek art there are many well-known representations of women placing items of clothing into chests or taking them out of chests [2]. To preserve a pleasant smell in the clothing, apples (Aristoph. Vesp. 1057, cf. Ath. 3,84a), for example, were placed in the chests. To protect clothing against moths and other insects (e.g. Aristoph. Lys. 730), malabathrum (Plin. HN 23,93), for example, was used. Clothing was washed at home in a vat or in the sea or a river (Hom. Od. 6,85–94). Soapwort and potash (potassium carbonate K_2CO_3), for example, were used as cleaning agents, or the clothes were boiled with an extract from wood-ashes; in addition, the Romans used urine, from which cleaning ammonia was derived.

4. ARCHAEOLOGICAL FINDS

Because of its perishable material, parts of cloth and clothing have only occasionally — except in the Nile valley — been preserved [1]; they show rich decoration with purely ornamental or figurative representations that also appear on clothing on, for example, vase-paintings, wall frescoes or terracottas (→ Textile art).

B. CULTURALLY SPECIFIC CLOTHING

1. MINOAN CRETE

Details of clothing in Minoan Crete derive mainly from depictions of cultural life; they show women wearing a tightly fitting jacket that left the breast exposed and had a high, turned-up collar, with a wide, bell-shaped skirt that extended to the ground and was held in place with a → belt. In the Middle Minoan Period the jacket loses its turned-up collar, and an arch-shaped apron covers the lower body, front and rear; a new element is the flounce-skirt made from rectangular strips of equal length, probably in different colours, that were sewn together with a tapering effect. The jacket is gathered under the breast with ties and in the Late Period displays short sleeves. The system of belting is varied, bulky in places or consisting of a straight, broad band. An unbelted one-piece garment with sleeves may have been worn by both men and women. Women left their heads uncovered but priestesses wore a tall, peaked covering. Men wore an apron that was put on in various styles (a long rectangle, at an angle and arch-shaped). A further characteristic of the apron is the so-called modesty pouch. In many cases the apron was held up by means of braces worn over the shoulders. Short trousers [1] for men are also attested. In addition there is a cloak-like garment that was wrapped around the body and tucked underneath the arms. In cult scenes a feather crown or a flat cap appears as head covering. In general, footwear is absent but shoes, or (high) boots, can be found on warriors.

2. PHOENICIA

Phoenician clothing — made from linen, flax or wool and frequently brightly coloured — came under foreign influence in the course of history. The early period was marked in particular by Egyptian patterns of dress. These include apron outfits for men and ankle-length or half-long clothes for women. We know that there were also cloaks with a → belt. The preferred form of ornamentation was geometric patterns, with figurative designs added in the 1st millennium BC. During the Persian period the Egyptian elements disappeared and closely-fitting, tunic-style clothes with sleeves became fashionable. After the Greek occupation of Phoenicia, Phoenician clothing was quickly Hellenized, though it seems that at least the male population of Carthage remained unaffected (cf. Plaut. Poen. 975f., 1008).

3. GREECE

On the Greek mainland Minoan clothing was adopted initially, although women's clothing evidently dispensed with the apron. In addition, men wore a one-piece garment that either reached to the ground or only covered the torso. Mentioned very early in literary sources (Hom. Il. 2,42, 262, 416 and *passim*), the → chiton, was the main garment for men, extending either only just below the groin or down to the knees; it was adopted by women in its longer form in the first half of the 6th cent. BC. The *chiton* consisted of two lengths of material that were sewn together down their long sides, creating a tube of material that the wearer

Clothing (Greek)

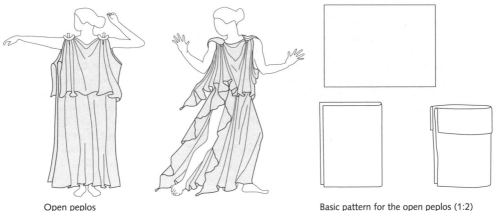

Open peplos

Basic pattern for the open peplos (1:2)

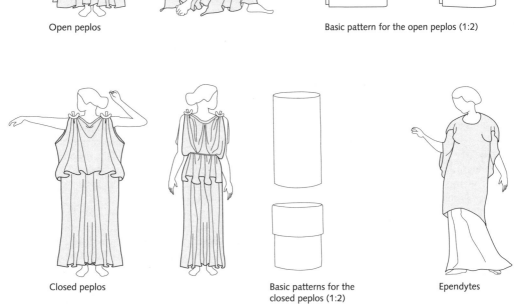

Closed peplos

Basic patterns for the closed peplos (1:2)

Ependytes

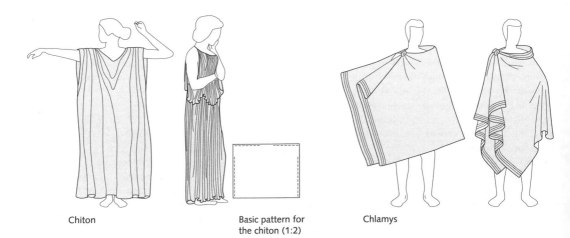

Chiton

Basic pattern for the chiton (1:2)

Chlamys

could slip into. Over the *chiton* women often wore the→ *peplos*, a long garment fastened at the shoulders, with extra length so that it had to be put on in such a way that one side was gathered in at the belt. The *pharos*, worn predominantly by princes, served as a cloak, as did the → *chlaina*, and later the *himation* (→ *Pallium*). A scarf, the → *epiblema*, appears principally on monuments of the 7th and 6th cents. BC as a supplementary item of clothing. In the high and late archaic period women wore a little cloak worn at an angle (Greek name probably *diploïdion*), that was taken under the left shoulder and tied on the right shoulder and upper arm, so that it dropped over the body in a radial bundle of folds. In the late archaic period women dispensed with the *peplos* and wore the long *chiton*; men at that time preferred the short *chiton*.

At the time of the Persian Wars the *peplos* came back into fashion amongst women; the *chiton* then became an undergarment, only to become the preferred item of women's clothing again at the beginning of the 4th cent. BC. The *ependytes* — a garment reaching down to the knees — also came into fashion in the 5th cent. BC; men and women used to wear it for everyday use as well as for festive occasions; another garment for festive events was the *xystis* (→ Festival dress). As well as these, other garments are known to us from literature (but hard to discern in art), such as garments from Cos (→ *Coae vestes*), Amorgos or Tarentum, Milesian cloaks etc. All of them were distinguished by the quality of the material, their colour and transparency and were highly regarded as luxury items. As male headware, the broad-brimmed → *petasos*, a hat for travellers, and the cap-like → *pilos* of tradesmen, herdsmen and simple folk, are all attested. Women covered their heads with a handkerchief, the → *kredemnon*, or with the *himation* pulled up; in the late Classical-early Hellenistic period the *tholia*, a conical hat with brim, came into fashion.

4. ROME

In the early period all Roman citizens of both sexes, as well as Roman allies admitted into the *formula togatorum*, wore as an overgarment the woollen → *toga*, which was of Central Italian-Etruscan origins and corresponded to the Greek himation The→ *stola* was introduced no later than the Augustan age as socially appropriate clothing for a married woman. The → *tunica*, with its front and back sections sewn together and with short sleeves (cf. → Cethegus), served as undergarment. Outside the home women wore two *tunicae* on top of each other (→ Dalmatica). Underclothes are mentioned only occasionally, such as e.g. the *subucula* (Varro, Ling. 5,131; 9,46) or the *indusium* (Plaut. Epid. 231, cf. Varro, Ling. 5,131); women would often wear both items (→ Subligaculum); and then there is the *campestre*, an apron that *i.a.* Roman youths wore in physical exercise on the Field of Mars, and the *cinctus* as well, which was worn under the toga in summer instead of the *tunica*. By way of cloaks, the → *paenula* was put on over the tunica and the → *lacerna* over the toga. Other cloaks were the → *pallium* for men, and the *palla* for women; the *alicula* (a shoulder cloak of late antiquity) should also be mentioned.

Some items of clothing were adopted from the Roman provinces, such as, for example, the *cucullus*, a hooded cloak; the *birrus*, a cloak similar to the *lacerna* but with a hood; the *braccae*, Gallic and Dacian trousers that reached down to the knees or to the ankles and were predominantly used as military clothing, and the *caracallus*, a cloak probably of Gallic origin, to which the Roman emperor M. Aurelius Antoninus (AD 211–217) owed his nickname → Caracalla because of his fondness for it. Other items of military clothing are for example the → *paludamentum*, the officers' cloak, and the → *sagum*, the soldiers' cloak. While these items of clothing can be determined from monuments of the Roman period, a more precise definition of some others is either difficult (e.g. → *Abolla*) or impossible (e.g. *trechedipnum*, Juv. 3,67).

→ Anaxyrides; → Bathing costume; → Barbaron hyphasmata; → Formal and festive costumes; → Fasciae; → Fimbriae; → Kausia, Kekryphalos; → Kemos; → Kosymbe; → Laena; → Manicae; → Mantellum; → Mastruca; → Mitra; → Needle; → Nimbus; → Paragaudes; → Periskelis; → Perizoma; → Pilleus; → Polus; → Recta; → Sabanum; → Saccus; → Sandals; → Soccus; → Strophium; → Taenia; → Tarantinon / -um; → Tiara; → Trabea; → Mourning dress; → Tribon; → Tunica; → Napkins; → Zeira; CLOTHING

1 H. BLOESCH, B. MÜHLETALER, in: AK 10, 1967, 130–132   2 E. BRÜMMER, Griech. Truhenbehälter, in: JDAI 100, 1985, 94–98.

A. ALFÖLDI, Insignien und Tracht der röm. Kaiser, in: MDAI(R) 50, 1935, 3–171; M. BIEBER, Charakter und Unterschiede der griech. und röm. Kleidung, in: AA 1973, 425–447; F. BLAKOLMER, Ikonographische Beobachtungen zu Textilkunst und Wandmalerei in der brz. Ägäis, in: JÖAI 63, 1994, Beibl. 1–28; A. BÖHME, Tracht- und Bestattungssitten in den german. Prov. und der Belgica, in: ANRW II 12.3, 423–455; L. BONFANTE, Roman Costumes. A Glossary and Some Etruscan Derivations, in: ANRW I 4, 584–614; Id., Etruscan Dress, 1975; L. CASSON, Greek and Roman Clothing, in: Glotta 61, 1983, 193–207; ST. DROUGOU, in: FS M. Andronikos, 1987, 303–316; D. GERZIGER, Eine Decke aus dem Grab der 'Sieben Brüder', in: AK 18, 1975, 51–55; H. R. GÖTTE, Stud. zu röm. Togadarstellungen, 1990 (Rev.: H. WREDE, in: Gnomon 67, 1995, 541–550); D. HARDEN, The Phoenicians, 1962, 144f.; F. KOLB, K.-Stücke in der Historia Augusta, in: Bonner Historia-Augusta-Kolloquium 1972/74, 1976, 153–171; L. KONTORLI-PAPADOPOULOU, Costumes, in: Aegean Frescoes of Religious Characters (Stud. in Mediterranean Archaeology 117), 1996, 86–93; G. LOSFELD, Essai sur le Costume Grec, 1991; A.-M. MAES, L'habillement masculin à Carthage à l'epoque des guerres punique (Studia Phoenicia 10), 1989, 15–24; SP. MARINATOS, K. (ArchHom A), 1967; Id., Kreta, Thera und das myk. Hellas, 1976, pl. 36.; M. C. MILLER, The Ependytes in Classical Athens, in: Hesperia 58, 1989, 313–338; A. PEKRIDOU-GORECKI, Mode im ant. Griechenland. Textile Fertigung und K., 1989 (Rev.: CHR. SCHNURR, in: Gnomon 64, 1992, 53–56); D. RÖSSLER, Gab es Modetendenzen in der griech. Tracht am E. des 5.

Clothing (Roman)

Tunica (woman's)

Tunica (man's)

Palla

Toga

Toga (back view)

Lacerna

Pallium

Laena

Cucullus

und im 4. Jh.v. u.Z.?, in: E. CH. WELSKOPF (ed.), Hellen. Poleis 3, 1974, 1539–1569; U. SCHARF, Straßen-K. der röm. Frau, 1994; S. SCHATEN, Drei Textilfrg. mit geom. Flechtbandornamenten in Sternform, in: Bull. de la Soc. d'Arch. copte 34, 1995, 71–75; B.-J. SCHOLZ, Unt. zur Tracht der röm. Matrona, 1992; A. STAUFFER, Textilien aus Ägypten aus der Slg. Bouvier. Spätant., koptische und frühislamische Gewebe. Exhibition Fribourg 1991/2, 1991; I. VOKOTOPOULOU, Führer durch das Arch. Mus. Theben, 1995, 88, 175.   R.H.

Clover (λωτός/lōtós, τρίφυλλον/tríphyllon, Lat. lotus, trifolium). Sometimes growing wild, sometimes cultivated, this important forage crop (in Columella 8,14,2 used also as food for tame geese) from the Leguminosae family is mentioned as early as Hom. Il. 2,776; 14,348; 21,351 and Hom. Od. 4,603. References to this lōtós in Theophr. Hist. pl. 7,8,3 and 7,13,5 (or lotus Verg. G. 2,84; Columella 2,2,20, as an indicator of good soil for growing cereals) as also Dioscorides 4,110 WELLMANN = 4,109 BERENDES are not sufficiently precise for a classification against the varieties that are known today. According to Plin. HN 18,144, lucerne (πόα Μηδική, Lat. medica, Medicago sativa L.), which is first mentioned by Aristoph. Equ. 606 as horse fodder, had been introduced from Media during the Persian Wars and since Varro, Rust. 1,43 was hailed (i.a. by Verg. G. 1,215; Columella 2,10,24 and Pall. Agric. 5,1) as being high-yielding and nutritious. The similar, arboreous snail clover (κύτισος, Lat. cytisus and cytisum, Medicago arborea L.) is accurately described by Aristot. Hist. an. 3,21,522b 27f. and Theophr. Hist. pl. 4,16,5; Theophr. Caus. pl. 5,15,4; Varro, Rust. 2,1,17 and 2,2,19; Verg. Ecl. 1,78 and G. 2,431; Plin. HN 13,130–134; Dioscorides 4,112 WELLMANN = 4,111 BERENDES as well as Columella 2,10,24 and 5,12 (on using and sowing it). The green or dried leaves were regarded as very good fodder. The crushed root of the mountain clover (montanum trifolium) was thought according to Columella 6,17,2f. = Pall. Agric. (= De veterinaria medicina) 14,18,2 to help against snakebite, if placed on the wound, as also its juice or sap mixed with wine. The frequently mentioned → fenugreek (τῆλις, βούκερως, αἰγόκερως, Lat. faenum Graecum, silicia or siliqua, Trigonella foenum graecum; e.g. Columella 2,7,1; Pall. Agric. 10,8) served as food for sheep but was also enjoyed by humans, both as food and as spice for wine (e.g. Columella 12,20,2 and 12,28,1).

F. ORTH, s.v. K., RE 11,585–591; V. HEHN, Kulturpflanzen und Haustiere (ed. O. SCHRADER), ⁸1911, reprinted 1963, 412–415.   C.HÜ.

Cloves The dried, peppercorn-like flower buds of Syzygium aromaticum (earlier known as Caryophyllus aromaticus L.) reached Rome from the Moluccas by way of India and Greece as garyophyllon (Plin. HN 12,7). With doctors of late antiquity such as Aetius Amidenus, i.a., the term karyóphyllon (Arab. karanful, It. garofalo

or garofano), probably derived from the Old Indo-Aryan katuphalam ('acrid fruit'), was quickly extended to carnations, especially Dianthus caryophyllus L. In the Middle Ages the gariophili were prescribed in the pharmaceutical book of Salerno Circa instans [1. 56f.] and i.a. in Thomas of Cantimpré 11,20 [2. 337] for clearing the head, as a scent, and for treating diarrhoea.
→ Spices

1 H. WÖLFEL (ed.), Das Arzneidrogenbuch Circa instans, diss. Berlin 1939   2 H. BOESE (ed.), Thomas Cantimpratensis, Liber de natura rerum, 1973.   C.HÜ.

Clovis I (Chlodovechus) Merovingian king; born AD 466, died 27 November 511. Son and successor (481 or 482) of Childeric, one of the Frankish kings in the region around Tournai; brother-in-law of Theoderic the Great; in 486 or 487 he defeated → Syagrius, the Roman governor in Gaul, and reached the Loire, the border with the West Goths. Between 492 and 494 he married the catholic Burgundian Chlothilde, and, after defeating the Alemanni at Zülpich (496 or 497), at Christmas 497 (498?, 499?) had himself baptized a catholic, unlike most Germanic kings, who were Arians. The baptism, said by → Gregorius of Tours, borrowing on the Constantine theme, to hark back to a promise made before the battle with the Alemanni, facilitated the integration of the Gallo-Romans into the growing empire of the Franks. Not only did the Roman civitates with their legal traditions (allegatio, insinuatio in the gesta municipalia) survive, but Gallo-Roman notables can even be found at the court of the king and in his entourage, as is attested by the early Merovingian royal charters; as charters of witness, these documents are, of course, in the Germanic legal tradition, but they contain Latin as well as Germanic names. The language and script of the charters show significant Roman influence. On the model of the imperial decree and the Roman private charter, the charter of witness develops into the dispositive charter, with a fixed format; it was in Gaul that Latin had been longest in daily use, and as 'Merovingian Latin' it becomes an important source as regards linguistic history; the writings that emerge from the Merovingian scriptoria and the royal chancellery derive from the later Roman cursive. The settlement with the Romans also facilitated a good relationship with the Roman Empire in the east, as is made clear by Emperor → Anastasius' granting of the honorary consulship in 508 in Tours. C.'s strengthening position is shown in 507 by his subjugation of the → West Goths under → Alaric, and of other, more minor Frankish kings in northern Gaul and Rheno-Franconia (509, 511). The strength of his rule over the whole of Gaul, uniting Romans and Gauls, is expressed in the removal of the royal residence to Paris (after 508), the holding of an imperial council in Orleans (511), the construction of a mausoleum in Paris and the recording of Frankish common law in the Lex Salica (508–511).

E. Ewig, Die Merowinger und das Frankenreich, 1988; R. Kaiser, Das röm. Erbe und das Merowingerreich, 1993; W. v.d. Steinen, Chlodwigs Übergang zum Christentum, in: MIÖG suppl. vol. 12, 1932 (ND 1963); J. M. Wallace-Hadrill, The Long-Haired Kings and Other Studies in Frankish History, 1982; E. Zöllner, Gesch. der Franken, 1970.   G.SP.

Cluentius Italian family name, especially in evidence in the 1st cent. BC (ThlL, Onom. 2, 505f.).
[1] C., L. Italic leader in the Social War, was defeated by Sulla in the second attempt to raise the siege of Pompeii and killed in 89 BC (App. B Civ. 1,218–221).
[2] C. Habitus, A. Roman knight from Larinum in Apulia, known from Cicero's oration *Pro Cluentio* in 66 BC. After the death of his homonymous father in 88 his mother Sassia married Statius Abbius Oppianicus. C. suspected his stepfather of attempting to murder him with the help of C. Fabricius and his freedman Scamander, and secured the conviction of all three of them in 74 (Cluent. 43–61). The trial of Oppianicus developed into an internal political scandal in Rome because both sides had obviously bribed senatorial jurors and as a result 70 prominent people involved were prosecuted by the censors (Cic. Verr. 1,38–40; Caecin. 28f. et al.; MRR 2,126) and C. received a censorial reprimand (Cluent. 117ff.). Oppianicus died in 72 in mysterious circumstances for which Sassia held her son C. responsible. In 66, through T. Accius, C. was charged by Statius Abbius Oppianicus, his younger stepbrother, of patricide, under the *lex Cornelia de veneficiis et sicariis,* but was successfully defended by Cicero, who sought in particular to refute the accusation of juror bribery in 74.

C. J. Classen, Recht — Rhetorik — Politik, 1985, 15–119; J.-M. David, Le patronat judiciaire au dernier siècle de la république romaine, 1992, 740, 784f., 852.   K.-L.E.

Clunia The important ruins of C. lie *c.* 40 km northwest of Uxama Argaela (now Osma near Coruña del Conde; CIL II p. 382). On Augustan coins the name is spelled Clounioq, later C. [2. 111ff.) and is probably Celtic ([1. 131]; a different view in [3. 1048]). C. played a part in the revolt by → Sertorius (75 BC: Liv. Per. 92; 72 BC: Exsuperantius 8; Flor. 2,10,9), in that of 55 BC (Cass. Dio 39,54) and that of → Galba in AD 68 (Suet. Galba 9,2; Plut. Galba 6,4). The assumption that C. then received the nickname Sulpicia derives only from coin evidence. [4. 449]. Equally uncertain is its patronage by Galba, as in CIL II 2779. C. was a → *municipium* (cf. the magistrates on coins and inscriptions; see also Plin. HN 3,18; 26f.), and a → *colonia* by at least the time of Hadrian (CIL II 2780). The population of C. belonged to the → Arevaci (Plin. HN 3,27; Ptol. 2,6,55). It was deserted during the Middle Ages [1. 131].

1 A. Schulten, Numantia 1, 1914   2 A. Vives, La Moneda Hispánica 4, 1924   3 Holder 1   4 A. Heiss,

Description générale des monnaies antiques d'Espagne, 1870.

A. Schulten, Fontes Hispaniae Antiquae, 1925ff., 4, 219–243; 5, 16; 8, 16; 19; 23; Tovar 3, 352f.   P.B.

Clupea ('Ασπίς; *Aspís*). Possibly pre-Phoenician town (Procop. Vand. 2,10,24) of the later Africa proconsularis, north-east of the peninsula Bon, today's Kélibia (Sources: Mela 1,34; Plin. HN 5,24; Ptol. 4,3,7f.; It. Ant. 57,6; Tab. Peut. 6,2; Stadiasmus Maris Magni 117 [GGM 1, 470]). Str. 17,3,16, Sil. Pun. 3,243f. and App. Lib. 519 call C. Aspis. Notwithstanding Ptol. 4,3,7f., C. and Aspis were not two different towns (cf. Sol. 27,8). Inscriptions: CIL VIII 1, 982–986; X 1, 6104; AE 1991, 1646–1658.

G. Camps, M. Fantar, s.v. Aspis, EB, 977–980; S. Lancel, E. Lipiński, s.v. Kélibia, DCPP, 245.   W.HU.

Clusinius
[1] C. Fibulus. was in 10 BC the centre of a famous inheritance trial involving the estate of Urbinia, who C.'s lawyer, T. → Labienus, claimed had been his mother, while the lawyer representing the other heirs, C. → Asinius [I 4] Pollio, argued that C. had been a slave of someone called Sosipater (Quint. Inst. 7,2,4f.; 26; Tac. Dial. 38,2; Charisius, Gramm. p. 98,3ff.B. = 77,15ff. K.).
[2] C. Gallus. Friend of Pliny the Younger, who addressed Epist. [see author's works] 4,17 to him (cf. the comm. of Sherwin-White *ad loc.*).

Syme, RP 2, 714.   D.K.

Clusium (earlier name *Camars*), Etruscan city on a hill over the Val di Chiana, now Chiusi (Liv. 10,25,11), Etruscan *Clevsins*. The reference in Verg. Aen. 10,655 *Clusinis advectus... oris* was puzzling even for historians in antiquity. The first settlement was characterized by widely scattered (κατὰ κώμας) habitats (cf. the spreading of necropoleis between the 9th and 6th cents.). C. enjoyed a heyday under → Porsenna, when the dispersed settlements were abandoned and a city centre developed. Framework of the colony Padania. Noteworthy are the buildings erected between the end of the 7th and the end of the 6th cents. as in Poggio Civitate (Murlo/Siena), modelled on a Greek-Oriental 'palazzo'. Also dating from the 6th cent. are rich graves in Poggio and Gaiella, underneath artistically constructed grave mounds, attributed to Porsenna because of the beauty of their ornamentation and large number of tomb chambers (Plin. HN 36,19,91). As early as the end of the 6th cent. luxury goods (like the François Vase) and artistic creations were being imported from Vulci and Tarquinia. If Porsenna's era was marked by the centralization of city life, in the following period the outskirts of the city were upgraded and populated (cf. also Liv. 5,36,3 for the early 4th cent. BC). From 87 BC a Roman *municipium*, *tribus Arnensis* (Plin. HN 3,52). As late as AD 540 C. was a fortified city (Procop. Goth. 2,11).

> G. CAMPOREALE, Irradiazione della cultura chiusiana arcaica, Aspetti e problemi dell'Etruria interna, 1974, 99–130; M. CRISTOFANI, Considerazioni su Pozzo Civitate (Murlo, Siena), Prospettiva 1, 1975, 9ff.
>
> M. CRISTOFANI, s.v. C., BTCGI, 1987, 283ff.   M.CA.

Clutorius Priscus Roman knight, author of a poem on the death of Germanicus, for which he was rewarded with money. When Drusus minor, Tiberius' son, was ill and C. boasted of having prepared a poem to mark his death also, the emperor had him executed in AD 21 (Tac. Ann. 3,49–51; Cass. Dio 57,20,3).

> H. BARDON, La littérature latine inconnue, 2, 1956, 74f.
>   D.K.

Cluviae Main centre of the → Carricini in Samnium, mentioned for events in 311 BC (Liv. 9,31,2f.); *municipium* since the 1st cent. BC, *tribus Arnensis*; birthplace of Helvidius Priscus (Tac. Hist. 4,5). Archaeological monuments: remains on the Piano Laroma at Aventino near Cásoli (Chieti); *opus incertum* and *reticulatum*; theatre in *opus reticulatum* with audience seating adjoining the city walls; thermal springs; *domus suburbana* with mosaics.

> A. LA REGINA, C. e il territorio Carecino, in: RAL 22, 1967, 87–99; A. PELLEGRINO, Il Sannio Carricino dall'età sannitica alla romanizzazione, in: ArchCl 36, 1984, 157–197.   G.U.

Cluvia Pacula (Facula in Val. Max. 5,2,1). Prostitute from Capua; by a decision of the Senate she had her property and freedom returned to her after 210 BC, for having secretly supplied food to Roman prisoners in the Second Punic War (Liv. 26,33,8; 34,1).   ME.STR.

Cluvius Italic family name (SCHULZE, 483), attested in Campania from the 3rd cent., in Rome for plebeians from the 2nd cent.
I. REPUBLICAN PERIOD   II. IMPERIAL PERIOD

I. REPUBLICAN PERIOD
[I 1] **C., C.** Praetor and probably proconsul of Macedonia or Asia around 104 BC (MRR 1,560).
[I 2] **C. (Clovius), C.** Mint master in 45 BC (RRC 476) and at the same time Caesar's prefect, probably responsible for land allotments in Gallia Cisalpina (Cic. Fam. 13,7; MRR 2,313); further identification, especially with the C.C. mentioned in the so-called → *laudatio Turiae*, is uncertain (MRR 3, 59).

> D. FLACH, Die sog. Laudatio Turiae, 1991.

[I 3] **C., Sp.** Praetor in 172 BC (Sardinia).
[I 4] **C. Saxula, C.** Praetor in 178 (?), Praetor peregrinus in 173 BC (MRR 1, 395, 408).   K.-L.E.

II. IMPERIAL PERIOD
[II 1] **P.C. Maximus Paullinus.** Senator whose temple grave was found near Monte Porzio in Latium. After a long praetorian career, appointed *cos. suff.* legate of Moesia superior and proconsul of Asia; had probably died before then (AE 1940, 99) [1. 105; 2. 146].
[II 2] **P.C.Maximus Paullinus.** Son of no. 1, *cos. suff.* 152 (AE 1971, 183; 1940, 99).
[II 3] **P.C.Rufus.** (Praenomen in an unpublished inscription from Rome, report I of Stefano Manzella). *Cos. suff.* before 65; he accompanied Nero on his journey to Achaea. Appointed legate of Hisp. Tarraconensis, probably by Galba; joined Otho. Accused of sedition before Vitellius, but accepted among the *comites* without having Tarraconensis taken from him. Took part in the conversations of Vitellius with Flavius Sabinus in December 69 (PIR² C 1206). Wrote a historical work used by Tacitus [3. 178f., 289–294].

> 1 W. ECK, RE Suppl. 14   2 ALFÖLDY, Konsulat   3 SYME, Tacitus.   W.E.

Clymene (Κλυμένη; *Klyménē*, Clymene).
[1] → Oceanid, wife of → Iapetus, who by her fathered → Atlas [2], → Prometheus and Epimetheus (Hes. Theog. 351; 507ff.; Hyg. Fab. praef. 11,31). In Euripides (Phaethon 1ff.; 45ff. DIGGLE; cf. also Ov. Met. 1,750ff.; Hyg. Fab. 152a; 154; 156) she is the mother of → Phaethon.
[2] → Nereid (Hom. Il. 18,47; Hyg. Fab. praef. 8), who according to Pausanias (2,18,1) had with → Dictys [1] an altar in Athens as saviour of Perseus. According to Virgil (Georg. 4,345) she was one of Cyrene's companions.
[3] Nymph, wife of Parthenopaeus (Hyg. Fab. 71).
[4] Daughter of → Minyas and Euryale, by Cephalus or Phylacus mother of Iphiclus (Hyg. Fab. 14; Paus. 10,29,6); also named as the mother of → Alcimede and → Atalante (Apollod. 3,105).
[5] Daughter of Catreus, wife of → Nauplius, mother of → Oeax and → Palamedes (Apollod. 2,23).
[6] Maidservant to → Helena [1] in Troy (Hom. Il. 3,144), according to Stesichorus (fr. 197 PMG) a Trojan prisoner.

> A. KOSSATZ-DEISSMANN, s.v. K. (1)–(4), LIMC 6.1, 68–70; K. LATTE, s.v. K. (1)–(4), (8), RE 11, 878–880.   R.HA.

Clymenus (Κλύμενος; *Klýmenos*, 'the famous').
[1] Epithet of → Hades-Pluto, in the Argive → Hermion(e). The Demeter temple there is said to have been erected by C. and his sister Chthonia: When → Demeter arrives in Argolis, she is ignored by their father Phoroneus, and Chthonia disapproves of her father's behaviour. As punishment the father is burned, together with the house, but she is brought to Hermione to erect a sanctuary to Demeter. Thus, C. (Ov. Fast. 6,757) and Chthonia became identified with the two gods, Persephone being regarded as C.'s wife (Paus. 2,35,4–11; Ath. 14,624e).   RA.MI.

[2] Son of Helios and husband of the Oceanid Merope, from whose union → Phaethon is born (Hyg. Fab. 154; reversal of the parents' gender contrary to tradition: → Clymene [1]).

[3] Cretan from Cydonia, descended from Ideaen Hercules, son of Cardis. He is said to have instituted games in Olympia 50 years after the Deucalian flood and set up an altar to the → Curetes and Hercules (Paus. 5,8,1). The ash altar of Hera (Paus. 5,14,8), as well as the Athena temple in → Phrixa (Paus. 6,21,6), are attributed to him.

[4] King of Orchomenus, son of Presbon or Orchomenus (Steph. Byz. s.v. Ἀσπληδών), husband of → Budeia, father of → Erginus. C. is murdered by the Thebans at a Poseidon festival in → Onchestus, whereupon his son avenges him (Paus. 9,37,1–4; Apollod. 2,67). In Pind. (Ol. 4,19) both father and son are Argonauts (→ Argonautae).

[5] Aetolian, son of → Oeneus and → Althaea [1] (Apollod. 1, 64; Antoninus Liberalis 2).

[6] Arcadian, son of Teleus (Parthenius 13) or Schoeneus (Hyg. Fab. 206). C. had several children by Epicaste, including → Harpalyce [2], whom he violated.

RA.MI.

Clyster see → Enema

Clytaemnestra (Κλυταμήστρα; *Klytaiméstra*, earlier form of the name Klytaimnestra/Κλυταμνήστρα; Lat. Clytaem(n)estra). Daughter of → Tyndareus and → Leda, sister of → Helena [1] and the → Dioscuri, wife of → Agamemnon, who killed her first husband → Tantalus, son of → Thyestes. She had several children by Agamemnon: → Chrysothemis [2], → Laodice [I 2] or → Electra [4], → Iphianassa [2] or → Iphigenia and → Orestes. Labouring under Aphrodite's curse of infidelity (Hes. fr. 176; Stesich. fr. 223 PMG) and after resisting for some time (Hom. Od. 3,266ff.), she lets herself be seduced by Aegisthus during the Greek campaign against Troy and has → Erigone [2] by him. When Agamemnon returns from Troy, he and his female prisoner of war → Cassandra whom he brought back with him are murdered by them, with accounts differing as to C.'s role and the weapons (sword, axe, net, veil) used (Hom. Od. 11,409ff.; Aesch. Ag. 1262; 1382; Aesch. Cho. 997f., Soph. El. 99, Eur. El. 154ff., Sen. Ag. 867ff.). She lives with Aegisthus in Mycenae (or Argos or Amyclae) and is murdered by Orestes, who was taken out of the country as a child and now returns to avenge his father (Hes. fr. 23a; Stesich. fr. 217; 219 PMG, Pind. Pyth. 11,37f.). The matricide motif in particular is developed by the tragedians (Aesch. Cho.; Soph. El.; Eur. El.; Sen. Ag.; Hyg. Fab. 117, 119). While Aeschylus depicts her as a far-sighted and calculating perpetrator, in Sophocles her coolness towards Electra and her joy at the reported death of Orestes, together with her existential insecurity following her husband's murder, are all highlighted. Euripides, on the other hand, leaves her ambivalent to events and bases her

motivation for murdering Agamemnon on his murder of her first husband and on his sacrificing of Iphigenia. Graves of C. and Aegisthus were shown outside Mycenae (Paus. 2,16,7). For later representations in art and literature see [1].

1 HUNGER, Mythologie, 15f., 20.

R. AÉLION, Euripide, héritier d'Eschyle, 1983, 2, 265–323; E. BETHE, s.v. K., RE 11, 890–893; S. MACEWEN, Views of Clytemnestra, Ancient and Modern, 1990; Y. MORIZOT, s.v. K., LIMC 6.1, 72–73.

FIG.: Id., s.v. K., LIMC 6.2, 35–38.   R.HA.

Clytia, Clytie (Κλυτία, Κλυτίη; *Klytía, Klytíē*, Lat. Clytia).

[1] Daughter of Oceanus and Tethys (Hes. Theog. 352).

[2] Daughter of → Pandareus from Crete, represented according to Pausanias (10,30,1f.) in the Cnidic → lesche in Delphi.

[3] Beloved of Helios (possibly identical to [1]), whom the latter abandons for → Leucothoe. The jealous C. betrays Leucothoe to her father, who has her buried alive. C. herself dies from sorrow and is transformed into a flower called heliotrope (Ov. Met. 4,206–270).

H. v. GEISAU, s.v. K., RE 11, 893f.   K.WA.

Clyti(a)dae (Κλυτιάδαι, Κλυτίδαι; *Klytiádai, Klytídai*). Family, which together with the Iamidae (→ Iamus) provided the seers in Olympia; through → Clytius [2], grandson of Amphiaraus, who is in turn the great-grandson of Melampus, the C. can be traced back to two of the central seers in Greek myth (Paus. 6,17,6). In the pre-Imperial period only Theogonus and his son Eperastus are known, by means of a statue in Olympia (Paus. loc. cit.).   F.G.

Clytius (Κλυτίος, Κλύτιος; *Klytíos, Klýtios*).

[1] Giant, who was killed either by Hecate with flaming torches or by Hephaestus with red-hot irons (Apollod. 1,37).

[2] Son of Alcmaeon and → Arsinoe [I 3]; grandson of Amphiaraus (Apollod. 3,87; Paus. 6,17,6). The soothsaying family of the → Clyti(a)dae in Elis can be traced back to C. (Cic. Div. 1,91).

[3] Argonaut, son of Eurytus of Oechalia (Apoll. Rhod. 1,86; 2,1043). C. was killed by Hercules in the conquest of Oechalia (Diod. Sic. 4,37).

[4] Son of Laomedon, brother of Priam, husband of Laothoe, father of Caletor (Hom. Il. 15,419; Apollod. 3,146; Apul., De deo Socratis 18).   AL.FR.

Clytus (Κλύτος; *Klýtos*) of Miletus, pupil of Aristotle [6] and author of *Perí Milétou* in at least two bks, quoted only by Athenaeus (12,540c; 14,655c). Perhaps used by Aristotle in the *Milēsíōn politeía*. FGrH 490 with comm.   K.MEI.

Cn. Abbreviation of the uncommon Lat. Praenomen *Gnaeus* (Old Lat. *Gnaivos*, Oscan *Gnaivs*, Etruscan *cneve*), from *(g)naevus*, 'birthmark', also abbreviated as *Gn.*

WALDE/HOFMANN, 1, 613; SALOMIES, 29f.   K.-L.E.

Cnacion (Κναχιών; *Knakión*). Mentioned only in the 'Great Rhetra' (Plut. Lycurgus 6,4, Pelopidas 17,6; → Sparta). Place name in Sparta, later equated to the river Oenus, today's Kelephina (Plut. loc. cit.; Lycoph. 550); not identifiable.   Y.L.

Cnemis (Κνημίς; *Knēmís*). Mountain in → Locris; together with Chlomon, the highest peak (938 m) in the chain that with its foothills forms a mosaic of valleys and passes connecting the narrow, east Locrian coastal band with the hinterland; in the south the C. reaches the lower Cephissus valley and the Copais plain. The C. represents the natural boundary between Locris Hypocnemidia and Locris Epicnemidia. Its formation is ascribed to the predominantly vertical tectonic movement that in the orogeny of the Early Tertiary Period created all the mountains of the region (Ghiona, Parnassus, Callidromus). References: Str. 9,2,42; 3,17; 4,1; Paus. 10,8,2; Plin. HN 4,27; Ptol. 3,14,9; Eust. ad Dionysii Periegesin 422; EM 360,33.

W. KASE et al., The Great Isthmus Corridor Route 1, 1991; W. A. OLDFATHER, s.v. K., RE 11, 909; PHILIPPSON/ KIRSTEN 1, 339ff.; PRITCHETT 4, 147ff.   G.D.R.

Cnemus (Κνῆμος; *Knêmos*). Spartan *nauarchos* (fleet commander) in 430/29 BC, destroyed Zacynthus in 430, conducted operations in Acarnania in 429 and was defeated at Oeniadae (Thuc. 2,66; 80–82; Diod. Sic. 12,47,4f.). C.'s formations suffered heavy losses in 429 at Stratus and Naupactus against the Athenians under Phormion. In the late autumn of 429 an assault that C. and his 'adviser' → Brasidas had planned against Piraeus was called off; Salamis was laid waste instead (Thuc. 2,83–94; Diod. Sic. 12,49).   K.-W.WEL.

Cnidus (Κνίδος; *Knídos*, Lat. *Cnidus*). City of the Carian or Dorian Chersonesus (now the Reşadiye peninsula). Dorian settlement (Hom. Il. 1,43; Hdt. 1,174); member of the Dorian Pentapolis. C. probably stood originally in the middle of the peninsula near today's Datça. Historical dates: About 580 BC it participated in the colonization of Sicily (Thuc. 3,88) and in the Hellenion in Naucratis (Hdt. 2,178); Persian in 546/5 (Hdt. 1,174). Around 550 Ionian treasury, 460 → lesche in Delphi. In 477 in the → Delian League, in 412 defection to Sparta, renewed Persian rule (interrupted at the start of the 4th cent.). In 394 → Conon's naval victory over the Spartan fleet near C.; under Maussollus the city was moved c. 370 to the western tip of the peninsula. In the 3rd cent. mostly Ptolemaic, 190 under Rhodian influence, 167 free, even within the Roman province of

→ Asia [2] (Plin. HN 5,104). From AD 263–467 constant disasters caused by violent earthquakes; in the early Byzantine period a suffragan diocese of (→ Aphrodisias [1]), six churches. In the middle of the 7th cent. C. was destroyed by the Arab fleet.

C.'s principal deity was → Aphrodite (on coins from the 6th cent. BC); in her sanctuary stood → Praxiteles' statue of Aphrodite (c. 360 BC; Plin. HN 36,20f.). Seated portrait of the Demeter of C. (c. 330 BC). Archaeology: Several temples, stoai, buleuteria, theatres in the upper part of the city and near the harbour, Hellenistic-Roman residences on terraced slopes; they are to be found on the island directly in front of C. In the north-west a naval harbour and in the south-east a commercial harbour (Str. 14,2,15).

From C. hailed → Agatharchides (historian and geographer), → Aeschylus [3] (rhetor), → Ctesias (doctor and historian), → Eudoxus [1] (mathematician), → Sostratus (architect). Roughly contemporaneously with → Hippocrates [6] on Cos, a distinct branch of scientific medicine (the so-called 'Cnidian School of doctors'; → Chrysippus [3]) was developed at the Asclepieum of C.

W. BLÜMEL, Die Inschr. von K., 1 (IK 41,1), 1992; H. A. CAHN, K. Die Mz. des 6. und 5. Jh.v.Chr., 1969; B. ASHMOLE, Demeter of Cnidus, in: JHS 71, 1951, 13–28; G. E. BEAN, J. M. COOK, The Cnidia, in: ABSA 47, 1952, 171–212; G. E. BEAN, Kleinasien 3, 1974, 142–161; N. DEMAND, Did K. really move?, in: Classical Antiquity 8, 1989, 224–237; J. ILBERG, Die Ärzteschule von K. (Berliner Verhandlungen der Sächsischen Akad. der Wiss. 76,3), 1925; I. C. LOVE, A Brief Summary of Excavations at K. 1967–1973 (Conference Ankara/Izmir 1973), 1978, 1111–1133; V. RUGGIERI, Tracce bizantine nella peninsula di Cnido, in: Orientalia Christiana Periodica 52, 1986, 179–201.   H.KA.

Cniva Gothic king who, together with other tribes, made forays over the Danube into Moesia and Thrace in AD 250, inflicted a severe defeat on the emperor Decius as he was advancing to relieve Philippopolis (Plovdiv) and, in breach of his agreement with the usurper Priscus, had the city pillaged. In their retreat Decius and his son Herennius took up position near Abrittus, but C. enticed the Roman army into a swamp, encircled and annihilated it. Both emperors fell. Their successor Trebonianus Gallus (251–253) had to allow the Goths to depart with the booty and moreover, had to pay an annual tribute. PIR C 1208.

H. WOLFRAM, Die Goten, ³1990, 55–57.   W.ED.

Cnopus (Κνῶπος; *Knôpos*). River in Boeotia; according to Nic. Ther. 889 it flowed into Lake Copais; schol. Nic. Ther. 889 also mentions an otherwise unknown polis C. that lay on the river → Ismenus (=C.?); it is from an area named Cnopia near Thebes (Str. 9,2,10: ἐκ τῆς Κνωπίας Θηβαϊκῆς) that the sanctuary of → Amphiaraus is said to have been transplanted to Oropus.

C. BURSIAN, Geogr. von Griechenland 1, 1862, 200; T. K.
HUBBARD, Remaking Myth and Rewriting History: Cult
Tradition in Pindar's Ninth Nemean, in: HSPh 94, 1992,
102–107; SCHACHTER, vol. 1, 19; P. W. WALLACE, Strabo's Description of Boiotia, 1979, 47.   P.F.

Coabis Road junction in the Jordan valley (Χωβα, Jdt
4,4; Χωβαι, Jdt 15,4), according to the *Tabula Peutingeriana* 12 miles from → Scythopolis and 12 miles away
from → Archelais, but in view of the total distance between those two locations (*c.* 50 miles) that cannot be
the case and so it is unlocated.

TIR/IP 105, s.v. C.   K.B.

Coactores The *coactores*, first mentioned in Cato (Agr.
150), were tasked with collecting revenue. They had an
intermediary function between creditors and debtors.
For the most part they were active at auctions, partly in
collaboration with *argentarii*. They conducted the *tabulae auctionariae* and received a fee that mostly
amounted to one per cent of the sale price. Several indicators suggest that their occupation disappeared in the
course of the 2nd cent. AD.

The theory that the *coactores* and the *coactores
argentarii* were identical is not convincing. The *coactores argentarii* sprang up in the 1st cent. BC and were
active at auctions as *coactores* and at the same time in
banking as *argentarii*. The *coactores*, on the other hand,
generally confined themselves to collecting money and
did not extend any credit. At auctions they undertook
the task of receiving money and delivering it to the vendors; in contrast to the *argentarii*, they did not lend
money to the purchasers. The father of the poet Horace
was a *coactor* and the grandfather of Vespasian, Titus
Flavius Petro, was a *coactor argentarius* (Suet. Vesp.
1,2). Caecilius Iucundus from Pompeii was an *argentarius* or a *coactor argentarius*, but certainly not a *coactor*.
→ Argentarius; → Auctio; → Banks (III); → L. Caecilius
Iucundus

1 J. ANDREAU, La vie financière dans le monde romain,
1987 2 M. TALAMANCA, Contributi allo studio delle ven-
dite all'asta nel mondo antico, in: Memorie dell'Accademia dei Lincei VIII 6, 1954, 35–251 3 G. THIELMANN,
Die röm. Privatauktion, 1961.   J.A.

Coae Vestes Luxury → clothing from the island of Cos,
with a transparent effect. They were known as early as
Aristotle (Hist. an. 5,19; cf. Plin. HN 4,62) and received
special mention during the Roman Imperial period. They were regarded as luxury clothing for demi-
mondaines (e.g. Hor. Sat. 1,2,101; Tib. 2,3,57) but
were also worn by men as light summer clothing. The
sheen, purple colouring and decoration in gold thread,
i.a. were highly esteemed. The fabric was woven from
the raw silk of the bombyx (→ Silk, → Butterfly), whose
cocoons produced only short threads that thus needed
additional spinning. Garments from Amorgos and

Tarentum were predecessors of the *coae vestes*, and
there were other forms of silken garments and transparent clothing as well, so that their authoritative and detailed identification in art is problematic.
→ Clothing; → Tarentine

H. WEBER, C. *v.*, in: MDAI (Ist) 19, 1969, 249–253;
R. KABUS-PREISSHOFEN, Die hell. Plastik der Insel Kos,
14. Beih., MDAI(A) 1989, 142–157.   R.H.

Coal-pan see → Heating

Coastline, changes in The course of coastlines and the
character of coastal landscapes are constantly being
changed by the interplay of eustatic variations in sea
level, tectonically caused instances of eruption and sub-
sidence, deposits of sediment from rivers, alluvia from
the sea, volcanoes and related bradyseism (e.g. in
Puteoli), sea currents, wind, breakers and tides. Bearing
this in mind can be important for evaluating particular
historical events. Thus, for example, the coastal strip at
→ Thermopylae that is now several km wide, thanks to
the sediment from several rivers, was an easy-to-defend,
narrow coastal pass in 480 BC when Spartans and Persians fought each other there. A determining factor for
the transfer of the principal residence of Macedonian
kings from → Aegae [1] to → Pella in the 4th cent. BC
may well have been, *i.a.*, the fact that Pella lay on the
Aegaean; formation of the deltas of → Axius and → Ha-
liacmon did not lead to the city's separation from the
sea until centuries later.

Because of the eustatic increase in sea level (since
antiquity about 1–2 m; today 1.5 mm per annum),
caused by the melting of ice masses during the geological warm period, one would have to expect all low-lying
buildings in antiquity to be under water now — as is
indeed the case with → Cenchreae, for example, the
eastern harbour town of Corinth. In the mouth of rivers
with a great deal of sediment, however, a contrary process predominates, extending the stretch of coastline
further outwards with the accumulated sediment. This
can be a desirable outcome for the residents, since — as
for example in the Nile delta — arable land is acquired
in the process; but it can also have negative consequences when it has a detrimental effect on the location's character and the lifestyle, as when harbour facilities get silted up, as was the case e.g. at → Ostia,
→ Utica, → Myus, → Priene, → Miletus and → Ephesus,
or when the alluvial soil becomes marshy as the ground
water level rises as a result of an increase in the sea level,
as happened e.g. in the delta of the → Padus (Po) at
→ Spina and → Ravenna. Basically it is a matter of natural processes that can indeed be affected by human factors also: thus, deforestation increases erosion and,
consequently, the amount of fluvial sediment carried by
rivers.

A. RABAN, Archaeology of Coastal Changes, 1988;
E. ZANGGER, s.v. Delta, Schwemmland, Strandverschie-
bung, in: H. SONNABEND (ed.), Mensch und Landschaft in

der Ant. (1999); H. SONNABEND, s.v. Küste, in: Id., ibid.; E. OLSHAUSEN, Einführung in die Histor. Geogr. der alten Welt, 1991, 202 n. 245 (bibliography) ; W. STORKEBAUM (ed.), Wiss. Länderkunden, vols. 1ff., 1967ff. (with several reprints).   V.S.

Cobades see → Cavades

Cobbler see → Shoe-maker

Cocalus (Κώκαλος; *Kόkalos*; Lat. Cocalus). Mythical king, who took over control of Sicily after the destruction of the → Cyclopes (Just. Epit. 4,2,2). He allowed → Daedalus [1], who was fleeing from the Cretan king → Minos, into the city → Camicus (in Paus. 7,4,6 Inykos), as also Minos who was pursuing him; the latter, however, he then had killed in a shower of hot water (schol. Hom. Il. 2,145; Apollod. [see authors/works] 1,14f.) that his daughters poured down on him through the bathroom ceiling (schol. Pind. N. 4,95); in Diodorus (4,77–79) C. himself kills Minos. C. gives the corpse to the Cretans with the explanation that their king fell into hot water (Diod. Sic. loc. cit.).   AL.FR.

Cocceianus see → Cassius [III 1]

Cocceius
[1] **C. Auctus, L.** Freedman of C. Postumius (Pollio). Architect (CIL X 1614), who constructed the road tunnels between Lake Avernus and Cumae and between Puteoli and Naples for M. Valerius → Agrippa [1] (Str. 5,5,245).

H. BENARIO, C. and Cumae, in: CB 35, 1959, 40–41; D. KIENAST, Augustus, 1982, 347 fn. 148, 348 fn. 153.   D.K.

[2] **C.C. Balbus.** *Cos. suff.* in 39 BC (InscrIt 13,1, p. 282; 291; 278; 135; 506; MRR 2, 386). As a supporter of M. → Antonius he was given the title of Imperator in Asia (IG II/III² 4110 [1. no. 124]).
[3] **L.C. Nerva.** *Cos. suff.* in 39 BC. Great-grandfather of the emperor (possibly from Narnia in Umbria, cf. Aur. Vict. Caes. 12,1; [Aur. Vict.] Epit. Caes. 12,1). Probably the son of C. in Cic. Att. 12,13,2 *i.a.* As a friend of Octavian (→ Augustus) as well as Mark Antony he was sent by the former to Syria with Caecina for negotiations with Mark Antony (App. B Civ. 5,251) in the summer of 41. He accompanied the latter to Italy and, with others, secured the Treaty of Brundisium in the autumn of 40 (App. B Civ. 5,252–272). Early in 37 C. travelled with → Maecenas to Brundisium for negotiations with Mark Antony once again (Hor. Sat. 1,5,27f.) and there they drew up the Treaty of Tarentum. C. owned a villa at Caudium (Hor. Sat. 1,5,50f. [1. no. 125]).
[4] **M.C. Nerva.** *Cos. suff.* in 36 BC, brother of C. [2]. According to coins from 41 BC *proq(uaestor) p(ropraetore)* of Mark Antony in the East (RRC 1, 525f. no. 517). In the Perugian War he sided with L. → Antonius

[I 4]. Octavian pardoned him out of regard for his brother (App. B Civ. 5,256). He then fought for Mark Antony in Asia and as *cos. designatus* was proclaimed Imperator (SEG 4, 604; ILS 8780). He was present at the Secular Festival of 17 BC as *XVvir sacris faciundis* (ILS 5050, 151; [1. no. 126]).

1 T.P. WISEMAN, New Men in the Roman Senate, 1971.   D.K.

[5] **M.C. Nerva.** Descendant of C. [4], from Narnia. *Cos. suff.* in AD 21 or 22. [1. 351f.], *curator aquarum* in 24 (Frontin. Aq. 102). In 26 he was the only senator to accompany Tiberius to Campania and Capri. There he committed suicide in 33 (Tac. Ann. 6,26; Cass. Dio 58,21,4). C. was a famous jurist (fragments collected in [2. 787]). PIR² C 1225 [3. 120].
[6] **(M.C.) Nerva.** Son of C. [5]. Jurist like his father, probably also a senator but not known to have held any office (PIR² C 1226) [3. 130].
[7] **M.C.Nerva.** Emperor from 96–98, see → Nerva
[8] **Sex. C. Severianus Honorinus.** *Cos. suff.* in 147 [4. 51]; Proconsul of Africa, probably in 162/3 [5. I 382]. He was honoured in Africa with a team of six horses; Apuleius delivered an oration before him (Apul. Flor. 37–40). His son was C. Honorinus (PIR² C 1230).
[9] **Sex. C. Vibianus.** Suffect Consul towards the end of the 2nd cent. He participated in the Secular Games in 204 as *XVvir sacris faciundis;* later proconsul of Africa (PIR² C 1232) [6. 166, 219].

1 SYME, RP 4   2 LENEL, Palingenesia 1   3 KUNKEL 4 VIDMAN, FO² 51   5 THOMASSON, Lat.   6 LEUNISSEN, Konsuln.   W.E.

Coccygium (Κοκκύγιον ὄρος; *Kokkýgion rós*). 'Cuckoo mountain', another name for the mountain Thornax, west of → Hermion(e) on the Argolid headland, with sanctuaries of Zeus and Apollo; today's Hagios Elias. References: Paus. 2,36,1f.; schol. Theoc. 15,64.

A. FOLEY, The Argolid 800–600 B.C., 1988, 184.   Y.L.

Cochlear(e)
[1] (χήμη, *chémē*, 'Spoon'). Smallest unit of Roman hollow measures, especially for medicines. Exceptionally, *cochlear(e)* is calculated differently: in the *Carmen de ponderibus* as $^1/_6$ of the *mystum* (1.9 ml); in Isidorus (Orig. 16,25) the *cochlear(e)* amounts to 2.3 ml.
→ Acetabulum; → Amphora; → Congius; → Culleus; → Cyathus; → Hemina; → Hollow measures; → Modius; → Quadrantal; → Quartarius; → Semodius; → Sextarius; → Urna

1 cochlear		11.4 ml
4 cochlearia	1 cyathus	45.5 ml
6 cochlearia	1 acetabulum	68.2 ml
12 cochlearia	1 quartarius	136.4 ml
24 cochlearia	1 hemina	272.9 ml
48 cochlearia	1 sextarius	546.0 ml

Dry measures:

8 sextarii	1 semodius	4.366 l
16 sextarii	1 modius	8.732 l
3 modii	1 quadrantal	26.196 l

Liquid measures:

12 heminae	1 congius	3.275 l
4 congii	1 urna	13.090 l
2 urnae	1 quadrantal	26.196 l
40 urnae	1 culleus	524.000 l

F. HULTSCH, Griech. und röm. Metrologie, ²1882; Id., s.v. C. (2), RE 4, 157; LAW, s.v. Measures and Weights, 3422–3426.　　　A.M.

[2] see → Cutlery

Cock see → Chicken

Cockfighting
A. SPREAD AND POPULARITY　B. ORGANIZATION AND PATTERN OF EVENTS

A. SPREAD AND POPULARITY
Cockfighting is attested from the 5th cent. BC to the Roman Imperial period (earliest evidence in Pind. Ol. 12,14, latest in Hdn. 3,10,3). It was especially popular with the Greeks [1. 117; 2. 82–92]: fighting cocks were considered an ideal example of the will to win (Ael. VH 2,28); it is in that light that they are depicted on the Panathenaean prize amphorae [3. 34] (→ Panathenaean amphorae); in Aesch. Eum. 861 they symbolize martial anger (the cock as 'the bird of Ares' in Aristoph. Av. 835), their aggressiveness was proverbial (cockfighting metaphors in Aristoph. Ach. 166; Equ. 494). In the first edition of the 'Clouds' Aristophanes had the two competing 'orations' (lógoi) challenge each other dressed up as fighting-cocks [4. 90–93; 5]. The Romans were not so fond of cockfighting, which they regarded as typically Greek and a childish game (Columella 8,2,5) [1. 122].

B. ORGANIZATION AND PATTERN OF EVENTS
Legally authorized cockfighting took place in Athens in the Dionysus Theatre from the end of the Persian Wars (Ael. VH 2,28), and all young men fit for military service were expected to watch (Lucian Anacharsis 37); cockfighting was, moreover, a popular recreational activity. It was held in games rooms (Aeschin. In Tim. 53), taverns or in open spaces, especially in gymnasia. Fighting-cocks were specially bred; those from Tanagra were considered particularly combative (Plin. HN 10,48). Fighting-cocks were carried about for hours at a time because it was believed that vibrations increased animals' strength (Pl. Leg. 7,789b-d), and they were fed garlic (or rubbed down with it: Hsch. s.v. σκοροδίσαι) so as to increase their aggressiveness (Xen. Symp. 4,9; schol. on Aristoph. Ach. 166 and Equ. 494). For the fight the cocks were fitted with iron spurs

(πλῆκτρον) (schol. on Aristoph. Av. 759), placed on tables or platforms and set upon each other. Sometimes the losing cock died (Dem. Or. 54,9); if it survived it belonged to the winner (Theoc. 22,71; Aristoph. Av. 70f. with schol.). Later on there were also cash prizes and wagers, and training of fighting-cocks came to be a profession (Columella 8,2,5: rix<i>osarum avium lanista, cuius patrimonium, pignus aleae, victor gallinaceus abstulit [1. 119f.]).

1 M. GWYN MORGAN, Three non-Roman blood sports, in: CQ 25, 1975, 117–122　2 E. PARASKEVAIDIS, Τὰ παίγνια τῶν ἀρχαίων Ἑλλήνων, in: Plato 41, 1989, 68–92　3 D.G. KYLE, Athletics in Ancient Athens, 1987　4 K.J. DOVER, Aristophanes' Clouds, 1968　5 O. TAPLIN, Phallology, phylakes, iconography and Aristophanes, in: PCPhS 33, 1987, 92–104.

J. DUMONT, Les combats de coqs furent-ils un sport?, in: Pallas 34, 1988, 33–44; H. HOFFMANN, H. in Athen, in: RA 1974, 195–220; K. SCHNEIDER, s.v. Hahnenkämpfe, RE 7, 2210–2215; G.R. SCOTT, History of Cockfighting, 1957; D.W. THOMPSON, A glossary of Greek birds, 1936, 33–37.　　　S.MÜ.

Cockroach see → Volume 4, Addenda

Cocles 'The one-eyed' (Enn. Scaen. 67f. V.² in Varro, Ling. 7,71; Plin. HN 11,150), used as a nickname. Cognomen of → Horatius C.

A. HUG, s.v. Spitznamen, RE 3A, 1828.　　　K.-L.E.

Cocondrius (Κοκόνδριος; Kokóndrios). Greek rhetor of undetermined date (probably Byzantine); a slim treatise on tropes (trópoi) is extant. These are at the beginning systematically divided into three groups (génē), namely trópoi referring to an individual word (e.g. onomatopoeia), to the whole sentence (e.g. allegory), or to both (e.g. hyperbaton). In elaboration C. does not adhere strictly to this system but deals with other types as well. For example, poets are quoted exclusively: Homer, as well as Alcaeus, the tragedians, and Theoc.
→ Style, figures of style; → trope

EDITIONS: WALZ 8, 782–798; SPENGEL 3, 230–243.　　　M.W.

Cocytus (Κωκυτός; Kōkytós, Lat. Cocytus).
[1] 'River of lamentation' (cf. κωκύειν, 'to weep, lament'). According to Paus. 1,17,5 from Homer onwards one of the rivers of the Underworld, named after the Thesprotic C. [1. 76]. It is fed from the → Styx and flows with the Pyriphlegeton into the → Acheron [2] (Hom. Od. 10,513f.); in Virgil the Acheron flows into the C. (Verg. Aen. 6,296f.). According to Pl. Phd., the C. flows around in a circle and empties into the → Tartarus (113b-c); it receives the souls of murderers (114a; cf. Orph. Fr. 222,5). To the C. the Orphic tradition attributes earth or coldness and the west (Orph. Fr. 123 and 125). In Roman poetry the C. is generally

described as black and slow-flowing (cf. Verg. G. 4,478f.; Verg. Aen. 6,132; Hor. Carm. 2,14,17f.).
→ Epirus; → Phlegeton

1 C. Sourvinou-Inwood, 'Reading' Greek Death. To the End of the Classical Period, 1995.   K.SCHL.

[2] River in Thesprotia/Epirus, flowing into the → Acheron [1] near the Nekyomanteion. According to Paus. 1,17,5 the C. was the model for the river of the Underworld C. [1] in Homer.

N. G. L. Hammond, Epirus, 1967; Philippson/Kirsten 2, 104–106.   D.S.

Code see → Cryptography

Codex
I. Cultural history   II. Law collections

I. Cultural history
A. Wood tablet-codex   B. Parchment and papyrus-codex

A. Wood tablet-codex
The codex (from *codex*, 'tree trunk', 'wood') was originally a stack of wooden tablets prepared for writing on. Writing-tablets, together with papyrus scrolls, are attested in Pharaonic Egypt from very early on, as also in the Near East (tablets are extant from at least the 8th cent. BC). They are also attested (likewise indirectly) from as early as archaic and classical Greece; the earliest extant finds in Greek date to the Hellenistic period. For the Greeks, however, the use of this writing medium was confined to documents that were intended for archiving, or everyday notes that were not likely to be erased. The → papyrus, which was introduced from Egypt, very quickly became the most used → writing medium, in the form of a → scroll for→ books, in various formats for official documents.

In Rome and the Roman world, on the other hand, tablets that were bound together into a block (→ *tabula*) were much more widely and diversely used, as is

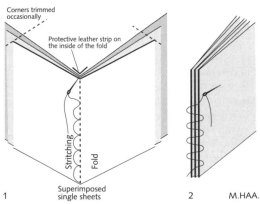

Structure of the Codex:
1. Structure of the individual layers: 'notebook' binding.
2. Combination of several layers (fascicles) to form the codex; corresponding more or less to modern bookbinding.

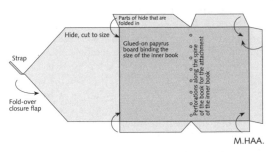

Cover of the Nag Hammadi codices; schematic representation of the inside.

evident from archaeological finds from the Imperial period (even earlier according to some sources: ORF, no. 8, fr. 173; Dion. Hal. Ant. Rom. 1,73,1; Liv. 6,1,2; Plin. HN 35,7): These tablets occur as *dealbatae*, whitened and written upon; *ceratae* (→ *cera*), with a sunken inner surface and filled with wax, upon which one wrote, or scratched, with a sharp point of metal → *stilus*; simple, rather thin tablets without an upper layer of wax, *non ceratae*, which were written on in ink with either a → *calamus* or a metal pen.

Generally, the tablets were combined in pairs to form a diptych. More than two tablets, however, could also be bound together into triptychs or polyptychs, the so-called *tabellae*, *pugillaria*, *codicilli*, that could be turned over like the pages of a notebook or a regular book. Tablets bound together into polyptychs of the last kind have been found in Herculaneum, dating back to no later than AD 79. They are carefully worked, written on along the short side of each *tabella*, and bound by a form of hinge with double thread. Two outer tablets served as a cover, as genuine codices were made from wood, quite similar to later codices made from → parchment or papyrus. As the careful preparatory work indicates, products of this kind were used less for everyday notes and jottings than for literary and especially important legal texts. Finds from Vindolanda in Britain show that, if made from very thin wood, such *tabellae* could be folded and bound accordion-style, so that one could leaf through the pages, albeit in pairs, as in a book.

It can be assumed that the codex was the original form of the Roman book, used in the archaic period for texts of early Latin prose (*annales pontificum*; → Annals, → *commentarii* of the magistrates, legal and literary works, like those of Cato the Elder, for example). Only from the 3rd–2nd cents. BC onwards did the papyrus scroll, already widely used by the Greeks, come into use by the Romans and it quickly replaced the codex in book production. This phenomenon is part of a general process of 'Hellenization' of Roman culture from the time of the Scipiones. During the period in which the scroll was the normal form of books the codex remained in use, as also amongst the Greeks, but was used for various purposes, such as jottings, occasional or everyday notes, or even for public or private documents.

B. Parchment and papyrus-codex

The more developed form of codex from parchment or papyrus, occurring more and more frequently from the 1st–2nd cents. AD onwards, certainly derived from the forms of the original tablet-codex: by the end of the 4th cent. AD they had finally superseded the scroll in book production. Everything points to it being the Romans who replaced wooden tablets with folded pages of parchment in codex production. After this form was established for all kinds of books, the codex was also produced in papyrus, the material typically used for scrolls, especially in Egypt and neighbouring countries where *charta* from papyrus was produced and exported. The old type of codex in tablets, however, remained in daily use (notebooks, jottings, school writing tablets) for some time to come.

From a technical point of view the normal codex consists of folded papyrus sheets (cut off from commercial rolls) or pages of parchment (from specially tanned animal skins, principally sheep or cattle), assembled in layers (fascicles), written on on both sides and bound with the fold at the book's spine. From the first cents. of its use (2nd –4th cents. AD) copies are often found with a single layer of varying thickness, while in others each layer consists of only one sheet. If the codex consists of several fascicles, they do not, in various copies, follow any overall, relatively consistent pattern; the fascicles can even vary within the one copy. Once standardized, the codex consists of several layers each generally having four folded sheets, or eight pages; but there are exceptions in every period. The oldest type of papyrus codex shows — when opened up with pages opposite each other — a contrasting arrangement of horizontal and vertical fibres; later on, however, the threads on both pages follow the same pattern. When the parchment codex is opened up, the inner side of the skin is the inner page, with the outer surface of the skin forming the outer pages (the so-called Rule of Gregory), an arrangement that developed either from the way the animal skin was folded before cutting or from a deliberate layering of individual sheets.

It has been assumed that — from at least the 2nd. cent. AD onwards — it was the Christians who favoured the scroll's replacement by the codex; other factors, instead, were more likely to be responsible, generally connected to social and cultural changes, in which Christianity happened to play an important part. The codex's success — its availability to the general public and for every kind of book — was finally established by its capacity: it could accommodate substantially more text than the scroll and could provide a unified shape to the canonical writings of the new religion, as well as to the large collections of laws and the body of authors' works from late antiquity — at a time of systematization of knowledge and texts. The book format of the codex survived from antiquity into the Middle Ages, during the course of which → paper caught up with parchment as a writing medium.

Codicology

A. Blanchard (ed.), Les debuts du c., 1989; A. K. Bowman, J. D. Thomas, Vindolanda: the Latin Writings-Tablets, 1983; G. Cavallo, Libro e cultura scritta, in: Storia di Roma IV, Caratteri e morfologie, 1989, 693–734; Id., Testo, libro, lettura, in: Ibid., P. Fedeli, A. Giardina (ed.), Lo spazio letterario di Roma antica, II, La circolazione del testo, 1989, 307–341; E. Pöhlmann, Einführung in die Überlieferungsgesch. und in die Textkritik der ant. Lit., vol. 1: Alt., 1994; G. Pugliese Carratelli, L'instrumentum scriptorium nei monumenti pompeiani ed ercolanesi, in: Pompeiana. Raccolta di studi per il secondo centenario degli scavi di Pompei, 1950, 266–278; C. H. Roberts, T. C. Skeat, The Birth of the C., 1983; W. Schubart, Das Buch bei den Griechen und Römern, ³1962; E. G. Turner, The Typology of the Early C., 1977.
                                                                GU.C.

Illustrated bibliography: H. Blanck, Das Buch in der Ant., 1992, 86–96.   M.HAA.

II. Law collections

A. General meaning   B. Codex Gregorianus and Hermogenianus   C. Official collections of constitutions

A. General meaning

Codex was initially the term for a book stitched together from → parchment leaves (*membrana*), in contrast to the *liber,* from a papyrus scroll, that was almost solely used up until the 4th cent. AD. The word *codex* derives perhaps from the fact that the books were held together with small sheets of wood. This form of book was especially suitable for reference works and was thus used in courts and in the administration for collections of Imperial decrees (→ *constitutiones*). Thence *codex* quickly became synonymous with such collections. Previously, in the legal world from as early as the late Republic, the *codex accepti et expensi* was the customary term for the domestic record of income and expenditure of the *pater familias* (also → *litterarum obligatio*).

B. Codex Gregorianus and Hermogenianus

The oldest collection of imperial laws that is termed a *codex* is the *Codex Gregorianus*, privately assembled by Gregorius, probably a *magister libellorum* from AD 284 to 290. This *codex* was published in Rome in 291 and contains the imperial constitutions since Hadrian, systematically organized into books and subject headings. The *Constitutionum libri XX* of Papirius Iustus (c. 170) may have been its model. The few remnants survive in the fragments in the Vatican, the→ Collatio, the → Consultatio, the lex Romana Burgundionum and the breviary (→ lex Romana Visigothorum). The constitutions up to 291 in the Codex Iustinianus probably have their origins in the Codex Gregorianus. As a private citizen, Gregorius may have changed the wording but is hardly likely to have changed the legal substance of the Imperial law. Towards the end of the 4th cent. expanded revisions are said to have been in circulation [1. 653, 670; 6. 391; 7; 8. 135].

→ Hermogenianus privately collected the constitutions for the years 291 to 294, which he had probably drafted himself, systematically arranged them under subject headings, edited them and published this Cod. Herm. (about a third of the size of the Cod. Greg.) in 295. About 1,000 rescripts are extant — in the same sources as the remnants of the Cod. Greg. Hermogenianus also produced two editions with supplements for 295 to 305 and for 314 to 319. Later supplements date from 364 and 365 [1. 665; 6. 392; 8. 36, 137].

C. OFFICIAL COLLECTIONS OF CONSTITUTIONS
The Codex Theodosianus was published on 15.2.438 as an official collection of Imperial constitutions from 313 to 438 for the *ius publicum, ius privatum* and Church law, was acknowledged from 1.1.439 in the East [5] and, after acclamation in the Senate (probably as early as 25.12.438), in the West as well [2. 1]. It was systematically arranged in 16 bks according to subject headings and chronologically within those headings. In terms of his original, much more extensive proposal (Cod. Theod. 1,1,5) Theodosius II had planned to codify jurisprudence, as well as the *leges generales* and *edicta*. The Commission made considerable use of its authority to abridge and amend the substance of laws. All but one seventh of the Codex Theodosianus, which originally contained *c.* 3,400 constitutions, can be reconstructed with the help of the breviary, which adds *interpretationes* of the laws, and the heavily worked-over fragments of the Cod. Iust. [2; 3; 6. 392; 9; 10].

Together with the Codex *Summa* (*De Iustiniano codice confirmando*, on Justinian's endorsement of the codex), the collection of imperial law from Hadrian to Justinian was published on 7.4.529 as the first part of the Corpus iuris, after the preparatory work of the codex already mentioned. POxy. 15, 1814 contains an excerpt of the section headings and the inscriptions 1,11–16 of this *codex vetus*. For its compilation, with the Codex *Haec* (*De novo codice componendo*: 'on the composition of a new codex'), Justinian appointed a commission of senior officials and jurists on 13.2.528. After a later commission had completed its work of adjusting the *codex vetus* to the digests that were published on 16.12.533 (Cod. Iust. 1,17,2) and updating it, the second edition (*codex repetitae praelectionis*) was published on 16.11.534, together with the Constitutio *Cordi* (*De emendatione codicis Iustiniani et secunda eius editione*: 'on the enlargement and the second edition') [4; 6. 392; 11].

→ Cuneiform, legal texts in; CODIFICATION

EDITIONS: 1 J. BAVIERA, FIRA II, ²1940 2 J. GOTHOFREDUS, C. Theod., 6 vol., 1665 3 TH. MOMMSEN, Theodosiani libri XVI ..., 1905 4 P. KRÜGER, Cod. Iust., 1877 5 Leges Novellae ad Theodosianum pertinentes, ed. P. M. MEYER ²1954 (nov. 1 of 439). BIBLIOGRAPHY: 6 A. BERGER, Encyclopedic Dictionary of Roman Law, 1953, repr. 1980 7 T. HONORÉ, Emperors and Lawyers, 1981, 114 8 D. LIEBS, Jurisprudenz im spätant. Italien, 1987 9 G. ARCHI, Teodosio II e la sua Codificazione, 1976 10 T. HONORÉ, The Making of the Theodosian Code, in: ZRG 103, 1986, 133–222 11 G. ARCHI, Problemi e modelli legislativi all'epoca di Teodosio II e di Giustiniano, in: SDHI 50, 1984, 341–354.
W.E.V.

Codex Hermopolis This name has been given to a papyrus scroll of 2 m in length discovered by S. GABRA in Tuna-el-Gebel, which contains 10 columns of a legal text in the Demotic language. The text dates from the 1st half of the 3rd cent. BC, but individual regulations could reach back to the time of the pharaohs; in POxy 46,3285 two fragments of a Greek version have survived, dating to the 2nd half of the 2nd cent. AD. Viewed in today's terms, the content can be divided into four sections: 1. Land utilization and leasing, leasing of enterprises (with an excursus on protest); 2. Deeds of maintenance; 3. Interference with the possessions of others; 4. The law of inheritance of the eldest son. This is not a systematic record of the full extent of civil laws, which is why the title 'Legal Code' chosen by the editor [1] is most probably incorrect. In any case, historians of law classify this work as belonging to the indigenous Egyptian law. SEIDL [2. 17, 19] regards it as a private work, a lemmatic commentary to a law (to be reconstructed therefrom), while WOLFF [3. 268ff.] regards it as a large Demotic law fragment whose Greek version was compiled for use by the → Chrematists. The Codex Hermopolis has also been interpreted as a scholarly legal publication compiled for use by the courts and as legal instruction for priests and public notaries [5. 357]. What is remarkable is the frequent use of the oath in civil proceedings. The Ger. trans. [4] should not be consulted without the detailed commentary [5].

1 G. MATTHA, The legal code of Hermopolis West, Cairo 1975 2 E. SEIDL, Eine demotische Juristenarbeit (Rez. Mattha), in: ZRG 97, 1979, 17ff. 3 H. J. WOLFF, Neue Juristische Urkunden, in: ZRG 97, 1979, 258ff. 4 ST. GRUNERT, Der Kodex Hermopolis und ausgewählte private Rechtsurkunden, 1982 5 T. Q. MRSICH, Rez. zu [4], in: ZRG 99, 1982, 357ff. 6 SCH. ALLAM, Zum Rechtsbuch von Hermopolis, in: Das Alt. 33, 1987, 177ff.
G.T.

Codex Salmasianus The Codex Parisinus Lat. 10318 (end of the 8th cent.) named after its former owner Claude de Saumaise (1588–1653), contains i.a. a collection of poems made in North Africa around AD 534. Alongside contemporary material such as the book of epigrams by → Luxurius, it also includes older texts (i.a. → Hosidius Geta, → Pentadius, → Pervigilium Veneris, → Symphosius).

EDITION: Anth. Lat. I, I: ed. D. R. SHACKLETON BAILEY, 1982 (without nos 7–18 RIESE).
BIBLIOGRAPHY: 1 A. J. BAUMGARTNER, Unt. zur Anthologie des C.S., 1981 2 W. SCHETTER, Kaiserzeit und Spätant., 1994, 451–465 3 M. SPALLONE, Il Par. Lat. 10318 (Salmasiano), in: Italia medioevale e umanistica 25, 1982, 1–71.
MA.L.

Codicilli The last will and testament written down as an informal document. In a codicil, only individual instructions could be laid down, but not the appointment or removal of an heir. Codicils were valid as an amendment to a testament if their establishment was reserved in an earlier testament or confirmed in a later one (*c. testamento confirmati*); non-confirmed codicils (intestate codicil) could only contain entails. A so-called codicillary clause of the content indicating that a testament should also be valid in case of formal errors, allowed the reinterpretation, to the extent possible, of a defective testament into a valid intestate codicil (Dig. 29,7; Cod. Iust. 6,36).

→ Inheritance, Law of; → Entail

> 1 H. HONSELL, TH. MAYER-MALY, W. SELB, 461f.
> 2 KASER, RPR I, 693f. U.M.

Codification see → Law, codification of

Codrus (Κόδρος; *Kódros*). Son of → Melanthus, a mythical king of Athens. In the list of Attic kings, his role is primarily to establish the connection to the Pylian colonists of Ionia. According to a tradition common in the 5th cent. BC, his father, a Neleid, came to Athens as a refugee and was made king by the last descendant of → Theseus; C. followed his father. His only notable act was his voluntary sacrificial death in order to save the city: when the Dorians attacked Athens and an oracle promises them victory if they were to capture C. alive, C., who disguised himself as a woodcutter, seeks a quarrel with the besiegers and is killed without being recognized; when they learn of the facts, they withdraw (Pherecydes, FGrH 3 F 154; Hellanicus, FGrH 4 F 125; Lycurg. Leocrates 84–86; cf. Pl. Symp. 208d).

The succession is reported in different ways. According to a version from the 5th cent. BC, C.'s son Medon becomes the successor and founds the dynasty of the Medontides (Hellanicus, FGrH 4,125). According to a different tradition, another son, Neleus, quarrels with Medon, leaves Athens with his brothers (prominently Androclus: Pherecydes, FGrH 3 F 155) and founds the Ionian cities with the Pylians who had fled to Athens; this tradition, according to which the Pylian settlers of Ionia had immigrated via Athens and which thus expresses the hegemony of Athens over Ionia, is already presupposed by the claim of the Peisistratids to be Pylians and Neleids just like C. (Hdt. 5,65). A third tradition has C. perish without offspring: the monarchy ends with him and his political successors are the → archons (Aristot. Ath. Pol. 3,3; Just. Epit. 2,7,1f.; Paus. 4,5,10).

C. has his cult in the Neleion together with Neleus and Basile (IG I³ 84; the location is not known). At least during the imperial period, his tomb was shown at the foot of the acropolis (IG II² 4258).

→ Colonisation II.

> KEARNS, 178. F.G.

Codrus Painter Attic red-figured vase painter, active around 440–420 BC. A bowl painter who maintained the workshop of Hieron and → Macron in the third generation. Whether he was a potter himself is not clear, but he certainly did the decoration himself. At times, the → Phiale Painter would sit next to him. His most important student was → Aeson [2], the last to run the workshop. In 425, as one of the first, the Codrus Painter (CP) reintroduced older means of style (Paris, LV G 458) and thus developed the style of archaism into the 'rich style'. There is also a conservative air in the selection of his subjects: the images of Athens' mythical past appear 'faithful to the state', such as the one including King Codrus from whom he derived his name (Bologna, Mus. Civ. PU 273), and 'uncritical of society' are the many ephebic images (London, BM E 83). Images in the Dionysian style, which at the beginning were only possible outside the workshop (→ Eretria Painter), only come to the fore quite late, such as in the image of Dionysus and Ariadne (Würzburg, M. v. Wagner Mus. L 491). Also typical are extremely fine relief lines and frequent explanatory notes.

> BEAZLEY, ARV, 1268–1272; VASE-PAINTERS, 1971, 471–472; BEAZLEY, ADDENDA, 356–357; A. LEZZI-HAFTER, Der Eretria-Maler, 1988, 86–88, 125–127, 193; CHR. SOURVINOU-INWOOD, The Cup Bologna PU 273: A Reading, in: Metis 5, 1990, 137–153. A.L.-H.

Coela (Κοῖλα; *Koîla*). The south-east coast of → Euboea (Hdt. 8,13f.; Dion. Chrys. 7,2; 7; Eur. Tro. 84; 90; Ptol. 3,15,25) that was feared because of its storms. In Str. 10,1,2; Val. Max. 1,8,10; Liv. 31,47,1; Oros. 6,15,11, C. is the southern part of the straits of Euboea up to Euripos.

> F. GEYER, Top. und Gesch. der Insel Euboia 1, 1903, 7ff.
> H.KAL.

Coelaletae (Κοιλαλῆται; *Koilalêtai*, Lat. *Coelaletae*). Ethnonym referring to two different Thracian tribes: the 'Greater Coelaletae' below the → Haemus (Plin. HN 4,41) and the 'Lesser Coelaletae' below the → Rhodope; in AD 21 they fought together with the Odrysae and Dii against the Romans (Tac. Ann. 3,38f.). The Thracian strategia Koiletike was situated there (Ptol. 3,11,9). C. are found several times as soldiers on inscriptions of the 1st cent. AD (cf. CIL XVI 33 of AD 86).

> CHR. DANOV, Die Thraker auf dem Ostbalkan ..., in: ANRW II 7.1, 1979, 21–185, especially 115ff.; M. Taceva, Istorija an ba 2, 1987, 168ff. I.v.B.

Coele (Κοίλη, also Κοιλή; *Koílē, Koílê*). Attic *asty* Deme of the phyle Hippothontis, from 307/6 to 201/0 BC of the Demetrias, with three *bouleutaí*, in the originally densely populated 'rocky Athens', which was, however, abandoned already in the 4th cent. BC [5], south-west of the Pnyx between the hill of nymphs and the Mouseion, near the Melitian gate [2. 168f.] at the *koilè hodós* [2. 180], where the tombs of → Cimon [1] (Hdt. 6,103) and the historian Thucydides (Marcellinus, Vita Thucydidis 17,55; Paus. 1,23,9) lay. C. offers one of the best preserved residential quarters of classical Athens [1; 3; 4].

→ Athens

1 E. CURTIUS, J. A. KAUPERT, Atlas von Athen, 1887, 17f., folio 3   2 W. JUDEICH, Die Top. von Athen, ²1931   3 H. LAUTER, H. LAUTER-BUFE, Wohnhäuser und Stadtviertel des klass. Athen, in: MDAI(A) 86, 1971, 109–124   4 H. LAUTER, Zum Straßenbild in Alt-Athen, in: Ant. Welt 13,4, 1982, 44–52   5 TRAVLOS, Athen, 159, 392.

TRAILL, Attica, 12, 21, 51, 68, 110 no. 68 table 8, 12; WHITEHEAD, Index s.v. Coele   H.LO.

Coele Syria (Κοίλη Συρία; *Koílē Syría*). Originally, the geographical term Coele Syria (CS), often used vaguely by authors in antiquity (the 'hollow' Syria; Aramaic *kōl* 'whole'?), may have referred to the entire part of → Syria west of the Euphrates; others, based on Strabo 16,15,4, see it in a more limited fashion as the area of Biqa* between Lebanon and Antilebanon. First mentioned by Ps.-Scyl. (GGM I 15–96, especially p. 78 c. 104), CS more often only includes South Syria, sometimes incorporating parts or the whole of Phoenicia. Usually excluded is the land east of the Jordan.

CS and Phoenicia form a Persian satrapy (2 Makk 3,5; 4,4 and passim). The Ptolemaic areas up to the Eleutherus are also referred to as CS. After the reorganization of Syria by Pompey, which had no specific consequences for its administration, the term is encountered even more often. For Josephus (Ios. Ant. Iud. 13,13,2 and passim), it expands to include the → Decapolis where those cities are thus designated in inscriptions and on coins of the 1st–3rd cent. AD. Under Septimius Severus (c. AD 200), a large north Syrian province CS including the → Commagene was established alongside *Syría Phoiníke*.

→ Damascus

G. BEER, s.v. K.S., RE 11, 1050–1051; E. BICKERMAN, La K.S., in: RBi 54, 1947, 256–268.   K.KE.

Coelius Plebeian gentilicium, also *Coilius*, in surviving manuscripts often confused with *Caelius* (SCHULZE 155; ThlL, Onom. 2, 523–525). Bearers of this name are documented since the 2nd cent. BC, usually belonging to the Tribus Aemilia.   K.-L.E.
I. REPUBLICAN PERIOD   II. IMPERIAL PERIOD

I. REPUBLICAN PERIOD

[I 1] **C. Antipater, L.** Possibly the brother of the senator C. Coelius C.f. [1; 2. 16], a highly educated scholar of law and rhetoric (Cic. Brut. 102; Dig. 1,2,2,40), considered the teacher and friend of L. Licinius Crassus (Cic. Brut. 102; de orat. 2,54). In the last third of the 2nd cent. BC, at least in part after 121 (death of C. Gracchus: HRR 1, fr. 50), he wrote the first historical mono-

graph in Rome and seven books about the second Punic War (title according to Cic. Orat. 230 *Bellum Punicum*; many prefer *Historiae*). This opus, dedicated to the grammarian L. Aelius Stilo (fr. 1; 24B), not only stands out with the depth of its material and a broad reference to the sources (apart from Fabius Pictor and Cato also the Hannibal-friendly work by Silenus), but also mainly by a lively and dramatic presentation which, following Hellenistic historiography, employs direct speech (fr. 16; 26), epic form elements (dreams: fr. 11; 34; storm at sea: fr. 40), and rhetorical art prose in the Asianic style (hyperbole: fr. 39; clauses rhythm: [3. 339]). Despite reservations, Cicero counts him among the *exornatores rerum*, who is clearly superior to his predecessors and successors (de orat. 2,54; leg. 1,6). He was imitated by Brutus (Cic. Att. 13,8), extensively referred to by Livy, especially in the books 21/22 [4; 5; 6], and placed above Sallust by the emperor Hadrianus (SHA Hadr. 16,6). Fragments: HRR 1, 158–177 and in [7].

1 SHERK 12, l. 27   2 E. BADIAN, The early Historians, in: T. A. DOREY(ed.), Latin Historians, 1966, 1–38   3 LEO, 336ff.   4 H. SRAGO, De L. Coelio Antipatro Livii in libro XXI auctore, 1927   5 P. G. WALSH, Livy, 1961, 124ff.   6 R. JUMEAU, Un aspect significatif de l'exposé livien dans le livres XXI et XXII, in: M. RENARD, R. SCHILLING (ed.), Hommage à J. Bayet, 1964, 309–333   7 W. HERRMANN, Die Historien des Coelius Antipater, 1979.

EDITION: W. A. SCHRÖDER, in: AAHG 39, 1986, 57–61
                                                                          W.K.

[I 2] **C., P.** *Praetor urbanus* in 74 BC, together with Verres (Cic. Verr. 2,1,130).

[I 3] **C. Caldus, C.** As a *homo novus* (Cic. de or. 1,117) and against fierce opposition, he was the first of his family to obtain the consulate . As a people's tribune in 107 BC, he accused P. → Popillius Laenas of high treason and during that action, introduced the secret ballot with a *lex tabellaria* for *perduellio* trials (Cic. Leg. 3,36 i.a.; coins of his grandson C. [I 4] RRC 437/1); possibly mint master in 104 (RRC 318); before 103, he successfully defended a client who had insulted the poet C. Lucilius on stage (Rhet. Her. 2,19); c. 99/98 he was praetor and propraetor in Hispania citerior; in 94, consul together with L. Domitius Ahenobarbus (MRR 2,12), in 93–87, proconsul in Gaul (MRR 3,59f.); he was augur and *Xvir sacris faciundis*.

[I 4] **C. Caldus, C.** Grandson of C. [I 3], whose portrait he had struck on his coins, mint master in 51 BC (RRC 437); quaestor in 50, took over the province Cilicia from Cicero in 50 (Fam. 2,15,4 and passim). His father was the *VIIvir epulonum* L. C. Caldus.

W. HOLLSTEIN, Die stadtröm. Münzprägung der Jahre 78–50 v.Chr., 1993, 361–369.

[I 5] **C. Vinicianus, M.** Quaestor around 56 BC, people's tribune in 53. At Caesar's side during the Civil War, praetor in 48 (?), he commanded two legions in Bithynia and Pontus in 47 with proconsular imperium (Career: ILS 883; MRR 3,60).   K.-L.E.

II. IMPERIAL PERIOD

[II 1] P.C.Apollinaris. *Cos. suff.* in 111 [1. 47]. Probably father of C. [II 3] (PIR² C 1239).

[II 2] P.C.Apollinaris. *Cos. ord.* in 169, probably son of C. [II 3].

[II 3] P.C.Balbinus Vibullius Pius. Son of C. [II 1]. Admitted as a patrician by Hadrian. His career is preserved in CIL VI 1383 = ILS 1063. *Cos. ord.* in 137 together with L. Aelius Caesar. For the origins of the family [2. 346].

[II 4] L.C.Festus. Admitted into the Senate by Hadrian; *procos. Ponti et Bithyniae, praef. aerarii Saturni, cos. suff.* in 148 (CIL XI 1183 = ILS 1079) [1. 51].

[II 5] L.C. Rufus. Possibly related to C. [II 4]. Probably *cos. suff.* at the end of 119, consular legate of Moesia superior in 120 (Inscr. Més. sup. 6, 195; PIR² C 1246) [3. 154f.]; consular governor of Germania inferior in the year 127 [4].

1 VIDMAN, FO² 2 CABALLOS, Senadores 3 W. ECK, in: Chiron 13, 1983, 147–159 4 W. ECK, I. PAUNOV, in: Chiron 27, 1997, 335–353. W.E.

Coemptio Probably the usual type of arrangement for setting up a marriage in which the → *manus* power relationship applied to the woman. *Coemptio* cannot simply be interpreted as the purchase of a bride (even as a practice in a very early phase of development) because it is connected to the formal transaction of the → *mancipatio*, which, at a very early stage separated the actual procedure from that of the conceptual image the term evokes. One can assume that originally, the bride's father 'transferred' the power over his daughter to the bridegroom. Later, the woman herself probably acted as the transferring part in the transaction. Under Justinian, the *coemptio* is no longer part of the system. The main source for the *coemptio* is Gai. Inst. 1. 113–115. There, a fiduciary *coemptio* to another man is also mentioned. It serves as a change of the female guardian (→ *tutela*).

KASER, RPR I, 77f. TREGGIARI, 25–28. G.S.

Coenus (Κοῖνος; *Koînos*).
[1] Son of Polemocrates, brother of → Cleander [3], probably from → Elimea, whose platoon of → pezetairoi he commanded; he was granted land by → Philippus II.. In 335/4 BC, C. married a daughter of → Parmenion. C. took part in all of Alexander's [4] battles from Europe to the → Hydaspes and was badly wounded at → Gaugamela. In eastern Iran, C. also acted independently, i.a. in the decisive battle against → Spitamenes. During the interrogation of his brother-in-law → Philotas, C. was one of the fiercest accusers (cf. Cleander [3]). By the → Hyphasis, C. appointed himself spokesman for the army, which refused to continue marching. A little later (325) he died, allegedly of natural causes, and was given a magnificent funeral.

BERVE no. 439 (uncritical); HECKEL, 58–64.

[2] In 324 BC near → Pasargadae, he joined Alexander [4] and a little later became satrap of → Susiana where he survived Alexander (Just. Epit. 13,4,14).

BERVE no. 440. E.B.

Coeranus (Κοίρανος; *Koíranos*).
[1] Belongs to the family tree of → Melampus (Hes. Cat. 136,3), but his exact position therein is not certain; father of the seer → Poly(e)idus (Pherecydes FGrH 3 F 112; Paus. 1,43,5).
[2] Charioteer for → Meriones; he saves → Idomeneus' [1] life by bringing a chariot to him at exactly the right moment, so that he instead of Idomeneus is hit by → Hector's spear (Hom. Il. 17,611–614). The motif of 'substitution death' is typical of Homer's epics [1].
[3] Lycian who is killed by → Odysseus instead of → Sarpedon (Hom. Il. 5,677).
[4] From Miletus or Paros; during a shipwreck between Paros and Naxos, dolphins save C. as the only one (more on the motif: → Dolphin [1]) out of gratitude for the fact that he had once purchased and liberated a group of dolphins which had been caught. Later, during his funeral, dolphins are again present (Archil. fr. 192 W; Demeas FGrH 502; Plut. Mor. 984f).

1 B. FENIK, Typical Battle Scenes in the Iliad, 1968, 187. RE.N.

Coercitio The authority of Roman magistrates to intervene where they judged the public order had been violated by citizens and non-citizens, restricting their rights and exercising sovereign power. This authority ranges from an interim order (*interdicta*) via the forced collection of public claims, the imposition of fines (*multae*), arrests (*vincula, prensio*), seizing of property (*pignoris capio*), [corporal] punishment (*verbera*), right up to the imposition of capital punishment (*c. plenissima, c. capitalis*, Dig. 7,1,17,1; 50,16,200). Even in the early republican period, *coercitio* was limited to specific areas of jurisdiction. Furthermore, the provocation laws (*leges Valeriae* and *Porciae de provocatione* of the years 509, 300 and 195 BC) — which had already been legendary since the early days of the Republic — give all Roman citizens the right to appeal to the public assembly if *coercitio* imposed by a magistrate threatened them with capital punishment, a right which later also applies to corporal punishment (Liv 2,8; 10,9; Cic. Rep. 1,40,63; 2,31,53), and the people's tribunes can intercede against all acts of *coercitio* by a magistrate. The criminal courts (→ *quaestiones*), too, which later replaced the comitial procedure, curb the range of the *coercitio* powers. Nevertheless, the *coercitio* is always an essential component for the magistrates of the → *potestas* in general and of an → *imperium* in particular, whereby the bearer of the imperium, within the bounds of his official military district, has greater authority against the Romans in exercising the *coercitio* (e.g. capital punishment as a disciplinary measure). Against non-Romans, all competent magistrates can impose, at their discretion, penal *coercitio* measures. Despite the freedoms inherent in the constitution, the magistrates as a judicial authority are, by virtue of their office, nevertheless required as a matter of principle to carry out an investigation (*inquisitio*) of the facts and to remain impartial. In the imperial period, this *extraordinaria cognitio* becomes the common form of criminal proceedings for the judicial activity of the imperial court. Via the later reception in legal history, it shaped today's laws on criminal proceedings.

→ Iurisdictio

MOMMSEN, Staatsrecht, 136–161; Id., Strafrecht, 35ff., 142ff., 260ff.; J. L. STRACHAN-DAVIDSON, Problems of the Roman Criminal Law 1, 1912, 96ff.   C.G.

Coeus (Κοῖος; *Koîos*, Lat. Coeus). The second of the six → Titans, son of → Uranus and → Gaia (Hes. Theog. 134; Apollod. 1,1,3). With the Titaness → Phoebe he begets two daughters, → Leto (Hom. h. Apollo 62) and → Asteria [2] (Apollod. 1,2,2; 1,4,1; Hes. Theog. 404ff.). He takes part in the titanomachy (Hes. Theog. 628ff.). C. has possibly given his name to the island of Cos (Tac. Ann. 12,61) and a River C. in Messenia (Paus. 4,33,5).

K. MAROT, Kronos und die Titanen, in: SMSR 8, 1932; M. MAYER, s.v. Koios, ROSCHER 2.1, 1265–1266.   EL.STO.

Coffered ceiling see → Lacunar; → Roofing

Cogidubnus, Cogidumnus Britannic client king (CIL VII 11: *rex magnus Britanniae* [1]) in Sussex (originally possibly king of the → Atrebates), who had authority over several *civitates* up to the Flavian period (Tac. Agr. 14,1) and presumably was among the 11 kings subjugated by Claudius (CIL VI 31537d).

1 J. E. BOGAERS, King C. in Chichester, in: Britannia 10, 1979, 243–254.

A. A. BARRETT, The Career of Tib. Claudius C., in: Britannia 10, 1979, 227–242.   C.KU.

Cognatio According to Roman law, the kinship established by a blood relationship, which also applies to non-agnates; the degree was determined by the number of mediated procreations or births. The *cognatio* gained legal importance with the *lex Cincia* (204 BC): the *cognati* up to the 6th degree of relationship (*sobrini*, great grandchildren from the same great-grandfather) were exempted from this law's ban on gifts. The *lex Furia* (beginning of the 2nd cent. BC) exempted these *cognati* from its restrictions, as well as in the 7th degree the children of *sobrini*. Later, the praetor granted the same [class of] persons the → *bonorum possessio intestati* if no civilian heir made a claim for the inheritance (Gai. Inst. 3,37). The *servilis cognatio*, based on one's birth as

a slave, was of no legal importance even if a manumission occurred later. Cf. Dig. 38,8; 38,10.

→ Agnatio; → Succession, law of; → Legatum

1 KASER, RPR I, 350f.   2 U. MANTHE, in: Gnomon 66, 1994, 525ff.   U.M.

Cognitio is derived from *cognoscere* and means an investigation or decision carried out when acting as a judge. In criminal proceedings, this term covers the investigation of a crime including the establishment of the facts (Dig. 47,20,3 pr.), as well as the interrogation of a person in remand (Dig. 1,16,6 pr.). In civil proceedings, *causae cognito* usually means a summary examination by a magistrate; as a form of proceedings, the *cognito* changes from an extraordinary type of proceedings (*extraordinaria c.*) to the exclusive type of trial (so-called cognition trial/proceedings).

1) The *causae* cognitio is a proviso in favour of an examination of the facts by the praetor himself, *causa cognita iudicium dabo* (Dig. 47,10,15,43); instead of restricting himself to the examination of the legal question relevant to the granting of a formula, the magistrate himself also examines the facts. Here, the prerequisites for the reliability of an accusation are often examined: for example if the praetor, for reasons of justice in an individual case, wants to grant a formula not provided for in the edict (e.g. Dig. 4,4,1,1); or in case of the *in integrum* → *restitutio*, of the *missio in bona*, in matters of guardianship or those regarding bail.

2) Since Augustus, the *cognitio extra ordinem* developed as a special type of court proceedings for legal situations which had previously not been actionable (entail, maintenance claims, etc.) in strict contrast (cf. Dig. 50,16,178,2) to the conventional formula proceedings in civil lawsuits. Instead of the conventional division into two parts (court magistrate for the section *in iure*, private *iudex* for the actual establishment of the facts), the cognition official as a government officer dealt with the entire process, which was now uniform. Time and again, one also comes across the *princeps* as a judge (even at the court of first instance). A decisive consequence of this uniformity is the emergence of an officialism (summons, failure to appear, enforcement of payment in kind, etc.). In the year 342, the formula proceedings are abolished once and for all (Cod. Iust. 2,57,1).

→ Ordo

I. BUTI, La 'cognitio extra ordinem', in: ANRW II 14, 1982, 29–59; J. M. KELLY, Princeps Iudex, 1957; G. I. LUZZATO, Il problema d'origine del processo extra ordinem I, 1965.   C.PA.

Cognomen In Roman and middle Italian personal names, the cognomen is the most recent part of the name and is usually placed last; it only came into general usage at the end of the Republic. In terms of its origin and character, the cognomen is an individual name which initially extends the → praenomen in its designation function and then, since the beginning of the imperial period, it increasingly replaces it. The word cognomen, in Plautus mostly still cognomentum (e.g. Persa 60), as a 'means to recognize identity' is derived from cognoscere and only in a secondary development was related to nomen as a 'co-name'. Among the aristocracy in Republican Rome and in Etruria, the individual cognomen was often passed on, thus becoming the family cognomen as a type of second → gentile which distinguished the stirpes of a gens (Dolabella, Scipio, Lentulus, Sulla, Cinna for the Cornelii). From the end of the Republic, the (individual) cognomen was usually conferred at birth; in that context, it was popular to use names with a good original meaning (Faustus, Victor). The older custom was the naming according to an individual characteristic, not necessarily a positive one (Cato 'smart guy', Blaesus 'stammerer', Censorinus [who was censor twice]).

Appellatives such as proper names (Helena) or derivatives thereof (Mart-ialis, Capitol-inus) could be chosen as cognomina. These appellatives were usually adjectives or substantives directly related to the name of the person (Faustus, Pictor), and more rarely they were metonymic names for special characteristics (Sura 'he with the striking calf', Felicitas 'she who should thrive'). It was particularly popular, especially after the generalization of the cognomen (see above), to choose already existing cognomina, especially those with a positive original meaning of the appellative base; individual cognomina became fashionable names that occurred frequently (Ianuarius after the first month of the year, Primus, Vitalis). In Republican Rome, most of the cognomen were of Lat. origin; some were taken from Greek or → Etruscan (Philo, Sophus: Greek Φίλων, Σοφός; Thalna: Etruscan name of the goddess Θalna; the proportion of Etruscan names has long been overestimated). In the imperial period, Greek cognomina (Hermes, Agatho, Cleopatra) are more common than Lat. ones; in addition, there were 'Barbarian' cognomen with Semitic, Celtic or Illyrian origins (Malchio, Blesamus, Epicadus).

For the c. 250 Etruscan cognomina (5th–1st cent. BC) and for the few Osc.-Umbr. cognomina, the same applies, mutatis mutandis, as for the Lat. cognomina of the Republic. Amongst the Etruscans, many cognomina are of Italic origin (Lusce, Crespe, Macre, Pacre from Lat. luscus 'cross-eyed', crispus 'curly', macer 'lean', Umbr. pacer 'gracious'). There, new citizens could also adopt the gentilicium of their patronus as a cognomen (in Au Tite Marcna, the patronus gentilicium Marcna is the cognomen of the new citizen Au[le] Tite).

→ Gens; → Personal names: Rome and Italy

KAJANTO, COGNOMINA; SOLIN/SALOMIES; H. SOLIN, Namen im alten Rom, in: E. EICHLER et al. (ed.), Namenforschung, 1995ff.; Id., Die griech. PN in Rom, 1982; H. RIX, Das etr. C., 1963.   H.R.

Cohors During early Republican times, the → allies placed units of 500 men under the command of the Roman army, which were later called cohortes and came under the command of a prefect of the relevant town. It remains unclear when the cohortes were integrated into the army as tactical units. Polybius called a cohort a unit consisting of three → maniples (Pol. 11,23; Battle of Ilipa 206 BC), but in his famous description of the Roman army, cohortes are not mentioned. Livy mentions cohortes in his representation of the campaigns in Spain during the 2nd cent. BC, sometimes in conjunction with maniples, but that is probably anachronistic. Archaeological investigations of the camp of → Scipio Aemilianus at Numantia indicate that, around 133 BC, the legions were still organized in maniples. Cohortes finally replaced maniples towards the end of the 2nd cent.; in Caesar's time, the cohors was the basic tactical unit of Roman infantry. It consisted of 480 men who were divided into six centuriae each under the command of a → centurio; however, the maniple continued to be used for administrative purposes. A legion consisted of 10 cohortes, and no later than under the Flavians, the first cohort of a legion was larger than the other cohortes, possibly twice the size. Under the Principate, a practice developed whereby, instead of a whole legion, only individual cohortes were temporarily transferred to a new base.

In Republican times, the cohors praetoria stood guard in front of the legion commander's quarters. Then, in 27 BC, Augustus created his own bodyguard (Praetorians) which consisted of nine cohortes of 500 men each, perhaps even 1,000 men, and which was under the command of a military tribune. Initially, the cohortes urbanae consisted of three, later of four cohortes, while the → vigiles comprised seven cohortes. The → auxilia were divided into cohortes of 480–500 men who were generally commanded by prefects. Probably under the Flavians, larger units (milliaria) were created which comprised between 800 and 1,000 soldiers.

In the army of Diocletian, cohortes, probably 500 men strong, continued to serve in the provinces. Under Constantine, the number of cohortes was reduced and the soldiers who served in them were given equal rank with the border troops (limitanei); in terms of their rank, though, they were classed as being below the field troops (comitatenses).

During Republican times, cohortes were also understood to be the personnel or household of a magistrate or a provincial governor, which often consisted of personal friends (e.g.. Cic. Att. 7.1.6.); this is the origin of the cohors amicorum — a formally defined circle of the princeps' friends.

1 G. L. CHEESMAN, The Auxilia of the Roman Imperial Army, 1914 (repr. 1971)   2 Y. LE BOHEC, L'armée romaine, 1989   3 M. DURRY, Les cohortes prétoriennes, 1938   4 P. A. HOLDER, Studies in the Auxilia of the Roman Army from Augustus to Trajan, 1980   5 L. KEPPIE, The Making of the Roman Army, 1984   6 H. M. D. PARKER, The Roman Legions, 1958   7 G. WEBSTER, The Roman Imperial Army, 1985.   J.CA.

Cohortatio see → Adlocutio

Coiedius Maximus Presidential procurator of Mauretania Tingitana under Marcus Aurelius and Verus, no later than the middle of 168; he took part in the conferring of civil rights of citizenship which is described in the *tabula Banasitana* (AE 1971, 534 = II.Mar. 2, 94).

W.E.

Coinage, standards of Relates to the systems of weights upon which ancient coinage was based.
A. GREECE B. ROME

A. GREECE

In the Greek coinage system (→ Money; → Minting), there were various standards; however, the designations of the nominal values and → weights were uniform and usually had the following ratios: 1 → talent = 60 minai, 1 → mina = 50 staters, 1 → stater = 2 drachmas, 1 → drachma = 6 → oboloi [1. 159]. The determination of ancient standards of coinage is based on the average weight of the largest possible number of well-preserved coins. Contrary to individually adjusted gold coins, ancient silver coins and those of base metal were minted *al marco*, i.e. a certain number of coins were produced from a certain amount of metal, which explains the variations in weight amongst individual pieces. Therefore, the standards of coinage assumed today are approximate values only [1. 154–55].

In the so-called Milesian standard of coinage (beginning of the 5th cent. BC), the drachma had a weight of *c.* 7 g [1. 155; 2. 185; 3. 390]. In the Aeginetan — the oldest standard of coinage in Greece — the drachma weighed about 6.2 g; the Aeginetan mina contained only 70 drachmas in contrast to 100 drachmas elsewhere [1. 155; 2. 185; 3. 11–12].

The most widely adopted standard of coinage was the Euboean-Attic with a weight for a drachma of 4.366 g; the main nominal value was the → tetradrachmon. Based on this standard of coinage, the → dareikos with the weight of the → didrachmon of *c.* 8.5 g was minted in gold and the Alexander coinage (a tetradrachm normally under 17 g) was minted in silver, which was in common use across the entire Mediterranean and in the east as far as Bactria. This standard influenced the Corinthian standard where the stater was not divided into two, but rather into three drachmas of *c.* 2.8 g each. In lower Italy and Sicily, the Corinthian stater was minted as a → nomos [3] [1. 155f.; 2. 185; 3. 46–48, 182f.].

The so-called Phocaean or Persian standard of coinage, also included the stater at the value of the → tridrachmon with originally 16.5 g, and then, from the end of the 6th cent. to the middle of the 4th cent. BC, with 15–15.9 g. The staters of → Croesus and the Persian → siglos were minted according to this standard, and also the staters, → hektai and other nominal values of the electron cities of Cyzicus, Phocaea and Mytilene (Lesbos); in Italy, the Phocaean colony of

Hyele minted to this standard [1. 156; 2. 185f.; 3. 501f., 512].

In the Chian standard of coinage found before 400 BC in Asia Minor and on the islands (Thuc. 8,101,1; Xen. Hell. 1,6,12: pay for soldiers on the fleet), the tetradrachm weighed *c.* 15.5 g. With the start of minting in Rhodes around 400 BC (tetradrachm *c.* 15.3 g), it is referred to as the Rhodian standard, also called Asia Minor standard because of its distribution in Caria, Ionia, the Troad and Mysia. In the course of time, the weight of this standard was reduced; the Hellenistic → cistophori, were tetradrachms minted in the kingdom of the Attalids from 166 BC, weighing around 12.35 to 12.7 g on average [1. 156f.; 2. 186; 3. 102f., 565f.; 4. 128].

Since 151 BC, a standard was introduced in the Phoenician cities of the Seleucid kingdom with a drachma weight of 3.63 g ($^5/_6$ of the Attic drachma) which in numismatics is often called the Phoenician standard of coinage. This, however, should rather be called the Ptolemaic standard of coinage because of its proximity to the Egyptian sphere of influence. Based on that standard, the shekel (→ Siglos) was minted during the Jewish uprising against Rome (AD 66–70) [1. 157; 3. 510f.].

B. ROME

In the Roman system of coinage, a uniform standard prevailed; however, the coin weights, based on the Roman pound with an assumed weight of 320–330 g [1. 157f.] or 327.45 g [5. 590–592], change over time. If one uses the solidi (→ Solidus) with a weight of 4.50 g as a base, which are adjusted *al pezzo* (individually) and of which there are 72 in a pound, it results in a pound of 324 g [1. 158].

In the Roman Republic with its duodecimal system of metal money, the following ratios existed: 1 → as = 2 semisses (→ Semis) = 3 trientes (→ Triens) = 4 quadrantes = 6 sextantes (→ Sextans) = 12 → unciae. In the decimal system, 1 → decussis = 10 asses, 1 → denarius (originally) 10 asses [1. 159f.].

From Augustus to the end of the 2nd cent. AD, 1 → aureus = 25 denarii = 100 → sestertii = 200 → dupondii = 400 asses. For the 3rd cent. AD, the ratios cannot be determined accurately because of high inflation [1. 160f.].

Since AD 324, after a uniform reorganization of gold minting across the empire, the following ratio resulted: 1 → solidus = 2 semisses = 3 → tremisses = 18 → miliarensia = 36 → siliquae [1. 161].

1 GÖBL 2 H. A. CAHN, Knidos. Die Münzfüße des 6. und 5. Jh. v.Chr., 1970 3 SCHRÖTTER 4 F. S. KLEINER, S. P. NOE, The Early Cistophoric Coinage, 1977 5 RRC 6 RIC (Einleitungen zu den Kaisern) 7 A Survey of Numismatic Research, 7 vols. 1961–1997. GE.S.

Coinage laws Statutory regulations issued by those authorized to produce coins (sovereigns, states), which relate to minting practice or money circulation in that state or its sphere of influence.
A. GREECE B. ROME

A. GREECE

1. The coinage decree of the Athenians (IG I³ 1453; ATL II D 14; [1]): the people's resolution about the unification of the coinage system as well as weights and measures in the → Delian League probably dates from the time around 449 BC. With this decree, the Ath. currency as well as Ath. weights and measures were to be the only valid ones in the League (s. §§ 8, 12 of the modern classification in [1] according to IG³), minting was to take place exclusively in Athens (§ 5) and foreign silver (money) was to be exchanged at a mandatory rate into Athenian money (§§ 5, 13). The decree emphasizes the predominance of Athens in the League and the prohibition of having one's own → minting facility is a restriction of the autonomy of the confederates.

2. Coinage convention between Mytilene (Lesbos) and Phocaea (Ionia; SGDI 213; Stv II 228): in this convention of the beginning of the 4th cent. BC, the two cities agree to common minting in → electron, for which in relation to both poleis one person is responsible whose task it is to alloy the gold. If this person intentionally adulterates the mixture, i.e. by adding too much silver to the gold, his punishment will be death (l. 13–15).

3. Athenian law about circulation of coins and → control of coins, 375/4 BC [2; 3]: the law determines that Ath. money has to be accepted if it is made of silver and it has the government minting stamp (l. 3/4). Between the tables of the money-changers on the Agora sat a government checker (→ dokimastḗs) who had to check foreign silver money submitted to him: if it had the same stamp as Attic money or was pure, i.e. of good silver, it had to be returned to the submitter; if, however, it had a core of bronze or lead, or if it had been counterfeited otherwise, it had to be cancelled and confiscated (l. 8–13). In the first quarter of the 4th cent. BC, foreign silver money often consisted of imitations of Athenian money, which were particularly common in commerce. The law also contains a detailed catalogue of penalties for violating these regulations.

4. Law of Olbia about the exchange of foreign currencies (Syll.3 218; IOSPE I² 24; IK 20,16): with this law from the 4th cent. BC, the city of Olbia regulates the circulation of money in commerce: import and export of minted gold and silver are permitted (l. 4/5), the exchange may only take place 'on the stone (table) in the square of the people's assembly' (l. 6–10). An essential determination lies in the fact that commerce in Olbia can only be carried out with the bronze or silver currency of the city, a contravention of the law attracts a penalty (l. 13–22). The exchange rate of the → Cyzicenes is fixed at 11 Olbian half staters, the value of all other gold or silver coins depends on 'how they come to

an agreement' (l. 24–29). The exchange dealings are free of any levies (I. 29–31). The prohibition of commerce in a foreign currency and the high fixed exchange rate for the Cyzicene → stater was intended to strengthen Olbia's currency.

5. References to minting laws can also be found in inscriptions which are not directly related to the coinage system itself. In the *sympoliteia* treaty between Smyrna and Magnesia [3] on the Sipylus from the 3rd cent. BC, it says: 'In Magnesia, too, one must accept the legal money of the city (Smyrna)' (OGIS 229, l. 55; IK 24,1,573, I. 55). In an honorary inscription at Sestus from the end of the 2nd cent. BC, a resolution of the *demos* [1] about the introduction of a local bronze minting is mentioned (IK 19,1, l. 43–49; [4; 5]). Around 96 BC, the Delphic Amphictyons (→ *amphiktyonía*) adopted the resolution that the Attic → tetradrachm be accepted at a value of four silver drachms (Syll.3 729, l. 2/3; FdD III 2, 1913, no. 139) whereby the Attic tetradrachm was to be protected against the devalued Achaean drachm and the Roman → victoriatus [6], which was also devalued.

B. ROME

1. The *Lex Clodia* of the year 104 BC again introduced the → quinarius (Plin. HN 33,46; RRC 610; 628f.; [7]).

2. With the *Lex Papiria* from the year 91 BC, reduction of the → as to the semiuncia standard was determined by law (Plin. HN 33,46; RRC p. 77f.; 611).

The → coinage reforms of the imperial period are also to be counted among the coinage laws: the price edict of emperor Diocletian (→ Edictum [3] Diocletiani) and the laws relating to → counterfeiting coins.
→ Money; → Coins, counterfeiting of; → Coinage reforms

1 CH. KOCH, Volksbeschlüsse in Seebundangelegenheiten, 1991, T 12 2 R.S. STROUD, An Athenian Law on Silver Coinage, in: Hesperia 43, 1974, 157–188 3 G. STUMPF, Ein athenisches Münzgesetz des 4. Jh.v.Chr., in: JNG 36, 1986, 23–40 4 H. v. FRITZE, Sestos. Die Menas-Inschr. und das Münzwesen der Stadt, in: Nomisma I, 1907, 1–13 5 TH. R. MARTIN, Sovereignty and Coinage in Classical Greece, 1985, 238–241 6 B. KEIL, Zur Victoriatusrechnung auf griech. Inschr., in: ZfN 32, 1914, 56–59 7 GÖBL, 48. GE.S.

Coinage reforms Changes in the coinage system which relate to the nominal value, the → coinage standard or the value structure of the coins.

1. The weights, measures and coin reform by → Solon in the year 594/3 BC was recorded by Aristot. Ath. Pol. 10. Solon reorganized the weights upon which later, c. 540 BC, early Athenian coinage was based. Thus, the Solonic reform cannot be called a coinage reform (CR) in the true sense [1].

2. After the end of the Civil Wars, → Augustus reorganized the Roman coinage system (24–21 BC): The → aureus (gold) weighed c. 7.96 g (with 41 in a

Roman pound). Equivalents to the aureus were: 25
→ denarii (silver) at *c.* 4 g (84 per pound), 100 → sestertii (brass) at *c.* 25 g (13 per pound), 200 → dupondii
(brass) at *c.* 12.5 g (25 per pound), 400 asses (→ As;
copper) at *c.* 11 g (30 per pound). The ratios of the
nominal values to each other remained until the end of
the 2nd cent. AD (RIC I², p. 3; [2]).

3. Under Augustus' successors, the weight of the
aureus was slightly reduced (Plin. HN 33,47); after
Nero's CR of the year AD 64, there were 45 aurei, each
with a weight of *c.* 7.2–7.4 g per pound, the denarius
sank to about 3.2–3.5 g, and its fineness, which under
Augustus had been 96–98 per cent silver, was now
around 93.50 per cent (RIC I², p. 3–5; [3]). The object
of the CR was to save precious metal in minting [4].

4. In AD 274, a CR took place under Emperor
→ Aurelianus [3]: he issued new silver money (in Rome)
whereby he had the population hand in the bad money
in order to eliminate confusion in the circulating media
(Zos. 1,61,3). These new coins are double denarii covered in a silver wash with an average weight of 3.9 g, on
the obverse the bust of the emperor with radiating
crown and on the reverse at the cut-off the characters
XXI for mintings of western mints or the Greek KB for
those of eastern mints (RIC 64, Rome: XXI; RIC 289,
Serdica: KA). It is disputed whether these characters
represent control marks, additional characters or value
marks ([5] rejects the interpretation as value marks and
presents a list of the theories argued thus far; in opposition [2. annotation 612]). It is possible to interpret the
characters as 20 units and to equate the double denarius
with 20 asses or the denarius with 10 asses as at the
beginning of Roman coinage from 211 to 133 BC [6].
The object of Aurelianus' CR was the stabilization of
the → Antoninianus/double denarius and the restoration of confidence in the money issued by the government.

5. For the CR of Emperor → Diocletianus see
→ Edictum [3] Diocletiani.

6. Emperor → Constantinus [1] I reorganized gold
minting by reintroducing the → solidus with a weight of
4.5 g, i.e. 72 per Roman pound (as opposed to 60 under
Diocletianus); this took place in AD 309 in Trier, AD
313 in his part of the empire and from 324 in the entire
empire (RIC VI, p. 100; RIC VII, S. 1). Aurei and solidi
were in circulation concurrently at a ratio of five aurei =
six solidi.

7. In AD 363, Emperor → Iulianus [11] reorganized
copper coinage: under Constantius [2] II and Constans
[1], the weight of the → centenionalis and → maiorina
coins introduced by them had been lowered several
times for the centenionalis from 3 g to 2 g, for the maiorina from 7.5 g to 3.5 g. Now, the specified weight
was 9.02 g (36 per Roman pound) or 3.38 g respectively (96 per Roman pound). On its reverse, the centenionalis had the circumferential legend SECVRITAS REI
PVBLICAE and an Apis bull; the maiorina carried on its
reverse the legend VOT/X/MVLT/XX [7; 8].

8. The East Roman emperor → Anastasius [1] I.
(491–518) with his CR of AD 498 and 512 attempted to
bring the copper → follis into a fixed value ratio to the
solidus. The copper coins introduced by him carried on
the reverse side the value designations M = 40
→ nummi, weight *c.* 9 g, K = 20 nummi, *c.* 4.5 g, and I =
10 nummi, *c.* 2.25 g. In 512, the weights were doubled
and, in addition, a five nummi piece (value E) with *c.*
2.25 g was minted. The follis with *c.* 9 g was equivalent
to 40 nummi. In 498, the solidus contained 16,800
nummi (420 folles), and in 512, 8,400 nummi (210 folles). The basis of Anastasius' CR was a coin fully made
of copper and not, as in earlier CR, made of → billon
[9].

→ Money; → Devaluation of money; → Coinage laws;
→ Coin production; → Coin minting

1 M.R.-ALFÖLDI, Riflessioni sulla riforma monetaria
cosidetta solonia, in: Bollettino di Numismatica 5, 1987,
9–17   2 GÖBL, 160   3 D.R. WALKER, The Metrology of
the Roman Silver Coinage. From Augustus to Domitian,
vol. 1, 1976, 17f.   4 L. TONDO, La riforma monetaria
neroniana, in: Riv. Italiana di Numismatica 78, 1976,
127–137   5 D. KIENAST, Die Münzreform Aurelians, in:
Chiron 4, 1974, 547–565   6 W. WEISER, Die Münzreform des Aurelian, in: ZPE 53, 1983, 279–295
7 M. MUNZI, Considerazioni sulla riforma monetaria dell'
Imperatore Giuliano, in: Annali istituto italiano di numismatica 43, 1996, 295–306   8 J.P.C. KENT, An Introduction to the Coinage of Julian the Apostate, in: NC 19,
1959, 117   9 M.F. HENDY, Stud. in the Byzantine Monetary Economy, c. 300–1450, 1985, 475–492.   GE.S.

Coinage system see → Money, money economy;
→ Coin minting

Coin counterfeit In other words: forgery. Unauthorized production or forced weight reduction of circulating coins to the detriment of the public by a party not
entitled to mint. It must be differentiated from the
manufacture or modification of old coins to the detriment of collectors. Coin counterfeit (CC) is as old as
minting coins. The oldest preserved forged coins are
imitations of Lydian electron coins of the early 6th cent.
BC [11. 35f.]. Forgeries undermined confidence in the
entire coinage (Dion. Chrys. 31,24).

Since the nominal value of an ancient coin corresponded to its metallic value and the strike guaranteed
it and, consequently, the nominal value, it was the objective of coin forgers to produce a coin with a superfi-
cially imperceptibly lower metallic value. The majority
are coins with a copper core (more rarely iron or lead)
and a very thin silver or (more rarely) gold plating
(→ Coin production). In the case of token coins there
was no need for the counterfeiter to manipulate the coin
metal because the profit lay in the difference between
metal and nominal value, which was otherwise realized
by the state. However, there are also Roman bronze
coins with an iron core.

Whether such plated coinages were forgers' products or state manipulation to stretch precious metal

supplies (often in times of crisis; cf. → coins, decline in the quality of) must be decided on a case-by-case basis. Opinions are in part controversial [5. 33–37]. A large number of the dies preserved from antiquity must be considered forgers' tools [7. n. 694]. It is unlikely that the plated Roman denarii of the 1st cent. BC and AD were official coinages [4; 12. 74–77]; this is contradicted by the → control of coins and the right to refuse forged coins. Literary reports on coin forging by the state[13. 473] — e.g., the gilded lead coins of Polycrates of Samos, the tin coinage of Dionysius [1] I of Syracuse — have only in part been confirmed by the coins themselves. Demosthenes emphasizes the frequency of silver coins with additions of lead or copper (Or. 24,114). Cases of illegal minting and CC by mint officials or employees were, for example, Diogenes [14] of Sinope [2], the minting of plated coins in Dyme about 200 BC (Syll.³ 530; [14]) and the background to the minters' uprising of → Felicissimus under Aurelianus [3] (SHA 38,2–4). The decree of AD 321 is directed against forging mint employees (Cod. Theod. 9,21,2). In the 4th cent. AD, one author even considered the official mints and mint employees as the main source of coin forgeries (Anon. de rebus bell. 3,1–3).

A more simple forgery technique was casting. Moulds for casting were produced by imprinting original coins in clay. Many coin casting forms have been found, especially from the inflationary period of the 3rd cent. AD. Some of the casts were tolerated emergency measures for remedying → shortages of small coins [1], such as the 'limes falsa' and the minimi of the 3rd cent. AD, which cannot be recognized as unofficial at first glance. However, true coin forgeries are the copper tin alloy casts of the Severian period (193–235) that simulate silver [12. 79f.]. Attempts to oppose CC were the serrated denarii (i.e. with sawed marginal notching) of the Roman Republic and the general → control of coins (cf. → nummularius; → Coinage laws).

Unauthorized removal of material by shaving (scalpere, radere) or clipping the margin (circumcidere) — which was easily performed on the thin coins and difficult to notice because of the absence of a marginal ring (Cod. Theod. 9,22,1 of 317; Ulp. Dig. 48,10,8) — and removal of the silver coating (Cod. Theod. 9,21,6 of 349) were equated with CC.

In Athens and most Greek cities capital punishment was imposed on CC according to Demosthenes (Dem. Or. 20,167; 24,212; the reference to Solon lacks credibility [14. 174f.]). Capital punishment was imposed on forging mint officials and employees in Dyme in about 200 BC [14]. Regarding Sulla's lex Cornelia de falsis of 82 BC, see → counterfeiting. This law considered counterfeiting as fraud (fraus). It remained the basis of fighting CC until the 4th cent. AD. Possibly only the imitation of gold and silver coins was prosecuted ([8. 244]; by contrast [10. no. 31,72–80]). In 319 Constantine [1] the Great once more determined penalties for forging coins dependent on gender and rank (Cod. Theod. 9,21,1). In 343 Constantine [2] II decreed death by burning as the penalty for forging gold coins (Cod. Theod. 9,21,5), Theodosius I had forgery of gold coins prosecuted as lèse majesté in 389 (Cod. Theod. 9,21,9) and, for the first time, explicitly made the imitation of bronze coins punishable in 393 (Cod. Theod. 9,21,10; [8. 251–253]).

→ Small coins, shortage of; → Coinage laws; → Coin production; → Coins, control of; → Counterfeiting; → Coins, debasement of; → Nummularius; COINS

1 M. R.-ALFÖLDI, Die »Fälscherförmchen« von Pachten, in: Germania 1974, 426–447 2 H. BANNERT, Numismatisches zu Biographie und Lehre des Hundes Diogenes, in: Litterae Numismaticae Vindobonenses 1, 1979, 49–63 3 W. CAMPBELL, Greek and Roman Plated Coins, 1933 4 M. CRAWFORD, Plated Coins — False Coins, in: NC 8, 1968, 55–59 5 G. DEMBSKI, Ein röm. Münzschatzfund aus Flavia Solva, in: NZ 90, 1975, 7–43 6 G. DEVOTO, Ripostiglio di Lucoli, il »gruzzolo« di un falsario di età repubblicana, in: Boll. di Numismatica 21, 1993, 7–99 7 GÖBL 8 PH. GRIERSON, The Roman Law of Counterfeiting, in: R. A. G. CARSON, C. H. V. SUTHERLAND (ed.), Essays in Roman Coinage, FS H. Mattingly, 1956, 240–261 9 H. F. HITZIG, s.v. Falsum, RE 6, 1909, 1973–1976 10 J. LLUIS Y NAVAS-BRUSI, La falsificación de moneda en el derecho romano, in: Numisma 30, 1958, 71–97; 31, 1958, 61–85; 32, 1958, 35–58 11 H. MOESTA, P. R. FRANKE, Ant. Metallurgie und Münzprägung, 1995 12 M. PETER, Eine Werkstätte zur Herstellung von subaeraten Denaren in Augusta Raurica, 1990 13 K. REGLING, s.v. Subaeratus, RE 4A, 1931, 471–474 14 G. THÜR, G. STUMPF, Sechs Todesurteile und zwei plattierte Hemidrachmen aus Dyme, in: Tyche 4, 1989, 171–183. DI.K.

Coin production

Up to the 16th cent., coin production (CP) hardly changed (BRAMANTE's minting press). Ancient coins are usually struck, less often cast. For the location of mints, their administration and organization see → minting. First of all, coin metal [18] must be made available by foundries. At least for precious metal coins, the purity of the alloy is the decisive determinant for their value. The coin metal was probably delivered already in an alloyed state (in ingots?). Serial marks of the Hellenistic → tetradrachms of Athens apparently identify different deliveries of silver. The coinage treaty between Mytilene and Phocaea of c. 400 BC (Stv 2,228) mentions an official responsible for the quality of the → electron. In the 2nd cent. AD in Rome, imperial freedmen were leaseholders of the foundry belonging to the mint (cf. CIL VI 791). In late antiquity, imperial officials checked and stamped the bars of precious metal.

The blank (coin plate) was normally cast. Casting could take place into moulds joined together by channels. Because of the considerable fluctuations in weight occurring here, precious metal coins were cast in open, uncovered plates having approximately hemispherical depressions which were filled to their rim. Such 'dimpled plates' made of clay occur in the entire Celtic area [22]. Further casting moulds for blanks were found in Israel (1st cent. BC; [16. fig. 1–2, 5]), Egypt [7] and

Cyprus (Ptolem. period). In classical Sicily (5th–4th cent. BC), blanks were cast into two-part individual moulds or, in the case of silver, it was drawn from the crucible with a type of spherical nose tong whereupon it quickly solidified into a blank form. The residues of the casting flash can still be detected on coins [7]. As required, the blanks were subject to further manual processing: removal of casting stems, filing or hammering of the edges, beating the blank flat to the desired thickness and size [3. 45–70]. The finished blanks were checked, usually *al marco*, i.e. a group of a certain number had to be equivalent to a unit of weight [3. 45–70], and gold coins, certainly the late Roman and Byzantine ones, *al pezzo*, i.e. there was a fixed weight for an individual blank. For the manufacture of coins with a core of base metal being silver plated, there were several methods: 1. Silver wash; 2. Plating: the copper blank covered in overlapping silver foils or silver granulate was heated up to the melting point of silver which then firmly bonded to the core [5; 18. 106–109]; 3. The silver in the alloy of the blank was 'driven out' by heating over a charcoal fire and then by dipping into a salt solution bath. The cutting or punching of blanks from silver and gold plate, practised in late antiquity, was rare before the 4th cent. AD (cross-marked coins of the Tectosages; Sassanids).

The manufacture of the stamping-dies has not been fully explained. For artistic special mintings, all dies were probably engraved individually by hand, which is also likely for the older Greek coins. In the manufacture of dies for mass minting, punches (upper dies; positive dies) with parts of the coin image or the legend could have been used already in pre-Roman times. For coins from late antiquity, there is proven evidence of letter dies. The discussion is still in progress [3. 7–27; 6; 10. 52f.; 14; 18. 95; 20]. Only a few Greek dies are preserved, more numerous are those from Roman times and late antiquity [15; 23]. In the 6th cent. BC, the coins were sometimes minted with several punches in several operations [14].

The minting-dies were made of bronze, iron with bronze plating at the die head or (in late antiquity) also of pure iron which was sometimes hardened to steel at the die head by repeated carbonizing. These dies were more wear-resistant than those made of bronze which wore down fairly quickly. The minting process itself can be reconstructed quite accurately. The lower die with the obverse image was inserted in a small anvil. In archaic and classical times, the oblong upper die with the reverse image (initially only the impression of a holding tool, incusum, cf. → quadratum incusum) was put into position without guidance; only for the → incusi coins was accurate placing necessary. From Hellenistic times, the tool was more frequently handled with fixed guiding and thus with a fixed rotational angle to the obverse side. To what extent the blanks were heated first in order to facilitate the minting process, has recently become the subject of debate again. The coin was now struck with one or several blows of a hammer onto the upper die, which is why the top of the upper die is always deformed.

The wear of minting-dies was dependent on several conditions (hardness of the head, height of the relief, size of the blank etc.). Experiments which try to establish the 'life expectancy' of ancient minting-dies are problematic, and attempts to calculate the minting volume of an emission from the number of dies are thus also problematic [3. 28–35; 19; 21]. Since, during minting, the upper and lower dies were subject to differing loads, they were abraded at a different rate. Worn dies were replaced as required while those still usable were retained for use on the other side of the coin (die coupling). Only from late antiquity, a scissor-like tool is known with obverse and reverse dies of equal size for minting gold coins.

Only base metal coins were cast, i.a. for minting into large → *aes grave* of the Roman Republic, Celtic coins in the poorly mintable alloy → Potin as well as counterfeits or emergency emissions (Limes falsa, see → Coin counterfeit).

There are hardly any written and only a few pictorial sources regarding the manufacture of coins. Worth mentioning are the comparison of the prophet → Mani (3rd cent. AD) between coining a word and minting a coin, a comparison accurately reflecting the conditions of the Persian court mint [11; 13], inscriptions of the city of Rome naming mint workers [1], a → tessera from Vienna, coins from Paestum, the Carisius denarius, a Sassanid seal stone/gem, a Merovingian → triens [10. fig. 3597–3600; 3612], a → contorniate, an Italic grave relief [2. fig. 397; 407] and a coin from Ancyra [18. fig. 77].

→ Money; → Incusi; → Coin counterfeit; → Minting; COINS; NUMISMATICS

1 M. R.-ALFÖLDI, Epigraphische Beitr. zur röm. Münztechnik bis auf Konstantin den Großen, in: Schweizerische Numismatische Rundschau 39, 1958/59, 35–48   2 Id., Ant. Numismatik, 1978, 28–34   3 M. M. ARCHIBALD, M. R. COWELLS (ed.), Metallurgy in Numismatics, 1993   4 P. BALOG, Notes on Ancient and Medieval Minting Technique, in: NC 15, 1955, 195–201   5 E. BERNAREGGI, Nummi Pelliculati, in: Riv. Italiana di Numismatica 67, 1965, 5–31   6 M. H. CRAWFORD, Hubs and Dies in Classical Antiquity, in: NC 141, 1981, 176–177   7 L. FISCHER, Zur ant. Prägetechnik, in: Dt. Mz.-Bl. 1942, 437–447   8 M. P. GARCIA-BELLIDO, Problemas técnicos de la fabricación de monedas en la antigüedad, in: Numisma 32, 1982, 9–50   9 Id., A Hub from Ancient Spain, in: NC 146, 1986, 76–84   10 GÖBL   11 R. GÖBL, Der Ber. des Religionsstifters Mani über die Münzherstellung, in: SAWW, Philol.-histor. Kl. 1968, 113ff.   12 G. F. HILL, Ancient Methods of Coining, in: NC 2, 1922, 1–42   13 H. HOMMEL, Ein ant. Ber. über die Arbeitsgänge der Münzherstellung, in: SM 16, 1965, 111–121 und 17, 1966, 33–38   14 S. KARWIESE, Zw. Punze und Amboß, in: Litterae Numismaticae Vindobonenses 3, 1987, 5–22   15 W. MALKMUS, Addenda to Vermeule's Catalog of Ancient Coin Dies, in: Journal of the Society for Ancient Numismatics 17/4, 1989, 80–85; 18/4, 1993, 96–105   16 Y. MESHORER, The Production of Coins in the Ancient World, 1970   17 F. MICHAUX-VAN DER MERSCH,

F. Delamare, Evolution de la technique de frappe des statères éginétiques, in: RBN 133, 1987, 5–33   18 H. Moesta, P.R. Franke, Ant. Metallurgie und Münzprägung, 1995   19 O. Mørkholm, The Life of Dies in the Hellenistic Period, in: C. Brooke i.a. (ed.), Stud. in Numismatic Method Presented to Philip Grierson, 1983, 11–21   20 W. Schwabacher, The Production of Hubs Reconsidered, in: NC 6, 1966, 41–45   21 D.G. Sellwood, Some Experiments in Greek Minting Technique, in: NC 3, 1963, 217–231   22 R.F. Tylecote, The Method of Use of Early Iron-Age Coin Moulds, in: NC 2, 1962, 101–109   23 C.C. Vermeule, Some Notes on Ancient Dies and Coining Methods, 1954.   DI.K.

Coins, control of

Coins, control of The checking of coins by special coin checkers (Greek *argyroskópos*, *argyrognṓmōn*, *dokimastḗs*, Lat. → *nummularius* a money-changer in general — or *spectator*, *probator* [1. 19]) played an important role in the protection against underweight value or counterfeit money (→ Coins, counterfeiting of). It is often mentioned in literature, in inscriptions and papyrus [1. 13–20, 24–28; 2. 1, 4–10; 5. 358–362], first in an inscription dated 550–525 BC from Eretria [1. 13]. Coin checkers were employees of private banks or were commissioned by the state [1. 20–28]; many were slaves. The checker examined the coins for genuineness, full weight and exchangeability; in performing his duty, he used the senses of sight, touch, smell, and hearing (Epict. 1,20,8; cf. Petron. Sat. 56: *nummularius, qui per argentum aes videt*), and he weighed coins [1. 16–18] (→ Money III. A.).

The Athenian → coins legislation of 375/4 BC [4] controlled the checking of coins by the official checker (*dokimastḗs*). He was required to return to their owners the foreign imitations of Ath. coins, which were numerous and quite good in those times, and to punch through and turn over to the council coins with a copper or lead core, as well as those of low grade alloy. Legal tender which had to be accepted were only those Ath. coins approved by the *dokimastḗs*. In Rome, a praetorian edict of 85/4 BC introduced the checking for denarii (Plin. HN 33,132). The coin checker had to record the amounts checked (Dig. 2,13,4). Emperor Iulianus [11] in AD 363 appointed *zygostátai* for the weighing of gold coins (Cod. Theod. 12,7,2; [1. 28–34]). In connection with larger payments, reference is occasionally made to checked coins [1; 5. 360–362].

Visible traces of checking are a chisel punch at the edge or small imprints of letters or geometrical and figurative symbols by which the core of the coins became visible. They can be found especially on early electron, Persian Sigloi, the tortoises of Aegina and silver coins from Macedonia, the Ptolemies and the Roman Republic (very rarely on gold coins). In the 1st cent. AD, approved bronze coins were given the countermark *PRO(batum)* (→ Small coin, shortage of). In Rome, bags of checked coins were sealed with lead or, between c. 150 BC-AD 100, provided with ivory *tesserae nummulariae* (→ Tessera) [2] threaded onto a cord.

1 R. Bogaert, L'essai des monnaies dans l'antiquité, in: RBN 122, 1976, 5–34   2 R. Herzog, Tesserae nummulariae, 1919   3 Id., s.v. Nummularius, RE 17, 1415–1456   4 G. Stumpf, Ein athenisches Münzgesetz des 4. Jh. v. Chr., in: JNG 36, 1986, 23–40   5 H. Willers, Ein Fund von Serrati im freien Germanien, in: NZ 31, 1899, 329–366.   DI.K.

Coins, debasement of

Coins, debasement of 'Debasement of of coins' refers to the manipulation of the valid coinage standard by the minting authority, usually the reduction of the precious metal content or quality and/or overall weight (gross weight) of a coin. Thus, debasement of coins meant that, from a certain amount of precious metal, a larger number of coins was minted than was provided for by the coinage standard.

Debasement of coins is to be distinguished from → counterfeiting of coins and from short-term monetary emergency measures (cf. for example Ps.-Aristot. Oec. 2,2,16, 1348b: iron coins; 2,2,20, 1349a: tin coins; 2,2,23, 1350a: bronze coins). Not to be equated with the decline in the quality of coins is a devaluation, i.e. the lowering by the mint master of the precious metal content of the units of a coin system, which was nothing but a redetermination of the coinage standard. Devaluation could be the result of a decline in the quality of coins, but could also be an emergency measure such as the reduction in the standards of silver minting in Tarentum, Heraclea, Thurii and Croton during the Pyrrhic War (280–275 BC). The restructuring of the Roman → denarius around 141 BC from 10 to 16 asses within the context of a law for curbing public expenditure also meant a devaluation of the bronze units. By contrast, an example of a debasement of coins is the decline in electron and silver minting by Carthage in the 3rd cent. BC as a result of manipulations carried out due to the pressure of the financial burdens caused by the wars against Rome and other opponents.

The system of imperial coinage began under Augustus, with fixed value ratios between the gold, silver, brass and copper units, collapsed after the middle of the 3rd cent. AD. After the reduction of the fine (silver coins) and raw weight (gold and silver coins) introduced under Nero in the year 64, a steady and persistent, long-lasting decline in the quality of coins. While the → aureus remained almost stable up to the time around AD 200, albeit with its weight being lowered slightly over time, its weight fell drastically in the first decades of the 3rd cent. until, after the middle of the cent., it no longer followed any standard and thus became a commodity. This development destroyed the fixed ratio of 1:25 between aureus and denarius. The denarius deteriorated already under Vespasian when its fine weight continued to fall and, at the end of the 2nd cent., it contained just over 50 per cent silver. In 215, Caracalla introduced the so-called → antoninianus, a silver coin which, apparently, was initially intended to function as a double denarius although its weight was the equivalent of only just over 1.5 denarii.

Subsequently, the new silver unit displaced the denarius, but its silver content fell steadily and, in the 60s of the 3rd cent., it was no more than a bronze coin with a silver component of a few per cent. The composition of brass also changed: valuable zinc was replaced by tin and lead. Brass lost its importance as a coin metal and, in the 60s of the 3rd cent., the last sesterces (→ sestertius) and asses (copper; → As) were minted. During the same period of time, the abundant local minting (ore coins) in the eastern provinces came to a standstill.

When, under Aurelianus (270–275), gold coins were minted to a standard again, fixed value ratios were not resumed, but rather it appears that gold coins remained a commodity with a fluctuating value. Diocletian fundamentally reformed the Roman coin system as well as the organization of coin minting (coin reform in 294, currency reform in 301). The → solidus, introduced under Constantinus I in 309, became the leading coin of late antiquity; it was a gold coin of stable weight (4.5 g) and a high-carat content. Silver coins, in general of less importance in the 4th cent., had a high silver content, but became steadily lighter. For the mass-minted copper coins of the 4th cent., some of which had a minimal silver content, several phases of the debasement of coins can be ascertained. Repeated attempts were made to stabilize the standard or to return to the original standard, but without success.

Since, in the coin systems of antiquity, material and nominal value are closely linked and the financial obligations to be fulfilled by the community or the ruler were the driving force of coin minting, availability and price of the precious metal were of great importance. A scarcity of precious metal had an effect on the standard to which the coins were minted.

The consequences of debasement of coins and of devaluation during the Roman Principate are difficult to understand and evaluate. In this context, the development of 'parallel currencies' in the form of service obligations (munera; → munus) and in kind (annona, → cura annonae; cf. also → adaeratio) is also worth mentioning. In view of incomplete sources, it is hardly possible today to adequately describe, in periods facilitating historical understanding, the complex interrelationships between the financing of rising public expenditure by an increase in the volume of coins with a simultaneous deterioration of the coins and price increases as well as their effects.

→ Money, money economy; → Devaluation of money; → Coin counterfeit; → Coinage; Coins, minting of

1 R. BLAND, The Development of Gold and Silver Coin Denominations, A.D. 193–253, in: C. E. KING, D. WIGG (ed.), Coin Finds and Coin Use in the Roman World (Studien zu Fundmünzen der Ant. 10), 1996, 63–100 2 L. CAMILLI, S. SORDA (ed.), L''Inflazione' nel quarto secolo D.C. Atti dell'Incontro di Studio Roma 1988, 1993 3 J.-M. CARRIE, Dioclétien et la fiscalité, in: Antiquité tardive 2, 1994, 33–64 4 L. H. COPE i.a., Metal Analyses of Roman Coins Minted under the Empire (British Museum Occasional Paper 120), 1997 5 M. CRAWFORD, Finance, Coinage and Money from the Severans to Constantine, in: ANRW II 2, 1975, 560–593 6 R. DUNCAN-JONES, Money and Government in the Roman Empire, 1994 7 J. C. EDMONDSON, Mining in the Later Roman Empire and beyond: Continuity or Disruption?, in: JRS 79, 1989, 84–102 8 C. HOWGEGO, The Supply and Use of Money in the Roman World 200 B.C. to A.D. 300, in: JRS 82, 1992, 1–31 9 Id., Ancient History from Coins, 1995 10 C. E. KING (ed.), Imperial Revenue, Expenditure and Money Policy in the Fourth Century AD (British Archaeological Reports Int. Ser. 76), 1980 11 Les 'dévaluations' à Rome. Époque républicaine et impériale (Coll. École Française de Rome 37,1; 37,2), 1978; 1980 12 G. MICKWITZ, Geld und Wirtschaft im röm. Reich des vierten Jahrhunderts n.Chr., 1932 13 W. WEISER, Die Münzreform des Aurelian, in: ZPE 53, 1983, 279–295.   H.-M.v.K.

Coins, finds of

A. INDIVIDUAL FINDS   B. DEVOTIONAL FINDS
C. FINDS IN GRAVES   D. TREASURE FINDS

A. INDIVIDUAL FINDS

Individual finds of coins that were not intentionally buried, can be categorized as random and settlement finds. The information yielded by a single coin is minimal. Even if it is certain that the coin represents a primary find, namely that it was already lost in antiquity at the find location, one can hardly derive any historical conclusions least of all chronological conjectures. Only the evaluation of a larger number of random finds within a geographical area allows statements on money circulation and economic relationships. The systematic compilation of coin finds in a settlement reflects the money circulation at that location, as well as its economic, military or political importance at various times.

B. DEVOTIONAL FINDS

Devotional finds consist of sacrifices to deities in holy springs and wells, as well as at river crossings. Frequently, the coins have accumulated over a long period of time and thus permit statements about the duration of cult activity. Building sacrifices are deposits in sanctuaries/shrines, such as the treasure of the Artemisium in Ephesus. These coins are important for archaeological dating.

C. FINDS IN GRAVES

Offerings of coins in ancient graves. They permit a relatively certain dating of the entire find complex.

D. TREASURE FINDS

Hoards which either contain coins that have been accumulated over a long period of time or the stock of coins available during a time of crisis. These coins are important sources for the circulation of money and the intensity of minting activity, for the importance of individual minting locations and trade relationships. The final coin of a hoard (i.e. the coin with the most recent minting date) does not indicate with certainty the point in time of concealment, it merely provides the terminus

post quem for it.
→ Burial; → Hoard(find)s; → Dedication/consecration;
→ Votive offering

M.R.-ALFÖLDI, Ant. Numismatik, 2 vols., 1978, 239–
242; K.CHRIST, Ant. Numismatik. Einführung und
Bibliogr., 1972, 91–100; GÖBL, 224–227; SCHRÖTTER,
416–418, s.v. M.   GE.S.

Coitio In Roman criminal law, a type of criminal association, e.g. between thieves and publicans, as mentioned by Ulpia (Dig. 4,9,1,1), but in particular, the
punishable election alliance (a defined case of election
fraud, → *ambitus*). Election alliances between candidates were probably regarded as harmless as long as
only personal relationships, friendships and clientele
connections were combined for common success in an
election. Distinctly different was the joint bribing of
electors on a large scale, against which the *lex Licinia* by
Crassus (55 BC) was directed, forbidding the *crimen
sodaliciorum* which not only made organized associations of electors an offence (→ *sodalicium*), but also the
coitio of candidates.

In a more general sense, *coitio* in Roman law is used
for any formal assembly of several persons, e.g. in societies or associations (→ *collegia*). In this context, Roman
lawyers explicitly mention a *ius coeundi*, namely a right
to form an association.

W.KUNKEL, Staatsordnung und Staatspraxis der röm.
Republik, II, 1995, 84.   G.S.

Colaeus (Κωλαῖος). A trader from Samos only mentioned in Hdt. 4,152 in connection with the founding
history of Cyrene (7th cent. BC). His ship was blown
off-course by the east wind beyond the Columns of Hercules (the Strait of Gibraltar) on the way to Egypt and
reached → Tartessus, which was previously unknown
to the Greeks.
→ Discovery, voyages of   K.BRO.

Col(o)bi (Κολοβοί, variant Κόλβοι). Ethiopian tribe
from the area around the southern part of the Red Sea,
named after the particular type of circumcision
common to them (Str. 6,773; Ptol. 4,7,28).   W.W.M.

Colchi Trading city on the south-eastern coast of India,
situated opposite → Taprobane (Ptol. 7,1,10; 7,1,95:
Kolchikòs kólpos). Peripl. m. r. 58f. made reference to
the fact that the coast of → Komarei up to and including
C. was important for pearl fishing. C. was probably the
city today known as Korkai.   K.K.

Colchis (Κολχίς; *Kolchís*, Lat. *Colchis*).

I. HISTORICAL OVERVIEW FROM EARLY TIMES
Area of the east coast of the Black Sea (→ Pontus
Euxinus) stretching as far as western Transcaucasia,
bordered to the north by the Great Caucasus and by
Meskheti to the south. The favourable climatic and soil

conditions (fertile river valleys, forests and a proliferation of natural resources) meant that advanced civilizations emerged in C. as early as the 3rd millennium BC.
Kulcha is mentioned in Urartian documents together
with the capital city *Ildamuša* (which flourished in the
8th cent. BC). Kulcha was probably destroyed at the
end of the 8th cent. BC by the → Cimmerii. Shortly after
this a new alliance of the Western Cartvelian tribes was
formed and a new state was also founded to the north of
the Čorochi estuary in the area today known as Western
Georgia (Hdt. 4,37; Str. 11,2,15–17; Xen. An. 5,6,37).
There was a King Saulaces here, according to Plin. HN
33,52; the kingdom was divided into militarily administered units ('Skeptouchiai'). On account of the high
population density and the political consolidation in C.,
the Greeks were only able to found a few, insignificant
colonies (→ Phasis, → Dioscurias, → Gyenus). In the
group of Greek myths about the → Argonauts, C. is the
gold-rich country of King → Aeetes (the son of Helios)
and → Medea. This was how it was remembered in the
ancient world. Under the → Achaemenids, C. was partially situated in the 13th and 14th satrapies (Hdt. 3,97;
7,79). Trade flourished in the Hellenistic era (metal
objects, linen, hemp and wax), particularly with the
southern Pontic colonies. In around 200 BC, C. was
assimilated into the Pontic kingdom (Str. 12,3,1; 28)
and shared the same fate as the rest of that kingdom
(→ Pontus).
→ Lazes

O.LORDKIPANIDSE, Das alte K. und seine Beziehungen
zur griech. Welt, 1985; S.SAPRYKIN, Pontijskoe carstvo,
1996, 160–166.   I.v.B.

II. THE BYZANTINE ERA
Following the fall of the old kingdom, new ethno-
political groups formed in C., one of which was that of
the (West Georgian) → Lazes, who considered themselves to be the descendants of the Colchians. This
group gradually gained in influence from the 4th cent.
AD onwards and increased their territorium (*Laziké*,
Λαζική). Under → Iustinianus I the previously insignificant coastal city of Petra Iustiniana became the central
point of the Byzantine rulership.
→ Georgia, Georgians; → Iberia [1]

H.BRAKMANN, O.LORDKIPANIDSE, s.v. Iberia II (Geor-
gia), RAC 17, 70ff.   K.SA.

Colentum Dalmatian island (today known as Murter,
Croatia), which belonged to the *conventus* of → Salona;
Plin. HN 3,140; Ptol. 2,13,3; Geogr. Rav. 408,13.

J.J.WILKES, Dalmatia, 1969, 487; S.ČAČE, Colentum
insula (Plinio Nat. Hist. 3,140), in: Diadora 10, 1988,
65–72.   D.S.

Collatia *Colonia Latina* of Alba Longa on the left bank of the Anio between Rome and Tibur. Occupied by the Sabini, conquered by Rome under Tarquinius Priscus. Well known on account of the rape of Lucretia by Sextus Tarquinius. A gateway in Rome is named after C. (cf. Paul Fest. 33,18ff.), as is the *via Collatina* (Frontin. Aq. 5). After the decline of the city (Plin. HN. 3,68), many grand *villae* were built in the area (archaeological discoveries). C. is identified with the fortress of Lunghezza on a hill to the left of the Anio, where finds have been made of architectural terracotta dating from around 500 BC and later. There are burial sites in the surrounding area dating from the Iron Age.

L. QUILICI, C., 1974; M. MONTALCINI, Precisazioni topografiche per il territorio di Lunghezza, in: Arch. Laziale 4, 1981, 166–170.   G.U.

Collatio legum Mosaicarum et Romanarum The possibly only incomplete comparison, as appearing in three MSS from the 9th and 10th cents., of selected Roman legal norms mainly concerning family law, the law of inheritance and most especially penal law (Coll. 6,71: *humana sententia, lex*: 'Legal opinion and the people's law') with corresponding OT norms (Coll. 6,71: *divina sententia; lex Dei*) can be dated on account of Coll. 5,3 to Cod. Theod. 9,7,6 to some time between 390 and 438 and must have been drawn up by an anonymous author, probably Christian rather than Jewish, under the possibly incomplete title *Lex Dei quam Deus praecepit ad Moysen* in at least 16 titles. The author, familiar with the law of Moses, is obviously aiming at Roman lawyers (Coll. 7,1: *scitote iuris periti*), in order to demonstrate to them the precedence (Coll. 7,1) of the *lex Dei* (law of God) of the OT over the parallel quotes more familiar to his audience (*leges humanae*, the law of Man) from real and fake writings by Paulus, Ulpianus, Modestinus, Papinianus, Gaius and both the Gregorianus and Hermogenianus codices. He was probably writing from a Christian perspective, an assumption supported by the closeness of his translation from the Pentateuch to those Latin versions (*versiones Latinae*) pre-dating Jerome, which seem to have been used by some Church Fathers [1. 131ff.].

EDITIONS: 1 TH. MOMMSEN, Collectio III, 1890, 107–198   2 PH. E. HUSCHKE, B. KÜBLER, Iurisprudentiae anteiustinianae reliquiae II 2, 1927, 327–394   3 J. BAVIERA, FIRA II, ²1940, 541–589.
BIBLIOGRAPHY: 4 M. LAURIA, Lex Dei, in: SDHI 51, 1985, 257–275   5 D. LIEBS, Jurisprudenz im spätant. Italien, 1987, 162.   W.E.V.

Collatio lustralis The *collatio lustralis* was probably originally known as the *collatio auri et argenti*, χρυσὸς καὶ ἄργυρος in the laws as *collatio, oblatio, aurum et argentum, pensio* or *functio auraria* (the term *lustralis* to describe the due date schedules appears for the first time in AD 379 in the Cod. Theod. 13,1,11). The *collatio lustralis* was introduced in late antiquity to replace older forms of state or local taxes on trade and commerce and was collected primarily from the municipal professional classes. Zosimus (2,38) ascribes the introduction of this tax, the destructive effect of which on families and towns 'was unimportant to the avaricious and extravagant Christian emperor', to Constantine, although some observations would indicate that it was first introduced in the territory ruled by Licinius, perhaps to compensate for the abolition of the *capitatio plebeia* for the general municipal population in 313 (Cod. Theod. 13,10,2). It must, in any case, have existed before 324, as Constantine waives it for the year of his vicennial celebrations (Chron pasch. 525 B.).

The papyri indicate that at least in Egypt the tax was collected on an annual basis from an early date, sometimes even monthly, which was more suited to the payment capacity of the smaller taxpayers than providing a larger sum every four or five years. In 410 (Cod. Theod. 13,1,20) this means of collection was made mandatory across the whole of the empire whilst maintaining the multi-year cycle. Those who had to pay were the municipal traders, artisans and craftsmen registered in the *matricula negotiatorum* (Cod. Theod. 16,2,15). The legal sources list groups of people active in the area of trade who were completely or partially exempted from the *collatio lustralis*: *navicularii*, veterans, professionals such as doctors, professors, even painting teachers (Cod. Theod. 13,4,4; 374), Christian clerics and gravediggers, also rural craftsmen, *coloni* etc. on estates belonging to the curia or to senators and also the curials themselves were exempt.

The collection was carried out according to a formal *indictio* initially dependent on those registered in the *matricula* by the local *curiae* (cf. eg. P. Oxy. 3577 of that year 342) and their chosen → *exactores* in addition to their assistants (P. Lugd. Bat. XXV 65). Towards the end of the 4th cent. (cf. Cod. Theod. 13,1,17 from the year) the *collatio lustralis* was collected as a matter of course within the framework of the corporations of traders and craftsmen by the *mancipes* they selected. From the time of Valentinian gold seems to have been preferred over silver as the metal of payment, which may have added to the impression gained from the literary sources of a particularly oppressive tax.

Anastasius released the east of the empire from the *collatio lustralis* in May 498 to applause from all quarters and allocated the proceeds—in cases where public trusts had been set up to raise the taxes—for municipal use. The loss of income to the coffers of the *sacrae largitiones* was compensated for by the rededication of income from the patrimonial estates of the *res privata*. In the succeeding western empires a tax was probably still levied in gold from craftsmen (Cassiod. Var. 2,26,30). It seems that in the 7th cent. in the east a *chrysargyron* was revived for a time, perhaps by Heraclius on account of the need for gold to finance his Persian campaigns; strangely, it could also be paid in kind.
→ Aurum coronarium; → Capitatio-iugatio; → Taxes

1 R. S. BAGNALL, Egypt in Late Antiquity, 1993, 153f., 158   2 P. A. BRUNT, Roman Imperial Themes, 1990, 336, 534   3 R. DELMAIRE, Largesses sacrées et res privata, 1989, 354–374 and passim   4 A. DEMANDT, Die Spätant., 1989, 77, 238, 301, 343, 350f., 381, 408   5 L. DE SALVO, Economia privata e pubblici servizi nell'impero romano. I corpora naviculariorum, 1992   6 J. DURLIAT, Les finances publiques de Dioclétien aux Carolingiens, 1990   7 Id., Les rentiers de l'impôt, 1993, 36f. 8 M. HENDY, Studies in the Byzantine Monetary Economy c. 300–1450, 1985, 175–178; 192–201   9 JONES, LRE 431f., 465, 871f. and passim   10 JONES, Economy, 35f., 41f., 170f., 176, 217f., 220f.   11 J. KARAYANNOPULOS, Das Finanzwesen des frühbyz. Staates, 1958, 129–137 12 J. MARTIN, Spätant. und Völkerwanderung, ³1995, 25, 68–70, 185   13 O. SEECK, RE 4, 370–375   14 F. TINNE-FELD, Die frühbyz. Ges., 1977, 137f. and passim   15 S. L. WALLACE, Taxation in Egypt from Augustus to Diocletian, 1938, 191–213.   E.P.

Collation see → Copy

Collectio Avellana Between 556 and 561 a private collection was made in Rome of 243 letters from the pope and the emperor, emperor's edicts and rescripts, official reports, synodal decrees and creeds (inventory with evidence [1. 274–281]). The name of the collection derives from a MS earlier kept in the Umbrian monastery Santa Croce di Fonte Avellana; it is today kept in Rome (Vat. Lat. 4916). The inventory goes back to a (lost) document, which constituted a semi-official product of the Church politics of the Roman pope → Hormisdas in the first schism between the western and eastern Church (→ Acacius[4]).

EDITION: 1 O. GÜNTHER, CSEL 35/1–2, 1895–98.
BIBLIOGRAPHY: 2 E. SCHWARTZ, Publizistische Slgg. zum acacianischen Schisma, 1934, 280–287   3 H. J. FREDE, s.v. Kirchenschriftsteller, VL 1/1, 1995, 406–414.
                                       C.M.

Collectiones canonum Collections of council decisions, later also papal letters of disciplinary content establishing normative standards (overview: [1]), which were quoted in lawsuits, councils and internal Church conflicts [3]. From the 4th cent. onwards, *collectiones canonum* [*c.c.*] were created in various places, including a collectio of Greek council texts in Antioch, which in partially divergent translation exerted a decisive influence on the West [2]. Of the numerous Latin *collectiones canonum* of the 5th and 6th cents. from Africa, Gallia, Spain and Italy, the collection of → Dionysius Exiguus represents a high point amongst canonical works. Critical editions of ancient *c.c.* are missing for the most part (an exception being the → Collectio Avellana), so the differences must be deduced from the editions of the individual texts. The first instances of *c.c.* subjected to comprehensive systemization following abandonment of the chronological order occur in the 6th cent.: the African *Breviatio canonum* of → Fulgentius Ferrandus, the *Concordia canonum* of → Cresco-

nius [5] — probably of Italian origin, the *Vetus Gallica* [6].

BIBLIOGRAPHY: 1 F. MAASSEN, Gesch. der Quellen und der Lit. des canonischen Rechts im Abendlande, 1870 2 ED. SCHWARTZ, commemorative publication 4, 1960, 159ff.   3 E. WIRBELAUER, Zwei Päpste in Rom, 1993 4 K. ZECHIEL-ECKES, Die Concordia c. des Cresconius, 1992   5 H. MORDEK, Kirchenrecht und Reform im Frankenreich, 1975.   E.W.

Collega *Collega* generally means the individual who is working together with others to arrange something (from *con* and *leg*), including, for example, the member of an association or a corporate body (Dig. 27,1,42; 46,3,101 pr., 50,16,85). In politics, a *collega* is in particular an official associate in court, administration and government (Dig. 50,16,173 pr.: *collegarum appellatione hi continentur, qui sunt eiusdem potestatis*).

The *collegae* in the republican offices of consul, praetor, censor, aedile, quaestor and tribune of the people are entitled and obliged to make independent decisions, but also to take part in ballots: decisions must not necessarily be made by committees of *collegae*, though each can intervene against the official act of another that is not yet legally valid (*intercessio*). In addition, on account of their higher rank, the consuls have the right to intercession (*ius prohibendi, intercedendi*) over the official acts of the praetors, aediles and quaestors; tribunes of the people can intercede in the official acts of all magistrates. Military action on the basis of an *imperium* is exempted from intercession. In reality, the *collegae* have to come to arrangements with each other (*comparatio*) and decide on the appropriate procedure (e.g. the drawing of lots, *sortitio*) and an appropriate allocation of duties on a case by case basis. The principle of collective responsibility also ensures valid representation even when one *collega* is missing. It is only the → office of censor that always requires two *collegae* to be in action at the same time. Under a dictatorship, the rights of intercession of any consular *collega* still in office are suspended; this can also happen in the case of extraordinary official powers, e.g. in the case of Sulla's post as *vir legibus scribendis et constituendae rei publicae* according to the Lex Valeria of 88 BC; this differs for example, however, from the case of the warranty of authority of the *tresviri constituendae rei publicae* by means of the lex Titia of 43 BC.

The historic development of the collective office at the head of government probably begins with the office of consul; although whether this is with a Lex Iunia of 510 BC (Liv. 1,59; Dion. Hal. Ant. Rom. 4,76) is debatable (Liv. 7,3,5). According to historical tradition, other political collective offices emerge in the 5th cent. BC: the → *tribuni plebis* and the → *aediles plebis* (494 onwards; Liv. 2,33; Dion. Hal. Ant. Rom. 6,90), the *decemviri legibus scribundis* (451 onwards; Gell. NA 14,7,5), the → *quaestores* (probably from 447 onwards; Liv. 4,4), the → consular tribunes (from 445 onwards; Liv. 4,6,8) and the → *censores* (from 443 onwards; Liv. 4,8). However, the study of the historical tradition leaves some questions unanswered. The demand of the plebeians for their representatives to participate in occupying higher offices, which is enforced from 399 in the case of consular tribunes, dates from the leges Liciniae Sextiae of 367 for the consulat and from the year 300 in the case of priesthoods (*pontifices, augures*), can actually only be implemented within a collective office structure. The office of → *praetor* introduced in 367 is initially specifically that of a single court magistrate — a *collega minor* for the consuls until the office of *praetor peregrinus* is added in 242 and various other *collegae* are added at a later stage. The curule aedileship created in 367 is always a collective office.

The principle of collective responsibility is also used in numerous 'multi-participant colleges' (*tresviri, quattuorviri* etc.) for various legal and administrative purposes; in terms of the formation of decisions, in this case it is not the principle of intercession that is the decisive factor, but instead, if appropriate, that of the majority decision. During the imperial period, in particular in late antiquity, the co-emperors appointed by an emperor were also seen as *collegae* and all were treated as equal in principle (Tac. Ann. 1,3; Eutr. 9,27); in this respect the emperorship cannot be totally classified as a monarchy.

→ Magistratus; → Collegium

JONES, LRE, 325; KASER, RPR 1, 302ff.; E. MEYER, Röm. Staat und Staatsgedanke, ⁴1975, 112ff.; MOMMSEN, Staatsrecht, 1, 27–61. C.G.

Collegium

[1] A *collegium* is a group of people coming together for religious, professional and social reasons. The legal basis for the *collegia* is set out in the Law of Twelve Tables (8,27 = Gaius Dig. 47,22,4): *his (sodalibus) potestatem facit lex, pactionem quam velint sibi ferre, dum ne quid ex publica lege corrumpant; sed haec lex videtur ex lege Solonis translata esse.* In terms of their internal organization, the *collegium* followed the model of the civic municipalities with magistrats, a council and *plebs*. The financial assets of the *collegium* included the income generated by members' contributions and also real estate and money donated as *fideicommissum*; there is even evidence that they had their own slaves (CIL XIV 367), who were the joint property of all members (*res communis*). In addition to the actual purposes for which they were founded, there are further objectives to be considered in relation to social and religious matters: the celebration of birthdays and taking care of the cult of the dead. Communal meals and the distribution of gifts of money (*sportulae*) to the members were part of the social life of the *collegium*, as well as group attendances at public events (*pompae*). Like the civic municipalities, the *collegium* chose influential people from the municipality or the state as *patroni*, who were sometimes high-ranking magistrates or members of the *ordo equester* or *senatorius* (cf. CIL XIV

250). There were also sometimes — as in the municipalities — *summae honorariae* to be paid for entry into the *collegium* or for the tenure of offices. Most that is known of the social life of the *collegium* is drawn from the discovery of inscriptions from → Ostia, which contained lists of members and also foundation texts and memorial inscriptions.

The Senate kept a watch on the *collegia*, particularly in respect of any undesirable political activity, which could lead to the disbanding of a *collegium* (→ Senatus Consultum de Bacchanalibus). In the late republican era several *leges* were passed, which governed the authorization and abolition of *collegia*. The *collegia compitalicia* in particular played an important role in the political conflicts in the post-Sullan era. In 64 BC, these *collegia* were banned by the Senate, only to be revived in 58 BC by means of a law passed by P. Clodius, which also allowed for the formation of new *collegia* (Cic. Pis. 8f.; Ascon. 8C). These *collegia*, into which slaves and freedmen were also accepted, continued to support Clodius' policies after the end of his tribuneship and, in so doing, contributed to the destabilization of the Republic. Most of the *collegia* were disbanded under Caesar (Suet. Iul. 42,3) and banned once again by Augustus (Suet. Aug. 32,1); Augustus passed a *lex Iulia*, which then determined under what conditions the formation of a *collegium* was permissible (CIL VI 2193 = ILS 4966). The *collegia funeraticia*, the principle point of which was to ensure a suitable → burial for their members, were generally allowed (cf. ILS 7212). Officially approved *collegia* included the supplementary *quibus ex s.c. coire licet* in their titles (according to CIL XIV 169 and *passim*). This category of *collegia* can particularly be found within the group of vocational colleges important to the state. During the principate there were also restrictions on the formation of new *collegia*; for example Trajan placed a general prohibition on the formation of *collegia fabrorum* in Bithynia (Plin. Ep. 10,34). In late antiquity, the *collegia* have particular importance as a form of organization through which the state could ensure that certain occupational groups were working in its favour (*navicularii, pistores, negotiatores suarii* etc.).

1 F.M. AUSBÜTTEL, Unt. zu den Vereinen im Westen des röm. Reiches, 1983   2 A. GRAEBER, Unt. zum spätröm. Korporationswesen, 1983   3 P. HERZ, Studien zur röm. Wirtschaftsgesetzgebung. Die Lebensmittelversorgung, 1988   4 A.W. LINTOTT, Violence in Republican Rome, 1968, 74–88   5 R. MEIGGS, Roman Ostia, ²1973   6 S. MROZEK, Les distributions d'argent et de nourriture dans les villes italiennes du Haut Empire romain, 1987   7 H.L. ROYDEN, The magistrates of the Roman professional collegia in Italy from the first to the third century A.D., 1988   8 F.M. DE ROBERTIS, Storia delle corporazioni e del regime associativo nel mondo romano I–II (undated)   9 L. DE SALVO, Economia privata e pubblici servizi nell'impero Romano. I corpora naviculariorum, 1992   10 B. SIRKS, Food for Rome, 1991   11 A. STUIBER, Heidnische und christl. Gedächtniskalender, JbAC 3, 1963, 24–33   12 J.P. WALTZING, Etude historique sur les corporations professionelles chez les Romains, 1895ff. P.H.

[2] C. poetarum. At the same time that the first Roman literature appeared in writing, there is evidence of a *collegium scribarum (et) histriōnum*, to which, after the success of a cult song by the performer → Livius Andronicus (207 BC or possibly 249, cf. [2] and Liv. 31,12,10 in the year 200) the Senate gave permission to assemble with the officials in the temple of Minerva on the Aventine Hill (cf. Fest. p. 446, details inexact). As the poets later met in the Templum Herculis Musarum on the southern end of the Campus Martius, there seems to have been a reorganization and transfer of the Collegium at the time of Fulvius Nobilior's censorship (179) (also due to the influence of Ennius). The reorganization meant that an older temple of Hercules was surrounded with a porticus and this was then dedicated to the group of Muses plundered from Ambracia in 189 [3. 332ff.]; the performers, whose social standing had fallen [4, 91ff.], were replaced by the poets. There is epigraphic evidence dating from the Augustan era of a magistrate's attendant as *magister scribarum poetarum* (s. [5; 6]). The members were mainly dramatists (Val. Max. 3,7,11, only mentioned here as *collegium poetarum*); they assembled round a statue of Accius erected in the venue of their meeting place, cf. Plin. HN 34,19. Recitations of plays took place here to compete for selection for the *ludi* and Maecius Tarpa was a much-feared judge (Hor. Ars P. 387; Sat. 1,10,37ff.), and there were also other types of 'unrestricted' readings by writers (Hor. Epist. 2,2,91ff.); Terence is supposed to have suffered the incessant protests of his rival Luscius and Martial amused himself with his writer friends in the *schola poetarum* (3,20,8ff.; 4,61,3f.) in this very place.

1 N. HORSFALL, The C.Poetarum, in: BICS 23, 1976, 79–95 (too sceptical) 2 C. CICHORIUS, Röm. Stud., 1922, 1–7 3 J. RÜPKE, Kalender und Öffentlichkeit, 1995 4 H. LEPPIN, Histrionen, 1992 (Literature 93, n. 12) 5 J. H. MORE, Cornelius Surus, in: GB 3, 1975, 241–262 6 S. PANCIERA, Ancora sull'iscrizione di Cornelius Surus magister scribarum poetarum, in: BCAR 91,1, 1986, 35–44.   P.L.S.

Colluthus (Κόλλουθος; *Kóllouthos*). A Greek native of Lycopolis in Egypt, who lived during the reign of Anastasius I (AD 491–518). Biography: Suda s.v. Κόλουθος, 3,1951, according to this Cod. Ambrosianus gr. 661; for the form of the name cf. [1, XI–XII]. Epic poet, author of a poem about the Calydonian Boar Hunt (*Kalydōniaká* in six bks.), of encomia (hymns of praise) in hexameters and of an epic poem *Persiká*, which may have dealt with Anastasius's triumphs over the Persians in the year 505 (cf. [4]).

His surviving work is a small epic poem in 392 verses, the 'Rape of Helen' (Ἁρπαγὴ Ἑλένης, discovered by Cardinal Bessarion in a southern Italian MS, and strangely not mentioned by the Suda [1. XIII–XIV]). It tells of events leading up to the Trojan War: the wedding of Peleus and Thetis, the judgement of Paris, his journey to Sparta, where he seduces Helen, the lament of Hermione about the mother who abandoned her and then the return to Troy. Various poetic themes appear in the epyllium, ranging from traditional epic about the bucolic landscape and the thrilling power of love to the realistic description of the despairing little Hermione. C.'s language imitates that of Homer, in the main, and is elaborate, learned and rich in comment and neologisms; his hexameters follow the same strict metric rules as those of his main influence, → Nonnus. C. is an accomplished artist, as are other epic poets in the 'school' of Nonnus (→ Tryphiodorus; → Musaeus): he follows the tradition of Hellenistic poetry in using the stylistic rules of *imitatio*, *variatio* and *oppositio in imitando*.

→ Epic; → Nonnus

EDITIONS: 1 E. LIVREA, 1968   2 P. ORSINI, 1972 3 O. SCHÖNBERGER, 1993.
BIBLIOGRAPHY: 4 A. CAMERON, The Empress and the Poet, in: YClS 37, 1982, 236–237, n. 82   5 G. GIANGRANDE, Review of [1], in: JHS 81, 1969, 149–154 6 G. GIANGRANDE, C.' Description of a Waterspout: An Example of Late Epic Literary Technique, in: AJPh 96, 1975, 35–41 (repr.: Scripta Minora Alexandrina, 1985, 295–301)   7 M. MINNITI COLONNA, Sul testo e la lingua di C., in: Vichiana, 8, 1979, 70–93   8 J. C. MONTES CALA, Notas críticas a C., in: Habis 18–19, 1987–1988, 109–115   9 M. L. NARDELLI, L'esametro di C., in: Jb. der österreich. Byzantinistik 32/3,1982, 323–333   10 V. J. MATTHEWS, Aphrodite's Hair: C. and Hairstyles in the Epic Trad., in: Eranos, 94, 1996, 37–39.   S.FO.

Collytus (Κολλυτός, also Κολυττός; *Kollytōs*, *Kollyttós*). Attic *asty* deme belonging to the Aegeis phyle in the centre of Athens south of the → Areopagus and west and south of the Acropolis, the dense urban development of which apparently blended into Melite (Eratosth. in Str. 1,4,7; [1. 169; 2. 16; 3. 55; 4. 276; 6. 27f.]); provided three (four) *bouleutaí*. The main street, the 'narrow' (στενωπός) C., was used as a marketplace (Phot. 375B; [1. 180]). Reference on the decree on demes IG II² 1195 l. 6ff., see [6. 128, 140, 187, 382]. There is evidence of rural (!) → Dionysia in C. with theatrical performances (Aeschin. In Tim. 157; Dem. Or. 18,180; 262 [6. 152, 213, 216, 220, 222]). C. was probably also the site of the sanctuary of Codrus, Neleus and Basile (IG I³ 84 [5]). An eponymous hero C. is mentioned by Steph. Byz. s.v. Διόμεια.

→ Athens

1 W. JUDEICH, Die Top. von Athen, ²1931   2 D. M. LEWIS, The Deme of Kolonos, in: ABSA 50, 1955, 12–17 3 H. LOHMANN, Atene, 1993   4 W. K. PRITCHETT, The Attic Stelai, in: Hesperia 22, 1953, 225–299   5 TRAVLOS, Athen 332–334, fig. 435f.   6 WHITEHEAD, Index s.v. C.

TRAILL, Attica 40, 59, 68, 110 no. 69, table 1; J. S. TRAILL, Demos and Trittys, 1986, 186.   H.LO.

Colometry The organization of lyric verses into metric cola (→ Metre) for the purposes of critical analysis or the text layout. Up until about 200 BC, lyric verses were written like prose, i.e. without paying attention to metric units (e.g. in the Berlin Papyri the *Pérsai* by Timotheus and the skolia PMG 917; also the tragic anapaests in PHibeh 24(a), 25, 179 i 4ff.). The introduction of colometry is linked to → Aristophanes [4] of Byzantium (Dion. Hal. Comp. 156; 221). Its earliest appearance is in a Stesichorus papyrus dating from the late 3rd cent. BC (PMGF 222b) and thereafter it is the usual rule in all MSS, with the exception of those showing musical notation.

Dion. Hal. ibid. indicates that besides Aristophanes there were also other metricians who organized their texts using colometry. Subscriptions in the MSS of two of Aristophanes' comedies (*Nubes, Pax*) explain that their colometry follows the analyses of → Heliodorus [6]; from this one can assume that the same is true of the rest of the comedies that have been preserved [3]. During the reign of Anastasius (AD 491–518), Eugenius [2] of Augustopolis set out the colometry of 15 different texts by Aeschylus, Sophocles and Euripides (Suda s.v. Εὐγένιος, ε 3394 ADLER).

Papyri by Pindar and the dramatists generally also contain the same colometry as the medieval tradition, which therefore harks back to the scholarly tradition of antiquity [2]. Deviations within the medieval tradition are mainly coincidental. → Demetrius [43] Triclinius was the first to attempt new analyses on the basis of the knowledge of metrics that he had gleaned from reading Hephaestion [1].

As late as the 19th cent., printed editions were still using the colometry from the MS sources, until A. BOECKH attained new insights into the structure of Greek lyric verse. Today it is recognized that the colometry of antiquity, although it is often satisfactory, is occasionally in need of revision; modern editions therefore arrange the texts according to their own metrical analyses.

In Latin the colometry of antiquity is generally only of relevance in the case of the *cantica* (→ Canticum) by → Plautus.

1 R. AUBRETON, Démétrius Triclinius et les recensions médiévales de Sophocle, 1949, 189–208 2 W. S. BARRETT, Euripides: Hippolytus, 1964, 84–90 3 N. DUNBAR, Aristophanes: Birds, 1995, 44–45 4 J. IRIGOIN, Histoire du texte de Pindare, 1952, 44–47 5 Id., Les scholies métriques de Pindare (Bibliothèque de l'École des Hautes Études 310, 1958), 17–34 6 R. PFEIFFER, History of Classical Scholarship I, 1968, 185–189. M.L.W.

Colon see → Punctuation

Colonae (Κολωναί; *Kolōnaí*).
[1] Attic *mesogeia* deme belonging to the Leontis phyle, provided two *bouleutaí*, on Mount Pentelicon [1. 372[17]] near Hecale [2. 64f.] or near Michaleza

[3. 131]. The Demotikon is Κολωνεύς and also Κολωνῆθεν.
→ Colonus

1 P. J. BICKNELL, Akamantid Eitea, in: Historia 27, 1978, 369–374 2 W. E. THOMPSON, Notes on Attic Demes, in: Hesperia 39, 1970, 64–67 3 J. S. TRAILL, Demos and Trittys, 1986, 61f., 131.

TRAILL, Attica 6, 47, 62, 69, 110 no. 70, 125, table 4.

[2] Attic *asty*(?) deme belonging to the Antiochis phyle, from 307/6 the Antigonis phyle and from 224/3 BC the Ptolemaïs phyle. It is unclear exactly where it was located. According to [1. 64f.; 2. 54, 92] on the Penteli close to the monastery in Mendeli, however unlikely to have been in Varnava (see [3]). Provided two *bouleutaí*. The Demotikon is Κολωνεύς and also Κολωνῆθεν.
→ Colonus

1 W. E. THOMPSON, Notes on Attic Demes, in: Hesperia 39, 1970, 64–67 2 TRAILL, Attica, 14, 26f., 30, 54, 62, 69, 111 no. 71, 125, tables 10, 11, 13 3 J. S. TRAILL, Demos and Trittys, 1986, 139 with n. 42. H.LO.

[3] (Κολωναί, Lat. *Colonae*). Town in the Troad, which was definitely located (Str. 13,1,18) near Beşik Tepe, 6 km south of → Alexandria [2] in the Troad ([2. 216ff.]; on the city fortifications see Xen. Hell. 3,1,13, cf. [2. 217]). Discoveries of ceramics indicate settlement at the end of the 7th cent. BC [2. 217]. In the early period, it supposedly belonged to Tenedos (Str. 13,1,47). C. probably belonged to the → Delian League, although the name is amended in ATL A 9 in 425/4 BC. In 400 BC, the town was captured by → Mania (Xen. Hell. 3,1,13), before she joined forces with the Spartans following the landing of → Dercylidas (Xen. Hell. 3,1,16). In 310 BC, C. was amalgamated with Alexandria in the Troad via the process of *synoikismós* (Str. 13,1,46).

1 L. BÜRCHNER, s.v. Kolonai (2), RE 11, 1110 2 J. M. COOK, The Troad, 1973 3 W. LEAF, Strabo on the Troad, 1923, 213–225. E.SCH.

Colonatus *Colonus* means farmer, specifically a tenant farmer — the tenant farmer of late antiquity who was tied to the land and was dependent on a landowner (→ Leasehold).
A. THE EARLY IMPERIAL PERIOD B. LATE ANTIQUITY

A. THE EARLY IMPERIAL PERIOD
The leasing of land was a practice already widespread in the time of the late Republic and in the early years of the Princate, along with the farming of the estates by → slaves (cf. i.a. Dig. 19,2; Columella 1,7). The length of the lease was generally set at five years (*lustrum*). In Italy, the lease was usually paid for in money; although there were also instances of partial payment in kind using produce from the estate (Dig. 19,2,19,3; 19,2,25,6; Plin. Ep. 9,37,3). As demonstrated by the frequent evidence in the sources of requests from *coloni*

for reductions of lease payments (Plin. Ep. 9,37,2; 10,8,5; regarding the legal requirements cf. Dig. 19,2,15), the economic situation of most tenant farmers was extremely precarious. Many *coloni* were permanently in debt to the landowners, who would then sell the security provided by the *coloni*, thus worsening the economic situation of the tenant farmers still further. A tenant farmer who continued to owe the interest on the lease, could be turned off the land; this probably did not occur often, as it was difficult to find suitable tenants (Plin. Ep. 3,19,6; 9,37,2). On expiry of the lease the landowners could look for new tenants; although a change of tenant was generally avoided (Columella 1,7,3). There is epigraphic evidence dating from as early as the 2nd cent. AD showing that some families of tenant farmers lived on the same estate for several generations. By the 3rd cent. at the latest, a lease contract was deemed to be extended by implication on the expiry of the lease if the contract had not been explicitly terminated (Dig. 19,2,13,11; 19,2,14; Cod. Iust. 4,65,16). In the 3rd cent. it was against the law to keep *coloni* on the land against their will (Cod. Iust. 4,65,11), which probably often happened when debts were incurred.

The situation of the *coloni* on the imperial estates in North Africa was regulated by means of the *lex Manciana*: the *coloni* had to hand over a proportion of the harvest (a third of the wheat, barley, wine and olive oil) and in addition they had to perform tasks (*operae*) for the *conductores* six days a year (CIL VIII 25902). This encouraged the cultivation of fallow land, as the *coloni* did not have to pay for a lease on this kind of land for several years (CIL VIII 25943). Information about a conflict between the *coloni* and the *conductores*, who wanted to increase the scope of the *operae*, is given in an inscription dating from the time of Commodus (CIL VIII 10570).

The idea, frequently put forward in research, that agriculture developed during imperial times from a slave-based system to one based on the Colonatus, probably bears little relation to reality: on the one hand, even in the earliest years of the principate the use of slaves in agriculture was the exception in many regions of the empire and, on the other hand, in areas where the use of slaves was still common during the early part of the Principate, this practice continued into late antiquity. The use of slaves or *coloni* depended on what labour was available in a particular region.

B. LATE ANTIQUITY

In late antiquity the characteristics of the *colonatus* changed. A proportion of the tenant farmers were tied to the land using legal means, a measure for which the motives were mainly fiscal (simplifying the collection of taxes; guaranteeing regular fiscal income). The *coloni* were entered in the tax registers under the name of the landlord; they were *censibus adscripti* (this is the origin of the term *adscripticius,* which is found in legal documents from the 2nd half of the 5th cent. onwards; in western legal documents the equivalent term is *origi-*

nalis). Tenant farmers who themselves owned land were entered in the registers under their own name and were themselves liable for tax (Cod. Theod. 11,1,14). The practice of tying to the land, which, in view of the shortage of labour, was in the interests of the landowners, was therefore maintained in areas in which → *capitatio* had been abolished (Cod. Iust. 11,52,1). Being tied to the land (*glebae adscriptio*) had disadvantages for the *colonus*, but it also protected him from expulsion by the landowner. The interest on the lease was mainly paid in kind (Cod. Iust. 11,48,5; for lease payment money cf. Cod. Iust. 11,48,20 pr.; 1).

The status of the *coloni* and *adscripticii* in civil law worsened in the 4th and 5th cents. They could only sell their own property (*peculium*) with the landowner's agreement (Cod. Iust. 11,50,2,3; 11,48,19) and could only have recourse to law against the landowner in cases of *superexactio* (claims of the interest on the lease being too high) or in criminal cases (Cod. Iust. 11,50,1; 11,50,2,4). Many landowners tried to influence their farmers' choice of religion; fugitive *coloni* risked beatings and being shackled (Cod. Theod. 5,17,1; Cod. Iust. 11,53,1). Nonetheless, the status of the *coloni* in civil law was never completely the same as that of the slaves. In the 6th cent., many *adscripticii* continued to turn to the court system for help (Nov. Just. Epit. 80 pr.; 1f.), something which was forbidden to slaves. There can, however, be no doubt that relations between the *colonus* and the *possessor* were characterized by their very imbalance. There are frequent complaints regarding exploitation and economic oppression of the *coloni* by the landowners (Aug. Epist. 247; Ioh. Chrys. Hom. Matth. 61 [62],3; Theod. Hist. eccl. 14,3; Vita Theod. Syc. 76).

The tying of the *coloni* to the land could in fact only be realized to a limited extent. Numerous *coloni* found employment in the army, in administrative positions or as clergy, although several laws tried to prevent this and the acceptance of *coloni* into the clergy was only possible with the permission of the landowner (Cod. Iust. 1,3,36 pr.). From 419, a fugitive *colonus*, whose return had not been demanded by the landowner for 30 years, gained his freedom (Cod. Theod. 5,18,1; imperial *coloni*: Nov. Val. 27). From 451 onwards there was a ruling in the West which meant that after 30 years a fugitive *colonus* had the status of *originalis* of the landowner on whose land he had settled (Nov. Val. 31), whilst in the East the 30 year limitation period was kept until the reign of Justinian (Cod. Iust. 11,48,22,3ff.; 11,48,23 pr.). The number of *adscripticii* probably decreased in the 5th cent.; and for this reason it was decreed by Anastasius that free men who settled on an estate became tied to the land after 30 years. They did not become *adscripticii*, and could still own property and take their landowner to court; only their freedom of movement was limited (Cod. Iust. 11,48,19; 11,48,23,1ff.; Nov. Iust. 162,2). There is a verified distinction between 'free' *coloni* and *adscripticii* from the 2nd half of the 5th cent.

The *colonatus* probably did not have as great a degree of importance to the agriculture of late antiquity as has long been ascribed to it by researchers: a culture of free smallholders continued to exist; slaves were employed on many large estates and free tenancy arrangements were maintained in many parts of the empire. The previously posited idea that the *colonatus* of late antiquity showed tendencies towards feudalization and that the coloni were the predecessors of the medieval serfs may these days be regarded as disproved.

1 J.-M. CARRIÉ, Le 'colonat du Bas-Empire': un mythe historiographique?, in : Opus 1, 1982, 351–370   2 J.-M. CARRIÉ, Un roman des origines: les généalogies du 'colonat du Bas-Empire', in: Opus 2, 1983, 205–251   3 D. EIBACH, Unt. zum spätant. Kolonat in der kaiserlichen Gesetzgebung, 1977   4 M. I. FINLEY, Private Farm Tenancy in Italy before Diocletian, in: Id., Property, 103–121; 188–190   5 D. FLACH, Inschr.-Unt. zum röm. Kolonat in Nordafrika, in: Chiron 8, 1978, 441–492   6 K.-P. JOHNE, J. KÖHN, V. WEBER, Die Kolonen in It. und den westl. Prov. des röm. Reiches, 1983   7 JONES, LRE, 795–808   8 A. H. M. JONES, The Roman Colonate, in: Past and Present 13, 1958, 288–303; repr. in: M. I. FINLEY (ed.), Studies in Ancient Society, 1974, 288–303   9 D. P. KEHOE, The Economics of Agriculture on Roman Imperial Estates in North Africa, 1988   10 J.-U. KRAUSE, Spätant. Patronatsformen im Westen des Röm. Reiches, 1987, 88ff.   11 A. MARCONE, Il colonato tardoantico nella storiografia moderna, 1988   12 P. W. DE NEEVE, Colonus. Private Farm-Tenancy in Roman Italy during the Republic and the Early Principate, 1984   13 B. SIRKS, Reconsidering the Roman Colonate, in: ZRG 110, 1993, 331–369.

J.K.

Colonea Fortress, town and bishop's seat in the province of Pontus in the north-east of → Asia Minor, developed and extended during the reign of → Iustinian I and defended against the Arabs in AD 778 and 940; part of Turkey since 1071 (today Şebinkarahisar). The area around C. had economic importance because of the alum mining carried out there (→ Alum) and was the centre of the → Paulician sect from the 7th to the 9th cents.

A. BRYER, D. WINFIELD, The Byzantine Monuments and Topography of the Pontos, 1985, 145–151.   AL.B.

Colonia Agrippinensis Present-day Cologne, principal city (Tac. Ann. 1,36,1; 37,2; 71,1) of the Ubii who moved from the Neuwieder Becken to settle in the area previously inhabited by the Eburones, following the *deditio* by Agrippa in 38 BC (Str. 4,3,4; Tac. Ann. 12,27,1; Germ. 28,4). Located on the gravel plain in the area today known as the old town (archaeology dates the *oppidum Ubiorum* to around the time of the birth of Christ). *Oppidum* (*Civitas*) *Ubiorum*, from AD 50 *Colonia Claudia Ara Agrippinensium* (about the name [1. 125f.]). The altar of the Ubii with an elected priest became the focal point of the ruler cult (*ara Ubiorum*: Tac. Ann. 1,39,1; 57,2) [1]. From about AD 10, the Tiberian *legio I* and the *legio XX Valeria victrix* wintered near *(apud)* this altar. These legions later (before AD 43) moved to Bonna and Novaesium. The siting of the early sections of the settlement is disputed; it is probable that the Marienburg, where there was an approximately four ha. stone encampment from the Flavian era, was already an important military focal point in *c.* AD 14, and Divitia perhaps an early bridgehead. There was no change within the settlement area during the time of Claudius [2]. Colonia Agrippinensis (CA) was probably the seat of the command of the Lower German army right from the beginning, and from *c.* AD 85, of the Lower German governor (a praetorium has been excavated) [3]; the naval command was based 3 km up the Rhine at the *classis Germanica* fort in Cologne-Marienburg.

At the instigation of his wife, Agrippina the Younger, born in *c.* AD 15 in the *oppidum Ubiorum*, Claudius promoted CA to a veterans' colony (Tac. Ann. 12,27,1 [4]). Despite occasional setbacks through disasters (e.g. extensive fire damage in AD 58 Tac. Ann. 13,57,3) and civil wars (particularly during the → Batavian Revolt) [5] the settlement grew into a flourishing economic centre by the middle of the 3rd cent. [6] with strong trading connections with the regions beyond the lines. The 96.8 ha area enclosed by the city walls [7] was home to *c.* 15,000 inhabitants in around AD 200 with *c.* another 5,000 living in the area outside the walls. There is archaeological and epigraphical [8] evidence of a right-angled street grid with a forum, capitol, praetorium, port and bridge on the Rhine, residential district, commercial enterprises (potteries, glass and leather goods); there were larger *villae* and numerous estates in areas on the edge of the settlement; the burial sites were ringed around the city walls, particularly in the areas near the main roads leading to the south, west and north.

The usurpation of → Vitellius began in CA on 2.1. AD 69 (Tac. Hist. 1,56ff.) and Trajan was installed as Augustus here on 27.1.98 (Eutr. 8,2,1). From 257, CA had its own mint (the mark of which was CCAA). In the autumn of 260, under the successor of the emperor Gallienus (cf. [1. 125f.]), the minor Saloninus, CA was unable to withstand the siege by the usurper Postumus and then became the starting point of the Gaulish Empire. Postumus' successor Victorinus was murdered here for personal reasons in 271 together with his son. CA enjoyed imperial support in the time of Constantine the Great (→ Divitia). CA never properly recovered from the ten-month-long looting in 355/356 (Amm. Marc. 15,8,19; layers of rubble); the last official construction work carried out in the name of the counter-emperor Eugenius was overseen by the Frankish Magister Militum Arbogastes, who crossed the Rhine in the winter of 392/393 in CA (CIL XIII 8262 [8. no. 188]). Having been destroyed many times in the 5th cent, CA was lost by the general Aegidius to the Franks in AD 456, who founded the first Frankish kingdom around Cologne under the leadership of Sigibert (in 511

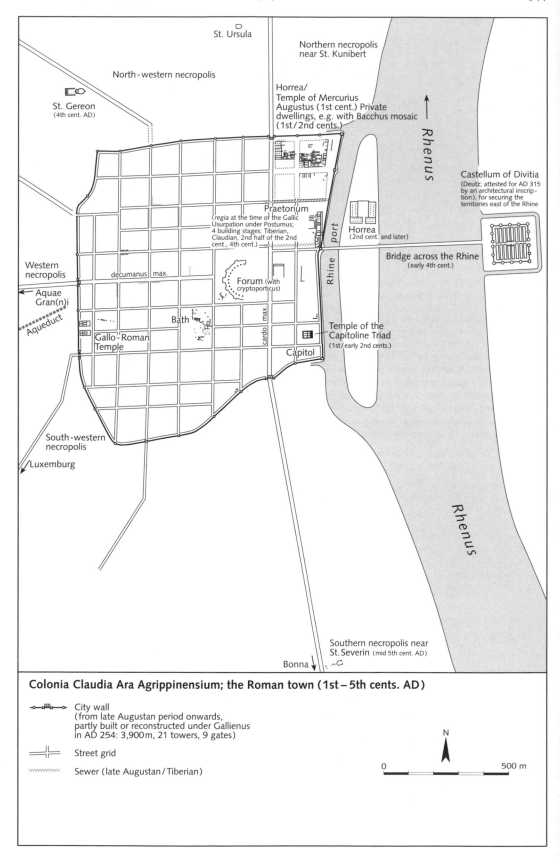

St. Ursula

Northern necropolis
near St. Kunibert

North-western necropolis

St. Gereon
(4th cent. AD)

Horrea/
Temple of Mercurius
Augustus (1st cent.) Private
dwellings, e.g. with Bacchus mosaic
(1st/2nd cents.)

Rhenus

Castellum of Divitia
(Deutz; attested for AD 315
by an architectural inscription), for securing the
territories east of the Rhine

Praetorium
(*regia* at the time of the Gallic
Usurpation under Postumus;
4 building stages: Tiberian,
Claudian, 2nd half of the 2nd
cent., 4th cent.)

Horrea
(2nd cent. and later)

Western
necropolis

decumanus max.

Bridge across the Rhine
(early 4th cent.)

Aquae
Gran(n)i

Forum (with
cryptoporticus)

cardo max.

Aqueduct

Bath

Gallo-Roman
Temple

Temple of the
Capitoline Triad
(1st/early 2nd cents.)

Capitol

South-western
necropolis

Luxemburg

Rhenus

Southern necropolis near
St. Severin (mid 5th cent. AD)

Bonna

Colonia Claudia Ara Agrippinensium; the Roman town (1st – 5th cents. AD)

City wall
(from late Augustan period onwards,
partly built or reconstructed under Gallienus
in AD 254: 3,900m, 21 towers, 9 gates)

Street grid

Sewer (late Augustan/Tiberian)

N

0   500 m

an *aula regia* for Theoderic I, the son of Clovis); Frankish coins appeared in *c.* 540. CA was a bishop's seat in the 4th cent. (the cathedral was probably already the bishop's church); important excavations have been carried out below St. Severin, St. Gereon and St. Ursula [9].

1 H. GALSTERER, Von den Eburonen zu den Agrippinensern, in: Kölner Jb. Vor- und Frühgesch. 23, 1990, 117–126   2 B. PÄFFGEN, W. ZANIER, Überlegungen zur Lokalisierung von Oppidum Ubiorum und Legionslager im frühkaiserzeitlichen Köln, in: FS G. Ulbert, 1995, 111–129   3 R. HAENSCH, Das röm. Köln als 'Hauptstadt' der Prov. Germania inferior (Geschichte in Köln 33), 1993, 5–40   4 W. ECK, Agrippina, 1993   5 D. TIMPE, Romano-Germanica, 1995, 71–78   6 E. FREZOULS, Gallien und röm. Germanien, in: F. VITTINGHOFF (ed.), Hdb. der Europ. Wirtschafts- und Sozialgesch. 1, 1990, 429–509   7 K. BACK, Unt. an der röm. Stadtmauer unter der Sakristei des Kölner Doms, in: Kölner Jb. Vor- und Frühgesch. 23, 1990, 393–400   8 B. GALSTERER, H. GALSTERER, Die röm. Steininschr. aus Köln, 1975 and addenda   9 E. DASSMANN, Die Anf. der Kirche in Deutschland, 1993, 104–140.

H. HELLENKEMPER, Arch. Forsch. in Köln seit 1980, in: Arch. in Nordrhein-Westfalen, 1990, 75–88; Id., Köln: Großstadt-Arch., in: Bodendenkmalpflege im Rheinland l, 1992, 24–29; Id. et al., in: H. G. HORN (ed.), Die Römer in Nordrhein-Westfalen, 1987, 459–519; Laufende Berichte in BJ und Kölner Jb. Vor- und Frühgeschichte.
                       K.DI.

MAPS: B. PÄFFGEN, S. RISTOW, Die Römerstadt Köln zur Merowingerzeit, in: A. WIECZOREK et al. (ed.), Die Franken — Wegbereiter Europas I, 1996, 145–159; in particular 146 and fig. 100; H. SCHMITZ, Colonia Claudia Ara Agrippinensium, 1956; H. HELLENKEMPER, Architektur als Beitrag zur Gesch. der CCAA, in: O. DOPPELFELD, Das röm. Köln I., Ubier-Oppidum und Colonia Agrippinensium, ANRW II4, 1975, 715–782; G. RISTOW, Religionen und ihre Denkmäler im ant. Köln, 1975; M. RIEDEL, Köln, ein röm. Wirtschaftszentrum, 1982; H. GALSTERER, Von den Eburonen zu den Agrippinensern. Aspekte der Romanisation am Rhein, in: Kölner Jb. für Vor- und Frühgesch. 23, 1990, 117–126.

Coloniae

A. DEFINITION   B. FOUNDING AND CONSTITUTION   C. CITIZENS' COLONIES   D. LATIN COLONIES   E. HISTORY

A. DEFINITION

A *colonia* was a settlement of citizens (with the addition of a greater or lesser proportion of non-citizens) for the military and political securing of Roman rule, later for providing for veterans and occasionally the Roman proletariat, almost always in a conquered city, the citizens of which would also be involved in the colony in some way (cf. the definition in Serv. Aen. 1,12).

B. FOUNDING AND CONSTITUTION

Coloniae are founded on the basis of the people's law by public officials, mainly *IIIviri coloniae deducen-*

dae, and then from the time of Marius they are increasingly founded by the military rulers and then the emperors. The colonists are recruited from volunteers, the use of force is only recorded occasionally. The expedition from Rome to the chosen location (*deductio*) was run along military lines. After measuring out the land and town area (→ *centuriatio*) the actual founding takes place according to *ritu Etrusco*, which is analogous with that of Rome [1]. The first buildings to be constructed are fortifications and public buildings. Private residences were built at a later stage (regarding Cosa cf. [2]). The *IIIviri* also pass the first colony statutes (*lex coloniae*). In contrast to earlier ideas that the previous population is generally driven out or oppressed, archaeological (Aquileia) and epigraphical (Brundisium) evidence tends to indicate that a considerable proportion is integrated into the new colony, even into the ruling classes.

C. CITIZENS' COLONIES

Coloniae civium Romanorum were at first very small; there was probably a standard number of 300 families of colonists, each of which was supposed to receive an area of land of two *iugera* (*bina iugera*), i.e. half a ha., an area on which it is scarcely possible to eke out a living. They were situated on the coast, although the expression *coloniae maritimae* (in Siculus Flaccus p. 99 TH.) is probably not a technical term. It remains unclear whether they played a role in coastal defences or if this is merely a conclusion drawn from the name. From the 2nd cent. BC (183 Mutina and Parma) the citizens' colonies become more similar to the Latin colonies in terms of number of settlers, land quota and location. The colonists in the citizens' colony remain full citizens, probably at first in their old Tribus, and the land assigned to them becomes property by Quiritarian law and thereby *censui censendo*. The allocation of land in citizens' colonies could therefore have an effect on the political composition of the Roman citizenry; this is probably the reason that the assignation quota for the colonists remained small; the preferred option was to provide them with → *ager publicus*, which did not affect the *census*. It is perhaps the case that in the beginning the citizens' colonies had very little chance of self-government, though if they did have a military role e.g. in coastal defence, they must have had their own magistrates. The command of the colonial *IIvir* cited in the → *lex coloniae Genetivae Iuliae* (103 CRAWFORD) for times when defence was necessary may, together with the *tumultus Italicus Gallicusve* (62) cited elsewhere in the law, reflect conditions in republican Italy. The senior officials in all colonies were initially *praetores* (Castrum Novum, CIL IX 5145), and later the customary *IIviri*. There is no evidence of general court decisions by Roman *praefecti iure dicundo*.

D. LATIN COLONIES

After the end of the Latin War in 338 BC, the policy of founding Latin colonies, which had previously been

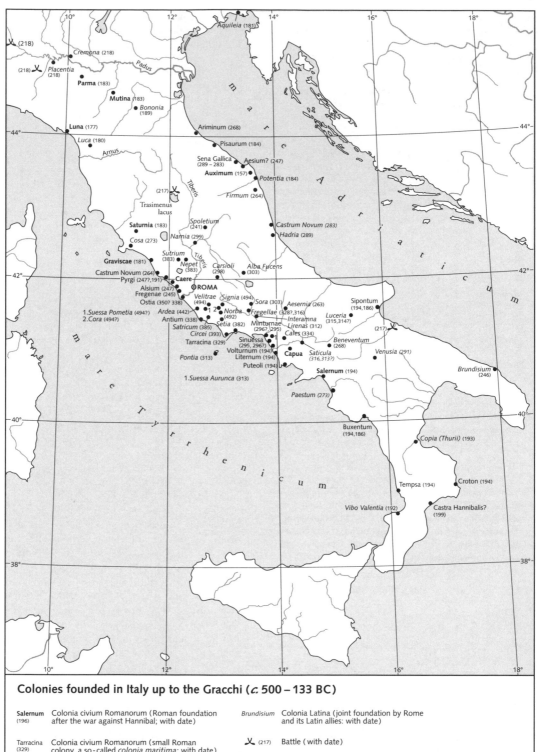

Colonies founded in Italy up to the Gracchi (*c.* 500 – 133 BC)

Salernum (196)	Colonia civium Romanorum (Roman foundation after the war against Hannibal; with date)	*Brundisium*	Colonia Latina (joint foundation by Rome and its Latin allies: with date)
Tarracina (329)	Colonia civium Romanorum (small Roman colony, a so-called *colonia maritima;* with date)	(217)	Battle (with date)

0   50   100   150   200   250   300 km

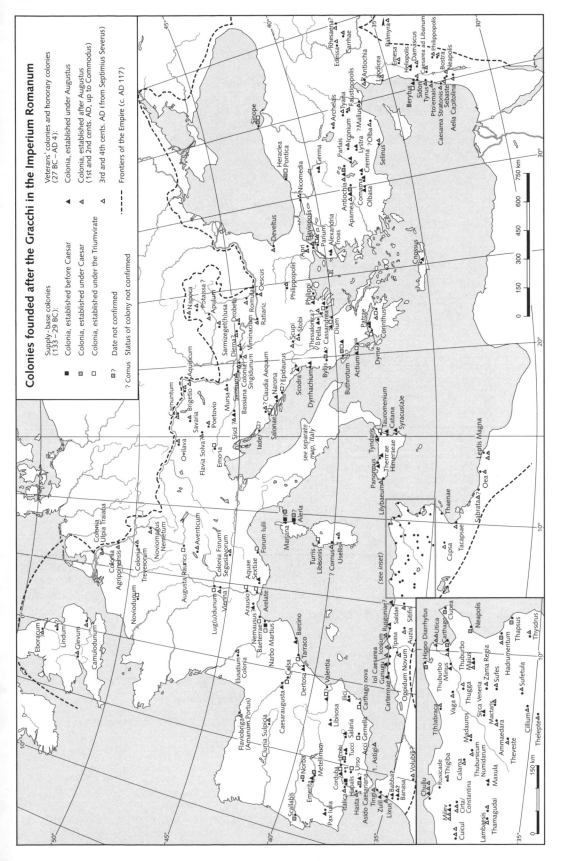

Colonies founded after the Gracchi in the Imperium Romanum

Supply - base colonies
(133 – 29 BC):

Colonia, established before Caesar ■

Colonia, established under Caesar ▣

Colonia, established under the Triumvirate □

? Date not confirmed

? Cornus Status of colony not confirmed

Veterans' colonies and honorary colonies
(27 BC – AD 4):

Colonia, established under Augustus ▲

Colonia, established after Augustus ▲
(1st and 2nd cents. AD, up to Commodus)

3rd and 4th cents. AD (from Septimius Severus) ▲

- - - - - Frontiers of the Empire (c. AD 117)

Colonies founded in Italy after the Gracchi

Supply-base colonies
(133 – 29 BC):

■ Colonia, established before Caesar

▣ Colonia, established under Caesar

□ Colonia, established under the Triumvirate

■? Date not confirmed

? Sora Status of colony not confirmed

Veterans' colonies and honorary colonies
(27 BC – AD 4):

▲ Colonia, established under Augustus

△ Colonia, established after Augustus
(1st and 2nd cents. AD, up to Commodus)

△ 3rd and 4th cents. AD (from Septimius Severus)

decided on and implemented by the Latin League, is continued alone by Rome. As in the case of the citizens' colonies, they are established on the basis of a people's resolution by Roman magistrates, usually *IIIviri*. Latin colonies are fortresses on the border with or actually in enemy territory such as Venusia or Aquileia: for this reason the colonies are much larger in terms of numbers of colonists and of territory than the early citizens' colonies. They are independent states (→ *civitates*) and Roman citizens, who make up the majority of the colonists, therefore lose their Roman citizenship when they settle in the colony (this is, however, revived, should they return to Rome). The Latin colonies have their own military units (*alae* and *cohortes*, some also have ships), which fight with the Roman allies (*socii*). The colonies also have their own → *census* for the deployment of these troops. As the social and political position of the individual colonist depended on his place in the local, rather than the Roman, *census*, when a Latin colony was founded new colonists were allocated land according to their rank (according to Liv. 40,34,2 in Aquileia the number of *iugera* allocated to the colonists was 50 for simple colonists, 100 for *centuriones* and as many as 140 for the *pedites*). There is no evidence of a split between privileged and less privileged Latin colonies.

E. History

During the 5th and 4th cents. BC, Rome and its Latin neighbours founded *coloniae* on confiscated land to provide for their own excess population and to secure conquered cities. Some of these were founded alone and some acting together within the scope of the *nomen Latinum*. → Ostia, Sutrium and Nepet, near the Etruscan border, probably go back to this period; their legal position at that time is, however, unclear. From 338 BC onwards, Rome founded citizens' colonies and Latin colonies for the reasons described above, and the numbers of colonists became larger and larger. For the most part, the founding of colonies in Italy stops in the 2nd cent. However, in Gallia Cisalpina the number of *coloniae* continues to increase, and when all the municipalities south of the Po receive citizenship in 90/89 BC, the Gaulish and Venetian *civitates* to the north have their status transferred to that of Latin colonies without *deductio* (Ascon. 3 C), a model, which continued to be widely followed in Gallia and Hispania under Caesar and Augustus. The first citizens' colonies outside Italy were the *colonia Iunonia* in Carthage, although this lost its colony statute after the fall of C. Gracchus in 121 BC, and then in 118 Narbo Martius, on the road from Italy to Spain. Dating from the time of Marius and Sulla, colonies providing for → veterans become common (cf. the legion numbers of Augustan colonies in the Narbonensis in Plin. HN 3,36). The deduction of Latin colonies had already ceased in the 1st cent. BC and the establishment of new colonies ceased completely in the 1st cent. AD. The last citizens' colonies were also deduced at the end of this cent. under Domitian

and Trajan. From this time on, towns already in existence (usually → *municipia*) were awarded the title of 'honorary colonies' (one of the last of these was Nicomedia under Diocletian, CIL III 326). In total there were eventually around 400 colonies. Just as they had a higher standing than the Municipia during the imperial period as *effigies parcae simulacraque populi Romani* (Gell. NA 16,13), those colonies which enjoyed → *immunitas* or even *ius Italicum* were regarded as more important than basic *coloniae*. Individual *coloniae* were also distinguished by an epithet, usually indicating an imperial founder. The *coloniae* were one of the most important channels of Romanization, which ensured that the area around the Mediterranean became an *orbis Romanus*.

1 C. MOATTI, Archives et partages de la terre dans le monde romain, 1993   2 P. BROWN, The world of late antiquity, 1971   3 G. ZACCARIA, Novità epigrafiche del foro di Aquileia, in: Epigrafia romana in area adriatica 1998.

SOURCES: Cicero, De lege agraria; M. H. CRAWFORD (ed.), Roman Statutes 1, 1996, no. 25, Lex c. Genetivae Iuliae,; Corpus agrimensorum, ed. by LACHMANN, BLUME and RUDORFF, Liber coloniarum
BIBLIOGRAPHY: H. GALSTERER, Herrschaft und Verwaltung im republikanischen It., 1976; B. GALSTERER-KRÖLL, Unt. zu den Beinamen der Städte des Imperium Romanum, 1972; L. KEPPIE, Colonisation and Veteran Settlement in Italy 47–14 BC, 1983; E. KORNEMANN, s.v. C., RE 4, 510–588 (list of *coloniae*); B. LEVICK, Roman Colonies in Southern Asia Minor, 1967; Misurare la Terra, 1984ff.; E. T. SALMON, Roman Colonization under the Republic, 1969; A. N. SHERWIN-WHITE, The Roman Citizenship, 1973; F. VITTINGHOFF, Röm. Kolonisation und Bürgerrechtspolitik unter Caesar und Augustus, 1950.
MAPS: E. KORNEMANN, s.v. C., RE 4, 510–588; F. VITTINGHOFF, Röm. Kolonisation und Bürgerrechtspolitik unter Caesar und Augustus, 1951; E. T. SALOMON, Roman Colonization under the Republic, 1969; H. GALSTERER, Herrschaft und Verwaltung im republikanischen Italien, 1976; L. KEPPIE, Colonisation and Veteran Settlement in Italy, 47–14 B.C., 1983.   H.GA.

Colonia Ulpia Traiana Roman colony on the left side of the Lower Rhine, modern Xanten, on a low terrace between two Rhine branches in an area only suited to a limited extent for cultivation. While early signs of settlement from the 4th or 3rd cents. BC indicate no continuity with the Roman period, a favoured central location of the → Cugerni already arose there at the turn of the millennium because of the proximity of the legion camp of → Vetera. According to Tac. Hist. 4,22,1, the settlement was set up in the 60s of the 1st cent. AD 'in the style of a → *municipium*'. After its destruction during the → Batavian Revolt (ash layer for AD 69/70), the → *vicus* was quickly restored. Between AD 98 andn 107, Trajan [1] elevated the settlement into the rank of a → *colonia*, and monumental construction followed. With 73 ha C.U.T. was the second largest town of the

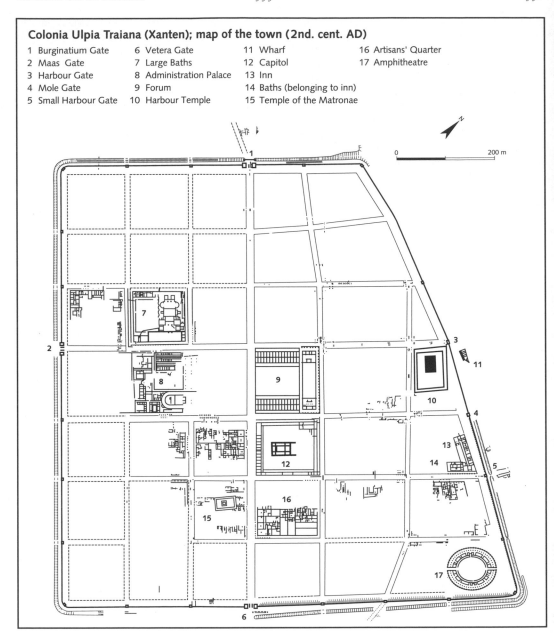

Colonia Ulpia Traiana (Xanten); map of the town (2nd. cent. AD)

1 Burginatium Gate	6 Vetera Gate	11 Wharf	16 Artisans' Quarter
2 Maas Gate	7 Large Baths	12 Capitol	17 Amphitheatre
3 Harbour Gate	8 Administration Palace	13 Inn	
4 Mole Gate	9 Forum	14 Baths (belonging to inn)	
5 Small Harbour Gate	10 Harbour Temple	15 Temple of the Matronae	

province Germania Inferior after → Colonia Agrippinensis (modern Cologne) (→ Germani [1] II. C.).

A 3.4 km-long wall with towers and gates served representational purposes and enclosed a settlement with a rectangular street grid. Apart from an amphitheatre (with stone expansion from the late 2nd cent. AD) that could hold *c.* 10,000 spectators, the Capitoline temple (one of the largest religious buildings of the province), the mercantile forum with a basilica and large thermal baths, all begun under Hadrian, are remarkable; also the 'port temple' in Mediterranean architecture and a Gallo-Roman colonnaded temple of the Matronae Aufaniae (→ Matres). The town benefited economically from the nearby military camp and trade passing through to Britannia. The territory belonging to C.U.T. appears to have been extensive. The town perished during the raids of the → Franks after AD 270, but was reconstructed *c.* AD 300 on a smaller scale and strongly fortified. After the 1st quarter of the 5th cent. the town decayed and was quarried.

ARCHAEOLOGICAL PARK

H. HINZ, Xanten zur Römerzeit, ⁴1977; Id., C. U. T., in: ANRW II 4, 1975, 825–869; U. HEIMBERG, A. RIECHE, C. U. T., 1986; C. B. RÜGER, Xanten, in: H. G. HORN (ed.), Die Römer in Nordrhein-Westfalen, 1987, 629–644; G. PRECHT, H.-J. SCHALLES, Spurenlese — Beitr. zur Gesch. des Xantener Raumes, 1989; H.-J. SCHALLES, Städte im Rheinland: Das Beispiel Xanten, in: L. WAMSER (ed.), Die Römer zw. Alpen und Nordmeer, 2000, 104–

107; H.-J. SCHALLES, Die Wirtschaftskraft städtischer Siedlungen am Niederrhein, in: T. GRÜNEWALD (ed.), Germania inferior, 2001, 431–463. RA. WI.

Colonides (αἱ Κολωνίδες). Town (or 'village', κώμη, Plut. Philopoemen 18,3) on the west coast of the Messenian Gulf near present-day Kaphirio [1] or possibly Vunaria (evidence of settlement) [2]. Minted coins during the Severian dynasty. References: Paus. 4,34,8; 12; Ptol. 3,16,7 (Κολώη). Inscription: IG V 1,1402–1404; SEG 11,996f. Coins: HN 432f.

1 R. HOPE SIMPSON, The Seven Cities Offered by Agamemnon to Achilles, in: ABSA 61, 1966, 125 2 E. MEYER, s.v. Messenien, RE Suppl. 15, 197. Y.L.

Colonization
I. GENERAL INFORMATION II. IONIC MIGRATION

I. GENERAL INFORMATION
A. DEFINITION B. THE COURSE OF COLONIZATION

A. DEFINITION
The term colonization is used to refer to several waves of settlement movements in the area around the Mediterranean in the period from the 11th cent. BC up to the Roman imperial era, which significantly alter the settlement geography of the Mediterranean world and have a decisive and lasting effect on the course of ancient history. In general the term colonization is not used to refer to the immigration in the 3rd and 2nd millenia of Indo-European tribes to Asia Minor, Greece and Italy or the spreading of Minoan and Mycenaean settlements around the eastern and parts of the western Mediterranean (→ Aegean Koine B.3 and B.4). Despite the partial paucity of literary and archaeological sources and substantial differences in the courses, causes and objectives of the respective waves of settlers' movements and establishment of colonies, it is still possible to determine the common characteristics of colonization: colonization starts in individual municipalities, the outline objective is generally known before the start of the expedition, the number of settlers is relatively low (probably generally between 100 and 200), and the newly established settlements are either completely or at least mainly economically and politically independent of the municipality from which the settlers originated. For this reason, colonization in antiquity must be regarded in a completely different light to modern 'colonialism', as the colonies in the ancient world were not set up by rival imperial powers with substantial military forces and, in particular, were not established with the objective of exercising dominance over large areas of territory in order to appropriate the raw materials and produce to be found there.

B. THE COURSE OF COLONIZATION
The first wave starts in Greece in the 11th cent. BC and leads to the settlement of the islands in the Aegean and also to the coast of Asia Minor between Smyrna and Miletus by the Ionians (see II below); at around the same time or possibly a little earlier, the Aeolians, who originated in Thessaly, settle the area to the north of the Ionian territory (→ Aeoles [1] D.: migration; → Aeoles [2]), and the area to the south of Miletus is settled by the Dorians (→ Doric Migration with map). According to the reference sources, a second wave of migration starts from the city states in Phoenicia at about the same time, which probably causes the Phoenician merchants to follow in the footsteps of Mycenaean traders via Cyprus, Crete and Sardinia into the west, and this leads to permanent settlements in the western part of North Africa, southern Spain and on the islands from the 8th cent. on (see III below); from the 6th cent., → Carthago, probably the most important Phoenician settlement, strengthens its presence in the south-western Mediterranean by means of numerous trading centres and settlements (Punic colonization).

The most extensive and significant wave in terms of its effect on the course of history is that generally referred to as the 'Great Greek Colonization', which starts in numerous Greek municipalities (excepting Athens) and at its peak between c. 750 and 580 BC probably leads to the doubling of the number of Greek city states around the Mediterranean. Key areas are southern Italy (→ Magna Graecia), Sicily, the northern Aegean and the area surrounding the Black Sea (see IV below). From the 6th cent., the colonization movements in the western Mediterranean overlap and there are increasing conflicts with the Carthaginians in Sicily and Spain and/or the Etruscans in northern and central Italy, areas which the Etruscans moved into in the 9th cent. and increased the numbers of their settlements substantially from the 7th cent. (see V below). Etruscan colonization in the south is ended with the naval battle against the Sicilian Greeks at → Cyme [2] (474 BC) and in the north with the incursions of the Celts. There is documentary evidence of Celtic migration in the 4th and 3rd cents. to Italy, south-eastern Europe and Anatolia, but very little archaeological evidence, and the migration can scarcely be viewed as a colonization operation (→ Celtic archaeology).

In the 5th cent., the character of colonization changes: whereas previously general trading interests, economic need or political problems were the spurs for establishing colonies, the primary reason for the settlements set up by colonists is now to maintain dominance over extended territories (although not to achieve this dominance in the first place). This can already be seen in the naval empire presided over by Athens (→ Delian League; → Klerouchoi [1]); the objective of military protection and the advancement of imperial administration becomes very significant in the many colonies established by Alexander [4] the Great and the Hellenistic kings (see below). Roman colonization pursues these objectives from the start (from the 4th cent. onwards) and does not take on the task of providing for veterans and the poorer sections of the population until the end of the 2nd cent. BC (→ *coloniae*). Whilst the colonies in the Hellenistic kingdoms did little to contribute to the Hellenization of the subjugated populations, the Roman colonies in the provinces were highly effective in ensuring the Romanization of the population of the empire (→ Romanization).   W.ED.

MAPS: B. D'AGOSTINO, Relations between Campania, Southern Etruria, and the Aegean in the Eighth Century B.C., in: J.-P. DESCOEUDRES (ed.), Greek Colonists and Native Population, 1990, 73–85; F. M. ANDRASCHKO, K. SCHMIDT, Orientalen und Griechen in Ägypten. Ausgrabungen auf Elephantine, in: FS H.G. Niemeyer, 1998, 46–67; P. BARCELÓ, Die Phokäer im Westen, in: FS H.G. Niemeyer, 1998, 605–614; J.-P. DESCOEUDRES (ed.), Greek Colonists and Native Population, 1990; H. MATTHÄUS, Zypern und das Mittelmeergebiet — Kontakthorizonte des späten 2. und frühen 1. Jt.v.Chr., in: FS H.G. Niemeyer, 1998, 73–91; H.G. NIEMEYER, The Phoenicians in the Mediterranean: A Non-Greek Model for Expansion and Settlement in Antiquity, in: J.-P. DESCOEUDRES (ed.), Greek Colonists and Native Population, 1990, 469–489; H.G. NIEMEYER (ed.), Phönizier im Westen (Madrider Beiträge 8), 1982; G.R. TSETSKHLADZE, F. DE ANGELIS (ed.), The Archaeology of Greek Colonisation. Essays Dedicated to Sir John Boardman, 1994.

II. IONIC MIGRATION
A. GENERAL B. HISTORICITY C. CHRONOLOGY
D. THE ORIGINS OF THE IONIANS IN ATTICA AND ATHENS E. ORIGINS IN OTHER REGIONS OF GREECE

A. GENERAL
The modern term 'Ionic migration' (IM) is used to describe the migration of Greeks from the mainland to Asia Minor, a movement which, according to ancient tradition, began in Athens and was organized and led by the sons of → Codrus (in summary Hdt. 1,145–147; Str. 14,1,3; Paus. 7,2,1–4); it was characterized by the great number of the participants and the fact that they originated from many parts of Greece (Pylians: Mimnermus fr. 9 WEST; Athenians originating from Pylos or Messenia like the Codrides: Hellanicus FGrH 4 F 125; Paus. 7,2,3; Ionians from Achaea: Hdt. 1,145f.; 7,94–95,1; Str. 8,7,1; Paus. 7,1,1–6; participants from other parts of Greece: Hdt. 1,146; comprehensive analysis of Ionian local traditions, institutions, personal and place names and names of months, cults and festivals in [16. part 1]). In the reference sources the movement is referred to as (*Ionikè*) → *apoikía* and also described in the same manner as the establishing of a colony. The cause of the IM is acknowledged as the struggle for the kingship in Athens among the sons of Codrus, which was won by Medon against Neleus and the other brothers (Hellanicus FGrH 4 F 125; Paus. 7,2,1; Ael. VH 8,5). The sources seem to point to the IM as taking place in the 4th generation after the fall of Troy or two generations after the return of the → Heraclidae (relative chronological analysis in [16. 307–324; 14. 326–330]). Based on the hellenistic chronologies detailing this relative sequence, it is calculated that the actual date for these events is in the 11th cent. BC ([16], and accordingly [20. 392–395]).

The sources of reference on the subject of the IM (listed in [16]) are fragmentary, often contradictory and certainly not consistent, and their historical content is assessed in a wide variety of ways by modern researchers. At the centre of the debate are the issues of historicity, chronology and the participation of Athens and other regions of Greece.

B. HISTORICITY
The settlement of the Aegean coastal areas in Asia Minor by Greeks emigrating from their mother country is today generally accepted as historical fact. The discoveries made in modern dialect research regarding the spread and development of the Ionian group of dialects make this the only possible explanation (cf. [19. 96–103; 124–133]; → Ionic).

C. CHRONOLOGY
The current position of archaeological research as regards the Cyclades, western Asia Minor and the offshore islands [17. 329–344; 20. 166–170] continues to support the dating of the Greek acquisition of land in Ionia in the Sub-Mycenaean and Proto-Geometric era [5. 785–790; 17; 18], i.e. in the 11th cent. BC, which therefore corresponds surprisingly well to calculations made by the historians of antiquity. Likewise, there is evidence of an extensive reduction in the number of settlements in most areas of the Peloponnese in the 11th cent. (end of Late Helladic III C Late and Sub-Mycenaean) (see below at end of section). On the other hand, the significance of Mycenaean finds in western Asia Minor [15; 9; 6; 12; 11] for the IM has been overestimated (by [3; 16; 20]. Mycenaean vessels, vase fragments and other individual objects in areas which subsequently belonged to the Ionians do provide evidence of contact with the Mycenaean world, but not necessarily the presence of Mycenaean settlers. Even in Ephesus, Mycenaean finds dating from the early 14th cent. BC and discovered in a (very disturbed) tomb and the proof of Mycenaean cult practices in the Artemisium [1. 27f.] cannot be regarded as evidence of the late Bronze Age settlement having a Mycenaean-Greek character, as they could also originate from individuals or groups in contact with Mycenaean culture, such as the inhabitants of a trading colony or a maritime trading centre in the middle of an otherwise completely Anatolian environment. Similar conclusions can be drawn regarding the 'beehive tomb' of Colophon (no longer extant today). In addition to the archaeological sources, more recent finds of Hittite texts make it unlikely that one could locate → Achijawa or another Greek settlement area in western Asia Minor at the time of the Hittite empire (cf. [7. 217–221; 2. map 3]).

The situation in south-west Anatolia was different: here Miletus, Iasos [5] and Müsgebi were completely Mycenaean settlements in the 14th and 13th cents. Minoan colonists had previously settled in → Miletus (and probably also in Iasos) (most recently [12]). Recent archaeological discoveries now make it seem highly probable [12] that Miletus was in fact also the town of Millawanda, which according to Hittite texts was (at least at times) under the influence of Achijawa [8]. This region's contacts with the Mycenaean mainland are probably reflected in the ethnic designations *mi-ra-ti-ja*, *ki-ni-di-ja*, *a-*64-ja* (= in all probability *a-si-wi-ja*) of the → Linear B texts of Pylos, which refer to women from Miletus, Cnidus and *Ἀσϝία (*Aswía*) = Ἀσία (*Asía*), whose low status suggests that the women arrived there via the slave trade. In Samos, the final Mycenaean finds date from the 13th cent. In Chios the important 12th-cent. settlement of Emporio was destroyed in the Late Helladic IIIC.

Overall, the evidence in western Asia Minor of contact with Mycenaean Greece provides as little proof of a Hellenization of western Asia Minor as the Mycenaean settlements in south-west Anatolia. What it does show, however, is that the colonization of Ionia occurred in an area that was already known to the Greeks.

D. THE ORIGINS OF THE IONIANS IN ATTICA AND ATHENS

In modern research, it is generally accepted as historical fact that the Ionians had their origins in Attica and Athens (overview in [14. 336]). The most important arguments for this case are phyle names shared by the Athenians and the Ionians, the shared custom of the celebration of the → Apatouria and almost completely consistent statements to be found in the literary sources (Hdt. 5,97,2; 7,94–95,1; 9,106,3 and *passim*; Thuc. 1,2,6; 1,12,4). For various reasons, however, this evidence is also regarded as the result of inventions or manipulation of older considerations in the interests of Attic politics ([3; 16]; 14; 20,367–404]; a vehement argument contradicting this [18]). Further evidence of early links between the mainland and the Ionians is demonstrated by the use in Homer (Hom. Il. 13,685) and Solon (fr. 4 D) of the ethnic designation *Iáones* and the country name *Iaonía*, which can be traced back to the older form of the Ionian name, *Ἰάϝονες (*Iáwones). This appears in the Linear B texts of Knossos as *i-ja-wo-ne* and can be interpreted (in KN bk 164,4) as the ethnic designation /*Iawones*/. Furthermore, the Near Eastern terms for the Greek nation as a whole derive from *Ἰάϝονες (Hebr. *jawan*, Egyptian *jwn(n)*, Pers. *yauna*), and must therefore have been formed before the disappearance of the Digamma (ϝ) or borrowed from a non-Ionian dialect. The argument for the derivation of *Íōnes* from *Iáwones, on the other hand, is not conclusive, as this could also have resulted from a new coinage associated with the eponymous hero *Íōn* [4].

E. ORIGINS IN OTHER REGIONS OF GREECE

The reduction mentioned above in the number of settlements in the Peloponnese at the end of the Mycenaean era is particularly marked in Achaea and Messenia (cf. [20. map 3]). In contrast, in Athens archaeological evidence points to an increase in population towards the end of the Mycenaean and Sub-Mycenaean eras [13; 20. 115–117 and fig. 3; 21. 60–75], which lends some credence to the statements in ancient sources to the effect that the Ionians originated in Messenia and Achaea. In relation to Messenia, the case for recognizing a degree of historicity in the ancient tradition regarding the at least partial origins of the Ionians in Pylos was particularly strengthened by the discovery of the palace of Ano Englianos which was clearly identified according to the Linear B texts as *puro/Pylos/* (→ Pylos), its destruction at the end of the 13th cent. and the subsequent rapid decline in settlements. This then brings into consideration the route via Athens mentioned in most of the sources — the reception of Pylian refugees, the takeover of the kingship in Athens by the Pylian royal house of the Neleids, the most famous member of which was → Codrus, the migration of the Pylians to Asia Minor led by Codrus' son → Neleus (family tree in Hellanicus FGrH 4 F 125) — but also the direct migration from Pylos to Ionia mentioned by Mimnermus (fr. 9 WEST) (cf. [18. 311]). On the other hand, the current status of archaeological research in Boeotia and Thessaly does not provide enough evidence to support the theory that the Ionians had their origins in Central Greece (as per [16]; guarded agreement in [18. 301]).

→ Ionic; → Iones

1 A. BAMMER, U. MUSS, Das Artemision von Ephesos, 1996 2 T. BRYCE, The Kingdom of the Hittites, 1998 3 F. CASSOLA, La Ionia nel mondo miceneo, 1957 4 J. CHADWICK, The Ionian Name, in: K. H. KINZL (ed.), Greece and the Mediterranean in Ancient History and Prehistory. Studies ... Fritz Schachermeyr, 1977 5 J. N. COOK, Greek Settlements in the Eastern Aegean and Asia Minor, in: CAH II³ 2, 1975, 773–804 6 E. B. FRENCH, Turkey and the East Aegean, in: C. ZERNER (ed.), Wace and Blegen, 1993, 155–158 7 O. R. GURNEY, Hittite Geography, in: H. OTTEN et al. (ed.), Hittite and Other Anatolian and Near Eastern Studies in Honour of Sedat Alp, 1992, 213–221 8 S. HEINHOLD-KRAHMER, s.v. Milawa(n)da, in: RLA 8, 188f. 9 CH. MEE, Aegean Trade and Settlement in Anatolia in the Second Millenium B.C., in: AS 28, 1978, 121–156 10 W. MÜLLER-WIENER (ed.), Milet 1899–1980, 1986 11 W.-D. NIEMEIER, The Mycenaeans in Western Anatolia and the Problem of the Origins of the Sea Peoples, in: S. GITIN et al. (ed.), Mediterranean Peoples in Transition: Thirteenth to Early Tenth Centuries B.C., 1998, 17–65 12 B. NIEMEIER, W.-D. NIEMEIER, Milet 1994–1995, in: AA 1997, 189–248 13 M. PANTELIDOU, Αἱ προιστορικαί Ἀθῆναι, 1975 14 F. PRINZ, Gründungsmythen und Sagenchronologie, 1979, 314–376 15 L. RE, Presenze micenee in Anatolia, in: M. MARAZZI et al. (ed.), Traffici micenei nel Mediterraneo, 1986, 343–358 16 M. SAKELLARIOU, La migration grecque en Ionie, 1958 17 F. SCHACHERMEYR, Die Ägäische Frühzeit 4, 1980 18 Id., Die griech. Rückerin-

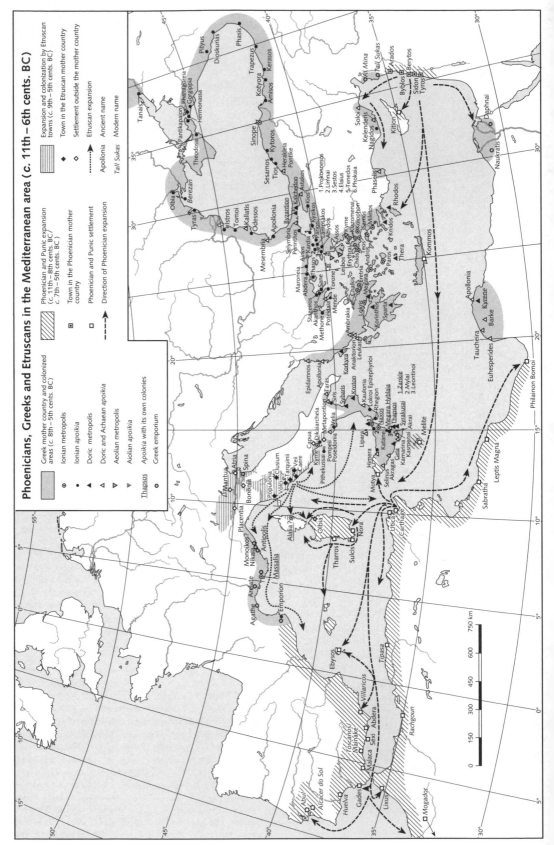

Phoenicians, Greeks and Etruscans in the Mediterranean area (c. 11th–6th cents. BC)

Greek mother country and colonized areas (c. 8th–5th cents. BC)

Ionian metropolis
Ionian *apoikia*
Doric metropolis
Doric and Achaean *apoikia*
Aeolian metropolis
Aiolian *apoikia*
Thapsos Apoikia with its own colonies
Greek emporium

Phoenician and Punic expansion (c. 11th–8th cents. BC / c. 7th–5th cents. BC)
Town in the Phoenician mother country
Phoenician and Punic settlement
Direction of Phoenician expansion

Expansion and colonization by Etruscan towns (c. 9th–5th cents. BC)
Town in the Etruscan mother country
Settlement outside the Etruscan mother country
Etruscan expansion
Apollonia Ancient name
Tall Sukas Modern name

1 Prokonnesos
2 Limnai
3 Sestos
4 Elaius
5 Tenedos
6 Phokaia

1 Zankle
2 Mylai
3 Leontinoi

0 150 300 450 600 750 km

Colonization: chronological synopsis

	Greek expansion		'Great Greek Colonization'				Phoenician expansion		Etruscan expansion
	Aeolian/Ionian/Doric Migration		Ionian apoikiai	Dorian apoikiai	Achaean apoikiai	Aeolian apoikiai	Phoenician city-states	Punians	Villanova Culture/City-states
	(Thessaly) (Achaea, Attica) (Peloponnese)		(Euboea, Miletus,...)	(Corinth, Megara,...)	(Achaea)	(Lesbos, Cyme,...)	(Byblus, Sidon, Tyre)	(Carthage/settlements in southern Spain)	(Caere, Tarquinii,...)

Time axis (left): 1200 BC – 1100 – 1000 – 900 – 800 – 700 – 600 – 500 – 400 – 300 – 200 – 100

Aeolian (Thessaly):
Lesbos, Tenedos, Coast of Asia Minor: Cyme?

Ionian (Achaea, Attica):
Cyclades: Ceos, Delos, Paros, Naxos, Amorgos
Coast of Asia Minor: Miletus,... Carian territory; Ephesus,... Lydian territory; Chios, Samos

Doric (Peloponnese):
Crete, Doric islands of the southern Aegaean
Coast of Asia Minor

Ionian apoikiai (Euboea, Miletus,...):
pre-colonization Euboean trade contacts ('Lefkandi') → Tyre, Al Mina, Amathous, Magna Graecia/Latium, Sicily/Sardinia
Magna Graecia, Acarnania/Epirus?, Sicily, Chalcidice, Propontis
Northern Aegaean, Propontis, Chalcidice, Pontos Euxeinos, Sicily
Pontos Euxeinos, Propontis, Western Mediterranean, Thracian Aegaean, Magna Graecia, Iberian Peninsula
Pontos Euxeinos

Dorian apoikiai (Corinth, Megara,...):
Acarnania/Epirus?, Sicily, Magra Graecia, Propontis
Propontis, Sicily, Magra Graecia, Acarnania/Epirus/Illyricum, Cyrenaeica, Chalcidice
Sicily, Acarnania/Epirus/Illyricum, Lipare, Cyrenaeica, Pontos Euxeinos

Achaean apoikiai (Achaea):
Magna Graeca
Magna Graeca

Aeolian apoikiai (Lesbos, Cyme,...):
Western and southern Troad = old and new Aeolis (Assos), Thracian Chersonese (Sestus, Madytus, Alopeconnesus), Northern Aegean (Aenus)

Phoenician city-states (Byblus, Sidon, Tyre):
Pre-colonization trade expeditions using Mycenaean and Cypriot (?) routes. 12th-cent. foundations attested by literary sources: Citium, Gades, Utica, Lixus. Emporia → Egypt, Cyprus, Crete, Aegean
Iberian Peninsula ('Tarshish-expeditions' = ?Tartessus, Tyre), Italy, Sardinia, Atlantic coast
Citium ('apoikia' of Tyre), 'emporia': Crete, Euboea, Aegean, Sicily, North Africa (Utica), Sardinia? (Nora)
Permanent 'emporia' and 'joint ventures': Egypt, Cyprus, Iberian Peninsula (i.a. Gadir, 'apoikia' of Tyre), Sicily, Mozia, Sardinia, southern Iberian Peninsula

Punians (Carthage/settlements in southern Spain):
Qarthadasht (Carthage, founded 814 BC; 'apoikia' of Tyre)
From the 7th cent., Carthage assumes responsibility for the protection of Phoenician emporia in the west
c. 560 'Punic expansion': Ibiza, Sardinia, Western Sicily, Iberian Peninsula, North Africa
Iberian Peninsula, Libyan hinterland, Conquest of Sicily, Western Sicily, (Corsica), Sardinia
247 BC, 238 BC, 206 BC, 146 BC

Villanova Culture/City-states (Caere, Tarquinii,...):
Southern Campania (Pontecagnano,...)
Po Plain (Bologna,...)
Po Plain: (Mantua, Bologna, Atria, Spina,...)
Campania: (Nola, Capua, Pompeii)
424 BC, 400 BC

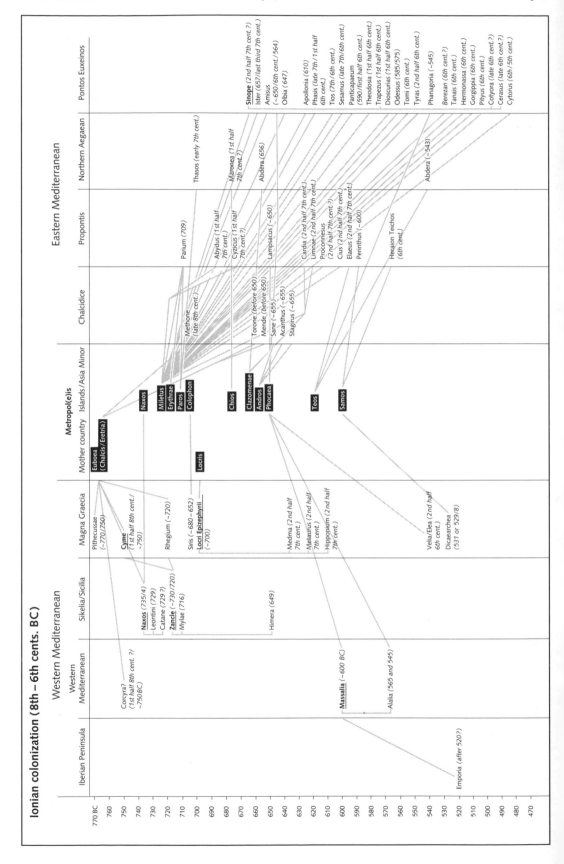

Ionian colonization (8th – 6th cents. BC)

Western Mediterranean

Eastern Mediterranean

Iberian Peninsula | Western Mediterranean | Sikelia/Sicilia | Magna Graecia | Mother country | Islands/Asia Minor | Chalcidice | Propontis | Northern Aegean | Pontos Euxeinos

Metropol(e)is

Euboea (Chalcis / Eretria)

Naxos
Miletus
Erythrae
Paros
Colophon
Locris
Chios
Clazomenae
Andros
Phocaea
Teos
Samos

Pithecussae (~770./750.)

Cyme (1st half 8th cent./ ~750.)

Naxos (735/4)
Leontini (729)
Catane (729 ?)
Zancle (~730/720)
Mylae (716)

Rhegium (~720)

Himera (649)

Siris (~680 – 652)
Locri Epizephyrii (~700)

Medma (2nd half 7th cent.)
Metaurus (2nd half 7th cent.)
Hippopium (2nd half 7th cent.)

Velia/Elea (2nd half 6th cent.)
Dicaearchea (531 or 529/8)

Corcyra? (1st half 8th cent. ?/ ~750 BC)

Massalia (~600 BC)

Alalia (565 and 545)

Emporia (after 520?)

Parium (709)

Thasos (early 7th cent.)

Methone (late 8th cent.)

Torone (before 650)
Mende (before 650)
Sane (~655)
Acanthus (~655)
Stagirus (~655)

Abydus (1st half 7th cent.)
Cyzicus (1st half 7th cent.?)
Lampsacus (~650)

Cardia (2nd half 7th cent.)
Limnae (2nd half 7th cent.)
Proconnesus (2nd half 7th cent.?)
Cius (2nd half 7th cent.)
Elaeus (2nd half 7th cent.)
Perinthus (~600)

Hexaion Teichos (6th cent.)

Maronea (1st half 7th cent.)

Abdera (656)

Abdera (~543)

Sinope (2nd half 7th cent. ?)
Ister (657/last third 7th cent.)
Amisus (~650/6th cent./564)
Olbia (647)

Apollonia (610)
Phasis (late 7th/1st half 6th cent.)
Tios (7th/6th cent.)
Sesamus (late 7th/6th cent.)
Panticapaeum (590/first half 6th cent.)
Theodosia (1st half 6th cent.)
Trapezus (1st half 6th cent.)
Dioscurias (1st half 6th cent.)
Odessus (585/575)
Tomi (6th cent.)
Tyras (2nd half 6th cent.)
Phanagoria (~545)
Berezan (6th cent.?)
Tanais (6th cent.)
Hermonassa (6th cent.)
Gorgippia (6th cent.)
Pityus (6th cent.)
Cotyora (late 6th cent.?)
Cerasus (late 6th cent.?)
Cytorus (6th/5th cent.)

770 BC
760
750
740
730
720
710
700
690
680
670
660
650
640
630
620
610
600
590
580
570
560
550
540
530
520
510
500
490
480
470

Doric colonization (8th – c. 6th cents. BC)

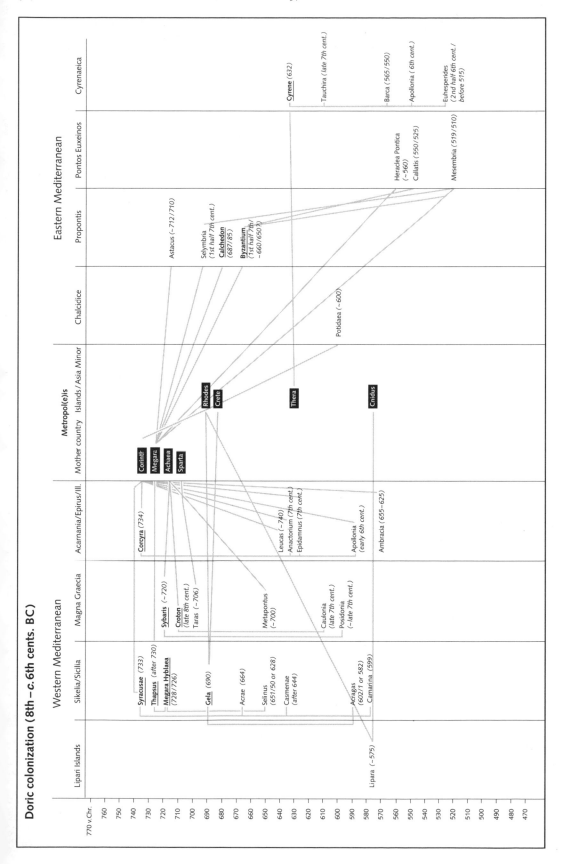

nerung im Lichte neuer Forschungen, 1983, 296–320
19 R. SCHMITT, Einführung in die griech. Dialekte, 1977,
96–103; 124–133 20 J. VANSCHOONWINKEL, L'Égée et
la Méditerranée orientale à la fin du deuxième millénaire,
1991 21 K.-W. WELWEI, Athen, 1992. S.D.-J.

III. PHOENICIAN COLONIZATION

The Phoenician expansion in the West at the end of
the 2nd millennium BC is based on the traditional trading links of the Late Bronze Age *Koine* of the Levant,
Cyprus and Anatolia with the Aegean and the central
and western areas of the Mediterranean. Following the
end of the crisis in the 12th cent. (→ 'Sea Peoples, migration of'), by which the Phoenician city states along the
Levantine coast — there are hardly any literary or archaeological records here — were affected to varying
degrees in terms of duration and intensity but for the
most part without serious consequences, the Phoenician expansion focussed on the rich silver, copper and
pewter deposits of Cyprus (→ Cyprus), Etruria
(→ Etruscans, Etruria), → Sardinia and the Iberian peninsula (→ Pyrenean peninsula). This provided the
highly specialized Phoenician artists and craftsmen
with raw materials and also promoted profitable intermediate trade (i.a. with Assyria; also the provision of
tributes). The Phoenicians rapidly won back the markets of the 2nd millennium in the central and western
areas of the Mediterranean. With their strong economic
position, the most important Phoenician cities of → Byblus, → Sidon and → Tyrus once again were able to determine the course of Phoenician politics in the Early
Iron Age.

There must have been strong and stable Phoenician
trading links with Egypt at an early stage, if the reports
of Wen-Amun (*c.* 1075 BC.) are to be believed: 50 ships
belonging to Sidon's trading fleet and 20 from that of
Byblus were used to exchange goods with Egypt. There
are undeniable written records detailing the Greek and
Roman versions of the history of the founding of the
earliest Phoenician towns and settlements: the founding
of Tyrus in 1198/1185 BC (Jos. Ant. Iud. 8,62 and Just.
Epit. 18,3,5), of → Citium at the beginning of the 12th
cent. (Verg. Aen. 1,619–626), of → Utica 1101 (Aristot.
Mir. 134; Plin. HN 16,216), of → Gades 1104/3 (Vell.
Pat.1,2,1–3) and of → Lixus (Plin. HN 19, 63), although the continuing absence of any archaeological
discoveries in the West should be borne in mind when
considering these references. Mythological heroic
deeds, such as the founding of → Salamis/Cyprus by
Teucer, the death of Hercules and the return of the Heraclids (→ Heraclidae), the downfall of the Athenian
monarchy or the fall of Troy (1184 BC) were obviously
chronological markers for the Phoenician expansion in
the Mediterranean, as following these events this began
at the start of the 12th cent.

The driving force behind the Phoenician expansion
was formed by the relatively small, proportionately
powerful and independent Phoenician city states, which
were dependent on → trade (II. Phoenicia) for their ex-

istence. This expansion, of which the political, economic and organizational structure and background scarcely changed in the following 500 years, was expressed in
two partially successive and partially overlapping archaeological phenomena. There is a large amount of
proof of the ubiquity from the start of the Phoenician
'merchant venturers' and craftsmen and their products
— which were luxury and prestige import goods for the
most part, and also (although at first only in the eastern
Mediterranean) the equally simple and obviously attractive ceramics — in the luxuriously furnished tombs
of nobles in Cyprus (Palaiopaphos-Skales, Salamis) and
the Aegean (Rhode, Cos, Samos, Crete, Euboea,
Athens, Corinth). Little by little, Phoenician trading
offices and workshops (*enoikismoi*) spread to the Cypriot and Greek settlements, and exploited both the
sources of raw materials and the local markets, as well
as cultivating close and enduring contacts with the
Levant.

As regards further westwards expansion during the
10th and 9th cents. into the central Mediterranean,
Italy, Sardinia, the Atlantic coast, Morocco and lastly
into the Iberian peninsula, the archaeological sources
are still only sporadic and confirm the picture of somewhat irregular, but not necessarily infrequent long-distance trading by the Phoenicians, the roots of which
stretch back into the Bronze Age. Attention can be
drawn here to the biblically referenced three-yearly
journeys undertaken by the kings → Hiram I (Tyre) and
Solomo (Jerusalem) to Tarshish, which is probably the
legendary kingdom of → Tartessus in southern Spain,
on the west coast above the Tyrian colony of Gadir (1
Kgs 10,22: 969–930 BC; Ez 27,12: 586 BC), an identification which, although plausible, is disputed.

Up until the 6th cent. there is archaeological evidence of a second phase (8th/mid 7th cent. BC) when
many Phoenician settlements (*emporia*), trading posts
and sanctuaries were established, generally on the periphery, with workshops and access to the sea, some of
them in close proximity to the centres of economic activity. For the most part, the hinterland consisted of
territory that was not subordinated in political or administrative terms or even subjugated; the Phoenician
partners were to some extent in a stronger position economically and technologically and to some extent they
were reliant on the cooperation of the indigenous aristocracy. Trading posts quickly developed into towns
with harbours, town walls, sanctuaries, necropoleis
and tophets, as e.g. on Cyprus, Mozia (Motya), Sicily
and Sardinia. At the same time, however, there are
exceptions such as e.g. → Pithecussae on Ischia, the
earliest Euboean settlement in the West (pre 750 BC),
which had a close relationship to the Tyrian colony of
Carthage (750–675 BC) and the Phoenicians lived here
as metics. The Phoenician settlements on the southern
Spanish coast were established in the first half of the 8th
cent. and experienced their largest growth in population between 720 and 700 BC, many were abandoned
again very early on and most underwent economic

recession and political reorganization in the mid 6th cent. The extraction of silver in the Río Tinto area declined and with the Phocaeans as the new trading partners in the area around Tartessus, Greek culture gained in influence.

According to tradition, → Carthago was founded in 814/3 BC by Tyrians (Timaeus, FGrH 566 F 60) as a 'new city' (Qarthadasht), mainly for domestic political reasons, and had special status as a colony (apoikía), which distinguished it from all other Phoenician settlements in the Mediterranean. Archaeological evidence is only traceable to the first half of the 8th cent. Over its 600-year history up until its destruction in 146 BC, Carthage developed into the leading and feared trading and naval power in the western Mediterranean and was the victor in many wars against Greece and Rome.
→ Phoenicia; → Phoenician archaeology

M.E. AUBET, The Phoenicians and the West, 1994; G.BUNNENS, L'expansion phénicienne en Méditerranée, 1979; W.CULICAN, The First Merchant Venturers, 1966; Id., Phoenicia and Phoenician Colonization, in: CAH² 3,2, 1991, 485–546; E.LIPINSKI, G.BUNNENS, s.v. Expansion phénicienne, DCPP, 166f.; A.ENNABLI (ed.), Pour sauver Carthage. Exploration et conservation de la cité punique, romaine et byzantine, 1992; E.GJERSTAD, The Phoenician Colonization and Expansion in Cyprus, in: RDAC 1979, 230–254; W.HUSS, Die Karthager, 1994; O.NEGBI, Early Phoenician Presence in the Mediterranean Islands: A Reappraisal, in: AJA 96, 1992, 599–615; H.G. NIEMEYER, Das frühe Karthago und die phöniz. Expansion im Mittelmeerraum (Veröffentlichungen der J. Jungius-Ges. der Wiss. Hamburg 60), 1989; Id., Die Phönizier und die Mittelmeerwelt im Zeitalter Homers, in. JRGZ 31, 1984, 3–94; W.RÖLLIG, Die Phönizier des Mutterlandes z.Z. der K., in: Phönizier im Westen (Madrider Beiträge 8), 1982, 15–30.   CH.B.

IV. THE 'GREAT' GREEK COLONIZATION
A. GENERAL   B. COURSE   C. CAUSES AND OBJECTIVES   V. ETRUSCAN COLONIZATION   VI. ALEXANDER THE GREAT AND HELLENISM

A. GENERAL
The colonization movement starts in the second half of the 8th cent. BC. The first colonies are → Naxos (near Taormina; 734 BC) and → Cyme [2], established at about the same time. Colonization continues in varying degrees of intensity up until about 500 BC, and in addition to the original colonies there are soon offshoot towns, either established independently by the colonies themselves or together with the original town from whence the colonists came.

There are no sources of information on colonization until Herodotus and Thucydides, but they provide valuable information about the west of the Mediterranean (Hdt. 1,163–167: Phocaeans; Thuc. 6,3–5: colonization of Sicily; dating as used here) and other regions (Hdt. 2,154 and 178f.: Greeks in Egypt; 2,33; 4,17f., 51–54, 78f.: Greeks around the Black Sea). Important information is also scattered through the geographical works of Strabo. There are also significant archaeological finds that, however, often do not correlate with tradition as handed down in literature, but do provide important information regarding ways of life, architectural styles and trading relations (detailed use in [1]).

B. COURSE
The starting points for the Great Greek Colonization are the approximate 20 Greek municipalities on the Greek mainland, the Aegean islands and the west coast of Asia Minor, which act as 'migration ports', where colonists from other municipalities and from inland probably assembled. A special role is played at the start by the Euboean towns of Chalcis [1] and Eretria [1], as well as Corinth and Megara, then later (from c. 650) also Miletus and Phocaea. Preferred areas are (in the order in which they were settled): Sicily (→ Naxos 734, → Syracusae 733, → Megara (Hyblaea) 728, Zancle/→ Messana c. 730–720), southern Italy (Cyme [2], → Sybaris, → Croton, → Rhegium, all end of the 8th cent.), the northern Aegean Chalcidice settled by Chalcis [1] (→ Methone end of the 8th cent., → Mende and → Torone pre 650), the sea routes to the west (→ Corcyra/Corfu end of the 8th cent.) and around the Black Sea (→ Propontis: Astacus [1] c. 710, Parium 709, as well as Selymbria, → Calchedon and → Byzantium in the first half of the 7th cent.). The settlement of the Black Sea area by Miletus starts shortly afterwards in the second half of the 7th cent. around the south coast, the south-western coast (as far as the Danube) and on the Crimean peninsula (first settlements: → Sinope, Ister [3], → Olbia, → Panticapaeum/Kertsh), as well as other colonies in the Propontis. The only settlement colony founded in North Africa is that of → Cyrene, founded by Thera/Santorini in 632, which subsequently founded → Barce in c. 550 and Euhesperides prior to 515. The most westerly settlement is that of → Massalia/Marseilles, founded by the Phocaeans from Asia Minor in around 600, which following the control of the Straits of Gibraltar by the Carthaginians, was to form the link to British tin deposits via the Rhone and the Loire and which itself also founded trading settlements: in northern Spain (→ Emporiae/Ampurias), possibly in southern France (Monoecus/Monaco, Nicaea/Nice, Antipolis/Antibes i.a) and definitely on Corsica (Alalia/ → Aleria) opposite the mineral-rich Etruscan coast, from which they were driven away by the Carthaginians in 540 and then moved to Elea (→ Velia). By the conclusion of the 'Great Greek' Colonization, there were between 150–200 new settlements around the Mediterranean and the Black Sea, including the subsidiary settlements established by the colonies.

C. CAUSES AND OBJECTIVES
The Greek colonization in the archaic era runs parallel with the formation of the → polis in Greece, but its existence cannot yet be presupposed at the beginning of the colonization in the 8th cent. It is therefore uncertain to what extent the early colonization expeditions can

have been organized on the part of the originating municipality by means of settlement resolutions, the provision of ships and the election of the *oikistes* (the leaders of the colonization expeditions), in order to reduce economic problems (the need for land, overpopulation). The founding of Cyrene as described by Herodotus (4,150–167) (not until *c.* 630 and instigated by an extreme drought) can therefore not in any way be regarded as a model case. It is more obvious to see the sponsors of early colonization as aristocratic individuals or groups, who, with varying prospects, left their original homeland either voluntarily or under duress in the situation of political upheaval and crisis — a shortage of land due to a growth in population and a concentration of landownership in the hands of a few aristocrats; the reduction in the authority of the aristocracy through the increase in importance of new sectors of society and the obligation to fit in with the emerging organization of the polis [2. 137]. Sparta's founding of Tarentum demonstrates the close relationship between a crisis in the aristocracy and colonization [3. 121–141]. The repercussions of solving problems in the colonies (administration, legal system, town planning) therefore seems to have actually promoted the formation of poleis in the mother country rather than copying it [4].

This all reveals a plethora of causes and objectives of colonization that do not fit together in one scheme. Note should be made, however, of the twin threads of trading interests (a favourite aristocratic activity) and the search for land (a necessary prerequisite for a colony's self-sufficiency), which run throughout the entire era of colonization. The earliest colonization starts in Chalcis [1] and Eretria [1], which have the closest links to the Levant and maintain trading posts there (Al Mina, Tell Sukas), and which with their first and also most northerly settlement in Italy (→ Pithecussae on Ischia in around 770) are primarily trying to gain access to Etruscan mineral deposits. Colonies are then swiftly established in Corcyra (by Eretria), Naxos, Zancle/→ Messana and Rhegium (by Chalcis), which are key stages of the sea route from the Corinthian Gulf to Pithecussae — a route followed by Corinth with the conquest of Corcyra, the founding of Syracusae and the subsequent establishment of colonies on the Adriatic coast (→ Leucas, → Ambracia, → Anactorium) and also by Megara and in particular the municipalities of Achaea, which founded Croton and Sybaris in the Gulf of Taranto. It was not by chance that Sybaris was located at the point of the shortest land link between the Gulf of Taranto and the Tyrrhenian Sea — which made it possible to avoid the dangerous navigation of the Straits of Messina and provided the colony with its proverbial riches — and tried to gain access to Central Italy with the founding of Posidonia/Paestum.

With the establishment of colonies in the Propontis, Megara made its mark on the sea route to the Black Sea at an early stage and created strong trading posts for itself in the shape of Calchedon and Byzantium, for trade which was certainly underway before the area was settled by Miletus. The location of the colonies established by Miletus on the southern coast of the Black Sea suggests that the idea was to obtain access to the mineral deposits of Anatolia; the settlements on the estuary of the large rivers flowing from inland Russia opened up the way to the North. Miletus' roughly simultaneous commitment in Egypt with a trading post (later accorded special privileges by → Amasis [2]) (→ Emporion) in → Naucratis created a trading area for Miletus which stretched from the Baltic to Nubia. It is therefore not surprising that Greek colonization, which began with the trading interest of the Euboeans, ends with the explicit interest in the Phocaeans' metal trade in Massalia and Aleria.

→ Apoikia; → Ktistes; → Metropolis; → Oikistes

1 J. BOARDMAN, Kolonien und Handel der Griechen, 1981
2 U. WALTER, An der Polis teilhaben, 1993 3 M. MEIER, Aristokraten und Damoden, 1998 4 I. MALKIN, Religion and Colonization in Ancient Greece, 1987.

J. BÉRARD, La colonisation grecque de l'Italie méridionale et de la Sicile, ²1957; Id., L'expansion et la colonisation grecques jusqu' aux guerres médiques, 1960 (extensive details of sources); C. ROEBUCK, Ionian Trade and Colonization, 1959; H. SCHAEFER, Eigenart und Wesenszüge der griech. Kolonisation, in: Heidelberger Jb. 4, 1960, 77–93; N. ERHARDT, Milet und seine Kolonien, 1983; J.-P. DESCOEUDRES (ed.), Greek Colonists and Native Population, 1990; G. R. TSETSKHLADZE (ed.), The Greek Colonisation of the Black Sea Area, 1998. Further literature dealing with individual locations. W.ED.

V. ETRUSCAN COLONIZATION

The expansion drive that started in the core Etruscan area between the Arno and the Tiber starts as early as the 9th and 8th cents. BC in the era of the → Villanova culture and follows a north-south axis [8]. In the north, it reaches Bologna (Felsina) [9] in the 9th cent. via settlements such as Fermo and Verucchio [4]. In the south, the expansion initially moves via the sea route with the establishment of colonies in Pontecagnano and Sala Consilina [5]. The more extensive colonization which started in the 7th cent. BC results in leagues of 12 cities north of the Apennines (Diod. Sic. 14,113,2; Liv. 5,33,8; Plin. HN 3,19,25 — Mantua, Bologna, Adria, Spina etc.) and in Campania (Nola, Capua, Pompeii etc.) [2; 3]. Like Spina, → Marzabotto is an example of a colony established in the late 6th and 5th cents. BC, based on a town planning design that owes a debt to Greek ideas (→ Hippodamus of Miletus) [7]. The expansion along the Tyrrhenian coast into the territory of the Ligurians (Genoa) and to southern France was limited by the striving for power of → Massalia (Marseilles), founded in around 600 by Phocaeans [1]. In contrast to Greek colonization, the individuals or municipalities behind the expansion are generally not known; any statement regarding the origins of the settlers can only be based on the alphabets and objects that they used [3]. In addition to the more agrarian-based settlements such as Marzabotto [7], the Etruscans also set up trading posts amongst the native population (Genoa) [1].

→ Etruscans, Etruria

1 L. AIGNER-FORESTI, Zeugnisse etr. Kultur im Nordwesten Italiens und in Südfrankreich. Zur Gesch. der Ausbreitung etr. Einflüsse und der etr.-griech. Auseinandersetzung, 1988   2 P. KRACHT, Stud. zu den griech.-etr. Handelsbeziehungen vom 7. bis 4. Jh.v.Chr., 1991   3 M. CRISTOFANI, Etruschi e altri genti nell'Italia pre-romana. Mobilità in età arcaica, 1996   4 M. FORTE (ed.), Il dono delle Eliadi. Ambre e oreficerie dei principi etruschi di Verucchio. Exhibition Bologna, 1995   5 P. GASTALDI, G. MAETZKE (ed.), La presenza etrusca nella Campania meridionale. Atti delle giornate di studio Salerno-Pontecagnano, 16–18 novembre 1990, 1994   6 R. DE MARINIS (ed.), Gli Etruschi a nord del Po I–II, 1986   7 F.-H. MASSA PAIRAULT (ed.), Marzabotto. Recherches sur l'Insula V, 3, 1997   8 M. PALLOTTINO, Etruskologie. Gesch. und Kultur der Etrusker, 1988   9 D. RIDGWAY, The Villanovan Cemeteries of Bologna and Pontecagnano, in: Journ. of Roman Archaeology 7, 1994, 303–316.   GE.BI.

VI. ALEXANDER THE GREAT AND HELLENISM

The alleged 70 (Plut. Mor. 328E) towns founded by Alexander [4] the Great during his campaign initially served — with the exception of → Alexandria [1], established in 331 — to provide for the veterans from Alexander's army and to secure dominance over the empire. It is disputed to what extent this was associated with the intention of spreading Greek culture and the Greek way of life, although these new colonies soon attracted other Greek settlers and became centres of Greek culture in the Middle East (Iran, Afghanistan, Pakistan and India; → Aï Chanum), built and organized along Greek lines. Alexander's successors in the Hellenistic kingdoms (→ Hellenistic politics, with map) followed this example, but also combined the founding of towns — often by the re-establishment of settlements already in existence or by the drawing together of several settlements — with the objective of reinforcing the structure of their rulership (naming the colonies after the ruler or members of the ruling family: Ptolemais, Seleucia, Antioch, Laodicea, Attalia, Cassandria etc.) and the promotion of the cult of the ruler (→ Ktistes).

After Alexandria, the only settlement established in Upper Egypt was → Ptolemais, founded by Ptolemy I. The settlement followed Greek patterns of organization (council, public assembly). The rest of Egypt remained a primarily 'rural area' (chóra), with scattered settlements of serving soldiers, who generally leased their farms to the indigenous population (→ Klerouchoi [2]).

In accordance with the extent and ethnic heterogeneity of the → Seleucid kingdom, in many parts of the realm there were military settlements with self-contained army units and towns with mixed Macedonian and Greek populations, which organized their administration themselves but were liable to tax and also served as bases for the administration of the kingdom. Settle-

ment activity was centred in North Syria (→ Antioch [1], Apamea [3], Laodicea, Seleucia in Pieria), in Asia Minor (Antioch [5] and [6], Apamea [2], Laodicea/Lycus), in Babylonia with the new capital of → Seleucia on the Tigris and in → Bactria/Central Asia. The settlements maintained close contact with the Greek world and occasionally received an influx of settlers from Greek cities (→ Euthydemus [2]), but they did not pursue a marked policy of → Hellenization in the surrounding area.

V. TSCHERIKOWER, Die hell. Städtegründungen von Alexander d.Gr. bis auf die Römerzeit, 1927; G. M. COHEN, The Seleucid Colonies, 1978; S. SHERWIN-WHITE, A. KUHRT, From Samarkhand to Sardis, 1993; R. BILLOWS, Kings and Colonists, 1995.

VII. ROMAN COLONIZATION

see → Coloniae (with maps)   W.ED.

Colonus (Κολωνός; Kolōnós, 'hill').

Attic asty deme of the Aegeis phyle, installed two bouleutaí, according to [4] by the C. [2]. Demotikon ἐκ Κολωνοῦ [6. 73³⁰]. → Sophocles came from C. and attests a cult of the eponymous hero C. (Soph. OC 54f., 888f.) [6. 208, 211].

→ Athens; → Colonae

1 J. M. CAMP, Die Agora von Athen, 1989   2 CHR. HABICHT, Athen, 1995, 151   3 E. HONIGMANN, s.v. Kolonos (2), RE 11, 1113f.   4 D. M. LEWIS, The Deme of Kolonos, in: ABSA 50, 1955, 12–17   5 TRAVLOS, Athen, 79   6 WHITEHEAD, Index s.v. Kolonos

TRAILL, Attica, 40, 68, 111 no. 72, table 2.   H.LO.

Colophon (Κολοφῶν; Kolophôn).

[1] Ionian city (Str. 14,1,3–5; Paus. 7,3,1–4) in Lydia, c. 13 km north of the harbour of → Notion. Ruins (acropolis, theatre, thermal baths) near today's Değirmendere. Temporarily at war with the Lydian kings, C. enjoyed great prosperity in the 7th/6th cents. BC (Aristot. Pol. 4,1290 b 15) and was notorious for its 'opulence' (Ath. 12,524b; 526a with Xenoph. fr. 3); regarding a feud with Smyrna, cf. Mimn. fr. 12 and Hdt. 1,150. After the overthrow of → Croesus under Persian domination, C. evidently lost its prosperity and paid only a modest contribution as a member of the → Delian League. Becoming Persian again for a while in 430 after factional fighting (Thuc. 3,34), C. then decided in 409 to ally itself once more with Athens (Xen. Hell. 1,2,4), only to fall under Persian domination again after 404. Under → Antigonus [1] in 302, C. was conquered by → Prepelaus for Lysimachus (Diod. 20,107,5), who later resettled the Colophonians to Ephesus (Paus. 1,9,7). Whether the Colophonians, who submitted to → Attalus [4] I. in 218 (Pol. 5,77,5), were reoccupying the original site or had settled in → Notion, which following the treaty between Rome and → Antiochus [5] III. had been exempt from paying tribute (Pol. 21,46,4; Liv. 38,39,8) since 188, has still not been re-

solved. *Resina Colophonia* or *colophonium* (Plin. HN 14,123; 26,104; Dioscorides, De materia medicina 1,92) was obtained from the pines on the heights surrounding C. The writers → Xenophanes, → Antimachus [3], → Nicander [4] and → Theopompus came from C., as also the iambic poet → Phoenix.

Inscriptions: SGDI 5611ff. Coins from the 6th cent. BC to Gallienus: HN 569ff.

About 13 km to the south of C., due east of Notion, lay the oracle sanctuary of Apollo of → Clarus.

L. BÜCHNER, s.v. Kolophon (2), RE 11, 1114–1119; V. SCHULTZE, Altchristl. Städte und Landschaften 2,2, 1926, 74ff.; L. B. HOLLAND, Colophon, in: Hesperia 13, 1944, 91–171; L. ROBERT, Les fouilles de Claros, 1954.
K.Z.

[2] In cuneiform texts (→ Script) a concluding annotation by the scribe that could contain the following: keyline (first line of the following tablet) and number of the tablet (both of these only in the case of serial texts); title of the work; number of lines; guarantee of authenticity (e.g 'copied from an original and checked against it'); details for presentation (origin, genre); name of the scribe and/or the owner; purpose of the script (e.g. 'for him to read ', but also 'for a long life'); divine invocation, combined with wishes for the well-being of the scribe and the tablet; curses against thieves and those who damage the tablet; date. Puzzling and playful formulae were very popular in the colophon.

H. HUNGER, Babylon. und assyr. Kolophone, 1968.
H.HU.

[3] see → Subscription

Colossae (Κολοσσαί; *Kolossaí*). City in south-west Phrygia, 4 km north-north-west of Honaz, significant already in the 5th cent. BC (Xen. An. 1,2,6; cf. Plin. HN 5,145), 15 km east-south-east of Laodicea, on the road through the Lycus valley between Sardeis and Celaenae. Coins have been attested from the late Hellenistic period onwards. The city was famous for its wool industry (Str. 12,8,16). St. Paul's letter to the Colossians points to an early Christian community. Home of a more or less unorthodox cult of the archangel Michael, who is said to have caused a curative spring to gush from a fissure in the earth (Hdt. 7,30); its famous church was destroyed in 1192/3 during Byzantine civil wars. C. was a suffragan diocese of Laodicea in Phrygia Pacatiane but was replaced in the Byzantine period by the Chonai settlement situated on higher ground.

BELKE/MERSICH, 122, 309–311; D. MÜLLER, Topographischer Bildkomm. zu den Historien Herodots, 1997, 163–165.
T.D.-B.

Colossal columns see → Monumental column

Colosseum
A. TERMINOLOGY AND HISTORY   B. ARCHITECTURE   C. FUNCTION

A. TERMINOLOGY AND HISTORY
Originally, the C. was called *amphitheatrum Flavium* (Flavian amphitheatre) after the imperial dynasty which had built it. The name *Colisaeus* appears for the first time in an epigram of the 8th cent. AD (Beda Venerabilis, PL 94,453); it derived from the neighbouring colossal statue of Nero (→ Colossus Neronis). Vespasian (Suet. Vesp. 11,1) had initiated the building of the C. in the valley between Esquiline, Palatine and Caelius, on the site previously occupied by the lake (*stagnum*) belonging to the famous → Domus Aurea. Titus inaugurated the C. in 80 AD (CIL VI 2059, *Acta fratrum Arvalium*; Suet. Tit. 7,3; Aur. Vict. Caes. 10,5). Supplementary building work was still undertaken under Domitian. Smaller repairs were carried out during the 2nd cent. AD (SHA Anton. Pius 8,2), a larger rebuild was required after a fire in AD 217, which had been caused by lightning (Chron. min. 1,147 MOMMSEN = Chronographus,354, p. 277; Cass. Dio 78; 25,2–3; SHA Heliogab. 17,8; SHA Alex. Sev. 24,3). In addition to its inauguration of AD 80, coins with images of the C. also celebrated its reopening in AD 222 as well as a restoration under Gordianus [3] III (SHA Max. Balb. 1,3–4). Further restorations are recorded for AD 250 or 252 (Isid. chronica 2, p. 463; Jer. Chron. p. 218; Amm. Marc. 4,10,14), 320 (Cod. Theod. 16,10), after 442 (CIL VI 32089), 470 (CIL VI 32091–2) as well as for *c.* 508 (CIL VI 32094).

B. ARCHITECTURE
The C. is built on level ground and, covering 3357 m², is the largest → amphitheatre ever built. Along its longitudinal axis, it measured 188 m, along its traverse 156 m; its height was 48,3 m. Five tiers offered room to about 50,000 spectators. It was comparatively easy to sink the foundations with their depth of 13 m into the former lake bottom; they were cast from concrete, and bore the foundation walls beneath the arena as well as the network of travertine pillars which supported the → cavea. The skeleton of travertine pillars was filled in with blocks of tufa or *opus testaceum* (→ Masonry), depending on the location. The façade was divided into four storeys; the first three were each made up of 80 arches, flanked by half-columns — in ascending order — of the Doric, Ionic, and Corinthian orders. The top storey consisted of an attica, divided by pilasters into 80 fields, in which windows alternated with bronze shields. The attica had three adjacent consoles with sockets for the wooden supports of the awning (*velarium*), used to shade the spectators from the sun. 76 of the 80 ground-floor entrance arches were numbered, thus enabling spectators to find their seats quickly; the four arches at the endpoints of the axes were particularly decorated and served as entrances for the magistrates or the performers. A special under-

ground passage led to the imperial box on the south side.

The → cavea was subdivided into tiers, in which spectators were seated according to their status and gender, as is indicated, *i.a.*, by inscriptions on the raised marble seats. Seating for senators was located above the podium which surrounded the arena; there, on marble steps, stood their → *subsellia*. The next three tiers—the *maenianum primum* (with eight rows), the *maenianum secundum imum* and the *maenianum secundum summum* — were reserved for the *equites*, further up for the *plebs*. Whereas the seats in these tiers were made from marble-clad brickwork, those in the highest tiers, the *maenianum summum in ligneis*, were made from wood; in this porticus, which encircled the cavea, there were eleven rows with seats reserved for women. Seats could be accessed via a cleverly thought-out system of vaulted passages, stairways and ramps, which in each case opened through richly decorated portals (*vomitoria*) onto one of three *praecinctiones* (→ Theatre) of the auditorium. Underneath the arena was a labyrinth of chambers and passageways, housing the props, as well as cages and stables for the animals, in addition to the weapons for the gladiators and much else. With the help of wooden elevators and trapdoors set into the floor of the arena, animals and props were produced on stage as and when appropriate.

C. FUNCTION

The opening of the C. was marked by a celebration which lasted for more than a hundred days; the programme included gladiator fights (→ *munera*), fights with wild beasts (*venationes*) and naval battles (*naumachiae*). The former two kinds of exhibition fights remain on the C.'s programme throughout the following years, but there is no further documentary evidence of naval battles after Titus. This indicates that the underground structures, which would have complicated the filling of the arena with water, were a later addition under Domitian. In the course of Christianization, *munera* and *venationes* increasingly lost their popularity with the imperial court; however, even though Honorius prohibited gladiator fights in the early 5th cent. AD, *munera* were still performed in the C. until at least 434. *Venationes* are even evident much later than that; the last animal hunt in the C. took place in AD 523 (Cassiod. Var. 5,42).
→ Amphitheatre (with ground plan and section/elevation of the C.); ROME

Anfiteatro Flavio: Immagine, Testimonianze, Spettacoli, 1988; P. COLAGROSSI, L'Anfiteatro Flavio nei suoi venti secoli di storia, 1913; G. COZZO, Il Colosseo, 1971; J.-C. GOLVIN, L'Amphithéatre Romain I/II, 1988; J.-C. GOLVIN, C. LANDES, Amphithéatres et Gladiateurs, 1990; R. REA, s.v. Amphitheatrum, in: LTUR I, 1993, 30–35.
I.N.

Colossus Neronis (Colossus Solis). C. 40 m high, bronze portrait statue of Nero in Rome (Plin. HN 34,45; Suet. Nero 31; Mart. epigr. 2), conceived as a counterpart to his 120 foot high portrait on canvas in the *horti Maiani* (Plin. HN 35,51), near the *vestibulum* of the → *domus aurea*. The commissioned artist was → Zenodorus; Pliny visited his workshop and saw a clay model of the Colossus Neronis (HN 34,46). After the → *damnatio memoriae* of Nero, the colossus was transformed into a statue of Sol (Plin. HN 34,45; Suet. Vesp. 18); according to another tradition, it was said to have been given the features of Titus and to have been moved to the *Via Sacra* (Cass. Dio 66,15,1). Hadrian had the figure placed in front of the Colosseum (SHA Hadr. 19,12) which, according to information from the → brick stamp in its base, happened after AD 123. Commodus is said to have tried to alter the statue to his own image or to his own imitation of Hercules (Cass. Dio 72,22,3; SHA Comm. 17, 9–10). In the Severian period the Sol aspect, especially in its Syrian-teleological character, was heavily emphasized, and this led to the colossus becoming an image of Sol's judgement on the destiny of mankind and the Roman Empire. The only authenticated representations are to be found on coins of Alexander Severus (RIC IV 2, 104 no. 410–411 pl. 8 no. 2; BMC Emp. VI Sev. Alex. no. 156–158 pl. 6) and Gordianus III.(Cohen V2 37 no. 165).

C. LEGA, in: LTUR 1, 295–298; RICHARDSON, 93–94.
R.F.

Colotes (Κωλώτης; *Kōlótēs*).
[1] Sculptor from Heraclea in Elis. C. was a pupil of → Phidias, and worked together with him, e.g. on the Zeus at Olympia. He worked principally in gold and ivory. In gold-ivory C. created an Asclepius in Kyllene and, according to Pliny (Plin. HN 35,54), an Athena in Elis, which according to Pausanias (Paus. 6,26,3), however, was attributed to Phidias; as this Athena's shield is said to have been painted by → Panaenus, a collective effort was probably involved. Ancient attribution to C. was unreliable; C. was also credited with a table decorated with gods and sporting scenes for the victors' crowns in the Heraeum of Olympia, but according to Pausanias (quoting an art historian as his source), this was ascribed to a C., who was a pupil of → Pasiteles from Paros. According to Pliny, C. also completed bronze portraits of philosophers. All identifications proposed on this basis remain speculative.

OVERBECK, no. 844–850; M. T. AMORELLI, EAA 4, 380–381 no. 1–2; P. MINGAZZINI, Il tavolo crisoelefantino di Kolotes ad Olimpia, in: MDAI(A) 77, 1962, 293–305; B. RIDGWAY, Fifth-Century Styles in Greek Sculpture, 1981, 169, 183; A. LINFERT, Quellenprobleme zu Alkamenes und Kolotes, in: Rivista di archeologia 12, 1988, 33–41.
R.N.

[2] Held by Diogenes Laertius to be amongst the 'highly regarded' pupils (10,25: ἐλλόγιμοι; *ellógimoi*) of → Epicurus; born in Lampsacus and presumably became a pupil of Epicurus there (between 310–306 BC); probably born around 320 BC. C. may have conducted an Epicurean school in Lampsacus. He was the recipient of letters from Epicurus, some fragments of which survive ([62]–[66]). (119) ²ARRIGHETTI = fragment 140–142 USENER). Epicurus recounts in one letter ([65] ²ARR. = fr. 141U) that C. had fallen at his feet during a lecture; he himself had reproached this act of prostration as unphilosophical (ἀφυσιολόγητον; *aphysiológēton*) but returned the veneration. One of C.'s pupils, Menedemus, is said to have gone over to the Cynics (Diog. Laert. 6,95) [1]. Nothing more is known of C.'s life.

Remnants of his writings show C. to be an author inclined to polemics. In his treatise 'One cannot live according to the teaching of other philosophers' (Περὶ τοῦ ὅτι κατὰ τὰ τῶν ἄλλων φιλοσόφων δόγματα οὐδὲ ζῆν ἔστιν) he criticizes *inter alia* Democritus, Parmenides, Empedocles, Socrates [2], Melissus, Plato, Stilpon, the Cyrenians and most of all Arcesilaus [3; 4]. Plutarch had read this dispute and judged it worthy of a response in his own 'Against C.' (Πρὸς Κωλώτην). C. also critically interpreted Platonic dialogues ('Against Plato's Lysis' (Πρὸς Πλάτωνος Λύσιν); 'Against Plato's Euthydemus' (Πρὸς Πλάτωνος Εὐθύδημον) [5; 6]), fragments of which have been found on the → Herculanian papyri. We learn of a treatise 'On Laws and Opinion' (Περὶ νόμων καὶ δόξης) [7]. In another treatise C. gave a critique of the key myth of the Platonic 'Politeia'. Cicero and later Macrobius (In Somnium Scipionis I 1, 9–2,4) and Proclus (In Pl. Resp. II p. 105,23–106,14; 109,8–12; 111,6–9; 113,9–113; 116,19–21; 121,19–25 KROLL) were prompted to rebut that critique.

1 SSR 2, 588–589; 4, 581–583   2 E. ACOSTA MÉNDEZ, A. ANGELI (ed.), Filodemo. Testimonianze su Socrate, 1992, 53–91   3 A. M. IOPPOLO, Opinione e scienza. Il dibatto tra Stoici e Accademici nel III e II secolo a. C., 1986, 183–185   4 P. A. VANDER WAERDT, Colotes and the Epicurean Refutation of Skepticism, in: GRBS 30, 1989, 225–267   5 W. CRÖNERT, Kolopes und Menedemos, 1906 (repr. 1965), 1–16, 162–172, 167–170, 170–171   6 A. CONCOLINO MANCINI, Sulle opere polemiche di Colote, in: CE 6, 1976, 61–67   7 E. KONDO, Per l'interpretazione del pensiero filodemeo sulla adulazione nel PHerc. 1457, in: CE 4, 1974, 43–56, especially 54f.
EDITIONS: H. USENER, Epicurea, ¹1887. repr. 1963, 1966   M. POHLENZ (ed.), Plutarch, Adversus Colotem; Non posse suaviter vivi secundum Epicurum (Plutarchi moralia 6/2, 1952; ²1959, 124–172, 173–215).
BIBLIOGRAPHY: H. VON ARNIM, s.v. Kolotes, RE 11, 1120–1122   R. WESTMAN, Plutarch gegen Kolotes. Seine Schrift 'Adversus Colotem' als philosophiegesch. Quelle, 1955   M. GIGANTE, Scetticismo e Epicureismo, 66–70, 93–98   T. DORANDI, Colotes de Lampsaque, in: GOULET 2, 1994, 448 (no. 180)   M. ERLER, Epikur. Die Schule Epikurs. Lukrez, in: GGPh² 4, 1994, 235–240.   M.ER.

Coloured weaving see → Textile art

Columbarium see → Funerary architecture

Columella
A. BIOGRAPHY   B. WORKS   C. LANGUAGE AND STYLE   D. TRANSMISSION AND LATER INFLUENCE

A. BIOGRAPHY
L. Iunius Moderatus C. came from Gades in the Baetica (Columella 8,16,9; 7,2,4) and belonged to the *ordo equester*. As an inscription from Tarentum shows, C. was a *tribunus militum* of the *legio VI Ferrata* (CIL IX 235 = ILS 2923). C. lived from the late Augustan period to the principate of Vespasian (1st cent. AD). His work, which was partly written during Seneca's lifetime (Columella 3,3,3) was appraised already by Pliny (HN 8,153; 15,66; 18,70; 18,303). His language and style demonstrate a good rhetorical education and a comprehensive knowledge of Cicero's works and Roman poetry. C.'s uncle, M. Columella, a property owner in the province of Baetica, was open-minded about new agricultural techniques. C. owned several wine-growing properties in Italy (Caere: Columella 3,3,3; Ardea, Carsioli, Alba: Columella 3,9,2).

B. WORKS
1. The treatise *Adversus astrologos* (Columella 11,1,31) has been lost.

2. The book *De arboribus*, on the other hand, is extant. It has been preserved in the MSS of *De re rustica* between books 2 and 3, but represents only a part of a separate, probably earlier work by C.

3. The plan of writing a book about religious practices pertaining to agriculture (Columella 2,21,5f.) was probably never realized.

4. C.'s main work, *De re rustica*, offers a comprehensive depiction of Roman agriculture; C. uses earlier authors and writings extensively, including the Carthaginian → Mago, → Cato, the handbook of Cornelius Celsus and not least the *Georgica* of Virgil, whom C. took seriously as a technical writer. In the *praefatio* to the *De re rustica* C. expresses two key thoughts: according to C., the increasing infertility of the soil, which his contemporaries saw as caused by the ageing of the earth, was a consequence of the introduction of slave labour and neglect of agriculture by land owners (Columella 1, praef. 1–3; cf. 2,1). At the same time, agriculture, which is linked to *sapientia*, is accorded high status (Columella 1, praef. 4); it is considered, as in Cato, as the most appropriate means of expanding one's assets. As important prerequisites for successful agriculture, C. cites technical knowledge, financial means and a will to work (Columella 1,1,1). Accordingly, the study of earlier literature is just as essential for a landowner as his presence on the property. C.'s criticism is directed primarily at large estates that cannot be intensively cropped, at the absence of owners of large estates and the employment of slaves unwilling to work.

The work is systematically structured, covers all essential areas of agriculture (cultivation of cereal crops: bk 2; wine-growing, olive trees, fruit trees: bks 3–5; cattle breeding: bks 6–7; poultry-farming and apiculture: bks 8–9; horticulture: bk 10) and, following Virgil's model, is written in verse. Added later were, first, bk 11 on the duties of the *vilicus and*, finally, bk 12 on the *vilica*: 11,1,2; 11,3,65). Book 11 moreover contains a detailed work calendar with astronomical and meteorological data, as well as an overview of tasks to be undertaken in specific months (11,2). The estates that C. describes were producing for the market and were thus dependent on good transport links to the cities. At the same time production for one's own needs should not be overlooked (4,30,1; 11,3,1; 12,3,6). Work to be done by slaves should be so organized as to allow the most effective supervision; to achieve that, the slaves should be divided into groups of 10 (1,9,5–8). Not only are working hours regulated (11,1,14–18; cf. 12,1,3; for tasks allowed on holidays: 2,21) but also the rate of work: a precise timeframe is prescribed for individual tasks (2,12,1; cf. 11,2,12f.; 11,2,26; 11,2,40; 11,2,44; 11,2,46). C. tries to motivate his slaves to work by treating them in a friendly manner. He recommends checking to see that they are well provided with food and clothing (1,8,15–18). All the same, a property's building should include, in C.'s view, an underground *ergastulum* for chained slaves (1,6,3; cf. 1,9,4f.). Fairly long comments are also devoted to leasing arrangements, which C. believes especially advisable for remotely located estates that are not easy to manage (1,7). Although C. is thoroughly knowledgeable about earlier technical writers (→ Agrarian writers), he was interested in criticizing earlier errors, evaluating his own experience and communicating new developments (cf. 3,7; 3,10; 7,2,4f.). C. was interested in higher revenue from agriculture, and so, in contrast to, e.g., Celsus, he does not only seek to avoid high costs but measure costs against returns (2,2,23f.). Income from agriculture was measured on the interest received through loans. C. believed that for wine-growing he could obtain a return of more than 6% on the money invested (3,3,8–15). This thoroughly intellectual approach is typical of C.: the traditional subject matter is explained in a rational manner, without any consideration of the *maiores*.

C. Language and Style

C. is linguistically and stylistically ambivalent: on the one hand he strives, as a 'Cicero of agronomy' (Martin), to secure a place for the subject in the educational canon; on the other, he uses colloquial and technical language, even some Late Latin tendencies (oblique indicative, vulgar weakening of the superlative: *eximie optimum*; *bene* instead of *valde*; *ne* in consecutive clauses; unclassical use of particles, co-ordination of disjunctives; colloquial pleonasms). The very frequent *personificatio* stands at the elements of intersection of the rural, technical and literary language. At the stylistic high points (cf., e.g., 1, praef. 3–33 or 4,8–

10) C. is able to carry the reader away with him. Repetition of words is painstakingly avoided — even beyond the boundaries of individual books. There is thus a surfeit of synonyms for plant forms, ploughing, sowing etc. Even changes in number and gender and simple/compound forms count as variation.

Despite the admiration of the humanists, modern judgement of bk 10 remains divided. The smoothness of construction, and the hexameter with Ovidian elision are probably to be seen as a critical continuation of Virgil. Instead of a poetic framework, there is one single subject/time line from autumn to autumn. C. ignores the dark side of rural life in favour of his optimistic world vision, but adapts to Virgil's *petit-bourgeois* setting.

D. Transmission and later influence

Even in antiquity C. was regarded as an authority in the field of agriculture; he is quoted by Pliny and Palladius and in works of late antiquity; in the early Middle Ages C. is mentioned by Cassiodorus and Isidore. The most important MSS are the Sangermanensis Petropolitanus 207 (S) and Ambrosianus L 85 (A; both from the 9th cent.); unfortunately both MSS reveal gaps, for which 10 of the R-mss from the 15th cent. appear to offer credible evidence, though admittedly with a tendency towards correction and normalization.

EDITIONS: 1 V. Lundström, A. Josephson, S. Hedberg et al., 1897–1968   2 I. M. Gesner, Scriptores rei rusticae veteres Latini, 1735   3 J. G. Schneider, Scriptores rei rusticae veteres Latini 2, 1794   4 H. Ash, E. S. Forster, E. H. Heffner, 1941–1955   5 W. Richter, 1981–1983.

BIBLIOGRAPHY: E. Christmann, Zur ant. Georgica-Rezeption, in: WJA 8, 1982, 57–67   Duncan-Jones, Economy, 33–59   R. Martin, Etat présent des études sur C., ANRW II. 32,3, 1985, 1959–1979   Id., Recherches sur les agronomes latins et leurs conceptions économiques et sociales, 1971, 287–385   Richter, ed. 3,569–656   W. Scheidel, Grundpacht und Lohnarbeit in der Landwirtschaft des röm. It., 1994   R. Suaudeau, La doctrine économique de C., 1957   K. D. White, Roman Farming, 1970.   E.C.

Column

I. Egypt and the Ancient Orient
II. Graeco-Roman Antiquity

I. Egypt and the Ancient Orient

As a statically significant building element, whether in wood or modelled from stone or brick, the column played different roles in Egypt and the Ancient Orient. In Egypt columns were a component of almost every form of architecture, from roof-bearing wooden posts in family residences to extravagantly shaped stone columns in temples and palaces. Having bases and capitals, the latter, too, betrayed the evolution from wooden columns. Columns frequently took on the shape of plants; they were probably always painted.

Columns were used sparingly in Hittite-Syrian-Palestinian territory; in temples and palaces they frequently served to support very wide entrance-ways. Of particular interest are the column bases in the shape of double animal figures [1. pl. 341]. In Mesopotamian territory columns were known as a building element in all periods but were very rarely used. Probably influenced by the pillars in the Urartian building style and transmitted via constructions in Median territory, columns became an essential characteristic of Achaemenid architecture, where they were used in enormous columned halls in the palaces of → Pasargadae, → Persepolis and → Susa. The richly decorated columns suggest Egyptian, Syrian and Greek-Ionic features.

1 PropKg 14.

D. ARNOLD, s. v. Säule, Lex. der äg. Baukunst, 2000, 221–225; R. NAUMANN, Die Architektur Kleinasiens von ihren Anfängen bis zum Ende der hethitischen Zeit, 1971, 126–144; G. R. WRIGHT, Ancient Building in South Syria and Palestine, 1985; M. C. ROOT, Art and Archaeology of the Achaemenid Empire, in: J. M. SASSON (ed.), Civilizations of the Ancient Near East, vol. 4, 1995, 2627 f.   H. J.N.

II. GRAECO-ROMAN ANTIQUITY
A. COLUMNS: TERMINOLOGY, STRUCTURE AND CONSTRUCTION TECHNIQUE   B. ORDERS OF COLUMNS   1. EARLY GREEK COLUMN SHAPES 2. DORIC ORDER   3. IONIC ORDER   4. CORINTHIAN ORDER   5. TUSCAN ORDER   6. COMPOSITE ORDERS   C. HALF-COLUMNS AND UNCANONICAL FORMS; RE-USED STONES

A. COLUMNS: TERMINOLOGY, STRUCTURE AND CONSTRUCTION TECHNIQUE
Column construction is a dominant theme in ancient Greek → architecture. In the Greek language area the column was generally termed κίων/kíōn or στύλος/ stýlos, in Lat. columna. In Greece and Rome, the column used in architecture was mainly made of stone or wood (oak, chestnut). The stone column consisted of a base (exception: Doric order), a shaft, occasionally monolithic but generally assembled from several drums pegged together (partly also bricked up), and a capital, consisting of abacus and → echinus [3], onto which the → epistylion (architrave) is then placed. (Obtaining, transporting, and setting in place giant, monolithic columns, like that of the High Archaic Apollonium in → Syracusae, 8 m tall, 2 m in diameter and weighing close on 35 tonnes, were much-praised achievements of ancient engineering skill.)The end of the column shaft, where the capital was to be fitted, was formed by the column neck (hypotrachelion), generally distinguished by multi-layered, ring-shaped grooves (anuli) or other forms of decoration.

The form of base, shaft and capital is an essential indicator of the order the column belongs to; even → Vitruvius, in bks 3 and 4, distinguishes different forms and types of temple mainly on the basis of the column shape and → proportions. Like the capitals and bases, the shafts, too, usually differ in shape: fluting tapering to a point in the Doric order; fluting ending in a smooth crosspiece in the Ionic and Corinthian orders. Unfluted or only partly fluted shafts are more frequently found from the Hellenistic period onwards (and become the rule in the Tuscan-Roman order). In a labour-intensive process (cf. the extant accounts for the construction of the Erechtheum on the Athenian Acropolis; → Building trade) a column's fluting — just like the → entasis — was completed only after erection of the column and its incorporation into the building framework; until then the shaft consisted of a coarsely prefabricated drum, with the precise fluting indicated, at the top and/or bottom, by means of a narrow, accurate stripe chiselled out before the column was erected. Mistakes in the fluting caused by a wrong strike of the chisel or through the stone being too brittle (especially in the case of marble) were not uncommon; such fractures were later meticulously repaired (e. g. on the Parthenon columns). Columns from rough poros were generally covered over with a final, thin layer of stucco. In most cases parts of the column were painted in colour (→ Polychromy). Various → optical refinements of the column also occasionally owe their existence likewise to filigree construction technique, such as e. g. the → inclination or variation in column diameter according to individual position (not uncommon in temple construction especially in the Doric order). Somewhat simpler in terms of technical construction were the columns in Roman profane construction, as for example in residential peristyles; here we find the unfluted Tuscan column, frequently built from brick and given a cement or stucco finish (Pompeii, Herculaneum).

B. ORDERS OF COLUMNS
1. EARLY GREEK COLUMN SHAPES
Column shapes in Greek antiquity before the fixing of the canonical orders (from the late 7th cent. BC) were predominantly influenced by Oriental and Egyptian forms with floral ornamentation. These are to be distinguished from the Minoan columns, reduced in abstract form to their load-bearing function, as found in the palaces of Crete and later also in the Mycenaean cultural sphere (Tiryns, Mycenae; → Mycenaean culture): a downwards tapering shaft that stands on a plinth and is topped with a bulbous capital and slab cover. In the historic Greece of the 8th and early 7th cents BC we predominantly find the initially mainly wooden supporting column with a raised plinth offering protection from an accumulation of moisture but without any capital, as seen in terracotta house models of varying styles; cf. also the 'Toumba Building' of → Lefkandi on Euboea.

2. DORIC ORDER
The theory of Vitruvius (4,1,2 ff.), that the specific forms of the Doric architectural order derived from the tenon- and mortise woodworking technique, has been discussed intensively and controversially in architectural construction research for more than 150 years now

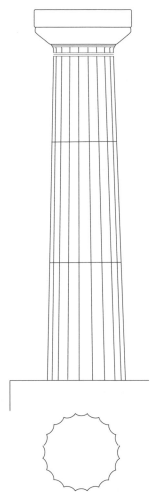

Doric column. Agrigento,
Temple of the Dioscuri
(480–460 BC).

— still without any tangible result. What is certain is
that, right from the beginning, the Doric order appeared fully developed in stone construction, which at
least suggests wooden precursors, details of which,
however, are unknown. The earliest extant Doric stone
construction is the Artemis temple of → Corcyra (late
7th cent. BC); to what extent the terracottas of the
temple of → Thermus, dating from around 630/620 BC,
are to be seen as predecessors or earlier stages in the
order's development from wood to stone construction
is still contested. The Doric order dominated temple
construction in the motherland and Western Greece in
the 6th and 5th cents BC, as also all other forms of
column construction in that period (halls, towers, fountain covers etc.) but is, on the other hand, somewhat
rare in Ionian territory (Athena temple of → Assus). The
upwards tapering Doric column is fluted (initially 16,
then 20, rarely 18 or 24 cannelures), the capital (con-

sisting of a padding-shaped echinus and square abacus
plate) separated from the shaft by several anuli. The
outline of the Doric column was initially thickset but
later became increasingly slender (starting with a ratio
for lower diameter to the top of the column of c. 1:4 to
c. 1:7 or even c. 1:8 in interior constructions). The Doric
order of architecture was abandoned in the Hellenistic
period as a representative individual form of column
construction (→ Angle triglyph problem) but was at the
same time incorporated in other functional contexts
(wall and façade architecture, peristyle). It became
more and more rare in Roman times and from the 2nd
cent. onwards AD is found only sporadically (and then
only as a museum retrospective of 'old' Greece, as for
example on Hadrian's Gate in Athens).

3. IONIC ORDER

The Ionic order of columns appears in monumental
stone constructions more than one generation after the
Doric, and is not even then fully developed, but initially
in rather uncanonical form. Archaeological research
partly explains this through the fact that the Ionic column was in the beginning used not as an element of
architectural composition, but as a stand-alone bearer
of votive offerings (→ Columns, monumental), as various early 6th-cent. BC 'Aeolian' capitals, each with
quite distinct floral ornamentation (as for example
from Larisa [6] on the Hermus or Neandreia), and other individual finds of early Ionic capitals would seem to
suggest. Only with the great Ionic temples of the mid
6th cent. BC at → Samos, → Ephesus and → Didyma
(→ Dipteros) do the Ionic column and the architectural
order as a whole seem to have found their canonical
form: probably an intentional bringing together of individual but now regulated and 'depersonalized' votives
into one construction, in the sense of an overall → ana-
thema — a process that fits in well with the complicated
political and cultural situation in the cities of Ionia and
Asia Minor in the decades before the middle of the 6th
cent. BC (for more on this see under → Temples).

The Ionic column consists of a multi-layered base
(which raises the column above the generally very flat
podium; cf. → Krepis [1]), a very slender shaft (bottom
diameter : column height between 1:10 and 1:13) with
rather slight tapering and the capital (pillow-shaped
echinus curling into volutes at the ends, with an → egg-
and-dart moulding as decorative support; the shape of
the volutes was pre-scratched with a compass-like
instrument). The Ionic base consists of a → spira (a cylinder richly profiled in parts) and on top a → torus similarly profiled and with a convex arch. A special form
developed in Attic architecture of the late 6th and 5th
cents. BC, consisting of a torus as a stand, a concavely
arching → trochilus on top of it and another torus on
top of that; this form spread widely on the Greek mainland. The fluting on the shaft (20–48, in the case of large
diameters later generally 36, in that of a smaller generally 24) ended in a flat crosspiece. In general the Ionic
order appears in strongly decorated form; in addition to
various forms of painting, specific decoration included

Columns and bases

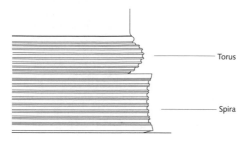

Torus

Spira

Samos: Temple of Hera (time of Polycrates)

Aeolic capital; Neandreia (early 6th BC)

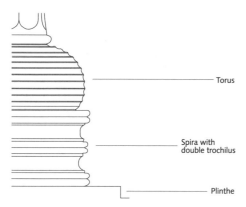

Torus

Spira with
double trochilus

Plinthe

Ephesos: Artemision (550 BC)

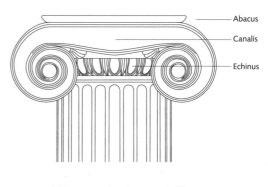

Abacus

Canalis

Echinus

Delphi: Porticus of the Athenians (478 BC)

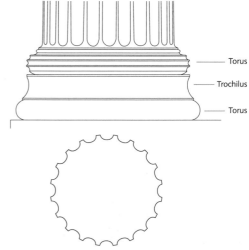

Torus

Trochilus

Torus

Ionic capital and base; Athens, Temple on the Ilissus
(448 BC)

Corinthian capitals

Phigalia, Temple of Apollo Epikoureios.
Reconstruction (420 BC)

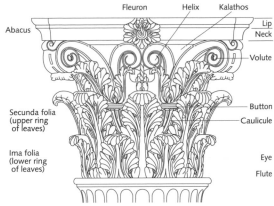

Fleuron   Helix   Kalathos
Lip
Abacus
Neck

Volute

Secunda folia
(upper ring
of leaves)

Button
Caulicule

Ima folia
(lower ring
of leaves)

Eye

Flute

Rome: Temple of Mars Ultor (2 BC)

Epidaurus, Tholos, K1 (360 – 310 BC)

Composite capital: Rome, Arch of Titus (AD 81)

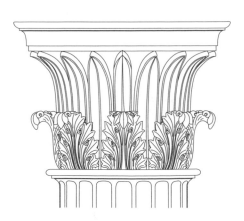

Athens; 'Tower of the Winds' (c. 160 BC)

Leptis Magna: Forum Novum (1st half of the 3rd cent. AD)

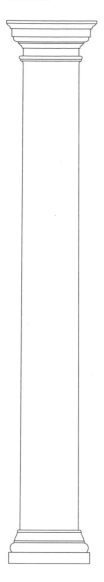

Tuscan half-column; Rome,
Colosseum (AD 80)

Openwork capital;
Constantinople, Hagia Sophia, west conch (6th cent. AD)

gilding and colourful intarsia on the capitals (e. g. paste fillings on the capitals of the Erechtheum on the Athenian Acropolis), as well as areas of relief on the column shaft (*columnae caelatae*) and on the column neck. The design of the Ionic column was transferred also to pillars and → antae.

4. CORINTHIAN ORDER

Strictly speaking, the Corinthian order is no more than a variation of the Ionic, with the capital being the only altered element; the base and shaft of the Corinthian resemble the Ionic column. Compared to the Ionic capital with its roll padding, the Corinthian capital, with its double row of acanthus leaves springing out of a basket-like body (kalathos) and the four curling volute stems taking shape from them on the corners (helikes) had the advantage of its equally shaped sides which

gave it a universal utility in serial construction; a corner problem, which was inherent in the Ionic column in particular (triagonal echinus with corner-volute), did not arise. The genesis of this type of capital has been very controversial; Vitruvius' attribution of its discovery to the sculptor → Callimachus [2] is an artistic anecdote (admittedly much repeated) without any historical foundation. Attempts to argue that the capital originated from columns supporting statues (Athena Parthenos) have been unconvincing.

The earliest known Corinthian capital was discovered in the first excavations at the temple of Apollo at Bassae (→ Phigalia) carried out in 1811/12; it was constructed around 420 BC and is now missing (its shape is transmitted through, however, and can be reconstructed from sketches by the excavators). Initially used exclusively in room interiors (tholoi of Delphi and Epidaurus, temple of Athena at Tegea), it first appeared in external construction at the choregic monument for Lysicrates on the southern slope of the Athenian Acropolis (335/4 BC), and thereafter with increasing frequency. In the late Hellenistic period, and especially in Roman architecture, the Corinthian column became the norm; the somewhat demure floral weave of the Greek capital gave way to the decorative profusion of the 'standard Corinthian capital' of the Roman Imperial period in the 1st and 2nd cents. AD. The leaf-chalice capital can be classed as a variant or special form of the Corinthian capital, consisting of a correspondingly functionally shaped *kalathos* with a row of acanthus leaves arranged in the shape of a chalice, as for example the capitals on the horologium of Andronicus ('Tower of the Winds') in Athens.

5. TUSCAN ORDER

The Tuscan column, widespread in Roman architecture and largely replacing the Doric order, was the product of an architectural synthesis of Etruscan and Greek elements that was probably completed in the 2nd cent. BC. The form's point of departure was the column of the Etruscan wooden temple, from which in the mid-Republican period the Roman podium temple derives a new architectural form even if linked to other orders (cf. → Temple). The Tuscan column consists of a mostly unfluted shaft rising from a smooth profile base derived from the Ionic-Corinthian order. The capital, with an initially bulbous but later streamlined echinus and with an abacus plate, recalls the Doric order; it was separated from the shaft by means of one or more massively profiled rings. The Tuscan column was particularly widespread in Roman profane architecture, for example on peristyles or façades. Strictly speaking, the Tuscan order belongs to the composite orders (see below B. 6.); its rich history of post-classical reception, however, warrants discussion in its own right (Co-LUMNS, ORDERS OF).

6. Composite Orders

Mixing the three Greek orders of columns was a phenomenon of Hellenistic architecture but was foreshadowed, even in the late Classical period, by the parallel use of several orders within one construction (→ Parthenon and Propylaea on the Athenian Acropolis; temple of Bassae near Phigalia). Initially it was not so much the shape of the individual columns or capitals that was affected as the context in which they were used. Thus, in the Roman *colonia* of Paestum (→ Posidonia), for example, we find a podium temple with Corinthian columns and Doric entablature. In Roman times, a fusion of Ionic and Corinthian column acquired the character of a new order ('composite order'): the kalathos with the acanthus shoots of the Corinthian order is, by virtue of its four-sided volute echinus, linked to the Ionic style of capital with an egg-and-dart moulding forming the bridge between the two. Even in the late Classical (Selinunte: mixture of Doric and Ionic forms) and Hellenistic (Labraunda) periods, however, there already are scattered instances of hybrid capitals.

C. Half-columns and uncanonical forms; re-used stones

A phenomenon of representative façade architecture is the emergence of blended columns and half-columns, the features of which overall follow the shapes and orders of columns. Early half-columns are to be found on the (window-fitted) west wall of the Erechteum on the Athenian Acropolis, and later on the façades and interiors of Macedonian and Thracian chamber graves, on plinths as well as on peristyles. Column shafts and capitals provide a broad field for uncanonical shapes, especially in the context of non-architectural → monumental columns : 'Snake columns', scalloped and spiral-shaped shafts are to be found, especially in late antiquity and early Christian architecture, as well as figured capitals that generally derived from the basic shape of the Corinthian or composite column. A rich source of new capitals, evolving from these, developed in Byzantine and Romanesque architecture. Starting in late antiquity, a quite distinct form of aesthetic eclecticism developed from the reuse of parts of columns (*inter alia* Rome, S. Stefano Rotondo).

On the reasons for ancient and post-classical use of individual column shapes and orders cf. also → Architecture; → Architecture, theory of; ARCHITECTURE, THEORY OF; COLUMNS; COLUMNS, ORDERS OF.

H. BAUER, Korinth. Kapitelle des 4. und 3. Jh. v. Chr. (MDAI(A), 3rd supplement/Beiheft), 1973; PH. BETANCOURT, The Aeolic Style in Architecture, 1977; O. BINGÖL, Das ion. Normalkapitell in hell. und röm. Zeit in Kleinasien, (MDAI(Ist), 20th supplement/Beiheft), 1980; CH. BÖRKER, Blattkelchkapitelle, 1965; H. BRANDENBURG, Die Wiederverwendung von Spolien und originalen Werkstücken in der spätant. Architektur, in: J. POESCHKE (ed.), Ant. Spolien in der Architektur des MA und der Renaissance, 1996, 11-39; H. BÜSING, Die griech. Halb-Säule, 1970; Id., B. LEHNHOFF, Volutenkonstruktion am Beispiel der Erechtheion-Osthalle, in: AK 28, 1985, 106-119; R. CHITHAM, Die Säulen-Ordnungen der Ant. und ihre Anwendung in der Architektur, 1987; B. FEHR, The Greek Temple in the Early Archaic Period: Meaning, Use and Social Context, in: Hephaistos 14, 1996, 165-191; E. FORSSMANN, Säule und Ornament, 1956; W. D. HEILMEYER, Korinth. Normalkapitelle (MDAI(R), 16th supplement/Ergänzungsheft), 1970; P. HELLSTRÖM, Dessin d'architecture hécatomnide à Labraunda, in: Le dessin d'architecture dans les sociétés antiques, 1985, 153-165; CH. HÖCKER, Architektur als Metapher. Überlegungen zur Bedeutung des dor. Ringhallentempels, in: Hephaistos 14, 1996, 45-79; Id., Sekos, Dipteros, Hypaethros — Überlegungen zur Monumentalisierung der archaische Sakralarchitektur Ioniens, in: Veröffentlichungen der J. Jungius-Ges. der Wiss. Hamburg 87, 1998, 147-163; T. N. HOWE, The Invention of the Doric Order, 1985; W. KIRCHHOFF, Die Entwicklung des ion. Volutenkapitells im 6. Jh. v. Chr. und seine Entstehung, 1988; H. KNELL, Der tuskan. Tempel nach Vitruv, in: MDAI(R) 90, 1983, 91-101; J. KRAMER, Stilmerkmale korinth. Kapitelle des ausgehenden 3. und 4. Jh. n. Chr., in: O. FELD (ed.), Studien zur spätant. und frühchristl. Kunst 2, 1986, 109-126; H. LAUTER, Die Architektur des Hellenismus, 1986, 253-276; B. LEHNHOFF, Das ion. Normalkapitell ..., in: H. KNELL (ed.), Vitruv-Kolloquium des DArV 1982, 1984, 97-122; H. L. MACE, The Archaic Ionic Capital, 1978; E. VON MERCKLIN, Ant. Figuralkapitelle, 1962; W. MÜLLER-WIENER, Griech. Bauwesen in der Antike, 1988, 217 s. v. Säule; J. ONIANS, Bearers of Meanings. The Classical Orders in Antiquity, the Middle Ages, and the Renaissance, 1988; F. PRAYON, Zur Genese der tuskan. Säule, in: H. KNELL (ed.), Vitruv-Kolloquium des DArV 1982, 1984, 141-147; J. RYKWERT, The Dancing Column. On Order in Architecture, 1996; T. G. SCHATTNER, Griech. Hausmodelle. Untersuchung zur frühgriech. Architektur (MDAI(A), 15th supplement/Beiheft), 1990; R. SCHENK, Der korinth. Tempel bis zum Ende des Prinzipats des Augustus, 1997; R. STADLER, Ein neues Kompositkapitell aus der Colonia Ulpia Traiana, in: Archäologie im Rheinland 1991, 1992, 83-85; E. M. STERN, Die Kapitelle der Nordhalle des Erechtheion, in: MDAI(A) 100, 1985, 405-426; R. A. TOMLINSON, The Doric Order: Hellenistic Critics, in: JHS 83, 1963, 133-137; V. TUSA, Il capitello dorico-ionico del Museo di Palermo, in: Atti 16. Congr. di storia dell'architettura, 1977, 179 f.; B. WESENBERG, Kapitelle und Basen. Beobachtungen zur Entstehung der griech. Säulen-Formen (BJ, 32nd supplement/Beiheft), 1971; Id., Beiträge zur Rekonstruktion griech. Architektur nach lit. Quellen, 1983.

C. HÖ.

Columna

[1] Antonini Pii. see → Columns, monumental

[2] Maenia. Monumental columns (→ Columns, monumental(erected in 318 BC, during the censorship of the plebeian, C. Maenius, consul in 338 BC, in the context of a major renovation of the → Forum Romanum in Rome (Plin. HN 34,20; Fest. 120L; Isid. Orig. 15,3,11); near the *curia Hostilia* (Cic. Sest. 8,18 et Schol Bob. ad loc.; 58,124 et Schol. Bob. ad loc.) in the area of the later arch of Septimius Severus. Defaulting debtors were denounced here by their creditors (Cic. Sest. 8,18; 58,124), and slaves punished for theft and other crimes (Cic. Div. Caec. 16,50).

> M. TORELLI, in: LTUR 1, 301–302; RICHARDSON, 94–95. R.F.

[3] Marci Aurelii Antonini. see → Columns, monumental

[4] Minucia. see → Columns, monumental

[5] Phocae. see → Columns, monumental

[6] Rostrata M. Aemilii Paulli. see → Columns, monumental

[7] Rostratae Augusti. see → Columns, monumental

[8] Traiani. see → Forum Traiani, see → Columns, monumental

Column basis see → Column

Column tomb see → Funerary architecture (III. C.2.); → Columns, monumental (II.-III.)

Colybrassus (Κολυβρασσός; *Kolybrassós*). Polis in Cilicia Trachea (Ptol. 5,5,8: Κολοβρασσός; Hierocles, Synekdemos 682,11: Ὀλυβρασός), on the basis of epigraphical evidence today's Ayasofya, 19 km to the north-east of Coracesium [1. 30f.]. City settlement with *bouleuterion* (?), temples, churches and military structures [2. 9f. (with a sketch map)].

> 1 K. TOMASCHITZ, Unpublizierte Inschr. Westkilikiens aus dem Nachlaß T.B. Mitfords, 1998   2 G. E. BEAN, T. B. MITFORD, Journeys in Rough Cilicia 1962 and 1963, 1965. K.T.

Comaetho (Κομαιθώ; *Komaithó*).

[1] Daughter of → Pterelaus, the mythological king of Taphos. She helped → Amphitryon, with whom she has fallen in love, in his battle against the Teleboeans from Taphos. She was, however, killed by him after he had conquered the island (Apollod. 2,60).

[2] Priestess of → Artemis Triklaria at the sanctuary of Laphria near Patrae. She and her lover → Melanippus have a sexual encounter in the temple, thus angering the goddess. In appeasement, a young boy and girl from abroad had to be offered up in sacrifice each year. This human sacrifice was abolished only after the arrival of → Eurypylus [5] (Paus. 7,19). FR.P.

Comana

[1] (Κόμανα; *Kómana*). City in → Cataonia (Str. 12,2,3), Hittite *Kummanni*; temple state of the goddess Ma-Enyo (Artemis Tauropolios; → Enyo; Roman → Bellona). Bishopric as early as the Severian period (2nd/3rd cents AD); today's Şar.

> W. RUGE, s.v. Komana, RE 11, 1127f.; HILD/RESTLE, 208f. K.ST.

[2] C. Pontica. (Κόμανα Ποντικά; *Kómana Pontiká*). Pontic temple state of Ma-Enyo with over 6,000 → hierodouloi (Temple prostitution; → Prostitution) and a trade fair that was especially important for the Armenians (Str. 12,3,32; 34; 36); situated on the upper reaches of the river → Iris [3] near Kılıklı (formerly Gömenek), where there is a hill settlement, a rocky outcrop with two stone graves and the remains of a Roman bridge that was built over by a weir (cf. the bridge mentioned by Cass. Dio 36,10,3). The high priest of C. P. was second in rank only to the Pontian king. From AD 34/5 a *politeía*, also called Hierocaesarea, of the province Galatia.

> W. H. WADDINGTON, E. BABELON, TH. REINACH, Recueil général des monnaies grecques d'Asie Mineure 1,1, ²1925, 106–111; D. R. WILSON, The Historical Geography of Bithynia, Paphlagonia, and Pontus in the Greek and Roman Periods, D.B. thesis, Oxford 1960 (typescript), 228–233; E. OLSHAUSEN, Der König und die Priester (Geographica Historica 4), 1987, 187–212. E.O.

Comanus (Κομανός; *Komanós*).

[1] C. from Naucratis. Greek grammarian of the 2nd cent. BC, who composed an exegetical work on Homer (an *hypómnēma*?; Aristarchus [4] of Samothrace challenged it in 'Against C.'/Πρὸς Κομανόν, schol. Hom. Il. 1,97–99; 2,798a; 24,110b). Identification with the homonymous Alexandrian politician → C. [2] is debatable, even if the grammarian is called 'the king's chief cup-bearer' in schol. Hes. Op. 97. The roughly 20 fragments reveal a respectable philological figure; most of them treat the meaning of Homeric words or expressions; one fragment treats the episode of hope (Elpis) in the vat (*píthos*) in Hesiod (schol. Hes. ibid., from an *hypómnēma*?). Grammatical terminology is discussed in fr. 19. Attribution of the grammatical fr. PYale 1,25 to C. is not very likely.

> A. R. DYCK, The Fragments of Comanus of Naucratis, in: SGLG 7, 1988, 217–262 (ed.); A. GUDEMAN, s.v. Komanos (2), RE 11, 1128–29; F. SOLMSEN, Comanus 'of the First Friends', in: CPh 40, 1945, 115f.; PFEIFFER, KPI, 261–262 with n. 27; A. WOUTERS, P. Yale 1. 25, in: The Grammatical Papyri from Graeco-Roman Egypt, 1979, 47–60. F.M.

[2] Son of a Ptolemaeus, from Alexandria, member of an important and wealthy family. In 188/187 BC he and his brothers were part of a delegation to Greece. C. was appointed → *próxenos* of Delphi. In 187, with the → court title of *tôn prṓtōn phílōn*, he served as *epistrátēgos* (?) with extraordinary powers to suppress the revolt of → Anchwennefer; he succeeded in August 186 (C. was at that time residing in Acoris/Hermoupolites, where he also owned a *dōreá* ('estate'), PRyl II 207 a 4). At about the same time, together with some others, he is attested as having been an officer with the same title in the district of Perithebas (SB I 599 (?)). In 169, together with Cineas [3], he played an important role in the → *synhédrion* of Ptolemy VI, when the powers of the regents Eulaeus [2] and → Lenaeus came to an end (Pol. 28,19). C. followed Ptolemy VIII to Cyrene and in 162/161 was dispatched by him with his brother Ptolemaeus as an emissary to Rome, where he successfully represented Ptolemy VIII's interests involving Cyprus (Pol. 31,28–31,1). C. is not identical to PP VI 16865, but SEG 9, 383f (Ptolemais, 158 BC) possibly refer to him.

H. HAUBEN, The Barges of the Komanos Family, in: AncSoc 19, 1988, 207–211; L. MOOREN, La hiérarchie du cour ptolémaïque, 1977, 74ff.; E. OLSHAUSEN, Prosopographie der hell. Königsgesandten 1, 1974, 54ff. no. 33; 83f. no. 59; J. D. THOMAS, The Epistrategos in Ptolemaic and Roman Egypt 1, 1975, 112f. W.A.

[3] Cilician, first a robber then a slave. Brother of Cleon [3] and with him a ringleader under → Eunus in the 1st Sicilian slave war (136–130 BC). As he tried to escape from Tauromenium, which was besieged by the Romans, C. was captured by P. Rupilius (according to Val. Max. 9,12,8 ext.1, after the fall of Enna [1. 61]) and took his own life in Enna in 132. Diod. 34,2,20f.

1 K. R. BRADLEY, Slavery and Rebellion in the Roman World, 1989, 49, 59, 61   2 G. MANGANARO, Ancora sulle Rivolte <servili> in Sicilia, in: Chiron 13, 1983, 405–409. ME.STR.

Comb (ὁ κτείς; *ho kteís*, Lat. *pecten*). Combs for wool and for the hair were known already in prehistorical Europe, Egypt and the Near East. They were made from a range of different materials (olive wood, boxwood, ivory, bone, later also from bronze and iron) and could also vary in shape (trapezoid or oblong). In the post-Mycenaean period they had two rows of teeth, with those on one side being more narrowly set teeth. Semicircular combs appeared in the archaic period. The Classical period in Greece and Rome preferred a straight comb with one or two rows of teeth. The middle section was of varying width and very often adorned with carved designs, inlays or pictures in relief, featuring simple ornamental and figurative or mythological images. The comb had a case in which the toothed edge could be inserted. As a feminine attribute, the comb also appeared as a votive offering for those goddesses especially linked to women such as Artemis Orthia, Athena (Callim. H. 5,31) and Aphrodite (Anth. Pal. 6,211). As an instrument of → personal hygiene the comb was indispensable; unkempt people were regarded as either being in mourning (Soph. OC 1261) or scruffy. Combs are extant from all periods of antiquity, but images of people combing their hair are not very common (e.g.

[1]); still women, and also Aphrodite [2], are often shown with a comb in their hand. Worth noting on Cypriot vases is the manner of carrying a comb from a band in the crook of the arm [3]. Comb-makers are mentioned in Latin inscriptions (CIL V 2543; 5812).

1 TRENDALL/CAMBITOGLOU, 20 no. 89 pl. 7,1
2 W. HORNBOSTEL (ed.), Kunst der Ant.: Schätze aus norddeutschen Privatbesitz, 1977, 180 no. 161
3 C. MORRIS, Combs on Cypriot Iron Age Pottery, in: RDAC 1983, 219–224.

S. MARINATOS, Kleidung, Haar- und Barttracht (ArchHom B), 1967; S. OPPERMANN, s.v. Pecten, KlP 4, 1972, 576f.; K. J. GILLES, German. Kämme und Fibeln des Trierer Landes, in: Archäologischers Korrespondenzblatt 11, 1981, 333–339; C. NAUERTH, Bemerkungen zu koptischen Kämmen, in: Stud. zur spätant. und frühchristl. Kunst und Kultur des Orients, 1982, 1–13; H. CUPPERS, Die Römer an Mosel und Saar, 1983, passim; G. DIACONU, Über die eisernen Kämme, in: Dacia 30, 1986, 181–189; H.-G. BUCHHOLZ, Ägäische Bronzezeit, 1987; J. WERNER, Eiserne Woll-Kämme der jüngeren Eisenzeit aus dem freien Germanien, in: Germania 68, 1990, 608–660. R.H.

Combabus (Κομβάβος; *Kombábos*) in the aetiological myth recounted by Lucian (De Dea Syria 17–27) is the founder of the temple of Atargatis in Hierapolis who introduced self-castration and women's clothing for the eunuchs (*gálloi*); for the motivation the author himself draws an analogy with the story of Phaedra and Hippolytus. Certainly the name C. suggests Cybebe (→ Cybele), a term for the Great Mother (Hdt. 5,102) cognate with the Hittite Kubaba, and *kybebos*, a term for the *gállos* (Semonides fr. 36 WEST); however, it is unclear here, as in other unrelated details, how much of that is invention on the part of (Ps.?–)Lucian.

E. LAROCHE, Koubaba, déesse anatolienne, et le problème des origines de Cybèle, in: Eléments orientaux dans la rel. grecque, 1960, 113–128. F.G.

Combe (Κόμβη; *Kómbē*, Lat. *Combe*). Daughter of the Phlian river-god Asopus and Metope; regarded since Hecataeus (FGrH 1 F 129), also called Chalcis, as the namesake of the eponymous city on Euboea (cf. Diod. Sic. 4,72; Zenob. 6,50). According to a tale recounted exclusively by Nonnus, C. was the mother of the seven Euboean Corybantes (→ Couretes; Nonnus, Dion. 13,135ff.). With them she fled from her husband Socus to Crete, Phrygia, and finally Athens to → Cecrops, who killed Socus, thus enabling the refugees to return to Euboea (in Ov. Met. 7,383, on the other hand, C. is transformed, while fleeing from her sons in the Aetolian Pleuron, into a bird, probably a *chalkís*, a hawk-like bird). C.W.

Comboiomarus (Conbolomarus, Combogiomarus). Celtic compound name 'with great fighting strength'? (SCHMIDT, 178). King of the Galatian Tectosages or Trocmi, who fought on the Seleucid side against Cn.

→ Manlius Vulso in 189 and had entrenched themselves on the mountains Olympus and Magaba (Liv. 38,19,2).

Combutis (Κόμβουτις; *Kómboutis*). Galatian leader following → Brennus [2] on the 279 BC invasion of Greece [1. 178]. C. and Orestorius were sent off together at the head of a strong contingent through Thessaly into Aetolia. There they committed great atrocities against the inhabitants of the city of Callion and suffered substantial losses on their return to Thermopylae at the hands of the Aetolians who had rushed in pursuit (Paus. 10,22,2–7).

1 SCHMIDT.   W.SP.

Comedy
I. GREEK II. LATIN

I. GREEK
A. BEGINNINGS B. EARLY FORMS OUTSIDE ATHENS C. ATTIC OLD COMEDY D. TYPICAL FEATURES OF OLD COMEDY E. FURTHER DEVELOPMENT OF COMEDY FROM THE END OF THE 5TH CENT. BC F. END OF OLD COMEDY; MIDDLE COMEDY G. FEATURES OF MIDDLE COMEDY AND THE TRANSITION TO NEW COMEDY H. NEW COMEDY

A. BEGINNINGS
The most plausible etymology of comedy is 'komos song'; *kômoi* (processions of groups of people or choruses) are depicted on vases from the early 7th cent. BC onwards; there appear, *inter alia*, dancers in leotards (partly padded on the waist and buttocks) and animal costumes (cf. the later animal choruses of Attic Old Comedy). Many pictures on vases also show the phallus-processions that according to Aristotle (poet. 4,1449a 10f.) were the origin of comedy.

B. EARLY FORMS OUTSIDE ATHENS
The Western Greek territory of Magna Graecia in Sicily and southern Italy formed an important breeding ground for the development of popular comic drama. According to Aristotle (poet. 3,1448a 30–34) the Dorians disputed — with dubious linguistic arguments ('comedy' from κώμη/'village', 'drama' from δρᾶν/'to take action') — Athenian invention of tragedy and comedy: the residents of the Peloponnesian Megara laid claim to an independent form of comedy older than the Attic kind (→ Susarion, whom Hellenistic sources place at the beginnings of Attic comedy (see below), is also said to have come from this same Megara), the residents of the Sicilian Megara Hyblaea pointed to their compatriot → Epicharmus, who was supposedly older than the earliest Attic comedy writers, → Chionides and → Magnes. The Hellenistic scholar Sosibius Lakon (FGrH 595 F 7) and the historian Semus of Delos (FGrH 396 F 24), moreover, confirm the existence of a popular farce that was widespread amongst the Dorians (under very dif-

ferent names: δικηλισταί, φαλλοφόροι, αὐτοκάβδαλοι, φλύακες, ἐθελονταί, ἰθύφαλλοι). This farce probably first reached literary heights with Epicharmus (who did not, however, call his plays κōmōidíai/κωμῳδίαι but *drámata*/δράματα). The rivals and successors to Epicharmus were → Deinolochus and → Phormis. Whether the Sicilian comic drama, like the Attic, used a chorus and whether it continued to exist beyond the end of the 5th cent. or was then replaced by plays of Attic style or origin is being debated [8. 159–161]. In any event, the → phlyakes vases demonstrate the continued existence of comic plays in Western Greek territory in the 4th cent.; those plays underwent a further literarization by → Rhinthon in around 300.

C. ATTIC OLD COMEDY
The rise of Attic comedy cannot be traced back with any certainty beyond the start of the 5th cent. BC (cf. Aristot. Poet. 5,1449a 38–b5). In later evidence a → Sousarion from the deme Tripodiscus of Megara (cf. PCG VII p. 661–665) is credited with being the inventor of Attic comedy. According to the *Marmor Parium* (FGrH 239 A 39), he was active between 580 and 560 BC (Sousarion test. 1 K.-A.); the five verses that are variously attributed to him, however, are not Doric, however, but Attic. The other items of evidence for a Megarian comedy are questionable, too, since underlying them are obviously contemptuous remarks by Attic comedy writers (Eupolis fr. 261 K.-A.; Aristoph. Vesp. 57; Ecphantides fr. 3 K.-A.) about crude 'Megarian jokes'. In poet. 3,1448a 31 Aristotle notes the claims of the Megarians to have been behind the invention of comedy (cf. above) but does not mention Susarion. What is probably the most convincing theory argues that comedy arose from a combination of popular Doric farces and the phallus-equipped *kômoi*; other theories attempt to make do with just one element of origin (cult dances, divine invocations in hymn, processions in animal-clothing, etc.) but then have difficulty in explaining specific elements of Old Comedy. Aristotle (Poet. 3,1448a 33) names → Chionides (who is reported to have won the first official comedy competition at the great Dionysia in 486 BC) and → Magnes (whose earliest victory is attested for 472) as the earliest two Athenian comedy writers. Scarcely anything from these two remains; so the years between 486 and around 455 are rather dark, until the moment → Cratinus (490/480 — after 423) appears on the scene, the earliest of the three most significant representatives of Old Comedy. At least three of his plays (test. 6 K.-A.) were performed at the Lenaean festival, at which there also was a state-organized dramatic contest from about 440 BC (→ *skēnikoí agónes*/→ Competitions, artistic). Cratinus was the first playwright in whose fragments a chief characteristic of Old Comedy is clearly recognizable: sharp political invective, the butt of which was very often the leading Athenian politician of the time, → Pericles. Parodies of myths, however, feature already in Cratinus' comedies. Cratinus is the most significant writer of

the first phase of fully developed Old Comedy (from about 455 to 430 BC); its second phase begins soon after 430 with the up-and-coming writers → Eupolis, → Aristophanes [3] and → Phrynichus and gradually merges into the preliminary shape of Middle Comedy (cf. below), when — from roughly the end of the 20s of the 5th cent. BC — far-reaching changes became evident. Other important writers of Old Comedy include → Telecleides, → Crates and → Pherecrates (cf. below), → Hermippus, → Amipsias and → Plato (45 writers' names from that period are known to us).

D. TYPICAL FEATURES OF OLD COMEDY

It is rooted in the political, cultural, and religious reality of Athens; apparently on at least two occasions there were political attempts to restrict its virtually limitless ὀνομαστὶ κωμῳδεῖν (*onomastì kōmōideîn*, 'mocking by name') (by Morychides in 440/39–437/36, and by Syracosius in around 415). Real representatives of contemporary Athens were unmistakably depicted on stage (generals, politicians, but also 'intellectuals' like Euripides and Socrates). The treatment of very real topics and the depiction of very real people could, paradoxically, also be mixed with elements and situations that were unreal, fantastic, fairy-tale-like or even absurd: grotesque kidnappings (Aristoph. 'Acharnians', 'Thesmophoriazousae'), adventurous flights into the heavens (Aristoph. 'Peace'), the founding of absurd-utopian communities (Aristoph. 'Birds'), marvellous descents into the underworld (Aristoph. 'Frogs') or conversely, the return of the dead (Eupolis, 'Demes'), with depictions of fool's paradise and the like. The fracturing and transcending of everyday reality also became manifest in the manifold beings embodied in the choruses of Old Comedy (→ Chorus): every kind of animal, but also weird personifications (chorus of Attic communities in the 'Demes' of Eupolis, of Delian League cities in the 'Poleis', of the Aegean islands in the 'Nesoi'). Even allegorical individuals appear (e.g. Comedy and Drunkenness in the 'Pytine' of Cratinus, War and Peace in the 'Peace' of Aristophanes). Corresponding to this manifold transcending of reality is the fracturing of theatrical illusion; a metatheatre appears almost automatically through the parabasis of the chorus (see below) in the middle of the play. The heroes of this comedy are scarcely conceived as inherently consistent individuals; instead they smoothly adapt to the most varied situations; they often do not receive personal names until late in the play (Dicaeopolis e.g. in Aristoph. Ach. first in V. 406). Old Comedy made use of many kinds of visual effects (costumes; props); its actors' masks display a much greater variety than found in tragedy (up to the New Comedy development of numerous types).

Much the same applies to the variety of linguistic devices: an abundance of very different speech registers is combined with a varied metrical pattern (from simple lines of dialogue verse to complicated lyrical forms). Nevertheless, this variety is presented in a range of fixed structural forms: the agon (between the main character

and the chorus or possible individual opponents) often takes place in the so-called → epirrhematic form (i.e. a definite sequence of spoken lines and sung or recited sections [7]); the → parabasis (as an interruption in the action) consists of a succession of spoken and sung choral sections in precise metrical forms, in the course of which the chorus steps out of its role in the plot and addresses the audience, partly as a direct mouthpiece for the writer (e.g. Aristoph. Ach. 628–664), but partly also in its own right (e.g. ibid. 665–718), and is thus able to criticize specific wrongs in the city; after the parabasis the action continues, often with a string of shorter parallel scenes (sometimes with very direct action: physical blows and the like), which demonstrate the brave behaviour of the main character and which are separated by lyrical intermezzi of the chorus; at the end stands the main character's triumph that often has a hedonistic flavour. Unlike in tragedy there occasionally are more than three speaking parts on the stage (cf. e.g. Aristoph. Ach. 40ff.); especially in the first half of the play the chorus is closely bound up in the plot; during and after the parabasis, however, it becomes less active and more of a commentator sympathetic to the hero. In addition to politics, sexuality (and along with it linguistic coprology) plays a large part in this comedy, which is shown *i.a.* by the stock costumes of the actors: the male figures are generally clad in tight-fitting leotards (with padded stomach and buttocks), with a short → chiton and especially with an oversized (usually erect) leather phallus. Finally, the wide range of references to tragedy (especially spoofs of Euripides) is characteristic; the important tragedy, however, lies not only in its potential for → parody; it also serves as model as comedy from the end of the 5th cent. (cf. above) gradually develops into a more closed dramatic form.

E. FURTHER DEVELOPMENT OF COMEDY FROM THE END OF THE 5TH CENT. BC

Even in the time of Old Comedy, along with the highly politicized plays of Cratinus, Eupolis, Aristophanes and other writers, there also was a more apolitical type of play; it appeared from the middle of the 5th cent. and was at first linked by Aristotle (Poet. 4,1449b 6–9) with the writer → Crates (shortly after Cratinus, around 425), who mostly did without mocking real personalities to concentrate on cohesive fictitious plots (μῦθοι, *mŷthoi*). After Crates, it was → Pherecrates (active 440/430 — around 410) who continued this form of comedy; it however probably was not sharply separated from the other, but regularly alternated with it: even many plays by Cratinus (cf. the 'Odysses') had little to do with contemporary Athens; others with politico-allegorical features (cf. Cratinus' 'Dionysalexandros' might have displayed a mixed form. After the 'Birds', the extant plays of Aristophanes tended to have a more cohesive plot; choral sections recede; after the 'Birds' no complete parabasis is discernible anymore. In his two extant plays from the period after 400 ('Ecclesiazousae' and 'Plutus') the role of the chorus is further reduced; in 'Plutus' only its entry (→ Parodos) is still developed; at all other points where the chorus has to appear, the text indicates with the direction χοροῦ (*choroû*, 'place for the chorus') that only *entr'acte* pieces were taking place, without any close connection to the play's plot. From here on this became the rule: in Menander's plays the chorus is present only with just such *choroû*-directions (i.e. as separators between the acts).

F. End of Old Comedy; Middle Comedy

Aristophenes' 'Frogs', performed in 405, were the last play that in form and content could be described as Old Comedy. Although many of the writers who were active before 400 (not least Aristophanes himself) were still producing comedies after 400, the years around 400 mark a breaking-point of distinct change, for which different reasons have been adduced: changes in the history of literary genres (influence of tragedy, see above), and politico-historical events (depoliticization of many aspects of life after the catastrophic defeat in the Peloponnesian War in 404; disappearance of great political figures worthy of mocking; dwindling confidence on the part of comedy writers in being able to have any effect on politics); both aspects need to be taken into account. Unfortunately this period of great change in comedy and the shift from 'Old' to 'Middle' (the term probably derives from the Alexandrian philologists who, thanks to their enormous library, could easily survey the development of comedy [9. 172–187]) are actually difficult to appreciate, as only scant remains of the comedy output between Aristophanes' 'Plutus' and the appearance of → Menander have survived, even though in numerical terms that output was not inferior to that of the preceding period (cf. Ath. 8,336d and the numbers of plays said to have been produced, e.g., by → Alexis and → Antiphanes). In spite of patchy source material two phases can still be discerned [9. 334–338]: a period of 'genuine' Middle Comedy (around 380–350) and a subsequent transitional phase to New Comedy (around 350–320).

G. Features of Middle Comedy and the transition to New Comedy

Between 400 and *c.* 370/60 BC, a distinct preference for mythical material is evident; often whole tragedies were rewritten as comedies (cf. the last two, non-extant plays of Aristophanes). Unlike in Old Comedy, the fantastic fairy-tale element is no longer a characteristic of these plays; instead, heroes, kings and even gods are now de-stylized to become figures of everyday Athenian life — with all the weaknesses that go with this [9. 204–241]. After the middle of the 4th cent. the myth-comedy disappears almost completely (perhaps because the comic potential deriving from the contrast between myth and the banality of everyday life seemed to have been exhausted); what remained was Attic bourgeois everyday life, which then became the norm in New Comedy (cf. below). The earlier linguistic and metrical variety disappeared along with the fantastic element in

the storyline: for a while in Middle Comedy a parody of the exuberant speech of the → dithyramb and the use of long anapaestic verses were cultivated, but these elements, too, then recede up to the middle of the 4th cent. [9. 241–280]; in the → metrics of New Comedy consist almost only of iambic trimeter and (to set off certain sections) trochaic tetrameter; in their diction they represent a slightly elevated version of everyday Attic speech.

The shattering of theatrical illusion and the meta-theatrical intrusions, as they were to be found in Old Comedy, also no longer appear (exception: occasional apostrophes to the audience by characters delivering monologues). Sexuality, previously very evident, disappears both in language (which becomes much more 'decent' after Aristophanes) and in costume: at a certain point in time that we can no longer determine, the Old Comedy leotard and its phallus were replaced by normal everyday clothing. Admittedly, in many New Comedy plays a sexual encounter (culminating in an unplanned pregnancy) triggers the comic action but this is merely reported in the introductory exposition. By the same token, → homosexuality, frequently and openly treated in Old Comedy, no longer has any place in New Comedy. Post-Aristophanic comedy, however, did not just lose earlier features but developed several new ones, in particular creating stock characters. Stereotypes begin to appear from roughly the middle of the 4th cent. (in some cases even earlier): the son from a good home who gets into trouble in a love affair; his more or less strict father who tries to protect him from escapades; from time to time the (sometimes resolute) mother; as contrast or mirror another family of a similar kind. Along with this 'middle-class' cast there is another, less middle-class, upon which the comic potential generally depends: the cunning slave, the beautiful hetaera, the boastful soldier (from the 2nd half of the 4th cent. more and more frequently encountered in the Greek world as a mercenary) as a vociferous rival to the middle-class son for the affections of the beautiful hetaera, the conceited-gossipy-inquisitive cook (hired for the banquets that usually take place in these plays), the avaricious, unscrupulous procurer or 'brothel-keeper' (often the real villain of this comedy), and not least the parasite (a roaming pauper or sidekick of a boastful soldier). The development of those stereotypes was largely fixed by Menander's time and was reflected in the creation of a wealth of distinct stage-→ masks (cf. Poll. 4,143ff.: nine for old men, eleven for young men, seven for slaves, three for old women, 14 for young women — totalling 44 in all; many copies are preserved in terracotta [14]). This cast of stereotypes then acted in a fixed pattern of fictitious (but quasi-real) plots that were developed in the first decades of the 4th cent., probably by thorough parodying of tragedy, and could finally be enacted without the constraint of a mythical framework [10]; the five-act pattern that then became typical of New Comedy was created from that process.

H. New Comedy

With the arrival of Menander (from 321) New Comedy was firmly established on the Attic stage. The productivity of its writers was scarcely any less than that of the preceding phase of comedy: its main representatives (→ Menander), → Diphilus and → Philemon each wrote about 100 plays. Along with those writers, › Apollodorus [5] of Carystus (a rival of Menander) and → Posidippus are also important representatives of the *Nea*. The really significant period for this form of comedy seems to have come to an end around the middle of the 3rd cent. BC, when the great writers Menander, Philemon etc. became classics who continued to be performed (cf. Philemon test. 16 K.-A.), but production of new comedies still continued for some time: over 50 writers' names are known from the 3rd cent. BC, well over 30 from the 2nd, at least 10 from the 1st, and at least six authors from the 1st to 3rd cents. AD are identified as writing in the style of the *Nea*. The comedy *agon* at the Athenian Dionysia was still attested up to around 120 BC [3. 397]: there is evidence of *agones* (though not always on a regular basis) at other locations during the 1st cent. BC (PCG II p. 1; 570; IV p. 77; 349; V p. 17). In the 1st cent. AD Emperor Claudius won such an *agon* in Naples with a play by his brother Germanicus (Suet. Claud. 11,3). *Agones* of the 2nd cent. AD are attested at Corinth (PCG II p. 483) and Boeotian Thespiae (PCG II p. 212; 311; 483). From the Imperial period we know of comic writers who did not perform their works but declaimed or published them — as perhaps Germanicus [2] did (Suet. Caligula 3,2); possibly also Apollinaris of Laodicea (4th cent. AD, cf. Sozom. Hist. eccl. 5,18,2) and Synesius, Dion 18 p. 278, 10 Terz.

I. Features of New Comedy J. The afterlife of Greek comedy

I. Features of New Comedy

In contrast to even Middle Comedy, politics almost never crop up anymore in the everyday plots of the *Nea* [11. 284f.]; problems within the middle-class family are depicted, together with clashes with those living on the fringes of middle-class society (pimps, hetaerae, soldiers). Mythological and unreal elements are abandoned in favour of a reality that the audience is familiar with. Comic action springs mainly from the interaction of the stereotypes developed by writers in the preceding decades (cf. above). In Menander these stereotypes are to some extent being personalized again; whether this was also the case with his rivals cannot easily be judged due to the fragmentary condition of their surviving works. Menander's plays in particular display a great interest in man's inner life (legacy from tragedy); gladly taking as their theme the interplay of man and → *tyche*, they carry 'humanity' as their message and strive to arouse emotions. Again the question has to remain open whether these were also characteristics of the comedy of Menander's rivals.

J. The afterlife of Greek comedy

The later influence of Old Comedy is identical to that of Aristophanes. Quotations from Middle Comedy are still to be found in miscellany-writers (especially Athenaeus) and lexicographers from the Imperial and Byzantine periods (→ Pollux, → *Antiatticist*, → Photius, › Suda); for the rest, however, knowledge of this phase of comedy disappeared so completely that generally not even the writers' names are known and Byzantine authors could only guess at who might belong to the comedy period that was transmitted to them as 'Middle' [9. 34–56]. New Comedy, by contrast, was very quickly taken up by Roman literature (for every extant or recognizable Roman comedy there is at least one Greek model that has been attested or is at least extremely probable); through the extant plays of Plautus and Terence, the Greek *Nea* became mother to all European comedy literature.

Editions: PCG (1983ff.). Bibliography: 1 E. Csapo, W. J. Slater (ed.), The Context of Ancient Drama, 1995 2 A. Koerte, s.v. Komödie (Greek), RE 11, 1207–1275 3 M. Landfester, Geschischte der griech. Komödie, in: G. A. Seeck (ed.), Das griech. Drama, 1979, 354–400 4 B. Zimmermann, Die griech. Komödie, 1998 5 A. Seeberg, From Padded Dancers to Comedy, in: A. Griffiths (ed.), Stage directions. Essays ... in Honour of E. W. Handley, 1995, 1–12 6 R. M. Rosen, Old Comedy and the Iambographic Tradition, 1988 7 Th. Gelzer, Der epirrhematische Agon bei Aristophanes, 1960 8 C. W. Dearden, Epicharmus, Phlyax, and Sicilian Comedy, in: J.-P. Descoeudres (ed.), Eumousia. Ceramic and Iconographic Studies in Honour of A. Cambitoglou, 1990, 155–161 9 H.-G. Nesselrath, Die attische Mittlere Komödie, 1990 10 Id., Parody and Later Greek Comedy, in: HSPh 95, 1993, 181–195 11 Id., The Polis of Athens in Middle Comedy, in: G. W. Dobrov (ed.), The City as Comedy, 1997, 271–288 12 W. G. Arnott, Alexis: The Fragments, 1996 13 R. L. Hunter, The New Comedy of Greek and Rome, 1985 14 L. B. Brea, Menandro e il teatro greco nelle terracotte liparesi, 1981.

H.-G.NE.

II. Latin

A. Variety of genres B. Origins C. Palliata 1. Characteristic features 2. Dramaturgy 3. Cantica D. Other genres E. Late forms

A. Variety of genres

Roman comedy, in its broader sense, includes not only literary genres such as → *palliata*, → *Togata* and *trabeata*, but also oral forms such as → *fescennini* versus, → *atellana* and → *mimus*, the last two of which were also being recorded in writing in the 1st cent. BC. The word *comoedia* was adopted from the Greek κωμῳδία and in both languages applies only to literary comedy.

B. Origins

Livy's account of the origin of the *ludi scaenici* in Rome (7,2) has been much discussed [2; 19]: 1. During a plague in 364 BC Etruscan dancers gave a performance with flute accompaniment. 2. Young Romans subsequently began to imitate them, singing 'crude' mocking verses to one another (*inconditis inter se iocularia fundentes versibus*). This obviously refers to the *fescennini*, or something similar. 3. From this arise musical *saturae* (*impletae modis saturae*), which were also accompanied by dancing (*motus*). 4. Finally it was → Livius Andronicus, who because of his own dependence on Greek comedy introduced a continuous plot (*argumentum*); that was the origin of 'plays' (*fabulae*). This step may be considered quite significant, since, as a result, more or less short Roman improvizations and sketches were then 'extended' by Greek plots into veritable stage productions. Livy's account — probably drawing on Varro [2] — shows that music and dance were attributed to the Etruscans, satirical verse to domestic traditions, and coherent plots to Greek comedy. Even if much of the detail — especially the form of the *satura* — is disputed and the influence of other 'oral' genres such as mime has to be taken into account, we can nevertheless see that the three elements mentioned by Livy are clearly identifiable, especially in Plautus' comedies but also in those of Terence — even though in sharply differing proportions. It can be no accident that several Roman theatrical terms come from Etruscan: *histrio* (actor), *ludius* (dancer), *persona* (mask), *subulo* (flute-player) [6; 19. 125f.].

C. Palliata

Along with tragedy, comedy was the most popular literary form in early Rome. The reason for that can be seen in the fact that right from the beginning it had to deal with a varied tradition of domestic comic genres and try to integrate them in a suitable way [3]. Insofar as it has literary roots, these derive from Greek comedy, and as it retains the Greek milieu it is named after the short Greek coat (*pallium*), → *palliata*. It is above all Greek New Comedy (*Nea*) that provided models for Roman writers. So far no influence from Old and Middle Comedy has been authoritatively demonstrated. This is only quite natural, as at the time of the *palliata* only New Comedy was still active with complete plays. Formal similarities with Old Comedy can be explained by the fact that it too came under the influence of 'verbal' farce. Roman soldiers were able to see New Comedy plays staged during their campaigns in Greek-speaking southern Italy and Sicily, with the result that they probably came to expect similarly amusing performances — but in their own language — at home as well. The first writer was → Livius Andronicus, who on commission from the aediles staged both a tragedy and a comedy in 240 BC. Coming from the Greek-speaking area in southern Italy, he was in a position to make Greek comedy accessible to Romans. Along with → Plautus and Terence (→ Terentius), whose 20 and 6

plays respectively are the only complete extant works of archaic Roman literature, other writers were → Naevius, → Ennius [1], → Caecilius [III 6] and lastly → Turpilius, with whom the *palliata* came to an end in around 100 BC. It lost its importance even with the death of Terence in 159 BC. The reason for the popular genre's disappearance may primarily be that the ever similar intrigues and the rarely varying set of characters gradually reached a point of exhaustion. Turpilius' obvious borrowing from → Menander did not bring fresh inspiration but, to the contrary, the end of the *palliata*.

1. Characteristic feature 2. Dramaturgy 3. Cantica

1. Characteristic features

While Greek New Comedy represents a mature stage of a fairly long literary development, making heavy demands on the audience's intellectual grasp and communicating a view on life, it is the great paradox of Roman comedy that it offers no reflection of the society of its time; it has a regulating effect and displays an imaginary dreamworld that captivates the public not because it can recognize its own world within it but as an alternative world freeing the audience from harsh reality [13. 42]. As Livy and his successors preferred New Comedy, the strange situation emerged of a late literary form being transposed into the embryonic stages of a foreign literature. Correspondingly, the *palliata* differentiates itself from Greek comedy by keeping contemporary socio-political events at some considerable distance. The plots are entirely fixed in an unreal setting that is recognizably Greek in its form but with a clear overlay of Roman locations and customs. Retaining the Greek milieu was a protective cover for expressing some daring subject matter that was unimaginable in Roman reality.

Its dominant element is the mockery with which the authority of the *pater familias* is treated: slaves usually triumph — generally in the interest of their young masters (*adulescentes*) — over the 'old men' (*senes*), and at times the *adulescentes* play a part in this, as they do at the end of Plautus' *Mercator* by sitting in judgement over the old men. Women, too, can be successful in their intrigues against men, as in Plautus' *Casina*. No less jarring is the situation when slaves (Plautus, *Persa* and *Stichus*) or even hetaerae (Plautus, *Truculentus*) gain the upper hand over free men. Another favourite object of mockery is the soldier, who was highly regarded in Rome. The frivolous trademark of Roman comedy-writers can also be seen in the last play that Terence wrote, the *Adelphoe* of 160 BC, at the end of which the young people and their slaves play cat and mouse with the hitherto unchallenged father Micio. If one were to say, quite rightly, that comedy here is shifting into satire [7. 38], that only shows that the 'oral' forms of the early period are still to be encountered in the late Terence, who was regarded as 'Greek'.

Thus, the *palliata* produces an unreal happening that transports the audience, especially those low on the social scale, into a dreamworld that was nevertheless at least tolerated and probably even partly enjoyed by the upper classes. The *palliata*, which was performed only on specific occasions, such as divine festivals, temple dedications, triumphal and funeral games, and which found itself in competition with tragedy [4. 115], also performed on those same occasions and, according to Horace (Hor. Epist. 2,1,165f.) much favoured by the Romans, may be compared to the customs of the → Saturnalia or the medieval carnival: for a very restricted timeframe, during its performance, potential conflicts could be channelled and curbed at one and the same time [17]. It should be noted, however, that the *palliata* was never revolutionary in its attitude towards slaves, and the conflicts were mainly set within the middle class.

2. DRAMATURGY

Compared to New Comedy, the dramaturgy of Plautine comedy is extremely undisciplined and that of Terentian still remarkably careless. The attempt to shape an individual scene to achieve the maximum effect works to the detriment of overall coherence. On the whole Roman audiences did not much question the logical consistency of plots or the significance of extrinsic connections. For a public mainly attracted to wit and humour, the momentary effect was all-important. Hence we have slaves launching into triumphal arias or managing to wangle fairly large sums of money, without the necessary preconditions ever becoming clear. The primacy of the comic event does not allow characters to develop or plots to unfold according to the laws of probability. In that respect even Terence is still fairly relaxed, even if he strives for a more consistent dramaturgy. After all he pursues the same goals as Plautus, even though on a higher plane.

3. CANTICA

The origin of the → *cantica* (especially plentiful in Plautus) represents a very difficult problem. They are completely the property of Roman comedians; 'what those brilliant writers have created from tame Greek models is in its form something absolutely new ... so that it cannot accurately be termed anything as a *singspiel, opera buffa*' [21. 169f.]. Contrary to the assumption that Roman tragedy took over the *cantica* from Hellenistic tragedy and passed it on to comedy [9. 321–373], it is probable that its origin and development were influenced by the Italian and southern Italian (Greek-speaking) 'oral' tradition (cf. [5. 205]). In any event there are no points of connection to Greek literary comedy.

D. OTHER GENRES

No other literary form of Roman comedy achieved the popularity of the *palliata*. Even if the *togata*, comedy in a Roman setting, had probably been created as early as Naevius, it did not gain ground until Terence's time, when a national → historiography began, though

still without achieving the significance of the *palliata*. Obviously it was not possible to present explicitly as Roman reality the daring material of Plautine and Terentian plays that had been set within a Greek environment. Moreover, the milieu of middle-class cobblers, barbers or millers was obviously perceived as little interesting. The same probably applied to the *trabeata*, created in the Augustan period by C. → Melissus, comedy in the elevated milieu of the knights, from whose cloak (*trabea*) it takes its name; it appears to have been destined to enjoy little success. Only comedy in the form of the *palliata*, removed from life's reality, proved to be successful — and that to a remarkable degree.

'Tragicomedy': a special form frequently seen in Plautus' *Amphitruo*, which the deliverer of the prologue calls a *tragicomoedia* (V. 59). Different influences have been conjectured (like that of the *hilarotragoidia*; → Tragedy), but this (artificial) word probably represents a joke alluding to the fact that the author has uncharacteristically used a a tragedy as his model [16. 23f.].

E. LATE FORMS

Already soon after Terence's death his and Plautus' plays were re-staged. The theatrical directors provided them with new prologues or endings and otherwise interfered with the texts. The years when Terence's plays were rerun are attested in the *didaskalia*. Stage performances of the *palliata* were still taking place in Cicero's day but, especially from the Augustan period, were outstripped by the popular forms of → mime and pantomime. With the reference to Fundanius in Hor. Sat. 2,8,19 we have at least the name of one comedy writer. Just as tragedy changed into being a recital drama in the Imperial period, this also happened to comedy, as attested by, e.g., Pliny the Younger (Epist. 6,21 on → Vergilius Romanus). It is understandable that the Church Fathers were not favourably disposed towards the genre, which however was still known to Augustine and Jerome [12]. In that period also belongs the prose-play → *Querolus sive Aulularia* that was intended for recital; it harks back to Plautus (to *Aulularia* in particular) and Terence. At that point, Roman comedy was finished.

COMEDY

1 W.G. ARNOTT, Menander, Plautus, Terence, 1975 2 TH. BAIER, Werk und Wirkung Varros im Spiegel seiner Zeitgenossen, 1997, 82–97 3 L. BENZ, Die röm.-ital. Stegreifspieltrad. zur Zeit der Palliata, in: ead, E. STÄRK, G. VOGT-SPIRA (ed.), Plautus und die Trad. des Stegreifspiels, 1995, 139–154 4 J. BLÄNSDORF, Voraussetzungen und Entstehung der röm. Komödie, in: [14], 91–134 5 Id., Plautus, in: [14], 135–222 6 G. BREYER, Etruskisches Sprachgut im Lat., 1993 7 T. A. DOREY, A Note on the Adelphi of Terence, in: G&R 9, 1962, 37–39 8 G.E. DUCKWORTH, The Nature of Roman Comedy, 1952 9 E. FRAENKEL, Plautinisches im Plautus, 1922 10 K. GAISER, Zur Eigenart der röm. Komödie, in: ANRW I 2, 1972, 1027–1113 11 R.L. HUNTER, The New Comedy of Greece and Rome, 1985 12 H. JÜRGENS, Pompa diaboli. Die lat. Kirchenväter und das ant. Theater, 1972

13 E. LEFÈVRE, Römische Komödie, in: M. FUHRMANN
(ed.), Die röm. Literatur, 1974, 33–62   14 Id. (ed.), Das
röm. Drama, 1978   15 Id., Versuch einer Typologie des
röm. Dramas, in: ibid., 1–90   16 Id., Maccus vortit bar-
bare. Vom tragischen Amphitryon zum tragikomischen
Amphitruo, AAWM 5, 1982   17 Id., Saturnalien und
Palliata, in: Poetica 20, 1988, 32–46   18 F. H. SAND-
BACH, The Comic Theatre of Greece and Rome, 1977
19 P. L. SCHMIDT, Postquam ludus in artem paulatim ver-
terat. Varro und die Frühgesch. des röm. Theaters, in:
G. VOGT-SPIRA (ed.), Stud. zur vorliterarischen Periode im
frühen Rom, 1989, 77–134   20 L. R. TAYLOR, The Opportunities for Dramatic Performances in the Time of
Plautus and Terence, in: TAPhA 68, 1937, 284–304
21 U.v.   WILAMOWITZ-MOELLENDORFF,   Menander,
Schiedsgericht, 1925   22 J. WRIGHT, Dancing in Chains:
the Stylistic Unity of the Comoedia Palliata, 1974.

EDITIONS (OTHER THAN PLAUTUS AND TERENCE):
CRF; E. H. WARMINGTON, Remains of Old Latin, 1935–
1940.   E.L.

Comes, comites
A. ROMAN REPUBLIC AND IMPERIAL PERIOD
B. BYZANTINE PERIOD

A. ROMAN REPUBLIC AND IMPERIAL PERIOD

Comes (from *com-* and *ire*, 'to go with') in its wider
sense is a companion, trusted friend, or one entrusted
with duties of aid and protection towards another (Dig.
47,10,1; 47,11,1,2). In public life, already in the Republican period *comes* means a member of the retinue
of a travelling official, especially a provincial magistrate
(Gr. ἑπόμενος; *hepómenos*); the *comes* himself may be
an official, a personal friend, slave, freedmen, client or
even a high dignitary (Suet. Iul. 42; Dig. 1,18,16).

In its special sense, from the beginning of the Imperial period *comes* denotes a member of the imperial
retinue (*comitatus*), initially its character not differing,
however, in any way from that of other functionaries.
But, as in the case of the emperor's relations and *amici*,
mere proximity to the emperor had a politicizing effect
on the position. In particular, there was a circle of advisers and functionaries around the emperor, and these
can be regarded as *comites* in a narrower sense. They
may, but need not, have belonged to the *consilium principis*, from Trajan's reign at the latest, the more or less
formally organized imperial court council (Cass. Dio.
52,33; Dig. 27,1,30).

In the context of the ceremonialization and the legal
formalization of relationships of court service and rank
in late antiquity, *comes* became a title denoting one of
the three ranks of the → *ordo dignitatum* (*comitivae
primi ordinis* = senators, *clarissimi; comitiva secundi*
and *tertii ordinis* = *equites/perfectissimi*, Cod. Iust.
12,13,1; Cod. Theod. 12,1, 127). Associated with the
comitiva primi ordinis are senatorial honours and
rights of immunity (Cod. Iust. 12,14; 10,48,12); the title is also granted emeritus to a wider circle of equestrian court officials and provincial administrators. Retired *decuriones* of the urban *curiae* became honorary
comitiva tertii (Cod. Theod. 12,1,127).

Comes also denotes particularly important official
positions of imperial trust, not only at court but also in
provincial administration, in civil and military administration, the latter in late antiquity being distinct from
the civil administration. In the courts themselves,
former equestrian positions acquire senatorial rank in
late antiquity, the holders of these offices then appearing almost exclusively in the two higher senatorial
ranks — those of the *illustres* and *spectabiles* — whereas simple senatorial rank — that of the *clarissimi* — in
general fell to civil government representatives in the
provinces.

At court, the following *comites* have the rank of *illustris*: (1) the *comes sacrarum largitionum*: the titles and
responsibilities of the offices in part varying markedly
in late Roman and early Byzantine official histories, at
different periods and with varying status responsible
for tax collection, customs duties, coinage, state enterprises, mines, monopolies and salaries (Not. Dign. Or.
13; Cod. Iust. 1,32); (2) the *comes sacri patrimonii*: at
various times responsible for *ad hoc* defined parts of
state wealth, generally at the personal disposal of the
emperor, especially landed properties (Cod. Iust. 1,34);
(3) the *comes rerum privatarum*: at various times responsible for relatively large parts of imperial/state
wealth, especially in the fiscal interests, placed as required under his keeping from the remit of the above-
named official spheres (Not. Dign. Or. 14; Cod. Iust. 1,
33); (4) the *comites domesticorum*: at various times
commanders of the imperial bodyguard at court (Not.
Dign. Or. 15). There are also several *comites* from the
second senatorial rank, *spectabilis*: (5) the *comites consistoriani* (members of the imperial → *consistorium*,
Cod. Iust. 12,10); (6) the *comites tribuni scholarum*:
commanders of the guards close to the court (Cod. Iust.
12,11); (7) the *comites et archiatri sacri palatii* (Cod.
Iust. 12,13).

Most frequently represented at court are *comites*
with equestrian rank (*perfectissimatus*) and a *comitiva
secundi ordinis*, as e.g. (8) *comites commerciorum*: responsible *i.a.* for trade in border provinces (Not. Dign.
Or. 13,6ff.); (9) *comites largitionum per omnes dioeceses*: subordinate to (1) above (Not. Dign. Or. 13,5);
(10) *comites metallorum*: responsible i.a. for the exploitation of mines (Not. Dign. Or. 13,11); (11) *comites
rationales*: responsible *i.a.* for the use of reserves, e.g.
from Egypt (Not. Dign. Or. 13,12); (12) *comites domesticorum equitum* or *peditum*: subordinate officers of
the imperial bodyguard (Not. Dign. Or. 15,9f.; Cod.
Iust. 12,12); (13) *comes domorum*: administrator of the
possesions used to meet the personal requirements of
the imperial family, especially the estates in Cappadocia, in the imperial chambers (Not. Dign. Or. 14,3;
Cod. Iust. 12,5,2); (14) *comes sacrae vestis*: responsible
in the imperial chambers for the 'wardrobe', at times,
however, more broadly for the organization of the
court (Cod. Theod. 11,18,1). (15) *Comes* (*tribunus*)
stabuli: responsible under the *Magister officiorum* for
horses and court transport; but at times had wider responsibilities (Cod. Theod. 11,18,1).

In the area of provincial government bureaucracy, in late antiquity the highest-ranking *comes,* (16) the *comes Orientis,* was *vicarius* of the *praef. praetorio Orientis* (Not. Dign. Or. 22); (17) a number of other *comites* were leaders of provincial governments (Cod. Iust. 1,40,3). (18) Some high but subordinate provincial officials, as *e.g.* the *comites thesaurorum,* subordinate to the *vicarii* of the dioeceses, bear the title *comes* (Cod. Iust. 12,23,2).

In the military, *comes militum sive militaris* denotes the commander above the *dux,* but below the *mag. militum* in rank and responsibility, as *e.g.* (19) the *comes militaris per Aegyptum* (Not. Dign. Or. 28). *Comes* is at the same time an honorary title denoting extraordinary military services (Not. Dign. Or. 1,35–37; Cod. Iust. 12,12).

→ Amicus; → Consilium; → Palatium

J. BLEICKEN, Verfassungs- und Sozialgesch. des Röm. Kaiserreiches 1, ²1981, 127ff.; JONES, LRE 366ff., 411ff., 607ff.; MOMMSEN, Staatsrecht, 2.1, 988–992; R. SCHNEIDER, Das Frankenreich, ²1990, 44ff.; P. SCHREINER, Byzanz, 1986, 46ff.   C.G.

B. BYZANTINE PERIOD
From the time of → Constantinus [1] I. Title reserved for higher officials and army commanders, especially for members of the permanent team of advisers (*consistorium*) newly created by him and organized into three *ordines*; from the 5th cent. it declined in importance. Until the 7th cent. the *comes sacrarum largitionum* was head of the exchequer, the *comes rerum privatarum* responsible for the imperial estates. After the 7th cent. the hellenized title κόμης (*kómēs*) is primarily reserved for military ranks, as for example the supreme commander of the theme (Byzantine military province) of Opsikion (in Bithynia), corresponding to the → στρατηγός (*stratēgós*) of the remaining themes. Other κόμητες (*kómētes*) are of lower rank, *e.g.* the κ. τῶν τειχέων (*tôn teichéōn,* guard of the palace walls), the κ. τοῦ σταύλου (*toû staúlou,* master of the imperial stables), the κ. τῆς κόρτης (*tês kórtēs*), a staff officer at the particular disposal of the στρατηγός (*stratēgós*). In general, κ. now denotes the leader of a basic unit (βάνδον; *bándon*) of the Byzantine army.

LMA 1, 71; ODB 1, 484f.; J. F. HALDON, Byzantine Praetorians, 1984; H.-J. KÜHN, Die byz. Armee im 10. und 11. Jh., 1991; N. OIKONOMIDÈS, Les listes de préséance byzantines des IXᵉ et Xᵉ siècles, 1972; P. B. WEISS, Consistorium und comites consistoriani, 1975.   F.T.

Cometas (Κόμητάς; *Kómētás*)
[1] Writer of epigrams, probably to be identified with the *grammatikós* of the same name in the middle of the 9th cent. in Constantinople. Four poems survive: in the poems Anth. Pal. 15,36–38 (the latter consisting of seven dodecasyllables) C. claims to have restored Homer's verses by punctuating them and rescuing them from 'useless rot', only to be mocked for it by the scholiast J (cf. → Constantinus [2] of Rhodus), in a marginal note

(in trimeters) to the 57 hexameters in which C. acclaims the rising of Lazarus (Anth. Pal. 15,40).

F. M. PONTANI, Lo scoliaste e Cometa, in: Studi in onore di A. Colonna, 1982, 247–53; AL. CAMERON, The Greek Anthology from Meleager to Planudes, 1993, 306, 308–11.   M.G.A.

[2] **C. Chartularius.** Otherwise unknown writer of epigrams from the *kyklos* of Agathias. Two of his poems have survived: an erotic poem (Anth. Pal. 5,265: on the poet's own situation as a forsaken lover) and an epideictic/bucolic poem (ibid. 9,586). He is probably to be identified with C. Scholasticus, author of four distichs on a skilful physician (9,597).

Av. and A. CAMERON, The Cycle of Agathias, in: JHS 86, 1966, 8.   M.G.A.

Comets see → Meteorology

Cometes (Κομήτης; *Komḗtēs*).
[1] Lover of → Aegiale(ia) wife of → Diomedes [1], the Achaean warrior at Troy. After Diomedes' return, C. tries to kill him; when Diomedes manages to save himself by finding refuge at an altar to Athena, C. leaves his homeland Argus (schol. Hom. Il. 5, 412). Mimnermus appears to have developed the structure of this myth as a parallel to the fate of → Agamemnon (fr. 17 G.-P.; cf. also Apollod. Epit. 6,9).
[2] According to Paus. 8,45,6 son of the Aetolian king → Thestius, brother of Prothous and → Althaea [1]. In connection with the quarrel after the Calydonian boar hunt C. and his brother are killed by their nephew → Meleager. Prothous and C., together with other participants in the boar hunt, were depicted on a tympanum of the temple to Athena in Tegea.   E.V.

Cominianus Lat. grammarian of the 1st half of the 4th cent. AD in Constantinople. He was the teacher of → Charisius, who relied extensively on him in his *Ars grammatica.* C.'s lost work, which served as a Latin textbook for Greeks [1. 123], was influenced by → Plotius Sacerdos. It may also have been used in the form of revised versions, by later authors, as e.g. → Dositheus, Anonymus Bobiensis and → Beda. Texts circulating under the name of 'Cominianus' during the Middle Ages should, however, be associated with his student Charisius.

1 HLL § 523.1.   P.G.

Cominium Town in *Latium adiectum*; the modern Val di Comino to the north of → Atina [1] (perhaps San Donato). During the 3rd Samnite War in 293 BC conquered by consul Sp. Carvilius Maximus (Liv. 10,39–44) and destroyed (perhaps in 291 by consul L. Postumius Megellus: Dion. Hal. Ant. Rom. 16,4,5). Probably not to be identified with C. Ceritum (Ocritum?), where Hanno learned of the defeat at → Beneventum in 212

BC (Liv. 25,14,14). Plin. HN 3,108 lists C. among the ruined towns of the Aequiculi. CIL X p. 507, 5143–56.

NISSEN 2, 669; G. DEVOTO, Gli Antichi Italici, ²1951, 118.

G.U.

Cominius
I. REPUBLICAN PERIOD   II. IMPERIAL PERIOD

I. REPUBLICAN PERIOD
Italic family name (ThlL, Onom. 2, 543); from the 2nd cent. BC its bearers belonged to the Roman equestrian class, and during the imperial period occasionally acceded to the Senate.

[I 1] C., P. Roman knight from Spoletium, and an acquaintance of Cicero; in 74 BC with his brother C.C. unsuccessfully accused L. Aelius Staienus (Cic. Clu. 100), and in 66 and 65 the people's tribune C. Cornelius [I 2], defended by Cicero, for *maiestas* (Ascon. 59–62C; Cic. Brut. 271); probably for that reason attacked in his turn by Catullus, friend of Cornelius (108).

J.-M. DAVID, Le patronate judiciaire au dernier siècle de la république romain, 1992, 827–829.

[I 2] C., Pontius. In 387 BC a messenger during the siege of the Capitol by the Gauls, said to have swum across the Tiber and so broken the blockade (Diod. Sic. 14,116,3f.; Liv. 5,46,8–10; Plut. Camillus 25 i.a.).

[I 3] C. Auruncus, Postumus. In annalistic tradition a patrician; consul I 501 BC and II 493, waged war against the Volsci. It is under his command that C. → Marcius is supposed to have received the epithet Coriolanus by taking Corioli (Liv. 2,33,4–9 i.a.). The dedication of the temple of Saturn on the Forum is also ascribed to him (Dion. Hal. Ant. Rom. 6,1,4).   K.-L.E.

II. IMPERIAL PERIOD
[II 1] C.C. Roman knight. Wrote lampoons on Tiberius, but due to the pleading of his senator brother was not condemned (Tac. Ann. 4,31,1; PIR² C 1261).

[II 2] M. Aurelius C. Cassianus. Senator, after a lengthy praetorian career (CIL VIII 7033 = ILAlg II 1, 617 concerns him), in 247/248 governor of Numidia and suffect consul (IRT 880) [1. 125ff.; 2. Vol. 1, 405, Vol. 2, 45].

[II 3] P.C. Clemens. Knight from Concordia. Numerous procuratorial offices, finally prefect of the fleets of Ravenna and Misenum under Marcus Aurelius (PIR² C 1266) [3. Vol. 1, 501ff.].

[II 4] T.C. Proculus. Senator, probably the brother of C. [II 1]; *procos.* of Cyprus under Claudius (PIR² C 1270) [2. Vol. 1, 296].

[II 5] C. Secundus. Praetorian legate of Pannonia inferior from 148–150 [2. Vol. 1, 113]; *cos. suff.* in 151 (military diploma, published by D. ISAC).

1 REBUFFAT, in: Libya Antiqua 15/16, 1978/79
2 THOMASSON   3 PFLAUM   W.E.

Comisene Border territory of Media, opposite Parthyene east of the Caspian Gates (the modern territory of Dāmghān). Although it had already been lost for a period to the Seleucids before the eastern campaign (*anábasis*) of → Antiochus [5] III, it did not finally fall to the Parthians (along with its central town of → Hecatompylus) until the 2nd cent. BC (cf. Str. 11,9,1). In the late Sassanid period the province (*šahr*) Kōmiš, which incidentally was probably never a Christian diocese [1], separated the provinces of Gurgān and Ray.

1 R. GYSELEN, La géographie administrative de l'empire sassanide, 1989, esp. 84   2 S. SHERWIN-WHITE, A. KUHRT, From Samarkhand to Sardis, 1993, esp. 89.

J.W.

Comissatio Traditional Roman drinking party, a regular accompaniment to a festive → *cena*, often lasting long into the night. For a long time it was reserved for men, but from the end of the Roman Republic women, too, could partake. The *comissatio*, a socially highly important form of gathering, reached Rome by the end of the 3rd cent. BC at the latest. The word is derived from the Greek word for revelry, κῶμος (*kômos*); its structure and rules corresponded to a large extent to those of the symposium (→ Banquet). Apart from the drinking, the entertainment consisted of informal and/or witty speeches, the host's *akroamata* (music, dance, drama, recitations) and interludes from the guests (riddles, games). Details of the *comissatio* are discussed by Plutarch in his *Quaestiones convivales*. Owing to occasional alcoholic excesses, the *comissatio* did not have a good reputation.

J. MARQUARDT, Das Privatleben der Römer 1, ²1886; A. MAU, s.v. C., RE 4, 610–619.   A.G.

Comitatenses The *comitatenses* were the units that constituted the mobile army of the late Roman Empire. Their name derives from the *comitatus*, the administrative machine that served the princeps and accompanied him on his travels. The *comitatenses* were not tied to any specific territorium, and could be joined to territorial troops permanently stationed in specific provinces (*limitanei* or *ripenses*). It is probable that → Diocletianus had raised a mobile army, but it was of limited size. However, → Constantinus enlarged the *comitatenses* and gave them new significance by on the one hand creating new units, on the other hand incorporating into them parts of Diocletian's mobile army and disbanding some of the border troops. The new mobile army comprised legions, some only 1,000 strong, newly created units called *auxilia*, and mounted *vexillationes*.

A statute of AD 325 underlined the formal distinction between *comitatenses* and border troops (Cod. Theod. 7,20,4). The *comitatenses* and the *limitanei* were granted a double tax exemption (for the soldier and his wife) after 24 years' service, and single tax exemption after 20 years' service; the *comitatenses*, however, enjoyed a privileged position upon early retirement on medical grounds. A statute of AD 372 (Cod. Theod. 7,22,8) stipulated that recruits should be called up either to the *comitatenses* or the *limitanei* on the basis of physical fitness.

The *comitatenses* were commanded by a *magister peditum* (infantry) and a *magister equitum* (cavalry). Under the Tetrarchy the *comitatenses* were divided into different armies, each with its own commander, aside from regional mobile armies created under *magistri equitum* and *comites rei militaris*. Units of these mobile armies were consequently distinguished from those units in the direct service of the princeps, called *palatini*. Soldiers from border units were often transferred to the mobile army without thereby receiving higher status; these soldiers, first mentioned in AD 365, were called *pseudocomitatenses*. Soldiers of the *comitatenses* were as a rule billeted in towns.

At the end of the reign of Theodosius I the mobile army of the eastern half of the imperium consisted of five units, of which two served under the emperor while the others were stationed in Thrace, Illyricum and in the eastern border region. Each of these units was commanded by a *magister utrius militiae*. In the west between 395 and 408 → Stilicho was the most influential commander; the most important mobile armies were stationed in Italy and Gaul.

The development of the mobile army did not at first entail any fundamental change in Roman military strategy. At first, the *limitanei* were still organized as they had been under Diocletian; but their status and effectiveness slowly declined, as emperors expended ever-increasing resources on the mobile army, which could react flexibly to military requirements as a high-prestige force.

1 D. HOFFMANN, Das spätröm. Bewegungsheer und die Notitia Dignitatum, 1969　2 JONES, LRE, 607–686.

J.CA.

Comitia In spite of Roman traditionalism, in the course of time the different forms of popular assemblies arising under the Roman constitution undergo a pronounced developmental change on the one hand and must, on the other, be considered in terms of their functional role at any one period. The following forms occur: the *comitia curiata*, the *comitia centuriata*, the → *concilium plebis*, the *comitia tributa* and the → *contiones*. It must also be said that, owing to fundamental methodical and factual reservations due to the relatively late date of the historical sources for the early periods of Roman history, no statement about the popular assemblies of this period can avoid a degree of uncertainty.

Comitia (from *com-ire*, 'to collect together'; singular — 'place of assembly'; plural »- electoral or decision-making bodies«) signifies the assembly of all eligible Roman citizens in the decision-making bodies set up to establish the collective will of the *populus Romanus*. Women, children, those declared to have forfeited their rights of citizenship and non-citizens could not partici-

pate in *comitia*. The *comitia* had only a decision-making or electoral function: they did not provide a forum for discussion or for hearing alternative proposals from the masses of the people. The latter was the function of the *contio*. Decisions capable of being made by the assembled plebs and affecting the entire Roman people, as instituted by the *lex Hortensia* of 287 BC, were made in a *concilium plebis*.

1. Probably the oldest form is that represented by the *comitia curiata*, whose origin the Romans traced back to Romulus (Dion. Hal. Ant. Rom. 2,12,14). It is uncertain whether this form originally had the comprehensive powers ascribed to it: conferring of royal power on the king, and later to bearers of imperial office in a *lex de imperio;* the election of magistrates; the sanctioning of laws and decisions over war and peace by petition of the king, later of the *interrex*, the *pontifex maximus* or a *consul*. It can, however, certainly be stated that the *comitia curiata* were an early form of tribally organized political life in Rome, contributing to the determination of the will of the entire state via a vote *curiatim*. It is not clear whether the 30 *curiae* were present as electoral bodies, as was the case later, nor, from the beginning, how they related to the, originally three, *tribus* organizations and to an early form of military assembly, where the basis for the other forms of *comitia* is generally accepted to be found. In any case, of powers that were perhaps originally more extensive, there remained only the right, in a ceremony of (purely) sacerdotal significance, to sanction laws and the election of magistrates already decided in other *comitia*, and to take decisions regarding adoption, emancipation and some aspects of wills (*testamentum calatis comitiis*) that originally also affected the interests of the *gens*. They can be shown to be still active in the late imperial period.

2. Historical tradition in the Augustan period, while tracing the *comitia centuriata* back to the institutions of King Servius Tullius (Liv. 1,42,5; Cic. Rep. 2,21), also seems to see them as representing a change from the *tribus*-based constitution towards urban districts based no longer on clan identity, but on territorial boundaries (Dion. Hal. Ant. Rom. 4,22). The 'Servian constitutional reforms' could in any case be seen as a shift of the political and institutional centre of gravity away from a type of city organization more or less dominated by influential clan assemblies, and towards one based more on an overall concept of statehood. This enabled *gentes* until then insufficiently represented, or even groups of citizens not belonging to *gentes* (*plebei*), to achieve a greater degree of influence, a development that might be seen to show affinities with the Athenian constitutional reforms of Cleisthenes in 509. All that can be said with any degree of certainty, however, is that the *comitia centuriata*, as a military assembly concerned with political issues (and which, probably for that reason, traditionally met on the → *campus Martius*), underwent various considerable changes in the course of the centuries, before taking on those forms

more familiar to us from the 2nd and 1st cents. BC (Pol. 6,14; Cic. Rep. 2,21). Thus we must think in terms of an initially only slight differentiation, between the *centuriae* of the *equites* (the mounted, upper-class warriors), of a *classis* (the heavily armed foot soldiers), and those *infra classem* (the lightly armed soldiery) inferior to both. The number of *centuriae* will also only gradually have developed towards the figure of 193. The relative importance of the groups of electors and the sequence in which they cast their votes changed. It must, however, be assumed that the centuries representing the combined groups of the propertied *equites* and the prosperous citizens were always numerically superior to those of the other voters; like the *ekklesia* of Athens before the reforms of Themistocles, the *comitia centuriata* had a timocratic structure (Servius *equitum ... numero separato ... reliquum populum distribuit in quinque classis ... eosque ita separavit, ut suffragia non in multitudinis, sed in locupletium potestate essent*, Cic. Rep. 2,22), even after a reform to be assumed sometime around the year 215 BC reduced the (*prima*) *classis* from 80 to 70 centuries.

Until the time of Cicero, the *comitia centuriata* comprised 18 equestrian centuries and 175 foot centuries as follows (*prima classis*: 70 *centuriae*; *secunda — quinta classis*: not fixed, either 20 or 30 *centuriae*, 90 in all; in addition five *centuriae tignariorum, fabrum, tubicinum, cornicinum, adcensorum velatorum*: Cic. Rep. 2,20). In general, the equestrian and *prima classis* centuries contained far fewer members than those of the following *classes*, but as electoral bodies not only had the same electoral weight, but in elections were also the first to cast the ballots allotted to them, in a system where voting always continued only until a majority of votes was established. In contrast, the *centuria adcensorum velatorum* comprised not only the great mass of the *proletarii* falling below the taxable minimum (1,500 *asses*), but also other, relatively poor members of the middle classes only barely liable for tax, making up a majority of the urban population of Rome. In practice, the centuries theoretically last to cast their votes never got as far as the ballot box.

The *comitia centuriata* made political decisions of central importance, such as those concerning war and peace, the election of the highest magistrates, the voting of statutes, juridical verdicts in comitial trials usually of political significance. On the one hand, this form of popular assembly clearly evinces an almost total lack of influence on the part of the impoverished masses; on the other hand, however, it also represents a restraint on the influence of aristocratic groups of senatorial and equestrian status in favour of the somewhat broader stratum of a propertied or otherwise modestly affluent 'middle class'.

3. The *comitia tributa* are possibly to be seen in connection with the above-mentioned reform of the *comitia centuriata* in around 215 BC. They were a new form of popular assembly, to be traced back to a newly configured *tribus*-based constitution (from then on four

tribus urbanae and 31 *tribus rusticae*), in which the Roman people, voting in 35 tribal electorates, elected the lower echelons of the magistrature (*aediles, quaestors*) and could vote on statutory proposals, if the magistrate responsible for summoning them thought fit. As the *tribus rusticae* comprise the property-owning citizenry of Rome, and the general mass of propertyless Roman citizens was concentrated in the *tribus urbanae*, the timocratic element in this form of popular assembly was also particularly pronounced. As the electorates cast their ballots simultaneously and were smaller in number, *comitia tributa* were easier to put into effect than *comitia centuriata*. This form of assembly is to be distinguished from the → *concilium plebis*, which, while also voting in *tribus*, could be summoned only by the people's tribunes, and only consider proposals put to it by them; this constitutes its only 'plebiscitary' distinction from the *comitia*.

The course of proceedings within the *comitia* was essentially determined by the magistrate authorized to summon them. By his *ius agendi cum populo* his was the prerogative for scheduling (*promulgatio*), formulating and drafting (*rogatio*) the proposals to be voted on (e.g. *legisactiones*), conducting the voting procedure, including its interruption or postponement, and assessing and announcing (*renuntiatio*) the outcome (*suffragia*). The fact that the *comitia* themselves could only vote on proposals presented to them, and not discuss them or put alternative proposals of their own devising, gave this procedure for reaching political decisions an authoritarian character. However, in saying that we must not overlook the legal opportunities for expressing and forming political opinion, for example in a → *contio*; and political gestures and demonstrations on the part of the populace were not always threatened with punishment, and certainly arose repeatedly in times of political crisis. Voting was originally by word of mouth, but after the *lex Papiria* of 131 BC there was a secret ballot. Each citizen received two tablets (*tabellae*), inscribed with UR (*uti rogas* = acceptance) or A (*antiquo* = rejection), and threw one of them into the urn (*cista*). In elections of officials the citizen himself wrote the name of his preferred candidate on a *tabella*. In comitial trials *tabellae* were distributed bearing the inscription A. (*absolvo*) or C. (*condemno*).

→ Centuria; → Tribus; → Curia

E. GJESTADT, Innenpolit. und mil. Organisation in frühröm. Zeit, in: ANRW I.1, 136–188; D. KIENAST, Die polit. Emanzipation der Plebs und die Entwicklung des Heerwesens im frühen Rom, in: BJb 175, 1975, 83–112; MOMMSEN, Staatsrecht, 3, 300ff.; L. R. TAYLOR, Roman Voting Assemblies from the Hannibalic War to the Dictatorship of Caesar, 1966; A. ROSENBERG, Unt. zur röm. Zenturienverfassung, 1911.   C.G.

Comitium see → Assembly buildings

Commagene (Κομμαγηνή; *Kommagēnḗ*). Region between the west bank of the → Euphrates [2] and the south-eastern slopes of the → Taurus, in south-eastern Turkey, approximately to be identified with the Turkish province of Adıyaman. The Taurus to the north separates it from the province of Malatya; to the west and the south there is a gradual transition to the provinces of Maraş and Gaziantep as far as the region of Jerablus (→ Karkemiš) on the border with Syria. In recent decades the landscape has been permanently altered by the damming of the Euphrates north of Mount Karababa, to form Lake Atatürk. International salvage excavations have provided a provisional impression of the history of settlement.

This began in the pre-ceramic Neolithic, and continued, strongly influenced by the southern Mesopotamian 'Ubaid and Uruk cultures, in the Chalcolithic. The early Bronze Age (3rd millennium BC) was marked by elements characteristic of local and regional cultures (ceramics: so-called Khirbet Kerak ware, painted Karababa ware, Syrian wares). From the beginning of the 2nd millennium BC the region drew the attention of the major powers of the ancient Orient: the Hittites, Egyptians, Assyrians and Babylonians as well as the Iranian ruling dynasties. The settlement of Samsat (Samosata) shows an almost continuous sequence of occupation from the Neolithic to the Seljuk period (excavation: N. ÖzGÜC).

In the Neo-Assyrian period C. is attested under the name *Kummuḫu* in Assyrian, Urartian and Neo-Babylonian, but not in Hittite or Luwian sources. It bordered on the late Hittite kingdoms of Malatya/Melid to the north, Maraş/Gurgum and Zincirli/Sam'al to the west and Karkemiš to the south (→ Asia Minor, Hittite successor states). The earliest mention of the land of Kummuḫu is in the reign of the Assyrian king Tukulti-Ninurta I (13th cent. BC) — but probably in confusion with Katmuḫi (Ṭur 'Abdīn) — but not again until the 9th cent. in the annals of the Assyrian king Assurnaṣirpal II when Kummuḫu continued as a loyal vassal of the Assyrians. In around 750 BC it submitted to the Urartian king Sardur II, who, owing to a period of weakness in the Assyrian Empire, was able to extend his power to the vicinity of → Karkemiš. In 743 a coalition of late Hittite kingdoms, led by Urartu and in which Kummuḫu took part, was defeated by Tiglatpilesar III; in 738 Kummuḫu submitted to the Assyrians again. Under Sargon II it recovered its status as a favoured Assyrian client, and after a revolt in Malatya/Melid the city of Melid was even awarded to Kummuḫu. In 708 BC Kummuḫu was the last independent late Hittite kingdom to become an Assyrian province, after having conspired with Urartu again. After the collapse of the Assyrian empire, between 607 and 605, Kummuḫu fell to the Neo-Babylonian empire under King Nebuchadnezzar II. It appears subsequently to have fallen under Median control. The capital city of the land of Kummuḫu, of the same name, is identified with Samsat, but this has not been confirmed by the latest excavations.

Between the disintegrating Seleucid empire, the advancing Parthians and Rome, which was spreading its power over Asia Minor, C. — like the neighbouring regions of Armenia, Cappadocia and Cilicia — was able to establish a kingdom, achieving independence in the middle of the 2nd cent. BC under a local ruler called Ptolemaeus, only to lose it definitively to the Romans in AD 18 or 72, under Antiochus [18] to the Romans. The son of Ptolemaeus was Samos, to whom the (re-) foundation of the city of → Samosata (Samsat) is attributed. The dynasty traced its origins, on the one hand, from the Orontides (→ Orontes), who originally ruled in Armenia and were dynastically linked with the Achaemenid royal house; on the other, there was a direct link to the Seleucid royal house via the wife of the Commagenian king Mithradates I Callinicus (*c.* 100–70 BC), Laodice Thea Philadelphus, daughter of the Seleucid ruler Antiochus [10] VIII Grypos.

Their son, Antiochus [16] I Theos (*c.* 70–36 BC), the most significant ruler of C., built for himself (and his father?) a 50 m-high, partially terraced funerary monument (tumulus), at the elevation of 2,150 m (Nemrut dağı) on the Nymphaeus (now Kahta çayı) near → Arsamea [2] (Eskikâhta). Colossal statues of Antiochus and Commagenian gods were set on the eastern and western terraces. In Hellenistic-Persian style, they follow the tradition of late Hittite funerary monuments. The cult reforms initiated by both rulers led to a syncretic Hellenistic-Iranian religion.

→ Asia Minor

D. H. FRENCH, Commagene, in: Asia Minor Stud. 3, 1991, 11–19; J. D. HAWKINS, s.v. Kummuḫ, RLA 6, 338–340; K. NASHEF, Die Orts- und Gewässernamen der mittelbabylon. und mittelassyr. Zeit (Répertoire géographique des Textes Cunéiformes 5), 1982, 171f.; M. J. MELLINK, The Tumulus of Nemrud Dağ and Its Place in the Anatolian Tradition, in: Asia Minor Stud. 3, 1991, 7–10; D. H. SANDERS, Nemrud Daği. The Hierothesion of Antiochos I. of Commagene, Vol. 1: Text, Vol. 2: Illustrations, 1996; R. D. SULLIVAN, The Dynasty of Commagene, in: ANRW II 8, 732–798; F. K. DOERNER, Kommagene, 1981; H. WALDMANN, Der kommagenische Mazdaismus, 1991; J. WAGNER, Dynastie und Herrscherkult in K., in: MDAI(Ist) 33, 1983, 177–224; F. K. DOERNER, T. GOELL, Arsameia am Nymphaios, 1963.   H.KÜ.

Commeatus *Commeatus* has two different meanings: it denotes either a limited leave of absence or suspension (as opposed to final dismissal, the *missio*), or specific logistical arrangements. The term *stellatura* denotes the misuse of either arrangement.

1. For soldiers, leave of absence meant being permitted to leave the vicinity of the standard (Tac. Hist. 1,46,4). *Commeatus* was wrongly confused with → *immunitas* or *vacatio munerum*, which signified exemption from the usual duties to be carried out by soldiers. The granting of such exemption was the prerogative of the centurions (Tac. Ann. 1,17,4; 1,35,1; Hist. 1,46,2ff; 1,58,1). In the Republican period, leave of absence was granted upon written request by the tribunes or the

army commander (Liv. 21,21; 28,24; 43,11). In order to prevent abuse, leaves of absence were precisely recorded (Veg. Mil. 2,19). In 323 Constantine forbade the granting of leave by officers of the decuriae or the cohorts (Cod. Theod. 7,12,1).

2. *Commeatus* comprises supplies, not including clothing (Liv. 32,27,2), grain or *frumentum*. Provisions such as meat, lentils, cheese and salt doubtless counted as *commeatus*, and perhaps weapons and horses. In a friendly country such goods were paid for and requisitioned; in hostile territory they were seized by the legions as war booty. In the Republican period the *frumentarii* were responsible for provisioning. Soldiers often fought hungry, as before the time of Caesar logistics were badly organized. During the Principate the provisioning of the legions was given close attention (cf. Veg. Mil. 3,3). The system had become very complex, and made it possible to transport provisions from farflung provinces — such as oil from the province of Baetica — to the legionary camps on the Rhine border. Supplying the army by land was difficult, but not impossible; the → *annona* and the fleet had important roles to play.

1 J. HARMAND, L'armée et le soldat, 1967, 179–194 2 A. LABISCH, Frumentum commeatusque, 1975 3 Y. LE BOHEC, L'armée romaine ²1990, 53 4 M. REDDÉ, Mare nostrum, 1986, 370–399 5 J. REMESAL RODRÍGUEZ, La annona militaris y la exportación de aceite bético a Germania, 1986. Y.L.B.

Commendatio

Commendatio (1) Recommendation of a person or thing (Dig. 4,3,37), (2) entrusting something for safekeeping (Dig. 50,16,136) and (3) offering evidence for an assertion (Cod. Iust. 6,22,2). (4) In the context of an informal arrangement, *i.e.* one in principle not legally enforceable by either party, *commendatio* is an act by which a client entrusts his affairs to a patron to be represented or resolved, committing himself in honour to a debt of gratitude (*se alicui in clientelam, fidem commendare*, Ter. Eun. 577; Petron. Sat. 140; Caes. B Gall. 4,27,7; Lex Visig. 5,3,8): a precursor in Roman law to the concept of commendation, central to feudal law in the Middle Ages. (5) In the political realm, *commendatio* is especially an address by which the Roman emperor recommended a *candidatus* for office to the popular assembly or, as early as Tiberius, to the Senate. As in the case of statutes proposed by the emperor, such recommendations were complied with without objection or alteration (Tac. Ann. 1,15: *sine repulsa et ambitu designandos*; *lex de imp. Vespasiani*, FIRA 1, S. 154–156: *quos magistratum potestatem imperium ... petentes senatui populoque Romano commendaverit ..., eorum ratio habeatur*).

→ Mandatum; → Clientes; → Patronus; → Magistratus

F. F. ABBOTT, History and Description of the Roman Political Institutions, ³1963, 276; KASER, RPR 2, 372; MOMMSEN, Staatsrecht 2,2, 921f. C.G.

Commentarii Continuous records (→ *acta*) in the nature of minutes, documenting the activities of official bodies and their agents (magistrates, *collegia*, city councils), but also perhaps commercial enterprises, *i.e.* large private households (Cic. Att. 7,3,7); but the term is not attested for actual balance sheets. The interests involved, and therefore the content (down to the private 'notebook', Cic. De or. 1,208), level of standardization and publication of records can vary greatly. Characteristic of the *commentarius*, as an individual record is that it is almost always part of a large series, that documentation and publication were not strictly required, except in the case of agreements, wills and → *leges*. Thus by the late Republic at the latest *commentarii* is used as a translation of the Greek → *hypómnēma* (cf. [1]), and may denote texts 'supporting oral delivery', drafts of speeches, notes for lectures, or reports designed to take the place of delivery in person (Cic. Brut. 164; Quint. Inst. 10,7,32; 3,8,68). This type of secondary documentation, and use of the term to describe 'a collection of cases', explains the use of *commentarii* to describe → commentaries on primary texts, especially in the legal sense (*commentarii in XII tabulas*) and in Christian → exegeses (on OT/NT).

Probably the earliest instance is the *commentarii pontificum*. The growing politicization of the priesthood after the → *lex Ogulnia* (300 BC) may have determined the interest in record-keeping in the middle of the 3rd cent. BC; members and rituals, down to observations of → portents were recorded; an extract in the form of a → *tabula* was published in front of the house of the *pontifex maximus* (cf. Cato Orig. HRR 77; [2. 167–172]). Similar registers are attested for other priestly colleges (*augures*: Cic. Div. 2,42; *quindecimviri s.f.*: Censorinus, DN 17,10f.; *fetiales*: Fest. 178,3–6L; *fratres Arvales*: acta). Documentation of members, perhaps amplified by reference to fictional antecedents, can have a prestige-enhancing effect; individual decisions and occurrences can acquire legitimizing force as precedents: apart from *commentarii*, no normative texts for the Roman priesthood have been discovered (for *libri sacerdotum* see [3]). Internal interests are decisive: the longest surviving quotation from the *commentarii pontificum* (Macrob. Sat. 3,13,10–12) gives a list of participants and especially the detailed menu for an inaugurative banquet; it demonstrates that the *commentarii* were arranged to accord with the years in office of the *pontifex maximus*. In many colleges a *commentariensis* can be attested (also for the *septemviri epulones*, CIL VI 2319).

Magistrates' personal journals seem to have been common in the late Republic (Cic. Sull. 40–45); even if their primary purpose was as a personal *aide-mémoire*, they acquired general significance, contributing to the written form of Senate decisions or statutes, composed by a small committee after the Senate session. Since the publication of official documents was limited, private *commentarii* may have been the primary form of written dissemination among the political elite. Systematized *commentarii* relay technical know-how to successors, sons or friends, with regard to the discharge of office and areas of expertise; they then take on the character of initiatory texts (Varro's *Eisagoge* for Pompey; Q. Cicero's *Commentariolum petitionis* for his brother; → Agrippa; → Frontinus; → Gaius). This technical aspect also characterizes those *commentarii* which, in the form of apologias and encomia, introduce the author to a wider public, and may be written in a correspondingly elaborate linguistic style (→ Caesar is an exception, cf. Hirt. Gall. 8, pr.; [4]); the concentration on discharge of office limits the autobiographical character of such works.

Generally speaking, it is not the *commentarii* themselves that have survived, but excerpts with the wording of particular decisions (perhaps with reference to the place where they can be found in the protocol codex, CIL XI 3614), consecutive summaries (*acta arvalia;* for their varying degree of compression see [5]; CIL VI 2004) and systematic collections (succession lists: CIL VI 1984). In assessing not only such epigraphic and/or literary publications, but also the *commentarii* that might, not always, underlie them, critical source-analysis of the motive for setting down the record is particularly indicated; neither 'clandestine literature' nor 'routine record-keeping' has proved to be sustainable as a working hypothesis.

→ Hypomnema

1 F. BÖMER, Der Commentarius, in: Hermes 81, 1953, 210–250   2 J. RÜPKE, Livius, Priesternamen und die annales maximi, in: Klio 74, 1993, 155–179   3 J. SCHEID, Les archives de la piété, in: La mémoire perdue 1, 1994, 173–185   4 J. RÜPKE, Wer las Caesars bella als Commentarius?, in: Gymnasium 99, 1992, 201–226 5 M. BEARD, Writing and Ritual, in: PBSR 53, 1985, 114–162.

LIEBENAM; F. SINI, Documenti sacerdotali di Roma antica 1, 1983.   J.R.

Commentariis, a From early times the official organization of the Roman Republican magistrature and pontifical colleges, frequently includes the specialized keeping and storage of minutes of negotiations, journals (*acta diurna*), documents, official notes and decrees (→ *memoria*, → *commentarii*, → *diplomata*, → *codicilli*, → *mandata*, → *hypomnemata*), collections of statutes or catalogues (*tabulae, regesta, notitiae*) (Varro, Ling. 6,88 — consuls; Cic. Verr. 1,1,71; Brut. 55 — provincial governors; Cic. Dom. 117—*pontifices*). The official titles of the subordinate employees responsible for the keeping and archiving of records changed. Different titles denote different status within the hierarchy, and the preposition *a* indicates an area of responsibility within a management structure: *a commentariis, ab actis, act(u)arii, chartularii, referendarii*. However, the official title and attribution of particular functions do not always allow precise conclusions as to the overall nature of the administrative tasks actually performed. In the Imperial period quite a large number of subordi-

nate officials, *a commentariis* probably always among them, was also required for court-related administrative duties in individual *officia* (later called *scrinia*). The same applies to prefectural administrations (Cod. Theod. 8,1,2). Here some of them may have very specialized duties, *e.g.* in the prison service vis-à-vis inmates (Cod. Theod. 9,3,6). In late antiquity, on the basis of their income (23 *solidi*) these counted as belonging to the class of *ducenarii,* thus the higher stratum of officials (Cod. Iust. 1,27,25). Generally speaking, the post of *a commentariis* was also represented in the *officia* of all provincial administrators and military commanders, either in the person of individual officials (*commentarienses*), with the *a commentariis* coming under a *princeps* (office manager), a *cornicularius* and other superiors in the hierarchy, or in the form of specialized *a commentariis* offices with several officials, as *e.g.* in the case of the *praef. praet. Africae*, with 12 officials (Not. Dig. Pass.; Cod. Iust. 1,27,25; Lydus, Mag. 3,8; 18).

→ Acta; → Actis, ab; → Archive; → Codex; → Commentarii; → Memoria

HIRSCHFELD 325; JONES, LRE 497, 522, 587; MOMMSEN, Staatsrecht, 1, 346ff.; 2, 1004ff.   C.G.

Commentary

I. GREEK

see → Hypomnema

II. LATIN

→ *Commentarii* (*commentarii*, also *commentarium*) were originally a non-literary assemblage of records concerning the affairs of a household, magistrate or priestly order. Among scholars, *commentarii* could denote the following: 1. corresponding to the Greek term → *hypómnēma*, a kind of 'notebook' (e.g. Cic. De or. 1,5; Brut. 164; cf. Gellius 16,8,3, who characterizes L. → Aelius' [II 20] *Commentarius de proloquiis* as follows: 'Aelius appears to have written this book as advice to himself rather than to inform others'); 2. a treatise (e.g. the *commentarii* in which L. → Ateius [5] Philologus displays his multi-layered scholarship: Suet. Gram. 10,5); 3. a 'commentary', i.e. a collection of glosses on a literary text. From the latter derives the specialist term still used today. The earliest commentary in this sense is perhaps L. Aelius' interpretation of the Song of the Salii (late 2nd/early 1st cent. BC: Varro, Ling. 7,2, with GRF fr. 1–3; → *Carmen saliare*). Other early examples are the commentaries of L. → Crassicius on C. → Helvius [I 3], Cinna's *Zmyrna* (Suet. Gram. 18.2) and that of C. Iulius → Hyginus on Cinna's *Propempticon* for Asinius Pollio (GRF fr. 1–2), and (perhaps) on the poetry of Virgil (GRF fr. 3–11). They were all written in the 2nd half of the 1st cent. BC, shortly after the works commented upon.

Many other similar texts followed, but most of them have either been lost or survive only in very abbreviated form (*e.g.* Pomponius → Porphyrio's commentary on Horace and Aelius → Donatus' [3] commentary on Terence). The earliest complete extant commentary on a Latin text, that of the grammarian → Servius on the poetry of Virgil, is from the early 5th cent. There was a widespread tradition in Servius' time of writing commentaries on Virgil [4; 5], and this enabled him to select from a great wealth of knowledge and opinion in writing his own commentary. In so doing, Servius fell back at least in part on the *variorum* commentary (touching on all themes) assembled by Aelius Donatus in the middle of the 4th cent.; nevertheless, Servius' work offers a cross-section through four centuries of Virgil scholarship.

The introduction to Servius' commentary provides a brief survey of themes that have become canons of the genre: the life of the poet, the title and character (*qualitas*) of his poem, his 'intention' and the number and sequence of books. The main part attempts to elucidate the text, line by line, often word by word, ascertaining Virgil's intended meaning. As one would expect in a work by a *grammaticus* (→ Grammarians III Rome), two out of three annotations concern linguistic questions: Servius is not only interested in explaining passages in the text whose sense might be obscure (including an astonishing number of passages whose word order he finds problematic), but also, usually implicitly, in assessing Virgil's use of language in terms of the grammatical rules prevailing in Virgil's time. Deviations from these rules are expounded and (for the most part) pardoned as 'archaisms' or 'tropes'. In the remaining part Servius touches on all possible subjects of interest: the structure of the text, particularly in passages where he is aware of variant readings [8]; borrowings from and imitations of Homer, Ennius and other Greek and Latin poets; Virgil's rhetorical skill; philosophical and religious teachings interwoven in the text; points of antiquarian or historical interest (in this respect notable deficiencies are occasionally apparent in Servius' historical knowledge: [9]). Many other commentaries on Latin literature, written to the same pattern, have survived in abbreviated form (e.g. Pomponius Porphyrio's commentary on Horace; Aelius → Donatus' [3] on Terence).

→ Commentarii; → Literary criticism; → Philology, Roman; → Servius; COMMENTARY

1 J. ASSMANN, B. GLADIGOW (ed.), Text und Kommentar, 1995   2 F. BÖMER, Der Commentarius, in: Hermes 81, 1953, 210–250   3 S. F. BONNER, Education in Ancient Rome, 1977, 227ff.   4 H. GEORGII, Die ant. Aeneiskritik, 1891   5 G. FUNAIOLI, Esegesi virgiliana antica, 1930   6 M. J. IRVINE, The Making of Textual Culture, 1994, 118ff.   7 E. RAWSON, Roman Culture and Society, 1991, 324ff.   8 J. E. G. ZETZEL, Latin Textual Criticism in Antiquity, 1981, 81ff.   9 Id., Servius and Triumviral History in the Eclogues, in: CPh 79, 1984, 139–142.   R.A.K.

Commerce

I. ANCIENT ORIENT (EGYPT, SOUTH-WEST ASIA, INDIA) II. PHOENICIA III. ETRURIA
IV. GREECE

I. ANCIENT ORIENT (EGYPT, SOUTH-WEST ASIA, INDIA)

Archaeologically attested since the Neolithic and documented since the 3rd millennium BC, long-distance or overland commerce — as opposed to exchange and allocation of goods on a local level according to daily needs — was founded on the necessity for ensuring the supply of so-called strategic goods (metal, building timber) not available domestically, as well as on the demand for luxury and prestige goods, or the materials required for producing them.

In historical times, the organization of commerce was as a rule in the hands of central institutions (palace, temple; exception: Assur's tin trade with Anatolia, → Kaneš), and its execution entrusted to commercial agents. There is widespread evidence of trading settlements, some of them with goods depositories, in distant locations (e.g. merchants from Assur in Kaneš, from Mari in Ḥalab/Aleppo, from Babylonia in Dilmun, from Palmyra in → Charax Spasinu, from Greece in → Naucratis). → International treaties protected the merchants from the whim of local rulers. The exchange value of goods often depended on non-economic factors. Apart from peaceful commerce, there was a role for organized military expeditions (e.g. up the Nile from Egypt to Nubia in search of gold) or systematic conquest with the aim of securing the required materials in the form of booty and tribute (e.g. Assyria during the 1st millennium BC — metals and horses for warfare, luxury goods). Textiles were almost the sole export of Mesopotamia; for other goods Mesopotamia was purely a transhipment centre. Egypt exported mainly gold, but also textiles and objects of high-value craftmanship.

Goods flowing into Mesopotamia came for the most part via way stations. In the Persian Gulf, → Dilmun was pivotal in the sea trade with Oman (where copper deposits and smelting remain to be confirmed archaeologically) and the → Indus cultures (wood, gemstones, perhaps also cornelian). Copper also came from Cyprus and Anatolia. Tin came via the land route through Iran to Susa, Ešnunna on the Diyāla and from there along the Euphrates to Mari and onward to northern and central Syria, or across the passes in the region of modern Suleimanie to → Assur and onward to Anatolia (Kaneš). Large quantities of building lumber were floated down the Euphrates to Babylonia from Syria and Lebanon. Experiences associated with this trade are reflected in the Epic of → Gilgamesh, commercial relations with the Iranian plateau in Sumerian epics. Syria and the Lebanon also provided carved ivories, purple textiles/clothing and wine. Long-distance transportation of grain was possible only by water, and so occurred only in situations of crisis. Egypt perhaps also acquired slaves from Syria; Babylonia from the north-east of modern Iraq.

Luxury goods reaching Egypt, Syria, Anatolia and Mesopotamia predominantly comprised cosmetics, fragrant oils, resins and other aromatic materials, spices: all originating in far-flung regions within the ambit of the Middle East. Sources are to a large extent silent regarding the provenance for silver and gold. The Egyptians acquired gold from Nubia. Silver came *i.a.* from Anatolia. → Lapis lazuli came from eastern Iran and Afghanistan. Commerce in prestige goods was to a great extent conducted in the form of exchange of gifts between rulers (attested *i.a.* in the → Amarna letters; gold to Babylonia).

During the 2nd and 1st millennia BC, emporia (→ Emporion) and city states on the Mediterranean coast (*i.a.* → Al-Mīnā, → Aradus [1], → Berytus, Byblos [1], → Ioppe, → Sidon, → Tyre, → Ugarit) played an important role in linking the Orient with the Aegean. In the Syrian-Mesopotamian world various locations bordering other states or at the interfaces of important trading routes fulfilled at various times a corresponding function: → Karkemiš on the upper Euphrates, → Ebla on the plain of Aleppo with links to Emar and Mari on the Euphrates; Assur (20th/19th cents. tin trade with Anatolia); in Babylonia, important bases for overland commerce were Ešnunna (20th–18th cents. to the Iranian plateau) and Sippar (Euphrates route to the northwest — Mari and Emar — and the south-east — Persian Gulf, Elam during the 19th–17th cents.). → Palmyra from early historical times and Ḥatra from the 1st to 3rd cent. AD were important bases for east-west traffic through the Syrian steppe. At various times, towns at the interface of important trading routes also developed into significant state centres, sometimes ruling over extensive tracts of territory (Mari in the 19th/18th cents.; Palmyra from the 1st cent. BC).

As late as the 1st millennium, overland commerce in the Middle East was done with donkey caravans (camels were not used until after the 2nd millennnium BC). The Nile, Euphrates, Tigris and Indus were of fundamental importance as transport routes for Egypt, Mesopotamia and India. Commerce between Egypt and the Levant (→ Byblos [1]) was carried out from the time of the Old Kingdom by seafaring ships, between the Aegean and Egypt during the 2nd millennium via Cretan Hierapetra, and by land along the Libyan coast to the Nile Delta (→ Aegean Koine). In the 6th cent. BC the sea route around the Arabian peninsula was controlled by Egypt. The passage through the Red Sea to Ethiopia (Punt) was already in use before this time. → Encouraged by Necho, Phoenician seafarers circumnavigated Africa (Hdt. 2,158). The route from southern Arabia along the west coast of Arabia is first attested under Solomon with the Queen of Sheba (→ Incense Road), and from there onwards via the → King's Way to Syria. The land route from Egypt ran via Raphia and Hazor, both of which served as staging-posts to central and northern Syria. Sea trade between India and Meso-

potamia into the 2nd millennium was via Dilmun in the Persian Gulf; from the 3rd cent. BC → Arabia played an important role in the India trade.

→ Barabara; → Ivory (carving); → Merv; → Patala

1 W. Helck, s.v. Handel, LÄ 3, 944–48　　2 H. Klengel, Handel und Händler, 1969　　3 C. Lamberg-Karlowsky, Trade Mechanisms in Indo-Mesopot. Relations, in: Journal of the American Oriental Society 92, 1972, 222–229.

J.RE.

II. Phoenicia

Phoenician presence and expansion in the Mediterranean, besides other factors and causes, was primarily associated with long-distance commerce, on the one hand the supply of raw materials and agricultural products, on the other hand the sale of building timber from Lebanon and refined finished products. From the beginning of the Iron Age at the end of the 11th cent. into the 6th cent. BC, organization and financial protection of commercial activities in the Mediterranean on the part of the Phoenician cities of Tyre, Sidon and Byblos was in the hands of the political executive. It was a stable system, essentially unchanged over the centuries, its origins residing in ancient and solid structures from the Middle Eastern Bronze Age. The report of the Egyptian ambassador Wen-Amun (1085–1060 BC) to the court of Zakar Baal, king of Byblos, as well as references in the OT (2 Sam 5; 1 Kgs 5–7, 9–10; 2 Chr 8–9, 20 [969–930 BC]; Jes 23 [end of the 8th/beginning of the 7th cent. BC]; Ez 26–28 [586 BC]) are valuable but meagre testimony from this period. Owing in part to their obscure origin, and given the reservations about their age and the degree to which they can be regarded as meaningful for the understanding of Phoenician commerce, they are disputed as sources.

The king controlled the necessary administrative structure and the monopoly for extracting and obtaining the particular raw materials plentifully available in this region, as well as their commercial exploitation. He had at his disposal outstanding craftsmen famed far and wide for their knowledge and skills, and he had legal and fiscal sovereignty over the harbours and territorial waters. Consortia of well-financed and influential private merchants and ship owners — commercial dynasties with diverse and extensive trade contacts and partners, independently organized but complementary to the king and working in close association and co-operation with his house and his commercial fleet — were the backbone of extensive enterprises, reaching out far beyond the Mediterranean region, and offering the prospect of profits and losses in equal measure. They either possessed or equipped considerable fleets, and offered effective financial protection against the risks and dangers associated with commerce. The phenomenon of 'gift exchange' and 'trade' in luxury items and valuables was a prerequisite of professional commerce. It fostered mutual alliances, and was used in dealings with commercial partners as a form of advance payment. The close interaction between Phoenician religion, state and monarchy was exemplified by the way the temple operated as a political and mercantile institution, even providing financial backing for commercial activities.

The city of → Tyre was celebrated for its sea power, its international significance for long-distance trade in the Mediterranean and its wealth. Splendour, magnificence and arrogance were held to be synoptic as it were with the misery provoked by its downfall, and both were the occasion of dramatic asseverations on the part of OT prophets. During the 9th–8th cents. BC, the high point and time of greatest expansion of Tyre's commerce to the east, agents for its commercial institutions operated in three commodity markets under its economic control, with the aim of securing supplies for the city and its tradesmen: in Israel, Arabia and Ophir, northern Syria and Cilicia, and Cyprus and the western Mediterranean region. Tyre purchased wheat, figs, honey, oil and resin in Judah and Israel; wool and wine in Damascus; sheep and goats in Arabia and Kedar; horses and mules in Togarma; saddle blankets in Dedan; malachite, rubies, purple dye, cloth, linen, embroidery and coral in Edom; textiles, carpets and rope in Harran, Kanna, Eden, Saba, Assur, Media and Kulmer; slaves, bronze vessels, iron, spices and calamus in Jawan, Tubal and Meshech; gold, silver, iron, tin, lead, ivory, monkeys and peacocks in Tarsis; fragrant oils, precious stones and gold in Saba and Ragma; iron and spices in Uzal; ivory and ebony in Rhodes (Ez 27,12–24). It is surprising, if explicable historically, that neither Cyprus as an ally of Tyre nor the copper trade is mentioned here.

In Homer (Il. 23,740–751; Od. 4,613–619; 13,272–286; 14,287–300; 15,414–483), for whom commerce is irreconcilable with the Greek concept of aristocracy and therefore contemptible (Od. 8,158–164), the Phoenicians, the 'Sidonians', are the trading people *par excellence* — in both the good and the bad sense. They are bold, excellent sailors, monopolize sea trade and navigate throughout the then known world. They possess their own ships and are a constant presence in the harbours of the Aegean, the Ionian Sea and the North African coast (Lemnos, Syros, Crete, Pylos, Ithaca, Libya, Egypt), but at the same time are a settled people, with house and land at home. Their handicrafts are celebrated without exception, objects of wonderment and desire. Homer has the Phoenicians performing casual, small-scale commerce of no significance: his is an idyllic conception, at the same time permeated with hostility, racism and fear of competition. One year they manage to sell off a ship-load of trash: they are exclusively profit-orientated, exploiting every opportunity to trade to their own advantage. They are pirates, abducting people and stealing children; they trade in slaves, but also in grain and wine. Homer does not mention Phoenician trading posts, permanent settlements or colonies.
→ Cyprus; → Phoenician archaeology

R. D. BARNETT, Ezekiel and Tyre, in: Eretz Israel 9, 1969, 6–13; J. D. MUHLY, Homer and the Phoenicians, in: Berytus 19, 1970, 19–64; G. BUNNENS, Commerce et diplomatie phéniciens au temps de Hiram I de Tyr, in: Journ. of the Economic and Social History of the Orient 19, 1976, 1–31; Id., La mission d'Ounamun en Phénicie. Point de vue d'un non-égyptologue, in: Riv. di Stud. Fenici 6, 1978, 1–16; Id., L'expansion phénicienne en Méditerranée (Inst. Belge de Rome 18), 1979; S. F. BONDÌ, Note sull'economia fenicia I: Impresa privata e ruolo dello stato, in: Egitto e Vicino Oriente 1, 1978, 139–149; H. G. NIEMEYER, Die Phönizier und die Mittelmeerwelt im Zeitalter Homers, in: JRGZ 31, 1984, 3–29; E. LIPIŃSKI, Products and brokers of Tyre according to Ezekiel 27, in: Stud. Phoenicia 3, 1985, 213–220; M. GRAS, P. ROUILLARD, J. TEIXIDOR, L'univers phénicien, 1989, esp. 79–127; M. E. AUBET, The Phoenicians and the West, 1996, esp. 77–118. CH.B.

III. ETRURIA

Etruscan objects are found from Spain to the Black Sea region, and from Poland to Carthage [5. 24f., 64f.]. Only in a few cases were the Etruscans themselves the bearers of these objects of gold, bronze and clay.

The Etruscan cities were politically independent, and it is therefore necessary to assume a different commercial orientation for each individual city. Those settlements with a coastal orientation had contacts particularly early: → Populonia, → Vetulonia, Vulci (→ Volcae), → Tarquinii, Cerveteri (→ Caere) and → Veii. The coastline in Etruscan times differed from today's in being less regular and characterized by lagoons that increasingly silted up, so that, for example, Vetulonia later had no direct access to the sea. The finds suggest that there were already early contacts with peoples north of the Alps [1. 1031ff.] and with Greece [10] (pre-colonial commerce). Seaborne trade, attested by finds on → Corsica, → Sardinia and → Sicily as well as in → Carthage, began as early as the 7th cent. BC [6]. The bronze finds from the 8th cent. BC, especially in the sanctuary of Olympia, remain problematic, probably representing offerings by Greeks returning home from the west rather than originating in Etruria itself [10]. A literary topos is the condemnation of Etruscan piracy by Greek sources; this throws additional light on competition with Greek seafarers [12]. Cerveteri, its strong maritime orientation indicated by its three harbours of → Alsium, Pyrgi and Punicum, was of particular significance in early trading relations. → Pyrgi played an important role with regard to trade with Carthage; further evidence for close relations with Carthage is the name Punicum. Tarquinia also had access to an important harbour, possessing in → Graviscae an → emporion along strongly Greek lines. Regisvilla (Regae), the port of Vulci (with a large amount of imported Attic ceramics and a significant bronze industry), has up to now been investigated only to a slight degree.

The especially common Etruscan bucchero canthari were probably brought into the Aegean by Greek merchants [9]. The spread of the → bucchero and of Etruscan-Corinthian ceramics, along with the bronze utensils, provides a picture of seaborne commerce to southern France with the Phocaean colony of → Massalia, founded around 600 BC and controlling onward trading with the Celtic tribes. In the background here were the important tin mines of Cornwall. As the Etruscan settlements in the interior gained in importance and prominence, northern Italy and the Celtic region north of the Alps became the focus of attention [1]. The Etruscan colonies of → Atria and → Spina, founded in the late 6th cent. BC on the Po plain, had along with Felsina (Bologna) the best connections with Athens, and were among those states having a mediating role in the introduction of Greek objects into the Celtic heartland [13; 14].

The quantities of Attic and other vases in Etruscan graves (→ Etrusci) allows us to estimate the scope of commerce at different periods [13]. Only the smallest proportion of objects traded finds its way into the archaeological record. The interest of Phoenician and Greek trading partners resided in the rich metal deposits (above all: iron) of the island of Elba (→ Ilva), the → Tolfa mountains and the Colline Metallifere. There was also trade in wine and oils, as is proved by the finds of Etruscan amphorae in settlements and shipwrecks on the southern coast of France [2]. Equally important raw materials such as → wood, → ivory and → glass, not to mention dyes for textile processing, only rarely survive. The same applies to → salt, which played an important role in preserving food and in stock breeding. Evidence for other foodstuffs such as grain, which the southern Etruscan cities were still obliged to supply in the 3rd cent. BC for the campaign of Scipio Africanus (Liv. 28,45), is almost totally lacking in the archaeological record. The products of the Etruscan bronze workshops, with especial emphasis on those of the Vulci craftsmen in the 6th and 5th cents. BC, are of great importance for assessing Etruscan long-distance commerce, and play a significant role as one of the foundations for Celtic chronology [14]. In the late period of the Etruscan city states, under the shadow of Roman expansion, trading relationships were in the main reduced to localized commerce and barter, and only a few indigenous products found their way beyond the Etruscan heartland.

→ Etrusci, Etruria (with maps)

1 L. AIGNER-FORESTI (ed.), Etrusker nördl. von Etrurien. Etr. Präsenz in Nordit. sowie ihre Einflüsse auf die einheim. Kulturen, Akt. des Symposiums Wien 1989, 1992   2 M. CRISTOFANI, P. PELAGATTI (ed.), Il commercio etrusco arcaico. Atti dell'incontro di studio, 1983, 1985   3 M. CRISTOFANI, Economia e società, in: G. PUGLIESE CARRATELLI (ed.), Rasenna. Storia e civiltà degli Etruschi, 1986, 79–156, esp. 124–156   4 M. CRISTOFANI, Gli Etruschi del mare, ²1989   5 Die Etrusker und Europa. Exhibition catalogue, Berlin, 1992   6 M. GRAS, Trafics tyrrhéniens archaïques, 1985   7 Id., La Méditerranée archaïque, 1995, 134–163   8 F.-W. VON HASE, Etrurien und das Gebiet nordwärts der Alpen in der ausgehenden Urnenfelder- und frühen Hallstattzeit, in: Atti del secondo congr. internazionale Etrusco, Florenz 1985, 1989, Vol. 2, 1031–1062   9 Id., Der etr. Bucchero aus Karthago. Ein Beitr. zu den frühen H.-Beziehungen im westl. Mittelmeergebiet, in: JRGZ 36, 1989, 327–410   10 Id., Présences étrusques et italiques dans les sanctuaires grecs

(VIIIᵉ-VIIᵉ siècle av. J.-C.), in: D. BRIQUEL, F. GAULTIER (ed.), Les Étrusques, les plus religieux des hommes. Actes du colloque international Paris 1992, 1997, 293–323   11 Id., Ägäische, griech. und vorderoriental. Einflüsse auf das tyrrhen. It., in: Beitr. zur Urnenfelderzeit nördl. und südl. der Alpen, Monographien des Röm.-German. Zentralmus. Mainz, 1995, 239–286   12 J.-R. JANNOT, Les navires étrusques, instruments d'une thalassokratie?, in: CRAI 1995, 743–778   13 P. KRACHT, Stud. zu den griech.-etr. H.-Beziehungen vom 7. bis 4. Jh. v.Chr., 1991   14 D. VORLAUF, Die etr. Bronzeschnabelkannen: eine Unt. anhand der technolog.-typolog. Methode, 1994.   GE.BI.

IV. GREECE
A. GENERAL   B. LONG-DISTANCE COMMERCE
C. MARKETPLACES AND COMMERCIAL CENTRES
D. FUNCTION OF MONEY AND LENDING   V. ROME

A. GENERAL
Commerce was pursued on a regular basis at all periods in ancient Greece, on a local and trans-regional level: in consumer goods such as food, craft-produced articles or animals; in luxury goods such as perfume, precious metals and costly textiles; but also in slaves. In the Mycenaean period Greek trading contacts spanned the entire Mediterranean region, but after c. 1200 BC Greek participation in long-distance trading activities appears to have declined dramatically; not until the 8th cent. BC did Greek long-distance commerce blossom again, with Greek merchants active alongside Phoenicians, Syrians and Etruscans in places such as → Al-Mīnā and → Pithecusae. There were, in addition, close connections with Egypt, where Greek merchants had their settlements in → Naucratis. Wine and olive oil were among the important export goods of the archaic era. Thus we have Charaxus, the brother of → Sappho, selling wine from Lesbos in Egypt (Str. 17,1,33). High profits were also made from trading expeditions to Spain (Hdt. 4,152). As early as the beginning of the 5th cent., grain imports were acquiring increasing significance for the Greek cities (Hdt. 7,147,2; Dem. Or. 20,30–33). From the 6th cent. BC onwards, wide-beamed ships with large square sails and considerable cargo space were in common use.

Archaeological evidence for Greek commerce rests largely on finds of pottery, indicating the presence of merchants from Greece or in close contact with Greeks. But pottery did not usually represent the most important good traded; ceramic vessels served above all as containers for bulk items such as wine or fish sauce. High-quality painted ceramic wares, which were often transported together with bulk items or luxury articles, were of comparatively low value.

B. LONG-DISTANCE COMMERCE
Long-distance commerce was largely pursued on a small scale by professional merchants (ἔμποροι); these emporoi received goods from producers in exchange for money or other goods, and then passed them on to consumers, who in turn paid for them with money or with

other goods. Such commerce was associated with considerable financial risk, and merchants often had to visit many ports in order to sell their wares. Literary sources depict the typical merchant as a free individual of modest means, travelling from market to market and selling various kinds of wares in small quantities. A merchant might own his own ship, but most entered into fixed-term partnerships with ship owners (ναύκληροι, → *naúklēroi*). This picture is in part confirmed from shipwrecks (such as the Giglio and Kyrenia wrecks), whose cargoes consist of a wide variety of different products.

Commerce was carried out on the basis of a variety of exchange mechanisms, among them buying and selling, barter (*e.g.* grain for wood, slaves for wine), as well as exchange of gifts. Transfer of goods in the absence of exchange, be it through war, → piracy, one-sided bestowal of gifts or robbery, must also be considered a characteristic of economic activity in Greece. Thus many of the slaves sold on Greek slave markets were prisoners of war or victims of piracy.

In general, merchants enjoyed little respect, especially in comparison with landowners living from the produce of the soil (Hom. Od. 8,159–164; Hes. Op. 618–694; Aristot. Pol. 1255b 40–1259a 36). The figure of the untrustworthy foreign merchant was a commonplace in Greek literature from Homeric times (Hom. Od. 15,415–484).

Participation of women in commerce was limited, on grounds of law or custom; normally they were excluded from larger-scale commerce, except under male control. Women most often traded in foodstuffs, cheap textiles and especially perfume. In the Hellenistic period, when more women had independent control over their own means, women are occasionally attested in inscriptions as being active in commercial life on a grand scale, often via agents. Slaves and freedpersons were frequently engaged in small-scale commerce, often as dependent agents of citizens and metics (*metoikoi*).

C. MARKETPLACES AND COMMERCIAL CENTRES

Exchange took take place in shops, in marketplaces, in ports and in sanctuaries. Places of trading varied considerably in size and significance; thus, on the one hand, there was the small → agora of a rather insignificant polis, on the other hand the large number of markets in places like Athens, Miletus, Delos, Alexandria and Rhodes. In such cities there were also specialist marketplaces such as the fish market in Athens (Aristoph. Vesp. 790). Most coastal cities built trading harbours with appropriate facilities on the quays, such as warehouses and offices for the merchants and the magistrates (→ Port facilities).

Some cities specialized in particular products (e.g. Cos for fine textiles, Athens for oil or cities on the Black Sea for fish). Such specialized marketplaces arose on account of their situation on trading routes or near centres of production and consumption, or by virtue of favourable political relations. Thus Corinth from ear-

liest times was the commercial centre between the Peloponnese and the rest of Greece, Athens in the classical period became an important commercial centre, and Hellenistic Rhodes profited from its position between Syria and the Aegean as well as its close ties with Egypt, which enabled it to develop into an important transhipment centre for grain. Delos, which in 166 BC acquired the status of a free port, was an important centre for the slave trade. The Greeks were also linked to central Europe and Asia by far-flung and complex trading networks.

Laws designed to regulate and demarcate commercial activities go back at least as far as the 6th cent. BC (Plut. Solon 24). Marketplaces were usually subject to taxation and regulation, and under the oversight of officials. In classical Athens as well as in Piraeus 10 → *agoranómoi* (ἀγορανόμοι) supervised the markets, supported by 10 *metronómoi* (μετρονόμοι), who supervised weights and measures, 10 officials who controlled the export trade (ἐπιμεληταί ἐμπορίου, *epimelētaí emporíou*) and up to 35 *sitophýlakes* (σιτοφύλακες), who had oversight of supply and prices on the grain market (Lys. 22,8f.); these officials were chosen by lot (Aristot. Ath. Pol. 51). In the 4th cent. BC there were also courts responsible for commercial disputes (Aristot. Ath. Pol. 59,5).

D. FUNCTION OF MONEY AND LENDING

Coinage was common in the Greek world from the 6th cent. BC. Although its primary function was not that of a means of exchange, it eventually played an extremely important role in commerce. Small silver coins were especially used in daily exchange in those places where the polis, by regular payment to soldiers, officials or craftsmen, ensured that there was always sufficient money in circulation. In the classical and Hellenistic periods the values of most traded goods were expressed in monetary terms.

Commerce was additionally facilitated by provision of → credits for purchasers or sellers. Many merchants lacked the financial means to pay for goods immediately themselves; they accordingly had resort to → loans. Towards the end of the 5th cent. BC the Athenians had developed a special form of → fenus nauticum (maritime loan system), particularly for the financing of long-distance commerce in grain or wine. The merchant or ship owner borrowed money at a high rate of interest to pay for the cargo, which then, often together with the ship, acted as security for the loan. Loan and interest were paid back at a fixed term, while piracy, shipwreck or the seizure of the ship or cargo annulled liability for repaying the loan. In the 4th cent. BC the high risk was compensated for by rates of interest of up to 30 per cent. Such agreements are attested for the most part for Athens by legal speeches (Dem. Or. 32,20; 33,4; 34; 35,10ff.; 35,51; 56,1; Lys. 32,6).

→ Money, money economy; → Grain trade, importation of grain; → Market; → Slave trade

1 J. BOARDMAN, The Greek Overseas, ³1980   2 FINLEY, Ancient Economy   3 F. MEIJER, O. V. NIJF, Trade, Transport and Society in Ancient Greece: A Sourcebook, 1992   4 MILLETT   5 P. MILLETT, Maritime Loans and the Structure of Credit in Fourth-Century Athens, in: GARNSEY/HOPKINS/WHITTAKER, 36–52   6 C. MOSSÉ, The World of the Emporium in the Private Speeches of Demosthenes, in: GARNSEY/HOPKINS/WHITTAKER, 53–63   7 A. J. PARKER, Ancient Shipwrecks of the Mediterranean and the Roman Provinces, 1992   8 H. PARKINS, C. SMITH (ed.), Trade, Traders and the Ancient City, 1998   9 ROSTOVTZEFF, Hellenistic World   10 D. SCHAPS, The Economic Rights of Women in Ancient Greece, 1979   11 S.v. REDEN, Exchange in Ancient Greece, 1995.   P.d.S.

V. ROME

A. REPUBLIC B. PRINCIPATE C. LATE ANTIQUITY
VI. BYZANTIUM

A. REPUBLIC

Until the 3rd cent. BC, commerce played a distinctly subordinate role as opposed to agriculture in the economy of central Italy. It was the beginning of coinage in the 3rd cent. BC (→ Coinage) and increasing contacts with the Hellenistic economic region that brought about a fundamental change in the backward economic structure of Rome. However, from the late 7th cent. onwards the Etruscan upper class imported high-value Greek ceramics into central and northern Italy; the Pyrgi gold tablets indicate the presence of Carthaginians on the Etruscan coast.

Sea trade in the western Mediterranean was at first the domain of Greek, Etruscan and especially Carthaginian merchants. The Roman-Carthaginian treaties (Pol. 3,21–26) reflect Carthaginian interests, but they demonstrate that the position of Rome in the western Mediterranean region was becoming stronger. At the time of the 1st and 2nd Punic Wars, not only did Rome become a sea power, but Roman merchants followed the legions to Africa in order to profit from the campaigns and the war booty (Pol. 1,83,7; 14,7,2f.). From at the latest the *lex Claudia de nave senatorum* (218 BC; Liv. 21,63,3) — a law forbidding senators and their sons from owning ships with a capacity of more than 300 amphorae — considerable financial means were going into commerce. The *societates publicorum* (→ Publicani), who leased taxes and duties, and were from time to time active in supplying the legions fighting in Spain, were important in this context (Liv. 23,48,9–23,49,3). With the destruction of → Carthage in 146 BC Rome had become the leading merchant power in the western Mediterranean. Domestic Italian commerce was no doubt facilitated during this period by Roman road-building activities.

As early as the 3rd cent. BC Italian traders were active in the area of the eastern Mediterranean, initially in the Adriatic and in order to protect them, Rome waged war against the Illyrians (Pol. 2,8–12). As early as 189 BC Roman and Italian traders in Ambracia on the east-ern Adriatic coast were exempted from harbour dues by a decision of the Senate (Liv. 38,44,4); in the northern Adriatic, Aquileia [1] developed into an important port (Str. 5,1,8). After the 3rd Macedonian War the Romans declared → Delos a free port, thus making the island the most important commercial centre in the eastern Mediterranean, while Rhodes lost its dominant commercial position (Pol. 31,7; Str. 10,5,4).

Superior forms of organization gave Italian traders the edge over their Greek counterparts. They traded actively not only in the provinces, but also beyond the territories held by Rome. Thus *c.* 114 BC Italian traders defended Cirta against → Jugurtha (Sall. Iug. 21,2; 26,1ff.); the presence of Roman and Italian traders in Asia Minor and Delos is attested by the massacres ordered by Mithridates (App. Mith. 22f.; Paus. 3,23,3ff.; cf. besides Cic. Ad Q. Fr. 1,1,6). In addition, Roman → *negotiatores* are mentioned for Gallia Narbonensis and later for the territories conquered by Caesar (Cic. Font. 11f.; Cenabum: Caes. B Gall. 7,3,1). Rome consistently defended the interests of these traders with military means (Cic. Leg. Man. 11).

The ostentatious lifestyle of the Roman upper class in the late Republic led to substantial imports of luxury goods from the east to Rome. Besides trade in agricultural products, which streamed out of the entire Mediterranean region to Rome, the export of wine from Italy to Gaul deserves particular mention; in particular the amphorae of the landowner Sestius from Cosa, marked with the stamp SES, attest to the considerable volume of this trade. The → slave trade too was very important during the 2nd and 1st cents. BC: Gauls in particular sold large numbers of prisoners of war or bond slaves to Italy, and many individuals from the eastern Mediterranean ended up on the slave market, in part as victims of piracy (Str. 14,5,2). The financial ethic of the Roman upper class excluded direct involvement of senators in commerce (Cato Agr. praef.); Cicero, on the one hand, characterizes small-scale commerce as disreputable, yet on the other gives a positive assessment of large-scale commerce (Cic. Off. 1,151).

B. PRINCIPATE

With the emergence of the Principate and with the *Pax Augusta*, the internal pacification of the Imperium Romanum, a new era began for Roman commerce; the security of travel, especially of shipping routes, and the development of the → infrastructure, such as the construction of harbours, gave new impetus to the exchange of goods. Keeping the large cities provisioned remained of central importance for trade throughout the region. Rome's supplies were organized by the → *cura annonae*; grain was imported from the provinces of Africa and Egypt; oil, wine and garum from the Spanish provinces. At the same time, a free market in grain survived in Rome. Military → logistics came under central administration, but the free market followed its routes and was established at its destinations. In addition, the mere purchasing power of Roman soldiers in far-flung stations represented a stimulus for local and pan-regional commerce.

Increasing urbanization, along with the widely mooted population explosion of the 1st and 2nd cents. AD, also had an impact on commerce. Luxury goods from the East, especially India, might have reached the Mediterranean by land via Palmyra or by the sea route to the ports on the Red Sea, continuing via the Nile to Alexandria (Str. 17,1,45; → India, trade with). Less extensive on the other hand was exchange of goods with the free Germans and northern Europe; important imports included slaves, skins and amber. Although merchants often sold their goods — and especially grain — where they could maximize their profits (Cic. Dom. 11; Philostr. VA 4,32; Manil. 4,165ff.), many of them traded with particular regions; as, for example, Flavius Zeuxis from Hierapolis, who sailed to Italy 72 times (IGR 4,841). Long-distance trade was carried out substantially via sea routes, as the costs of land transport were appreciably higher than by sea; cost ratios for transport by sea, inland waterborne transport and land transport were approx. 1:4,9:28. Under these circumstances harbours and ports such as Gades (Str. 3,5,3), Puteoli (Str. 5,4,6) and Alexandria (Str. 17,1,7; 17,1,13) were economic centres of pan-regional importance.

Impressive as long-distance commerce in the Imperium Romanum was, it should not be overlooked that the major part of commerce, in total not quantifiable, took place in a local and regional framework. Producer-trading (agricultural and commercial) satisfied to a great extent the mutual needs of city and rural *territorium*. The establishment and organization of countless urban and rural markets (*nundinae*; cf. Plin. Ep. 5,4; 5,13; 9,39; → Market) supported the more or less constant flow of goods carried by specialist merchants. To some extent, such local markets took place only seasonally and in conjunction with feast days or court sessions (Dion. Chrys. 35,15ff.). Prices often varied widely from city to city, especially after harvest failures, which led to rises in grain prices (Dion. Chrys. 46,10).

It is difficult to assess the influence of taxes and duties (→ Taxes; → Customs duties) on commerce. The central message of K.HOPKINS' 'taxation-commerce model' [14] is, however, interesting: tax-exporting provinces (e.g. Asia, Gallia) must also export products to the tax-recipient regions (e.g. border provinces with a high military presence), in order to garner the ready currency necessary for the next round of taxation. The Roman system of customs duties does not appear on the whole to have represented any marked burden on commerce. The Imperium thus had at its disposal an instrument that, while satisfying its thirst for revenue, could also provide stimuli by way of privileges, temporary reliefs, definitive tax exemption, etc. High customs duties were levied at the borders (up to 25 per cent of the value of goods at the eastern border). This, however, had no harmful effect on the passage of goods, insofar as it was as a rule luxury goods that passed over the frontiers into the empire.

Nothing concrete can be said on the subject of merchants' incomes; no source provides any such calculation. The mere fact that goods were transported over long distances attests to the financial success of mercantile enterprises. The big fortunes were not as a rule made from commerce, even though members of the Roman upper class drew a part of their wealth from indirect participation in this branch of the economy. Some members of pan-regional or inter-provincial commercial organizations, such as, for example, *negotiatores* of the *corpus/collegium cisalpinorum et transalpinorum* or members of the *collegia nautarum,* may likewise have amassed considerable wealth. Rare details of prices permit no conclusions as to the profits of the merchants, as they give no information on the difference between buying and selling prices.

C. LATE ANTIQUITY

During the 3rd cent. AD conditions for commerce changed markedly. Above all, border conflicts to the north and east, causing destruction in many parts of the Imperium Romanum, made regular commerce impossible, at least on a temporary basis. Scholars agree that a marked decline in population was associated with these developments. The collapse of the monetary systems — especially the decline in the silver content of the denarius (→ Devaluation of money) and price increases (→ Prices) — is viewed as an indicator of economic decline. On the other hand, it must not be assumed that these economic changes affected all regions of the Imperium Romanum in the same manner, and commerce as a whole. Some cities and regions manifested definite economic prosperity; mention need only be made here of the cities of Side and Perge on the south coast of Asia Minor, flourishing tracts of Egypt, and Roman Britain, for which a long period of peace began just at the beginning of the 3rd cent. AD. The consolidation of the borders, far-reaching reforms in administration, taxation and currency, combined with attempts at tying prices to wages, assure a changed context for commerce from the time of Diocletian.

→ Money, money economy; → Imports/Exports; COMMERCE

1 W. AMELING, Karthago, 1993, 147–151   2 E. BADIAN, Publicans and Sinners, 1972, 67–81   3 J. M. BLÁZQUEZ, J. REMESAL, E. RODRÍGUEZ, Excavaciones arqueológicas en el Monte Testaccio (Roma), 1994   4 P. A. BRUNT, The Equites in the Late Republic, in: Id., The Fall of the Roman Republic, 1988, 144–193   5 D'ARMS   6 D'ARMS/ KOPFF   7 H.-J. DREXHAGE, Preise, Mieten/Pachten, Kosten und Löhne im röm. Ägypten, 1991   8 ESAR 9 J. M. FRAYN, Markets and Fairs in Roman Italy, 1993 10 P. GARNSEY, C. R. WHITTAKER (ed.), Trade and Famine in Classical Antiquity, 1983   11 K. GREENE, The Archaeology of the Roman Economy, 1986   12 J. HATZFELD, Les trafiquants italiens dans l'orient hellénique, 1919 13 P. HERZ, Studien zur röm. Wirtschaftsgesetzgebung. Die Lebensmittelversorgung, 1988   14 K. HOPKINS, Taxes and Trade in the Roman Empire, in: JRS 70, 1980, 101–125   15 G. JACOBSEN, Primitiver Austausch oder freier Markt? Unters. zum Handel in den gallisch-germa-

nischen Prov., 1995, 48–64   16 JONES, Economy
17 JONES, LRE, 824–872   18 L. DE LIGT, Fairs and Markets in the Roman Empire, 1993   19 F. DE MARTINO,
Wirtschaftsgesch. des alten Rom, 1985   20 F. MEIJER,
O. VON NIJF, Trade, Transport, and Society in the Ancient
World, 1992   21 J. NOLLÉ, Nundinas instituere et
habere, 1982   22 G. REGER, Regionalism and Change in
the Economy of Independent Delos, 314–167 BC, 1994
23 J. REMESAL, Heeresversorgung und die wirtschaftli-
chen Beziehungen zwischen der Baetica und Germanien,
1997   24 ROSTOVTZEFF, Roman Empire   25 E. SIDE-
BOTHAM, Roman Economic Policy in the Erythra Tha-
lassa 30 BC AD 217, 1986   26 B. SIRKS, Food for Rome,
1991   27 A. TCHERNIA, Italian wine in Gaul at the end of
the Republic, in: GARNSEY/HOPKINS/WHITTAKER, 87–
104.
      MAPS: T. Frank, An Economic Survey of Ancient
Rome, Vols. I–VI, ND 1975   F. de Martino,
Wirtschaftsgesch. des alten Rom, 1985   F. Vittinghoff
(ed.), Europäische Wirtschafts- und Sozialgesch. in der
röm. Kaiserzeit, 1990, esp. 20–160; 375–752.   H.-J.D.

VI. BYZANTIUM

A. LITERATURE AND SOURCES B. CHRONOLOGY
C. OVERALL ECONOMIC BACKGROUND TO COM-
MERCE D. FORMS OF COMMERCE AND TYPES OF
MERCHANT   E. MAIN COMMERCIAL PRODUCTS
F. REVENUES   VII. EARLY MIDDLE AGES

A. LITERATURE AND SOURCES

No overall investigation of Byzantine commerce
exists. Documentary sources for the period in question
are almost entirely absent. Historical texts from the
period since AD 600 contain only isolated hints. Despite methodological difficulties, hagiographies (→ vitae
sanctorum) and the seals of the commerciarii (customs
agents) are important sources. Our knowledge therefore remains highly episodic and random.

B. CHRONOLOGY

Commerce in the border zones of the ancient world
attained a final peak with the restoration of the unified
empire under Justinian. It was, however, overwhelmingly restricted to the Mediterranean region, while
trade with Asia and → India was essentially in the hands
of the → Sassanids; as regards trade north of the Alps
and Pyrenees, the Byzantines were at best suppliers. The
wars in the Balkans against Avars and Slavs and in Asia
Minor against the Sassanids led to severe obstruction of
land routes from as early as 570, but it was not until the
middle of the 7th cent. that the Arab advance as far as
the Aegean also brought about considerable restrictions
to seaborne trade, thus defining a clear chronological
boundary in this region.

C. OVERALL ECONOMIC BACKGROUND TO COM-
MERCE

In Justinian's empire the focus of commerce, as in
previous centuries, remained in the east. This was determined by the density of the urban network, the size of
the population, and the fact that the trade routes from

Africa and Asia culminated there. Moreover many
areas were not yet subject to the process of desertification owing to climate changes, as known to us today. As
a trade center, the city In the Balkans within a space of
30 years (570–600) and in Asia Minor c. 650 with the
Arab advance, entirely lost its significance as intermediary point linking internal and external commerce. Not
only the effects of war but also epidemics and earthquakes brought about a rapid reduction in both the
urban and the rural population. The importance of the
Black Sea remains substantially unknown (furs, fish,
amber — this last evidently not particularly important
for Byzantium). Behind the protection of its impreg-
nable walls, Constantinople during this period increasingly developed into a hub for sea- and landborne commerce. Commerce profited from the excellent Roman
road system, overseen and painstakingly maintained by
a dedicated department of the Byzantine state. The
compilation of the so-called Rhodian Sea Law during
the course of the 8th cent. demonstrates that, in spite of
the Arab presence, seaborne trade had not entirely suc-
cumbed, especially on the local level. A largely 'neutral'
Cyprus also played an important commercial role in
this connection. In so far as commerce took the form of
trading in goods for gold, then thanks to the gold solidus it rested on a firm base, accepted even in Asia and
Africa.

D. FORMS OF COMMERCE AND TYPES OF
MERCHANT

The importance of commerce in Byzantium depended primarily on the far-flung network of contacts surviving from late Roman antiquity, and only slightly
impaired even by the political collapse of the Justinian
imperium. 7th century sources thus report commercial
relations between Alexandria and the British Isles. The
Ceylon report of Cosmas (only later termed a 'traveller
to India', → Cosmas Indicopleustes) mentions 6th-cent.
Byzantine-Sassanid rivalry in the East Asian trade.
Finds of coins along the course of the → Silk Road attest
to a direct or indirect Byzantine presence. Chronicles
speak of short- or long-term commercial agreements
with the Avars, the Turkic peoples of Central Asia, the
Sassanids, and later even the Arabs. After the late 6th
cent. the Byzantines themselves were apparently less active as long-distance merchants, instead receiving goods
at particular locations within the empire (esp. in Constantinople or cities near the borders) and organizing
the wholesale trade. Arabs (or members of the Islamic
community) built a mosque in Constantinople as early
as the 8th cent., indicating regular commercial activity.
Commercial activities associated with the so-called
commerciarii (customs and tax agents) played a not
insignificant role during the 7th and 8th cents. This species of commerce, which was, however, more associated with state-supervised trading in kind at times of
crisis, and military logistics, is still a subject of controversy in research circles.

Apart from trading in gold for goods, trade by barter for natural products generally took on increasing significance from the 7th cent. onwards, even within the Byzantine Empire. The rise of trade fairs (annual markets) in association with church festivals (Ephesus, Trimithos in Cyprus) was important for early internal commerce, for which evidence is hard to find.

E. Main commercial products

Grain was always paramount in importance and volume, esp. in supplying the metropolis of Constantinople (at first from Egypt, later from Thrace and the Black Sea region). The political goal of preventing hunger riots at the heart of the empire was crucial for this trade.

Oil was used not only as a foodstuff for the population; it was also essential for lighting the churches. Fish and fish products (dried fish, fish eggs) were a basic foodstuff in maritime regions. Wine, in particular sweet wine, was an export product, as amphorae (→ Transport amphorae) in shipwrecks bear witness. Cheese and dried meat were also exported. Important products for the regional internal market (attested early for Constantinople) were vegetables and fruit. The timber trade acquired particular importance especially during this period, owing to the construction of warships; iron was important for the production of weapons, not only on behalf of the state, and was also passed on to outlying peoples who supported Byzantium against its enemies. The Byzantine Empire, and Constantinople in particular, was a focus for luxury products, whether for domestic use at court (and by the social strata associated with the court) or for onward sale. Most prominent among these products were the various kinds of silk (i.e. silk from China or Central Asia, and from the 6th cent. also silk produced in Byzantium). The demand for spices in western and northern Europe was entirely met by imports from Byzantium. Fine wood (*i.a.* from Africa) was also used in Byzantium before 800, but onward sale cannot be assumed. In general, until the 8th/9th cents. there is no evidence yet in the west for most of those products whose origin from the 10th cent. onwards appears to be Byzantium; or there was already the opportunity for obtaining supplies directly without the intermediary of Byzantium.

F. Revenues

Tax revenues accruing to the Byzantine state from commerce were (despite widespread opinion to the contrary) considerably inferior to those from land-ownership, and amounted to hardly more than five to 10 per cent of total tax revenues. The tax on commerce during the period in question was called the *octava* and amounted to about 12.5 per cent of value, but assessment of these data is still a matter of controversy.
→ Money, money economy; COMMERCE

1 G. F. BASS, E. H. VAN DOORNINCK, Yassi Ada. A Seventh-Century Byzantine Shipwreck, 1982 2 D. CLAUDE, Der Handel im westl. Mittelmeer während des Frühmittelalters, 1985 3 J. FERLUGA, Mercati e mercanti fra Mar Nero e Adriatico: il commercio nei Balcani dal VII al XI secolo, in: Mercati e mercanti nell'alto medioevo, 1993, 443–489 4 M. F. HENDY, Studies in the Byzantine Monetary Economy c. 300–1450, 1985 5 J. KODER, Gemüse in Byzanz, 1993 6 A. E. LAIOU, s.v. Commerce and Trade, ODB I, 489–491 7 D. G. LETSIOS, Νόμος Ῥοδίων ναυτικός. Das Seegesetz der Rhodier, 1996 8 M. LOMBARD, Les métaux dans l'ancien monde du Vᵉ au XIᵉ siècle, 1974 9 R. S. LOPEZ, The Role of Trade in the Economic Readjustment of Byzantium in the Seventh Century, in: Dumbarton Oaks Papers 13, 1959, 69–85 10 H. MAGOULIAS, The Lives of the Saints as Sources of Data for the History of Commerce in the Byzantine Empire in the Sixth and Seventh Centuries, in: Kleronomia 3, 1971, 303–330 11 N. OIKONOMIDES, Silk trade and production in Byzantium from the sixth to the ninth century: the seals of the Kommerkiarioi, in: Dumbarton Oaks Papers 40, 1986, 33–53 12 A. P. RUDAKOV, Ocherki vizantijskoj kul'tury po dannym grecheskoy agiografii, (repr.) 1970, 138–174 13 P. SCHREINER, s.v. Handel (in Byzanz), LMA 4, 1898–1903 14 Id., Zivilschiffahrt und Handelsschiffahrt in Byzanz, in: R. RAGOSTA (ed.), Le genti del Mare Mediterraneo, Vol. 1, 1981, 9–25 15 J. L. TEALL, The Grain Supply of the Byzantine Empire 330–1025, in: Dumbarton Oaks Papers 13, 1959, 87–139.
P.S.

VII. Early Middle Ages

In 1937 H. PIRENNE [7] formulated the thesis that it was the Muslim conquests, cutting off access to Mediterranean and Oriental commerce, that caused the collapse of the economic structures of the ancient world and with it the ruralization of the north-west, in particular the Carolingian Empire. His thesis has since undergone some modification in favour of conceptions of gradual structural change and territorial shifts from the 5th cent. onwards. Research in many areas has contributed to this: archaeologists with excavations of commercial sites (Haitabu, Birka, Dorestad, Hamwih), numismatists by refining their methods of interpreting the vastly increasing amount of archaeological material on a commercial-historical basis, economic historians with new insights into the role of manorially based commerce, and finally the use of anthropological theories of early commercial practice and exchange and central place theory.

During the centuries of transition from late antiquity to the early Middle Ages, large-scale processes of political and ecclesiastical transformation in the western imperium and/or its successor empires and their neighbouring regions dictated to a large extent the form and effect of commercial activity, here understood as everyday exchange of goods as distinguished from gifts given on the basis of reciprocity and ceremonial exchange. Apart from the centralization of western Christianity on Rome and the formation of the greater Frankish kingdom, two events created important conditions for gradual change in commercial structures: the expansion of the Avars and Slavs in Eastern Europe (6th cent. onwards), which obstructed long-distance trade between the Baltic and the Black Sea, the Balkans and the

Adriatic, and had as a consequence a re-orientation towards the sea route to the Rhine estuary and the river routes through Gaul to Marseille; and the Arab conquest of the Mediterranean coasts from Egypt to Spain (7th/8th cents.), and the subsequent blockade of the sea routes via Byzantium. The long term-results of this new configuration were the harmonization of conditions of exchange in the regions either side of the north alpine imperial borders, and a movement of commercial maritime activities to the Channel coasts and the North Sea, with links to the Scandinavian north-east and the Mediterranean south.

On the individual level, as early as the 6th cent. links were beginning to be formed between Jewish, Greek and Syrian long-distance traders and the new regional rulers (protection, exemption from customs duties), as well as new export links across the Channel and to the east. These tendencies were accentuated during the decades of upheaval from the late 7th cent. onwards. Intensifying commercial relations with the coast of Britain and with their North Sea and Baltic neighbours were largely borne by the Friesians and Anglo-Saxons, but also by the Franks. Besides traditional goods (slaves, wine, oil, spices), raw and finished industrial products from the domestic hinterland (ceramics, millstones, cloth, weapons, glass) were increasingly traded. The high-born rulers explicitly encouraged this commerce, their interest in intensifying trade and thereby expanding market and money exchange coming ever more clearly to the fore.

Despite an evident proliferation of regulations, as the capitularies of the earlier Carolingians in particular bear witness (regulation of coastal trade and trade on the eastern border, bridge and road construction, customs regulations, market encouragement and control, coinage reforms, weights and measures ordinances, export bans, criticism of profiteering, emergency prices), no systematic application of commercial norms can be detected; statutory regulation of commercial activities themselves (purchase, price, credit) remained entirely absent. This, however, does not alter the fact that, with the emergence of the north-west coastal commercial area and its close associations with river traffic and the commercial/industrial hinterland, the foundations (outside Italy) for the secular rise of the medieval city were laid.

1 H. ADAM, Das Zollwesen im fränkischen Reich und das spätkarolingische Wirtschaftsleben, 1996 (VSWG Supplement 126)   2 P. CONTAMINE i.a., L'économie médiévale, 1997, 41–80   3 H.-J. DREXHAGE, s.v. Handel, RAC 13, 519–574   4 P. GRIERSON, Commerce in the Dark Ages: a Critique of the Evidence, in: Transactions of the Royal Hist. Soc., 5th ser., V/8, 1959, 123–140   5 R. HODGES, Dark Age Economics, 1982   6 Mercati e mercanti nell'alto medioevo, 1993   7 H. PIRENNE, Mahomet et Charlemagne, 1937   8 H. SIEMS, Handel und Wucher im Spiegel frühma. Rechtsquellen, 1992   9 Untersuchungen zu Handel und Verkehr der vor- und frühgesch. Zeit in Mittel- und Nordeuropa, Vol. 1–6, 1985–1989 (AAWG)   10 A. VERHULST, Der Handel im Merowingerreich: Gesamtdarstellung nach schriftlichen Quellen, in: Antikvariskt arkiv 39, 1970, 2–54.   LU.KU.

Commercium primarily refers to commerce, but also to the right of productively engaging in certain legal transactions concerning the turnover of goods (Ulp. 19,5: *emendi vendendique invicem ius*) or to the status of being subject to private business law. The Latins of the Latin League had been entitled to *commercium* with the Romans since ancient times. Although it did not open all types of transactions to them, it gave them the important *mancipatio* (including the *testamentum per aes et libram*, (Ulp. 19,4). *Latini colonarii* and other *peregrini* could receive the commercium as an award. This practice partially extended the scope of the *ius civile* to non-citizens, a significant fact in the time before civil rights were universally granted in the *constitutio Antoniniana* (AD 212).

The term *commercium* is also embedded in the formula for the *interdictio* of the squanderer through the praetor: *ea re commercioque interdico* (Paulus, Sent. 3,4a,7). Private law could not extend to things that were removed from trade (*res extra commercium*; Inst. Just. Epit. 2,20,4; Dig. 20,3,1,2), such as sacred objects (*res divini iuris*), common property (*res communis omnium*) or state property (*res publica*). A different case altogether was an individual's lack of *commercium* concerning a specific item. In this case, the person in question could not gain possession of the item except through inheritance (Dig. 31,49,2; 41,1,62; 45,1,34). But if the heir lacked *commercium* for an item that did not belong to the *testator*, he then owed the common market value of the said item to the legatus (*aestimatio*; Dig. 31,49,3). Similarly, a stipulation debtor was liable if he lacked *commercium* (Dig. 45,1,34).

A. GUARINO, C. e ius commercii, Le origine quiritarie, 1973, 266–282; M. KASER, Ausgewählte Schriften I, 1976, 271–309; KASER, RPR I²; A. N. SHERWIN-WHITE, The Roman Citizenship, ²1973; WIEACKER.   P.A.

Commissioned poetry comes into being when a poet accepts an explicit (not merely implied) request by a power not identical with the → author (regarding rejection → *recusatio*) and is therefore always → occasional poetry. The request can come from a deity (inspiration), a ruler (→ court poetry), another individual (a), or a community (b). (a) Ancient tradition holds that Simonides of Ceos was the first to produce paid commissioned poetry (CP) with his *epinikia* in the 6th cent. BC (Schol. Aristoph. Pax 697b H.), followed by Pindar and Bacchylides [2. 46f.]. The trend towards professional poetry since the end of the archaic period drew criticism of what was perceived to be a perverted focus on material success. Aristophanes and Plato [3. 138–146] are early such critics, but later examples exist as well (Juv. 7,87 on Statius). Strict poetological maxims of this nature have shaped modern research, which tends to disregard the fact that request and payment have always played a critical role in a poet's existence since Homer's time [1]. The success of occasional poetry is a result of the poetic art to integrate heteronomous ideas. (b) Attic Tragedy is defined as occasional poetry because of its performance under the conditions of the agon which determined its outer framework [5. 19–29]. In Attic Tragedy, the citizens of the *polis* found a reflection of the constitutive elements that characterized their community [1], and for this the poets were rewarded. In Rome, occasional poetry was used in early times for the production of religious state celebrations: in 207 BC, the Senate appointed Livius Andronicus to compose a processional song for the 'expiation' of *prodigia* (Liv. 27,37,7). A publicly commissioned celebration song had been part of secular festivals ever since the *Ludi Tarentini* in 249 BC. In 17 BC, Horace accepted the commission for the *carmen saeculare* 6,32323,149 [4. 115–118].

1 J. M. BREMER, Poets and their Patrons, in: H. HOFMANN, A. HARDER (ed.), Fragmenta dramatica, 1991, 39–60 2 A. P. BURNETT, The Art of Bacchylides, 1985 3 J. DALFEN, Polis und Poiesis, 1974 4 E. DOBLHOFER, Horaz in der Forsch. nach 1957, 1992 5 J. LATACZ, Einführung in die griech. Trag., 1994. U.SCH.

Commius Celtic name ('nicely dressed'?) [1. 335–336]. Caesar installed the Atrebatian C. as king in 56 BC after conquering his tribe. When C. was sent to Britain in 55 BC to persuade the local tribes of entering an alliance with Caesar, he was first put into chains but released upon Caesar's arrival. He served Caesar as leader of the cavalry and as negotiator in Britain and in Gallia and in return was granted rulership over the → Morini and others (Caes. B Gall. 4,21,6–8; 27,2–3; 35,1; 5,22,3; 6,6,4; 7,76,1).

In 52 BC, C. changed sides and attempted to come to the aid of → Vercingetorix in front of Alesia. Following this, he proceeded to lead the Belgae in several battles against the Romans. An attack on his life instigated by T. → Labienus left him severely wounded yet able to escape. In 51 BC, he and → Correus joined forces in the last great revolt against Caesar, for which he recruited Germanic troops. After Correus' defeat and death, he fled to the Germans and continued the fight alone until he finally gained assurance from M. → Antonius that he could reside at a designated location without ever having to lay eyes on a Roman again (Caes. B Gall.7,75,5; 76,3–6; 79,1; 8,6,2; 7,5; 10,4; 23,3–7; 47–48; Cass. Dio 40,42,1; 43,3). After a short time, he appears to have fled to Britain with part of his tribe (Frontin. 2,13,11). His name appears on the coins of the → Atrebates of the mainland as well as of the south-east of Britain, coins that were produced by his sons Tincommius, Epillus and Verica, among others [2. 427–428; 3. 35–54].

1 EVANS 2 B. COLBERT DE BEAULIEU, Monnaies Gauloises au nom des chefs ment. dans les Communautes de César, in: Hommages A. Grenier, 1962, 419–446 3 R. P. MACK, The Coinage of Ancient Britain, 1964.

S. C. BEAN, The coinage of the British Atrebates. The sons of C., in: Act. XIe Congr. int. numismatique, vol. 3, 1993,1–5; F. MÜNZER, s.v. C., RE 4, 770–771. W.SP.

Commodianus Christian Latin poet of unknown origin (it is doubtful that the name in the title of the *Instructiones* = Inst. 2,35, *nomen Gasei*, is original and that it refers to the real Gaza; it could be regarded as a display of modesty by the 'sinner' according to Amos 1,6f.). The dating varies between the 3rd cent. (mention of *Gothi*, Carmen apologeticum 810, problematic loss of faith during the persecution of Christians, cf. the discussion in Africa under Cyprianus after 250) and the 5th cent. (reference to the seizure of Rome by Alaric in 410?). In 480, C. is mentioned by Gennadius (Vir. ill. 15). The earlier dating is more plausible considering the archaic dogma, the polemics against 'Judaist idolatry' (Inst. 1,37), and the consistent chiliasm (in regard to Rome's battles with the newly emerged empire of the Sassanids?). Furthermore, the decidedly anti-classical form and language of the poems which were written predominantly in accentuated hexameters (→ Metrics) reveal a hostile attitude towards the Greco-Roman culture, not inability (cf. → Tertullian's prose style). Literary records: (1) Two bks of *Instructiones* with 45 and 35 short acrostical mnemonic poems respectively. Bk. one offers apologetic arguments against 'heathens' (e.g. Inst. 1,15, euhemeristic arguments against the cult of Hercules in Rome, with reference to Verg. Aen. 8,184–305) and against Jews, bk. two contains practical rules of conduct for Christians (e.g. 2.8 on *miles Christi*). (2) The *Carmen apologeticum* (or *Carmen de duobus populis*, sc. about the Jews and the Christians; 1,060 hexameters) contains harsh criticisms of 'heathen' cults and of lax morals, presents a strictly ascetic position, and threatens the end of the world as an expression of god's wrath. C. frequently refers to the Bible but is also acquainted with classical Roman writings, especially Virgil.

ED.: J. MARTIN, CCL 128, 1960; A. SALVATORE, 1965–1968 (instructiones 1–2).
LIT.: L. KRESTAN, s.v. C., RAC 3,248–252; K. THRAEDE, Beiträge zur Datier. C.', in: JbAC 2, 1959, 90–114; J. FONTAINE, Naissance de la poésie dans l'occident chrétien, 1981, 39–52; D. NORBERG, La versification de C., in: Munera philologica et historica Mariano Plezia oblata, 1988, 141–146. K.SM.

Commodus Roman emperor in AD 180–192. Son of Marcus Aurelius and Faustina II. He was born on 31 August 161 in a villa near Lanuvium. His twin brother T. Aurelius Fulvus Antoninus died at the age of four (PIR² A 1512). His name was originally L. Aurelius Commodus. On 12 October 166 he and his brother both received the title of Caesar: L. Aurelius Commodus Caesar. He was thereby designated as the natural successor, and the ideological concept of → adoptive emperorship was avoided altogether. For the same purpose, he was admitted into all priestly colleges and designated as *princeps iuventutis* (HA Comm. 12,1; 2,1). In 175, Marcus Aurelius took him to the Danube in the war against the Germans. After Avidius Cassius' revolt, C. accompanied his father to the east for the purpose of securing the rulership. On their return on 23 December 176, C. — now already equipped with the title of *imperator* — and his father celebrated a triumph over the Germans and Sarmatians (HA Comm. 2,4; 12,5). *Cos. ord.*177. At the age of 15, C. was the youngest consul ever to have been nominated until that time. In the same year, perhaps on 1 January, he was awarded the *tribunicia potestas*. From that time on, he was also named *Augustus* and → *pater patriae*; the complete name being Caesar L. Aelius Aurelius C. Augustus. The only title withheld from him was *pontifex maximus* (cf. e.g. RMD III 185), emphasizing his role as his father's co-emperor. Before again taking C. to the Danube into the battle against the Germans in 178, Marcus Aurelius married C. to Bruttia Crispina (Cass. Dio 71,33,1; HA Comm. 12,6). Before his death, he recommended C. to the friends who had gathered and to the army commanders.

Having become *cos. II* in 179, C. served five additional times as consul during the time of his single rule (after 17 March 180). He received eight emperor acclamations (*imp. VIII*186); after 182, he bore the victor's title of Germanicus maximus, after 184, he was Britannicus as well. After late 182/early 183, he bore the epithet Pius, and after 185, with the overthrow of the praetorian praefectus Perennis, Felix as well (HA Comm. 8,1). After 180, he bore the following name: Imperator Caesar M. Aurelius Commodus Antoninus Augustus, which pointed to the close connection with his father. In the first few months of the year 191 [1. 866ff.], he changed his name to Imperator Caesar L. Aelius Aurelius Commodus Augustus in order to align himself with the figure of L. Verus and his brand of emperorship.

After Marcus Aurelius' death, C. remained at the border of the Danube for only a short time. He made peace with the Marcomanni, Quadi, Dacians and Burii, supposedly in defiance of his father's military advisors. But this interpretation depends on the question whether Marcus Aurelius had actually planned to establish two new provinces north of the Danube (cf. [2. 389ff.; 3. 473ff.; 4. 254f.]. The borders remained quiet during his rule. However, unrest emerged in Gallia, Upper Germany, Africa and Dacia, the most serious of which became known as *bellum desertorum* [5. 367ff.]. C. himself had little or no interest in leading the empire. Even the decision for peace may largely have been a result of his wish to return to Rome and to conduct his life there according to his private interests. Accordingly, he left politics and the empire to others during most of his rule, first only to the praetorian praefects Tarrutienus Paternus and Tigidius Perennis as well as to the *cubicularius* Saoterus, then to M. Aurelius Cleander, finally to the praetorian praefects Eclectus and Aemilius Laetus and his *concubina* Marcia. Saoterus, Cleander and Eclectus had previously been slaves. While Perennis first insti-

gated the removal of Saoterus, then the removal of Paternus, he was exposed himself by C. supposedly because of a mutiny among British troops. Cleander was sacrificed by C. to an intrigue instigated by the *praef. annonae* Aurelius Papirius Dionysius.

As the first emperor 'born to the purple' (cf. Hdn. 1,5,6) and much in contrast to his father, C. found himself in a tense relationship with the Senate from early on, at the latest since the conspiracy of 182 in which his sister Lucilla had participated. Many senators were executed (again starting in 187 and in the year 192), so were several high-ranking knights, primarily praetorian praefects, but also members of the imperial family, including his wife, Bruttia Crispina. Many lived in fear of his unpredictable outbursts. Some of the executions evidently were motivated by lack of money, due on the one hand to the actions of his favourites, on the other hand to his extreme passion for fights in the amphitheatre. C. even presented himself in the arena in the guise and with the attributes of Hercules (Cass. Dio 72,17-19). His religious mysticism drew him to many cults such as that of Isis, Serapis, Mithras and Iupiter Dolichenus, some of which even appeared on Roman imperial coins. C. regarded himself as *auctor pietatis* (BMC Emp. IV 809. 818). Above all, however, he worshipped Hercules, whom he tried to resemble ever more closely until he finally became 'Hercules Romanus' (Cass. Dio 72,15,6. 20,2f.). The Senate accepted him as a god and established a *flamen Herculaneus Commodianus* for him. The city of Rome was renamed after C., as if he had been the founder, as Colonia Lucia Aurelia Nova Commodiana, and the Senate, the population of Rome as well as local decurions received his name (cf. ILS 400). On 31 December 192, C. was removed through an intrigue by Eclectus, Aemilius Laetus and Marcia: the wrestler Narcissus strangled him in his bath after poison had not worked. It is doubtful whether the murder of C. was, as the sources suggest, an improvised reaction to C.'s plan to murder the *consules ordinarii* of 193. It is more likely that it was a carefully prepared conspiracy (cf. [6. 81ff.]). At first, the memory of C. was erased (→ *damnatio memoriae*), but his body was laid to rest in the *mausoleum Hadriani* by Pertinax (CIL VI 902). The erasure of his name was revoked when → Septimius Severus included him in his genealogy and declared him divine (HA Comm. 17,11).

1 C. Letta, in: Latomus 54, 1995 2 G. Alföldy, in: R. Klein (ed.), Marc Aurel, 1979 3 A. R. Birley, in: see 2 4 Id., Marcus Aurelius², 1987 5 G. Alföldy, in: BJ 171, 1971 6 A. R. Birley, The African Emperor Septimius Severus, 1988².

F. Grosso, La lotta politica al tempo di Commodo, 1964; H. G. Pflaum, La valeur d'information historique de la vita Commodi à la lumière des personnages nommément cités par le biographe, in: Bonner Historica-Augusta-Colloquium, 1970, 1972, 199ff.; M. R. Kaiser-Raiss, Die stadtröm. Münzprägung während der Alleinherrschaft des C., 1980.
COINS: BMC Emp. IV, 641ff.
STATUES AND PORTRAITS: M. Wegner, Das röm. Herrscherbild II 4, 1939.; Fittschen/Zanker, I 81ff. W.E.

Communication

A. Preliminary remarks   B. The spread of
Greek and Latin in antiquity   C. From oral
to written culture   1. Law and rhapsody
2. Scribe   3. Inscriptions   4. Written recording of laws   D. Inscriptions and monuments as aids for education and propaganda   E. Rhetoric

A. Preliminary remarks

The study of communication 'deals with the problems of interhuman communication and all related phenomena' [1]. It has a broad agenda which cannot be
considered here in all of its diverse aspects. This article
focuses on the eminent aspect of linguistic communication whose widespread manifestations can only receive selective attention. Ancient theories of signs and
philosophical theories of communication (→ Philosophy of language), for instance, will not be addressed.

B. The spread of Greek and Latin in an-
tiquity

The communicative capacity of a language depends
primarily on its (geopolitically determined) reach. The
most widely used languages during the Roman imperial
period, Greek and Latin, both of high cultural significance, originally emerged under very different conditions on their path to success. Early Greek consisted of
several local dialects that were intelligible amongst each
other. From the 8th to the 5th cents., waves of colonization originated from the city states and swept to all
coastal regions of the Mediterranean, the Propontis and
the Black Sea (founding of new city states; → Colonization), and contributed to the further spread of Greek.
The Ionic dialect originated from Chalcis, Eretria, Phocaea and Miletus, and took hold on the Black Sea, on
the Propontis, in Campania, in northern Sicily and in
southern Gallia. Doric spread through Northern Africa
(Cyrenaeica), in southern Sicily, and in Calabria, while
Aeolic spread through Lucania and Campania. Furthermore, Greek spread from these widely scattered city
states more or less deeply into the hinterland. During
the course of the 5th cent., the Attic-Ionic dialect became predominant. It became the administrative language in the Macedonian kingdom in the 4th cent.. Following Alexander the Great's conquest, this public
form of Greek (→ Koine) became the language of the
Greek cities founded by him or founded after his death
in Asia Minor, Syria, Mesopotamia and Egypt, as well
as the administrative language in the kingdoms of the
→ Diadochi [2; 3]. The elites of the conquered peoples,
at least, were forced to learn the Greek language and
had to strive towards cultural approach. Thus, the
Greek koine grew into a kind of lingua franca in the
eastern parts of the Roman Empire and in the western
Greek colonies. The Romans acknowledged that the
Greeks were in the lead culturally, a fact that motivated
upper-class Romans to strive towards bilingualism
from the beginning of the Republic until about AD 250

and allowed the Greek city states in the subjugated
regions to largely govern themselves.

Latin, on the other hand, began as the language of
the then small and insignificant city of Rome, founded
around 600 (the Varronic founding date of 753 BC is no
longer accepted today [4. 28, 51–54]), without any dia-
lectal relationships to other Italian languages, perhaps
with the exception of Faliscan. During the rapid spread
of Roman dominance, the Latin language also spread to
all the regions where Romans had taken hold, by way of
the troops being stationed there, the settlement of
Roman colonies in the subjugated areas, and the establishment of Latin as the administrative language. The
predominance of Latin did not come to an end until its
transition into the Romance languages [5]. It was revived again in the European Middle Ages as the language of the Church and of intellectuals.

The domination of Greek and Latin combined with
the bilingualism of the Roman upper class that lasted
for more than 300 years served to facilitate not only the
administration of the many peoples that were joined
during the Roman imperial period, but also the communication of the foreign peoples amongst each other,
aside from its economic influence.

The spread of the two languages was greatly aided
by high quality means of transportation. Originally, the
Greeks' main means of transportation had been the
ship. The organizational genius of the Romans, on the
other hand, resulted in a network of well-built roads
(→ viae publicae) not only for the immediate surroundings, or Italy, but in all conquered areas, during the
imperial period even in those regions still dominated by
the Greek language. Equipped with milestones, the
Roman roads stretched from Britain to Syria and from
Spain to Germania and the Balkans. There is no reference to a central administration for road construction
(curatores viarum) until the Republic's last cent. [6].
The roads not only served the movement of troops but
also → commerce and, especially during the imperial
period, aided in the quick and well-organized dissemination of news. Messenger service (cursus velox) was
only used for the transmission of military and administrative information, not for private letters. Later, a service for the transport of goods (cursus clabularis) was
established (→ cursus publicus). Passenger service required imperial permission letters (→ diploma).
Hadrian expanded the establishment of state postal
routes to all provinces (→ Postal services). In the later
imperial period, more and more private individuals
used the state passenger service. The speed of the cursus
publicus was about 75 km per day given relatively favourable weather and road conditions (e.g. on mostly
flat ground); additional detailed information and
sources in [7; 8; 9]. From the 4th cent. on, roads were no
longer always in good condition, not even when the
emperor himself was travelling on them [10. 88].

C. From oral to written culture

The original form of communication in Rome and in the Greek city states was purely oral. One must consider that these cities occupied a very limited area in early times. All citizens could easily walk from the periphery to the city centre to reach the agora or the forum. The Greek → alphabet (or rather the at first regionally different attempts at adapting the Phoenician alphabet to Greek) probably came into being in the first half of the 8th cent. The form and sequence of the letters in the Latin alphabet was adopted from the Etruscans, who in turn used the Greek alphabet with slight variations, around the end of the 7th cent. However, writing did not begin to play a significant role in the Greek and Latin cultural realms until cents. later, both in internal as well as external communication.

An important form of internal communication was jurisdiction, which is — concerning Greece — a particularly interesting object of study in its transition from oral to written culture. The first manifestations of writing aside from archaic poetry are inscriptions stemming from the realm of law.

1. Law and rhapsody

Literary records refer to → Zaleucus from the Greek colony of Locri in southern Italy (1st half of the 7th cent. BC) as the first to have committed laws to writing (Ephoros, FGrH 70 F 138–139 = Str. 6,1,8). He is also mentioned by Aristotle, together with → Charondas of Catana, who came along a little later and whose laws were introduced in Rhegium as well as in the other Chalcidic colonies of lower Italy and Sicily, even spreading through Asia Minor (Str. 12,2,9 regarding the city of Mazaca in Cappadocia). Ephorus (FGrH 70 F 139), on the other hand, traces the origin of Zaleucus' legislation to Crete, Sparta and Athens. He names Crete as (FGrH 70 F 149 = Str. 10,4,19; cf. Aristot. Pol. 2,10–12, 1271b–1274b) the residence of the Spartan legislator → Lycurgus, where he was introduced to Rhadamanthys' and Minos' tradition of jurisdiction by → Thaletas (or Thales), a poet and musician well versed in law (the two professions were not separated in early times). While a sceptical view of the mythical and tendentious details in this source is well justified, the statement that the legislature of Zaleucus and Lycurgus depended on Cretan sources nevertheless contains a core of historical truth [11. 139–155] (cf. Hdt. 1,65; Aristot. Pol. 2,12,6, 1274a). The archaeological finds confirm this assessment. According to L.H. Jeffery [12. 43, 76, 188–189, 209 No 7; 11. 141], Crete possesses many more relics of legal inscriptions than any other Greek region. Some of these inscriptions stem from the 7th cent. BC, all of them go back to oral tradition.

A personality such as Thaletas embodies the characteristics of the wise man in his combined qualities of poet, musician and legal expert (μελοποιὸς ἀνὴρ καὶ νομοθετικός: Ephorus in Str. 10,4,19). According to archaic thinking, the divinely inspired → rhapsodes expressed his eminent position and function as the leader of souls through his ability to memorize things from far in the past by giving early events and wise sayings a melodic form that was easy to remember. Verses, maxims and the rhetorical speech of later times were all known to educate psychagogically, an effect that was regarded as highly significant until the end of antiquity [13. 1–13, 16–20] (cf. Plut. Lycurgus 4,2–3).

The texts suggest the existence of an oral tradition for legislature which was handed down from generation to generation (similar to what is known in the Scandinavian region [11. 144]): Strabo (12,2,9) tells of the Cappadocian city of Mazaca, which had adopted the laws of Charondas, and reports that there existed the office of a singer of laws (νομῳδός, nomoidós) who also had to explain the laws. Stobaeus, who used excerpts from the prooemium of Charondas for his legislature (Anthologium 4,2,24 Hense, vol. 2, p. 154 l. 22 — p. 155 l. 2), tells of a requirement contained therein that all citizens had to learn this prooemium by heart and could be called upon to recite it after the singing of the paean at public festivals (probably in musical form), so that its recommendations would be well committed to memory. Aelianus (var. 2,39) also mentions that freeborn Cretan children had to learn the laws — embedded in melodies — by heart, so that the music could unfold its guiding power over the soul ([11. 144f.; 13. 10–13; 14. 436–441]; cf. Mart. Cap. De nuptiis 9,926, Ps.Aristot. Problemata 19,28,919b–920a). As far as the Roman region is concerned, Cicero (Leg. 2,59,5) reports from his own childhood that the → Tabulae Duodecim, the first written Roman laws (mid-5th cent. BC), had to be memorized by boys ut carmen necessarium (roughly: 'like a formula one had to know' [trans. K. Ziegler], although the translation of carmen into 'formula' does not quite do justice to the original sacred and magical aspect of the word).

2. Scribe

The existence of oral rhapsodic traditions in the legal and administrative realms finds further support in official titles such as hieromnémones ('those who have memorized the sacred rites') and mnémones ('those who remember'), titles that were later applied to scribes and archivists (Aristot. Pol. 6,8, 1321b 39). In a few inscriptions that bear testimony to these official titles, the difficult transition from oral to written culture is revealed (on the following, cf. [15]). A Cretan inscription [16] dating from about 500 BC obligates Spensithius and his sons 'to record for the city in Phoenician (or red) writing everything that concerns public affairs, both sacred and human, and to memorize them (mnamoneúein)', for which they received board and freedom from any impositions. This scribe shared an equal rank with the highest city officials (kósmoi), he held his post for life and could transfer it to his sons. Such preferential treatment can be explained by the fact that the ability to read and write was still very rare, at least in this apparently small and unknown city which is home to the inscription, even though inscriptions had existed for a while (since the 7th cent. on Crete).

A person equipped with this rare knowledge (although no longer endowed with the ethical and religious aura of the rhapsodes) held a position of extraordinary power. A good example of this is Maeandrius, the secretary of the tyrant → Polycrates of Samos: after the fall of his master he placed exorbitant demands on the citizens of Samos, which however brought ruin on him (Hdt. 3,123; 142–148). Around the same time, the → scribe was also highly respected among the Etruscans: when the Roman C. Mucius Cordus Scaevola entered the enemy camp in order to kill the Etruscan king Porsenna, he instead struck dead the scribe who was seated on the elevated commander's chair next to the king, dressed in almost equal splendour (Liv. 2,12,7).

Other Cretan inscriptions (from → Gortyn) also retained the antiquated professional title of *mnámōn* for scribes or secretaries of various officials [15.84], a title still left from the oral epoch (inscriptions of Gortyn, col. 9,32 and 11,52–53 [23]) and indicative of a significance they still held in Aristotle's writings (see above). Two inscriptions on the Ionian Erythrae [17. 1 no. 1 and 17] contain rules that strictly limit the secretary's period of office with the intention of preventing abuse of the power that came with the knowledge of documents. At the same time, these inscriptions reveal that a certain number of literate individuals was available to hold these offices in the small city of Erythrae from the 4th cent. at the latest [15. 89–91].

3. INSCRIPTIONS

It is still debated whether or not and at what time the centrally placed inscriptions were accessible to the majority of citizens, in other words, to what degree the population knew how to read and to write. We can assume that a high cultural level was achieved in the first four centuries of the Roman imperial period due to the relatively wide distribution of convenient writing materials (→ Papyrus; → cera). It is doubtful, however, that the lower classes were able to do more than laboriously decipher a few words and write their own names. In regard to laws (and also to honorary inscriptions), both the Greek and the Roman realms maintained for a long time that a law was officially enacted only after it was read publicly. Then, the law was chiselled on a stele of rock, engraved on metal plates, or written on whitewashed wooden boards in black or red paint and displayed in public. As we can gather from an inscription from Teos (470–460 BC; cf. [18]), the public reading of previously published law inscriptions had to be repeated under certain circumstances, evidencing the fact that a certain percentage of the population was illiterate. Over time, duplicates (at first mostly made of wood) were kept in archives, among which the imperial archives stood out due to their strict organization.

4. WRITTEN RECORDING OF LAWS

The written recording of laws had the advantage of largely protecting jurisdiction from arbitrary alterations by influential individuals or factions, regardless of the fact that common people could not read them. From the 5th cent. on, but often even earlier, city communities handed over to scribes sacred and customary laws which had originally been handed down orally and, in Greece, in rhapsodic form to be recorded in writing. The functional designations *hieromnémōn*, *mnámōn*, *poinikastás*, *grapheús* or *grammateús* in inscriptions or literary texts emphasized now the memory, now the literacy, now the archivist work of the officials in question, while the functions themselves were always the same. Written recordings enabled a wide distribution of laws (for example those of Charondas) and made it possible that the Roman Law of Twelve Tables referred to the legislature of → Solon (Liv. 3,31,8; 32,1–6; Gell. NA 20,1,4; Cic. Leg. 2,23,59; 25,64).

The written recording and publication of the Law of Twelve Tables and other laws was the result of a decade-long argument between the patricians and the people's tribunes, and must be regarded as a plebeian achievement (Liv. 3,31,7–37,4). Little is known about scribes or secretaries from early Roman times. A single record concerns the scribe Cn. → Flavius [I 2], whose election to the office of curule aedile in 304 was rejected because scribes were not allowed to exercise such a function. Following this, he is said to have resigned his occupation and subsequently was confirmed as aedile (Gell. NA 7,9,2–5; Liv. 9,46,1–12). The knowledge gained as scribe enabled Cn. Flavius to write a book about the proceedings in court cases, information which previously had only been accessible to the nobility. He also initiated the publication of the → calendar on the forum on whitewashed wooden boards, indicating the days when court cases could take place.

It is furthermore significant that the Senate's decision of 186 BC on the Bacchanalia contains the first law that had to be publicly displayed in all of Italy, not just in Rome (→ senatus consultum de Bacchanalibus).

D. INSCRIPTIONS AND MONUMENTS AS AIDS FOR EDUCATION AND PROPAGANDA

Aside from their legal significance, inscriptions also played an important role in education and propaganda until the end of antiquity [14. 441–444]. The popular honorary inscriptions which the cities decided upon and paid for and which were often combined with the erection of a statue, a bust, or an honorary sign, often served educational purposes as well: they were supposed to be an incentive for fellow citizens to earn similar rewards for themselves. Moral maxims such as the sayings of the → Seven Sages were 'published' on inscriptions. They were first displayed in the temple area of the Delphian Apollo in duplicate form: once in a short series of five maxims, then, starting no later than the 3rd cent., in a series of 140 maxims. The long series was copied by → Clearchus [5] of Soli, a student of Aristotle's, who had the series chiselled into a stele of stone in a Greek city located on the Oxus in Bactria (today's Afghanistan) and erected in a central location [19]. The long series was also displayed in stone in Miletoupolis in Mys around 300 BC, while the short series had already found its place in the gymnasium of Thera in the

4th cent. These are only individual surviving examples of the widely common practice to use inscriptions as a means for the collective guidance of souls. Such inscriptions sometimes resulted from private initiative, such as (according to Ps.-Pl. Hipparch. 228d–229b) the herms by → Hipparchus [1] (6th cent. BC) that were erected along roads, and especially the monumental philosophical inscription by the Epicurean → Diogenes [18] in Asia Minor's Oenoanda (2nd cent. AD) [14. 441–444].

Imperial propaganda had a preference for inscriptions but also used different monuments of stone: buildings (→ Ara Pacis Augustae), triumphal arches and pictorial columns (e.g. Trajan's and Marcus Aurelius' columns in Rome). Regarding propaganda inscriptions, the single one that must be mentioned is the summary of Augustus' deeds (*Res gestae Divi Augusti*), which originally was engraved on two iron pillars in front of Augustus' mausoleum in Rome (lost today). A well-preserved copy with Greek translation was found engraved in stone in Ancyra (Ankara) and the remnants of two other copies were found in Apollonia in Pisidia (Greek translation only) as well as in Antioch (Pisidia; Latin text only). We can assume that copies of the *Res gestae* could be found originally in all bigger cities of the Roman empire. Busts and statues of each of the emperors, perhaps also of their wives and children, were very common, not to mention the numerous pictorial coins and coin legends. It is doubtful that the messages on the coins could always be understood by the masses [20. 254–257]. All of these manifestations fulfilled a function similar to that of today's mass media.

E. RHETORIC

In the 5th cent. BC in Greece, a new means of communication emerged whose long-lasting significance for the Mediterranean cultures cannot be overstated: → rhetoric, a collection of rules concerning argumentation, disposition and style of a speech, and also concerning the arousal of affects in the listener. Enhancing gestures (→ Gestus) and changes in the tone of voice were carefully practised. If deemed necessary for a court case, crying, underaged children of the defendant or other such dramatic elements were brought onto the rostrum, so that a speech was not only an acoustical and aesthetic experience, but became a veritable spectacle. The combination of rational with irrational elements could result in a distortion or relativist qualification of the true facts: the objectively weaker side could appear to be the stronger side of the argument through rhetorical means. The technical aspects of speech therefore became indispensable tools in public court cases and in political speeches in front of the public assembly, both in the Greek and Roman areas. The art (τέχνη, *téchnē*) was taught by the sophists in Greece in the 5th cent., wandering teachers who were not content with private lessons but gave demonstrative speeches about a variety of topics and spoke to the gathering masses at public assemblies or at the numerous Greek religious festivals.

They enjoyed great success and were richly rewarded. The success with the public never abated in all of antiquity. Starting no later than in the 2nd cent. BC, private schools of rhetoric flourished in many Greek cities. The upper class regarded these schools in combination with the also private grammar schools as an indispensable supplement to the generally elemental instruction in the Hellenistic → gymnasion.

In Rome, rhetoric was met with hesitant acceptance; it gradually became one of the subjects for upper-class instruction not until the middle of the 2nd cent. Even in the Latin realm, lessons were first held in Greek by Greek teachers (at times prisoners of war [21]) and relied on Greek textbooks. The beginning of the 1st cent BC saw the first attempts to teach rhetoric in Latin, but they were put to an end by the edicts of censors (92 BC; cf. Gell. NA 15,11) in response to upper-class fears that Latin instruction of rhetoric would make it accessible to the common people who would thereby gain greater influence in public life. However, this did not prevent Latin rhetorical instruction from becoming common soon thereafter, namely with Cicero (106–43 BC). Cicero's speeches became a subject of instruction, his textbooks *De inventione, Partitiones oratoriae* and *Topica* contained Greek teaching materials in Latin terminology. The anonymous *Rhetorica ad Herennium*, written around 50 BC, is another example of the unstoppable breakthrough of Latin rhetoric. Yet even towards the end of the Republic, Greek rhetors still came to Rome in large numbers, and the members of the upper class routinely sent their sons to Greece and into the Greek cities of Asia Minor to receive the finishing touches in rhetorical skill. A good education in rhetoric now frequently replaced the advantages of aristocratic birth and wealth, and in the imperial period gave professional rhetors the chance to advance into the highest state offices. Even philosophers who followed Plato's dislike of rhetoric were soon forced to admit that philosophical instruction could not get by without rhetoric, considering that the guidance of souls was part of it [22. 44–52; 13. 184–189; 14. 452]. Rhetoric combined with grammar and occasionally philosophy were the few educational subjects that were still taught after the decline of the Hellenistic gymnasium in the imperial period by teachers who were employed by the cities according to an imperial rule [22. 215–261].

→ Letter; → Gestures; → Prayer; → Intertextuality; → Cryptography; → Literary activity; → Communications; → Recitations; → Spectacles; → Competitions, artistic

1 R. SCHNELLE, s.v. K.-Forsch., HWdPh vol. 4, 897f. 2 K. STRUNK, Vom Mykenischen bis zum klass. Griech., in: H.-G. NESSELRATH (ed.), Einl. in die griech. Philol., 1997, 135–155 3 R. BROWNING, Von der Koine bis zu den Anfängen der modernen Griech., in: H.-G. NESSELRATH (ed.), Einl. in die griech. Philol., 1997, 156–168 4 K. CHRIST, Röm. Gesch., 1980 5 J. KRAMER, Gesch. der lat. Sprachen, in: F. GRAF (ed.), Einl. in die lat. Philol., 1997, 115–162 6 L. M. HARTMANN, s.v. Cura, RE 4, 1767 7 G. REINCKE, s.v. Nachrichtenwesen, RE 16,

1496–1541   8 W. KUBITSCHEK, s.v. Itinerarien, RE 9, 2308–2363   9 R. CHEVALLIER, Voyages et déplacements dans l'Empire Romain, 1988   10 H. HALFMANN, Itinera principum. Gesch. und Typologie der Kaiserreisen im Röm. Reich, 1986   11 G. CAMASSA, Aux origines de la codification écrite des lois en Grèce, in: M. DETIENNE (ed.), Les savoirs de l'écriture en Grèce ancienne, 1988, 130–155   12 L. H. JEFFERY, Archaic Greece. The City-States c. 700–500 B.C., 1976   13 I. HADOT, Seneca und die griech.-röm. Trad. der Seelenleitung (Quellen und Studien zur Gesch. der Philos. 13), 1969   14 Id., The Spiritual Guide, in: A. H. ARMSTRONG (ed.), Classical Mediterranean Spirituality, 1986, 436–559   15 F. RUZÉ, Aux débuts de l'écriture politique: Le pouvoir de l'écrit dans la cité, in: M. DETIENNE (ed.), Les savoirs de l'écriture en Grèce ancienne, 1988, 82–94   16 L. H. JEFFERY, A. MORPURGO-DAVIES, Ποινικαστάς and Ποινικαζεν: BM 1969.4-2.1, A New Archaic Inscription from Crete, in: Kadmos 9, 1970, 118–154   17 IEry   18 P. HERRMANN, Teos und Abdera im 5. Jh.v.Chr., in: Chiron 11, 1981, 1–30   19 L. ROBERT, De Delphes à l'Oxus: Inscriptions grecques nouvelles de la Bactriane, in: Comptes rendus de l'Académie des inscriptions et belles lettres, 1968, 416–457   20 H. KLOFT, Rel. und Geld. Funktionale und kommunikative Aspekte des Münzgeldes, in: G. BINDER, K. EHLICH (ed.), Religiöse K. — Formen und Praxis vor der Neuzeit. Stätten und Formen der K. im Alt. VI (Bochumer Alt.wiss. Colloquium vol. 26), 1997, 243–257   21 J. CHRISTES, Sklaven und Freigelassene als Grammatiker und Philologen im ant. Rom (Forschungen zur ant. Sklaverei vol. 10), 1979   22 I. HADOT, Arts libéraux et philosophie dans la pensée antique (Études Augustiniennes), 1984   23 R. F. E. WILLETTS, The Law Code of Gortyn, 1967.

G. ACHARD, La communication à Rome, 1991 (Petite Bibliothèque Payot 211, 1994); C. COULET, Communiquer en Grèce ancienne, 1996; Stätten und Formen der K. im Alt. I–VI, Bochumer Alt.wiss. Colloquium vol. 13, 16, 17, 23, 24, 26, 1993–1997.   I.H.

Communications

I. ANCIENT ORIENT   II. CLASSICAL ANTIQUITY

I. ANCIENT ORIENT

In the ancient Orient, oral and written messages (→ Letter) were transmitted by messengers. Messengers handled the supra-regional diplomatic traffic (e.g. the → Amarna letters between Egypt and Palaestine, Cyprus (→ Alaschia), Syria, the Hittite kingdom, Mittani, Assyria, Babylonia and Elam), forwarded political or military news (at times gained through espionage), handled interior administrative communication, and transmitted (private) information in the area of commerce. Aside from the messenger systems governed by the state, news was also transmitted by special representatives when needed or by commercial travellers.

In Mesopotamia, messages were written on clay tablets and then handed over to caravans for transport [1. 419]. During the 3rd dynasty of Ur (21st cent. BC), a well-organized messenger system served communication within and between the different provinces of the kingdom, as well as with outside regions. Travellers

entrusted with the transmission of messages received rations in the form of natural produce as travelling provisions and for use during rests or other stops along the way. The effective communication system of the Ur III period [2. 295–315] was supported by the use of donkeys as transport animals and through a network of roads with rest stations, probably constructed by King Šulgi. The palace archives of → Mari (19th/18th cents. BC) bear testimony to extensive communications traffic esp. regarding political and military information in old Babylonian times. The letters [3;4] delivered by messengers to the various royal courts (in central Syria, northern Syria, Babylonia, and Elam) contained, for instance, reports about an adversary's or partner's political intentions and moods, about the condition of the military units, and also about the movement of troops. The information was often gained from the recipient's confidants, as well as from more or less professional spies and informers [5. 38–40].

Records of correspondences found in Ninive (→ Ninus [2]) document the acquisition and transmission of political and military news from the border area between Assyria and Urartia during the time of the New Assyrian King Sargon II (722–705 BC) [6; 7]. A royal representative residing in the border area used a messenger to send the information gathered from scouts and informers about military operations and alliances, as well as internal political affairs of the Urartians, to the royal court, where it was analyzed [8]. The so-called → royal roads with special rest and exchange stations for the messengers [9] supported a well-organized and functioning messenger system for the transmission of information.

1 D. O. EDZARD, s.v. Karawane, RLA 5, 414–421   2 W. SALLABERGER, Ur III-Zeit (OBO 160/3), 1999, 121–390   3 R. W. FISHER, The Mubassir, Messengers at Mari, in: G. D. YOUNG (ed.), Mari in Retrospect, 1992, 113–120   4 B. LAFONT, Messagers et ambassadeurs dans les archives de Mari, in: D. CHARPIN, F. JOANNÈS (ed.), La circulation des biens, des personnes et des idées dans le Proche-Orient ancien, 1992, 67–183   5 J. SASSON, The Military Establishments at Mari, 1969   6 K. DELLER, Ausgewählte neuassyr. Briefe betreffend Urarṭu zur Zeit Sargons II., in: P. E. PECORELLA, M. SALVINI (ed.), Tra lo Zagros e l'Urmia, 1984, 97–122   7 G. B. LANFRANCHI, S. PARPOLA, The Correspondence of Sargon II, vol. 2, 1990   8 R. FOLLET, 'Deuxième Bureau' et information diplomatique dans l'Assyrie des Sargonides, in: Riv. degli studi orientali 32, 1957, 61–94   9 K. KESSLER, 'Royal Roads' and Other Questions of the Neo-Assyrian Communication System, in: S. PARPOLA, R. M. WHITING (ed.), Assyria 1995, 1997, 129–136.

E. OTTO, s.v. Bote, LÄ 1, 846–847; M. VALLOGGIA, s.v. Nachrichtenübermittlung, LÄ 4, 288–291; S. A. MEIER, The Messenger in the Ancient Semitic World, 1988.   H.N.

II. CLASSICAL ANTIQUITY
A. DEFINITION B. TRANSMISSION OF MESSAGES
1. STATE TRANSMISSION 2. PRIVATE
TRANSMISSION 3. METHODS AND SPEEDS OF
LOCOMOTION C. DISSEMINATION OF
INFORMATION D. THE ACQUIRING OF
INFORMATION 1. POLITICAL AND MILITARY
INFORMATION 2. GEOGRAPHICAL AND TACTICAL
MILITARY INTELLIGENCE

A. DEFINITION

The concept of communications comprises all technical and organizational installations and processes used for the transmission, dissemination, and gathering of any type of information. Aside from oral and written messages, Greek and Roman antiquity also made use of information that could be grasped and transmitted optically.

B. TRANSMISSION OF MESSAGES
1. STATE TRANSMISSION

The transmission of information governed by the state comprised the three forms of messages named above and served the purpose of transporting them using a variety of methods. Compared to modern means of communication, only few technical aids for the forwarding of information were known in antiquity. The transmission of oral and written messages therefore relied almost exclusively on messengers. Different ancient states used various specialized ways to organize their messenger systems in order to grant their governments efficient systems of forwarding information. The use of other, more technical procedures seems to have played a much smaller role in ancient communications.

a) MESSENGERS

Communication between the Greek poleis was achieved with the aid of ἡμεροδρόμοι/hēmerodrómoi, 'day runners' (Hdt. 6,105) who could cover long distances as indicated by their name, or δρομοκήρυκες/ dromokérykes, 'express messengers' (Aen. Tact. 22,3; Aeschin. 2,130). Generally, they travelled on foot. For the quick transmission of important messages over long distances, or for the transport of money, persons and festival delegations, Athens used special triremes of the fleet, the so-called 'sacred' state ships Salaminía and Páralos (Thuc. 3,77,3; 8,74,1).

In Rome, functionaries and state representatives used specialized state personnel for the transmission of official messages and correspondence. During Republican times, private messengers were used as well. The latter either came from the households of magistrates (Cic. Fam. 2,7,3) or were members of the large associations of leaseholders, the → publicani (Cic. Att. 5,16,1). State couriers included the → statores, viatores (→ viator), geruli ('carriers', in addition to the viatores messengers of magistrates from the capital, CIL VI 32294, and bearers of letters and files: Cod. Theod. 11,30,29; 31), cursores ('runners', 'couriers'), the emperors' ta-

bellarii (→ tabellarius), soldiers, and since the 4th cent. esp. the → agentes in rebus. All of these messengers were employed on behalf of the different departments of the Roman administration, as indicated in the inscription for a optio tabellariorum officii rationum from Rome (roughly: 'group leader of messengers for the financial office': CIL VI 8424a).

b) SPECIAL SYSTEMS

Records of special systems for the transmission of messages exist for a few ancient states ruled by dictators, who in some cases ruled over very large regions. Research refers to these institutions in an anachronistic manner as → postal services or state postal services. The three best-known systems are the Persian, documented for Cyrus [2] II (→ Angaria), founder of the empire, the Ptolemaic, revealed on papyri from the 3rd and 2nd. cents. BC, and the Roman imperial system, the → cursus publicus. There are also indications that specially established communications connections existed for the Asia Minor regions of Antigonus [1] Monophthalmos (Diod. Sic. 19,57,5) and for Macedon in the 2nd cent. BC (Liv. 40,56,11).

c) TECHNICAL METHODS

In contrast to today, the use of technical aids in the transmission of messages in ancient times was limited to → fleets and → armies; the sources indicate hardly any civilian methods at all. Even the military only used certain methods in special situations or in certain geographic regions. A few less extravagant means such as encryption methods in messages (→ Cryptography) were probably used by private citizens as well.

When it came to short distances, written messages could be sent with the aid of projectiles: on spears (Caes. B Gall. 5,48) or in arrow shafts (Aen. Tact. 31,26f.). Furthermore, we know of the use of animals as news transmitters. Not only dogs (Aen. Tact. 31,32) but also birds were used, esp. pigeons and swallows (Plin. HN 10,34). Birds in particular were not only used as carriers of written messages, but also as simple harbingers, for instance as a sign of the impending arrival of travellers [1]. Due to the small number of records we cannot clearly determine to what extent carrier pigeons were used. In the military, the use of pigeons may have been limited to special emergency situations (such as the siege of Mutina: Plin. HN 10,53; Frontin. Strat. 3,13,7f.).

Aside from military commands (→ signa), signalling or → telegraphy transmitted simple messages by using optical or acoustical signals such as warning signals or calls for help through fire signals (Hom. Il. 18,207–214) on the one hand, or, on the other hand, it transmitted differentiated messages through light signals by way of the so-called synchronous telegraph or Polybius' letter code (10,44–47). The Roman army apparently did not much engage in such complex signalling for the transmission of messages. Veg. Mil. 3,5 shows the use of simple signal masts.

2. Private transmission

Since a postal service in the modern sense did not exist in antiquity, the senders themselves were responsible for organizing the sending of private letters and parcels. They had to find trustworthy individuals who travelled the desired route and were willing to take the additional freight with them. All travellers en route for business or private reasons were candidates, esp. merchants and hauliers. Soldiers gave their letters addressed home or to friends stationed elsewhere to comrades who had business at the desired destination. Even Cicero and his correspondents evidently had to rely on travellers to deliver their mail, esp. over long distances (cf. e.g. Cic. Fam. 4,9,1; 4,10,1; Cic. Att. 5,20,8), although wealthy households generally had their own messengers. There were also professional couriers who offered their paid services (→ tabellarius). The same conditions for the transmission of messages also applied to the Christian Church [2. 206–256]. Bishops used either their own slaves and servants for sending letters, or members of their presbyterium, or other travelling intermediaries whenever possible. Church authors complained about the frequent long delays in communication (e.g. Paul Nol. 20,1) which were a result of inconsistent transmission.

3. Methods and speeds of locomotion

Ancient messengers normally did their job of bringing messages on foot. This fact is indicated by designations such as the Greek hēmerodrómoi or the Latin cursores (see above II. bk.1.a). Furthermore, sources only mention the exact method of locomotion in cases of unusual speed. A normal traveller on foot covered on average of 20–30 km per day. Professional couriers, on the other hand, were expected to cover longer distances per day, esp. on shorter assignments. Cicero received letters on the same day in Astura, located 52 km away from Rome (Cic. Att. 12,39(37),1). Ovidius (Pont. 4,5,7) assumed that a messenger could cover the distance from Brundisium (Brindisi) to Rome (534 km) in nine days, thus travelling at a rate of 59 km per day. Messengers were faster, esp. over long distances, if they could use means of transportation that could be exchanged regularly. The cursus publicus made this possible during the Roman imperial period. An example from the 4th cent. AD is the magister officiorum Caesarius, who travelled in great haste from Antioch to Constantinople in six days (1088 km), thus covering 181 km a day in a cart (raeda), usually harnessed to mules (Lib. Or. 21,12–16). Top speeds such as this could only be beaten by riders who frequently changed horses. According to Procop. Arc. 30,3–5, in this way riders were able to cover 10-day journeys (c. 300 km in one day). Such speeds were recorded because they were highly unusual and therefore cannot serve as a basis for calculating the average required time for ancient message transmission [3]. The time required could vary greatly from case to case, even in private delivery. Aside from the method of locomotion which was mainly dependent on the significance of the messages as well as

that of the recipient, the time required also depended on the distance, the condition of the route, the season, and — in official communication — on the manner in which business was conducted in particular offices, where documents were often delayed. Particularly large variations in time were also found for routes that included travel by sea [4. 402–403].

C. Dissemination of information

The dissemination of information comprises the transmission of general or current information to a specific or unspecified number of persons. If information is transmittted by order of the state, it could entail the sudden necessity of communicating facts to the population on the one hand, or on the other hand, regular announcements. In both cases, oral as well as written announcements or a combination thereof can be considered. Oral announcements were made in general by the town crier (κῆρυξ/kêryx, Lat. praeco) [5] if not by the official representatives themselves. They were made depending on the occasion, for example at assemblies of the citizenry, at festivals, in the theatre, on public squares (esp. in front of office buildings or sanctuaries) and could occur either spontaneously or regularly. Written announcements, on the other hand, offered the advantage of not being tied to the moment and did not require the presence of many persons.

For this reason, general announcements were first made available to the public — esp. when a response was desired — in written form through notices on whitewashed plates (Greek leúkōma, Lat. album: → Writing utensils) at popular locations (loco celeberrimo), in Egypt on → papyrus. In general, decisions made by the public assembly and the council meetings of communities, for example concerning newly elected magistrates, → senatus consulta as well as edicts by the Roman emperors, were published on such non-durable material. Only a small part of public announcements such as laws, international treaties, and festival calendars were set down on durable material (stone, bronze). Documents that were publicly preserved in this way served more than just administrative purposes. They enjoyed a timeless significance and their high-profile publication often served political purposes [6]. Documents exist for the Ptolemaic kingdom and the Roman empire that retrace the sequence of publications of an edict from the emperor to the periphery [7. 97–127]. It appears that the Roman emperors and the Senate regularly and voluminously informed the governors in the provinces about important decisions. It was the responsibility of the provincial governors to inform the population through edicts. The governor of Egypt, for example, either sent a circular letter with the order to publish an edict to the leaders of regional administrations, to epistrategoi or strategoi, or directly addressed the order to individual strategoi. The municipia and colonies of Italy, on the other hand, not always received general directions directly. They were responsible for obtaining their own information through their magistrates and delegates [8]. According to Suetonius (Iul. 20,1), Caesar introduced the publication of events that occurred in public courts and assemblies, the *acta populi* (→ *acta*), in the city of Rome in 59 BC, as well as the publication of Senate records, the *acta senatus*. These publications were probably not provided by way of a → newspaper, but more likely on a display [9].

Leaflets were distributed mostly for political purposes (Cass. Dio 51,10,2). Similarly, pictorial displays — the posters of today — were carried along in triumphal marches. Advertisements, on the other hand, for election candidates, sales ads, or announcements of gladiatorial games (→ *munus*), were usually painted on house walls; many of these were found in → Pompeii (s. CIL IV with suppl. 2 and 3; for a useful selection [10]).

D. THE ACQUIRING OF INFORMATION
1. POLITICAL AND MILITARY INFORMATION

For the purpose of collecting strategic political and military information about other, generally unfriendly states, the different ancient governments used the same organs and institutions: they primarily relied on friendly and allied peoples, client states, hospitality (esp. → *proxenía*), delegations (→ *legatus*), deserters, exiles, hostages, professional informers and spies (→ espionage) [11], merchants, and intercepted correspondence. Ancient records evidence these practices for classical Greece [12] as well as for the time of Alexander the Great [13] and the Imperium Romanum [14; 15]. Furthermore, ancient rulers also conducted interior investigations to protect themselves from conspiracies. In order to do so, they relied on confidants and favourites, in the Roman Empire on bodyguards, special troops and military ranks, as well as on *speculatores* (scouts), → *frumentarii*, → *agentes in rebus*.

2. GEOGRAPHICAL AND TACTICAL MILITARY INTELLIGENCE

For the reconnaissance of unknown or enemy territory, ancient governments tried to recruit knowledgeable local guides such as shepherds or hunters. The officers themselves often worked out the tactical and strategic reconnaissance esp. in the preparation of a battle, otherwise, this was accomplished by special patrols, riders, reconnaissance teams, or individual scouts (σκόποι/*skópoi*, → *exploratores*).

→ Letter; → Cursus publicus; → Communication; → Land transport; → Postal services; → Navigation; → Espionage; → Traffic

1 H. FISCHL, Die Brieftaube im Alt. und MA, Programm des kaiserl. humanistischen Gymnasiums Schweinfurt für das Schuljahr 1908/09, 1909, 1–38 2 D. GORCE, Les voyages, l'hospitalité et le port des lettres dans le monde chrétien des IVᵉ et Vᵉ siècles, 1925 3 A. M. RAMSAY, The Speed of the Roman Imperial Post, in: JRS 15, 1925, 60–74 4 JONES, LRE, vol. 1 5 J. OEHLER, s.v. Keryx, RE 11, 349–357 6 W. ECK, Administrative Dokumente. Publikation und Mittel der Selbstdarstellung, in: Id., Die Verwaltung des Röm. Reiches in der hohen Kaiserzeit, vol. 2, 1998, 359–381 7 F. VON SCHWIND, Zur Frage der Publikation im Röm. Recht, ²1972 8 W. ECK, Zur

Durchsetzung von Anordnungen und Entscheidungen in der hohen Kaiserzeit, in: Id., Die Verwaltung des Röm. Reiches in der hohen Kaiserzeit, vol. 1, 1995, 55–79 9 P. WHITE, Julius Caesar and the Publication of Acta in Late Republican Rome, in: Chiron 27, 1997, 73–84 10 K.-W. WEEBER, Decius war hier…, 1996 11 J. A. RICHMOND, Spies in Ancient Greece, in: G&R 45, 1998, 1–18 12 C. G. STARR, Political Intelligence in Classical Greece, 1974 13 D. ENGELS, Alexander's Intelligence System, in: CQ 30, 1980, 327–340 14 N. E. J. AUSTIN, B. RANKOW, Exploratio, 1995 15 A. D. LEE, Information and Frontiers, 1993.

W. RIEPL, Das N. des Alt., 1913; A. C. LEIGHTON, Secret Communication among the Greeks and Romans, in: Technology and Culture 10, 1969, 139–154; G. ACHARD, La communication à Rome, 1991; S. LEWIS, News and Society in the Greek Polis, 1996. A.K.

Communio Joint ownership of an object in Roman law.

A. PAST HISTORY B. PRINCIPATE C. INFLUENCE

A. PAST HISTORY

The most important circumstances that led to the formation of a *communio* entailed a community of purchasers (*societas quaestus*) or a community of heirs. Regarding both, the *communio* did not gain acceptance until late, towards the end of the Republic. Before that, multiple heirs were joined in a community of *ercto non cito* (after *erctum ciere*: to make a division), as we know from the papyrus find of 1933, containing Gaius, *Institutiones* 3, 154a, b. It originally meant a community of property that excluded individual ownership by its members with the purpose of assuring the continuation of the control over the property by a → *pater familias* among several sons sharing equal rights. The term *consortium* ('community of fate') expresses the close alliance within the communities not only regarding property but also regarding family law. A *consortium ercto non cito* could also be formed outside of inheritance law and without the existence of family relationships through a civil action similar to the → *in iure cessio* or the old Roman → adoption. The community formed on this basis was a *societas omnium bonorum*, binding all present and future property. However, the Law of Twelve Tables (5th cent. BC) already provided for an *actio familiae erciscundae*, a suit aiming at the division of family property (Dig. 10,2), and it is possible that a *consortium* between unrelated individuals emerged from the continuation (legally: the new creation) of the community among those members who did not want any conflict.

B. PRINCIPATE

In classical Roman law, the *communio* was the only legal possibility for several persons to jointly own something. Each owner was entitled to a non-material share (*pars pro indiviso*, Dig. 50,16,25,1) of the property, which could be sold and mortgaged. A single member of the *communio*, however, could not take charge of the entire property and was not allowed to cut out a material part of the property (such as a plot of land) for individual use. In practical terms, the members of the *communio* were forced into agreement. Legally, each member had the right to veto (*ius prohibendi*, Dig. 8,2,27,1; 10,3,28) any one-sided measures taken by another. If no agreement could be reached, the only recourse was a suit to dissolve the *communio*: the *actio communi dividundo* (Dig. 10,3). It led — similar to the earlier *actio familiae erciscundae* — to the liquidation of the *communio* according to the terms set forth by the judge (→ *adiudicatio*). It was also the basis for a real division of the property or for the assignment of the property to the single ownership of one of the previous members. The latter required not only a decision concerning property rights but also a liquidation according to the law of contract, for example, granting the right of compensation when member A receives a more valuable part of the liquidated property than member B. The suit to dissolve the *communio*, therefore, was aimed legally at the creation of new terms (such as newly formed ownerships) as well as obligations (such as payments).

C. INFLUENCE

In late antiquity, the *ius prohibendi* was narrowed down. In its place, a law of majority rule was introduced and, for the same purpose, the *actio communi dividundo* was expanded to resolve conflicts without having to liquidate the *communio*. Furthermore, under Justinianus, a communio that was not governed by a *societas* was designated as a 'quasi-contract' so that emerging payment claims based on contract law could be better explained in a *communio* that lacked articles of partnership (Inst. Iust. 3,27,3). In modern times, the *communio* was finally rejected in favour of a joint right of ownership that did not entail a non-material share in single objects. The joint handling of ownership prevailed concerning partnership law and concerning the community of heirs (e.g. §§ 719, 2033 Art. 2 BGB). The *communio* continues to exist in cases of co-ownership (such as married persons co-owning the plot with the family residence).

KASER, RPR I, 99–101, 590–592; H. HONSELL, TH. MAYER-MALY, W. SELB, Röm. Recht, ⁴1987, 149–151; F. WIEACKER, Societas I, 1936; COING I, 293f.; G. MAC-CORMACK, The actio communi dividundo in Roman and Scots law, in: A. D. E. LEWIS, D. J. IBBETSON (ed.), The Roman law tradition, 1994, 159–181. G.S.

Comparatio publica was probably not a technical term at first (therefore also *c. venalitium, c. specierum*). It referred to the public purchases of provisions for the Roman State, primarily concerning military equipment and public grain supplies (→ Logistics, → *cura annonae*). Comparatio publica (CP) did not become a legal category until the Cod. Theod. (under headings 11,15). There, it is designated as a highly regulated type of business including sales obligations (in modern law: contract obligations) and exact price regulations. In real terms, however, the CP already existed in Republican times (Liv. 2,9,34; 10,11). It was the only way for the state to meet the growing need to supply the city populations with grain.

S. BRASSLOFF, s.v. C.p., Re 4, 781–784. G.S.

Comparison In ancient rhetoric, the terms εἰκών/*eikón* (literally 'image', 'illustration': often for short comparisons), παραβολή/*parabolé* (especially for similes) as well as Latin *simile, similitudo* cover diverse phenomena dominating a word, sentence or even a text that create a relationship between two facts or spheres of the imagination. The primary function of emphasis placed the comparison close to the → topos (Quint. Inst. 4,1,70), and the *exemplum* (5,11,22; but cf. Cic. Inv. 1,49), the *figurae sententiarum* (Cic. De or. 3,201 = Quint. Inst. 9,1,31; → figures).

A theory of comparison was first presented by Aristotle in his 'Rhetoric' (3,4,1406b), where he distinguishes short (suitable for prose) and elaborate (reserved for poetry) comparison and defines the latter both by delimitation against and partial equation with → metaphor. The comparison supposedly differed from it because of the insertion of a comparative particle ('such as'). The → *Rhetorica ad Herennium* (4,45,59–48,61) places the comparison with *imago* ('image') and *exemplum* ('example') among the intellectual figures (however, the metaphor is linked with verbal ornamentation; but cf. Cic. De or. 3,39,157) and names four functions of the comparison: ornamentation, proof, frank statement and realization (*ornandi, probandi, apertius dicendi, ante oculos ponendi causa*). The likeness of the comparison need not be complete but must rather refer to individual aspects (Cic. Inv. 1,49 adds probability as a condition). Quintilianus [1], in the passages cited, provides the most detailed treatment of the comparison (more references in Greek and Latin literature: [1. §847]).

The mode of the relationship between the two facts is not substitution (*immutatio*), but that both areas/facts are preserved and paralleled by a comparative particle. Usually, image recipient and sender are clandestinely related to each other through a *tertium comparationis* that can be defined more closely but is not stated explicitly. Even if the paradox character distinguishing the metaphor can be weakened by the obviousness of its composition, the comparison exhibits all the functions of the metaphor in all forms of language usage: aesthetisization, realization and emphasis 'by appealing to the general experiences of natural and human life' [1. §843].

Expanded comparisons, i.e. those that constitute a larger text unit and have been part of the traditional stock of poetry since the Homeric epics [2; 3], may unfold — with or without a comparative particle — a great dynamic of their own since not every aspect of the simile can be related to an aspect of what is compared.

This creates a semantic surplus that constitutes the poetic nature of the comparison (examples: Hom. Od. 23,233–240; Luc. 1,150–157).

→ Metaphor

1 LAUSBERG §§422–425 (Beweismittel), 843–847 (ornatus) 2 M.H. McCALL, Ancient Rhetorical Theories of Simile and Comparison, 1969 3 R. RIEKS, Die Gleichnisse Vergils, in: ANRW II 31.2, 1981, 1011–1110. C.W.

Compendiariae

Compendiariae (from Lat. *pictura compendiaria*, an advantageously short way of painting; 'abbreviated' painting). Ancient technical term, often translated as 'quick painting'. The manner, the application and the influence of this Greek painting technique of the late 4th cent. BC is still debated due to the lack of detailed explanations in the sources (esp. in Plin. HN 35, 110; Petron. Sat. 2). The debate includes a number of methods: impressionist 'paint spot painting'; the use of a kind of sketching; a partial representation of single elements through compositions of overlapping and clipping; a generally fast work method that combines all of these techniques. All of these methods can be found on period ceramics and in later Roman Campanian → wall paintings. Carelessly hatched contours and a busy ductus in certain places seem to indicate a specialized way of using the brush for design as well as for modelling, for instance in the paintings of the 'Persephone tomb' in Vergina (→ Aegae) attributed to → Nicomachus, a 'fast painter' as well. *Compendiariae* should also be understood in an economic sense: a small work effort could create a big effect in the painting, thereby leading to a financial advantage for the painter.

M. ANDRONIKOS, Vergina, 2, 1994; J.J. POLLITT, The Ancient View of Greek Art, 1974, 266–273; A. ROUVERET, Histoire et imaginaire de la peinture ancienne, 1989, 119, 228–255; I. SCHEIBLER, Griech. Malerei der Ant., 1994, 69f. N.H.

Compensatio

Compensatio *Compensatio* (charging to account) was a rather complicated institution in Roman law. The basic idea, however, is simple: when two parties involved in a court case have claims against each other, the claims are not treated separately, but are offset one against the other — as far as the amounts cover each other. Both claims are thereby paid off, so that the complaint becomes groundless and the defendant can no longer sue for his counter-claim. The complication in Roman law resulted from the different legal procedures connected to the different reasons leading to claims.

Gai. Inst. 4,61–68 illustrates *compensatio* in the framework of *bonae fidei iudicia*, which refers to the types of civil cases that were developed by the praetors and thus were placed under the rule of good faith (*bona* → *fides*). The judge's discretion was based on the possibility of relying on the *bona fides* and entailed his authority to offset claims against each other that originated from the same legal relationship (*ex eadem causa*): since the plaintiff sued according to the wording of the formula *ex fide bona* appropriate to his request, the judge could interpret the request in such a way that the plaintiff only demanded in good faith what he deserved after the legal relationship was completely sorted out. Since the judgement would have resulted in a cash amount in any case (*condemnatio pecuniaria*), the opposing claims were of the same nature and therefore could be offset against each other without any problem. Of course, the counter-claim had to be uncontested or proven (solvent).

Classic Roman law dealt with two special cases in a similar way: 1) A banker (→ *argentarius*) could not enforce independent claims against a client, only the amount overdrawn in the account. The banker had to keep this in mind when stating the reason and the object of his request (→ *intentio*); otherwise he completely lost the case (*pluris petitio*, Gai. Inst. 4,68). 2) Whoever took over the property of an insolvent debtor in return for the promise of paying the creditors a certain quota of their claims (*bonorum emptor*, → *bona*) had to accept the rule that the *compensatio* entailed the full amount of the counter-claim, not just its quota, concerning claims of the insolvent party belonging to the *bona* (*agere cum deductione*, complaint with deduction, Gai. Inst. 4,65). In such a case, the counter claim was neither required to be equivalent nor due for payment. However, the *bonorum emptor* was not in danger of sanctions due to *pluris petitio*.

Compensatio apparently did not exist in any real sense regarding the *iudicia stricti iuris* (complaints according to strict law), only in the sense of an indirect duty towards the plaintiff to agree with the *compensatio* in a → *pactum*. The praetor could refuse the complaint (*actionem denegare*) if the ability to materially offset the claim was obvious and the insistence on a complaint gave the appearance of harassment. As a further addition, Marcus Aurelius (according to Inst. Just. Epit. 4,6,30) is attributed with the inclusion of an *exceptio doli* (statement of fraud) into the charge, to authorize the examination of an equivalent counter-claim due for payment by the → *iudex*. Should the *exceptio* turn out to be founded, the complaint was to be rejected according to the general rules. But in this case, the plaintiff was perhaps granted the special exception of limiting his complaint in front of the *iudex*.

Justinian standardized and reformed the *compensatio*: the sentence was now limited to the balance of the liquid claims (Cod. Just. Epit. 4,31,14). Thus, the defendant was freed from the original claim against him to the amount of his counter claim *ipso iure*. The *compensatio* did not develop into an institution governing material law until the 19th cent. The common-law designation of *compensatio lucri cum damno* for the balance of interests in general indemnity law has no connection to the *compensatio* of Roman law. On the other hand, *compensatio* was already a common term in antiquity for the exclusion of claims against a person who inflicted damage through negligence, if the damaged party itself was negligent as well (Dig. 16,2,10 pr.).

KASER, RPR I, 644–647 H. HONSELL, TH. MAYER-MALY, W. SELB, Röm. Recht, ⁴1987, 272–276. G.S.

Comperendinatio describes according to Gai. Inst. 4,15 an agreement of the parties to appear on the day after next before a *iudex* (Fest. 355,1; Prob. 4,9: *in diem tertium sive perendinum*; for Roman calculations of court dates cf. Gell. NA 10,24,9), as had already been provided for in the Twelve Tables. It did not require the form of a stipulation because the consequences of missing it were considered sufficient as a sanction. How the transition from the procedure *in iure* to *apud iudicem* specifically came about in the formular procedure is unclear, because the *comperendinatio* is no longer explicitly mentioned in detail and the word increasingly takes on the general meaning of an adjournment. In the comitial criminal procedure (→ *quaestio*), *comperendinatio* also designates the time intervals between the four court dates (Cic. Dom. 45).

→ Ampliatio; → Denuntiatio

D. JOHNSTON, Three Thoughts on Roman Private Law and the Lex Irnitana, in: JRS 77, 1987, 70–77; KASER, RZ, 274; U. MANTHE, Stilistische Gemeinsamkeiten in den Fachsprachen der Juristen und Auguren der Röm. Republik, in: K. ZIMMERMANN (ed.), Stilbegriffe der Altertumswissenschaften, 1993, 70. C.PA.

Competitions, artistic see → Volume 4, Addenda

Compitalia
A. TERM B. REPUBLICAN PERIOD C. AUGUSTAN REFORM

A. TERM

The junction of three or more roads is called a *compitum* (ThlL, s.v. 2075, 77ff.). It was the site of altars, chapels and other monuments (also called *compita*) at which farmers and their servants prayed *in fundi villaeque conspectu* (Cic. Leg. 2,27) to the Lares, offered sacrifices and where adjoining residents met for consultation (Trebatius in Serv. Georg. 2,382). Whatever older ideas one may assume to lie behind this custom (on this debate: WISSOWA-SAMTER [4. 224ff.]), the earliest attested cultural practices and concepts of the *compitum* and the Compital Lares are based on the junction of roads, landed property and those who live on it and, therefore, are celebrations of rural village communities (hence always Compital Lares in the plural) whose climax was the festival of the Compitalia. In the late Republic they were still announced by the praetor using an ancient formula (Gell. NA 10,24,3; Macrob. Sat. 1,4,27) eight days in advance in December (as a movable feast cf. Varro, Ling. 6,25; 29) and, so, took place a 'few days after the Saturnalia' (Dion. Hal. Ant. Rom. 4,14): known dates are 31 December 67, 1 January 58 and 2 January 50 BC (Ascon. p. 65 C; Cic. Pis. 8; Cic. Att. 7,7,3). The rural Compitalia have the character of a village year end's festivity (*finita agricultura*: Schol. Pers. 4,28) in which only the estate administrator was

permitted to perform cult duties otherwise reserved to the owner (Cato Agr. 5,3) and in which (as in the → Saturnalia) an extra ration of wine (Cato Agr. 57) was distributed among the servants. As proclaimed feast days (*feriae conceptivae*), they were adaptable to the rhythm of farming and celebrated by the persons actually working in the house and on the farm but not the nominal owners. The rural Compitalia were a communal thanksgiving for the past year and a prayer for the coming year, a defence against harmful forces, a purification and a particularly exuberant celebration— increasingly the latter so that they eventually declined into a festivity for servants and slaves because the owners kept away (characteristically Cic. Att. 7,7,3) [1. 32ff.]

B. REPUBLICAN PERIOD

Allegedly the Compitalia of the city of Rome were instituted by King Servius → Tullius (Plin. HN 36,204): the city was subdivided into four districts (*tribus*, 'villages'), with each 'village' receiving a leader (as supervisor of the strict *tribus* regulations). For cultural bonding, adjoining neighbours had to establish Compitalia chapels at all *compita*. These neighbours annually offered a communal sacrifice in which all slaves participated (Dion. Hal. Ant. Rom. 4,14; Macrob. Sat. 1,7,34ff.). In fact, during the late Republic there were *magistri vicorum* (with the right to wear the *toga praetexta*: Cic. Pis. 8; Liv. 34,7,2), who presided with increasing duties over Compital colleges in their *vicus* (this can be illustrated by probably analogous conditions in Campania and on Delos: [2. 586ff.; 1. 43ff.]. The main duty of these *magistri* and their *collegia* was the preparation and conduct of the Compitalia festivity and the associated games whose popularity compelled an extension to three days (Fest. p. 304f.; from January in the Calenders of Philocalus and Polemius Silvius). Respectable and free citizens increasingly withdrew (Liv. 34,7,2: *infimum genus*) from these *collegia* while their political influence (cf. Q. Cic., de petitione consulatus 30) and the opportunities for abuse led to a temporary abolition after 64 BC [3].

During the Compitalia wool effigies were hung up at the *compita* before daybreak (*noctu*: Fest. p. 108) in numbers equal to heads in the *compitum* community: male and female effigies for free persons and little balls for slaves (Fest. p. 273). In these *sacra publica* (Varro, Ling. 6,29; Fest. p. 284), sacrificial cakes contributed by each household were offered (Dion. Hal. Ant. Rom. 4,14,3f.). Sacrifices of pigs [7. 411; 2. 590ff.] are not attested for the Compitalia but are for other Lares cults, perhaps also other *compita* rituals. Likewise, sacrifices of garlic buds and poppy capsules for Mania (sing. in Macrob. Sat. 1,7,35) ([4.214f.] with Varro, Sat. Men. 463 B. intermingled with the making of the *effigies*) were not part of the Compitalia [8]. Games (*ludi compitalicii*: Cic. Pis. 8; Ascon. p. 6f. C) and opulent banquets (Verg. Catal. 5,27f.; Dion. Hal. Ant. Rom. 4,14,4 — Cicero enjoyed walks and a hot bath: Att. 2,3,4) completed the festival.

C. Augustan reform

The declining and politically abused compital colleges and their events were reorganized in 7 BC by Augustus in the context of his reorganization of Rome into 14 regions with 265 *vici = compita* (Plin. HN 3,66; [5]): the Lares, of which there were now two, were associated with the *Genius Augusti* and became the core of the imperial cult. During the Compitalia the popular, now three-day long games were officially promoted (Suet. Aug. 31; Calp. Ecl. 4,125f.).

Interpretations of the Augustan period considered the Lares Compitales the deified souls of the deceased or gods of the Underworld for whom images were hung up during the Compitalia to deflect from the living (Fest. p. 108; p. 273). How long these images, which could function secondarily as a kind of census, remained up and what was done with them is unknown. The principle of 'one image per person' (*tot effigiesquot capita*) contradicts thoughts of a substitute for human sacrifice (as in [6]) but demonstrates that it revolved around the people living and working in a community (therefore, the Lares Compitales must be secondary to the *Lar familiaris*).

The Compitalia as a festival of the presence of all persons in a community (ritual constitution of a community with purification, thanksgiving, prayer and celebration) tied to the place of daily life and work surely extends back into the earliest times of human community. With the increasing dissolution of the association of life and work and the growth of slavery, they became a festivity of the lower classes, servants and slaves but were still of sufficient interest to Augustus to be associated with the imperial cult after reorganization.
→ Lares; → Collegium; → Magister; → Cult; → Ludi; → Genius

1 F. Bömer, Unt. über die Religion der Sklaven in Griechenland und Rom, I 1957   2 Ph. Bruneau, Recherches sur les cultes de Délos à l'époque hellénistique et à l'époque impériale, 1970, 586ff.   3 J. M. Flambard, Clodius, les collèges, la plèbe et les esclaves, in: MEFRA 89, 1977, 115ff.   Id., Collegia compitalicia, in: Ktema 6, 1981, 143ff.   4 K. Meuli, Altröm. Maskenbrauch, in: MH 12, 1955, 206ff. (= Gesammelte Schriften, 1975, 85ff.) 5 G. Niebling, Laribus Augusti magistri primi, Historia 5, 1956, 303ff.   6 E. Samter, Familienfeste der Griechen und Römer, 1901, 111ff.   7 G. Wissowa, Religion und Kultus der Römer, ²1912, 171ff.   8 E. Syska, Stud. zur Theologie des Macrobius, 1993, 232f.   U.W.S.

Complega Celtiberian town, only mentioned in App. Hisp. 42f. in association with the Roman campaigns of 181–179 BC. A. Schulten [2. 136] identified C. with → Contrebia (C. a Celtic variant, not identical with → Complutum, as [1. 795]) still has.

1 E. Hübner, s.v. C., RE IV, 794f.   2 A. Schulten, Numantia 1, 1914.

Tovar 3, 340.   P.B.

Complutum Celtiberian town, whose location near Alcalá de Henares was determined from ruins and inscriptions (CIL II p. 410; Suppl. p. 941). The name of C. is probably Iberian according to Holder [1. 1087] but Roman according to Hübner [2. 795] ('City of Rain'). Its inhabitants belonged to the → Carpetani (Ptol. Geog. 2,6,56). C. only became important in the Christian period (Paul. Nol. 31,607; Prudent 4,41ff.; Chron. min. 3,648), especially as a diocesan town [3. 444].

1 Holder 1   2 E. Hübner, cf. C., RE IV, 795 3 A. Schulten, Fontes Hispaniae Antiquae 9, 1947.

Tovar 3, 238.   P.B.

Compluvium According to Varro (Ling. 5,161) and Vitruvius (6,3,1f.) the customary formation of the roof opening of all types of the → atrium in the Roman → house. The funnel-shaped roof surfaces of the *compluvium*, which slope inward, conduct rainwater into the → impluvium, a basin at the atrium's centre. In the older *displuvium* the roof surfaces slanted outwards.

E. M. Evans, The Atrium Complex in the Houses of Pompeii, 1980; R. Förtsch, Arch. Komm. zu den Villenbriefen des jüngeren Plinius, 1993, 30–31.   C.HÖ.

Compsa, Cossa Town of the Hirpini in the *regio II* on the border to Lucania, modern Conza della Campania (Province of Avellino). Located on a height by the upper → Aufidus, at the crossing to the Sele valley (Sella di Conza). Involved in the Second Punic War, Hannibal's base of operations after Cannae (216 BC), but it was reconquered by Fabius Maximus (214 BC). In the Social War on Rome's side (Vell. 2,16). *Municipium* of the *tribus Galeria*. Cults of the *Mater Deum* and *Iupiter Vicilinus in agro Compsano* (Liv. 24,44,8). Epigraphy: CIL IX, p. 88, 963–993, Roman sarcophagi, episcopal seat; the walls were destroyed by Charlemagne, other monuments by various earthquakes after 980.

Nissen, 2, 821; Ruggiero, 2, 563; M. R. Barbera (ed.), C. e l'alta valle dell'Ofanto, 1994.   G.U.

Comum Chief town of a Ligurian tribe of the Golasecca culture, inhabited since the 12th cent. BC (necropolis of the Ca' Morta), modern Como. Strong influence of the Celtic Insubres [1. 207f.] of the Padana. Control of the *lacus Larius* and one of the most important passes across the Alps. Reached by the Romans in 196 BC (Liv. 33,36f.), C. became a 'fictive' Roman *colonia* in 89 (based on the *lex Pompeia*: Str. 5,1,6). Expanded by one of the Scipiones (83 or 77 BC) and refounded by Caesar as Novum Comum (59 BC) [2. 441], C. became a *municipium* of the *tribus Oufentina* in *regio XI* in 49. In the late Imperial period, C. was a military base with a *praefectus classis* at the *lacus Larius* (Not. Dign. 42,9).
→ Golaseccca

1 G. LURASCHI, C. oppidum, RAComo 152–155, 207f.
2 Id., Foedus, ius Latii, civitas, 1979.

Novum C., 1993.   A.SA.

Concha Latin for shell, snail (Greek κόγχη/kónchē),
also describes shell-shaped vessels or large drinking-
bowls as well as the snail-shaped horn of Triton (Verg.
Aen. 6,171; Plin. HN 9,9). In early Christian literature
concha designates the upper half-dome of the → apse
and the water basin used for baptisms and baths.

G. MATTHIAE, s.v. Conca, EAA 2, 779.   C.HÖ.

Conciliabulum Conciliabulum (from concilium) in the
legal meaning is an assembly place or, more often, just
the venue (locus ubi in concilium convenitur, Fest. p.
33) at which citizens gathered for the proclamation of
laws, levying etc. The word describes a settlement with
elementary self-government in the territory of one of
the tribus rusticae. In the context of the ager Romanus
we hear of per fora et conciliabula (Liv. 25,22,4;
39,14,7 etc.), which — as in the lex Poetelia of 358 —
provides an excellent parallel to the nundinae in the city
of Rome. In late Republican laws it occurs together
with → praefectura, forum, vicus, castellum territori-
umve (cf. documentation in [1]). Presumably, these are
not essentially different forms of settlement but different aspects (administrative-judicial centre, market
town, fortification), which can also refer to the same
place although not necessarily: not every conciliabulum
is also a praefectura. Many earlier conciliabula on
Roman territory were transformed in the last cents. of
the Republic into → municipia (Frontin. Str. 19 L.).

1 RUGGIERO 2, 566.

MOMMSEN, Staatsrecht 3, 798f.; H. GALSTERER, Herrschaft und Verwaltung im republikanischen Italien, 1976,
26–35.   H.GA.

Concilium Concilium (from con-calare) is an assembly
(Fest. p. 38) that has been called; also used in a transferred sense (Cic. Tusc. 1,72; Lucr. 3,805).

1. In political usage, concilium frequently differentiates a popular assembly without legal consequences
from constitutional → contiones and → comitia (is qui
non universum populum, sed partem aliquam adesse
iubet, non comitia, sed concilium edicere iubet, Gell.
NA 15,27,4; Liv. 9,45,8). It was also used in the meaning of contio or comitia and then more often in association with populi and plebis (Cic. Sest. 65; lex Iulia
municipalibus 132/FIRA 1,150). In the Imperial period
the distinct meaning of concilium was lost.

2. In the struggle of the orders of the early Republic
an organization of the plebs formed, the concilium plebis, which served to pass resolutions within the plebs as
well as electing officials (tribuni and aediles plebis) (Liv.
2,56,2f.; 2,60,4f.). Occasionally in the earlier period,
probably after an approving sententia of the Senate

(Liv. 2,56,16; also 3,55 regarding the lex Valeria Hora-
tia de plebiscitis of 449 BC) and unrestricted since the
lex Hortensia of 286 BC, resolutions of the plebs (plebis
scita) assembled in a concilium plebis were granted the
same binding effect as the leges populi of the comitia
centuriata. The word came to mean the same as → comitia tributa. A magistrate equipped with the ius agendi
cum populo presided over this assembly and, before its
opening, auspices had to be obtained in the same
manner as for the comitia centuriata (Liv. 1,36,6;
5,52,16f.; Cass. Dio 37,2f.; Dig. 1,2,2).

3. The concilium provinciae was the customary form
of an assembly of towns and peoples in a Roman province at the behest of the governor and under the formal
leadership of the priest responsible for the imperial and
state cult (Cic. Verr. 2,154; Tac. Ann. 15,21f.; lex civ.
Narb. 25/FIRA 1,201f.; Dig. 17,14,1). This assembly
was not used for passing autonomous resolutions as
some pre-Roman precursors were (e.g., the synodoi of
the Greek sympoliteiai or koina or the assemblies of all
tribes of Gaul — Liv. 36,28,7; Frontin. Str. 3,2,6; Caes.
B Gall. 6,13), but rather for a discussion of provincial
affairs, joint loyalty addresses and petitions, the
appointment of delegations to the emperor (Dig. 50,7;
Cod. Iust. 10,65,5) as well as festivities and games associated with the state and imperial cults. In Christian late
antiquity the concilia provinciarum no longer had a cult
function. Furthermore, they — unlike what was possible before the constitutio Antoniniana of AD 212,
which made all provincials equal citizens — had gained
a certain power of their own within the context of the
provincial administration (Cod. Theod. 12,12,16: civitatum postulata, decreta urbium, desideria populorum
liquido tua sublimitas recognoscit ad imperialis officium pertinuisse responsi; likewise Cod. Iust. 10,65,5).

4. Analogous to the concilia provinciarum, the concilia ecclesiastica, i.e., the 'synods' of the Church,
formed as early as the 3rd cent. AD, but then increasingly after the official toleration of Christianity, in the
province for the election of the metropolitan bishops or
under their leadership (can. IV 'de ordinatione episco-
porum' of the concilium Nicaenum/COeD 1ff.). Even
before Constantine the Great there were super-regional
councils, but under his government they acquired significance for Church organization throughout the empire (Cod. Iust. 1,2,1). The first concilium oecumeni-
cum is the one called by this emperor in Nicaea in AD
323 (Euseb. Vita Const. 3,17ff.).

MOMMSEN, Staatsrecht 1, 191ff.; 3/1, 143ff., 321ff.,
394f.; F. F. ABBOTT, A History and Description of Roman
Political Institutions ³1963, 251ff., 302; E. MEYER, Röm.
Staat und Staatsgedanke, ⁴1975, 85f., 406; JONES, LRE
763f.; K. BAUS, H. JEDIN, Von der Urgemeinde zur frühchristl. Großkirche, 1965, vol. 1, 395ff.   C.G.

Conclamatio An old element in Roman mortuary customs: when the eyes of the deceased were closed the
attending relatives repeatedly called his name (Serv.
Aen. 6,218; Luc. 2,23; Sen. Dial. 9,11,7; with the same

meaning Ov. Tr. 3,3,43 *clamor supremus* ; Ps.-Quint. Decl. mai. 8,10 *conclamata suprema*). Since this word also describes the ordinary death lament (e.g., Tac. Ann. 3,2,2; *Oratio imperatoris Hadriani* in CIL 14, 3579, 19; Sen. Ep. 52,13 and *passim*), a lot of evidence cannot be clearly attributed. This custom, which was obviously no longer understood in the historical period, was rationalized as an attempt to wake persons in a state of apparent death (Serv. Aen. 6,218; implicitly already in Quint. Decl. min. 246,4). The calling of the dead's name was (later?) repeated until cremation or interment (Serv. Aen. 6,218; cf. Verg. Aen. 6,506).
→ Burial

H. BLÜMNER, Die röm. Privataltertümer, 1911, 483; W. KIERDORF, Totenehrung im republikanischen Rom, in: Tod und Jenseits im Altertum, 1991, 71–87 (73); J. M. C. TOYNBEE, Death and Burial in the Roman World, 1971, 44.   W.K.

Conclusio see → Partes orationis

Concolitanus (Κογκολιτάνος; *Koncholitános*). Celtic name, 'he whose heel is broad' [1. 182]. Jointly with → Aneroëstes, king of the → Gaesati. He was captured by the Romans after the Celtic defeat at Telamon in 225 BC (Pol. 2,22,2; 2,31).

1 SCHMIDT.   W.SP.

Conconnetodumnus Celtic composite name of unclear meaning, 'he who strikes deep wounds'? [1. 74–75; 2. 219]. Together with → Cotuatus, C. was the leader of a band of Carnutes who in 52 BC, killed and looted the merchants resident in → Cenabum, including the *eques* C. → Fufius Cita (Caes. B Gall. 7,3,1). C. is not identical with the Congonnetodubnus attested in Saintes (CIL XIII 1040; 1042–1045) [2. 181].

1 EVANS   2 SCHMIDT.   W.SP.

Concordia The personification and deification of harmony analogous to the Greek → Homonoia (Cic. Nat. D. 2,61; ThlL, Onom. 2, 555–558 s.v. C.). C. is attested on one of the *pocula deorum* (*Cucordia. pocolo*) [1]. Worship of c. is attested in Rome from the 4th cent. BC. The decisive phases in her history are associated with the search for internal unity (cf. the *concordia ordinum*). A first temple was allegedly dedicated to her in the northwest corner of the Forum in 367 BC by → Camillus to celebrate the end of the 'struggle of the orders' (Plut. Camillus 42,4) [2]. In the same location the consul L. Opimius dedicated a temple in 121 BC after the bloody persecution of the Gracchi, which propagandistically interpreted the elimination of the Gracchi as the restoration of internal peace but opponents considered it cynical (Plut. C. Gracchus 17,8; App. B Civ. 1,120; mockingly Aug. Civ. 3,25). Generally, this building is considered a renovation of Camillus' [3] temple; in 7 BC it was restored by Tiberius as C. Augus-

ta. Since Vespasian the → Arvales routinely performed the *indictio* of the festival of Dea Dia there. Today only the podium and the threshold of the cella are visible. Already in 304 the aedile Cn. Flavius allegedly dedicated an *aedicula* (chapel) nearby for the restoration of internal harmony (Liv. 9,46,6; Plin. HN 33,19). Another temple of C. was promised by the praetor L. Manlius in 218 during an army revolt in Gaul (Liv. 22,33,7). It is uncertain if the temple of C. Nova promised by the Senate for Caesar in 44 BC was ever built (Cass. Dio 44,4).

The temple built by Livia in her porticus was devoted to the understanding of C. as the goddess of interfamiliar harmony that had been expanded into the political sphere (Ov. Fast. 6,637f.) [4]. In the Imperial period her cult was also widespread outside of Rome. Therefore, she is frequently depicted in Roman art (numerous coins). Regarding the Judeo-Christian perception of C. cf. [5].

1 R. WACHTER, Altlat. Inschr., 1987, 465–467   2 MOMIGLIANO 89–104.   3 DUMÉZIL, 406   4 J. SIMPSON, Livia and the Constitution of the Aedes Concordiae, in: Historia 40, 1991, 449–455   5 K. THRAEDE, s.v. Homonoia, RAC 16, 176–289.

A. M. FERRONI, G. GIANELLI, s.v. C., LTUR 1, 316–321; T. HÖLSCHER, s.v. Homonoia/C., LIMC 5.1, 478–498; DUMÉZIL, 402–408; E. SKARD, C., in: H. OPPERMANN, Röm. Wertbegriffe, 1967 (1931), 173–208.   R.B.

Concubinatus In Roman law a permanent union between man and woman without *affectio maritalis*, i.e. without the intention of both parties of permanently entering a legal bond for forming a household, procreating and raising children. Since the marital laws of Augustus, the *concubinatus* increasingly became a form of living together if marriage was prohibited. Thus, senators and their descendants were prohibited under the *l. Iulia de maritandis ordinibus* from marrying a freedwoman, actress or daughter of an actor. Freeborn Romans could not enter into a marriage with an adulteress. Finally, soldiers were prohibited from marriage for reasons of military discipline until the time of Septimius Severus, likewise provincial officials from marrying women from the administered province. In those cases the *concubinatus* provided a solution. Upon the soldiers' discharge, their concubines were frequently legitimized as wives. The *concubinatus* was even found in the highest circles. The *concubinatus* of the emperors Vespasian (Suet. Vesp. 3) and Marcus Aurelius (SHA Aur. 29,10) are recorded. However, liaisons with slaves were not a *concubinatus* but as → *contubernium*; they were subject to their own evaluation. On the other hand, the 'mistress' of a married man was regarded as *concubina*.

Despite the social acceptance of the *concubinatus*, it had no legal consequences until late antiquity. In particular, the woman did not have the *honor matrimonii* (the wife's position of honour), as specifically emphasized by legal writing (Dig. 39,5,31 pr.; Dig. 25,7,4). Therefore, her children were extramarital (→ *spurius*) though that did not preclude a right to inheritance from the father: an *epistula Hadriani* (119, BGU I 140) is interpreted to mean that the children of soldiers even had a non-testamentary right to inheritance. Since a *concubina* had no paternal powers and could not convey them, children were born 'under no power' (*sui iuris*) but were in need of guardianship, presumably of an officially appointed guardian.

Constantine attempted to fight *concubinatus* with prohibitions (Cod. Theod. 4,6,2 and 3) but the tendency of *concubinatus* to approximate marriage as closely as possible in late antiquity was stronger. This only applied if the partners were unmarried and the man remained associated with only one *concubina*. The children of such liaisons were specially elevated as *liberi naturales* from the (other) *spurii* (now also *vulgo quaesiti*). The option of legitimization was created for them, i.e. equal status with legitimate children, initially in the case of after-the-fact marriages of the parents (Cod. Iust. 5,27,5ff.). Justinian (Nov. 74 in 538) further introduced a legitimization by an act of imperial mercy which was, e.g., granted when no legitimate children were present and the mother of the *liberi naturales* was no longer alive so that a marriage had become impossible. In Nov. 18 he introduced a legal right to inheritance for the benefit of the surviving *concubina* and her children if the husband was not survived by a member of a legitimate family founded by him.

KASER, RPR I, 328f., II, 183f.; P.M. MEYER, Der röm. Konkubinat, 1895 (repr. 1966); B.RAWSON, Roman concubinage and other de facto marriages, in: TAPhA 104, 1974, 279–305; S.TREGGIARI, Concubinae, in: PBSR 49, 1981, 59–81. G.S.

Concussio The Digests (Title 47,13) label cases of a forced granting of benefits to an officeholder as *concussio* (blackmail). Possibly, this is a further development of the reclamation procedure (→ *repetundarum crimen*). Punishable behaviour in office due to *concussio* was not prosecuted by a *iudicium publicum* but by *extraordinaria* → *cognitio*. Therefore, it was probably only considered an independent offence in the Imperial period (2nd cent. AD). The sources present pretending a (higher) official authority, orders of a superior and threats of an unfounded suit as means of *concussio*. Apparently, *concussio* was also committed by subordinate officials since threats of punishment for committing it were differentiated into *honestiores* (deportation) and *humiliores* (capital punishment) (Paulus, Sent. 5,25,12). The severity of this penalty is obviously based on the hope of a deterrent effect and probably the spread of corruption.

V.GIUFFRÉ, La 'repressione criminale' nell' esperienza romana, 1993, 134f.; H.F. HITZIG, s.v. C., RE VII, 840. G.S.

Condatomagus City of the → Ruteni in Aquitania at the confluence of the Tarn and the Dourbie, called Aemiliavum since the 3rd cent. AD (therefore modern Millau), modern La Graufesenque. Significant pottery production, especially *terra sigillata*, exported in the 1st cent. AD, gradually superseded by Lezoux (→ Arverni). Monuments: many workshops, two *fana*, *nymphaeum*. Inscriptions ('kiln registers ') from C. are an important source of the economic history of the ancient pottery industry.

A.ALBENQUE, Les Rutènes, 1948; F.HERMET, La Graufesenque, 1934; R.LEQUÉMENT, in: Gallia 41, 1983, 476–479; R.MARICHAL, Les graffites de La Graufesenque, 1988. E.FR.

Condemnatio In criminal proceedings the sentencing of the accused (Cic. Verr. 2,75). In civil proceedings the *condemnatio* is according to Gai. Inst. 4,43 that part of the proceeding formula that grants a private judge in the context of the suit brought forward (→ *intentio*) and the statement of facts (→ *demonstratio*) the power to sentence or acquit (*qua iudici condemnandi absolvendive potestas permittitur*). It is only required in payment suits. Gai. Inst. 4,48ff. further states that *condemnatio* relates to a sum of money (*condemnatio pecuniaria*). This restriction (which was only finally abandoned under Justinian, Iust. inst. 4,6,32) by sentencing a monetary fine may be a reminiscence of the legal cases in the early period in which the dispute was mainly about the payment and only indirectly about facts. The *condemnatio* could take different forms. If it aimed at a fixed sum an *intentio* predetermined its amount. However, if it aimed at an *incerta pecunia*, the judge was at liberty to estimate the amount, *condemnatio infinita* (*aestimatio litis*), or a maximum amount was stated to him, *condemnatio cum taxatione*. In some suits the judgement was a multiple of the value of the object of the dispute. If the formula contained the *clausula arbitraria*, a payment in kind was suggested in an interim notification of assessment. If the defendant paid as a result, he was acquitted.

→ Arbiter

H.BLANK, Condemnatio pecuniaria und Sachzugriff, in: ZRG 99, 1982, 303–316; KASER, RZ, 241, 256; W.WALDSTEIN, Haftung und dare oportere, in: FS Wesener, 1992, 519–530. C.PA.

Condicio A *condicio* (condition, as in the modern § 158 German Civil Code (BGB)) permitted the effectiveness of a business arrangement to depend on a future and uncertain event, e.g. the duty to repay a material loan 'if and when the ship returned from *Asia*'. In Roman law *condiciones* could be attached to most legal arrangements. However, the *actus legitimi* (Dig. 50,17,55) were incompatible with conditions and ineffective as conditional business. The Romans in particular understood the delaying effect of the *conditio* at the occurrence of which an arrangement would become effective as decisive. Until then there was a pending state (*condicio pendet*), occasionally with preliminary effects, e.g., in the conditional novation (Dig. 23,3,80). If a seller again transferred a conditionally transferred item, the second disposition was (only) void when the *condicio* occurred. Claims that had a delaying condition could be amended or waived (Dig. 46,2,14,1; 46,4,12). The occurrence of a dissolving condition terminated the effectiveness of an initially valid business. Legal positions such as freedom, → *patria potestas*, or the right of inheritance did not permit dissolving *condicio*. Property under a dissolving condition was recognized during the classical period.

In the *condicio potestativa* (in contract to *condicio casualis*) the entitled person in a business could influence the occurrence of the *condicio*. Occasionally, a beneficiary would only acquire endowments under a negative *condicio potestativa* at his death. This was avoided with the *cautio Muciana* (→ *cautio*).

Impossible or illegal conditions voided a transaction. In the case of legates the Sabinians and later jurists considered an impossible or illegal *condicio* as not having been imposed. The Roman doctrine of *condicio* was reintroduced in the late Middle Ages, but the principle of the retroactive effect of the occurrence of a condition, which was established by Bartolus, was only overcome in the 19th cent.

W. FLUME, Rechtsakt und Rechtsverhältnis, 1990; A. MASI, Studi sulla condizione nel diritto romano, 1966; H. PETER, Das bedingte Rechtsgeschäft, 1994.   P.A.

Condictio

A. TYPE OF SUIT IN THE IUS CIVILE   B. SETTLEMENT FOR ACQUISITION WITHOUT LEGAL BASIS C. TYPES OF CONDICTIO   D. CONTENT OF THE CLAIM

A. TYPE OF SUIT IN THE IUS CIVILE

Sentencing to a particular payment could be achieved with the → *legis actio per condictionem* after the 3rd cent. BC: *certa pecunia* based on a *lex Silia*, other *certae res* based on a *lex Calpurnia* (cf. Gai. Inst. 4,17 b–19). The *condictio* ('announcement') is merely a procedural designation: the court date was not granted immediately but only after the expiry of an 'announced' term of 30 days to allow the debtor the option of compliance without court procedure.

The *certum* in this suit is, in the first place, a payback guarantee for an informal loan (→ *mutuum*), i.e. in money or as seed. Since the suit does not name a reason for the obligation, it was also suitable for other payback guarantees, e.g., after erroneous fulfilment of a non-existent obligation. Furthermore, in the classical period the *condictio* became the suit for fulfilment of the abstract debt promise in the → *stipulatio* if its object was a *certum*. In that case the condiction formula (now the type of suit in the formulary procedure) was prefaced, as a document from Pompeii shows, by a → *praescriptio* that noted the stipulation (*ea res agatur de spon-*

sione [1. 143, 147]). Furthermore, the *condictio* was applied to the → *litterarum obligatio* (a claim from the housebook of the *pater familias*) because it was treated as a fictive loan (Cic. Q. Rosc. 4,13; 5,14).

B. SETTLEMENT FOR ACQUISITION WITHOUT LEGAL BASIS

The jurists of the Principate discussed the *condictio* in detail for the acquisition of assets without legal basis and in the process laid the foundation for the condiction theory in modern civil law (e.g., §§ 812ff. BGB). Pomponius (Dig. 50,17,206) formulated the claim for justice based on *condictio* in the most general terms: *iure naturae aequum est neminem cum alterius detrimento et iniuria fieri locupletiorem* ('By the law of nature it is fair that no one become richer by the loss and injury of another'). In this generalization the teachings of the jurists followed a tradition of legal philosophy that extends back to the Stoa (Cic. Off. 3,21 and also [2]). However, the Roman jurists did not found an institution for a general settlement of equity. Rather, based on its strict legal inheritance (→ *ius*) the classical *condictio* was preserved as a restriction to clearly definable, specific factual circumstances.

At the core of the classical *condictio* are facts that are based on a *datio*, originally the acquisition of Quiritic property. The only true exception is the *condictio furtiva*: a 'claim to deliverance' that was in practice restricted to the material value. It was due to the owner from a thief. All cases of *condictio*, have in common as the *veteres* (before the 1st cent. BC) already recognized, that someone acquired something *ex inusta causa* (Dig. 12,5,6). → *Causa* must be understood with a double meaning as both a cause and (equalization) purpose in this case. The *datio* as precondition of the main group of *condictio* was considerably expanded in the course of development: during the high classical period it is equal to, e.g. the waiving of debt (→ *acceptilatio*) as well as acquisition by occupancy, commingling or consumption. In particular, it was possible to pay the enrichment to the creditor based on instructions to a third party (→ *delegatio*, Dig. 16,1,8,3). However, granting of a *condictio* in the case of payment for services without legal basis was disputed (cf. the report of Ulp. Dig. 12,6,26,12).

C. TYPES OF CONDICTIO

Classical Roman law differentiated three types of *condictio* with respect to a *datio sine causa*: the most important was the *condictio indebiti* for cases of erroneous payments for a non-existing debt (Dig. 12,6). If the payment was not intended for cancelling a debt (*solvendi causa*), a *condictio* could still be considered if the debtor based on an informal agreement expected a counter-payment that was not owed but that was then not made (later the innominate contract). This *condictio ob rem* was called the *condictio causa data causa non secuta* (Dig.-Titel 12,4) in the post classical period. The third type is the *condictio ob turpem vel iniustam* causam (Dig.-Title 12,5). If a payment was made against the *datio ob rem* and, therefore, the *condictio ob rem* was precluded, return of the payment could still be demanded because of *turpis causa* (contrary to custom) or the illegality of the recipient. However, *condictio* was again precluded if both partners in the agreement had acted contrary to law or custom: *in delicto pari melior causa erit possidentis* (in case of offence by both sides, the *causa* of the one in possession is better, Dig. 12,7,5 pr. and 3,6,5,1). This principle was an expression of the concept that the granting of governmental legal protection should not be used to enforce claims contrary to custom — while the 'owner' (*possidens*) only has a factual and not a legally recognized advantage because of the *causa* contrary to custom. Some special cases that do not fit into the scheme described were summarized by Justinian's compilers as *condictio sine causa*. These included a *condictio incerti* because an (abstract) obligation was entered into without legal basis and a *condictio ob causam finitam* when an initially existing obligation ceased after the fact. The *condictio ex lege* (Dig. 13,2,) and *condictio generalis* (Dig. 12,1,9), which occur in the Digest, hardly relate to the classical *condictio*.

D. CONTENT OF THE CLAIM

What was originally acquired because of the *condictio* was generally to be surrendered rather than the (still) available enrichment. A limitation in liability because of the *condictio* only appears to have been recognized in cases of void gifts among spouses and acquisition by a ward without the participation of the guardian because of the loss or diminishment of the matter received.

1 J. G. WOLF, Aus dem neuen pompejanischen Urkundenfund: Die Kondiktionen des C. Sulpicius Cinnamus, in: SDHI 45, 1979, 141–177 2 C. WOLLSCHLÄGER, Das stoische Bereicherungsverbot in der röm. Rechtswiss., in: Röm. Recht in der europäischen Tradition, Symposion für F. Wieacker, 1985, 41–88.

KASER, RPR I, 592–600; H. HONSELL, TH. MAYER-MALY, W. IBID., Röm. Recht, ⁴1987, 350–356; W. PIKA, Ex causa furtiva condicere im klass. röm. Recht, 1988. G.S.

Condrusi Germanic people, listed by Caesar (B Gall. 2,4,10) among the *Germani cisrhenani* together with the → Eburones, Caerosi and Paemani; lived as clients of the → Treveri (ibid. 4,6,4) between them and the Eburones (ibid. 6,32,1). The *Condroz* region on the river Maas between Namur and Liège, which is called *pagus Condrustus* in medieval documents, recalls the C.

G. NEUMANN et al., s.v. C., RGA 5, 78–80. K.DI.

Conductores see → Locatio conductio

Condylum (Κόνδυλον; *Kóndylon*). Fortification in the southern Olympus on a bypass around the valley of the Tempe that runs through → Gonnus, probably to be equated with Gonnocondylus, and located near modern Tsurba-Mandria. When Philip V released Perrhaebia in 196 BC, he kept C. with the place name Olympias until 185 (Liv. 39,25,16). A garrison of Perseus was stationed in C. in 169 BC during the Third Macedonian War.

B. HELLY, Gonnoi, 1973, Index; F. STÄHLIN, Das hellenische Thessalien, 1924, 8f. HE.KR.

Confarreatio According to Gai. Inst. 1,112, the term *confarreatio* is based on the fact that during this religious act a *farreus panis* (a bread made of emmer but not spelt) was sacrificed by the bridal couple to *Iuppiter farreus* (→ far). Apart from the → coemptio and a one-year valid duration of the marriage (*usus*), the *confarreatio* was the third option of establishing the → manus (male power) over the wife. This effect was probably an ancillary result of the *confarreatio* while the highly festive conclusion of the marriage probably took centre stage in the ceremony. It took place before 10 witnesses, the priest of Jupiter (*flamen Dialis*, → flamines) and the highest priest (*pontifex maximus*). Such a lavish ceremony was presumably reserved for patricians or the nobility. In the end, the *confarreatio* was only employed for the marriages of priests. Whether Gai. (2nd cent. AD) is describing an already entirely defunct ceremony is uncertain. A marriage based on the *confarreatio* was divorced by a *diffarreatio*, again probably with a priestly ritual (Plut. Quaest. Rom. 50).

TREGGIARI, 21–24. G.S.

Confederations see → States, confederacies of

Confessio Literally a confession, but in the modern sense also an acknowledgement. It led immediately to the enforcement proceeding instead of a sentence according to the principle that the confessing party should be considered as having been sentenced: *confessus pro iudicato habetur (est)* (Dig. 42,2,1; 3; 6; Cod. Iust. 7,59,1). However, there were exceptions:

1) In criminal proceedings a defendant confessing to certain grave crimes (e.g., *crimen laesae maiestatis*: the most famous case being Jesus before Pilate, Mk 15,2ff.) was treated as sentenced. All that was left to him was a plea for mercy, *deprecatio*, to the proconsul (cf. Dig. 48,18,1,27). In the case of less serious crimes there was an apparent limitation to an (optional) consideration of the evidence just as an examination of the truthfulness of a confession was permissible (Dig. 48,18,1, 17; 23; 27).

2) In a civil trial the type of procedure must be distinguished: in the *legis actiones* procedure, a *confessio* (which was also possible by silence) before the magistrate (*in iure*) resulted in owing a particular sum or having to return the object (according to Gai. Inst. 2,24 this is the basis of → in iure cessio), the immediate applicability of the foreclosure suit of the *legis actio per manus iniectionem* (Gai. 4,21ff.) or before the *arbi-*

trium litis aestimandae. In the formular procedure the *confessio in iure* and the *confessio apud iudicem* must be differentiated according to the sources. Little is known about the latter, but a confession before a judge probably functioned as proof of the confessed issue though it could be modified (Dig. 42,2,2). The *confessio in iure* had to be recorded in the → *litis contestatio* to unfold its effect (modern technical term: 'preclusion') in the scope of what was admitted. The judge then immediately passed sentence — without considering evidence (Dig. 42,2,3; 5) — or restricted the proceeding to questions not confessed. In the context of the *lex Aquilia* an *actio confessoria* is mentioned (Dig. 9,2,23,11) that possibly developed from the *arbitrium litis aestimandae* and which became the subject of the judicial proceeding after the defendant's admission in cases of an undetermined value of the damaged object. In the → *cognitio* procedure the confession increasingly becomes the proof — though with a gradual transition in the details.

W. LITEWSKI, Confessio in iure e sententia, in: Labeo 22, 1976, 252–267; D. NÖRR, Zur Interdependenz von Prozeßrecht und materiellem Recht am Beispiel der lex Aquilia in: Rechtshistor. Journ. 6, 1987, 99–116; C. PAULUS, Einige Bemerkungen zum Prozeß Jesu bei den Synoptikern, in: ZRG 102, 1985, 437–445; N. SCAPINI, La confessione nel diritto romano I, 1973, II, 1983; D. SIMON, Unt. zum Justinianischen Zivilprozeß, 1969, 202.   C.PA.

Confirmatio see → Argumentatio

Confluentes
[1] Modern Koblenz, traffic node and commercial port, at the confluence (*ad* C.) of the Moselle and the Rhine, on the Mainz-Cologne road along the Rhine Valley and the routes leading from Trier over the Hunsrück mountains and Maifeld to the Rhine (CIL XVII 2,675). A straight pile frame bridge crossed the Rhine to Ehrenbreitenstein from 49 BC (dendrochronology [1]). The Moselle bridge with stone pillars on a pile frame is dendrochronologically younger (AD 104/176). A late Tiberian/early Claudian fort, which was abandoned in AD 70, and a *vicus* towards the Rhine are hypothesized to have been in the old city. On the east side of the Rhine the cohort camp of Koblenz-Niederberg (2.8 ha) secured the link between the bridge and the limes in the 2nd/3rd cents. The little-known settlement in the old city survived until its destruction by Germanic raids around 260. After that C. was located on the Rhine limes and was protected by an irregular fortification in the old city, which was garrisoned with *milites defensores* and still existed in 354 (Amm. Marc. 16,3,1), (8.5 ha) (Not. Dign. Occ. 41,24). About the mid 5th cent. C. was already Frankish. A large Gallo-Roman sanctuary on the west slope of the Kühkopf (1st cent. to *c.* 400) is remarkable.

1 ECK, 20f.

H.-H. WEGNER, Koblenz, in: H. CÜPPERS (ed.), Die Römer in Rheinland-Pfalz, 1990, 418–424.   K.DI.

[2] In Raetia. According to the Not. Dign. Occ. 35, a *praefectus numeri barcariorum Confluentibus sive Brecantia* is attested, modern Koblenz at the confluence of the Aare and the Rhine. STAEHELIN [1] believes that the settlement was located at the inflow from the upper lake into the lower lake near Constance, but according to BERGK [2] the settlement was located at the mouth of the Rhine into Lake Constance, modern Rheineck.

1 F. STAEHELIN, Die Schweiz in röm. Zeit, 1948, 313   TH. BERGK, Zur Gesch. und Top. der Rheinlande, 1882, 98.   H.C.

[3] see → Lugdunum

Confusio In the *confusio* (the 'merging') the same person is both debtor and creditor or owner and holder of a limited material right, e.g. a usufruct. In Roman law *confusio* led to the extinction of the claim or the right. The late classic jurists (3rd cent. AD) occasionally use the term *consolidatio* for *confusio* without creating material distinctions. The effect of the *confusio* could not be prevented by the will of the parties. However, the Roman jurists occasionally assume a duty to refound the claim or right. The opinion of the Proculians (→ Law schools) that the → *noxalis actio* against the owner of a slave who caused damage is revived when the damaged party, who has in the meantime acquired the slave, sells him to a third party (cf. Gai. Inst. 4,78 towards the end) does not belong in this context: Since the compensation obligation of the owner arose again as a personal obligation with owning the property, the Romans did not use the term *confusio* with reference to the injured party the damaged person. The contrary opinion of the Sabinians, according to which the damaged person, who is reselling, has no compensation claim against the buyer, is not justified with a *confusio* but probably rests on the consideration that his interest in compensation had materialized with the sale.

P. KIESS, Die confusio im klassischen röm. Recht, 1995.   G.S.

Confutatio see → Argumentatio

Conger (γόγγρος; *góngros*, sometimes, e.g., Ath. 8,356a: γρύλλος; *grýllos*), a marine eel, a sea fish that was popular like the → eel and, therefore, expensive (Plaut. Mil. 760; Persa 110; cf. information in Ath. 7,288c). Aristotle mentions two species that differ in colour (Hist. an. 8,13, 598a13), their unusual length, thickness and smoothness, the large stomach and the tallow-like fat. The conger feeds on fish including its own species and octopuses but, in turn, is the prey of moray eels and crabs (cf. Plin. HN 9,185). According to Aristot. Hist. an. 8,15,599b6, it hibernates. The female's pregnancy becomes apparent by placing it in fire (Hist. anim. 6,17, 571a28–b2).
→ Fishes

KELLER II, 360.   C.HÜ.

Congiarium Derived from *congius* (a liquid measure), the term *congiarium* designated in the Republican period the distribution of wine and oil organized by Roman officials, but under the Principate the distribution of money to the *plebs urbana*. The term *congiarium* is rarely used in the context of extra payments to soldiers (*donativum*; CIL VIII 18042). In the course of the 2nd cent. AD, the term *congiarium* is replaced by the term *liberalitas* and in the 4th cent. by *largitio*. The distribution occurred on the occasion of triumphs, the accession of a *princeps*, the *tirocinium* of the heir apparent, the *decennalia* (celebrated by Septimius Severus in AD 202 and Constantine in AD 315), as a testamentary bequest of a deceased *princeps* and on other occasions. Based on literary and epigraphic evidence, memorial coins and the list of the Chronographus of AD 354, it was possible to identify the *congiarium* of the first three cents. AD and their frequency, the sums paid out (from 75 denars in the 1st cent. to 250 denars in the mid 3rd cent.) and the composition of the coins (silver or gold). Literary texts and reliefs of the Arch of Constantine as well as the coins issued on these occasions beginning with Nero confirm the importance of the *princeps'* presence at the *congiarium*. The legend CON, CONG, CONGIAR or CONGIARIVM is associated with a donation scene. The recipient of the gift ascends the steps of the podium (*suggestum*) on which the *princeps* is seated and extends a corner of his toga to receive the coins that were counted with a counting-board by a helper. Coins by Nero, Titus, Nerva and later Marcus Aurelius show Minerva with a helmet in the centre. On other coins the personification of a standing *liberalitas* appears, recognizable by her typical attributes, the counting-board and the cornucopia.

Since the reign of Hadrian the legend *liberalitas* is sometimes associated with a distribution scene, sometimes with a representation of *liberalitas* herself. The reliefs on the Arch of Constantine in Rome shows the distributions of Marcus Aurelius and Constantine while setting them in the context of the imperial fora. The last *congiarium* in Rome is dated to the rule of Theodosius (13 June 389).

→ Donativum; → liberalitas

1 D. VAN BERCHEM, Les distributions de blé et d'argent à la plèbe romaine sous l'Empire, 1939 2 J.-P. CALLU, La politique monétaire des empereurs romains de 238 à 311, 1969 3 M. CORBIER, Trésors et greniers dans la Rome impériale, in: Le système palatial en Orient, en Grèce et à Rome, 1987, 411–443 4 H. KLOFT, Liberalitas Principis, 1970 5 F. MILLAR, Les congiaires à Rome et la monnaie, in: A. GIOVANNINI (ed.), Nourrir la plèbe, 1991, 43–65 6 G. SPINOLA, Il '*congiarium*' in età imperiale, 1990 7 P. VEYNE, Le pain et le cirque, 1976
8 C. VIRLOUVET, Tessera frumentaria. Les procédures de la disribution du blé public à Rome, 1995
9 R. VOLLKOMMER, *Liberalitas*, LIMC 6.1, 1992, 274–278 and 6.2, 141–143.   MI.CO.

Congius Based on an amphora (= 8 *congii*), *congius* designates a Roman volume measure for liquids and is equal to 3.275 l, which is standardized when filled with water or wine at 80 pounds at 327.45 g each, so that a *congius* of 10 pounds weighs about 3.275 kg. The 'Farnesian' *congius*, which was produced in AD 75 under Vespasian and shows the abbreviation *p(ondus) X* (for 10 pounds) in the inscription, was just below the standard with 3.265 l (ILS 8628). Regarding the subdivision of the *congius,* cf. → *cochlear.* The *chous* is equated with the Roman *congius.*

→ Amphora; → chous; → Calibration; → Measure of volume

F. HULTSCH, Griech. und röm. Metrologie, ²1882; Id., s.v. C., RE IV, 880–881; H. Chantraine, s.v. Quadrantal, RE XXIV, 667–672; O. A. W. DILKE, Mathematik, Maße und Gewichte in der Antike, 1991.   A.M.

Conjecture see → Emendation of texts

Conjugation see → Inflection

Connacorix (Κοvvακόριξ; *Konnakórix*). Galatian with a Celtic name [1. 182; 2. 155], in 73 BC a commander of → Mithridates in → Heraclea (Memnon 29,4; 34,4; 35,1–4; 7; 36=FGrH 3 no. 434).

1 SCHMIDT. 2 L. WEISGERBER, Galatische Sprachreste, in: Natalicium. FS J. Geffken, 1931.   W.SP.

Conon (Κόνων; *Kónōn*).
[1] Athenian, in 413 BC commander in Naupactus, after 411/10 repeatedly *stratēgós*. C. was bottled up in 406 by the Peloponnesian fleet in the port of Mytilene and lost 30 ships (Xen. Hell. 1,6,14–23; Diod. Sic. 13,77–79). After Athens' victory at the → Arginusae he was freed. Since he did not participate in the battle, he was not deposed and sentenced to death like the other generals (Xen. Hell. 1,6,38–7,1). He escaped the destruction of the Attic fleet at Aegospotami in 405 and fled to king → Euagoras [1] (Xen. Hell. 2,1,28f.; Diod. Sic. 13,106,6) at Cyprus. From there C. contacted the satrap Pharnabazus and the Great King since Sparta was at war with Persia after 400 because of the Greek towns in Asia Minor. The Great King ordered the building of a fleet and C. became its admiral (*naúarchos*) in the spring of 397. After extensive preparations, from the spring of 296 C. operated from Caunus in the southeast of the Aegean and captured Rhodes (Androtion FGrH 324 F 46; Diod. Sic. 14,39,1–4; 79,5–8; Hell. Oxy. 12, 3; cf. 18 CHAMBERS). In August 394 the Persian fleet under C. destroyed Spartan maritime power in the battle of Cnidus (Xen. Hell. 4,3,11f.; Diod. Sic. 14,83,5–7). The Spartan harmosts and garrisons were driven out of Asia Minor and the islands (Xen. Hell. 4,8,1f.; Diod. Sic. 14,84,3f.). In the spring of 393 Pharnabazus and C. attacked Laconia with a large fleet, occupied Cythera and supported the anti-Spartan alliance near Corinth. Pharnabazus returned to Asia while

C. entered Piraeus with the Persian fleet and supported Athens' efforts to renew its power in the Aegean by rushing the reconstruction of the 'long walls' (Xen. Hell. 4,8,1–9; Diod. Sic. 14,84,4f.; 82,2f.; IG II 2 1656–1664; TOD 107 A; SEG 41,102). Thereupon, in 392 Sparta entered into peace negotiations with the Persian satrap Tiribazus and offered the surrender of the Greek cities in Asia Minor. The Athenians in turn sent delegates to Sardeis, which C. joined but the peace negotiations failed. C. was imprisoned by Tiribazus (Xen. Hell. 4,8,12–16; Diod. Sic. 14,85,4) but escaped to Euagoras in Cyprus where he died soon after (Lys. 19,39–41).

As the founder of Athens' renewed power, victor of Cnidus and liberator of the Greeks from the Spartan yoke, bronze statues of C. were erected in Athens, Samos and Ephesus. C. was the father of the important stratēgós → Timotheus.

P. FUNKE, Homónoia und Arché, 1980; D. A. MARCH, Konon and the Great King's Fleet, 396–394, in: Historia 46, 1997, 257–269; B. S. STRAUSS, Athens after the Peloponnesian War, 1986.

[2] Athenian, grandson of C. [1], son of Timotheus, served repeatedly in the 2nd half of the 4th cent. as a trierarch and was stratēgós of Piraeus in 334/3 and 333/2 (IG II² 2970,5; SEG 22,148). In 319 after the occupation of Piraeus by the Macedonians he went as a delegate with Phocion and Clearchus to Nicanor (Diod. Sic. 18,64,5). DAVIES, 511f.   W.S.

[3] C. of Samos. Astronomer and mathematician in Alexandria under → Ptolemaeus III, Euergetes and a friend of → Archimedes [1]. The latter posthumously dedicated to him the treatise directed at their mutual friend and student of C., → Dositheus [3], De Quadratura parabolae ('The squaring of the Parabola') and regretted that C. had died too young to have offered the proof to his writings on spirals (De lineis spiralibus, praef. p. 3,13 HEIBERG). Therefore, C.'s writings on the Archimedean spiral mentioned by → Pappus are not considered authentic. → Apollonius [13] of Perge cites him as a predecessor in the theory of conic sections but notes that he lacked the necessary care in providing proof when criticizing (the otherwise unknown) Nicoteles of Cyrene.

As an astronomer C. collected solar eclipse observations in Egypt (Sen. Q Nat. 7,3,3, cf. Catull. 66,3) and wrote seven volumes De astrologia (Prob. Verg. Ecl. 3,40) to which perhaps the → parapegma mentioned in Ptol. Phaseis 67,7 H. (cf. Catull. 66,2; Plin. HN 18,312) belongs. He supposedly conducted his observations on star risings in Italy and Sicily but his authorship of the work De Italia, which Serv. Aen. 7,738 mentions, is not considered as secured.

C. became famous for his 'discovery' of the stellar constellation Coma Berenices (Πλόκαμος Βερενίκης, 'The Lock of Berenice') between Leo, Virgo and Bootes: → Berenice [3] II., the spouse of Ptolemy III, dedicated

the hair on her head in the temple of Venus Arsinoe Zephyritis before a campaign of her husband against Syria in 246 BC to his happy return (Hyg. Poet. Astr. 2,24 l. 1002 VIRÉ). The hair disappeared and C. found it again in the sky. The poet → Callimachus wrote a katasterismos (→ Stars, legends about) on this topic and concluded his Aítia with it. → Catullus made this a poem of its own (Carm. 66) that became the model for all later constellation panegyrics.

A. REHM, s.v. Konon [II], RE XI,1338–1340; GUNDEL, 107f.   W.H.

[4] Greek mythographer, probably 1st cent. BC/ 1st cent. AD. A longer summary of his 'tales' by Photius (Bibl. cod. 186) is preserved (Dihēgéseis; dedicated to Archelaus [7] Patris, king of Cappadocia from 36 BC-AD 17). They include 50 mythographical tales (rhetorical elaborations of foundation stories, aetiologies, love tales, and various mythical events). According to Photius they were composed in a pleasing and graceful Attic style that was occasionally considered too complicated for ordinary readers. Attribution of the mythographical fragment POxy 3648 (2nd cent. AD) to the original of C.'s Dihēgéseis rests on solid arguments. C. also composed a Herakleía and a work on Italy.

EDITIONS: FGrH 26; R. HENRY, Photius, Bibliothèque 3, 1962, 8–39 (with trans. and notes).
BIBLIOGRAPHY: A. HENRICHS, Three Approaches to Greek Mythography, in: J. N. BREMMER (ed.), Interpretations of Greek Mythology, 1987, 242–277; E. MARTINI, s.v. K. (9), RE 11, 1335–1338. F.M.H.

Conope (Κωνώπη; Kōnṓpē). Place in Aetolia near modern Angelocastro at the southern edge of the Achelous plain, new foundation between 287 and 281 BC as Polis Arsinoeia in honour of Arsinoë [II 3], the wife of Lysimachus. A favourable location on a ford of the Achelous (Str. 10,2,22), member of the Aetolian koinon (→ Aitoloi, map). Epigraphy: IG IX 1,131–133; SEG 17,269–272; 25,625; 34,468f.; 40,457 [1].

1 G. KLAFFENBACH, in: SPrAW 1936, 360–364.

C. ANTONETTI, Les Étoliens, 1990; D. STRAUCH, Röm. Politik und Griech. Trad., 1996, 264f. D.S.

Consabura Remains of this probably Celtic town [1. 1105] near Consuegra south of Toledo (CIL II p. 431; [3. 177]). Frontin. Str. 4,5,19 mentions C. in the context of the war with Sertorius in 78 BC. Other attestations: Plin. HN 3,25; Ptol. 2,6,57; It. Ant. 446,6; Geogr. Rav. 313,15; CIL II 2,2166; 4211.

1 HOLDER 1 E. HÜBNER, s.v. C., RE IV I, 889 3 A. SCHULTEN, Fontes Hispaniae Antiquae 4, 1937.

TOVAR 3, 222–224. P.B.

Consanguinei Siblings with a common father (uterini share the mother). According to Roman civil law consanguine sisters had a legal right of inheritance while agnatic relatives of a higher degree of relationship (aunts, nieces etc.) were excluded from intestate inheritance (Gai. Inst. 3,14; Inst. Iust. 3,2,3a).

→ Agnatio; → Succession, law of

H. L. W. NELSON, U. MANTHE, Gai Institutiones III 1–87, 1992, 65f.   U.M.

Conscience The modern term 'conscience' as the awareness of good and evil in one's acts has an approximate though not exact linguistic equivalent in Greek συνείδησις (syneídēsis, also τὸ συνειδός/to syneidós, σύνεσις/sýnesis) and Latin conscientia. The term syneídēsis is rarely used from the 5th to 2nd cents. BC but becomes more frequent after the 1st cent. BC. Three basic meanings must be differentiated: 1) the 'awareness' of one's own, mostly negatively evaluated behaviour; 2) the (moral) conscience; 3) one's 'internal' conscience. Conscience internalizes the moral judgements of society and religion and effects the historical transition from shame to guilt, from result to intent as moral standards (Soph. Ant. 265f.; Democr. B 297 DK; Men. Monostichoi 597). In Hellenistic philosophy introspection, self-observation, and self-examination became part of the way of life. The younger Stoa identified conscience with reason (ἡγεμονικόν, hēgemonikón), the higher self of man, and demanded purification of the conscience with mental exercises (Epict. Dissertationes 3,93–95; M. Aur. 5,27).

The Latin term conscientia is also used more frequently with the increased use of syneídēsis in the 1st cent. BC, repeatedly in Cicero and throughout in Seneca (for attestations see ThlL). Conscientia is even more equivalent to the modern meaning of conscience than syneídēsis and often refers to the 'Inner'. Cicero conceptualizes conscience as a law of nature and coined the term 'pang of conscience' (morderi conscientia, Cic. Rep. 3,22; Cic. Tusc. 4,45). In Seneca the differentiation of bona (Sen. Epist. 12,9; 43,5) and mala conscientia (Epist. 105,8; Benef. 3,1,4), good and bad conscience, are part of the fixed vocabulary of guiding the soul. The ability to feel shame is a basic condition for moral progress (Sen. Epist. 25,2).

Philo of Alexandria (about 25/10 BC-AD 40) elevated to syneidós (occasionally also syneídēsis) to a key term in his theology as the internal judge over good and bad behaviour divinely implanted into humans (Phil. Quod deterius potiori insidiari soleat 146).

The self-examination of Hellenistic philosophy flowed into Christian penance. The pure conscience demanded by God is no longer achieved by one's own purity and innocence but required humility, fear and a plea for the forgiveness of sins (Cor 4,5; 11,31; Lactant. Div. inst. 6,24,20; Aug. Serm. 20,3). An erroneous reading of the LXX derived from Origen and accepted by Jerome turns syneídēsis, read as syntérēsis ('preservation'), into the 'spark of conscience' (scintilla conscientiae; Hier. in Hesecielem 1,6–8 according to Orig. Homiliae in Ezechielem 1,16). This text resulted in

varying interpretations of the two terms in the terminologically oriented interpretation of scholasticism, which transformed syntérēsis into sy(i)ndérēsis: conscientia on the one hand is the ability to differentiate good and evil in individual cases, syndérēsis on the other hand is the ability to clearly recognize general principles (Thomas Aquinas, Summa theologica I, quaestio 79, articulus 12f.; 1 II quaestio 94, articulus 1).

GRAECO-ROMAN: E. R. DODDS, The Greeks and the Irrational, 1951; I. HADOT, Seneca und die griech.-röm. Tradition der Seelenführung, 1969; P. HADOT, Exercices spirituels et philos. antique, ³1993; M. KÄHLER, Das Gewissen, 1878; G. MOLENAAR, Seneca's use of the term conscientia, in: Mnemosyne 4, 1969, 170–180; O. SEEL, Zur Vorgesch. des Gewissensbegriffs im altgriech. Denken, in: FS Franz Dornseiff, 1953, 291–319 CHRISTIAN: A. CANCRINI, Syneidesis. Il tema semantico della con-scientia nella Grecia antica, 1970; H. CHADWICK, Betrachtungen über das G. in der griechischen, jüdischen und christlichen Tradition, 1974; H. OSBORNE, Syneidesis, in: Journal of Theological Studies 32, 1931, 167–179; Id., Syneidesis and synesis, in: CR 45, 1931, 8–10; T. C. POTT, Conscience, in: The Cambridge History of Later Medieval Philosophy, 1982, 686–704; G. RUDBERG, Cicero und das Gewissen, in: Symbolae Osloenses 31, 1955, 95–104; J. STENZELBERGER, Syneidesis, Conscientia, Gewissen, 1963; M. WALDMANN, Synteresis oder Syneidesis?, in: Theologische Quartalsschrift 118, 1938, 332–371; F. ZUCKER, Syneidesis — Conscientia, 1928.
                                                                                          F.R.

Conscientious objection Conscientious objection (CO) constitutes any rejection of military or war service independent of motivation, i.e. in the case of conscripts avoiding the mustering and not appearing for service, in the case of active soldiers refusing commands, desertion, mutiny or switching sides. Unlike desertion (which in the Roman army occurred because of fear of punishment and the harshness of the service and discipline, cowardice and demoralization, but also because of a better material offer from the other side), CO is at least in some cases recognizable as an ethically-morally, religiously or politically motivated rejection of war or armed service and its possible consequences. For example, Musonius Rufus noted in the civil war situation of the Year of Four Emperors in AD 69 the bona pacis ac belli discrimina ('the blessings of peace and the hardships of war ') (Tac. Hist. 3,81).

CO was not tolerated in Rome; relief (vacatio) from military service was only granted in a few exceptional cases. The first politically and socially motivated CO was supposedly granted in 495/4 BC (Liv. 2,27,10ff.). However, certain attestations only exist for the period after 275 BC, e.g., the wars against Pyrrhus (Val. Max. 6,3,4), Hannibal (Liv. 24,18,7ff.; 2,000 men involved), Perseus (Liv. 43,14,3f.) and in Spain (Pol. 35,4,1ff.; App.Hisp. 49). The first known individual case of CO is C. Vettienus, who in 90 BC cut off the fingers of his left hand so that he would not have to fight in the → Social War [3] (Val. Max. 6,3,3). Self-mutilation as well as flight and disappearance (Suet. Tib. 8; Dig. 49,16,4,11) were the customary methods of CO attested among conscripts up to late antiquity (Suet. Aug. 24,1; Dig. 49,16,4,12; Amm. Marc. 15,12,3; Cod. Theod. 7,13,4; 7,13,5; 7,13,10), while active soldiers deserted or in extreme cases committed suicide (Dig. 28,3,6,7; 48,19,38,12). CO declined during the early Principate with the emergence of a professional army, but forced recruitment led to conflicts.

Christians did not generally refuse military service, since the position of leading bishops on this point was contradictory. It is disputed if CO occurred because of a general dislike of (potential) killing or for fear of idolatry ('image worship' because of the non-Christian imagery; cf. the *imperatoris imagines*, Veg. Mil. 2,7). The Christian empire of late antiquity treated CO and desertion as crimes because it was dependent on the military service of all men.

For CO in the Greek world, → *deilías graphé*; *lipotaxíou graphé*.

→ Desertor

1 M. Clauss, s.v. Heerwesen (Heeresreligion), RAC 13, 1073–1113   2 W. Gerlings, Die Stellung der Alten Kirche zu Kriegsdienstverweigerung und Krieg, in: Osnabrücker Jahrbuch Frieden und Wissenschaft 4, 1997, 155–166   3 H. Hegermann, s.v. Krieg III, TRE 20, 25–55   4 J. Helgeland, Christians and the Roman Army from Marcus Aurelius to Constantine, in: ANRW II 23.1, 724–834   5 J. H. Jung, Die Rechtsstellung der röm. Soldaten, in: ANRW II 14, 882–1013   6 Th. Kissel, Kriegsdienstverweigerung im röm. Heer, in: Antike Welt 27,4, 1996, 289–296   7 Kromayer/Veith   8 J. Rüpke, Domi militiae, 1990   9 E. Sander, Das Recht des röm. Soldaten, in: RhM 101, 1958, 152–234   10 L. J. Swift, War and the Christian Conscience I: The Early Years, in: ANRW II 23.1, 835–868   11 L. Wierschowski, Kriegsdienstverweigerung im röm. Reich, in: AncSoc 26, 1995, 205–239   12 Id., Roma naturaliter bellicosa? — Kriegsdienstverweigerung und Fahnenflucht im Röm. Reich, in: Osnabrücker Jahrbuch Frieden und Wissenschaft 4, 1997, 131–154.   L.WI.

Conscripti (from *conscribere* in the specific sense of' to write together' or 'to add in writing', 'to register') generally means persons entered into a register. Thus, *conscripti* means the *cives Romani* entered in a list of citizens, also the registered colonists of a *colonia*, the soldiers and officials entered into the matriculation rolls of a military unit and, finally, the tax payers entered into *census* lists (Liv. 1,12,8; 37,46,10; Suet. Iul. 8; Dig. 50,16,239,5; Cod. Iust. 6,21,16; 11,48,4).

In the combined word *patres conscripti*, *conscripti* refers to the more clearly recognizable plebeian group that was accepted into the Senate during the final phase of the struggle of the orders (before the *lex Hortensia* of 287 BC) but who were not furnished with all the rights due to patrician senators. Activities closed to them may have included, e.g., the approval of laws (*auctoritas senatus*). Festus (p. 7 M.) may be understood in this meaning: *nam patres dicuntur qui sunt patricii generis,*

conscripti qui in senatu sunt scriptis adnotati. Livy (2,1) offers a different, more legendary interpretation. The assumption that *conscripti* merely characterized the newly accepted senators for reasons of tradition — and not for political reasons, which would have continued the conflict — is more probable. Just as the duration of Senate membership and the rank of offices was noted, so the antiquity of nobility still had a rank-differentiating effect on procedural and ceremonial rules even after the complete equalization of patricians and plebeians in 287 BC, e.g., in the speaking order in the Senate (Liv. per. 11; Cass. Dio, fr. 37,2, lib. IX; Diod. Sic. 21,18,2).

→ Tabulae publicae; → Censuales; → Senatus; → Patricii; → Plebeii

F. F. Abbott, A History and Description of Roman Political Institutions, ²1963, no. 267; Mommsen, Staatsrecht 3, 835f.   C.G.

Consecratio Verbal noun of *consecrare*, 'to dedicate, to declare as *sacrum*'; a legal act by magistrates — often together with → *pontifices* — in which the consecrated object was withdrawn from worldly/human use. A specifically Roman procedure, since in Roman understanding temples, cult images, altars and cult instruments did not have an 'autogenous' sacred quality. A differentiation by content between *consecratio* and → *dedicatio* is occasionally alleged for the Republican period (e.g. [1. 399]), but the two terms were used synonymously since the late Republic (Dig. 24,1,5,12; SHA Hadr. 13,7). *Consecratio* is documented in various contexts:

1. *Consecratio* of altars, temples, properties, cult images, money, etc. (cf. Festus p. 424) in connection with constituting or expanding public sanctuaries (*sacra publica*; cf. Dig. 1,8,6,3; Gai. Inst. 2,2,4). Like numerous other religious institutions, the procedure of *consecratio* is attributed by Roman annalists to King → Numa (Liv. 1,21,1ff.), who created a ('well-ordered') *urbs* divided into profane and sacred zones by *consecratio* after Romulus had created the first preconditions for the organization of a political community by drawing the boundary of the → *pomerium*. In the Republican period, with the abolition of the monarchy, the competence of *consecratio* was transferred to the highest Roman officials. It could also be transferred by a resolution or a *lex* for specific objects to former officials (Cic. De domo 44–52). Up to the Principate the *consecratio* constituted the last step in establishing new cultic sites — e.g., after a → *votum* before a battle — as part of the religious activities of Rome's political elite. The emperors built and consecrated all later significant temples. They were after all the only ones who were able to grant permission for the transformation of public into consecrated properties (*loca sacra*) (Dig. 1,8,9,1–3). The Roman *consecratio* procedure was later received by the Catholic Church in a modified Christian form (cf. Inst. Iust. 2,1,8: *sacra sunt, quae rite et per pontifices deo consecrata sunt* ...) [2. 30f.].

2. As *consecratio bonorum, consecratio* was part of a criminal (capital) procedure or political → *coercitio*, by expropriating (mostly) properties through consecration to the benefit of a public temple. The *consecratio bonorum* was performed by people's tribunes (Liv. 8,20,8; Cic. De domo 123; Plin. HN 7,143f.). The *consecratio capitis* falls into this area as part of a cursing or self-cursing formula that did not enter legal practice or language (cf. Liv. 3,48,5; Plin. Pan. 64).

3. Formally and by content different from the previous types is the *consecratio* of deceased emperors in the context of their deification. This *consecratio* was a resolution by the Senate (passed upon a request from the succeeding emperor) that declared the deceased a *divus* [3]; in the later period the *consecratio* occurred together with the burial (→ Ruler cult).

1 A. MUTEL, Reflexions sur quelques aspects de la condition juridique des temples en droit romain classique, in: Mélanges offerts à L. Falletti, 1971, 389–412   2 J.L. MURGA, La venta de las 'res divini iuris' en el derecho romano tardio, 1971   3 CH. SAUMAGNE, La lex de dedicatione aedium (450–304) et la divinitas Christi, in: Studi in onore di E. Volaterra, 1971, 383–407.

W. KIERDORF, *Funus* und *consecratio* Zu Terminologie und Ablauf der röm. Kaiserapotheose, in: Chiron 1986, 43–69; F. SALERNO, Dalla *consecratio* alla *publicatio bonorum*, 1990; G. WISSOWA, s.v. C., RE IV 1, 896–902.
C.F.

Consensus

Consensus is the unanimous will of the parties of a contract (→ *contractus*). In Roman law it was the basis of the binding character of buying (→ *emptio venditio*), contracts of lease, work and employment (→ *locatio conductio*), of commission (→ *mandatum*) and association (→ *societas*). The 'invention of' *consensus* as the central element of a system of civil law is one of the 'grandest juridical achievements, and one of the most influential for further development' [1. 180]. The liability resulting from *consensus* necessitates neither a specific form nor an advance nor performance. The principle of *consensus* combines in a unique way specific notions of Roman law with the necessity of deciding on business involving persons from outside the citizenry: the notion of *consensus* developed from the → *praetor peregrinus*, the court official responsible for litigation with non-Romans, who were not admitted to the business transactions covered by *ius civile*. However, it is based on the Roman idea of → *fides*. Therefore, contracts resulting *from consensus* became enforceable *ex fide bona* ('from good faith').

In classic Roman law of the Principate, the notion of *consensus* achieved an importance going well beyond the four consensual contracts (see above). E.g., the error of one party in the strictly formal transaction of → *stipulatio* made it void (*Inst. Iust.* 3,19,23); in a similar way, *consensus* was required for real and literal contracts (→ *contractus*). Even for the contraction of marriage, which was not considered a contract proper, *consensus* was required in the form of *affectio maritalis* (mutual wish to marry; Ulp. *Dig.* 24,1,32,13; 35,1,15).

After setbacks in early medieval law, the principle of *consensus* was expanded even further under the influence of fully developed Church law. Eventually, in the contractual theories of natural law in the 17th and 18th cents., it became the most important foundation not only of law, but of the whole notion of state.

1 M. KASER, Röm. Privatrecht. Ein Studienbuch, ¹⁶1992.

G. GROSSO, Il sistema romano dei contratti, ³1963.   G.S.

Consentes Dei Roman name for a group of twelve deities, six male and six female, presumably from the etymological root *'con-sens' ('being together') [1]. They corresponded to the 12 Olympians of Greece from at least the time of Varro [2], but the name, including an archaic plural form *deum consentium*, points to greater antiquity. Their temple (*aedes deum consentium*: Varro, *Ling.* 8,70) must be the *porticus deum consentium* at the north end of the Forum and its two groups of six golden statues each (Varro, *Rust.* 1,1,4) those which Vettius Agorius → Praetextatus restored in 367 (*CIL* VI 102 = *ILS* 4003) [3]. The selfsame group was occasionally venerated in the provinces (Dacia: [2. 124f.]), and in the → *interpretatio Romana* they found a counterpart in the group of twelve anonymous divine advisors of Etruscan Jupiter (Tinia; Varro, cited in Arnobius 3,40, cf. A. Caecina in Sen. Q Nat. 2,41) [4. 31].

1 LEUMANN, 523   2 CH. R. LONG, The Twelve Gods of Greece and Rome, 1987, 235–243   3 NASH 2, 241   4 PFIFFIG.   F.G.

Consentia Town at the confluence of the → Crathis and the Basentus (Plin. HN 3,72), modern Cosenza. From its strategically favoured position C. controlled the routes to Sybaris and the Tyrrhenian Sea. The earliest date is given by Strabo (6,1,5), who mentions C. as the metropolis of the Bruttian League (founded in 356 BC), but a small number of bronze oboli bearing the legend KOS (or KWS), traditionally dated to 400–356 BC, appear to push back the date. In 330 BC it was taken by Alexander the Molossian, who was buried there after falling to the Lucanians at Pandosia (Liv. 8,24,4; 14; 16; Str. loc. cit.). In the Second Punic War C. several times switched allegiance between Rome and Carthage, eventually capitulating in 204 BC (Liv. 23,30,5; 25,1,2; 28,11,13; 29,38,1; 30,19,10). C. was involved in the slaves' revolt of 73 BC (Oros. 5,24,2) and in 40 BC was sacked by Sextus Pompeius (App. B Civ. 5,56; 58). *Colonia* under Augustus, *regio* III (Lib. colon. 1,209,16); famous for the site of the grave of → Alaric (died in AD 410) in the bed of the Busento near the town, which, however, has not been found. (Jord. Get. 30,158). The few archaeological remains left after a history of continuous settlement include stones from the old city wall built into the Norman keep, a necropolis of the late 4th cent. and a cult of Hercules. C. was mentioned in the *elogium* of Polla (*CIL* XI 6950) as one of the *stationes* along the *via Annia* (*It. Ant.* 105,4; 110,7).
→ Bruttii

BTCGI 5, 431–441 s.v. Cosenza; P.G. GUZZO, I Bretti, 1989, 80f.; M. PAOLETTI, Occupazione romana e storia della città, in Storia della Calabria antica, 1994, 481–485.
M.C.P.

Consentius Name of a 5th-cent. Lat. grammarian, perhaps from Narbo (Narbonne), which he refers to in his Ars (GL 346,5; 348,35). He was either identical with or related to → Sidonius Apollinaris, curator palatii under Avitus (455–456). Of the latter C. we know that, like his father the poet and philosopher, he certainly came from Narbo; that he wrote both Latin and Greek verse; and that thanks to his outstanding knowledge of Greek he was despatched as ambassador to Constantinople (related esp. in Sid. Apoll. Carm. 23; Epist. 8,4; 9,15). The grammarian C. wrote two treatises De nomine et verbo and De barbarismis et metaplasmis [2]; the latter is important for its examples of vernacular speech. Both treatises were part of an ambitious Ars grammatica. As grammarian he was drawn on for most of the medieval collections, examples being the Ars Ambrosiana, Malsacanus, Cruindmelus, Tatuinus, Anonymus ad Cuimnanum, Clemens Scotus, Erchembertus and Ermenricus.

EDITIONS: 1 GL 5, 338–404 2 M. NIEDERMANN, 1937.
BIBLIOGRAPHY: 3 SCHANZ/HOSIUS, 4,2, 49. 56. 58. 210–213 4 O. SEEK, G. GOETZ, s.v. C. 1–3, in RE 4,911f.
P.G.

Considius Italian proper name (SCHULZE, 158, 456; ThlL, Onom. 2, 566f.) attested from 1st cent. BC, so C. [I 1] below is probably unhistorical.
I. REPUBLIC II. EMPIRE

I. REPUBLIC
[I 1] C., Q. People's tribune 476 BC. A later tradition that he proposed an agrarian law with his colleague T. Genucius and initiated a process against the consul of 477, T. Menenius, for not helping the Fabii at the Cremera (Liv. 2,52; Dion. Hal. Ant. Rom. 9,27,2) is of doubtful authenticity.
[I 2] C., Q. In 74 BC was judge in the case against Statius → Abbius Oppianicus; in 70 removed from the one against Verres (Cic. Verr. 1,18). He held a large fortune (Cic. Att. 1,12,1) and granted comprehensive loans, which he did not cancel during the internal political conflicts of 63, so that a debt crisis was averted, and he was praised in a senatorial motion (Val. Max. 4,8,3). In 59 during the Vettius affair he voiced open criticism of Caesar in the Senate for oppressing the corporation (Cic. Att. 2,24,4; Plut. Caes. 14,13–15).

NICOLET 2,848f.; T.P. WISEMAN, New Men in the Roman Senate 139 B.C.- A.D. 14, 1971, 225f.

[I 3] C. Longus, C. Praetor before 54 BC; in 53(?)–50 governor of Africa (MRR 3,61); in 50 made an unsuccessful application for the consulate (Cic. Lig. 2); a Pompeian, he was sent in 49 as legatus pro praetore to Africa (ILS 5319), and fought C. → Scribonius Curio there (Caes. B Civ. 2,23,4). In 46 he was killed by Gaetulian auxiliaries after the battle of Thapsus (Bell. Afr. 93,1f.).
[I 4] C. Nonianus, M. Praetor by 54 or 50 BC at the latest, was originally assigned Cisalpine Gaul as propraetor in 49 and was one of Pompey's supporters in Campania (Cic. Fam. 16,12,3; Att. 8,11B,2).
[I 5] C. Paetus, C. Son of C. [I 3] above and a supporter of Pompey, he was captured by Caesar in Africa in 46 BC but then pardoned (Bell. Afr. 89,2). That he was mint master the same year (RRC 465) is doubtful.
K.-L.E.

II. EMPIRE
[II 1] Senator of praetorian rank, who accused Pomponius Secundus of befriending → Aelius Gallus in 31 (Tac. Ann. 5,8,1); possibly identical with or at least definitely related with C. Proculus, who in 33 on the accusal of Q. Pomponius, the brother of P. Secundus, was sentenced by the Senate and executed (Tac. Ann. 6,18,1); cf. PIR² C 1278, 1281.
[II 2] C. Aequus. Roman knight; in 21 falsely accused the praetor Magius Caecilianus; punished by the Senate at the behest of Tiberius (Tac. Ann. 3,37,1).
[II 3] C. Proculus. → C. [II 1] above. His sister Sancia was banished (Tac. Ann. 6,18,1).
W.E.

Consilium 1. c. propinquorum: relatives and friends were a traditional source of advice (Gell. NA 17,21) for the pater familias when he had to adjudicate family matters for wife and children (Val. Max. 5,9,1; Sen. Clem. 1,15). Calling such a family council was not obligatory, although an unjust decision drew censorial reproof (Cic. Rep. 4,6). 2. c. magistratuum: the senior magistrature would summon a consilium to advise them on judicial and administrative matters. The fact that a decision was preceded by a council was published (Cic. Att. 4,2,5). Courts martial also decided after deliberation (Livy 29,20,5). Governors appointed a consilium of citizens and senators to express an opinion on administrative and legal questions. In the procedure for appointing a court in iure the praetor regularly consulted lawyers. 3. c. principis: from Augustus on a consilium was appointed, at first drawn by lot from the Senate but later openly designated by the emperor, as a standing body; as well as senators there were experts of equestrian rank. Hadrian's crown council (according to SHA Hadr. 18,1) included Celsus, Iulianus and Neratius Priscus. Even Tiberius called on Cocceius Nerva (Tac. Ann. 4,58; 6,26) and Domitianus Pegasus (Iuv. 4,77) to serve as his lawyers. Under Marcus Aurelius the comites turned the consilium into a general staff. From the time of Septimius Severus outstanding lawyers like Papinian, Paulus and Ulpian could rise to the rank of praefectus praetorio, so becoming permanent members of council. Diocletian's reforms changed court procedure: the crown council became the → consistorium, standing in the emperor's presence.

W. Liebenam, s.v. C., *RE* 7, 915–922; F. Amarelli, Consilia principum, 1983. W.E.V.

Consistere is a legal term for, i.a., the place of residence as distinct from → *origo*. This can be the home address or → *domicilium* (*Cod. Iust.* 3,19,1); furthermore, we read at Dig. 5,1,19,2: *at si quo constitit, non dico iure domicilii, sed tabernulam pergulam horreum armarium officinam conduxit ibique distraxit egit*: 'but if he has settled anywhere — I speak not of the right of residence, but if he has rented a small shop, a stall, a store, a warehouse or a workshop and carried on a business or worked there'. In that case the merchant has to conduct his defence (*defendere*) there, i.e. he can be sued there just as he can at his home address. The word could also refer to the place of assembly of a *collegium*. P.A.

Consistorium can mean a place of assembly (*consistere* means to discuss a topic: Cic. Fin. 4,72). From the time of Constantine [1] the Great it came to apply to the group of close collaborators of the emperor previously called the → *consilium principis* (as in *sacrum consistorium*, sometimes also *auditorium*, Greek θεῖον συνέδριον: Cod. Iust. 1, 14,8; [Aur. Vict.] Epit. Caes. 14). The *consistorium* serves for deliberations about political and administrative matters as well as, when the need arises, court procedures and the particularly solemn sanctioning of imperial laws (Cod. Iust. 1,14,8 & 12). The modus operandi of the *consistorium* was formalized, but in the last resort it was dependent on the will of the emperor, as was the constitution of the committee. According to the requirements of the situation, those attending the meeting could include: (1) Specially appointed members, *comites consistoriani*, in the 6th century with the rank of *spectabiles* (Cod. Iust. 12,10). (2) *Ex officio* members: *magister officiorum, quaestor sacri palatii, comes sacrarum largitionum, comes rerum privatarum* and other *proceres nostri palatii* (Cod. Iust. 1,14,8 pr.). (3) Other co-opted officials or persons trusted by the emperor. Therefore, the *consistorium* is usually the institutional setting for the various high-ranking public officials and courtiers to achieve practical and political influence for their interests, views and expertise — despite its importance varying with the emperor's style of government, from military and authoritative to administrative and civilian (cf. Amm. Marc. 25,4,7 & 30,8,1ff.).
→ Consilium (principis); → Constitutiones

Kaser, *RZ*, 232ff.; Jones, *LRE*, 333ff.; Mommsen, Staatsrecht, 2.2, 988f. C.G.

Consolatio see → Consolatio as a literary genre

Consolatio ad Liviam (Epicedion Drusi) In about 1450 a MS that has since been lost was brought to Rome, which is the source [1] for the work preserved in several MSS of the latter half of that century, as *P. ... Ovidii Nasonis ... ad Liviam de morte Drusi*. This poem

was included in editions of Ovid from 1471 onwards. It takes the form of an address to → Livia Drusilla: the death of her son Nero → Claudius Drusus in Germany in 9 BC is lamented (1–166) and the funeral rites described (167–264 or 298), before it reverts to largely traditional consolatory themes (265 or 299–474). The → *Elegiae in Maecenatem* may contain allusions to this work. A reference to the temple of Castor and Pollux in Rome (283–288) suggests a composition date after 6 AD. The probable imitation of Ovid's poems of exile puts the *terminus post quem* at AD 12. The restrained language of this insipid poem, its dignified style and metric quality argue against its being post-Augustan. There are some awkward transitions. This poem scarcely seems to be the work of → Ovid himself (a view contradicted in [2] below), though the language shows his influence.
→ Elegy

Editions: → Appendix Vergiliana.
Commentary: H. Schoonhoven, The Pseudo-Ovidian Ad Liviam de morte Drusi, 1992.
Bibliography: 1 M.D. Reeve, The Tradition of Consolatio ad Liviam, in Revue d'histoire des textes 6, 1976, 79–98 2 G. Baligan, Appendix Ovidiana, 1955, 95–97.
J.A.R.

Consolatio as a literary genre
A. General B. Content C. Principal works
D. Influence

A. General
→ Mourning and consolation are basic elements of the human condition. Should anyone encounter misfortune from the death of a friend or family member, banishment, loss of health, of property or of freedom, then friends and relations try to alleviate sorrow or improve morale by offering comfort and encouragement. Therefore, consolatory scenes and motives occur already in older Greek poetry (e.g. Hom. *Il.* 5,381–402; Archil. fr. 13 W.; Eur. Alc. 416–419). What is specifically meant by *consolatio* as a literary genre, though, are writings of a philosophic bent, whose authors either try to dissuade individuals from grieving in the face of misfortune, or proffer general counsel on overcoming adversity. Their point of departure is the Sophists' (→ Sophistic) belief in the convincing power of dialectic discourse. Its expression in a tone of aggressive rebuke is probably based on a Cynical → diatribe which other philosophers adapted for their writings intended for the therapy of the soul.
C.G.

B. Content
Of the wide range of consolatory themes (Cic. Tusc. 3,81) only writings on exile (cf. → Exile, literature of) and on the occasion of bereavement (*consolatio mortis*) stand out clearly. Exile in the early empire is taken up by → Seneca the Younger (Dial. 12: *Ad Helviam*), → Musonius Rufus (Diss. 9) and → Plutarch (*Perì phygês*: Mor. 599a–607f), all apparently in imitation of Hellenistic precursors. The central thought is that a 'change of

abode' is no evil in itself and even with the disadvantages of poverty and degradation that frequently accompany it should not dismay a man of understanding.

Especially effective was the rich field of *consolatio mortis*, to which all the principal schools of philosophy had contributed: the → Peripatos with the concept of 'moderate sorrow' or *metriopatheia*; the → Academy with the reflection that death released the soul of earthly care and led it to a better life; → Epicureanism with its methods of distraction (*avocatio*) and the recalling (*revocatio*) of pleasing aspects and activities (cf. Cic. *Tusc.* 3,33); the → Stoa particularly with the ideal of freedom from the → affects (*apátheia*) and the scorning of *fortuita*, the workings of chance, as irrelevant to happiness; the → Cyrenaics and others with the recommendation of *praemeditatio malorum*, the imagined anticipation of evil, to ward off unexpected blows of fate. Apart from the pseudo-Platonic dialogue of *Axiochus* all works we have — irrespective of the stance of the author contain arguments of different provenance. A good introduction is the *Consolatio ad Apollonium* attributed to Plutarch (Plut. *Mor.* 101e–122a), authentic according to [1. 39–42]. Some writings proffer two separate lines of argument: on the one hand, that there has been no unsurmountable pain and damage to the bereaved, on the other, that for the person mourned by them death has not been a misfortune, or may even be the transition to a better existence. The reasoning is supported by examples, particularly *exempla* of those who have endured comparable sorrow in an exemplary manner (e.g. Sen. Dial. 6,12,6–15,3).

C. PRINCIPAL WORKS

Among Hellenistic works of consolatory literature that of the academy philosopher → Crantor 'On Grief' (*Perì pénthous*) was, despite the title, based on a particular case; it was to exercise considerable influence. → Panaetius urged his Roman friend Q. Aelius [I 16] Tubero, to learn it by heart (Cic. Acad. Pr.,135); the compiler of the *Consolatio ad Apollonium* used it extensively; so did Cicero when, on the occasion of → Tullia's death, he addressed a *Consolatio* to himself (fr. 4a VITELLI); this in turn influenced Seneca (Dial. 6), → Jerome (Ep. 60) and → Ambrose (Exc. Sat. 1). Seneca has the richest material in his addresses to Marcia and to Polybius (Dial. 6; 11) as well as three letters (Ep. 63; 93; 99). Plutarch's short consolation addressed to his wife (Mor. 608a–612b) belongs, despite its personal tone, to the philosophical tradition. Of the monographs against the fear of death none remain complete; excerpts of more comprehensive works do, however, suffice to convey a fair impression of their worth (Lucr. 3,830–1094; Cic. Tusc. 1).

D. INFLUENCE

The line of argument and the topoi of consolatory literature had wide-ranging influence on related literary genres. This shows in private letters of consolation from the Ciceronian correspondence (Fam. 4,5, Sulpicius Rufus to Cicero; 5,16; not Ad Brut. 1,9), as well as in many a poetic epicedion (→ Consolatio ad Liviam 343–470; Stat. Silv. 2,1,208–237) and the occasional funerary epigram (e.g. EpGr 650; CLE 1567). Consoling arguments are also contained in the Greek handbooks of funerary speeches at the height of the imperial period (Ps.-Dion. Hal. Rhet. 6,5; Men. Rhet. pp. 413f.; 418–421 SPENGEL).

While the Roman → *laudatio funebris* (funeral oration) was devoid of consolatory content until well into the Empire [2. 82–86], typical pagan elements are to be found in the burial speeches of Ambrose (exc. Sat. 1; Obit. Valent. 40–53), although as in the burial speeches and letters of consolation composed by the Cappadocian Church Fathers (Greg. Naz. Or. 7,18–21; Ep. 223; Basil. Ep. 5f.; 300–302; Greg. Nyss. Or. in Meletium, Opera 9, pp. 454–457) they are infused with Christian thought [2. 87f.; 3; 4]. Similarly we find explicit examples in Jer. Ep. 60 and Ambrose Ep. 8 FALLER, while in other Christian writing (e.g. Paul. Nol. Ep. 13; Jer. Ep. 39) the motives of old consolations are recognized only with difficulty. Their reception in the Middle Ages and early in the modern era is worthy of notice.

→ CONSOLATIO AS A LITERARY GENRE

1 J. HANI (ed.), Plutarque: Consolation à Apollonios, 1972 2 W. KIERDORF, Laudatio Funebris, 1980 3 Y.-M. DUVAL, Formes profanes et formes bibliques dans les oraisons funèbres de St. Ambroise, in *Entretiens* 23, 1977, 235–291 4 J. F. MITCHELL, Consolatory Letters in Basil and Gregory Nazianzen, in *Hermes* 96, 1968, 299–318.

C. BURESCH, Consolationum a Graecis Romanisque scriptarum historia critica, in Leipziger Stud. 9, 1887, 1–170; CH. FAVEZ, La consolation latine chrétienne, 1937; C. C. GROLLIOS, Seneca's Ad Marciam. Trad. and Originality, 1956; H.-TH. JOHANN, Trauer und Trost, 1968; R. KASSEL, Unt. zur griech. und röm. Konsdationsliteratur, 1958; K. KUMANIECKI, Die verlorene *Consolatio* des Cicero, in Acta Classica Universitatis Scientiarum Debreceniensis 4, 1968, 27–47; P. VON MOOS, Consolatio, 1971/2 (for medieval reception).   W. K.

Console Modern term, derived from French, for a horizontal support protruding from a wall or pillar, and serving as a ledge for an arch, statuary, or as the base of a corbel or → geison. As multi-storey buildings became more frequent with the increasing range of constructional forms available to Hellenistic architects, the console could form the transition to the roof of a building while still serving as a structural element of the multistoreyed façade. The combination of console and corbel that began to appear in the eastern Mediteranean in the 2nd cent. AD made the structurally distinct elements of horizontal console and any block it supported a single unit. In the Augustan architecture of the Concordia temple in Rome the varied effects of light and shade produced by the abundance of ornaments on its generous forms marked the highest point of the console-geison as a decorative element. The console is also found as a purely functional element in the architecture of the Roman Empire, and is frequently painted onto murals or occasionally applied to them three-dimensionally in stucco.

H. v. HESBERG, K.-Geisa des Hell. und der frühen Kaiserzeit, suppl. 24 MDAI(R), 1980; H. LAUTER, Die Architektur des Hell., 1986, 253–259; W. v. SYDOW, Die hell. Gebälke in Sizilien, in MDAI(R) 91, 1984, 239–358.

C.HÖ.

Consonant see → Phonetics

Constans

[1] **Flavius Iulius C.** Roman Emperor, born *c.* 320 AD, the youngest son of Constantine [1] and Fausta, elevated to Caesar on 25 December 333 and at about the same time betrothed to Olympias, the daughter of → Ablabius [1]. From 9 September 337 Augustus. At a meeting of the brothers in Pannonia (Julian Or. 1,19a) C. received Italy, Illyricum and Africa (Zon. 13,5). He refused to acknowledge the guardianship of his eldest brother Constantine [2] II [1]. Constantine II, who was in possession of the north-western provinces, was quick to demand changes to the territorial divisions (Zon. 13,5), attacking northern Italy in 340 but losing both the battle and his life when confronted by C.'s generals at Aquileia. C. stayed in Naïssus at the time (Cod. Theod. 12,1,29; 10,10,5; Zon. 13,5). After a temporary stay in Milan he fought the Franks along the Rhine in 341–42, soon afterwards inspecting Britain (Amm. Marc. 27,8,4; 28,3,8; Lib. Or. 59, 141). C. appears by dint of long periods of absence — such as the hunts he took accompanied only by his German bodyguard (Zos. 2,42,1) — to have lost control of his court. On the instigation of Marcellinus, his *comes rei privatae*, on 18 January 350 the half-barbarian officer → Magnentius was proclaimed Caesar. C. attempted flight, but was killed by Gaiso at Helena (Elne) in the Pyrenees (Aur. Vict., Epit. Caes. 41,23). The circular building of Centcelles should not be considered as his mausoleum [2]. C., who unlike his brothers had been baptized, legislated against the pagans (Cod. Theod. 16,10,2f.), persecuted the → Donatists (Optat. 3,3) and was a committed follower of Athanasius [3]. From the orthodox side it is said of him that he respected the independence of the Church (Hosius apud Athan. Hist. Ar. 44,6). *PLRE* 1, 220 no. 3.

1 H. R. BALDUS, Ein Sonderfall höfischer Repräsentation der spätconstantinischen Zeit, in R. GÜNTHER, S. REBENICH (eds.), E fontibus haurire, 1994, 255–262 2 R. WARLAND, Status und Formular in der Repräsentation der spätant. Führungsschicht, in *MDAI(R)* 101, 1994, 175–202, 192ff. 3 J. MOREAU, C., in JbAC 1, 1959, 180–184.

KIENAST, ²1996, 312f.

B. BL.

[2] **C. (Constans) II.** Byzantine emperor (641–668), nephew of → Heraclius, nicknamed 'Pogonatos' (the Bearded), fought against the Islamic Arabs and against

the Slavs, gave the establishment of military provinces (themes) decisive impetus (q.v.). From 663 reigned in Syracuse in Sicily, where he was murdered.

ODB 1, 496f.

F.T.

[3] In 409/10 when ordered to take Africa for the usurper → Attalus he failed when faced by → Heraclianus, who had remained loyal to Honorius, and was killed (*PLRE* 2, 310).

[4] Son of the usurper → Constantine [3] III, a monk before being made Caesar in 408 and Augustus in 409 or 410. As Caesar he took Spain, withdrawing to fight the Germans, but leaving his father's old *magister militum*, → Gerontius, in charge and entrusting barbarian troops of the Honoriaci to guard the Pyrenean passes. Both betrayed his trust. When he attempted to advance into Spain once more in 410, he was defeated by Gerontius and was killed near Vienna while fleeing (*PLRE* 2, 310).

[5] in 412 was *magister militum per Thracias*, and in 414 consul in the East. It is disputed whether he is identical with the correspondent of Synesius (Epist. 27) [1.281f.] *PLRE* 2, 311.

1 V. HAEHLING.

H.L.

Constantia

[1] **Flavia Iulia C.** Daughter of Constantius [1] I and Theodora, half-sister of Constantine [I], betrothed in 312 to → Licinius (Lactant. *De mort. pers.* 43,2). The wedding took place early in 313 when Constantine and Licinius met in Milan (Lactant. *De mort pers.* 45,1; Euseb. Hist. Eccl. 10,5,3; Anon. Vales. 13; Zos. 2,17). The issue of this marriage was a son, Licinianus Licinius, born in July 315. In 316 she accompanied her husband in his war against her half-brother, and fled with him from Sirmium to Adrianople (Anon. Vales. 17). In the second war she acted as mediator for her husband's capitulation (Aur. Vict. Epit. Caes. 41,7; Anon. Vales. 28). Although Licinius and later his son were executed, in 325 and 326 respectively, C. retained her influential position as *nobilissima femina* at the court of Constantine. She allegedly counselled the faction of Eusebius of Nicomedia at the Council of → Nicaea (Philostorgius, Hist. Eccl. 1,9–10) and even on her deathbed attempted to influence Constantine in favour of the Arians (Rufinus Hist. 10,12). After her death, she was commemorated on coins (RIC 7, 571) and by the renaming of the harbour of Maïuma near Gaza in her honour (Euseb. Vita Const. 4,38; Sozom. Hist. Eccl. 2,5,7). *PLRE* 1, 221 no. 1.

H. A. POHLSANDER, C., in Anc. Soc. 24, 1993, 151–167.

B. BL.

[2] → Constantina

[3] Posthumous daughter of → Constantius [2] II by his third consort → Faustina. Born 361/2. Sent to Gaul in 374 to marry the emperor → Gratianus (Amm. Marc. 21,15,6; 29,6,7) but died when she was about 20. Gra-

tianus (died August 383) subsequently remarried (Zos. 5,39,4). Her remains were transferred to Constantinople in 383 (Chron. min. 1, 244). *PLRE* 1, 221 no. 2.

Constantianus

[1] Brother-in-law of → Valentinian I. He led the fleet of the Euphrates in 363 in Julian's Persian campaign (Amm. Marc. 23,3,9; Zos. 3,13,3). In 370 when *tribunus stabuli* in Valentinian's Gaulish campaigns he was killed in an ambush (Amm. Marc. 28,2,10). *PLRE* 1,221.   w.p.

[2] *Comes sacri stabuli* ('supervisor of the imperial stables'), Byzantine general in the war of → Justinian I against the Goths; from 536 in Dalmatia; after the dismissal of → Belisarius in 540 in Ravenna; requested the emperor summon him home from Italy in 543 or 544; in 551 he and general Scholasticus were defeated at Adrianople by a force of Slavs (PLRE 3 A, 334–337 no. 2).   f.t.

Constantina Eldest daughter of Constantine [1] the Great, she was married in 335 to → Hannibalianus and presumably not meant to be made Augusta until after Constantinus'death (Philostorg. Hist. Eccl. 3,22). After the murder of Hannibalianus she lived in the part of the empire ruled by Constans [1]. She was involved in Vetranio's elevation to Caesar in 350 and in the following year married her cousin → Gallus, by then Caesar. She reigned with him in Antioch and took active part in matters of government. Ammianus Marcellinus describes her as a tyrannical 'Megaera' or Fury (Amm. Marc. 14,1,2). In 354 she died on the journey to her brother Constantius, with whom she sought to mediate in the crisis about Gallus. The variant form of the name, Constantia, is to be rejected because of ILCV 1768 (PLRE 1, 222 no. 2).

B. Bleckmann, C., Vetranio und Gallus Caesar, in: Chiron 24, 1994, 29–68.   b.bl.

Constantinople (*Constantinopolis*).
I. Site   II. Topography   III. History

I. Site

Imperial residence, founded in 324 by → Constantine [1] the Great on the site of → Byzantium. Bounded to the north by the Golden Horn, with the → Bosporus [1] to the east and the → Hellespont to the south, the city could only be attacked from one side by land. By virtue of its site it dominated trade and commerce between Europe and Asia, between the Aegean and the Black Sea (→ Pontos Euxeinos; Hdn. 3,1,5; Pol. 4,38–45).

II. Topography

The city plan did not follow the customary imperial layout, but alternated thoroughfares and occasional cross-streets in a fan-like pattern with large areas left free for building [1]. The most important traffic arteries

were those running along the banks of the Propontis and the Golden Horn respectively, together with the Mese that forked in the city centre, coming from the Augusteion from the east. When the city was extended outwards by Theodosius II (AD 402–450), making a comparison with the seven hills of Rome possible, he divided it into 14 *regiones* and 322 *vici*. A description of the topography and a list of the most important buildings of that period is given in the *Notitia urbis Constantinopolitanae* [2].

The inner city included some large squares. The Augusteion (no. 5 on the plan) [2. 232], freely accessible from the Mese, was the seat of imperial and ecclesiastical power, with the Great Palace (no. 5b) and the senate (no. 5c) to the south-east (Zos. 3,11,3; Procop. Aed. 1,10,5–9; Ioh. Mal. 321,8–12), the Basilica (no. 5d) to the north-west (Procop. Aed. 1,11,12), the Baths of Zeuxippus (no. 5e) to the south-west (Ioh. Mal. 321,12f.) and the → Hagia Sophia (no. 5a) and the patriarchal residence to the north-east. Numerous statues of the imperial family were erected here [3. 158ff.]. From about 500 there is evidence of busy commerce here. By the 7th cent. the Augusteion was becoming less of an → agora and more the forecourt of the Hagia Sophia [4. 44ff.]. The Forum of Constantine (no. 8) [2. 234, 236] was the true agora, the centre point of city life and the marketplace that Constantine the Great originally intended: it rose the second of the city hills, a circular paved square, surrounded by two-storey arcades with equestrian statues, and with two gate structures (Zos. 2,30,4). In its centre there rose the Column of Constantine (no. 8a) [3. 173ff.], to the north-west was the senate, on the south side the Nymphaeum (no. 8b), and in the east the tribunal (no. 8c). The vaulted base of the column of Constantine was perhaps converted into a chapel dedicated to St Constantine in the 9th cent. (no. 8d; cf. [5]). Every description of a procession mentions the Forum of Constantine, and the column and chapel especially as stations on that route. It was also the place where the inhabitants would naturally gather, as they did in the great earthquake of 533 (Chron. pasch. 629,10–15).

The Forum of Theodosius (no. 9) [2. 235] to the south of the city's third hill by the Mese, was also known as the Taurus Forum, and served in early Byzantine times as a reception area. Not before the 8th cent. is there evidence of trading here. The Arcadius Forum or Xerolophus opposite the Lycus valley on the Mese is likwise built on a mound. Whether it was rebuilt after the earthquake of 740 is unknown. The hippodrome (no. 6) that Septimius Severus (193–211) had built earlier (Ioh. Mal. 292,12) was rebuilt by Constantine on the model of the Roman Circus Maximus (→ Circus C.; Zos. 2,31,1; Ioh. Mal. 321f.; Chron. pasch. 528) to accommodate 30,000 spectators. As well as being used for contests and races, the hippodrome also saw political assemblies and propaganda rallies of 'Blues' or 'Greens' (→ *factiones*). Formerly the seat of a *proconsul*, from 359 the city was ruled by a *praefectus urbi* or

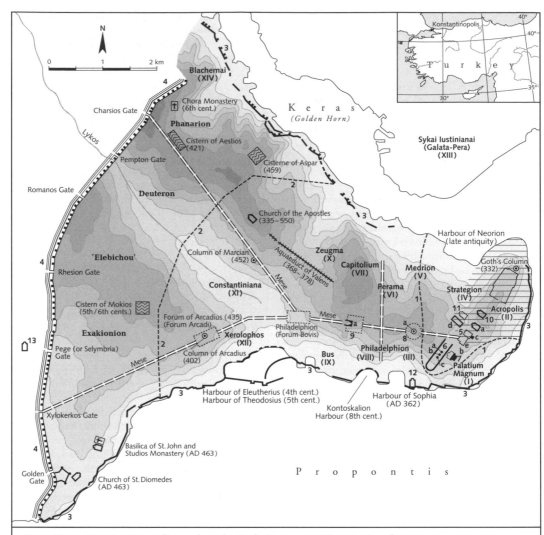

N

0 1 2 km

Blachernai (XIV)

Chora Monastery (6th cent.)

Charsios Gate

Phanarion

Cistern of Aestios (421)

Lykos

Pempton Gate

Cisterne of Aspar (459)

K e r a s (Golden Horn)

Romanos Gate

Deuteron

Church of the Apostles (335–550)

Sykai Iustinianai (Galata-Pera) (XIII)

Harbour of Neorion (late antiquity)

'Elebichou'

Column of Marcian (452)

Zeugma (X)

Aquaeduct of Valens (368–378)

Capitolium (VII)

Medrion (V)

Goth's Column (332)

Rhesion Gate

Constantiniana (XI)

Perama (VI)

Strategion (IV)

Acropolis (II)

Cistern of Mokios (5th/6th cents.)

Forum of Arcadius (435) (Forum Arcadi)

Mese

Philadelphion (Forum Bovis)

Mese

Philadelphion (III)

Palatium Magnum (I)

Exakionion

Xerolophos (XII)

Philadelphion (VIII)

Pege (or Selymbria) Gate

Column of Arcadius (402)

Bus (IX)

Mese

Harbour of Eleutherius (4th cent.)

Harbour of Theodosius (5th cent.)

Kontoskalion Harbour (8th cent.)

Harbour of Sophia (AD 362)

Xylokerkos Gate

P r o p o n t i s

Basilica of St. John and Studios Monastery (AD 463)

Golden Gate

Church of St. Diomedes (AD 463)

Konstantinopolis

T u r k e y

Byzantium - Constantinopolis: archaeological site - map with extant and reconstructed monuments (up to the 8th cent. AD)

Area of the pre-Christian acropolis (Byzantium)

1. Wall at the time of Septimius Severus (2nd cent., conjecture)

2. Constantinian wall (conjectural line)

3. Constantinian sea wall (oldest parts near the palace precinct; after AD 196)

4. Theodosian wall (main wall, outer wall, moat; completed c. AD 413)

5. Tetrastoon (Severan, 2nd cent., later Augusteion)

   a. Hagia Sophia

   b. Imperial palaces

   c. Senate

   d. Administrative basilicas

   e. Baths of Zeuxippus

6. Hippodrome (AD 203; expanded after AD 324)

   a. Obelisk from Karnak (15th cent. BC) on marble base with reliefs (c. AD 390)

   b. Serpent column from Delphi (479 BC)

   c. Obelisk in stonework (c. AD 400?)

7. Palace of Lausus (5th/6.th cents.)

8. Forum of Constantine / Forum Constantini (early 4th cent.)

   a. Remains of Column of Constantine (AD 328)

   b. Nymphaion (not shown)

   c. Tribunal (not shown)

   d. Chapel of Constantine (not shown)

9. Forum of Theodosius / Forum Tauri (AD 372 – 393)

   a. Remains of the triumphal arch

10. Hagia Eirene (after AD 740, with parts of the Justinianic atrium and narthex, after AD 532)

11. Remains of the church of St. Mary Chalkoprateia (5th cent.)

12. Central-plan building of the church of Sts. Sergius and Bacchus (AD 527 – 536)

13. Church of the Virgin Mary at Pege (AD 555/56)

Zeugma Constantinian *regio* (I-XIV)

Elebichu District

=== Main streets

Preserved or partially preserved

Reconstruction

0 10 20 30 40 50 60 70 m

eparch, who resided near the Forum of Constantine. Lack of building land was tackled by a special edict governing permitted constructions, height and spacing. To reduce the number of building plots and to provide cheap accommodation for the poor there were tenements five or even six storeys high. Even though the inhabitants were seemingly powerless to influence state policy, the pressure exerted by the two principal factions, the 'Blues' and the 'Greens', on state and even imperial administration was considerable. The union of these otherwise feuding parties was what led to the → Nika Revolt of 532.

Supplying the huge capital with adequate drinking water from the hilly country to the north-west, often across great distances, was an enormous achievement (→ Water supply, → Water pipes). → Constantius [2] II laid a pipeline and built a number of large cisterns. From 363–373 Valens built an aqueduct, large parts of which still remain; a few years later Theodosius I (379–395) drew in another from the north. Even so water consumption had to be restricted by decree again and again. In addition, huge open cisterns and covered tanks were built under public and private buildings; they served as reservoirs and helped stabilize the buildings in earth tremors (e.g. Yerebatan Sarayı). To ensure a secure supply of provisions for the inhabitants, new docks had to be built and existing ones added to along the Golden Horn and at the grain harbour on the Propontis coast (→ Victualling, → Agriculture). Artisans were found mainly in the Mangane ward and north of the Mese. An industry of special importance for the state economy was the production of → silk, once living specimens of the silkworm had been smuggled from China to Constantinople in 551. As well as the large cathedrals within the city, monasteries and more churches were built beyond the city walls from about 380. In the 5th cent. the number of monasteries within the walls increased considerably, particularly in the more sparsely built-upon south-west and the Lycus valley.

From the first, Constantine the Great saw C. as the cultural hub of his empire. Aesthetic criteria always weighed heavily in the city planning of the emperors; this was a significant factor in the placing of countless monuments and statues in public places, the building of colonnades, the construction of public buildings and churches, and their ornamentation with mosaics, murals, sculptures and the like, some of which were treasures plundered from the rest of the known world. In the basilica beside the library, itself founded in 357, a university was established, which in turn was moved to the capitol in 425. It developed into the most important seat of learning in the city and in the empire. Not only were law, grammar, rhetoric and philosophy taught here, but the traditions of classical antiquity were maintained.

→ Byzantium (incl. maps); CONSTANTINOPLE

1 A. BERGER, Die Altstadt von Byzanz in der vorjustinianischen Zeit, in *Poikila Byzantina*, Varia 3, 1987, 7–30

2 O. SEECK, Notitia urbis Constantinopolitanae, in: Id. (ed.), *Notitia Dignitatum*, 1876 (repr. 1962, 1983), 227–243   3 F. A. BAUER, Stadt, Platz und Denkmal in der Spätant., 1996, 143–268   4 R. GUILLAND, Ét. de top. de Constantinople byzantine 2, 1969   5 C. MANGO, Constantine's Porphyry Column and the Chapel of St. Constantine, in C. MANGO, Stud. on Constantinople 4, 1993, 103–110.   I. v. B.

W. MÜLLER-WIENER, Bildlex. zur Top. Istanbuls, 1977; G. OSTROGORSKY, Gesch. des byz. Staates, 1975. MAPS: R. JANIN, Constantinople Byzantine, 1964; W. KLEISS, Top.-arch. Plan von Istanbul, 1965; C. MANGO, Le développement urbain de Constantinople (IVᵉ-VIIᵉ siècles), 1985; W. MÜLLER-WIENER, Bildlex. zur Top. Istanbuls, 1977.

III. HISTORY

After his victory in AD 324, Constantine's intention was first to extend → Byzantium as his monument, then to make it his capital, confirming his status by a symbolic new foundation. The 'pagan' taint of Rome disqualified that city, although it retained its rank and privileges. Older works of art and architecture would, as was customary in late antiquity, be incorporated from throughout the empire into the over-dimensioned city concept. Constantinople was to have a capitol, a mint, praetorium, hippodrome, forums (principally the Augusteion, and the Forum of Constantine with its still extant columns), (*miliareum aureum*, μίλιον; *milion*; main thoroughfare) and a palace complex. The renaming of the town as Constantinople probably occurred in 324, and its consecration on 11 May 330. The Roman urban model indirectly influenced C. by way of tetrarchs' residences such as → Thessalonica and → Nicomedia. The new foundation of the city did coincide with an end to persecution, but despite its Christian characteristics it was still not intended as the literal embodiment of the new religious policy. The most important cathedrals were indeed started by Constantine but were completed only later: Hagia Eirene (no. 10 on the map), → Hagia Sophia (no. 5a), later to become the spiritual centre of the orthodox world, and the Apostles' Church, demolished in 1462 because of instability, the site of the emperor's tomb.

In 412 the construction of a new wall (still extant; no. 4) with 96 towers on the landward side doubled the area enclosed from 6 km² under Constantine to around 12 km². The population of the town and its hinterland fell between the 6th and 8th cents., only to increase until in the 11th cent. it once again surpassed half a million people. In 1300 there were 100,000 inhabitants; before the Turkish conquest in 1453 no more than 40,000 remained.

From its foundation it was the seat of government, first of the entire empire and then of its eastern division and from the time of → Theodosius I always the residence of the emperor. Despite successive fires, plagues and earthquakes it remained throughout the Middle Ages a city of modern dimensions, the imperial capital, defining the realm politically, commercially, spiritually and culturally. Its walls withstood attacks and sieges from Persians, Avars, Arabs, Bulgars and Rus, until in 1204 Constantinople was taken by the knights of the fourth 'Crusade' under the command of Venice. The destruction and comprehensive looting extended to numerous monuments and signalled the end of the city's dominance and wealth. Nor would the city again enjoy political influence after the reign of Michael VIII ended in 1282. After a long siege Sultan Mehmed II stormed the town on 29 May 1453.

→ Byzantium (incl. maps); CONSTANTINOPLE

H.-G. BECK, Konstantinopel. Zur Sozialgesch. einer früh-ma. Stadt, in Byz. Zeitschr. 58, 1965, 11–45; B. BLECK-MANN, Konstantin der Große, 1996, 109–119; G. DAG-RON, Naissance d'une capitale, 1974; A. DEMANDT, Die Spätantike, 1989, 75f.; R. JANIN, Constantinople Byzan-tine, ²1964; C. MANGO, Le développement urbain de Con-stantinople, 1985; C. MANGO, G. DAGRON (eds.), Con-stantinople and Its Hinterland, 1995; W. MÜLLER-WIE-NER, Bildlex. zur Top. Istanbuls, 1977; Id., Die Häfen von Byzantion-Konstantinupolis-Istanbul, 1994; M. RESTLE, s.v. Konstantinopel, Reallex. zur byz. Kunst 4, 1990, 366–737. G. MA.

Constantinopolis see → Constantinople

Constantinus

[1] C. I. 'the Great', Roman emperor from AD 306–337. Born c. 275 (Euseb. Vita Const. 4,53; Aur. Vict. Caes. 41,16; [Aur. Vict.] Epit. Caes. 41,15, differently Euseb. Vita Const. 2,51) at Naïssus (Anon. Vales. 2) the son of Constantius [1] I and of Helena. After his father was made Caesar, Constantine served on the staff of → Di-ocletian and of → Galerius (Pan. Lat. 7[6] 5,3; Lactant. De mort. pers. 18,10; Anon. Vales. 2). In 305 he left the court of Galerius to join his father, now western Augus-tus, at Gesoriacum (Boulogne), shipping then to Britain to fight the Picts. On the death of Constantius on 27 July 306 in Eburacum (York), C. was immediately pro-claimed Augustus by the legionaries of the expedition-ary force. Galerius as senior Augustus was unable to counter this contravention of the rule of succession of the → tetrarchy, but still only recognized C. as Caesar. At the end of 307 C. married Fausta, the daughter of → Maximianus Herculius, and had his father-in-law, who had resumed active political life, again raise him to Augustan rank, without, however, breaking openly with Galerius (Pan. Lat. 7[6]). After Maximian's abor-tive attempt to seize power in Arles in 310, C. no longer considered himself bound to the Herculian house, but instead fictitiously claimed descent from the emperor → Claudius Gothicus to give himself a legitimacy inde-pendent of the tetrarchy (Pan. Lat. 6[7] 2,1–5).

While his colleagues Licinius and Maximinus Daia were locked in stalemate attempting to press their claims on the territory of Galerius, who had died in 311, C. seized the opportunity to increase his territory con-siderably by a campaign against → Maxentius, who ruled Italy and Africa. In the spring of 312 he smashed Maxentius' north Italian forces in battles at Susa, Turin and Verona, marching on Rome that autumn, and on 28 October defeating Maxentius at the Milvian bridge. Prominent senators like → Ceionius [8] were demon-stratively given promotion despite their support of Maxentius, and the Senate in return explicitly con-firmed support of his position as first among the Cae-sars, above Maximinus Daia (Lactant. De mort. pers. 44,11). In the spring of 313 he met Licinius in Milan, in order to give him his half-sister → Constantia [1] in marriage. On this occasion, the two rulers agreed on the outline of the policy on Christianity that had been prac-tised in C.'s part of the empire since 312 and which was primarily directed against the anti-Christian policy of → Maximinus Daia. The terms of the treaty were pub-lished only after Maximinus was defeated at Nicomedia (Lactant. De mort. pers. 48,2–12; Euseb. Hist. eccl. 10,5,2–14).

Once Licinius had won Maximinus' share of the empire for himself, the division and organization of joint rule led to tension with C. that not even the com-promise of assigning Italy to → Bassianus [3] could re-solve. However, it probably took until 316 rather than 314 before C. was able to defeat Licinius in the first of the civil wars at → Cibalae and the *campus Ardiensis*, agreeing to peace talks only because his own supply lines were threatened. Licinius had to cede the entire Balkans except for the Thracian diocese. On 1 March 317 in the town of Serdica (now Sofia) that would remain his seat until 322, C. raised his two sons → Cri-spus and Constantine [2] II to Caesars, whereas Licinius was allowed only a single Caesar. A second war with Licinius broke out when C. trespassed on Licinius' ter-ritory when fighting a Gothic incursion. In a combined operation, in which the fleet under Crispus and the army both advanced along the coast towards the straits, C. succeeded in beating Licinius at Adrianople and Chrysopolis, forcing him to capitulate at Nicomedia in the summer of 324.

The accession to supreme ruler was celebrated by the assumption of the title *victor* (instead of the term *invic-tus* with its pagan connotations), the renaming of Byzantium as Constantinople *ob insigne victoriae* (Anon. Vales. 30) and the adoption of the diadem as part of the insignia of imperial power. During the vic-tory celebrations on 8 November 324, Constantius was elevated to Caesar and Fausta and Helena to Augustae. Dynastic policy soon suffered a severe setback when C. shortly after the murder of Licinius in 325 had his own son Crispus put to death, followed by his consort Fausta early the following year. Only in 333 and 335 did he make new Caesars of Constans [1] and his neph-ew Dalmatius. The four Caesars were active in separate parts of the empire, enjoyed only a modicum of power and were strictly controlled by officials appointed by the central power. The assigning of a *praef. praetorio* to the Caesars (another *praef. praet.* held office in Africa), was an important step towards the establishment of regionalized praetorian prefectures.

Stemma of the family of Constantine the Great

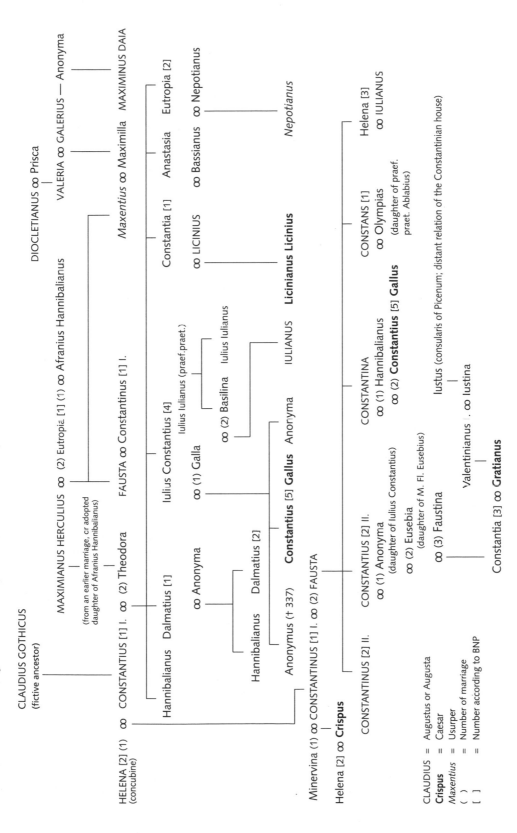

The long reign of C. saw the institutional development into a late antique state finally accomplished, in part by the formation of the four major court offices (though Licinius is credited with creating the office of *magister officiorum*), as well as the conversion of the elite troops that fought the civil war into a mobile force under the command of a *magister militum* or *equitum*.

Externally C. succeeded in securing the frontiers. In the first years of his reign in 310 he crowned his victory over the Franks with the building of a bridge at Cologne. Along the lower Danube, once he had built a bridge at Oescus in 328, he laid out a line of fortresses, at the same time assuming the title of *victor ac triumphator*; in 332 the Goths were defeated by C. [2] Caesar and forced into an alliance, and in 334 conflicts among the Sarmatians were exploited so as to strengthen the Roman position on the lower Danube. His final years as emperor were devoted to preparing for war on the Sasanids. In 335 his nephew Hannibalianus was elevated to *rex regum* in order to retain Armenia and the neighbouring kingdoms as client states of Rome. As C. himself was setting out to campaign against the Persians, he died on 22 May 337 at Nicomedia.

The impact that his reign has had on world history lies in the emperor's sympathy for Christianity, although opinions on the 'Constantinian turning-point' are polarized. His personal religious convictions are not accessible to the historian. His own testimony (particularly Euseb. Vita Const. 4,9) seems to show that in later life he considered the Christian God his protector and patron, a guarantor of victory. This is scarcely the result of any conversion, for example one caused by the vision he experienced in 312, quite distinct accounts of which are given by Lactantius (De mort. pers. 44,5) and Eusebius (Vita Const. 1,28–30). Once he had distanced himself from the tetrarchy, C. had no further reason to proceed with persecution, even before Galerius issued his Edict of Toleration in 311. From 310 the emperor's self-representation betrays an element of solar monotheism which is still characteristic even after the rapprochement with Christianity — no later than 324 — as witness his colossal statue in Constantinople with its radiate crown. From the first years of his reign in the west he was in contact with the bishops of Cologne, Trier, Arles and Córdoba, seeking their advice in 312 when he took over Africa and Italy and was faced with the internal problems posed by the large proportion of Christians in Africa. In the Donatist controversy C. primarily contributed with the organizational support for the Synods of Rome (313) and Arles (314) towards the setting-up of a superordinate structure for the Church, but failed in the attempt to reconcile the conflicting parties (→ Donatists). In the dispute with Licinius, C. tended towards a philosophic monotheism (RIC 7,364 no. 36; silver medallion of Ticinum with its Chi-Rho monogram).

With the assumption of the eastern provinces where Christians had been prosecuted for years and renewed prosecution by Licinius threatened, C. had to take sides, as in the dispute between Orcistus, inhabited mainly by Christians, and Nacolea [1]. Despite considerable confiscation of temple property and even the closing of some temples, pagan cults were still permitted (Lib. Or. 30,6). In the controversies that racked the eastern Church, particularly the quarrel about → Arius, C. strove to achieve maximum integration and so supported the Council of Nicaea (325) in efforts to draw up a suitable form of creed to restore church unity. When C. tried to recall Arius to Alexandria, after the latter had first been excommunicated in Nicaea only to be reinstated in 327–328 by the Synod of Nicomedia, he faced opposition from Athanasius, who became Bishop of Alexandria from 328 and whom he banished in 335. These attempts to achieve religious unity have been wrongly interpreted as apostasy to Arian belief, particularly as C. let himself be baptized on his deathbed by Bishop Eusebius of Nicomedia who had Arian sympathies. As the first Christian emperor he soon became a mythical figure. The Eastern Orthodox churches celebrate his feast on 21 May (PRLE 1, 223–224 no. 4).

1 A. CHASTAGNOL, L'inscription Constantinienne d'Orcistus, in MEFRA 93, 1981, 381–416.

T.D. BARNES, Constantine and Eusebius, 1981; Id., The New Empire of Diocletian and Constantine, 1982; B. BLECKMANN, Konstantin der Große, 1996; J. BLEICKEN, Constantin der Große und die Christen, 1992; G. BONAMENTE, F. FUSCO (eds.), Constantino il Grande dall'antichità all umanesimo, 2 vols., 1992–1993; TH. GRÜNEWALD, Constantinus Maximus Augustus, 1990; K.M. GIRARDET, Kaisergericht und Bischofsgericht, 1975; KIENAST, ²1996, 298–303; H. KRAFT (ed.), Konstantin der Große, 1974; J.L. MAIER, Le dossier du donatisme I. Des origines à la mort de Constance II (303–361), 1987; E. SCHWARTZ, Kaiser Constantin und die christl. Kirche, ²1936.

[2] **C. II.** Son of C. [1], Roman emperor (Augustus) 337–340. Born 316 in Arles, on 1 March 317 elevated to Caesar in Serdica. Sent to Trier in 328, he fought the Franks and Alemanni (AE 1934, 158); in 332 he was entrusted by his father with operations against the Goths (Anon. Vales. 31; Julian Or. I 9d), but returned to Trier later (Athan. *c.* Ar. 87). Although he was the eldest of the three surviving sons of Constantine [1], his brothers Constantius [2] II and Constans [1], conceded him no more than formal precedence when they all assumed the title of Augustus on 9 September 337 (CIL III 6963 and 7207). In possession of Spain, Gaul and Britain, he attempted to force a fresh territorial division on Constans and was killed on 29 April 340 (Cod. Theod. 11,12,1) fighting his brother's generals at Aquileia (Aur. Vict. Epit. Caes. 41,21; Zon 13,5). *PLRE* 1, 223 no. 3.

KIENAST, ²1996, 310f. B. BL.

[3] **Flavius Claudius C. III.** Western emperor, usurper, 407–411. Proclaimed Augustus while a common soldier in Britain. He claimed to be descended from → Constantinus [1]; elevated his son → Constans [4] to

Caesar and then to Augustus; and made → Gerontius his *magister militum*. Achieved mastery over Britain, Gaul (repulsing the Germans and securing the frontier on the Rhine) and, through the agency of his son Constans, Spain. Gerontius defected in 409. He temporarily gained the acceptance of → Honorius, but in 411 his *magister militum* → Edobicus was defeated by → Constantius [6] III. C. subsequently surrendered, and was killed in captivity near Ravenna (PLRE 2, 316f.).

[4] Politician in the East. Praetorian prefect in 447, 456 and 459; in 457 *cos.*, *patricius*. In 447 concerned himself with repairing earthquake damage to the walls of Constantinople; in 464–65 he was envoy to the Persian king. *PLRE* 2, 317f.

v. HAEHLING, 97f.   H. L.

[5] Thracian, a Byzantine general who served → Justinian I against the Goths in Italy under → Belisarius; successful from 535–37, but executed in 537/8 for attacking Belisarius. PLRE 3 A, 341f. no. 3.

[6] C. IV. Byzantine emperor (668–685), son of, from 654 co-caesar with, and then successor to Constans [2] II; forced the Caliph Muawiya, who besieged Constantinople from 674–78, finally to agree to a 30–year truce, but had to let the Bulgars settle south of the Danube. The council he summoned to Constantinople in 680–81 settled the Monothelete controversy.

LMA 5, 1376; *ODB* 1, 500f.

[7] C. V. Byzantine emperor (741–776), son of Leo III and successor to him; in 743 successfully opposed his brother-in-law and rival → Artabasdus. He ordered religious images to be removed, presumably as a reaction to the plague of 746–47, permitting only the worship of the cross, which like his father he saw as the one clear symbol of the victory and salvation of Christianity. The Synod of Hiereia he called in 754 confirmed his iconoclastic stance. His domestic policy laid the emphasis on military and business reforms, as well as an active building programme. He could boast some foreign successes, particularly against the Bulgars. His memory was grossly defamed by iconodules.

LMA 5, 1376; *ODB* 1, 501; I. ROCHOW, Kaiser Konstantin V., 1994.

[8] C. VI. Byzantine emperor (780, or 790–797), son of Leo IV and → Irene, who acted as regent for her nine-year-old son after Leo's death. In 790 he forced his mother to surrender power and proceeded against the iconodulia which had been sanctioned by the 787 Council of Nicaea.He was forced to recognize her as co-empress in 792; it was only in 797 that she finally deposed and blinded him.

R.-J. LILIE, Byzanz unter Eirene und Konstantin VI. (780–802), 1996; *LMA* 5, 1376 (& 644f., s.v. Irene); *ODB* 1, 501f.

[9] C. VII = Constantine VII Porphyrogenetus. Byzantine Emperor, born 906, died 959, son and heir of Leo VI (died 912). He rose to power only after the rule or regency of others, the last of whom was his father-in-law → Romanos I Lakapenos, in 945. He became known as a patron of scholarship and especially of a new historical-antiquarian interest that took the form of making compilations. The term 'Encyclopedist', commonly used for this trend, is now being questioned [1]. Furthermore, earlier assumptions that he had contributed his own writings to the apparatus of scholarship have had doubt cast upon them [2]. This is as true of the legend-rich, encomiastic *vita* of his grandfather Basil I as of the treatise of statemanship *De administrando imperio* and the so-called book of ceremonies, an uneven and incomplete compendium made on his orders and supplemented after his death (for a critical fresh edition of an important section see [4]), whose use in the practice of court ceremonial can hardly be assumed [3].

1 P. ODORICO, La cultura della συλλογή, in *Byz. Zeitschr.* 83, 1990, 1–21   2 I. ŠEVČENKO, Re-reading Constantine Porphyrogenitus, in Byzantine Diplomacy, 1990, 167–195   3 A. MOFFATT, The master of Ceremonies' Bottom Drawer, in Byzantinoslavica 56, 1995, 377–388   4 J. F. HALDON, Const. Porph., Three treatises on Imperial Military Expeditions, 1990.

H. HUNGER, Literatur 1, 360–367.

[10] C. VIII. Byzantine emperor (1025–28), the brother of, from 962 co-ruler with, and finally successor to Basil [4] II. He was the last male representative of the Macedonian dynasty that persisted until 1055 through his daughters → Zoë and Theodora, together with their consorts and lovers.

ODB 1, 503f.

[11] C. IX. Byzantine emperor 1042–1055, second husband of Zoë, the daughter of Constantine VIII; an unwarlike ruler, given to self-indulgent luxury, but a patron of the arts and sciences. Although well-disposed to the Papal envoys in 1054, he could not settle their quarrel with Patriarch Michael I Keroullarios of Constantinople.

ODB 1, 504; *LMA* 5, 1378; W. CONUS-WOLSKA, Les Écoles de Psellos et de Xiphilin sous Constantin IX Monomaque, in Travaux et Mémoires 6, 1976, 223–243; Id., L'École de droit et l'enseignement du droit à Byzance au XIe siècle: Xiphilin et Psellos, in Travaux et Mémoires 7, 1979, 1–103 (for the emperor's policy on education).

[12] C. X. Byzantine emperor (1059–67) from the Asia Minor magnate family of the Doukas, squandered the state finances on favourites and proved incapable of coping with the difficulties affecting the nation that had arisen with the incursions of the Seljuk Turks.

LMA 5, 1378; *ODB* 1, 504.   F.T.

Constantius

[1] C. I, Flavius Valerius C., C. or M., Caesar (293–305) and Augustus (305–306), in later times nicknamed Chlorus; born c. 250 in what would become Dacia Ripensis. On the staff of the Illyrian soldier emperors, first *protector*, then *tribunus*. Under the rule of → Carinus attained equestrian rank as *praeses Dalmatiarum* (Anon. Vales. 1; SHA Car. 17,6). It seems likely that even before 293 (thus Aur. Vict. Caes. 39,24; Eutr. 9,22,1), and in fact before 289, when he was *praefectus praetorio* to → Maximianus, he had to divorce his first wife → Helena, in order to marry Theodora, daughter or step-daughter of the western Augustus. Six children resulted from this second marriage (→ Constantine, family tree). On 1 March 293 C. was probably in Milan when proclaimed Caesar (→ Tetrarchy), faced with the immediate task of defeating the usurper → Carausius and defending the frontier of the Rhine. His preferred residence was Trier. In the summer of 293 he finally drove Carausius from his Gallic bridgehead (Pan. Lat. 8[5], 6–7), but it took until 296 to regain Britain, once the *praef. praet.* Asclepiodotus had defeated Carausius' successor → Allectus. The series of victories over Franks and Alemanni enumerated in Pan. Lat. 6 (7),6 (invasion of Frankish homeland, victories in the territory of the Lingones and near Vindonissa) evades precise dating; perhaps between 300 and 304 [1. 61]. When Diocletian and Maximian abdicated, their respective Caesars were promoted, the Herculian C. becoming senior Augustus to the Jovian Galerius by virtue of his age. Accompanied by his son Constantine, he set out for Britain from Gesoriacum (Boulogne) in 305 and fought against the Picts. He died at his headquarters in Eburacum (York) on 25 July 306. As the Christians in his part of the empire were a tiny minority, nothing is known of any persecution. Because of this, Christian histories of the time of Constantine later spread the story that C,, too, sympathized with Christianity (Euseb. Vita Const. 1,13ff.). PLRE 1, 227–228 no. 12.

KIENAST, ²1996, 280–282.

[2] C. II. Roman emperor (Augustus) from 337–361. Born 7 August 317, the son of Constantine [1] and Fausta, on 8 November 324 made Caesar. He was probably sent to Gaul in 332 and shortly thereafter to Antioch (Zon. 13,4,10) where a campaign against the Persians was being prepared. After the death of Constantine C. led the funeral ceremonies (Euseb. Vita Const. 4,70). That he was responsible for the murder by soldiers of most members of the cadet branch of the house of Constantine is claimed by tendentious sources opposed to C. (cf. Julian Ep. ad Ath. 270c; Zos. 2.40; Amm. Marc. 21,16,8). C. at any rate tolerated the deed (Eutr. 10,9,1). Together with his brothers Constantine II and Constans he was elevated to Augustus on 9 September 337.

By the territorial division we assume was agreed at a conference in Viminacium in 337, C. was given Thrace, Asia Minor and the dioecesis Oriens. Until 350 he confined himself mostly to Antioch, organizing from there the defence of the eastern frontier; despite much fighting in Mesopotamia (344 battle of Singara: Lib. Or. 59,99–120) he achieved no decisive success. News of → Magnentius' and → Vetranio's usurpations reached him early in 350, but he could not march westwards before that autumn, after Shapur II had raised the siege of Nisibis. After fruitless negotiations at Heraclea in September, he was able, at a meeting with Vetranio at Naïssus on 25 December 350, to persuade him to step down. On 15 March 351 in Sirmium he had his cousin Constantius Gallus made Caesar, and despatched him to the eastern frontier, so that he could himself continue the struggle against Magnentius. The battle of Mursa, fought on 28 September 351 at a cost of 54,000 casualties, was a defeat for Magnentius, although it was not until August 353 that C. gained full control of the empire following his defeat of Magnentius at Montsaléon in Gaul and the latter's subsequent suicide. Successful campaigns against the Alemanni (354–356) and Sarmatians (357–358) compensated only in part for the weakening of the frontier defences during the civil war.

His efforts to shape a system like Constantine's, with multiple rulers and subordinate Caesars, thus countering attempts to usurp power, failed. In Antioch Gallus proved too independent and C. had him killed at the end of 354. His other cousin, → Iulianus, later to be known as Julian the Apostate, who had been appointed Caesar and sent to Gaul in 355 shortly after suppressing the usurpation of Silvanus, was raised to Augustus in Paris at the beginning of 360. Occupied by his struggle with the Persians, C. was unable to march against Julian before the autumn of 361, dying en route on 3 November 361 at Mopsucrene in Cilicia.

C. tended towards the moderate (Homoean) variety of Arianism. He sought to help it prevail over the Nicene tendency (→ Athanasius, → Hilarius), a policy the exact opposite of the one adopted by → Constans [1] and culminating at the failed Council of Serdica in 343. Confirmed by his victory at Mursa of divine approval for his mission, C. forcibly tried to impose a single creed throughout the empire, finally by means of the simultaneous councils held in Rimini and Seleucia in 359 which were to accept a creed hammered out by a small commission in the presence of the emperor shortly before (Athan. Nic. Syn. 8,3). His religious policy has been labelled with terms such as 'state Church' or 'caesaro-papism' [1]. After some sharp measures directed at the pagans (Cod. Theod. 16,10,4–6) he returned to a tolerant course, because of the impression made on him by his visit to Rome in 357 and his wish to reach understanding with the Senate. PLRE 1, 226 no. 8.

1 C. PIÈTRI, La politique de Constance II, in L'Église et l'empire au IVᵉ siècle, 1989, 113–172.

T. D. BARNES, Athanasius and C., 1993; KIENAST, ²1996, 314–317; R. KLEIN, C. II. und die christl. Kirche, 1977; Id., Die Kämpfe um die Nachfolge nach dem Tode Constantins des Großen, in Byz. Forsch. 6, 1979, 101–150; C. VOGLER, Constance II et l'administration impériale, 1980.

[3] **Flavius C.** From 324–327 *praef. praetorio* for Constantine [1], perhaps in Antioch, in 327 consul. He may have been sent by Constantine to negotiate with the Augustus → Licinius immediately before 316 (Anon. Vales. 14). *PLRE* 1, 225 no. 5.

[4] **Iulius C.** Son of C. [1] from his marriage to Theodora, and so half-brother to Constantine the Great. The assumption that he spent the early part of Constantine's reign in exile is a questionable one (cf. rather Lib. Or. 18,8). Only in the final years of the latter's life was C. raised to patrician rank achieving the consulate in 335. After the death of Constantine he was killed by soldiers as a possible pretender and his fortune sequestered by Constantius [2] II (Julian Ep. ad Athen. 270c; 273b). Of his children the future Caesar Constantius [5] Gallus (from marriage to Galla) and the future Emperor Julian (mother Basilina) both survived. PLRE 1, 226 no. 7.

[5] **C. Gallus.** as Caesar Flavius Claudius C. born 325, the son of C. [4] and Galla. After the family massacres he received a Christian upbringing in exile. On 15 March 351 his grandfather Constantius [2] II raised him to the rank of Caesar in Sirmium and married him to → Constantina. His doings in Antioch, which culminated in serious conflict with the curiales and the civil authorities, were exaggerated by Ammianus Marcellinus as tyrannical (14,1). Because of differences over his authority as Caesar, Constantius had him recalled and then executed in Flanona at the end of 354 (Amm. Marc. 14,11). *PLRE* 1, 224 no. 4.

KIENAST, [2]1996, 318.   B. BL.

[6] **C. III.** Had served his way up from the ranks; probably from 410, or 411 at the latest, he was *mag. mil.*; *cos.* 414, 417, 420; *patricius* from 414–15. He defeated → Constantinus [3] III, forced the Goths into Spain in 415, and so stabilized the western empire. He won powerful influence over → Honorius. In 417 he married → Galla Placidia; was raised to Augustus in 421, but not recognized in the east. Died in 421; father of → Valentinianus III (PLRE 2, 321–325).   H. L.

[7] **of Antioch.** See → John Chrysostom

[8] **of Lugdunum.** (cf. Sid. Apoll. Epist. 3/2,3: *religione venerabilis*; 2/10,3: *eminens poeta*). In AD 475 in the *Vita S. Germani Autisidoriensis* [1; 2] he traced the life of Bishop Germanus of Auxerre (died *c.* 445) in nominal style tending towards abstraction. An innovation was the aretalogical account of the journeys that Germanus undertook, emulating Jerome's *Hilarion* in indefatigably working miracles. The *Vita* served as a model [2. 232–234]; added to in the first half of the 9th cent., it was used by Heiric of Auxerre in 875 as the basis for the ambitious metric *Vita* of Carolingian times [3,1. 358–361].

EDITIONS: 1 R. BORIUS, 1965   2 W. LEVISON, in *MGH Scriptores rerum Merovingicarum* 7, 225–283. BIBLIOGRAPHY: 3 W. BERSCHIN, Biographie und Epochenstil im lat. MA, 1 & 3, 1986 & 1991.   W. B.

Constellations see → Volume 4, Addenda

Constitutio see → Status [1]

Constitutio Antoniniana Decree of → Caracalla (AD 212), by which he extended Roman citizenship to almost all members of the empire (Cass. Dio 77,9,5; Dig. 1,5,17); cf. Aur. Vict., Caesares 16,12, who mistakenly attributes that action to → Marcus Aurelius instead of M. Aur. Antoninus Caracalla. Whether the much-discussed PGiss. 40 I contained the edict is questioned by [1]. The problem of the *[de]diticii*, who in the papyrus were apparently excluded from → citizenship or from the rights and privileges that it entailed, is possibly explained by the so-called Tabula Banasitana (AE 1971, 5344): the Mauretanian leaders granted citizenship by Marcus Aurelius had to continue paying taxes. Cassius Dio (77,9,4–5) emphasizes that Caracalla was motivated by financial considerations when he doubled the inheritance tax, which only Roman citizens had to pay. Other reasons (e.g. the desire to unify the empire's legal system) are occasionally advanced by modern researchers. A direct consequence of the Constitutio Antoniniana was that the *nomen gentile* of Emperor Aurelius became the most popular in the empire.

1 H. WOLFF, Die C.A. und Papyrus Gissensis 40 I, 1976.

A. N. SHERWIN-WHITE, The Roman Citizenship, [2]1973, 380ff.   A. B.

Constitution (πολιτεία/*politeía*, Latin *res publica*), constitutional theory.
I. NAME   II. CONCEPT AND TYPOLOGY   III. DEVELOPMENT OF THE TYPOLOGY

I. NAME

The Greek word → *politeía* (Antiph. 3,2,1; Thuc. 2,37; Pl. Resp. 8,562a; Aeschin. 1,5; Aristot. Pol. 3,1279a), which Plato [1] also paraphrases as κατάστασις τῶν ἀρχῶν καὶ ἀρχόντων ('appointment of offices and officeholders', Pl. Leg. 6,751a) and Aristotle [6] with τάξις τῶν τὴν πόλιν οἰκοώντων ('regulation for the town's residents', Aristot. Pol. 3,1274b 34) is equivalent to the English term constitution, i.e., the state's form of government. *Politeía* may also mean → citizens' rights (Hdt. 9,34), the totality of the citizens (Aristot. Ath. Pol. 54,3), the lifestyle of the community (Dem. Or. 19,184) or simply its government (Thuc. 1,127; Dem. Or. 18,87) [1.37–123]. Cicero uses the Latin terms → *res publica*, → *civitas* and *genus rerum publicarum* (Cic. Rep. 1,31,47, 1,33,50, 1,34,51, 1,28,44) for *politeia*.

II. CONCEPT AND TYPOLOGY

The understanding of *politeia* as the government form of a → polis has been reflected since the 5th cent. BC in the terminology of constitutional typology. The three main types of constitutions were → *monarchia*, → *oligarchia* or → *aristokrat* and → *demos* [1] or → *iso-*

nomia ('equality before the law', Hdt. 3,80–83; 1,242–249). In the first two the term is derived from the number of those governing, but the terms *demos* or *isonomia* for democracy (*demokratía*: Hdt. 6,43; Antiph. 6,45) show that formation of the concept may also express the criterion of all citizens' claim to → government [7.7–69]. The opposite of *isonomia* is → *tyrannís* (h. Hom. 8,5; Aesch. PV 736; Aristoph. Nub. 564) which describes an autocrat's arbitrariness that is controlled by no law. Therefore, constitutional typology permits a reconstruction of the concept of constitution.

III. DEVELOPMENT OF THE TYPOLOGY

The development of constitutional typology followed the development of ancient → political philosophy. In Herodotus the speakers in the debate about constitution discussed three main types of constitution from the perspective of the corruptibility of the rulers which leads to a violation of the existing common → laws and customs (Hdt. 3,80–83). The background to this debate is the understanding of Attic democracy as *isonomía*, which was institutionally implemented by → Cleisthenes [2] as a defensive reaction against the preceding tyranny [13]. In the factional discussions of the late 5th cent. BC in Athens, moderate democrats sought continuity with Solon [1] through the slogan → *pátrios politeía* ('V') [3.1–25].

→ Plato's [1] intervention into the political debate gave it a new irreversible direction [1.385–432]: in the 'Republic' (*Politeía*), Plato assumes the constitutional typology as a given but expands the use of the term by also applying *politeía* metaphorically to the 'governance of the soul'. As well, he replaced the quantitative criterion of the number of governing persons by a qualitative one (Pl. Resp. bk. 8–9; [4.21–71; 5.263–285]): apart from aristocracy as the rule of the best (striving for justice), there is timocracy (striving for honour), oligarchy (wealth), democracy (freedom and equality) and tyranny (force and arbitrariness). However, Plato's differentiation of one just form of government (ὄντως πολιτεία/*óntōs politeía*) from the many unjust forms, with the latter being the degeneration of the former, is of fundamental importance. He introduced the state's objective, → justice (identical with geometrical equality) as the criterion for a constitution and founded the tradition in political thought that sought to construct the 'best constitution' (*arístē politeía*). Plato radicalized this thought in his *Politikos* by no longer recognizing 'improper constitutions' as 'constitutions' at all (Pl. Plt. 303c; Plat. Leg. 8,832c: *stasioteía* instead of *politeía*). The best constitution was expressed in the rule of reason (*noo-kratía*, 'government of the → intellect', cf. Pl. Leg. 4,713e–714a, but without this expression) whose government is measured by justice as the common good (*to koinón*, Plat. Leg. 4,715a-c) (loc. cit.; [6.258–292]). As a result, Plato formulates the first 'constitutionalism' (cf. → POLITICAL THEORY II).

Aristotle [6] combines pre-Platonic and Platonic constitutional theory by differentiating three correct

forms that are guided by the common good (*basileía*/ monarchy, *aristokratía* and *politeía*) from their degenerated forms (*tyrannís*, *oligarchía* and *demokratía*; Aristot. Pol. 3,6–7). He adapted the constitutional typology of oligarchy and democracy with a view towards the constitutions of his time according to the sociological criterion of property — the rich versus the poor (ibid. 3,8). In particular, he refined the typology in the context of a reconceptualization of political philosophy (ibid. 4,1) by analyzing variants within a type and its institutions to help existing poleis achieve greater stability by combining institutions (→ 'Mixed constitution') (ibid. 3,8; 3,11; 5,8–9; [10.52–63]). In the light of the greater stability that differentiated Rome from the Greek states, the historian → Polybius [2] introduced the idea of a mixed constitution as a historiographical model (bk. 6; [2.40–95]). Based on Plato's concept of the decay of constitutions, Polybius assumed a cycle of constitutional change (Pol. 6,7,5–6,9,2) that may be delayed by a mixed constitution (6,10).

Based on these Greek models, → Cicero (*De re publica* and *De legibus*) attempted to combine the aspects of stability and the 'best constitution' (*optimus status civitatis*, Cic. Rep. 1,20,33): Rome in the period from the Monarchy to the Gracchi combined the advantages of the three classical constitutional types (Cic. Rep. 2); it was also the 'best state' because the consensus of the population about the sharing of power was supported by justice (ibid. 2; 3; 8,219–244; 3,14,108–121).

→ Augustine's criticism of Cicero's ideal of the state (Aug. Civ. 19,21 ff.) omits any constitutional typology: he measured the Roman *res publica* against the Christian concept of justice and denied it the name *res publica* (loc.cit.; [9; 14.158–170]). In the context of the Platonic approach, → Boethius at the end of antiquity associated the three classical constitutional types with the three forms of musical 'mean' (*medietas*) (Boeth. De institutione arithmetica 2,45; [12]) and, as a result, prepared the way for a comparable interpretation of constitutions by J. BODIN in the 16th cent. (*Six livres de la république* 6,6; → POLITICAL THEORY II).

→ Aristokratia; → Civitas; → Demokratia; → Justice; → Rulership; → Mixed constitution; → Oligarchy; → Plato [1] (G.3.); → Politeia; → Political philosophy; → Res publica; → State; → Tyrannis; ARISTOCRACY; DEMOCRACY; POLITICAL THEORY (II); CONSTITUTION; CONSTITUTIONAL TYPES

1 J. BORDES, Politeia dans la pensée grecque jusqu' à Aristote, 1982 2 K. VON FRITZ, The Theory of the Mixed Constitution in Antiquity, 1954 (on Polybius) 3 H. FUKS, The Ancestral Constitution, 1953 4 A. HELLWIG, Adikia in Platos Politeia, 1980 5 W. KERSTING, Platos 'Staat', 1999 6 A. LAKS, The Laws, in: CH. ROWE et al. (ed.), Cambridge History of Greek and Roman Political Thought, 2000, 258–292 7 CH. MEIER, Entstehung des Begriffs Demokratie, 1970 8 A. NESCHKE, Justice et Etat idéal chez Platon et Cicéron, in: M. VEGETTI (ed.), La Repubblica di Platone nella tradizione antica, 1999, 79–105 9 Id., La cité n'est pas nous, in: [8], 219–244 (on

Augustine) 10 W. Nippel, Mischverfassungstheorie und V.realität in Ant. und früher Neuzeit, 1985 11 H. Ryffel, Μεταβολὴ πολιτειῶν. Der Wandel der Staatsv., 1949 12 M. L. Silvestre, Forme di governo e proporzioni matematiche: Severino Boezio e la ricerca dell' *aequum ius*, in: Elenchus 17.1, 1996, 95–109 13 G. Vlastos, Isonomia, in: Id., Studies in Greek Philosophy, vol. 1, 1995, 90–111 14 P. Weber-Sch, Einführung in die ant. polit. Theorie, 1976. A. NE.

Constitutiones This term, deriving from the Republic's administrative and judicial practices, was not customarily applied to Imperial edicts (*edicta*), judgements (*decreta*) and written administrative and legal decisions (*epistulae*) until the 2nd cent. AD (Gai. Inst. 1.5). It also included imperial commands (*mandata*: Plin. Ep. 10,111), decrees (*orationes*: Dig. 23,2,60,3) and other instructions personally signed by the emperor, such as acts of clemency (*adnotationes*: Cod. Iust. 9,16,4 of 290). The *lex de imperio* (→ *imperium*, → *civitas*) did not originally extend imperial authority to lawmaking in general. The strict interpretation that imperial legal actions did not have the same validity as laws had to be disposed of (cf. Cod. Iust. 1,14,12,2 of 529) before the enabling law could also be seen as the basis for legitimizing at least imperial decrees, edicts and written instructions (Gai. Inst. 1,5; Fronto, Epist. 1,6 p. 14 Naber). In the 3rd cent. the same justification led to a further extension of the *lex*. Then every imperial wish expressed in writing became law (Ulp. Dig. 1,4,1). In the Dominatus *constitutiones* and *lex* were used synonymously (Cod. Theod. 1,1; Cod. Iust. 1,14), in the sense of *lex generalis* (Cod. Theod. 1,1,5; Cod. Iust. 1,14,7, 440; 12.1, 529; Cons. 7.3), *sanctio pragmatica* ([1.] *constitutiones* 1.1, of 438) and *lex personalis* ([1.] Nov. Val. 8,2 of 441). The *constitutiones* then came to be published in collections or formally sanctioned as → *codex*. A fairly small collection of 16 *constitutiones* from the years 333–408, mostly pertaining to Church law, is named, after its first publisher, *constitutiones Sirmondianae* [2]. Probably the most famous of all *constitutiones* is Caracalla's grant of citizenship in the *Constitutio Antoniniana*.

Editions: 1 Novellae Valentinianae, in: Leges Novellae ad Theodosianum pertinentes, ed. P. M. Meyer, ²1954. 2 Th. Mommsen, Theodosiani libri XVI cum Constitutionibus Sirmondianis, vol. II, 1905, 907–921.
Bibliography: 3 P. Jörs, s.v. c. principum, RE 7, 1106–1110 4 D. Liebs, Das Gesetz im spätröm. Recht, in: Gesetz in Spätant. und frühem MA, AAWG III 196, 1992, II. W.E.V.

Constitutiones apostolorum see → Apostolical constitutions

Construction drawing see → Building trade

Construction technique
I. Near East and Egypt II. Greece and Rome

I. Near East and Egypt
A. Near East B. Egypt

A. Near East
From the earliest times clay was the most important building material in Mesopotamia, along with reeds in the marshlands of the extreme south. With only a few exceptions, stone architecture, in a fairly strict sense of the term, is not found either in Babylon, which was lacking in raw materials other than limestone lodes, or in Assyria. When stone was used it was mainly for functional purposes, e.g. in laying foundations. Only in late Assyrian monumental architecture from the 8th cent. is there any appreciable component of stonemasonry, stemming perhaps from the influence of stonemasons from Phoenician-Syrian border areas of the Assyrian Empire where stone had played a more important role in architecture, just as in Asia Minor (Hittites) and later in Iran (Achaemenids). Little is known about quarries and stone extraction, apart form occasional representations in late Assyrian relief sculptures. The Babylonian method of using reeds in building corresponds very closely to the technique that can still be found in southern Iraq today; even the production of clay bricks has scarcely changed over the millennia. The first, handfashioned bricks date from around 8000 BC; bricks shaped in mould are to be found from the second half of the 8th millennium. Brick production consists of several phases: extracting the clay from pits, preparation of the clay mixture, shaping the bricks in wooden moulds and drying them. As large quantities of water were needed to produce the bricks, production centres were generally located in the vicinity of canals or rivers. Chaff was used to thin the mixture out. The preferred time of year for tile manufacture was in May and June: the drying process then took only a few days. July and August were the usual months for construction. Because of the lack of combustible material, fired tiles were expensive and used sparingly, chiefly in areas that were very susceptible to dampness. Wood in Mesopotamia was used principally for roofing. For shorter lengths, indigenous palm trunks or poplars sufficed, but for large columns in monumental architecture suitable woods (*i.a.* cedar and pine) had to be imported from the mountain areas of Zagros, Taurus, Amanus and Lebanon.

B. Egypt
Construction techniques are largely distinguished here in terms of a particular form of architecture. Profane buildings with a limited life span were constructed from bricks, whether fired or unfired, and wood or reeds, whereas sacred and funerary buildings that were intended to have a more permanent existence were made predominantly of stone. The early period is still characterized by brick architecture, even in tomb building. The use of stone increases from the 3rd dynasty

onwards, in conjunction with the development of metal tools. In the Old Kingdom the preferred material was limestone but hard rock was also used, e.g. as dressing blocks for the pyramids. The stone sizes were initially small but were later larger in keeping with the growing dimensions of buildings. The huge building projects of the 4th dynasty provide guidelines as to the way in which construction technique and management were to develop later. Nevertheless, the Middle Kingdom witnessed a temporary return to stone architecture. Large temples of the New Kingdom were initially constructed from limestone, but sandstone predominated later. Hard rock was preferred in the 25th and 30th dynasties.

Stones were broken away with the use of wedges but hard rocks were initially worked on as freestanding units. The use of copper saws and the final preparation of the surface with grinding stones and a quantity of emery are both attested. The stones were then transported mostly on water, thereafter moved with sleds and rollers. Yardsticks and measuring ropes were used for measuring the fit on the building site; the unit of measurement was the royal ell (52.5 cm). In rocky soil no special foundations were necessary, just some excavation to bed in the bottom layer of stones. In alluvium, on the other hand, deep foundation trenches were dug, though, up until the New Kingdom, with stones that were too small, thus creating a danger of collapse. Buildings were erected from large blocks of varying size that were adjusted to fit only at the moment of assembly and this led to an irregular pattern of joins. Wide gaps in the inner wall were filled in with stone and mortar. On larger construction jobs materials were lifted up by means of ramps, and in the process successive banks of sand could extend up the entire building. The finishing and polishing of the walls proceeded from top to bottom.

→ Architecture; → Building trade; → Quarries

D. ARNOLD, s.v. Construction technique, LÄ 1, 1975, 664–667; Id., Building in Egypt. Pharaonic Stone Masonry, 1991; O. AURENCHE, L'origine de la brique dans le Proche Orient ancien, in: M. FRANGIPANE, H. HAUPTMANN, M. LIVERANI, P. MATTHIAE, M. MEL-LINK (ed.), Between the Rivers and over the Mountains. Archaeologica Anatolica et Mesopotamica Alba Palmieri Dedicata, 1993, 71–85; P. R. S. MOOREY, Ancient Mesopotamian Materials and Industries, 1994, 302–362.   U.S.

II. GREECE AND ROME
A. DEFINITION AND PARAMETERS B. GREECE
1. MATERIALS 2. TOOLS, TRANSPORT
3. CONSTRUCTION C. ROME D. NEIGHBOURING
CULTURES

A. DEFINITION AND PARAMETERS
Since the 19th cent. the materials and construction techniques (CT) of Greek and Roman → Architecture have been a favourite subject of study in the fledgling archaeological field of building research; going beyond art and achitecture of the 19th cent., this eagerness to acquire knowledge focussed in particular on ancient Rome and in the process became linked to the technical ambitions of contemporary architecture in the 19th and 20th cents. As sources for information on CT, apart from the numerous traces of ancient work practices to be found on buildings, building sites or quarries, we have literary and epigraphical transmission, at times very detailed, as well as occasional finds of tools and graphical depictions (e.g. the relief at the Haterii grave). Until now research has concentrated on practical and technical aspects; going beyond that, however, it must be noted that developments and variations in ancient CT were closely connected to the social and economic circumstances of ancient societies. Without knowing the social and political role of its developers and the highly specialized craftsmen-entrepreneurs (→ Building trade), Greek stone block architecture, for example, is as hard to fathom as Roman cement casting techniques, the revolutionary effectiveness of which can be explained simply in the fact that a whole army of unskilled labourers could then be employed under the supervision of specialist engineers and carpenters (→ Architect; Materiatio). For other aspects of CT not covered in more thematic detail here: → Vaults and arches, construction of; → Funerary architecture; → Dome, Construction of domes; → Masonry; → Optical Refinements; → Column; → Quarries; → Roofing (each with a specialized bibliography); for planning and statistics → Building trade.

B. GREECE
1. MATERIALS
The most important building materials were stone and → wood, along with mud or clay → bricks that were either fired or dried in the open, → terracotta, various metals as well as → stucco, mortar and other bonding materials. Only in its representative and military forms (→ Fortifications) did Greek → architecture consist of monumental stone block edifices, constructed for the most part from a generally poorly preserved combination of wood, clay and quarried stone-building techniques. The preferred stone was πῶρος (pôros), a regionally variable hard limestone, together with → marble; varieties of harder stone such as granite and basalt were used, mostly as rubble for foundations and fillings but sometimes also in a composite design, e.g. in the use of different coloured stones for decorative effect (Erechtheion and Pillar of King Eumenes in Athens). It became necessary to develop quarries around 600 BC as new representative forms of public building (→ Temple) developed that needed larger blocks in such quantity that they could no longer be covered by residual boulders or fieldstones; from the 6th cent. BC pieces of marble, in particular, were amongst the most sought-after → natural resources. Wood was used not only for wall jambs in wickerwork or clay/quarry stone buildings and in early wooden temple constructions (→ Temple), but even in periods of advanced stone-building techniques it was an indispensable building material for roof-

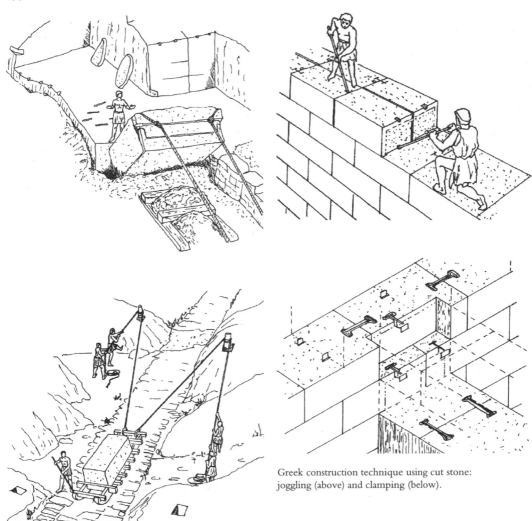

Greek construction technique using cut stone: joggling (above) and clamping (below).

Greek construction technique using ashlars: quarrying (above) and transport of building material (below).

ing and load-bearing constructions, bridges, false ceilings, supports, half-timbering and all interior areas. In addition, wood was ever present in the building process, in scaffolding, cranes, dowelling, various means of transport and other tools. Indigenous conifers (spruce, pine, cypress), oak or poplar were predominantly used; the great demand, for other purposes as well, made wood a first class export-import item.

Even in early Greek architecture loam and clay were used as mortar, as a filling and sealing compound or as material for architectural pieces (mouldings, piping, → tiles). Despite their limited durability, clay bricks that were dried in the open were used until well into the 4th cent. BC, even for city walls, essentially for reasons of cost. Fired wall bricks began to be used in Greece from c. 400 BC, but on a frequent basis only in the Hellenistic period; fired shaped pieces for clay pipes,

→ acroteria, metope plaques, and especially roofing tiles, mouldings, water spouts and ridging pieces are common in Greek CT from c. 700 BC (→ Architectural sculpture; → Terracotta). — Apart from tool manufacture, the metals most commonly used in Greek construction material were → iron, → bronze and → lead. Fashioned from bronze, and also from iron from the 6th cent. BC, were nails, studs and dowelling, hooks and reinforcements (e.g. architrave of the propylaeae of the Athenian acropolis), but especially the clamps with which the individual stone blocks were joined together; these were cast from lead. Precious metals and glass flux were occasionally used as sumptuous decoration (capitals of the north hall of the Erechtheion on the Athenian Acropolis). Clay was commonly used as a bonding material, also as plaster (partly mixed with chaff); lime or gypsum mortar came into use in the Hellenistic period, waterproof plaster mortar as early as the 6th cent. BC (Corinth, temple of Asclepius) and was used in underwater buildings (→ Harbour installations) and → cisterns. Stucco interior decoration consisted mainly of light gypsum mortar; fine marble stucco, with which poros buildings were coated in a c. 5

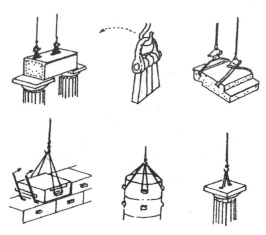

Greek construction technique: various lifting devices

mm layer, was a mixture of lime, sand and marble powder.

2. TOOLS, TRANSPORT

Stone was worked with hammers, mallets, wedges, chisels and drills to achieve various grades of fineness, freshly hewn blocks were cut up with saws. Round building items (bases, cylindrical sections, capitals of → columns) were turned or shaped on large potter's wheels. Amongst the building tools used were steel nails and dividers for marking cuts (→ Tracing (in full size)), angle irons, plumblines, rasps, as well as templates for shaping guidelines, and dye for marking. Scaffolding, cranes and pulleys sometimes were sophisticated mechanical constructions. Strong, high-tensile ropes were especially important not only for fixing → curvature but also for transporting and shifting building parts. Transporting materials from the quarry to the building site could well be a significant cost factor for small buildings (Asclepius temple, Epidaurus) and at times occurred as a gesture of magnanimous generosity (transport of whole buildings as a construction kit to their ultimate location, e.g. the Eumenes Stoa in Athens). Land transport of large and heavy building components took place by means of wagons, on wooden rollers or through special wooden rolling panels and cylindrical assemblies, as → Chersiphron probably used for the up to 70 tonne components of the archaic Artemisium of Ephesus; it was oxen that were primarily used as draught animals. Sea transport was customary for longer distances, provided there were harbours that were close to the quarries and building sites and had appropriate loading and unloading facilities.

3. CONSTRUCTION

For foundations unworked rock was preferred; otherwise, the shape of artificial foundation structures depended on the size of the building and the terrain. Residences often had a foundation of nothing more than packed rubble. Deep foundations are rare and limited to very bad building surfaces (Delphi, Tholus in the Marmaria); grill, strip and point foundations were common, pile foundations were less common and used to stabilize sections of the terrain bearing especially heavy loads. Foundations quite often contained material from earlier buildings and consisted of packed quarry stone and, in the classical period, of ashlars too, joined together cleanly or cut to fit. Only the → euthynteria, gently rising above ground level, was levelled off and fixed with clamps; on it was raised the stepped → krepis with the → stylobate as base for columns or walls. The construction of vertical → masonry did not depend on materials; wooden columns, wicker or clay brick walls stood on low bases or socles as protection from surface moisture. In stone constructions the blocks were initially fitted only roughly with quarry stone filler (Mycenaean 'Cyclopean masonry'), later more tightly sealed, either in isodomic, pseudo-isodomic or polygonal form, in which, especially on city walls (→ Fortifications) in the late classical and Hellenistic periods, the surface structure and the pattern of joins could assume a really artistic character. Stonemasonry could be either solid or parallel-coursed; parallel-coursed walls were filled with gravel and, to help stability, regularly joined up with layers of stone that ran across the courses.

In stone block and column construction blocks that had been pre-measured in the → quarries were measured up again at the building site and marked to show their planned position but, while being moved were left in → bosses to protect against damage; individual carrying bosses, lewis holes, recesses for lifting tongs, or a wolf grip facilitated transport with the use of cranes and levers. Columns and architraves were monolithic only in the 6th cent. BC; the use of cylindrical columns and architraves made from two or three parallel stones (→ Epistylion) considerably simplified transport and removal. To achieve a better fit, the contact surfaces of stone blocks and cylindrical columns were minimized by → anathyrosis and the sections locked with clamps or the columns secured with dowels. Chips and splintering were especially frequent with brittle marble and were repaired by patching. Only at the end of the move were → bosses, edge protectors and edge flaps removed, though they were sometimes kept in place for artistic purposes to give an uncompleted effect. Finally, following guidelines on the lowest, sometimes uppermost cylindrical section, the columns were given → cannelure, stone sections were decorated, and all capital and entablature areas were painted (→ Polychromy). Large numbers of → optical refinements, like → curvature of the stylobates (that sometimes permeated the whole building, e.g. in the → Parthenon), → inclination and → entasis of the columns, made the construction task considerably more difficult and demanded precision of an extremely technical nature.

C. ROME

In Roman antiquity essential principles of Greek construction materials, like the wood-clay-quarry stone technique for undemanding, functional architecture

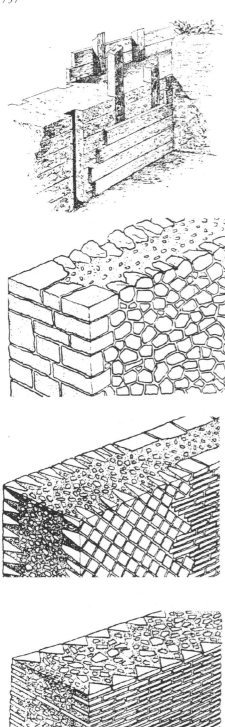

Roman construction technique: construction of a core made of *opus caementicium* (above), and various facings of tuffa (middle) and brick (below).

(e.g. commercial or military buildings) and the stone block technique that was transmitted via Etruria, continued to be used; tufa, soft, easy to work and easy to transport, available naturally everywhere and often used for Italian stone buildings, had to have its porous surface worked to a very high degree but at the same time did not require many of the protective measures that the Greeks used in transporting their brittle stone. The consistency and colouring of the tufa often permit assignation to particular quarries and, in addition, a chronological time frame for a building or its period of construction, as individual quarries were often used only for a few decades. One specific feature of Roman construction material is the frequent optical emphasis on technical-constructional building components, e.g. of the foundations or the substructures, as the result of a Roman conception that culture was able to overcome Nature (→ Architecture). Furthermore, from the 2nd cent. BC innovations appeared that highlight the especially close nexus between technical change, the development of new types and shapes of building, the politico-ideological framework and the social and logistical organizational structures in the → building trade. For the various technical building innovations in infrastructural and military buildings: → Fortifications; › Harbour facilities; → Canals, construction of; → Canalization; → Lighthouses; → Roads and bridges, construction of; → Dockyards. For technical aspects of interior decoration: → Fresco; Wall paintings.

The arrival of cement casting (for its development, sources and technical details of its use and production → *opus caementicium*), with its almost universal malleability, thanks to timber facing, and its virtually unlimited durability and load-carrying capacity, offered a cheap, readily available and quick-to-produce building material, the employment of which needed, moreover, only a few highly specialized experts for the planning, the building site logistics and the making of the wooden formwork, plus a large number of unskilled personnel. The dramatically increasing use of fired → bricks, also in the 2nd cent. BC, offered similar advantages (architectural adaptability, durability, cheap and quick manufacture and use by large armies of unskilled labour) and, in addition, *opus caementicium* served as a durable and load-bearing bonding material. Above all, cement casting enabled the construction of new building shapes, and new building styles as well; → vaults and arches as well as the casting of → domes are frequently to be found as forms of → roofing; prerequisites here were special cement mixtures with reduced weight from an admixture of volcanic pumice, and artistic, wooden formwork for pouring moulds (→ Materiatio). Storeyed buildings, similar to apartment blocks, became feasible in this way (in Rome residences grew to up to seven storeys; → House); bridges (→ Roads and bridges, construction of) and → water pipes with considerably wide spans in places traversed valleys and rivers on high piles.

From the very beginning the unadorned cement was dressed with a decorative coating of tiles or tufa (→ Masonry). Despite unresolved problems of chronology, the different forms of dressing constitute a potential means of dating buildings or individual stages in building. From the late Republic brick buildings were increasingly regarded as needing adornment and were dressed with pre-polished travertine, marble or other varieties of hard stone. Status-seeking in the imperial period produced a real demand for luxury materials and that in turn led to the use of increasingly extravagant dressings and increasingly precious varieties of stone, even in structural complexes (porphyry, granite and basalt even for columns, entablatures and stone blocks; colour was especially appreciated (→ Polychromy). In a similarly extravagant fashion even the flooring of buildings was decorated (→ Pavimentum); various tiling techniques, expensive sheets of covering and → mosaics were the rule in public buildings of the Roman imperial period.

D.NEIGHBOURING CULTURES

Up until now the construction material of cultures neighbouring the Graeco-Roman world have been under-represented as a subject of study and research. Throughout, a Hellenocentric or Roman-centric view has prevailed, assuming more or less strong influences of Greek or Roman construction material on neighbouring cultures and thence going on to infer some putative degree of cultural independence. In individual cases this is appropriate; thus Roman construction material, for example — like Roman technology generally — served as a first-class means of Romanization, of the cultural subjugation of conquered territories. Overall, however, this perspective is problematic, in that it postulates a one-sided and passive process of reception and does not seek to ask either whether techniques developed in these neighbouring cultures might have been adopted by the Greeks and Romans, or to what extent adaptations of technique in the neighbouring cultures were part of a consciously eclectic appreciation of their culture. For technical building characteristics of neighbouring cultures, see: Etruscan, Iberian, Phoenician, Scythian and Thracian archaeology.

G. LUGLI, La tecnica edilizia romana, 1957; R. MARTIN, Manuel d'architecture grecque, 1, Matériaux et techniques, 1965; A. ORLANDOS, Les matériaux de construction et la technique architecturale des anciens Grecs, 2 vols, 1966/68; A. BURFORD, The Greek Temple Builders at Epidauros, 1969; B. FEHR, Plattform und Blickbasis, in: MarbWPr 1969, 31–67; F. RAKOB, Hell. in Mittelitalien: Bautypen und Bautechnik, in: P. ZANKER (ed.), Hell. in Mittelitalien, Kongr. Göttingen (1974), 1976, 366–386; J. J. COULTON, Greek Architects at Work, 1977; H. DRERUP, Zum Ausstattungsluxus in der röm. Architektur, ²1981; F. RAKOB, opus caementicium und die Folgen, in: MDAI(R) 90, 1983, 359–372; J. M. CAMP II., W. B. DINSMOOR JR., Ancient Athenian Building Methods, 1984; J. P. ADAM, La construction romaine. Matériaux et techniques, 1984; R. GINOUVÈS, R. MARTIN, Dictionnaire méthodique de l'architecture grecque et romaine, 1, Matéri-

aux, techniques, 1985; E. M. STERN, Die Kapitelle der Nord-Halle des Erechtheion, in: MDAI(A) 100, 1985, 405–426; G. BRODRIBB, Roman Brick and Tile, 1987; W. MÜLLER-WIENER, Griech. Bauwesen in der Ant., 1988; G. GRUBEN, Fundamentierungsprobleme der ersten griech. Großbauten, in: Bathron, FS H. Drerup, 1988, 159–171; A. HOFFMANN et al. (ed.), B. der Ant., Kongr. Berlin (1990), DiskAB 5, 1991; H.-O. LAMPRECHT, opus caementitium: Bautechnik der Römer, ⁴1993.   C.HÖ.

Consualia The two festivals (*feriae*) of the → Consus, the C., fell on 21 August and 15 December. On 21 August a form of harvest festival was celebrated: the *flamen Quirinalis* and the Vestals sacrificed first crops from the harvest at the underground altar of the Consus. Then the priests organized games with draught horses and mules; pastoral games are also mentioned (the rape of the Sabines is said to have taken place during these games). We know nothing of the second festival; probably the grain stores were ritually opened up on that day.

DUMÉZIL, 168; LATTE, 72; P. POUTHIER, Ops et la conception divine de l'abondance dans la religion romaine jusqu'à la mort d'Auguste, 1981; G. WISSOWA, Religion und Kultus der Römer ²1912, 202.   J.S.

Consul(es) The word *consul* is of uncertain etymology (possibly originating from *con*- and *sal*- = 'hastily get together' or from *con*- and *sell-/sedl-* = 'sit down together with' or 'sit down next to'). The historical tradition (Liv. 1,60,3–4), firmly established in the late Republican period, that following the expulsion of the last king Tarquinius Superbus in 510 BC there were two *consules*-colleagues at Rome's head is uncertain, because of some contrary indications in the same historical transmission. Initially, *consules* were probably assigned as advisers to a *praetor maximus* (Fest. 249 L.; Liv. 3,5–9) who was elected for a fixed period. Later on, the highest magistrature happened to divide itself evenly into larger committees, not only into the extraordinary 10–man college of the 12 Tables Law (→ Tabulae Duodecim) of 451–449 BC, but also in the → consular tribunate that was predominantly practised between 445 and 367 (Liv. 4,7,1ff.). After the Licinian-Sextian laws of 367 BC (Liv. 6,34–42), however, the two-man college of the *consules* appears established, as a result of the plebeians' long fought-for claims of equality with the patricians that were met only through the consulate.

The official competencies of the two *consules*-colleagues were so strong in the Republican period that Polybius (6,11,11–12) saw in them a kind of royal power: they encompassed all decision-making powers of the State that did not, by virtue of their origin or by law, belong to the → Senate, → public assemblies, specific courts or specific → magistrates with their own competencies. They consisted of the power of constraint (*imperium domi*), command of the Roman army (*imperium militiae*), the right to intervene in all unfinished official transactions of a *consules*-colleague and all subordinate magistrates (i.e. the praetors, aediles, quaestors; not the censors), the right to propose laws and the right to nominate candidates for elections to the public assembly, the right to convene, address and propose items for sittings of the Senate (*ius agendi cum senatu, cum populo*), as well as the right in an emergency to fill a vacancy left by a colleague (*sufficere*) and appoint a *dictator* (if need be against the will of an incumbent *consul*-colleague). Exercise of the consular power was limited by the right of intervention held by the other colleague or by a people's tribune (→ Tribunus). Every Roman citizen had the right to appeal to the public assembly against a consul's punitive judgements affecting life or liberty (*provocatio*). These limits to the powers of office, as also the yearly election of *consules* by the *comitia centuriata*, were clearly designed with the aim of sharing powers and putting a check on power in normal times. Exceptionally, however, the *consules* had the power, according to constitutional tradition—even if partly contested (Sall. Catil. 51,25ff.)—to take extralegal emergency measures with the authorization of the Senate (*senatus consultum ultimum*). Also — as a departure from the regulatory annuality of *consules*-office (Liv. 3,21) — the period of office could be extended on an exceptional basis (*prorogatio imperii*), as in the case of Marius (Cic. Sest. 37f.: Liv. 8,23,12), for example. Together with other departures from the constitution, this occurred in late Republican Rome, though not for the first time—as a measure of unquestionable political necessity .

From the beginning of the imperial period, the *consules*-office was overshadowed by imperial sovereignty, although it admittedly remained the highest office of state in a formal sense. Thus, for instance, calendar years were named after the *consules* then in office, and its formal status was retained in the traditional insignia of magisterial power (12 lictors with *fasces* and *secures, sella curulis, toga praetexta* i.a.) but thereafter only *candidati principis* were elected *consules*, and the exercise of office had to subordinate itself completely to the dictates of imperial power, which from then on held the controlling initiative, previously held principally by the *consules*, with all important foreign policy, military, financial, legal and manpower issues (Tac. Ann. 1,1–4). Thenceforth, the office changed from being a constitutional sharing of power during the Republican regime to being merely a career stepping-stone within the imperial-aristocratic hierarchy; the office of consul was sought after instead, because of the access to the highly regarded and financially rewarding 'consular' offices of provincial government and, in late antiquity, in the imperial seat of government and the court administration. Already under Caesar, without there being any emergency, a multiple occupancy of office was introduced with two *consules ordinarii* and several pairs of purely honorary *consules suffecti* serving in the one year of office; over time the intervals were shortened from four months to one month. In late antiquity, by being placed on the same footing as the *praefecti prae-*

torio, the *magistri militum* and the *praefecti urbi* holding office in Rome and Constantinople, the *consules* were displaced from even their titular positions of primacy (Cod. Iust. 12,3,3; 12,4 tit.); their office, however, essentially survived in name until AD 537 (Nov. Just. Epit. 49).

J. BLEICKEN, Verfassungs- und Sozialgesch. des röm. Kaiserreiches, 60ff., 303ff.; JONES, LRE, 532f., 558f.; MOMMSEN, Staatsrecht 1, 8ff., 2, 174ff., 702ff.　C.G.

Consularis as a substantive designates a former → *consul* or a senator who was accorded the honour of a former *consul*, later used adjectivally to designate the powers, entitlements and responsibilities of a serving or former *consul*. Since the office of *consul* was the highest office of state in the Republic and nominally (i.e. eponymously) also in the imperial period, former consuls were accorded precedence, in the Senate's order of speaking and voting, after each of the consuls still in office but ahead of senators holding the rank of praetor, tribune, aedile or quaestor. Consular rank, which could be conferred by the Senate, and later also by the emperor, in recognition of services rendered without having had to exercise the consulate previously, was later a prerequisite for election as *censor*, as *dictator* and for appointment to some of the highly regarded — proconsular — offices of provincial government in, for example, Africa, Achaea and Asia, but in the period when there was a distinction between imperial and senatorial provinces, the latter frequently had an administrator with proconsular authority, the former — because of their independence from the proconsular *imperium* of the emperor — never had one.

→ Proconsul; → Senatus; → Cursus honorum

JONES, LRE, 106f.; MOMMSEN, Staatsrecht, 2, 74ff., 145 and 243ff.; 3, 966.　C.G.

Consular tribunes more accurately in Lat. *tribuni militum consulari potestate*, were probably elected for the first time in 443 BC (Liv. 4,7,1f.) — soon after the two-year-long government of the *XII viri legibus scribundis* (in 450/449) — initially by the *comitia centuriata*, so as to share consular powers of office among more than two colleagues. Livy takes the view that a larger number of bearers of the *imperium* were needed because of the several war fronts at that time. Other authors see this institution as an expression of the competing interests in the class struggle between patricians and plebeians (Pompon. Dig. 1,2,2,25). An argument in favour of that view is the fact that it was only in 404 that a plebeian became consular tribune (Liv. 5,12,2f.), and against it, i.a., that 'simple' military tribunes of that period were appointed with the annual levy of the army (*legio*) from the population as a whole and a patrician background — unlike the system for consular office up until the *leges Liciniae Sextae* of 387 BC — was not a prerequisite. Those laws established an equal sharing of the consulate, introduced a praetorship and did away with the institution of consular tribune, which was by then obviously unnecessary. In the 56 years of its constitutional validity there was always a majority of colleges of consular tribunes — versus 22 of consuls.

The consular tribunes were elected by the public assembly after the consent of the Senate (Dion. Hal. Ant. Rom. 11,60) and had the same powers — but not the same entitlements (e.g. to a triumph and to sit and hold rank in the Senate) — as the consuls. They numbered at least three, frequently four, never five and probably six at most; though at times officials with censorial authority were probably also counted as belonging to the college of consular tribunes.

In the late Republican period (in 53/2) the reintroduction of the institution was considered for a while but never came about (Cass. Dio 40,45,4).

F. F. ABBOTT, A History and Description of Roman Political Institutions, ³1963, no. 194–196; MOMMSEN, Staatsrecht 2.1, 181–192.   C.G.

Consultatio veteris cuiusdam iurisconsulti The educational document was probably produced in Gaul as late as the 5th cent. AD. In an expert commentary, the points of view in a case involving a written settlement of an estate amongst the heirs (and their siblings) are analyzed and commented on in keeping with the rhetorical doctrine on status. Possible difficulties affecting the parties and those acting on their behalf, the purpose of the trial, the suit itself, the conduct of the trial, and third parties, in so far as they had any bearing on the trial and its outcome, are worked through systematically and substantiated with quotations from the Cod. Gregorianus, Cod. Hermogenianus, the Pauli sententiae and the Cod. Theodosianus.

EDITIONS: P. KRÜGER, Collectio III, 1890, 199; J. BAVIERA, FIRA II, ²1940, 591.
BIBLIOGRAPHY: K. H. SCHINDLER, Consultatio, in: Labeo 8, 1962, 16–61.   W.E.V.

Consultus Fortunatianus (C. Chirius F. derives from a misunderstood title of a work: enchiridion/enchiriadis). Author of a Lat. manual Ars rhetorica in three bks in the form of question and answer. In bks 1 and 2 the inventio is discussed (status, partes orationis), with emphasis on the doctrine of status, and in bk. 3 dispositio, elocutio, memoria and pronuntiatio. Probably to be dated in the 5th rather than the 4th cent. AD [6], the work represents a comprehensive and highly systematic compendium, deriving from the declamatory school (p. 2,20) and is in the → Hermagoras-tradition of the status ('issues') doctrine transmitted by earlier editors but, at the same time, quite obviously draws from Latin sources in other sections [3. 45 ff.; CALBOLI, ed., 21 ff.]. Despite considerable circulation in manuscript (as a text in schools; link with Aug., De rhetorica; used extensively by Cassiodorus), the work, which at the end of the 8th cent. still formed part of a representative

introduction into the → artes liberales (Par. Lat. 7530), became increasingly less important during the Middle Ages, when Boethius' De differentiis topicis held sway, but was then eagerly transcribed again by the humanists when a different concept of rhetoric was in fashion.

EDITIONS: HALM p. 79–134; L. CALBOLI MONTEFUSCO, Ars rhetorica, 1979 (with quotations; bibliography).
BIBLIOGRAPHY: 1 H.-W. FISCHER, Unt. über die Quellen der Rhet. des Martianus Capella, diss. 1936, especially 88 ff.   2 M. C. LEFF, The topics of argumentative invention in Latin rhetorical theory from Cicero to Boethius, in: Rhetorica 1,1, 1983, 23–44, especially 36f.
3 K. MÜNSCHER, s.v. F. 7, in: RE 7,1, 44–55   4 A. REUTER, Unt. zu den röm. Technographen F., Julius Victor, Capella und Sulpitius Victor, in: Hermes 28, 1893, 73–134   5 W. SCHÄFER, Quaestiones rhetoricae, diss. 1913, 82ff.   6 U. SCHINDEL, HLL § 616–617.1.
TRANSMISSION: 7 G. BILLANOVICH, Il Petrarca e i ret. lat. min., in: IMU 5, 1962, 103–164 (with bibliography) 8 R. GIOMINI, I Principia rhetorices di Agostino ..., in: Filologia e forme letterarie. Studi F. Della Corte 4, 1987, 281–297.   W.-L.L.

Consus is god of the harvest of the grain crop. His name is derived from condere ('harvest'). His festival was the → Consualia, his underground altar was in the valley of the Circus, south of the foot of the Palatine. The C. inscription transmitted by Tertullian (De spectaculis 5,7) can hardly have come from this altar and does not seem very old. Goddesses involved in protecting the grain crop (Seia, Segetia, Tutilina) were also venerated at the same location. In 272 BC, after his triumph over Tarentum, L. Papirius Cursor constructed a temple [1] on the Aventine to C., whose inaugural festival (natalis) under Augustus took place on 21 December.

1 A. ZIOLKOVSKI, The Temples of Mid-republican Rome, 1993, 24.

DUMÉZIL, 168f.; G. WISSOWA, Religion und Kultus der Römer, ²1912, 201ff.   J.S.

Contarii were auxiliary cavalrymen armed with a heavy lance (contus) about 3.5m long. They held the lance across the withers of the horse, with both hands either on top of or underneath the lance, and were thus not protected by a shield. This lance was probably adopted from the Sarmatians. From the time of Trajan or Hadrian there were separate units of C., as for example the ala I Ulpia contariorum milliaria. Although the C. initially wore no armour, they probably contributed to the development of mailed cavalry.

1 J. W. EADIE, The development of Roman mailed cavalry, in: JRS 57, 1961, 167–73.   J.CA.

Contestani(a) Area and tribe between Cartagena and Júcar in the province of Murcia and Valencia; the name appears to be Celtic [1. 1107]. C. is mentioned in the context of the Sertorius war (Liv. fr. bk. 91), also in Plin. HN 3,19f.; Ptol. 2,6,14,61; see also [2. 131; 3. 222].

1 HOLDER 1   2 A. SCHULTEN, Fontes Hispaniae Antiquae 1, ²1955   3 Id.., Fontes Hispaniae Antiquae 6, 1952.

L. CONESA, Contestania ibérica, 1972; TOVAR 3, 31.   P.B.

Contest of Homer and Hesiod (Αγὼν Ὁμήρου καὶ Ἡσιόδου/Agṑn Homéru kaì Hēsiódou, Latin Certamen Homeri et Hesiodi).

The 'Contest of Homer and Hesiod' (CHH), which is only related in one MS (Cod. Laurentianus Graecus 56,1), is part of the ancient anecdotal-biographical tradition surrounding famous poets and thinkers (cf. → Biography). This work, a compilation of prose and hexameter verse, was written during or shortly after the reign of emperor Hadrian (AD 117–138) (presumably during the → Second Sophistic) since the author mentions the oracle of the Delphic → Pythia [1] to Hadrian regarding the true descent of Homer (→ Homer [1] II.A.-B.) in lines 33–43. However, the tradition of a poetic competition between → Homer [1] and → Hesiod is probably much older. Heraclitus [1] (22 B 56 DK) is familiar with the legend of Homer's death at the end of the CHH; Thgn. 425 f. contains a variant of verses 78–79 of the CHH. In the poetic competition between Aeschylus [1] and Euripides [1] in the 'Frogs', Aristophanes [3], appears to assume that the CHH is familiar [10].

The Museíon, written by the sophist → Alcidamas in the 4th cent. BC, cites the author of the CHH as the source for his account of Hesiod's death (l. 239 f.). Two papyri (Flinders Petrie Pap. XXV, 3rd cent. BC; Pap. Michigan 2754, 2nd/3rd cents.) discovered around 1900 contain long excerpts of an account that agrees with the MS of CHH down to details, with the second papyrus concluding with the words 'from the writing of Alcidamas on Homer'. According to [15], both papyri contained excerpts from Alcidamas' Museíon, which was supposedly also used as the main source by the compiler of the preserved CHH. However, Alcidamas did not invent the tale of the CHH. Rather, a major point of the traditional narrative — that Homer distinguished himself in 'improvising' (σχεδιάζειν/schediázein) in a competition with Hesiod — helped his purpose: to demonstrate the advantage of improvising while speaking. Contrary to [13], [10] wishes to locate the idea of a poetic agon between Homer and Hesiod in the 6th cent. BC, which is characterized by → rhapsode competitions; he largely attributes their details, as present in the CHH, to Alcidamas. [6] notes a parallel tradition in Plutarch's [2] 'Banquet of the Seven Sages' and in Dion [I 3] of Prusa's '2nd Royal Speech'.

The CHH contains three main parts: (1) 1–62: the origin of Homer; (2) 63–214: the CHH at the funerary games for Amphidamas of Chalcis; (3) 215–338: the deaths of the two poets. The original tale of the poetic competition appears to have been taken from a statement by Hesiod (Hes. Op. 639 f.) that he had once won the poetic prize at the funerary games for Amphidamas in Chalcis with a hýmnos. However, the contest as it is consists of several subdisciplines in which it is always

Hesiod who challenges Homer. First Homer answers questions regarding the philosophy of life in hexameter verse, then he completes hexameter couplets begun by Hesiod, and finally both poets provide model examples of their poetic art: Homer from the Iliás and Hesiod from the Érga. Contrary to expectations, the judge Pandes decides for the peaceful poetry of Hesiod and against the war-like epics of Homer. The CHH is part of the history of the reception of Homer and Hesiod in antiquity. Though biographical in orientation, it makes critical statements on the respective 'value' of the two works.

→ Agon (s. addenda); → Hesiod; → Homer [1]; → Competitions, artistic

1 J. VAHLEN, Der Rhetor Alkidamas, in: SAWW philol.-histor. Klasse, Bd. 43, 1863, 491–528.

EDITIONS: 2 T. W. ALLEN, Homeri Opera, Bd. 5, 1969 3 F. NIETZSCHE (ed.), Der Wettkampf zw. Homer und Hesiod, in: Acta Societatis Philologae Lipsiensis 1871, 1 f. 4 A. RZACH, Hesiodi Carmina. Accedit Homeri et Hesiodi certamen, 1902, 433–450. LITERATURE: 5 B. GRAZIOSI, Competition in Wisdom, in: F. BUDELMANN, P. MICHELAKIS (eds.), Homer, Tragedy and Beyond. FS P. E. Easterling, 2001, 57–74 6 K. HELDMANN, Die Niederlage Homers im Dichterwettstreit mit Hesiod (Hypomnemata 75), 1982 7 K. HESS, Der Agon zw. Homer und Hesiod, diss. Zurich 1960 8 Y. KAWASAKI, The Contest of Homer and Hesiod and Alcidamas, in: Journ. of Classical Studies (Japan) 33, 1985, 19–28 (Japanese with Engl. abstract) 9 F. NIETZSCHE, Der Florentinische Tractat über Homer und Hesiod, ihr Geschlecht und ihren Wettkampf, in: RhM 25, 1870, 528–540; 28, 1873, 211–249 10 N. J. RICHARDSON, The Contest of Homer and Hesiod and Alcidamas' Mouseion, in: CQ 31, 1981, 1–10 11 E. ROHDE, Studien zur Chronologie der griech. Litteraturgesch., in: RhM 36, 1881, 380–434 (especially 419 f.) 12 W. SCHADEWALDT, Legende von Homer dem fahrenden Sänger, 1942, 42–54 13 M. L. WEST, The Contest of Homer and Hesiod, in: CQ 17, 1967, 433–450 14 Id. (ed.), Hesiod, Works And Days, 1978 (with commentary) 15 E. VOGT, Die Schrift vom W. H. H., in: RhM 102, 1959, 193–221 16 U. VON WILAMOWITZ-MOELLENDORFF (ed.), Vitae Homeri et Hesiodi, 1916, 34–45.   W.D.F.

Conthyle (Κονθύλη; Konthýlē).

Attic mesogeia deme of the phyle Pandionis, from 224/3 BC of Ptolemaïs; one → bouleutḗs; the location is uncertain (Mazareïka? [2; 3. 43]). According to [1. 601ff.], C. formed the cultural association of Tricomi together with Erchia and Cytherus. Sources: Aristoph. Vesp. 233; Phot. s.v. Κοθύλη.

1 P. J. BICKNELL, Clisthène et Kytherros, in: REG 89, 1976, 599–603   2 M. PETROPOLAKOU, E. PENTAZOS, Ancient Greek Cities 21. Attiki, 1973, 157 no. 25 3 TRAILL, Attica 43, 62, 69, 111 no. 73, table 3, 13.   H.LO.

Contio

Contio, from 'co-ventio' (general meaning: public gathering) means in a special sense an assembly of Roman citizens convened by a magistrate, not to take decisions but for information and explanatory purposes. It was the precursor of a public assembly that later on had as its rationale the holding of a vote, elections or formal legal proceedings in the *comitia*. It had no fixed structure but followed the pattern of later, decision-making proceedings. In the case of legal proceedings in the *comitia*, three *contiones* had in fact to precede each instance. It may be taken as given that every enfranchised citizen had the right to speak freely. Even controversial items could be placed on the agenda (example: Liv. 34,1–8). The purpose of a *contio* was to allow public discussion of political and legal issues to take place in an orderly, undemagogic fashion and thereby, in particular, to prevent any unruly gatherings (*contiones turbulentae, seditiosae*) from taking place outside the forum or beyond the authorized time frame (Cic. Rep. 2,29).

The general decline in political significance of public assemblies in Rome after the introduction of the principate, towards the end of the 1st cent. AD, meant a corresponding loss of purpose of the *contiones* also, but not their disappearance altogether. This was particularly true outside Rome, where, in cities constituted in the Greek or Roman model, duly convened and authorized *contiones* and → *comitia* could take place, whenever necessary, in an orderly fashion to discuss city issues, hold elections and take decisions (Dig. 48,19 e contr.). Only for Rome and other reserved areas did the power of *creatio* of the magistrates rest with the emperor. Public assemblies of soldiers convened by a commander constituted another category of *contio*, an extraordinary case of the *contio apud milites habita* covered by the constitution, namely the army gatherings taking place in politico-military crises, which as early as the Republican period, for example, elected a commander-in-chief in an emergency (Liv. 25,37) and which in the late Imperial period were always summoned by an imperial command (*declaratio augusta*) (Amm. Marc. 20,4; 26,2).

F. F. Abbott, A History and Description of Roman Political Institutions, ³1963, 251ff.; Mommsen, Staatsrecht 3, 305; L. R. Taylor, Roman Voting Assemblies, 1966, 13–38. C.G.

Contiomagus *Vicus* of the *Contiomagienses* (AE 1959,76) belonging to the *civitas Treverorum* near a crossing of the Saar on the Roman road Divodurum—Mogontiacum at today's Pachten (part of Dillingen an der Saar). Of cultural significance is a theatre building with names inscribed on the stone seats (BRGK 58, 1977, 476, 27). Destroyed in AD 275/76, C. was reconstructed at the beginning of the 4th cent. as a rectangular citadel (1.9 ha.).

G. Schmidt, Das röm. Pachten, 1986.

Contionacum A palace complex was developed at Konz bei Trier, above the point where the Saar joins the Moselle, in the middle of the 4th cent. AD and used as a palace until the early 5th cent.; identified as the summer palace C. where Valentinianus I issued several decrees in AD 371 (Cod. Theod. 2,4,3; 4,6,4; 9,3,5; 11,1,17); Auson. Mos. in 369 probably also refers to C.

A. Neyses, Die spätröm. Kaiservilla von Konz, 1987. F.SCH.

Contorniati Modern technical term for antique medallions, minted or cast mainly in the Rome mint but possibly in private workshops also, with a highly beaten edge (Italian *contorno*) and a deep-cut groove, mostly of brass, less commonly from bronze, with an average diameter of 40 mm. The symbols on the reverse, frequently a palm branch and the monogram PE [2. Part 2, 242–306], are for the most part engraved later, sometimes inserted with silver in niello technique. C. date to the 4th and 5th cents. AD [2. Part 2, 7ff.; 4].

On the obverse of the *contorniati* are to be found the likenesses of, for example, Alexander the Great, Horace, Sallust and Roman emperors, especially Nero, Trajan and Caracalla or Divus Augustus; on the reverse mythological representations e.g. from the Alexander tradition, as well as competition and circus scenes [2. Part 1]. As to the symbols, the palm tree is certainly a symbol of victory but interpretation of the monogram PE is still in dispute, possibly *P(raemiis) FEL(iciter receptis)* as a good luck sign for the owner [1. 30ff.; 2. Part 2, 309ff.; 4].

The purpose of the *contorniati* is still not unambiguously clear. A. Alföldi [1; 2] saw them primarily as a propaganda tool of pagan urban Roman aristocracy. It is nevertheless clear that they were influenced by the iconography of the non-Christian past and, *i.a.*, were distributed at the games by leading magistrates on taking up office [4]. Precursors of the *contorniati* are coins with a hammered edge (→ Sestertius, → Dupondius, → As) that were also used as board counters [3; 4].

1 A. Alföldi, Die K. Ein verkanntes Propagandamittel der stadtröm. heidnischen Aristokratie in ihrem Kampfe gegen das christl. Kaisertum, 1942/3   2 A. Alföldi, E. Alföldi, Die Kontorniat-Medaillons, Teil 1, 1976, Teil 2, 1990   3 Göbl, Vol. 1, 31   4 M. R.-Alföldi, Ant. Numismatik, Teil 1, 1978, 214f. GE.S.

Contour see → Painting; → Vase painters

Contra Term for military posts on Roman military roadways, especially in Upper Egypt and in the Lower Nubia that was dependent on Rome, that were opposite the places whose names were linked with *contra*, on the other side of the Nile: 1. C. *Copto* opposite Coptus (Itin. Anton 159). 2. C. *Lato* opposite Esna (ibid., 165). 3. C. *Apollonos* opposite Edfu (ibid., 165). 4. C. *Thumis* opposite a so far unknown town between Edfu and Kom Ombo (ibid., 160). 5. C. *Ombos* opposite Kom Ombo (ibid., 160). 6. C. *Syene* opposite Assuan (ibid., 167). 7. C. *Taphis* opposite Tafa (ibid., 164). 8. C. *Talmis* opposite Kalabsha (ibid., 164). 9. C. *Pselcis* opposite Dakka (ibid., 164). R.GR.

Contraception The gynaecological writings in the *Corpus Hippocraticum* (→ Hippocrates, with a list of works and abbreviations) are mainly concerned with female fertility. The one exception to this rule represents a prescription with an allegedly contraceptive effect; its basic substance μίσυ/*mísy* (possibly copper ore) was claimed to be able to prevent conception for a year if dissolved in water and taken orally ([Hippoc.] Mul. 1,76; 8,170 L. and Hippoc. Nat. Mul. 98; 7,414 L.) [1]. Even if this is the only 'contraceptive' — in the modern sense of the word — in the Hippocratic body of writing, it would nevertheless be wrong to think that that was all there was to the subject of contraception in antiquity. As conception was thought to be a gradual process in which the seed 'settled' in the womb (cf. Aristot. Gen. an. 737a 21) and was slowly 'cooked' (cf. [Hippoc.] Genit./Nat. Puer. 12,7,486 L.), the difference between contraception and abortion was fuzzy in antiquity. Medicines that could also be taken as → abortifacients were usually recommended as multi-purpose expulsive agents, so that 'inducing a late menstruation 'represented a euphemism for an abortion in the early stages of pregnancy, and indeed even infanticide was sometimes regarded as a decidedly late abortion (→ *abortio*, → *abortiva*, → Abortion).

The medical writer → Soranus, whose 'Gynaecology' was written in the time of Trajan and Hadrian, constitutes an exception: he was in favour of contraception (understood as any form of intervention preventing the union of the male seed with the female) rather than abortion (defined as destruction of the seed), because it represented a safer method of birth control (1,20,60). The medicines that he prescribed were supposed to have a cooling and obstructive effect to prevent the male seed from penetrating the womb, or a warming and irritating effect to expel the seed. These contraceptive medicines were administered vaginally or by means of soaked sponges as pessaries. The substances used included pomegranate skin, ginger, olive oil, vinegar and various resins that influenced the acidic balance in the vagina and thus created a hostile environment for the sperm.

Apart from medicines, however, other techniques of contraception were also available, including contraceptive positions during intercourse, coitus interruptus (probably the 'landing in the grassy meadows' of Archilochus, P. Colon 7511 = SLG 4782), attempting to hold back the semen, and procedures for expelling the semen from the womb immediately after intercourse, such as, for example, jumping up and down, douching or inducing sneezing (Sor. 1,20,61). In [Hippoc.] Genit. 5 (7,476 L.) it is maintained that a woman who does not wish to become pregnant can expel the seed of both partners whenever she so wishes. Even amulets and invocation practices were employed; one such incantation, preserved on a papyrus from the 4th cent., speaks *i.a.* of getting a frog to swallow sweet peas soaked in menstrual blood, with every pea swallowed guaranteeing one year free of conception (PGM 36, 320–332).

The difficulty in assessing the totality of ancient contraceptives lies in the fact that polypragmasy was the rule in ancient medicine. Since people turned to a widely varying range of treatments, and probably to incantations and amulets at the same time also, it would have been extremely difficult in the case of successful contraception to establish with certainty which individual measure had achieved the desired effect and was thus worthy of recommendation to others [2].

There were various reasons for taking contraceptive measures. There was a view that prostitutes held the body of knowledge in relation to contraception and that doctors later learned from them [3]. A further potential source of information may have been → midwives, but it is uncertain whether they had a relatively large clientele in antiquity. Certainly women whose economic value depended on their not falling pregnant would have had an interest in contraception. Even women who were not prostitutes, though, will have needed to know about contraception if they intended to have extramarital intercourse or, within marriage, to have a period free of conception, in between pregnancies. Soranus condemned women whose interest in contraception stemmed only from a concern to preserve their beauty or to conceal an adulterous liaison, but he conceded that contraception was warranted if the womb was too small for a pregnancy and the woman's health would be at risk if she became pregnant (Sor. 1,20,60). We cannot say for certain what the degree of interest was in contraception in antiquity; in view of the high rate of infant mortality, people would probably have been far more concerned to improve the chances of conception. As a method of birth control (→ Family planning), infanticide was preferred to contraception and abortion: parents then had the opportunity to determine the sex and state of health of their child before deciding whether or not to bring it up.

→ Family planning; → Woman; → Birth; → Gynaecology; → Children, exposition of

1 J. RIDDLE, Contraception and Abortion from the Ancient World to the Renaissance, 1992, 74–76   2 K. M. HOPKINS, Contraception in the Roman Empire, in: Comparative Studies in Society and History 8, 1965, 124–151   3 B. W. FRIER, Natural Fertility and Family Limitation in Roman Marriage, in: CPh 89, 1994, 318–333.

L. A. DEAN-JONES, Women's Bodies in Classical Greek Science, 1994; M. T. FONTANELLE, Avortement et contraception dans la médecine gréco-romaine, 1977; H. KING, Hippocrates' Women, 1998.   H.K.

Contraction see → Phonetics

Contracts

I. General points II. Ancient Orient, region
with cuneiform script III. Pharaonic Egypt
IV. Judaism V. Classical Antiquity

I. General points

A contract is an agreement between two or more
persons (possibly implicit) for the purpose of a legal
result (e.g., a purchase as exchange of goods against
money). Relative to the purpose of the transaction, contracts that in legal terms directly refer to the purpose,
the 'abstract' legal transaction, which is independent of
it, and the 'ad hoc legal transaction' must be differentiated. A legal procedure is abstract if the legal effect is
legally not linked to the result that the parties are attempting to achieve (e.g., recognition of a debt without
characterizing it as a purchase price debt) [1.1382]. A
legal process is described as ad hoc if it is used to achieve
another process while directed by its original purpose
(e.g., the design of the purchase debt as a loan in a purchase on credit; a fundamental discussion in [3]). The
issue of the required form must be separated from the
contract definition (→ Documents I). The coming into
force and effect of the contract must also be differentiated. The consensual contract that comes about
through a declaration of intent was only known to fully
developed Roman law (see below, V.), it required a tangible factor (on down payments, see → arra) or an affirmation. At times the conclusion of contracts, as well as
other legal transactions, was accompanied by formal
acts but no legal formalism of the Roman kind is evident in non-Roman antiquity (on the history of legal
formalism, see below). Despite the frequency of the
written form, writing alone was not sufficient as the
basis of a contract, but a specific, contract-creating element was required. In contrast to present practice, the
contract granted no claim to fulfilment. However,
non-fulfilment violated the rights of the other party and
entitled it to action against the contract partner. Thus,
the contract indirectly worked towards fulfilment. The
specific appearance of the contract was characterized
by the fact that in the end there was only a limited
number of conceivable and adequate regulations [2].

1 W. Kunkel, s. v. Συγγραφη, syngrapha, RE 4 A, 1376-
1387 2 T. Mayer-Maly, Die Wiederkehr von Rechtsfi-
guren, in: Juristenzeitung 26, 1971, 1–3 3 E. Rabel,
Nachgeformte Rechtsgeschäfte Mit Beiträgen zu den
Lehren von der Injurezession und vom Pfandrecht, in:
ZRG 27, 1906, 290–335; 28, 1907, 311–379 (= Id.,
Gesammelte Aufs, Vol. 4: Arbeiten zur altgriech., hell. und
röm. Rechtsgesch. 1905–1949, 1971, 9–104).

II. Ancient Orient, region with cunei-
form script

Contracts in → cuneiform script are known in
chronologically and regionally varying numbers
(→ Cuneiform, legal texts in) and in differing types in
terms of legal history from the early 3rd millennium BC
to the turn of BC and AD, in some cases several hund-

reds and even thousands. The earliest contracts preserved in writing concern the sale of fields and date from
the early dynastic period (29th/28th cents. BC). Contracts were especially used to document the holding of
rights in important objects such as real estate (e.g., leasing fees for land; mortgage on real estate; → leasehold)
and money matters (e.g., → loans and marriage contracts — in the latter the marriage per se was not the
issue!). The preserved Aramaic contracts of the 1st millennium — which were written on perishable → writing
materials (leather, papyrus) and, therefore, are fewer in
number — are mainly from Jewish groups (→ Document IV). Therefore, they can neither be considered as
testimonials of a cuneiform legal order nor — given the
broad distribution of → Aramaic — as testimonials of
an 'Aramaic ' legal order (contrary to [7.557]). The
binding effect of the contracts depended on specific factors (e.g., [9]), supplemented or replaced by a (promissory) oath [5]. They were not dependent on written
documentation. Formalities accompanying the contract are well documented [8]. Numerous → international treaties are known from the public shpere.

III. Pharaonic Egypt

As elsewhere, legally binding agreements pre-existed
written history (early 3rd millenium BC). They are
mostly recorded on → papyrus, but in large numbers in
hieratic writing only from the workers' settlement of
Dar al-Madina, from the time of Ramses and after the
7th cent. BC (to the Roman period) in demotic script
and language (→ Demotic law). Apart from occasional
fragments, legal transactions of the Old and Middle
Kingdoms were only preserved because documents
were copied as hieroglyphic inscriptions in the upper
building parts of private tombs for the purpose of documenting rights gained by the tomb owner (on the evidence, e.g., [2; 11.63–66]). → Ostraca were rarely used
to record contracts.

The 'principle of mandatory remuneration' is critical
for contract theory: acquiring ownership in things required that the purchaser give the buyer a proper remuneration [10.45–50]. Therefore, a contract required a
preceding real action or an → oath. Starting in the late
New Kingdom, the promissory oath was only used for
confirmation of the binding nature but not to create it
[11.49–51; 10.37f.]. There were a great many types of
contracts in Egypt (e.g., [1.86–104]). The only treaty of
state preserved — as a hieroglyphic inscription — is the
Egyptian version of peace treaty following the battle of
→ Qadesh (1258 BC).

IV. Judaism

Neither the Torah nor the Talmud contain a technical term for contract (→ Jewish law). Old Hebrew contracts are not known, but contracts among Jews — especially in Greek and Aramaic — are (→ Document IV).
The existence of contracts is also attested in the Torah
and Talmud. A contract was originally brought about
through a real and later a fictional performance or the

form, i.e., as a real (e.g., Gen 23,13–16) or literal contract (e.g., Jer 32,44). Witnesses or a promissory oath were used for affirmation [6.292–294]. No special significance is allotted to contracts in ancient Israel, given the ethnic kinship structure, because legal relationships were primarily regulated through provisions in kinship law or resulted from prohibited actions towards third parties [4.92].

1 W. BOOCHS, Altägyptisches Zivilrecht, 1999 2 H. BRUN-
NER u.a., s.v. Papyrus-Verzeichnis, L 4, 672–898
3 M. COHN, s.v. V., J Lexikon 4/2, 1927, 1202–1205
4 Z. W. FALK, Hebrew Law in Biblical Times, 1964
5 J. HENGSTL, Rechtl. Aspekte der Adler-Schlangen-Fabel
im Etana-Epos, in: G. SELZ (ed.), FS B. Kienast (2003)
6 F. HORST, Der Eid im AT, in: Evangelische Theologie 17,
1957, 366–384 (=Id., Gottes Recht, 1961, 292–314)
7 E. LIPINSKI, The Aramaeans. Their Ancient History,
Culture, Religion, 2000 8 M. MALUL, Studies in Mesopotamian Legal Symbolism, 1988 9 E. PRITSCH, Zur juri-
stischen Bed. der šubanti-Formel, in: H. JUNKER (ed.), At.
Stud. FS F. N (Bonner biblische Beitr. 1), 1950, 172–187
10 E. SEIDL, Rechtsgesch. der Saiten- und Perserzeit,
²1968 11 Id., Einführung in die äg. Rechtsgesch. bis zum
Ende des NR, 1957 12 K. ZIBELIUS-CHEN, s.v. Staats-
vertrag, L 5, 1222 f.   JO. HE.

V. CLASSICAL ANTIQUITY

In commercial societies characterized by intensive trade, such as those of Classical Greece, the Hellenistic world and Rome, the binding nature of agreements (from ordinary → purchases and the → work contract to → international treaties) is of central importance. Therefore, the legal significance of the contract is one of the elements that underpin the structure of the Greek and Roman legal order.

In Greek law the term → synthḗkē is closest to a modern understanding of a 'contract', but it is not as closely defined and often only analogous to a 'notarized' contract (→ syngraphḗ). In any case, it has no critical significance for the legal consequences of an agreement. The term → synállagma, which only generally means 'mutual exchange' without sketching out resulting legal consequences, is even more imprecise. In fact, in Graeco-Hellenistic legal thought the category of the contract is unsuitable for extrapolating immediate effects. The starting-point of the relevant Greek idea in the context of private agreements is instead the enforcement to which a 'debtor' is exposed. It can either result from direct submission to access by enforcement, which is accomplished by the → práxis clause in public or private → documents. Alternatively, it is based on an impermissible act (blábē; cf. → blábēs díkē), committed by the 'debtor' when he does not react according to the agreement to the 'creditor's' transfer of assets, which was made for the purpose of receiving remuneration (→ Purpose-specific empowerment). Greek law did not know a claim to the promised payment or compensation instead of the payment, but only indirect constraint to behaviour in compliance with the agreement in order to avoid enforcement [1; 2; 3]. Therefore, the agreement of the parties (→ homología) even in a documented transaction was not directed towards the jointly determined legal obligation but the acknowledgement that the liability-generating fact in the text was true.

It was Roman law that developed the contract (Latin → contractus) as a general and fundamental concept of civil law. In the 2nd cent. AD, the jurist Gaius [2] (Gai. Inst. 3,89) differentiated four types of contract: they are created by agreement (→ consensus), making a payment (a real contract, such as a → loan; → mutuum), the use of verbal formulas (verbis, especially the → stipulatio) or the rather rare written contract (→ litterarum obligatio). If an obligation was incurred from the contract, it was directly related to the performance. According to content, contracts were differentiated according to whether the obligation (→ obligatio) was directed towards dare ('giving', especially 'conferring'), facere ('doing') or praestare (to 'vouch' for something else, e.g. as a surety, praes) (Gai. inst. 4,2). In a court action regarding the performance, the obligated party was always sentenced to a money payment (→ condemnatio sc. pecuniaria). In a contract based on a simple agreement, which was only recognized for four types (→ consensus), the performance obligation was determined by the principles of trust and good faith (bona → fides II). Simple verbal agreements (→ pactum) were not contracts and, therefore, not actionable as being outside the canon of recognized contracts. However, in a careful further development of the law, the praetor (→ ius B. honorarium) could effect fulfilment in select cases, which in late antiquity resulted in the development of a general doctrine of 'innominate' contracts. The Roman concept of the contract has persistently affected Continental legal history.

→ International treaty; → Contract fidelity; CLAIM; CAUSA→; DEBT LAW; CONTRACT

1 H.-A. RUPPRECHT, Kleine Einführung in die Papyruskunde, 1994, 113 f. 2 WOLFF, 143 3 J. HERRMANN, Ver-
fügungsermächtigungen als Gestaltungselemente ver
schiedener griech. Geschäfte, in: Id., KS, 1990, 59–70.

KASER, RPR, Vol. 1, 522–527; HONSELL/MAYER-MALY/
SELB, 294–344.   G. S.

Contractus In Gai. Inst. 3,88 contractus constitutes, with delicts, one of the two higher branches of the whole Roman law of obligations. This has led many analysts to translate contractus simply as 'contracts'. Originally, however, contractus was really not limited to a commitment as a contract but actually meant literally only 'to incur (an obligation)'. In the period of the principate contractus was indeed understood to be linked to an agreement (consensus, conventio) (Dig. 2,14,1,3). Even then, however, not every agreement would necessarily lead to a contractus. As no complete contractual freedom prevailed in Roman law, the creation of an obligation remained linked to definite conditions of objective law. By itself, agreement suffficed only for the four recognized consensual contracts

(→ *consensus*). As further grounds for the creation of obligations from *contractus*, Gai. Inst. 3,89 ends up listing: *re* (through the action itself), *verbis* (by use of prescribed verbal formulae) and of much less practical importance *litteris* (→ *litterarum obligatio*). 'Real' contracts under Roman law were loan for consumption and replacement (→ *mutuum*), loan for use and return (*commodatum*), deposit for safekeeping (→ *depositum*) and mortgage (→ *pignus*). Handing over the item(s) once agreement to the transfer had been reached constituted a contractual obligation for its return (Dig. 44,7,1,2–6). By far the most important practical example of verbal contracts is the → *stipulatio*. Beyond that, Gai. Inst. 3,95a; 96 instances only the *dotis dictio*, which, compared to the *stipulatio*, was actually an unnecessary process in the grant of dowry (→ *dos*), and the *promissio operarum*, a freedman's undertaking on oath to perform services for his employer. In contrast to the *contractus*, the → *pactum* was an agreement that did not have the effect of creating obligations. By late antiquity, however, the *pacta* had drawn closer and closer to the *contractus* and at the end of the Middle Ages the *pactum* had replaced the *contractus* as the dominant concept of non-delictual (later: non-legal) obligations. The phrase *pacta sunt servanda* dates from that time.

> KASER, RPR I, 522–527; G. GROSSO, Il sistema romano dei contratti, ³1963; S. E. WUNNER, C., 1964. G.S.

Contra paganos see → Polemics

Contrebia (Celtic for 'communal dwelling' [1. 1109]). Fortress retreat of the Celtiberian → Lusones [1. 136]. Its location cannot be accurately established; probably not identical with today's Daroca, C. was nevertheless nearby, in the Hiloca valley south-west of Zaragoza ([1. 136; 2. 212]; see also the conjectures in [4. 247]). Epigraphical evidence is almost entirely lacking (only CIL II 4935?), but, on the other hand, coins have been found with Iberian legends [5. 93]. C. is mentioned fairly often in the context of the Celtiberian wars (181 BC: Liv. 40,33; App. Ib. 42 [*Complega* probably = *Contrebia*]; Diod. Sic. 29,28; 33,24 [*Kemelon* probably = *Complega*]. 143 BC: Aur. Vict. 61; Val. Max. 2,7,10; 7,4 ext. 5; Ampelius 18,14; Vell. Pat. 2,5,2; Flor. Epit. 1,33,10. 77 BC: Liv. fr. book 91; cf.. [2. 212–214; 6. 34f., 181]). C. was militarily important (→ Complega).

It should not be confused with C. Leucada, which is mentioned only for 76 BC (Liv. fr. B. 91). The epithet is Celtic [7. 192]. As to the town's location north of → Numantia cf. [6. 189; 1. 128].

> 1 A. SCHULTEN, Numantia 1 2 Id., Fontes Hispaniae Antiquae 3, 1925ff. 3 HOLDER 1. 4 Enciclopedia Universal Ilustrada 15 5 A. VIVES, La Moneda Hispánica 2, 1924 6 A. SCHULTEN, Fontes Hispaniae Antiquae 4, 1937 7 Holder 2.
> TOVAR 3, 414–416. P.B.

Control (political) see → Censores; → Collega; → Dokimasia; → Ephoroi; → Euthynae

Control-marks Suitably smaller symbols (images, monograms, ciphers, alphabetical letters, abbreviations of names) to identify particular issues, dates of stamping or workshops, as an additional control measure on coinage, near the coin image and legend. Control-marks appeared in the 4th cent. BC (supplementary coin images), increasingly so in the Hellenistic period (monograms) and also in the Roman Republic. Instead of the monograms and abbreviations, names of officials came to be more or less written out in full in some cases (Hellenistic period; Roman Republic). In a series of Roman issues between 110 and 67 BC the control system was particularly pronounced; individual coinage was even distinguishable in part through symbols, letters or ciphers (e.g. Calpurnius [I 20] Piso Frugi, 67 BC). The control system was also sophisticated in Roman coins of late antiquity, when from the late 3rd cent. details of mints and workshops, often with other symbols added, appeared in constantly varying form.

> 1 T. V. BUTTREY, The Denarii of P. Crepusius and Roman Republican Mint Organization, in: ANSMusN 21, 1976, 67–108 2 M. H. CRAWFORD, N. Fabi Pictor, in: NC 1965, 149–154 3 Id., Control-Marks and the Organization of the Roman Republican Mint, in: PBSR 34, 1966, 18–23 4 C. A. HERSH, Sequence Marks on Denarii of Publius Crepusius, in: NC 1952, 52–66 5 Id., A Study of the Coinage of the Moneyer C. Calpurnius Piso L. f. Frugi, in: NC 1976, 7–63 6 H. ZEHNACKER, Moneta. Recherches sur l'organisation et l'art des émissions monétaires de la Republique romaine, Vol. 1, 1973, 91–195. DI.K.

Controversiae Practice speeches for legal cases (*genus iudiciale*); with the → *suasoriae* (*genus deliberativum*), one of the two forms of → *declamatio*. Initially serving primarily to prepare for court orations (Quint. 2,10,7), *controversiae* became, as the most demanding form of practice (Tac. Dial. 35), the culmination of oratorical training in the imperial period. Early Greek precursors are the model speakers of Sophistic antilogic [3. 110–114]; individual themes of *controversiae* amongst the earliest Roman rhetoricians (e.g. Cic. Inv. 2, 144) point directly to Hellenistic models. The term *controversiae* was first used in the Augustan period (Sen. Controv. 1 praef. 12).

Still practised by Cicero as a private technique for speech training (Sen. Controv. 1,4,7), they developed, under the political conditions of the Principate, into a quasi-literary genre with a claim to a high level of artistry; they were intended for a public audience (showpiece declamation: Sen. Controv., Ps.-Quint. Declamationes maiores) but continued to be used for school purposes as well (e.g. practice of the status system, → Rhetoric; school declamation: Ps.-Quint. Declamationes minores [5. XVI; 2. 1–2]).

In their extant form the *controversiae* consist of a summary heading, the law relevant to the *causa*, an

→ *argumentum* (statement of the theme) and the exposition of the theme. The subject matter ranges from historical, pseudo-historical and mythological model cases to convoluted romantic-fantastic pieces of fiction with a regular repertoire of typical characters (tyrannicides, pirates, priestesses, prostitutes, disowned sons and the like). Specific to the *controversiae* are subtle sub-features of the issue at contention (*divisiones*) and biassed elaborations of the sketchy *argumenta* (*colores*).

Together with the *suasoriae*, the *controversiae* remained an element of rhetoric-dominated higher education in schools right to the end of late antiquity (Himerius; Libanius; Ennodius, Dictiones 14–28). In the Middle Ages the *controversiae* fell into disuse as rhetorical training; they were replaced in universities by the legal *disputatio*. The extant *controversiae* were received as literature; their fanciful subject matter was used as moral allegories (*Gesta Romanorum*) and encouraged poetic elaboration: the short story in verse *Mathematicus* of Bernardus Silvestris (12th cent.) evolved from Declamatio maior 4. With the general revival of classical rhetoric in the Renaissance the *controversiae* were again used as an educational tool (cf. Erasmus, *De ratione studii*; Rudolf Agricola's *De inventione dialectica, c.* 1485). A modern illustration of the dark fascination of their often grotesque features is P. QUIGNARD's literary biography → *Albucius* (1990; cf. Sen. Controv. 7, praef.).

1 S. F. BONNER, Roman Declamation in the Late Republic and Early Empire, 1949 (ND 1969) 2 J.DINGEL, Scholastica materia, 1988 3 J.FAIRWEATHER, Seneca the Elder, 1981 4 F.H. TURNER, The Theory and Practice of Rhetorical Declamation from Homeric Greece through the Renaissance, 1972 5 M.WINTERBOTTOM, The Minor Declamations Ascribed to Quintilian, 1984 6 L. A. SUSSMAN, The Declamations of Calpurnius Flaccus, 1994.   TH.ZI.

Contubernium in the basic meaning of the word meant a communal lodging of soldiers; it applied either to a tent camp during an *expeditio* or to barracks in a fixed encampment (Tac. Ann. 1,41,1). Two extensions of meaning developed from that: the term was used for a group of soldiers sharing a lodging, and from that it was used to describe a shared sense of trust and solidarity among those soldiers (Suet. Tib. 14,4; Caes. B Civ. 2,29). This included the officers. The *contubernium* seems not to have been a tactical unit, although in Vegetius (Veg. Mil. 2,13) the *contubernium* is used as a synonym for *manipulus*. At first the *contubernium* consisted of eight men (Ps.-Hyg. 1), later 10, who were under the command of one of them, the *decanus* (Veg. Mil. 2,8; 2,13). In Leo the Tactician (Tact. 20,194) the *contubernium* involved 16 men.

1 H. VON PETRIKOVITS, Die Innenbauten röm. Legionslager, 1975.   Y.L.B.

Contumacia Derived from *contemnere* (to despise; this meaning of the word survives today in the contempt of court of British law). In Roman law the *contumacia* meant above all the defendant's failure to obey a legal summons in the exercise of *extraordinaria* → *cognitio*. No similar use of the word *contumacia* is encountered before the introduction of this procedure in the Principate and of the *contumacia*, probably under Claudius. Admittedly a comparable function existed in earlier civil proceedings after the XII Tables (5th cent. BC) in a judge's ruling for one party against the other party that had not appeared (→ *addicere*). The → *vocatio in ius* of the XII Tables was, however, only a private summons, and even a default in the *in iure* procedure amounted simply to a concession to the private claims of the other party. Non-appearance in response to a summons at the expiry of the *cognitio,* on the other hand, was disobedience to the officials of the imperial courts, if not to the emperor himself. Before the *contumacia* existed, however, a highly complicated procedure had to be gone through, in which the party had to be appropriately summonsed three times before the judge could issue a ruling (Ulp. Dig. 5,1,68–73). Even then, though, a ruling in favour of the defaulting party was still possible, if his case was *bona causa*, that is to say had a better legal basis to it. If the ruling was against the defaulter, however, he had no legal redress: *si appellat non esse audiendum, si modo per contumaciam defuit* ('his appeal shall not be heard if he was absent only by virtue of *contumacia*', Dig. 5,1,73,3). Justinian extended the *contumacia* to defaulting plaintiffs.

KASER, RZ, 376–379; H.HONSELL, TH. MAYER-MALY, W. SELB, Röm. Recht, ⁴1987, 557.   G.S.

Conubium In Rome being eligible to marry (*conubium*) was a prerequisite for a legally valid marriage. Both partners had to have the *conubium*: *Conubium est uxoris iure ducendae facultas. Conubium habent cives Romani cum civibus Romanis: cum Latinis autem et peregrinis ita, si concessum sit. Cum servis nullum est conubium* ('*Conubium* is the legal ability to marry a woman. Roman citizens have the *conubium* to marry each other but, only by special dispensation, to marry Latins and other foreigners . There is no *conubium with slaves*'; Ulp. 5,3–5). That description omits to mention certain impediments to marriage, existing even amongst Roman citizens, that, it must be said, had largely lost any significance by the time of the principate: not until the *lex Canuleia* (445 BC) was *conubium* between patricians and plebeians introduced. To some free people, however, the *conubium* was still denied, i.e. members of Italian municipalities with a lesser form of citizenship (*civitates sine suffragio*) and freedpersons (*libertini*). Roman freedpersons who were full citizens were unable to enter into a valid marriage with members of those groups. Italian residents received the *conubium* no later than the end of the Social Wars (91–89 BC). Roman freedpersons were finally granted the *co-*

nubium in the *lex Papia Poppaea* of Augustus (cf. Dig. 23,2,23; 44). Even then, however, marriages between members of senatorial families and freedpersons were still invalid.

Like citizenship and the → *commercium*, *conubium* could be conferred upon those people or groups who did not enjoy it originally. Grants of the *conubium* to Italian communities (Liv. 8,13; 23,4) and — from the imperial period — to veterans on discharge from military service (*missio honesta*) for marriage to non-Roman women (ample material in CIL XVI) are attested. The *conubium* was spread more widely with the extension of citizenship during the imperial period. The *conubium* lapsed with the loss of full citizenship rights (→ *deminutio capitis*). A marriage contract was thus invalidated. Relationships without the *conubium* were → *concubinatus* and, with slaves, the → *contubernium*.

The most important consequence of *conubium* was for children born in legitimate marriages: they were freeborn Roman citizens. Marital property rights from the → *dos* were available only to married people with *conubium*.

KASER, RPR I² 75, 315   H. HONSELL, TH. MAYER-MALY, W. SELB, Röm. Recht ⁴1987, 388f.   TREGGIARI, 43ff. M. HUMBERT, Hispala Fecenia et l'endogamie des affranchis sous la République, in: Index 15, 1987, 131–148.

G.S.

Conventus (Pl. -us; literally 'get-together'; Greek διοίκησις/*dioíkēsis*, αγορά/*agorá*, σύνοδος/*sýnodos*). In the Roman provinces *conventus civium Romanorum* describes both court districts with their respective main seats as well as the court assemblies that were held there on fixed days with the governor presiding ([1.470; 12.222²⁷]; regarding *conventus* in general cf. Str. 13,628; regarding the *conventus* order in the Augustan period, Plin. HN 5,105–126; on the procedure of a *conventus* in Apameia [2] Dion. Chrys. 35,15; IGR 4,1287, cf. [2.101]; on archiving the decisions, which contributed to the continuity of → provincial administration (II.), cf. [3.103]). A *conventus* was established both for administrative purposes and the legal organization of the provinces.

The first conventus locations are found in Sicily *c.* 200 BC. Ethnic units were deliberately broken up [3.237]. The first planned division of territorial *conventus*, which occurred between 129 and 90 BC in the province of → Asia and was still confirmed by Cicero (Cic. Fam. 3,8,4; 13,53,2; Cic. Att. 6,2,4; 5,15,3; [11.206]), is attested in a letter by an unnamed proconsul to the Milesians between 56 and 50 BC (IPriene 106; [4]). Caesar reported on his *conventus* court tour through the *conventus* locations in Illyricum and Gallia cisalpina (Caes. BGall. 1,54,3; 5,1,5; 5,2,1; 6,44,3; 7,1,1; Suet. Iul. 30,1; 56,5). In the province Hispania seven *conventus* with their main locations are known (Plin. HN 3,18). They were already established under Augustus ([5; 6.57f.]; not under Vespasian, thus [7]) and the most important were Tarraco (Plin. HN 3,23;

[5]), Corduba (Plin. HN 3,10; [8]) and Astigi (Plin. HN 3,12; [9]; [10]).

In the Imperial period the *conventus* were increasingly replaced by *koiná* (→ *koinón*) in the East and by *concilia* (→ *concilium*) in the West, since these assemblies were entrusted with sacral functions (cf. → imperial cult) and more strongly involved the native elite. → Government VIII.

1 KASER, RZ, ²1996   2 G. P. BURTON, Proconsuls, Assizes and Administration of Justice under the Empire, in: JRS 65, 1975, 92–106   3 A. J. MARSHALL, Governors on the Move, in: Phoenix 20, 1966, 231–246   4 SHERK No. 52, p. 272–276   5 G. ALFÖLDY, in: CIL II 14, ²1995, pp. XIIIf. 6 L. A. CURCHIN, Roman Spain, 1991   7 P. LE ROUX, in: AE 1984, 553   8 A. STYLOW, in: CIL II 7, ²1995, pp. XVIII–XX   9 A. STYLOW, in: CIL II 5, ²1998, pp. XVIII–XX   10 S. J. KEAY, The C. Tarraconensis in the Third Century A.D.: Crisis or Change?, in: A. KING, M. HENIG (eds.), The Roman West in the Third Century, 1981, 451–486   11 L. ROBERT, Hellenica, Bd. 7, 1949   12 W. DAHLHEIM, Gewalt und Herrschaft, 1977.

ME.STR.

Convivium see → Banquet

Cook The Greek term μάγειρος (*mágeiros*) covers three different functions: that of the sacrificing priest who slices the throat of the sacrificial animal, that of the butcher who cuts the sacrificial animal up and that of the cook who prepares a meal. In the Homeric and archaic periods the culinary function cannot be distinguished from the others. In the classical period the term *mágeiros* describes a culinary specialist, a cook, and *mágeiroi* are found cooking at State, i.e. public, sacrifices, e.g. at the Posideia festivals (→ Poseidon) on Delos (*mágeiroi* are mentioned in the financial accounts of the *hieropoioí* (→ Sacrifices)), in Elis on the occasion of the Olympic competitions and at the meals (→ Table culture) in the → Prytaneion of several cities. In addition, they performed as cooks at a large number of private sacrificial festivals that were regularly arranged by associations or private individuals. In large sanctuaries such as those of Delos and Delphi, for example, cooking staff were made available to the pilgrims; these cooks were called ἐλεοδύται (*eleodýtai*, Ath. 4,172f–173b) in Delos, καρυκκοποιοί (*karykkopoioí*, 'sauce makers', Ath. 4,173d) in Delphi. The faithful were able to take a *mágeiros* to prepare the meat at local sanctuaries.

From the 4th cent. BC cooks are found looking after meals in private homes. There are two types of these private cooks: for the most part they are engaged at the marketplace for a particular occasion; this is the type of cook in Graeco-Roman comedy. In Athens they come from all parts of the world. Some of them are famous: 'Agis of Rhodes was the only one who knew how to cook fish briefly, Nereus of Chios prepared a steamed sea eel fit for the gods, Chariades of Athens specialized in the white *thríon* (fig leaves filled with eggs, milk, bacon, cheese etc), Lamprias invented black sauce, Aphthonetos, sausages, Euthynos, a lentil dish' (Euphron in Ath. 4,379d-e; others in Ath. 9,403e). The second type is the cook who is accommodated in the → *oíkos* household as a domestic employee, that is to say a slave.

Other terms for cook also crop up: the sole function of an ὀψοποιός (*opsopoiós*) is to prepare good meals; the term δειπνοποιός (*deipnopoiós*) has the same narrow meaning. In his critique of luxury, Clemens [3] of Alexandria mentions the existence in many homes of specialists in pastries, jams and beverages (Clem. Al. Paidagogos 2,1,2,2; 2,1,4,1; 2,2 passim).

In Rome the cook (*coquus*, German *Koch* is a loan word from Vulgar Latin *coco*) was initially entrusted with the preparation of food in its entirety (meat, grain, bread-making); from the 2nd cent. BC, however, his work began to be regarded as an art and increasingly that of a specialist. Amongst the staff there was a hierarchy: at the head stood the *archimagirus*, the head cook, who was assisted by a second cook (*vicarius supra cocos*) and the kitchen juniors (*coci*). Trimalchio's cook can perform magic with every part of a pig: 'from the womb a fish, from the bacon a wood pigeon, from the ham a turtle dove, from a haunch a hen' (Petron. Sat. 70,1–2).

E. M. RANKIN, The Role of the Mageiroi in the Life of the Ancient Greeks, 1907; K. LATTE, s.v. mageiros, RE 27, 393–395; J. ANDRÉ, L'alimentation et la cuisine à Rome, 1961, (Ger.: Essen und Trinken im alten Rom, 1998); H. DOHM, Mageiros. Die Rolle des K. in der griech.-röm. Komödie (Zetemata 32), 1964; G. BERTHIAUME, Les rôles du mageiros, 1982. P.S.-P.

Cookery books
I. NEAR EAST AND EGYPT II. GREECE AND ROME

I. NEAR EAST AND EGYPT
Although there is copious epigraphical and graphic evidence for a highly developed → table culture at the courts of oriental rulers in antiquity, cooking recipes are known to us so far only from Mesopotamia: 34 from the 18th cent. BC (gathered from three clay tablets), one from the 6th/5th cents. BC. They offer practical instructions in the manner of medical prescriptions.

The reason why the recipes were preserved in writing is not clear. They deal predominantly with stewed poultry and other meat, together with two recipes for poultry pies. The recipes do not give details of quantities but occasionally an expression 'according to taste' is used for adding spices. As a flavour enhancer, Mesopotamian cuisine uses a fish sauce like the Lat. *liquamen*. The addition of sheep's fat to the broth — helping to raise the cooking temperature and adding to the flavour of the meat — has parallels in later Near Eastern cooking. Preparation of meals in Egypt is attested by, i.a. wall paintings and reliefs, as well as plastic representations (serving figures).

1 J. BOTTÉRO, Textes culinaires Mésopotamiennes, 1995 2 Id., s.v. Küche, RLA 6, 277–98 3 W. J. DARBY et al. (ed.), Food: The Gift of Osiris, 1977 4 H. A. HOFFNER, Alimenta Hethaeorum, 1974 5 F. JUNGE, s.v. Küche, LÄ 3, 830–33 6 S. SUBAIDA, R. TAPPER, Culinary Cultures of the Middle East, 1994. J.RE.

II. GREECE AND ROME
To start with, the term 'cookery book' is unsuitable for the Graeco-Roman world. It would be better, like E. DEGANI [1], to speak of → 'gastronomic writing', as gastronomy and culinary matters cropped up as motifs in Greek poetry as early as the archaic period. Semonides of Amorgus (middle of the 7th cent. BC) describes a cook's bragging (fr. 24 WEST); Hipponax (end of the 6th cent.) has a glutton appear (fr. 126,2 DEGANI). → Ananius is the real discoverer of gastronomic poetry, followed by → Epicharmus. Appetite is a witty topic throughout Old Comedy and it was in that period also that the first descriptions of a fantasy land of food are to be found (Pherecrates 137 K.-A.). This tendency is further strengthened in Middle Comedy, cf. the descriptions in the *Prōtesílaos* of → Anaxandrides (fr. 41 K.-A.) and in the *Aúgē* of → Eubulus [2] (fr. 14 K.-A.).

Real cookery books (CB) appeared in the second half of the 5th cent. BC. Most of them are, however, completely lost; we have scanty fragments of some of them. The work of Mithaicus of Syracuse (Ath. 12,516c; 7,282a; Poll. 6,70; Pl. Grg. 518b), for example, is said to have consisted of a simple collection of recipes. Glaucus of Locri (Ath. 7,324a; 9,369b) also provided recipes, as well as some views on the culinary art, which, in his view, something to be practised by slaves (Ath. 14,661e). Hegesippus of Tarentum (Ath. 12,516c-d; 14,643f) left behind a list of ingredients for preparing a particular dish (*kándaulos*). → Epaenetus [2] and Artemidorus [4] from Tarsus (1st cent. BC) were likewise authors of general CB. Other works were specialized, like that of Dorion (1st cent. BC) on fish, that of Chrysippus of Tyana (middle of the 1st cent. AD), of Harpocration of Mendes (1st cent. AD) and of → Iatrocles [3] on pastries. Finally, remarks on cooking are encountered in dietary prescriptions within medical works. Books on the culinary art were often written to be read aloud or to be read at banquets.

Sometimes only the names are known of authors who composed a *Deípnon* ('Banquet'); an exception is → Archestratus [2] of Gela (2nd half of the 4th cent. BC), whom Athenaeus 62 fr. quotes. His poem *Hēdypátheia* (roughly: 'enjoyable life') is full of pieces of advice; Athenaeus calls him the Hesiod or Theognis of gourmets (Ath. 7,310a). Another significant author of the end of the 4th cent., → Matron of Pitane, composed a parody, *Deípnon Attikón*, that takes the form of a genuine battle in which food represents the enemy that has to be attacked and overcome.

The Roman era produced some culinary treatises, including that of Apicius (→ Caelius [II 10]), a contemporary of Emperor Tiberius. His extant work *De re coquinaria* ('On cooking') was composed in the 4th cent. AD.

Antique discussions of culinary art are much more than just recipe books; they convey a whole system of food perceptions, in which the boundaries between religion, medicine, nutrition and society, poetry, humour and instruction are quite fluid.

1 E. DEGANI, On Greek Gastronomic Poetry, in: Alma Mater Studiorum 1990, Vol. 1, 51–61, 1991, Vol. 2, 164–175.

J. ANDRÉ, L'alimentation et la cuisine à Rome, 1961 (Ger.: Essen und Trinken im alten Rom, 1998); F. BILABEL, s.v. K., RE 11, 932–943; A. DALBY, Siren Feasts. A History of Food and Gastronomy in Greece, 1996 (Ger.: Essen und Trinken im alten Griechenland, 1998); J. WILKINS et al. (ed.), Food in Antiquity, 1995; J. MARTIN, s.v. Deipnonliteratur, RAC 3, 658–666.   P.S.-P.

Cooking, art of see → Cookery books; → Cook

Coon (Κόων; *Kóōn*). Trojan, oldest son of → Antenor [1]. In the attempt to avenge his brother → Iphidamas on Agamemnon, C. injures Agamemnon's arm but is killed by him. As a result of the injury, Agamemnon is forced to leave the fight (Hom. Il. 11,248ff.; 19,53). The scene was depicted on the → Cypselus chest (Paus. 5,19,4).

P. WATHELET, Dictionnaire des Troyens de l'Iliade, 1988, no. 196.   MA.ST.

Cooptatio (from *co-optare*: 'to co-opt') can mean the acceptance of a person into a *gens*, a client relationship, a society (*collegium*), or into a public corporation (*corpus, corporatio, collegium*), (Liv. 2,33,2; Suet. Tib. 1,1–2; Plin. Ep. 4,1,4; Cic. Verr. 2,2,120; Dig. Iust. 50,16,85 *tres faciunt collegium*; Lex col. Genetivae 67=FIRA 1, 177ff.; SC de collegiis, FIRA 1, 291: *coire, convenire, collegiumve habere*).

In the political arena, *cooptatio* refers to a type of supplementary election that was legitimate but frequently extraordinary. (1) Beginning in the Republican period but above all during the Imperial period, the → Senatus itself had, on principle, the right to decide on the *cooptatio* of new members (Cic. Leg. 3,27; Liv. 4,4,7). But generally, a → *lectio senatus* was conducted by the → Consul or the → Censor during the Republican period, later by the emperor. (2) Similarly, → *decuriones* could co-opt the members of a *curia*, even though they were usually designated by community magistrates (Cic. Verr. 2, 2, 120; Plut. Sulla 37; Lex Iulia municipalis 83–88=FIRA 1, 147; the *adscriptio* of late antiquity into the *album decurionum* as a duty of public law: Cod. Iust. 10,32,62).

(3) The state colleges for priests were primarily filled by way of *cooptatio*. Only important officials (e.g. the *pontifex maximus*) were elected or, in the imperial period, nominated by the emperor (Dion. Hal. Ant. Rom. 2,73; Liv. 3,32, 3; Cic. Leg. agr. 2,7,16; Cass. Dio 51,20). Another type of *cooptatio* existed for magistrates and tribunes: (4) consuls could replace an absent

colleague through the *cooptatio* of another and could co-opt a *dictator* as a temporarily superordinated third colleague, although the consent of the *comitia* was generally required (Liv. 2,2,11; 3,19,2; contested). Furthermore, consuls could temporarily replace subordinate magistrates (such as praetors, aediles, and quaestors) by virtue of their authority. In this case, it was not required to repeat the public election in any case (cf. Gell. NA 13,16,1; Liv. 3,29,2f.). However, censors were excluded from this rule (Liv. 9,34,25). (5) Tribunes of the people could unconditionally co-opt others for absent colleagues (Liv. 3,64,10).

→ Creatio

KASER, RPR, 1, 302ff.; W. LANGHAMMER, Die rechtliche und soziale Stellung der Magistratus municipales und der Decuriones, 1973, 196; MOMMSEN, Staatsrecht, 1, 215ff., 221f.; 3.2, 854.   C.G.

Copa see → Appendix Vergiliana

Copae (Κῶπαι; *Kôpai*). Boeotian town located on a hill on the north-eastern shore of a lake named after it. The town was already listed in the catalogue of ships (Hom. Il. 2,502, Str. 9,2,18; Paus. 9,24,1), today's Kastron (formerly Topolia). Populated since Proto-Geometric periods, the ancient remnants are mostly covered by modern buildings. The region of C. comprised the north-eastern bay of Lake C. with the still unidentified, late Mycenaean fortress called Gla (Palaiokastro) today and its surrounding area, bordering on Acraephia in the south (IG VII 2792; SEG 30,440). As a member of the Boeotian League (map: → Boeotia, Boeotians), C. supplied a → Boeotarch since 446 (?) BC alternately with Acraephia and (after 424) Chaeronea (Hell. Oxy. 19,3,394–396). It was governed in the form of a polis headed by an archon [2. 283; 3], minting its own coins at times in the 4th cent. [1. 344].

1 HN 2 R. SHERK, The Eponymous Officials of Greek Cities I, in: ZPE 83, 1990, 249–288 3 FOSSEY, 277–281, 288–290.

J. M. FOSSEY, The Cities of the Kopaïs in the Roman Period, in: ANRW II 7.1, 560–562; Id., Mycenean Fortifications of the North East Kopaïs, in: OpAth 13.10, 1980, 155–162; N.D. PAPACHATZIS, Παυσανίου Ελλάδος Περιήγησις 5, ²1981, 160–163.   M.FE.

Copais (Κωπαΐς; *Kōpaís*). Northern Boeotian basin, formerly with a lake that had no drain above ground. The rivers → Cephis(s)us [1] (therefore Κηφισίς (*Kēphisís*), Hom. Il. 5,709; Paus. 9,24,1) and Melas as well as the streams and revmata from the surrounding mountains flowed into it. It was named after the city of → Copae on the north-eastern shore; the existence of different regional parts named after the main cities along the shore is documented [2. 16]. The area of the C. plain comprised c. 350 km², the expansion of the lake had strong seasonal variations and did not exceed c. 250 km². The lake was drained in 1883–1892: formerly it had drained through numerous katavothra (underground water drains) [4. 27–32] along the eastern shore into Lake Paralimni, Lake → Hylice (Str. 9,2,20), and into the Gulf of Euboea; the katavothra of the north-eastern Bay of Copae were regarded as particularly important since they supposedly received the Cephissus, whose water resurfaced in → Larymna (Str. 9,2,18).

The highly fertile plain of C. was densely populated since earliest times [1. 264–373; 3. 16–80]. As early as the mid 2nd millennium BC, the Minyae of → Orchomenus constructed devices for the protection from floods (dykes, canals) and for land expansion (polder) [2; 3]. Settlements were created on the plains as well and the canal was navigable. Occasionally, this effective system was disturbed by catastrophes (for instance by floods [3. 106–116, 119–134; 4. 19–25], obstructions of the katavothra, earthquakes, Str. 9,2,16), but always repaired again, until it finally collapsed and the lake became marshy towards the end of the 1st millennium. New efforts towards drainage were undertaken by Alexander the Great (Str. 9,2,18 [5. 76f.]; Steph. Byz. s.v. Ἀθῆναι; Athênai) and in the Roman imperial period [3. 135–144]. The population declined sharply during Hellenistic and Roman times. The eels of Lake C. were a desired commodity (Paus. 9,24,2), so was the reed (Theophr. Hist. pl. 4,10f.; Theophr. Caus. pl. 5,12,3; Plin. HN 16,168–172).

1 FOSSEY   2 J. KNAUSS et al., Die Wasserbauten der Minyer in der Kopais, 1984   3 Id., Die Melioration des Kopais-Beckens durch die Minyer im 2. Jt.v.Chr., 1987   4 A. SCHACHTER (ed.), Essays in the Topography, History and Culture of Boiotia, 1990   5 P. W. WALLACE, Strabo's Description of Boiotia, 1979.

H. KALCYK, B. HEINRICH, The Munich Kopais-Project, in: J. M. FOSSEY (ed.), Boeotia antiqua 1, 1989, 55–71; S. LAUFFER, Kopais Unt. zur historischen Landeskunde Mittelgriechenlands 1, 1986; Id., s.v. Große Katavothre, in: LAUFFER, Griechenland, 337f.; Id., s.v. Kopais, in: LAUFFER, Griechenland, 240.   M.FE.

Cophen (Κωφήν; *Kōphén*: Arr.; Κώφης/*Kóphēs*: Diod., Dionys Per., Str.; *Cophes*: Plin. HN). Western tributary of the river → Indus [1], old Indian *Kubhā*, today's Kabul.

K. KARTTUNEN, India and the Hellenistic World, 1997, 112.   K.K.

Copia Personification of fullness, depicted with the horn of plenty (Plaut. Pseud. 671; 736; → Amalthea), later also called *cornucopia* (Amm. Marc. 22,9,1). C. with the horn of plenty appears on the coins of two cities with the name *Colonia C.*, which not necessarily indicates the existence of a cult [1; 2]. C. is also mentioned in an inscription from Avennio (today's Avignon, CIL XII 1023). According to Ovid (Met. 9,85–88), C. received the horn filled with fruit and flowers, which Hercules had broken off the → Achelous, from the Naiades.

1 G. WISSOWA, Religion und Kultus der Römer, ²1912, 332   2 H. L. AXTELL, The Deification of Abstract Ideas in Roman Literature and Inscriptions, 1907, 43.

F. BÖMER, Metamorphosen B. 8–9 (comm.) 1977, 277; M. HERNANDEZ INIGUEZ, s.v. C., LIMC 3.1, 304; P. POUTHIER, Ops et la conception divine de l'abondance dans la religion romaine jusqu'à la mort d'Auguste, 1981.   R.B.

Copies
A. ORIGINAL AND COPY   B. TECHNIQUE
C. GREECE   D. ROME

A. ORIGINAL AND COPY

In archaeological literature, any reproduction of classical and Hellenistic sculptures that is faithful in form to the original is regarded as a copy, even if the copy does not completely correspond in size, material, or degree of completion. Copies in the broadest sense are a main characteristic of ancient art production which was based on slow change of style, on the familiarity with the iconography of passed epochs and a deep respect towards them: innovations were judged as gradual improvements of recognized works; the concepts of 'plagiarism' and 'fakes' did not exist in ancient art production. An understanding of the copies primarily depends on the knowledge of the specific cultural requirements that dictated the degree of closeness to the original as well as the technical execution. The long-established research practice of using copies from the Roman period to reconstruct Greek originals is controversial and often regarded with scepticism today. The production of copies must be regarded as an essential element of an artistic period with its own intrinsic value (1st cent. BC — 3rd cent. AD), in which it supplied the main body of visual art in addition to portraiture and reliefs. Copies covered a wide spectrum from faithful reproductions to reconstructions and recreations involving archaism, classicism, and eclecticism. It is characterized by syncretism in form and motive in a culture that was oriented towards the past.

B. TECHNIQUE

The technical ability of ancient sculptors to produce exact copies relied on casting and on the use of callipers. → Lysistratus (4th cent. BC) is attributed with the invention of the plaster cast. Still extant from the Hellenistic period are plaster moulds for the serial production of → toreutic works and small art objects (Begram, Memphis, Athens). Records of large-scale plaster casts exist from Baiae (1st cent. AD); they were constructed with the aid of moulds made from gypsum or elastic bitumen. During the copying process, callipers were used to transfer a few peripheral measuring points from the cast to the stone. The volume, however, was rarely measured. The repertoire of casts for copies was limited due to high costs. Furthermore, due to the risk of damage, marble originals were rarely copied, but almost exclusively bronze work. Reconstructions in marble therefore were subject to modifications: protruding parts were equipped with supports, limbs became more voluminous due to the lower load-bearing capacity of the stone, and free-flowing parts of robes and flowing hair could not be moulded at all. The reproduction of eyelids and eyelashes from bronze had to be freely recreated in marble. Only in rare cases, these could be imitated in inserts made from different materials.

C. GREECE

Repetitions already existed in archaic sculpture. They were subject to the norms of contemporary representational patterns (kouroi) and popularized familiar images of deities. They are not counted as copies; their temporal distance to the original is irrelevant. The earliest copies that refer back to centuries earlier are documented for the 2nd cent. BC in Asia Minor and Delos. In Pergamum, iconographically simplified or stylistically innovated reproductions of classical works from the Acropolis in Athens (Athena Parthenos) served to create a connection to the significance and to the context of the originals. At the same time, one could find small-scale terracotta copies as well as the first exact marble copies in residences (Diadumenos from Delos, *c.* 100 BC).

D. ROME

The adoption of Greek culture by the Roman upper class in the late Republican period at first included access to original works. This led to an increased demand in the residential as well as public areas in the 1st cent. BC that was largely satisfied through copies (Cicero's letters; → Herculaneum, Villa dei Papiri). The choice of models and the appearance of the copies were determined by the supply and the context of the furnishings. Certain standards of what was regarded as appropriate furnishings (*decor*) made it possible to achieve a variety of thematic effects with few repeatedly used types. In Dionysian ensembles, copies were sometimes used more than once, for instance in mirror images, or were modified to sculptures on fountains. Greek portraits were used in galleries of herms, statues of gods were reduced to busts, and statues of athletes were placed into alcoves. The closest connection to Greek visual arts is evident in Roman portrait statues whose bodies were shaped after Greek statues. Copies with references to the original masters were rare; accordingly, the *opera nobilia* by → Pasiteles were not used as a catalogue of copies but as educational literature. Decorative needs were predominant even in archaist, classicist, and eclectic reproductions of Greek sculpture (*lychnoýchoi*: stands for lamps and trays as 'dumb waiter'). Small bronze copies were regarded as genuine works of art (Corinthian bronze) and often passed off as originals.

The large demand for decorative statues brought Greek sculptors who had worked in Delos, Rhodes, or Athens in the 1st cent. BC to Rome and Naples where one could already find warehouses, the trading of copies, and restoration shops in the early imperial peri-

od. However, during the height of the copying trade in the 2nd cent. AD, copiers worked mostly in Athens, Ephesus, and Aphrodisias. Copies in bronze were rare but more numerous than the surviving stock would indicate. Altogether, the formerly high number of Greek bronze originals was surpassed by an even higher number of marble copies which repeated a few models hundreds of times.

A stylistic history of copies should include the changing use of originals by the copiers and the changing tastes of the periods expressed in the details. The copiers rarely made changes in composition or design, but often modified the surface and the folds in robes and in hair. Early copies show a precise reproduction of the flesh and greater faithfulness to detail. Since the time of Hadrian (early 2nd cent. AD), details in the body shapes were simplified, robes became more elaborate, and backsides were neglected. The supports for statues — indispensable for marble copies of bronze originals — evolved from simple tree stumps to independent creations with more and more details. In the early 3rd cent. AD, a general change in the reception of images led to the quick end of copying.

→ Fakes

G. LIPPOLD, Kopien und Umbildungen griech. Statuen, 1923; F. MUTHMANN, Statuenstützen und dekoratives Beiwerk an griech. und röm. Bildwerken, 1951; A. RUMPF, in: Archäologie 2, 1956, 81–132; G. LIPPOLD, EAA 2, 804–810; H. LAUTER, Zur Chronologie röm. Kopien nach Originalen des 5. Jh., 1966; P. ZANKER, Klassizistische Statuen, 1974; M. BIEBER, Ancient Copies, 1977; B. S. RIDGWAY, Roman Copies of Greek Sculpture. The Problem of the Originals, 1984; J.-P. NIEMEIER, Kopien und Nachahmungen im Hellenismus, 1985; C. HEES-V. LANDWEHR, Die antiken Gipsabgüsse aus Baiae, 1985; K. PRECIADO (ed.), Retaining the Original. Multiple Originals, Copies and Reproductions (Studies in the History of Art 20), 1989; P. ZANKER, Nachahmung als kulturelles Schicksal, in: CH. LENZ (ed.), Probleme der Kopien von der Antike bis zum 19. Jahrhundert, 1992, 9–24; E. BARTMAN, Ancient Sculptural Copies in Miniature, 1992; C. GASPARRI, L'officina dei calchi di Baia, in: MDAI(R) 102, 1995, 173–187; E. K. GAZDA, Roman Sculpture and the Ethos of Emulation. Reconsidering Repetition, in: HSPh 97, 1995, 120–156; D. WILLERS, Das Ende der antieken Idealstatue, in: MH 53, 1996, 170–186. R.N.

Coponius Roman family name (SCHULZE, 168, 276, A.7; ThlL, Onom. 2, 587), related to *copo* 'innkeeper' in popular etymology (Mart. 3,59), attested since the 1st cent. BC.
[1] C., C. Cicero praised him and his brother T.C. as *adulescentes* in 56 BC (Balb. 53; Cael. 24). In 53 BC, he was *praefectus* in Syria, in 49 BC, praetor and mint master under Pompey (RRC 444), and in 48, as propraetor, he lost his fleet in a storm at sea. He is probably identical to the C. who was proscribed in 43 and who owed his life to his wife's plea for clemency from Mark Antony (App. B Civ. 4,170) as well as the *vir e praetoriis*

gravissimus and Munatius Plancus' enemy in 32 (Vell. 2,83,3).

T. P. WISEMAN, New Men in the Roman Senate 139 B.C.-A.D. 14, 1971, 226. K.-L.E.

[2] Roman sculptor; created 14 statues for the porticoes of the Pompeius Theatre in Rome in 55 BC, some of them still extant. Those are characterized by the → personifications of the peoples conquered by Pompey.

F. COARELLI, Il complesso pompeiano del Campo Marzio e la sua decorazione scultorea, in: RPAA 44, 1971–72, 99–122; OVERBECK, no. 2271 (sources). R.N.

[3] Roman *eques*; in AD 6, he was sent to Judaea as *praefectus*. He governed it as part of the province of Syria. He had the *ius gladii*, but as *praef.* was subordinate to the legate of Syria (Jos. BI 2,117f.; Ant. Iud. 18, 2,29–31). W.E.

Copper
I. DEFINITION AND PROPERTIES II. THE NEAR EAST III. GREECE IV. ROME V. CENTRAL EUROPE VI. COPPER DEPOSITS AND SMELTING METHODS

I. DEFINITION AND PROPERTIES
Pure copper is relatively rare in nature. Also, it quickly turns into secondary minerals through oxidation and therefore was hardly available as a usable material for early cultures. It was obtained through the smelting of copper ores. In metal form, copper can be processed and worked on in many ways. From early on, a large part of the processed copper was used to create alloys with → tin, → lead, and zinc, which are superior to pure copper in technical usability. Metallic copper can be formed particularly well. However, tool blades made from copper could not be hardened for working on even harder materials, such as stone. Copper was also useful for forging sheet metal and for beating metal into receptacles and reliefs. Metal casting, on the other hand, was difficult, since copper only melts at 1080° C, which requires a tremendous technical effort. Pliny differentiates between *aes caldarium*, which could not be hammered but was melted, and *aes regulare* (copper sticks), which was worked with the hammer and was also known as *aes ductile* (Plin. HN 34,94). JO.R.

II. THE NEAR EAST
The history of copper use goes back to the 8th and 7th millennia BC. Aside from small finds of natural, pure copper, many places where copper ore was found were known since prehistoric times, particularly in Asia Minor (Ergani Maden), the Caucasus/Transcaucasia, and in the region of the Persian Gulf (esp. Oman), inner-Iran, Cyprus, Palestine (Feinan), and Egypt (Sinai, eastern desert). Copper was traded in the form of ore, ingots, and finished products. The earliest imports of copper from Syria, the Near East, and Cyprus to Egypt took place in the time of the 18th and 19th dynasty (*c.*

1500–1200 BC). The oldest datable objects that were forged cold from pure copper are known from the 7th millennium and stem from Anatolia and northern Mesopotamia (Çayönü, Tell Maghzaliya). From not much later, possibly from the same period, stem hot forged copper artefacts; smelting is documented in this area for the 6th millennium.

Until early in the 4th millennium, copper was only used for small objects (pearls, needles, pendants). Prior to the introduction of → bronze in the beginning of the 3rd millennium, metallurgy of pure copper was predominant, and even towards the end of the 3rd millennium, unalloyed copper was used for large-scale sculptures. But since the early 4th millennium, an increasing number of objects was made from arsenic copper (hoard of Naḥal Mišmār/Dead Sea), an alloy which was probably produced accidentally as a result of a certain type of ore, later the result of an intentional process (by adding minerals rich in arsenic). It is possible to distinguish the arsenic copper tradition from the bronze tradition down into the 2nd millennium BC. Further alloys from the 4th and 3rd millennia BC are lead copper and (rarely) silver copper as well as antimonium copper. The variety of artefacts made from copper and its alloys (e.g. jewellery, weapons, tools, receptacles, large-scale sculptures) does not, however, clearly indicate that a connection existed between the specific alloyed metals used and the types of products made from them.
→ Metallurgy

R. J. FORBES, Metallurgy in Antiquity, 1959, 290–377; P. R. S. MOOREY, Ancient Mesopotamian Materials and Industries, 1994, 242–278. R.W.

III. GREECE
Copper technology came from the east and reached Greece in about the 4th millennium. It did not, however, play as significant a role there as in the Near East, since → bronze quickly became the material of choice. In Greece and its surrounding areas, copper was largely replaced by bronze due to a better casting ability in the production of weapons, tools, jewellery items, and statuettes, also in the more traditional production of sheet metal and wire.

IV. ROME
In Roman times, copper was produced in large quantities as a metallic raw material, but completely lost its use as a production material since it was exclusively used for the production of various types of copper alloys. Even thin-walled receptacles were made from tin bronze, tools were rarely forged from copper any longer, instead cast from bronze or brass. Only coins of lower value were minted from copper. This development can be traced back to the Etruscan period, where bronze technology reached a high peak and copper objects became the exception. Copper was of high significance in early Roman history as a standard of value and as a means of payment, which, as Pliny points out,

is evident in a multitude of terms: *tribuni aerarii*, → *aerarium*, *obaerati*, *aere diruti* (Plin. HN 34,1).

V. CENTRAL EUROPE

North of the Alps, the use of copper clearly began later than in Eastern Europe, where numerous copper objects were found from the mid 4th millennium BC (Bulgaria, Romania). The finds from former Yugoslavia and the Ukraine are from slightly later (late 4th millennium BC). In the 3rd millennium BC, the use of copper stretched across the entire Central and Western European region, serving primarily as material for the production of tools and weapons. The mid 2nd millennium led here as well to a replacement of copper by bronze, until copper no longer had any significance at all as a raw material for the production of utensils.

VI. COPPER DEPOSITS AND SMELTING METHODS

The first raw materials used for smelting copper were weathering products of copper and its primary ores such as azurite, malachite, atacamite or chrysocolla, which stand out because of their intensive green and blue colours. Very early records show their use as gems for making pearls and as colouring agents. The development of various techniques of ore smelting probably occurred in the context of → pottery productions and began in the 8th millennium BC, but did not become widely used until the 4th millennium. These techniques made it possible to transform secondary weathering products and, later, the numerous primary ores as well into metallic copper. Deposits of copper ores are widely spread and can be found throughout all regions. Since the 3rd millennium, mining concentrated on the large copper deposits in Sinai and in Wādī l-ʿAraba, in Anatolia, on Cyprus, and later on the deposits in Romania, Spain, and the Alps. We know that in the European Bronze Age and especially in the Roman period, the copper supply for large areas was already obtained from only few central deposits, which indicates that the metal trade must have held a special economic significance. In ancient literature, copper deposits are mentioned repeatedly, for instance for Spain, whose deposits supposedly surpassed all other known deposits in quantity as well as quality (Turdetania in the province of Baetica: Str. 3,2,8; cf. 3,2,3; 3,2,9; Plin. HN 34,4), also for Italy (Plin. HN 34,2; Alps: Plin. HN 34,3; Temesa, Bruttium: Stat. Silv. 1,1,42), for Macedonia (Vitr. De arch. 7,9,6), for Asia Minor (Str. 13,1,51), and especially for Cyprus (Str. 14,6,5; Plin. HN 34,2; 34,94; Jos. Ant. Iud. 16,128). In the Roman period, the deposits on the island of Euboea were already exhausted (Str. 10,1,9; Plin. HN 4,64).

The smelting of copper ores was achieved through a process of reduction, in which the copper ore was first roasted and thereby oxidized, and then reduced to metallic copper with the aid of charcoal. In this manner, a copper was produced which contained a few percent of impure materials. In late antiquity, the purity of copper was increased to values exceeding 99% through highly developed smelting methods. The large number of different copper ores that occur in combination with arsenic and antimony make it possible for archaeologists to infer the origin of the copper from specific deposits through the impurities of the processed copper and its alloys. In certain regions, the concentrations of arsenic, antimony, or nickel reached values of over 10%, which led researchers to the assumption that arsenic bronze was produced intentionally in the early period of copper metallurgy. In actuality, however, we are dealing with unintentional additions of copper ores that were particularly rich in arsenic, antimony or nickel.

→ Mining; → Bronze; → Metallurgy

1 P. T. CRADDOCK, Early Metal and Mining Production, 1995   2 CH. ÉLUÈRE (ed.), Découverte du métal, 1991   3 J. F. HEALY, Mining and Metallurgy in the Greek and Roman World, 1978   4 S. JUNGHANS, E. SANGMEISTER, M. SCHRÖDER, Metallanalysen kupferzeitlicher und früh-bronzezeitliche Bodenfunde aus Europa, 1960   5 R. MADDIN (ed.), The Beginning of the Use of Metals and Alloys, 1986   6 J. D. MUHLY, Copper and Tin, 1973   7 J. RIEDERER, Bibliographie zu Material und Technologie kulturgesch. Objekte aus Kupfer und Kupferlegierungen, in: Berliner Beitr. zur Archäometrie 7, 1982, 287–342   8 B. ROTHENBERG, The Ancient Metallurgy of Copper, 1990   9 R. F. TYLECOTE, The Early History of Metallurgy in Europe, 1987   10 R. F. TYLECOTE, A History of Metallurgy, 1976.   JO.R.

Copreus (Κοπρεύς; *Kopreýs*).
[1] Son of → Pelops. He transmits to → Hercules the tasks ordered by → Eurystheus, who fears personal contact. For this reason, Homer reverses the normally descending genealogical line in hero epics and refers to C. as 'the worse father of the better son' (Hom. Il. 15,639–641). In Eur. Heracl., C. demands in Eurystheus' name the release of the → Heraclidae, who are seeking asylum from the Attic king → Demophon [2]. According to Apollod. 2,5,1, Eurystheus had cleansed C. from a blood guilt. The name is not originally derived from *kópros*, 'excrement', 'manure' but is related to the larger meaning of 'manure farm', 'livestock stable' [1]; apparently, the pejorative meaning has been a secondary development [2].
[2] Boeotian, receives the godly horse → Areion from → Poseidon and gives it to → Hercules (Thebais fr. 8 BERNABÉ).

1 R. JANKO, The Iliad. A Commentary. vol. 4: Books 13–16, 1992, 298   2 B. MADER, s.v. Kopreus, LFE   3 M. SCHMIDT, s.v. Kopreus, LIMC 6.1, 99–100.   RE.N.

Coprus (Κόπρος; *Kópros*). Attic *paralia*-deme of the phyle Hippothontis, with two *bouleutaí*. Probably identical with the synonymous (river?) island (νῆσος τῆς Ἀττικῆς, Schol. Aristoph. Equ. 899; Hsch. s.v. K.), but not identical with Gaiduronisi (Patroklu Charax) [1]. [2. 52; 3. 178; 4] assume that C. was located east of Eleusis.

1 E. HONIGMANN, s.v. Kopros, RE XI 2, 1365f.
2 TRAILL, Attica 21 with n. 26[bis], 52, 69, 111 no. 74, table
8 3 TRAVLOS, Attika 4 E. VANDERPOOL, New Evidence
for the Location of the Attic Deme Kopros, in: Hesperia
22, 1953, 175f.   H.LO.

Coptic Latest form of the → Egyptian language, used
for Christian literature in Egypt from *c.* AD 300 until
the Middle Ages, written in the Greek alphabet with the
inclusion of several additional letters adopted from
→ Demotic. Two main dialects thereof (Sahidic, later
Bohairic) were prevalent in all of Egypt. In addition,
four other dialects existed, three of which (Achmimic,
Subachmimic or Lycopolitan, Oxyrhynchitic or 'Middle Egyptian') were recorded only to the 5th cent., while
only one (Fayumic) still appeared for a longer time.
Coptic literature is strongly tied to religion (Bible,
Apocryphal literature, Church Fathers, Church history), the works having largely been translated from
Greek. Legal documents and letters were also strongly
patterned after the Greek models in regard to formulas
and style, the language itself is interspersed with many
Greek loan words. Furthermore, several Gnostic and
Manichaean works have survived from the 4th and 5th
cents. Pre-Christian, indigenous elements can still be
found in the magical texts, otherwise only in rare cases
(Cambyses novel).

W.E. CRUM, A Coptic Dictionary, 1939; M. KRAUSE,
Ägypten in spätantik-christlicher Zeit, 1998; H.J.
POLOTSKY, Grundlagen des koptischen Satzbaus, 2 vols.,
1987, 1990.   J.OS.

Coptic cursives see → Writing, styles of (Cursive)

Coptic Uncial see → Uncial

Coptus Main city of the 5th upper Egyptian district
(besides Ombos and Qūṣ), Egyptian *gbtw*, which became Greek κοπτός (*koptós*), Copt. *kebt* and Arab. *qift*.
Important starting-point for expeditions into the Wadi
Hamāmat and the Red Sea. Located in C. were temples
for → Min (main god), → Isis (also referred to as 'Widow of Coptus') and → Horus; records also indicate a
cult of Geb. Colossal stone statues of Min stem from the
early 1st dynasty. Protective decrees in the later Old
Kingdom exempted temples and chapels from taxes.
The surviving buildings are primarily Ptolemaic and
Roman; there are remnants of an oracle chapel from the
period of Cleopatra VII. The best-preserved temple in
al-Qalū'a is dedicated to Isis. In the Ptolemaic period,
C. enjoyed an economic peak due to foreign trade in
ports on the Red Sea (Myos Hormos, Berenice). In the
Roman period, C. served as a military base and was
destroyed by Diocletian following a revolt (AD 292).
Still, the city remained an important trading place until
the Arab period.

1 H.G. FISCHER, Inscriptions from the Coptite Nome,
1964   2 H. KEES, s.v. Koptos, RE XI 2, 1367–1369
3 L. PANTALACCI, C. TRAUNECKER, Le Temple d'El-Qalūa
1, 1990   4 C. Traunecker, Coptos, 1992.   JO.QU.

Copy
A. INTRODUCTORY COMMENTS
B. COPYING-TECHNIQUES   C. PUBLICATION
D. DEVELOPMENT IN THE MIDDLE AGES

A. INTRODUCTORY COMMENTS
Copy should be understood in two ways: on the one
hand, it refers to the copying of a literary work beginning with the first version and throughout the various
writing phases, including the alteration of the text into
book form. On the other hand, it refers to the copies of a
book intended for its systematic, 'publisher driven' dissemination. Copy thus refers to both the working
methods of ancient authors and to the realm of book
production.

B. COPYING-TECHNIQUES
There are only few indirect records about the work
methods of ancient writers and these are often hard to
interpret. Of great importance is therefore the letter by
Pliny the Younger (3,5), in which he describes the scientific work methods of his uncle, Pliny the Elder. On the
basis of this letter and other sources (Lucian, *Quomodo
historia sit conscribenda* 48; Marcell., Vita Thucydidis
47e, Plut. *De tranquillitate animae* 464e — 465a) it is
possible to gain an impression of how Pliny the Elder as
well as other ancient writers carried out their work. It
began with the reading of a book, *adnotationes*, then
excerpts were collected and dictated to a *notarius* (stenographer), who transferred them to *pugillares*, plates
made from wood or wax, pages of papyrus or parchment, and from these onto papyrus scrolls (later into a
codex made from papyrus or parchment). The reconstruction above is confirmed concretely and tangibly in
a highly unique document, the P Hercul. 1021. This
scroll contains the first version or design of the *Academicorum historia* by → Philodemus of Gadara, the
Greek philosopher of the Epicurean School in the 1st
cent. BC, unless we are dealing with a collection of pure
excerpts. A comparison of these two sources makes it
possible to retrace at the least the early stages of a literary work in antiquity: either a writer read his sources,
marked (*adnotare*) the places that seemed important for
the preparation of his work with a sign, created
excerpts and wrote them, possibly even by himself, onto
pugillares (plates of wood or wax). Or he dictated them
to a stenographer, who transferred them onto a scroll.
The result was the first, still incomplete version of the
work. The author's work progressed in a number of
steps: new research and further considerations resulted
in more material which was noted in the margins of the
previously collected parts or it could also be added to
the verso of the scroll. Appendices, supplements, and
linguistic or stylistic improvements found their place
either on the margins and on the empty places of the
recto or on the verso. These interventions were not
made by the author himself, at least not in Philodemus'
and Pliny's case and probably as in many other cases,
but instead were written down by a scribe or the profes-

sional *diorthōtés*. Before the text was copied or dictated for the creation of a fair copy in preparation for publication, the collected material could be reworked and rearranged prior to receiving the last visual finishing touches. These 'intermediate versions' were apparently called *hypomnēmatiká*. Similar conclusions can be drawn from an analysis of the colophons of several papyri from Herculaneum (P Hercul. 1427, 1506 and 1674), which contain books of rhetoric by Philodemus, as well as from a few passages in Galen (*in Hipp. art. comm.* 3,32; 18a,529 K.) and from the Neoplatonic commentators of Aristotle (Ammonius in Aristot. Cat. 4,3–13 Busse). Scholars have concluded that the difference between *hypomnēmatiká* and *syntagmatiká* concerned form more than content, at least in certain circles: therefore the provisional (*hypomnēmatiká*) and the final (*syntagmatiká*) version of a work were terminologically distinguished. It is highly unlikely that each time a *hypomnēmatikón* formed the intermediate step from the provisional version or the draft to the fair copy. It is more probable that the second phase could often be avoided, or rather was an alternative to the first. An author could order the written version of his work either by compiling a formless conception or a *hypomnēmatikón*, either one of which was directly transferred into the final version.

The creation of a literary work therefore entailed the use of the file-card box only rarely and to a limited degree, and only in the beginning phase, that is for the collection of excerpts. We must distinguish between at least two phases of authoring an ancient work, and the first one is not the same for all authors: 1.1. First drafts which were based on a prior collection of excerpts that had possibly been written on small plates or *pugillares*. 1.2. *Hypomnēmatiká*, meaning temporary drafts, in which the material had not yet received the last finishing touches. 2. The final version or fair copy (*hypómnēma, sýntagma*) of the text which usually preceded the actual publication, the *ékdosis*. The *ékdosis* is the version of the work which the author regarded as completed and which he made available to the public with all the risks surrounding publication (*ekdidónai*) in a society that did not know about copyright in the modern sense. The steps leading from the first compilation of a text to its publication were therefore as follows: study of the sources and collection of excerpts,→ first compilation in the form of a draft and/or a preliminary version, → transfer into a fair copy, → handing over the MS to a publisher for publication.

Dictation played a major, perhaps even a predominant role during the compilation of the work as well as in the production of the publication for commercial distribution. The MSS that appear to have been written down by the author himself and the indirect sources indicating the author's own hand reveal quite clearly that poets evidently preferred writing themselves, while the prose writers commonly used a system of dictation, perhaps even exclusively. The above insights, however, should not be generalized since they involve a wide arena and are tied to many different conditions, methods and personal or subjective circumstances.

Occasionally, both methods (the author's own hand as well as dictation) can be found in the same author at the same time. This statement is not only true for the writing of poetry and prose or the transitional phases of a work from original text to book. In Roman circles, especially in the literary circles influenced by Neoteric and Alexandrian movements, poetry was written down increasingly by the authors themselves in the late Republican period and in the early imperial period. Prominent voices turned against the rampant use of dictation that occurred not only in scholarly and technical/scientific works of prose but also in poetry, for example Quintilian (Inst. 1,1,20): dictation should be regarded with suspicion, since it required the author's long and careful examination more than writing by one's own hand. Also, young and inexperienced authors may be tempted by dictation to publish careless and largely improvised works.

C. PUBLICATION

Now, the text was ready for publication. A popular method for poetic works was to read the text first to a group of friends, then to the public. If it was successful, the author could either publish his work himself or — much more commonly — entrust it to a publisher who ordered the copies, assumed the production costs (in some cases with financial assistance from the author or his patron), and took care of the distribution.

The most famous publisher in antiquity was probably Atticus, a friend of Cicero's who had even granted him a type of copyright, considering of course that his publication activity was not limited exclusively to Cicero's works. In his workshops, Atticus employed a number of highly qualified scribes (*librarii*) and proofreaders (*anagnostae*), whose service helped him to issue high-quality publications. The publisher was responsible for the reproduction of the work in several copies. In order to shorten the time of *duplicatio*, the texts were copied by a group of slaves. One or two copies served as models for reproduction. A MS could be divided amongst several scribes, who each produced a fair copy of a certain part that corresponded to one or more books. It is much harder to determine whether this phase of book production was dictated as well. The hypothesis that several traditional MSS — the *codex Sinaiticus* of the Bible is the best known — were written down from dictation recently found support in new arguments. The arguments are based on an analysis of two components characteristic for copy by dictation: 1. The use of the term that refers to the transfer of a text and 2. The cooperation of several persons. An essential confirmation of dictation is the practice of collation, in which groups of two worked together. A lector read the text or the MS to be compared out loud, a proof-reader followed the reading in the copy and made the necessary corrections. Collation was a common practice in the use of dictation in ancient scholastic circles and contributed finally to the increasingly important role of stenography in public and literary life. Dictation made the copying of texts in the publication business much easier and sped up distribution, even considering that work was done in small groups who tripled or quadrupled the texts. A document of this method is a letter that was handed down only in Syrian language by the Katholikos, the patriarch of Baghdad, Timotheus I (727/8–832) and which indicates that at least Timotheus and his circle preferred the method of copying from dictation. The removal of any mistakes in the 'publication phase' was the responsibility of the proof-readers (*diorthōtés, anagnosta*), who examined each individually copied or dictated copy. In special cases, the author himself or a scholar could examine the copies, a practice which often led to improvements in content and increased the quality of the books. The accuracy and quality of the copies was probably not always perfect, since they depended primarily on the conscientiousness of the publishers and the ability of the proof-readers. Corrections were probably made by two people, one of which read the text being copied out loud while the other followed the text in the copy and made the corrections. In the first few cents. of the Roman empire, slaves were gradually replaced with free scribes and proof-readers who did piecework and were compensated for their work according to the number of copied lines (stichometry) they produced. Piecework, however, resulted in an increasing deterioration in the quality of MSS.

After the book was copied and completely proofread, only the task of distribution was left, which was often seen to by the publisher himself who sometimes was also the bookseller.

D. DEVELOPMENT IN THE MIDDLE AGES

In the Byzantine and Latin Middle Ages, the same methods continued to be used aside from a few significant innovations. Two remarkable changes had occurred in the meantime. On the one hand, autography was increasingly preferred and was further developed, at least in several cultural branches from the 11th and 12th cents. This development was caused and aided by the fact that notaries wrote documents in their own hand and by the professional practices of notaries in general. Furthermore, this was the period in which *scriptoria* emerged where not only the MSS of contemporary authors were copied but also those of 'classical' authors, in an attempt to safeguard their survival.

A methodical innovation can be found in Thomas Aquinas, who is an important example for the description of an author's work methods in the Latin Middle Ages. Thomas Aquinas himself wrote a series of notes on individual pieces of paper (autograph). A fellow monk who worked as a scribe copied these notes by dictation (apograph), then the copy was carefully examined by the author and his friends. Only then, a fair copy of the text was written on parchment or paper fascicles which were bound as a codex or MS and intended for the library. We have less information about what happened in the East, where autography was on the increase as well. No dependable and detailed example for the work methods of a Byzantine author has survived. Presumably there were not great differences to the systems of the Latin world. A further change occurred in the Greek East: in the Occident, copies were usually made for the purpose of book production that met the requirements of religious, secular, or monastic circles, but in the East, a large number of individual initiatives led to the ordering of private copies from individual scribes for the production of copies from high-level intellectuals but also from less significant scholars. One peculiarity of occidental universities was, finally, the so called *pecia*-system. The *apógraphon* of an author was used as the basis for official *exemplaria* texts which in turn served as models for all other copies. Each specimen was divided into several layers (*peciae*) which were simultaneously copied by professional scribes or were loaned out to students in return for a fee, so that the students could create their own copies for individual use.

→ Book; → Scribe

T. DORANDI, in: ZPE 87, 1991, 11–33; Id., in: W. KULLMANN, J. ALTHOFF (ed.), Vermittlung und Tradierung von Wissen in der griech. Kultur, 1993, 71–83; T. KLEBERG, Bokhandel och bokförlag i antiken, 1962, 13–83; A. PETRUCCI, in: C. QUESTA, R. RAFFAELLI (ed.), Il libro e il testo, 1984, 397–414; D. REINSCH, in: D. HARLFINGER (ed.), Griech. Kodikologie und Textüberlieferung, 1980, 629–644.   T.D...

Copyright A legally entrenched copyright protected by penalties did not exist in Greek and Roman antiquity ([1]; cf. [2]). → Plagiarism was considered reprehensible but had no legal consequences. The occurrence described in Vitr. 7 praef. 4–7 according to which → Aristophanes [4] of Byzantium exposed the victors of a poetic competition in Alexandria as plagiarists, who were then punished by the king, is an exception. Similarly, the wish of → Martial [1] (1,52, cf. [3] ad loc.) that a plagiarist of his poems should be punished according to the *lex Fabia de plagiariis*, is an expression of frustration, not of legal reality.

The right of authors to their texts could only be secured through measures concerning the content, for example, by appending a → *sphragís* [3] (cf. → *subscriptio* II.; [4; 5]) or acrostichic comments (→ Acrostich; Cic. Div. 2,112: *Q. Ennius fecit*) [4]. The best protection against plagiarism probably was an intensive public discussion of the work and the resulting public knowledge of at least a considerable portion of the text.

→ Copy; → Autograph; → Book (C.); → Forgeries; → Sphragis [3]; → Author

1 K. ZIEGLER, s. v. Plagiat, RE 20, 1956–1997, esp. 1967 f. 2 M. ROSE, Authors and Owners, 1993   3 M. CITRONI (ed.), M. Valerii Martialis Epigrammaton liber I, 1975 (with commentary)   4 W. KRANZ, Sphragis, in: RhM 104, 1961, 3–46; 97–124   5 G. CERRI, Il significato di sphragis in Teognide e la salvaguardia dell'autenticità testuale nel

mondo antico, in: Lirica greca e latina (Annali dell' Ist. Universitario di Napoli, Sezione Filologico Letteraria 12), 1992, 25–43   6 E. VOGT, Das Akrostichon in der griech. Lit., in: A&A 13, 1967, 80–95.   U.SCH.

Cora Latin city on the western slopes of the *montes Lepini* above the Pontine plain, connected to the *via Appia*, today's Cori (province Latina). Colony of Alba Longa; participated in the founding of the *lucus Dianae* near Aricia. Outpost on the border to the Volsci, *prisca colonia Latina* (c. 501 BC, Liv. 2,16,8); silver coins. Destroyed by Sulla, then *municipium* of the *tribus Papiria*. Archaeological monuments: remnants of a city wall with towers, walls of the acropolis in *opus polygonale* with post-Sullanic restorations in *opus incertum* (round towers), several terraces in *opus polygonale* for protection against landslides; the so-called little temple of Hercules (well preserved), a four-columned pseudoperipteros (1 BC). Further down, remnants of the Temple of Castor and Pollux (CIL X 6505f.), Corinthian prostylos with six travertine columns on a high tufaceous podium; below C., the Ponte della Catena with an arch (Republican period). There are several *villae rusticae* in the surroundings. Epigraphical evidence: CIL X, p. 645, 6505–52.

A. VON GERKAN, Die Krümmungen im Gebälk des dor. Tempel in Cori, in: MDAI(R) 40, 1925, 167–180; P. BRANDIZZI-VITTUCCI, Cora, 1968.

Coracesium (Κορακήσιον; *Korákésion*). City in Cilicia Trachea (Plin. HN 5,93; Ptol. 5,5,3; Stadiasmus maris magni 207; Hierocles, Synekdemos 682,8), in Byzantine times Καλὸν ὄρος/*Kalón óros* (also *Candeloro i.a.*), today's Alânya. Scyl. 101 referred to C. as *pólis*. The city resisted Antiochus III in 197 BC (Liv. 33,20,4f.) and served Diodotus Tryphon, the Seleucid rebel, as a basis against Antioch VII (Str. 14,5,2). According to Plut. Pompey 28,1, the Cilician pirates were defeated in a naval battle near C. (a different account: App. Mith. 96,442). C. was a diocese of Pamphylia I.

S. LLOYD, D. RICE-STORM, Alânya (Alaᵓiyya), 1958.
K.T.

Coral (Hellenistic κοράλ(λ)ιον (*korállion*), κουράλ(λ)ιον (*kourállion*), Latin *curalium, corallium*).

A. GENERAL COMMENTS   B. CELTIC CULTURE

A. GENERAL COMMENTS
    The fact that coral does not consist of plants but of the calcareous skeletons of minuscule anthozoan coelenterates has only been known since the 19th cent. Theophrastus (De lapidibus 38), Pliny (HN 32,21–24, cf. Isid. Orig. 16,8,1), and Dioscorides (5,121 WELLMANN = 5,138 BERENDES) praise especially red coral, which was found near Naples, Trapani, on the islands of Huyères, and on the Aeolic islands. Darker coral is

mentioned as *lace* by Plin. HN 32,21 in reference to the Persian Gulf and the Red Sea. Ov. Met. 4,744–752 explains the hardening of coral in air as an effect of Medusa's head which turns things into stone. It was used as medicine in a variety of ways (Dioscorides loc. cit. on its astringent and cooling effects; Plin. HN 32,24 and Celsus, Ned. 5,6ff.). Coral jewellery and amulets (cf. Plin. HN 37,164: the *Gorgonia* = coral supposedly shields from lightening and whirlwinds) have survived only in rare cases.   C.HÜ.

B. CELTIC CULTURE
    Coral (*corallium rubrum*) was a precious material for → jewellery in the Celtic culture of the late Hallstadt and early La Tène period (6th/5th cents. BC). Due to its striking red colour it was endowed with apotropaic significance. Pearls, pendants, inserts esp. for fibulas, metal receptacles, and weapons (→ Helmets, → Swords) were made from coral. It was imported from the Mediterranean coasts and processed in the Celtic region; raw coral was found in a few settlements. In the 4th/3rd cents. BC, coral was gradually replaced by → Cenamel (blood enamel).

→ Hallstatt culture; → Celtic archaeology; → La Tène culture

A. WIGG, Koralle und Email als Einlage bei Metallarbeiten, in: R. CORDIE-HACKENBERG et al., Hundert Meisterwerke keltischer Kunst, 1992, 207f.   V.P.

Coralis (Κόραλις λίμνη (*Kóralis límnē*), erroneously often found as Κάραλις (*Káralis*) [1. 3]). One of the most important lakes of central Anatolia between Lycaonia and Pisidia, today's Beyşehir Gölü. Only Str. 12,6,1 refers to it by the name of C.; in the Byzantine Middle Ages, it is usually called *Pousgoýse límnē* (Πουσγούση λίμνη). The drain of the lake flows through the south-eastern *Trogítis límnē* (today's Suğla Gölü), which is significantly smaller and largely drained today, and it irrigates as Çarşamba Suyu the plain south of → Iconium [2].
    It must be distinguished from the *Cabalitis palus* named in Liv. 38,15,1 (correctly, as opposed to the traditionally used name of *Caralitis palus*; today's Söğüt Gölü) on the Lycian-Carian border [1. 74].

1 J. TISCHLER, Kleinasiat. Hydronymie, 1977   2 BELKE, 44, 117, 218, 237.   K.BE.

Coralius (Κωράλιος; *Kōrálios*, Κουράλιος; *Kourálios*). River north-east of → Coronea. The river's banks were home to the Boeotian central sanctuary of Athena Itonia (Alc. 3 D.; Alc. 4). Callim. H. 5,64 calls it *Kurálios*. Str. (9,2,29; 33; 9,5,14; 17) confuses the C. and the other river by the same name near the sanctuary of Athena Itonia in Achaea Phthiotis with the Kuarios, a tributary of the river Peneius in Thessaliotis.

P. W. WALLACE, Strabo's Description of Boiotia, 1979, 116.   P.F.

Coralli (Κόραλλοι; *Kóralloi*). Tribe in the region of the → Getae, documented in literature only for the last cent. of the Roman Republic and the 1st cent. of the Imperial period (Ov. Pont. 4,2,37; 8,83; Str. 7,5,12). Appianus (Mith. 293) mentions the C. separately from the Iazyges and Thracians, but more likely meant the Sarmatae or Scythae instead.

> M. FLUSS, s.v. K., RE XI 2, 1377.   I.v.B.

Corasium (Κοράσιον; *Korásion*). Harbour in the Cilicia Trachea. Together with → Korykos [2], to which it was connected through *korasiodrómos* (messenger service), C. reached great prosperity in late antiquity without becoming a polis or a diocese; today's Susanoğlu.

> H. Hellenkemper, F. Hild, Neue Forschungen zu Kilikien (Denkschriften der Österreichischen Akad. der Wissenschaften: Philosoph.-Hist. Klasse 186) 1986, 311f.   F.H.

Corax (Κόραξ; *Kórax*).
[1] Mountains to the east of Aetolia, today's Giona in the Nomos Phokis, 2484 m high; Str. 7 fr. 6; 9,3,1; 10,2,4; Liv. 36,30,4; 37,4,7.

> PHILIPPSON/KIRSTEN, vol. 1, 650.   D.S.

[2] see → Siegecraft
[3] **C.** In ancient rhetoric tradition, C. and Tisias (T.) from Syracuse were regarded as the inventors and founders of rhetoric, the practical, learnable and teachable *téchnē rhētorikḗ* based on experience. The two were also known as the first to teach this art (→ *téchnē*) for payment (Quint. Inst. 2,17,7). Due to contradictory traditions, it is very difficult to determine which exact role either C. or T. played in this regard [2. 53]. As far as T.'s students are concerned, the names of → Lysias, the son of the Syracusean Cephalus (RADERMACHER (=R.) B 2,3), and → Isocrates (R B 2,4,5) are mentioned. C.'s students were first T. (Sopater, Comm. on Hermogenes 5,6,14; Walz B 2,9 R.), then → Gorgias [2] of Leontini [2. 1, 55, 221]. Cicero (De or. 3,81) dismisses C.'s students altogether as 'quarrelsome, annoying and noisy troublemakers'.

It seems to be clear that rhetoric was created in Syracuse during the years after the fall of the tyrannis and the re-establishment of democracy (466/5 BC). Cicero (Brut. 2,46) explains with reference to Aristotle that C. and T. authored an *ars* ('art') and *praecepta* ('rules') (cf. Cic. De or. 1,91) because of the civil actions which were once again instituted in Syracuse after a long time. The *ars* must therefore have concerned the speech of the courts (*génos dikanikón*), a fact which can also be observed in a few prolegomena (introductions) and comm. on rhetoric (for example Sopater, Hermogenescomm. WALZ 5,6,14; s. [1. 59])). Theophrastus (A 5,17 R.) and a few authors of prolegomena and comm. (esp. Anon. WALZ 4,11,14ff., Ioannes Doxopatres, WALZ 4,12,14ff. = H. RABE, Prolegomenon Sylloge (P.S.) 4, p.

25,17ff. R.; WALZ 2, p. 119,16ff. = P.S. 9 p. 126,5ff. R.; Troilos, WALZ 6,48,26ff. = P.S. 5 p. 52,3ff. R.; Anon. WALZ 7,6) who presumably refer to a report by the historian Timaeus from Sicily only know of C. as the founder of rhetoric and the creator of a *téchnē*. According to this report, C. had been the influential vassal of › Gelon [1] and › Hieron [2] and attempted in the democracy to influence the people through his speech as he did his masters before. For this purpose, he established certain rules and thus became the inventor of a *téchnē* for popular and consulting speeches, the *génos dēmēgorikón*, later *symbouleutikón* [2. 54].

Plato never mentions C. In the *Phaedrus*, where Plato discusses Sophist rhetoric, T. appears together with Gorgias of Leontini, Empedocles' student, as a representative of the theory that probability (*eikós*) is more important than truth in → rhetoric, and above all as capable of making small things appear large and large things appear small; this is supposedly part of his instruction-book as well (→ Rhetoric, textbooks of) (273a 6–c 5). Besides Plato, Isocrates never mentions C. either [1. 60].

Aristotle (Rh. 1402a 17–26) claims that C.'s entire *téchnē* consists of the probable (*eikós*). In the *Sophistici elenchi* 183b 25–34, he ties the improvements in rhetorical *téchnē* to the following sequence: 'Following the first ones' is Teisias, then Thrasymachus, and then Theodorus; but these 'first ones' remain unnamed. Aside from C., he may refer to Empedocles, whom Aristotle supposedly called the inventor of rhetoric (cf. Quint. Inst. 3,1,8) in his *Sophistḗs* according to Diogenes Laertius (8,57) and Sext. Emp. (Adversus mathematicos 7,6). According to Cicero (Inv. 2,6f.), Aristotle refers to T. as *princeps* the first one in his *synagōgḗ technôn*, a summary of all previous rhet. *téchnai* (R . A 5,8, [2. 53]), and as the *inventor* ('inventor') of rhetoric.

According to Quint. Inst. 2,15,4, the definition of rhetoric as πειθοῦς δημιουργός (*vis persuadendi*), meaning the 'master of persuasion/convincing' [3. 27–32] was known among others as the rhetoric of Gorgias of Leontini (Pl. Grg. 453a 2). This definition was used by Isocrates, presumably a student of T.'s (B 2,4,55 R.), and by Gorgias, who, however, may have understood it differently as *vis (dýnamis)*, the 'power, possibility' to persuade. According to several prolegomena, T., C. and their students defined rhetoric in the way mentioned above, but according to other prolegomena, it was only C., and, again according to yet others, it was only T. (B 2,13 R.).

The prolegomena attribute C. with the invention of symbouleutic speech (→ *genera causarum*), esp. its structure, *dispositio*. There is no mention of him dealing with court speeches at all (R. A 5,16, B 2,23, 24, [1. 60f.; 54–57]). However, the number and the terms for the different parts of speech do not correspond in the prolegomena. These complex arguments lead MARTIN to the conclusion that the main part of the structure found by C. is the *symbouleýein*, the giving of advice, which the latter had already practised with kings; now it is framed by the prooemium and the summary (*anakephaleýōsis*), which became important in order to arouse or calm the affects of the people [2. 57f.].

1 G. A. KENNEDY, The Art of Persuasion in Greece, 1963 2 J. MARTIN, Antike Rhet., 1974 3 O. A. BAUMHAUER, Die sophistische Rhet., 1986.

A. GERCKE, Die alte τέχνη ῥητορική und ihre Gegner, in: Hermes 32, 1897, 341–381; L. RADERMACHER, Stud. zur Gesch. der griech. Rhet., in: RhM 52, 1897, 412–424; K. BARWICK, Die Gliederung der rhet. TEXNH und die horazische Epistula ad Pisones, in: Hermes 57, 1922, 1–62; D. A. G. HINKS, Tisias and Corax and the Invention of Rhetoric, in: CQ 34, 1940, 61ff.; ST. WILCOX, The Scope of Early Rhetorical Instruction, in: HSPh 53, 1942, 121–156, hier 137; Id., Corax and the Prolegomena, in: AJPh 64, 1943, 1–23; G. A. KENNEDY, The Earliest Rhetorical Handbooks, in: AJPh 80, 1959, 169–178. O.B.

Corbio

[1] Ancient city in Latium on the north-eastern foothills of *mons Albanus*, perhaps today's Roccapriora. It became involved in the Roman wars with the → Aequi: conquered by Cincinnatus in 458 BC (victory at *mons Algidus*), taken back by the Aequi, then destroyed by consul C. Horatius Pulvillus in 457 (Liv. 3,30). Near C., T. Quinctius Capitolinus defeated the Aequi in 446. Archaeological monuments: a few remnants, Imperial Roman *villa*.

A. NIBBY, Analisi storico-topographico-antiquaria della carta dei'dintorni di Roma 2, 1837, 21–24; NISSEN 2, 596. G.U.

[2] City of the → Suessetani near → Tarraco [1. 51, 209; 2]. C. is mentioned only once in Liv. 39,42,1 in the context of the Celtiberian Wars: in 184 BC, C. was conquered and destroyed by A. → Terentius Varro. Its location is unknown, conjectures are offered in [3. 504]. The name is Celtic [4. 1117].

1 A. SCHULTEN, Fontes Hispaniae Antiquae 3, 1935 2 Id., s.v. Suessetaner, RE A IV 2, 588 3 Enciclopedia Universal Ilustrada 15 4 HOLDER 1.

TOVAR 3, 435. P.B.

Corbulo see → Domitius [II 11]

Corcyra

[1] (Κόρκυρα, *Kórkyra*, Lat. Corcyra; the island of Corfu).

A. NAME B. GEOGRAPHY C. HISTORY D. ARCHAEOLOGY

A. NAME

The northernmost of the Ionian islands, always referred to as C. on coins and local inscriptions, but in literature and other inscriptions (IG II–III² 96; SEG 25, 354) also called Κέρκυρα, Lat. *Corcyra*, today officially *Kérkyra*. The name *Corfu* has been in common use since the 10th cent. and stems from the Greek word *Koryphé* ('summit'), named after the fortress overlooking the medieval and the modern city.

B. GEOGRAPHY

The island is 62 km long, 3,5 to 28 km wide and covers an area of *c.* 585 km². Shaped like a crescent, it approaches the Epirote mainland in the north and the south within 2 to 8 km. Since antiquity, the most important settlements are located on the east side with its many bays, whereas the steep cliffs on the west side are exposed to the open sea. The highest mountain is Pantocrator in the north-east with a height of 906 m. Due to the high rainfall (the highest in Greece), C. enjoys lush vegetation and rivers that flow all the year round. C. had a → Peraea on the mainland, which today is Albanian (Thuc. 3,85) [8. 284].

C. HISTORY

C. has been populated since the Palaeolithic period, although little is known about C.'s early history: The settlements (e.g. Aphiona, Cephale, Ermones) were located in the west and in the north of the island, in the early Bronze Age there was immigration from the mainland (Illyria) [2], but there are no indications that contacts existed to the Mycenaean world of Greece. C. is not named expressly in the Homeric epics, but beginning no later than the 5th cent. BC (Thuc. 1,25,4), C. is identified by its inhabitants as Scheria, home of the → Phaeaces. The first Greek settlers came from → Eretria [1]. Around 750, they drove out the Libyrnians who resided there (Plut. Mor. 293ab; Str. 6,2,4). Probably around 734, a Corinthian colony was established on the east side of the island under Bachiadus (→ Bacchiadae) Chersicrates [13. 62–70; 11. 163 no. 3]. Alone, or perhaps together with Corinth, C. founded additional colonies in north-western Greece: → Leucas, → Anactorium, → Apollonia [1], and Epidamnus (→ Dyrrhachium) [13. 209–217]. In the 7th and 6th cents., C. had the strongest Greek fleet (victory in 664 over Corinth in the first known naval battle of Greece), it ruled the Ionian Sea and the commerce in the Adriatic [7]. C. did not take part in the battles of the Persian Wars.

The fight for Epidamnus [3. 60–62], founded by C. together with Corinth, was one of the reasons that led to the → Peloponnesian War, prior to which C. had formed an alliance with Athens [13. 282–293]. In this war, conflicts surrounding exterior politics ended in bloody partisan battles between representatives of the oligarchy and the democracy, with the former emerging victoriously [3. 88–94, 368f.]. Timotheus' successful interventions resulted in C.'s membership in the Second → Athenian League in the year 375 BC (StV 262f.) [18], but this event was followed by further violent interior strife [3. 94–96] that led to a temporary withdrawal from the alliance with Athens. C. was able to maintain its independence until it was conquered by → Cleonymus in 303. Thereafter, it was ruled by different masters (→ Agathocles [2], → Pyrrhus, → Demetrius [2] Poliorketes). In 228 BC, the Illyrian garrison under Demetrius of Pharus surrendered to the Romans. C. came under the protection of Rome (Pol. 2,9–12) and became the first Greek city to belong to the Roman territory. C.'s location between Italy and Greece contributed to the economic development of the island, with many Roman emperors stopping off there (esp. in → Cassiope). When the empire was divided in AD 395, C. was annexed to the east. The first known bishop was Iovianus in the 1st half of the 5th cent. AD. He was the builder of a basilica with five naves in the ancient city [19. 7–10]. C. was prey to looting by the Ostrogoths (551) and invasions by the Slavs (7th cent.), although the island's population remained Greek [14].

D. ARCHAEOLOGY

Considering its historical significance, there are few visual remains today, although the results of newer excavations reveal the wealth and the economic importance of C. The ancient city with the name of C. — the only *pólis* on the island — was located 3 km south of the medieval and modern city on the peninsula of Analipsi (or Kanoni) ([4; 15. 118–130]; maps: [6. 337; 16. 185]). Directly adjacent to the ancient city were two harbours (silted up today) whose shipyards (*neória*) are now uncovered: In the north-east is 'Port Alcinous' (commercial port; map: [5. 59]), in the west and in the laguna of Chalikiopulos is located the 'Hyllaic port' (naval port) [6]. Adjacent to the south of 'Port Alcinous' is the paved agora, in its midst is the basilica built from ancient reused stones. South of the agora (today's Phigareto) were the workshops and trading area [10; 16]. Of the many temples in the city area (e.g. Hera Acraea, Apollo Korkyraios, Dionysus), the most important is the Temple of Artemis with the famous Gorgo pediment from the early 6th cent. BC, located west of the agora (maps: [11. 14; 15. 128f.]). The northern city walls ran along the narrowest place between the Bay of Garitsa and the Hyllaic port, and in the south apparently right below the acropolis on the hill of Analipsis [5. 59]. The necropoleis to the west and the north (Bay of Garitsa) of the ancient city are important due to their (late) geometric and archaic material ('grave of Menecrates'). The archaeological remnants that are worth mentioning for the island are the harbour town of Cassiope and a Doric temple near Roda in the north. Coins: [1; 12]. inscriptions: [8; 17].

1 BMC, Gr (Thess.-Aetolia) 115–167, Gr (Corinth) 112 2 G. ARBANITOU-METALLINOU, Οικισμός της εποχής του Χαλκού στους Ερμονες Κέρκυρας, in: AD 44–46 A, 1989–1991 (1996), 209–222 3 H.-J. GEHRKE, Stasis, 1985 4 H. KALETSCH, s.v. Palaiopolis, in: LAUFFER, Griechenland, 502f. 5 P.G. KALLIGAS, Κέρκυρα, ἀποικισμός καὶ ἔπος, in: ASAA 60, 1982, 57–68 6 A. KANTA-KITSOU, Ausgrabungen auf Kerkyra, in: AD 47 B 1, 1992 (1997), 337–340 (Modern Greek) 7 F. KIECHLE, Korkyra und der Handelsweg durch das Adriatische Meer im 5. Jh.v.Chr., in: Historia 28, 1979, 173–191 8 P. MELA, K. PREKA, D. STRAUCH, Die Grabstelen vom Grundstück Andrioti auf Korkyra, in: AA 1998, 281–303 9 PHILIPPSON/KIRSTEN 2, 202–290, 422–455 10 K. PREKA-ALEXANDRI, A Ceramic Workshop in Figareto, in: BCH Suppl. 23, 1992, 41–52 11 G. RODENWALDT et al., Korkyra, 2 vols., 1939/1940 12 RPC, 274 13 J.B. SALMON, Wealthy Corinth, 1986 14 SOUSTAL, Nikopolis, 178–181 15 R. SPEICH, Korfu und die Ionischen Inseln, 1982 16 A. SPETSIÉRI-CHORÉMI, Un dépôt de sanctuaire archaïque à Corfou, in: BCH 115, 1991, 183–211 17 D. STRAUCH, Aus der Arbeit am Inschr.-Corpus der Ionischen Inseln, in: Chiron 27, 1997, 209–254 18 C. TUPLIN, Timotheos and Corcyra, in: Athenaeum 62, 1984, 537–568 19 D.D. TRIANTAPHYLLOPULLOS, s.v. Kerkyra und die Ion. Inseln, RBK 4, 1–63.

H. KALETSCH, s.v. Kerkyra, in: LAUFFER, Griechenland, 323–328. D.S.

[2] **C. Melaina.** (Κόρκυρα μέλαινα; *Kórkyra mélaina*, Lat. *Corcyra nigra*, 'Black C.'). Island off the Dalmatian coast, today Korčula (Croatia). Called 'black' probably because of its forest in contrast to another island of the same name in the south. Around 600 BC, a colony was founded by citizens from → Cnidus (Scylase 23; Scymnus 427f.; Str. 7,5,5, Plin. HN 3,152), another colony was established originating from → Issa in the 4th/3rd cents. BC (SEG 43, 348; StV 451). During the Imperial period, it was governed by → Salona [1].

1 G. ALFÖLDY, Bevölkerung und Ges. der röm. Prov. Dalmatien, 1965, 107.

L. BRACCESI, Grecità Adriatica, ²1979; J.J. WILKES, Dalmatia, 1969; Id., The Illyrians, 1992. D.S.

Corduba The modern Córdoba on the bank of the Guadalquivir (→ Baetis), which is navigable from C. to its mouth; the city lies at the centre of a region of highly fertile soils. C. also owes its significance to favourable transport links, the old *via Herculea*, and the surrounding mining industry. The region contained important centres of the Tartessian culture in pre-Roman times (Colina de los Quemados, Montoro). The consul → Claudius [I 17] founded the Roman city in 152 BC in the context of the Celtiberian wars. During the Civil War it supported Caesar, and later Pompey. C. became the capital of the province of Baetica; its inhabitants belonged to the Galeria tribe. Its impressive town plan is meanwhile well-known to us (cf. map). Celebrated personalities of Roman history, such as the two → Senecas and → Lucanus, were born here, and in a later period bishop Ossius, one of the central ecclesiastical figures of the 4th cent., an indication of the importance of C. in late antiquity. The West Gothic kings Agila and Athanagild made vain attempts to conquer the city, which was able to resist with the aid of the Byzantines. Not until AD 584 was Leovigild able to capture it. C.'s golden age did not come until after the Arab conquest in the 10th cent., when it became the seat of the caliphate of the Ummayads.

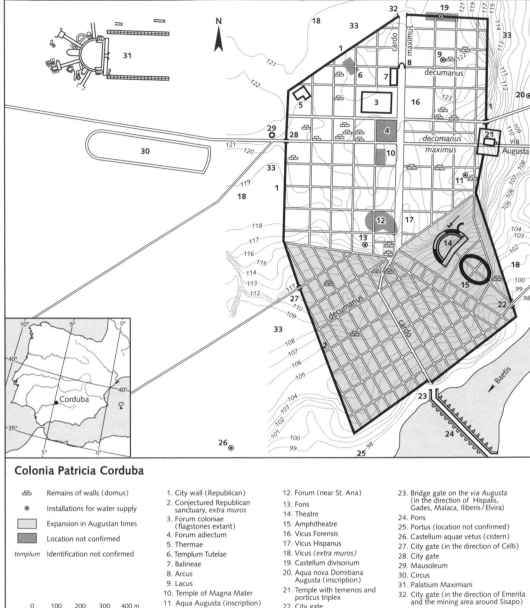

Colonia Patricia Corduba

🏛 Remains of walls (domus)	1. City wall (Republican)	12. Forum (near St. Ana)	23. Bridge gate on the *via Augusta* (in the direction of Hispalis, Gades, Malaca, Iliberis/Elvira)
⊙ Installations for water supply	2. Conjectured Republican sanctuary, *extra muros*	13. Fons	
▢ Expansion in Augustan times	3. Forum coloniae (flagstones extant)	14. Theatre	24. Pons
▢ Location not confirmed	4. Forum adiectum	15. Amphitheatre	25. Portus (location not confirmed)
	5. Thermae	16. Vicus Forensis	26. Castellum aquae vetus (cistern)
templum Identification not confirmed	6. Templum Tutelae	17. Vicus Hispanus	27. City gate (in the direction of Celti)
	7. Balineae	18. Vicus (*extra muros*)	28. City gate
	8. Arcus	19. Castellum divisorium	29. Mausoleum
	9. Lacus	20. Aqua nova Domitiana Augusta (inscription)	30. Circus
	10. Temple of Magna Mater	21. Temple with temenos and porticus triplex	31. Palatium Maximiani
	11. Aqua Augusta (inscription)	22. City gate	32. City gate (in the direction of Emerita and the mining area around Sisapo)
			33. Necropolis

0   100   200   300   400 m

H. v. HESBERG, Cordoba und seine Architekturornamentik, in: W. TRILLMICH, P. ZANKER (ed.), Die Monumentalisierung hispanischer Städte zw. Republik und Kaiserzeit, 1990, 283–287; A. STYLOW, Apuntes sobre el urbanismo de la Córdoba romana, in: ibid., 259–282; TOVAR, 1, 86–92; R. WIEGELS, Die Tribusinschr. des röm. Hispanien, 1985, 30–33.   P.B.

MAPS: A. VENTURA, J. M. BERMÚDEZ, P. LEÓN, Análisis arqueológico de Córdoba Romana, in: P. LEÓN ALONSO (ed.), Colonia Patricia Corduba, Coloquio internacional, Córdoba 1993, 1996, 87–128, here: 111   A. IBÁÑEZ CASTRO, Córdoba hispano-romano, 1983.

Corellia C. Hispulla. Daughter of Corellius [2]; married to one Neratius; Corellius [1] was her son. PIR² C 1296.   W.E.

Corellius

[1] **L. Neratius C. Pansa.** *Cos. ord.* AD 122; son of Corellia Hispulla, a daughter of C. [2], and probably of one of the *Neratii* from Saepinum; related to the family of Domitius Apollinaris, *cos. suff.* 97 [1; 2. 487, 598].

[2] **Q. C. Rufus.** Perhaps from Laus Pompeia [3]. Suffect consul probably in AD 78; governor of Germania superior in 82; according to Plin. Ep. 1,12,6f. an oppo-

nent of Domitian, but not openly. He was commissioned by Nerva to buy up and distribute land in Italy (Plin. Ep. 7,31,4). Probably in 98 he killed himself by refusing food. A friend of Pliny the Younger (PIR² C 1294) [2 passim; 4. 38]. A coin from Hierapolis bearing his name is probably not an indication of a proconsulate in Asia (cf. [5. 117f.]).

1 Camodeca, in: EOS 2, 112f.   2 Syme, RP 7
3 Alföldy, in: EOS II 355f.   4 Eck   5 Weiser, in: EA
20, 1992.   W.E.

Corfinium Main centre of the Paeligni, on the Aternus; the modern Corfinio (province of L'Aquila). In 90 BC under the name Italia or Italica (Diod. Sic. 37,2,4; Str. 5,4,2; Vell. Pat. 2,16,3) capital of the rebellious Italici; coinage bearing the legend *viteliu*. *Municipium, tribus Sergia*; affected by the Civil War (Caes. B Civ. 1,16–23). *Regio IV* (Plin. HN 3,106). Intersection of the *via Valeria, via Claudia Valeria* and *via Minucia* (It. Ant. 310). Archaeological remains: remains under San Pelino e Pentima; walls, *forum, curia*; thermal baths (CIL IX 3152–54). Traces of two temples, theatre, amphitheatre, *macellum Lucceianum* (CIL IX 3162), cisterns; *campus* (237 × 143 m) outside the city, adjoining *piscina* (51 × 34 m); aqueduct leading from Aternus. Necropolis from the 5th cent. BC; Roman mausolea. Cults: Vetedina, Pelina, Minerva, Venus, Ceres, Magna Mater and Attis, Bellona, Liber Pantheus, Isis, Fons.

N. Colella, Corfinium, 1933; M. A. Sydenham, The Coinage of the Roman Republic, 1952, no. 617–624, 634; G. Paci, in: Epigraphica 42, 1980, 31–64; F. van Wonterghem, Superaequum, 1984; Id., Der Campus, in: ZPE 54, 1984, 195ff.; M. Buonocore, Corfinium, Suppl. It. 3, 1987, 93ff.; EAA 2, Suppl. 2, 1994, 296–298.   G.U.

Corinna (Κόριννα; *Kórinna*). Lyric Greek poet of the 5th cent. BC (?), probably from Tanagra in Boeotia (Paus. 9,22,3). The Suda gives various birthplaces, and has her a pupil of Myrtis and contemporary of → Pindarus, whom she is said to have defeated. Other, rather improbable, biographical anecdotes link her with Pindar. Although the Suda speaks of five bks., and many sources assign C. to the canon of nine lyric poets, her work was not published by the Alexandrians. There is also no surviving reference to her of any kind until the 1st cent. BC (FGE 341). Our knowledge of her work is principally based on the two papyrus fragments PMG 654 and 655. The orthography of both fragments corresponds to that of Boeotian inscriptions from 320–250 BC, which engendered a debate on her actual dates that has not been settled to this day. Assigning her to the 3rd cent. BC by Lobel has found many adherents [1]. The fragments contain Ionic and Glyconic metres, and are composed in a plain, paratactic style; the language in general corresponds to the artificial language of Greek lyricism, with a sprinkling of dialect. The themes of the fragments are local legends: PMG 654 contains two poems, one of them about a song contest between

→ Cithaeron and → Helicon, the other a speech by the seer Acraiphes to the river-god Asopus, in which he explains the disappearance of his nine daughters. PMG 655 is from a → partheneion [2. 102–103], and tells (in the first person and possibly in choral form) of the pleasure occasioned by fine stories (καλὰ Ϝεροῖα, 2) told by the city orator about Cephisus and Orion. This fragment appears to belong to a book entitled 'Tales' (Ϝεροία > εἴρω, ἐρέω? *cf*. PMG 656). Other attested titles are 'Boeotus', 'Seven against Thebes', 'Euonymiae', 'Iolaus', 'Journey home' (Κατάπλους) and possibly 'Orestes' (690 PMG).
→ Women authors

1 E. Lobel, Corinna, in: Hermes 65, 1930, 356–365
2 E. Stehle, Performance and Gender in Ancient Greece, 1997.
Editions: PMG   D. A. Campbell, Greek Lyric 4, 1992, 18–69.
Literature: D. E. Gerber, Greek Lyric Poetry since 1920, in: Lustrum 36, 1994, 152–162   D. L. Page, Corinna, 1953 (repr. 1963).   E.R.

Corinth, Gulf of (Κορινθιακὸς κόλπος; *Korinthiakòs Kólpos*). According to Str. 8,2,3, the Gulf of C. (the eastern section of which is today called Gulf of C., the western section 'Gulf of Patras' [Πατραϊκὸς κόλπος], was held to begin at the estuary of the Achelous or the Evenus on the coast of central Greece and Araxus (today the Cape of the same name Ἄκρα Ἄραξος) on the Peloponnesian coast, at a width of 10 km and a maximum depth of 133 m. The two coastlines approach each other at Antirrhion and Rhion to within *c*. 2 km (ancient reckoning: 5 *stadia*/ 925 m, Str. *loc. cit.*; maximum 7 stadia/1295 m, Thuc. 2,86,4, similarly Agathemerus 24; less than *milia passuum*/1480 m, Plin. HN 4,6; 10 stadia/1850 m, Ps.-Scylax 35) with a threshold depth of 68 m. In the eastern section of the Gulf of C., which was also called the 'Crisaean' (Κρισαῖος κόλπος, *cf*. Thuc. *loc. cit.*) or 'Delphic Gulf' (Δελφικὸς κόλπος, *cf*. Ps.-Scylax, *loc. cit.*), they diverge again, the floor of the Gulf reaching a maximum depth of slightly more than 850 m, to terminate at the → Isthmus after a total distance of 127 km at the west coasts of Boeotia and Megaris in two deep bays, the north-easternmost of which was probably known as the 'Alcyonian Sea' (Ἀλκυονὶς θάλαττα; Alkyonìs). For the distance around the Gulf of C. from the Achelous or the Evenus to Araxus, Str. *loc. cit.* gives 2,330 *stadia* (431,05 km) or 2,230 (412,55 km); from the isthmus to Araxus 1,030 *stadia* (190,55 km). The north coast of the Gulf of C. is a subsiding coastline, with few alluvial plains and many bays. The shoreline was thus not useful as a communications route. The pattern was rather that a number of routes ran from the interior southwards to the shore, to be continued by sea. The southern coast on the contrary is relatively uniform, with several coastal plains and north-extending delta formations; here an east-west route hugged the coast from early times.

Although attempted several times in vain in antiquity (Periander, Demetrius [2] Poliorcetes, Caesar, Caligula, Nero, Herod [16] Atticus), the joining of the Gulf of C. to the Saronic Gulf by means of a canal through the southern end of the Isthmus of Corinth was only accomplished in 1893. However, the link was already accomplished from the 6th cent. BC by means of a slipway for transporting ships (*diolkos*).

PHILIPPSON/KIRSTEN 3, 65–70.   E.O.

Corinthian alloy

Corinthian alloy *Corinthium aes*, according to Plin. HN 34,6–8 an alloy of → copper, → gold and → silver, with an artificial patination that made it gleam like gold. Attempts to identify Corinthian alloy (CA) with so-called 'black gold' and 'niello' are not convincing, as only a lesser sort of CA was dark in colour. The term CA was always associated with legendary invention, names of old masters, and dubious authenticity. Juridical sources (Dig. 32,100,3), however, distinguish CA from plain bronze, referring to costly tableware that was still being produced in the early imperial period (Paus. 2,3,3). *Corinthiarii*, who appear only in the imperial household, were probably custodians of CA rather than its manufacturers.

Greek statuettes and vessels decorated in relief and assigned or faked with the names of old masters were also called CA. In literature from Cicero to the middle imperial period this type of article symbolized extravagant luxury and an immoderate passion for art. Verres is said to have ruined himself on the basis of it; Augustus is mocked for it, Trimalchio caricatured.

E. POTTIER, DS 1,2, 1507–1508; A. MAU, s.v. Corinthium aes, RE 4, 1233–1234; H. JUCKER, Vom Verhältnis der Römer zur bildenden Kunst der Griechen, 1950; I. CALABI LIMENTANI, s.v. Corinthiarius, EAA 2, 838; D.M. JACOBSON, M.P. WEITZMAN, What Was Corinthian Bronze?, in: AJA 96, 1992, 237–247; A.R. GIUMLIA-MAIR, P.T. CRADDOCK, Corinthium aes (Antike Welt 24, Sonderheft), 1993; D.M. JACOBSON, M.P. WEITZMAN, Black Bronze and the Corinthian Alloy, in: CQ 45, 1995, 580–583.   R.N.

Corinthian League

Corinthian League Modern term for the union of Greek states brought into being in 338/7 BC at an assembly in Corinth by → Philippus II of Macedonia after the battle of → Chaeronea (338 BC). The league evidently included all Greek states with the exception of Sparta, and was associated with a treaty establishing a 'general peace' (→ *koinè eirénè*). The members' oath and list of league members have survived in part in the form of an inscription (IG II² 236 = TOD 177; further information in Dem. Or. 17). The customary obligations of the treaty among its co-signatories also included a declaration of loyalty to the kingdom of Philip and his successors. Measures to be taken against infringements of the treaty had to be decided by the members' assembly (*synhédrion*), and carried out under the leadership of the *hègemón* ('leader'; certainly Philip

himself). The figures next to the names of the members are supposed to represent their proportional share in the military arm of the league and in membership of the *synhédrion*. By linking a general peace with the obligation to recognize his leadership and with proportional representation — as is also to be found in → Boeotia — Philip created a procedure for efficient enforcement of the general peace, and at the same time gave his hegemony over the Greeks a form that was more acceptable to them.

The decision of the Corinthian League (CL) to wage war against the Persians and give Philip supreme command was presumably a consequence of the terms of the treaty. After Philip's death (336), Alexander [4] was presumably recognized as his successor *ex officio* in the position of *hègemón*, and entrusted with command in the war against the Persians. The *synhédrion* of the CL condemned Thebes after its revolt against Alexander in 335 (Arr. Anab. 1,9,9). The island states of the Aegean were annexed to the CL (*e.g.* Chios: Syll.3 283 = TOD 192), but not the Greek states in Asia Minor, although they became allies of Alexander. After the revolt of the Greeks in 331/30 (→ Agis [3]), Antipater [1] referred the matter to the *synhédrion*, which in turn referred it on to Alexander (Diod. Sic. 17,73,5f.). It is probably at that time that Sparta was annexed to the CL. In Alexander's absence, a 'general supervisory commission' (*hoi epì tèi koinêi phylakêi tetagménoi*) fulfilled his function as *hègemón* (Dem. Or. 17,15). The CL appears to have disintegrated after Alexander's death, the Hellenic League of 302 BC seeing itself as its renewed form (IG IV² 1,68; → Antigonus [1]).

1 J.A. O. LARSEN, Representative Government in Greek and Roman History, 1955, ch. 3   2 T.T. B. RYDER, Koine Eirene, 1965, ch. 7 and appendix 10.   P.J.R.

Corinthian Standard see → Coinage, standards of

Corinthian vases

Corinthian vases
A. GENERAL B. RESEARCH C. VESSEL FORMS AND ILLUSTRATIONS D. STYLISTIC DEVELOPMENT

A. GENERAL

Painted ceramic wares of supra-regional importance were produced in → Corinth from the Late Geometric period. The high point of Corinthian vase-making, with exports to all regions of the ancient world related to trade and the foundation of Greek cities, was in the 7th and the 1st half of the 6th cent. BC. The technological basis for this success was the development of the regulated three-stage firing process by Corinthian potters.

B. RESEARCH

Following the ground-breaking work of H. PAYNE, distinction is made between → Proto-Corinthian vases, 'transitional style', Early Corinthian (EC), Middle Corinthian (MC) as well as Late Corinthian I and II (LC I,

Vessel shapes in Corinthian pottery

A Amphorae   1 Neck amphora   2 Belly amphora

B Pitchers, Hydriae   1 Trefoil-lipped oinochoe   2 Trefoil-lipped oinochoe   3 Oinochoe, conical shape   4 Hydria   5 Bottle

C Kraters   1 Column krater (EC)   2 Column krater (LC)

D Drinking vessels, Plates   1 Kylix   2 Kylix   3 Plate   4 Lekanis

E Oil and unguent receptacles, Pyxides
1 Alabastron
2 Ring aryballos
3 Aryballos
4 Aryballos
5 Amphoriskos
6 Exaleiptron
7 Pyxis, concave shape
8 Pyxis, convex shape without lid
9 Pyxis, convex shape
10 Pyxis in shape of woman's head

F Figure receptacles   1 Siren   2 Leg   3 Komast   4 Hare   5 Ram

→ Vessel shapes (with ill,); Laconian vase painting (with ill.)

M. HAA.

II) [1. 363–395]. To some extent, the dating of Corinthian vases (CV) is still slightly problematic [1. 429–434], being based primarily on groups of finds from Greek cities in Sicily and lower Italy for which foundation dates have come down to us; finds from other localities are also relevant [1. 675–678]. The most recent research by NEEFT produces the following chronology: EC: 620/615–595; MC: 595–570; LC I: 570–550; LC II: after 550; although on the basis of the finds at Sindos TIVERIOS suggests *c*. 550 as an end date for MC. Attribution of CV to painters and studios has had mixed results, but with AMYX we now have a basis for the study of all aspects of CV.

C. VESSEL FORMS AND ILLUSTRATIONS

The clay of CV is soft, yellowish and occasionally greenish. Misfirings were frequent, the slip usually being burnt to a dull black. Rich use was made of the supplementary colours red and black, used for the first time in Corinth. Outlines are frequently present, primarily for human figures, often in association with black-figure technique [1. 541–543]. Painted vessels are generally small in format, seldom being taller than 30 cm [1. 435]. Especially common are perfume jars (→ Alabastron, → Aryballos [2]), the → pyxis, the → krater, the → oinochoe, and bowls. Pyxides with moulded women's heads, [1. 451–453], the ring aryballos [1. 446] and the flask-shaped vessel with illustrations of women's celebrations [1. 510f.; 653–657] are Corinthian specialities. As in → East Greek pottery, CV too includes many painted vessels in the form of animals, plants and parts of the body [1. 512–533; 2]. Inscriptions are less frequent than in Attic black-figure work, and of especial note is the rarity of signatures (→ Chares [5], → Timonidas). Geometric captions are primarily in the form of mythological names [1. 556–593]; inscribed texts are mostly dedicatory formulae, rarely names [1. 593–600]. In CV the typical and most frequent decoration is the animal frieze, used already in proto-Corinthian and continuing into LC. Of the heroes, Heracles figures frequently, in addition to the Trojan hero-cycle (esp. Achilles, Ajax, Aeneas, Hector); gods are rare, the most common being Artemis, Athena, Hermes and the Dioscuri [1. 617–625]. The most frequent themes from human life are scenes of battle, riders and feasting [1. 646f.]. Interpretation of the 'large-bellied dancers', a common theme from the EC onwards, is a matter of dispute [1. 651f.]. Sporting themes are strikingly rare [1. 647–651].

D. STYLISTIC DEVELOPMENT

Stylistic development in CV is not always easy to define, especially as the proportions of the vessels scarcely change, in contrast to Attic black figure ware. Perfume jars are the most frequent EC painted ware, but the columned crater, in antiquity called the 'Corinthian crater', is also developed (→ Eurytius Crater) [1. 378]. Narrative illustration and animal friezes are typically combined, the lion being the preferred 'beast

of prey' in the friezes (after the Assyrian model); the inscribed rosette is used as ornamentation. The animal figures are more accomplished in the MC than in the EC. The most frequent 'beast of prey' is now the panther; variety is introduced into the background ornamentation, which forms a dense, wallpaper-like pattern. New vase forms are the small amphoriskoi and the convex pyxis. Alongside less carefully executed works (→ Dodwell Painter) there are some of great quality (→ Cavalcade Painter; → Timonidas). In LC I the for the most part carelessly executed animal friezes continue to appear only on pyxides and perfume jars; dotted patterns are popular as background ornamentation. But masterpieces still appear, especially in large vessels such as the Amphiaraus Crater, the → Astarita Crater or the paintings of the → Tydeus Painter. A striking aspect is the increased imitation of Attic black figure ware in pictorial themes (increase in mythological scenes) and vessel forms (adoption of the Attic → lekythos and oinochoe), as well as optical effect (reddish coating over the otherwise yellowish vase surface, corresponding to Attic patterns). In LC II only ornamental vessels and vessels painted in the silhouette technique are still produced. After this, apart from the few high-quality red figure CV, the vases of the 'Sam WIDE group', decorated with outline drawings and used for cult purposes, are particularly to be noted [1. 395].

CV represent one of the most significant vase genres of antiquity, and from the 7th cent. BC onwards exerted a strong influence on other artistic traditions: especially on Attic vases of the 7th and early 6th cents. BC (→ Black-figured vases I.), Boeotian and also Etruscan vase painting (Black-figured vases II.).

→ Geometric vase painting; → Red-figured vase painting

1 AMYX, CVP   2 W. R. BIERS, Mass Production, Standardized Parts, and the Corinthian »Plastic Vase«, in: Hesperia 63, 1994, 509–516.

AMYX, Addenda; H. PAYNE, Necrocorinthia, 1931, 35–209; M. TIVERIOS, Archa. Keramik aus Sindos, in: Makedonia 1986, 70–85.   M.ST.

Corinthian War A war named after the area of military operations around → Corinth; triggered by a border conflict between Locrians and Phocians in 395 BC, and brought to an end by the → King's Peace in 386. Sparta as an ally of the Locrians invaded the Phocians' ally Boeotia, which entered into a military alliance (*symmachia*) with Athens. After the Spartan defeat outside → Haliartus in 395 (death of → Lysander), Corinth and Argos joined the Athenian-Theban *symmachia* (StV II² 225). An allied advance against Laconia in 394 ended with the defeat at the Nemea stream. The Spartan king → Agesilaus [2], recalled from the war against the Persians, won a victory at → Coronea. After the overthrow of Sparta's maritime dominance by the Persian fleet under the Athenian → Conon [1], Persia openly supported the alliance at Corinth. The dispute there developed into a minor war, in which neither Sparta's capture of the harbour at → Lechaeum nor the destruction of a Spartan → *móra* by the Athenians → Iphicrates and → Callias [5] led to a decisive victory. After expelling pro-Spartan aristocrats, Corinth entered into a → *sympoliteia* with Argos. Peace negotiations initiated by Sparta in 393/2 and 391 failed.

In the resumed war, in 390 Sparta gained important successes on land by Agesilaus and by the commanders → Thibron and Teleutias in the Aegean. In 389 Athens sent → Chabrias to Corinth, and → Thrasybulus into the northern Aegean in an attempt to restore Athenian hegemony there. After Thrasybulus' death in 388, → Agyrrhius and Iphicrates continued the war at sea; the Spartans → Gorgopas and Teleutias undertook privateering campaigns from Aegina against the Piraeus and the Attic coast. In 388 → Antalcidas came to an understanding with the Persian king, and by means of his military victories on the Hellespont forced Athens to send ambassadors to → Tiribazus. After the King's Peace, pronounced in 387 and sworn in 386, the cities in Asia Minor, Clazomenae and Cyprus were awarded to the Persians; all other Greek cities were to be autonomous. Athens received Lemnos, Imbros and Scyros. The Boeotian League and the *sympoliteia* of Corinth and Argos were dissolved under pressure from Sparta.

P. Funke, Homónoia und Arché, 1980; E. Meyer, Gesch. des Alt. 5, ⁴1958, 224–269; B. S. Strauss, Athens after the Peloponnesian War, 1986.   W.S.

Corinthium aes see → Corinthian alloy

Corinthus/Corinth (Κόρινθος; *Kórinthos, Corinthus*, the modern Corinth).

I. Position   II. History   III. Structural remains

I. Position

The city lies on the second and third terraces above the coastal plain (40–95 m above sea level), *c.* 2 km from the coast; its original location was presumably on a delta originating from the time *c.* 250,000 years ago when the Gulf of Patra and the Gulf of Corinth still constituted a lake [1]. The city wall enclosing the imposing isolated limestone mass of the fortified Akrokorinthos (575 m) had an outer perimeter of some 12 km (not including the inner fortress wall), to which must be added the two salient walls, 2 to 2.5 km long, to the likewise fortified harbour at → Lechaeum. It has an area of some 600 ha., by far the largest area of a city in Greece; to this must be added the walled-in space between the city and the harbour at Lechaeum, an area half as large again. The territory included the surrounding land to the west, the south and especially the southeast, plus the → Isthmus and the territory south of the → Gerania mountain including the Peiraeum peninsula (nowadays Perachora), taken from Megara in the 6th cent. BC and comprising for the most part Late Tertiary neogene massifs, limestone in the south-east. C. possessed two harbours, Lechaeum on the → Gulf of Corinth and → Cenchreae on the Saronic Gulf. Its outstanding position with regard to communications, and its dominating strategic location at the gateway of all roads from the north to the Peloponnese and at the intersection of east-west maritime routes across the Isthmus, in combination with its magnificent fortress mountain, assured C. great importance throughout antiquity.

II. History
A. Early history and archaic period
B. Classical and Hellenistic period   C. The Roman colony   D. Late antiquity and Byzantine period

A. Early history and archaic period
Although the name C. is pre-Greek, and several prehistoric, especially Neolithic, settlements are known in the close vicinity (with a pronounced interruption of settlement in the Middle and Late Helladic) [2], and prehistoric finds have now also been made within the area of the city [3], the foundation of the historic city appears to belong to the period after the → Doric Migration, and to have originated in Argos. After modest beginnings, a considerable economic and political upturn began in *c.* 725 BC; this is attested archaeologically by the appearance and spread of Proto-Corinthian and Corinthian pottery, historically by the large number of important colonies (Potidaea, Leucas, Corcyra, Anactorium, Ambracia, Apollonia, Epidamnus, Syracuse) [4]. The early strength of C. as a maritime power is emphasized in Thuc. 1,13. C. already appears as a Greek city in Hom. Il. 2,570 (also ibid. 13,664). Political dominance in the early period lay with the Heraclid noble family of the → Bacchiadae, who were overthrown by → Cypselus [2]. The tyranny of Cypselus and his son → Periander (*c.* 620/610–550/540 BC) [5; 6] brought a new period of prosperity with the extension and consolidation of the colonial empire. The overthrow of the tyranny, possibly with the aid of Sparta, was followed by a qualified oligarchy. C. joined the → Peloponnesian League, playing an important role as the only significant naval power, and retaining its independence especially by virtue of good relations with other cities, primarily Athens. Owing to its central location, in 481 BC C. became the assembly point for the Greeks allied in defence against the Persian danger; this alliance is consequently called the → Corinthian League. Large contingents from C. took part in the → Persian Wars, at Artemisium, Salamis, Mycale and Plataeae.

B. Classical and Hellenistic period
The growing power of the Athenians and their expansion to the west presented a severe threat to the existence of C., and in the 'Hellenic War' (458–446) led

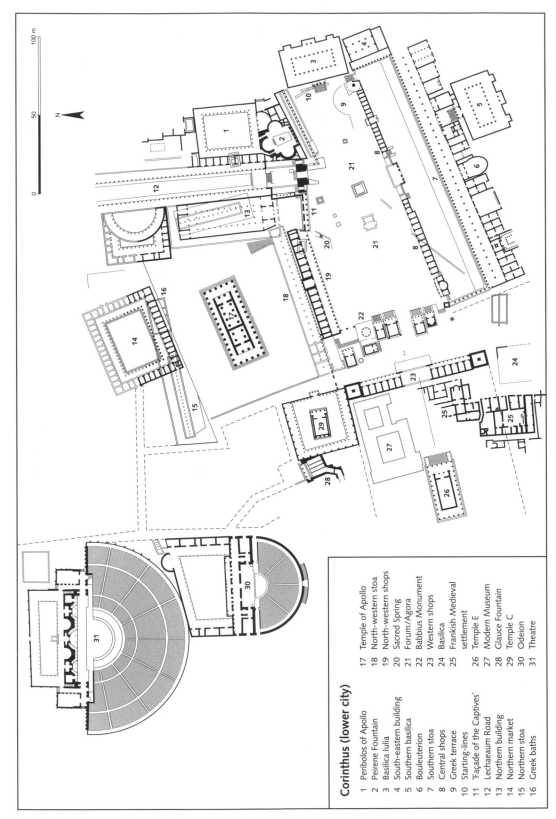

Corinthus (lower city)

1 Peribolos of Apollo
2 Peirene Fountain
3 Basilica Iulia
4 South-eastern building
5 Southern basilica
6 Bouleuterion
7 Southern stoa
8 Central shops
9 Greek terrace
10 Starting-lines
11 'Façade of the Captives'
12 Lechaeaum Road
13 Northern building
14 Northern market
15 Northern stoa
16 Greek baths

17 Temple of Apollo
18 North-western stoa
19 North-western shops
20 Sacred Spring
21 Forum/Agora
22 Babbius Monument
23 Western shops
24 Basilica
25 Frankish Medieval
   settlement
26 Temple E
27 Modern Museum
28 Glauce Fountain
29 Temple C
30 Odeion
31 Theatre

to the first period of hostilities with Athens. The same circumstances led to the Corinthian complaint to Sparta, triggering the → Peloponnesian War, in which C. also suffered serious defeats and losses. Immediately after the war, the atmosphere changed completely. C. repeatedly refused help to Sparta, and in 395 BC joined Athens, Bocotia and Argos in a confederacy against Sparta, leading to the so-called → Corinthian War (395–386). After a bloody democratic revolution in 392 C. lost her independence and entered a → synoikismós with → Argos. In the → King's Peace of 387/6 this union had to be dissolved, and after an aristocratic coup C. allied itself again with Sparta. The intense fighting around C. in connection with the Theban campaigns into the Peloponnese (370–362) under Epaminondas caused C. to withdraw from the Peloponnesian League and to make peace with Thebes; this led to a pronounced economic upturn.

In reminiscence of the league of 480 BC, Philip II again named C. as the seat of his 'League of the Greeks', which was dissolved after the → Lamian War (323/2). From then on C. was under Macedonian occupation, and in the period of the → Diadochi allied itself successively with Polyperchon, Ptolemy I, Cassander and Demetrius [2] Poliorcetes. C. was the lynchpin of Demetrius' son Antigonus [2] Gonatas' rule over the Peloponnese, interrupted briefly by the secession of his nephew Alexander [9]. In 243 BC Aratus [1] succeeded in occupying citadel and city by means of a carefully prepared attack, and C. immediately joined the Achaean Confederacy (Plut. Aratus 18–24; Pol. 2,43,4–6). The conquests of Cleomenes III, of which C. was one, compelled Aratus to cede C. again to Antigonus [3] Doson as the price of an alliance (223/2 BC). After the 2nd Macedonian War C., now free again, joined the Achaean Confederacy (→ Achaeans, with map). C. was the main centre of the final resistance against Rome, and had to pay for that fact with the most terrible catastrophe in its history, complete destruction by the Romans under L. → Mummius in 146 BC. The population was put to death or sold into slavery [7], the territory in part awarded to Sicyon, but in the main adopted as Roman *ager publicus*. But the city was probably not abandoned [8].

C. THE ROMAN COLONY

C. was newly founded by Caesar in 44 BC as the Roman citizen colony *Colonia Laus Iulia Corinthus* [9], and settled with freedmen and veterans. It quickly developed again into one of the most magnificent cities of Greece, and became the seat of the governor of the province of Achaea [10; 11]. A Jewish community and an early Christian community are confirmed by the visit of the Apostle Paul in AD 50/1 [10. 107–118]. Bishops are first firmly attested in the 2nd cent. The Roman emperors promoted C. primarily by buildings; *e.g.* Hadrian with an aqueduct from the valley of the Stymphalus [12]. In AD 267 C. was severely laid waste by the Herulians.   Y.L.

D. LATE ANTIQUITY AND BYZANTINE PERIOD

Thanks to its Pauline tradition and its function as metropolis of the province of Achaea, from the beginning of the 4th cent. AD C. was the ecclesiastical and administrative centre of the Greek mainland. The presence of its bishops is accordingly attested at almost all the important councils (but not that of 325 in Nicaea). Destruction by earthquakes in 365 and 375 as well as by → Alaricus [2] in 395 was followed by large-scale reconstruction projects [13]. Earthquakes (521/2, especially 550/1) and epidemics (542) so weakened the settlement that by the end of the 6th cent. at the latest, in the aftermath of the Avaro-Slav invasion, it appears to have been largely abandoned (residual settlement on the citadel in the 7th cent.). But C. was soon (probably already under → Constans [2]) once again a Byzantine base, and capital of the → theme of Hellas, from the beginning of the 9th cent. the theme of Peloponnesus. Brisk settlement activity began again at this time [14]; though no longer based on the ancient road network, trade flourished (ceramics, glass, silk-weaving). In 1147 Roger II transported the silk-weavers to Sicily. During the 13th and 14th cents. C. came under a succession of Frankish masters, until in 1458 the Turks finally put an end to Byzantine rule in C. For the numerous and important archaeological remains from the Byzantine period see [14 with plan].   E.W.

III. STRUCTURAL REMAINS

Owing to the destruction of 146 BC structural remains in C. are rare. Apart from various sections of the city wall, they comprise primarily the famous pillars of the temple to Apollo (map no. 17) from the last quarter of the 6th cent. BC, on the hill to the north above the market, as well as on the north side of the agora (no. 21) the underground well-house of a sacred spring (no. 20; with an oracular sanctuary), all covered by Roman structures, with many surviving and reused walls, especially those of the large market halls and spring houses.

At the centre of the city is the agora (no. 21): an open space (c. 65 × 165 m) is skirted to the north and south by large pillared halls with shops, workshops and public buildings, forming to the south a magnificent complex on two terraces (laid out in the period of Philip II, c. 340/335 BC). Behind it and to the north, east and south are large basilicas, while the west side is closed off by a row of temples [16]. A broad, straight avenue (no. 12) leads from the harbour at → Lechaeum through a monumental gate structure [17] onto the north side of the agora. As well as a large → basilica (end of the 1st cent. BC) and another market building, this street contains a sanctuary of Apollo (no. 1) and the Peirene spring, last magnificently restored by → Herodes [16] Atticus (no. 2; used as early as the 7th cent. BC). Other temples lie behind a further row of pillared halls behind the west side of the agora; here also the Glauke spring-house (no. 28), cut from the rock and now much dilapidated. To the north-west of the Glauke spring-house an Odeum (no. 30; 1st cent. AD) and a large theatre (no. 31) (constructed in the 5th cent. BC, completely reconstructed at the time of the foundation of the Roman colony, repaired by Hadrian); to the north of this by the city wall the sacred precinct of Asclepius with finds from the 7th cent. BC onwards; also the large Lerna spring-house. On the way out towards the citadel a part of the potters' quarter and remains of the sanctuary of Demeter and Persephone/Kore have been excavated (Paus. 2,4,7) [18].

The best-known structure on the citadel (Acrocorinth) is the 'upper Peirene' spring-house, alongside it the temple of Aphrodite, which is said to have had over 1,000 → hierodules. Further pillared halls, market buildings, thermal baths, living quarters (also Byzantine), including quite large villas and several churches i.a. have been excavated for the most part to the north of the hill with the temple to Apollo. Sources: Str. 8,6,20–23; Paus. 2,1,1–5,4. Inscr.: IG IV, 210–413; CIL III 534–545; 6098–6100; 7268–7277; 13692–13696; 14405a [19]. Coins: HN², 398–405.   Y.L.

1 D. J. W. PIPER et al, Quaternary History of the Gulfs of Patras and Corinth, in: Zschr. für Geomorphologie 34, 1990, 451–458   2 C. BLEGEN, Korakou, a Prehistoric Settlement near Corinth, 1921   3 L. KOSMOPOULOS, The Prehistoric Inhabitation of Corinth 1, 1948   4 C. MORGAN, Corinth, the Corinthian Gulf and Western Greece during the Eighth Century B.C., in: ABSA 83, 1988, 313–338   5 S. I. OOST, Cypselus the Bacchiad, in: CPh 57, 1972, 10–30   6 V. PARKER, Zur griech. und vorderasiat. Chronologie des 6. Jh.v.Chr. unter bes. Berücksichtigung der Kypselidenchronologie, in: Historia 42, 1993, 385–417   7 H. VOLKMANN, Die Massenversklavungen der Einwohner eroberter Städte in der hell.-röm. Zeit, 1961, 30f., 88   8 J. WISEMAN, Corinth and Rome I: 228 B.C.-A.D. 267, in: ANRW II 7.1, 1979, 438–548   9 C.K. WILLIAMS, The Refounding of Corinth, in: S. MACREADY, F. H. THOMPSON (ed.), Roman Architecture in the Greek World, 1987, 26–37   10 D. ENGELS, Roman Corinth, 1990   11 A. J. S. SPAWFORTH, Roman Corinth, in: A.D. RIZAKIS (ed.), Roman Onomastics in the Greek East (Meletemata 21), 1996, 167–182   12 Y.A. LOLOS, The Hadrianic Aqueduct of Corinth, in: Hesperia 66, 1997, 271–314   13 T. E. GREGORY, in: Hesperia 48, 1979, 264–280   14 D. M. METCALF, in: Hesperia 41, 1973, 180–251   15 D. I. PALLAS, s.v. Korinthos, RBK 4, 759–807   16 C. K. WILLIAMS, A Re-evaluation of Temple E and the West End of the Forum of Corinth, in: S. WALKER, A. CAMERON (ed.), The Greek Renaissance in the Roman Empire, BICS Suppl. 55, 1989, 156–162   17 C. M. EDWARDS, The Arch over the Lechaion Road at Corinth and Its Sculpture, in: Hesperia, 63, 1994, 263–308   18 N. BOOKIDIS, R. STROUD, Demeter and Persephone in Ancient Corinth, 1987   19 B. D. MERITT, A. B. WEST, J.H. KENT, Corinth VIII, 1–3 (Greek and Latin inscriptions), 1931–1966.

W. ELLIGER, O. VOLK, s.v. Korinthos, LThK³ 6, 378f.; T. E. GREGORY, s.v. Corinth, ODB 1, 531–533; R. JANIN, s.v. Corinthe, DHGE 13, 876–880; J. KODER, s.v. Korinthos, LMA 5, 1444f. (Lit.); Id., s.v. Morea, LMA 6, 834–836; E. MEYER, s.v. Korinthos, RE Suppl. 12, 514–516; D. I. PALLAS, s.v. Korinthos, RBK 4, 746–811 (bibliography up to 1990); H. S. ROBINSON, s.v. Corinth, PE, 240–243; J.B. SALMON, Wealthy Corinth, 1984; R. SCHEER,

s.v. Korinthos, in: LAUFFER, Griechenland, 338–343; E. WILL, Korinthiaka, 1955; C. K. WILLIAMS, s.v. Corinto, EAA², 301–303; Hesperia (regular reports of American excavations); Corinthian Results of Excavation, 1929ff. (continuing publication).   Y.L. and E.W.

Coriolanus Marcius C., Cn, received the epithet C. for his deeds of heroism in the capture of Corioli in 493 BC (Liv. 2,33,5). The unyielding patrician's proposal to exploit a famine in order to render the plebs submissive led to his banishment in 491, and to his attempt to return home at the head of the Volsci enemy. According to tradition (Liv. 2,39–41; Dion. Hal. Ant. Rom. 8,14–36), his mother Veturia and wife Volumnia persuaded him to turn back before the gates of Rome, and this cost him his life. The historical core of this romantically embroidered heroic tale lies in the threat to Rome's existence posed by the mountain tribes of the Volsci at the beginning of the 5th cent. In the figure of C., oral tradition may have preserved the memory of some 'mercenary leader', as attested in the person of Poplios Valesios on the approximately contemporary → Lapis Satricanus.

A. REICHENBERGER, Die Coriolan-Erzählung, in: E. BURCK (ed.), Wege zu Livius, 1967, 382–391.   W.ED.

Corioli City of the Volsci in *Latium adiectum*, perhaps to be located near Monte Giove. Home city of → Coriolanus; C. is mentioned in connection with the events of 490 BC (Liv. 2,39; 3,71). Ceased to exist in the course of the 5th cent.; no traces left at the time of Pliny (HN 3,69).

S. GSELL, Top., Jahr, 180f.; A. NIBBY, Analisi storico-topographico-antiquaria della carta de'dintorni di Roma 1, 1837, 512f.; NISSEN 2, 631.   G.U.

Corippus, Flavius Cresconius Latin epic poet (6th cent. AD) from Africa. After poetic beginnings in the province he first found recognition with a panegyric → epic, also of historical importance (→ Panegyrics), about the suppression of a revolt of nomadic tribes by Justinian's commander Iohannes Troglita (*Iohannis*, 8 bks. = *Ioh.*); he recited the 1st bk. c. 550 in Carthage. His career as a 'wandering poet' [1] led him to Constantinople, where in 566/8 he presented a panegyric epic on → Iustinus II (*Laudes Iustini*, 4 bks. = *Laud.*). An alleged *panegyricus* to the quaestor and magister Anastasius is merely the *praefatio* to a lost panegyric epic [3. 211ff.]. The library catalogues of Lorsch and Murbach (9th cent.) list three biblical epics by one Cresconius, who may be identical with our C. [4. 371ff.]. In his *Ioh.*, C. adopts narrative structures from the *Aeneid*, but here and in the *Laud.* continues → Claudian's form of the panegyric epic, i.a. with *praefationes* thematizing the recitative situation. In his use of language and his narrative skill, C. shows himself to be the last great practitioner of the Roman epic [2; 6]. His influence survived into the early Middle Ages [7], and his *Laud.* attracted frequent commentaries during the 16th–18th cents. [5]. In spite of several medieval attestations only two MSS are in existence: Trivult. 686, 14th cent. (*Ioh.*); Matrit. 10029, 10th cent. (*Laud.*).

EDITIONS: M. RUIZ AZAGRA, 1581 (*Laud.*); P. MAZZUCCHELLI, 1820 (*Ioh.*); *Ioh.*: J. DIGGLE, F. R. D. GOODYEAR, 1970; M. A. VINCHESI, 1983 (bk. 1 trans., comm.); AV. CAMERON, 1976 (trans., comm.); U. J. STACHE, 1976 (K); S. ANTÈS, 1981; A. RAMÍREZ DE VERGER, 1985.
BIBLIOGRAPHY: 1 A. CAMERON, Wandering Poets, in: Historia 14, 1965, 470–509 2 W. EHLERS, Ep. Kunst in Corippus' *Johannis*, in: Philologus 124, 1980, 109–135 3 H. HOFMANN, Review on: S. ANTÈS, ed. 1981, in: Mnemosyne 40, 1987, 209–219 4 Id., Corippus as a Patristic Author?, in: VChr 43, 1989, 361–377 5 Id., Cornelius van Arckel und sein Corippus-Komm., in: Philologus 134, 1990, 111–138 6 M. LAUSBERG, *Parcere subiectis*: Zur Vergilnachfolge in der *Johannis* des Corippus, in: JbAC 32, 1989, 105–126 7 D. SCHALLER, Frühkarolingische Corippus-Rezeption, in: WS 105, 1992, 173–187.
H.HO.

Coriscus (Κορίσκος; *Korískos*) from Scepsis; a Socratic often mentioned *c.* 375–350 BC alongside → Erastus (Str. 13,1,54); accompanied Plato to Hermias at Assus; recipient of the sixth of Plato's letters. Father of Neleus, to whom Theophrastus bequeathed the body of Aristotle's writings. Stobaeus passes down an apophthegm on death by C. in his old age (Stob. 3,7,53 = T 9 LASSERRE).

F. LASSERRE, De Léodamas de Thasos à Philippe d'Oponte. Témoignages et fragments, 1987.   K.-H.S.

Cormorant *Phalacrocorax carbo* (L.), a dark-feathered, fish-eating, goose-sized member of the web-footed group (*steganopodes*), mentioned in Aristot. Hist. an. 7(8),593b 18–22 as the so-called 'raven' (κόραξ; *kórax*), and as breeding in trees. The *phalacrocorax* ('bald-headed raven') in Plin. HN 10,133, at that time native to the Balearics, used to be identified as the cormorant [1. 196f.], but is nowadays thought to be the hermit ibis or crested ibis (*Comatibis eremita*), now extinct in Europe. A synonym found in Plin. HN 11,130 is *corvus aquaticus*. The Middle Minoan Hagia Triada fresco on Crete shows a (partially destroyed) cormorant (not a pheasant!) being stalked by a (wild)cat [2. vol. 1, 166 fig. 17].

1 LEITNER 2 KELLER.   C.HÜ.

Cornelia
I. REPUBLICAN PERIOD   II. IMPERIAL PERIOD

I. REPUBLICAN PERIOD
[I 1] Younger daughter of P. Cornelius Scipio Africanus and Aemilia Tertia, b. *c.* 190 BC; *c.* 176/5 she married Tiberius → Sempronius Gracchus. Of her 12 children only three survived early childhood: Tiberius, Gaius and Sempronia.

C. is known as 'Mother of the Gracchi' (CIL VI 31610), with whose politics she was already associated in antiquity [1. 108–120; 127; 2. 48–89]. In a partly popular, partly elite tradition, the sources give an uneven picture of C.'s views and influence. She is said to have approved the Gracchi's plans, supported or even pushed them (Plut. Tib. 8,4; Plut. Gaius 4,1–3; 13,2; Diod. Sic. 34,25,2); others speak of a moderating influence, even of a distinct rejection of at least some of the political plans of the younger Gracchus, while avoiding an open break (Plut. Gaius 13,2). This latter tendency is shown in the fragments of C.'s letters handed down by Nepos; doubt has, however, been justifiably cast on their authenticity [1. 120–124]. Ancient sources are almost unanimous, viewing C. as a Roman matron with an exemplary lifestyle [3. 65–70], a tradition that can probably be traced back to her son Gaius [1. 118–120; 127–132], and is still discerned in sources of the imperial period (Tac. Dial. 28,1–3; Val. Max. 4,4;): C. devoted herself entirely to the upbringing of her sons, whose deaths she later bore with the utmost fortitude (Plut. Gaius 19,1–3; Sen. Consolatio ad Helviam 16,6; ad Marciam 16,3); after the death of her husband in 153 she remained 'virtuous' and unmarried; she is said to have 'even' declined a proposal from Ptolemy VIII Euergetes II (Plut. Tib. 1,7). C. was highly cultured (Cic. Brut. 211; Quint. Inst. 1,1,6; Plut. Gaius 13,1), interested in art and sociable (Plut. Gaius 19,1–3), and appears, at least after her move to Misenum, to have led a very independent life within the constraints of the time. A statue with inscription was erected in her honour, probably still in the Republican period [1. 128–131; 2. 66–70].

1 L. BURCKHARDT, J. V. UNGERN-STERNBERG, C., Mutter der Gracchen, in: M. DETTENHOFER, Reine Männersache?, 1994, 97–132 2 B. KRECK, Unt. zur polit. und sozialen Rolle der Frau in der späten Republik, 1975 3 B. V. HESBERG-TONN, Coniunx Carissima, 1983.

[I 2] Daughter of Cornelius Sulla by his first wife Ilia (Plut. Sulla 6). Wife of Q. Pompeius Rufus (*cos.* 88 BC), by whom she had two children: Q. Pompeius Rufus (people's tribune 52) and Pompeia. She was a capable businesswoman, and bought Marius' villa at Misenum for a low price, reselling it later at a substantial profit to Licinius Lucullus (Plut. Marius 34,4).
[I 3] Daughter of L. Cornelius Cinna; married to the young C. Julius → Caesar, by whom she had a daughter Julia. She died *c.* 68 BC (Suet. Iul. 1; 6; Plut. Caesar 1,1; 5,3).
[I 4] Daughter of P. Cornelius Scipio Nasica. After the death of her first husband P. Cornelius Crassus, in 52 BC she married Cn. → Pompeius, whom in 48 she accompanied on his flight to Egypt, where she had to witness his murder. She later returned to Rome (Plut. Pomp. 55,1; 74,1–75,1; 76,1; 80 Luc. 8,577–595a; 637–662).

[I 5] C. Fausta. Daughter of → Sulla; at first married to C. Memmius, then after her divorce from him *c.* 54 BC to T. → Annius [I 14] Milo. She was rumoured to be 'immoral', and to have committed adultery with C.→ Sallustius Crispus (Macrob. Sat. 2,2,9; Gell. NA 17,18). H.S.

II. IMPERIAL PERIOD

[II 1] Wife of C. Norbanus Flaccus, *cos.* 24 BC; daughter of L. Cornelius Balbus (CIL VI 16357; PIR² N 167).

[II 2] Daughter of Scribonia and P. Cornelius (Scipio), *cos. suff.* 35 v.Chr.; her half sister was Augustus' daughter Iulia; married to Paullus Aemilius Lepidus, *cos. suff.* 34; she died in the year of the consulate of her brother P.C. Scipio; Propertius wrote *elegiae* 4,11 on her death (PIR² C 1475) [1. 110f.; 246ff.].

[II 3] From the family of the → Scipiones; wife of L. Volusius Saturninus, *cos. suff.* AD 3; mother of Q.V. Saturninus, *cos. ord.* 56 (Plin. HN 7,62), RAEPSAET-CHARLIER no. 270 [1. 298].

[II 4] Wife of Calvisius [8]; accused under Caligula of having influenced the army in Pannonia, she committed suicide with her husband (Cass. Dio 59,18,4; PIR² C 1479) [3].

[II 5] *Virgo vestalis maxima*, condemned under Domitian for incest, and buried alive (Plin. Ep. 4,11,6–13; Suet. Dom. 8,4; RAEPSAET-CHARLIER nos. 274, 275).

[II 6] C. Cratia. Daughter of Cornelius Fronto [2. 214f.]; married to Aufidius [II 7]; mother of three sons (PIR² G 219; RAEPSAET-CHARLIER no. 282).

[II 7] C. Orestilla. or Orestina. Wife of Calpurnius Piso; taken away from her bridegroom by → Caligula during the wedding ceremony, and banished two years later (Cass. Dio 59,8. 7; Suet. Calig. 25; RAEPSAET-CHARLIER no. 285; [3. 23ff.] *cf.* AE 1992, 186 = CIL VI 41050).

1 SYME, AA   2 MUSTILLI, in: Epigraphica 2, 1940   3 KAJAVA, in: Arctos 18, 1984.   W.E.

Cornelianus

[1] Addressee of Pliny Ep. 6,31, cf. [1]. PIR² C 1301.

1 A.N. SHERWIN-WHITE, Comm. ad loc.

[2] *Ab epistulis Graecis* in the imperial chancellery under Marcus Aurelius and Commodus. Phrynichus dedicated his eclogues to C., and acclaimed him as reviving classical rhetoric (pp. 55, 306, 474–75, 482, 492–93 RUTHERFORD). He can probably not be identified with the C. named in Fronto (ad Am. 1,1; 1,2, *cf.* [1. 29–30]). PIR² C 1303.

1 E. CHAMPLIN, Fronto and Antonine Rome, 1980.

G. W. BOWERSOCK, Greek Sophists in the Roman Empire, 1969, 54–55.

[3] Probably L. Attidius C., probably Italic; *cos. suff.* between AD 180–182 (CIL VIII 10570 = ILS 6870). Died 198 (CIL VI 2004,5; 8). PIR² A 1342; PIR² C 1304.

LEUNISSEN 129, 355, 371.   M.MEI. and ME.STR.

Cornelius Name of one of the oldest and most celebrated Roman patrician families; during the Roman Republic the largest and most extensive *gens*, giving its name to the *tribus Cornelia*. Its patrician branches probably stem from the Maluginenses, frequently attested in the 5th cent. BC (C. [I 57–58]); the sequence was probably as follows: in the 5th cent. the Cossi [I 20–22]; in the 4th cent. the Scipiones [I 65–85], Rufini [I 62] and Lentuli [I 31–56]; from the 3rd cent. the Dolabellae [I 23–29], Sullae [I 87–90], Blasiones [I 8–10], Cethegi [I 11–15] and Merulae [I 60–61]. Membership among the patrician families is dubious in the case of the Cinnae [I 17–19], Mammulae and Sisennae [I 86]. The plebeian branch included the Balbi [I 6–7] and all the Cornelii, who achieved citizenship through Sulla or later (see below, C. [I 1]), *e.g.* the Galli and the Nepotes. The patrician Cornelii celebrated their own feasts (Macrob. Sat. 1,16,7) and tended to bury their dead (Cic. Leg. 2,56f.; Plin. HN 7,187), as demonstrated by the tomb of the Scipios on the *via Appia* in Rome; Sulla (C. [I 90]) was the first to be cremated. The most substantial branch was that of the Lentuli, the most celebrated that of the Scipiones. The family's most celebrated members: P.C. Scipio Africanus ('the Elder Scipio'), C. [I 71]. P.C. Scipio Africanus ('the Younger Scipio'), C. [I 70] L.C. Sulla the *dictator*, C. [I 90].

I. REPUBLICAN PERIOD   II. IMPERIAL PERIOD

I. REPUBLICAN PERIOD

[I 1] Cornelii. Those freed by L.C. [I 90] Sulla, said to be more than 10,000; formerly slaves of the people he proscribed, and given citizenship by him (ILS 871, organized in a college?; Ascon. 75C; App. B Civ. 1,469; 489).

S. TREGGIARI, Roman Freedmen during the Late Republic, 1969, 171.

[I 2] C., C. Quaestor *c.* 71 BC; people's tribune 67. A supporter of Pompey, he introduced several statutory proposals strongly opposed by the conservative wing of the Senate: a prohibition on lending to ambassadors of foreign *nationes*, a stricter regime against corruption, laws to be dispensed exclusively by the popular assembly (accepted in modified form), jurisdiction of the *praetor* to be solely on the basis of his edict. A case of *maiestas* consequently brought against him was set aside in 66 (→ Cominius [I 1]), but proceeded with in 65, on which occasion C. was successfully defended by Cicero. Fragments of the lost speech *Pro Cornelio* and Asconius' commentary represent the primary source for C.

M.T. GRIFFIN, The Tribune C. Cornelius, in: JRS 63, 1973, 196–213.

[I 3] C., C. Roman *eques*, Catilinarian; in 63 BC conspired to murder Cicero, but — probably as a reward for denunciations — remained unpunished (Sall. Catil. 28,1–3; Cic. Sull. 18; 52).

[I 4] C., C. Seer, said to have prophesied the outcome of the battle of Pharsalus, in 48 BC (Gell. NA 15,18).

[I 5] **C. Arvina, P.** Consul 306, defeated the Samnites (Liv. 9,43,1–22). 304 *censor*, 288 *cos. II*.

[I 6] **C. Balbus, L.** The first consul (40 BC) to be a non-citizen by birth. He came from Gades, and received Roman citizenship from Pompey for his services in the battle against Sertorius in 72. He became an *eques* and served under Caesar in 61 as *praef. fabrum*; 60 in Rome he worked to bring about the so-called 1st Triumvirate, and had himself adopted by Theophanes of Mytilene, a friend of Pompey; then he briefly served again with Caesar in Gaul (or Rome?) as *praef. fabr*. In 56 he was accused of illicit presumption of citizenship, and successfully defended by Crassus, Pompey and Cicero (*Pro Balbo*). He subsequently represented Caesar's interests and before the outbreak of the Civil War became with C. → Oppius more or less Caesar's representative in Rome. In 50/49 he tried to win Cicero to Caesar's cause, did not take part in the Civil War, and later applied himself to bringing about reconciliation, especially the pardoning of Cicero. After the death of Caesar he allied himself with Octavian, who in 40 made him *cos. suff.*, certainly for services rendered. He was patron of Gades and Capua and was still alive in 32. He was a friend of Cicero and Varro, and induced → Hirtius to bring out the 8th book of *De bello Gallico* (Hirt. Gall. 8,1) .

NICOLET 2, 853–855.

[I 7] **C. Balbus, L.** (the Younger). Nephew of C. [I 6], like him from Gades and from 72 BC a Roman citizen. From 49 he was with Caesar (often on diplomatic service), 47 in Alexandria, 45 in Spain; 44 quaestor, 43 proquaestor in Hispania ulterior; in 40 he was again a pro-magistrate (propraetor?) in Spain. 21/20 proconsul in Africa (victory over the Garamantes). In 19 he triumphed, the first to do so who had not been born a Roman, and at the same time the last private individual (InscrIt 13,1,87). In 13 in Rome he dedicated a stone theatre built by himself. C. wrote a → Praetexta and was the author of *Exēgētiká* [1]. PIR² C 1331.

1 SCHANZ/HOSIUS I, 141, 146, 351.

[I 8] **C. Blasio, Cn.** Consul 270 (triumph over Rhegium), *censor* 265, *cos. II* 257 (Sicily).

[I 9] **C. Blasio, Cn.** 199–196 BC proconsul with *imperium extra ordinem* in Hispania Citerior (*ovatio*, MRR 1,336), *praetor* 194 (Sicily), ambassador 196 (MRR 3,63).

[I 10] **C. Blasio.** *Praetor* during the 140s (?) BC (SHERK 34). MRR 3,64 (dating).

[I 11] **C. Cethegus, C.** Proconsul in Spain 200 BC (Liv. 31,49,7), 199 aedile, 197 consul (triumph over the Insubres and the Cenomani, MRR 1,332f.); as censor in 194 the first to introduce separate seats for senators at the games (Ascon. 69C); 193 ambassador to Africa. Elogium: InscrIt 13,3, no. 64 [I. 211–219].

1 A. DEGRASSI, Scritti vari di antichità 1, 1962.

[I 12] **C. Cethegus, C.** Catilinarian, senator 63 BC; after Catilina's exit from Rome he remained there as the most radical of the ringleaders, and was to murder Cicero (Cic. Cat. 4,13; Sall. Catil. 43,2–4 with characterization); after a house-search (find of weapons) and incriminations by the Allobroges he was arrested, and on 5 December 63 executed in Tullianum (Sall. Catil. 55,6).

[I 13] **C. Cethegus, M.** The first significant bearer of the name; *flamen* until c. 223 BC, *pontifex* from 213 until his death in 196, aedile 213, *praetor* 211 (Sicily), *censor* 209 (proceeded severely against defeatists and those refusing to serve), 204 consul, 203 proconsul in upper Italy, where he defeated Mago (Liv. 30,18,1–5). Already acclaimed by Ennius (Ann. 304–308 SK., Cic. Brut. 57–59) as an orator (*suaviloquente ore*).

[I 14] **C. Cethegus, P.** As consul in 181 BC with M. Baebius [I 10] Tamphilus enacted the first law against obtaining office by devious means (MRR 1,383f.).

[I 15] **C. Cethegus, P.** As a senator in 88 BC anathematized by Sulla, but later pardoned; in the 70s he played an important role in Roman internal politics as a notorious intriguer (Cic. Clu. 84f.; Parad. 5,40 *et al.*; MRR 3,64).

[I 16] **C. Chrysogonus, L.** → Chrysogonus.

[I 17] **C. Cinna, L.** Consul 127 BC (MRR 1,507).

[I 18] **C. Cinna, L.** the opponent of Sulla; son of C. [I 17]. His early career is unknown; he was *praetor* by 90 BC at the latest. He fought as a legate in the Social War, probably under the command of Cn. Pompeius Strabo (Cic. Font. 43; Liv. Per. 76). Although known as a supporter of Marius, in 88 L.C. [I 90] Sulla tolerated his election to consul for 87 on condition of his sworn undertaking not to touch Sulla's laws. Immediately upon entering office, he attempted against the opposition of his colleague C. → Octavius to circumvent Sulla's laws (naturalization of freedpersons, the franchise for new citizens, return of Marius); he was eventually violently forced out of Rome, and L.C. [I 61] Merula elected (illegally) in his place. Cinna responded by assembling troops and the exiled supporters of Marius around him, and took Rome. Octavius was killed in the process.

The following three years, the so-called *dominatio Cinnae* (Cic. Att. 8,3,6) or the *Cinnanum tempus* (Cic. Dom. 83 *et al.*), were later seen, probably with only partial justification, as a time of naked terror (Cic. Brut. 227: *sine iure fuit et sine ulla dignitate res publica*); largely at the instigation of Marius, many politically prominent opponents of the Cinna-Marius camp were murdered, Sulla's laws rescinded and Sulla himself declared an enemy of the state. After Marius' death in January 86 Cinna ruled virtually alone in Rome. His regime was primarily maintained by the knights and new citizens he favoured, but in general he attempted to stabilize the political and economic order. His continuing occupancy of the consulate 86–84 (86 with Marius, after Marius' death with L. → Valerius Flaccus, 85/84 with Cn. → Papirius Carbo) met with opposition. In 85, in expectation of Sulla's return from the east, Cinna began arming, but early in 84 he was killed by mutinous troops in Ancona. In 85 Caesar married Cinna's daughter Cornelia [3].

E.BADIAN, Waiting for Sulla, in: JRS 52, 1962, 47–61; CHR. BULST, Cinnanum Tempus, in: Historia 13, 1964, 307–337; H.BENNETT, Cinna and his Times, 1923; CHR. MEIER, Res publica amissa, 1966, 229ff.

[I 19] C. Cinna, L. Son of C. [I 18], and like him an opponent of Sulla; brother-in-law of Caesar. After 78 BC with Sertorius in Spain, c. 73 back in Rome; praetor only in 44 through Caesar; he was not one of the conspirators, but behaved so ineptly that at Caesar's funeral the enraged mob confused the people's tribune C. Helvius Cinna with him and killed the tribune (MRR 2,320f.).

[I 20] C. Cossus, A. Military tribune 437 BC, consul 428, consular tribune 426, celebrated for his single combat with king Lars → Tolumnius of the Veientes, whose arms he offered to Jupiter Feretrius as → spolia opima (Liv. 4,19f. et al.); the year of the deed and the position held by C. were already matters of dispute in antiquity (MRR 1,59), but under Augustus acquired internal political significance (M. → Licinius Crassus, cos. 30 BC).

[I 21] C. Cossus, A. As dictator in 385 defeated the Volsci and triumphed (Liv. 6,11–14). He is subsequently said to have quelled the unrest of the plebs by arresting M. → Manlius Capitolinus (Liv. 6,15–16).

[I 22] C. Cossus Arvina, A. 353 and 349 mag. equitum, 343 consul; he was said to have been saved during the 1st Samnite War by the self-sacrifice of P. Decius [I 1] Mus, to have won a victory and triumphed (Liv. 7,32; 34–38 etc.): perhaps all annalistic invention; 332 cos. II, 322 dictator (victory and triumph over the Samnites unhistorical), 320 fetialis.

CORNELII DOLABELLAE
Patrician branch of the Cornelii, attested since the 3rd cent. BC; the cognomen 'small hatchet' derives from dolabra (WALDE/HOFMANN I³, 364; KAJANTO, Cognomina 342).

E.BADIAN, The Dolabellae of the Republic, in: PBSR N.S. 20, 1965, 48–51 (with genealogy).

[I 23] C. Dolabella, Cn. Aedile 165 BC, praetor 162 at the latest, consul 159 (law de ambitu, Liv. Per. 47).

[I 24] C. Dolabella, Cn. Fleet commander to Sulla 83–82 BC (advised against the attack on Rome), consul 81, proconsul in Macedonia 80–77 (MRR 3,65), triumph; subsequently accused of extortion by the young Caesar (Tac. Dial. 34; Vell. Pat. 2,43,3 et al.; [1. 71]); acquitted after being defended by C. Aurelius [I 5] Cotta and Q. Hortensius.

[I 25] C. Dolabella, Cn. Praetor 81 BC, proconsul in Cilicia 80–79; upon his return convicted of extortion, his proquaestor C. Verres having heavily incriminated him [1. 69].

1 ALEXANDER.

[I 26] C. Dolabella, L. Praetor c. 100 BC, governor in Spain 99–98, triumph over the Lusitani (InscrIt 13,1,85).

[I 27] C. Dolabella, P. Consul 283 BC (victory at Lake Vadimo over the Senones and the Etruscans, triumph); ambassador to Pyrrhus 280/79 (MRR 1,188; 192f.).

[I 28] C. Dolabella, P. Praetor 69 or 68 BC, then proconsul of Asia (MRR 2,139).

[I 29] C. Dolabella, C. Probably the son of C. [I 28]; son-in-law of Cicero. He was defended by Cicero in two court cases early on, and in 50 BC himself accused Ap. Claudius [I 24] Pulcher. At this time he took as his second wife Cicero's daughter → Tullia, without Cicero's approval; he divorced her in 46. At first without political ambition, but with a lavish lifestyle, in 49 C. D. joined Caesar and fought alongside him in Greece. Upon his return to Rome C. D. had himself adopted by a plebeian, and in 47 became people's tribune. In the popular tradition, he began to agitate for the relief of debts and the lowering of rents, and (like his model P. Clodius [I 4] Pulcher, to whom he raised a statue, Cic. Att. 11,23,3) engaged in gang warfare with his opponent L. Trebellius, ultimately ended by M. Antonius [I 9], Caesar's deputy in Italy, only at the insistence of the Senate, and only with force. Caesar nevertheless took C. D. along on his African and Spanish campaigns in 47/46, and then against the opposition of C. D.s adversary M. Antonius appointed him cos. suff. for the year 44 and thus his successor in office. After the Ides of March he was confirmed in his consulate by the murderers of Caesar as well as by Antony, and suppressed unrest by the pro-Caesar plebs in Rome. In the redistribution of the provinces in April C. D. was allocated Syria, and in July received a five-year imperium proconsulare. That same autumn he set out on a Parthian campaign, reached Asia at the beginning of 43 and once there had the governor C. Trebonius killed in Smyrna. In February, the Senate therefore declared him an enemy of the state. C. D. meanwhile began armed preparations against Caesar's murderer C. Cassius [I 10], who held Syria, but on the march through Cilicia was encircled in Laodicea by Cassius and had himself killed.

M.H. DETTENHOFER, Perdita Iuventus, 1992.

[I 30] C. Epicadus. Freedman of Sulla, perhaps his librarian; completed Sulla's memoirs and wrote De cognominibus, De metris and probably also an antiquarian work (Suet. Gram. 12; SCHANZ/HOSIUS 1,581).

CORNELII LENTULI
Important branch of the patrician Cornelii, attested from the 2nd half of the 4th cent. BC and far into the imperial period. The cognomen probably does not derive from lens 'lentil' (Plin. HN 18,10), but from the diminutive of lentus 'lethargic' (KAJANTO, Cognomina 249). During the early imperial period the gens usurped the cognomina of other branches of the Cornelii, which had perished (Cossus, Maluginensis, Scipio, see below II).

Genealogies: G. V. SUMNER, The Orators in Cicero's Brutus, 1973, 143; SYME, AA, stemmas XXI and XXII; PIR 2², S. 328 (imperial period).

[I 31] C. Lentulus. (praenomen unclear). 137 BC (?) *Praetor* (?) in Sicily, was defeated by slaves under → Eunus (Flor. 2,7,7); possibly to be identified with C. [I 38].

[I 32] C. Lentulus, Cn. Took part as a military tribune in the battle of Cannae; 212 BC quaestor in Lucania, 205 aedile, 201 consul (command over the fleet at Sicily), 199 *IIIvir coloniae deducendae* to Narnia, 196/95 member of the commission of ten to Greece; augur from before 217 until his death in 184.

[I 33] C. Lentulus, Cn. 161 BC ambassador in Cyrene, 146 consul.

[I 34] C. Lentulus, Cn. Consul 97 BC (MRR 2,6).

[I 35] C. Lentulus, L. The earliest representative of the branch. Consul 327 BC (fought against the Samnites); is supposed in Livy (9,4,7-16) to have counselled capitulation at Caudium in 321 (an invention), *dictator* 320.

[I 36] C. Lentulus, L. In 206 BC received a consular *imperium* in the war with the Carthaginians in Spain, although he had previously held no office (and accordingly in 200 celebrated only an *ovatio*, MRR 1,324); in 205 aedile (?, MRR 3,66) with his brother C. [I 32], but during this year and the next remained in Spain. 199 consul, insignificant campaigns in Upper Italy (until 198). In 196 he went as ambassador to Antiochus in Syria (Pol. 18,49ff.; MRR 1,337).

[I 37] C. Lentulus, L. In 168 BC brought the news of victory from Pydna to Rome; probably identical with the *praetor* of 140, and perhaps with C. [I 38] (MRR 1,501f.).

[I 38] C. Lentulus, L. Consul 130 BC

[I 39] C. Lentulus, L. *Praetor* (year unknown), proconsul (of Asia?) 82 BC (SIG³ 745; MRR 2,68).

[I 40] C. Lentulus, P. *Praetor* 214 BC, *propraetor* in western Sicily until 212; in 201 is supposed to have opposed the Carthaginian peace petition (App. Lib. 62-64).

[I 41] C. Lentulus, P. 172 BC ambassador in Greece, in 171 fought against Perseus; 169 curule aedile (first appearance of African carnivores at the games in Rome, Plin. HN 8,64 etc.); in 168 after the battle of Pydna he was a member of the legation to negotiate with Perseus (Liv. 45,4,7); as *praetor urbanus* in 165 entrusted with the task of recovering illicitly held state lands against compensation, and if necessary buying private land in addition (Cic. Leg. agr. 2,82; Granius Licinius p. 8f. CRINITI). 162 *cos. suff.*, 156 at the head of a legation to the East; *princeps senatus* from 125 (Cic. Div. Caec. 69; Leg. agr. 2,82 *et al.*). As an old man in 121 he took part in the conflict with C. Gracchus and was wounded (Cic. Cat. 4,13; Phil. 8,14 *et al.*).

[I 42] C. Lentulus, Ser. 172 BC ambassador to Greece, 169 *praetor* (Sicily).

[I 43] (C.) Lentulus Batiatus. (or Vatia), C. Owner of a gladiator school in Capua, from which in 73 BC some slaves escaped under the leadership of → Spartacus (Plut. Crass. 8).

[I 44] C. Lentulus Caudinus, L. Consul 275 BC; while his colleague M'. Curius [4] Dentatus defeated Pyrrhus, he fought the Samnites, apparently with success, triumphed and adopted the victor's epithet *Caudinus* (InscrIt 13,1,41; MRR 1,195), which he bequeathed to his sons C. [I 45, 46].

[I 45] C. Lentulus Caudinus, L. Consul 237 BC, censor 236, *princeps senatus* probably 220, *pontifex* before 221, *pontifex maximus* 221-213.

[I 46] C. Lentulus Caudinus, P. Consul 236 BC; triumphed over the Ligurians (InscrIt 13,1,77).

[I 47] C. Lentulus Caudinus, P. Probably the son of C. [I 46]; 210 BC under Scipio in Spain, aedile 209, *praetor* (Sardinia) 203; as *propraetor* in 202 went from there in his ships to Africa. Member of commissions of ten: in 196 to Greece and Asia Minor and in 189-188, again to Asia Minor (MRR 1,363).

[I 48] C. Lentulus Clodianus, Cn. Adopted son of C. [I 34]; in 89 BC fought in the Social War under Cn. Pompeius Strabo (MRR 3,67); mint master (?) in 88 (RRC 345); in 82 returned with Sulla to Rome (Cic. Brut. 308; 311); *praetor* by 75 at the latest; as consul in 72 introduced a law on the validity of Pompey's awards of citizenship (Cic. Balb. 19; 32-33), and proceeded against the provincial administration of Verres. He suffered a heavy defeat against → Spartacus (Sall. Hist. 3,106), but nevertheless in 70 became *censor* with his consular colleague L. Gellius, the two of them expelling 64 senators from the Senate. In 67 Pompey's legate in the war on piracy; in 66 he supported Manilius' law giving command in the East to Pompey (Cic. Leg. Man. 68); patron of Oropus and Temnus (Cic. Flac. 45); a not untalented orator (Cic. Brut. 230; 234).

[I 49] C. Lentulus Clodianus, Cn. Son of C. [I 48]; ambassador in 60 (to Gaul), *praetor* 59 (chairman of *quaestio de maiestate*, MRR 3,67).

[I 50] C. Lentulus Crus, L. An opponent of Caesar. In 61 BC chief accuser in the case against P. Clodius [I 4] Pulcher for sacrilege (Cic. Har. resp. 37 etc.); as *praetor* in 58 he took Cicero's part; in 51 he applied in vain for the priestly position of a *XVvir sacris faciundis*. 49 consul with C. Claudius [I 9] Marcellus. At the outbreak of the Civil War Caesar sought unsuccessfully to draw him to his side. In January he left Rome, and in March went with Pompey to Greece, then to Asia, where he recruited two legions (Caes. B Civ. 3,4,1; also releasing Jews, Ios. Ant. Iud. 14,228 *i. a.*) and overwintered with the other opponents of Caesar in Thessalonica. In 48 as proconsul he took part in the battle of Pharsalus, then fled via Rhodes and Cyprus to Egypt, where he was captured and killed after Pompey (Caes. B Civ. 3,104,3; MRR 2,276).

[I 51] C. Lentulus Lupus, L. Curule aedile 163 BC; in 162-161 ambassador to Greece, *praetor* 159 (SC de Tiburtibus, ILS 19), consul 156, 154 condemned for extortion (Val. Max. 5,9,10); nevertheless 147 *censor*, *XVvir sacris faciundis* in 143, *princeps senatus* from 131 until before 125; after his death mocked for his way of life by the poet → Lucilius in his 1st book of satires. MRR 1,447.

[I 52] C. Lentulus Marcellinus, Cn. Quaestor and mint master in 76 or 75 BC (in Spain?, RRC 393); perhaps 68 people's tribune (?, MRR 3,68); 67 *legatus pro praetore* under Pompey in the war on piracy off the coast of Africa (hence patron of Cyrene, SIG³ 750); 60 *praetor*; *propraetor* in Syria 59–58. 56 consul, coming out as a patron of Cicero, opponent of Clodius (as already in 61); he was an energetic spokesman for the senatorial elite in their vain resistance against Pompey, Caesar and Crassus (Cic. Brut. 247). After his consulate he retired and probably soon died. He was *VIIvir epulonum* and married to → Scribonia, Augustus' first wife.

[I 53] C. Lentulus Niger, L. *Flamen Martialis*, probably before 69 BC (*Cf.* Macrob. Sat. 3,13,11), until his death in 56. *Praetor* by 61; unsuccessful bid for the consulate for 58; in 56 judge in the Sestius case (Cic. Vatin. 25).

[I 54] C. Lentulus Spinther, L. (Allegedly so called owing to his similarity to an actor of the same name, Plin. HN 7,54; Val. Max. 9,14,4), brother of C. [I 50]; follower of Pompey. Quaestor and mint master 74 BC (?, RRC 397 and MRR 3,69); curule aedile 63 (supported Cicero against the Catilinarians), praetor 60; governor in Hispania citerior 59, with the support of Caesar (whom he possibly also had to thank for the pontificate *c.* 60); consul 57 (accomplished Cicero's recall, Cic. Sest. 107 and *passim*, law regarding the transfer of Rome's grain supply to Pompey), proconsul in Cilicia 56–53 (*imperator*, triumph 51); in 49 fought against Caesar, by whom he was captured and pardoned at Corfinium; returned to Pompey. In 48 fought at Pharsalus, was at Rhodes in 47 and subsequently killed, probably at Caesar's behest.

[I 55] C. Lentulus Spinther, P. Son of C. [I 54], from 57 BC *augur*; during the Civil War possibly not an open opponent of Caesar, after the Ides of March joined Caesar's murderers, became quaestor in 44, in 43 served as *proquaestor pro praetore* in Asia (actions against Dolabella, Cic. Fam. 12,14; 15; coinage: RRC 500); 43–42 *legatus* under Cassius (operations against Rhodes and Myra), died soon after Philippi in 42.

[I 56] C. Lentulus Sura, P., the Catilinarian. 81 quaestor, 74 praetor, 71 consul, but in the great purge of the Senate in 70 was expelled from the Senate by the censors because of his lifestyle. In 65/64 he allied himself with Catilina; praetor again in 63, seen as the leader of the Catilinarians in Rome. He attempted to win over a legation from the Allobroges, but was betrayed by them to the consul Cicero and arrested. After a hearing in the Senate on 3 December he had to relinquish his praetorship, and on 5 December on Cicero's orders was executed along with four other conspirators (Sall. Catil. passim).

CORNELII MALUGINENSES

Patrician branch of the Cornelii, particularly prominent in the 5th and 4th cents. BC and attested into the

2nd cent.; the *cognomen* was adopted again by the C. Lentuli during the early imperial period (see C. [II 30]).

Genealogy: MÜNZER, s.v. Cornelius, RE 4, 1290.

[I 57] C. Maluginensis, Ser. Six times consular tribune between 386 BC and 368; *magister equitum* to the *dictator* T. Quinctius 361 (Liv. 7,9,3).

[I 58] C. Maluginensis Uritinus, L. Consul 459 BC (triumph over the Volsci, InscrIt 13,1,67); in 450 his son M. was a member of the college of the *decemviri* (MRR 1,46).

[I 59] C. Merenda, Ser. In 275 BC distinguished himself at the taking of Caudium; consul in 274 (MRR 1,196).

[I 60] C. Merula, L. As *praetor* in 198 BC suppressed a local slave revolt; 194 *triumvir coloniae deducendae* (Tempsa), 193 consul (defeated the Boii at Mutina, but was not permitted a triumph).

[I 61] C. Merula, L. *Flamen Dialis*, praetor by 90 BC, *cos. suff.* 87 for the exiled L.C. [I 18] Cinna; after the return of the Marians laid down that office and the priesthood, which then remained unoccupied for 75 years; committed suicide prior to court proceedings against him (MRR 2,47).

[I 62] C. Rufinus, P. *Cos. I* 290 BC; with his colleague M'. Curius [4] Dentatus brought the Samnite War to a conclusion (triumph), then — before 285 — *dictator*, *cos. II* 277 (conquered Croton); notorious for his greed, in 275 he was expelled from the Senate by the censor Fabricius for the possession of 10 pounds of silver tableware (MRR 1,196).

[I 63] C. Rutilus Cossus, P. Dictator 408 BC, consular tribune 406.

[I 64] C. Scapula, P. Consul 328 BC (Liv. 8,22,1).

CORNELII SCIPIONES

Most celebrated branch of the *gens* (probably going back to the Maluginenses or C. [I 57]); most influential at the time of the Punic Wars. At the end of the Republic it was absorbed by the Cornelii Lentuli, who also revived the *cognomen* (*cf.* C. [I 67]) during the imperial period (see C. [II 32, 33]) [1. 244–253]. Their well-known family tomb was on the *via Appia* in front of the Porta Capena (Cic. Tusc. 1,13), where the bodies were deposited unburnt in sarcophagi in underground chambers (Plin. HN 7,187). It was discovered in 1614, and in 1780 completely uncovered (published by G. B. PIRANESI), the finds (inscriptions, sarcophagi, sculptural decoration) for the most part going to the Vatican museums. The elder Africanus (C. [I 71]) is supposed to have set up a bust of the poet → Ennius there (Cic. Arch. 22; Liv. 38,56,4; Plin. HN 7,114) [2]. Epigraphical *elogia*: ILLRP 309–317; see genealogy and [1, stemma XIX].

1 SYME, AA   2 F. COARELLI, Il sepolcro degli Scipioni a Roma, 1988.

The Cornelii Scipiones and their family relations (3rd/2nd cents. BC)

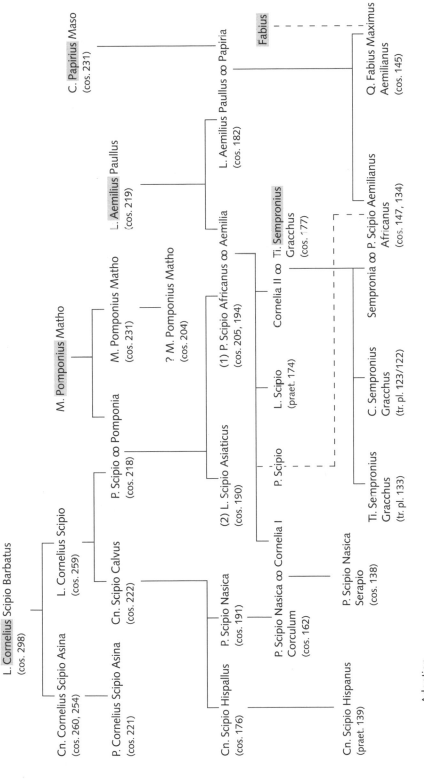

- - - = Adoption

= Gentes

[I 65] **C. Scipio, L.** Aedile before 259 BC, consul 259 (conquest of Aleria on Corsica; took Sardinia with the exception of Olbia, which was courageously defended by the Carthaginians; triumph?); *censor* 258; dedication of the temple of Tempestas in gratitude for the fleet's having been spared. Oldest poetic *elogium* on the Scipio tombs (ILLRP 310, with no mention of the triumph).

[I 66] **C. Scipio, L.** Son of the elder Scipio Africanus (C. [I 71]); in 192 BC captured by Antiochus [5] III, who released him in 190 after according him honourable treatment (details obscure, Liv. 37,34; 36f.). 174 praetor, but in the same year expelled from the Senate by the censors (Liv. 41,27,2).

[I 67] **C. Scipio, P.** By tradition the first bearer of the individual *cognomen*, as he is said to have served as a 'staff' to his blind father (Macrob. Sat. 1,6,26). According to tradition he was consular tribune in 395 BC; all his other offices are uncertain.

[I 68] **C. Scipio, P.** Brother of C. [I 77], he was consul in 218 BC. He was on his way to Spain when he heard of Hannibal's march on Italy; sending the major part of his army on to Spain under his brother, he himself returned to Italy (Pol. 3,49,4). In the autumn of 218 he was defeated and wounded by Hannibal on the Ticinus; with his colleague T. → Sempronius Longus he suffered another heavy defeat on the Trebia (Pol. 3,64–75; Liv. 21,45–56). In 217 he went as proconsul to Spain, where in 211 he fell while fighting the Carthaginians; he was succeeded by his son P.C. [I 71] Africanus.

[I 69] **C. Scipio, P.** Eldest son of P.C. [I 71] Scipio Africanus; *augur* in 180 BC, before 168 he adopted the son of L. Aemilius [I 32] Paullus, later to become the Younger Africanus [I 70]. Owing to a weak constitution he was not politically active, but did write speeches and a book on Greek history (Cic. Brut. 77 [1]). Inscription ILLRP 311 on the Scipiones tomb does not relate to him.

1 SCHANZ/HOSIUS 1,176.

[I 70] **C. Scipio Aemilianus Africanus (Numantinus), P.** b. 185/84 BC the second son of L. Aemilius [I 32] Paullus; adopted as a child by the son of the Elder Africanus (C. [I 71]), P.C. [I 69] Scipio. In 168 took part in the battle of Pydna (Plut. Aem. 22) under the command of his (birth-) father, and from the spoils received the library of king → Perseus (Plut. Aem. 28). Back in Rome, he formed a friendship with → Polybius, who became his mentor (famous account of their first meeting and characterization of the young Scipio in Pol. 31,23–30). In 151 he fought as military tribune in Spain under L. → Licinius Lucullus, and won the *corona muralis* (Vell. Pat. 1,12,4). In 150 he was sent to Africa to requisition elephants for the Spanish theatre of war, while there renewing the patronal relationship established by the elder Africanus with the Numidian king Massinissa. An attempt to mediate between Numidians and Carthaginians failed. 149/48 served as military tribune under M'. → Manilius in Africa, and again

achieved the highest military distinctions (*corona graminea*, Plin. HN 22,6–13). In 148 he returned to Rome in order to have himself elected aedile, but at the urging of the people and eventually with the agreement of the Senate, who exempted him from the rules of the *cursus honorum*, was elected consul for 147 and made expressly responsible for the war against Carthage. In early 146, against prolonged and determined resistance, his troops stormed the city. Carthage was utterly destroyed, and a curse placed on any resettlement. The inhabitants were sold into slavery; the treasures plundered by the Carthaginians from Sicily and Lower Italy were returned (Cic. Verr. passim; Syll.3 677). By means of a Senate commission, Africa was organized as a Roman province (Africa). Scipio held lavish games, celebrated a brilliant triumph in Rome, and like his grandfather was honoured with the name Africanus.

Probably during the years 144/3 [1. 491–495] Scipio undertook an embassy to the Greek East aimed at the settling of disputes and the combating of piracy, first to Egypt then via Rhodes to Syria, and as far as Babylon and Ecbatana on the frontier with the Seleucids and Parthians (Lucil. 465); his return took him via Pergamum to Greece. His companion was the philosopher → Panaetius (Cic. Acad. 2,5).

In 142 Scipio became *censor* with L. Mummius (restoration of the *pons Aemilius* and embellishment of the Capitol). The anecdote that Scipio altered the text of the censors' closing prayer, praying no longer for the expansion of the Empire but only for its preservation (Val. Max. 4,1,10a), is unhistorical. In 137 he supported the law of the people's tribune L. Cassius [I 17] Ravilla, extending the secret ballot in the people's courts. In 136 he prevented acceptance of the peace negotiated by Scipio's brother-in-law Tib. → Sempronius Gracchus and concluded by C. → Hostilius Mancinus with the Numantians. This hurt Gracchus, and in part forms the basis for Scipio's later resistance to the Gracchan reforms. In 134 Scipio was again made consul, the ban on iteration being set aside, and took over command in Spain. Despite a lack of support from Rome (use of volunteers and his own clients in the army, App. Ib. 363–365), he started the siege of Numantia, which in 132 was starved into capitulation, whereupon he triumphed in Rome and received (unofficially) the epithet Numantinus. He justified the murder of Tib. Gracchus and also in 131 prevented C. → Papirius Carbo from lifting the ban on iteration and continuation for the people's tribunate (Cic. Lael. 96; Liv. Per. 59). In addition, by means of a resolution of the Senate, he deprived the Gracchan agrarian commission of its power of decision over the division of state land in the hands of allies, transferring it to the consuls, who were hostile to the Gracchi. Scipio thereby made himself highly unpopular among the supporters of reform; when in 129 he was found dead at his home from unknown causes, suspicion was immediately cast on the followers of the Gracchi or even his own wife Sempronia, the Gracchi's sister. His burial was arranged by his nephews Q.

→ Fabius Maximus and Q. Aelius [I 16] Tubero; the funeral oration was written by C. → Laelius. The place of burial is unknown.

There is no doubt that Scipio had cultural interests — he was a patron of Terence (Suet. Vit. Ter. 1; 3, *cf.* Ter. Ad. prol. 13–21) and Lucilius (594 MARX) — and an extensive grounding in Greek culture, but this did not make him a philhellene or cause him to neglect the interests of Roman power. Polybius, the main source for his life (bks. 31–39), and from whom later sources (especially Appian) draw, stylizes him as a sensitive politician who was already aware of the transience of Roman power (especially Pol. 38,21–22); later tradition, especially Cicero in *De re publica*, where Scipio is the main speaker, expanded this picture in an unhistorical way to surround Scipio with a fictive circle of humanely and conservatively inclined Roman friends, the so-called 'Scipionic Circle' [2]. Fragmentary speeches: ORF I⁴, 122–134.

1 H. B. MATTINGLY, Scipio Aemilianus' Eastern Embassy, in: CQ N.S. 36, 1986, 491–495 2 H. STRASBURGER, Der 'Scipionenkreis', in: Hermes 94, 1966, 60–72.

A. E. ASTIN, Scipio Aemilianus, 1967; J.-L. FERRARY, Phil-hellénisme et impérialisme, 1988; CAH 8, ²1989, Index s.v.

[I 71] C. Scipio Africanus, P. Son of [I 68], b. 236 BC; took part in the battles of Ticinus 218 and Cannae 216 against the Carthaginians (Liv. 21,46,7ff.; 22,53). In 213 he was aedile, and in 210 a consular *imperium* was conferred on him after the death in Spain of his father and uncle C. [I 77], although he had previously been neither a praetor nor a consul, and he went to Spain. In 209 he captured Carthago Nova (the modern Cartagena; here supposedly the first elevation of a Roman commander to *imperator* by acclamation, Pol. 10,40), in 208 north of the Baetis (Guadalquivir) defeated → Hasdrubal Barkas, who escaped to the north. In 206 at Ilipa (north of Seville) he defeated → Mago and Hasdrubal son of Gescon, bringing about the collapse of Carthaginian power in Spain. After quelling a mutiny among his troops he went to Africa, there meeting → Syphax and → Massinissa and winning over the Numidians. Elected consul for 205 he wanted to take the war into Africa, and this was allowed after considerable resistance by the Senate (Liv. 28,40–45). He first took Locri in southern Italy, his defence of the scandalous behaviour of his legate there, Q. → Pleminius, and alleged unmilitary comportment temporarily presented a danger to his own standing (Liv. 29,6–9; 16–22). In 204 he landed on African soil at Utica, in 203 joined Massinissa and defeated Hasdrubal and Syphax, the latter being taken prisoner. After an armistice and peace negotiations with the Carthaginians had failed, and Hannibal had returned from Italy, in 202 came the decisive battle of Zama, in which Hannibal was defeated (Pol. 15,5–16; Liv. 30,29–35). A peace treaty having been concluded, Scipio triumphed in Rome and was honoured with the name Africanus (Pol. 16,23; Liv. 30,45,6f. *et al.*).

Scipio's successes soon led to resistance among the Roman nobility, led by M. Porcius → Cato. Thus, although in 199 becoming censor and *princeps senatus* (repeated in 194 and 189), he did not appear prominently. In 194 he wanted to be given supreme command as consul II against Antiochus [5] III, but he failed in the Senate (Liv. 34,43). He proceeded in 190 to support his brother C. [I 72] as legate in the undertaking against Antiochus. Although he took no part in the battle of Magnesia in 190, he negotiated the peace with the king (Liv. 37,45,11–19). The two brothers had scarcely returned to Rome when accusations were made that they had misappropriated part of the settlement payment or been bribed by the king (Pol. 23,14; Liv. 38,50–53 [according to Valerius Antias]; Gell. NA 4,18; 6,19 [from Cornelius Nepos]). The factual details and chronology of the disputes they had with their opponents, which were to last for years, are not entirely understood, but an early aspect was Scipio's accusation before the Senate. In 187, in spite of his support, his brother was condemned for corruption, but on the initiative of Tib. → Sempronius Gracchus the fine was not applied. Another legal action against Scipio followed in 184, but was abandoned when he retired to his estate at Liternum in Campania, where he died and was buried in 183.

Scipio was married to the daughter of L. Aemilius [I 32] Paullus; his elder daughter Cornelia married P.C. [I 83] Scipio Nasica; the younger Cornelia became the wife of Tib. Sempronius Gracchus and mother of the two people's tribunes Tib. and C. → Sempronius Gracchus.

H. H. SCULLARD, Scipio Africanus, 1970; Id., Roman Politics 220–150 B.C., ²1973, 290–303 (trials).

[I 72] C. Scipio Asiagenes, L. Younger brother of P.C. [I 71] Scipio Africanus. He took part as legate in his brother's campaigns in Spain, Africa and Sicily (207–202 BC), and in 193 was praetor in Sicily. In 191 he fought under M'. Acilius [I 10] Glabrio at Thermopylae. In 190 as consul he was given supreme command against Antiochus [5] III (Liv. 37,1,7–10); his brother accompanied him as legate, and was seen as holding actual responsibility for the campaign. After the conclusion of peace in 189 C. returned to Rome, triumphed in 188 and adopted the cognomen Asiagenes (or Asiagenus; Asiaticus is not attested until the Augustan period). In 187 his family's opponents instituted proceedings against him, accusing him of having been bribed by Antiochus, and his political career came to an end; in 184, in connection with the trial of his brother, his horse of state was taken away from him by the censors M. Porcius → Cato and L. → Valerius Flaccus.

J. P. V. D. BALSDON, L. Cornelius Scipio, in: Historia 21, 1972, 224–234.

[I 73] C. Scipio Asiagenes, L. Grandson of [I 72]; probably mint master 106 BC (RRC 311), *augur* from 88, praetor by 86; in 85 fought as proconsul in Macedonia (MRR 3,71). As consul in 83 he had to surrender to L.C. [I 90] Sulla after his army deserted to Sulla (MRR 2,62). After another attempt at resistance he was proscribed by Sulla but escaped to Massilia (MRR 2,65 n. 1).

[I 74] C. Scipio Asina, Cn. (Invented explanation of the 2nd cognomen in Macrob. Sat. 1,6,29). Consul 260 BC, taken by the Carthaginians at Lipara, later exchanged; consul II 254 (successes in Sicily, capture of Panormus); triumph 253 (MRR 1,210).

[I 75] C. Scipio Asina, P. Probably the son of C. [I 74]; consul 221 (subjugation of the Istri), *interrex* 217.

[I 76] C. Scipio Barbatus, L. The earliest bearer of the name buried in the ancestral tomb; possibly seen as the family's progenitor (peperino sarcophagus, now in the Vatican: NASH 2, fig. 1131). Aedile 301?, consul 298, fought in Etruria; according to the (later?) *elogium* (ILLRP 309) 'he took Taurasia and Cisauna, Samnium, and subjected all Lucania'. Propraetor 295, censor 280 (?), *pontifex maximus* from before 304 until after 280.

E. T. SALMON, Samnium and the Samnites, 1967, 260f.; R. WACHTER, Altlat. Inschr., 1987, 301–341.

[I 77] C. Scipio Calvus, Cn. Brother of C. [I 68]; 222 BC consul. When in 218 Hannibal succeeded in crossing the Rhône, S.C. was sent on by his brother to Spain, in order to hinder the arrival of Carthaginian reinforcements. At first he fought there alone, then from 217 as proconsul very successfully with his brother, until in 211 first his brother, then he himself was defeated and killed by the Carthaginians (Liv. 25, 34–36). He was succeeded by his nephew P.C. [I 71] Scipio Africanus.

J. BRISCOE, in: CAH 8, ²1989, 56–59.

[I 78] C. Scipio Hispallus, Cn. Son of C. [I 77]; *pontifex* 199 BC, *praetor* 179, consul 176, died the same year (InscrIt 13,1,49; Liv. 41,15f.).

[I 79] C. Scipio Hispanus, Cn. Son of C. [I 78], as praetor in 139 BC expelled Chaldaeans and Jews from Rome (Val. Max. 1,3,3). *Elogium*: ILLRP 316.

[I 80] C. Scipio Maluginensis M. Praetor 176; did not go to his province, and because of this was rebuked by the censors (Liv 41,15,10; 27,2).

[I 81] C. Scipio Nasica, P. Father of C. [I 83]; in 204 BC brought the → Mater Magna from Ostia to Rome (Liv. 29,14,8ff.); 194 *praetor* in Hispania Citerior; as consul in 191 defeated the Boii and triumphed (Liv. 36,38–40); in 189 and 184 he applied in vain for the censorate; in 181 as *IIIvir coloniae deducendae* he participated in the founding of Aquileia (Liv. 39,55,6; 40,34,3).

[I 82] C. Scipio Nasica, P. Praetor 93 BC, married to Licinia, daughter of the orator L. → Licinius Crassus; his son of the same name was adopted by Q. Caecilius [I 31] *c.* 64.

[I 83] C. Scipio Nasica Corculum, P. Son of C. [I 81]; 168/67 BC took part under L. Aemilius [I 32] Paullus in the war against Perseus (his account of his own exploits as a source for Plut. Aem. 15–22). 165 praetor; 162

consul, but owing to a religious error in the elections had to abdicate along with his colleague (InscrIt 13,1,51). As censor in 159 he set up Rome's first water clock (Plin. HN 7,115), and had unauthorized statues removed from the Forum (Plin. HN 34,30). As *cos. II* in 155 he subjected the Delmatae and triumphed (Liv. Per. 47). In 154 he prevented a permanent theatre from being built in Rome (Liv. Per. 48). He vigorously advocated clemency for Carthage. In 150 he organized the resistance against → Andriscus in Greece. 150 *pontifex maximus*, 147 and 142 *princeps senatus*. Known also as an orator and for his legal expertise (Cic. Brut. 79).

M. GELZER, KS 2, 1963, 39–79.

[I 84] C. Scipio Nasica Serapio, P. Son of C. [I 83]; *praetor* by 141 BC (defeat by the Scordisci ?, MRR 3,72); in 138 as consul detained briefly by the people's tribunes for disregard of their rights. When in 133 Ti. → Sempronius Gracchus sought to force his re-election as people's tribune, and the incumbent consul P. → Mucius Scaevola did not intervene, Scipio on his own authority called on the Senate to follow him for the 'salvation of the state', and led the Senate opposition and their followers against Ti. Gracchus, who was killed in the commotion (Rhet. Her. 4,68; Liv. Per. 58; Plut. Ti. Gracch. 19f. *et al.*). Afterwards, to escape the displeasure of the people over the death of Gracchus, Scipio led a legation to Asia, and died in Pergamum in 132. *Pontifex maximus* from 141(?) to 132 (Plut. Ti. Gracch. 21).

[I 85] C.Scipio Nasica Serapio, P. Son of C. [I 84]; praetor by 114 BC, consul 111; died in office (MRR 1,540).

[I 86] C. Sisenna, L. Praetor 78 BC; the historian → Sisenna.

CORNELII SULLAE

The family is attested since the 3rd cent. BC; it disappeared in the 1st cent. AD with C. [II 60] (*cos.* 52). The cognomen Sulla is probably of Etruscan origin [1.106], according to ancient tradition a reference to red facial spots (Plut. Sulla 2,1), or by family tradition an abbreviated form of 'Sibyl' (Macrob. Sat. 1,17,27; → C. [I 88]).

1 KAJANTO, Cognomina

Genealogy: MÜNZER, s.v. Cornelii, RE 4, 1515; PIR 2², 362.

[I 87] C. Sulla, Faustus. Son of the dictator C. [I 90] and Caecilia [I 7] Metella; b. before 86 BC; his praenomen and that of his twin sister Fausta was said to symbolize the good fortune of his father. He was a follower of → Pompeius and betrothed to the latter's daughter → Pompeia (Suet. Iul. 27,1; Plut. Pomp. 47,4). As military tribune under Pompey in 63 he stormed the Temple in Jerusalem, in 60 gave magnificent games in honour of his father (Cass. Dio 37,51,4); he became *augur* before 57 (Cass. Dio 39,17,2); in 56 his coinage (RRC 426) celebrated his father and Pompey; quaestor 54; in 52 he received the commission to rebuild the Curia Hostilia (Cass. Dio 40,50,2f.). During the Civil War in 49–47 as *proquaestor pro praetore* he was on Pompey's side, escaped from the battles of Pharsalus (48) and Thapsus (46), was then captured and killed by P. → Sittius (Bell. Afr. 95).

[I 88] C. Sulla, P. Praetor 212 BC; was first to hold the *ludi Apollinares* (after a probably manipulated prophecy from the Sibylline Books) (Liv. 25,12,3–15; 27,23,5).

[I 89] C. Sulla, P. As a relative of the dictator he enriched himself by the proscriptions (Cic. Off. 2,29). In 65 BC he was *consul designatus* with P. Autronius [I 2] Paetus, but accused *de ambitu* by the son of the failed candidate L. → Manlius Torquatus; as a result neither of the winning candidates was able to take up his post, and they were both expelled from the Senate (Cic. Sull. 11,49f.; Sall. Catil. 18 *et al.*). He retired to Naples (Cic. Sull. 17,74), and is said to have participated in the so-called 1st Catilinarian conspiracy (Cic. Sull. 67 *et al.*). In 62 he was again accused *de vi* by L. Manlius Torquatus because of his associations with Catilina, and defended and acquitted by Q. → Hortensius and Cicero, who was deeply in debt to C. (Gell. NA 12,12,2f.). In 57 his house served as headquarters for P. Clodius [I 4] in his struggle against T. Annius [I 14] Milo (Cic. Att. 4,3,3). C. was on Caesar's side in the Civil War, and in 48 defended the camp at Dyrrhachium against the Pompeians (Caes. B Civ. 3,51ff.). At Pharsalus he commanded the right wing of the Caesarian forces (Caes. B Civ. 3,89,2; 99,4; App. B Civ. 2,317). He was able to enrich himself again from the sale of the property of Caesar's ostracized opponents (Cic. Off. 2,29; Fam. 15,19,3). His death was not regretted (Cic. Fam. 9,10,3; 15,17,2).

D. H. BERRY (ed.), M.T. Cicero: Pro P. Sulla oratio, 1996.
K.-L.E.

[I 90] C. Sulla Felix, L. b. 138 BC, of an old patrician family of only moderate means, which had not been politically prominent since the Samnite wars (→ Cornelius [I 62] Rufinus). After a dissolute youth, an inheritance from his stepmother enabled him to embark on a career befitting his station. Elected quaestor in 107, he fought successfully under consul → Marius as leader of an equestrian troop in the Numidian war. In that campaign, skilful diplomacy enabled him to persuade king → Bocchus [1] to deliver up his son-in-law → Jugurtha thus effectively bringing the war to an end (Sall. Iug. 102–113). In 104 and 103 he served as legate or as military tribune under Marius in the war against the Germanic tribes in Gaul; in 102, probably with the approval of Marius, he transferred to Q. → Lutatius Catulus in Upper Italy. In spite of initial lack of success against the Cimbri, in 101 at Vercellae he contributed significantly to Marius' victory. But his attempt to have himself elected praetor for 98, bypassing the office of aedile, failed. It was not until 97 that he attained the praetorship by bribery (for dates *cf.* [4]). In 96 on behalf of the Senate as proconsul in Cilicia he installed Ariobarzanes [3] as king of Cappadocia, advanced as far as the Euphrates and initiated the first diplomatic contacts between Rome and the Parthians; while he was there, a Chaldaean seer is supposed to have prophesied a great future for him (Plut. Sulla 5). After his return (probably in 92) an accusation of extortion came to nothing, because the Senate wished to use Sulla against Marius. This is also indicated by the group of statues of the delivery of Jugurtha to Sulla, erected on the Capitol in 91 by Bocchus and by will of the Senate, and thus characterizing Sulla as the victor in the Numidian War [3. 114–121]. A serious rift with Marius was prevented by the start of the → Social War, in which Sulla as legate again demonstrated his military abilities, following the example of his forefathers in taking on the war against the Samnites (App. B Civ. 1,51).

With the support of the Metelli he was elected consul for 88, allied himself with powerful families (he married as his 4th wife Caecilia [7] Metella, the widow of M. Aemilius [I 37] Scaurus, while his son married the daughter of his co-consul Q.→ Pompeius Rufus), and as the leading exponent of senatorial policy was entrusted with the war against Mithridates. The people's tribune P.→ Sulpicius Rufus countered this realignment of forces with a plan to incorporate new citizens in Italy into all the 35 Roman tribes, in order to create a new political base. The consuls' attempt to prevent this by using religious pretexts to impose a suspension of business (→ *iustitium*) failed; Sulla withdrew to join his army at Nola. There he received the news that the execution of the war against Mithridates had been transferred to Marius. When Sulla in a supposedly conciliatory speech indicated that another army would be going into wealthy Asia, the soldiers demanded a march on Rome, whereupon all the officers with the exception of one quaestor (probably L. → Licinius Lucullus) refused to obey. Rome was taken against vigorous opposition, opponents of Sulla declared enemies of the state, Sulpicius killed, his laws revoked and his followers hunted down, Marius managing to escape to Africa. The laws enacted at that time under military pressure (App. B Civ. 1,59,266f.: the Senate's assent to legal bills presented by the tribunes, legislation only via the → *comitia centuriata*, enlargement of the Senate) are not mere foreshadowings of later laws of the *dictator* Sulla; there is also mention of a law regarding colonization (Liv. epit. 77) and a law on debt. Under pressure from his followers, Sulla sent his army to Nola and permitted the election of consuls for the year 87. His declining popularity was demonstrated by the election of his adversary, L. Cornelius [I 18] Cinna, and the failure of his attempt to transfer the army of proconsul Cn. Pompeius Strabo to his colleague in office Q. Pompeius Rufus. Sulla contented himself with an oath from Cinna not to undertake any hostile action, and crossed over to Greece,where troops belonging to Mithridates were already present.

Sulla's strategy is scarcely fathomable. He seems to have wanted to spare his army, and at the same time enrich his troops in order to forge himself a compliant instrument to use in his struggle against the regime of Cinna. For, although Mithridates in the so-called 'Asian Vespers' had had some 80,000 Romans and Italians killed, Sulla failed to rush against him; he sent back Q. → Braetius Sura, legate of the governor of Macedonia, who had already achieved successes against the king's commander Archelaus [4]. On the other hand he allowed the army sent by Cinna and the Senate under consul L. → Valerius Flaccus to march unhindered against the king. When this army, under C. → Flavius Fimbria, nevertheless defeated Mithridates and confined him in Pitane, Sulla's fleet under Lucullus knowingly allowed him to escape by sea. Sulla, who in the meantime had taken the Piraeus and Athens and defeated the king's forces in two clashes in Boeotia (86), did not force a conclusive battle on Mithridates, and granted him a favourable peace at Dardanus (85): obliged to surrender his conquests and pay 2,000 talents, he remained unpunished and in possession of his empire, even gaining the status of a Roman ally (App. Mith. 56–58). But from the cities of Asia Sulla demanded 20,000 talents and high payments to his soldiers.

In early 83 Sulla, who while still in Asia had broken off all dealings with the Roman Senate after the death of Cinna (84), crossed over to Brundisium in a state of open rebellion, and was immediately joined by political friends (Q. Caecilius [I 31] Metellus; M. → Licinius Crassus), former enemies (P. Cornelius [I 15] Cethegus) and defectors (L. → Marcius Philippus; C. → Verres with the war-chest of consul Cn. → Papirius Carbo; Cn.→ Pompeius with three legions of his father's veterans). Although, to mollify the hostile mood in Italy, Sulla respected Cinna's citizenship laws, he needed more than a year to assert his authority with battles on the Tifata mountain (83), at Sacriportus (summer 82) and finally before Rome at the Porta Collina (1 November 82).

In undisputed possession of Rome, Sulla set out to regulate the Republic he had contributed to ruin. Given the fact that the constitution rested on the *mos maiorum* and on precedent with a flexibility familiar to him since youth, his measures based on the formal use of traditional institutions can be seen as legal, and therefore Sulla may be regarded to this day as the 'last Republican' [8], or as a statesman seriously concerned about the Republican constitution [7]. The Senate had declared his actions as consul and proconsul (88–82) to be in accordance with the law, and his appointment as *dictator* by means of a *lex Valeria* enacted by the *interrex* L. → Valerius Flaccus still operated within the framework of the constitution. The vague description of the function of the *dictator* (*rei publicae constituendae* = 'establishment of the state') could legitimize any measure (see [12]), even the → proscriptions, which by the use of lists of those who could be killed with impunity turned indiscriminate murder into organized massacre. In all, 4,700 mainly rich people fell victim (Val. Max. 9,2,1), among them 40 senators and 1,600 *eques* (App. B Civ. 1,95,442). Their possessions were confis-

cated and for the most part sold at a discount to friends of Sulla (→ Chrysogonus); their sons and grandsons were declared unfit for public office. This last measure of 'hereditary punishment', entirely alien to Republican law, almost leads one to conclude that Sulla's laws passed by the *comitia centuriata* in 81 were also and primarily designed to ensure the security of Sulla himself (*cf.* [13] and [6. 256]).

The body of laws displays three aims: the strengthening of the Senate, the weakening of all subsidiary seats of power (people's tribunate, people, magistrates) and the comprehensive protection of the 'system' for its beneficiaries: in the Roman public assembly the 10,000 freed slaves (Cornelii) of those who had been proscribed, and the veterans settled in confiscated sections of Italian cities. Of central significance was the enlargement of the Senate from 300 (but effectively c. 150) members to 600, mainly from the Italian equestrian class and owing their lives, their Senate seats, or both, to Sulla. To this Senate he transferred 1. control over all political and some criminal offences in what were now seven jury courts (→ *quaestiones*), 2. heightened supervision over governors in the provinces, whose administration he additionally regulated in detail by a *lex de repetundis*, 3. control over legislation by subjecting the proposals of the people's tribunes to the consent of the Senate. By this measure, the restriction of the people's tribunes' right of veto and their exclusion from further office, he sidelined the tribunate as a political authority, just as he had used the *quaestiones* to distance the people from the judicial process related to political crime. Tightening the rules relating to careers in public office, which were now obliged to run from the quaestorship via the praetorship to the consulate, with minimum age requirements and restrictions with respect to iteration (→ *cursus honorum*), he raised the number of quaestors to 20 and decreed their automatic entry into the Senate, thus depriving the censors (whom he did not remove) of their influence over its make-up. In order to avoid long-term military commands abroad, the praetors, whose number he raised to eight, and the consuls were to go to the provinces determined by the Senate once their particular year of office was ended: a rule that was already broken in Sulla's lifetime, and had to fail as the number of provinces increased.

Enjoying the support of 'his' Senate and the veterans, Sulla retired as *dictator* probably in the year 80 (for the date [10. 74f.]; 81 is proposed by [11. 205]), supposedly laying himself open to any charge, and in 80 as consul with Metellus Pius formally rejoined the ranks of the nobility. Once his term in office was ended he retired to Puteoli as *privatus*, still keeping a political ear to the ground, and died there in 78 from an already long-standing illness.

A conclusive assessment of Sulla the person and his achievement is scarcely possible, as the main sources, Appian and Plutarch, depend strongly on Sulla's (lost) autobiography [2. 401; 3.], Livy and the post-Livyan tradition base themselves on Cornelius Sisenna's favourable portrayal, and the picture provided by Cicero is strongly subjective [5]. In spite of his marked arrogance and superstitious belief in his good fortune (*fortuna, felicitas*; he was easily led by prophecies and dreams, from 81 bore the name 'Felix', was portrayed as 'darling of Venus' — Epaphroditos — and named his children Faustus and Fausta), Sulla probably never aspired to lifetime dictatorship or monarchy, but wanted to secure for himself an eminent position within the wider framework of a republican order. Fear of another civil war ensured that his constitution survived for a while, even if his political heirs (especially → Pompeius) in 75 and 70 reinstated the rights of the people's tribunes [9]. He may well have solved the immediate, pressing political problem at home, provision for the veterans, but he did not achieve any lasting legal settlement, so that the militarization of politics continued. In foreign politics, Sulla further destabilized the precarious situation in the East; for his mild treatment of Mithridates and ruinous plundering of Asia Minor reinforced the king's lust for expansion and exacerbated the piracy problem. In fighting successfully against both of these, Pompey attained a position of prominence that led to his conflict with Caesar, the next Civil War, and finally to the fall of the Republic.

1 E.BADIAN, Lucius Sulla, 1970   2 Id., s.v. Sulla, OCD
³1996, 400f.   3 H.BEHR, Die Selbstdarstellung Sullas, 1993   4 T.C.BRENNAN, Sulla's Career in the Nineties, in: Chiron 22, 1992, 103–158   5 H.DIEHL, Sulla und seine Zeit im Urteil Ciceros, 1988   6 U.HACKL, Senat und Magistratur in Rom.., 1982   7 TH.HANTOS, Res publica constituta, 1988   8 A.KEAVENEY, Sulla, the Last Republican, 1982   9 U.LAFFI, Il mito di Sulla, in: Athenaeum 45, 1967, 177–213, 255–277   10 MRR 3, 1986, 73–76
11 R.SEALEY, Sulla, in: CAH 9, ²1994, 165–207
12 R.WITTMANN, Res publica recuperata, in: D.NÖRR, D.SIMON (ed.), Gedächtnisschrift für W. Kunkel, 1984, 563–582   13 D.J.WOOLLISCROFT, Sulla's Motives, in: Liverpool Classical Monthly 13/3, 1988, 35–39.   W.ED.

II. IMPERIAL PERIOD

[II 1] Bishop in Rome AD 251–253. Owing to his forbearance towards those lapsed Christians who under → Decius had observed the sacrifices, an anti-bishop → Novatianus was elected (CSEL 3/2, Epist. 44–52). Banished in 252; later revered as a → martyr.

P.I.KAUFMAN, Church, Book, and Bishop. Conflict and Authority in early Latin Christianity, 1996, esp. 53f.; B.MONDIN, s.v. Cornelius, Dizionario Enciclopedico dei Papi, 1995, 24f.   C.F.

[II 2] Prosecutor of Mamercus Aemilius Scaurus in AD 34; not a senator. probably in that same year banished to an island (Tac. Ann. 6,29,3f.; 30,1).
[II 3] P.C. Anullinus. Senator from Iliberris in Baetica. His long career brought him the suffect consulate *c.* 175, the consular governorship of Germania superior probably at the end of the reign of Marcus Aurelius and the proconsulate in Africa in AD 193. Took part in the Civil Wars at the side of Septimius Severus; *praef. urbi*

and *cos. II* 199 (CIL II 2073 = 5506 = ILS 1139 = II² 5, 623); close friend of Septimius Severus [1. 71f.; 2. vol. 1, 99ff.; 3; 4].
[II 4] P.C. Anullinus. Son of C. [II 3]. Patrician. *Cos. ord.* 216; *salius Palatinus* and *augur* (PIR² C 1323).
[II 5] Ser. C. Cethegus. *Cos. ord.* in AD 24. probably proconsul in Africa at the end of Tiberius' reign (CIL VIII 23264; PIR² C 1336) [5. 115ff.].
[II 6] L.C. Cinna. Quaestor in 44 BC with Dolabella in Asia; went over to Mark Antony; *cos. suff.* 32 BC; SCHEID [6. 23ff.] him the report in Sen. Benef. 4,30 and Clem. 1,9. *Frater Arvalis* (PIR² C 1338 concerns him. C. [II 7] was according to SCHEID his younger brother; elsewhere regarded as his son. Either the son of Pompey's daughter or married to her [7. 46ff.].
[II 7] Cn. C. Cinna Magnus. Related to Pompey, *cf.* C. [II 6]. Whether he or C. [II 6] was spared by Octavian is a matter of dispute (cf. C. [II 6]). Alleged conspiracy against Augustus (Sen. Clem. 1,9; Cass. Dio 55,14ff.) [7. 266]. *Cos. ord.* AD 5. His estate went to Augustus (Sen. Clem. 1,9,12; PIR² C 1339).

1 ECK, Statthalter   2 CABALLOS, Senadores   3 ALFÖLDY, in: Fundberichte Baden-Württemberg 12, 1987, 305ff.; 14, 1989, 289ff.   4 B.E.THOMASSON, Fasti Africani, 1996   5 VOGEL-WEIDEMANN   6 SCHEID, Recrutement   7 SYME, AA 46f.

[II 8] Sex. C. Clemens. Son of one Sex., *tribus Palatina*, from Caesarea in Mauretania. *Cos. suff.* between *c.* 161 and 169, governor of the Tres Daciae *c.* 171/2 (CIL VIII 9365 = ILS 1099) [1. 103ff.].
[II 9] Cn. Pinarius C. Clemens. Perhaps from Spain; admitted to the Senate under Nero. *Cos. suff.* perhaps in AD 70. Legate in the army of Upper Germany *c.* 72–74; → *ornamenta triumphalia* for successes in the *agri Decumates* on the right bank of the Rhine (*cf.* CIL XIII 9082 = ILS 5832). Buried at Hispellum (CIL XI 5271 = ILS 997) [2. 35–37; 3. Vol. 1, 102f.].
[II 10] C. Dolabella. Close friend of Octavian; in 30 BC he was in close contact with Cleopatra, and informed her that she would be included in the triumphal procession in Rome (Plut. Ant. 84,1). Possibly mentioned in Quint. Inst. 6,79 as Augustus' close friend (PIR² C 1345).
[II 11] Cn. C. Dolabella. Probably the grandson of C. [II 12]. Related to → Galba, and for this reason friends of Galba advised him to adopt Dolabella (Plut. Galba 23). → Otho banished him to Aquinum (Tac. Hist. 1,88,1). After the death of Otho he left his place of banishment, and Plancius Varus denounced him to → Vitellius, who had him killed (PIR² C 1347 [4. 231 A. 506].
[II 12] P.C. Dolabella. Son of C. [II 10]. Patrician. *Cos. ord.* AD 10 (CIL VI 1384). Consular governor of Illyricum Superius = Dalmatia under Augustus and Tiberius until *c.* 20 [5. I 89]; his troops kept the peace at the time of Augustus' death (Vell. Pat. 2,125,5). Proconsul of Africa 23/24; he defeated → Tacfarinas definitely, but Tiberius refused him the triumphal insignia (Tac. Ann. 4,23–26). In AD 27 in the Senate he accused

Quinctilius Varus, with whom he was related; he often presented bills in the Senate designed to provide for more effective administration in the provinces, along lines favoured by Tiberius (PIR² C 1348) [6. 85ff.].

[II 13] Ser. C. Dolabella Metilianus Pompeius Marcellus. Son of C. [II 14]. Patrician. His career is contained in CIL IX 3154 = ILS 1049. *Cos. suff.* in AD 113, (PIR² C 1350 [7. 48, 108; 8. 107].

[II 14] Ser. C. Dolabella Petronianus. *Cos. ord.* in AD 86. Son of C. [II 11]. PIR² C 1351; [7. 44].

[II 15] M.C. Fronto. *Cos. suff.*142; → Fronto

[II 16] C. Fuscus. Of senatorial origins, he embarked on an equestrian career. In AD 68 he brought his home town over to → Galba's side [9. Vol. 4, 128f.]. Procurator in Illyricum; friendship with Vespasian; the Ravenna fleet after defecting from → Vitellius chose him as its prefect (Tac. Hist. 3,12). Praetorian prefect under Domitian; in Juv. 4,112 portrayed as a member of Domitian's *consilium*. In 86/87 commanded an army against the Dacians, which was annihilated by them (PIR² C 1365 [10. 46ff., 53ff.]).

[II 17] C.C. Gallicanus. Proconsul of Baetica 79/80 (AE 1962, 288). Legate of Lugdunensis in 83, *cos. suff.* 84. Trajan transferred to him the task of setting up the alimentary institution in *regio* VIII (PIR² C 1367).

1 PISO 2 ECK, Statthalter 3 CABALLOS Senadores 4 W.ECK, Senatoren, 1970 5 THOMASSON 6 VOGEL-WEIDEMANN 7 VIDMANN FO² 8 W.ECK, RE Suppl. 14 9 SYME, RP 10 K.STROBEL, Die Donaukriege Domitians, 1989. W.E.

[II 18] C. Gallus. Creator of the Roman love elegy, b. 69/68 BC (Hier. Chron. Ab Abr. 1990; for his birthplace: [4. 6–12]). He rose from modest circumstances (Suet. Aug. 66,1) as a friend of → Augustus (Prob. Verg. Ecl. praef. p. 328,2 HAGEN) and → Asinius Pollio (Cic. Fam. 10,32,5); thus he is supposed to have engaged himself for Virgil's farm (Prob.). He commanded successfully in the Alexandrine war (Dio Cass. 51,9), and in 30 BC became first prefect of Egypt (Suet., ibid.). Owing to extreme self-aggrandizement in word and image (Dio Cass. 53,23; *cf.* CIL III 14147,5 [7]) as well as imprudent remarks (Ov. Tr. 2,446) he fell into disfavour with Augustus and, threatened with a trial, in 27 (Hier.) or 26 (Dio Cass.), took his own life.

Probably in 45 B.C. (according to Cic. Tusc. 3,45; *cf.* [13. 216–218]) he published a hexameter poem after Euphorion (Serv. Ecl. 6,72; Verg. Ecl. 10,50) on the 'Grynian grove' ([4. 77–83; 10. 43–46] *et al.* suppose it to be a part of *Amores*, but cf. Serv. Ecl. 10,1), to which Virgil pays tribute in the dedication to his 6th Eclogue (V. 64–73). Four books of elegies, *Amores*, are to the actress Cytheris (under the name *Lycoris*); Gallus began them under Caesar [1. 151ff.; 13. 213ff.], and with them founded the specifically Roman genre of the → elegy (Ov. Tr. 4,10,53; *cf.* especially [6]): a papyrus [1] has confirmed that Gallus portrayed himself as servant of a *domina*, and saw his poetry as a tool of courtship [13. 227ff.]. One elegy, in which he compared himself with Milanion as a model of obedience (*obsequium*), can still be traced in Virgil's 10th Eclogue (cf. Serv. Ecl. 10,46) and Prop. 1,1 and 1,8 A [*cf.* especially 10; 5; 14]. Parthenius wrote his mythological Ἐρωτικὰ παθήματα (*Erōtikà pathēmata*) for Gallus.

→ Virgil is supposed to have removed *laudes Galli* from Georgics 4 (Serv. Ecl. 10,1; Georg. 4,1). → Propertius pays tribute to the dead poet (2,34,91f.); Ovid is bolder (Am. 3,9,63f.); → Quintilian thinks less of him (Inst. 10,1,93: *durior Gallus*). During the Renaissance verses were attributed falsely to him [12. 1349f.]. He became an object of expert interest again especially through [11] and sensational finds of inscriptions (e.g. on the obelisk in front of St. Peter's) and a papyrus [1; 7; 13; 3]. In spite of his fate, Gallus has not yet been discovered as a subject of poetry; he is the eponymous hero only in a novel that serves as an introduction into Roman private life [2].

1 R.D. ANDERSON, P.J. PARSONS, R.G.M. NISBET, Elegiacs by Gallus from Qasr Ibrim, in: JRS 69, 1979, 125–155 2 W.A. BECKER, Gallus, (1838) ³1863 3 J. BLÄNSDORF, Der Gallus-Papyrus — eine Fälschung?, in: ZPE 67, 1987, 43–50 (against F.BRUNHÖLZL, in: CodMan 10, 1984, 33–40) 4 J.-P. BOUCHER, C.C.G., 1966 5 G.B.CONTE, Il genere e i suoi confini, 1980, 11–43 6 F.JACOBY, Zur Entstehung der röm. Elegie, in: RhM 60, 1905, 38–105 7 L.KOENEN, D.B. THOMPSON, Gallus as Triptolemos on the Tazza Farnese, in: Bulletin of the American Society of Papyrologists 21,1984, 111–156 8 G.E. MANZONI, Foroiuliensis poeta, 1995 9 L.NICASTRI, Cornelius Gallus e l'elegia ellenistico-romana, 1984 10 D.O. ROSS, Backgrounds to Augustan poetry, 1975 11 F. SKUTSCH, Aus Vergils Frühzeit, 1901 12 A. STEIN, F.SKUTSCH, s.v. Cornelius 164; in: RE 4,1, 1342–1350 13 W. STROH, Die Ursprünge der röm. Liebeselegie, in: Poetica 15, 1983, 205–246 14 Id., in: Tredici secoli di elegia latina, 1989, 53–62 15 G.GRIMM, in: JDAI 85, 1970, 158–170 (on a possible portrait bust). W.STR.

[II 19] C. Labeo. Author of works on religion, such *De diis Penatibus*, *De diis animalibus*, 'On the oracle of Clarian Apollo'. Christian authors such as Arnobius and Augustine polemicize against him. 3rd rather than 2nd cent. (PIR² C 1373; *testimonia* and fragments collected by [1]).

[II 20] C. Laco. Equestrian *assessor* on Galba's staff in Hispania Tarraconensis; as Galba's praetorian prefect he had great influence. Banished after Galba's death; killed on the orders of Otho (PIR² C 1374).

[II 21] (C.) Latinianus. Financial procurator of Moesia inferior in 105; praesidial procurator of Raetia until 116, relieved that same year ([2]; RMD III 155). Father of C. [II 22].

H. WOLFF, Ein neues Militärdiplom aus dem Straubinger Vicus vom 16. August 116 n.Chr. (in print).

[II 22] L.C. Latinianus. Son of C. [II 21]. Praetorian governor of Pannonia inferior [3. Vol. 1, 112], consular legate of Pannonia superior in AD 126 [4. 74ff.]; proconsul of Asia towards the end of Hadrian's reign (SEG

35, 1365 = AE 1986, 671). Dig. 48,5,28,6 relates to him.

[II 23] Imperator Caesar Ulpius C. Laelianus Augustus. → Laelianus

[II 24] Cn. C. Lentulus. Son of one L. *Cos. ord.* 18 BC (PIR² C 1378) [5. 286ff.].

[II 25] Cn. C. Lentulus Augur. Son of one Cn. *Cos. ord.* 14 BC. Augustus' legate in battles on the Danube, perhaps *c.* 10–6 BC; for his successes he received the *ornamenta triumphalia* (Tac. Ann. 4,44,1; for dates [5. 290ff.; 6. Vol. 6, 435ff.]. *Procos. Asiae* 2/1 BC [3. vol. 1, 207]. Member of the college of → augurs and *arvales*. In AD 14 he accompanied Drusus to Dalmatia to suppress the mutinies of the legions. Under Tiberius frequently active in the Senate, sensitive to the wishes of the Princeps. In 24 AD emerged he safely from a trial for *maiestas*; died in 25. The great fortune he had obtained through Augustus reverted to the Princeps, as frequently happened in the case of → *liberalitates* (Tac. Ann. 4,44,1; Suet. Tib. 49,1; Sen. Ben. 2,27,1. PIR² C 1379). On his fortune [7. vol. 1, 475ff.].

[II 26] Cossus C. Lentulus. *Cos. ord.* 1 BC. As proconsul of Africa for two years *c.* AD 6–8 he defeated the Gaetules. For this he received the *ornamenta triumphalia* and the victor's name Gaetulicus. Member of the *XVviri sacris faciundis* (IRT 301); city prefect *c.* 33–36; close friend of Tiberius (PIR² C 1381) [5. 297ff.]. His sons C. [II 27] and [II 29].

[II 27] Cossus C. Lentulus. Son of C. [II 28] *Cos. ord.* 25; his son of the same name *cos. ord.* 60. Probably legate of the army of Upper Germany between 25 and 30 ([8. 8f.]; PIR² C 1381).

[II 28] L. C. Lentulus. *Cos. ord.* 3 BC; *flamen Martialis*. Whether he was proconsul of Africa is uncertain, and derived only from Inst. 4,25 (PIR² C 1384 [9. 249ff.; 10]).

[II 29] Cn. C. Lentulus Gaetulicus. Son of C. [II 26], brother of C. [II 27]. Praetor *peregrinus* 23, *cos. ord.* 26; XV*vir sacris faciundis* (EOS I 603ff.). Commander of the army of Upper Germany for 10 years from *c.* 29–39 (Tac. Ann. 6,30,2f.; *cf.* [11. 127ff.]). Although related by marriage to Seianus and accused by Abudius Ruso, nothing happened to him. Under Caligula probably involved in a *putsch* against the ruler, or so the official version goes (CIL VI 2029d= 32346h [12. 210f.; 8. 10ff.]. Married to Apronia, whose father was legate of the army of Lower Germany *c.* 28–34. Wrote occasional poetry and erotic epigrams (PIR² C 1390). His son was Cn. C. Lentulus Maluginensis, *cos. suff.* 55 (PIR² C 1391).

[II 30] Ser. C. Lentulus Maluginensis. *Cos. suff.* AD 10. Although *flamen Dialis*, in 22 he asked to be admitted to the ballot for the proconsulate of Asia; but this was refused (Tac. Ann. 3,58f.). Died in 23. His sister was married to Seius Strabo, Seianus' father [5. 297].

[II 31] P.C. Lentulus Marcellinus. Son of one P.; *cos. ord.* 18 BC (PIR² C 1396 [5. 287]).

[II 32] P.C. Lentulus Scipio. *Cos. suff.* AD 2 (PIR² C 1397 [5. 252, 297f.]).

[II 33] P.C. Lentulus Scipio. Son of C. [II 32]. *Praetor aerarii* in AD 15; legate of the *legio IX Hispana*, with whom in Africa 21–23 he took part in the actions against Tacfarinas. *Cos. suff.* 24. Proconsul of Asia under Claudius, probably 41/42 (EA 6, 1985, 17ff.). Married to Poppaea Sabina, about whom he expressed himself diplomatically in the Senate in AD 47 (Tac. Ann. 11,4; PIR² C 1398). His son was C. [II 49].

[II 34] C. Lupus. Proconsul of Crete-Cyrene under Tiberius; *cos. suff.* 42. Although *amicus* to Claudius, killed by him at the instigation of Suillius Rufus (PIR² C 1400).

[II 35] C.C. Minicianus. *Eques* from Bergomum, friend of Pliny; one of the first known *curatores rei publicae* (CIL V 5126 = ILS 2722; PIR² C 1406).

[II 36] M.C. Nigrinus Curatius Maternus. *Eques* from Liria in Tarraconensis. Admitted to the Senate by Vespasian; governor of Aquitania; *cos. suff.* 83 (*cf.* CIL XIV 4725); consular legate to Moesia, then to Moesia inferior *c.* 85–89; distinguished himself in the wars on the Danube; 95–97 legate to Syria, where he was a member of a faction opposed to Nerva (Plin. Ep. 9; 13,10f.). Relieved of his post, he retired back to Liria (CIL II² 14, 124; *cf.* 125–127 [12. 139ff.; 13 Vol. 1, 105f.]).

[II 37] P.C. Orestinus. Son of P.C. Scipio [II 47]. *Comes* to Tiberius or Germanicus (AE 1992, 186); probably the father of Cornelia [II 7] (AE 1992, 186=CIL VI 41050).

[II 38] A.C. Palma Frontonianus. *Cos. ord.* in 99, which leads us to conclude that he was closely associated with Trajan. Consular legate to Hispania Citerior *c.* 101, and roughly 104/5–108 to Syria. From there in 105/106 he annexed Arabia as a new praetorian province; for this he received the triumphal insignia and a bronze statue on the Forum Augusti (Cass. Dio 68,16,2); whether ILS 1023 is to be ascribed to him appears uncertain. 109 *cos. ord.* II. At the end of Trajan's reign suspected of aspiring to imperial power. In the first months of Hadrian's rule he was executed by resolution of the Senate; the grounds for his condemnation are unclear (PIR² C 1412 [14. Vol. 4, 297ff.]).

[II 39] Sex. Subrius Dexter C. Priscus. On the full name [15. 154]. *Cos. suff.* probably in AD 104. Took part in the case against Varenus Rufus (Plin. Ep. 5,20,7). Proconsul of Asia 120/121. Plin. addressed Epist. 3,21 on the death of Martial to him. One of his ancestors was perhaps Q.C. Priscus, legate to Galatia under Tiberius (AE 1981, 827). On the Cornelii Prisci [16. 92ff.].

1 P. Mastandrea, Cornelio Labeone, un neoplatonico latino, 1979   2 Fink, Military Records on Pap. no. 63 II 26   3 Thomasson   4 W. Eck, M. Roxan, in: FS H. Lieb, 1995   5 Syme, AA   6 Id., RP   7 P. A. Gianfrotta, in: EOS   8 Eck, Statthalter   9 E. Champlin, in: ZPE 62, 1986   10 B. E. Thomasson, Fasti Africani, 1996   11 D. Krömer, in: ZPE 28, 1978   12 Scheid, Recrutement   13 K.-H. Schwarte, in: BJ 179, 1979   14 Caballos, Senadores   15 W. Eck, in: Chiron 13, 1983   16 Id., in: Epigraphica 41, 1979.

[II 41] **Cn. Arrius C. Proculus.** Praetorian governor of Lycia-Pamphylia c. 138–140, *cos. suff.* 145 (PIR² C 1422).

[II 42] **Q.C. Proculus.** On the full name PIR² C 1423 [1. 106ff.]. *Cos. suff* 146; *procos. Asiae* probably 161/162 [2. 216].

[II 43] **Cn. C. Pulcher.** *Eques* from Epidaurus. Procurator of Epirus under Trajan; under Hadrian *iuridicus* in Egypt. Knew Plutarch and Epictetus (PIR² C 1424) [3. vol. 1, 178f.; 4. Vol. 4, 26f.].

[II 44] **L.C. Pusio.** His career known up to legionary command (c. 54–56 [5. 149ff.]). *Cos. suff.* at the beginning of Vespasian's reign [1. Vol. 1, 108f.].

[II 45] **L.C. Pusio Annius Messala.** Son of C. [II 44]. *Cos. suff.* 90; *septemvir epulonum*, proconsul of Africa c. 103/104 [1. Vol. 1, 110f.].

[II 46] **Q.C. Quadratus.** Brother of C. [II 15]. *Cos. suff.* 147 (PIR² C 1426 [6. 51]).

[II 47] **Sex. C. Repentinus.** *Eques* who progressed from *advocatus fisci* via various offices in Rome to become praetorian prefect under Antoninus Pius and Marcus Aurelius; he eventually received the rank of a *clarissimus vir* (PIR² C 1428 [7. 43ff.]). His son probably C. Repentinus, senator. Married Didia Clara, daughter of Didius Iulianus. When the latter briefly took power in 193 he appointed Repentinus *praef. urbi* (EOS 2, 730). PIR² C 1472.

[II 48] **P.C. Scipio.** Quaestor in Achaea AD 1 or 2. (AE 1967, 458 [8. 252]). Perhaps identical with him the senator of the same name who achieved the rank of praetorian proconsul (AE 1992, 186).

[II 49] **P.C. Scipio Asiaticus.** Son of C. [II 33]. *Cos. suff.* 68. He probably received the *cognomen* Asiaticus in reminiscence of the victory over Antiochus III. There is no question of his having been born during his father's proconsulate in Asia (*cf.* C. [II 33]). PIR² C 1440.

[II 50] **P.C. (Scipio) Salvidienus Orfitus.** Patrician. On his kinship [9. 199ff.]. Quaestor to Claudius; *cos. ord.* 51; *procos. Africae* probably 62/3 (IRT 341). Accused in the Senate by Aquilius Regulus and executed (PIR² C 1444; [10]).

[II 51] **Ser. C. Scipio Salvidienus Orfitus.** Son of C. [II 50]. *Cos. suff.* perhaps before 82. According to Suet. Dom. 10,2, executed as *molitor rerum novarum* (PIR² C 1445).

[II 52] **Ser. C. Scipio Salvidienus Orfitus.** Son of C. [II 51]; *cos. ord.* 110; *praef. urbi* under Hadrian and Antoninus Pius (PIR²C 1446; [11]).

[II 53] **Ser. C. Scipio Salvidienus Orfitus.** Son of C. [II 52]. *Cos. ord.* 149; *procos. Africae* probably 163/4 (IRT 232); Apuleius made a speech in his honour (PIR² C 1447; [10]. His son of the same name became *cos. ord.* in 178 (PIR² C 1448).

[II 54] **Q.C. Senecio Annianus.** Senator who came from Carteia in the province of Baetica; via a proconsulate in Pontus-Bithynia he became suffect consul, probably in the Antonine period (CIL II 1929 [12. 201f. n. 570]: not *suff.* in AD 116).

1 CABALLOS, Senadores   2 ALFÖLDY, Konsulat   3 PFLAUM   4 SYME, RP   5 W. ECK, in: BJ 1984   6 VIDMAN, FO²   7 G. CAMODECA, in: ZPE 43, 1981   8 SYME, AA   9 VOGEL-WEIDEMANN   10 B. E. THOMASSON, Fasti Africani, 1996   11 VIDMAN, in: EOS   12 W. ECK, in: Chiron 13, 1983.   W.E.

[II 55] **C. Severus.** Augustan epic poet, from whom 16 fragments are extant (two probably in prose). The poem about kings, attributed to him by his friend Ovid (Pont. 4,16,9; *cf.* 4,2,1), may have been the first part of a long verse chronicle called *Res Romanae* (Probus, Gramm. 4,208 quotes a half v. under this title). The 25 vv. on the death of Cicero quoted in Sen. Suas. 6,26 perhaps come from the later part of this work. If Quint. Inst. 10,1,89 speaks of him in general as *versificator quam poeta melior*, he nevertheless praises the quality of the 1st book of his poem on the Sicilian War of 38–36 BC (perhaps unfinished). A description of Etna referred to by Seneca (Ep. 79,6; according to him recurring later as Ovid's description in Met. 15,340ff.), may have been part of this work.

→ Carmen de bello Aegyptiaco

H. DAHLMANN, Cornelius Severus, in: AAWM 6, 1975; COURTNEY, 320.   ED.C.

[II 56] **Cn. Pinarius C. Severus.** Son of C. [II 9]. Patrician. *Cos. suff.* 112 (PIR² C 1453 [1. vol. 1, 114ff.]).

[II 57] **Faustus C. Sulla.** *Cos. suff.* AD 31. Married to Domitia Lepida, thus stepfather of Valeria Messalina, widow of the emperor Claudius (PIR² C 1459 [2. 267]).

[II 58] **L.C. Sulla.** *Cos. ord.* 5 BC with Augustus (PIR² C 1460).

[II 59] **C. Sulla Felix.** Descendant of the *dictator* Sulla. *Frater arvalis;* died in AD 21 [3. 117ff.]. Father of C. [II 61] and [II 60].

[II 60] **Faustus C. Sulla Felix.** Son of C. [II 59]. *Cos. ord.* 52; half-brother to Valeria Messalina; brother-in-law to Claudius, whose daughter Antonia he married. *Frater Arvalis.* Rival to Nero; in 58 banished to Massilia, and in 62 killed there on the orders of Nero (PIR² C 1464 [3. 251ff.]).

[II 61] **L.C. Sulla Felix.** Probably son of C. [II 59]. *Cos. ord.* in AD 33. Son-in-law to Germanicus; perhaps briefly married to Agrippina (PIR² C 1465 [2. 172]).

[II 62] **P.C. Tacitus.** → Tacitus.

[II 63] **Q.C. Valens Cu[...] Honestianus Iunianus.** Praetorian legate of Numidia c. 210/13 [4. 109; 5].

1 CABALLOS, Senadores   2 SYME, AA   3 SCHEID, Recrutement   4 W. ECK, RE Suppl. 14   5 B. E. THOMASSON, Fasti Africani, 1996.   W.E.

Cornelius Bocchus Mentioned by Pliny the Elder as the source for parts of his *Naturalis historia* (Plin. HN 16,216; 37,24; 97; 127); Solinus also repeatedly draws on a C.B. as a source for chronological details (cf. Solin. 1,97; 2,11; 2,18); still the identity of this C.B. with that referred to in Pliny (suspected by [1. XIV]) cannot be proved [2. 646f.]. The inscriptions CIL II 35 and 5184

(=ILS 2920 and 2921) from Lusitania (1st cent. AD), according to which a Lucius CB was *flamen provinciae* and *tribunus militum legionis III Augustae,* however probably do relate to Pliny's source. PIR² C. 1333.

1 TH. MOMMSEN, C. Iulii Solini collectanea rerum memorabilium, ²1895   2 SCHANZ/HOSIUS, vol. 2.
M.MEI. and ME.STR.

Cornelius Gallus see → Cornelius [II 18]

Cornelius Longinos (or C. Longus). Author of two mediocre epigrams: the dedication, written after a Leonidian model (Anth. Pal. 6.300), of a few modest gifts by a farmer to Aphrodite (6.191) and the description of a painting (Anth. Plan. 117). Nothing is known about the poet, who may have been a contemporary of Gaetulicus (1st half of 1st cent. AD).

FGE 67–70.   E.D.

Cornelius Sisenna see → Sisenna

Cornicines The *cornicines* were military musicians (*aeneatores*). They played the *cornu,* a wind instrument curved into a circle and made of bronze; the distinction from the *bucina* is difficult. These soldiers were taken from among the poorest citizens and were already represented in the Servian centuriate (Liv. 1.43). On their own the *cornicines* gave the standards the command to change position, and jointly with the → *tubicines* the signals in battle (Veg. Mil. 2.22;3.5). Under the Principate the *cornicines* were held in higher regard than in the Republic, as their mention in Jos. (Bell. Iud. 5.48) shows.

1 O. FIEBIGER, s.v. Cornicines, RE 4. 1602–1603.
Y.L.B.

Corniculum, cornicularii In the Republican period the *corniculum* was one of the → *dona militaria* (Liv. 10,44,5; Suet. Gram. 9; CIL I² 709 = ILS 8888); in the Principate the *cornicula* were then no more than insignia of rank. The exact meaning of the word is disputed. It is derived either from *cornus* (cornelian cherry) or from *cornu* (horn). Accordingly it meant either two small spears (cf. Pol. 6,39) or else small horns which hung from the helmets. The *cornicularii* represented the elite of the → *principales* and undoubtedly carried out administrative duties, since civil *cornicularii* are attested (Val. Max. 6,1,11; Suet. Dom. 17,2 and Frontin. Str. 3,14,1). They are found at the head of the *officia* of all the more senior officers, in the navy (the *praef. classis*), among the auxiliary troops, in the legions (with the *tribuni,* the *praef. castrorum* and the *legati*), in Rome (with the *praef. vigilum,* the *praef. annonae,* the *praef. urbi* and the *praef. praetorio*) as well as with the *procuratores.*

1 DOMASZEWSKI/DOBSON   2 V. MAXFIELD, The Military Decorations of the Roman Army, 1981.   Y.L.B.

Cornificius Plebeian family name (on coins also Cornuficius, RRC 509); in origin probably the name of a trade (SCHULZE, 417), historically attested from the 1st cent. BC.

[1] **C., L.** Son of C. [2], follower of Octavian (→ Augustus) in 43 BC, as people's tribune, he accused M. Iunius Brutus of the murder of Caesar (Plut. Brut. 272), in 38 and 36 fought as legate (?) against S. → Pompeius in the Adriatic and in Sicily (App. B Civ. 5,339f.; 360ff; 462ff.; Vell. Pat. 2,79,4). In 35 he was consul (MRR 2,406), then proconsul of Africa and triumphed in 32 (MRR 2,419). He renovated the temple of Diana on the Aventine (Suet. Aug. 29,5), which from then on was named after him (ILS 1732). PIR² C 1503.

J.-M. DAVID, Le patronat judiciaire au dernier siècle de la république romaine, 1992, 893.

[2] **C., Q.** People's tribune in 69 BC, praetor *c.* 66 (?) applied unsuccessfully for the consulate (Ascon. 82C) 63 together with Cicero; in 63 he guarded the Catilinarian C. Cornelius [I 12] Cethegus (Sall. Catil. 47,4) and in 62 reported in the Senate on the scandal of P. Clodius [I 4] (Cic. Att. 1,13,3).   K.-L.E.

[3] **Q. C.** Son of C. [2], augur probably since 47, at the latest 46 BC (CIL 6,1300a; Cic. Fam. 12,17f.; [3. 292]). In 48/47 as *quaestor pro praetore* in Illyricum, 46 in Cilicia, praetor probably in 45 [3. 306], 44–42 as proconsul in Africa, where he was killed outside Utica on the side of Caesar's murderers (Cic. Phil. 3,26; Fam. 12,22; App. B Civ. 327f.; cf. Jer. Chron. a.ABr. 1976 [3. 327f.]). He was an orator (Cic. Fam. 12,18,1), probably an Atticist (Fam. 12,17,2), and as a poet belonged to the circle of the Neoterii (Catull. 38; Ov. Tr. 2,436).

1 F.L. GANTER, Q.C., in: Philologus 53, 1894, 132–146   2 W. STERNKOPF, Die Verteilung der röm. Prov. vor dem Mutinischen Krieg, in: Hermes 47, 1912, 321–401   3 MRR 2   4 E. RAWSON, Roman Culture and Society, 1991, 272–288   5 COURTNEY, 225–227   6 FPL³, 1995, 224f.   CHR.KU.

[4] **C. Longus.** A Roman scholar active in the third quarter of the 1st cent. BC (he quoted Cic. Nat. D. and was in turn quoted by Verrius Flaccus). He wrote at least three books about early religious history, which Priscian and Macrobius knew under the title *De etymis deorum* (or *Etyma*) and which were also quoted by → Verrius, → Arnobius, and → Servius Danielis.

GRF 473–480.   R.A.K.

Cornus

[1] (It. Ant. 84,1; Corni: Anonymous of Ravenna 5,26; Guido 64; at Ptol. 3,3,7). Carthaginian settlement on the west coast of Sardinia, eighteen miles from each Tharros and Bosa, today S'Archittu (Cuglieri). Founded at the end of the 6th cent. BC, C. was extended to become a city protected by strong walls, which Liv. 23,40f. calls the *caput eius regionis,* capital city of that thickly wooded region (the Montiferru). In the summer of 215 BC the battle between T. Manlius Torquatus and

Ostus, the son of Ampsicora, an ally of Hannibal, took place there. The defeated Sardic-Punic forces withdrew into the city, but the Romans were successful in conquering this last *receptaculum* of the rebels. Probably from the early Imperial period a *municipium* of the *tribus Quirina* and a *colonia* in the 2nd cent. AD. Inscriptions from the time of emperors Hadrian, Septimius Severus and Gratianus testify to a *flamen* and a *sacerdos provinciae* for the imperial cult. In AD 379–383 the *Thermae aestivae* and the nearby *fons* were restored; aqueduct in *opus vittatum mixtum* of the 2nd/3rd cents. AD. In the Byzantine period we find near C. the city of Columbaris with its baptisterium of St John, with two basilicas and an episcopal complex, possibly the seat of the diocese of Sanafer, which was represented by Bishop Boniface at the Council of Carthage in 484. A Boethius Cornensis *episc(opus)* is still remembered in the Lateran Council of 649. The bishop's seat seems to have been moved from Bosa to C. in the mid 11th cent.

> A. MASTINO, C. nella storia degli studi, 1982; R. ZUCCA, C. e la rivolta del 215 a.C. in Sardegna, in: L'Africa Romana 3, 1986, 363–387; Id., Un vescovo di C. (Sardinia) del VII secolo, ibid, 388–395; L. PANI ERMINI, A. M. GIUNTELLA, Complesso episcopale e città nella Sardegna tardo romana e altomedievale, in: Scavi e ricerche 7, 1989, 77–80. A.MA.

[2] Name of a species of bush occurring in southern and central Europe (κράνον, *kránon* or κράνεια, *kráneia* at Hom. Il. 16,767 and Theophr. Hist. pl. 3,12,1–2; κύρνος, *kýrnos* in Hsch.) with two types: 1) the early flowering variety *Cornus mas* (cf. Plin. HN 16,105 and *passim*) with its red, pleasant-tasting stone fruit (κράνειον, *kráneion*, Theophr. Hist. pl. 4,4,5), the cornelian cherries, the pig food of Circe (Hom. Od. 10,242); 2) the variety flowering in the summer *Cornus sanguinea* (*Cornus femina*, Plin. HN 16,105; θηλυκράνεια, *thēlykráneia*, Theophr. Hist. pl. 1,8,2) with black, inedible fruit. The wood, rightly called *hartriegel* 'hard bar' in German, had been used since antiquity to make, among other things, wheel spokes (Plin. HN 16,206), sticks [1. 37] and the shafts of spears (Plin. HN 16,186). A legend in Paus. 3,13,5 maintains that the Trojan Horse was made of it. A spear made of it is said to have killed Priam's son Polydorus (Verg. Aen. 3,22ff.). Many names of villages and countryside areas are associated with κράνεια or *cornus*, as is the original name for → Corsica with κύρνος (*kýrnos*).

> 1 H. BAUMANN, Die griech. Pflanzenwelt, 1982. C.HÜ.

Cornutus

[1] Friend of the poet → Tibullus, to whom he dedicated *elegiae* 2 and 3 of his 2nd book.
[2] **Cornutus Aquila.** Praetorian imperial governor of Galatia in 6 BC [1. 253].
[3] Cognomen of many senators (PIR² II p. 375).

> 1 THOMASSON, I. W.E.

[4] **L. Annaeus Cornutus.** (First name only in Charisius, Gramm. 162,9). Born in Leptis (Africa), he lived in Rome under Nero as a famous Stoic philosopher and scholar; exiled between AD 63 and 65 (Cass. Dio 62,29,2f.). Teacher of → Persius, who dedicated *satura* 5 to him, and of → Lucan(Vita Persii); he knew → Silius Italicus (Charisius, Gramm. 159,27). C. was remembered in Persius' will, organized his unpublished works and handed them over to → Caesius Bassus for publication (Vita Persii). An Ἐπιδρομὴ (*Epidromḕ*) τῶν κατὰ τὴν Ἑλληνικὴν θεολογίαν (θεωρίαν codd.) παραδεδομένων (summary of the traditions of Greek theology), an allegorizing explanation of the names and representations of Greek gods intended as a school book, is preserved. Further subject matter of his writings: a) on the Aristotelian categories, b) Περὶ ἑκτῶν (title in POxy. 3649, ed. 1984), c) Virgil commentary and a tract about Virgil, d) *De figuris sententiarum*, e) *De enuntiatione vel orthographia*, f) Ῥητορικαὶ τέχναι (Textbook on rhetoric). An anonymous rhetorical tract, which was also edited in the name of a Cornutus (text in SPENGEL-HAMMER 1,352–398) is not his; scholia to Persius and → Juvenal handed down in his name actually belong to the Middle Ages.

> EDITIONS: C. LANG, 1881 (Epidrome); GRF (add), 167–209.
> BIBLIOGRAPHY: D. NOCK, s. v. Kornutos, in: RE Suppl. 5. 995–1005; R. S. HAYS, L.A.C. Epidrome, diss. Austin 1983; P. MORAUX, Der Aristotelismus bei den Griechen 2, 1984; G. W. MOST, C. and Stoic Allegoresis, in: ANRW II.36,3, 1989, 2014–2065 (with bibliography). J.LE.

Coroebus (Κόροιβος; *Kóroibos*).

[1] Hero founder of Tripodiscus in the Megaris. The legend is told in Callim. Fr. 26–31 in connection with an Argive *aition* according to the local historians Agias and Dercylus (FGrH 305 F 8 to) [1]: → Linus, the son of Apollo and → Psamathe, is torn apart by dogs, and Psamathe is killed by her father → Crotopus. As a punishment Apollo sends a child-murdering demon, the *Poineé* or → Ker, to Argus. When the brave C. kills the monster, the god sends a further plague, whereupon C. goes to Delphi to do penance. There he receives a tripod and is ordered to establish a temple and a settlement on the spot where it falls to the ground, leading to the founding of Tripodiscus ('small tripod'). C.'s grave in Megara with a depiction of his victory over the *Ker* is described by Paus. 1,43,7f. (cf. the alleged tomb epigram Anth. Pal. 7,154 = FGE 1456ff.). Ov. Ib. 575f. and Stat. Theb. 1,557–668 are influenced by Callimachus. For the cultural background of the legend cf. [2].
[2] Phrygian, son of Mygdon (Eur. Rhes. 539), suitor of → Cassandra and useless ally of Priam, killed by Neoptolemus, Diomedes (Ilias Parva fr. 16 EpGF = 15 PEG; Quint. Smyrn. 13,168ff.) or Peneleus (Verg. Aen. 2,424f., cf. 341ff.) at the fall of Troy. According to Paus. 10,27,1, represented in the painting by Polygnotus in the → *lesche* of the Cnidians in Delphi [3]. Proverbially a fool (Callim. Fr. 587; Zenob. 4,58; Serv. Aen. 2,341; Eust. 1669,46).

[3] Athenian, inventor of pottery according to Plin. HN 7,198.

1 G. MASSIMILLA, Callimaco: Aitia, libri primo e secondo, 1996, 299–302   2 K. HANELL, Megarische Studien, 1934, 85–87   3 E. D. SERBETI, s.v. Koroibos (1), LIMC 6.1, 103.   A. A.

[4] According to Plutarch (Pericles 13,4) the → architect who began the construction of the → Telesterion in → Eleusis (completed after his death by → Metagenes and Xenocles); C. as an architect involved in Eleusinian building projects is also mentioned epigraphically in IG I³ 32 (probably c. 450 BC). Vitruvius (7 praef. 16f.) and Strabo (9.1.12) however name → Ictinus as the architect of the Telesterion; in spite of numerous painstaking interpretations of the sources, the contradiction remains unresolved to the present day.

H. SVENSON-EVERS, Die griech. Architekten archa. und klass. Zeit, 1996, 237–251.   C. HÖ.

Corolamus Minor king of the → Boii with a Celtic name [1. 184]. In 196 BC he killed the consul M. → Claudius [I 12] Marcellus (Liv. 33,36,4–8), who was operating in the Boian region in northern Italy.

1 SCHMIDT.   W. SP.

Corona

[1] see → Wreaths
[2] see → Decorations, military; → Dona militaria
[3] see → Constellations

Corone (Κορώνη; Korōnē). City on the west coast of the Messenian Gulf, modern Petalidi, c. 30 km south west of Kalamata, at the foot of Mount Mathia (modern Lykodimo) with numerous ancient remains, including parts of the city wall. After Messenia had been freed from Spartan rule by the Boeotians under Epaminondas, a new Boeotian city was allegedly founded (it is impossible to decide conclusively whether there was an older C. [1]); after 184 BC member of the Achaean League (Liv. 39,49,1; Plut. Philopoemen 18,3; coins). In the 2nd cent. AD C. belonged temporarily to Sparta. The place is still mentioned in Hierocles, Synekdemos 647,15 bishop's seat in the Middle Ages. The name C., however, had in the meantime been transferred to the city on the site of the old city of Asine.

The temple of Apollo Corynthus eighty stadia south of C. that is described by Paus. 4,34,7 was excavated on the coast near Longa [2] with four temples succeeding one another chronologically, and with subsidiary buildings from the Archaic to the Roman periods. Evidence: Paus. 4,34,4–6; Str. 8,4,5f.; 9,2,29; Ptol. 3,16,8; Steph. Byz. s.v. Κορώνεια. Inscription: IG IV 619; 1605; V 1.1392–1401; SEG 11,993–995; 14,336; 15,224; 16,291. Coins: HN, 418, 433.

1 F. KIECHLE, Pylos und der pylische Raum in der ant. Tradition, in: Historia 9, 1960, 51f.   2 F. VERSAKIS, Τὸ ἱερὸν τοῦ Κορύνθου Ἀπόλλωνος, in: AD 2, 1916, 65–118.

N. KALTSAS, s.v. Messenia, EAA², 638; G. S. KORRES, s.v. Koroni, PE, 463; E. MEYER, s.v. Messenien, RE Suppl. 15, 195f.   Y. L.

Coronea (Κορώνεια; Korṓneia). Boeotian city 2 km east of modern Agios Georgios, c. 4 km north of modern C. (formerly Kutumala) on a low promontory (244 m) on the south-eastern edge of a very fertile plain stretching northwards as far as the southern shore of the former Lake → Copais, then south of C., narrowing to a valley, reaching deep into the northern side of the → Helicon [1] and opening up access to an important pass crossing to Thisbe in Boeotia. In the north-eastern part of the plain at the Metamorphosis church near modern → Alalcomenae [1] (formerly Marmura) [1; 2. 330f.; 11. vol. 2. 85–89] or immediately to the north of the ancient city mountain [8. 285, 345; 13] was the Boeotian central sanctuary to Athena Itonia belonging to C. (→ Iton) [12. vol. 1, 117–127, vol. 3, 5f.], where also the annual federal celebrations of the Pamboiotia were held (Str. 9,2,29; Paus. 9,34,1). Only minimal traces of the ancient city of C. are still extant: remains of a polygonal encirclement wall [9. 128–131] and a few Roman buildings filled in with reused stones; the theatre is thought to have been on the eastern slope of the city mountain [2. 325–327; 15. 114].

Scattered finds testify a settlement on the site since the Neolithic period. The C. mentioned in Homer's catalogue of ships (Hom. Il. 2,503) and by Hecat. FGrH 1 F 117 belonged from the very beginning to the Boeotian tribal association (Hdt. 5,79,2); independent minting of coins c. 2nd half of 6th cent. BC until 480, 456–446, c. 386–374 and after 335 (HN 345). From c. 446 BC C., together with its two neighbouring cities of → Lebadea and → Haliartus, formed one of the eleven districts of the newly constituted Boeotian League (→ Boeotia, with map) and, alternating with them, provided a → Boeotarch (cf. Hell. Oxy. 19,3,392–394). Initially independent again after the disbanding of the confederacy in 386, C. (possibly in the form of the re-established federal district) was from c. 374 until the destruction of Thebes in 335 under Theban or, between 352 and 346 (Diod. Sic. 16,35,3; 58/1; Dem. Or. 5,21; 6,13; 19,112; 141; 148; 325; 334), under Phocian control; after that C. was a member of the restored Boeotian League until that was disbanded in 146 BC.

Owing to its strategically favourable position at the crossroads of the main road on the south bank of Lake Copais and the pass leading south over the Helicon, C. was the scene of two decisive battles in the classical period: in 447 BC the defeat of Tolmides ended Athenian supremacy in central Greece (Thuc. 1,113,2; Diod. Sic. 12,6,1f.) and in 394 the Spartan king Agesilaus defeated the Boeotians and their confederates (Xen. Hell. 4,3,16–21; Xen. Ages. 2,9–19; Diod. Sic. 14,84.1f.; Plut. Agesilaus 18f., 605e–606b; Paus. 3,9,13) [1; 11. vol. 2, 85–95]. In the Hellenistic period C. was always a centre of Boeotian resistance against the Romans (Pol. 20,7,3; 27,1.8f.; 5,1–3; Liv.

33,29,6–12; 36,20,2–4; 42,46,7–10; 63,3; 67,12), but was spared from ultimate destruction by a Roman senatorial decree in 170 BC (Liv. 43,4,11; SEG 19, 374). After a period of decline, there was a new upswing in the 2nd cent. AD attested through numerous improvement measures promoted by Roman emperors (SEG 32, 460–471; 35, 405) [3; 6]. In AD 531 C. was destroyed by an earthquake (Procop. Goth. 4,25,17), but is attested later than this as a bishop's seat [5]. Inscriptions: IG VII 2858–3053; SEG 43, 205; [2. 326–329; 4; 7. 482–485; 10. 253–273].

1 J. BUCKLER, The Battle of Koroneia and its Historiographical Legacy, in: J. M. FOSSEY (ed.), Boeotia antiqua 6, 1996, 59–72   2 FOSSEY   3 J. M. FOSSEY, The Cities of the Kopais in the Roman Period, in: ANRW II 7.1, 1979, 566–571   4 Id., The City Archive at Koroneia, in: Id. (ed.), Stud. in Boiotian Inscriptions, 1991, 5–26   5 R. JANIN, s.v. Coroneia, DHGE 13, 914   6 J. KNAUSS, Die Melioration des Kopaisbeckens durch die Minyer im 2. Jt.v.Chr., 1988, 139–144   7 D. KNOEPFLER, Sept années de recherches sur l'épigraphie de la Béotie, in: Chiron 22, 1992, 411–503   8 R. SCHEER, s.v. Koroneia, in: LAUFFER, Griechenland   9 F. G. MAIER, Griech. Mauerbauinschriften 1, 1959   10 OLIVER   11 PRITCHETT   12 SCHACHTER   13 T. G. SPYROPULOS, Ἀνασκαφή παρὰ τὴν Κορώνειαν Βοιωτίας, in: Praktika 1975, 392–414   14 Id., Ἰτώνιον, in: AAA 6, 1973, 385–392   15 P. W. WALLACE, Strabo's Description of Boiotia, 1979, 114–117.

PHILIPPSON/KIRSTEN 1,2, 449f.; N. D. PAPACHATZIS, Παυσανίου Ελλάδος Περιήγησις 5, ²1981, 211–220; M. H. HANSEN, An Inventory of Boiotian Poleis in the Archaic and Classical Periods, in: Id., Introduction to an Inventory of Poleis, 1996, 90f.   P.F.

Coronis

[1] (Κορωνίς; Korōnís, accusative also Κόρωνιν; Korōnín). Daughter of the Lapith → Phlegyas, mistress of → Apollo, by him mother of → Asclepius. Through his messenger, the raven, Apollo discovers that C., pregnant by him, has slept with → Ischys and wants to marry him (Hes. Aeolidae fr. 60; Pind. Pyth. 3,5–20). According to Pindar (Pyth. 3,27–29), Apollo in his omniscience needs no messenger. He kills Ischys and has C. and other women killed by → Artemis. He saves Asclepius from the flames in which the body of C. is being burned and hands the child to the centaur → Chiron to bring up (Pind. Pyth. 3,25–46; Apollod. 3,10,3; Pherecydes FGrH 3 F 3); according to Pausanias (2,26,3–6), Asclepius was born in Epidaurus and saved by Hermes. C. was worshipped by a cult in Titane in Sicyonia (Paus. 2,11,7) and in Epidaurus, where, according to an epigraphically preserved paean by → Isyllus, she was called Aigla (IG IV 950). Through the spread of the cult of Asclepius in Messenia the local heroine → Arsinoe [I 1] was made the mother of the god, but the Delphic oracle confirmed C. as his mother (Paus. 2,26,6f. cf. 4,3,2 and Hes. fr. 50). According to Ovid (Met. 2,542–547; 599–632), Apollo regrets his deed and seeks in vain to revive C. The originally white bird which brought him the bad news message is changed into a black raven (cf. Callim. Fr. 260, 56–61).

C. LACKEIT, s.v. Koronis, RE 11, 1431–1434; J. LARSON, Greek Heroine Cults, 1995, 61–64; E. SIMON, s.v. Koronis, LIMC 6.1, 103f.; M. L. WEST, The Hesiodic Catalogue of Women, 1985, 69–72.   K.WA.

[2] see → Punctuation

Coronius C. Titianus *Vir perfectissimus*, governor of the *provincia vetus* of Epirus between AD 293 and 305 (AE 1993, 1406).   W.E.

Coronta (Κόρωντα, Κορόνται; *Kóronta, Koróntai*). City in → Acarnania near modern Chrysovitsa, with finds dating to Mycenaean times, mentioned only at Thuc. 2,102,1, member of the Acarnanian Koinon, destination of the Peloponnesian *theorodokoi* (SEG 36, 331 l. 49–51). Inscriptions: IG IX 1², 2, 427–433; 603f.; AD 25 B 2, 1970, 297; 26 B 2, 1971, 321; 40 B, 1985, 140; SEG 29. 473.

PRITCHETT, vol. 8, 102f.; D. STRAUCH, Röm. Politik und Griech. Tradition, 1996, 274.   D.S.

Coronus (Κορωνός; *Korōnós*). Ruler of the → Lapithae, son of → Caeneus; C.'s son Leonteus, together with Polypoetes, led the contingent of the Lapiths before Troy. Homer mentions C.'s name in the catalogue of ships in order to give prominence the little-known Leonteus; in early mythology C. was probably associated with the → legend of the Argonauts, where Apoll. Rhod. also mentions him (1,57f.). A story which possibly reflects historical events is reported at Apollod. 2,154: according to it, C. quarrelled with the Dorians in the Hestiaeotis and together with → Aegimius [1] met his end through Hercules.

K. SEELIGER, s.v. Koronos, ROSCHER 2, 1390–1391.   E.V.

Coropissus (Κοροπισσός; *Koropissós*). City in → Isauria, possibly the *statio* Coriopio of the Tab. Peut. 10,3, probably modern Dağpazarı (formerly Kestel), 64 km north west of Seleucia on the Calycadnus. Imperial *pólis* with (later) city wall; diocese [1; 2].

1 HILD/HELLENKEMPER 1, 313f.   2 M. GOUGH, s.v. Dağ Pazarı, PE, 256.   K.T.

Corpili (Κορπῖλοι; *Korpîloi*). Thracian tribe east of the lower course of the → Hebrus (Str. 7a,1,48). The Thracian *strategia* of Corpilice (Ptol. 3,6,9) also extended over the earlier territory of the → Apsinthii as far as → Aenus [1] (Str. 7a,1,58). In 188 BC the C. took part in the uprising against the troops of Cn. Manlius Vulso together with the Caeni and Maduateni (Liv. 38,40,7).

CHR. DANOV, Die Thraker auf dem Ostbalkan. ..., in: ANRW II 7.1, 1979, 21–185, esp. 84f.; M. TAČEVA, Istorija na bălgarskite zemi 2, 1987, 58ff.   I.v.B.

Corporation see → Associations

Corpus Caesarianum Modern name for the chronologically organized collection of → Caesar's own *commentarii* or those reporting on his wars. Bks. 1–7 (58–52 BC) and 8 (52/51) of the *Bellum Gallicum* (BG), 3 bks. *On the Bellum civile* (49/48; BC), *Bellum Alexandrinum* (48/47; BAl), *Afric(an)um* (47/46; BAfr), *Hispaniense* (45; ending mutilated; BHisp). The almost fully preserved collection already existed in the present form at the time of Suetonius (Suet. Iul. 56,1); Caesar's *commentarii* were handed down to the Middle Ages in this form only. Elucidation on the history of their development is given by internal evidence and the letter to Balbus written by → Hirtius [1], probably at the end of 44 BC, which is placed in the collection before the 8th bk. of the BG, but was conceived as a foreword to the entire Corpus Caesarianum (CC). Hirtius, who worked in Caesar's chancellery, announces in the form of an *excusatio* that he intervened in Caesar's oeuvre (*me mediis interposuerim Caesaris scriptis*) because he wanted to complete the series of campaign reports (*commentarii*) up to Caesar's death himself. The different authors — we have to assume more than one on linguistic grounds — of the three last bks. show that Hirtius' († 21.4.43 BC) work was not finally edited. While BG 8 certainly and the BAl, closely associated with BC 3, probably originate from Hirtius, the linguistically isolated BAfr could be an eyewitness report requested by him. BHisp has at its beginning a transition that gives the impression of an editorial (); Caesar's oration, giving a revue of his life since his quaestorship and representing his army as the bearer of his cause even after his death (42), provides a finale to the entire CC. It is L. → Cornelius [I 9] Balbus who is most likely to have been responsible for this final editing and publication.

Linguistically the post-Caesarian *bella* are linked to the BG the general tradition of → *commentarii* (e.g) and to the giving of dates down to the day means of presentation of tragic → historiography (esp. depictions of battles). Where, above all in BAfr and BHisp, narrative progress or linking of several strands of action are marked monotonously by *tum ... interdum ... interea,* there is a clear deterioration from Caesar. His anonymous narrator, however, characterized only as a participant in Caesar's wars, is maintained. When the authors wanted to identify themselves, the only method at their disposal was disproportionate representation of themselves as protagonists. On this hypothesis, L. → Munatius Plancus is author of the BAfr, and a Spanish cavalry officer Clodius Arguetius (Arquitius?) author of the BHisp.

The CC offers the opportunity of examining the processes of historical adoption and differences in the quality of craftsmanship within a very small space. For the publishers of the collection and the first recipients these differences seem to have been subordinate to the need to possess a piece of coherent literature, written from one point of view, with which they could identify.

EDITION: → Caesar.
COMMENTARY: R. SCHNEIDER, BAfr, 1905; G. PASCUCCI, BHisp, 1965.
BIBLIOGRAPHY: K. BARWICK, Caesars Commentarii und das C.C., 1938; L. CANALI, Problemi della prefazione irziana, in: Maia 17, 1965, 125–140; Id., Osservazioni sul C.C., in: Maia 18, 1966, 115–137; J. MALITZ, Die Kanzlei Caesars, in: Historia 36, 1987, 51–72; J. RÜPKE, Wer las Caesars bella als commentarii?, in: Gymnasium 99, 1992, 201–226.　　　　　　　　　　　　　　　J.R.

Corpus Hermeticum

A. OVERVIEW　B. HERMETIC TREATISES　C. ASCLEPIUS　D. EXCERPTS　E. AUTHORS　F. TEACHINGS OF THE HERMETIC TEXTS

A. OVERVIEW

There had been a comprehensive body of writings in Egypt, produced in the name of the god → Hermes, who has been identified with the Egyptian god Thot (Theuth, Thout), the god of wisdom and the art of writing, since the Hellenistic period. The Corpus Hermeticum (CH) included not only the so-called technical writings of astrological, alchemistic, magic and medical content [1], but also religious and philosophical texts. There are 17 Greek treatises, the Lat. *Asclepius* (Ascl.) and 29 Greek excerpts (exc.) from the anthology of → Stobaeus (further testimonia and fragments in Lactantius, Cyrillus, Iamblichus, Zosimus, *et al.*). This collection is supplemented by three Coptic texts from the papyrus discoveries of Nag Hammadi (NHCod. VI 6–8), by the so-called *Hermetic Definitions* (DH, Armenian), a few new excerpts from an Oxford MS (Clark. 11) and two fragments (A, B) from a Viennese papyrus.

B. HERMETIC TREATISES

One of these fragments proves the existence of Hermetic collections in the 2nd/3rd cents. AD: fragment B 4–5 contains the numbering of a 9th and 10th treatise; cf. Cyrillus c. Jul. PG 76. 548B, who names an Athenian (!) compiler of 15 Hermetic writings. The preserved texts refer to the so-called *Genikoi Logoi* (CH XIII 1; exc. III 1 VI 1; NHCod. VI, 6 63.2, Viennese fragment B 6; CH X purports to be an extract from these), *Diexodikoi Logoi* (Cyrillus c. Jul. PG 76, 553A, cf. NHCod. VI, 6 63,3) and others, the content of which seemed to be of an introductory nature [2. 97–194]. There are few external points of contact for the dating. In addition to the Viennese papyri mentioned (2nd/3rd cents. AD), there is the quotation of the hymn in the → *Poemandres* (CH I 31) in a Christian papyrus (PBerl. 9794) from the end of the 3rd cent. The first mentions of the name Hermes Trismegistus are found in → Athenagoras (Suppl. 28.4) and → Philo of Byblus (FGrH 790 F 2,17). The first quotations from Hermetic writings are in → Tertullianus (Adversus Valentianos 15,1; De anima 2,3; 28,1; 33,2; cf. Ps.-Iustinus, Cohortatio ad Graecos 38,2). Therefore the 1st to 3rd cents. AD is assumed to be the period in which the Hermetic philosophical texts emerged. It seems likely, however, that the extant 17 treatises were not compiled until the 10th/11th cents. in Byzantium [3].

The existing MSS from the 14th to 16th cents. all go back to one single archetype. In 1463 MARSILIO FICINO undertook the first Latin translation of the CH (I–XIV) based on MS A (Laurentianus 71,33) choosing the title of *Pimander*. The first Greek edition of all 17 treatises was produced in 1554 by ADRIANUS TURNEBUS, who appended Stobaeus' excerpts II A, I and a section from Ascl. 27 in the Greek original (Stob. 14,52,47) to the not yet numbered treatises I–XIV. In his bilingnual edition, FLUSSAS (François Foix de Candalle) counted these Stobaeus texts and an excerpt from the Suda of 1574 as the 15th treatise. This numbering is maintained to the present day, even though the corresponding texts of CH XV have been put in their original position, so that the 15th to 17th treatises count as XVI–XVIII.

C. ASCLEPIUS

The Latin *Asclepius* has been handed down among the works of → Apuleius (first ed. 1469). This is a very free Lat. trans. of the Greek Λόγος τέλειος (*Lógos téleios*) from the 2nd/3rd cents. AD; remains of the Greek original in Lactantius, Cyrillus, Stobaeus, et al. The translation must date from before 410, as Augustine quotes rather long passages from it in his *De civitate Dei*. A Coptic translation of part of the Greek text (=Ascl. 21–29) is preserved in NHCod. VI 8 (originated *c*. AD 350). It contains an apocalyptic prediction of the decline and revival of Egypt and its religion. The final prayer (Ascl. 41) is in Coptic translation in NHCod VI 7 and in the papyrus Mimaut (Louvre 2391 = PGM III 591–609) in Greek form.

D. EXCERPTS

In addition to excerpts from CH II, IV, X and Ascl., Stobaeus hands down further items of text of varying length. Among them is the extensive exc. XXIII with the title of Κόρη Κόσμου (→ *Kórē Kósmou*). The find of → Nag Hammadi has given us a new, hitherto unknown, Hermetic writing in Coptic translation under the title of 'On the Ogdoad and Ennead' (NHCod. VI 6). It depicts spiritual ascension to the eighth and ninth spheres of heaven by means of hymns and prayers. The 'Hermetic Definitions' contain short dogmas on god, the world and man (cf. exc. XI 2). The Armenian translation was probably produced in the 6th cent., while the oldest MSS date from the end of the 13th cent. According to MAHÉ [4. II 407–436], these dogmas, which he believes are derived from the Egyptian tradition of wisdom, belong to the oldest level of Hermetic philosophical literature (from 1st cent. BC.); the later treatises then developed from such gnomologies. Emphasis on the Egyptian origins of the Hermetic texts characterizes more recent research [5; 2; 4].

E. AUTHORS

The Hermetic texts are pseudo-epigraphical literature. We have no knowledge about the authors and their environment (suppositions in [2. 155–195]). They use the literary fiction that Hermes instructed his sons in the distant past and had these discussions written down on steles in the Egyptian sanctuaries (s. exc. XXIII 5–7; NHCod. VI,6 61,18–63,32; Ps.-Manetho in Sync. 72 WADDELL, 208–11; Iambl. De myst. VIII 5). In addition to Hermes' dialogues with Tat (CH II A: text lost; IV, V, X, XII, XIII, Ascl., exc. I–XI, NHCod. VI 6) and with Asclepius (CH II, VI, VIII, IX, XIV, Ascl., DH) there are texts (and letters) addressed to King Ammon (CH XVI, XVII, Ascl., exc. XII–XXI) and conversations in which Isis reveals to her son Horus the wise sayings of Hermes (exc. XXIII–XXVII). Hermes is also taught by the highest spirit (*nous*) himself, who also appears as 'Poemandres' or 'good demon' (→ *Agathós Daímōn*) (CH I, III [?], XI, cf. CH XII). CH VII is a 'mission speech' to all people (cf. CH I 28) and CH XVIII a rhetorical exercise in praise of the kings (see exc. XXIV 1–5).

F. TEACHINGS OF THE HERMETIC TEXTS

The real aim and essential content of all Hermetic writings is the recognition of god as the creator of the world and mankind (cf. CH I 3). He who acknowledges god is pious and good and attains salvation (CH I 27, VI 5, X 15, exc. II bk. 2). Ignorance, on the other hand, means badness and ruin for mankind (CH VII, X 8, XI 21, Ascl. 22). The Hermetics see themselves as an elite that meets with lack of understanding among the masses (CH IX 4, XIII 13, exc. XI 4). Hermetic texts never grow tired of stressing the difference between creature and creator (CH XIV): god is incorporeal, perfect, eternal, invisible and unwavering (exc. I–IIA). He is truth, he is the father (or of dual gender, cf. CH I 9, V 9, Ascl. 21) and the good (CH II 14–17, VI 1, X 3, XIV 9). As such he creates everything through his spirit, because he wants to become visible in his creatures (CH V, XI 22, XII 21, XIV 3, Ascl. 41). Man in particular is created for the purpose of acknowledging and praising god (CH III 3, Ascl. 9). Mid-Platonic doctrines, probably from the Alexandrian school of philosophers, were primarily drawn on as the basis for these teachings, often in simplified form (additionally also astrological doctrines, CH II 6–7, V 3–4, exc. VI). Tending towards Platonic doctrines, CH II, for instance, drafts a theory of space as the comprehensive energy (*enérgeia*) to prove the existence of God and his spirit (*nous*) (cf. Ascl. 34) CH XI develops a theory on → *aion* which is ultimately based on Pl. Ti. 37d (cf. Ascl. 30–31). Particularly the doctrine of matter and ideas as formative powers is often in the background (CH I 4–8, Ascl. 14, exc. IX, XV).

In this adoption of philosophical doctrines the Hermetic authors are not, however, aspiring to a uniform system. There are, indeed, countless contradictions among the Hermetic texts, e.g. on the question of whether god created the world alone (CH XI 11–14,

XIV 4) or with the aid of an intermediary (CH I 9, XVI 5, exc. II A 14, NHCod. VI,8 75,8–17)[6]. Judgement of what the world is also differs. As a creation of god the cosmos is a perfect god in its order and variety (CH V, VIII 2, Ascl. 8), in which there is no death in the sense of actual passing away (CH VIII, XII 15–18, exc. IV 13), on the other hand it was created by comparison with god, material and only an image (CH VI 4 therefore even calls it the 'abundance of badness', while IX 4 confines this to the earth). This tension, which needs to be clearly separated from Gnostic attitudes, is characteristic of Hermetic texts. The cosmos and in particular heaven should be praised as the work of god, but man must not lose himself in it and its sensually perceivable materiality (CH IV 5, Ascl. 15). For there is a danger that he will direct his desires towards the visible (CH I 19–20, XII 3) and in this way be prey to the power of the demons and fate (CH IX 3, XVI 15–16). Thus all Hermetic texts have in common a polemic against physicality and sensual perceptions (CH VII, XIII 6). Doctrine about souls is also not uniform; in some texts the Platonic division into three is adopted (CH XVI 15, exc. IIB 6, III 7, XVII), in others spirit (*lógos*), soul and pneuma are distinguished (CH X 13–16, XII 13–14). The question of whether all people possess spirit (*nous*) (CH I 22, XII 12) or not (CH IV 3) is also handled differently. In CH X 7–8, exc. XXIII 39–42 animals are included in the cycle of incarnations, in CH X 19–20 this is denied. Some texts teach a post-mortal judgement and punishments for the soul (exc. VII, Ascl. 27–28), others see punishment in injustice itself (CH I 23, X 20).

The Hermetic authors adopted various images from their religious environment to describe the act of recognising god. This recognition, which can take place only after preparatory instructions, is therefore described as a baptism of the spirit (CH IV) and as a rebirth and deification (CH XIII, in I 26 only after death, cf. X 7, XII 12) [7]. It is understood as an ecstatic vision or spiritual ascent (CH X 4–5, XI 20, XIII 11; Ascl. 29; NHCod. VI,6); the extent to which personal experience forms the basis is disputed. The origin of this metaphorical language is sought in the → syncretism of the 2nd/3rd cents. AD, the proportion of Hellenistic-Jewish theologoumena apparently being greatest [8; 9]. Points of contact with Christian or Christian-Gnostic formulations and thoughts can be explained by this common root [but see 10].

→ Hermetic writings

1 A.-J. Festugière, La Révélation d'Hermès Trismégiste, 1949–1954, I 89–308 2 G. Fowden, The Egyptian Hermes, 1986 3 J.F. Horman, The text of the Hermetic literature and the tendencies of its major collections, diss. Hammond, 1974 4 J.-P. Mahé, Hermès en Haute-Égypte I–II, 1978–1982 5 F. Daumas, Le fonds égyptien de l'hermétisme, in: Gnosticisme & monde hellénistique, 1982, 3–25 6 J.-P. Mahé, La création dans les Hermetica, in: Recherches Augustiniennes 21, 1986, 3–53 7 K.-W. Tröger, Mysterienglaube und Gnosis in C.H. XIII, 1971 8 C.H. Dodd, The Bible and the Greeks,

1935, 99–200 9 H. J. Sheppard et al., s.v. Hermetik, RAC 14, 1988, 794–5 10 J. Büchli, Der Poimandres. Ein paganisiertes Evangelium, 1987.

EDITIONS AND TRANSLATIONS: R.v.d. Broek, G. Quispel, C.H., 1991; C. Colpe, J. Holzhausen, C.H., 1997; B.P. Copenhaver, Hermetica, 1992; P.A. Dirkse, J. Brashler, D.M. Parrott, NHCod. V,2–5 and VI, 1979, 341–451 (NHCod. VI,6–8); J.-P. Mahé (see above 6), I 61–87, I 157–167, II 355–405 (NHCod. VI,6–8 and DH); Id., Fragments hermétiques dans les Pap. Vind. gr. 29456r° et 29828r°, in: Antiquité païenne et chrétienne, 1984, 51–64; C. Moreschini, Apul., opera III (BT), 1991, 39–86; A.D. Nock, A.J. Festugière, C.H. (Budé, 4 vols.), 1945–54 (definitive text); J. Paramelle, J.-P. Mahé, Extraits hérmetiques inédits dans un manuscrit d'Oxford, in: REG 104, 1991, 109–139; W. Scott, Hermetica I–IV, 1924–1936.

BIBLIOGRAPHY: H. D. Betz, Schöpfung und Erlösung im hermetischen Fragment 'Kore Kosmou', in: Gesammelte Aufsätze I, 1990, 22–51 (first 1966); A.-J. Festugière, Hermétisme et mystique païenne, 1967; S. Gersh, Theological doctrines of the lat. Asclepius, in: Neoplatonism & Gnosticism, 1992, 129–166; A. González Blanco, Hermetism. A bibliographical approach, ANRW II 17.4, 2240–97; W. C. Grese, C.H. XIII and early Christian literature, 1979; J. Holzhausen, Der Mythos vom Menschen im hell. Ägypt. Eine Studie zum 'Poimandres', 1994; J. Kroll, Die Lehren des Hermes Trismegistos, 1914; R. Reitzenstein, Poimandres, 1904; A. Wlosok, Laktanz und die philos. Gnosis, 1960; Th. Zielinski, Hermes und die Hermetik, in: ARW 8–9, 1905–6, 321–72 and 25–60.   J.HO.

Corpus Hippocraticum see → Hippocrates

Corpus iuris *Corpus iuris* (CI) is used in Liv. 3,34,7 for the Twelve Tables and in Cod. Iust. 5,13,1. pr. (AD 530) for the whole of Roman law. In Const. Omnen § 1 (533) *totum corpus* means Justinian's work of reform mentioned in Const. Deo auctore § 11 (530) and, with its parts (*institutiones, digesta seu pandecta, cod. Iustinianus repetitae praelectionis*) in Const. Cordi § 5 (534). Justinian himself did not institute any measures for the official collection of the *novellae* after 535. They were first included by the glossarists in the collected work they named the CI: *digestum vetus, infortiatum, digestum novum.Codex (I–IX), Volumen (parvum)* with *tres libri codicis* (X–XII), *Institutiones, Authenticum* (IX *Collationes*) and the *Libri feudorum* (as Coll. X since the 13th cent.). *Corpus iuris civilis* is the name of the first one-volume collected edition of the *corpus iuris* provided by D. Gothofredus in 1583.

P. Weimar, Legistische Lit. der Glossatorenzeit, in: Handbuch der Quellen und Lit. der neueren europ. Privatrechtsgesch. I, 1973, 155ff.   W.E.V.

Correction see → Copy; → Correction marks

Correction marks An ancient text could be corrected in at least two ways: a) a διορθωτής (*diorthōtḗs*), a professional *corrector*, collated the copy with the original. This intervention was sometimes indicated by the monogram δι = δι(ώρθωται), 'corrected' [1. 15. n. 85,13] (→ Publication). b) A reader (not necessarily a professional corrector, but often a lay man) collated the copy with another sample. Two or more correctors could work on the same copy [3]. A wrong correction was indicated as ἀποδιόρθωμα (*apodiórthōma*) (PSI 12, 1287,11–14).

The intervention of an ancient corrector is recognizable by the divergent writing, the different ink and the (secondary) position of the correction in relation to the original text. The correction systems varied; the letters or words were deleted with a sponge [Ist n. 50, 63] or were placed between round brackets (περιγράφειν: [Ist n. 15, 25, 63, 76]; PHerc. 1021, col. 23, 27–29), crossed out with a horizontal or diagonal stroke (διαγράφειν: [Ist n. 24]), expunged using dots [Ist n. 63] or a small line above, below or on each side [Ist n. 34]. These methods were often combined [Ist n. 6, 67, 72]. The corrected text was added between the lines and framed by dots (ἐπιστίζειν: [Ist n. 16, 29]). The position of two words (or verses or strophes) was reversed by β α written above them.

Omissions were often inserted with the *ancora* sign: *ancora superior* ↑or *ancora inferior*↓; the siglum ἄνω (*supra*) or κάτω (*infra*) indicated whether the omission had been inserted in the top or bottom margin [4]. Errors or omissions were nevertheless often left uncorrected. In cases of doubt the corrector used the siglum Z or ζη = ζή(τει) [Ist n. 34]. If this sign was used by a professional scholar, he could also cite the source for his correction or a variant on the text handed down [Ist n. 15, 27, 34].

In the Latin and Greek Middle Ages the correction method hardly changed and the symbols used mostly remained the same. The spread of parchment, however, encouraged the method of erasure as an efficient correction technique [5].
→ Critical signs; → Text, emendation of; → Text, corruption of; PALAEOGRAPHY; PAPYROLOGY

1 E. G. TURNER, Greek Manuscripts of the Ancient World, ²1987, 15–16   2 R. BARBIS, in: Akten des 21. internationalen Papyrologenkongresses, 1997, 57f.   3 K. MCNAMEE, in: Proc. of the 16ᵗʰ International Congr. of Papyrologists, 1981, 79–91   4 Id., Sigla and Select Marginalia in Greek Literary Papyri, 1992   5 M. MANIACI, Terminologia del libro manoscritto, 1996, 189–192.   T.D.

Corrector The word *corrector* (from *corrigere*, 'correct') designates in general the critic who imposes censure or punishment, or the reorganizer, e.g. a pedagogue, overseer, official or politician with duties of this kind (Plin. Pan. 1,6,2; Sen. Dial. 4,10,7; Amm. Marc. 31,4,9).

From the time of Trajan the name *corrector* was given to a senatorial legate of the emperor who was sent to a province with a special mission, e.g. *ad ordinandum statum liberarum civitatum* (Plin. Ep. 8,24). Arising from this already in the 3rd cent. AD is a form of regular provincial administrative office, (Dig. 1,18,20: *legatus Caesaris, id est praeses vel corrector provinciae*), the incumbent of which had to be, even according to the order of rank of late antiquity, of senatorial rank (*clarissmimus*), although he was below other *rectores*: the *praesides*, the *consulares* and the few *proconsules* and other *spectabiles* in provincial governments (Cod. Iust. 1,49). In the *notitia dignitatum* (*orient.* and *occident.*, *indices*) the following *correctores* were mentioned for their period: in the eastern legal district two *correctores* (for the provinces of Augustamnica/Egypt and Paphlagonia) next to 40 *praesides*, 15 *consulares*, two *proconsules* (in Asia and Achaea), the *comes Orientis* and the *praef. Augustalis* in Egypt. In the west three (for the provinces of Savia/Pannonia, Apulia et Calabria, Lucania et Bruttii) as well as 31 *praesides* (of which seven in Italy), 22 *consulares* (of which eight in Italy) and a *proconsul* (in Africa). The duties of the *correctores* were in principle the same as for higher-ranking provincial administrators (Cod. Theod. 1,16 and 22; Cod. Iust. 1,40 and 45).

JONES, LRE, 45, 525ff.; LIEBENAM, 482f.   C.G.

Correus Celtic(?) name of a chieftain of the → Bellovaci, 'dwarf'? [1. 339–340]. In 51 BC, together with → Commius, C. led the last large revolt of several Gaulish tribes against Caesar, which was also supported by Germanic troops. After initial success in beating the Rome-friendly → Remi and by avoiding an open battle with the Romans through clever tactics, an ambush laid by C. ultimately failed. The Gauls were beaten and C. fell in battle (Caes. B Gall. 8,6–21; Oros. 6,11,12–14). The name also appears on a British gold coin [2. 1134f.; 3. 153].

1 EVANS   2 HOLDER, 1   3 R. P. MACK, The Coinage of Ancient Britain, 1964.   W.SP.

Corsica (Κύρνος; *Kýrnos*). Mediterranean island, surrounded in the north and west by the *Mare Ligusticum*, in the east by the *Mare Thyrrhenum* and in the south by the *fretum Gallicum* separating C. from Sardinia. The ancient names for the island might represent the renaming of an indigenous (Corsican?) toponym by Greeks (possibly from Euboea) and Romans (cf. the roots *kurn-/korn-*, still widespread in C.). Settlements on C. are documented from the 8th millennium BC. In the Neolithic period contacts with Sardinia and the Etruscan and Ligurian coasts. Pinnacle of the Aeneolithic culture of Terrina near Aleria. In the Aeneolithic period the megalithic culture (dolmen, menhirs and menhir statues) emerged on C. In the Bronze Age fortified settlements emerged (castles with towers). Contacts with cultures on the Italian peninsula of the later Iron Age, often negotiated by Sardinia, did not lead to urbanization in

C.; this was first introduced by a Phoenician settler community c. 565 BC. According to Hdt. 1.165–167, settlers from Phocaea in Asia Minor moved into the region around Alalia and built a city centre there. At the time of the siege of Phocaea by the Persian Harpagus c. 545 BC some of the inhabitants left the city, sailed to Alalia and settled there. With their commerce and piracy, the new settlers caused such lasting disruption to the Etruscan-Punic economical hegemony in Etruria and Sardinia that the Etruscans (esp. Caere) and Carthaginians joined forces and equipped 120 ships to destroy Alalia. However, the Phoenicians anticipated the allies with a surprising successful action. The Greeks left C. and settled in Velia in Campania, while the Carthaginians could now freely rule over Sardinia and the Etruscans controlled C. Alalia was Etruscanized at the beginning of the 6th cent., possibly by a military expedition led by Velthus Spurinna from Tarquinia. Rome took an early interest in C. (cf. the report on the exile of Galerius Torquatus in Alalia: Theopilus 1 FGrH 296; failure of Romans to found a city: Theophr. Hist. pl. 5,8,2; the Etruscan inscription by *Klautie* (Claudius) on an Attic kylix from 425 BC from the necropolis of Casabiada).

The Roman conquest of C. proceeded in two stages: first L. Cornelius Scipio took Aleria in 259 BC and subjugated a few Corsican tribes, then the consul Ti. Sempronius Gracchus extended Roman rule in 238–237 BC at least theoretically to Sardinia and C., from 227 BC combined into the province of *Sardinia et C.*. The indigenous population repeatedly rose up against Rome. In the 1st cent. BC, Roman *coloniae* were founded in C. In c. 100 Marius founded the *colonia Mariana* in northeastern C., where the Vanacini (CIL X 8038) lived. Between December 82 and 1 January 80 Sulla led a division of *coloni* to Aleria. During the civil wars, C. went over from Pompey to Caesar. Between 40 and 38 Sex. Pompey occupied C. with his legate Menas; the island finally fell to the future Augustus and remained with him until reorganization of the province in 27 BC, when the province of *Sardinia et C.* was assigned to the Senate, which had it governed by a proconsul with the rank of a praetor. Constitutionalization of the province of C. by separating it from Sardinia took place in AD 6, when Augustus personally took on the administration of Sardinia, or in AD 67 on the occasion of the return of Sardinia to the Senate. From AD 69, it seems, C. was governed by a procurator. According to Tac. Hist. 2,16, Decimus Pacarius, the governor of C., sided with Vitellius, resulting in an internal rebellion that cost him his life. Diocletian's administrative reform kept C. as a province under a *praeses*. At the beginning of the 5th cent. AD C. was conquered by the Vandali. In 536 it was won back by Byzantine troops.

→ Aleria; → Mariana

J. JEHASSE, L. JEHASSE, La nécropole préromaine d'Aléria, 1973; J. DUCAT, Herodote et la Corse, in: Hommages à F. Ettori, 1982, 49–82; PH. PERGOLA, Corse, in: Topographie chrétienne des cités de la Gaule, 1986, 95–105; M. GRAS, Marseille, la bataille d'Alalia et Delphes, DHA 13, 1987, 161–181; O. JEHASSE, Corsica classica, 1987; C. VISMARA, Funzionari civili e militari nella Corsica romana, in: Studi per L. Breglia 3, 1987, 57–68; S. A. AMIGUES, Une incursion des Romains en Corse d'après Théophraste, H.P.V 8,2, in: REA 92, 1990, 79–83; J. LEHASSE, L. JEHASSE, La Corse antique, 1993; J. CESARI, Corse des origines, 1994. R.Z.

Corsote (Κορσωτή, *Korsōté*). Xen. An. 1,5,4 mentions C. as a large city situated in the desert south of the confluence of the Chaboras (→ Habur) and the Euphrates. He describes it as being surrounded by the river → Mascas, probably more of a canal. Attempts to locate it near Bāǧūz or Hirbat ad-Dīnīya are dubious.

R. D. BARNETT, Xenophon and the Wall of Media, in: JHS 73, 1963, 3–5. K.KE.

Corstopitum Settlement in the valley of the North Tyne, modern Corbridge. During the conquest by Agricola (AD 77–84) a large base was erected here, subsequently replaced by a camp further to the east (destroyed by fire c. 125). After Hadrian's Wall was erected 7 km to the north, C. was extended to become a supply base. In the early 3rd cent. C. played a decisive role in connection with the campaigns of Septimius Severus. An important city adjoining the base arose here in the 3rd and 4th cents. [1].

→ Limes; → Britannia

1 M. BISHOP, J. N. DORE, Corbridge, 1988 2 E. B. BIRLEY, Research on Hadrian's Wall, 1961, 149f. M.TO.

Cortona (Κρότων; *Krótōn*, (ἡ) Κυρτώνιος; *(hē) Kyrtónios*, Κόρτωνα; *Kórtōna*, Γορτυναία; *Gortynaia*; Corythus, Etruscan *curthute*).

[1] Etruscan city on a hill north of the *lacus Trasumenus*, modern Cortona. In connection with the legend of → Dardanus, the son of Corythus, C. aroused particular interest among Hellenistic scholars (cf. Verg. Aen. 3,167ff.; 7,206ff.; Serv. Aen. 1,380; Plin. HN 3,63). Its origin is recorded in Hdt. 1,57 as Pelasgian, but in Hellanicus (FGrH 4 F 4) as Tyrrhenian, linked to the oriental origins of the Etruscans. A thirty-year peace with the Romans in 310 BC is recorded in Livy (9,37,12). C. became part of the *tribus Stellatina*, *regio VII* and in the Imperial period belonged to the *XV populi Etruriae*; nothing is known of the geographical extent of its territory (a *cippus* with the inscription *tular rasnal* gives no further elucidation). Arrangement of the graves and rich burial gifts are evidence of a *gens*-based social structure.

P. BRUSCHETTI, Nota sul popolamento antico del territorio cortonese, in: Ann. Acc. Etr. Cort. 18, 1979, 85ff. G. COLONNA, Virgilio, Cortona, e la leggenda etrusca di Dardano, in: AC 32, 1980, 1ff. M. CRISTOFANI, s.v. C., BTCGI, 1987, 422ff. A. CHERICI, in: C., 1987, 139ff. Id., in: P. ZAMARCHI GRASSI, La Cortona dei Principes, 1992, 3ff. M.CA.

[2] Plin. HN 3,24 names the Cortonenses among the *stipendiarii* of the *conventus Caesaraugustanus*; this makes C. a peregrine community. Its location is unknown; modern Cardona [1. 431] or Odón in the province of Teruel are possibilities.

1 A. SCHULTEN, Fontes Hispaniae Antiquae 8, 1959.

TOVAR, 3, 410.   P.B.

Coruncanius, Ti. Consul in 280 BC, first plebeian *pontifex maximus* in 254, first issued *responsa* publicly and in association with legal instruction (Dig. 1,2,2,35), did not, however, produce any writings (Dig. 1,2,2,38).

WIEACKER, RRG, 528, 535.   T.G.

Corvinus
[1] Friend of the poet → Juvenal, who dedicated *satura* 12 to him.
[2] Mentioned by Juvenal as an exiled senator (1,108).
[3] C. Celer. Municipal quaestor in Oea in Africa (Apul. Apol. 101).   W.E.

Corvus
[1] The invention of the *corvus* ('raven') is attributed to C. Duilius, *cos.* in 260 BC and victor over the Carthaginians in the battle of Mylae. It was a boarding-plank attached to the bow of the ship, steered with the aid of a pulley and a rope. When it was thrown on to the enemy ship, a metal hook remained fixed to the deck; this was a way of damaging the enemy's rigging, which allowed the Roman soldiers to enter the ship (Pol. 1,22,23). With the invention of the *corvus* the tactic of boarding was given precedence over ramming.

1 L. POZNANSKI, Encore le *coruus*; de la terre à la mer, in: Latomus 38, 1979, 652–661   2 M. REDDÉ, *Mare nostrum*, 1986, 100 and 661.   Y.L.B.

[2] see → Constellations

Corydallus (Κορυδαλλός, *Korydallós*). Attic *asty* deme of the Hippothontis phyle, from 200 BC of Attalis, the mountains of the same name (Str. 9,14; 23; Diod. Sic. 4,59,5; Ath. from 9,390ab; Ael. NA 3,25 [2]); one (?) *bouleutḗs*. The deme centre suspected [2] near Palaiokastro/Palaiochora. The so-called 'heroa' [1; 2. 10ff.] are farmsteads, not the sanctuary of the Kore Soteira attested by Ammonius (*Perì diapheroýsōn léxeōn* 84, s.v. Κόρυδος VALCKENAER).

1 E. HONIGMANN, s.v. Korydallos, RE 10, 1447   2 A. MILCHHOEFER, Erläuternder Text, in: E. CURTIUS, J. A. KAUPERT, Karten von Attika 2, 1883, 10ff.

TRAILL, Attica 12, 52, 70, 111 no. 75, table 8, 14.   H.LO.

Coryphasium (Κορυφάσιον, *Koryphásion*). Rocky cape at the north end of the Bay of Navarino in Messenia; in the Classical period this was the site of the city of → Pylos with a sanctuary of Athena Coryphasia

(Paus. 4,36,1f.). The port of Pylos is not identical to the Osman-Aga lagoon (Divari), but can be found in the Bay of Navarino. Evidence: Thuc. 4,3,2; 118,4; 5,18,7; Diod. Sic. 15,77,4; Str. 8,3,7; 21; 23; 27; 4,1f.

E. MEYER, s.v. Messenien, Re Suppl. 15. 201f.; PRITCHETT 1, 1965, 6–29.   Y.L.

Corythus (Κόρυθος, *Kórythos*).
[1] Epiclesis of Apollo, see Kory(n)thos.
[2] Eponym of the Corytheís deme in Tegea (Paus. 8,45,1).
[3] Son of Zeus and → Electra [3], the daughter of Atlas. Tyrrhenian king. Founder of C. (or Cortona or Cora: Plin. HN 3,5,63), an Etruscan city (Sil. Pun. 4,720), which was also identified with Tarquinii [1], Lat. Corythus. The Italic version of the myth has C.'s sons → Iasion and → Dardanus [1] setting out from there for Samothrace and Troy (Verg. Aen. 3,167ff.). C. is also recorded as the husband of Electra, who is the mother of Dardanus by Zeus (Hyg. Poet. Astr. 2,21).
[4] Son of → Paris and → Oenone or → Helena [1]. He comes to Troy as a helper, falls in love with Helen and is therefore slain by his father (Parthenius 24).
[5] Arcadian king, foster father of → Telephus (Apollod. 3,104).

1 N. M. HORSFALL, Corythos, in: JRS 63, 1973, 68–79.
                                                  RE.ZI.

Cos (Κῶς; *Kôs*, Lat. *Cos*).
I. GEOGRAPHY AND SETTLEMENT   II. HISTORY
III. ARCHAEOLOGY   IV. CULTURAL INFLUENCE

I. GEOGRAPHY AND SETTLEMENT
Island in the eastern Aegean, off the south-west coast of Asia Minor, the second largest of the Doric islands (298 km²). A fertile plain in the north contrasts with a barren, sparsely populated mountainous area in the south (highest elevation the Oromedon, 850 m; in the south-west the Latra, 425 m).
In the Neolithic period (finds in a cave near the modern town of Kephalos) C. was populated by people from Asia Minor. A second migration phase can be established in the early and mid Bronze Age (seraglio in the modern town of C.). *In around.* 1600 BC Minoan colonists established themselves in C., but their presence ended *c.* 1450 BC owing to mainland Mycenaean immigration. Numerous traces are preserved from the Mycenaean period in C. (seraglio, necropoleis of Langada and Eleona, fortification walls at the *castro* of Palaiopyli). Immigration of the Doric population (→ Doric Migration) probably took place in around 900 BC; according to Hdt. 7,99,2 (cf. Paus. 3,23,6) these Dorians came from Epidaurus, which is supported by archaeological finds (e.g. the type of burials).

II. HISTORY
A. CLASSICAL PERIOD B. HELLENISTIC PERIOD
C. ROMAN PERIOD

A. CLASSICAL PERIOD

Together with Halicarnassus, Cnidus and the Rhodian cities of Lindus, Ialysus and Camirus, C. formed the Doric Hexapolis (Hdt. 1,144,3), whose central sanctuary was at → Cnidus. In the wake of Persian expansion in Asia Minor at the beginning of the 5th cent. BC the tyrant Scythes ruled in C. together with his son Cadmus, who then renounced the tyranny (Hdt. 7,163f.). C. was not involved in the → Ionian Revolt of 494 BC and was for a time under the rulership of the Carian dynast → Artemisia [1], under whose aegis contingents from C. fought at Salamis on the side of the Persians (Hdt. 7,99,2). Subsequently C. was a member of the → Delian League with a tribute of five talents which signified prosperity (ATL 1,326f.; 509; 3,213; 242). In the → Peloponnesian War C. at first remained neutral. The Spartan commander Astyochus took advantage of a devastating earthquake in the year 412/11 BC (Thuc. 8,41,2) to capture the island. Won back for Athens in 411 BC by → Alcibiades [3] (Thuc. 8,108,2), after the battle of Aigospotamoi (405 BC) Cos allied itself to Sparta, on whose side it remained until it changed allegiance again to the Athenians after the naval battle of Cnidus (394 BC) (Diod. Sic. 14,84,3).

B. HELLENISTIC PERIOD

In 366/5 BC, as part of a → synoikismós, the founding of the city of C. took place on the site of the modern island capital at the eastern end of the large plain on the north coast (Diod. Sic. 15,76,2). In the so-called → Social War [1] (357–355 BC) it broke away from Athens with the support of → Maussollus of Halicarnassus in alliance with Rhodes, Chios and Byzantium (Diod. Sic. 16,7,3; 21,1). After that, first Maussollus and later Pers. dynasts took over rulership of C., until one of Alexander [4] the Great's fleets liberated the island in 333 BC (Arr. Anab. 2,5,7; 3,2,6; Curt. 3,7,4) and a Macedonian garrison was installed. In the Hellenistic period (from 309 BC.: Diod. Sic. 20,27,3) C. was predominantly under Ptolemaic rule, with interruptions by the temporary dominance of the Antigonids (after the naval victory of → Antigonus [2] Gonatas over a Ptolemaic fleet at C. in 261/0 BC).

C. ROMAN PERIOD

In the wake of Roman expansion in the eastern Mediterranean, C. came under the rulership of Rome in 197 BC and from then onwards proved to be a loyal partner to the alliance, without breaking its economic and cultural contacts with Alexandria. In 88 BC, during the 1st Mithridatic War, C. was successful in persuading the Pontic king to leave by handing over precious temple treasures, some of them Jewish (Jos. Ant. 14,112,) and other valuables (App. Mith. 23–27; cf. Tac. Ann. 4,14). In 41 BC → Antonius [I 9] procured a leading political position similar to that of a tyrant for the Coan Nicias, which was terminated in 31 BC by the future Augustus. C. lost its status as a *civitas libera* and became part of the province of → Asia [2]. Under Tiberius ambassadors from C. applied for the renewal of the ancient law of asylum for the Asclepius sanctuary (Tac. Ann. 4,14). In AD 53 Claudius granted C. the *immunitas* (Tac. Ann. 12,61) which lasted until it was revoked by → Diocletian (284–305). In *c.* AD 140 C., together with other Aegean islands and cities in Asia Minor, was struck by a great earthquake, which resulted in extensive aid measures on the part of the emperor → Antoninus [1] Pius. From the means made available at this time new public buildings were erected in the city of C.; magnificently decorated houses appeared. After an earthquake in 469 (Priscos fr. 43) the city was rebuilt again, but almost completely destroyed by the earthquake of 584 (Agathias of Myrina, 2,16,1–6 DINDORF).

III. ARCHAEOLOGY

Archaeological finds in the city of C., founded in 366 BC, testify to a prosperity probably essentially based on commerce. C. was regularly laid out according to the Hippodamian system (→ Hippodamus) with streets crossing one another at right angles. Numerous mosaics in private houses document also personal prosperity. From the public buildings of the Hellenistic and Roman periods many temples, columned halls, gymnasiums, thermal baths, remains of the Hellenistic city wall, and also a stadium with an excellently preserved starting device are extant. Outside the city of C. there are ancient remains near Cephalus (temple, theatre), Cardamena (temple, theatre) and Asfendiu (sanctuary of Demeter).

Undoubtedly the most famous archaeological site on C. is the sanctuary of → Asclepius *c.* 4 km south-west of the city. It was constructed *c.* 350 BC on the site of a grove of Apollo Cyparissius (discovered in 1902 by the German archaeologist R.HERZOG; since then German and Italian excavations). Owing to the revolutionary medical work of the Coan physician → Hippocrates [6], C. had by that time already gained a reputation as an outstanding medical centre. The Asclepieum had been erected on three terraces above a spring containing iron and sulphur, with large open staircases and columned halls. In the Roman period the complex was extended with temples and thermal baths. Numerous inscriptions from the Hellenistic and Roman periods document the importance of the Asclepieum as a prominent health resort and cult site. Apart from the aid given to the sick, there was also medical research undertaken there.

IV. CULTURAL INFLUENCE

In addition to the medical school, C. was also home to an astrological school, founded in the 3rd cent. BC by the Babylonian priest → Berosus (Vitr. De arch. 9,6,2). Well-known Coans were the poet Philetas (4th/3rd cents. BC), who also worked as a tutor at the Ptolemaic royal court in Alexandria, the Hellenistic grammarian

→ Nicanor, the doctors → Dexippus [3], → Heraclides [25], → Thessalus and C. → Stertinius Xenophon, the personal physician of the emperor Claudius, and also → Ariston [4] and [5].

R. HERZOG, Koische Forsch. und Funde, 1899; Id., Kos. Ergebnisse der dt. Ausgrabungen und Forsch., 1932; P. HAIDER, s.v. Kos, in: LAUFFER, Griechenland, 348–351; C. and C. MEE, Kos, 1984; R. W. PLATON, E. L. HICKS, The Inscriptions of Cos, 1891; S. M. SHERWIN-WHITE, Ancient Cos, 1978; G. SUSINI, Nuove scoperte sulla storia di Coo, 1956; M. G. PICOZZI, s.v. Kos, PE, 465–467.

H.SO.

Cosa(e) (Κόσσαι; *Kóssai*). Settlement in a fortified location above the sea in the territory of Vulci, *colonia* in 273 BC (Plin. HN 3,51; Vell. Pat. 1,14,6), reinforced in 196 BC (Liv. 32,2,7; 33,24,8), modern Ansedonia. Oddly, Verg. Aen. 10,168 associates it with Aeneas, but the Etruscan ethnicon *cusate* and earlier Etruscan influence may have caused confusion (possibly there was an Etruscan town near modern Orbetello). After 90 BC a *civitas Romana*, abandoned in the 5th cent. AD because of a plague of rats (Rut. Namat. 1,285ff.). Remnants of the town with towers remain.

F. E. BROWN, C., 1980.

M.CA.

Cosconia Gallitta Daughter of Cornelius Lentulus Maluginensis, *cos. suff.* in AD 10; wife of the praetorian praefect Seius Strabo [1. 307ff.]. PIR² C 1528.

1 SYME, AA.

W.E.

Cosconius Plebeian family, attested since the 3rd cent. BC (ThlL, Onom. 2,663f.).
I. REPUBLICAN PERIOD II. IMPERIAL PERIOD

I. REPUBLICAN PERIOD
[I 1] C., C. Fought successfully in 89 BC in the Social War in Apulia (as praetor or legate?, Liv. Per. 75), proconsul in Illyria from 78–76 (Cic. Clu. 97 etc.); perhaps identical with the C. mentioned in Valerius Maximus(8,1 para. 8).
[I 2] C., C. As praetor he was in 63 BC the record-keeper during the Senate deliberations against the Catilinarians (Cic. Sull. 42). In 62 proconsul in Hispania ulterior (Cic. Vatin. 12), died in 59 as a member of the five-man collegium for Caesar's agrarian legislation (MRR 2, 192).
[I 3] C., C. Friend of Cicero, people's tribune in 59 BC, aedile in 57, judge in the trial against P. → Sestius in 56, praetor in 54 (?), proconsul in Macedonia about 53–51 (MRR 2, 233, n. 1; 3, 77); probably identical with the C.C. killed in 47 by Caesar's veterans (Plut. Caes. 51,1).
[I 4] C., M. Praetor in 135 BC in Macedonia (war against the Scordisci, Liv. Per. 56), where he was also proconsul until 132 (?) (MRR 3,77).
[I 5] C., Q. Witness of the poet Terence's death during a storm at sea in 159 BC (Suet. Vita Terentii 5), probably identical to the grammarian mentioned in Varro (Ling. 6,36; 89) and Solin 2,13 (?).

SCHANZ/HOSIUS 1, 119, 584f.

K.-L.E.

II. IMPERIAL PERIOD
[II 1] C. Gentianus. Governor of Moesia inferior in the early years of Septimius Severus.

LEUNISSEN, 198f., 250f.

W.E.

Cosilinum *Statio* on the *via Popilia* (Tab. Peut. 7,1), after which Sala Consilina is named, in the *liber regionum* of 120 *praefectura Consiline in provincia Lucaniae*. Inhabited market site (Cassiod. Var. 8,33) near an old spring (Marcellianum). In the 5th cent. AD an episcopal seat. The old fortification mentioned in Pliny (Plin. HN 3,95) may possibly be associated with Padula in the Tanagro valley (thus already in [3]), where a fortified embankment was found on a hill and prehistoric graves in the valley (archaic graves of the 7th–5th. cents. and Lucanian ones of the 4th–2nd cents. BC).

1 D. ADAMASTEANU, Vie di Magna Grecia, 1963, 57 2 E. KIRSTEN, Süditalienkunde 1, 1975, 463–466 3 NISSEN, 2, 904 4 V. PANEBIANCO, s.v. Padula, EAA 5, 1963, 815–816.

U.PA. and H.SO.

Cos(s)inius Italic proper name, attested with and without doubling of the s (SCHULZE, 159; ThlL, Onom. 2.667f.).
I. REPUBLICAN PERIOD II. IMPERIAL PERIOD

I. REPUBLICAN PERIOD
[I 1] C., L. Praetor (?) in 73 BC, fell in battle against Spartacus (Sall. Hist. 3,94; Plut. Crassus 9,4f.).

F. RYAN, The Praetorship of Varinius, Cossinius and Glaber, in: Klio 78, 1996, 376.

[I 2] C., L. Speaks as dialogue partner in Varro (Rust. 2) on cattle breeding, probably identical to a L.C. mentioned by Cicero between 60 and 45 BC (Att. 1,19,11; 13,46,4 and *passim*), who was also a friend of Atticus.

NICOLET 2, 856f.

K.-L.E.

II. IMPERIAL PERIOD
[II 1] P. C. Felix. Consular governor of Pannonia inferior in AD 252 (CIL III 3421; AE 1953, 12).

J. FITZ, Die Verwaltung Pannoniens III, 1994, 1044ff.

[II 2] C. Marcianus. Senatorial governor of Numidia under Gordian III (AE 1967, 563).
[II 3] C. Maximus. Senator, perhaps from Cuicul or Carthage (PIR² C 1531).
[II 4] C. Rufinus. Suffect consul, proconsul of Asia, perhaps at the end of the 2nd/ beginning of the 3rd cent. AD (IGR IV 1162).

LEUNISSEN, 203.

W.E.

Cosmas (Κοσμᾶς; *Kosmâs*).

[1] C. and Damianus. Doctor saints and patrons of healing. The Greek Synaxarion (ed. by H. DELEHAYE) contains three different pairs of saints with these names: 1) the sons of Theodata, who were born in Asia Minor and buried in Pelusium, whose feast day is 1 November; 2) the Roman martyrs stoned during the rule of → Carinus (283–285), whose feast day is 1 July; 3) the Arab martyrs killed with their three brothers under the emperor Diocletian (284–305) in Cilician Aegae, whose feast day is 17 October. The history of the pair from Asia Minor is best attested and probably the earliest but the legends of all three pairs of brothers, especially the episode with a 'transplantation' of the leg of a black person on a Roman patient, were intermingled. Also, they had to share 1 November as feast day with the other two pairs of Christian doctor saints, i.e., Pantaleon and Hermolaus as well as Cyrus and Iohannes of Menuthis. The significance of all of these patrons of healing becomes evident when looking at their pagan predecessors and competitors: Aegae (the temple of → Asclepius) and Menuthis (the temple of → Sarapis) were renowned cult centres of pagan healing arts and the church of Sts C. and Damianus in Rome stood on the *forum pacis*, a prestigious meeting place of Roman doctors. However, it is doubtful if the doctor saints should be considered Christianized → Dioscuri. The legends emphasize that they had received a good medical training and mainly differed from pagan doctors by not charging a fee for their medical services. The cult of C. and Damianus was widespread in the 5th cent. and eventually replaced in the Latin world by the cult of the other *anárgyroi* ('unpaid healers') as patrons of healing.

1 O. DEUBNER, Kosmas und Damian, 1907   2 L. RÉAU, Iconographie des saints médecins Côme et Damien, 1958   3 M. HAIN, K. und D., Kultausbreitung und Volksdevotion, 1967.   V.N.

[2] C. Indicopleustes. (Κοσμᾶς Ἰνδικοπλεύστης; *Kosmâs Indikopleústēs*). Merchant of Alexandria, who in the 1st half of the 6th cent. AD travelled in East Africa, Arabia and allegedly India and Taprobane (Sri Lanka). He probably was a monk when he wrote a *Christianikè topographía* (Χριστιανικὴ τοπογραφία) in 12 books. In the debate on the idea of a spherical Earth, which in his opinion was 'pagan', C. defended a biblical world view, according to which the Earth has the shape of Moses' tabernacle (Ex 26) — a rectangular disc over which the world is constructed.

It is less the purpose than its numerous asides that make C.'s work a historically valuable source. Though Phot. 36 dismisses them as 'fanciful' (μυθικώτερος), lively descriptions treat the flora and fauna of India (pepper, coconut, rhinoceros, giraffe, hippopotamus) and the goods traded with Taprobane. The usually reliable descriptions of the countries visited preserve, e.g., copies of Ptolemaic inscriptions [1; 2]. Information on the dates of the Christmas celebration, baptismal rites and the spread of Christianity are of significance for ecclesiastical history.

1 OGIS I 54, 199   2 H. BENGTSON, KS, 1974, 327–333.

88 PG, 51, –470; W. WOLSKA-CONUS, La Topographie chrétienne, 1962 (essays); Id., La Topographie chrétienne de Cosmas Indicopleustès, 3 vols., 1968–1973 (ed., French trans., commentary); HUNGER, Literatur 1, 520–521, 528–530.   K.BRO.

[3] (Κοσμᾶς Μελῳδός; *Kosmâs Melōidós*; also C. Hagiopolites, K. Ἁγιοπολίτης; *K. Hagiopolítēs*, or C. of Jerusalem, C. of Majuma). Bishop and composer of hymns, born in the 2nd half of the 7th cent. AD, died in 750 in Majuma near → Gaza. According to partly diverging information in the *vitae*, the father of → Iohannes [33] of Damascus, finance minister at the court of the → caliph in → Damascus, ransomed the young C. from slavery and adopted him. Presumably before 700, but according to some sources only in 736, the brothers retreated to the monastery Mar Saba near Jerusalem. Around 743 C. became bishop of Majuma where he remained until his death. C. is considered one of the most important composers of hymns in the Byzantine church of the 8th cent. The focus of his work lies in the field of canonical poetry, which reached its apex in the 8th cent. Scholia on the poems of → Gregory [3] of Nazianzus attributed to him are also preserved but their authenticity is not secured.

→ Canon

EDITIONS: PG 98, 455–524 (canones); PG 38, 339–680 (Scholia in S. Greg. Naz.); W. v. CHRIST, M. PARANIKAS, Anthologia Graeca carminum Christianorum, 1871.
BIBLIOGRAPHY: A. KAZHDAN, S. GERO, K. of Jerusalem, in: ByzZ 82, 1989, 122–132; A. KAZHDAN, K. of Jerusalem. 3: The Exegesis of Gregory of Nazianzos, in: Byzantion 61, 1991, 396–412.   K.SA.

[4] Otherwise unknown writer of an epideictic distich, which Pyrrhus, the son of Achilles, voices during the sacrifice of Polyxena (Anth. Plan. 114). The lemma description of C. as *mēchanikós* ('engineer') was plausibly corrected to *monachós* (BRUNCK), but equation with the monk C. [2] Indicopleustes remains to be proved.   M.G.A.

Cosmetics In Greek and Roman antiquity there was a huge demand for essences, oils and pomades. As part of their skin care men lotioned themselves to keep their skin soft and tender (Ath. 15,686). Lotioning extended from the head over the entire body and it was a widespread custom to apply lotion several times a day, with a different lotion being used for each part of the body (Ath. 12,553d). Without lotion one was considered dirty. According to tradition, animal fats and butter were the first substances used for this purpose (cf. Plut. Mor. 1109b). Lotions and cosmetics were kept in special vessels and little boxes, some of which have been preserved with their contents from the Greek and Roman periods [1]. The great demand for cosmetics products in antiquity resulted in an extensive body of literature (cf. Ov. Medic.). Thus, the doctor Criton (about AD 100) supposedly composed a four-volume work on cosmetics. The production and use of lotions in Minoan and Mycenaean culture is known from the decipherment of → Linear B tablets and excavations (e.g., 'House of the Oil Merchant' in Mycenae, the 'Ointment Kitchen' of Kato Zakro). Homer speaks in particular of lotioning the hair and the body after bathing, with olive and rose oil being the most important substances; Hom. Od. 18,172; 179; 196 also suggests the use of facial make-up. Since the 8th cent. BC precious oils and lotions were imported from the Orient, which led in the 6th cent. BC to the futile attempt in Athens and Sparta to suppress the sale and production of lotions.

Greek women used white lead (*psimythion*) to give a pale facial colour and *anchousa*, which was extracted from alkanet, for their cheeks; the eyelids received a dark liner (Xen. Oec. 10,2). Fingernails and the palms were dyed red with henna (Dioscorides 1,65). Furthermore, an abundance of lotions and oils was available for application to the hair and body for both fragrance and general care. Rose oil, *malobathron*, spikenard oil, *amarakinos* (a mixture of oil, myrrh and marjoram) were among the most popular.

In Republican Rome the luxury of cosmetics and *unguenta exotica* (exotic lotions) led to a (futile) ban as early as 189 BC (Plin. HN 13,24). A Roman woman of the imperial period had a great number of diverse cosmetics available of which the best known were: white lead, chalk, 'Melian earth' for whitening, → *purpurissum* and *rubrica* as rouge, *stibium* for darkening the eyelashes and brows (cf. Juv. 2,93f.). → *Lomentum* (soaked bean meal, s. Mart. 3,42; 14, 60; Juv. 6,461) was popular for covering wrinkles and in combination with ground snails it made the skin soft and tender (Plin. HN 30,127). Both sexes used beauty plasters made of fine thin leather (*splenia*) (Mart. 8,33,22; Ov. Ars am. 3,201), with men using them, for example, to cover scars (Plin. HN 12,129).
→ Body care

1 AA 1984, 54.

D. BALSDON, Die Frau in der röm. Ant., 1979, 288–293; S. LASER, Medizin und Körperpflege (ArchHom 3.2), 1983, 153–164; R. JACKSON, Cosmetic Sets from Late Iron Age and Roman Britain, in: Britannia 16, 1985, 165–192; P. FAURE, Parfums et aromates de l'Antiquité, 1987; G. DONATO (ed.), The Fragrant Past. Perfumes and Cosmetics in the Ancient World. Exhibition Atlanta 1989; E. PASZTHORY, Laboratorien in ptolem. Tempelanlagen. Eine naturwissenschaftliche Analyse, in: Antike Welt 19, 1988, H. 2, 3–20; Id., Salben, Schminken und Parfüme im Alt., 1990.   R.H.

Cosmogony see → World, creation of the

Cosmology
A. MEANING OF THE WORD   B. ORIGINS AND TRANSITIONS   C. THE MESOPOTAMIAN HERITAGE   1. OMINA   2. CREATION MYTHS   3. ACHIEVEMENTS OF BABYLONIAN ASTRONOMY   4. MEDICAL THEORIES   D. GREEK COSMOLOGY   1. THE PRE-SOCRATICS   2. THE GEOMETRIZATION OF COSMOLOGY   3. THE MOTION OF THE CELESTIAL BODIES   E. ROMAN COSMOLOGY   F. TRANSITION TO THE MIDDLE AGES

A. MEANING OF THE WORD
Teachings regarding the order of the world, from Greek *kósmos* (κόσμος) and *lógos* (λόγος). *Kósmos*: the alignment, the regulated interrelationship of things in a whole, order. Originally the word was used for a military, institutional or governmental order (Homer, Hesiod). Herodotes and Thucydides used *kósmos* for the constitution of a state, Democritus and Aristotle for the type of state, and the Pre-Socratics for the world order. Plato frequently used *kósmos* as a synonym for the firmament, the universe and the 'whole'. *Lógos*: 'word, speech, list, explanation, proof' (→ logos).

B. ORIGINS AND TRANSITIONS
The development of cosmological concepts can only be understood in relation to the exchange of mythological and scientific knowledge between the Ancient Orient and Greece. Herodotes' description of Egypt and Babylon expresses his great admiration for the achievements of their scholars. Learned Greeks considered a trip to Egypt or Asia Minor a precondition for acquiring knowledge. However, it is more difficult to answer what knowledge was received by what route in the Greek area. Most transmission models assume a spreading of Ancient Oriental (Babylonian, Egyptian) myths and their rationalization by Greek scholars in the 7th and 6th cents. BC, after which the many variants of Greek cosmogony (teachings of the origins of the world) and cosmology developed from the myths. This opinion can be questioned on two fronts: (a) Greek knowledge of Oriental myths is documented by numerous quotes (e.g., Plato's creation myth in the 'Timaeus'), but that does not mean that the development of Greek cosmology was sparked by a rationalization of the myths alone. The other great domains of knowledge in the Near East (→ Astronomy and → medicine) have at least as large a share. (b) For a number of reasons it is untenable to view the initial phase of cosmology as the age of a one-time transfer of knowledge rather than a continuously developing state of knowledge in parallel cultures with a lively flow of information — an exchange that continued into the Roman period:

(1) Since the 6th cent. BC, a competent astronomy developed exclusively in Babylon. Systematic observations were only recorded in Mesopotamia but became the basis of the first scientific theories of stellar motion. At the time of the earliest systematic theory of the cosmos in Plato's 'Timaeus' and the later first geometric

models of stellar movement by → Eudoxus [1] and → Callippus [5] (4th cent. BC), none of these Mesopotamian observations were quoted or even performed on their own. There is not a trace of evidence for the required systematic collection of astronomical data in Classical Greece.

(2.) Even at an early time the Pythagoreans and Plato noted the significance of numerical ratios in describing planetary movements. These proportions were only used in Babylonian astronomy and not in Egypt. At the latest → Hipparchus [6] took over the unchanged dimensions of these numerical ratios from the Babylonians. Quantification in Greek astronomy profited from a transfer of knowledge but not from independent, systematic observations. In the astronomy of → Ptolemy (2nd cent. AD) — the apex of Ancient astronomical theorizing — the Babylonian inheritance is apparent. He used the Babylonian hexagesimal system, the numerical parameters of solar and planetary theories are identical to those of the Babylonians, and many of the quoted observations were derived from Babylonian sources. On the other hand, nowhere in Babylonian documents on astronomy are there approaches to representing the arithmetic schemes of astronomy with geometric models. The permanent challenge to the Greek science of the cosmos consisted in using geometry to represent an empirically extremely exact theoretical calculation scheme.

C. THE MESOPOTAMIAN HERITAGE
1. OMINA

A significant number of Babylonian clay tablets deal with the circumstances that determine the fate of a state's community and its king. Fundamental ideas about cosmological relationships can be derived from them. The → omen literature, which attempted to elucidate the formally fixed destiny of the state by means of rules, came into existence no later than the 2nd millennium BC. Omina always took the form 'when such and such an event occurs, then the fate of the king or state is destined in such and such a manner'. The most important group of events that entered into the Babylonian omina were astronomical events such as eclipses or certain planetary constellations in the skies, as well as meteorological events. This was expressed in a very global, cosmic understanding of causal relationships and introduces the themes of Greek natural philosophy: astronomy and the science of the elements. Just as astronomic events were more than just special constellations of the stars in the firmament, meteorological events also had a direct influence on the well-being of the state: both were signs from the gods. These cosmological circumstances determined the destiny of the state and, therefore, the fate of each individual. However, the linkage of events by omina should not be considered to be deterministic: omina described circumstances that favour particular developments but do not force them.

2. CREATION MYTHS

Just like the omen texts, the creation myths of the Ancient Orient link the idea of an all-penetrating power of divine action and forces (recognizable in indicators, the position of the stars and the basic forms of weather) to events on earth. The links were represented in myths and explained in several variants: the changing seasons and corresponding growth and decay of plants was equated in the myths with a disquieted goddess descending into the Underworld, causing plants and animals to hibernate before reawakening them to life when she rose back to the world above again. The creation myths varied basic themes: (a) a god acquires or has power, (b) he uses this power to create order from a chaotic initial state by separating opposite states, often earth and water, from each other (→ World, creation of the).

3. ACHIEVEMENTS OF BABYLONIAN ASTRONOMY

Questions of cosmology concern the order, changes and causal links of events in the universe. In the first place this means events that determine life: the position of the stars and the environment. The effect of the sun's movements on daily life is obvious. The separation of day and night is part of every creation myth and with it the definition of time.

No later than the 6th cent. BC, Babylonian astronomers developed mathematical schemes with which they were able to describe certain phenomena with rules and to predict them with great accuracy. The most important were phenomena of the horizons: the day ended with sunset, at the same time the next day began. Months as the next larger calendar unit begin on the evening of the moon's first appearance after new moon (→ Calendar). The year began with spring at the beginning of a month, which was initially empirically determined but from the 5th cent. BC on was calculated according to mathematical schemes. The movements of the → planets were initially described according to their appearances on the horizon as days on which they either appeared after too much proximity to the sun on the eastern horizon or were overpowered by an approaching sun in the west and then remained invisible for several days. Calculation of the beginnings of the months was a real astronomical challenge because it was strongly dependent on the complex movements of the moon. Calculation succeeded by means of arithmetic tables that were supported in a piecemeal fashion by the linear relationships of numerical entries and fundamental periodicities of the movements of celestial bodies. Thus, the horizon phenomena of the moon and the appearance of the planets were also related to their apparent disappearance and reappearance in the sun's proximity.

The successful empirical basis of Babylonian astronomy were archives with long, systematically kept observations of phenomena of interest and the motion of the sun, moon and planets under the stars. These observation reports are known since the 7th cent. BC and maintained their written form of expression to an astonishing degree across political and cultural events until the Roman conquest (last tablets about 60 BC). No later than the 6th cent. BC the Babylonian astronomers discovered that the moving stars always moved in one zone in the heavens, the zodiac. From this time the locations of all stars are related to the path of the sun (ecliptic coordinates). These coordinates and times were the basic numerical data of ancient astronomical theory. The Babylonians succeeded in discovering regularities in this data that were then described in simple arithmetical relationships. The fundamental parameters of Babylonian astronomy consisted of periodicities of heavenly phenomena and findings of the fundamental relationships between them. The high esteem in which the Greeks held cosmic harmonies originated in the numerical relationships of Babylonian astronomers.

4. MEDICAL THEORIES

→ Medicine is the second scientific activity that is equally important in considering cosmic relationships and developed with different emphasis in Babylonia and Egypt. Extensive collections of prescriptions and treatment methods are preserved from both cultures and have roots that extend far into the past (3rd millennium BC). Like the early omen texts, medical texts have a strict syntactical structure and consist of a diagnostic opening section, followed by a middle part with formulations for making medicine, then a direction for treatment and occasionally concluding remarks on the prognosis for successful treatment. The regular relationship between diagnosis and therapy links indicators — not causes — of the disease with the therapeutic measure. They lie in a complex web of interdependence that partially extends outside the human body. Disease is the result of violations of divine commandments. These cosmological ideas underlie the assumption that human well-being depends on distant heavenly constellations.

D. GREEK COSMOLOGY
1. THE PRE-SOCRATICS

Thales, Anaximander and Anaximenes, who lived in the 6th cent. BC in Miletus, are considered the first Greek scholars. They lived on the periphery of the mighty Persian Empire when the sciences, especially astronomy, reached the peak of their development there. According to a representation by Aristotle (Metaph. 1,3), the 'Pre-Socratics' rejected the mythical and religious nature interpretations of their ancestors. The rise and decay of the world was explained in early → natural philosophy (*physikḗ*) by a growth metaphor; the purpose is to discover order (*kósmos*) in nature (φύσις/*phýsis*), determine its essence and explain its origin. The idea of the cosmos as a structure of the whole linked by the elements directly associates its order with the harmonies of which the Pythagoreans spoke using the verb ἁρμόττειν (*harmóttein*, 'compose'), meaning harmonies borrowed from music and based on numbers. Many early doctors and almost all Pre-Socratics

located the *phýsis* of humans in the general context of the *kósmos*. The early medical texts of the *Corpus Hippocraticum* often reflect ancient oriental views of cosmically caused diseases. In writings such as 'On the Nature of Man' and texts on meteorological phenomena ('Airs, Waters, Places'; → Hippocrates), therapeutic success depends on knowledge of the universe (τὸ ὅλον, *to hólon*), while harmony between the human body and the environment is a precondition of health.

2. THE GEOMETRIZATION OF COSMOLOGY

The 'Timaeus', a late dialogue of → Plato, is the oldest preserved text that systematically treats the structure of the world, the movement of the stars, the structure of matter and their changes including mineralogical and zoological facts. Different components of the oriental concept of nature were synthesized with Pre-Socratic speculation. The creation myth of the 'Timaeus' and the dialogue are Plato's 'probable' representation of the world, which was created by a → *dēmiourgós* [3], a 'craftsman'. The created order follows harmonic principles that equally determine the construction of the smallest elements of matter and the principles of the movements of the celestial bodies. The special meaning of the 'Timaeus' lies in the fact that Plato set cosmology on a course in which the means of geometry were used for the construction of regularities and explanation of the fundamental properties of the world. Plato did not develop an astronomical theory as a solution but formulated a research programme that Greek science was only able to bring to a preliminary conclusion around 500 years later.

Aristotle assumed the eternity of the cosmos and stellar → motion and concludes there is an unmoved moving force (κινῶν ἀκίνητον, Aristot. Met. 1212b 31) that moves the cosmos from the outside. The greatest contribution of Aristotle's cosmology is the development of a theory of motion: the natural motion of the celestial bodies is circular and eternal; heavy bodies fall without influence of external forces towards the centre of the earth. This basic concept supported the hypothesis of a geocentric cosmology. Since Aristotle the geometric method has dominated in cosmology. Somewhat before → Euclid [3], the author of the 'Elements', → Autolycus [3] of Pitane (before 310 BC), composed the oldest completely preserved geometric-astronomic treatise.

It is unclear when the spherical shape of the earth was discovered. Plato was already convinced of a spherical shape without justifying it. Aristotle argued (Aristot. Cael. 2,14) that the shadow of the earth is always circular on the lunar surface and, therefore, the earth must be a sphere. This was hardly disputed. The spherical shape of the stellar sphere is likewise not apparent in the visual perception of an observer on earth. The Egyptians visualized the sky as a flat roof, which was often depicted as the goddess Nut stretched out over the land. Babylonian astronomers understood the heavens with their daily revolution to be a sphere no later than the 5th cent. BC, which is explained by the Babylonians already using abstract concepts such as a system of co-ordinates on spheres. The concept of a position of the stars with the earth at rest made the assumption of a revolving stellar sphere almost inescapable.

Plato defended the central location of a round earth at the centre of the cosmos in similar manner to → Anaximander. Aristotle's theory of motions formulated the physical reasons for a geocentric location of the earth: if it were to revolve around the sun (which is at the centre of a resting sphere of fixed stars), then the earth would have to turn around its own axis once daily. However, this motion could not be reconciled with Aristotle's theory of motions. Freely moving bodies above the earth's surface, such as clouds or dropped stones, would have to remain behind the motion of the earth's surface, which they manifestly did not.

Euclid postulated a complex halving of the visible heavens above the horizon in different → seasons. Assuming a fixed star sphere of finite size, it follows in strict geometric terms that an observer on earth must be at or close to the centre of this sphere. If the observer was clearly off centre in the sphere, the horizon would have to reveal a heaven that did not halve the stellar sphere. This is one of the most sustainable arguments for a geocentric cosmology. It is repeated by the most diverse authors and even features in the 16th-cent. discussion of Copernician theory.

→ Aristarchus [3] of Samos (320–250 BC) became famous because of a critique by Archimedes [1] in the treatise 'The Sand Reckoner' and a brief comment by Plutarch for having proposed a heliocentric cosmology. Since Aristarchus stood at the beginning of the phase of geometrizing the cosmos and physical consideration played no role for him, it is conceivable that he was able to escape the concentrated argument in favour of a geocentric universe. In the first book of the 'Almagest', → Ptolemy discussed in detail the possibility of a heliocentric universe and rejects it so convincingly that Copernicus was only able to evade it using rhetorical tricks in his treatise De Revolutionibus. The assumption that other ancient authors propounded a heliocentric cosmology does not stand up to documentary evidence. Heraclides [16] Ponticus is also incorrectly described as a defender of heliocentrism in the context of Simplicius' Commentary on Aristotelian 'Physics' and → Calcidius' Commentary on Plato's 'Timaeus'.

3. THE MOTION OF THE CELESTIAL BODIES
→ Eudoxus [1] of Cnidus (c. 428–347 BC) attempted to explain the motions of the planets on the basis of geometrical hypotheses in which the sun, moon and planets moved on homocentric rings (i.e., they are arranged with a common centre) that are interposed in a mobile manner and whose centre is the earth, which is at rest. Deficiencies in principle resulted in the homocentric planetary model never being seriously pursued.

The next great step in the development of geometric models for stellar movements was performed by the mathematician → Apollonius [13] of Perge (265–170 BC), followed by the astronomer → Hipparchus [6] of

Nicaea (190–120 BC). Beginning with an investigation of the duration of the seasons, they developed a geometric model in which a secondary smaller circle on the periphery of which the sun moved was guided by a primary larger circle. Hipparchus attempted to apply a model of similar construction to planetary motion but failed. Only Ptolemy succeeded in the 2nd cent. AD. in solving the complicated methodological problems of planetary models. The epicycle theory of planetary motion was the standard model of mathematical astronomy until the work of KEPLER.

In his work 'Planetary Hypotheses' Ptolemy made an attempt to determine the relative spatial dimensions of the stars based on mechanical considerations. Ptolemy determined that the geometric theories should obey the principles of an ether-filled space. The stars were described as immutable bodies that are made of ether, do not age and move uniformly in circles. They only perform a single, voluntary motion. Every body, whether on earth or in the skies, can assume a natural motion, but only bodies on earth can be removed from their natural motion by force and coerced into changing their location.

E. ROMAN COSMOLOGY
Roman cosmology is closely linked to the tradition of the seven → artes liberales. The resulting popularization of Greek cosmological concepts resulted in a wide dissemination of cosmological knowledge but with the complex mathematical-geometric foundations being relegated to the background. Various textbooks offered a summary of the structure of the cosmos as well as the most important themes and terms.

→ Pliny the Elder (23–79 BC) composed the most exhaustive Roman representation of the structure of the cosmos and its internal relationships. He treated cosmological themes (as did many later medieval authors) in his 'Natural History' (Naturalis historia) in individual chapters on different topics. Book 18 treats a special characteristic of his astronomy: the theory that retrograde planetary motions were caused by the power of the sun's rays but without explaining the mathematical-geometrical methods and principles underlying this model. → Martianus Capella (c. AD 410–439) composed 'The Marriage of Philology to Mercury', an allegoric survey of ancient cosmology in eight books and the most widely read introduction to the Seven Liberal Arts. Apart from a general description, he treated the approximate orbiting times of the planets, interesting constellations and the varying lengths of day and night in a superficial manner. His description of the motion of Venus is difficult to understand but during the early Middle Ages it provoked interpretative attempts in which the planets Mercury and Venus moved in paths around the sun. This source is of great importance to the Copernican turn towards a heliocentric cosmology.

The Commentary of → Macrobius (AD 360–after 422), Commentarii in somnium Scipionis, on the approach in Cicero's cosmology to Plato's 'Timaeus' was one of the most widely read astronomical texts of the Middle Ages. In his representation of the general Greek cosmological model with a round earth at the centre, surrounded by seven celestial spheres, the last of which is the bearer of the 10 celestial circles, he emphasized the necessity of the regularity and circularity of celestial motions as well as the mandatory use of numbers for the world order.

→ Calcidius (about 400) composed an influential Commentary on the 'Timaeus' (*In Timaeum commentarius*), a free translation of the Plato commentary by Theon of Smyrna. This description of the heavens and planetary motion differed from those of other authors, especially because he placed the sun in the series of planets between the moon and Mercury. Another difference was his comparatively strong interest in the geometric background and the possibilities of the 'Greek' cosmological model, but he was unfamiliar with that of Ptolemy. Otherwise, he treated the customary themes of a manual, such as the spherical shape of the earth and the universe, eclipses, the order of the celestial circles and the motion of the planets.

F. TRANSITION TO THE MIDDLE AGES

From the 6th to the 12th cents., the texts of Greek mathematical astronomy, especially the 'Almagest', were unknown in Europe. The decline of astronomical and cosmological knowledge in the 6th cent. was followed by a revival of interest in the 8th (Beda, 673–735). The texts of Cassiodorus, Isidore and Beda were influential, but none provide a complete image of cosmological relationships. Six Roman texts defined the knowledge of the early Middle Ages: Aratus' [4] 'Phaenomena' (in translation by Germanicus, Cicero or Avienus), Hyginus' 'Astronomia' and the cited texts of Pliny, Macrobius, Martianus Capella and Calcidius. Platonism gained great influence in the Middle Ages that extended to the 16th cent. as a result of Calcidius' Commentary on the 'Timaeus'.

→ Astronomy; → Astrology; → Calendar; → Planets; → Mathematics; → Moon; → Sun; → World, creation of the; → Chronography; → Time, theories of; COSMOLOGY

D. J. FURLEY, The Greek Cosmologists, 1987; B. S. EASTWOOD, Astronomy in Christian Latin Europe C. 500 C. 1150, in: Journ. for the History of Astronomy, 28, 1997; D. GOLTZ, Studien zur altoriental. und griech. Heilkunde: Therapie — Arzneibereitung — Rezeptstruktur, 1974; G. E. R. LLOYD, Magic, Reason, and Experience, 1979; O. NEUGEBAUER, A History of Ancient Mathematical Astronomy, 1975; J. NORTH, Astronomy and Cosmology, 1994; E. REINER, Astral Magic in Babylonia, 1995; A. J. SACHS, H. HUNGER, Astronomical Diaries and Related Texts from Babylonia, vol. 1ff., 1988ff.   GE.G.

Cosmopolitanism The theory of cosmopolitanism (etymology: *kósmos*, 'world', and *polítēs*, 'citizen') had already been developed in the pre-Hellenistic period by the sophist → Hippias [5] of Elis (late 5th cent. BC), who disputed the authority of positive law in favour of unwritten laws. → Democritus [1] of Abdera declared that the entire earth was open to the wise man and that the home of a good soul is the universe (fr. 247 DK). If one wishes to believe Cicero (Tusc. 5,108), Socrates, a contemporary of Democritus, also considered himself a 'citizen of the World' (*mundi incolam et civem*).

The term experienced its true flowering during Hellenism when the traditional polis order was placed in doubt. Theoretical reflection became reality: philosophers, especially Cynics and Stoics, travelled much, understood themselves as cosmopolitans and no longer considered their exile as a negative. → Diogenes [14] of Sinope declared that he had no house or native city but that he was a citizen of the world (κοσμοπολίτης, SSR V B 263) because 'the only true citizenship is the one realized in the cosmos '(Diog. Laert. 6,72). His student → Crates of Thebes said: 'My fatherland includes more than just a wall and a roof / the entire earth is city and house to us / it is open to us to inhabit it '(Diog. Laert. 6,98). The same assessment of cosmopolitanism is also found in another Socratic school: → Aristippus [3] of Cyrene, who said of himself: 'I will not bind myself to one city but live everywhere as a stranger' (Xen. Mem. 2,1,13), and → Theodoros Atheos, who considered the world to be his fatherland (Diog. Laert. 2,99).

It is disputed to what extent the cosmopolitanism of the Cynics and the Cyrenaics was primarily a negative mental attitude, i.e., that being a citizen of the world primarily meant no ties to a fatherland and being devoted to an impassioned individualism, or if it also contained the positive feeling of belonging to a universal human community as was the case with the Stoics. In any case, there was an intellectual tradition linking Cynicism to the Stoa that was related in two works: the *Politeía* of Diogenes [14] of Sinope, which undermined the foundations of the *pólis* and the work of the same name by → Zeno of Citium, which demanded that people should stop living apart in cities and instead should consider themselves as the citizens of one city and one people that only knows one way of life and one social order (Plut. De fortuna Alexandri 6,329a-b). To → Chrysippus [2] the universe appeared as one great city, governed by the gods, inhabited by humans and subject to natural law (SVF III, 333–339). Later, → Panaetius (2nd cent. BC) took one step back by believing that the existence of separate states could be reconciled with efforts for the protection and safety of the common society of all human beings (Cic. Off. 1,149). Stoic cosmopolitanism continued into the imperial period. Seneca (De vita beata 5), Epictetus (Diatribe 2,10,3) and Marcus Aurelius (4,4; 6,44) considered the universe their home while the world was seen as one great city. However, this cosmopolitanism had to compete with the new concept of the world and humanity that arose with Christianity. In it all humans were equal in Christ. Paul said (Col 3,11): 'There is neither Greek nor Jew, circumcision nor non-circumcision, Barbarian, Scythian, bond nor free man. Christ is all and in all.'

H.C. BALDRY, Zeno's Ideal State, in: JHS 79, 1959, 3–15; SSR IV, 537–547, n. 52; I. LANA, Tracce di dottrine cosmopolitiche in Grecia prima del cinismo, in: RFIC 29, 1951, 193–216; 317–338; G.B. LAVERY, Never Seen in Public: Seneca and the Limits of Cosmopolitanism, in: Latomus 56, 1997, 1–13; J.L. MOLES, Cynic Cosmopolitanism, in: R.B. BRANHAM, M.-O. GOULET-CAZÉ (ed.), The Cynics. The Cynic Movement in Antiquity and its Legacy, 1996, 105–120.	M.G.-C.

Cosmos see → Cosmology; → World

Cossaei (Κοσσαῖοι; *Kossaîoi*). A mountain people of the Zagros that was divided into tribes, approximately in the area of modern → Luristan, cf. Latin *Cossiaei* (Plin. HN 6,134); *Cossaei* (Curt. 4,12,10). *Kossaía* as the name of a region is found in Diod. Sic. 17,111,5. The relationship to the *Kíssioi* and the *Kissía* region (Hdt. 5,49; 5,52; Diod. Sic.11,7,2) remains uncertain. The C. were probably identical to the Cassites (*Kaššu*) whose clans infiltrated → Mesopotamia after the 17th cent. BC. Subsequently, a durable Cassitic dynasty, which retained certain Cassitic features despite rapid Babylonization, established itself until the 12th cent. BC in Babylonia. Remains of the Cassitic language can still be demonstrated in Assyrian inscriptions of the 1st millennium. Under the Achaemenids the C. were largely independent but they were subjugated in 324/3 BC by Alexander [4] the Great (Arr. Anab. 7,15,1–3; Diod. Sic. 17,111,4–6; Plut. Alexander 72,4). Later Cossaean troops were integrated into Alexander's army (Arr. Anab. 7,23,1; Diod. Sic. 17,110; Str. 11,13,6). In 317 BC Antigonus I passed through the territory of the C. (Diod. Sic. 19,19,3), who were described as wild cave dwellers, and suffered losses.

J.A. BRINKMAN, s.v. Kassiten, RLA 5, 464–73.	K.KE.

Cossura (Κόσσουρα, Κόσ(σ)ουρος; *Kóssoura, Kós(s)ouros*, Lat. *Cossura, Cossyra*). Vulcanic island between Sicily and Africa, modern Pantelleria, before the Punic Wars under Carthaginian rule, in the First Punic War temporarily, after 217 BC finally conquered by Rome and attached to the province of Sicilia. The partially Phoenician inscriptions of coins demonstrate that the population was Punic for a considerable time later. Remains from the Prehistoric to Byzantine periods.

S. TUSA, La Sicilia nella preistoria, 1983, 274ff.; Id., Attività ricognitiva a Pantelleria, in: Kokalos 39/40, II.2, 1993/4, 1547f.	GI.F.

Cossus Cognomen, maybe of Etruscan origin and probably initially a praenomen (SCHULZE, 158, 519; KAJANTO, Cognomina 178). Nickname of one of the oldest branches of the Cornelii (→ Cornelius [I 20–22]). Meaning as the nickname 'woodworm' is uncertain [1],

in the early imperial period also a praenomen of some Cornelii Lentuli (Cornelius [II 26–27]).

1 WALDE/HOFMANN 1,281	K.-L.E.

Cossutia Daughter of a wealthy equestrian with whom Caesar became engaged probably for financial reasons [1. 16], but whom he divorced because of his office as priest [2. 14] (Suet. Iul. 1,1).

1 G. WALTER, Caesar, 1955	2 W. WILL, Caesar, 1992.
ME.STR.

Cossutianus Capito Senator at least from 47 BC; in 57 sentenced by the Senate because of extortion in his province, perhaps Lycia-Pamphylia (Tac. Ann. 13,33; 16,21; [1]). As son-in-law of Ofonius Tigellinus was readmitted to the Senate where he accused Antistius Sosianus and Thrasea Paetus (PIR² C 1543).

1 SYME, RP 2, 1150ff.	W.E.

Cossutius Roman family name, attested since the 2nd cent. BC [1. 189–203]. Several artists belonged to this *gens*.
[1] The → architect C., whom Vitruvius (7, praef. 15ff.) called a *civis romanus*, probably under → Antiochus [6] IV Epiphanes (ruled 176/5–164 BC) in → Athens 'took over the construction of the Olympieion using a large measure according to Corinthian symmetries and proportions '(Vitr. De arch. 7, praef. 17). The late archaic new construction of the Zeus temple, which was begun under the Peisistratids as a Doric → dipteros, remained unfinished and was transformed by C. into a building of the Corinthian order, which also remained incomplete and was only finished and inaugurated under → Hadrian (Cass. Dio 69,12,2). Vitruvius regretted that C. had left no writings, but concluded from this fact that construction had advanced so far that written documentation was no longer required for completion.

1 RAWSON, Family.

A. GIULIANO, s.v. C., EAA 2.; E. RAWSON, Architecture and Sculpture: The Activities of the Cossutii, in: PBSR 63, 1975, 36–48; R. TÖLLE-KASTENBEIN, Das Olympieion in Athen, 1994, 17–74, 142–152.	C.HÖ.

[2] Kossutios Cerdo, M. Greek sculptor, *libertus* of C. He signed two copies of a classical Pan type found in Rome. Their dating to the 1st cent. BC is disputed as is his identification as a Marcus Kossutios of Aphrodisias.

D. ARNOLD, Die Polykletnachfolge, 1969, 49–54; 247; E. RAWSON, Architecture and sculpture. The activities of the Cossutii, in: PBSR 43, 1975, 36–47.

[3] C. Menelaus, M. Greek sculptor and *libertus*. Known from a now lost signature, he is usually identified as Menelaus, allegedly a student of → Stephanus, who was active in the 1st cent. BC, and creator of the eclectic group 'Orestes and Electra'.

E. RAWSON, Architecture and sculpture. The activities of the Cossutii, in: PBSR 43, 1975, 36–47.; P. ZANKER, Klassizistische Statuen, 1974, 57–58. R.N.

Costoboci (Κοστοβῶκοι; *Kostobôkoi*, Paus. 10,34,5; Κοστουβῶκοι; *Kostoubôkoi*, Cass. Dio 71,12,1; *Costoboci*, SHA Aur. 22,1; *Costobocae*, Amm. Marc. 22,8,42; *Castaboci/Castabocae*, ILS 1327). A people of Dacian (Thracian?) origin that lived on the eastern margin of the Carpathians. In AD 170, the C. took part in the Marcomanni Wars against Rome. A raid took them through Dacia (cf. CIL III 14214 = ILS 8501) into Greece where they were defeated in → Phocis (Paus. 10,34,5; cf. ILS 1327). The Asdingi inflicted a crushing defeat on them in 171/2 (Cass. Dio 71,12,1).

A. PREMERSTEIN, s.v. Kostoboken, RE 11, 1504–1507; P. OLIVA, Pannonia and the Onset of the Crisis, 1962, 276–278; I. I. RUSSU, Les Costoboces, in: Dacia N.S. 3, 1959, 341–352. J.BU.

Cotenna (Κότεννα; *Kótenna*). City in eastern Pamphylia. The name C. is possibly related to the Katenneis tribe that inhabited the mountainous region above Side and Aspendus [1]. In sympolity with Erymna, its western neighbour [2]; bishopric of Pamphylia I (with metropolis in Side) [3; 4. 242]. Modern Gökbel (formerly Menteşbey, Gödene).

1 ZGUSTA, 240f., 294 2 M. ZIMMERMANN, Untersuchungen zur histor. Landeskunde Zentrallykiens (Antiquitas 1/42), 1992, 137 3 J. DARROUZÈS, Notitiae episcopatuum Ecclesiae Constantinopolitanae, 1981 4 G. FEDALTO, Hierarchia Ecclesiastica Orientalis 1, 1988, 242.

G. E. BEAN, s.v. K., PE, 467. F.H.

Cothocidae (Κοθωκίδαι; *Kothōkídai*). Attic *paralia* deme of the Oeneis phyle, from 307/6 to 200 BC of the Demetrias, with two *bouleutaí*. Probably *c.* 6 km north-east of Eleusis near Hagios Ioannis in Goritsa north of Aspropyrgos, the provenance of tomb inscription IG II² 6481 [1; 2. 49]. → Aeschines [2] was from C.

1 E. HONIGMANN, s.v. K., RE 11, 1516 2 TRAILL, Attica 9, 19, 49, 62, 68, 111 no. 76, table 6, 12. H.LO.

Cothurnus (ὁ κόθορνος; *ho kóthornos, cot[h]urnus*). The Greek cothurnus was a high-shafted soft leather boot that fitted tightly to the leg and foot (and, by extension, was used as a synonym for an adaptable person in Xen. Hell. 2,3,30–31). It was wrapped with bands or tied at an opening at the front. The cothurnus is mentioned as women's footwear (Aristoph. Eccl. 341–346; Lys. 657), but was worn in particular by elegant youths at a symposium and → komos. It was the preferred footwear of Hermes, Diomedes, Odysseus, Theseus and Iolaus, who wore it as a walking-shoe; associated by Aristoph. Ran. 45–47 (cf. Paus. 8,31,4) with Dionysus. The other significance of the cothurnus was as theatre

footwear. Originally probably without a sole but Aeschylus introduced a sole that became higher over time [1]. In the 2nd cent. BC the cothurnus was given high wooden soles that almost became stilts during the Roman imperial period so that Lucian (Nero 9), for example, mocked them as wooden stands (*okríbantes*, cf. Ov. Am. 3,1,45). Occasionally, the cothurnus had a 'Lydian' connotation (Ov. Am. 3,1,14; Hdt. 1,155,5) in ancient literature. The *neurobátēs* (νευροβάτης), a kind of high-wire artist whom Carinus had perform in AD 284/5 (SHA Car. 19,2), also wore the cothurnus.

1 K. KNOLL, H. PROTZMANN, Die Antiken im Albertinum, 1993, 45f. no. 24.

O. LAU, Schuster und Schusterhandwerk in der griech.-röm. Lit. und Kunst, 1967, 127–130; N. HIMMELMANN, Ein Ptolemäer mit Keule und K., in: N. BASGELEN (ed.), FS J. Inan, 1989, 391–395. R.H.

Cotini Celtic people that settled in the 1st cent. AD with other small tribes to the north of the → Marcomanni and → Quadi. Renowned as miners, they apparently owed the Quadi tribute. Apart from mining iron ore, it may be assumed that they manufactured weapons. Their location is disputed but it was probably in central Slovakia near the Slovakian Ore Mountains. In the Marcomanni Wars the C. sided with the Romans (Cass. Dio 72,12) and were later settled between the Danube and the Drava (Tac. Germ. 43,1; Ptol. 2,11,11).

J. DOBIÁŠ, The History of Czechoslovak Territory before the Appearance of the Slavs (Czech with English summary), 1964, 174; 182; 370. J.BU.

Cotiso King in the lower Danube region about 40 BC., according to Flor. 2,28 of the Dacians (according to Suet. Aug. 63,2 of the Gaetae). Florus and Horace (Carm. 3,8,18) report that he suffered a defeat at the hands of the Romans, probably in 30/29 (cf. [1]). Information by Antony that Octavian planned to establish a family relationship with C. is probably just a rumour (Suet. ibid.).

1 A. MÓCSY, Der vertuschte Dakerkrieg des M. Licinius Crassus, in: Historia 15, 1966, 511–514.

A. MÓCSY, Pannonia and Upper Moesia, 1974, 23f. D.K.

Cotta Cognomen in the *gens Aurelia* (→ Aurelius [I 2–12 and II 13]).

KAJANTO, Cognomina 106. K.-L.E.

Cottia Wife of the consul Vestricius Spurinna, to whom Plin. Ep. 3,10 is addressed. Possibly from the Transpadana [1].

1 SYME, RP 7, 488, 542f. W.E.

Cottiae *Mutatio* ('horse-changing post') between Ticinum and Augusta Taurinorum (It. Ant. 340,3; It. Burd. 557,5), modern Cozzo. Branch to Vercellae (Tab. Peut. 4,1; cf. Geogr. Rav. 4,30; CIL XI, 3281–3284); *miliarium* (CIL V, 8063); *municipium* (CIL XI, 416).

NISSEN, 2, 176; MILLER, 226; RUGGIERO, 4, 1254.   G.BR.

Cottius Celtic name derived from *cot(to)* — 'old' [1. 186–187; 2. 184].
[1] M. Iulius C. Son of king M. Iulius Donnus, ruler of the Alpes Cottiae, which bear his name (Str. 4,1,3; 4,6,6; Vitr. De arch. 8,3,17; Suet. Tib. 37,3; Cass. Dio 60,24,4). During the Augustan alpine campaigns in 15/14 BC, he initially appears to have resisted the Romans but then submitted and was finally accepted by Augustus into the equestrian officialdom of the empire. In the inscription of the arc of Segusio (Susa), which was erected in 8/9 BC in honour of Augustus, he bears the title *praef. civitatium* of 14 named tribes (CIL V 7231), of which six belong to the subjected tribes on the Tropaeum Alpium (CIL V 7817), as well as unnamed tribes. C. administered his realm for life in Roman service and saw to the building of a pass road (cf. CIL XII 5497). He was supposedly interred in Susa (Amm. Marc. 15,10; Plin. HN 3,138).

1 EVANS   2 SCHMIDT.

J.PRIEUR, La province romaine des Alpes Cottiennes, 1968; G.WALSER, Studien zur Alpengesch. in ant. Zeit, 1994.

[2] M. Iulius C. Son of C. [1], who was probably praefect as the heir of his father but then was granted the title of king by Claudius in AD 44, which was probably also associated with an enlargement of his territory (Cass. Dio 60,24,4; cf. CIL V 7269). After his death in AD 63, Nero permanently transformed his realm into a Roman province (Suet. Nero 18; Eutr. 7,14,5; Jer. Chron. 184b; Aur. Vict. Caesares 5,2; Cassiod. Var. 685; Chron. min. p. 138 MOMMSEN).
[3] Son of → Vestricius Spurinna.

Cotton The German word *Baumwolle* (= tree wool) is analogous to the Greek nomenclature ἔριον ἀπὸ ξύλου, ἐριόξυλον. Cotton is the soft seed hairs of cultivated species of the genus *Gossypium* (the cotton plant) in the mallow family (Malvaceae). The cotton plant, usually an annual shrub, can reach a height of up to 2 m, which is why ancient authors sometimes spoke of it as a tree. A walnut-sized, capsule-like fruit develops from the flower and in the autumn soft, white seed hairs, the actual cotton, emerge from it. The ripe capsules were harvested and then dried.

Herodotes (3,106) claims India as the cotton plant's land of origin and describes it as a wild tree whose wool surpasses sheep's wool in beauty and quality. Theophrastus and Pliny also comment on the origin and appearance of the cotton plant (Theophr. Hist. pl. 4,4,8; 4,7,7; Plin. HN 12,38–39), which grew on the Persian Gulf according to these authors. According to

Strabo (15,1,20), Nearchus reported that clothes were made of cotton in India. It remains unclear if the βύσσος *(byssos)* mentioned in Pausanias (5,5,2; 6,26,6; 7,21,14) as growing in Elis and being processed in Patrae was cotton.

1 E.J.W. BARBER, Prehistoric Textiles. The Development of Cloth in the Neolithic and Bronze Ages with Special Reference to the Aegean, 1991, 32f.   2 BLÜMNER, Techn. 1, 199f.   3 WAGLER, s.v. B., RE 3, 167ff.   4 J.P. WILD, Textile Manufacture in the Northern Roman Provinces, 1970, 17–19.   A.P.-G.

Cottyto (Κοτυτώ; *Kotytố*; variant *Kótys*/Κότυς, *Kottố*/Κοττώ; Lat. Cottyto).
A. GENERAL   B. THE CORINTHIAN-SICILIAN CULT
C. THE THRACIAN CULT

A. GENERAL
Traditionally considered variants of the name of a Thracian-Phrygian goddess who was honoured in orgiastic rites and whose festivity, the Kotytia, was celebrated in Corinth and Sicily in the Greek world [1]. However, it is probable that the Corinthian-Sicilian cult was part of the calendar of rural celebrations and should be differentiated from the putative Thracian cult [2].

B. THE CORINTHIAN-SICILIAN CULT
According to the Suda (s.v. Κότυς; Θιασώτης Κότυος), Cotys was in Corinth ἔφορος τῶν αἰσχρῶν; the *daimon* C. is also associated by Hesych. s.v. C., with that city. This Corinthian cult was characterized by obscenity and transvestism (Eupolis fr. 88; cf. 93 PCG). Reports on the daughters of Timandreus, of whom one, Cot(y)to, was worshipped by the → Heraclids, may contain an aetiological myth (schol. Theoc. 6,40a; cf. schol. Pind. Ol. 13,56b). In Sicily the proverb *harpagá Kotyt(t)íois* referred to a celebration, the Cotyt(t)ia, during which cake and nuts were attached to branches and torn off by participants (Plut. Proverb. Alex. 78; cf. → *eiresiónē*). Recently, it was discovered that the celebration, known as Κοτυτίον (*Kotytíon*), was important in → Selinous (SEG 43,630 A 7). The conclusion is that a locally important Dorian cult of Cot(y)to was associated with the fertility of the soil and the purity of the community.

C. THE THRACIAN CULT
Only Strabo (10,3,16 citing Aeschylus' *Edonoi*, fr. 57 RADT) believes that the Cotytia as well as the Bendidea (→ Bendis) were a Thracian celebration analogous to ecstatic Phrygian rituals. Therefore, the 'Thracian' C. may be based on a misinterpretation of Aeschylus by Strabo or a pseudo-archaeologia of the other by Aeschylus. The commentators on the *Báptai* of Eupolis do not mention Thrace with reference to the C., nor is there Thracian archaeological evidence for the C.. An identification with Artemis is speculative.
→ Eupolis; → Hellotis

1 K. SCHWENN, s.v. Kotys (1), RE 11, 1549–1551
2 M.H. JAMESON et al., A Sacred Law from Selinous,
1993, 23–26. R.GOR.

Cotuatus Celtic composite name from *cot* — 'old'
(EVANS, 340–342). Leader of an army of Carnutes, who
in 52 BC attacked and murdered Roman merchants in
Cenabum together with Conconnetodumnus. As a
deterrent, Caesar had him cruelly executed (Caes. B.
Gall. 7,3; 8,38).
→ Conconnetodumnus W.SP.

Cotyora (Κοτύωρα; *Kotýōra*). Port town on the south
coast of → Pontus Euxinus, assumed to be near Ordu,
where remains of an ancient harbour pier are located.
The 'Ten Thousand' of → Xenophon rested there for 45
days before they took to the sea in the west. Under Pharnaces I (185–160/154 BC), C. was united in a *synoikismós* with Cerasus in Pharnacaea and declined to a small
town (πολίχνη, Str. 12,3,17) (Arr. Peripl. p. eux. 24;
Peripl. m. Eux. 34). E.O.

Cotyrta (Κοτύρτα; *Kotýrta*). Spartan → *períoikoi* town
on the west coast of the Parnon penninsula (→ Parnon),
maybe modern Daimonía, where Mycenaean finds
have been recorded in quantity. References: Thuc.
4,56,1; Steph. Byz. s.v. K. Epigraphy: IG V 1,961–967;
1013; SEG 2,173–175; 11,899. Y.L.

Cotys (Κότυς; *Kótys*).
I. HELLENISTIC PERIOD II. IMPERIAL PERIOD

I. HELLENISTIC PERIOD
[I 1] Important king of the → Odrysae 383/2–360/59
BC (Suda s.v. C.; characterization in Ath. 12,531e–
532a), successor to Hebryzelmis [1]. C.'s diplomatic
and military skill — suppression of the uprisings of
Adamas (Aristot. Pol. 1311b) and Miltocythes (Dem.
Or. 23,115) — led to a consolidation and expansion of
the kingdom of the Odrysae. With the help of his son-
in-law, the Athenian mercenary leader → Iphicrates
(Dem. Or. 23,129; Ath. 4,131a; Nep. Iphicrates 3,4),
and later (Dem. Or. 23,132) with the support of Charidemus [2] (Dem. Or. 23,149–150), C. fought a long
war with changing fortunes against Athens for possessions on the Chersonesus and the Propontis (Dem. Or.
23, passim; cf. Nep. Timotheus 1,2), so that an initially
good relationship with Athens (granting of citizenship:
Dem. Or. 23,118) turned into the opposite (Dem. Or.
23,114). At the end of his rule, C. possessed almost the
entire Chersonesus (Demo. Or. 23,158–162) and intervened in Macedonian rivalries for the throne (Diod. Sic.
16,2,6). Citizens of Aenus murdered C. (Aristot. Pol.
1311b; Dem. Or. 23,119; 163; Aeschin. In Tim. 51).
His son → Cersobleptes succeeded him as ruler
[1. 218–231; 2].

C.'s economic measures are attested by Aristotle
(Oec. 1351a) and in the inscription of Pistiros [1. 317].
C. minted silver and gold coins [3. 112–125]. The name

C. on vessels of the Rogozen hoard has been associated
with this king (cf. SEG 37,618; 40,580).

1 Z.H. ARCHIBALD, The Odrysian Kingdom of Thrace,
1998 2 A. FOL, Die Politik des odrys. Königs K.I., in:
E. CH. WELSKOPF (ed.), Hellenische Poleis 2, 1974, 993–
1014 3 U. PETER, Die Mz. der thrak. Dynasten (5.–
3. Jh.v.Chr.), 1997.

[I 2] Thracian king, son of Rhaizdus, honoured at
Delphi 276/5 (?) BC as a → *próxenos* (Syll.³ 438). Identification with C., the father of → Rhascuporis in
IGBulg 1,389 and 5,5138 (MORETTI, 122; cf. SEG
31,652) is disputed [1. 5].
[I 3] Odrysian king, son of a certain Seuthes (Liv.
42,51,10f.) [1. 5], with a brilliant personality (Pol.
27,12; Diod. Sic. 30,3). Ally of → Perseus in the 3rd
Roman-Macedonian War (171–168 BC; Liv. 42,29,12;
51,10; 57,6; 58,6; 43,18,2; Eutr. 4,6,2). The incursion
of Autlesbis and Corragus into Odrysian Marene (Liv.
42,67,3–5) forced C. to defend his realm. In 168 BC he
participated in the battle of Pydna against Perseus of
Macedonia (Liv. 44,42,2). In 167 political alliance with
Rome (Pol. 30,17; Liv. 45,42,5–12; Zon. 9,24). Inscription Syll.³ 656, which is usually attributed to him, is in
part also attributed to C. [I 4] (cf. SEG 32,1206)
[2. 75–77, 91–93, 98–100]. On coinage: [3. 33f., 84].
[I 4] Founder of the Odrysian-Astaean (→ Astae) dynasty with capital in Bizye, ruled c. 100–87 BC. As a
Roman ally, C. prevented the usurpation of the Macedonian throne under the governorship of C. Sentius
(Diod. Sic. 37,5a; Liv. Per. 70). C.'s successor was Sadalas I [cf. 1. 6].
[I 5] King of the → Astae and Odrysae loyal to Rome,
who in 57 BC bribed L. Calpurnius [I 19] Piso to kill the
king of the → Bessi, Rabocentus (Cic. Pis. 84). In 48 C.
sent his son, Sadalas II with Thracian horsemen to support Pompey (Caes. B. Civ. 3,4,3; 36,4; Luc. 5,54; Cass.
Dio 41,51,2; 63,1) [2. 121; 4. 189–191]. On coinage:
[3. 40–53, 88–89].
[I 6] Son of Sadalas II and Polemocrateia (IGR 1,775;
Cass. Dio 47,25,1 irrt), grandson of C. [I 5] (cf. [1. 6]).
After his father's murder, C. was raised in Cyzicus
(App. B Civ. 4,75,319–320) and installed in 28 BC as
the Astaean-Odrysian king. Brother-in-law of → Rhoemetalces I, who later became guardian of C.'s son Rhas-
cusporis II (Cass. Dio 54,20,3; 34,5). C. was probably
killed during the warfare of the Macedonian governor
M. Primus in 22 BC in Thrace (Cass. Dio 54,3,2). PIR²
C 1553; SEG 34,701 [2. 123–126; 4. 192–191; 5. 212–
213].
[I 7] Father of Rhascusporis I, who founded the
Sapaean dynasty in 48 BC (IG II/III² 3442) [5. 212f.].
[I 8] Sapaean king c. 42–31 BC; son of Rhascusporis I,
grandson of C. [I 7]; honoured in Athens (IG II/III²
3443); predecessor and brother of Rhoemetalces I.
PIR² C 1552 [5. 212–213; 6].
[I 9] Son of Rhoemetalces I., installed by Augustus
about AD 12 as Odrysian-Sapaean king, married to
Antonia [7] Tryphaena (Str. 12,3,29). Ovid (Ov. Pont.

2,9), Antipater of Thessalonica (Anth. Plan. 75) and Tacitus (Tac. Ann. 2,64,2) praised C. As *árchōn* in Athens C. built a stoa in Epidaurus (Paus. 2,27,6; IG II/III² 1070 = Agora 15,304). The jealousy of his uncle Rhascusporis III, who was disadvantaged in the division of the realm, led — despite intervention by Tiberius — in AD 18/19 to C.'s murder. His part of the realm was inherited by his children under the guardianship of Trebellenus Rufus (Tac. Ann. 2,64–67; 3,38,3; 4,5,3; Vell. Pat. 2,129,1). PIR² C 1554 [1. 6; 2. 133–137; 4. 200–204; 6].

[I 10] Son of C. [I 9] and Antonia [7] Tryphaena, who grew up in Rome. In AD 38 he was installed by Gaius (→ Caligula) as king in Lesser Armenia and part of Arabia (Tac. Ann. 11,9,2; Cass. Dio 59,12,2; Ios. Ant. Iud. 19,8,1; Syll.³ 798; IGR IV 147). PIR² C 1555 [1. 6; 4. 207–209; 6].

> 1 V. BEŠEVLIEV, PN bei den Thrakern, 1970   2 CHR. M. DANOV, Die Thraker auf dem Ostbalkan von der hell. Zeit bis zur Gründung Konstantinopels, in: ANRW II 7.1, 1979, 21–185   3 Y. YOUROUKOVA, Coins of the Ancient Thracians, 1976   4 R. D. SULLIVAN, Thrace in the Eastern Dynastic Network, in: ANRW II 7.1, 1979, 186–211   5 M. TACEVA, Corrigenda et addenda, in: Terra antiqua Balcanica 2, 1987, 210–213   6 PIR² VI, Stemma 22.
>
> U.P.

II. IMPERIAL PERIOD

[II 1] **Tiberius Iulius C. I.** Bosporan king, son of Aspurgus, brother of → Mithridates VIII, who abandoned Rome. C. fought him with C. Iulius [II 16] Aquila and was installed in AD 45 by Claudius [III 1] as king of Bosporus (Tac. Ann. 12,15–21; Cass. Dio 60,28,7). He conquered the territory of the Achaeans south of → Gorgippia (IOSPE 2,37). He introduced the imperial cult in the → Regnum Bosporanum (IOSPE 2,32).

> V. F. GAIDUKEVIČ, Das Bosporan. Reich, 1971, 339–343.

[II 2] **Tiberius Iulius C. II.** Bosporan king AD 124–133; son and successor of → Sauromates; → Hadrian gave him the → Chersonesus [2] to ward off Scythian raids (→ Scythae) (IOSPE 2,27).

> V. F. GAIDUKEVIČ, Das Bosporan. Reich, 1971, 350.

[II 3] **Tiberius Iulius C. III.** Bosporan king, AD 228–233, son of → Rhescuporis III, governed in 228–230 together with → Sauromates III.
→ Regnum Bosporanum

> V. F. GAIDUKEVIČ, Das Bosporan. Reich, 1971, 354.
>
> I.v.B.

Council meetings of increasing complexity served in ancient society to reduce and regulate conflict for the purpose of enabling collective action. Independently of the respective constitutional form, council meetings (CM), whose members were usually drawn from economically powerful and socially respected circles, supported the → ruler in decision-making (cf. → *basi-*

leús, → *gerousía*; the Roman senate under the monarchy), formulated a consensus of peers in the aristocracy (→ *Áreios págos*; → *senatus*) and prepared the resolutions of the popular assembly in democracies and republics (cf. → *ekklēsía*; → *comitia*; → assemblies) (→ *boulḗ*). CM were convened in a regulated form and at certain places (→ Assembly buildings). A special form of the CM was the gathering of representatives of superregional ethnic groups (→ *amphiktyonía*; → *koinón*; → states, confederations of), usually at locations of cultic significance (→ Delphi; → Dodona; → Panionium), and political federations (→ Athenian League, → Corinthian League; → Peloponnesian League), whose leadership committees consulted and passed resolutions (→ *synhédrion*).
→ Assemblies   W. ED.

Counterfeiting The fundamental Roman law regarding counterfeiting was the *lex Cornelia testamentaria nummaria* of 82 BC. (Ulp. Dig. 48,10,9). It prohibited admixtures of low-grade metal to gold ingots, the counterfeiting of silver coins or the issuing of fake ones, threatening freemen with banishment for these deeds and slaves with capital punishment. By extending the interpretation of this law, the counterfeiting of gold coins was also recorded in the Principate; even the rejection of gold and silver coins bearing the head of the emperor was subject to this law (Paulus, Sent. 5,25,1). In the post-Constantinian period (since the 4th cent. AD) counterfeiters were prosecuted for high treason.
→ Counterfeit coins

> MOMMSEN, Strafrecht, 672ff.; R. TAUBENSCHLAG, s.v. Münzverbrechen, RE 16, 455–457; PH. GRIERSON, in: A. G. GARSON (ed.), Essays in Roman Coinage Presented to H. Mattingly, 1956, 240ff.   DI.S.

Countermarks Small, generally round or square stamps with ciphers, letters or an image embossed on a coin at a later date. From the earliest periods of → minting, countermarks have been found on Greek, Roman and Byzantine coins right through to coins struck in modern times. The purpose of countermarking was to introduce foreign money to one's own currency area as a valid method of payment, and to make one's own money either reusable in the marketplace or to upgrade its value. Extremely well-worn coins that had been in circulation for a long time also were countermarked.

The first coins embossed with countermarks were the → electron coins of the Lydian and Persian kings in the 6th/5th cents. BC in Sardis [1]. These were private and unofficial countermarks [2. 27–37] that possibly were to guarantee fine metal content. Such countermarks are also to be found on coins from Aegina (6th/5th cent.), Elis, Athens (5th/4th cent.), Pamphylia, Pisidia and Cilicia (4th cent.) as well as on drachms and hemidrachms from Byzantium minted according to the Persian weight standard (*c.* mid 4th cent. BC). Coins of Ptolemy I and Ptolemy II frequently show countermarks of such kind.

In Hellenistic times official countermarks of cities or rulers are to be found on silver and bronze coins, while gold coins present rare exceptions [2. 37–45]. Countermarking of foreign silver coins served to integrate these into the local market; the reason was mostly a shortage of precious metal.

Countermarks are frequent on coins from the Roman Empire [3. 28–43] and municipal mintings of the Roman east [4]; in such cases ciphers as countermarks often give the coin a new value. On the countermarks of the Roman legions see legionary → coins.

1 C. M. Kraay, Archaic and Classical Greek Coins, 1976, 15–16　2 G. Le Rider, Contremarques et surfrappes dans l'Antiquité grecque, in: Numismatique antique: problèmes et méthodes, 1975, 27–56　3 BMCRE I　4 C. J. Howgego, Greek Imperial Countermarks, 1985.

Schrötter, s.v. Gegenstempel, 211f.　GE.S.

Court (Greek ἀυλή/aulé, Lat. *aula, comitatus*).
A. General　B. Hellenism　C. Principate
D. Late antiquity　E. Reception

A. General

Like territorial monarchy, → *monarchia*, the court as 'the extended residence' of a monarch is a post-classical phenomenon of ancient history that does not appear until the end of the political dominance of municipal community life. The courts, which originated in the → *oíkos* of a Greek nobleman and the → *domus* of a Roman nobleman were, in contrast to those 'houses' no longer incorporated into the city community, but established themselves as autonomous centres of political decision-making and rule over cities, peoples and empires. The opportunities for influence, wealth and status that resulted from personal proximity to a king or emperor attracted members of the aristocratic upper classes to the court, although they there often had to compete with groups of people of lower social status. The communication conditions at the court, the importance of the favour of the ruler, the instability of the position obtained and the flattery and intrigues involved in striving for upward mobility and securing positions were already observed and criticized by contemporaries as specific to court life (cf. Pol. 4,87,3f.; 5,26,12f.; Luc. 8,493f.; Amm. Marc. 22,4,2). The development of court splendour and the fostering of science and art helped to raise the outward status of the monarch; in contrast to later European history, however, no independent upper-class court culture arose in antiquity that would have surmounted the municipal political characteristics of the classical period: the ancient equivalent of 'courtlyness' (Middle High German *höveschheit*, Middle Latin *curialitas*) remained 'urbanity' (Greek ἀστειότης, *asteiótēs*; Lat. *urbanitas*).

B. Hellenism

→ Palace grounds, sometimes splendidly and spaciously arranged, often formed the spatial framework for the courts in newly established towns that were the official residences of monarchs (Alexandria, Seleuceia, Antioch, Pella, Aegae, Pergamum etc.). The most important group in courtly society aside from the relatives of the king were his 'friends' (φίλοι, *phíloi*) whose common feature was their Greek or, especially in the case of the Antigonids, also Macedonian origin, who otherwise however were recruited through open selection for their personal qualities from the municipal upper classes, and from the ranks of artists, writers and scientists. They formed the constant retinue of the king from his 'council' (συνέδριον, → *synhédrion*) that met every morning to the symposium in the evening. From their ranks provincial governors, military leaders and envoys were chosen for duties outside the court. Additional people at the court were more intensively involved in organizational duties: the king's bodyguard responsible for his protection (σωματοφύλακες, *sōmatophýlakes*), the central secretary's office (ἐπιστολογραφεῖον, *epistolographeîon*) and the extensive serving staff, often consisting of slaves and → eunuchs. The initially mainly egalitarian relationship between the kings and their 'friends' that resulted from the shared foreign rule over an indigenous population and the competitive situation between the courts became more hierarchical from the beginning of the 2nd cent. BC onwards. At the Ptolemaic and Seleucid courts, and also to some extent at the Macedonian court, a system arose of up to eight → court titles that integrated the entire upper class entrusted with administrative functions into a rank order structured according to its formalized closeness to the monarch. Contrary to this, persons of low social status, some of whom were eunuchs, were brought into the inner sanctum of the kings as a reaction to the increasing political autonomy of courtly society, visible in courtly factions, often centred around individual 'friends' who at times even became a danger to the kings.

C. Principate

In contrast to the Hellenistic royal courts, the Roman imperial court arose within a municipal class of nobility whose hierarchy was based on senatorial rank classifications. The spatial framework of the court was a complex of two palace buildings with large rooms which in the course of the 1st cent. AD occupied the Palatine (→ Mons Palatinus), the most aristocratic residential area of Rome, and was called by its name (*palatium*). Characteristic of the social composition of court society is the fact that the closest retinue of the emperor in the 1st cent., apart from members of his family, consisted to a large extent of persons of lower status in the aristocratic hierarchy, gradually even primarily of imperial slaves and → freedmen. Their status, which was based on imperial favour, was frequently linked with positions in the court organizational structures that had recently arisen. The equestrian prefects of the praetorian guard (→ *praefectus praetorio*), the leaders of the central offices for finances (*a rationibus*), correspondence (*ab epistulis*) and petitions (*a libellis*), as well as other persons in the extensive imperial service of the palace, valets perhaps (*cubicularii*), were able (in a similar manner to the women of the imperial household) at times to attain positions of decisive political influence and great wealth. The contact between the emperor and the majority of members of the senatorial-equestrian aristocracy which occurred at the court was initially limited to the traditional forms of interaction of the aristocratic household, morning greetings (→ *salutatio*) and the evening → banquet (*convivium*) that extended to comprehensive functions frequently involving the entire aristocracy and to the occasional calling of the imperial council (→ *consilium*). Friends (*amici*, → *amicitia*) of the emperor were, in a non-specific manner, all the members of the senatorial-equestrian aristocracy (who appeared at court), and in a narrower sense, those who had a closer relationship to him. In Imperial Rome there was no hierarchic ranking corresponding to the system of court titles of the Hellenistic period. Rather, in the course of the 2nd cent., the discernible temporary integration of the leading members of the senatorial aristocracy into the daily life of the emperor went hand in hand with the prevailing of the traditional social hierarchy also at the court.

D. LATE ANTIQUITY

A decisive feature of the imperial courts in late antiquity is their great distance from the city of Rome and the emancipation from the latter's senatorial society resulting from this. With the development of new residences in Constantinople, Milan, Ravenna and other cities in the empire, the organizational court structures of the early imperial period developed into extensive centres for the civil and military administration of the empire which replaced the traditional Roman magistratures in their political functions. Their leaders — the *praepositus sacri cubiculi* responsible for internal court matters, then the *magister officiorum*, the *quaestor sacri palatii*, the *comes sacrarum largitionum*, the *comes rerum privatarum* and the two *magistri militum praesentales* — together with others made up the official imperial council (→ *consistorium*).

Parallel to this, a different court ceremonial was established from the period of Diocletian (around AD 300) onwards that took place, for example, at the → *adoratio purpurae* or at festive banquets. It surrounded the emperors with a religious aura, distanced them from their surroundings and at the same time manifested the given social rank order at the court. Organizational structures and ceremonial hierarchies were in this way thwarted by an informal hierarchy structured according to imperial closeness and favour, visible in the way rival groups influenced imperial decisions. The social recruitment of the closest imperial circles and the top offices at the court was characterized by

the great lack of persons of noble birth. The chamberlains (*cubicularii*) who because of their function had the greatest chances for closeness to the emperor, were almost exclusively → eunuchs, former slaves of foreign origin. In contrast to the Principate, the leading imperial functionaries were, however, through the offices they fulfilled accepted into the highest social classes, which meant that the late imperial courts became places of exceptional social mobility. The attempt by Constantine [1] the Great to establish a rank order structured on the basis of formalized closeness to the emperor or according to *comites primi, secundi* and *tertii ordinis* and in this way to found a hierarchization of the upper class comparable to the court ranking system of the late Hellenistic period was unsuccessful. With the status laws of Valentinian I (372), a modified senatorial rank order according to *clarissimi, spectabiles* and *illustres* or *illustrissimi* was, however, established as the principle of the hierarchy of the upper class (→ Court titles C.).

E. RECEPTION

The importance of the courts of late antiquity to the development of European court centres in the Middle Ages and the early modern period has to a large extent not yet been researched. A direct continuous link to ancient courts can be seen in Byzantium and the papal Curia and also to some extent in the Merovingian empire. Attempts at establishing conscious connections with the symbolism of rule of late antiquity, with ceremonial regulations and designations of court offices such as can be established for the Frankish-German empire of the 9th and 11th cents. or for Italian Renaissance princes helped to legitimize rule; the adapted forms, however, went hand in hand with changed content and functions. The topoi of ancient court criticism were continued to be frequently cited in the Middle Ages and in the early modern period. Correspondingly, a typological comparison of ancient courts with courts in the Middle Ages and the early modern period demonstrates structural similarities, particularly with regard to the transfer of power from the ruler to the persons working in his direct environment and in relation to the communication structures resulting from this. A fundamental problem for the courts of antiquity, the competition between monarch and aristocracy, can be seen in a similar manner only at the royal courts of the Middle Ages, discernible in the employment of ministerials who were not free men. On the other hand, the European courts in the age of Absolutism were characterized by the extensive integration of the aristocracy into the milieu of the monarch and in this way by the possibility of influencing political and social status relationships in court ceremony. This indicates that the connecting-points the different eras can be explained mainly on the basis of equivalent solutions to problems in the organization of large royal households and in pre-modern autocracy that do not require the assumption of direct links.

→ Aristocracy; → Comes, comites; → Friendship; → Ruler; → Rulership; → Court titles; → Slavery; → Administration

A. GENERAL: E. LÉVY (ed.), Le système palatial en Orient, en Grèce et à Rome, 1987; A. WINTERLING (ed.), Ant. Höfe im Vergleich, 1997.
B. HELLENISM.: BERVE 1, 10-84; E. BIKERMAN, Institutions des Séleucides, 1938, 31-50; G. HERMAN, The Court Society of the Hellenistic Age, in: P. CARTLEDGE et al. (ed.), Hellenistic Constructs, 1997, 199-224; L. MOOREN, The Aulic Titulature in Ptolemaic Egypt, 1975; H. H. SCHMITT, s.v. Hof, Kleines Lexikon des Hellenismus, ²1993, 253-259; G. WEBER, Dichtung und höfische Gesellschaft, 1993.
C. PRINCIPATE: A. ALFÖLDI, Die monarchische Repräsentation im röm. Kaiserreiche, 1970; FRIEDLÄNDER 1, 33-103; MOMMSEN, Staatsrecht 2.2, 833-839; SALLER, 41-78; A. WALLACE-HADRILL, The Imperial Court, CAH 10, ²1996, 283-308; A. WINTERLING, Aula Caesaris, 1999.
D. LATE ANTIQUITY: HOPKINS, Conquerors, 172-196; H. LÖHKEN, Ordines dignitatum, 1982; O. TREITINGER, Die oström. Kaiser- und Reichsidee nach ihrer Gestaltung im höf. Zeremoniell, 1938; A. WINTERLING (ed.), Comitatus, 1998.
E. RECEPTION: R. A. MÜLLER, Der Fürstenhof in der frühen Neuzeit, 1995; W. PARAVICINI, Die ritterlich-höf. Kultur des MA, 1994; P. E. SCHRAMM, Kaiser, Rom und Renovatio, ³1962; P. SCHREINER, Charakteristische Aspekte der byz. Hofkultur, in: R. LAUER, H. G. MAJER (ed.), Höf. Kultur in Südosteuropa, 1994, 11-24; A. WINTERLING, Höfe, in: Id. (ed.), Antike Höfe im Vergleich, 1997, 11-25; Id., Vergleichende Perspektiven, in: ibid. 151-169.   A.WI.

Court poetry Its origin at the court of a king or prince was constituted for the content of court poetry (CP) in the narrower sense. As part of the court society (each differently constituted) the author contributes, with or without an explicit commission, to the legitimisation of rule by shaping power structures through his literature or, simply through his writing, by expanding these with a cultural dimension. The earliest example is the naming of the Aeneads in the Iliad; especially significant in this regard is the CP of the Greek choral lyricists (→ Pindarus, → Bacchylides, → Simonides) at the courts in Sicily and Greece and then in Hellenism (especially Alexandria) [1]. In the case of Latin authors, on the other hand (e.g. → Statius, → Martialis), one can speak of CP only to a limited extent as Republican components survived into the Principate [2]. Greek authors in Imperial Rome, however (e.g. → Crinagoras), pass on the conventions of CP from the Greek royal courts.
→ Propaganda

1 G. WEBER, Dichtung und höfische Ges., 1993 (fundamental)   2 E. FANTHAM, Roman Literary Culture: from Cicero to Apuleius, 1996.   U.SCH.

Court ranks see → Court, see Court titles

Court titles
A. ANTECEDENTS IN THE ANCIENT ORIENT
B. HELLENISM   1. GENERAL   2. PTOLEMAIC EGYPT
3. SELEUCID KINGDOM   C. ROMAN EMPIRE AND
LATE ANTIQUITY   D. BYZANTIUM

A. ANTECEDENTS IN THE ANCIENT ORIENT
Court titles (CT) and court ranks in antiquity, used for the description and creation of personal proximity of members of courtly society to the → ruler or to the hierarchical rank classification of the upper class involved in administration, are a consequence of the emergence of territorial monarchies from the time of Alexander [4] the Great and the resulting organization of → courts as centres of political rule. The question of ancient Oriental antecedents and models for the CT of antiquity must be answered with the aid of the two essential characteristics of the court ranking system in the direct successors of the ancient Oriental empires, i.e. the Hellenistic monarchies: CT are not linked to offices; the court rank and CT of a person end with the death of the person who bestowed them. In view of these premises, the pre-Hellenistic monarchies in the Mesopotamian-Syrian area are excluded as models, as title and office here appear to be linked and as for example the table of the Assyrian king has place only for office bearers. In the Persian empire of the → Achaemenids numerous titles are common. Several resemble or are similar to the Hellenistic CT but the term 'relatives of the king' designates real not fictitious relations [1] of the Persian king, and titles are always linked with offices and functions: a nobleman's title derives from his being in the king's service. Achaemenid models for the organization of Greek courts of tyrants in the ancient and classical period (cf. Pl. Ep. 7,334c, where *phíloi* ('friends') and *syngeneîs* ('relatives') of Dion [I 1] of Syracuse are mentioned) are possible (cf. [2]), but not necessary as these manifestations can also be interpreted merely as basic parallels.

In the Egypt of the pharaohs, on the other hand, there was already in the Old Kingdom a strong tendency not just to develop a ranking and title system that differentiated closeness to the ruler, but also to devalue the office in favour of the title and to link the functions and competencies to the title instead of to the office. The decline from the 12th dynasty onwards of the fine distinction between the titles, or rather: ranks that had been achieved led to a chain of ranking titles that was identical for all members of court and that was therefore not suitable for describing concrete offices. Pure rank descriptions were still known in Egypt under Persian rule [3]. These, however, probably did not serve as models for Ptolemaic CT.

1 J.-D. GAUGER, Zu einem offenen Problem des hell. Hoftitelsystems, in: FS J. Straub, 1977, 137-158   2 V. FADINGER, Griech. Tyrannis und Alter Orient, in: K. RAAFLAUB (ed.), Anfänge polit. Denkens in der Antike, 1993, 263-316   3 W. HUSS, Ägyptische Kollaborateure in persischer Zeit, in: Tyche 12, 1997, 131-143.

W. HELCK, Untersuchungen zu den Beamtentiteln des ägyptischen Alten Reiches, 1954; Id., Zur Verwaltung des Mittleren und Neuen Reiches, 1958, 281 ff.; W. KLAUBER, Assyrisches Beamtentum nach Briefen aus der Sargonidenzeit, 1910; LÄ 2, s.v. Hofrang, 1237; 5, s.v. Rang, 146 f.; 6, s.v. Wedelträger, 1161–63; J. RENGER, s.v. Hofstaat, RLA 4, 435–446; J. WIESEHÖFER, Das antike Persien, 1993.   A.ME.

B. HELLENISM

1. GENERAL

The Hellenistic CT of the Antigonids (→ Antigonus) in Macedonia, of the Attalids (→ Attalus) of Pergamum, of the Ptolemies (→ Ptolemaeus) and Seleucids (→ Seleucus), followed the example of the empire of Alexander; titles such as φίλος (phílos, 'friend'), σωματοφύλαξ (sōmatophýlax, 'bodyguard') and συγγενής (syngenés, 'relative') initially and well into the 3rd cent. BC had a genuine background through close relationships to the monarch. The titles could be revoked and were in principle not hereditary, but de facto personal contacts bring additional members of a family into the closest circle of the king. Morning greetings, shared meals and the accompanying of the king on his journeys gave rise to political influence which was used for political, military and diplomatic tasks. The trend in the Hellenistic kingdoms was not uniform, as, e.g., the local aristocracy that was not called upon by other rulers was available to the Macedonian Antigonids. The formalization of CT that was also discernible at the turn of the 3rd to the 2nd cent. BC among the Ptolemies and Seleucids cannot be observed in a similar manner amongst the Antigonids and Attalids.

2. PTOLEMAIC EGYPT

In Ptolemaic Egypt the CT basically remained — as in all the successor states of the empire of Alexander — individual titles throughout the 3rd cent. although the keeping of a title during absence from court already represented the first step in the linking of court title and office. It was not until the reign of Ptolemy V that CT, probably through a single administrative decree, were introduced as class designations for groups of officials and the offices linked with the CT (before 197/4 BC). The fact that someone belonged to a group was foregrounded, and this is clear from the use of the partitive genitive (τῶν φίλων, tōn phílōn, meaning that the bearer of a title belonged to the 'group of friends'). Six titles are attested or to be assumed (rank order from bottom to top): τῶν διαδόχων (tōn diadóchōn), ἀρχισωματοφύλαξ (archisōmatophýlax), τῶν φίλων (tôn phílōn, τῶν πρώτων φίλων (tôn prótōn phílōn), τῶν σωματοφυλάκων (tôn sōmatophylákōn), συγγενής (syngenés). In the difficult situation under Ptolemy V who came to the throne as a child, this system of CT consolidated the relationship with the officials: on the one hand their office put them into a (fictitious but designated) close relationship with the king and linked them to him more closely, and on the other hand their prestige and authority in the country were boosted. More-over, the system of CT also formed a type of protective shield for the guardians of the underage king.

The differentiation of CT progressed. In 155 BC the CT 'from the group of archbodyguards' (tôn archisōmatophylákōn) can be found, and before 140 the CT 'from the group of people whose rank is equal to the first-class friends ' (tôn isotímōn toîs prótois phílois) appears and in around 120 'from the group of people whose rank is equal to the relatives' (tôn homotímōn toîs syngenésin). The rank order in the extended system was probably (from top to bottom): 'relatives', 'those equal in rank to the relatives', 'friends of the first class', 'those equal in rank to the friends of the first class', 'archbodyguards', 'friends', 'diadochi', 'bodyguards'. There is uncertainty about the emblems of court rank as they have not been passed down to us; we can however assume that they were used in a manner similar to the other monarchies (see, however, GVI 1152,25f.; 1508,9f. with [1. 446 A. 2]). CT can also be combined with a personal address (the 'relative' as 'brother', adelphós).

The changed structure of the titles is evidence of their increasing devaluation which people initially sought to counter by further differentiating the system and then, however, by reducing the number of titles to the three highest ones; for not much later most of these titles disappear again: in the 1st cent. BC the only titles still used were those of the 'relatives', 'those equal in rank to the relatives' and of the 'friends of the first class'.

The pursuit of titles ultimately led to a levelling out as lower and lower grades of officials were given higher titles (the trend appears to have gone faster and more consistently in Egypt than in the external estates of the Ptolemies). However, as the CT of the lower ranks rose, the CT of their superiors also had to be increased (157/6 and 135/4 are important turning points).

Differentiation of the apparatus of officialdom went hand in hand with CT. Particularly amongst the stratēgoi (στρατηγοί) it becomes clear that the extent and significance of the administrative district determined the level of the CT. The CT also changed with the field of work so that promotions can be detected through titles. The highest offices (and hence CT) were held by the epistratēgoi (ἐπιστρατηγοί) and the governor of Cyprus, for who military functions were connected with civil supervision of several regions.

1 L. ROBERT, Noms indigènes, 1963.

CHR. HABICHT, Die herrschende Ges. in den hell. Monarchien, in: Vierteljahresschrift für Sozial- und Wirtschaftsgesch. 45, 1958, 1ff.; L. MOOREN, in: Proc. XIVth Int. Congress of Papyrologists, 1974, 233ff.; Id., The Aulic Titulature in Ptolemaic Egypt, 1975; Id., La hiérarchie de cour ptolémaique, 1977; M. TRINDL, Ehrentitel im Ptolemäerreich, Diss. 1942.   W.A.

3. SELEUCID KINGDOM

The title and ranking system at the Seleucid court was administered by the bureaucracy (1 Macc 10,65). As in Hellenistic Egypt, the CT in the upper ranks were expressed as kinship relationships: the 'relative' (*syn-genḗs*) and the 'one brought up together with him' (*sýntrophos*: MAMA 3,62) were addressed by the king as 'brother' (*adelphós*) (2 Macc 11,22). For the lower ranks, degrees of personal closeness to the king were employed: 'friends of the first rank' (*prṓtoi phíloi*), 'treasured friends' (*timṓmenoi phíloi*) and 'friends' (*phíloi*) (OGIS 255; 256; WELLES 45; 1 Macc 10,20 with 65); members of the overall rank of 'friends' formed a corps (Pol. 30,25 (31,3),7; cf. 30,26 (31,4),9). It was possible to pass through the rank levels from 'friend' to 'relative' (1 Macc 10,20; 65; 89). Whether and how titles were linked with attributes (purple gown, gold jewellery, gold tableware for eating and drinking) does not become clear from the main source for this issue (1 Macc 10,20; 62–65; 89; 11,57f.). The question also must remain unanswered to what extent the rather looser structure of the Seleucid kingdom in comparison with the Ptolemaic empire characterized its title and ranking system and whether the giving of a Greek personal name by a king to a non-Greek (which is attested only once) was also part of this [1. 150, cf.132].

The bestowing of a court title could be preceded by gifts to the title giver (1 Macc 11,24–27; cf. 13,34ff.); it could be combined with giving gifts to the person raised in status, with enfeoffing him, or with his appointment to an office (1 Macc 2,18; 10, 20; 65; 89; 11,26f.; 57). Titles, attributes and material gifts were not hereditary; they could be taken back by the donor and, like other privileges, required confirmation by successors (1 Macc 10–11; 2 Macc 4,38). Although a CT was not a pre-requisite for participation in court life (Ath. 155b), title holders did, however, form the core of court society, waited on the king, lived with him and advised him in peace and war (Pol. 5,56,10; 83,1; 8,21,1; 29,27; Diod. Sic. 34,1; 16; Ios. ant. Iud. 12,263); they could, how-ever, also fulfil a role in the administration of the king-dom far from the court, carry out a military command against an enemy or even exercise a reign that, although loosely connected to the bestower of the title, was *de facto* independent (1 Makk 10–11). In crisis situations the personal fate of title bearers could be connected with that of the bestower (OGIS 219,15; Liv. per. 50; Ios. Ant. Iud. 13,368).

1 S. SHERWIN-WHITE, A. KUHRT, From Samarkhand to Sardis, 1993.

E. BIKERMAN, Institutions des Séleucides, 1938, 40–50.
A.ME.

C. ROMAN EMPIRE AND LATE ANTIQUITY
As early as the Republican period, the term *titulus* could be used for describing high official positions (e.g. *t. consulatus*: Cic. Pis. 9,19) and generally an honour-able status and merits attained (e.g. *perpetrati belli t.*: Liv. 28,41,3). With the beginning of the Imperial period there arose, in addition to the Republican → *cursus honorum* and the status rights of the senatorial and

equestrian class, a 'courtly' system of honourable court services and awards. It was used for both members of the imperial *familia* in a civil-law sense and the officials who were constantly in the entourage of the king, whether they were from the equestrian class or from the senatorial class, with the organization of court func-tionaries and domestic staff becoming increasingly di-verse in the course of time. The model of the Hellenistic royal courts and their ceremonies was imitated in the process, as can be seen from a circle of friends (*amici*), advisers and close followers (*consiliarii*, later *consisto-riani*, *comites*, → *comes*, corresponding to *hetaîroi*, *he-pómenoi*) whose rank depended on honour. In contrast to Hellenism, however, it was necessary under the Roman emperors of the Principate to co-ordinate the system of court offices, positions of honour and trust with a system of 'Republican' rank classes (*senatores*, *equites*) and offices (*cursus honorum*). This was achieved a) through equal titular ranking of the im-perial administrative functionaries in the narrower sense and the traditional Republican officials (the *lega-tus pro consule* of an imperial provincial administrator corresponded in rank to the *proconsul* of a senatorial province), b) through imperial raising of court func-tionaries to the status of knights or senators, often after they had been in Republican office, only in a purely honorary sense and for a short time and c) — with the beginning of the → Dominats — through the creation of a uniform order of public offices and ranks (*ordo dig-nitatum*); the → court in these instances was regarded as the centre of all state activity and hence also as the source of all acknowledgement of political achieve-ments or claims for recognition.

This order from late antiquity found expression in various legal regulations: e.g. coherently in the Codex Theodosianus of the 4th cent. (B. 6) and the → Codex Justinianus (B. 12), also coherent legal expression. Since the reign of Constantine I in the 4th cent. there also was an order of the *comites* of the emperor that included numerous imperial offices and contained three grades of rank (Eus. Vita Const. 4,1); it also continued to exist later in many of its aspects. An additional el-ement was the title *patricius* (Zos. 2,40) that was up-dated by Constantine to provide an exceptional highest honour. To the main, generally continuous elements also belonged, however, the three main rank classes of the — functionally changed, but still existing — senato-rial orders (*illustres*, *spectabiles*, *clari*) and a level of *dignitates* ('offices') below them, amongst whom the *perfectissimi* were at the top, followed by other levels through to a simple *egregius* within a formally still ex-isting *ordo equester* (Cod. Iust. 12,31).

Within the *illustres* the following grading occurred from *c.* 400: at the top were the active office bearers of the first senatorial rank class (*in actu positi illustres*), followed by those who did not hold office but belonged to the entourage of the emperor and held the symbol of a higher office, then by the *i.* with *cingulum* not called to the court, those *i.* present at court, but without *cingu-*

lum and the *i.* absent from court and without *cingulum*. Office bearers (*administratores*) and even people who held no office but who were entrusted with military or civil duties always were higher in rank than holders of purely honorary positions (*honorarii*) (Cod. Iust. 12,8,2). The ranking criteria 'power to act' and 'closeness to the court' discernible in this had, however, also existed before. Since the Diocletianic-Constantinian imperial reforms (end of the 3rd to the beginning of the 4th cent. AD) about 20 of the highest active civil and military imperial officials in each part of the empire belonged to the first senatorial rank class. To the *spectabiles* belonged mainly the emperor's advisers, many representatives of the highest imperial officials and the heads of the court chanceries. In the third rank level of the 'simple' senators we find mainly the provincial governors. All subordinate official functions of a higher service at the imperial court used to be filled by members of non-senatorial *dignitates*. The system of CT was linked with a differentiated system of privileges (graded exemptions from the legal → *munera*, special judicial treatment, material contributions and public honours of various kinds; cf. in detail: Cod. Iust. 1,28ff. and 12,1ff.).

→ Illustris vir

1 ALFÖLDI   2 JONES, LRE, 366ff., 411ff., 607ff.
3 A. WINTERLING (ed.), Ant. Höfe im Vergleich, 1997
4 H. LÖHKEN, Ordines Dignitatum, 1982   5 R. SCHARF,
Comites und comitiva primi ordinis, 1994   6 W. HEUL,
Der constantinische Prinzipat, 1966.   C.G.

D. BYZANTIUM

As in ancient times, CT also in the Byzantine empire (4th–15th cent. AD) are to be understood, in contrast to offices, as pure honours not connected with any set activity or function. But here too, there was not always a clear distinction between titles and designations of office.

The original cognomen *Caesar* (Καῖσαρ, *Kaîsar*) first became part of the title of the emperor; in the Diocletianic system of the → tetrarchy from AD 293 it was the term for the two 'sub-emperors' in the east and west. After 550 it was used as the highest CT for imperial co-rulers or designated successors to the throne, usually an emperor's sons [1. 363].

→ Constantinus [1] I, by association with the Roman principate, created the high-ranking CT *patricius* (πατρίκιος) that could be freely bestowed and that survived into the 11th cent. [3. 1600].

In late antiquity the titles *illustris* (ἰλλούστριος; *illoýstrios*), *spectabilis* (περίβλεπτος, *períbleptos*) and *clarus* or *clarissimus* (λαμπρότατος, *lamprótatos*) were the names given to the three ranking grades of the senatorial class. From the time of Constantine [1] I, members of the imperial family frequently bore the title *nobilissimus* that in later cents. was generally used as a high-ranking court title (νωβελίσσιμος) [3. 1489f.].

To the relatively minor office of the *cura palatii* (responsible for the palace building) was linked the CT κουροπαλάτης (*kouropalátes*) that was first bestowed by → Justinianus I on his nephew and later successor Justine II [2. 1157].

The purely Byzantine CT μάγιστρος (*mágistros*) was not created until a relatively long time after the cancellation of the high office of *magister officiorum;it* is attested from the 9th cent. onwards [2. 1267].

The consulate that had *de facto* been reduced to a honorary title already in the imperial period appears in Byzantium as the court title → *hýpatos* (ὕπατος, with the higher ranks δισύπατος, *dishypatos* and ἀνθύπατος, *anthýpatos*).

In the → *Kletorologion* of Philotheos, a handbook on court etiquette from AD 899 [3. 1661f.], the CT discussed above are accorded the following rank order (from top to bottom): *kaísar, nōbelíssimos, kouropalátes, mágistros, anthýpatos, patríkios, dísypatos, hýpatos*. Here, the specific insignia (βραβεῖα, *brabeîa*) bestowed when the award was given, are also described.

1 ODB 1   2 ODB 2   3 ODB 3.

ODB 1, 623; R. GUILLAND, Titres et fonctions de l'Empire byzantin, 1976; W. HEIL, Der konstantinische Patriziat, 1966; N. OIKONOMIDÈS, Les listes de préséance byzantines des IXe et Xe siècles, 1972; STEIN, Spätröm. R. I–II; F. WINKELMANN, Byz. Rang- und Ämterstruktur im 8. und 9. Jh., 1985.   F.T.

Covinnus See → War chariot

C-Painter see → Siana cups

Crab see → Crustaceans

Cradle see → Volume 4, Addenda

Crafts, Trade

I. ANCIENT ORIENT AND EGYPT   II. IRAN
III. CELTIC-GERMANIC AREA   IV. ETRURIA
V. CLASSICAL ANTIQUITY

I. ANCIENT ORIENT AND EGYPT

Crafts in Egypt, in Syria-Palestine and in Mesopotamia can be best categorized by the materials employed: stone, bone and other animal products, clay and glass, metals, wood, wool and flax and leather, as well as reed and plant fibres. These were used to make objects of the most varied kinds, from cooking-pots to finely worked pieces of jewellery. For the building trade, stone, clay, reed and wood were important. For the investigation of the various forms of crafts, three types of sources, each providing different information can be consulted: concrete archaeological discoveries, pictorial representations of objects and artisans and written documents.

The degree of preservation of the archaeological discoveries depends on the material and the region. All craft products are better preserved in the Egyptian desert than in the Nile Valley or generally in the Asian part of the Middle East. Particularly impressive is the degree of preservation of leather, reed, rope and linen. Ceramics are well attested in the entire region. Vessels, statues and other objects made of stone that tended to be more common in Egypt and Syria-Palestine than in Mesopotamia are well preserved. Precious finds such as gold jewellery were only made in tombs and under unusual conditions. Finds such as the intact tomb of Tutankhamen (14th cent. BC), the royal cemetery of Ur (mid 3rd cent. BC) and the tombs of the late Assyrian queens of Kalhu (9th cent. BC) show not just technical competencies on the part of the artisans, but also what great fortunes were spent on private representation. A large number of these treasures were robbed as early as antiquity, some of them even just after the tomb had been erected. In Egypt the architecture is mostly stone. Unlike in Mesopotamia, buildings made of unfired clay bricks are not preserved here. Evidence of tools is common in Egypt, but rare in other places. Only a small number of workshops have undergone precise archaelogoical examination.

Although there are Mesopotamian depictions e.g. of textile workers or potters, no technical information worthy of note can be gleaned from them. Syrian-Palestinian iconographic finds also tend to be sparse.

There are many written testimonies to business transactions with self-employed tradesmen or workshops in Mesopotamia; these provide information about the quantity of imported raw materials and the finished export products; this we can, for example, gain information about the materials that were required to produce a war chariot. Evidence of the sale of artisans' products in Egypt is indeed available, but regrettably it is not from related archives of individual workshops. Examination of these sources is still in the early stages. Evidence for the Syrian-Palestinian area is poor, as in the iconographic field, although the excellent capabilities e.g. of the Phoenicians in textile weaving, carpentry or metalwork, are well known from texts.

The objects required for basic needs were mainly produced in private households; institutions like palaces or temples relied on entire workshops to cover their needs. It appears that in Mesopotamia the artisans connected with the temple or palace also did work for private customers, whereas the evidence for Egyptian tradesmen suggests that they were linked to a private household or the state. It is also probable that already at that time these tradesmen had private paid jobs on the side. A large number of artisans were involved in the enormous building projects in periods of political flourishing. The construction and embellishment of completely new capital cities like Achet-Aton (→ Amarna) in Egypt or Dūr-Šarrukīn in Assyria must have required the skills of thousands of qualified workers; a large number of unskilled workers were also required to assist them. Unfortunately none of these projects are documented in the textual sources.

The technical competencies of the tradesmen in the Middle East were thought to be considerable already in antiquity. Artisan products were exchanged for raw materials in trade with the surrounding areas. This trade created the prerequisites for the Greek world to be influenced by Middle Eastern styles and techniques, particularly in the middle of the 2nd millennium and in the 8th cent. BC.

1 R. DRENKHAHN, Die Handwerker und ihre Tätigkeiten im alten Äg., 1976   2 A. LUKAS, Ancient Egyptian Materials and Industries, ⁴1989   3 P. R. S. MOOREY, Ancient Mesopotamian Materials and Industries: The Archeological Evidence, 1994.   M.v.M.

II. IRAN

The uniform Achaemenid courtly art style that developed in a relatively short time was due to a programme on the part of the great kings that merged many disparate artistic elements from 'the lands of one lord' to form a whole that would emphasize the *pax achaemenidica* in a polyethnic great empire. The presence of artisans can be deduced not just from the objects but is also mentioned in Darius [1] I's 'fortification inscription' from Susa [3. DSf] and the Elamite treasury tablets from Persepolis [1; 2]. Amongst the Persian goods and art objects that reached the West, glass, textiles, vessels made of metal, jewellery and furniture were especially desired; they presuppose the existence of the corresponding crafts. From the Sassanid period we know of the forced settlement of specialized workers (prisoners of war) in the empire and of the building of royal workshops under special supervision. In the hierarchy of the municipal population, according to the evidence of the Nestorian synod of 544 in → Gundeshapur, the 'foreman of the (royal) artisans' had the highest status amongst the laymen, even higher than the foremen of the associations of free artisans that were organized 'like guilds'. Well known were the textile and building trades, as well as toreutics, carpet manufacture and jewellery making.

1 G. G. CAMERON, Persepolis Treasury Tablets, 1948   2 R. T. HALLOCK, Persepolis Fortification Tablets, 1969   3 R. G. KENT, Old Persian, 1953   4 M. C. MILLER, Athens and Persia in the Fifth Century B.C., 1997   5 N. PIGULEVSKAJA, Les villes de l'état iranien aux époques parthe et sassanide, 1963, 116ff., 159ff.   6 A. TAFAZZOLI, A List of Trades and Crafts in the Sassanian Period, in: AMI 7, 1974, 191–196   7 J. WIESEHÖFER, Das ant. Persien, 1994, Index s.v.   8 H. E. WULFF, The Traditional Crafts of Persia, 1966.   J.W.

III. CELTIC-GERMANIC AREA

With regard to Celtic-Germanic crafts, almost all sources available that can provide insight into individual branches of the trades, the materials and also the methods of production are archaeological ones; hence to date little is known about the structure, organization, social position etc. of the artisans.

From the Bronze Age onwards and particularly in the Celtic Iron Age (→ Hallstatt and → La Tène Culture) workshop sites, artisan districts in settlements and occasionally also artisan tombs are known which reveal themselves through their building structures and lavish and specialized facilities (ovens, stoves, potter's wheels etc.), waste materials (bone remnants, wrongly burnt ceramics, slag etc.), products and above all through special tools. There is evidence of potters, smiths working with bronze, iron and precious metals, woodworking tradesmen (cartwrights, coopers, carpenters, shipbuilders, turners), bone carvers (needles, combs), textile tradesmen, leather artisans, and glass, amber and jetworking artisans. In the Celtic area a great deal of contact with the south can be established, as e.g. in the case of the construction tradesmen with a knowledge of the clay brick construction method on the → Heuneburg or the granulation technique in the case of goldsmiths. For the Germanic area we rather have to assume that simple crafts existed within a village framework that were partly characterized by influences from Celtic crafts and that also continued to exist right through to the imperial period of the first cent. AD.

→ Germanic archaeology; → Celtic archaeology; → Bricks

CH. ELUÈRE (ed.), Outils et ateliers d'orfèvres des temps anciens, 1993; J.-P. GUILLAUMET, L'artisanat chez les Gaulois, 1996; G. JACOBI, Werkzeug und Gerät aus dem Oppidum von Manching, 1974; H. JANKUHN et al. (ed.), Das Handwerk in vor- und frühgesch. Zeit, 2 vols., 1981/3; S. SIEVERS, Die Kleinfunde der Heuneburg, 1984.

V.P.

IV. ETRURIA

The preserved sources give us a very complex picture of Etruscan trades. The few written documents, such as Pliny (HN 35,152), speaking of the Corinthian nobleman → Demaratus [1] who brought tradesmen with him to Tarquinia, are late. Etruscan bronze household devices had a certain reputation (Critias at Athenod. 1,28b; Pherecrates at Athenod. 15,700c). Only a few Etruscan artists are known by name. Vulca of Veii, who created the cult image of the Capitolinian Jupiter in Rome in the late 6th cent. BC as a commissioned work, is one of the few exceptions (Plin. HN 34,34). The valuables in the burial sites of → princes' tombs were commissioned works. With the strengthening of the middle class in the 6th cent. BC, the first signs of broad-ranging production can be discerned. All artisan fields experienced an upswing at the beginning of Greek colonization. New methods, the result of Greek or Phoenician influences, are to be found repeatedly in certain trade branches.

From the 8th cent. onwards the fast-turning potter's wheel was used. The vessels in the Etruscan geometric style strongly imitate imported Greek ceramics. This also applies to the vase styles that followed in time. We can subsequently assume that there also were immigrant artisans (e.g. → Caeretan hydrias). The painters of the tomb frescos were closely linked with the vase painters. The typical Etruscan → bucchero ceramics were first developed in Cerveteri in imitation of metalwork (2nd quarter of the 7th cent.) and continued in a degraded form (bucchero grigio) until the 4th cent. BC. Other Etruscan towns like Chiusi and Orvieto were from the 6th cent. BC leaders in the manufacture of the stamp-decorated bucchero pesante. The six technique, that in Athens was only used to a limited extent continued to have an influence on the Etruscan sovradipinta technique for a long time (→ Red-figured vases). The manufacturing centres of vernice-nera ceramics were more in the south of the Italian peninsula. The pewterized ceramics of the Hellenistic period from the Orvieto-Bolsena region that imitate metal vessels and that were manufactured for tombs are remarkable.

The goldsmith's craft with its highly developed technique of filigree and granulation learned from the Phoenicians was of particular importance.

Etruscan toreutic artists were outstanding representatives of their profession. Their range of products comprised a large number of the most varied devices (especially hand mirrors), from furniture and cart fittings to vessels that were partly already being manufactured in series (beked jugs). Equally important from the 8th cent. BC were the weapon workshops that even at the time of Scipio Africanus (Liv. 28,45) still supplied the Roman army with equipment (namely in → Arretium/Arezzo).

The work of carpenters, cartwrights and shipbuilders can only be judged through pictorial sources. The depictions of furniture on wall paintings, vases etc. convey an image of crafts that in imitation of Greek forms supplied → furniture for sophisticated requirements. Evidence of both transportation wagons and war chariots exists amongst the items that have been found.

The coroplasts occupied a special position as Etruscan temple roofs, usually made of wood, were equipped with clay sheets decorated with reliefs and fully sculptured figures made of clay (→ terracotta) that served as protection against the weather. In addition to coroplastic works ('married-couple sarcophagi', statues et al.) we find those made of stone, especially the tomb sculptures in Tarquinia, Vulci and Chiusi in the ancient period and later in Volterra (alabaster) with the aid of fine workshops. Of central significance are the subterranean → hypogaea with their rich internal architecture chiselled out of tufa (especially Cerveteri and Chiusi). From the middle of the 6th cent. BC, Etruscan glyptics, for which special drilling techniques were a prerequisite, set in. We know little about textile and leather work, that was probably mostly done for private use.

→ Etrusci, Etruria

L. BONFANTE, Etruscan Dress, 1975; M. BONGHI JOVINO (ed.), Produzione artigianale ed esportazione nel mondo antico. Il Bucchero etrusco, Atti Milano 1990, 1993; G. COLONNA, Il maestro dell'Ercole e della Minerva. Nuova luce sull'attività dell'officina veiente, in: OpRom 16, 1987, 7–41; M. CRISTOFANI, I bronzi degli Etruschi,

1985; M. CRISTOFANI, M. MARTELLI (ed.), L'oro degli Etruschi, 1985; M. EGG, Ital. Helme. Stud. zu den ältereisenzeitl. Helmen It.s und der Alpen, 1986; U. FISCHER-GRAF, Spiegelwerkstätten in Vulci, 1980; E. FORMIGLI, G. NESTLER, Etr. Granulation. Eine ant. Goldschmiedetechnik, 1993; F.-W. VON HASE, Früheisenzeitl. Kammhelme aus It., in: Ant. Helme. Slg. Lipperheide und andere Bestände des Antikenmus. Berlin, 1988, 195–211; S. HAYNES, Etruscan Bronzes, 1985; Y. HULS, Ivoires d'Etrurie, 1957; M. MARTELLI, La ceramica degli Etruschi. La pittura vascolare, 1987; A. NASO, Architetture dipinte. Decorazioni parietali non figurate nelle tombe a camera dell'Etruria meridionale (VII–V sec. a. C.), 1996; F. PRAYON, Frühetr. Grab- und Hausarchitektur, 1975; G. M. A. RICHTER, Engraved Gems of the Greeks and the Etruscans, 1968, especially 173–213; E. RYSTEDT, C. WIKANDER, Ö. WIKANDER, Deliciae Fictiles. Proc. of the First International Conference on Central Italic Architectural Terracottas at the Swedish Institute in Rome 1990, 1993; S. STEINGRÄBER, Etr. Möbel, 1979; Id. (ed.), Etr. Wandmalerei, 1985; P. ZAZOFF, Etr. Skarabäen, 1968.   GE.BI.

V. CLASSICAL ANTIQUITY
A. GENERAL   B. CULTURE AND THE ECONOMY
C. TRAINING AND WORKING CONDITIONS IN THE
TRADE   D. LOCATION AND TECHNICAL EQUIPMENT
OF THE WORKSHOPS   E. ARTISANS AND CLIENTS
F. WAGES   G. SOCIAL STATUS   H. LITERATURE
AND PHILOSOPHY   VI. BYZANTIUM

A. GENERAL
Although the political structures changed fundamentally in the course of antiquity, the working conditions in the crafts and the social position of craftsmen remained essentially unchanged: for the production of consumer items and the creation of works of art, crafts were of decisive importance, mechanical instruments were only used to a small extent and in many branches there were no pioneering technical innovations. The public despised the artisan but had a high regard for his products (Plut. Pericles 2,1). There was no clear distinction between artisans and artists in today's sense; the terms τέχνη (téchnē) and ars designate the work of both the artisan and the artist. In addition to the literary texts and the inscriptions, which do not shed light on all aspects of the ancient crafts equally, the numerous workshop images on Attic vases and the Roman grave reliefs (especially from Italy and Gaul) are also important as evidence to draw upon.

B. CULTURE AND THE ECONOMY
Apart from isolated and hence self-sufficient households, private production was not able to fully meet the need for artisan products. Although private production in the household continued in all ages of antiquity (tools and devices: Hom. Il. 23,831ff.; Cato Agr. 5,6; 31; 37,3; textile manufacture: Hes. Op. 536ff.; Verg. G. 1,293f.; 1,390ff.; Suet. Aug. 73; Columella 12,3,6), professional crafts were vital for economy and society from archaic times to late antiquity; on the one hand, the population of the towns depended on consumer goods such as vessels, textiles and furniture or on foodstuffs like bread, and on the other, many people in urban centres found work and derived an income from the trades. Agriculture also required to a great extent the competency of craftsmen (cf. Hes. Op. 430; Cato Agr. 14; 16) or their products (Cato Agr. 22; 135; Varro, Rust. 1,16,3). Trade initially played only a subordinate role in the supply of products of the crafts because an artisan normally sold his products in the workshop directly to the customers. In many regions small workshops produced goods for local needs, while production centres of supraregional importance also emerged — in ceramic manufacture during the ancient and classical period for instance near Corinth and Athens: and in the Roman period near → Arretium, as well as in southern and central Gaul.

In Homeric society artisans were among the few foreigners who were welcome in the community as they had special capabilities (Hom. Od. 17,381ff.); only specialized wandering artisans could produce prestigious objects for the upper class. Cult statues, votive offerings and sculptures, gold and silver crockery, and temple or wall paintings were often created by foreigners not only in small rural settlements but also in towns in which many artisans worked. The mobility of these artisans was not eclipsed by the emergence of town crafts but continued to characterize the work and life of many sculptors, builders and miners. Economic crises, changes in general taste, as well as legal measures as for instance the ban decreed by → Demetrius [4] of Phalerum on the erection of lavish tomb statues in Athens (Cic. Leg. 2,66) were able to abruptly and adversely effect the stock of orders of these artisans. On the other hand, the implementation of relatively large construction projects required the recruitment of a corresponding number of well-trained workers; in this way building plans were dependent on how many workers were available. The Roman army, which was equally reliant on tradesmen and engineers for the manufacture of armour, weapons and siege devices, as well as for the construction of lodging and supply routes (→ fabri), in the republican period had its own units of craftsmen and technicians under the command of the praefectus fabrum (Veg. Mil. 2,11). To ensure the population's supply, artisans in late antiquity were forbidden to change their job or to give up their workshop; several occupations were hereditary so that sons were compelled to take up the work of their fathers. Numerous decrees concerned particularly the bakers in Rome who belonged to the corpus pistorum (Association of Bakers) and had to supply bread for distribution among the population (Cod. Theod. 14,3). In other towns the compulsory measures of the administration were likewise directed at the bakers (Antioch: Lib. Or. 1,205–210; 1,226f.).

Based on the structure of the ancient economy, increasing production of certain goods could lead to a drop in prices and hence also to the departure of artisans (cf. Xen. Vect. 4,6). The incomes of artisans and the quality and price of their products were to a large extent protected; there was, however, a lack of unions between the artisans that would have effected efficient organization of the production and sale of the products. Not until late antiquity did *corpora* develop that were primarily meant to regulate the relationships between the administration and the individual artisans.

For simple artisans a certain degree of versatility was necessary because most manufacturing processes (house building, making of furniture) required the processing of materials of different kinds. Artisans in smaller towns were from time to time forced to produce different kinds of goods — e.g. iron ploughshares, sickles, knives, nails and keys — to obtain sufficient orders for their workshop. The element of competition that was also found in other fields of ancient life contributed to the quality of the crafts and to the financial success of the artisans. Thus Hesiod, writing on the subject, states that one potter resented another potter, one carpenter another carpenter (κεραμεὺς κεραμεῖ κοτέει καὶ τέκτονι τέκτων; Hes. Op. 25), and that towns organized competitions for potters, as is attested by the grave inscription of one Bacchius, who won several wreaths (IG II² 11387). There are also several indications of financial competition between artisans in different towns; according to Athenaeus, artisans in Rhodes attempted to manufacture metal vessels at more favourable prices than the Athenians in order to win over new groups of buyers (Ath. 469b).

Through fashioned consumer goods, artisans had an influence on the cultural development that could scarcely be overlooked. Attic ceramics were an important medium for pictorial representations; the potters and vase painters in this way shaped the visual worlds of the Greeks and made a fundamental contribution to the interpretation of traditional myths or everyday social constellations. In addition, the workshop in a village or town was also a place of social communication; Socrates is said to have held many of his discussions in the workshop of the cobbler Simon next to the Agora of Athens (Diog. Laert. 2,122; cf. Xen. Mem. 4,2,1; Hes. Op. 492f.).

C. Training and working conditions in the trade

Training in the craft was done by an experienced artisan, often by the father or another relative (Pl. Prt. 328a). Not only the myth of → Daedalus [1] (Apollod. 3,15,8) but also numerous inscriptions and literary references point to the fact that it was often traditional for a craft to be carried on within a family and for the son to take over the workshop. As can be seen from workshop scenes on Attic vases, it was common for children to work. If an artisan had no sons he could adopt a boy or buy a slave child. Only for Ptolemaic and Roman Egypt is there firm evidence of the practice that children who did not belong to the family or who were slaves were trained in a craft (cf. e.g. POxy. 275; 725); on the basis of comments regarding the teacher-pupil relationship in the field of sculpting and painting, however (Plat. Men.

91d; Plin. HN 36,16f.), it is to be assumed that this was also practised in other regions and eras.

The duration of training depended, on the one hand, on the individuals ability to learn and on the on the expectations of the master. The training began with insignificant tasks. In the potter's workshop a boy might for example have turned the potter's wheel while the master shaped the vessel; proverbially it was considered foolish to begin potting with the → pithos (Pl. Grg. 514e). Although a fully-trained architect, potter, sculptor, painter, smith or shoemaker was a master of all production stages, it can be established that in the workshops individual assistants specialized in certain work processes. The increasing use of special terms for certain artisans does not, however, mean that whole workshops were specialized in a corresponding manner. Without doubt there was great discipline in the craft so as to avoid damage to tools and materials as well as injuries; this was especially the case if fire, heavy weights or sharp tools were used in carrying out the trade.

A well-trained slave could expect to be freed and then also had the opportunity to employ free workers or even to own slaves. Status differences were almost meaningless in view of the demands of the trade; in e.g. the eastern colonnade of the Erechtheion, no difference can be established between the work of free artisans and slaves. Women (wives, daughters, female slaves) were perhaps employed in the trade in larger numbers than we can tell from the few testimonies (cf. Xen. Mem. 2,7 and a female vase painter: red-figured hydria, BEAZLEY ARV 571,73).

Working hours for activities outside the home probably depended on the length of the day; many activities could also be carried out with artificial light. Numerous artisans worked in a confined and unhealthy environment; their workload could lead to illnesses and physical deformities. In the building trade it was, despite the use of large cranes and pulleys as well as heavy wagons to transport the stone blocks, still the task of the artisans to move the building materials through their own physical strength, especially as the wheelbarrow was still unknown.

D. Location and technical equipment of the workshops

The ancient workshop normally comprised the people, tools and materials necessary for production. The location of the workshop — and hence also the building itself — was only of secondary importance; depending on the current task, an artisan could move his workshop to another place. In several branches of the trades the location of the workshops depended on the availability of raw materials and fuel. Good clay suitable for the manufacture of ceramics was found close to Corinth and Athens and was the prerequisite for the production of ceramics in these towns; near Arretium, too, the local clay deposits were used. Metalliferous ores were in many cases mined and smelted in remote regions

(→ Mining); here settlements for the miners then developed, as e.g. in the Laurion area in Attica or in Vipasca in Roman Spain (CIL II 5181 = ILS 6891). Centres of metalworking were also located in ports; iron ore from Elba was brought to Puteoli and processed there (Diod. Sic. 5,13,1f.). In textile production, too, a concentration of workshops in regions in which high quality raw materials were obtained can be observed (wool: Patavium, Str. 5,1,7; 5,1,12; linen: Tarsus, Dion Chrys. 34,21–23; Byssus: Patrae, Paus. 7,21,14). In many larger towns most of the branches of the trades were represented; in Athens, potters who made terracotta figures, shoemakers, bronze smiths and stonemasons who worked marble were located in the crafts district near the Agora; in Pompeii bakers, weavers, fullers, blacksmiths, potters and builders lived and worked throughout the city. Inscriptions attest to the fact that this also applies to Rome.

The ancient workshops were of varied size: blacksmiths, jewellers or weavers probably worked alone or with only a few assistants, as Attic vase pictures and Roman funerary reliefs from Italy and Gaul show; the workshop was often directly associated with the artisan's residence and served at the same time as his shop. In a potter's workshop or a bronze foundry, on the other hand, six or more artisans could easily be employed. There is only seldom evidence of larger workshops in classical Greece (Lys. 12,8; 12,19: 120 shieldmakers; Dem. Or. 27,9: 2 → *ergastéria* with 32 and 20 slaves; cf. Dem. Or. 36,4), though they were common in some branches of Roman commerce such as the large brickyards.

The ancient crafts were by their very nature strongly rooted in tradition. No technical progress was made that would have been able to fundamentally change working procedures. Nevertheless, new artisan techniques repeatedly emerged, as for example the manufacture of relief-decorated ceramics with the help of moulding-bowls in the Hellenistic period, glass-blowing in the 1st cent. BC or brickfiring in the early Principate. Even within the established tradition of the trades there were opportunities for innovations, as can be especially seen from the evidence for the working of → glass. In the field of bronze-working, the hollow-casting procedure must have been considered a significant step forward since it allowed, for the first time, the production of life-size bronze statues. A craft that required training was essentially based on a wealth of invention, knowledge and manual skill rather than on lavish technical equipment. Increasing demand did not lead to technical changes or the establishment of large businesses, but to the equipping of new workshops in which work was done using traditional techniques. From time to time it is certainly the case that several artisans together used high-capacity installations; in Gaul several potters had their clay goods fired in one potter's oven. Again and again the conclusion has been drawn from the short remarks of Xenophon (Xen. Cyr. 8,2,5f.) that there was mass production through in-

creased specialization, but the actual goal of specialization in the trades was not to increase productivity but to improve quality. According to Augustine, an additional advantage of specialization was that it shortened the training period (Aug. Civ. 7,4).

E. ARTISANS AND CLIENTS

Artisans did not work only for sale to anonymous customers but often on commission, which applies particularly to sculpture and the building trade; in this field public orders played an important part. In such cases the artisans had to take into consideration the expectations of the clients. As a workshop painting shows, the customers monitored the completion of the statues (red-figured bowl, Berlin SM, Beazley ARV 400,1). The members of building committees were probably in a position to make competent judgements about architectonic designs; therefore their influence on public building work should not be underestimated.

When orders were given, the artisans and clients agreed on materials, the size, style, price and date of completion (cf. for instance CIL I² 698 = ILS 5317); the artisan was liable for any damage to the materials supplied or for wasting them (Dig. 9,2,27,29). For the 5th cent. BC, contracts between private clients and artisans are mentioned only rarely; Andocides for example claims that Alcibiades forced the painter → Agatharchus to work for him although he had to fulfil contracts with other clients (And. 4,17). With regard to classical Greece, business reports show that the craftsman was strictly bound by the contractual conditions; aside from all the details of construction work, precise stipulations regulated the length of the working day, the number of tradesmen, their salaries, the resolution of conflicts between the individual groups of tradesmen and measures to be taken if deadlines were exceeded. The artisans who supervised the large building projects and coordinated the large number of different stages of the work were called *architéktōnes* (ἀρχιτέκτωνες, 'architects'), a title that is only attested for the building trade and that indicates the very high status of the carpenters (τέκτων, *téktōn*) in the ancient building trade. If the community awarded work directly and, as in Athens in the 5th cent. BC, paid per day (or per piece of work), the individual artisan's continuing employment depended on the consent of the architect responsible; in view of this situation, the artisans could, if need be, threaten to discontinue the work. There is evidence of the downing of tools in Ptolemaic and Roman Egypt as well as in Asia Minor as the result of a shortage of materials or food supplies or the failure to pay wages.

F. WAGES

There are insufficient sources concerning the payment of trade work. Compared with the pay of a hoplite, the daily pay in Athens during the 5th cent. BC of a tradesman who was not fully trained was somewhat lower, that of a qualified tradesman somewhat higher than a hoplite's. For the quarries and mines of the *prin-*

cipes a wage rate applied that depended more on the age of the worker than on the type of work, with the highest wage corresponding to the pay of a Roman soldier. The → *Edictum Diocletiani* (7,1–63) does show the relationships between the wages in the various branches of the trades, but on the basis of the sources it is not possible to make a comparison with the pay of a soldier in the year 301. Artisans normally earned enough to ensure a relatively good standard of living but they could not become wealthy. The linen weavers in Tarsus were not even in a position to produce the 500 drachmas needed for acquiring citizenship (Dion. Chrys. 34,23); still, several anecdotes passed down to us from Pliny (Plin. HN 34,37; 35,62; 35,88) and also votive offerings and tomb monuments show that individual artisans — among these primarily qualified sculptors and painters — grew rich and even displayed their affluence. An example of this is the large tomb monument of the baker Eurysaces at the Porta Maggiore in Rome with reliefs that vividly depict work in a bakery.

G. Social status

In antiquity, a definite prejudice existed towards people who performed physical work (βάναυσοι, *bánausoi* or *sordidi*); repeatedly ancient literature mentions that deformity of the body, disease and premature death due to the exertion of incessant work that allowed no leisure for public activity or activity pertaining to the Muses, as well as financial and social dependence characterized the life of tradesmen (Xen. Mem. 2,8; Oec. 4,2f.; cf. Aristot. Pol. 1278a; 1337b). The low status accorded the *bánausoi* was nowhere as strongly marked as in Sparta (Xen. Lac. 7,1f.) and in democratic Athens where politicians who had links with the trade could be reproached for that; in Corinth the tradesmen were, according to Herodotus, despised the least (Hdt. 2,167). In Rome too, the social disapproval of physical paid work and of the trades was widespread: according to Cicero, all tradesmen performed dirty work as there could be no freedom in a workshop (*Opificesque omnes in sordida arte versantur; nec enim quicquam ingenuum habere potest officina*; Cic. Off. 2,150; cf. Dion Chrys. 7,110ff.). Nonetheless, that many tradesmen in Roman times mentioned their occupation on grave inscriptions was, however, also the result of the fact that — unlike in Greece — it was common in Rome to give precise details of the social status of the deceased. There are many additional indications that artisans reacted to the public contempt with a self-confidence based on their knowledge of the trades. The autographs that served to label a commercial good, but often also demonstrated the artisan's pride in his achievement, are especially worthy of mention here. Attic votive reliefs and vase paintings depict very well the way in which potters and vase painters saw themselves: one vessel depicts vase painters at work being crowned with garlands by goddesses (red-figured hydria, around 470 BC, Beazley ARV 571,73). Even though only a few tradesmen held public office, membership of cult clubs or professional associations did, however, offer them the chance to realize their social and political ambitions. In public, artisans certainly undertook collective activities in the early Principate: the *fullones* (→ Fuller) of Pompeii erected a statue for Eumachia and named themselves in the inscription belonging to it (CIL X 813 = ILS 6368).

H. Literature and philosophy

Early Greek literature offers numerous descriptions of the work of artisans and mentions many tradesmen by name; the skill of artisans plays a decisive part in the plot of the Homeric epics (cf. Hom. Il. 18,368–617; Od. 5,243–261; 8,492f.; 23,183–204); in the allegories too, artisans' techniques appear (Hom. Od. 9,384–394; cf. Hes. Theog. 862–866). Hephaestus and Athena teach humans their *téchnē* (Hom. Il. 15,410ff.; Od. 7,109ff.; 23,160). The dignity of technical work is due to the origin of the *téchnai* as coming from the gods. At the same time the ambivalence towards the trades was based on the view that the work of an artisan could be detrimental to humans (Hes. Op. 60–75) or serve to deceive and overpower a stronger party (Hom. Od. 8,266–332). In antiquity there was no theoretical analysis of trade production; in various contexts, however, philosophers have made the work of artisans a theme of their work. In discussing the myth of Prometheus in his 'Protagoras', Plato justifies the need for trade work by the fact that man with his natural equipment — 'naked, barefoot, uncovered and unarmed' — needs the *téchnai* to survive (Pl. Prt. 320d–322d). In the context of a question concerning language theory, he investigates the use of tools in detail (Pl. Crat. 387a–390d; cf. also Plt. 279a–283a on textile production). Aristotle, in his observations on the various forms of knowledge and the central question of coming into existence, discusses the act of production (ποίησις, *poíēsis*; Aristot. Eth. Nic. 1140a; metaph. 1032a–1033b), that essentially means transferring a preconceived form (εἶδος, *eídos*) to an available substance (ὕλη, *hýlē*). In the zoological writings this position serves to explain the phenomenon of the conception of ideas (Aristot. Gen. an. 729b–730b; cf. 735a; 740b), so that here the movement of the hand that effects the tool and hence the object of the work is considered to be fundamental in the manufacturing process. In political theory the low repute of the artisans is expressed in the view that they should not belong to the citizenry of a polis (Pl. Leg. 846a–847b; Aristot. Pol. 1328b).

1 O. Behrends, Die Rechtsformen des röm. Handwerks, in: H. Jankuhn (ed.), Das Handwerk in vor- und frühgesch. Zeit (AAWG 122), 1981, 141–203   2 Blümner, Techn.   3 A. Burford, Craftsmen in Greek and Roman Society, 1972   4 Id., The Greek Temple Builders at Epidauros, 1969   5 J. Crook, Law and Life of Rome, 1967   6 H. Cuvigny, The Amount of Wages Paid to the Quarryworkers at Mons Claudianus, in: JRS 86, 1996, 139–145   7 R. Duncan-Jones, The Economy of the Roman Empire, ²1982   8 P. Garnsey (ed.), Non-Slave Labour in the Greco-Roman World, 1980   9 B. Gralfs, Metallverarbeitende Produktionsstätten in Pompeji, 1988

10 W. V. HARRIS, The Organisation of the Roman Terracotta Lamp Industry, in: JRS 70, 1980, 126–145   11 J. F. HEALY, Mining and Metallurgy in the Greek and Roman World, 1978   12 H. JANKUHN (ed.), Das Handwerk in vor- und frühgesch. Zeit (AAWG 122), 1981   13 JONES, LRE, 858–864   14 N. KAMPEN, Image and Status: Roman Working Women in Ostia, 1981   15 H. LOANE, Industry and Commerce of the City of Rome 50 B.C.-A.D. 200, 1938   16 B. MAYESKE, Bakeries, Bakers, and Bread at Pompeii, PhD diss. University of Maryland, 1972   17 D. P. S. PEACOCK, Pottery in the Roman World, 1982   18 H. V. PETRIKOVITS, Die Spezialisierung des röm. H., in: H. JANKUHN (ed.), Das Handwerk in vor- und frühgesch. Zeit (AAWG 122), 1981, 63–132   19 G. PRACHNER, Die Sklaven und Freigelassenen im arretinischen Sigillatagewerbe, 1980   20 R. H. RANDALL JR., The Erechtheum Workers, in: AJA 57, 1953, 199–210   21 F. DE ROBERTIS, Lavori e lavorati nel mondo romano, 1963   22 E. SCHLESIER, Ethnologische Aspekte zu den Begriffen 'Handwerk' und 'Handwerker', in: H. JANKUHN (ed.), Das Handwerk in vor- und frühgesch. Zeit (AAWG 122), 1981, 9–35   23 A. STEWART, Greek Sculpture, 1990   24 STRONG/BROWN   25 J. M. C. TOYNBEE, Death and Burial in the Roman World, 1971   26 S. TREGGIARI, Roman Freedmen during the Late Republic, 1969   27 Id., Urban Labour in Rome: Mercennarii and Tabernarii, in: P. GARNSEY (ed.), Non-slave Labour in the Greco-Roman World, 1980, 48–64   28 A. WALLACE-HADRILL, Houses and Society in Pompeii and Herculaneum, 1994   29 J. B. WARD-PERKINS, Marble in Antiquity, 1992   30 R. S. YOUNG, A working-class district, in: Hesperia 20, 1951, 135–288   31 G. ZIMMER, Griech. Bronzegußwerkstätten, 1990   32 ZIMMER.   A.B.-C.

VI. BYZANTIUM

A. SOURCES AND LITERATURE   B. THE CRAFTS IN THE CONTEXT OF ECONOMIC TRENDS   C. FORMS OF ORGANIZATION OF THE ARTISANS   VII. EARLY MIDDLE AGES

A. SOURCES AND LITERATURE

The available sources make a portrayal of the trades difficult. This applies particularly to details regarding the nature and distribution of the individual branches of the trades. Only from Egyptian papyrus documents do we have sufficient evidence through to the 7th cent., but these cannot be transferred to the other parts of the empire. Rather sporadic details are given in the Lives of the Saints (→ vitae sanctorum) and by the chronicler → Theophanes.

B. THE CRAFTS IN THE CONTEXT OF ECONOMIC TRENDS

A distinction must be made between private individual artisans (τεχνίτης, technítēs) who were in many cases also the vendors of their wares, i.e. business people, and the artisans (some of whom were slaves) in the monopoly state businesses (silk trade companies, weapon manufacture, arsenals, working of precious metals in the coin factories) that had been set up in the large towns, especially Constantinople. The brisk building activity (→ Building trade) under Justinian, especially

the redesigning of Constantinople, represents a high point for all branches of the trades (Procop. Aed.).

The decline of the cities from the 2nd half of the 6th cent. also brought with it a significant decline in the diversity of trade activities. Only Constantinople was not much affected by this, but also in those settlements that had dwindled to being castra, the number of artisans needed to supply the population remained. Particularly important here were the construction artisans needed for the building and improvement of defence facilities; the tilling of fields was also not possible without the specialized smith trade. All concrete names for trade occupations (e.g. in the letters of → Theodoros Stoudites, 8th/9th cents.) relate in all probability to Constantinople alone.

C. FORMS OF ORGANIZATION OF THE ARTISANS

The artisan associations of late antiquity are mentioned through to the time of Justinian (Digests, Procop. Arc., inscriptions from Korykos). The next express mention of organizations is not found again until the Book of the Eparchs by → Leo VI from 911/912. This long period of time prompts us to ask whether the associations of the 10th cent. continued the professional associations of late antiquity and whether there were any trade associations in the 7th and 8th cents. at all. The problem is probably only relevant to the capital city of Constantinople anyway, as in most of the other fort-like settlements artisans were indeed necessary but no forms of organization were required because of their small numbers. The structure of the professional associations in the 10th cent. also shows, in comparison with late antiquity, no differences so fundamental that a completely new beginning would seem probable. Notes from the chroniclers, indicating that the emperors drew upon the assistance of the artisans for state matters, also indicate that there was no complete break with tradition. Particularly noteworthy in this respect is the written and oral oath taken at the appointment of Constantine VI as co-regent (776) in which also οἱ τῶν ἐργαστηριακῶν (Theophanes 449,25–450,7 DE BOOR) participated. The prerequisite for this — also given the linguistic expression — is that there were trade associations.

1 W. BRANDES, Die Städte Kleinasiens im 7. und 8. Jahrhundert, 1989, especially 149–152   2 H. MAGOULIAS, Trades and Crafts in the Sixth and Seventh Centuries as Viewed in the Lives of the Saints, in: Byzantinoslavica 37, 1976, 11–35   3 A. I. ROMANCUK, Chersonesos und sein ländliches Territorium im 8./9. Jahrhundert, in: H. KÖPSTEIN, F. WINCKELMANN, Studien zum 8. und 9. Jahrhundert in Byzanz, 1983, 35–45   4 P. SCHREINER, Die Organisation byz. Kaufleute und Handwerker, in: Untersuchungen zu Handel und Verkehr 6 (AAWG), 1989, 44–61   5 A. STÖCKLE, Spätröm. und byz. Zünfte, 1911.   P.S.

VII. EARLY MIDDLE AGES

There are four trends that characterize the institutions, fields and forms of trade work from the 6th to the

9th cent. AD: the shift in the focus from the *civitates* to pre-urban or rural centres of rule (→ Domains, palatinates, fortified castles, bishops' churches, monasteries; also market and commercial centres), the way in which the regions on both sides of the former Roman imperial borders started to come into line, the decline in certain artisan standards (→ Glass) on the one hand, and the way in which other techniques became more elaborate and widespread (water mills, weapons) on the other hand, as well as the beginnings of new commercial centres (Frisian-Flemish cloths, Badorf ceramics, basalt millstones in the volcanic Eifel etc.). Recent research concerning the archaeology of settlements and industries, linguistic research, and such concerning legal, financial, technical and art history research has contributed to this picture. It however still lacks the conceptual rounding off — with regard to central contrastive concepts, for instance autarky market, city country, work performed at home-trades, regular employment-contract work, tax service, freedom servitude, wandering-settled, consumer goods artwork — that would allow us to understand the diversity of the manifestations.

Overall, we do not have sufficient information about trades in the early Middle Ages to allow for more than a simple understanding. The little information we have from written sources or excavation finds from the 6th–9th cents. does not suffice, either in number or in breadth, to cover the trades field as a whole or to see how it fitted into the social or commercial framework, to say nothing of establishing urban or regional profiles.

As a starting-point for rising commercial activity, these were new regal, ecclesiastical and aristocratic centres of rule (more than 500 large stone buildings in 8th–9th cent. France; weapon, manuscript and liturgical centres), centres of coastal and river trade (with seasonally present refinement workers) and villical facilities for further commercial processing and the extraction of materials (grain mills, malt kilns/breweries, blacksmith shops, weaving and spinning centres (*genitia*), potters' workshops, smelting ovens, salt boiling factories). Here we see a pattern of dependent services by enfeoffed people, i.e. services that were carried out by workers who were not free (*ministeria, servientes*), from the monk as clerk to the *aurifaber* within the monastery who did the rounds as an enfeoffed slave much in demand, and the ore digger in the mountain forest and the ferryman at the ford who all lived a life of servitude. Although in Carolingian times there is increasing evidence of targeted sales to (high-status) customers or at local, regional and distance trading markets, it appears that only rarely were there business stratifications of settled businesses in the sense of a doubly free market relationship (purchase of materials and sale of products).

In the early medieval process of handing down and transforming the ancient *mechanicae* canon, in spite of increasing links with applicability and the monastic *opus manuum* command, any sign is lacking that artisan activities were understood as *opera* or *artes* distinct from agriculture, household work and trade, or that some of them were more highly regarded than others. Concerning the way in which they were viewed, the important issues remained the individual *opera*, the proximity to the ruler and the level of service. In the same way, the attitude of the aristocracy and the Church marked by an ambivalence of contempt and admiration towards the trades, influenced the individual *artifex/faber*. No special recognition was accorded the particular skill as individual achievement; decisive is the place of the anonymous work in Church worship or the aristocratic structure of pageantry; even subtly decorated jewellery or treasures are guilelessly melted down when required. We should give up our notion that the *geldoniae* that existed since the 8th/9th cents. — local oath allegiances to defend against current dangers that were combatted by the Church — went back to the → *collegia* of late antiquity or the Germanic sacrificial cults. Since the early 11th cent. it was the traders (*mercatores*), not the artisans (*artifices*), who started to join associations and form professional groups.

1 Artigianato e tecnica nella società dell'alto medioevo occidentale, vol. 1–2, 1971   2 H. JANKUHN (ed.), Das Handwerk in vor- und frühgesch. Zeit, vol. 1–2, 1981/83 (AAWG)   3 U. KOCH (ed.), Die Franken, Wegbereiter Europas, vol. 2, 1996   4 A. DOPSCH, Wirtschaftsentwicklung der Karolingerzeit, vol. 2, 1922, 137–186   5 K. EBERLEIN, Miniatur und Arbeit, 1995   6 D. HÄGERMANN, Technik im frühen Mittelalter, in: W. KÖNIG (ed.), Propyläen Technikgeschichte 1, 1991, 315–505   7 H. ROTH, Kunst und Kunsthandwerk im frühen MA, 1986   8 F. SCHWIND, Zu karolingerzeitlichen Klöstern als Wirtschaftsorganismen und Stätten handwerklicher Tätigkeit, in: L. FENSKE (ed.), Institutionen, Kultur und Gesellschaft im MA (FS J. Fleckenstein), 1984, 101–123.
LU.KU.

Cragaleus (Κραγαλεύς). Son of → Dryops in the land of Dryope. C., who is wise and just, is chosen by → Apollo, › Artemis, and › Hercules to act as arbitrator in their dispute about the Epirote city → Ambracia. Apollo demands the city for himself because his son rules the land of Dryope. Artemis demands it because she had liberated the city from a tyrant, and Hercules because he defeated the Celts, the Thesproteans and the Epiroteans. C. awards the city to Hercules and in return is changed into a rock by Apollo (Antoninus Liberalis 4). C. is also the eponym of the Cragalides who provided an → Amphiktyonia for the protection of the Delphian Oracle, which was destroyed in 590 BC (Aeschin. Leg. 3,107ff.).
AL.FR.

Cragus (Κράγος). Mountains in Lycia west of the lower Xanthus (Str. 14,3,5, known today as Yan Dağ). Patara, Telmessus, Tlos, and Xanthus i.a. belonged to the area that was named after C., as documented on late Hellenistic coins and in imperial inscriptions (IGR III 488).

1 W. RUGE, s.v. K., RE 11, 1567.

H. A. TROXELL, The Coinage of the Lycian League, 1982.
U.HA.

Cranaus (Κραναός; *Kranaós*). Attic hero; also, the personification of Attica's rough and rocky ground. C. ruled during the time of the Deucalionic flood (→ Deucalion). His wife was Pedias (= 'plains') of Lacedaemon (Marmor Parium, FGrH 239 A 4) [1]. In the myth, he has three daughters: Cranae, Cranaichme and Atthis (Apollod. 3,186). C. functions as arbitrator in the conflict between Athena and Poseidon (Apollod. 3,179). Pindar refers to Athens as *Cranaaí* (Pind. Ol. 13,38), Attica's inhabitants called themselves *Cranaoí* (Hdt. 8,44). C. is forced by → Amphictyon [1] to give up his rulership. He dies in the deme of Lamptrae (Paus. 1,31,3). Perhaps statue A in the western gable of the Parthenon in Athens [2].

1 G. BERGER-DOER, s.v. K., LIMC 6.1, 108f.
2 L. WEIDAUER, Eumolpos und Athen, in: AA 1985, 195–210. RE.ZI.

Crane Γέρανος (*géranos*), Lat. *grus* or *gruis* refers to the common crane (*Grus grus*), but *grus Balearica* in Plin. HN 11,122 refers to the demoiselle crane (*Grus virgo* [1. 131f.]; also, cf. 10,135 *grues minores* or *vipiones*). The bird's main characteristic is its long legs (Lucil. 168). Spring and autumn migrations of the crane were closely watched in the Mediterranean area since it flew over the region, but did not brood there (Hom. Il. 2,460; Aristot. Hist. an. 8(9),10,614b 18–26; Plut. Lucullus 39,5; wedge formation in Cic. Nat. D. 2,49; Mart. 9,13,7 and 13,75; migration from Thrace across the Bosporus to Egypt and Ethiopia: Ael. NA 2,1 and 3,13). A mythic story exists about a fight with the → Pygmies (Hom. Il. 3,3–6; Plin. HN 10,58; Babr. 26). The crane was claimed to keep itself awake at night with a stone in its claw (Plin. HN 10,59 and *passim* up to Isid. Orig. 12,7,15) and supposedly took on ballast before crossing the sea (Aristoph. Av. 1137; Plin. HN 10,60). The crane's courtship displays (cf. Plin. HN 10,59) were known from tame cranes. The bird was valued at times as a delicacy in Rome, (Hor. Sat. 2,8,87; Gell. NA 6,16,5; Stat. Silv. 4,6,9), especially if fattened (cf. Varro, Rust. 3,2,14), contrary to the Greeks who took it to be inedible (Epicharmus near Ath. 8,338d). Cranes were caught with snares and nets (Enn. Ann. 556; Hor. Epod. 2,35) or with hidden bait pasted inside a hollowed squash with the juice of mistletoe (Dionysii Ixeuticon 3,11; [2. 42f.]). The bird was considered to be sacred to Demeter (Porph. De abstinentia 3,5) because its appearance in the spring marks the right time for sowing (Hes. Op. 448), and it follows the plow (Theoc. 10,31). Images on coins [3. pl. 6,3; 6,6 and 6,7] and ancient gems [3. pl. 22,2; 22,12; 22,17 and 24,8] demonstrate the popularity of the beautiful bird.

1 LEITNER   2 A. GARZYA (ed.), Dionysii Ixeuticon libri, 1963   3 F. IMHOOF-BLUMER, O. KELLER, Tier- und Pflanzenbilder auf Mz. und Gemmen des klass. Alt., 1889, repr. 1972.

KELLER 2, 184–193; TOYNBEE, 231–233. C.HÜ.

Cranii (Κράνιοι). City west of → Cephallenia, east of the main city today named Argostoli. It supported Athens in the → Peloponnesian War: Thuc. 2,30; 33; 5,35; 56; Str. 10,2,13.

P. KALLIGAS, Ἱερὸ Δήμητρας καὶ Κόρης στὴν Κράνη Κεφαλλονιᾶς, in: ArchE, 1978, 136–146; R. SPEICH, Korfu und die Ion. Inseln, 1982, 263–265. D.S.

Crannon (Κραννών). City in the Thessalian Tetras Pelasgiotis, located through findings on inscriptions at *c.* 22 km south-west of → Larisa [2]. Settled since Neolithic times, it bore the place name of Ephyra since the Mycenaean period (Str. 8,3,5). From no later than the 6th cent. BC on, C., home of the Scopadae family, belonged to the eight most important Thessalian cities. In the early 4th cent., it was ruled by the tyrant Deinias of Pherae, and in 352, C. fell under Macedonian rule. In 322, the victory of Antipater near C. brought an end to the → Lamian War (323/2; Diod. Sic. 10,16ff.). In the year 215, Philip V ordered the naturalization of 214 citizens from C. in Larisa (IG IX 2,517).

C. HABICHT, Epigraphische Zeugnisse zur Gesch. Thessaliens unter der maked. Herrschaft, in: Ancient Macedonia 1, 1970, 273ff.; K. LIAMPI, Die Münzprägung von Krannon, in: Πρόγραμμα περιληφές ανακοινώνεων Διεθνές συνέδριο για την αρχαία Θεσσαλία. FS D. Theochari 1987, 1992, 59f.; F. STÄHLIN, Das hellenische Thessalien, 1924, 111f. (Sources). HE.KR.

Crantor (Κράντωρ; *Krántōr*) of Soli. Academic philosopher of the early 3rd cent. BC. Studied with → Xenocrates and → Polemon. He surrounded himself with a considerable number of students (Diog. Laert. 4,24). It is unclear whether he was scholar of the → Academy for a short period of time. His favourite student was → Arcesilaus [5]. Little has survived of his voluminous and varied writings (Diog. Laert. 4,24: 30,000 lines). The writing 'On Mourning' (Περὶ Πένθους) was famous and decisive for the genre of consolation literature. A few fragments thereof are still extant — Cic. Acad. 1,135 comments on them: *aureolus ad verbum ediscendus libellus* ('a golden booklet for memorization'). In the context of the renewed appreciation for Plato, C. was the author of the first commentary on Plato's 'Timaeus', wherein he followed Speusippus and Xenocrates on the fundamental issues of interpretation and took an independent position only on specific individual points (such as the question of the soul's constitution: he focused on its role in understanding). He is the creator of the two-directional ordering of the Platonic sequence of numbers according to powers of the numbers two and three in the shape of a Lambda. Horace still regarded C. as the authoritative source for questions of → ethics (Hor. Epist. 1,2,3f.). Like Polemon, the natural holds normative significance for C. His theory of goods appears in the guise of popular philosophy in Sext. Emp. adv. math. 11,51–58): the greatest share of *eudaimonia* (→ Happiness) is attributed to *arete* (→ Virtue), followed by health, pleasure and wealth.

TESTIMONIA AND FR.: H. J. METTE, Zwei Akademiker heute: Krantor von Soloi und Arkesilaos von Pitane, in: Lustrum 26, 1985, 8–40.
BIBLIOGRAPHY: H. J. KRÄMER, Die Spätphase der Älteren Akademie, GGPh² 3, 151–174.   K.-H.S.

Crassicius Pasicles (Pansa), L. Originally from Tarentum, he was enslaved but later freed. His working years were the thirties and twenties BC, first as an assistant for mimeographers, then as grammaticus in modest circumstances. His commentary on → Helvius Cinna's *Zmyrna* brought him popularity and attracted students from respected families (for example Iullus → Antonius [II 1], son of the triumvir). But at the height of his success he closed his school and followed the sect of the Stoic-Pythagorean philosopher Q. → Sextius. It is not known when he changed his name *Pasicles* to *Pansa* (Suet. Gram. 18).

R. A. KASTER, Suetonius, De Grammaticis et Rhetoribus, 1995, 196–203; T. P. WISEMAN, Who was Crassicius Pansa?, in: TAPhA 115, 1985, 187–196.   R.A.K.

Crassus Cognomen, first used as an epithet for abnormal tallness, occasionally with the implication of the figurative meanings 'rough, uncouth, crude', soon also used as a surname. In the republican period, the name was used by the Aquilii, Calpurnii, Canidii, Claudii, Licinii, Otacilii, Papirii, Veturii; in the imperial period by the Galerii, Iulii and Sulpicii. The most significant individuals of this name belonged to the Plebeian → Licinii Crassi (L. Licinius C., cos. 95 BC, the orator; M. Licinus C., cos. 70 and 55 BC, the triumvir).

A. HUG, s.v. Spitznamen, RE 3A, 1828; KAJANTO, Cognomina 244.   K.-L.E.

Crataeis (Κραταιΐς). According to Homer (Od. 12,124), C. is the mother of → Scylla. Hesiod (fr. 150 Rz.; Acusilaus fr. 5, FHG 1, 100), on the other hand, refers to → Hecate as Scylla's mother. Ancient historians attempted to explain this discrepancy in the sources in two ways: on the one hand, a genealogy was established which identified Hecate as the mother of C. and C. as the mother of Scylla (Semus of Delos, fr. 18a, FHG 4, 495). On the other hand, the name of C. was interpreted as an epiclesis by Hecate (Apoll. Rhod. 4,828). These interpretations allow the assumption that C. belongs to the same realm as Hecate — the underworld.   FR.P.

Cratea (Κράτεια, Κράτια). City in Bithynia, known today as Gerede, newly founded as Flaviopolis in the Flavian period (end of the 1st cent. AD). It was the main city of the South Paphlagonian border area in the Gerede Basin and was annexed to Galatia in *c.* 275/4 BC, and in 179, annexed to Paphlagonia (Land of Gaizatorix; Str. 12,3,41). In 6/5 BC, it became → Bithynia et Pontus and was part of Paphlagonia under Diocletia-

nus (late 3rd cent. AD), later part of Honoria. Documented as a diocese since AD 342/3.

K. STROBEL, Galatien und seine Grenzregionen, in: E. SCHWERTHEIM (ed.), Forsch. in Galatien (Asia Minor Stud. 12), 1994, 29–65; K. BELKE, Paphlagonien und Honorias, 1996, 239f.   K.ST.

Craterus (Κράτερος, Κρατερός; *Kráteros, Kraterós*).
[1] Son of Alexander of Orestis. Under Alexander [4], he commanded a → *táxis* of the → *pezétairoi* at the → Granicus (334 BC), and near → Issus (333) and → Gaugamela (331), he commanded the entire regiment. C. held a leading command against the → Uxii and the Ariobarzanes [2], as he also did in the wars in → Hyrcania and Areia [1] after Darius' death [3]. He played an important role in the coup against → Philotas (Curt. 6,8,2–17; 11,10–19). C. had initiated the spying on Philotas in the year 322 (Plut. Alexander 49). C. carried out highly significant tasks in → Sogdiana, eastern Iran, and in north-west India (especially at the 'Hydaspes'), after having been promoted to → *hipparchos*. On the march along the Indus, he commanded one half of the ground troops while → Hephaestion [1], C.'s bitter enemy (Plut. Alexander 47), commanded the other half. While Alexander marched through → Gedrosia, C. led the elephants and the troops who were unfit for war on an easier route but also took along three *táxeis* for the suppression of revolts along the way. During the victory celebrations in → Susa, C. married Princess Amestris, but separated from her after Alexander's death. From the city of Opis, C. and the dismissed veterans were sent to Macedonia in order to replace → Antipater [1], with whom Alexander wanted to get even. Antipater apparently denied C. access. At the time of Alexander's death (323), C. stood in Cilicia, was excluded from the negotiations in Babylon (→ Diadochi, period of the), and received an honorary office lacking any real substance.

The → Lamian War forced Antipater to seek C.'s help (Diod. Sic. 18,12,1). C. married his daughter → Phila who gave birth to his son C. [2]. He crossed over to Asia together with Antipater for the battle against → Perdiccas. Defeated by → Eumenes [1], C. fell in the battle (321/20). C. glorified his role in one of Alexander's lion hunts in a bronze group sculpture by → Lysippus and Leochares. C. [2] displayed the work in Delphi.

BERVE 2, no. 446; HECKEL, 107–33; P. PERDRIZET, Venatio Alexandri, in: JHS 19, 1899, 273–279.   E.B.

[2] Son of C. [1] and → Phila, born in 321 BC. Half-brother of → Antigonus [2] who entrusted C. with Corinth and Chalcis *c.* 280. C.'s command was later expanded to include Euboea and the Piraeus, and after the → Chremonidean War, in which he successfully defended the Isthmus against Areus [1], it was further expanded to include Attica and its garrisons. C. died *c.* 250 and was succeeded by his son Alexander [10] became his successor. Cf. also C. [3] and C. [1] (end).

CAH² 7,1, Index s.v. K.   E.B.

[3] **C. 'the Macedonian'** Author of a 'collection of (Ath.) referenda' (*Psēphismátōn synagōgḗ*) in at least nine bks., which was probably part of the systematic research of documents by the early → Peripatos (Aristot. Politeiai; Theophr. Nomoi etc.). C. organized the documents chronologically and commented on them: bk. nine deals with the year 411/10 BC (fr. in Plutarchus, Stephanus of Byzantium, as well as Scholia to orators and comedians). It is still contested whether he is identical to C. [2], half-brother of Antigonus [2], who ruled since *c.* 280 as governor over the Peloponnese in Corinth for Antigonus.

EDITION: FGrH 342 with comm.
BIBLIOGRAPHY: O. LENDLE, Einführung in die griech. Gesch.- Schreibung, 1992, 275.   K.MEI.

[4] **C. from Antioch**, professionally active *c.* 129/117 BC as the personal physician and *archiatros* (→ Archiatros) of → Antiochus [9] VII. He also functioned as *sidetes* and as a leading member of his council (OGIS 256 = IDélos 1547). Aside from his duties as physician, he also held the office of valet to Queen → Cleopatra [II 14] Theano, and, in the role of *tropheús,* supervised the education of her son, the future → Antiochus [11] IX. Philopator.   V.N.

Crates (Κράτης; *Krátēs*).

[1] Athenian, the poet of the Old Comedy who began giving performances *c.* 450 BC [1. test. 7]. Previously an actor with → Cratinus [1], [1. test. 2 and 3]. Certain sources claim that he wrote seven plays [1. test. 1 and 2], other sources claim eight [1. test. 4]. Altogether nine titles of plays have survived (although the Μέτοικοι 'The Metoikoi' and Πεδῆται 'The Prisoners' may be wrongly attributed to him). On the list of Dionysian winners, C. is listed chronologically after Cratinus and Diopeithes [1. test. 9]; according to Aristophanes [1. test. 6], his public success was inconsistent. Aristotle [1. test. 5] points to C. as the first Attic writer of comedies who refrained from a mockery of contemporary politics and created complete fictional plots. In this regard, C. (as did his 'successor' → Pherecrates) appears as a significant predecessor of the apolitical Attic comedies of the 4th cent.; he was also regarded as extremely funny [1. test. 2]. The altogether 60 fr. (four of which are uncertain) allow only scant conclusions about the content of the plays. The Γείτονες ('The Neighbours') was supposedly the first Attic comedy that featured drunkards; the Θηρία ('The Animals') took up the theme of the legendary land of milk and honey, a theme that tended to reoccur in the Old Comedy (cf. Ath. 6,267e): two (allegorical?) figures meet, one of which envisions a simple and natural life, the other a luxurious, effeminate life (fr. 16; 17), while the chorus of animals admonishes people to stop eating their flesh (fr. 19). In fr. 46 (the play is unknown), a physician speaking Doric appears.

1 PCG IV, 1983, 83–110.

[2] There was doubt about the existence of this second author of comedies with the name C. (cf. C. [1]), but an inscription has raised the probability [1. test. *2]. Two of the four titles of plays that have been handed down under the name of this C. (Θησαυρός, 'The Treasure', Φιλάργυρος, 'The Miser') point to an author of the Middle or even the New Comedy. No fr. have survived.

1 PCG IV, 1983, 111.   H.-G.NE.

[3] **C. of Athens.** Academic philosopher of the 3rd cent. BC. In 276/5, after the death of his close friend → Polemon, he became scholarch of the → Academy for several years. C. did not gain prominence through his own teachings, but strove instead to preserve the traditional Platonic teachings (just like his teachers Polemon and Crantor), (cf. Cic. Acad. 1,9,34). Among his students were → Arcesilaus [5] and → Bion [1] of Borysthenes. In 287, he functioned as negotiator for Athens and succeeded in ending the siege by Demetrius [2] Poliorcetes (Plut. Demetrius 46,3–4).   K.-H.S.

[4] **C. of Thebes.** Cynical philosopher, Diogenes [14] of Sinope's student, probably alive from 368/365–288/285 (Diog. Laert. 6,85–93 whose *vita* is the source for most of the biographical information places his main working years in the 113th Ol. = 328–325 BC). A member of one of the richest families in Thebes, C. became one of the best known Cynics. Several reports exist about his 'conversion' to Cynicism according to which he relinquished his entire fortune and exclaimed the famous sentence: 'C. has liberated the C. of Thebes'. Disadvantaged by nature — he had a hunchback which drew the mockery of gymnasium members — he followed → Hipparchia's wish and married her. She was a young girl from a wealthy family in the Thracian city of Maronea; her brother Metrocles was already a student of C.'s. With the marriage, Hipparchia assumed the mantle of Cynic (τρίβων/ *tríbōn*) and followed her husband everywhere. According to the records, the two had sexual intercourse in public and led what disgusted contemporaries regarded as a 'marriage of dogs' (κυνογαμία/*kynogamía*). C. and Hipparchia had a daughter and a son with the name of Pasicles. C. died in Boeotia and was buried there.

C. led the life of a Cynic: he wore a thick coat in the summer and rags in the winter in order to practise self-control (ἵν' ἐγκρατὴς ᾖ, Diog. Laert. 6,87). When asked what benefits he had gained from philosophy, he answered: 'A daily ration of beans and an untroubled mind' (Diog. Laert. 6,86). He claimed that his homeland was responsible for his bad reputation and the poverty that fate could not rob from him; he called himself a fellow citizen of Diogenes, who is invulnerable to the attacks of envy. He entered private residences and promoted the teachings of Cynicism, gave advice and admonishments, and came to be called the 'door opener' (Diog. Laert. 6,86). He was less rigorous than Diogenes and enjoyed the reputation of a philanthropist. He was called in to arbitrate family disputes and was revered as a 'household god' (*lar familiaris*: Apul. Florida 22).

C.'s students were Metrocles, Hipparchia, Zeno of Citium, Cleanthes [2], Bion [2] of Borysthenes, and perhaps Theombrotos, Cleomenes, and Menippus of Gadara as well. His literary work, which became the stylistic standard for the cynical style (*kynikòs trópos*: a mixture of fun and seriousness called *spoudaiogéloion*; → cynicism), was extraordinarily voluminous, especially in the realm of poetry. He distinguished himself through his tragedies written in highly philosophical style — if we can believe Diogenes Laertius — and through his elegies (a parody of Solon is directed at the Pierian muses), parodies of Homer, and especially through a hexametrical poem 'The Beggar's Sack' (*Péra*, the utopian design of an ideal Cynical city), a 'Hymn to Fertility', a *Ephēmerís* (a diary), 'letters' (stylistically similar to Platonic letters yet completely different from the pseudepigraphic letters by 'C.') as well as a 'Praise of Lentils'. Diogenes Laertius and Emperor Iulianus referred to his works as *Paígnia* ('playful poetry'). His talent for parody greatly influenced → Timon of Phleius, the author of the *Silloi*.

→ Cynicism

EDITIONS: SSR II 523–575 (sect. V H), comm. IV 561–566; Late Helladic 11, 164–173 (fr. 347–369); E. MÜSE-LER, Die Kynikerbriefe, 1. Die Überlieferung 2. Krit. Ausg. mit dt. Übers. (Stud. zur Gesch. und Kultur des Alt. 6–7), 1994.
TRANSLATIONS: L. PAQUET, Les Cyniques Grecs. Fragments et témoignages (Philosophica 4: Éditions de l'Université d' Ottawa), 1975; Id., (ibid. 35) 1988, 103–113 (expanded and corrected edition); Id., Le livre de poche. Classiques de la philos., 1992 (foreword: M.-O. GOULET-CAZÉ), 166–175.
BIBLIOGRAPHY: U. CRISCUOLO, Cratete di Tebe e la tradizione cinica, in: Maia 232, 1970, 360–367; D. R. DUDLEY, A History of Cynicism from Diogenes to the 6th Century A.D., 1937 (repr. 1967), 42–53; M.-O. GOULET-CAZÉ, Une liste de disciples de Cratès le Cynique en Diogène Laërce VI 95, in: Hermes 114, 1986, 247–252; R. GUIDO, La figura e gli insegnamenti di Cratete di Tebe in Giuliano Imperatore, in: Rudiae 4, 1992, 117–134; A. A. LONG, Timon of Phlius: Pyrrhonist and Satirist, in: PCPhS 204, 1978, 68–91; V. PÖSCHL, K., Horaz und Pinturicchio, in: Acta Antiquitatis Academiae Scientiarum Hungaricae 39 (1982–1984), 1987, 267–273.   M.G.-C.

[5] **C. of Mallus.** (Cilicia). Grammarian and philosopher at the Attalid court in Pergamum, 1st half of the 2nd cent. BC, contemporary of Aristarchus [4], teacher of Panaetius (Str. 14,5,16). The Suda refers to him as a 'Stoic philosopher' (x 2342). In 168/7, the Attalides sent him to Rome. After a fall, he was forced to stay there longer than he had intended and, in the meantime, gave public speeches that exerted a significant influence on the emerging philological/exegetical practice in Rome (Suet. Gram. 2,1–4).

In antiquity, C. was known under the epithets 'the Homeric' (*Homērikós*) and 'the critic' (*Kritikós*: Suda). The latter was probably chosen by himself with polemic intent regarding the narrow interests of Alexandrian grammarians (Sext. Emp. adv. math. 1,79). The first epithet refers to his work as a philologist of Homer which is well documented in extant fr. (primarily Homer scholia and Eustathius, collection: [7. 39ff.], to be completed by Scholl's Indices, and F19, 30, 42, 53 and T10 M.; new fr. in POxy. 2888 and 3710, and perhaps Apollonius Sophistes papyrus 1217 Pack², in this context cf. Comanus fr. 21* DYCK). The Homer scholia document the titles *Diorthōtiká* or *Perì diorthóseōs* ('critical comment.'; cf. Suda x: διόρθωσις) and *Homēriká* ('problems in Homer'). The former must have been devoted primarily to issues surrounding textual criticism, while the *Homēriká* probably dealt with astronomical and geographical questions (with reference to allegoresis); these two areas are, however, often closely joined together in C.'s works. C. discusses and resolves problems concerning exegesis and textual criticism using the traditional methods of Hellenistic philology, and indicates a particular interest for passages dealing with geography and astronomy. Characteristic of C. is the postulate that one can already detect evidence of scientific concepts in Homer which were not discovered in Greek science until much later. Among them can be found, in particular, the notion that the cosmos has a spherical shape with the earth at the centre: the part of the globe that was not covered by the continents was taken up by the outer sea, which C. identified as the Homeric Oceanus — the setting of Odysseus' journeys. He applied the same postulate of scientific understanding to other poets as well.

C. also worked on Hesiod (schol. Hes. Theog. 126 and 142, Op. 529–531; Vita Dionysii Periegetae 72, 56 KASSEL, in: [1]), Alcman (in Suda α 1289), Stesichorus (Ael. NA 17,37), Pindar (schol. Pind. N. 2,17c), Euripides (fr. in the schol.: 57f. W., fr. 49–51 M.), and Aratus [4] (in the corpus of the ancient comm. on the poet: Ach. Tat. 1,11 DI MARIA, schol. Aratus Phainomena 1 [p. 44ff. MARTIN], 62, 254–55). It is unclear whether C. devoted to them special commentaries. Given the content, all of the references in the fr. on Aratus can be traced back to the works of Homer [2].

Of great significance for the modern history of ancient philology and textual exegesis are the fr. in Varrus, Ling. 8,63 and 68; 9,1 (in this context, cf. [9. 2–48]), where C. and Aristarchus [4] discuss the role of → anomaly and → analogy in the inflection of words: the discussion deals with the criteria for linguistic correctness. Unclear are the questions of how significant this discussion was for antiquity, whether it actually took place, or if we are dealing with an argumentative trick by Varro or a misunderstanding of his sources (regarding this cf. [3]). C.'s theories about the role of hearing and of sound in the evaluation of poetry are discussed by → Philodemus in his work 'On Poems', which is partially extant in the Herculanean papyri (Περὶ ποιημάτων: bks. one, two and five). Here, it becomes clear that C. was a central figure in the Hellenistic discussion of poetics. C. was probably the source for large parts of the first two books on the debate between Philodemus and his adversaries: a group of 'philosophers'

(Epicurean?), a group of 'critics', Heraclides Ponticus, Andromenides, Heracleodorus, Pausimachus (a reconstruction of the work's structure, the fr. from bks. one and two in [14]). This material partially reappears in bk. five (PHercul. 228, fragmentary 1, PHercul. 1425 Coll. xxivff.: see [4]).

C. was probably interested in Attic → glossography. The attribution of the work Περὶ Ἀττικῆς διαλέκτου ('On the Attic Dialect') to C. is, however, contested, since we know of an Athenian glossographer with the homonym of C. (FGrHist 362, with an ed. of a part of the fr. and addenda to vol. IIIb, 406ff.; [9. 48ff.]); cf. [13] (with an updated list of fr.).

C. is cited in the Prolegomena de comoedia and in the scholia of Aristophanes by Tzetzes. We may, however, be dealing with pseudepigraphic fr. [5].

Some of the fragments that cannot be assigned clearly may originate from geographical or astronomical monographies or from paradoxographical works (the fr. S. 66 and 71f. W., in parts newly ed. in [8]).

C.'s students, besides → Panaetius, were: Tauriscus, Alexander of Miletus, Hermias, Zenodotus of Mallus as well as Herodicus (cf. T3, 11–14 and fr. 18 M.); the PBerolinensis 21 163 (ed. [6]) perhaps also mentions a Dionysius.

→ Aristarchus [4] of Samothrace; → Crates [7] of Athens; → Panaetius; → Zenodotus of Mallus

1 R. KASSEL, in: C. SCHÄUBLIN (ed.), Catalepton. FS B.Wyss, 1985   2 P. MAASS, Aratea, 1892, 167ff.
3 D. BLANK, in: S. EVERSON, Language, 1994, 149ff. (with bibliography)   4 C. MANGONI, Filodemo, Il quinto libro della Poetica, 1993   5 W. J. W. KOSTER (ed.), Prolegomena de comoedia, 1975, XXVIIIf.   6 M. MAEHLER, in: R. PINTAUDI (ed.), Miscellanea Papyrologica, 1980, 152, 156f.   7 C. WACHSMUTH, De Cratete Mallota, 1860
8 H. J. METTE, Sphairopoiia, 1936 (with bibliography and ed. of parts of the fr.)   9 Id., Parateresis, 1952 (with ed. of a part of the fr.)   10 R. PFEIFFER, History of Classical Scholarship from the Beginnings to the End of the Hellenistic Age, 1968   11 E. ASMIS, Crates on Poetic Criticism, in: Phoenix 46, 1992, 138–69   12 J. I. PORTER, Hermeneutic Lines and Circles: Aristarchus and Crates on the Exegesis of Homer, in: R. LAMBERTON, J. J. KEANEY (ed.), Homer's Ancient Readers, 1992, 67–114   13 M. BROGGIATO, Athenaeus, Crates and Attic Glosses: A Problem of Attribution, in: D. C. BRAUND, J. M. WILKINS, Athenaeus and His Philosophers at Supper: Reading Greek Culture in the Roman Empire 2001   14 R. JANKO, Philodemus, On Poems 1 (2001).   MA.BR.

[6] of Tarsus. Academic philosopher in the later 2nd cent. BC whose teachings are unknown. He became leader of the → Academy after Carneades the Younger (Philod. Academicorum index 30,5) and remained scholarch to his death in 127/6, unless already displaced in 129/8 by → Cleitomachus [1]. Diog. Laert. 4,67 completely ignores his position as scholarch.   K.-H.S.

[7] of Athens. A C. ὁ Ἀθηναῖος is mentioned in the Suda ει 184 (s.v. Εἰρεσιώνη = Pausanias Atticista ε 17 PEA = F 1 FGrH) and in schol. Soph. OC 100 (= F 4 FGrH). The first source refers to him as the author of a treatise 'On

Sacrificial Ceremonies in Athens' (Περὶ τῶν Ἀθήνησι θυσιῶν, cf.also Suda κ 2706 s.v. κυνήειο = F 2 FGrH). A C. without any characterizing epithet is mentioned as the author of a work 'On the Attic dialect' (Περὶ τῆς Ἀττικῆς διαλέκτου) in at least five bks. (F 6–13 FGrH) which was used by Athenaeus. There is no clear proof for or against the assumption that the two authors are identical. The dating of the Athenian C. in the 1st cent. BC is based essentially on the fr. of the Atticist work and assumes that the two authors are one and the same (some researchers attribute it to → C. [5] of Mallus). Also, a much earlier dating of the writing about Athenian cults has been proposed (4th/3rd cent. BC.). The question therefore remains unanswered.

EDITION: FGrH 362.
BIBLIOGRAPHY: K. LATTE, Zur Zeitbestimmung des Antiatticista, in: Hermes 50, 1915, 387–88; F. JACOBY, s.v. K. (12), RE 11, 1633–34; Id., FGrH III B, comm. on 362, 220–224; PFEIFFER, KP I, 296 no. 64; H. J. METTE, Parateresis. Unt. zur Sprachtheorie des Krates von Pergamon, 1952, 48–53.   F.M.

Cratesiclea (Κρατησίκλεια). Wife of Leonidas II, mother of → Cleomenes [6] III, who was strongly in favour of his reform plans. Following her son's flight to Ptolemy III, she went to Egypt as a hostage and was executed there in 219 BC after the failure of Cleomenes' coup (Plut. Cleomenes 6,2; 7,1; 22,3–10; 38,2–12).   K.-W.WEL.

Cratesipolis (Κρατησίπολις; Kratēsípolis). Wife of Alexander [8], married before 314 BC. After her husband was murdered in 314, she succeeded in establishing herself in the area he ruled, the centres of Corinth and Sicyon (Diod. Sic. 19,67) and maintained power with the aid of → Polyperchon (Diod. Sic. 19,74). In 308, C. handed the rule of her cities to Ptolemy I (Diod. Sic. 20,37), outwitting the mercenaries on Acrocorinth in the process (Polyaenus, Strat. 8,58), and retired to Pagae, where Demetrius [2] Poliorketes wanted to pay her a visit in 307 BC (Plut. Demetrius 9).   BO.D.

Crateuas (Κρατεύας; Krateúas). Rhizotómos 'root-cutter', 'herb man'; [6. test. 7 and 8]) of the 2nd/1st cent. BC. He was assumed to be the pharmacologist of → Mithridates VI Eupator simply because he is attributed with assigning the name of mithridátia (6. test. 2) to a plant, although there is no proof for it in the phytonymy. It was also assumed that he went to Thapsus [3. 1644], but this was a mistake since the fr. in question [6. test. 16] points to Sicily [1; 2. 206, 529 and appendix]. The portrait of the Codex Vindob. med. gr. 1, f. 3ᵛ has been regarded as authentic [5. 1139.62–65].

C. is claimed to have authored three works on medicine [6. test. 3], all organized alphabetically [6. 139–144]: 1) A rhizotomikón (test. 23) in three bks. (test. 20) on plants; 2) a work about materials obtained through mining (metalliká; test. 4) and aromatic substances (arōmata) [4. 4]; 3) polychrome plates of analyzed plants without any text [4. 5] intended for public use [4. 21]. All of this information may refer to a single work (see already in [3. 1645]) which appears to be lost today but excerpts of which could be the 10 fragments of the Codex Vindob. that bear the name of C. (edition in [6. 144-146]). In traditional records, we find the incorrect assumption that the plates constitute the first illustrated herbarium of antiquity [4. 20].

→ Pedanius Dioscorides appears to have adopted — directly or indirectly — more from C. than he admits [4. 11-20], even though he holds the opinion that C. 'passed over numerous useful substances and plants even though he seems to belong to those who have done the best analyses of the material' (test. 7). Galen claims to have consulted him (test. 4 in [5]) and cites him among the authors who should be studied if one wants to gain a knowledge of medicine (test. 3 and 6).

Supposedly, the illustrations of the alphabetical list by Dioscorides in the Codex Vindob. reflect those by C. In this context, it is assumed that there was an intermediary [4.20-30] who today is dated in the period of *c.* AD 200, although the only indication for this firmly established attribution in the literature is the fact that fragments under the name of C. can be found next to these illustrations.

→ Galen

1 I. CAZZANIGA, in: Helikon 4, 1964, 287-289 2 A. CRUGNOLA, Scholia in Nicandri Theriaka, 1971 3 E. KIND, s.v. K. 2, in: RE 11, 1644-1646 4 M. WELLMANN, Krateuas, 1897 5 Id., s.v. Dioskurides 12, in: RE 5, 1131-1142 6 WELLMANN 3, 139-144. A.TO.

Crathis (Κρᾶθις; *Kráthis*).

[1] River in Achaea on the Peloponnesus, today known as Crathis (formerly the river of Akrata). Its springs are located on the Chelmos (Aroania). Water still flows continuously today, into the sea at Cape Akrata on the western part of a fertile plain. The western arm forms the waterfall of the Styx. References: Hdt. 1,145; Str. 8,7,4; Paus. 7,25,11f.; 8,15,8f. Y.L.

[2] Arcadian mountains, eastern continuation of the *Aroania ore* on which we find the spring of the C.[1] near Zarouchla (Paus. 7,25,11; 13). Paus. attests the existence of an Artemis Pyronia sanctuary there. 8,15,9.

PHILIPPSON/KIRSTEN 3, 216-223. E.MEY. and E.O.

[3] River in Bruttium that rises near → Consentia and flows into the sea near Thurii, today known as Crati. Legend held that its water could be used to dye the hair of people and animals blond (Eur. Tro. 228; Ael. NA 12,36; Aristot. Mir. 169). The valley of C. formed the main connection between inner Bruttium and the plains of → Sybaris. The river received its name from Achaean colonists after the name of a river in their homeland (Hdt. 1,145); according to other sources (Ael. NA 6,42), the name was derived from the name of a shepherd's boy who was revered in Sybaris. In 510 BC, the shores of the C. were the site of the devastating defeat of the Sybarites in the battle against → Croton. According to Diod. Sic. 12,9,2 (cf. Str. 6,1,13), the victorious party changed the flow of the C. to run over the ruins of Sybaris, a claim which cannot be proven archaeologically. In regard to the temple of Athena Κραθία (*Krathía*), cf. Hdt. 5,45. The identification of the C. with the bull on the coins of Sybaris is questionable.

G. GIANELLI, Culti e miti della Magna Grecia, 1924, 123f.; P. G. GUZZO, Le città scomparse della Magna Grecia, 1982, 46, 102; Id., L'archeologia delle colonie arcaiche: Storia della Calabria antica, 1987, 147. M.C.P.

Cratinus (Κρατῖνος; *Kratînos*).

[1] Son of Callimedes, important poet of the Attic Old → Comedy.

A. BIOGRAPHICAL INFORMATION

The first appearance of C. is documented for the late 450s BC [1. test. 4ab; cf. test. 5]; his death probably occurred between 423 (*Terminus post quem*: his last piece, the *Pytíne*/'The Bottle'; cf. [1. test. 3]) and 421 (in Aristoph. Pax 700-703, he is allegedly dead [1. test. 10]); he allegedly lived to be 94 years old [1. test. 3]. In about 30 years at the stage, he apparently wrote 21 plays [1. test. 1 and 2a]; as many as 29 titles are extant, although some of these may be double titles ('Εμπιπράμενοι ἢ 'Ιδαῖοι/'The Inflamed or the People of Ida', Διονυσαλέξανδρος ἢ 'Ιδαῖοι). C.'s first (Dionysian-?) victory is calculated to have occurred 'after the 85th Ol.' (= 440-39 and 437-46), [1. test. 2a]. Altogether, the documents indicate six first place wins in the Dionysia [1. test. 5], and three in the Lenaia [1. test. 6], which bespeaks an impressive record of success. He lost twice against → Aristophanes [3] (in the Lenaia of 425 and 424), [1. test. 7ab]; the latter mocked C.'s vanished artistic ability (Aristoph. Equ. 526-536 = [1. test. 9]) but suffered a painful defeat in 423 with 'Clouds' against C.'s *Pytíne* [1. test. 7c].

B. WORKS

The fr. allow the following conclusion about content: the → *Archílochoi* created after → Cimon's death (cf. fr. 1), ('Αρχίλοχοι, 'Archilochus and his followers'?) dealt with poets (fr. 2). The *Dionysaléxandros* (Διονυσαλέξανδρος, 'Dionysus in the role of Alexander', that is, in the role of Paris, the Trojan) from probably 430 BC became comprehensible due to a papyrus hypothesis (test. i). In the form of a mythological allegory, it blamed Pericles (here in the form of Dionysus, who perhaps wore the 'onion head' of Pericles as an identifying mark [2]) for the → Peloponnesian War. In the *Drapétides* (Δραπέτιδες, 'Runaway Women'), Theseus apparently played a role (fr. 53. 61); the seer Lampon was ridiculed as a glutton (fr. 62). The *Thrâittai* (Θρᾷτται, 'Thracean Women', around 430) brought Pericles, the 'onion-headed Zeus' (fr. 73), onto the stage himself and mocked the younger → Callias (fr. 81); the chorus was apparently formed by Thracean worshippers of the goddess → Bendis (cf. fr. 85). The *Malthakoí*

(Μαλθακοί) exposed a chorus of 'weaklings' (cf. fr. 105) to ridicule. The mythical play Νέμεσις ('Nemesis', with political connotations?) dealt with the birth of Helena from an egg laid by Nemesis, who had been impregnated by Zeus and which Leda 'incubated' as the fostermother (fr. 115). The Odyssês (Ὀδυσσῆς, 'Odysseus and his companions') dramatized → Odysseus' adventure with the Cyclops. It may have originated in a period when political mockery in comedies was either forbidden or restricted (439–437 BC?). The Panóptai (Πανόπται, 'The All-Seers') appear to anticipate the sophist theme of the 'Clouds' by Aristophanes [3], (cf. fr. 167).

The Plútoi (Πλοῦτοι, 'The Givers of Wealth', titans that formed the chorus, cf. fr. 171) was apparently the first in a sequence of Old Comedy plays that glorified a life of riches in the golden age (cf. fr. 176). The Pytínē (Πυτίνη, 'Bottle'), C.'s last and most famous play, ingeniously made fun of the poet's own fondness for drink: his allegorical wife, the comedy, threatens to sue him for neglect (test. ii; cf. fr. 193–195) but friends reunite the estranged couple (cf. fr. 199) and C. begins to write again (cf. fr. 208–9). The play Seríphioi (Σερίφιοι, 'The People of Seriphus') was written at about the same time and presents a part of the Perseus myth. The Cheírōnes (Χείρωνες, 'Chiron and his Centaurs') juxtaposed the old and better times — Solon the deceased functioned as their representative (fr. 246)? — with the new and worse times (cf. fr. 256f.). The same theme could be found in the Nómoi (Νόμοι, 'Laws') where Pericles (fr. 258) and Aspasia (fr. 259) were attacked as representatives.

C. INFLUENCE

Since the Hellenistic period, C. was regarded as the most important representative of the Old Comedy together with → Aristophanes [3] and → Eupolis [1. test. 17, 18, 27, 28, 30, cf. test. 20, 21ab]. His emergence was seen as an important epoch in the development of comedy as he gave the genre a more distinct form and turned it into a vehicle for political mockery and public criticism [1. test. 19]; this would make him the actual creator of political comedy. The sharpness of his criticisms was noted in particular [1. test. 17, cf. test. 18. 25], and his writing style was compared with that of Aeschylus [1. test. 2a]. Hellenistic scholars focused on him as much as on Eupolis and Aristophanes [1. test. 22, 23]. A special piece by the grammarian Callistratus on the Thrâittai [1. test. 39] is documented, the existence of a comm. by Didymus [1] Chalcenterus can be inferred [1. test. 41], whereas the existence of a writing 'On Cratinus' (Περὶ Κρατίνου) by Asclepiades [8] of Myrleia is unconfirmed [1. test. 40]. In the imperial period, C. was regarded as the main representative of good old Attic [1. test. 24, 30, 43]. Compared to Aristophanes, however, he was regarded as too one-sided a writer of political invectives who may have created good openings but did not succeed in carrying them through [1. test. 17]. Criticisms of this nature probably contributed to the fact that C.'s work did not survive the end of antiquity. Meanwhile, fragments of several plays (Dionysaléxandros, Kleobulínai, Plútoi; unconfirmed for Seríphioi and Hórai) have surfaced.

→ Comedy

1 PCG IV 112–337   2 M. REVERMANN, Cratinus' Διονυσαλέξανδρος and the Head of Pericles, in: JHS 117, 1997, 197–200   3 G. BONA, Per un' interpretazione di Cratino, in: E. CORSINI (ed.), La polis e il suo teatro 2, 1988, 181–211.

[2] C. the Younger. Attic comedy writer of the 4th cent. BC (fr. eight and 10 point to the second half of the cent.). Of eight surviving titles, four suggest mythological subjects (Ὀμφάλη/'Omphale'; Χείρων/ 'Cheiron'; Γίγαντες/'The Giants' and Τιτᾶνες/'The Titans' may refer to the same play), the others hint at typical topics of the New Comedy: Θηρωμένη ('The Hunted'); Ταραντῖνοι ('The Citizens of Tarentum'); Ψευδυποβολιμαῖος ('The Wrongly Accused One'); Πυθαγορίζουσα ('The Disciple of Pythagoras') points to a mockery of philosophers (cf. the mockery of Plato in fr. 10).

1 PCG IV, 1983, 338–345.   H.-G.NE.

[3] Comes sacrarum largitionum (→ comes B) and professor of law (antecessor) in Constantinople during Justinianus' time, member of the commission for the compilation of the → Digesta (Constitutio Tanta § 9).

PLRE III, 362   SCHULZ, 350   T. HONORÉ, Tribonian, 1978, 148f..   T.G.

Cratippus (Κράτιππος; Krátippos).
[1] of Athens. According to Dionysius of Halicarnassus (De Thucydide 16), he was roughly a contemporary of → Thucydides and also the one who continued his work. The table of contents from his historical work which spanned at least to 394 BC is recorded in Plutarch (mor. 345c-e). Some researchers (e.g. [1; 2; 4; 5; 6]) claim that C. was a significant historian of the 4th cent. BC and the author of the → Hellēnikà Oxyrhýnchia, others (e.g. ED. SCHWARZ, ED. MEYER, F. JACOBY) refer to him as a 'late fraudulent author who used the guise of a contemporary to gain respect for his concoction' (especially JACOBY): the basis for this debasement and the changed dating are (presumably) certain odd statements C. made about the speeches and the death of Thucydides in FGrH 64 F 1.

EDITION: FGrH 64 with comm.
BIBLIOGRAPHY: 1 H. R. BREITENBACH, s.v. Hellenika Oxyrhynchia, RE Suppl. 12, 383–426 (fundamental) 2 P. PÉDECH, Un historien nommé Cratippe, in: REA 72, 1970, 31–45   3 G. A. LEHMANN, Ein Historiker namens Krattipos, in: ZPE 23, 1976, 265–288   4 S. ACCAME, Cratippo, in: Miscellanea Greca e Romana 6, 1978, 185ff. 5 P. HARDING, The Autorship of the Hellenika Oxyrhynchia, in: The Ancient History Bulletin 1, 1987, 101–104 6 K. MEISTER, Die griech. Geschichtsschreibung, 1990, 65ff. (bibliography).   K.MEI.

[2] of Pergamum. He was first a student of Antiochus [20] of Ascalon's. After his death (68 BC), he went over to Peripatos. He began his work in Mytilene but moved to Athens c. 46 where he taught Cicero's son from the year 45 on. Cicero valued him as a *Peripateticorum ... princeps* (Cic. Tim. 1). However, this does not mean that he was scholarch; that office was held at the time by Andronicus [4] and Boethos. As far as C.'s teachings are concerned, we only know of one statement about prophecy (Cic. Div. 1,5; 70f.).

P. MORAUX, Der Aristotelismus bei den Griechen I, 1973, 223–56; H.B. GOTTSCHALK, in: ANRW II 36.2, 1095ff.
H.G.

Craton (Κράτων). Greek rhetor, roughly a contemporary of the older Seneca, known as a bitter enemy of the dominant style of → Atticism during his time. Seneca the Older recorded a few utterances that attest to C.'s honest humour in the face of Emperor Augustus (contr. 10,5,21f.). Considering this fact, as well as his openly stated animosity towards the imperial confidant Timagenes, C. must have belonged to Augustus' inner circle.
M.W.

Cratylus (Κρατύλος; *Kratýlos*). Best known → Heraclitean, probably from Athens. Aristotle attributes C. with a radical rephrasing of → Heraclitus' statement that one cannot step into the same river twice (22 bk. 91 DK). C. supposedly claimed that one cannot step even once into the same river (Aristot. Metaph. 1010a 7ff. = 65 4 DK). This statement is understood as the idea that everything is always in motion and subject to change in every way, also as a denial of any possible identity. According to Aristotle, the lesson of the river led to C.'s sceptical attitude towards epistemology. Constant change and motion would make it impossible to attain knowledge about things or to produce valid statements. In Plato's 'Cratylus', C. represents the thesis that for each object, there exists a naturally correct name, that is to say a name that describes the essence of the thing it names. It is unclear if this thesis is compatible with C.'s lesson of the river [1].

C.'s most important contribution to the history of Greek philosophy lies in his influence on Plato, who presumably encountered the lesson of the river through C. (cf. Aristot. Metaph. 987a 29ff.).

1 G.S. KIRK, The Problem of Cratylus, in: AJPh 72, 1951, 225–253.

S.N. MOURAVIEV, s.v. Cratylos (d'Athènes?), GOULET 2, 503–510; D.J. ALLEN, The Problem of Cratylus, in: AJPh 75, 1954, 271–287.
G.BE.

Creatio (from *creare*: 'to create', 'to generate') has the meaning of 'appointing' or 'calling' in regard to private functions (*tutor*: Dig. 26,7,39,6) as well as public offices (→ *magistratus*: Dig. 48,14,1 pr.). It is used as a synonym but not as completely identical in meaning with *nominatio* and *vocatio* and at times is joined with *lectio, electio* (CIC. Verr. 2,2,49; Tac. Agr. 9; Dig. 1,11,1, pr.) or *cooptatio* (Liv. 2,33,2; 3,64,10). The term implies that an act of installation took place which contributes to the legitimacy. The general principle of *creatio* is valid for all political (administrative, legal, military) offices, for the most important priestly offices of the Roman republic and the imperial period (Dig. 50,8,2,7; Vell. Pat. 2,12,3) as well as for emperors. Senators, on the other hand, were not 'created' in this sense but only 'legated', at first by the consuls, and since the 4th cent. by the *censores* (however, see Liv. 4,43,3; App. B Civ. 1,100 and Cic. Div. 2,23). Requirements for *creatio* could be: Roman citizenship, free birth, legal competence, lack of infamy, previously held offices, minimum age, minimum wealth, social rank. The *creatio* was implemented by the following authorities through various procedures:

a) The senate: in the republican period, it appoints the members of commissions and legations elected by the senate, probably by the senate's president (Liv. 33,24,5–7). In the imperial period, the senate can co-opt members and elect or appoint magistrates as long as the emperor does not use his right of selection and appointment (Gai. Inst. 1,3,4 and 5; Inst. Iust. 1,2,5f.)

b) The public assembly: the *comitia centuriata* elect and appoint office bearers and priests, the *comitia tributa* elect and appoint the people's tribunes and other officials through those officials who supervise the election and announce the results (*renuntiatio*; Liv. 1,60,4; 6,41,6 and 9; Cic. Leg. 3,10).

c) Magistrates: on the basis of an *imperium*, a magistrate could, if necessary, enact the *creatio* of a colleague or of a subordinate magistrate; a consul or praetor could even enact the *creatio* of a *dictator* (Liv. 2,2,11; 2,18,6–8; 3,64,9f.; 32,27,5). All magistrates could and had to install legally designated representatives of officials and subordinate officials as long as they were not chosen by the people (Suet. Iul. 7; Dig. 1,21,1). Even extraordinary magistrates can receive the right of *creatio* for magistrates, such as the dictators Sulla and Caesar as well as the *triumviri* in 43 BC (App. B Civ. 1,99; Cass. Dio 41,36,1; 47,66,55).

d) The emperor: formally, he only installs the legates and official who are subjects of his *imperium*, while the election and appointment of the office bearers including the *candidati principis* first still rests with the public assembly (Suet. Aug. 40), later with the senate as well, and finally only with the senate (Gai. Inst. 1,3,4). With the loss of republican-senatorial traditions, the emperor actually and gradually gains the right of directly appointing all civil and military officials (Dig. 48,14,1: *ad curam principis magistratuum creatio pertinet*; Novell. Anthemius 3,1). Beginning in the principate, but more so in late antiquity since Diocletianus, legitimately created emperors install a subordinate emperor's colleague or sub-emperor when needed, a development which probably grew out of the fact that extraordinary magistrates had the right of *creatio*.

e) The army assembly (*exercitus*) and other symbolic representatives of the state (*proceres palatii, senatus, populus*). The occurrences of proclaiming Roman emperors (Eutr. 9,1) which disregarded the rights of the senate (and of the public assembly) took place occasionally in the principate, but more frequently since the time of the 'soldier emperors' (3rd cent. AD). Even though these acts occurred under varying circumstances, they reveal that various symbolic representatives of the state can participate in the transition of power due to their military importance or political authority based on their special responsibility for the entire state in certain situations.

f) The organs of constitutional cities (Cod. Iust. 10,68,1) or registered associations and corporations (Dig. 3,4,1).

→ Candidatus; → Comitia; → Cooptatio; → Dictator; → Ingenuus; → Magistratus; → Renuntiatio

F. F. ABBOTT, A History and Description of Roman Political Institutions, ³1963, 277; W. ENSSLIN, Der Kaiser in der Spätant., in: HZ 177, 449ff.; JONES, LRE 321ff.; W. KUNKEL, Staatsordnung und Staatspraxis der röm. Republik, 1995, vol. 2, 36, 198; E. MEYER, Röm. Staat und Staatsgedanke, ⁴1975, 200f.; MOMMSEN, Staatsrecht 1, 213ff., 221ff., 646ff.; 2, 418ff., 675ff., 733, 915ff., 1147; 3, 217ff.   C.G.

Credit see → Loan

Creditor Whoever is entitled to a claim from a relationship of debenture (→ *obligatio*) is a *creditor*. The obligated party is called the debtor, → *debitor*. According to Roman understanding, a *creditor* cannot simply transfer his rights without certain qualifications (→ *cessio*). The word *creditor* was often used in a succinct sense, referring to a creditor secured by → hypothecary law. This is the basis for the *iure creditoris vendere* (Dig. 17,1,59,4) concerning the sale of the seized items, in which the selling creditor rightfully excludes a guarantee in order to avoid a seller's liability to the buyer. On default (*mora creditoris*) → *mora*.   R.WI.

Crematio (Burning at the stake) was a form of Roman capital punishment. The execution may originally have been left to the injured party and his agnates (→ *agnatio*) in a kind of 'channelled' private revenge. In that case, the criminal proceedings served only to establish the prosecutor's right to carry out the private punishment. This is probably how we should understand Gaius' report in his comm. on the Twelve Tables (Dig. 47,9,9), which states that this law (pl. 8,10) ordered execution by fire for premeditated arsons: *igni necari iubetur* (interpretation according to [1], but critical thereof [2; 3]). The imposition of *crematio* corresponded with the principle of talion (→ *talio*) in that it aimed at a mirror effect between punishment and crime. In later times, *crematio* is imposed for other crimes as well, as a 'public punishment'. It was imposed for high treason in the republic (Liv. 3,53; Val. Max. 6,3,2) and in

the principate, then probably for crimes against the crown as well (*crimen laesae maiestatis*; Paulus, Sent. 5,29,1). In the period of classical jurisprudence, *crematio*, crucifixion (→ *crux*), and beheading (→ *decollatio*) were regarded as the most serious punishments of all (*summa supplicia*, according to Callistratus Dig. 48,19,28 pr., *c.* AD 200). These punishments were imposed exclusively, or generally, on unfree persons and on members of the lower classes (*humiliores*). There are numerous documentations of *crematio* for late antiquity. This phenomenon may be a result of Constantine's abolition of crucifixion. The way that *crematio* was executed is described by Tert. Apol. 50: The (usually naked) offender is tied to a stake; then the wood piled around or under him is set on fire.

1 W. KUNKEL, Unt. zur Entwicklung des röm. Kriminalverfahrens in vorsullanischer Zeit, 1962, 42ff. 2 B. SANTALUCIA, Diritto e processo penale nell' antica Roma, 1989, 42f.   3 WIEACKER, RRG, 254 with n. 86.

G. MACCORMACK, Criminal Liability for Fire in Early and Classical Roman Law, in: Index 3, 1972, 382–396; DULCKEIT, SCHWARZ, WALDSTEIN, § 12 I 3; TH. MAYER-MALY, s.v. vivicomburium, in: RE 9A, 497f.   G.S.

Cremera Stream that runs south-east from Baccano past Veii and flows into the Tiber near Fidenae. Historically significant at the time of the alliance between Veii and Fidenae: it helped to connect these two cities with each other and with the coast and thereby restricted Rome's freedom of movement. This fact is probably the reason for the historical war of Rome against Veii, wherein the C. is documented as the site of the battles with the Fabii and also as the site of their end (Liv. 2,49ff.; Dion. Hal. Ant. Rom. 9,15).   M.CA

Cremna (Κρῆμνα, Lat. *Cremna*). Important Pisidian fortress and city of Hellenistic origin (κρημνός = 'precipitous'). Coins from *c.* 100 BC [1]. Around 35–30 BC, C. was conquered by Amyntas [9] of Galatia (Str. 12,6,4). Under Augustus, veterans were settled there and the name became *Colonia Iulia Augusta Felix Cremnensium* [2] from then on. C. was one of the most prosperous 'Pisidian' colonies with abundant minting of coins until Aurelianus' time (270–275) [1]. Under Probus, it was the last stronghold of Lydius, the Isaurian leader of the *brigands*, was taken after a heavy siege (Zos. 1,69f.; on works about sieges [3]). In late antiquity and the Byzantine period, C. was a suffragan diocese of Perge. Ruins exist near Çamlık (formerly Girme = C.).

1 AULOCK 2, 36–40, 106–145   2 B. LEVICK, Roman Colonies in Southern Asia Minor, 1967   3 S. MITCHELL, The Siege of Cremna, in: D. H. FRENCH, C. S. LIGHTFOOT (ed.), The Eastern Frontier of the Roman Empire, 1989, 311–328   4 W. RUGE, s.v. Kremna, RE 11, 1708.   P.W.

Cremona First Lat. *colonia* (Pol. 3,40,5) north of the Po in the region of the Cenomani [1. 57]. Italic bridgehead against the Insubres and Boii (Tac. Hist. 3,34) as well as against Hannibal (Liv. 21,25 etc.). In 190 BC, it was newly settled (Liv. 37,46) and became an important road junction of the *via Postumia* and the site of a large market (Tac. Hist. 3,30). In the year 90 BC, it became *municipium* of the *tribus Aniensis*, in 81 probably capital of the *prov. Gallia Cisalpina*. In 41 BC, C. suffered heavily from confiscation and land redistributions [3. 20f.] benefiting the veterans of the future Augustus; *colonia* of *regio X* (Plin. HN 3,130; Ptol. 3,1,31). Together with Bedriacum, C. became involved in the conflicts of the year AD 69. First, it served as the base of the Vitellians against Otho and was then plundered by the Flavians (Tac. Hist. 3,33). C. was rebuilt under Vespasianus but never again reached its former importance. In late antiquity, it served as a base for troops and military service (Not. Dig. 9,27.42,55). In the year 605 it was destroyed by the Langobardi (Paul. Diac. Hist. Lang. 4,28).

1 N. NEGRONI, Indigeni, etruschi e celti nella Lombardia orientale. C. Romana, 1985   2 A. BERNARDI, C., 1985   3 P. J. TOZZI, Storia padana antica, 1972

G. PONTIROLI, Cremona e il suo terrritorio, Atti del Centro Studi dell' Italia Romana 1, 1969, 163f.; Id. (ed.), C. romana, 1985.   A.SA

Cremutius Cordus

Roman historiographer (and senator?) of the Augustan-Tiberian period. He incurred L. → Aelius [II 19] Seianus' hatred and was accused in AD 25 before the senate *lege maiestatis*, because he had glorified Caesar's murderers Brutus and Cassius in his *Annales*. After an honest defence, he took his own life by refusing food. His writings were confiscated and burned in Rome and in the empire. However, his daughter Marcia, the recipient of Seneca's consolatory discourse, was able to save several books. Under Caligula, a new, 'purged' edition appeared (Sen. Consolatio ad Marciam 1,2–4; 22,4–7; Tac. Ann. 4,34; Suet. Tib. 61,3; Suet. Calig. 16,1; Quint. Inst. 10,1,104; Cass. Dio 57,24,2–5). C.'s work was characterized by a republican spirit and dealt with the → civil wars (since Caesar's death?) and with at least the beginnings of Augustus' rule; the sparse fragments including a piece on Cicero's death can be found in the HRR 2, 87ff.

H. BARDON, La littérature latine inconnue 2, 1956, 162ff.; L. CANFORA, Studi di storia della storiografia romana, 1993, 221ff.; H. TRÄNKLE, Zu Crem. Cor., in: MH 37, 1980, 231–241.   D.K.

Creon

(Κρέων; *Kréōn*, Lat. Creon, Creo).
[1] Regent and King of Thebes, son of Menoeceus, brother of → Iocaste, married to Eurydice. His daughter → Megara is the first wife of Hercules. His son Haemon is engaged to → Antigone [3], the other son, → Menoeceus, sacrifices his life for Thebes (Eur. Phoen. 834ff.; 1310ff.; Stat. Theb. 10,628ff.). Originally, C. was a filler character — the name means 'ruler' — and his character varies strongly from poet to poet. In Soph. OT, he is the adversary of → Oedipus: he functions as a mes-

senger from Delphi (87ff., cf. Sen. Oed. 212ff.; ibid. 511ff. where C. also reports Laius' words from the underworld), defends himself against the unjustified reproach of usurpation (Soph. OT 513ff., cf. Sen. Oed. 668ff.) and takes over the government after the king blinds himself (Soph. OT 1422ff.). In Soph. OC 728ff., C. uses false promises and then violence in the attempt to force the return of Oedipus, who had been banned and is wandering aimlessly, but whose return is required for the victory of Thebes. In Soph. Ant., he is the antagonist of the heroine Antigone: his law forbidding the burial of → Polynices under threat of capital punishment against transgressors was supposed to deter traitors (Soph. Ant. 182ff.) and lawbreakers (ibid. 655ff.), but violated divine law (ibid. 450ff.). As a suspicious (ibid. 289ff.; 1033ff.), high-handed, and obstinate (ibid. 726ff.) tyrant, deaf to public opinion (ibid. 504ff.; 690ff.; 733) and to the admonishments of Haemon and Teiresias, he ends up paying for the transgression that he recognized too late (ibid. 1261ff.) with the loss of his son and his wife. In Eur. Phoen., C. takes care of the city's defence against the army of the → Seven against Thebes (Eur. Phoen. 697ff.) but loses Menoeceus (see above) and banishes Oedipus, the cursed (ibid. 1585ff., cf. Stat. Theb. 11,665ff.). C.'s attainment of royal dignity changes him drastically into a cruel tyrant. As such, he forbids the burial of all Argives (Stat. Theb. 11,648ff., cf. Eur. Supp. 467ff.). But Theseus then wages war against Thebes, kills C. and enforces the burials (Stat. Theb. 12,752ff.).

[2] King of Corinth, father of → Creusa [3]. Bride of → Iason, killed with a poisoned dress by → Medea, whom Iason had deserted. C. grants Medea the fateful postponement of her banishment (Eur. Med. 271ff.; Sen. Med. 179ff.) and burns to death from the touch of Creusa's poison-torn body (Eur. Med. 1204ff.; depiction on vases and Medea sarcophagi).

→ Oedipus; → Theban myths

G. BERGER-DOER, s.v. Kreousa (2), LIMC 6.1, 120–127; V. EHRENBERG, Sophokles und Perikles, 1961 (Engl. 1954), 67ff. = H. DILLER (ed.), Sophocles, 1967, 95ff.; M. M. HIJMANS-VAN ASSENDELFT, Aliquot de Creontis Thebani persona in litteris Latinis annotationes, in: Acta Classica 3, 1960, 77–85; F. HUMBORG, s.v. K., RE Suppl. 4, 1048–1060; R. P. WINNINGTON-INGRAM, Sophocles, 1980, 117ff.   CL.K.

Creophylus

[1] (Κρεόφυλος; *Kreóphylos*). Appears in the ancient legend of Homer as one of the → Homeridai, either Homer's friend (Pl. Resp. 600b = [2. Test. 3]) or his son-in-law (schol. Pl. Resp. 600b = [2. Test. 4]). He originally stemmed from either Samos (thus Callim. Epigr. 6 = [2. Test. 7]; Str. 14,638 = [2. Test. 8]), or Ios (thus Certamen Homeri et Hesiodi p. 44, 28 WIL. = [2. Test. 2]; Vita Homeri Procli p. 26, 26 WIL. = [2. Test. 9]) or Chios (thus Suda = [2. Test. 6]; schol. Pl. Resp. 600b = [2. Test. 3]). Supposedly, he was the author of the → *Oichalías hálōsis* (in Callimachus, Proclus i.a.).

From C.'s descendants on Samos (guild of rhapsodes in competition with the → Homeridai of Chios? [4]), → Lycurgus is said to have received the Homeric epics in Sparta.

EDITIONS: 1 U.v. WILAMOWITZ-MOELLENDORFF (ed.), Vitae Homeri et Hesiodi, 1916 and passim   2 PEG.
BIBLIOGRAPHY: 3 A.RZACH, s.v. K., RE 11, 2150–2252   4 W.BURKERT, Die Leistung eines Kreon Kreophyleer, Homeriden und die archa. Heraklesepik, in: MH 29, 1972, 76–77.   J.L.

[2] (Κρεώφυλος). Historian mentioned in a Rhodian arbitral award [1. Z. 120]. Of his 'Annales of Ephesians' (Ἐφεσίων ὧροι), only two passages have survived, one on the founding legend of Ephesus (Ath. 8,62 p. 361c-e) and one on the Medea myth (schol. Eur. Med. 264). C., whose work is written in Ionian dialect and must be dated between this drama by Euripides (431 BC) and the arbitral award (c. 196 BC), is regarded as the oldest author to write about Ephesus. Sources: FGrH 417.

1 IPriene, no. 37.   K.BRO.

Crepereius
[1] C. Gallus. Agrippina [3] the Younger's confidant, killed in AD 59 in the shipwreck organized by Nero in the Gulf of Baiae (Tac. Ann. 14,5,1).
[2] L.C.Proculus. Suffectio consul and proconsul of an unknown province (PIR² C 1573); according to [1. 27ff.], perhaps proconsul on Cyprus.

1 M.LE GLAY, CCEC 1986, no. 6.   W.E.

Crepundia A piece of jewellery or a toy, usually metal, for small children in Rome. Besides the bulla (→ Ages), children wore several such miniatures as an → amulet, strung on a chain and worn around the neck or over the shoulder. The *crepundia* were also used to identify abandoned children and were kept in a *cistella* (little chest) together with other children's items (Plaut. Cist. 634ff., Plaut. Rud. 1151ff.).
→ Amulet; → Jewellery

E.SCHMIDT, Spielzeug und Spiele im klass. Altertum, 1971, 18–21 incl. fig. 1.   R.H.

Cres (Κρής). Eponym of the island of → Crete. The contradictory myths mirror the island's various archaic institutions and mythologems. C. is regarded as the son of Zeus and an Idaeic nymph, but also as the protector of newborn Zeus (in this context he is addressed as Curete or as the King of the → Curetes); his son is → Talos. He is an autochthonous king and the bringer of culture, but also a lawmaker like → Minos, who influenced the late Spartan lawmaker → Lycurgus as well (Ephoros, FGrH 145; Diod. Sic. 5,64,1; Steph. Byz. s.v. Κρήτη).   F.G.

Crescens
[1] Freedman of Nero's, who in AD 69 held a banquet for the citizens in Carthago on the occasion of Otho's installation as emperor (Tac. Hist. 1,76,3; PIR² C 1576).
[2] Cynical philosopher from the mid–2nd cent. who attacked Justin as well as Christianity (Justin. Apol. 2,3; Euseb. Hist. eccl. 4,16).   W.E.

Cresconius In the 6th cent. AD, he probably arranged (in Africa or Rome) a systematic collection (*Concordia canonum*) of synodal laws (*Canones*) and papal decisions (*Decretales*), based on the collection of → Dionysius Exiguus. An extended version with the inclusion of texts from Gaul exists from the Carolingian period (so-called Gaulic Cresconius).

EDITION: PL 88, 829–942 (critical ed. is missing)
BIBLIOGRAPHY: H.MORDEK, s.v. C., LMA 3, 345f.   J.GR.

Cresilas Bronze sculptor of Cydonia. According to the evidence of inscriptions on existing socles, C. worked c. 450–420 BC in Delphi, Hermione and Athens. He created the most famous portrait of → Pericles in antiquity, 'worthy of the epithet Olympian' (Plin. HN 34,74). It was regarded as identical with the portrait statue of Pericles seen by Pausanias on the acropolis and which is clearly identified in copies. A statue by C. depicting a mortally wounded figure (*volneratum deficientem*) was described by Pliny and is usually equated with the bronze statue depicting Diitrephes hit by arrows, mentioned by Pausanias on the acropolis, yet without the name of the artist. The socle on the acropolis, with the consecration of Diitrephes' son may belong to it, but this is debated because the socle today is palaeographically dated to the mid–5th cent., while Pausanias refers to Diitrephes as a strategist from 414–411 BC. Due to the uncertain dating, suggestions for an identification based on copies must be deemed questionable (so-called Protesilaus).

C. apparently took third place in an artists' contest for four Amazon statues in Ephesus, after → Polyclitus and → Phidias. Among the Amazon statues that survived in copies (→ Amazones), the attribution to C. varies between the Sciarra-type and the Capitol-type. Pliny's note about a Ctesilaus who created a wounded Amazon and a Doryphorus probably refers to C. All other attributions (Athena of Velletri, the so-called Diomedes) are speculative.

OVERBECK, no. 870–876, 946; G.RICHTER, The Sculpture and Sculptors of the Greeks, 1950, 233–237; LIPPOLD, 172–174; A.RAUBITSCHEK, Dedications from the Athenian Akropolis, 1949, 131–133, 510–513; J.MARCADÉ, Recueil des signatures de sculpteurs grecs, 1, 1953, 62–64; P.ORLANDINI, EAA 4, 405–408; B.SCHMALTZ, Zu den Ephesischen Amazonen, in: AA 1995, 335–343; R.BOL, Amazones Volneratae, 1998, 87–93 and passim.   R.N.

Cresphontes (Κρεσφόντης).

[1] Heraclidus (→ Heraclidae), husband of → Merope. In the lottery for the Peloponnese, C. uses a trick to gain Messenia. After a short reign, he falls victim to a revolt. His only surviving son, → Aepytus [4], avenges him (on the motif: → Orestes) and secures the paternal throne for himself (Paus. 4,3,3–8; 8,5,6–7).

[2] Son of [1] in Euripides' tragedy of the same name, in which C.'s mother almost kills him by mistake while avenging the murder of his father.

> M. A. HARDER, Euripides' K. and Archelaos, 1985, 1–122; J. FREY-BRÖNNIMANN, P. MÜLLER, s.v. K., LIMC 6.1, 131–132. RE.N.

Crestones (Κρηστῶνες, Κρηστωναῖοι, Γραστῶνες). Thracian tribe located south-east of the Mygdonia and in the south up to Lake Bolbe (Aristot. Mir. 122). Xerxes marched through their land on his approach from › Acanthus [1] to › Therme. The stream Echeidoros which rises near the C. could not provide enough water for his army (Hdt. 7,124; 127). At that time, the C. were led by a Bisaltaean king, which may point to the existence of an anti-Persian military alliance (Hdt. 8,116). The C. lived in small towns together with the → Bisaltae and the → Edones (Thuc. 4,109). It appears that they were subjugated by the Macedonian king → Alexander [2] I (Thuc. 2,99) after the Persian satrapy of Thracia had dissolved. In the 1st cent. BC, the → Paeones are mentioned in place of the C. (Str. 7a,1,41).

> A. FOL, T. SPIRIDONOV, Istoričeska geografija na trakijskite plemena, 1983, 170f. I.v.B.

Creta et Cyrenae After the conquest by Q. Caecilius Metellus (69–67 BC; Liv. per. 100; Plut. Pompey 29), → Crete was organized as a double province together with → Cyrenae (Roman province since 74 BC), (C. et C.). A short-term separation between the two occurred as a result of M. Antonius' declaration of independence (43 BC). In 27 BC, Augustus re-established the old order (senatorial province). The seat of the government was → Gortyne. After the Diocletian reorganization, the double province was dissolved (Cyrenae went to Libya Pentapolis). An important document for the legal privileges of Greeks is the edict of Cyrene by Augustus from 7–6 BC (FIRA I no. 68).
→ Crete

> G. PERL, Die röm. Provinzbeamten in Cyrenae und Creta zur Zeit der Republik, in: Klio 52, 1970, 319–354; W. ORTH, Ein vernachlässigtes Zeugnis zur Gesch. der röm. Prov. C. et C., in: Chiron 3, 1973, 255–263; I.F. SANDERS, Roman Crete, 1982, 3–15. H.SO.

Crete (Κρήτη, *Krētē*, Latin *Creta*).
A. SETTLEMENT GEOGRAPHY B. ARCHAIC PERIOD
C. CLASSICAL AND HELLENISTIC PERIOD
D. CRETE UNDER ROMAN RULE E. LATE ANTIQUITY AND BYZANTINE PERIOD

A. SETTLEMENT GEOGRAPHY

C. is the largest Greek island, with an east-west extension of 250 km and a north-south extension of max. 60 km. The narrowest part is the Isthmus of Hierapytna in the east. The island's topography is shaped by its mountains. Three large mountain ranges dominate: in the west the 'White Mountains' (→ *Leúka órē*, 2,482 m), in the centre the → Ida Mountains (Piloritis, 2,456 m) and in the east the → Dicte Range (highest elevation 2,147 m) with the Lassithi Plateau (mountains as the characteristic geographical element of C.: Str. 10,4,4). Since the mountains extend to the coast in the south, the gentle slopes of the north and east coasts (especially Suda Bay near Chania and the Gulf of Mirabello in the east) are the preferred sites of settlements and harbours. An exception to the rule of predominantly coastal, northern and eastern settlement is the fertile Mesara Plain in south-central C. Though used for economic purposes, the mountains primarily had a cultic function (Ida). The climate, which was already praised by ancient authors (Theophr. Hist. pl. 9,16,1–3), is characterized by hot summers and rainy winters, with the west receiving considerably more precipitation though it did not become a preferred settlement area in antiquity. The island's topography did not permit larger settlements. This explains the large number of ancient towns; since Homer (Hom. Od. 19,174) C. has proverbially been the island of 90 (later 100) towns — in fact there were almost 60 independent communities during the classical period.

In about 2000 BC the celebrated → 'Minoan' culture, named after the legendary king → Minos of → Knossos, flowered on C. The architectural evidence of this earliest European civilization are — apart from many other finds — the four great palaces of Knossos, Phaistos, Malia and Zakro with their extensive settlement territories. The palaces were more likely repeatedly destroyed by natural catastrophes than by human action — and then rebuilt each time. A final catastrophe, which brought the palace period to its end in most of C. about 1450 BC (this period lasted a few decades more in Knossos), is probably not to be associated with a presumably earlier volcanic eruption on Santorin and a resulting tidal wave [1] [2].

B. ARCHAIC PERIOD

After a brief Mycenaean interlude, a new chapter in Cretan history began in the 11th cent. with the immigration of the Doric population. However, the Minoan past remained a fixed component of the collective memory of the Greeks and, as an identity-providing component, it justifies the inclusion of Minoan culture in Greek history together with the island's geographical

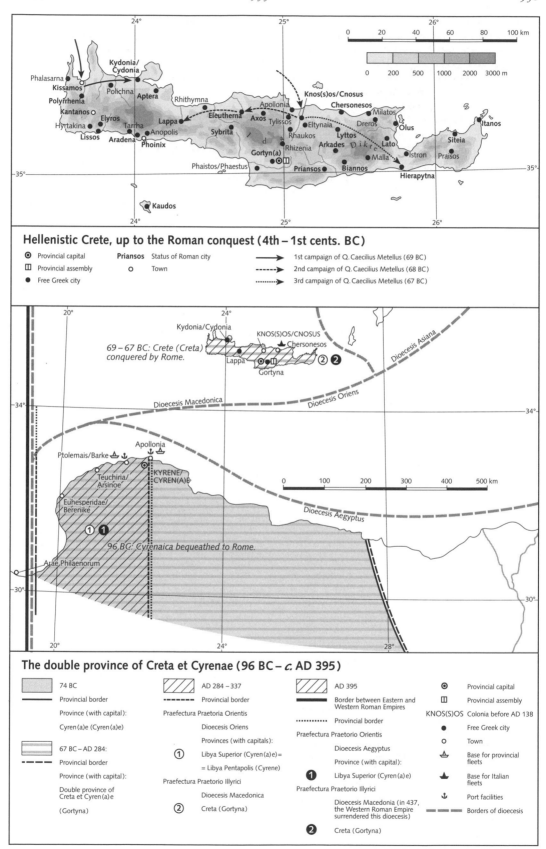

Hellenistic Crete, up to the Roman conquest (4th – 1st cents. BC)

- ◉ Provincial capital
- ▥ Provincial assembly
- ● Free Greek city

Priansos Status of Roman city
- ○ Town

- → 1st campaign of Q. Caecilius Metellus (69 BC)
- ---→ 2nd campaign of Q. Caecilius Metellus (68 BC)
- ·····→ 3rd campaign of Q. Caecilius Metellus (67 BC)

The double province of Creta et Cyrenae (96 BC – c. AD 395)

▦ 74 BC	
Provincial border	
Province (with capital):	
Cyren(a)e (Cyren(a)e)	
▤ 67 BC – AD 284:	
Provincial border	
Province (with capital):	
Double province of Creta et Cyren(a)e	
(Gortyna)	

AD 284 – 337
Provincial border
Praefectura Praetoria Orientis
Dioecesis Oriens
Provinces (with capitals):
① Libya Superior (Cyren(a)e) =
= Libya Pentapolis (Cyrene)
Praefectura Praetorio Illyrici
Dioecesis Macedonica
② Creta (Gortyna)

AD 395
Border between Eastern and Western Roman Empires
········· Provincial border
Praefectura Praetorio Orientis
Dioecesis Aegyptus
Province (with capital):
❶ Libya Superior (Cyren(a)e)
Praefectura Praetorio Illyrici
Dioecesis Macedonica (in 437, the Western Roman Empire surrendered this dioecesis)
❷ Creta (Gortyna)

- ◉ Provincial capital
- ▥ Provincial assembly
- KNOS(S)OS Colonia before AD 138
- ● Free Greek city
- ○ Town
- ⚓ Base for provincial fleets
- ⚓ Base for Italian fleets
- ⚓ Port facilities
- ═ ═ Borders of dioecesis

location. The idea of a Cretan thalassocracy (Hdt.
1,171; 3,122; Thuc. 1,4,8) and of Minos as one of the
great law makers (Cic. Rep. 2,12; Tac. Ann. 3,26) are
part of later reminiscences. The Dorian-style constitutions and social order of the Cretan cities show strongly
archaic traits with rigid hierarchies. Usually, a warrior
aristocracy comparable in some respects to Sparta in its
organization and mentality ruled over a subjugated
original population (on Cretan ethnogenesis, Hom. Od.
19,172ff.; Diod. Sic. 5,64,80) that had the legal status
of Klarotes or Mnoites. Ancient philosophers of government often praised Cretan institutions (Pl. Leg.
631b; 634d; Aristot. Pol. 1264a 39ff.; 1271b 18ff.;
however Pol. 6,45–47). In terms of settlement geography a relocation of the towns into the interior and onto
secure heights can be observed during the Dorian take-
over (example Lato).

C. Classical and Hellenistic period

In the classical period the island was largely marginal. C. was neither involved in the Persian Wars (despite
requests, Hdt. 7,145,2; 169–171) nor the Peloponnesian War since no Cretan city was a member of one of
the large federations. In terms of legal history, the
record of the famous town law of → Gortyne (about
450 BC) is important. In the Hellenistic period C.
played a more central role. The internal Cretan conflicts
that may be assumed to have existed in the classical
period (and were specifically expressed in a contract
between Knossos and Tylissus in the mid 5th cent. BC)
continued (Pol. 6,46,9) with Knossos and Gortyne taking leading roles. These conflicts were internationalized
since the large Hellenistic powers, especially the Antigonids and the Ptolemies, but also the Attalids, attempted to include the strategically located island in their
power spheres. On the other hand, the Cretan towns
were also interested in receiving support from the large
powers. The resulting tensions were not diffused by
founding a Cretan → koinón (probably already in the
1st half of the 3rd cent. BC). Ephemeral single purpose
alliances — such as the one concluded in 222 BC between Knossos and Gortyne (Pol. 4,53,4) — were unable to stabilize the volatile relationships among states.
In the 2nd cent. BC Gortyne established itself as the
foremost power on C. In the Hellenistic period Cretans
were in demand as mercenaries by external powers who
particularly appreciated their qualities as archers and
military tacticians (Pol. 4,8,11; Plut. Philopoimen
13,6). Cretans were also feared as pirates but their turn
to → piracy should primarily be regarded as a consequence of social problems. This activity strongly contributed to the generally negative reputation of Cretans
in the Ancient World (Callim. H. 1,8; Pol. 6,46; Tit 1,2).

D. Crete under Roman rule

After the Roman conquest in 67 BC (Liv. Per. 100;
Plut. Pompeius 29), Augustus made C. part of the new
double province → Creta et Cyrenae. Gortyne became
the provincial capital with its buildings and infrastruc-

ture being the best indicators of C.'s cultural and economic revival in the Roman Imperial period. Gortyne
became a centre of early Christianity. In AD 58 the
Apostle Paul visited the town (Acts 27,7) and installed
Titus as its first bishop (Titus Basilica of the 6th cent.).
As a consequence of Diocletian's reforms in the late 3rd
cent. AD., C. was reorganized as a province of its own.
→ Creta et Cyrenae (with map); → Minoan culture and
archaeology; → Minoan religion

1 S. Marinatos, The Volcanic Destruction of Minoan
Crete, in: Antiquity 13, 1939, 425–439 2 H. Lohmann,
Die Santorin-Katatstrophe — ein arch. Mythos? in:
E. Olshausen, H. Sonnabend (ed.), Naturkatastrophen
in der ant. Welt. Stuttgarter Kolloquium zur Hist. Geogr.
des Alt. 6, 1996 (Geographica Historica 10), 1998, 337–
358.

J. Bowman, K., 1965; M. W. B. Bowsky, Eight Inscrip-
tions from Roman Crete, in: ZPE 108, 1995, 263–280;
P. Brulé, La piraterie crétoise hellénistique, 1978;
A. Chaniotis, Die kret. Berge als Wirtschaftsraum, in:
E. Olshausen, H. Sonnabend (ed.), Gebirgsland als
Lebensraum. Stuttgarter Kolloquium zur Hist. Geogr. des
Alt. 5, 1993 (Geographica Historica 8), 1996, 255–266;
Id., Die Verträge zw. kret. Poleis in der hell. Zeit, 1996;
A. Evans, The Palace of Minos at Knossos, 4 vols.,
1921–1936; P. Faure, La Crète aux cent villes, in: Kretika
Chronika 13, 1959, 171–217; Id., Recherches de top-
onymie crétoise, 1989; F. Gschnitzer, Abhängige Orte
im griech. Alt., 1958; A. Guarducci, Inscriptiones Cre-
ticae I–IV, 1935–1950; A. J. Haft, The Myth that Crete
Became, 1981; G. L. Huxley, The Minoans in Greek
Sources, 1968; E. Kirsten, Das dor. K., 1, 1942; S. Kreu-
ter, Außenbeziehungen kret. Gemeinden zu den hell.
Staaten im 3. und 2. Jh.v.Chr., 1992; S. Link, Das griech.
Kretas, 1994; J. W. Myers et al., Aerial Atlas of Ancient
Crete, 1992; A. Petropoulou, Beitr. zur Wirtschafts-
und Gesellschaftsgesch. Kretas in hell. Zeit, 1985; I. F. Sanders, Roman Crete, 1982; T. A. B. Spratt, Travels and
Researches in Crete, 2 vols., 1865; St. Spyridakis, Cre-
tica. Studies on Ancient Greece, 1992; H. van Effenterre, La Crète et le monde Grec de Platon à Polybe,
1948; R. F. Willets, Aristocratic Society in Ancient
Greece, 1955; Id., Cretan Cults and Festivals, 1962; Id.,
Ancient Crete, 1965; M. Zohary, G. Orshan, An Outline of the Geobotany of Crete, in: Israel Journal of Bota-
ny, Suppl. 14, 1965, 1–49.   H. SO.

Maps: D. Gondikas, Recherches sur la Crete Occidentale, 1988; I. F. Sanders, Roman Crete, 1982; K. Busch-
mann et al., Östl. Mittelmeerraum und Mesopot. Von
Antoninus Pius bis zum Ende des Parthischen Reiches
(138–224 n.Chr.), TAVO B V 9, 1992; A. H. M. Jones,
The Cities of the Eastern Roman Provinces, ²1971, 351–
362; E. Kettenhofen, Östl. Mittelmeerraum und Mesopot. Die Neuordnung des Orients in diokletianisch-kon-
stantinischer Zeit (284–337 n.Chr.), TAVO B VI 1, 1984;
Id., Östl. Mittelmeerraum und Mesopot. Spätröm. Zeit
(337–527 n.Chr.), TAVO B VI 4, 1984; A. Laronde, La
Cyrénaïque romaine, des origines à la fin des Sévères (96
av. J.-C.–235 ap. J.-C.), in: ANRW II 10.1, 1006–1064.

E. Late Antiquity and Byzantine period
The island's administrative affiliation with
→ Cyrene (→ Creta et Cyrenae) was terminated under
→ Constantine [1] I the Great and C. became part of the
diocesis Macedonia. It is unknown if C. became a
→ theme in the course of the reorganization of Byzantine
administration in the 7th cent. Otherwise, C.
shared the fate of the other Aegean islands [1], attacks
by Vandals (457) and Slavs (623) were short-term episodes.

However, the coup-like conquest of the island by
expelled Spanish Arabs under Abū Ḥafṣ (between 824
and 827/8) marked a clear break. Arab rule proved stable,
and the island was only reconquered in 961. CHRISTIDES
[2] describes the cultural situation and the Arab-
Greek symbiosis. As far as the Byzantine central
government was concerned, the Aegaean was left open
to the raids of Arab pirates for centuries [3. 35ff.,
111ff.]. In 1204 the island was conquered by the Venetians
who made it one of their most important bases
in the Levant trade.

1 E. MALAMUT, Les îles de l'Empire Byzantine: VIIIᵉ-XIIᵉ
siècles, 2 vols., 1988 2 V. CHRISTIDES, The Conquest of
Crete by the Arabs, 1984 3 H. AHRWEILER, Byzance et la
Mer. La marine de guerre, la politique et les institutions
maritimes de Byzance aux VIIᵉ-XVᵉ siècles, 1966.   J.N.

Cretheus (Κρηθεύς, as *ke-re-te-u* already Mycenaean).
The son of → Aeolus [1] and Enarete (Apollod. 1,51),
founder and ruler of → Iolcus. After the death of his first
wife → Sidero, he married his ward Tyro, the daughter
of his brother → Salmoneus and the mother of Pelias
and → Neleus with Poseidon, with whom he begat
→ Aeson [1], Phere and → Amythaon (Hom. Od.
11,235ff.; Hes. fr. 30,29ff.; Apollod. 1,90ff.; 96); Val.
Fl. 5,476ff. also makes → Athamas a son of C.; Pind.
Nem. 5,26 speaks of a daughter → Hippolyte [3]. An
association of C. with the Peloponnese (Crathis, a river
near Aegae [1]) must be rejected.

1 M.L. WEST, The Hesiodic Catalogue of Women, 1985,
141ff.

P. DRÄGER, Argo pasimelousa, I, 1993, 81f., 108ff., 334f.
    P.D.

Creticus Cognomen (originally the epithet of a victor)
in the family of the Caecilii Metelli (→ Caecilius [I 23]
and [II 16]) and of Mark Antony [I 8] C.   K.-L.E.

Creusa (Κρέουσα; *Kréousa*, Latin Creusa).
[1] Daughter of Gaia and Oceanus, who bears → Hypseus
and Stilbe to the river god Peneius (Pind. Pyth.
9,14f.; Diod. Sic. 4,69).
[2] The youngest daughter of → Erechtheus and → Praxithea.
Apollo begat → Ion [1] with her, whom she
abandons but whom Hermes took to Delphi. C. marries
→ Xuthus (Hes. fr. nova 10a 20ff.), who becomes king
of Athens after Erechtheus' death. When consulting the
Delphic oracle because of their childlessness, the couple

finds Ion again. C. later bears → Dorus and → Achaeus
[1] (Eur. Ion; Apollod. 1,50) to Xuthus.
[3] Daughter of the Corinthian king → Creon [2]. When
→ Iason [1] wants to marry her, she is assassinated by
his abandoned wife → Medea. Her name is sometimes
also recorded as → Glauce [2].
[4] Daughter of → Priamus and → Hecabe (Hyg. Fab.
90), spouse of → Aeneas [1] to whom she bears Ascanius.
During the conquest of Troy she is removed (Verg.
Aen. 2,736ff.; Paus. 10,26,1; somewhat different in
Lycoph. 1263ff.).

G. BERGER-DOER, s.v. K. (1)–(3), LIMC 6.1, 117–118;
120–121; 127–128; TH. KOCK, s.v. K. (2)–(5), RE 11,
1825.   R.HA.

Creusis (Κρεῦσις). Boeotian port on the → Corinthian
Gulf in the bay of Livadostro, belonging to Thespiae
(Str. 9,2,25; Liv. 36,21,5; Paus. 9,32,1). Near the coast
are the remains of a fortress linked to a quay system. C.
had increased importance as a port during the Spartan-
Theban conflicts before 371 BC (Xen. Hell. 4,5,10;
5,4,16f.; 6,4,3f.; Xen. Ag. 2,18). In the 2nd and 1st
cents. BC C. was an important Roman harbour (Liv.
36,21,5; 42,56,5).

FOSSEY, 157–163; G. GAUVIN, J. M. FOSSEY, Livadhostro:
un relevé topographique des fortifications de l'ancienne
K., in: P. ROESCH, G. ARGOUD (ed.), La Béotie antique,
1985, 77–87.   K.F.

Crexus (Κρέξος). Named together with Timotheus and
Philoxenus as a poet of dithyrambs (Ps.-Plut. De musica
1135c). He allegedly introduced to dithyrambic poetry
the style of Archilochus and the tragedians of partially
speaking and singing iambic meters to the accompaniment
of the lyre (λέγεσθαι/ᾄδεσθαι παρὰ τὴν κροῦσιν)
(1141b; also Philod. De musica 4,5).   F.Z.

Cricket German 'Grille', Pliny's *gryllus* (HN 29, 138)
probably is the field cricket, *Gryllus campestris*, which
runs backwards (thus Nigidius Figulus), digs into the
ground and chirps at night with its wings (*stridere*). As a
paste, a cricket (dug out with its earth) helps against ear
aches. It is drawn from its earthen hole using an ant tied
to a hair as bait [1. 132]. Isid. Orig. 12,3,8 conveyed
this information to the Middle Ages. It is uncertain if
the wingless, locust-like insect *trixalis* in Plin. HN
30,49 is a cricket because Ael. NA 6,19 only says that
the *trōchallís* is 'not silent'.

1 LEITNER.   C.HÜ.

Crimen
A. PUBLIC CRIMINAL PROSECUTION B. RELATIONSHIP
TO CIVIL LAW C. IMPERIAL PERIOD

A. PUBLIC CRIMINAL PROSECUTION
The legal technical category in classical Roman jurisprudence
of the Principate applied to public criminal

procedures (*iudicium publicum*) where crimes were prosecuted based upon accusation (→ *accusatio*). As with civil legal forms in Roman Law, it is not a characteristic routine legal transaction but should rather be understood as a means of attack and defence in a trial (→ *actio*, → *exceptio*). The meaning of the term *crimen* predominantly lies in the procedural field. Therefore, *crimen* appears most frequently in the sources in connection with suits or empowerments to sue, sometimes virtually in place of the *accusatio*. The crime that is prosecuted in the *iudicium publicum* is called the *crimen publicum*, e.g. in a rescript of emperor Gordian (AD 242, Cod. Iust. 8,34,3). The relationship of *crimen* to its procedural pursuit is particularly clear in the contrast of *crimen publicum* and *crimen extraordinarium*, e.g., in the constitution of emperor Septimius Severus in AD 196 (Cod. Iust. 3,15,1): *quaestiones eorum criminum, quae legibus aut extra ordinem coercentur* (criminal procedures that are conducted according to laws or outside the conventional procedural order).

B. RELATIONSHIP TO CIVIL LAW

The linguistic use of *crimen* is not always strictly technical. This even applies to the fundamental differentiation between *crimen* as the subject of a public procedure and → *delictum*, an injustice prosecuted in a civil suit. Gai. Inst. 3,197 occasionally calls a theft of goods under 'civil law' a *crimen furti*. In the age of the Law of the Twelve Tablets (5th cent. BC) *delicta privata* still prevailed. In the early period a public prosecution can only be assumed with certainty for crimes against the community, such as high treason and treason (→ *perduellio*), or against the sacred order. As a possible example of sacral crimes, Liv. 3,55,7 states: Whoever violates the sacrosanctity of the people's tribune, his 'head' is forfeit to Jupiter, he is 'outlawed' and his wealth is given to the temple of Ceres, Liber and Libera (*eius caput Iovi sacrum esset, familia ad aedem Cereris Liberi Liberaeque venum iret*). All other grave crimes such as murder and arson remained the subject of civil law prosecutions, i.e. were understood as *delicta* (*privata*), until the 1st cent. BC. [1; 2]. However, the exact delimitation between civil and public law in the early period is disputed in secondary literature. After the judicial reform of Augustus (*lex Iulia iudiciorum publicorum*, 17 BC) serious crimes committed against private citizens, such as murder, rape and kidnapping, became *crimen publica* in Roman Law. Finally, since the 2nd cent. AD, severe forms of theft, such as cattle rustling (*crimen abigeatus*, Dig. 47,14), theft in public baths or at night (*furtum balnearium, nocturnum*, Dig. 47,17) and burglary (→ *effractor*, Dig. 47,18), were prosecuted by the public.

C. IMPERIAL PERIOD

The last cited cases of prosecution were not part of the *ordo iudiciorum publicorum*, that is of legally regulated crimes. Rather, the use of the cognition proceeding (→ *cognitio*) in criminal law led to the introduction of *crimen* under Imperial law and even customary law (the latter mentioned by Macer Dig. 47,15,3 pr.). The *crimen extraordinaria* not only put private delicts 'under state control' but also extended criminal law to include new facts. These are the 'unbounded legality' [3] of crimes against majesty (*crimen laesae maiestatis*) in the Imperial period [4]: after Augustus had this crime regulated again in the *lex Iulia de maiestate* (probably 27 BC), infractions unknown to the *lex* were sanctioned in criminal law, in a proceeding *extra ordinem*: insulting mention of the Imperial person and name, insults to his statue or image, military disobedience towards the emperor, and consulting astrologers or soothsayers about the emperor's future (cf. especially Paulus, Sent. 5,29,1). The character of this criminal deed as *crimen extra ordinem* is further revealed in the 'freedom' of this procedure: a formal accusation was no longer required but mere notification (or rather denunciation), by anyone — including slaves — was sufficient for criminal prosecution. The decision regarding the punishment was increasingly left to the decision-maker in each individual case. An opening for differentiating the punishment according to social status as member of the *humiliores* or → *honestiores* [5] was created.

The broad scope of the judge's discretion in determining the severity of punishment remained an important peculiarity of the *crimen extraordinarium* even in Justinian's codification. Otherwise the differences between *crimen publica* and *crimen extraordinaria* were largely blurred in late antiquity. The Digest titles regarding the *crimen extraordinaria* (47,11) are a historical reminiscence just like those on *publica iudicia* (48,1). The fragments reproduced there also show that late classical jurists (after 200), especially → Marcianus, were concerned with a systematization of the entire criminal law. A product of this is in particular the development of the subjective element in *crimen*: the universal requirement is intentional perpetration (*dolus*, cf. [6]).

1 W. KUNKEL, Unt. zur Entwicklung des röm. Kriminalverfahrens in vorsullanischer Zeit, 1962 2 DULCKEIT, SCHWARZ, WALDSTEIN, § 12 I 3 3 MOMMSEN, Strafrecht, 951 4 B. SANTALUCIA, Diritto e processo penale nell'antica Roma, 1989, 118 5 R. RILINGER, Humiliores-Honestiores, 1988, 207ff. 6 V. GUIFFRÈ, La 'repressione criminale' nell' esperienza Romana, ³1993, 165ff.
G.S.

Criminal procedure see → Volume 4, Addenda

Crimisus (Κριμισός). River in West Sicily (*Crinis(s)us*, Verg. Aen. 5,38; *Crinisos*, Vibius Sequester 1,44), at which → Timoleon defeated the Carthaginians in 340/339 BC (Plut. Timoleon 25 with Diod. Sic. 19,2,8). Also, one of the rivers in Segesta (Fiume Freddo, Belice destro, Belice sinistro) as is suggested by the legend that the river god C. begat → Aegestus with the Trojan woman Egesta (Verg. Aen. 5,36ff.). On coins from Segesta C.

appears as a dog; a human representation is also known (Ael. VH 2,33), cf. [1].

1 G. MANGANARO, s.v. Criniso (sic), EV 1, 933f.

GI.MA. and K.Z.

Crinagoras (Κριναγόρας) of Mytilene. Born about 70 BC, he probably did not die before AD 11 (Anth. Pal. 7,633, cf. 9,283). C. was an influential man in his native town. His participation in several delegations from his town to Rome is attested in inscriptions: in 48 or 47 and in 45 (IG XII 35a; 35b), in 26/25 to Tarragona in Spain (to Augustus, IG XII 35c). He was also highly regarded in Rome where he belonged to the circle around Octavia, the sister of Augustus. C. is one of the significant poets of epigrams in the 'Garland' of Philippus (Anth. Pal. 4,2,8). 51 poems of good quality are preserved, generally without exaggerated stylistic sophistication but representing an important historical source: they are mostly opportunistic poems (often to accompany presents) that always reflect personal experiences and contemporary events with references to famous persons of that age. His flattering intention at times acquires grotesque traits: Anth. Pal. 9,224 is dedicated to a goat that deserves acceptance among the stars because it gave its milk to Caesar Augustus, ibid. 9,562 to a parrot that escaped into a bush and was teaching all the birds how to greet the emperor. Parthenius of Nicaea wrote an elegy in honour of C. (one verse is preserved, SH 624).

GA II 1, 198–231; 2, 210–60.

M.G.A.

Crinas from Marseilles (→ Massalia), physician, who came to Rome in the time of Nero (Plin. HN. 29,9). He gained renown when he combined astronomy with medicine by orienting the diet plans for his patients according to the course of the stars. When he died, he left 10 million sesterces after having already spent the same sum on repairing the walls and other defences in his native town.

V.N.

Crinis (Κρῖνις). Stoic logician, author of an 'Art of the Dialectic' (Διαλεκτικὴ τέχνη; cf. Diog. Laert. 7,62; 68; 71; 76). An allusion in the Epict. Dissertationes 3,2,15 dates his active phase to the period after → Archedemus [2] of Tarsus (late 2nd cent. BC) and his death before the philosophical career of Epictetus (early 2nd cent. AD).

B.I.

Crioa (Κριώα). Attic *asty* (?) deme of the Antiochis phyle. With one *bouleutaí*, after 307/6 BC two *bouleutaí*. Location uncertain, but the genealogical links between the eponymous hero Crius (schol. Aristoph. Av. 645) and Pallas suggest proximity to Pallene [1; 2. 373²]. The funerary inscription IG II² 6108 of the wife of a Κριωεύς is from Kypseli.

1 E. HONIGMANN, s.v. K., RE 11, 1866 2 P. J. BICKNELL, Akamantid Eitea, in: Historia 27, 1978, 369–374.

TRAILL, Attica 23, 54 with n. 27, 59, 69, 111 no. 77, tab. 10; J. S. TRAILL, Demos and Trittys, 1986, 139.

H.LO.

Crisa (Κρῖσα). City in West Phocis (Κρῖσα: Hom. Il. 2,520; Hecat. FGrH 1 F 115a; Pind. Isthm. 2,18; Soph. El. 180; Str. 9,3,3; Paus. 10,37,5; Plin. HN 4,7; Frontin. Str. 3,7,6; schol. Pind. Pyth. 1 hypoth.; Ptol. 3,14,4; Hsch. s.v. K.; Κρίσσα/η: Hom. H. Apollon 282; Eust. in Hom. Il. 526; Κίρσα: Alc. fr. 121 D.), toponym of the alluvial plain bounded in the SE by Cirphis and Parnassus (Κρισαῖον πεδίον: Hdt. 8,32; modern plain of Itea) on the bay of the Corinthian Gulf. C. lies on a rock spur (cf. Pind. Pyth. 5,37: Κρισαῖος λόφος; H. Hom. Apollon. 282ff.) south of modern Chryso, where a pre- and protohistorical settlement was located near the chapel of Hagios Georghios (late Mycenaean period, fortified by a surrounding Cyclopean wall, possibly the 'divine Crisa' of Hom. Il. 2,520). The port of Kirrha was located about 1.5 km south of C. along the coast on the western mouth of the Pleistus. The visible remains on the southern edge of the Magula of Xeropigadi (again Kirrha today) are attributed to it. They confirm settlement at this site since the early Bronze Age, a flowering in the Middle Helladic period and decline in the Mycenaean period (to the benefit of C.). The wealth and strategic importance of the pre- and protohistorical settlements are due to the plain's fertility, the proximity to the sea and a location on the intersection of regional land and maritime routes.

In ancient tradition C. and Kirrha were equated (cf. Paus. 10,37,5; Etym. m. s.v. K.). The town that was destroyed at the end of the First Sacred War (→ Delphi, → Sacred Wars) soon became C. (Str. 9,3,3; Frontin. Str. 3,7,6; Pind. Pyth. 1 hypoth.), which is why this conflict is also known as the 'Crisan War' (Κρισαῖος/ Κρισαικὸς πόλεμος, cf. Str. 9,3,3) and was soon called Kirrha (Diod. Sic. 9,16; Aeschin. 3,107–113; Paus. 10,37,4; Plut. Solon 11; Polyanus, Strat. 3,5; Marmor Parium FGrH 239 F 37) — therefore, the name of the region as the 'plain and sea of Kirrha' (τὸ Κιρραῖον πεδίον καὶ λιμήν, Aeschin. loc. cit., cf. Ps.-Scyl. 37). The lack of later archaeological evidence suggests the destruction of C. Kirrha functioned as the 'anchorage' (ἐπίνειον) of Delphi (Paus. 10,37,4). Archaeological finds from the classical, Hellenistic, Roman and Byzantine periods (now called Chryson) and literary documentation (Paus. loc. cit.; Ptol. 3,14,4 for the Imperial period) prove settlement continuity despite destruction in 339 (Aeschin. 3,123) and 281 BC (Iust. 24,1,4f.). The hostile attitude of Crisa/Kirrha towards Delphi contributed to its reputation as a godless town (Aeschin. 3,107; Callisthenes FGrH 124 F 1). At the end of the First Sacred War the plain was declared a 'sacred zone' dedicated to Apollo (Aeschin. 3,107f.; Dem. Or. 45,149–155; Polyaenus Strat. 3,5; Str. 9,3,4; Paus. 10,37,4; CID I, 10).

G. DAVERIO ROCCHI, La 'hiera chora' di Apollo, la piana di Cirra e i confini di Delfi, in: M.-M. MACTOUX (ed.), Mél. P. Lévêque 1, 1988, 117–125; L. DOR et al., Krisa,

1960; E.W. Kase, A Study of the Role of Krisa in the Mycenaean Era, in: AJA, 75, 1971, 205f.; F. Schober, Phokis, 1924, 32–34; TIB 1, 195.   G.D.R.

Crispinus

[1] Originally from Egypt, perhaps formerly a slave. In Iuvenal 4,108 he is mentioned as a participant in Domitian's consilium on the Albanum (cf. [1. 532, n. 76]: perhaps *praef. annonae*; [2. 69f.]: courtier). Since Martial 7,99 is addressed to him, he was in any case an influential man at Domitian's court (PIR² C 1586).

1 Syme, RP 7   2 B.W. Jones, The Emperor Domitian, 1992.

[2] A. A[..]cius C. (IEphes. III 517; VII 3045) see A. → Larcius Crispinus.   W.E.

Crispus

[1] Flavius Iulius C. The eldest son of Constantine [1] from the liaison with Minervina, born *c.* AD 300; elevated together with his half-brother Constantius [2] II and Licinianus Licinius to the rank of caesar on 1 March 317 in Serdica. Unlike his brother he also became a *princeps iuventutis* in the same year and in 318 he was the first of the newly elevated caesars to be made consul. C., who was obviously groomed to be the successor, was sent to Gaul with his own *praef. praet.* after his elevation as caesar. He married Helen, an otherwise unknown woman named Helena (Cod. Theod. 9,38,1). After successful battles against the Franks and Alamanni, C. commanded the fleet in the second war against Licinius in 324 (Anon. Valesianus 23; 26f.) and defeated Amandus, Licinius' admiral, near the Hellespont. Though extraordinarily honoured after the victory over Licinius, C. was suddenly executed in 326 at the command of his father (Amm. Marc. 14,11,20). His stepmother Fausta was executed soon after. The Graeco-Roman tradition in late antiquity explained the undoubtedly linked murders with the → Phaedra motif (Zos. 2,29,1–2; Aur. Vict. Epitome de Caesaribus 41,11–12; Philostorgius Hist. eccl. 2,4a; Zon. 13,2,38–41). PLRE 1, 233 no. 4.

Kienast, ²1996, 305f.; H. Pohlsander, C., in: Historia 33, 1984, 79–106.   B.BL.

Critias (Κριτίας; *Kritías*) of Athens, born about 460 BC, descended from an old Attic noble family, on his mother's side he was an uncle of → Plato. Like → Alcibiades [3] he belonged to the circle around → Socrates. Politically he belonged to the antidemocratic forces: in 415 he was accused of participating in the mutilation of the → Herms, in 411 he was a member of the oligarchic council of the 400 (→ Tetrakosioi). After the democratic restoration he stayed in Thessaly until 404, after the Athenian defeat in 404 he was one of the leaders of the terror regime of the 30 tyrants (→ Triakonta). In 403 he was killed in battle against the democrats under Thrasybulus near Munichia (Piraeus).

Like → Ion [2] of Chios, C. occupied himself with a multitude of literary genres: a hexametric poem is dedicated to → Anacreon [1] (88 B 1 DK), in an elegy he describes the inventions of various countries (B 2), another is addressed to Alcibiades, in which the name of the addressee causes him to replace the pentameter with an iambic trimeter (B 4). Fragments on the Spartan constitution are preserved (B 6f.) from his 'State Constitutions' in elegiac distichs. It has not been completely clarified if C. also wrote tragedies because two titles ('Peirithous' and 'Sisyphus') are ascribed by tradition partly to Critias, partly to Euripides [1]. Scholarship has largely accepted the thesis of Wilamowitz [1] which reconstructed for C. a tetralogy consisting of 'Tennes', 'Rhadamanthys', 'Peirithous' and the satyr play 'Sisyphus' [2]. 'Peirithous' (TrGF 43 F 1–12) deals with Hercules' journey to the Underworld and the liberation of Theseus; a longer fragment of 'Sisyphus' is preserved (F 19), in which an explanation of the origin of laws and a rationalistic theory of the origin of religion is presented.

C. composed more state constitutions (88 B 30–38 DK: Athens, Thessaly, Sparta), aphorisms (B 39), dialogues (B 40f.), a treatise 'On the Nature of Love and the Virtues' (B 42) and proems to political speeches (B 43) in prose.

1 U. v. Wilamowitz-Moellendorff, Analecta Euripidea, 1875, 166   2 A. Lesky, Die trag. Dichtung der Hellenen, ³1972, 525.

M. Centanni, Atene assoluta: Crizia dalla tragedia alla storia, 1997; A. Dihle, Das Satyrspiel 'Sisyphos', in: Hermes 105, 1977, 28–42; Diels/Kranz 2, 371–399; TrGF I 43; B. Gauly et al. (ed.), Musa tragica 1991, 108–125; Guthrie 3, 298ff.   B.Z.

Critical signs see → Volume 4, Addenda

Critius (Κρίτιος; in written sources: Κριτίας). Bronze sculptor in Athens. C. is always mentioned together with Nesiotes. His prime was in 448–444 BC, Pliny's date is too late. C. was a contemporary of → Hegias [1]. In antiquity his style was considered antiquated and dry. He became famous as the master of the → Severe Style (1st third of the 5th cent. BC) with his statues of → Harmodius [1] and → Aristogeiton, the Tyrannicide group, which in 477/6 BC was set up in the Agora to replace a group by → Antenor [2] that had been taken by the Persians in 480 BC. Since it was simultaneously reproduced in several media, it was possible to identify it in Roman marble copies (Naples, MN). It is disputed to what extent C. was guided by the example of Antenor. Preserved fragments of the original base with parts of the inscription mostly relate to the group by C. On the Acropolis four statue bases with the signatures of C. and Nesiotes are preserved. Of these the statue of the armed runner Epicharinus, which Pausanias still saw, was created after 480 BC; the dedication of Hegelochus represented an Athena Promachos and another a rider. However, the C. boy, a marble statue from the Acropolis dated about 480 BC, was attributed to C. for doubtful stylistic reasons. Pausanias and Pliny link a sculptor school of five generations to C.

OVERBECK, nos. 443; 452; 453; 457–463; 469; LIPPOLD, 106–108; A. RAUBITSCHEK, Dedications from the Athenian Akropolis, 1949, 120–123; 160–161 a; 513–517; W. FUCHS, in: EAA 4, 410–415; B. RIDGWAY, The Severe Style in Greek Sculpture, 1970, 70–83; 90–91; S. BRUNNSAKER, The Tyrant-Slayers of Kritios and Nesiotes, 1971; J. KLEINE, Unt. zur Chronologie der att. Kunst von Peisistratos bis Themistokles, in: MDAI(Ist) Beih. 8, 1973, 67–78; B. FEHR, Die Tyrannentöter, 1984; W. H. SCHUCHHARDT, C. LANDWEHR, Statuenkopien der Tyrannenmörder-Gruppe, in: JDAI 101, 1986, 85–126; STEWART, 135–136; 251–252.   R.N.

Critodemus (Κριτόδημος). Astrologer of the Hellenistic period, named by Pliny the Elder together with → Berossus, by Firmicus Maternus with the oldest representatives of Greek astrology, mainly used by → Vettius Valens (however, the horoscopes mentioned by Valens in connection with C. extend into a later period, in part into the 2nd cent. AD), then also by Hephaestion (2,10,41–46), Rhetorius and Theophilus of Edessa. His work Ὅρασις (*Hórasis*/'Vision'), the beginning of which was copied by Valens 3,9,3 = 9,1,5, exhibits a mystical-poetic style, discusses climacteric years (*klimaktéres*), life span, violent ends (*biaiothanasía*) and planet districts (*hória*: the 'summary' only refers to this CCAG VIII 3,102). The title Πίναξ/*Pínax* ('Table') mentioned by Heph. 2,10,41 probably just refers to a table rather than an entire work. A collection of fragments is essential.

SOURCES: P. SCHNABEL, Berossos und die babylon.-hell. Lit., 1923, 118–120 (Index of fragments); Fr. 13: CCAG VIII 1,257–261 (a somewhat deviating text: W. HÜBNER, Grade und Gradbezirke, 1995, 215–258); Fr. 17: CCAG VIII 4,199–202.
BIBLIOGRAPHY: F. BOLL, s.v. Kritodemos, RE 11, 1928–1930; O. NEUGEBAUER, H. B. VAN HOESEN, Greek Horoscopes, 1959, 185f.   W.H.

Critognatus (Ecritognatus). Celtic composite name with variant readings: 'knows trembling' or 'born to attack' [1. 78–79; 2. 185].

Arvernian nobleman, who in 52 BC extolled his fellow combatants in besieged Alesia to hold out when the absence of the Gaulish relief army caused serious provisioning difficulties. Caesar (B Gall. 7,77,2–16) relates the full wording of C.'s speech as an example of Gaulish cruelty because he called for eating the bodies of the old and the infirm rather than falling into eternal Roman servitude.

→ Alesia

1 EVANS 2 SCHMIDT.

B. KREMER, Das Bild der Kelten bis in augusteische Zeit, 1994, 191–195.   W.SP.

Critolaus (Κριτόλαος).

[1] of Phaselis, peripatetic head of a school in the 1st half of the 3rd cent. BC [1; 2] and one of the most important peripatetic philosophers of the period between → Straton and → Andronicus [4] (Testimonies in [3]). He accompanied → Carneades and → Diogenes [15] of Babylon in 156/5 BC in the philosphers' delegation to Rome. C. defended the Aristotelian theories of the eternity of the World and the fifth element (of which he assumed the soul was made; → Elements, theory of). He also included real things and appearances among the highest good. C. criticized the Stoic distinction of caution as a permissible 'good feeling' (εὐπάθεια) and fear as an impermissible passion as being purely linguistic. Nevertheless, C.'s determination of the ethical goal as 'the natural fulfilment of life in prosperity' (τελειότης κατὰ φύσιν εὐροοῦντος βίου, fr. 20 WEHRLI) reflected the Stoic → Zeno. In rejecting the view that rhetoric is an art [3. 70], he followed Plato and claimed that → Demosthenes [2] benefited from Aristoteles' rules.

1 H. V. ARNIM, s.v. K. (3), RE 9, 1930–1932 2 R. GOULET, s.v. Critolaos de Phaselis, in: GOULET 2, 521–522 3 WEHRLI, Schule, vol. 10, ²1969, 40–74.

F. OLIVIER, De Critolao Peripatetico, 1895; F. WEHRLI, K. von Phaselis, in: GGPh², 1983, 588–591.   R.S.

[2] Achaean, *stratēgós* in 147/6 BC with extraordinary powers. Together with → Diaeus he drove the Achaean Confederacy into the catastrophic Achaean War using anti-Roman demagoguery and died in the battle of → Scarphea against Q. → Caecilius [I 27] Metellus (Pol. 38,10–13; Diod. Sic. 32,26; Paus. 7,14f.).

J. DEININGER, Der polit. Widerstand gegen Rom in Griechenland, 1971, 224–234.   L.-M.G.

Criton (Κρίτων; *Krítōn*).

[1] Wealthy friend of → Socrates and of the same age, also from the Alopece demos (Pl. Ap. 33d; Pl. Crit. 44b; Xen. Mem. 2,9,2; 2,9,4); discussion partner of Socrates in Plato's 'Criton' and 'Euthydemus' and in Xen. Mem. 2,9,1–3. In Plato's 'Criton' he unsuccessfully advises Socrates to flee his prison. The Epicurean → Idomeneus claimed that not Criton but Aeschines [1] of Sphettus had done this (Diog. Laert. 2,60; 3,36). Diogenes Laërtios (2,121) lists the titles of 17 dialogues composed by C. → Socratics.

SSR VI B 40–51; DAVIES 336.   K.D.

[2] Attic writer of comedies, who in 183 and 167 BC won second place at the Dionysian agon [1. test. 1. 2]. The titles of four pieces are preserved (Αἰτωλός/'The Aetolian', Ἐφέσιοι/'The Epheseans', Μεσσηνία/'The Messenian Woman', Φιλοπράγμων/'The Industrious Man') and three fragments: in fr. 1 a soldier appears to speak, in fr. 3 a parasite appears to be described (or speak?).

1 PCG IV, 1983, 346–348.   H.-G.NE.

[3] Sculptor from Athens. Together with Nicolaus he created in the mid 2nd cent. AD several canephores (→ Kanephoroi) as architectural supports that were found near Rome. Replicas are known from Athens.

LOEWY, no. 346; G. LIPPOLD, Kopien und Umbildungen griech. Statuen, 1923, 58; A. SCHMIDT-COLINET, Ant. Stützfiguren, 1977, 26–29; E. SCHMIDT, Zu einigen Karyatiden in Athen, Rom und London, in: AA 1977, 257–274; A. STEWART, Attika, 1979, 168; R. BOL, in: Forsch. zur Villa Albani. Katalog der ant. Bildwerke, 2, 1990, no. 178–180.   R.N.

[4] Sculptor from Athens. C. is probably the copyist of the signed statue of a bull-slaying Mithras in Ostia, of which a replica is known from Rome. The dating is disputed, therefore an equation with C. [3] is questionable.

L. GUERRINI, in: EAA 4, 415–416, no. 3.   R.N.

Criu Metopon (Κριοῦ μέτωπον, 'Ram's Forehead'). The designation of the two southernmost peaks of the Taurian → Chersonesus [2]: Cape Capyc and Cape Ai Todor (Plin. HN 4,86; Ps.-Scymn. 953; Ptol. 3,6;2) opposite Cap Carambis in Paphlagonia. According to legend the golden ram carried → Phrixus from there to the Colchi (Ps.-Plut. De fluviis 14,4).

V. D. BLAVATSKIJ, Očerki noennogo dela v antičnih gosudarstvah severnogo Pričernomor'ja, 1954, 133f.   I.v.B.

Crius (Κριός, Κρῖος or Κρεῖος, 'Ram').
[1] The third of the six titans, son of → Uranus and → Gaia (Hes. Theog. 134). Together with the goddess Eurybie he begat → Astraeus, → Pallas and → Perses (Hes. Theog. 375) [1. 390]. According to Pausanias (7,27,11) a river in Achaea was named after C.
[2] Seer, who lived in Sparta at the time of the Dorian migration. The ram god Carneus (→ Karneia) was worshipped in his house. His daughter met the Dorian scouts when getting water and led them to her father who told them how to conquer the town (Paus. 3,13, 3–5).
[3] King of → Euboea [1]. His son supposedly robbed → Delphi twice and was killed by → Apollo (Paus. 10,6,6).
[4] Teacher of → Phrixus. He informed him of the attacks of his stepmother Ino (cf. [2]). After C. has fled with him to → Colchis, he is sacrificed and his golden skin is hung up in a sanctuary. This is a variant of the Legend of the Golden Fleece (Diod. Sic. 4,47,5; → Argonauts). This tale allows one to recognize the memory of an ancient Peloponnesian god who transforms himself info other gods or humans after the abandonment of the animal-formed gods.

1 P. GRIMAL, Dictionnaire de mythologie grecque et romaine, 1951, 390, Stammbaum 32   2 Id., s.v. Athamas, ibid., 56f.

H. v. ARNIM, s.v. K. (1)8, RE 11, 1866–1869; K. SCHERLING, s.v. Kr(e)ios, RE 11, 1705–1707.   EL.STO.

[5] see → Constellations

Crixus Together with → Spartacus a leader of the great slave rebellion in 73 BC. After C. left the main army in early 72, his troops were defeated and he was killed in Apulia by the consul L. Gellius [4] and the propraetor Q. Arrius [I 4] (Sall. Hist. 3,96 M.; Liv. Per. 95f.; App. B Civ. 1,540–543 et al.).   K.-L.E.

Crobylus (Κρωβύλος). Writer of comedies in the 4th cent. BC, with 11 fragments preserved: two can be assigned to the comedy Ἀπαγχόμενος ('He Who Hangs Himself'), two to Ἀπολείπουσα (or –λιποῦσα, 'The Woman Who Left (the Man) ') and three to Ψευδυποβολιμαῖος ('The False Substitute').

1 PCG IV, 1983, 350–355.   B.BÄ.

Crobyzi (Κρόβυζοι). Large Getic subtribe (→ Getae) living between the Athrys (modern Jantra), the lower Oescus (modern Iskar) and the → Pontus Euxinus (Hecat. FGrH 1 F 170; Arr. Anab. 1,1; 1,3; Ptol. 3,10,4). In their land (Κροβυζική) the rivers Athrys, Noes and Artanes (modern Vit?, Hdt. 4,49) flowed. After the collapse of the kingdom of the → Odrysae, it seems to have expanded to the south to the northern slope of the → Haemus (Str. 7,5,12). Phylarchus (FGrH 81 F 20) reports of Isanthes, a legendary king of the C. Together with the Getae the C. worshipped → Zalmoxis (Hellanicus FGrH 4 F 73). They shared Scythia minor (modern Dobrudža) with the Scythae and the Greeks (μιγάδες Ἕλληνες/ 'Mixed Greeks', Ps.-Scymn. 754ff.), whose culture strongly influenced them.

A. FOL, T. SPIRIDONOV, Istoričeska geografija na trakijskite plemena, 1983, 36f., 113–115; D. M. PIPPIDI, D. BERCIU, Din istoria Dobrogei 1, 1965, 90ff.; A. AVRAM, Unt. zur Gesch. des Territoriums von Kallatis in griech. Zeit, in: Dacia 35, 1991, 103–137.   I.v.B.

Croceae (Κροκέαι). Place in South Laconia (modern Κροκεές, Krokeés), famous because of the green porphyry (lapis Lacedaemonius) quarried about 3 km to the south-east and highly prized in the Roman Imperial period. Attestation: Paus. 3,21,4; Str. 8,5,7; Plin. HN. 36,55; Steph. Byz. s.v. Krokea.

R. BALADIÉ, Le Péloponnèse de Strabon, 1980, 203–207; M. and R. HIGGINS, A Geological Companion to Greece and the Aegean, 1996, 54f.; C. LE ROY, Lakonika, in: BCH 85, 1961, 206–215; G. A. PIKOULAS, CIL III, 493 (Κροκεὲς Λακωνίας), in: Horos 6, 1988, 75ff.; B. POULSEN, A Relief from Croceae, in: T. FISCHER-HANSEN et al. (ed.), Recent Danish Research in Classical Archaeology, 1991, 235ff.; H. WATERHOUSE, R. HOPE SIMPSON, Prehistoric Laconia. Part I, in: ABSA 55, 1960, 103–107.   Y.L.

Crockery Images (reliefs, mosaics, paintings, especially illustrated books) help in understanding the crockery used in the course of a meal [1]. For example, a mosaic from Antioch ('House of the Buffet Supper') shows a set table with much crockery: bowls in various shapes, rectangular and round, tableware, egg cups or bowls for sauces and wine cups. Already in antiquity drinking vessels were carefully differentiated from crockery (*vasa potoria/vasa escaria*: Dig. 33,10,3,3).

Texts also provide useful information on the form, decoration and function of the objects (e.g., they note the *boletaria*, bowls for mushrooms) but they are very dispersed and difficult to interpret: it is not very easy to attach the ancient terms to depicted or preserved items. The same form may also have had multiple functions at the table but also in other contexts.

The richest tables had very complete sets of crockery (*ministerium*, σύνθεσις: 'service') that included tableware, drinking vessels and all indispensable items for a good dinner (Paul. sent. 3,6,86). Otherwise, crockery was more modest and less opulent. Meals were often heavily staged. The feast of Trimalchio (Petron.) is a caricature but, nevertheless, telling: bowls and presentation plates (*ferculum*) took an important place in its course: they were brought in by servants with much ceremony (paintings in a house near the Lateran in Rome) [2], loaded with various dishes, appetizers, vegetables and meat, the arrangement of which alone could be a spectacle. These bowls could be very large (the largest preserved ones exceed a diameter of 60 cm) but the sizes were probably standardized: a potter's bill of La Graufesenque (France) differentiates *catini* (i.e. bowls for servants) of one foot (*pedales*), a half foot (*semipedales*) and a third foot (*trientales*) [3] size. Both round bowls of about 30 cm diameter and others of a lesser size (*c.* 10 cm) which probably carried other objects are known. The less frequent oval bowls were made of many different materials (silver, bronze, sometimes plated with tin or silver, terracotta or glass) ranging from 10 cm to more than 50 cm length. The largest among them used to serve poultry and fish are shown in mosaics and paintings. The oval bowls are not very deep. Likewise, round bowls are either flat or only slightly concave. Both are often united in the same ensemble. Basins, often ribbed, were used for serving. The vessels filled with food on the table had very different shapes, as is evident in paintings from Pompeii: sometimes they are flat with a vertical edge, sometimes more strongly concave; in those cases they are true bowls or even buckets (*situla*). However, it is difficult to determine their exact function: according to their size and appearance the basins were perhaps used to allow guests to wash their hands; the pails were often used for wine but also filled with fruit. Small dishes (*acetabulum*) permitted presenting the much appreciated sauces. Salt was often offered in small open vessels, spices in jars, often in the shape of vases (amphoras) or small statues with intricate small devices for opening and closing. Some of these objects had a double function:

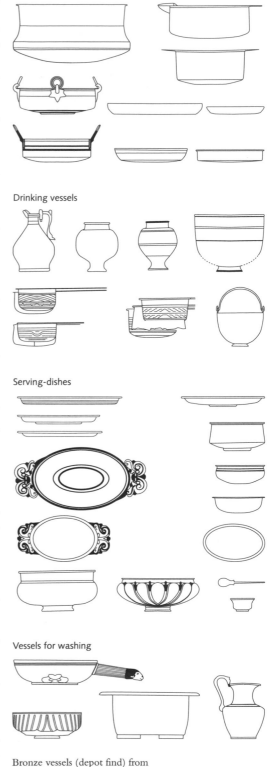

Cooking vessels

Drinking vessels

Serving-dishes

Vessels for washing

Bronze vessels (depot find) from Augusta Raurica/Augst (Roman).

silver egg cups in Pompeii and in Boscoreale become small stands when turned over. There are no personal pieces such as plates.

Some terracotta or metal tableware is present three- or four-fold as finds and texts show (inventory of a silver hoard, Berlin PM 8935, mid 1st cent. AD) [4].

→ Table Utensils

1 F. BARATTE, La vaisselle de bronze et d'argent sur les monuments figurés romains, in: Bulletin de la Société nationale des antiquaires de France, 1990, 89–107 2 G. CASSINI, Pitture antiche ritrovate accanto il v. ospedale di S. Giovanni, 1783 3 R. MARICHAL, Les graffites de La Graufesenque, Gallia, 47. ed., 1988 4 F. DREXEL, Ein ägypt. Silberinventar der Kaiserzeit, in: MDAI(R) 36/7, 1921/1922, 34–57.

F. BARATTE, La vaisselle d'argent en Gaule dans l'antiquité tardive, 1993; W. HILGERS, Lat. Gefäßnamen, 1969; S. MARTIN-KILCHER, Services de table en métal précieux du 1er au 5e siècle après Jésus-Christ, in: F. BARATTE, K. PAINTER (ed.), Trésors d'orfèvrerie gallo-romains, 1989, 15–190; L. SCHWINDEN, Ein neugefundener Silberteller mit Graffiti aus der röm. Villa von Wittlich, in: Funde und Ausgrabungen im Bezirk Trier, 1989, 19–29; D. E. STRONG, Greek and Roman Gold and Silver Plate, 1966. F. BA.

Crocodile 1) Nile crocodile; *Crocodilus niloticus Cuv.*; first described by Hdt. 2,68 (κροκόδειλος, Egyptian also *chámpsas*); *crocodilus*, Isid. Orig. 12,6,19; Egyptian *msḥ*. It is about 8 m long (more than 11 m according to Ael. NA. 17,6), it has a rather short tongue (Aristot. Part. an. 2,17,660b 27–29; Plut. De Is. et Os. 75). Lifting the skull together with the immobile upper jaw in the apparent resting position gave the impression that only the upper jaw is mobile (Plin. HN 8,89; 11,159; cf. Hdt. 2,68; Aristot. Hist. an. 1,11,492b 23f.). As lung breathers (Aristot. Hist. an. 1,1,487a 22) crocodiles lay eggs (Plin. HN 8,89) that they supposedly brood alternately (Plin. HN 10,170, but correctly Cic. Nat. D. 2,129), staying in the water at night (Cic. Nat. D. 2,124). They have a close association with the 'crocodile bird,' a river-bank bird (τρόχιλος/*tróchilos*, *Pluvianus aegyptius*) (Hdt. 2,28; Ael. NA 3,11; 12,15; Apul. Apol. 8), and with → dolphins [1] but on hostile terms because as competitors they allegedly cut open their bellies with their sharp back fin (Plin. HN 8,91; Solin. 32,26). Crocodiles reach an age of 60 years (Ael. NA 10,21) and multiply very fast because they are rarely killed (Diod. Sic. 1,35; cf. n. 22,15,15–20), unless their eggs are broken by the → *ichneumon* (Diod. Sic. ibid.).

Crocodiles were caught with bait on a fishing rod (Hdt. 2,70; Diod. Sic. 1,35), with nets (Diod. Sic. 1,35) or a harpoon (Ael. NA 10,24; Str. 17,814). In 58 BC 5 crocodiles were displayed for the first time in Rome (Plin. HN 8,96), Augustus had 36 crocodiles killed in the Circus Flaminius (Cass. Dio 55,10). Elagabalus [2] had a pet crocodile (SHA Heliogab. 17,28,3). Symmachus reported in his letters about unsuccessfully keeping crocodiles for his games (Symm. Ep. 9,141; 151; 6,43) [1. 212f.]. According to Hdt. 2,69; 90; Str.

17,811; Diod. Sic. 1,89 the crocodile was sacred to some Egyptians, especially in → Arsinoe [III 2] [2. 292f.] but not to the inhabitants of → Elephantine and Apollonopolis (Hdt. 2,69; Ael. NA 10,21). Numerous mummified and interred holy crocodiles (Cic. Tusc. 5,18; Cic. Nat. D. 1,82; 101; 3,47; Juv. 15,2; Tert. adversus Marcionem 2,14) are preserved in modern museums.

In therapeutic practise it was recommended to use the fat as an ointment against fever and to use the fragrant entrails against any kind of facial blotch (Plin. HN 28,107–111; cf. 121 and Scribonius Largus 14). Stuffed crocodiles were hung up in Roman salve shops (GLM p. 52 R. *ad pigmentarios*). The crocodile also occurs in fables (Aesop. 37 HAUSRATH; Phaedr. 1,25; cf. Ael. VH 1,4). Asterius [2] is the first to mention crocodile tears after eating a human (in Phot. p. 503), in Latin for the first time Ps.-Hugh of St. Victor, De bestiis 2,8 [4. 60]. Crocodiles are often found in Roman art, e.g., fighting pygmies in a Pompeian mural [1. fig. 113]; other attestations in [1. 213; 3. 161f., 354, 375–377, 384]. The crocodile is also common on coins and jewellery [5. pl. 6,29–31; 14,1; 15,4; 22,46–48].

2) The slender-snouted crocodile of NW and West Africa (*C. cataphractus Cuv.*) is perhaps mentioned in Plin. HN 5,9.

3) The mugger crocodile (*C. palustris Cuv.*) of India was known to Hdt. 4,44; Ael. NA 12,41; Plin. HN 6,75 and, without being named, to Str. 15,690 and 695f.; Paus. 4,34,3 and Curt. 8,9,9 (30).

4) The gharial (*Gavialis gangeticus Gm.*) of the Ganges river with its long snout was considered sacred in India according to Ael. NA 12,41.

5) Whether Ctesias (Phot. bibliotheke 45a 20ff.; Ael. NA 5,3) intended the saltwater crocodile (*C. porosus Gray*) cannot be decided.

→ Lizard

1 TOYNBEE, Tierwelt 2 RÄRG 3 REINACH, RP 4 Hugo de Sancto Victore, Opera omnia, vol. 3 (PL 178), 1879 5 F. IMHOOF-BLUMER, O. KELLER, Tier- und Pflanzenbilder auf Mz. und Gemmen des klass. Alt., 1889, repr. 1972.

H. GOSSEN, A. STEIER, s.v. Krokodil, RE 11, 1947–56; KELLER, vol. 2, 260–270. C. HÜ.

Crocon (Κρόκων). Mythical king who ruled in the border area of Eleusis and Athens (Paus. 1,38,2). He was married to Saisara, a daughter of → Celeus. According to the Eleusian myth he was a son of → Triptolemus. Triptolemus was usually considered a son of Celeus and Metaneira (cf. Apollod. 3,102). The eponymous hero was accepted into the sacred Eleusian family. The name C. is derived from the cultic action of the κροκοῦν/*krokoûn*, laying of wool threads into the right hand and on the left foot of the *mystes*. The family of the Croconides built a sanctuary of → Hestia in the 4th cent. and sued the Coeronides, who claimed lineage from Coeron, an illegitimate son of Triptolemus.

Crocus

[1] (Κρόκος). *Stratēgós* (*autokrátōr*; → Lochos) of Cyprus during the Egyptian civil war 131–124/3 BC.

R. BAGNALL, The Administration of the Ptolemaic Possessions outside Egypt, 1976, 259; L. MOOREN, The Aulic Titulature in Ptolemaic Egypt, 1975, 191f. no. 0354.

W.A.

[2] The genus Crocus (the word κρόκος/*krókos* is Pre-Greek with Semitic analogues) has its greatest diversity in Anatolia with 32 species. The extraordinary splendour of the colour of mass occurrences in the mountains (first on the bed of the Gods on Mount Ida, Hom. Il. 14,348, with the yellow endemic *Crocus gargaricus* [1. 74f.]); the use of the stamen as spice, medicine, dye and perfume and its popularity as a cultivated and garden plant secured the crocus general fame in mythology and daily life in all of Graeco-Roman antiquity (references in [2]; on making salves add Theophr. De odoribus 27 and 34). Apart from using wild species, the fall-flowering violet saffron, *Crocus sativus L.*, with its particularly large stamen was cultivated. It was probably produced by selection from the S Aegean *Crocus cartwrightianus* [1. 55–57]. Saffron is described in detail in Theophrastus Hist. pl. 6,6,10 (cf. [3. 192–194]; figures: [1. fig. 29 a; 4. 153]. Pliny (HN 21,137–139) particularly praises *crocus* as medicine. The 'thorny' crocus of Theophr. Hist. pl. 7,7,4 is the false saffron (safflower, *Carthamus tinctorius L.*).

1 B. MATHEW, The Crocus — A Revision of the Genus Crocus (Iridaceae), 1982   2 F. ORTH, s.v. Safran, RE 1A, 1728–1731   3 S. AMIGUES, Théophraste. Recherches sur les plantes, 3, 1993   4 H. BAUMANN, Die griech. Pflanzenwelt, 1982   5 Id., Greek Wild Flowers and Plant Lore in Ancient Greece, translated and augmented by W. T. and E. R. STEARN, 1993.

B.HE.

Croesus (Κροῖσος; *Kroîsos*, Latin Croesus).

A. HISTORIC PERSON

Lydian king (*c.* 560–547 BC), last of the Mermnad dynasty (→ Mermnadae). The most important source remains → Herodotus' Lydian Logos (Hdt. 1,6–94), even though he preserved little that is Ancient Anatolian. C.'s mother was Carian (→ Caria), that of his brother Pantaleon Ionian (Hdt. 1,92). A queen is never mentioned.

As prince Croesus was the mercenary captain and governor in → Adramyttium (FGrH 90 F 65), later perhaps co-regent at the side of his father → Alyattes and finally his successor (cf. Hdt. 1,92). Although he was heir designate, the way to the throne was murderous (cf. Plut. Mor. 401e). In gratitude C. later donated a golden statue in Delphi to his protective deity Artemis/Magna Mater, at least (1,51) can be interpreted that way. Artemis was equally honoured by Lydians, Carians and Greeks.

Croesus concluded a treaty of friendship with the Ionians of the islands (Hdt. 1,27). He was the first to make the Greek cities on the mainland of Asia minor pay taxes (Hdt. 1,6; 27); before him there were only punitive expeditions and tribute collection. Two mainland cities received a special status: Ephesus and Milet. The Milesians remained friends and allies (Hdt. 1,22; 141). Ephesus, which was governed by C.'s nephew → Pindar was besieged by C. but was able to preserve its freedom by placing itself under the protection of Artemis (Polyaenus, Strat. 6,50). As in the sanctuaries in Troy and Didyma, C. also acted as a refounder or donor: the Artemisium retained its ancient Anatolian character; a subsidiary sanctuary existed in → Sardeis.

C. gained his proverbial wealth from mines in the Pergamum region (Aristot. Mir. 834). However, he probably acquired gold for minting through the Milesians from the Black Sea region (cf. Aristeas FGrH 35 F 4).

C. was a great conqueror. Herodotus (1,28) provides a catalogue of all his subjects. The boundary of his empire towards → Media was the river Halys (Hdt. 1,103), but only in its upper reaches Mazaka/Pteria? (modern Kayseri). C.'s military practise was traditional: carefully tested oracles were consulted (→ Delphi), the actual warfare transferred to the crown prince, a pitched battle was sought, conquered cities were cursed (Str. 13,1,42), the inhabitants were deported (Hdt. 1,76).

Sandanis, a Lydian with a Luwian name, attempted in vain to keep C. from going to war against → Cyrus [2] (Hdt. 1,71). C. concluded alliances with Egypt, Babylon and Sparta (Hdt. 1,69; 77). Cappadocia (Median Katpatuka, Greek Cilicia) was stated as the objective. C. was defeated in two battles (Hdt. 1,73–85). It cannot be determined with certainty if C. was killed or pardoned. C.'s years of government — 14 years (2×7) and 14 days (Hdt. 1, 86) — are probably of magical derivation.

C. H. GREENWALT, JR., Croesus of Sardis, in: J. M. SASSON (ed.), Civilizations of the Ancient Near East II, 1995, 1173–1183; D. G. HOGARTH, Lydia, in: CAH III ²1960, 501–524.

PE.HÖ.

B. CROESUS IN GREEK AND LATIN TRADITION

Already early in the 5th cent. BC, 50 years before Herodotus' famous C. story (s. A.), imagery and literary testimonials attesting to a deep Greek interest in the figure of C. are documented. C. appears especially in Delphi — because of his generous dedications — as the model of the pious ruler (Pind. Pyth. 1, 94; Bacchyl. 3, 23–62), who reacts to his 'tragic' overthrow by → Cyrus [2] with the 'heroic' [1. 8] act of self-immolation (Amphora of Myson, 490 BC: C. on the pyre [2]; Bacchyl. loc. cit.: solution of the problem in theodicy by having Apollo extinguishing the burning pyre with a rainstorm and removing C. to the Hyperboreans). There is indication of a C. tragedy in the 1st half of the 5th cent. (see [1. 10]; [3]: trilogy, in which C. must pay for the shortcomings of → Gyges (?); by contrast [4. 329]).

Herodotus was the first to consider the cause of C.'s tragic fate in terms of his ethical misdeeds or misjudgement (especially Hdt. 1, 29–33; 34,1; 86–91): the same 'blindness' and 'haughtiness' (*hýbris*), with which C. considers himself in conversation with Solon (1, 27–31; 32,1) to be the most fortunate man and causes him grasp prevents him from grasping Solon's warning against the 'envy of the gods' (*phthónos tôn theôn*) and the frailty of human fate, causing him to misinterpret the Delphic oracle and to engage in the fateful attack on Cyrus. Only on the pyre (Hdt. 1, 86–91) did he recognize the 'truth' of Solon's view of life; because he relates his conversation with Solon, he is pardoned by Cyrus and becomes his wise councillor (see also Hdt. 1, 207) [4; 5. 11ff.].

Subsequently, the example of C. enjoyed great popularity among Greek and Roman authors (s. Plut. Solon 27,1; compilation of passages [6; 8. 455]). Apart from use of the material in mirrors of princes and panegyrics of rulers, (Xen. Cyr. 7,2,9–29; Lib. Or. 18,74: Iulianos [11] Apostata) two main tendencies are evident in interpretation: admonition against the vicissitudes of human fortunes (e.g. Diod. Sic. 9, 2–4; Plut. Solon, 27: *sóphrosýnē* of Solon) and the cynical (or stoic) contrast of wealth and fortune (e.g. Lucian, Charon 9–13). In the modern period the material was resumed by the opera, for example, by R. KEISER Der hochmütige, gestürzte und wieder erhabene Croesus ['The Vain, Humbled and Restored Croesus'] ([7]; performed: Hamburg 1710 and 1730) — with an explicit didactic objective on the 'impermanence of worldly honours and wealth' (ibid.). The tradition of C.'s legendary wealth continues to this day (attestation see [8. 465f.]).

→ Herodotus; → Hybris; → Cyrus; → Solon

1 W. BURKERT, Das Ende des Kroisos Vorstufen einer herodoteischen Geschichtserzählung, in: Ch. Schäublin (ed.), Catalepton. FS B. Wyss, 1985, 4–15   2 E. SIMON, Die griech. Vasen, 1976, 107f. with fig. 133   3 B. SNELL, Gyges und Kroisos als Tragödienfiguren, in: ZPE 12, 1973, 197–205   4 D. ASHERI, Erodoto, Le storie, vol. 1, 1988, XLVff.; CVIIff.; 281ff.; 320f.   5 P. OLIVA, Solon— Legende und Wirklichkeit (Konstanzer Althistorische Vorträge und Forsch. 20), 1988, 11–17; 84f.   6 Id., Die Gesch. von Kroisos und Solon, in: Das Altertum 21, 1975, 175–181   7 U. SCHREIBER, Die Kunst der Oper, vol. 1, 1988, 160f.   8 F. H. WEISSBACH, s.v. Kroisos, RE Suppl. 5, 1931, 455–472.

I. FRINGS, Der Weise und der König: Solon und Kroisos bei Herodot und Lukian (Xenia Toruniensia 2), 1996.

CHR.SCH.

Crommyon (Κρομμυών or Κρεμμυών). Fortified port in the East of Corinthian territory on the Saronian Gulf south of the → Gerania mountains, 120 stadia (*c.* 21 km) from → Corinth (Thuc. 4,45,1), probably near modern Hagios Theodori. According to legend Theseus killed the Crommyonian sow there. In the Classical period Crommyon was fortified. Evidence: Scyl. 55; Str. 8,6,22; Paus. 2,1,3; Xen. Hell. 4,4,13; 5,19; Steph. Byz.

s.v. Krommyon; Hierocles, Synekdemos 645,14. Epigraphy: IG IV 195f.   Y.L.

Cromna (Κρῶμνα) Milesian → *apoikía* East of Sesamos (later → Amastris [4]) on the Paphlagonian Black Sea coast, modern Tekkeönü. C. claimed to be the birthplace of Homer (Ὅμηρος Κρομνεύς [1]). C. 300 BC C. was integrated into a *synoikismós* with Amastris, which then took over the claim and in the Imperial period minted (ps.-autonomous) coins with the portrait of Homer and the inscription Ὅμηρος Ἀμαστριαν(ός) [2].

1 L. ROBERT, Études anatoliennes, 1937, 262–265   2 Id., À travers l'Asie Mineure, 1980, 415–417.   C.MA.

Cromnus (Κρῶμνος, Κρῶμνα, Κρῶμναι, Κρῶμοι). Place in the Arcadian region of Cromnitis on the road from Megalopolis to Messene, 11 km south of Megalopolis, possibly on a hill *c.* 2 km north-east of modern Paradisia (Παραδείσια). Incorporated into the foundation of Megalopolis. Attested in Paus. 8,3,4; 27,4; 34,5f.; Xen. Hell. 7,4,20–28; Callisthenes, FGrH 124 F 13; Steph. Byz., s.v. Κρῶμνα.

J. ROY et al., Two Sites in the Megalopolis Basin, in: J. M. SANDERS (ed.), ΦΙΛΟΛΑΚΩΝ, 1992, 190–194.   Y.L.

Cronion (Κρόνιον). A hill with pine growth (123 m) above the Altis in → Olympia with a Cronos cult only attested in literature (priesthood of the Βασίλαι/ *Basílai*): Xen. Hell. 7,4,14; Pind. Ol. 1,111; 5,17; 6,64; 9,3; Paus. 5,21,2; 6,19,1; 20,1f.; Dion. Hal. Ant. Rom. 1,34,3.   E.MEY. and E.O.

Cronius (Κρόνιος; *Krónios*).

[1] Platonist (Syranus, In Aristot. Metaph. 109,11) of the Pythagorizing tendency, mostly called a Pythagorean, (perhaps older) contemporary and friend (Porph. De anthro nympharum 21) of → Numenius, about the mid 2nd cent. AD. As a rule C. is only mentioned with him but frequently before him and generally shares his opinion. C. was read in the school of Plotin (Porph. Vita Pythagorica 14); he composed hypomnemata (ibid., probably no commentaries on whole writings) and a treatise 'On rebirth' (Περὶ παλιγγενεσίας, Nemesius, De natura hominis 2,114). Most testimonia concern the teachings of the soul: like Numenius and → Harpocration [1] C. did not hold the soul but rather matter responsible for evil (Stob. 1,375,14ff. W.). He also considered any incorporation (metempsychosis) of the soul evil (ibid. 380,16ff.) and denied one in animals (Nemesius, De natura hominis 2,114).

C. treated at least individual passages or questions in Plato's 'State' and 'Timaeus', in the former the 'Marriage Number' (Procl. in Plat. Rep. 2,23,6ff. K.) and the Myth of Er (ibid. 2,109,7ff.). That it was found in a work attributed to Zoroaster is explained by C. with → Er being → Zoroaster's teacher; here we see C.'s interest in non-Greek traditions. The question of the sense in which the cosmos came into being derives from 'Timaeus' (ibid. 2,22,20ff.). Another interest was → allegory: C. attempts to show that Homer's cave of the Nymphs can only be understood allegorically (Porph. De antro nympharum 2–3).

TESTIMONIA: E. A. LEEMANS, Numenius van Apamea, 1937, 153–157.
BIBLIOGRAPHY: J. DILLON, The Middle Platonists, 1977, 379–380.   M.FR.

[2] Son of the *epistratēgós* Callimachus [8], (older?) brother of a Callimachus, *syngenēs* either in 56 or 50 BC, then *syngenēs* and *epistratēgós*. He probably followed directly after his father, holding office after March 39.

PP I/VIII 194 b; L. M. RICKETTS, The Epistrategos Kallimachos and a Koptite Inscription, in: AncSoc 13/4, 1982/3, 161–165; esp. 164 with n. **; J. D. THOMAS, The Epistrategos in Ptolemaic and Roman Egypt 1, 1975, 109 no. XIII.   W.A.

Cropidae (Κρωπίδαι; *Krōpídai*). Attic *mesogea* deme of the Leontis phyle, a *bouleutēs*, also attested as Κρωπιάς or Κρῶπες (Steph. Byz. s.v. Κρωπιά), Κρωπίδης demoticon. Cropia was probably the name of the region [2. 2019]. Κλωπίδαι, which is also attested on inscriptions (Aristoph. Equ. 79) [2], possibly belonged to Aphidna [3. 90f., 116 no. 19; 4. 55, 62]. In 431 BC → Archidamus [1] travelled to Acharnae through C., which is located by [3. 47; 4. 131] to the west of Ano Liosia (Thuc. 2,19). With Eupyridae and Peleces, C. formed a 'three village unit' (τριχωμία, Steph. Byz. s.v. Εὐπυρίδαι) [5. 185⁴⁶].

1 C. W. J. ELIOT, The Coastal Demes of Attica, 1962, 150 n. 31   2 E. HONIGMANN, s.v. Kropia, RE 11, 2019   3 TRAILL, Attica 47, 62, 69, 111 no. 78, table 4   4 J. S. TRAILL, Demos and Trittys, 1986.   5 WHITEHEAD.
                                                        H.LO.

Cross, legend of the Holy see → Helena [2]

Croton (Κρότων, *Krótōn*, Lat. *Croto[n]*). City founded in around 733 BC by Achaean colonists under → Myscellus from Rhypae, in response to a Delphic oracle, on the eastern coast of → Bruttium in southern Italy (Antiochus, FGrH 555 F 10). In the 6th cent. BC, C. expanded at the expense of its neighbouring colonies: important milestones were the capture and destruction of Siris in the middle of the 6th cent, the defeat against Locri on the Sagra in 548 and the destruction of Sybaris in 510 BC (Hdt. 5,44; 6,21). C. controlled a large territory between the rivers Neaethus in the north and Tacina (Thagines) in the south and extended to the Crotonian colony Terina on the Tyrrhenian Sea; to its *chóra* belonged Crimisa, near today's Punta Alice, founded by Philoctetes (Lycophr. Alexandra 913; Str. 6,1,3). At the end of the 6th cent. BC, → Pythagoras worked in C. and founded a school there (Liv. 1,18,2; Iust. 20,4,2ff.). Other people who came from C.: → Alcmaeon [4],

→ Cylon [2]. At the end of the 5th cent., C. established an Italiot league based in → Heraclea [10] for the protection against the Italic peoples. C. was conquered by Dionysius I, then besieged by the → Bruttii, and finally destroyed by → Agathocles [2] in 295 BC. In the Pyrrhic War (→ Pyrrhus) C. was occupied by the Romans for the first time in 277 BC; it was abandoned towards the end of the Second → Punic War. A Roman colony developed in 194 BC.

C. lay in a plain surrounded by hills at the mouth of the Aesarus, which served as a harbour; initial settlement *katà kōmas* ('in villages'). An extended circular wall was built in the 5th cent. BC. The city consisted of three settlement cores. The street grid probably dates to the end of the 7th or beginning of the 6th cent BC. A belt of necropoleis lies on the hills surrounding the city centre: in Vela, on the hill S. Giorgio, in S. Francesco, on the hill Viscovatello, and in Carrara. Votive objects attest to a sanctuary, possibly dedicated to Hera, outside the walls at Vigna Nuova. Cult sites have been found outside the city at today's Capo Colonna, at S. Anna di Cutro and Giammiglione di Scandale. The Roman colony withdrew to the hill of Castello in today's historical centre; necropoleis from the Imperial Period cover large areas of the eastern parts of the city of the Greek period.

Crotone. Atti del XXIII Convegno di Studi sulla Magna Grecia Taranto 1983, 1986, 4; BTCGI 5, 472–521; M. SASSI, Tra Religione e scienza, in: S. SETTIS (ed.), La Calabria antica, 1988, 565–587; M. GIANGIULIO, Ricerche su Crotone arcaica, 1989; M. OSANNA, *Chorai* coloniali da Taranto a Locri, 1992, 167–200; A. MUGGIA, L'area di rispetto nelle colonie magno-greche e siceliote, 1997, especially 64–69.   A.MU.

Crotopus (Κρότωπος; *Krótōpos*). King of Argos (cf. → Coroebus [1]), son of Agenor, father of Sthenelas and Psamathe (Paus. 2,16,1). C.'s grave lay in Argos, where later on a temple of Dionysus was erected (Paus. 2,37,7). After killing Python, Apollo visits C. in expiation (Stat. Theb. 1,570). Psamathe bears the god a son, → Linus. C. condemns her to death when he learns of her relationship with Apollo. The latter punishes Argos with a plague (Conon, FGrH 26 F 1 19).   RE.ZI.

Crow In antiquity seven varieties of the crow family (Corvidae) were identified: 1. the common raven (κόραξ/*kórax*, Lat. *corvus*; *Corvus corax* L.); 2. the carrion crow and hooded crow (κορώνη/*korōnē*, Lat. *cornix, cornicula*; *C. corone* L. and *C. cornix* L.) and probably also the gregarious nester, the rook (*C. frugilegus* L.); 3. the → jackdaw (κολοιός/*koloiós*, βωμωλόχος/*bōmōlóchos*, Lat. *monedula* or *graculus*; *Coloeus monedula*); 4. the → jay (κίσσα/*kíssa*, κίττα/*kítta*, Lat. *pica*; *Garrulus glandarius*); 5. the → magpie (*Pica pica*), linguistically not distinguished from no. 4; 6. the Cornish chough (κολοιὸς κορακίας/*koloiòs korakías*, *Pyrrhocorax pyrrhocorax*) and 7. the Alpine chough (*pyrrhocorax, P. graculus*). Only the three most important of these will be discussed here:

In antiquity the carrion crow and hooded crow were neither distinguished from each other nor from the rook. Their care of their young was regarded as exemplary, as the male fed the brooding female (Aristot. Hist. an. 6,8,564a 15–18; cf. Ael. NA 3,9), and both parents fed the young even after they were able to leave the nest (Aristot. Hist. an. 6,6,563b 11–13; Plin. HN 10,30; Basil. Hexaemeron 8,6,6; Ambr. Hexaemeron 5,18,58). Because of their heavy head the sightless young (Aristot. Gen. an. 4,6,774b 26–28) were said to leave the egg tail first (Plin. HN 10,38; Dionysii Ixeuticon 1,10). In winter they were to be found close to cities (Aristot. Hist. an. 8(9),23,617b 12f.), though not on the acropolis (Ael. NA 5,8) or in Athens itself (Plin. HN 10,30; cf. Aesop. 213 H.). They were rare in Africa (Aug. Epist. 118,9). They cracked nuts by dropping them from the sky onto a rock below (Plin. HN 10,30). They were friendly with herons (Aristot. Hist. an. 8(9),1,610a 8; Plin. HN 10,207) and grazing cattle (Ov. Am. 3,5,21–24). They did not get on well with the little owlet, the bird of Athena/Minerva (→ Owls) (Aristot. Hist. an. 8(9),1,609a 8–12; Plin. HN 10,203; Ov. Fast. 2,89 and Am. 2,6,35: armiferae cornix invisa Minervae; Ael. NA 3,9) or with the goshawk (Ael. NA 6,45) or the weasel (Aristot. Hist. an. 8(9),1,609a 17; Plin. HN 10,204). They were said to reach an age nine times greater than that of humans (Hes. fr. 171 RZACH; Ov. Am. 2,6,36: illa [sc. cornix] quidem saeclis vix moritura novem), like → Nestor (schol. Juv. 10,247; Priap. 57 and 61,11; Plin. HN 7,153), to be good carriers of mail (Ael. NA 6,7 with the anecdote of the grave of a tame crow that had belonged to an Egyptian king) and able to be trained to imitate the human voice (Varro, Ling. 6,56). The hooded crow was regarded as a bird of prophecy and a weather forecaster (Plaut. Asin. 260; Plin. HN 18,363; Isid. Orig. 12,7,44 with a quotation from Verg. G. 1,388), though this was refuted by Cic. Div. 2,78 and Nat. D. 3,14; Prudent. Contra Symmachum 2,571 and Isidore loc. cit. It also appears in fable (Aesop. 212; 358 and 415 H.; Hor. Epist. 1,3,19) and proverbs (e.g. schol. Cic. Flac. 46; Mur. 25).

The Cornish chough has a long, red (φοινικόρυγχος/ phoinikórynchos) beak that arches downwards and is mentioned only in Aristot. Hist. an. 8(9),24, 617b 16f. as one of the three varieties of jackdaw.

The Alpine chough, to be found in the Alps, is correctly described by Plin. HN 10,133 as black with a yellow beak.

H. GOSSEN, A. STEIER, s.v. Krähe, RE 11, 1556ff.; KELLER vol. 2, 91–114. C.HÜ.

Crucifixion see → Damnatio ad crucem

Crumerum Military camp and vicus on the Danube embankment road east of Brigetio in Pannonia superior, now Nyergesújfalu (Komárom, Hungary). The site was established at the end of the 2nd cent, and in the 2nd/3rd cents. was the base for the cohors V Callaeco-

rum Lucensium (CIL III 3662–3664), in the 4th cent. for the equites promoti (Not. Dign. Occ. 33,30). Rebuilt in the period of Constantine and fortified with corner turrets (It. Ant. 246,2; 266,8; Not. Dign. Occ. 33,9,30; CIL III 3662–3666, 10602; Κοῦρτα in Ptol. 2,11,5; 15,4).

C. PATSCH, s.v. C., RE 4, 1726; A. GRAF, Übersicht der ant. Geogr. von Pannonien, 1936, 94; TIR L 34 Budapest, 1968, 50 (bibliography); S. SOPRONI, s.v. C., in: J. FITZ (ed.), Der röm. Limes in Ungarn, 1976, 43. J.BU.

Crus Nickname ('lower leg') referring to a peculiarity of the legs; cognomen in the family of the Cornelii (→ Cornelius [I 50]) Lentuli.

A. HUG, s.v. Spitznamen, RE 3A, 1828; KAJANTO, Cognomina 225. K.-L.E.

Crusis (Κρουσίς; Krousís). This region named in Hdt. 7,123,2, Thuc. 2,79,4, Str. 7, fr. 21 and Steph. Byz. s.v., lay to the north of → Bottice on the north-west coast of the Chalcidic peninsula between cape Megalo Karaburnu and Nea Kallikrateia. Its coastal towns Aenea, Smila, Scapsa, Gigonus and Haisa are mentioned already in Hecataeus and in Herodotus' account of Xerxes' campaign, and attested, in some cases from 452/1 BC, in others only from 434/3 (together with the inland localities of Cithas and Tinde), as members of the → Delian League. Most of them defected in the course of 432, but some were very quickly won back again. Only Aenea, Scapsa and possibly Tinde are named as surviving in the 4th cent. BC, and only Aenea beyond the Hellenistic period.

F. PAPAZOGLOU, Les villes de Macedoine à l'époque romaine, 1988, 415–421; M. ZAHRNT, Olynth und die Chalkidier, 1971, 195–198. M.Z.

Crusta, Crustae Ancient technical term used in → construction technique. According to Vitruvius (2,8,7 and passim), a term for the frames or facings of walls made from cast cement (→ opus caementicium), later used generally for the covering of floors, roofs and walls with → stucco, marble, travertine or → mosaic. In → toreutics crusta also refers to the relief-adorned 'jacket', the 'shell' surrounding the body of the receptacle proper.

GEORGES 1, s.v. c., 1775f.; A. RUMPP, s.v. C., KlP 1, 1336; H.-O. LAMPRECHT, Opus Caementicium Bautechnik der Römer, ⁴1993, 38–44. C.HÖ.

Crustaceans

A. GENERAL

The class Crustacea of the arthropod family, to be found, in many varieties, mainly in the sea but also in freshwater. The Greeks called them 'soft-shelled' (μαλακόστρακα/malakóstraka, Aristot. Hist. an. 1,6,490b 10–12 and passim; Speusippus in Ath.

3,105b; erroneously as ὀστρακόδερμα/*ostrakóderma*, Ael. NA 9,6 following Aristot. Hist. an. 7(8),17,601a 17f., where these names are meant, however to distinguish different types of crab). The Romans used *contecta crustis tenuibus* (Plin. HN 9,83) or *crustis intecta* (Plin. HN 9,43) or *crustata* (Plin. HN 11,165) to describe the soft-shell quality. Eustathius uses *mollitestia* to translate the term (7.2) in the 'Hexaemeron' of Basilius. Trying to differentiate ancient varieties in the literature from the 5th cent. is difficult. Aristotle and apparently — because of the culinary importance — Greek doctors (5th and 4th cents.) provide a great deal of good information. Details touch on the characteristic variations of legs, which sometimes included the pincers, the thin armour that surrounds the soft, fleshy body and has to be shed and replaced at regular intervals, the absence of any voice, its often predatory eating habits, its metabolism, reproductive system and gill breathing. Various types of crustaceans were differentiated, furthermore also cray fish, → lobsters, shrimps and woodlice/sow bugs.

B. CRABS

Of the order of the decapoda ('ten feet'), subdivision crabs, Brachyura (crabs), καρκίνος/*karkínos*, Lat. *cancer* (the origin of which Isid. Orig. 12,6,51 falsely derives from the mussel, *concha*), less common names καρκίνιον/*karkínion*, καρκινίδιον/*karkinídion*, καρκινοειδές/*karkinoeidés*, Sicilian κάρχας/*kárchas*.

C. FAMILY OF THE RECTANGULAR CRUSTACEANS

Living on land, especially in tropical and subtropical countries, the following have been attested: 1) the marbled rectangular crab, *Grapsus marmoratus* Fabr., on a lapis lazuli gemstone [1. pl. 24,31], 2) the *Gonoplax rhomboides*, on a red jasper [1. pl. 24,30], 3) the beak-crab, *Corystes dentatus*, on a vase from Caere [2. 2, fig. 145], 4) the river crab (*Astacus astacus*), frequently on coins (e.g. [1. pl. 8,6 and 7]), important in popular medicine and agriculture (for deterring pests), 5) the oyster crab, πιν(ν)οτήρης/ *pin(n)otérēs*, πιν(ν)οφύλαξ/ *pin(n)ophýlax*, *Pinnoteres pisum*, which (with a shell length of 10–18 mm) lives, for example, inside wing shells and is said to die with them. No real symbiosis takes place. The creature was, however, a prime example for Chrysippus' [2] Stoic concept of nature (fr. 729a SVF 2,207 = Ath. 3,89c-e), which Plutarch (De sollertia animalium 30 = Mor. 980a-c) derides. In Soph. fr. 113 N. it serves as a metaphor for something tiny (carnelian: [1. pl. 24,25]).

D. FAMILY OF THE BOW-CRAYFISH

These live mostly on stones or walls in water. We have been able to identify 1) the *cancer marinus*, καρκίνος θαλάσσιος/ *karkínos thalássios*, 2) the North Sea or common crab (*Cancer pagurus* L.), καρκίνος Ἡρακλεωτικός/*karkínos Hērakleōtikós*, 3) the *Xantho florida*, depicted on both a Parisian and a Viennese carnelian [1. 24 and 32].

E. FAMILY OF TRIANGULAR CRUSTACEANS (?)

With the varieties γραῦς/*graûs* and πάγουρος/ *págouros*. Their capture with enticing music is described in Ael. NA 6,31 and in 9,43, their behaviour during sloughing. Gp. 5,50,1 mentions their efficacy in combatting pests. Descriptions of all representative varieties are given in Batr. 294–300 and Aristot. Hist. an. 4,2,525b 16ff. Realistic depictions are to be found on frescoes, plates, vases, coins and gemstones. According to Gregory of Tours (De cursu stellarum 8) the famous lighthouse of Pharus was constructed on top of four crustaceans hewn into stone.

F. FAMILY OF CARCINIA

Καρκίνια/*karkínia* are described in detail at Aristot. Hist. an. 4,4,529b 20–530a 7 and 5,15,548a 14–21. The varieties of hermit crabs can be defined in terms of the shells of their host snails νηρείτης/*nēreítēs* or στρόμβος/ *strómbos* [2. 2,489].

G. FAMILY OF UROPODS

To these probably belongs, *Eriphia spinifrons*, depicted on two gemstones [1. pl. 24,33]. Representative of sea cray fish are the cray fish, κάραβος/*kárabos*, *locusta*, or the spiny lobster (*Palinurus vulgaris*) and the slipper lobster (*Scyllarus arctus*), κάραβος ἄρκτος/ *kárabos árktos* or καραβίς/*karabís*. A good description of the behaviour of the crayfish with its red colouring, long body with a tail-shaped rear end, 5 sets of rear legs and an enlarged right pincer is given in Aristot. Hist. an. 5,17, 549a 14–b 28. Representations are to be found not only in the minor arts but also in mosaics from Pompeii and England [2. 2, fig. 124 und 147].

H. FAMILY OF TRUE CRABS

The principal representative of the true crabs (ἀσταικοί) was 1) the lobster (ἀστακός/*astakós*, Lat. *cammarus*), *Homarus vulgaris*. It was caught in most areas of the Mediterranean (but, according to Ael. NA 4,9, not the Black Sea) as a popular dish not just of the nobility. The description in Aristot. Hist. an. 4,2,526a 11–b 18 is very detailed. In Plin. HN 32,147 it is a typical sea creature. 2) The river crayfish or brook crayfish, known as ὁ ἐν τοῖς ποταμοῖς ἀστακός/*ho en toîs potamoîs astakós* and Lat. *astacus*, has been paid scant attention but is depicted on a coin from Astacus in Bithynia [1. pl. 8,7]. In Plin. HN 9,97, it is mentioned only as a variety of crustaceans 3). According to Ael. NA 14,9, the flesh of the λέων/*léōn*, Lat. *leo* (*Neophrops norvegicus*; common in the northern Adriatic), mixed with rose oil to make an ointment, was said to be a beautifying agent.

I. SHRIMPS

(The suborder of shrimps, Natantia; καρίδες/ *karídes*, Lat.*squillae*). A distinction was made between 1) the edible variety *Palaemon squilla*, καρὶς κυφή/*karis kyphé*, which appears on coins [1. pl. 8,10–14] and gemstones [1. 24,32; 26,49]; 2) the stone shrimp described in Ael. NA 1,30, *Palaemon serratus*; 3) the sand shrimp, *Crangon vulgaris* (?), μικρὸν γένος καρίδων/ *mikròn génos karídōn* in Aristot. Hist. an. 4,2,525b 2 and καριδάριον/*karidárion* (Anaxander fr. 24 K.); 4) the whip shrimp, *Peneus caramote* (?) in Ath. 7,306c (καρίδων γένος/ *karídōn génos*), which is said to have been depicted several times in the minor arts. All shrimps were called καρίς/*karís*, κούρις/*koúris* or κῶρις/ *kóris*, by Ath. 3,106b folk-etymologically derived from κάρα. The absence of pincers and their elongated body shape are characteristic. They were a popular dish in the comic writers and were used as fishing bait and as duck fodder for breeders of livestock.

J. STOMATOPODS
The order of stomatopods (*Mysis*) is probably what is meant by κραγγόνες/*krangónes* in Aristot. Hist. an. 525b 21–31. The κολύβδαινα/*kolýbdaina* = θαλάσσιον αἰδοῖον/*thalássion aidoîon* (*Squilla Desmarestii*), which Aristot. Hist. an.4,7,532b 23–26 describes, belongs here too.

K. WOODLICE/SOW BUGS
→ Woodlouse

L. FLEA CRABS
(Order Amphipoda; καρκινάδες/*karkinádes*). Several varieties of these, from both sea and river, were known of. The parasitic varieties mentioned in Aristot. Hist. an. 4,4,530a 27–29 should probably be included with them, too.

M. SUBCLASS BARNACLES/CIRRIPEDS
Cirripedia, βάλανοι/*bálanoi*, Lat. *balani*. Identifiable amongst these are 1) *Balanus cylindricus*, a large, dark variety in Egypt (Ath. 3,87f), 2) *Balanus tintinnabulum*, the balanid (?), to be found in the sea on cliffs and in marshy places. The Naples Mosaic [2. 2, fig. 124] shows at least one example on the left edge.

N. SUBCLASS COPEPODS
(The subclass Copepoda; φθεῖρες/*ptheîres*). These small crustaceans sit as parasites on the gills and fins of fish. The ψύλλος/*psýllos* and the οἶστρος/*oístros* probably belong with them, but the latter [3. 1,168] is classified there as *Cecrops Latreillii* from the family of fish lice.

1 F.IMHOOF-BLUMER, O.KELLER, Tier- und Pflanzenbilder auf Münzen und Gemmen des klass. Alt., 1889, repr. 1972 2 KELLER 3 H.AUBERT, F.WIMMER (ed.), Aristoteles Thierkunde, 1868 (translation).

F.MARX, s.v. Assel, RE 2, 1744; H.GOSSEN, s.v. Hummer, RE 8, 2538ff.; B.HAVINGA, Krebse und Weichtiere, 1929.
C.HÜ.

Crustumerium (*Crustumeria*, *Crustumium*), modern Crustumeri. Town in Latium on the hill of the Marcigliana Vecchia in a region settled since the early Iron

Age. According to contradictory tradition it is a very early foundation: colony of Alba (Diod. Sic. 7,5,9; Dion. Hal. Ant. Rom. 2,36,2), Siculan foundation (Cassius Hemina, cf. Serv. Aen. 7,631), Sabine (Plut. Romulus 17,1) or Etruscan foundation (Paul. Fest. 48). Subjugated by Rome in 500 BC, it gave its name to the *tribus Crustumina*. Varro (Ling. 5,81) mentions a *secessio Crustumerina*. According to Plin. HN 3,68, a famous Latin *oppidum* of times long gone

L.QUILICI, ST. QUILICI GIGLI, C., 1980.   M.CA.

Crux Little is known about the origin and spread of crucifixion in ancient legal systems. There is probably no evidence for it in classical Greece [1]. Herodotus (1,128; 4,43; 202) reports on it as a form of execution among the barbarians, Polybius (1,24,6) among the Phoenicians. Little likely is the idea of the Romans adopting it directly from the Phoenicians [2] (differing views in [3; 4]). Crucifixion however does come to be used as capital punishment among the Romans from about 200 BC (cf. Plaut. Mil. 359). The → *tresviri capitales* probably introduced the punishment for slaves at that time as a deterrent against the sharply increasing crime rate [5] (fundamentally opposite views in [6]). Some 300 years later in Tac. Hist. 4,11, crucifixion is still the *servile supplicium*, i.e. the highest penalty for slaves.

The crucifixion of non-Roman, free residents of the provinces, attested since Cicero (e.g. Verr. 2,5,72), may have been due to both local practises and the fact that it 'worked' as a punishment for slaves. Inciting rebellion (→ *seditio*), with which Jesus of Nazareth was charged, was among the serious crimes for which crucifixion was imposed. In late antiquity crucifixion, together with being burnt to death (→ *crematio*) and beheading (→ *decollatio*), was being listed as the supreme penalty (*summum supplicium*) for Roman citizens (Paulus, Sent. 5,17,2) as well. Late classical legal fragments from the 1st half of the 3rd cent. that had been incorporated into the Digests and had accurately said as much were subsequently changed, because of Christian respect for death on the cross: instead of crucifixion the gallows (*furca*) were named, which Constantine had ordered as a replacement for crucifixion (after 314).
→ Damnatio in crucem

1 K.LATTE, s.v. Todesstrafe, RE Suppl. 7, 1606ff. 2 E.CANTARELLA, I Supplizi capitali in Grecia e a Roma, 1991, 186ff. 3 F.RABER, s.v. Crux, KlP 1, 1337 4 H.F. HITZIG, s.v. Crux, RE 4, 1729 5 W.KUNKEL, Unt. zur Entwicklung des röm. Kriminalverfahrens in vorsullanischer Zeit, 1962, 75ff. 6 W.NIPPEL, Aufruhr und 'Polizei' in der röm. Republik, 1988, 46.

J.BLINZLER, Der Prozeß Jesu ⁴1964; O.BETZ, Probleme des Prozesses Jesu, ANRW II 25.1, 565ff.   G.S.

Cruxifixion see → Damnatio in crucem

Crya (Κρύα; *Krýa*; Καρύα; *Karía*, Ptol. 5,3,2; *Crya fugitivorum*, Plin. HN 5,103; now Taşyaka). Fortified town in the Rhodian Peraea on the south-west coast of Asia Minor in Lycia on the gulf of Telmessus, 2,4 km west-north-west of Fethiye. Sources: Mela 1,16; Steph. Byz. s.v. Krya

> G. E. BEAN, s.v. Taşyaka, PE, 886; Id., Kleinasien 4, 1980, 31, 34; Id., P. M. FRASER, The Rhodian Peraea, 1954, 55f.; GGM 1, 494f. no. 258f.; P. ROOS, Topographical and Other Notes on South-Eastern Caria, in: OpAth 9, 1969, 59–93; TAM 1, 151.　　　　H.I.O.

Crypta, Cryptoporticus From the Greek κρυπτή (*krypté*); in the description of the Nile barge of Ptolemy IV, transmitted in Athenaeus 5, 205a, it designated a closed walkway lit by windows. In Lat. texts *cryptoporticus* could cover various items of architecture such as cellars (Vitr. De arch. 6, 8), vaults (Juv. 5, 106) or even subterranean, vaulted cult or grave structures. In modern archaeological terminology the term *cryptoporticus* is used synonymously with *crypta*; this compound word from *crypta* and → *porticus* that comes to us only from Pliny (Ep. 2,17,20; 5,6,27f.; 7,21,2) and Sidonius (Ep. 2,2,10f.) referred to long, vaulted walkways which — often as part of the garden design — represented a part of the Roman → villa devoted to leisure (sometimes also encountered in public buildings, e.g. in the large theatre and the 'Building of Eumachia' at Pompeii). They could be built above ground, entirely underground or only partly sunken; in the summer they served as a cool retreat, and thus, for those climatic reasons, generally had very small doors, but were occasionally luxuriously furnished and illuminated with sophisticated systems of lighting.

> F. COARELLI, C., Cryptoporticus, in: Les Cryptoportiques dans l'Architecture Romaine, conf. Rome 1972 (1973), 9–20; R. FÖRTSCH, Archäologischer Komm. zu den Villenbriefen des Jüngeren Plinius, 1993, 41–48.　　C.HÖ.

Cryptography
A. SAFEGUARDING UNENCODED MESSAGES
B. ENCODING WITH LETTERS AND NUMBERS
C. OTHER METHODS

A. SAFEGUARDING UNENCODED MESSAGES
Even in antiquity there existed a great many ways of encoding information to keep it secret. Each form of secret writing was supposed to be accessible only to those who were initiated into it. The most detailed extant account of methods of sending secret messages is provided by the Greek specialist on warfare → Aeneas [2] Tacticus from the first half of the 4th cent. BC (Aen. Tact. 31,1–35). Most of that account is devoted to different modes of delivering unencoded messages. In what follows, Aeneas describes various techniques for disguising and concealing the text without altering it in any way, e.g. by tattooing the scalp of the messenger and then letting the hair grow again, by writing on a tablet before a layer of wax is laid over it, or by the use of special, invisible ink that needed to be treated in a particular way later on to make the text legible. The form of mirror writing transmitted in Isidore (Isid. Orig. 1,25) also belongs to this category.

B. ENCODING WITH LETTERS AND NUMBERS
Aeneas mentions only two methods of enciphering messages: 1. Marking letters within a book or document that is to be delivered: the addressee reads the secret message by following the sequence of marked letters (Aen. Tact. 31,2–4). 2. Using a number of dots instead of vowels, with the number of dots corresponding to the vowel's place in the alphabet; i.e. one dot for α, two dots for ε etc. Aeneas offers the following example: Διονύσιος καλός = Δ:: :.: N ::: Σ:: :.: Σ Κ.Λ::Σ (Aen. Tact. 31,31).

Another ancient encyphering technique, known to us from the time of Caesar and Augustus, is that of substituting other letters or ciphers. With his close associates Caesar is said to have used a secret form of writing in which each letter of the alphabet is replaced by the third coming after it, i.e. an A is replaced by a D. (Suet. Iul. 56,6; Gell. NA 17,9,1–5). Regarding this topic, Gellius also refers to a commentary of the grammarian Probus (Gell. NA 17,9,5: *De occulta litterarum significatione in epistularum C. Caesaris scriptura*). Augustus used a simpler code in which B stands for A, C for B etc., but double A for X (Suet. Aug. 88).

We also know of other more complicated substitution systems. The Greek number code, which is based on substituting the 24 letters in the Greek alphabet with their generally acknowledged numerical value, was apparently derived from an oriental tradition. If the sum of the ciphers of a word or a στίχος (*stíchos*, roughly 'standard line') was the same, people spoke of isopsephia (roughly 'equal number of units') [1. 307–319]. These codes were used, for example, for proper

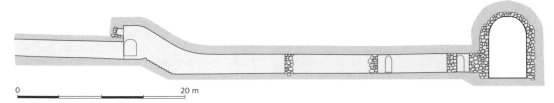

Tivoli, Villa Hadriana.
Crypta below the Temple of Aphrodite.

names in signatures or for shorter words: ἀμήν *amén* = α' + μ' + η' + ν' [1 + 40 + 8 + 50] = 99 = koppa [90] theta [9]. Later on, the number code included the possibility of reversing the sequence of letters, e.g. within 3 groups of 9 letters each (α-θ etc.) with the addition of the three additional signs stigma, koppa and sampi in place of δ, ι, ϙ.

C. OTHER METHODS

Only a few sketchy attempts have survived from antiquity of any system of encoding that replaces whole sections of clear text with a code, as for example Cicero's use of cover names in some of his letters (Cic. Att. 2,20,5).

One form of a substitution or encryption system that alters the sequence of textual elements is to be found in the → skytale that writers from the Imperial period attributed to the Spartans.

Other methods of cryptography, transmitted predominantly from the Middle Ages but in existence, at least in part, some time earlier, are: the removal of vowels or their replacement by the consonant following them in the alphabet; the use of foreign alphabets, e.g. that of Greek, instead of Latin; the invention of special cryptographic alphabets. In magic texts the normal alphabet is frequently replaced by a fantasy alphabet composed of astrological and alchemistic signs together with normal letters of the alphabet. In mystical cryptography individual letters of the alphabet have a particular symbolic meaning, depending on the context: Y is used by the Pythagoreans for ὑγίεια (*hygíeia*, health), and the letter T (τ, *tau*) in Christian texts symbolizes the cross [2. 1765].

→ Communications

1 V. GARDTHAUSEN, Griech. Paläographie II 2, 1913, 298–319 2 M. GUARDUCCI, Dal gioco letterale alla crittografia mistica, in: ANRW II 16.2, 1736–1773. A.K.

Cryptoporticus see → Crypta, Cryptoporticus

Ctesias (Κτησίας, *Ktēsías*) of Cnidus
A. LIFE B. WORKS

A. LIFE
Historian in terms of literary genre, but in modern terms a novelist. C. came from an old family of doctors and lived as personal physician at the court of Artaxerxes [2]II for several years (405–398/7 BC). On his behalf he made contact with → Evagoras [1], the Athenian → Conon [1], as well as with Sparta.

B. WORKS
C. composed a *Períodos* (a geographical treatise) and an *Indiká* with a range of factual reports. C. became famous, however, for his large, 23-volume *Persiká* written in Ionic dialect. Although this work, modelled on the *Helleniká,* has not been preserved, such large fragments have reached us through Diodorus,

Nikolaus of Damascus and Photius (FGrH 688) that we can certainly reconstruct it and attempt a literary and historical classification.

The *Persiká* encompassed the history of the Orient from the legendary king → Ninus, the founder of the Assyrian kingdom, up to the eighth year of the reign of Artaxerxes [2] II (398/7). The work consists of the *Assyriaká* — i.e. three volumes of Assyrian history (with surprisingly little information on Babylon) and three of Median history — as well as the *Persiká* proper. C. adopted from → Herodotus [1] the model of dividing up Oriental history according to the dominant peoples (Assyrians, Medes, Persians). The work ended with a list of kings 'from Ninus and Semiramis to Artaxerxes II' (FGrH 688 F 33).

C. emphasizes that — unlike his predecessor Herodotus, whom he regards as a liar — he saw things with his own eyes or heard them himself from the Persians. Contrary to expectations, that methodology — with explicit reference to the Herodotean *autopsía* — does not, however, result in any great historical value. The history of Assyria from Ninus to Sardanapal (1240 years; according to Hdt. 520 years; they both date the Trojan War to c. 1270–1240 BC) does indeed offer some literary highlights (→ Assurbanipal), but is either freely invented or (more likely) taken from sources of low historical reliability. There are many factual errors: thus, for example, Nineveh — contrary to Herodotus — is set on the Euphrates. This is a good example of C.'s pure argumentativeness and his capricious zeal to depict everything differently. C. treated Median history similarly. It was not so much the study of official lists that led him to double the period of Median sovereignty to 300 years, as his determination to prove Herodotus wrong. Even the historical value of his information on the period from → Cyrus [1] to → Xerxes is slight. Nowhere does C. offer anything better than what we have from Herodotus. Cyrus is described hardly any better than any of his Assyrian subjects. Not even genuine Iranian legends are provided. C. had little interest in the politics of the Persian kingdom and did not draw on good sources in this field either. For the atmosphere at court (harem intrigues), on the other hand, C. is first-rate.

In the 4th cent. BC, C. was regarded as the author of oriental history *par excellence*. Isocrates, Plato and Aristotle read him, → Theopompus wanted to compete with him, → Ephorus, Heraclides of Cyme and → Dinon used his work or continued it.

J. BONQUET, Ctesias' Assyrian King-List, in: AncSoc 21, 1990, 5–16; F. JACOBY, s.v. Ktesias, RE 11, 2032–2073; F. W. KÖNIG, Die Persika des Ktesias, 1972; A. MOMIGLIANO, Ktesias, 1931 (= Id., Ausgewählte Schriften 1, 1998, 77–109); N. WILSON, Photius: The Bibliotheca, 1994. PE.HÖ.

Ctesibius

[1]

A. LIFE AND WORK   B. INVENTIONS

A. LIFE AND WORK

A Greek mechanic and inventor of the first half of the 3rd cent. BC, who came from Alexandria (Vitr. De arch. 9,8,2; Philo of Byzantium, Belopoiika 67) and worked there, C. was the founder of → pneumatics.

In an epigram (Ath. 497d), C.'s contemporary Hedylus mentions a hydro-acoustic double horn of plenty, with which C. is said to have adorned a statue of the 'divine Arsinoe'. Arsinoe [II 3] II., who had been the wife of Ptolemy II Philadelphus since 277 BC, was deified in 274; coins from as early as c. 270 depict that statue. Thus, C. lived and worked under Ptolemy I and II in the → Mouseion in Alexandria. In 159 BC, a public water clock was installed in Rome using the regulator principle invented by C. (Plin. HN 7,215); attribution by Aristocles (Ath. 174 b-e) of the invention of the hydraulis (→ Musical instruments) to an Egyptian barber from the 2nd cent. named C. is certainly based on a misunderstanding.

C.'s work (Hypomnémata mēchaniká or Commentarii) was probably still available to Vitruvius (Vitr. De arch. 1,1,7; 10,7,5). It is possibly that it was from this text that the story derives telling how, as the son of a barber in Alexandria, C. discovered the solidity and energy of air, the principle underlying most of his inventions, when he constructed a mirror adjustable in height that was hanging by a rope for his father's salon; it was connected to a ball of lead as counterweight by a rope leading over a pulley; the rope slid up and down in a narrow tube and emitted a whistling noise with the flow of air in and out (Vitr. De arch. 9,8,2–7).

Philo of Byzantium (Belopoiika 77f.) was able to report as an eyewitness of C.'s invention and dramatic experimental presentation of the 'air valve' (ἀερότονον) that was dependent on that principle, and would draw on accounts of others for the description of the 'metal valve' (χαλκότονον) that was invented and tested only after his own parting of ways with C. (ibid. 56; 67). Following C.'s work closely, Vitruvius describes the construction of water clocks (Vitr. De arch. 9,8,4–7), the hydraulis (Vitr. De arch. 10,8) and the Ctesibii machina (Vitr. De arch. 10,7,1–3; cf. Philo of Byzantium, Pneumatika 1).

B. INVENTIONS

C.'s machina is a fountain-like water sprinkler, wrongly thought of by its creator as an air-pump, providing a continuous stream of water through a pressure tank fitted with check valves. Two cylinders with pistons that are each operated through a lever fixed on to a rod stand in two separate water containers; through their flap valves, they function in alternation as sucking and pressure pumps and pump air (as well as water) that forces the water out into the pressure tank through a vertical pipe (as Philo and Vitruvius explain). In a later, enlarged and improved version for fighting large-scale fires, both cylinders stand in one large water tank; the pistons are operated over a rod with a see-sawing lever and move in opposite directions at the same time; the outlet valve fitted onto the standpipe for the jet of water can be turned in any direction; the compressed air in the pressure tank acts specifically to counterbalance the pneumatic pressure. Fire hoses of this kind remained in use until the arrival of steam and motor hoses in the 20th cent.

C.'s water, winter or night clock (ὡρολόγιον/ hōrológion) derived from the principle of the older clepsydra (→ Clocks) that was used in legal proceedings for measuring the time allocated to a speaker. This involves a container with inlet and outlet for water, but without any timing display, as is used in → automata in which floats that are moved by changes in water level operate cogs and other transmission mechanisms. Linked to that was the division of daylight time into 12 (variable) hours on a sundial that C. then analogously transferred to night time (from sundown to sunrise). For the constant night-long inlet of water into the catchment container he led the inflow from the public water supply into an overflow container, from which, as a result of constant water pressure the water could steadily drip out through an opening at the bottom. A more exact control developed through a cone-shaped float that fitted exactly into the cone-shaped opening of the water supply and permitted a balance between the reservoir level and the water inlet. The water level in the reservoir, the clepsydra proper, is then indicated by a float that is fitted with a rod that has a figure-shaped end, working as a pointer. This points at hour markings on a revolving cylinder; those markings are gradated according to the various lengths of hours depending on the month.

Alternatively, instead of the gradations in hours, C. adjusts the water flow to fit the length of hours of days; for this he replaces the opening at the base of the reservoir tank that has a round disc with an eccentric opening; with its turning (ideally by one part in 365 per day) the height of the water outlet, and thus the level of water pressure that controls the outflow velocity, can be varied. The horologia anaphorica (Vitr. De arch. 9,8,8; 'sunrise clock' — a form of self-moving → astrolabium) represent a later innovation, in which by means of a string fitted with a counterweight, the movement of the float over a shaft turns a net (rete) of lines of hours in front of a (bronze) disc, to be adjusted daily, with engraved celestial revolutions (and constellations).

The torsion catapults that had been developed under Dionysius [25] the Elder in Syracuse and then improved, through size standardization, in costly trials under the first two Ptolemies in Alexandria, were very susceptible to weather because of their corded strands wound on two racks; C. therefore tried to correct that and came up with two variations, the first of which, the 'air-driven' type, was based on his knowledge of pneumatics. In this → catapult the tension on the two arms of the bow is achieved by the pressure of (compressed) air caused through the build-up of tension in bronze cylinders from piston rods linked to each of the bow arms. With the 'bronze-driven' type, on the other hand, the tension in the bow arms is achieved by means of several bronze leaf springs layered on top of one another. For technical reasons neither of the two forms had any lasting success, while the torsion catapults, even in standardized sizes, remained in use well beyond antiquity.

→ Hero; → Mechanics; → Philo of Byblus

1 A. G. DRACHMANN, Ktesibios, Philon and Heron, 1948
2 Id., The Mechanical Technology of Greek and Roman Antiquity, 1963   3 B. GILLE, Les mécaniciens grecs, 1980
4 F. KRAFFT, Heron von Alexandria, in: K. FASSMANN (ed.), Die Großen der Weltgeschichte 2, 1972, 333–377
5 E. W. MARSDEN, Greek and Roman Artillery, 2 vols., 1969–71   6 A. SCHÜRMANN, Griech. Mechanik und antike Gesellschaft, 1991.   F.KR.

[2] see → Phaedon from Elis

Ctesicles (Κτησικλῆς; *Ktēsiklês*).

[1] Author of *Chroniká* in at least 3 vols. in the Hellenistic period, quoted only by Athenaeus (6, 272c: census in Athens under Demetrius [4] of Phalerum 317/6 BC; 10, 445c-d: death of Eumenes [2] I. in 241). WILAMOWITZ [1] and JACOBY (comm. on FGrH 245) argue for his identification with Stesicleides of Athens, author of an *Anagraphè tōn archóntōn kai Olympioníkōn* ('Listing of officials and Olympic winners') quoted in Diogenes Laertius (2,56).

1 U. VON WILAMOWITZ-MOELLENDORFF, Antigonos von Karystos (Philolog. Untersuchungen 4), 1881, 335.

EDITION: FGrH 245 with comm.   K.MEI.

[2] Sculptor. C. was known as having created a marble statue in the Heraeum of Samos, which according to a comedy story-line of the late 4th cent. BC is said to have sent a youth into erotic aberrations.

OVERBECK, no. 1372; EAA 4, 418 no. 1.   R.N.

[3] Hellenistic painter of the first half of the 3rd cent. BC from Asia Minor? Anecdotally Plin. HN 35,140 praises his portrait painting of the Seleucid queen → Stratonice, in which C., by way of revenge for lack of recognition, presented her in a compromising situation. She nevertheless had it exhibited at the harbour of Ephesus. Nothing more is known of this probably talented painter.

G. CRESSEDI, s.v. Ktesikles (2), EAA 4, 418; G. LIPPOLD, s.v. Ktesikles (4), RE 11, 2077.   N.H.

Ctesidemus Second-rate Greek painter (according to Plin. HN 35,140), who worked around and after 350 BC and was the teacher of → Antiphilus [4]. Extant works are a battle painting, the sack of Oechalia, and a portrait of Laodamia; nothing is known of their style.

G. LIPPOLD, s.v. Ktesidennos, RE 11, 2077.   N.H.

Ctesiphon (Κτησιφῶν; *Ktésiphôn*).

[1] Athenian, son of Leosthenes from Anaphlystus, supporter of → Demosthenes [2], whom he had successfully, though technically pre-empting official endorsement (→ Euthynae), proposed in 337/6 for a crowning. → Aeschines [2] lodged a protest against this that was unambiguously rejected in 330 at the 'crown trial' (Aeschin. In Ctes.; Dem. Or. 18; Plut. Mor. 840C and 846A). C. was also one of the emissaries to queen Cleopatra in Epirus (Aeschin. In Ctes. 242).

PA 8894; DEVELIN 1731; LGPN 2, s.v. Ktesiphon (5).   J.E.

[2] Greek name for the capital of the Arsacid and Sassanid empire (→ Arsaces; → Sassanids) from the 2nd cent. BC — 7th cent. AD (Parthian/Pahlavi: *tyspwn*, Arabic: *Ṭaysabūn*). Hailed as the Eastern counterpart to Rome; part of the *c.* 30 km² large city complex at al-Madāʾin (with, *i.a.*, → Seleucia, Vēh Ardašīr) on the northern Babylonian Tigris.

First mentioned in 221 BC as a place name/village name on the left bank of the Tigris (Pol. 5,45), C. had become a major city by the 1st cent. AD at the latest (Str. 16,1,16; Plin. HN 6,30,122; 6,31,131). It was attacked by Roman forces on several occasions, successfully (116: Trajan, 165: Verus, 198: Severus, and 283: Carus) and unsuccessfully (262: Odainath of Palmyra, 363: Julian, 628: Heraclius). After the conquest by Ardair (226), C. became the Sassanid coronation city and capital [4] as well as seat of the Nestorian Katholikos (i.a. Synode of 410) and a Jewish exilarch.

In 637 C. was conquered by Muslim forces; it started to decline after the founding of Baghdad (762), where the material from the old royal residence partly destroyed by al-Manṣūr were reused [4]. Only the Tāq-e Kisrā from the 6th cent., the largest arch of antiquity, has survived to this day. So far, there have hardly been any excavations.

1 J. M. FIEY, Topography of al-Madāʾin, in: Sumer 23, 1967, 3–38   2 A. OPPENHEIMER, Babylonia Judaica in the Talmudic Period (TAVO Suppl. B47), 1983, 179–235
3 R. McC. ADAMS, Land behind Baghdad, 1965, 61–83
4 J. KRÖGER, s.v. Ctesiphon, EncIr 6, 1994, 446–8.   S.HA.

Ctesippus

[1] see → Socratics

[2] Son of the Athenian *stratēgós* → Chabrias from Aexone, for whom Demosthenes [2] fought against the motion by Leptines for repeal of the *atéleia* (→ Liturgies) in 354 BC (Dem. Or. 20,75; 82). C. is attested as trierarch (IG II² 1623,72f.: 334/3 BC; in IG II² 1604,87 [377/6] perhaps the grandfather) and → *choregos* (IG II² 3040; in the 320s according to [1. 24]). C.'s obstinate behaviour is the target of comic mockery (Diphilus F 37 PCG V; Timocles F 5 PCG VII; Men. Fr. 303 KÖRTE; Ael. NA 3,42). After his father's death in 357 → Phocion unsuccessfully tried his hand at bringing C. up (Plut. Phocion 7). DAVIES 561 (on PA 8885 and 15086).

1 D. M. LEWIS, Notes on Attic Inscriptions II, in: ABSA 50, 1955, 1–36. BO.D.

Ctimenae (Κτιμεναί; *Ktimenaí*). Capital of the → Dolopes in the vicinity of Lake Xynias, probably near today's Cydonia and not today's Ktimenai (formerly Anodranitsa). Conquered in 198 BC by the Aetolians allied with Rome (Liv. 32,13,10); thereafter Angeia was the capital of the Dolopes.

B. HELLY, Incursions chez les Dolopes, in: I. BLUM (ed.), Topographie antique et géographie historique en pays grec, 1992, 48ff.; F. STÄHLIN, Das hellenische Thessalien, 1924, 148f. HE.KR.

Ctimene (Κτιμένη, *Ktiménē*).

[1] → Odysseus' youngest (or younger [1]) sister. She was brought up together with → Eumaeus and sent to Same to be married (Hom. Od. 15,363ff.: only place tò mention siblings of Odysseus).

[2] Daughter of the Locrian Phegeus from Oenoë; C. is said to have been seduced by → Hesiod and to have given birth to → Stesichorus, which caused her brothers Amphiphanes and → Ganyctor [2] to kill Hesiod in revenge (Vita Hesiodi p. 50 WILAM.).

1 A. HOEKSTRA, A Commentary on Homer's Odyssey, vol. 2, 1989, 255. RE.N.

Cuballum see → Volume 4, Addenda

Cubicularius (from *cubiculum*, literally 'bedchamber', also 'private living space', cf. Varro, Ling. 8,54) could denote a domestic slave, a personal servant, but also someone responsible for guarding access to a *persona publica* (Dig. 50,16,203). Officials from as early as the Republic had *cubicularii* in that sense (Cic. Verr. 2,3,8) and emperors from the very beginning had them as personal servants and confidants in their private domain (Suet. Iul. 4,1; Suet. Dom. 17,2). The higher ranks of the emperor's staff were occupied primarily by eunuchs (Zos. 4,37), and the lower orders apparently by non-eunuchs (Cod. Iust. 12,25). Generally there was only one *cubiculum* (sometimes two, one each for the emperor and empress: Not. Dign. Or. 1,9; Not. Dign. Occ. 1,8; Cod. Iust. 12,5,5); the functional structure varied. With the ceremonial elevation of the emperor (*sacrum cubiculum*) introduced from the time of Diocletian (Eutr. 9,26) the senior *cubicularius* (*praepositus s.c.*) and his deputies (*primicerius* and *castrensis s.c./comes domesticorum*) came to play a central role at court. They performed various services, such as *paedagogia* for the *castrensis* ('page duties'; Cod. Theod. 8,7,5; Cod. Iust. 12,59,10,5), and that of *curae palatiorum* (ceremonial duties; Cod. Iust. 12,16) for the *ministeriales dominici* ('chamberlains': Cod. Iust. 12,25) and the *cubicularii*. The *spatharius*, as commander of the watch, the *saccelarius*, as treasurer, and the *comes sacrae vestis* (Cod. Theod. 11,18,1) were also high-ranking *cubicularii*. *Cubicularii* had privileges both

during their service (slaves were given the status of free men on admission to the service) and after they left the service (general exemption from special taxes and manual and compulsory labour, Cod. Iust. 12,5).
→ Palatini

ALFÖLDI 25ff.; JONES, LRE 566ff.; MOMMSEN, Staatsrecht 2, 834ff. C.G.

Cubitus denotes the elbow, i.e. the forearm up to the tip of the middle finger and, along with the usual Roman unit of measurement, the *pes*, was used as the 'ell', amounting to 1 ¹/₂ feet (444 mm). In Greek the *cubitus* is translated as πῆχυς (*pêchys*) .
→ Measures; → Pes

F. HULTSCH, Griech. und röm. Metrologie, ²1882, 76f., 98; H. NISSEN, Metrologie² = HB Altertumswiss. I², 1892, 838, 865; A. OXÉ, Die röm. Meile eine griech. Schöpfung, BJ 131, 1926, 213–244, especially 233ff. A.M.

Cubulteria Samnite city (tribal name*Kupelternum* on Oscan coins), *civitas foederata* after the Second Punic War, and *municipium* with *IIviri* after the Social War. In AD 599 elevated to a bishopric. C. is thought to be *c.* 2 km north of Alvignano near the churches S. Ferdinando or S. Ferrante.

G. COUQUER (ed.), Structures agraires en Italie Centro-méridionale (Collection de l'École Française de Rome 100), 1987, 149f.; H. SOLIN, Le iscrizioni antiche di Trebula, Caiatia e C., 1993, 145–173. M.BU.

Cuckoo (κόκκυξ/*kókkyx*, since Hes. Op. 486; Suda s.v. κοῦκκος/*koûkkos*, Lat. *cucul(l)us* first at Plaut. Trin. 245, then at Plin. HN 18,249; 28,156 and 30,85; *coccyx*: Plin. HN 10,25), the well-known brood parasite and migratory bird that appears early in Greece (Dionysius, Ixeutika 1,13, [1. 11]). The cry that gives rise to its name (verb: κοκκύζειν/*kokkýzein*, Hes. loc. cit.) was just as striking as its practise of depositing an egg (rarely are there two) in the nests of various small birds (in Aristot. Hist. an. 6,7,564a 2 the ὑπολαΐς/*hypolaḯs*, probably a warbler). Aristotle (Hist. an. 6,7,563b 14– 564a 6) countered the view that the → goshawk (*hiérax*) changed into a cuckoo in summer with a number of convincing arguments, including the fact that the former was actually a bird of prey (with hooked claws). From the fact of its meagre output of eggs Aristotle deduced that the cuckoo had a cold nature (Gen. an. 3,1,750a 11–17) and a related cowardice that was manifested in its flight from pursuing birds. Placing the egg in the alien nests of the φάψ/*pháps* (dove), ὑπολαΐς/*hypolaḯs*, κόρυδος/*kórydos* (crested lark) and χλωρίς/*chlōrís* (greenfinch) was interpreted as cunning as a consequence of its cowardice (Aristot. Hist. an. 8(9),29,618a 8–31). In that passage, various details of the removal of the host bird's young are discussed as well. Ael. NA 3,30 supplies the observation that the cuckoo places an egg only in nests where the eggs resemble its own. To the details taken from Aristotle, Plin.

HN 10,25–27 only adds that the flesh of the C. has an especially good taste. A cuckoo was depicted on the shield of → Hera, because Zeus had first approached his future wife in this guise on mount Thornax, the 'Cuckoo Mountain' (óros Kokkýgion, Paus. 2,36,1) (Paus. 2,17,4).

1 A. GARZYA (ed.), Dionysii Ixeuticon libri, 1963.

D'ARCY W. THOMPSON, A Glossary of Greek Birds, 1936, repr. 1966, 151–153; LEITNER, 93; KELLER, 2,63–67.
                                                                    C.HÜ.

Cucumber The large annual varieties of the generally tropical family of Cucurbitaceae with sizeable berries all come from the Near East. In antiquity the different varieties were often confused with one another. The real cucumber Cucumis sativus L. (σίκυς; síkys, σίκυος; síkyos, ἀγγούριον; angoúrion, Lat. cucumis) is encountered in Plin. HN 19,64–66 as a vegetable grown in hothouses (intra specularium munimenta) to ensure a constant fresh supply for Tiberius. Theophr. Hist. pl. 7,1,6 describes the process of leaving the seeds in milk mead (lac mulsum) for two days before sowing to make them sweeter. The small green cucumbers in Italy are distinguished from the large green, yellow and black 'flesh cucumber' (unknown variety!). The cucumber grows in every shape (according to Theophr. Hist. pl. 7,3,5) and towards nearby water. Plin. HN 20,3–12 describes the medicinal applications of individual varieties, especially as treatment for eye diseases.

According to Plin. HN 19,68, the Greeks knew three varieties, the Spartan, the Skytalic (cylindrical) and the Boeotian, though in his source (Theophr. Hist. pl. 7,4,6) those details refer to the honey-melon, Cucumis melo L. Plin. HN 19,67 describes the latter as a golden-yellow 'cucumber', allegedly originating from Campania, with the name of melopepo (μηλοπέπων).

Also regarded by Pliny as a cucumber was the watermelon, Citrullus vulgaris Schrad., these days more frequently grown in the south (HN 19,65 under the name pepo, πέπων; cf. Plin. HN 20,11, Theophr. Hist. pl. 7,3,5 and Dioscorides 2,135 p. 1,206 WELLMANN = 2,163 p. 226f. BERENDES). The squirting cucumber Ecballium elaterium L. appears in Plin. HN 19,74 and 20,3–6 (as a source of elaterium, used e.g. to counter opacity of the eye; cf. also Dioscorides 4,150 p. 2, 292–296 WELLMANN = 4,152 and 155 p. 449–451 BERENDES) as cucumis silvestris. Like these, the colocynth, Citrullus colocynthis, also has poisonous fruit. It is probably the bottle gourd (the calabash), from which storage containers were made, that is meant by σικύα Ἰνδική (κολοκύντη in Ath.2,58f or cucurbita in Plin. HN 19,69–71 and passim).The real pumpkin, Cucurbita pepo L., was only introduced from America in the 16th cent.   C.HÜ.

Cugerni see → Volume 4, Addenda

Cuicul Small Berber town in Numidia between Cirta and Sitifis, now Djemila. Attested forms of the name: Κούλκουα, Ptol. 4,3,29; Cuiculi, It. Ant. 29,1; Culchul, Tab. Peut. 2,4; Chulchul, Geogr. Rav. 39,25. A veteran colony was established under Nerva (CIL VIII Suppl. 3, 20713) which contributed substantially to C.'s upswing. In the 5th cent., C.'s importance declined. Significant ruins have survived: temples (Venus Genetrix, Liber, Saturnus, Frugifer, Gens Septimia), theatre, forums, basilicas, arches, thermal baths, wells, private homes (with remarkable mosaics), churches. Inscr: CIL VIII 1, 8300–8348; 2, 10894–10904; Suppl. 2, 20135–20179; CRAI 1915, 316–323; 1943, 376–386; AE 1971, 179 no. 510; 1989, 290 no. 893; 1992, 531 no. 1889; [1. 338–340].

1 Bull. Archéologique du Comité des Travaux Historiques, 1946–1949.

Y. ALLAIS, Djemila, 1938; P.-A. FÉVRIER, Djemila, ²1978; C. LEPELLEY, Les cités de l'Afrique romaine [...] II, 1981, 402–415; L. LESCHI, Djemila, 1953; E. LIPIŃSKI, s.v. Djemila, DCPP, 133; P. MONCEAUX, C. chrétien, in: Atti della Pontificia Accademia Romana di archeologia III. Memorie 1,1, 1923, 89–112, fig. VIIf.   W.HU.

Culex 'The Mosquito', Lat. short epic poem (→ Epic), dedicated to Octavian as a Virgilian pseudepigraphon (v.1) and received as an early work by Virgil since Lucan [1. 157ff.; 6] Suetonius' Life of Virgil; it is, however, more likely to come from the Tiberian period [1. 57ff.; 7]: a mosquito stings a sleeping shepherd and thus saves him from a snake but is killed by him; it recounts the tale to him in a dream from the underworld and receives a proper burial in appreciation. Bucolic setting and epic parody (→ Parody) are the striking features [2]; as an → allegory the work would refer to Augustus (pastor) and Marcellus (culex) [5]. Its authenticity (for discussion [1. 1ff., 241ff.]) is ruled out by retrospective allusions to the totality of Virgil's work (Bucolica, vv.42–97 = morning; Georgica, vv.98–201 = noon; Aeneis, vv.202–414 = night) [7]. The text has been transmitted in the → Appendix Vergiliana in a corpus of late antiquity.

EDITION: W. V. CLAUSEN, Appendix Vergiliana, 1966, 15–36.
BIBLIOGRAPHY: 1 D. GÜNTZSCHEL, Beiträge zur Datierung des C., 1972 (bibl. 209ff.) 2 D. O. ROSS, The C. as Post-Augustan Literary Parody, in: HSPh 79, 1975, 235–253 3 J. RICHMOND, in: ANRW II.31,2, 1981, 1125–1130 (research report) 4 M. BONJOUR, s.v. C., EV 1, 1984, 948f. 5 W. AX, Die pseudovergilische Mücke, in: Philologus 128, 1984, 230–249; 136, 1992, 89–129 6 G. ZANONI, Testimonianze antiche sul C., in: MD 19, 1987, 145–168 7 G. MOST, The 'Virgilian' C., in: Homo Viator. FS J. Bramble, 1987, 199–209 8 A. SALVATORE, Virgilio e Pseudovirgilio, 1994, 211–285.   P.L.S.

Culina Lat. term for kitchen. In Greek antiquity, an independent room in the → house with hearth and other infrastructure (smoke outlet, drainage) for preparation of meals was unknown for a long time; generally, the hearth served as a focal point in the main room of a house and was at the same time the centre of social communication. Kitchens in a more narrow sense, as functionally-defined, separate room components, are to be found first in the late Classical houses of Olynthus, then increasingly as independent rooms in Hellenistic houses (Dura Europos, Delos, Priene), where this reflected, in a striking way, a change in the relationship between private and public areas in residential architecture.

In the oldest Roman houses cooking was done in the → atrium; in rural districts this custom was maintained, with the result that there the main room of the house could be called a *culina* (Varro, Rust. 1,13,2; Vitr. De arch. 6,9,1f.). From the 2nd cent. BC it was almost a regular feature of well-to-do Roman urban homes to have a small room with brick hearth (with smoke leaving through the window), often connected to the → latrine; the size of such rooms in Pompeii varied between 6 and 20 m². Furnishings and size of the room became indicators of social standing (cf. Sen. Ep. 114,26). In the limited space of multi-storey rental apartments, people generally cooked on a transportable oven in the living room; there was no space there for a separate *culina*.

E. BRÖDNER, Wohnen in der Antike,²1993, 40–41; W. HOEPFNER, E. L. SCHWANDNER, Haus und Stadt im klass. Griechenland, 1986, 54; 245; 273; K. W. WEEBER, Alltag im Alten Rom, 1995, 219–221.　　　　C.HÖ.

Culleus *Culleus* properly designates a leather sack made of cowhide; it was used by the Romans as the largest unit for measuring fluid capacity (especially with wine). Probably originally based on the volume of the stitched cowhide, the *culleus* amounts to 524 l; 20 *amphorae*, 40 *urnae* or 160 *congii* constitute the *culleus*, with 1 *congius* corresponding to 3,275 l.
→ Amphora; → Congius; → Measure of volume; → Urna

F. HULTSCH, Griech. und röm. Metrologie, ²1882; F. OLCK, s.v. C. (no. 2), RE 4.2, 1901, 1746–1747; O. A. W. DILKE, Mathematik, Maße und Gewichte in der Antike, 1991.　　　　A.M.

Culpa Under Roman law an obligation to pay damages always required guilt (*culpa*, negligence, or → *dolus*, criminal intent).

In interpreting the *lex Aquilia* (probably 286 BC), jurisprudence developed a distinction between the forms of guilt, *dolus* and *culpa*: *culpa* is the offence against an objective standard of care (*diligentia*, care on the part of a *diligens/bonus pater familias*). *Culpa* was also used to describe guilt in general. The Roman penal code knew only few crimes that were punishable also in the case of negligence.

In the case of *bonae fidei iudicia* there initially was liability only for fraudulent breach of faith (*dolus malus*). Later on, liability was also established — depending on the type of contract — for other offences

against *bona fides*. In the Principate these were distinguished with the terms *dolus* and *culpa*, the latter then being divided into *culpa* (*levis*) and *culpa lata*. (In late antiquity, → *custodia*- (supervision) liability was seen as the liability for *culpa levissima*.)

Liability for *culpa* could be made conditional (Ulp. Dig. 9,2,27,29). Elective guilt (*culpa in eligendo*) constitutes a contractual liability for involved helpers. If liability is established for offences against the subjective standard of *diligentia quam in suis* (termed *culpa in concreto* in non-Roman Latin), this can mean either a more severe liability for → *dolus* (Dig. 16,3,32) or a concessional one for *culpa*: e.g. with *dos* (dowry), *tutela* (guardianship), *societas* (society). Classical jurisprudence maintained a case-based approach to handling *culpa*; only in the late Classical and Byzantine periods do we find standardization and a unifying formulation of theory. *Culpa* in Roman law marks the starting-point of liability for the imposition of damages for negligence under modern law.
→ Damnum

KASER, RPR I, 503–513, 346–357; H. HONSELL, TH. MAYER-MALY, W. SELB, Röm. Recht, ⁴1987, 229–238; A. WACKE, Fahrlässige Vergehen im röm. Strafrecht, in: RIDA 26, 1979, 505–566.　　　　R.GA.

Cult
I. GENERAL　II. ANCIENT ORIENT　III. GREEK AND ROMAN RELIGION　IV. BIBLICAL

I. GENERAL
Cult encompasses the entirety of ritual tradition in the context of religious practise. Via Christian usage, the term derives from the *cultus deorum* ('divine worship') named already in Cicero, and corresponds to the Greek *thrēskeía*; like the latter (and the Latin *caerimonia*, 'rites'), it can in pagan language stand simply for 'religion' in general and thus refer to the absolute predominance in pagan Greek and Roman religion of ritual actions over faith. There, as in the religious cultures of the ancient Mediterranean (including ancient Israel), the focus is on the blood → sacrifice of domestic animals, accompanied by → prayer and → libation (which can also be independent actions); a specific development of the Greek world seems, by contrast, to be the cult of → mysteries.　　　　F.G.

II. ANCIENT ORIENT
Cult in the ancient oriental cultures manifests itself in archaeological and written evidence. Especially in the cuneiform cultures of Mesopotamia, Asia Minor (→ Hattusa) and Syria a very large number of → ritual texts are available that enable us to comprehend in detail individual cult rituals and their structure ('syntax'). Together with myths and epics they offer additional data about the structure of cult rituals. Moreover, detailed information can be inferred from c. 100,000 cuneiform administrative records that have been published to date from the Babylonian → hemer-

ologies from the 3rd to 1st millennia BC, as well as the inscriptions of Egyptian pharaohs, about the sacrifice materials, cult objects, the groups of people participating in the cult ritual (*i.a.* → rulers, → priests) and favourable days for ritual activities. Festival cycles and calendars can be reconstructed with great precision. Archaeological evidence (partly preserved → temples and temple outlines, graphical depictions on cylindrical seals, bas-reliefs, and other picture panels such as wall paintings and cult objects, a rather large number of which (particularly ceramic ones) have been preserved — e.g. incense stands or libation vessels) completes our picture of ancient oriental cult.

Ancient oriental cult basically resulted from all aspects of everyday life. The sources available to us, however, cast light predominantly on official cult. In the ancient oriental view the ruler was responsible for the proper conduct of the cult [1. 839]. His role in the cult reflected his elevated position in the social structure. Important features of the public cult event are above all the large number of festivals (→ Feasts) and ceremonial → processions (→ Akītu Festival) in which the ruler plays the central role. Through the collaboration of divinity and ruler the cosmic order is made manifest and created anew. Thus, in the cult event all sections of society are bound together in worship of the god(s). In that sense, cult had the effect of creating identity for the community. Myths that are recited as *hieroi logoi* in a cult ritual (→ Enūma eliš) remind people that the cult practises have been instituted by the gods [1. 839].

For the ancient oriental mind the principal purpose of daily cult was to ensure that the gods were provided with food, clothing and shelter [6. 183–98; → Atraḫasis]. That is why → sacrifice and the offering of cult paraphernalia (i.a. divine clothing, tools) stand at the heart of cult ritual. Together with cult songs (→ Songs) and → prayers, the sacrifices however also served to attract the attention of the gods to mankind.

→ Altar; → Amulet; → Burial; → Divination; → Gestures; → Hieros Gamos; → Yahwe; → Purification; → Asia Minor, Religion; → Cult image; → Magic; → Mesopotamia, Religion; → Syria, Religion; → Ziggurrat

1 W. Barta et al., s.v. Kult, LÄ 3, 839–59   2 G. van Driel, The Cult of Assur, 1969   3 V. Haas, Geschichte der hethitischen Religion, 1994   4 B. Landsberger, Der kult. Kalender der Babylonier und Assyrer, 1915   5 S. M. Maul, Zukunftsbewältigung: eine Untersuchung altoriental. Denkens …, 1994   6 A. L. Oppenheim, Ancient Mesopotamia, ²1977   7 W. Sallaberger, Der kult. Kalender der Ur III-Zeit, 1993   8 TUAT vol. 2, 1988, 163–452.   J.RE.

III. Greek and Roman Religion

A. Sources and ancient thought   B. Time
C. Place   D. Cult recipients   E. Rites
F. Participants

A. Sources and ancient thought

The main sources for Greek and Roman cult are the literary texts that from Homeric times onwards recount cult activities (sacrifice, prayer, oaths etc.) as part of fictional narrative; from the time of the Linear B texts (as main evidence for cult in Bronze Age Greece), there also are inscriptions and, lastly, iconographic and archaeological finds. Literary and epigraphical texts tend to both record only the extraordinary and omit the everyday as being all too familiar, while iconographic and archaeological finds are hard to interpret in the absence of relevant texts. Indigenous reflection on cult details seems to begin, in a practical way, with the cult performance, in so far as individual cults and rites can have their basis in aetiological myths. Such myths can assume an important role with local historians or ancient geographers (→ Strabo) and travel writers (→ Pausanias), and are at the forefront of Greek cult writing proper [1]; even the Romans M. Terentius → Varro (*Antiquitates rerum divinarum*, dedicated to the Pontifex Maximus C. Iulius Caesar) and, less directly, → Verrius Flaccus (*De significatu verborum*, preserved in the partly double epitomization by Festus and Paulus Diaconus) belong to that tradition. Particularly, the later reflection tends towards systemization and the formulation of theories, and is often uncritically adopted by modern research (→ Chthonic deities). The Christian polemics against pagan cult focus especially on offensive and unusual rituals and categorically reject animal sacrifice.

On the other hand, there are the sacred laws (*leges sacrae*), attested from the late Archaic period, that codify individual cults, entire cult complexes or local cult calendars for politico-administrative reasons (LSCG and Suppl., LSAM, [2]); such laws have also been preserved, if more rarely, from Italian towns but not from Rome, where the records kept by priests, the so-called *libri pontificales*, performed that role [3]. Since the Renaissance modern research has largely concentrated on antiquarian details (Meursius: [23, 39f.]; [4; 5]). Constant parameters of cult are the particular time, the particular place, the (superhuman) recipient, the particular activity, and the particular attitude of the participants — expressed most of all in the concept of purity (→ Purification).

B. Time

Ancient cult was on the one hand connected with festival days — with those of individual cities which usually involved a sacrifice and a → procession (*pompé*), but also with those of larger or smaller social groupings, from the Panhellenic festival to that of individual *gentes*, — and, on the other hand, to extraordinary events that caused a group or individual to turn to the gods. This would happen, e.g., to avert a disaster, foretold or already present (plagues, famines, sieges and the like), to give thanks for help rendered or, from the Hellenistic period, to commemorate an exalted living individual (→ Ruler cult). From the late Archaic period the regular festivals were recorded in festival calendars, the main purpose of which was not so much the diary function as the setting down of state expenses (→ Nicomachus), while the Roman festival calendar that was put on public record by M. Fulvius Nobilior in the early 2nd cent. BC and subsequently codified had more of a representative function [6].

C. Place

The location of the cult was usually sacred, thus removed from customary places and generally with its boundaries demarcated. For the domestic cult, a niche in the wall or a simple, small altar would suffice for demarcation. Within cities, just as in open spaces, special areas were marked out and designated by surrounding walls (→ Temenos) and boundary stones; another regular feature is the → altar, often also a temple, and — particularly outside the cities — a special group of trees (→ Grove) or a spring; special localities — mountain peaks, grottoes — could become places for cult. (After a more potent sanctification, especially from a lightning strike, also those places were demarcated that were so inaccessible to humans that cult was impossible there [→ Abaton]).

D. Cult recipients

Each cult addressed a superhuman counterpart — gods, demons, heroes, deceased ancestors, whose particularities were also defined by the cult. Hymn and prayer recount the myth and efficacy of this counterpart. Specific features or details of the sacrifice were correlated with specific recipients, in that sacrificial offerings were a form of pre-payment; votive offerings, by contrast, express thanks for services rendered; apotropaic rites were appropriate for baneful beings; different libation for different beings (e.g. water, milk, and olive oil for the deceased); the type, colour and sex of a sacrificial animal depended on the recipient: animals outside the usual triad of cattle, sheep and pigs — such as goats, dogs, donkeys, birds — were reserved for special beings; female animals were often used for goddesses, black animals for dwellers of the underworld. In that sense the cult made a decisive contribution to the profile of the supra-human recipient; if living people (especially rulers) received cult, this had the profiling effect of differentiating and distancing them from other mortals.

E. Rites

From the Bronze Age, animal sacrifice (→ Sacrifices, [7; 8]) was the central ritual of Graeco-Roman antiquity. Following ancient views, the burning of bones and parts of the flesh served to feed the gods, and absence of sacrifice brought their existence into question (Aristoph. Av.); the fact that the gods ended up receiv-

ing the worthless part, and humans the edible flesh, had led as early as Hesiod's 'Theogony' to the aetiological myth of → Prometheus cheating the gods out of their sacrifices. While this feeding (or in Rome a meal taken together by gods and humans) was usually not really acted out (though the sacrificial portions could still be laid on the hands or knees of the idols [9. 40f.]), individual sacrifices were played out as real hospitality towards the gods, who were present in their statues (*theodaisía*, Lat. → *lectisternium*). With other types of ancient sacrifice [10] the animal or another offering was completely burned (holocaust), or sometimes also completely destroyed by immersion in water.

Beside animal sacrifice we also find non-bloody kinds of sacrifice —following Theophrastus' theory of culture and sacrifice, wrongly thought to be the older form in antiquity [11], in which the crop from trees and fields was offered up, often as a first-fruit sacrifice at, for example the start of the harvest, so as to allow the god to partake before the humans. Libations and prayers accompanied the sacrifice but also took place as independent ritual acts. Libation, the ritual pouring of particular liquids (most of all wine — sacrifice was not possible without wine —, but also water, milk, honey and olive oil), marked the different phases of the sacrificial proceedings but could also, e.g. for the marking of holy stones, take place in burial cult or magic; the semantics of different liquids structure the sacrificial proceedings or contribute to the recipient's profile [12].

In animal sacrifice, a → prayer, which like every rite has its own fixed structure, was delivered by the priest or master of the sacrifice before the slaughter of the victim, but could also be addressed to the divinity independently of any sacrifice; the essential element is that ancient prayer was always spoken aloud [13; 14]. The curse and the oath — as self-cursing — are not easily separated from prayer [15; 16]; poetically structured, the → *hymnus* is the functional equivalent of prayer.

F. Participants

A critical aspect of every sacrifice — the individual form of which might vary greatly depending on the locality and the occasion — is the fact that this ancient cult function always reflected the self-image and hierarchic structure of the organizing body; dispensing with the usual social hierarchy is, indeed, one of the features that mark the extraordinary character of the rituals of the → mystery cults. In that sense cult is almost always a group event, not something performed by an isolated individual (even if, by way of exception, the individual can act by himself in prayer, in cursing — from Hom. Il. 1,33ff. — and in magic ritual) with the presence of a religious specialist, the → priest, not being strictly necessary for the proper conduct of the cult. Private cult or cults at remote locations in Greece and Rome could do without his presence, while the presence of priests at state cults in Greek cities, just as in Rome, was the expression of the state's commitment to the cult.

Just as the location of the cult was set apart through its particular sanctity, so too were the cult participants exalted through special ritual purification. Preparatory ritual cleansing was necessary for every participant (for that purpose wash-basins were to be found at the entrance of ancient sanctuaries, and Verrius drives *delu-brum* 'sanctuary' from *luere* 'washing'). Sexual relations and contact with birth or death caused temporary exclusion or required special ritual cleansing before taking part in the cult again (→ Purification). Certain categories of people (women or men, slaves, foreigners) could be excluded altogether. The sign of sacralization was usually a garland, the shape of which was cult-specific [17]. Often a special form of dress was necessary; bare feet, white garments (or negatively a ban on coloured clothing), or, for women, hair worn open, were widespread as indicating a cultic state far removed from the ordinary. An extreme form of this was the → nudity that was practised in some cults; it had an initiatory background and indicated a transitional stage between two phases in life [18]. Another extreme aspect was the special formal attire of the priests, such as that of the Eleusinian hierophant and the Roman *flamen Dialis* (→ *flamines*); it raised the wearers up out of the rank of ordinary citizens as lifelong intermediaries between man and divinity [19] (while the clothing of the buyers of priesthoods in Hellenistic cities of Asia Minor, purple garment and golden garland, only promoted the rise in status as a selling point [20]).

Participation in cult not only expresses group identity, but it also to creates new groups. The polis and its subdivisions (*phratría, gens*), as well as links transcending the polis (amphictyonies; the Panhellenic cult in Olympia and Delphi; all Latini), expressed the fact of their belonging together in the cult. The same applied to outsiders, such as the various non-Greek groups in Athens (from the Classical period onwards, → Bendis) or in Delos, and the expatriate associations in cities of the Hellenistic East, all of whom expressed their identity in the cult of their local divinity; likewise, cults that transcended location, such as the mystery cults of Eleusis (Pl. Ep. 7) and Samothrace or the cults of Dionysus, Isis or Mithras, could create a specific group identity. Such groups often formed local cult associations whose function, especially in the Hellenistic and Imperial world, could extend far beyond communal cult practice and could range from the creation of new social ties for strangers (Apul. Met. 11) to groups philosophizing together (as in the case of Plato's Academy as *thíasos* of the Muses), so that communal cult worship can be interpreted a culturally specific focus of new forms of social organization [21; 22]; even the early Christian communities can be seen as groups linked by common cult worship that, as was the case with the mysteries, did not take place in public (Plin. Ep. 10,96,7). Conversely, refusal to take part in the cult, especially in the communal sacrifice, indicated a breach of solidarity and a declaration of being an outsider. This was the case with the vegetarian Pythagoreans of the 4th cent. BC and the early Christians.

1 A. TRESP, Die Fragmente der griech. Kultschriftsteller, 1914   2 J. v. PROTT, L. ZIEHEN, Leges Graecorum sacrae e titulis collectae, 2 vols. 1896/1906 (repr. 1988) 3 G. ROHDE, Die Kultsatzungen der röm. Pontifices, 1936 4 P. STENGEL, Opferbräuche der Griechen, 1910   5 Id., Die griech. Kultusaltertümer, ³1920   6 J. RÜPKE, Kalender und Öffentlichkeit. Die Geschichte der Repräsentation und rel. Qualifikation von Zeit in Rom, 1995   7 F. T. VAN STRATEN, Hiera kala. Images of Animal Sacrifice in Archaic and Classical Greece, 1995   8 O. REVERDIN, B. GRANGE (ed.), Le sacrifice dans l'antiquité, 1981 9 GRAF   10 W. BURKERT, Opfertypen und ant. Gesellschaftsstruktur, in: G. STEPHENSON (ed.), Der Religionswandel unserer Zeit im Spiegel der Religionswiss., 1976, 168–187   11 W. PÖTSCHER, Theophrastos. Περὶ Εὐσεβείας, 1964   12 F. GRAF, Milch, Honig und Wein. Zum Verständnis der Libation im griech. Ritual, in: Perennitas. Studi Angelo Brelich, 1980, 209–221   13 H. S. VERSNEL, Religious Mentality in Ancient Prayer, in: Id. (ed.), Faith, Hope and Worship, 1981, 1–64   14 S. PULLEYN, Prayer in Greek Rel., 1997   15 L. WATSON, Arae. The Curse Poetry of Antiquity, 1991   16 R. HIRZEL, Der Eid, 1902 17 M. BLECH, Stud. zum Kranz bei den Griechen, 1982 18 M. J. HECKENBACH, De nuditate sacra, 1911 19 M. BEARD, J. NORTH (ed.), Pagan Priests. Rel. and Power in the Ancient World, 1990   20 M. SEGRE, Osservazioni epigrafiche sulla vendita di sacerdozio, Rendiconti dell'Istituto, in: Lombardo 69, 1936, 811–830; 70, 1937, 83–105   21 P. BOYANCÉ, Le culte des Muses chez les philosophes grecs. Études d'histoire et de psychologie religieuse, 1936   22 F. POLAND, Geschichte des griech. Vereinswesens, 1909   23 L. MÜLLER, Geschichte der Philologie in den Niederlanden, 1869.   F.G.

IV. BIBLICAL

A. OLD TESTAMENT/ EARLY JUDAISM   B. NEW TESTAMENT/EARLY CHRISTIANITY

A. OLD TESTAMENT/ EARLY JUDAISM

Cult (as a regulated form of direct contact with the divine, serving both as divine worship and, through it, the promotion and sanctification of human existence) developed in the Old Testament-Jewish-Christian tradition by adapting cult practise to correspond to the divine and human images of the bearers of tradition. Originally barely distinguishable from the cult of its oriental neighbours, cult in Israel (especially in the theology that prevailed after the exile [587–539 BC]) displayed the following characteristics:

a) Monolatrist emphasis: the non-pictorial veneration of JHWH (→ Yahweh) asserts itself with increasing demands for exclusiveness. b) Centralizing tendency: the cult finds its focus in the sacrifice of domestic animals (late Old Testament-early Judaism, especially as expiatory sacrifice); in Josiah's reforms (around 622 BC) this sacrifice is unified and linked to the Temple of Jerusalem (2 Kgs 22f.; cf. Deut.). With the reorganization of the temple cult in the Persian period, the sacrificial cult becomes reserved for the (Zakodite) priests, with the high priest at their head, while the 'Levites' provide ancillary services; Jewish temples are also attested in Egypt: 6th/5th cents. BC at Elephantine, 2nd cent. BC, 1st cent. AD at Leontopolis. c) Commemorative dimension: through the calendar cycle the cult makes clear JHWH's acts of salvation towards his people (especially at Passover in memory of the Exodus). d) Ethical component: the cult criticism of the prophets (Amos, Isaiah et al.), → Psalms and Wisdom press for a social and moral attitude corresponding to the original cult intention. The Jewish movements of resistance against Seleucid (from 167 BC) and Roman domination (AD 66–70; 132–135) saw themselves motivated also by damage to the integrity of the cult and are accompanied by cult restoration (e.g. 164 BC reconsecration of the temple).

Disputes about legitimate cult led to the formation of Jewish factions: the → Sadducees, who were linked to the temple aristocracy, saw their allegiance as only to the biblical Torah cult; the Pharisees/→ *Pharisaei* were influential in emphasizing interpretation of ritual and, indeed, they extended priestly laws of purification to every-day life; the → Qumran community withdrew from the temple because they challenged the legitimacy of the Hasmonean priestly caste and of ritual practise, and developed — though without abandoning sacrifice cult — a practise that concentrated on scripture reading, cleansings and meal ritual. Temple cult disappeared after the destruction of Jerusalem and its temple by Titus in AD 70. Further cult development is marked by pharisaic-rabbinic emphasis on scripture readings and prayer.

B. New Testament/Early Christianity

The relationship between the Jesus movement/early Christianity and Jewish cult was characterized by both distance and affinity: → Jesus and the Palestinian community presuppose Jewish cult practice and emphasize following the prophetic tradition, the primacy of divine and neighbourly love (Mk 12,28–34 and *passim*). It was, however, in the non-ritually transmitted intimacy with the heavenly Father that Jesus anchored the salvation through the Kingdom of God (*basileía toû theoû*) that he himself heralded and proleptically performed. In thereby binding the relationship with God to divine initiative — like John the Baptist before him — he distanced himself from temple cult; against its optimistic view of salvation he brought forward the fact of God's eschatological claims at the cleansing of the temple (Mk 11,15–19; Jn 2,13–17). Already for Hellenistic Jewish Christianity the Jewish temple cult had become obsolete as means of salvation (e.g. Acts 7,47–50). The demarcation against pagan cult was more marked (e.g. 1 Cor. 10,19–22; Min. Fel. 32,1–3). The intellectual object of 'worship in spirit and truth' (cf. Jn 4,20–24) caused the preoccupation with sacred sites and concrete cult objects on the whole to recede. Nevertheless the cult, specifically in its Old Testament character, did retain a presence in early Christian literature (paradigmatically in Hebr and in the Epistle of Barnabas) and had a varied influence (cult and sacrifice metaphor, cult typology and allegory, cult-analogous eschatolofical

motifs), especially in soteriology, ecclesiology and ethics (e.g. Rom. 12,1: *logikè latreía*, 'logical C.'; 1 Pet. 2,5–10). Thus, basic cultic experience and models of interpretation of cult remained alive in early Christianity.

Focussing on baptism (that had developed into a rite of initiation) and the Eucharist, a genuine Christian cult gradually developed, from its earliest beginnings on the periphery of Jewish ritual (also under the influence of → mystery cults, in particular with the forms of initiation and meal ritual, as well as the premises for interpreting the sacrament). Its meaning and function is embodied in the confession of belief in the death for our salvation, the resurrection and the pneumatic presence of the → Kyrios Jesus Christ. With this conceptual transformation (especially in the threshold phase with the old Church), terminology (sacrifice, priest, altar etc.) and concrete forms of symbolism (sacred dates, actions, locations etc.) of the outdated cult practices, theologically reviewed and ethically applied, gain a new lease of life (e.g. the first epistle of Clement 43f.; Didache 14; Justin Dial. 117; Hippolytus, Traditio apostolica 4). The pagan environment was able to understand the Christian community as a cult association; but the latter's non-participation in public cult and the peculiarity of Christian worship aroused suspicions of impiety and murky secret rites (donkey cult, excesses, cannibalism etc.).

→ Cult image; → Sacrifices; → Ritual/Rites; → Temple

R. ALBERTZ, Religionsgesch. Israels in at. Zeit, 2 vols., ²1996/97; K. BACKHAUS, Kult und Kreuz. Zur frühchristl. Dynamik ihrer theologischen Beziehung, in: Theologie und Glaube 86, 1996, 512–533; R. J. DALY, Christian Sacrifice. The Judaeo-Christian Background before Origen, 1978; B. EGO, A. LANGE, P. PILHOFER (ed.), Gemeinde ohne Tempel. Zur Substituierung und Transformation des Jerusalemer Tempels und seines Kultes im AT, ant. Judentum und frühen Christentum, 1999; H.-J. KLAUCK, Herrenmahl und hell. Kult, ²1986; A. SCHENKER, TH. KWASMAN, K. BACKHAUS, s.v. Kult, LThK³ 6, 505–509.　KN.B.

Cult associations see → Associations

Culter (Greek μάχαιρα, *máchaira*). Originally the → knife, specifically the knife of butchers and therefore the butchering tool in → sacrifices (Hom. Hym. Apoll. 535f. for *máchaira*). On Greek and Roman representations, the *hiereús* or the *victimarius* has the sacrificial knife brought to him on a tray or holds it in his hand. The *culter* was used to open the carotid artery of the sacrificial animal and to cut out its intestines. The sacrificing *victimarius* was also called *cultrarius* after the sacrificial knife. Furthermore, the *culter* was the attribute of oriental peoples who were famous for their courage in battle (→ Amazons; → Sword).

→ Knives; → Razor

G. ROUX, Meurtre dans un sanctuaire sur l'amphora de Panagurišté, in: AK 7, 1964, 30–40; F. FLESS, Opferdiener und Kultmusiker auf stadtröm. histor. Reliefs, 1995, 19–20; 73–74.　R.H.

Cult Façade The term cult façade (CF) is used to designate the typically Phrygian monument of → Cybele. It consists of a façade chiselled into rock with an alcove for the statue of the goddess. The monuments are pointed towards sunrise. The older CF go back to the 8th cent. BC, when Phrygia was a powerful state. In the 6th cent., when Phrygia was already under Lydian rule, another group of CF was built. The façade of the 'Midas Monument' belongs to the older group. It is the best-preserved monument and can be found close to the ancient city of Midas near the modern village of Yazılı Kaya.

C.H. E. Haspels, The Highlands of Phrygia. Sites and Monuments, 1-2, 1971;; M.J. Mellink, s.v. Midas-Stadt, RLA 8, 1993-1997, 153-156.   FR.P.

Cult image
I. Ancient Orient   II. Phoenicia   III. Greece and Rome

I. Ancient Orient
A. General comments   B. Egypt
C. Mesopotamia   D. Palestine   E. Syria, Anatolia

A. General comments
In the Near East, idols which functioned as cult images (CI) could be found in central temples, peripheral sanctuaries, private houses, and sometimes on open-air sanctuaries and cult alcoves. Their material consistency, appearance, and size varied depending on their origin and the context of their use.

B. Egypt
CI of gods already existed in earliest times. They could be anthropomorphic (anthr.), theriomorphous, or of mixed shape, and were created as inanimate objects by craftsmen in a workshop ('gold house'), later to be animated through the ritual 'opening of the mouth'. They were made of stone or metal or as composite images made of wood covered by silver, gold, and/or elektron plating with inlays of semi-precious stones or ivory. The CI functioned as the body of the deity and formed the centre of everyday and festival cults. The religion of → Amenophis [4] IV brought a renunciation of the CI which is indicated in the fact that → Aton was not represented as a statue.

C. Mesopotamia
From the end of the 3rd millennium at the latest, gods were worshipped, i.a., in the shape of anthr. CI. The sometimes life-sized composite statues of the temples consisted of a wooden core with silver, gold, and/or elektron plating in which eyes, hair, etc. were inlaid with stone, semi-precious stones, or fritt (cf. for example [4.67A]). In the workshop, the craftsmen worked under the inspiration of their patron gods and built the statue whose creation could be regarded as the earthly birth of the deity. After the rituals 'washing of the mouth' and 'opening of the mouth' had been performed, the deity took part in earthly life through its CI. Outside of the temples, the gods were present in stone statues, divine symbols, and divine standards. In private cult, domestic gods were set up in the house in the shape of clay figurines.

D. Palestine
We have to assume the existence of clay or stone CI. already for the earliest period (21st-16th cents. BC). Metal statues of the mid Bronze Age (1st half of the 2nd millennium) primarily consisted of naked goddesses, which were replaced by enthroned or fighting gods in the late Bronze Age (15th -13th cents.) During the 1st millennium BC in Israel and Juda, gods continued to be worshipped, i.a., in the shape of anthropomorphic CI i.a. Partial documentation exists for bronze statuettes with gold or silver plating as well as for painted large-scale terracottas. Large composite figures from Gaza are found in a neo Assyrian relief of › Tiglatpileser III (744-27), [4. 65]. Small terracottas were common in the realm of private piety. The renunciation of image worship by the Judaic → Yahwe community is contested as far as dating, cause, development, and scope are concerned, but it is apparent in the OT's critique, polemics, and ban of images. It can be traced from the articulation of an anti-iconic programme up to its implementation, which took place much later.

E. Syria, Anatolia
Evidence of anthr. CI made of stone (Nevali Çori) already exists for the aceramic Neolithic period (c. 8th millennium). For the Syrian centres of the 3rd and 2nd millennia BC (→ Ebla, Emar etc.), there is evidence both of metal and composite statues (the latter being textually documented). CI made from precious metals are mentioned in the annals of Ḥattusili I. Extant from the period of the great empire (→ Ḥattusa II) are small bronze figurines with inlays, some with inset arms and legs and horned cone-shaped hats; descriptions of pictures from the time of Tudḥalija IV supplement the iconographic details and the lists of materials used in composite figures. Late Hittite art evolved differently in the various Hittite successor states (→ Asia Minor, Hittite successor states) and i.a. brought about large stone statues as well as small metal statues.
→ Sculpting, technique of; → Horned crown; → Gold-ivory technique; → Yahwe; → Juda and Israel

EGYPT: 1 J.Assmann, D.Wildung, s.v. Gott, Götterbild, LÄ 2, 671-674, 764f. 2 W.Barta, W.Helck, s.v. Kult, Kultstatue, LÄ 3, 839-848, 859-863.
MESOPOTAMIA: 3 A.Berlejung, Die Theologie der Bilder, 1998   4 A.H. Layard, Monuments of Nineveh 1, 1849   5 J.Renger, U.Seidl, s.v. Kultbild., RLA 6, 307-314.
PALESTINE: 6 C.Uehlinger, s.v. Götterbild, Neues Bibel-Lex. 1, 1991, 871-892   7 Id., Anthropomorphic Cult Statuary in Iron Age Palestine and the Search for Yahweh's Cult Images, in: K.van der Toorn (ed.), The

Image and the Book, 1997, 97–155.
Syria, Anatolia: 8 V. Haas, Gesch. der hethit. Rel., 1994. A.BER.

II. Phoenicia

Important old CI from the Phoenician and Punic realm were entirely or essentially non-iconic (for example, the CI of → Astarte/→ Aphrodite of → Paphus), true to the tradition of the → baitylia, the picture-less stone monuments endowed with numinous power typical for Semitic cultures. Extant are, among others, remnants and traces of the CI triad in the Phoenician temple of → Kommos (Crete) and of a CI in Sarepta (Sarafand, Lebanon). The customs, however, were not consistent. CI that followed Greek (and Egyptian) models (for example, → Heracles, → Melqart) are documented on coins and reliefs or have been copied as votive images (clay and bronze statuettes).
→ Phoenician Archaeology

S. Ribichini, Poenus advena. I dei fenici e l'interpretazione classica, 1985; P. Warren, Of Baetyls, in: OpAth 18, 1990, 193–206. H.G.N.

III. Greece and Rome
A. Theology 1. Introduction 2. Greece 3. Rome B. Archaeology 1. General 2. Historical development IV. Christian

A. Theology

1. Introduction

In contrast to the votive statues donated (publicly or privately) to sanctuaries (→ anáthēma), CI were part of the → cult. In this context, they were the object of various ritualistic practises that could only be carried out in the official cult by specially authorized persons (officials or priests). Probably in response to the polemical writings of Christian authors against so-called 'idolatry' (cf. i.a. Tert. De idolatria; Arnob.; Aug. Civ.) that focused on the aspect of 'image worship' in ancient polytheistic religions, older theologians, who were strongly influenced by 19th cent. Christian culture, also regarded the existence of CI as a central characteristic of ancient religions (i.a. [1; 13]).

2. Greece

The cults served by CI varied according to the nature of the cult image and the myth of the represented gods: dressing, feeding, and washing are documented for many CI, but only small and transportable CI were suitable for being carried along in → processions [4; 7; 8; 16]. The sacred nature of the CI was usually due to their old age and the legends resulting thereof, according to which they had, perhaps, 'fallen from the sky' (cf. for example Paus. 1,26,7; 9,12,4), or it was a result of the way they were displayed and/or decorated in the sanctuaries [5]. The manner in which priests, officials, and temple visitors were allowed to communicate with the CI was generally subject to rules (although perhaps not always). Depending on the type of cult and deity, it may have been allowed and customary for temple visitors to touch and kiss the CI (Hercules in Agrigent: Cic. Verr. 2,4,94), but equally customary were bans on touching (Diana/Artemis of Segesta: Cic. Verr. 2,4,77) and even the restriction of access to a certain group of people who were allowed to see CI (priestesses: Eileithyia in Hermione, Paus. 2,35,11; Ceres/Demeter in Catina: Cic. Verr. 2,4,99).

Little is known about the emergence of iconographies with canonical significance for Greek CI, especially since the oldest wooden CI are not extant. However, research has indicated that a given relationship between myth, ritual, and CI could be maintained even when a cult was exported into other regions and cultures where it was received and altered (Tauric Artemis: [9]; Artemis of Ephesus: [6]). The most voluminous collection of descriptions of Greek CI are the writings by Pausanias.

3. Rome

In older research, which predominantly referred to Varro (in Aug. Civ. 4,31), it was maintained that the Romans 'originally' had no CI since they were not acquainted with any myths comparable to those of the Greeks and thus did not know any anthropomorphic gods [14. 50ff.; 18. 32f.]. However, following the construction of the → Capitolium in the 6th cent. BC and the creation of a CI for the Capitolinic Triad (Jupiter, Juno, Minerva) by a (supposedly) Etruscan artist (Plin. HN 35,127: Volca), the majority of the later emerging public cult sites were furnished with CI. The practises performed with the CI (dressing, feeding: → lectisternium, cleansing), especially of the Graecus ritus, resembled those of the Greek models. The most prominent example of a non-anthropomorphic Roman CI is the black (meteor) stone from the → Mater Magna cult imported in 205–04 BC from Pessinunte (cf. Liv. 29,10,7; Amm. Marc. 22,9,5). The Roman CI were regarded as sacra publica ('public cult objects') and had to be specially consecrated by officials and pontifices (later also by the emperors), (→ Consecratio; → Votive offerings).

It is hard to determine what role the Romans played in introducing the use of CI to the indigenous peoples in Western and Northern Europe, since possible (older) wooden CI are not extant. It seems likely that the → 'Romanization' of indigenous institutions and cults frequently brought about new forms that however were carried out with Roman means (regarding Spain cf. [15]). It is similarly unclear to what extent the colonies founded by Rome contributed to the diffusion of Roman types of CI (on the Capitolinic Triad: [12]).

Christianization resulted in a break from using CI in European religion (see below IV.). Mostly due to the Jewish tradition of a non-pictorial (non-iconic) notion of God, all forms of CI were at first categorically rejected. However, following the → veneration of saints, acts which are comparable with ancient practises (esp. ritual baths) were performed on the statues of saints by the early Middle Ages at the latest [2; 17].

1 F. BACK, De Graecorum caerimoniis in quibus homines deorum vice fungebantur, diss. Berlin 1883   2 E. BEVAN, Holy Images. An Inquiry into Idolatry and Image Worship in Ancient Paganism and Christianity, 1940   3 BURKERT 4   H. U. CAIN, Hell. Kultbilder Rel. Präsenz und museale Präsentation der Götter im Heiligtum und beim Fest, in: M. WÖRRLE, P. ZANKER (ed.), Stadtbild und Bürgerbild im Hell., 1995, 115–130   5 H. CANCIK, H. MOHR, s.v. Religionsästhetik, HrwG 1, 121–156   6 R. FLEISCHER, Artemis von Ephesos und verwandte Kultstatuen aus Anatolien und Syrien, 1973   7 B. GLADIGOW, Epiphanie, Statuette, Kultbild. Griech. Gottesvorstellungen im Wechsel von Kontext und Medium, in: Visible Rel. 7, 1990, 98–111   8 Id., Präsenz der Bilder, Präsenz der Götter. Kultbilder und Bilder der Götter in der griech. Rel., in: Visible Rel. 4/5, 1985/86, 114–127   9 F. GRAF, Das Götterbild aus dem Taurerland, in: Ant. Welt 10/4, 1979, 33–41   10 F. HAMPL, Kultbild und Mythos. Eine ikonographisch-myth. Unt., in: F. KRINZINGER et al. (ed.), Forsch. und Funde, FS B. Neutsch, 1980, 173–185   11 K. KOONCE, ΑΓΑΛΜΑ and ΕΙΚΩΝ, in: AJPh 109, 1988, 108–110   12 B. H. KRAUSE, Trias Capitolina: ein Beitr. zur Rekonstruktion der hauptstädtischen Kultbilder und deren statuentypologischer Ausstrahlung im röm. Weltreich, diss. 1989   13 E. KUHNERT, De cura statuarum (Berliner Stud. für klass. Philol. 1,2), 1884 (repr. 1975)   14 LATTE 15 A. NÜNNERICH-ASMUS, Architektur und Kult — Beispiele ländlicher und urbaner Romanisierung, in: H. CANCIK, J. RÜPKE (ed.), Reichsrel. und Provinzialrel., 1997, 169–184   16 I. B. ROMANO, Early Greek Cult Images and Cult Practices, in: R. HÄGG, N. MARINATOS, G. C. NORDQUIST (ed.), Early Greek Cult Practice, 1988, 127–133   17 P. SAINTYVES, De l'immersion des idoles antiques aux baignades des statues saintes dans le christianisme, in: RHR 108, 1933, 144–192   18 G. WISSOWA, Rel. und Kultus der Römer, ²1912.   C.F.

B. ARCHAEOLOGY

1. GENERAL

In classical archaeology, CI designates the representation of a deity in or in front of the temple consecrated to it. We do not have a specific ancient term. The CI is a scientific classification and must be studied as a special type of idol according to archaeological criteria. It is a complete sculpture and — usually entirely, at times only partially — anthropomorphic. It was transferred into paintings or reliefs only in domestic cults (→ *lararium*), in regional cults of the ancient periphery (Thracian horseman), or in cult communities of the Imperial period (Mithras Reliefs). Ancient cults required the presence of the deity in the CI which, in turn, was housed in the temple. The temple could be occupied by several deities (cult partners) which were joined in CI groups. Additional deities could later join in (*synhedroi*), in Hellenism it was often a → *basileús*, in the imperial period a member of the imperial family. Further idols in the temple were usually different in form, always set up differently than the CI, and regarded as votive objects.

The CI was not regarded as identical with the deity but as its visualization. It guaranteed and emphasized the notion that the deity was accessible and it communicated the power of the deity in an artistic way. This was accomplished through the use of overwhelmingly large shapes (→ Colossus), through illustrations on the base and on the accessories that clarified the myth, through the use of precious materials (gold, ivory, precious wood), and through impressive distinctions between body, hair, and robe. Ritual washing and dressing, → lectisternium and theoxeny often required a small format, while the festive → epiphany of large CI was supported through the special use of lighting, proportions and spatial arrangement of elements designed to create distance (gates, bases, curtains). Shining eyes made of precious stones, hair made of reflecting precious metals and ephemeral decorations brought the deity to life. The experience of the deity's presence through the CI is witnessed in reports about granted requests, conversations, nodding of the head, sexual intercourse, and declarations of love. The abduction of the CI was regarded as equivalent to the destruction of the community, and in a similar sense, it was comforting to take it along after expulsions. The secure connection between the deity and its place found expression in the reverence for ancient forms and iconography (→ Xoanon), while any modernization of the CI rarely took place. The CI created and preserved the appearance of the local deity, thus being disseminated in votive objects, memorialized on coins and document steles, or copied when the cult spread out further.

2. HISTORICAL DEVELOPMENT

A) GREECE

Only few original CI have survived in fragments, even fewer in their original context. Research is thus based on the descriptions in written sources and the pictures on local coins. A small number of CI can be identified in copies from the imperial period (Apollo Philesios, see → Canachus [1]; Athena Parthenos). The late 8th cent. BC witnessed the creation of the first CI and that of the oldest preserved original → sphyrelaton (Apollo, Dreros). All of the ancient CI known of through literary sources were of small format and shaped as xoanon with or without a lining of gold, bronze, or ivory, in not always entirely human shapes, but always attired in real robes (Hera of Samos, Artemis of Ephesus, Athena Chalkioikos in Sparta).

Large formats and bronze statues were rare (Apollo Philesios, Apollo Amyklaios) and there is no evidence of marble statues. At the end of the 6th cent. BC, the first acroliths (→ Akrolithon) emerged in Magna Graecia in the 5th cent. They together with the gold-ivory statues (→ Gold-ivory technique) constituted a type of monumental design unique for CI, and determined the appearance of the chief gods over centuries. The formats vary from large to colossal in size. their appearance being colourful and expensive. Gold-ivory statues shape the image of deities with white skin and hair that gleams of gold (Ivory Athena, Rome, MV); essences gave the deities a pleasant smell. Divine attributes such as goodness, grace, majesty were expressed through artistic means and caused a religious experience. Regarded as zenith were the colossal gold-ivory statues of Athena Parthenos and of Zeus in Olympia by → Phidias, both of which were seen as expressing the complete essence of godliness; the staging of the Zeus statue was rehearsed in Olympia in a workshop. The CI only played a limited role in the transformation of the divine image during the late classical period. We still find hieratic poses, but genre motifs do not appear in the CI. Representations of Aphrodite which were created through portraiture of artists' models (→ Praxiteles) are therefore judged in many different ways.

The Hellenistic period continued with the colossal size and the use of a variety of materials on acroliths and marble paintings with accessories from other materials (Priene, Claros, Aegira). In regard to form, both classicist and archaic elements are popular. The iconography of Zeus, Asclepius, and Athena maintains its orientation towards the classical period, even in peripheral cultures (Solunte, Ai Chanum); it becomes canonical and exerts Greek influence on the CI of foreign deities (Serapis; Cybele). A number of partially extant CI groups appear standing or enthroned in a manner typical of family pictures (Messene, Lycosura).

b) ROME

Not much more is known about CI in early Rome and in the Italian landscapes than the mention of xoana and Etruscan-style terracotta cult images (Jupiter in Rome, 6th cent. BC). In the course of general Hellenization, the earliest CI in Greek style can be found in Rome from the late 3rd cent. BC onwards. Since they were always donated by a commander or a magistrate, the earliest examples stem from → war booty. In the 2nd cent. BC, they were created by Greek artists in Rome (artist family of the Timarchids); few fragments of the usually colossal acroliths are extant (*Fortuna huiusce diei*, *Fides*). Due to the many temples donated by the military, there was a great demand with the iconography of the many personifications (Honos, Virtus, Spes, Clementia) rarely being particularly developed. In the rest of Italy, acroliths and marble colossi also were common (Diana in Nemi, Feronia in Terracina). In the imperial period, the CI of Jupiter in the city of Rome is prescribed for the entire empire. Other CI are only known from pictures on coins and appear to have been derived from Greek types. Due to cultic reasons, we find here predominately seated images. The Roman preference for numerous epithets finds its correlative in a greater abundance of attributes. Most of the newly created CI are devoted to the *Divi Augusti* and *Divae Augustae* and are reproductions of Zeus statues and Fortuna or Venus statues in larger-than-life marble works. CI played an important role in Christian and pagan apologetics. From the 4th cent. AD on, CI were secularized as works of art, moved from the dismantled temples into public buildings (Constantinople), or 'executed' through destruction.

CULT IMAGE

V. MÜLLER, s.v. Kultbild, RE Suppl. 5, 472–511; H.P. LAUBSCHER, Hell. Tempelkultbilder, diss. Heidelberg 1960 (typescript); I. B. ROMANO, Early Greek Cult Images, 1980; H. FUNKE, s.v. Götterbild, RAC 11, 659–828; W. SCHÜRMANN, Unt. zu Typologie und Bedeutung der stadtröm. Minerva-Kultbilder., 1985; B. GLADIGOW, Präsenz der Bilder, Präsenz der Götter, in: VisRel 4–5, 1985f., 114–127; H. G. MARTIN, Röm. Tempelkultbilder, 1987; C. VERMEULE, The Cult Images of Imperial Rome, 1987; B. ALROTH, Greek Gods and Figurines, 1989; B.H. KRAUSE, Trias Capitolina, diss. Trier 1989 (typescript); B. GLADIGOW, Zur Ikonographie und Pragmatik röm. Kultbilder, in: Iconologia sacra, 1994, 9–24; H. U. CAIN, Hell. Kultbilder, in: Stadtbild und Bürgerbild im Hell., 1995, 115–130; E. I. FAULSTICH, Hell. Kultstatuen und ihre Vorbilder, 1997; E. HÄGER-WEIGEL, Griech. Akrolith-Statuen des 5. und 4. Jh.v.Chr., 1997; A. A. DONOHUE, The Greek Images of the Gods. Considerations on Terminology and Methodology, in: Hephaistos 15, 1997, 31–45.
R.N.

IV. CHRISTIAN

Christianity at first follows Judaism in its strict rejection of images and their cultic worship (Ex. 20,4f.). However, since Jesus Christ is understood to be the 'image of God' (2 Cor. 4,4; Col. 1,15), it is impossible to avoid the theological reflection of his human image. Consequently, after various preliminary steps, → Iohannes [33] of Damascus (Contra imaginum calumniatores orationes tres, esp. 1,14–16) develops an actual theology of the image (icon) in *c.* 730 which is finally adopted by the Eastern Church after long-lasting conflicts (iconoclasm, → Syrian dynasty) during the 7th Ecumenical Council of 787 in Nicaea (reinforced as definitive by empress Theodora in 843): since the nature of God and the nature of man are joined together in Jesus Christ (so called *perichōrēsis*), his image also expresses the actual invisible divinity. One must, however, distinguish between the glorification of the image (*proskýnēsis katà timén/timētikè proskýnēsis*) and the worship of God (*proskýnēsis katá latreían/ alēthinē latreía*). While Christianity at first very generally reproached the pagan world because its practise of 'idolatry', it now found itself clarifying its own cultic behaviour towards image and God in a complex terminology. One could interpret the worship of relics of martyrs and other saints as a preliminary step in the Christian treatment of CI, esp. the worship of the relic of the cross that was supposedly found by → Helena [2], the mother of Emperor Constantine I (a terminological differentiation was already made in the martyrium of → Polycarpus of Smyrna [†156] 17,3: to worship the son of God — to love the martyrs).

B. KOTTER (ed.), Die Schriften des Johannes von Damaskos, vol. 3 (Patristische Texte und Studien 17), 1975; H. G. THÜMMEL, Bilderlehre und Bilderstreit, 1991.
M.HE.

Cumae see → Cyme

Cumani, Comani Extinct Turkic people from the Kipchak group. Their self-designation was *Kun*, Slavic *Polovcy*, German *Polowzer*, or *Falben*; referred to as 'Falbi' in the Middle Ages. The C. are documented to have lived in the Volga Basin since the late 9th cent. In the middle of the 11th cent. AD, they invaded the region of the modern Ukraine, laid waste Hungary in 1071–72, extinguished the → Patzinaks in 1091, represented a constant threat for Russia between 1060 and 1210, and were defeated in 1239–40 by the Mongols. They served as intermediaries for the Byzantines in the commerce between the Black Sea and the Russians. Ruled by the 'Golden Horde', they became a basic element of the modern Turkic peoples in the Pontic-Russian steppe regions. A part of the C. went to Hungary, where they maintained their traditional religion as *Kúnok* until 1350.

Cumanic belongs to the predecessors of the modern kipchak Turkic languages. It is documented in the *Codex Cumanicus* (c. 1294–1340; Bibliotheca Marciana, Venice), which is a heterogeneous collection of Latin-Persian-Cumanic and German-Cumanic glossaries and of Cumanic versions of individual parts of the Latin liturgies that was probably brought together by Genoese merchants and German Franciscans.

G. HAZAI, s.v. Kumān, EI 5, 373a-b; G. KUUN (ed.), Codex Cumanicus, 1981. CL.SCH.

Cunaxa (Κούναξα; *Koúnaxa*). City on the left shore of the Euphrates river mentioned only by Plut. Artaxerxes 8,2. In its vicinity, → Cyrus [3] the Younger lost the battle and his life against his brother → Artaxerxes [2] II in the autumn of 401 BC. According to Plut., the city was 500 stadia away from Babylon, but according to Xen. An. 2,2,6, the distance was 360. Thus, until today the city's location cannot be clearly ascertained (Tell Kuneise?).

H. GASCHE, Autour des Dix Mille: Vestiges archéologiques dans les environs du 'Mur de Médie', in: P. BRIANT (ed.), Dans les pas des Dix-Mille, 1995, 201–216, esp. 201; O. LENDLE, comm. on Xen. An. (bk. 1–7), 1995, s.v. Kunaxa J.W.

Cuneiform, legal texts in

A. GENERAL POINTS B. DETAILS C. RECEPTION
D. HISTORY OF RESEARCH

A. GENERAL POINTS

Legal texts in cuneiform (LTC) are named after the → cuneiform script which had emerged towards the end of the 4th millennium BC in Mesopotamia, spread through the entire Near East, and was used to record the legally relevant proceedings in this area. Similar to Latin writing, cuneiform script in itself does not give any indications about the cultural or legal background of a written document. The use of the plural for 'LTC' is therefore appropriate. Only in Mesopotamia itself, the written documents comprise the entire time span from the invention of cuneiform script until gradual replacement in daily use by → Aramaic and then by Greek starting in the 1st millennium BC.

The state of the documents from the various systems of laws varies drastically; within each, we find that the different types of businesses and the different types of sources are represented unevenly. C. 80% of the extant cuneiform material consist of legal or administrative documents and of letters. The share of legal documents varies from only a few documents (e.g. Ebla: 10–15 of 15,000 texts; → Hattusa: c. 200 of several thousand texts) to c. 30% of texts in the Old Babylonian material. They consist primarily of business and trial documents and to a much smaller extent of legislation, such as *i.a.* the Old Babylonian *mēšarum* file ('Seisachtheia'), of collections of laws, and → international treaties. In addition, there exist indirect legal sources such as official and private letters, administrative documents, royal inscriptions, → wise sayings , → omens, hymns, and epics.

The different historical periods distinguishable for → Mesopotamia are also clearly defined in the history of law. The first (Old Sumerian) documents originated in the period of the early dynasty (until 2330 BC). Following the empire of Akkad (c. 2330–2190), which is less fruitful also as far as legal history is concerned, we have more than 30,000 clay plates from the New Sumerian period (21st cent.), among them more than 1,000 contracts and trial documents, and furthermore the first record of the Sumerian and Old Babylonian *Codices*. The question whether the latter are by their nature laws has yielded a controversial argument but should be negated. So far, over 7,000 contracts and trial documents, several thousand letters, the Codex → Hammurapi, the most voluminous of the *codices*, as well as acts of royal legislation ('Seisachtheia') have been published from the Old Babylonian period (c. 2000–1595). In contrast, the roughly contemporary Old Assyrian period has yielded few written documents from the Assyrian core territory in northern Mesopotamia. The mid Babylonian period is also only sparsely recorded compared to the mid Assyrian period. The most eminent legal document of this time is the 'mid Assyrian book of law' (c. 1100 BC). Several legal documents exist from the new Assyrian as well as from the new Babylonian periods, also a fragment which is discussed as a 'new Babylonian law'. The last legal documents in cuneiform script belong to the Seleucid and Arsacid periods (3rd–1st cents).

Outside of Mesopotamia, the legally documented cultural periods are shorter. The oldest known city so far with voluminous textual findings is → Ebla (c. 2300). Few legal documents stem from → Mari, which was destroyed by Hammurapi. From → Kaneš, an old Assyrian trade colony in Anatolia, there exist over 20,000 texts that originated in the period between c. 1900–1700 BC (primarily from the 19th cent). Among them are many legal documents that reflect old Assyrian and local law. The → Hittite law of Anatolia can be reconstructed primarily from the 'Hittite Laws' and from documents that today would be counted under public law (e.g. deeds of land gifts; office instructions). Additional groups of documents of significant volume and relevance for the history of law are extant primarily from → Elam (c. 26th — 6th cents.), from the Hurri(ti)c royal houses of Arrapḫa and Nuzi (c. 1460–1330; → Hurrians), furthermore from → Alalaḫ (18th and 15th cents.) and → Ugarit (c. 1400–1200), but hardly any from → Urartu (c. 825–640).

B. DETAILS

Clay plates were the material typically used for writing LTC. Codifications are unknown since the legislation concerns individual matters, and none of the collections of legal norms that were in use comprises the entire system of laws. This latter resulted primarily from everyday documents which recorded personal, family, and material law (→ Marriage; → Family; → Manumission; → Woman), and, more importantly, the commercial transactions which were needed in the active economy (Antichresis; Order; → Surety; → Loan; Contract of employment; Division (of inheritance); (Commerce)-Association; → Purchase; → Tenancy; → Leasehold; → Security; Gifts; Exchange; Settlement; Safekeeping; Work Contract). Business documents were for the most part evidentiary documents, possibly also dispositive documents. In general, witnesses were used, among them the writer of the document; as security, one sometimes used the (promissory) → oath, the → curse, and the (possibly bloody) contract punishment. As is customary today, documents were sealed through the use of signature. On the outside, the documents predominantly came in the form of double documents (cover plate surrounding the interior plate) up to Neo-Babylonian times. It is certainly possible that this form influenced the arrangement of the (later) Greek double documents. The stylization of the documents followed certain forms, in which we can trace local differences and changes over time. A common form was the (often abstract) certificate of commitment. At times we can recognize symbolic acts that indicate the completion of a legal matter (e.g. cutting the seam of a robe), but there is no evidence that Roman-type formalism was practised. A general archiving of legal documents was unknown, but public as well as private → archives did exist. The procedure used in these also is recorded in numerous documents. The details differ in all respects depending on the different systems of laws.

C. RECEPTION

All LTC belong to the 'pre-scientific' laws (prior to Roman jurisprudence), that is, they are lacking in theoretical background and are held up entirely by the practises of scribes. This does not lessen their legal significance but must be considered in the exegesis regarding terminology and practises. The → scribes practised legal phrases by copying model contracts and compendia of forms, and were clearly competent enough to fulfil the daily legal needs. In the later reception of LTC, specifically regarding the history of law, we must distinguish between, on the one hand, the practise of possibly using 'plagiarized' clauses and business types — which can only be proven by way of comparison — and on the other hand, the literary tradition of collecting laws and other writings that is traceable all the way into the Bible (cf. e.g. [5]).

D. HISTORY OF RESEARCH

From the end of the 19th cent., soon after the cuneiform script was deciphered, there appeared editions of documents and collections of translations ([4. 210ff.]; TUAT 1: collections of laws; TUAT 3: documents in a survey of cultural comparisons), as well as the first summarizing representations [4. 51ff.]. The publication of the *Codex Ḥammurapi* in 1902 strongly stimulated the research of LTC and the publication of documents. We must, however, differentiate between number of texts discovered, texts published in autographs, and texts that have been published with commentary and translation. Since many documents stem from illegal excavations, only a certain amount of editing has occurred for holdings that are connected. The state of publication and the abundance of material will not allow an exhaustive representation of LTC in the foreseeable future, even though a large number of studies exist concerning individual questions of legal history, with more of them appearing constantly.

→ Civil law

1 S. GREENGUS, Legal and Social Institutions of Ancient Mesopotamia, in: J. M. SASSON (ed.), Civilizations of the Ancient Near East 1, 1995, 469–484 2 R. HAASE, Einführung in das Studium keilschriftl. Rechtsquellen, 1965 3 Id., Die keilschriftl. Rechts-Sammlungen in dt. Fassung, 1979 4 V. KOROŠEC, Keilschrift, in: HbdOr, suppl.-vol. 3, 1964, 49–219 5 E. OTTO, Rechtsgesch. der Redaktionen im Kodex Ešnunna und im Bundesbuch, 1989 6 M. SAN NICOLÒ, Beitr. zur Rechtsgesch. im Bereiche der keilschriftl. Rechtsquellen, 1931.

BIBLIOGRAPHIES AND REFERENCE BOOKS: R. BORGER, Hdb. der Keilschriftlit. 3, 1975; RLA (with numerous legal lemmata); M. SAN NICOLÒ, É. SZLECHTER, in: SDHI 16, 1950–1962, 1996 (triannually); G. CARDASCIA, S. LAFONT, in: Revue Historique de Droit Français et Étranger 75, 1997.   JO.HE.

Cuneiform script is the old Mesopotamian writing system whose spread reached west into → Asia Minor (19th–13th cents. BC), into the Caucasus (→ Urartu, 9th–7th cents.), and south-west to → Syria (since the 24th cent., → Ebla) and Palestine, temporarily also into Egypt (→ Amarna letters). Cuneiform script (CS) was written from the left to the right. The 'wedge' shape of the individual stroke elements of the signs resulted from the act of pressing the stylus into moist clay, but the transfer of this 'wedge'-shape to inscriptions on stone also brought about the modern term of CS (cf. Latin *cuneus*, 'wedge'). In the beginning ('invention' of the CS

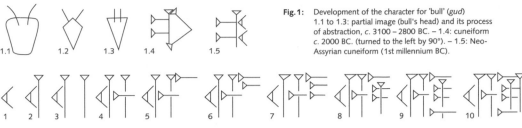

Fig. 1: Development of the character for 'bull' (*gud*)
1.1 to 1.3: partial image (bull's head) and its process of abstraction, c. 3100 – 2800 BC. – 1.4: cuneiform c. 2000 BC. (turned to the left by 90°). – 1.5: Neo-Assyrian cuneiform (1st millennium BC).

Fig. 2: Sequence of wedges in writing the character *ù* (c. 2000 BC).

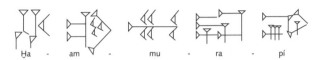

Ha - am - mu - ra - pí

Fig. 3: Name of King Ḫammurapi in syllabic script (c. 1750 BC).

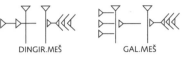

DINGIR.MEŠ   GAL.MEŠ

Fig. 4: 'The great gods' DINGIR.MEŠ GAL.MEŠ, in Akkadian, written with the Sumerograms DINGIR, 'god', and GAL 'great', and the logogram MEŠ = plural (1st millennium BC).

at the end of the 4th millennium BC in South Mesopotamia), we find predominantly pictorial signs; however, in the course of few generations, these signs were abstracted into linear shapes, whereby signs were now put together from single strokes, the so-called *Winkelhaken* (lit. 'angle-hooks' — two wedges so combined as to form an angle) and indented circles for ciphers, (fig. 1). The sequence in which the different elements in a sign were written was fixed (as is the sequence of lines in the Sino-Japanese system; fig. 2).

The original inventory contained signs for words, ciphers, and units of measurement. By way of phonetic abstraction (for example, a slight variation of *gi*/'reed' was also used for Sumerian *gi*/'to return'), a system of syllables emerged (in which the value of the syllable *gi* was entirely abstract) with the types of v(owel) (for example, *a, e, i, u*), c(onsonant)v (for example, *ba, bu*), vc (for example, *ab, ub*), and cvc (for example, *bar, bul*). CS did not complete the next step of forming an alphabet (the notation of mere consonants); but the syllabography of CS with its precise notation of vowels was of superior clarity compared to scripts consisting of consonants only.

Texts in CS are rarely written in purely syllabographic form (syllabographic script: fig. 3; logographic script: fig. 4). CS is characterized by a mixed system of word signs and syllable signs (comparable to the Japanese use of Chinese characters and *kana* syllabic signs). Since it is impossible for syllabography to represent two consonants in initial or final position (e.g. *tra-*, *-art*) or three in medial position (*-astra-*), one had to find a makeshift solution when writing words in languages that contained such consonant clusters: Hittite *ši-pa-* for *spa-* or *As-ta-ar-ta-* for Greek *Strato-*(*nike*). For a span of 3,000 years, CS served as a means of rendering Sumerian and Akkadian, and — at different times — other languages as well: → Hurrian, → Amorite, Cassitic (→ Cossaei), → Hittite and related Indo-European languages, → Elamite and → Urartian. Ugaritic → al-

phabetical script (14th–13th cents. BC) was an offspring of CS in form. → Ancient Persian cuneiform also is a CS in matters of form (not system). The total number of CS signs that were in use varied depending on the time period; for instance, only c. 600 signs were still used in Assyria in the 1st millennium BC (compared to the c. 1,000 signs used in the 3rd millennium). However, the scribes in e.g. Old Assyria (20th–19th cents.) and Old Babylon (19th–17th cents.) were able to get by with a minimal system of 70–80 signs, if necessary.

CS experienced a significant palaeographical development from the early 3rd millennium to the end of the 1st millennium, in that the CS in Assyria and Babylon took on their own individual styles from the 2nd millennium onwards. We also find individual variations of CS in peripheral regions, esp. in the Hittite kingdom (→ Hattusa). Differences also exist between monumental CS (on stone) and strongly cursive forms (for instance in letters).

→ Script

1 B. ANDRÉ-LEICKNAM, C. ZIEGLER (ed.), Naissance de l'Écriture, ⁴1982   2 D. O. EDZARD, s.v. Keilschrift, RLA 5, 544–68   3 M. GELLER, The Last Wedge, in: ZA 87, 1997, 43–95   4 M. KREBERNIK, H. J. NISSEN, Die Sumer.-akkad. Keilschrift, in: H. GÜNTHER et al. (ed.), Schrift und Schriftlichkeit, 1994, 274–88 (incl. bibliography)   5 E. REINER, How We Read Cuneiform Texts, in: JCS 25, 1973, 3–58.   D.O.E.

Cunobellinus Briton king (*Britannorum rex*, Suet. Calig. 44) between c. AD 10–40/43. Son of → Tasciovanus. The interpretation of his coins reveals that C., starting from Verulamium, succeeded in gaining control over most of south-east Britain and in establishing his rule in Camulodunum in the region of the → Trinovantes (Essex) without provoking Roman intervention. His death may well have changed the situation, as the primary goal of the Claudian invasion (AD 43) was to conquer the kingdom of C. (Cass. Dio 60,20). The notion that C. can be identified generally as the king of Catuvellauni is based only on textual conjectures by Cassius Dio.

→ Adminius; → Caratacus

S. FRERE, Britannia, ³1987, 27–47; R. P. MACK, The Coinage of Ancient Britain, ³1975.   C.KU.

Cup see → Pottery, shapes and types of

Cupid see → Eros

Cupido see → Eros

Cupra Maritima City on the coast in Picenum (*regio V, tribus Velina*) near La Civita, north of modern Cupra Marittima. CM derived from a sanctuary for the goddess Cupra that is of pre-Roman origin; *IIviri* are documented. Archaeological remnants: A forum from the Augustan period, fragments of consular lists.

G. PACI (ed.), Cupra Marittima e il suo territorio in età antica (Atti del Convegno, maggio 1992), 1993 (Picus Suppl. 2).   S.M.M.

Cura

[1] Personification of worry (ThlL, Onom. 2,753). In Horace's first Roman Ode, C. is a black, ghostly companion of man (Hor. Carm. 3,1,40: *post equitem sedet atra C.*). Aeneas encounters the 'avenging worries' (*ultrices Curae*) at the gate of Hades (Verg. Aen. 6,274 and Serv. Aen. on this passage). According to Hyginus Fab. 220, C. formed man from a piece of earth. Saturn determines that man belongs to C. in life and to Jupiter after death. The fable is of Greek origin [1]. In all probability, evidence for C. exists on a *poculum deorum* (CIL I² 442: *Coira pocolo* [2]). The idea of C. as a personified figure has also been adopted in German literature (Goethe, Hans Sachs) [3].

1 J. BERNAYS, Ges. Abh., 1885, 2, 320   2 R. WACHTER, Altlat. Inschr., 1987, 465   3 M. HAUSER, Der röm. Begriff C., diss. Basle 1954, 84–88.

P. FEDELI, s.v. C., EV 1, 961f.   R.B.

[2] **Cura, curatores.** In the Roman Republic, *cura* generally designated the carrying out of public duties in the political and legal realms. More specifically, it referred to tasks that were not automatically and regularly under the purview of the ordinary magistracies (→ *magistratus*). They could be assigned to annual magistrates as additional tasks or to specially elected extraordinary officials. At first, there was no precise terminology for the holders of *curae*. Instead, various designations could be used such as *IIIviri agris dandis assignandis* or *curator restituendi Capitolii* (Varro in Gell. NA 2,10,2). The constitution required a popular vote for the appointment of special emissaries, and typically the designation not of an individual person but of a *collegium* of several men (*IIIviri, Vviri, Xviri*) for the office. The

transfer of the *curatio annonae* to Pompey was therefore an exception reflecting the changed political situation. All in all, *cura* came to be used as a general designation of the responsibility for the *res publica*, whereby also the position of *princeps* could be aggrandized propagandistically and ideologically since Augustus.

Already in the last phase of the Roman Republic, the term *curatores* was occasionally applied to special emissaries. In particular, we encounter the designation of *curator viarum* in reference to an independent task without link to any other office, and in reference to an additional task given to an ordinary magistrate (CIL I² 808 = ILLRP I² 465; CIL I² 744 = D. 5800 = ILLRP I² 465a). Beginning with Augustus, *curatores* become a common phenomenon in Rome itself, as well as in the other cities managed by Rome. Augustus installed *curatores* of senatorial rank in order to give continuity to certain limited public and administrative necessities in the city of Rome. At the same time, this was a means to tie more senators into official activities which gave them a chance to gain prestige.

The *curatores viarum*, the only *curatores* to be active outside of Rome, were appointed from 20 BC on, when Augustus assumed the *cura viarum* himself [4. 25ff.]. They were organized as a collegium and were jointly responsible for all of the main state highways in Italy. Beginning only in the Claudian period, each *curator* was assigned a specific road. From that time on, seven or eight *curatores* were active simultaneously [5]. They were responsible for road repairs; in the case of the *via Traiana*, the first *curator*, Pompeius Falco, also led the new construction (ILS 1035). However, the name of the builder on milestones and building inscriptions is always that of the emperor. The main task of the *curatores* was the delegation of the construction work to contractors and the procurement of financing through the *aerarium* or the cities. Apparently, the *curatores viarum* were nominated by the *princeps* on the basis of a senatorial decision, as is documented for the *curatores aquarum* (Frontin. Aq. 100,1); later, the Senate no longer took part in the appointments.

The other *curatores* for the city of Rome were also appointed in this manner well until the Claudian period. In 11 BC, three *curatores aquarum* were appointed as managers of the Roman municipal water supply. They received the troop of 240 slaves that had been put together by Agrippa as workers. Claudius then enlarged the troop by 460 more slaves. But even this substantial number of personnel was only used for occasional repairs, larger construction projects always being given to contractors. The personnel was responsible in particular for ensuring the daily supply of all parts of the city by adjusting the flow. A detailed insight this can be found in Frontinus' *De aquis urbis Romae* [1; 6].

The *curatores locorum publicorum iudicandorum*, who initially were responsible for the public lands in Rome, also were Augustan. This *cura* was changed and broadened under Claudius at the latest, and eventually comprised the *cura aedium sacrarum et operum loco-rumque publicorum* [5]. Although the *collegium* initially consisted of five *curatores*, it seems that only two consular *curatores consularis* were appointed from the mid 1st cent. AD [10]. Their responsibility was the supervision of the public lands as well as the maintenance of temples and public buildings; the work itself, however, was leased to independent contractors. The *curatores alvei Tiberis* operated in a similar fashion. They were appointed in the first few years of Tiberius' rule and were responsible primarily for keeping the shore of the Tiber clear and for assessing the public lands after floods [11]. All *curatores* were subordinate to the emperor's directives, which is evident among other things in the constant or temporary appointment of *procuratores* from the equestrian class.

Similar to Rome, other Roman cities also appointed more and more *curatores* for special tasks of various types through the council of decurions, as *e.g.* for the supply of food, for holding games, and also for the water supply ([3]; cf. also ILS III 2, 684–686).

Two types of *curatores* were appointed by the emperor in the cities outside of Rome until the end of the 3rd cent.: the *curatores kalendarii*, who were responsible for the interest income of the community, and the *curatores rei publicae* or *civitatis*, who were appointed by Domitian first in Italy, later also in the provinces. They were of senatorial, equestrian, or only municipal status. It was their duty to supervize the property and the finances of the cities; they did not, however, take the place of the municipal magistrates [9]. The largest number of them is known from Italy, where there were no state officials who would regularly appear on the spot [4. 190ff]. In some provinces, *curatores* were relatively numerous, for example in Asia [2] or Africa, although the first *curator* was not documented there until the period of Commodus [7]. Only in the early 4th cent., the *curator rei publicae* was transformed from an imperial emissary to the highest municipal magistrate who was appointed by the council of decurios itself.
→ Cura annonae

1 CHR. BRUUN, The Water Supply of Ancient Rome, 1991 2 G.P. BURTON, The Curator Rei Publicae: Towards a Reappraisal, Chiron 9, 1979, 465ff. 3 M. CORBIER, De Volsinii à Sestinum, Cura aquae et évergétisme municipal de l'eau en Italie, REL 62, 1984, 236–274 4 W. ECK, Die staatliche Organisation Italiens in der Hohen Kaiserzeit, 1979 5 Id., *Cura viarum* und *cura operum publicorum* als kollegiale Ämter im frühen Prinzipat, Klio 74, 1992, 237ff. = Id., Die Verwaltung des Röm. Reiches in der Hohen Kaiserzeit 1, 1995, 281ff. 6 Id., Organisation und Administration der Wasserversorgung Roms, in: Id., Die Verwaltung des Römischen Reiches in der Hohen Kaiserzeit 1, 1995, 161ff. 7 G. L. GREGORI, Un nuovo senatore dell'età di Commodo, in: ZPE 106, 1995, 269–279 8 M. HAUSER, Der röm. Begriff cura, 1954. 9 F. JACQUES, Le privilège de liberté, 1984 10 A. KOLB, Die kaiserliche Bauverwaltung in der Stadt Rom, Gesch. und Aufbau der *cura operum publicorum* unter dem Prinzipat, 1993 11 J. LE GALL, Le Tibre, fleuve de Rome dans l'antiquité, 1953.   W.E.

Cura annonae
I. REPUBLICAN PERIOD II. PRINCIPATE AND IMPERIAL PERIOD III. ORGANIZATION IV. LATE ANTIQUITY AND BYZANTINE PERIOD

I. REPUBLICAN PERIOD
The duty of the *cura annonae* (CA) lay in the organization of the food supply for the population of the city of Rome. In its fully developed form, the CA designates the collection of grain as a tax (predominantly in Egypt and Northern Africa), the transport of the grain to Rome as well as the storage and free distribution thereof to about 200,000 people in the city. Due to its strong population growth in the 2nd and 1st cents. BC, Rome became increasingly dependent upon grain shipments from the provinces. Over time, the Republic intervened in Rome's grain supply more and more: from the reorganization of the province of Sicily in the year 210 BC, grain was collected on the island as a tax, and from the year of 146 BC, the province of Africa had to provide grain as well. The grain that was obtained in this way, however, then had to be divided between the city of Rome and the legions. The grain laws by C. Gracchus determined a fixed, low price (6 $1/_3$ *as* pro *modius*) for the sale of grain to Roman citizens and also prescribed the construction of public storehouses for grain. The distribution of grain was unpopular with the senators; it was even revoked from 81–73 BC. But the emphatic demands of the *plebs urbana* finally made an improved grain supply indispensable. The *lex Clodia frumentaria* from 58 BC abolished payment for grain distributed by the Republic. In the month of September of 57 BC, after violent excesses by the *plebs urbana,* the Senate transferred extensive authorities to Pompey for securing the grain supply of Rome for a time period of five years. In the following years, the number of grain recipients grew substantially, until Caesar reduced it in 46 BC from *c.* 320,000 to 150,000. Under Augustus, the number of grain recipients again rose to 320,000 until the year of 5 BC. In 2 BC, a *recensus* of the citizens was held in order to once again reduce this number. Since then, the number remained constant at 200,000. When Constantinople became the eastern capital in the 4th cent. AD, free grain was distributed there as well.

II. PRINCIPATE AND IMPERIAL PERIOD
Augustus soon recognized that he had to improve and supervise the distribution of grain. During a supply shortage in 22 BC, Augustus took charge of the CA in response to the urging of the *plebs urbana* following the model of Pompey. The supervision of the grain supply was first transferred to two prior praetors and later to two consulars. During Augustus' last ruling years, however, an *eques* was appointed *praefectus annonae* for the first time. This prefecture belonged to the most important offices in the early Principate that could be held by *equites*. An administration developed which could issue authorization vouchers (*tesserae frumentariae,* → Tickets and tokens) and which compiled lists of

those who were authorized to receive grain rations. A ration of 5 *modii* (*c.* 33 kg) per month was almost sufficient for two people. The grain distributions did, however, not benefit all of the *c.* 800,000 residents of Rome. One possible criterium for the authorized receipt of free grain was not implemented: the distribution was not aimed primarily at the needy. Only residents of Rome were considered, while slaves, women and (at least until Trajan) children under age eleven (or perhaps fourteen) were excluded. Among the possible criteria for the authorization of receipt, Roman origin, an entry on a list with a fixed number of places, or the status of a freeborn have been considered. The consequences that these restrictions brought with them completely depended upon the size of Rome's city population. 200,000 male authorized recipients older than eleven years take the place of *c.* 600,000 free Roman citizens of both sexes and all ages. It is highly improbable that the free population of urban Rome was significantly larger than that. Nevertheless, the criteria for the authorized receipt of grain were of importance. The mortality in Rome was high and the population only remained constant because of a significant influx of people. Freedpersons and immigrants often were the same people. The problem was not so much the exclusion from a list of authorized persons, but the orderly registration of the immigrants and their descendants into the *plebs frumentaria*. A large part of the grain consumed in Rome was thus made available to the free population through political measures. It was probably not sufficient, however, to completely cover the needs of many families, and additional grain had to be purchased on the market.

III. Organization

During the Principate, the largest part of the grain distributed in Rome came from Northern Africa and Egypt, although, during late antiquity, the Egyptian grain was used to supply Constantinople. The grain was collected as a tax, less frequently as a leasehold for public land or, especially in Northern Africa, as income from the land ownership of the *princeps*. From time to time, grain in addition to that collected as a tax was bought on the market. The sea shipments from Northern Africa or from Egypt were organized by the administration. Since only a few hundred shiploads were needed, private shipowners (*navicularii*) could handle the transport. The *principes* tried to secure this service also in years of grain shortage when private commerce held the promise of bigger profits by way of binding the shipowners to the *annona* through privileges that were linked to obligations, with the result that the *navicularii* eventually came under public control just like the bakers. During the Republic and the early Principate, the grain was first brought to Puteoli, from where it was transported in smaller ships to the mouth of the Tiber. The harbour of Ostia was extended after AD 42 under Claudius and later under Trajan. At the same time, large storage houses (*horrea*) were built in Ostia and Rome

for storing public as well as private grain. Thus, Ostia became Rome's most important harbour for the supply of grain.

Initially, grain was distributed once a month, probably at different locations in the city. Since the middle of the 1st cent., the distributions were concentrated at the *Porticus Minucia*. Grain was distributed there throughout the whole month; each authorized citizen could pick up his ration once in this time span at the gate (*ostium*) assigned to him. Altogether, there were 45 gates; thus, 150–200 grain recipients daily must have been serviced at each gate. Septimius Severus was the first to supplement the grain rations with olive oil. Under Aurelianus, food distributions also included pork and wine, which, however, required its own administrative apparatus. Furthermore, under Aurelianus, bread was distributed instead of grain; thus, bakers and bakeries came under stricter public supervision. The *Porticus Minucia* now proved to be too small and bread soon had to be distributed daily at many different locations (*gradus*, thus *panis gradilis*).

→ Bakeries; → Nutrition; → Grain laws; → Grain; → Malnutrition

1 P. Garnsey, Famine and Food Supply in the Graeco-Roman World, 1988   2 A. Giovannini (ed.), Nourir la plèbe, 1991   3 P. Herz, Studien zur röm. Wirtschaftsgesetzgebung — die Lebensmittelversorgung, 1988   4 Jones, LRE, 695–705   5 W. Jongman, R. Dekker, Public Intervention in the Food Supply in Pre-Industrial Europe, in: P. Halstead, J. O'Shea (ed.), Bad Year Economics: Cultural Responses to Risk and Uncertainty, 1989, 114–122   6 H. P. Kohns, Versorgungskrisen und Hungerrevolten im spätant. Rom, 1961   7 H. Pavis D'Escurac, La préfecture de l'annone. Service impérial d'Auguste à Constantin, 1976   8 G. Rickman, The Corn Supply of Ancient Rome, 1980   9 B. Sirks, Food for Rome: The Legal Structure of the Transportation and Processing of Supplies for the Imperial Distributions in Rome and Constantinople, 1991   10 E. Tengström, Bread for the People. Studies in the Corn-Supply of Rome during the Late Empire, 1974   11 D. van Berchem, Les distributions de blé et d'argent à la plèbe romaine sous l'Empire, 1939   12 C. Virlouvet, Famines et émeutes à Rome des origines de la République à la mort de Néron, 1985.

W.J.

IV. Late antiquity and Byzantine period

During the time of inflation under Diocletian, taxes in the form of natural produce developed into the *annona*, the most significant form of income for the treasury. The *annona*'s significance decreased since the consolidation of the currency system under Constantine the Great. In the mid Byzantine period, *annôna* (ἀννῶνα) could even refer to natural product taxes in the form of money payments or wages paid partially in food supplies.

H. Geiss, Geld und naturwirtschaftliche Erscheinungsformen im staatlichen Aufbau It. während der Gotenzeit, 1931; A. Cercati, Caractère annonaire et assiette de l'impôt foncier au Bas-Empire, 1975.

G.MA.

Curator rei publicae The office of the *curator rei publicae* (CRP) is first documented for the turn of the 1st to the 2nd cent. AD and is one of the imperial offices held by the equestrian class. It corresponds roughly to the office of the λογιστής (*logistés*; Cod. Iust. 1,54,3; Dig. 1,22,6) known from Hellenistic times. If appointed by the emperor (Dig. 50,8,12), the CRP assumes the responsibilities of a state procurator (Dig. 1,19, tit. *de officio procuratoris Caesaris vel rationalis*) — if necessary — in the technically autonomous foreign *civitates* or in the *municipia* and *coloniae* governed by Roman law, in case the cities fail to fulfil their tax or other obligations to the *fiscus*. The CRP exists since Constantine I as a part of the internal office structure of the city, and is responsible for the imposition and execution of local taxes to the empire (Dig. 50,4,18,9). The CRP must not be confused with the office of a *defensor civitatis* that emerged in late antiquity and was designed for a different purpose.

→ Cura; → Defensor civitatis

JONES, LRE 728ff.; KASER, RZ 156f.; LIEBENAM, 481ff.; E. MEYER, Röm. Staat und Staatsgedanke, ⁴1975, 422.
C.G.

Cures Sabine city on the left bank of the Tiber, 24 miles from Rome on the *via Salaria*. C. is the hometown of two Roman kings (Titus Tatius, Numa Pompilius), the designation of the Romans as *Quirites* (Str. 5,3,1), and also the name of the *mons Quirinalis* (Varro, Ling. 5,51). The Romans conquered C. under M'. Curius Dentatus (290 BC). As a *municipium*, C. was incorporated into the *tribus Sergia*. Sulla and Caesar deduced *coloniae* to C. It belonged to *regio IV* (Ov. Fast. 2,135; Str. 5,3,1) and was called C. *Sabini* in the imperial period. It became an early Christian bishop's seat. Destroyed by the Langobardi. The name can be traced in S. Maria degli Arci (*arx*) and in Correse (city, river, pass). A simple settlement of huts beginning in the 9th cent. BC, from the 7th cent. on spreading to both hills, defended through trenches. Archaeological findings: → *cippus* with archaic Sabine inscription, temple, forum, theatre, Roman thermal baths; *villae* with cisterns in the surroundings. Inscriptions: CIL IX 4952–5012.

M.P. MUZZIOLI, C. Sabini, 1980; T. LEGGIO, Da C. Sabini all'abbazia di Farfa, 1992; A. GUIDI, in: EAA, 2. Suppl. 1994, II, 342.
G.U.

Curetes (Κουρῆτες; *Kourêtes*, Lat. *Curetes*). Mythological beings who protect the infant → Zeus from his father → Kronos by hitting their spears against their shields in order to drown out his screams (Callim. H. 1,51–53; Apollod. 1,1,6f.) or to deter the father (Str. 10,3,11). Most sources locate the scene in the cave of → Dicte on Crete, others locate it on → Ida [1] (e.g. Epimenides, FGrH 457 F 18, Aglaosthenes of Naxos, FGrH 499 F 1f., Apoll. Rhod. 1,1130, cf. Callim. H.

1,6–9). In one variation of the latter version, it says that the umbilical cord fell off while the C. carried Zeus to the cave. The rock of Omphalos was regarded as proof of this (Callim. H. 1,43f., Diod. Sic. 5,70,4). The mythological cave is a spatial representation of the 'time before': the C. are claimed to have been born from the earth (Str. 10,3,19), grown tall after a heavy rain (Ov. Met. 4,282), cf. → Spartoi, and sacrificed children to Kronos (Ister, FGrH 334 F 48). In accordance with this is the motif of milk and honey used to nourish Zeus: these were the foods from the time before the invention of bread; the bees of Dicte/Ida were blessed, unimpressed even by the most unfavourable weather conditions (Diod. Sic. 5,70,5); the social harmony of bees is directly related to this mythological time (Verg. G. 4,149–155).

The C. inhabited caves and ravines. They invented shepherding and beekeeping, hunting, archery, and neighbourly help (Diod. Sic. 5,65,1–3) — a period prior to the polis. As divine beings that were connected to the earth, they were also regarded as prophetic (Apollod. 3,3,1; Suda s.v. κουρήτων στόμα). → Epimenides of Crete is said to have been called the new Cures (Plut. Solon 12,7, 165d). The C. are youthful (Lucr. 2,633–639); Zeus, as he was worshiped on Dicte, was depicted beardless (EM 276,19 s.v.), and in the Hellenistic hymn from the temple of Palaikastro [1] he is referred to as *mégistos koûros* [2]. The tympana and bronze shields of the orientalizing period that were found in the cave on the mountain of Ida [3] point to the fact that the dance during the yearly celebration of Zeus' birth (Antoninus Liberalis 19) was performed in the archaic period by armed young men, the *koûroi*, in reference to the obvious etymology of the C. (Str. 10,3,11; cf. Hom. Il. 19,248). Performances such as these apparently continued into Hellenistic times (Dion. Hal. Ant. Rom. 2,70,3). It has been assumed that this complex may indicate the existence of a cultic community of young warriors who carried out an initiation ritual [4]. However, this thesis can hardly be regarded as an explanation for the myth of the C.

The Dictaean hymn that was sung around an altar has Zeus 'jump' (*thóre*) into beds (?; or vessels), herds, the harvest, cities, ships, youth, and into Themis. The dance was apparently understood as an incitement of the god and as a reference to his birth [5]. In the hymn, Curus is addressed as 'leader of the Daemones' (V. 4), that is, of the C. whose mythological relationship to the 'time before' has been replaced by a direct connection to domestic wealth and public welfare. In this form, the cult of the C., particularly as protectors of herds and guarantors of oaths is very common throughout Crete. There are also no clear indications that relationships exist to initiation rites in other contexts containing a cult of the C. In Messenia, burnt offerings were made to the C. which suggest a connection with the fertility of nature (Paus. 4,31,9). On Euboea, they were identified with the → Cyclopes and praised as the first bearers of *chalka hopla* ('brazen weapons') that gave Chalcis its name (Str. 10,3,19; Epaphroditus in Steph. Byz. s.v. Ἀἴδηψος; *Aídēpsos*, but cf. also Archemachos, FGrH 424 F 9). Their cult in Olympia was associated with a local Idaean cave (Pind. Ol. 5,17f.; Paus. 5,7,6). The cult in Ephesus (cf. Syll.3 353,1; IEph 47,7, 1060,9 etc.) and in other cities in Ionia and Caria, the most remarkable outside of Crete, was connected to an alternate version, according to which the C. protected the children of → Leto from Hera (Str. 14,1,20, also, Diod. Sic. 5,60,2f.; but cf. Apollod. 2,1,3). An early cult is also known on Thera (IG XII 3, 350).

In spite of these records that prove a wide spread of cultic activity (also in the early Hellenistic Cyrene: SEG 9, 107f., 110), the C. served primarily as place-markers in the endless revisions of mythological traditions in order to satisfy the needs of the times. Early on, their connection to the → nymphs who fed Zeus led to a genealogy that relates them as playful dancers to the Oreades and to the → Satyrs (Hes. fr. 123 M-W). As musicians, they were connected already in the *Phoronis* (EpGF fr. 2a, p. 154) with the servants of the Great Mother, the Phrygian Corybantes. Euripides associates them with the *bákchoi* (Eur. Bacch. 120–134; fr. 472,14) both as servants of Dionysus' father and as ecstatic dancers. This view of the C. as (ecstatic) musicians, 'virtually satyrs of Zeus', is what prompted Str. 10,3,9–18, probably based on Posidonius (FGrH 468 F 2). Another common identification focused on the role of the C. as divine servants: Demetrius of Scepsis, probably the source of Str. 10,3,19–22 p. 471–473C, was one of those who assumed that the C. were identical with the Corybantes who had been brought from Phrygia to Crete — a view which certainly influenced the Cretans themselves (SGDI 5039,14). He, however, was also familiar with the conjecture that both of them stemmed from the Idaean → Daktyloi and that some of the → Telchines were C. as well. The most controversial debate in antiquity, however, probably dealt with the completely unrelated question regarding the identity of the Aetolian C. mentioned by Hom. Il. 9,529f. (cf. Ephoros, FGrH 70 F 122, cf. Str. 10,3,1–8).

1 ABSA 15, 1908–09, 339   2 M.L. WEST, The Dictaean Hymn to the Kouros, in: JHS 85, 1965, 149–159   3 F.CANCIANI, Bronzi orientali e orientalizzanti a Creta nell' VIII e VII secolo a.C., 1970   4 BURKERT, 168, 202, 392   5 NILSSON, GGR 1, 322f.

F.SCHWENN, s.v. Kureten, RE 11, 2202–2209.   R.GOR.

Curia Pre-Roman station servicing the road connections from the Upper Rhine to the Alpine passes (Bernardino, Spluegen, Julier) that lead towards Italy, today known as Chur. The place was most likely a Roman *vicus* from the time of the Augustan Alpine campaign. Despite the important traffic location, the Romanization between Lake Constance and the Alps was weak [1. 67–72]. Archaeological finds: modest Roman finds in the 'Welschdörfli'. In the 4th cent. AD building of the late antique fort in its vicinity early Christian installations. Bishop's seat since the 5th cent.

1 G.WALSER, Der Gang der Romanisierung in einigen Tälern der Zentralalpen (Stud. zur Alpengesch.), 1994.

W.DRACK, R.FELLMANN, Die Römer in der Schweiz 1988, 380–384; A.HOCHULI-GYSEL, Chur in röm. Zeit aufgrund der arch. Zeugnisse (Beitr. zur Raetia Romana), 1987, 109–146.   G.W.

Curiae The *curiae* belong to the most important institutions of archaic Rome. The most generally accepted etymology of *curiae* today is the derivation from **coviria*= 'association of men'. For the modern dating of its origin it is important to consider that the composite *curia* is not a general Indo-European term but a term specific to Italy. From this one must conclude that the *curiae* did not emerge until after the Indo-European language family broke apart. However, the information that the original home of the *curiae* was on the Palatine (Tac. Ann. 12,24) indicates that these 'associations of men' came into being already in the early phase of Roman culture.

The *curiae* were associations of individuals that can be traced in multifarious ways in the religious and political life of later epochs. But even for the Romans, the origins and the contours of their old functions were covered in a fog of legends and in uncertain interpretations of continuing rites: Romulus, e.g., is claimed to have divided the population into 30 *curiae* (Liv. 1,13,6; Plut. Romulus 14). It is extremely difficult to clarify the exact occasions for the creation and the organizational principles of these first *curiae*. Of the 30 that existed in classical times, only seven are known by name: Rapta, Foriensis, Veliensis, Velitia, Acculeia, Faucia, Titia. Research suggests that the first four were named after localities, the last three after associations of individuals.

The worship of Juno was the common element for all of the *curiae*. The cultic practises of the *curiae* required not only the presence of priests, but also expressly the presence of women and of children whose parents had to still be living (Dion. Hal. Ant. Rom. 2,22,1). Each *curia* possessed its own building which was also called *curia*. In these assembly rooms, the religious rites were carried out and the communal banquets took place. It appears that, besides Juno, each *curia* worshipped its own deity whose cult belonged to the *sacra publica*. For the purpose of exercising this function, a *flamen curialis* was chosen (Fest. p 56 L). In mid February of each year, the *curiae* celebrated the *fornacalia*, a festival that celebrated the community of the members of the *curia*, with each *curia* practising this ritual in a different way. The right of admission also granted that person the recognition of belonging to the *curia* (Ov. Fast. 2,513–530; Plin. HN 18,8). Later on, it was decided that February 17th was the holiday for Romans who no longer knew their *curiae*, a day that received the vernacular name of *stultorum feriae*.

For the leadership and general supervision of the communal activities, the members of the *curiae* elected a → *curio*. The criteria required of a potential candidate for this office are highly revealing: only men over the age of 50 without any physical impairments and of considerable wealth could be elected (Dion. Hal. Ant. Rom. 2,21,3). This catalogue of requirements occupies an intermediary position within the evolution of institutions: age and physical integrity underscore the continuation of demands typical for earlier societies, since these criteria do not reflect individual status and achievement, while the material criterion is not conceivable without a clear social differentiation and its consequences for the incorporation of the individual into a social hierarchy. From all this it follows that the office of *curio* gave expression to a transition in institutions: the social status of the individual no longer depended only on age, yet the high age requirement functioned as an effective barrier against the concentration of power which could have resulted from an inheritance mechanism.

The trend towards a more strictly institutionalized exercise of power led to the appointment of a *curio maximus* from the ranks of the *curiones* who acted as chief supervisor of the *curiae's* activities. The leaders of the *curiae* were apparently also regarded as guarantors that decisions would be carried through. For this purpose, each *curio* was assigned a *lictor* as clerk (Gell. NA 15,27,2). It would appear that this development was also the basis for the creation of a new process in the transfer of military authority. Into the Republican period, the → *comitia curiata*, who sat on the *comitium*, were responsible for confirming the *imperium* of the higher magistrates through the *lex curiata*. In modern research, the predominant view holds that we are dealing with an archaic form of legitimizing power for the *rex* onto which new mechanisms were superimposed in later times, without the institutionally conservative Romans having to let go of the old rites. Already early in the Republican period, the *curiae* had largely lost their political relevance and were regarded as legal relics of an earlier time.

T. J. CORNELL, The Beginnings of Rome, 1995; B. LINKE, Von der Verwandtschaft zum Staat, 1995; G. PRUGNI, Quirites, in: Athenaeum 75, 1987, 127–161.   B.LI.

Curialis, Curiales

[1] *Curialis* (from *curia*) is the term used for both individual members of the local council and the council in its entirety as an institution (*decuriones*; Dig. 29,2,25,1; 37,1,3,4; 50,16,239,5).
→ Curia; → Decuriones
[2] *Curalis* was the name given to the members of the municipal Curial class, i.e. the members of families who on the basis of family descent (*curiali obstricti sanguine*; Cod. Iust. 10,32,43), or, on the basis of the official duties of the heads of their families (Cod. Iust. 10,32,62) could and should take on the duties of a member of the council and municipal office holder as *curiales*, and in late antiquity even had to do so if they fulfilled certain conditions, and in particular if they were very wealthy (*curialis nexus*: Cod. Iust. 10,32,63,1; generall tit. 32).

[3] *Curiales* in late antiquity were civil servants at the imperial court (*curia*); the word is used as synonymous with *palatini, aulici* or *comitatus* (Amm. Marc. 21,12,20; Salv. Gub. 3,50).

JONES, LRE 572ff., 737; LIEBENAM 226ff., 489ff.   C.G.

Curiata lex Legally binding decision of the *comitia curiata* (organized by *curiae*) — probably the oldest type of Roman popular 's assembly. The early form can hardly be deduced from the sources (cf. Cic. Rep. 2,25). Presumably, all questions of the succession of influential families, religion, citizenship, military call-ups (*legio*), taxes, the inauguration of kings and priests and later the responsibilities of the offices were regulated by *leges curiatae* (Liv. 1,17,8f.; 1,22,1). In the struggle of the orders, elections and the administration of justice did not, however, devolve upon the people until the assemblies of the people as a whole formed in the early Republic (*comitia centuriata*) or the plebs in *comitia tributa* (*concilia plebis*). During the period of the middle and late Roman republic it was mainly the latter who took on the people's legislation so that in the 1st cent. BC only the following areas remained subject to the *curita lex*: admission of a person to a *gens* and dismissal from it (Gell. NA 5,19,9), the authorization of wills made by ancient procedure *calatis comitiis* (*curiatis*) (Gai. Inst. 2,103), the ceremonial inauguration of the already elected, appointed or coopted *pontifices, augures* and the Vestals (Cic. Rep. 2,9,16; Fest. p.462) as well as the top magistrates with *imperium* (Liv. 3,27,1; 4,14,1; Gell. NA 13,15,4) elected by the *comitia centuriata*. According to Cicero (Leg. agr. 2,29) the *lex curiata* did not constitute the legitimation of office, having merely a morally strengthening effect. This reveals the gradual decline in the constitutional importance of the *curita lex* , just as does the meeting of 30 lictors and three augures common at the time, symbolic of the meeting of the former 30 *curiae* (Cic. Leg. agr. 2,31). In spite of the reduction in political significance of the comitial procedure in early imperial times, the ceremonial function of the *curiata lex* did not disappear entirely, but its duties in the law relating to wills and testaments and the gentes gradually passed to court proceedings or to imperial rescript practice (Gai. Inst. 2,101–108; 4,17; Cod. Iust. 6,23,9; 8,47,2,1).
→ Comitia; → Curia

F. F. ABBOTT, A History and Description of Roman Political Institutions, ³1963, 18ff., 249ff.; KASER, RPR 1, 678; 2, 207, 481; B. LINKE, Von der Verwandtschaft zum Staat, 1995; MOMMSEN, Staatsrecht 3, 89ff., 316ff.   C.G.

Curiatus Italian surname (SCHULZE, 355); according to Roman legend, Rome's war against Alba Longa under King Tullus Hostilius was decided through the fight between the triplet Curiatii brothers of Alba and the triplet Horatii brothers (→ Horatius) of Rome, with the former being killed (Liv. 1,24f.; Dion. Hal. Ant. Rom. 3,16–20). After the destruction of Alba, the family is said to have moved to Rome and accepted by the Patricians (Liv. 1,30,2; Dion. Hal. Ant. Rom. 3,29,7). The consul recorded in the *fasti* for 453 BC, member of the 1st collegium of the decemvirs for the drafting of the 12 Tables, P.C. Fistus Trigeminus (MRR 1,43f.; 45), is probably not historically correct; the politically unimportant Plebian family of the Curiatius traced itself back to him in the 2nd/1st cent. BC (RRC 223; 240; Cic. Leg. 3,20; Val. Max. 3,7,3). K.-L.E.

Curictae (also *Curica*, Tab. Peut.; Κυριϰτιϰή, Str. 2,5,20). Island off the Dalmatian coast (now Krk, Croatia) with two towns: Curictae (Κούριϰον, Ptol. 2,16,13) near what is today the town of Krk and Fertinates (Φουλφίνιον, Ptol. loc.cit.) near modern Omisalj. Contested by the armies of Pompey and Caesar (Caes. B Civ. 3,10,5), since Augustus part of Illyricum. Claudius awarded the residents the *ius Italicum* (Plin. HN 3,139, *tribus Claudia*).

G. ALFÖLDY, Bevölkerung und Gesellschaft in [...] Dalmatien, 1965; J.J. WILKES, Dalmatia, 1969. D.S.

Curio

[1] Cognomen in the *gens Scribonia* (→ Scribonius).

ThlL, Onom. 2, 757–760; KAJANTO, Cognomina 318. K.-L.E.

[2] *Curio* is the name traditionally given to the head of each of the 30 *curiae*, the old class of the Roman people between the *tribus* and the *gentes*. The *curiones* is assisted in his religious role by a *flamen curialis*; at the head of the *curio* was a *curio maximus* (Liv. 27,8,1; CIL VIII 1174) elected by all the people. We cannot delineate in detail and with certainty the presumably wide range of duties of the *curio* in the early period of Rome; in the later period the *curio* continued to perform important religious services within the gentes' *sacra* and the *sacrum* of their *curia*, particularly at the Fornicalia festival in February (Varro, Ling. 5,83; 6,46; Ov. Fast. 2,527). In the late Republic they represented the *curiae* at the *comitia curiata* called by a magistrate or the *curio maximus* in the case of certain matters relating to the gentes and wills and testaments and provided religious support for elections by means of a *curiata lex*, unless 30 *lictores* acted symbolically anyway (Cic. Leg. agr. 2,29ff.).

→ Curiae; → Curiata lex; → Tribus

F. F. ABBOTT, A History and Description of Roman Political Institutions, ³1963, 18ff., 252ff.; LATTE, 143, 399f.; MOMMSEN, Staatsrecht 3, 89f. C.G.

Curiosi (from *curiosus* 'prudent', 'eager to learn') was the name given in late antiquity to civil servants of the imperial court of the up to 1,300 *agentes in rebus* (Cod. Iust. 12,20,3) who were given various special duties to perform locally for the central imperial government, as well as in the provinces or in foreign countries. As a

special group, the *curiosi* are defined as *agentes in rebus in curis agendis et evectionibus publici cursus inspiciendis* (Cod. Iust. 12,22,2) who above all have to prevent improper use of government posts (Cod. Iust. 12,22,4) and examine infringements of the law established by them (*crimina*) in the provinces and report these to the relevant provincial governors (*iudices*) (cf. Cod. Iust. 12,22 tit. *de curiosis*). In their investigatory and 'informer' duties they worked independently of local officials (*nihil prorsus commune aut cum iudicibus aut cum provincialibus habeant*), but were not to meddle in their areas of responsibility (Cod. Iust. 12,22,4). At the office of the *magister officiorum*, a *curiosus cursus publici praesentalis* heads the *curiosi* in all provinces (Not. Dign. Or. 11,50f.; Not. Dign. Occ. 9,44f.)

→ Cursus publicus; → Magister officiorum

W. BLUM, C. und Regendarii, diss. 1969; JONES, LRE 578ff. C.G.

Curiosum urbis Romae List of the sights of the 14 municipal districts (*regiones*) of Rome. Aside from the core Constantinian *Curiosum urbis Romae*, a more recent, more intensely interpolated *Notitia* and a *Classis commixta* have been passed down to us.

A. NORDH, Prolegomena till den romenska regionskatalogen, 1936; Id., Libellus de regionibus urbis Romae, 1949; HLL 5, 1989, § 520. K.BRO.

Curium (Κούριον). Town on the southern coast of → Cyprus, according to Hdt. 5,113 and Str. 14,6,3 founded by → Argus [II]. Remains of settlements from the Bronze Age. The first mention of a king is in the time of → Asarhaddon 673/2 BC. At the battle of Salamis in 480 BC, King Stasanor went over to the Persian side. The last king, Pasicrates, who was on the side of Alexander the Great, took part in the siege of Tyrus in 312 BC [4]. Diocese in late antiquity.

In the city area, fortification walls, thermal springs, Roman private houses with mosaics, a theatre and a large basilica from the 5th cent. AD have been excavated [1]. Extensive necropoleis in the east and south. In the west there is a stadium from the 2nd cent. AD on the road to the important sanctuary of Apollo Hylates 4 km away. The ancient → temenos with its large altar was furnished in Imperial times with a stone temple, banquet rooms, baths and a palaistra [2; 3; 4].

1 D. SOREN, J. JAMES, Kourion, 1988 2 D. BUITRON-OLIVER et al., The Sanctuary of Apollo Hylates (Stud. in Mediterranean Archaeology 109), 1996 3 D. SOREN, The Sanctuary of Apollo Hylates at Kourion, Cyprus, 1987 4 J.H. and S.H. YOUNG, Terracotta Figurines from Kourion in Cyprus, 1955.

MASSON, 189–201 no. 176–189; T.B. MITFORD, The Inscriptions of Kourion, 1970; E. OBERHUMMER, s.v. K., RE 11, 2210–2214; H.W. SWINY, An Archaeological Guide to the Ancient Kourion Area and the Akrotiri Peninsula, 1982. R.SE.

Curius Plebian gentes name, attested from the beginning of the 3rd cent. BC onwards (ThlL, Onom. 2, 760–762).

[1] Otherwise unknown proconsul between 47 and 45 BC (contact of Cic. Fam. 13,49).

[2] C., M. People's tribune in 198 BC, objected to the election of T. → Quinctius Flamininus as consul (Liv. 32,7,8).

[3] C., Q. In 70 BC, as a former quaestor (?), he was expelled from the Senate (MRR 2,127); later he was a follower of Catilina, and in 63 through his lover → Fulvia he betrayed the conspiracy to Cicero (Sall. Catil. 23,2ff.; 26,3; 28,2; Suet. Iul. 17).

[4] C. Dentatus, M' From a previously undistinguished family (cognomen because he was supposedly born with teeth, Plin. HN 7,68), consul in 290 BC, 284 (suff.), 275, 274. In the 1st Consulate he defeated the Sabines (given half-citizenship) and ended the 3rd Samnite War (dual triumph, MRR 1,183f.). In 283 he vanquished the Senones in Upper Italy where the colony of Sena Gallica was then established (Pol. 2,19,9–12). In 275 he was victorious over Pyrrhus (MRR 1,195); his triumphal march included elephants for the first time (Flor. Epit. 1,13,28). As censor in 272 he commenced construction of the second oldest aqueduct to Rome, the → Anio vetus, but he died in 270 before it was completed (Frontin. Aq. 1,6). His proverbial incorruptibility and modesty were idealized by the elder → Cato as a model and this shaped the later sources.

G. FORNI, Manio Curio Dentato uomo democratico, in: Athenaeum N.S. 31, 1953, 170–240.   K.-L.E.

Curriculum see → School

Curse
I. ANCIENT ORIENT, EGYPT, OLD TESTAMENT
II. GREECE AND ROME

I. ANCIENT ORIENT, EGYPT, OLD TESTAMENT
In the ancient Orient, the curse is considered to be a magically effective utterance by which the speaker destroys enemies or objects of their sphere, excludes them from the community or at the very least reduces their vitality. How effective this is depends upon the status of the speaker, the social context and the use of set phrases.

There is no evidence of colloquial curses in the Near East and hardly any from Egypt. In the Near East set curse phrases are preserved from the mid 3rd millennium onward in various languages (Akkadian and Sumerian; Aramaic, Hebrew [6. 561–593]) particularly as a component — mostly as the final section — of inscriptions on buildings, votive offerings, boundary stones, steles, sarcophagi etc. Those who do wrong to the inscription bearer are cursed. The same applies to Egypt, where curses appear in texts warning against damaging tombs, sacrificial foundations and other monuments. In Egypt both private and royal monu-

ments can be protected with curses but, contrary to the legend of 'the curse of the Pharaohs', they are never found in the tombs of New Kingdom kings. The threats are of punishments in this world (social ostracism, physical punishments, death) and damnation in the hereafter. The type and executors of the threatened punishments change in the course of time: in the Old Kingdom the curses delight in threatening the judgement of the gods, whilst in late antiquity obscene curses are particularly common. Those cursed include — as in Mesopotamia — not just all the names generally given to wrongdoers but also future rulers responsible for maintaining the institution and capable of abolishing or harming it. In Western Asia, the most common type of curse follows the pattern: wishing that divinity XX do this and that to the wrongdoer (especially annihilation of the descendants and diseases).

In view of the limited options for jurisdiction, the curse plays an important role as a substitute for legal sanctions (in Egypt [1]) in the case of documentary and contractual conditions (as in Mesopotamia) as well as also for offences that are not punishable by law.

In the Old Testament curses are pronounced in a prospective manner in order to strike future criminals who remain unknown, to secure social support and peace, and thus regularly at religious celebrations (Deut. 27,14–26). Set curse phrases play an important role especially in the → international treaties from Mesopotamia, Anatolia and Syria [5. 132–186]. As Israel applies the ancient Oriental custom of the mutually sworn treaty between sovereign and vassal to the god-people relationship, the curse patterns that belong to this are adopted for perjury, but are mostly supplemented by series of blessings (Deut. 28,15–69 with 1–14). The related symbolic act of self-cursing (Deut. 29,11) was carried out apparently without saying a word. Set curse phrases also appear in incantations and rites to ward off danger as an accompaniment to magical acts (Egypt), especially to ward off black magic (Mesopotamia). The growing conviction in the course of time of Jehovah's exclusive right of disposal over human life leads in later sections of the Old Testament to curses only appearing to be legitimate with the will and in the name of God. Using God's name in vain in a curse was a violation of the Ten Commandments.

1 J. ASSMANN, When Justice Fails: Jurisdiction and Imprecation in Ancient Egypt and the Near East, in: JEA 78, 1992, 146–162 2 S. MORSCHAUSER, Threat-Formulae in Ancient Egypt, 1991 3 F. POMPONIO, Formule di maledizione della Mesopotamia preclassica, 1990 4 J. SCHARBERT, ThWAT 1, 437–451   5 TUAT 1 6 TUAT 2.   K.J.-W. and K.KO. and M.KR.

II. GREECE AND ROME
A curse (ἀρά, dirae) in the Greek and Roman world was the vehemently expressed wish that bad things — generally disease or death — befall another person; if he seeks the help of the gods, these will often be subterranean deities. The curse is on the one hand a means used

by society or individuals to proceed against real or imagined wrongdoers who would otherwise be untouchable or against those for whom one seeks the most drastic punishment possible, and on the other hand, especially in situations of competition and envy it is a means of eliminating competitors (particularly in injury-invoking magic), and ultimately in the → oath as a self-curse it is the strongest possible security against breaching the oath.

The curse as a punishment usually ensures the help of the gods and is therefore similar to a → prayer; as a result Homer also calls the priest *arētēr*, 'curser'. When the young → Phoenix abducts the concubine of his father, the latter uses the → Furies to place upon him the curse of childlessness, and 'subterranean Zeus' and Persephone grant his invocations (Hom. Il. 9,453–457); the same deities grant the curse of → Althaea against Meleager (Il. 9,566–572). While the curse here proves effective in family disputes, later curses of unknown murderers [1], thieves etc, are occasionally found as texts written on lead tablets in the temples of chthonian deities [2]. Aside from these are official curses such as that of the priests and priestesses of Athens on the enemy of the state → Alcibiades (Plut. Quaest. Rom. 44,275d) or the curses contained in inscriptions of the town of Teos against a series of wrongdoers (so-called *Dirae Teorum* [3]). The Anatolian tomb curses of the imperial period represent a special group — where the deceased defends himself against the sullying or misuse of the tomb [4]. In literary usage curse poems, such as those of Callimachus and Ovid *Ibis*, serve to disparage literary enemies [5].

The curse as a means of fighting competition finds expression in private magic in the curse table (*tabellae defixionum* [6; 7], → Defixio) — since the 5th cent. BC lead tablets are inscribed with texts in which the subterranean deities are invoked for assistance. They are mostly deposited in tombs, occasionally also in wells, rivers or the sea, often together with voodoo dolls [8]; the → magic papyri of late antiquity provide detailed scenes. Whereas in Athens of the 5th and 4th cent. BC the curse was generally procedural, later the curse was applied in love and horse-racing. In the Attic procedural curse the wish is especially for incapacity for testimony, at the circus for a spectacular accident, in love for unbridled passion, and in other contexts, at least later, also for illness or death. The curse therefore provides in all these areas an explanation for negative manifestations (for instance Cic. Brut. 50,217 or Hier. Vita S. Hilarionis 21).

→ Magic

1 L. ROBERT, La Collection Froehner, 1936, no. 77 2 H. VERSNEL, Beyond Cursing. The Appeal to Justice in Judicial Prayers, in: C. A. FARAONE, D. OBBINK (ed.), Magika Hiera, 1991, 60–106 3 TOD, 23 4 J. H. M. STRUBBE, Cursed be He that Moves My Bones, in: [2], 33–59 5 L. WATSON, Arae. The Curse Poetry of Antiquity, 1991 6 A. AUTODOLLENT (ed.), Defixionum tabellae, 1904 7 J. G. GAGER (ed.), Curse Tablets and Binding Spells from the Ancient World, 1992 8 C. A. FARAONE, Binding and Burying the Forces of Evil. The Defensive Use of 'Voodoo Dolls' in Ancient Greece, in: Classical Antiquity 10, 1991, 165–205.

W. SPEYER, s.v. F., RAC 7, 1160–1288; F. GRAF, Gottesnähe und Schadenzauber, 1996.   F.G.

Cursive see → Writing styles

Cursor Cognomen ('runner, courier') in the *gens Papiria*.

KAJANTO, Cognomina 361.   K.-L.E.

Cursus honorum designates the professional rise through the ranks of Roman politicians in a series of honorary offices (Cic. Fam. 1,9,17; 3,11,2; Amm. Marc. 22,10,6), in a special sense it is the name given to a complex of legal regulations for politicians of the Roman republic, who, starting with official stages that justify a seat in the Senate, wish to reach via a series of offices the highest senatorial rank, that of consul, i.e. a former consul. The whole process involves rules on a) the acquisition of membership in the Senate by holding an office that gives entry to it, b) the sequence of offices, c) the minimum time interval between the offices and d) the respective minimum age of the applicants. The purpose of the rules is to ensure equality of opportunity of the political class in competition for the highest state offices by limiting especially the forms of political ambition and official self-promotion (*ambitus*) and in this way to strengthen the functional capacity of the hierarchically organized structure of offices and the status of the rank of senator.

The rules generally arose in conjunction with the elections of the middle and later Roman republic, especially in consequence of the 'lightning careers' of young *nobiles* who appear politically threatening in and after the 2nd Punic War — the first reference to which is to be found in 180 BC in the *lex Villia annalis* that at the very least specified the minimum age (Liv. 40,44,1); however, before this 10 years of military service was already required as a prerequisite for application for high office (Pol. 6,19,4). Although some aspects of the *cursus honorum* remain unresolved, after 180 it included the aedileship, praetorship and consulate, furthermore — probably since the time of the Gracchi — also a people's tribunate for applicants from the *plebs*. Sulla's reforms (Cic. Leg. 3,3,9) incorporate in the *cursus honorum* — probably for the first time (Tac. Ann. 11,22) — the quaestorship as well as the offices of the *aediles, praetores* and *consules* that were already gradually being filled and exclude the people's tribunate; it could in any case never have become part of the regular *cursus honorum* because it was restricted to the *plebs*, although anyone who held the office had the right to a seat in the Senate (Gell. NA 24,8,2; App. B Civ. 1,28).

Republican cursus honorum at the time of Cicero

1st stage: quaestorship (minimum age: 31)
            20 quaestors (since Sulla)
            Interval (2 years)

2nd stage: aedileship (minimum age: 37)
            4 aediles (under Caesar: 6 aediles)
            Interval (2 years)

3rd stage: praetorship (minimum age: 40)
            10 praetors (since Sulla;
            12 praetors under Caesar)
            Interval (2 years)

4th stage: consulate (minimum age: 43)
            2 consuls

At the time of Cicero the minimum age for quaestors was 31, aediles 37, praetors 40 and consuls 43 with compulsory intervals of two years each between the offices (App. B Civ. 1,100,466; Cic. Off. 2,17,59; Cic. Fam. 10,25,2; Phil. 5,7,47;), see fig. The censors, dictators, purely military leadership offices, legates, promagistrates and members of administrative, priestly or judicial colleges from the duumvirate to the centumvirate were not included in the regular *cursus honorum*. However, before, between and after the stages of the *cursus honorum* in the actual sense, additional military and civilian offices could determine the career of a Roman politician. At the end of the Republic the transfer of exceptional powers, for instance for Pompey, Caesar or Octavian, led to the rules being temporarily disregarded (Plut. Pompey 14,1; App. B Civ. 3,88,361; Suet. Aug. 27), and in the imperial period they lost their earlier importance as a means to allocate roles within the upper class because the offices were ultimately filled according to the will of the emperor, despite continuing elections by the people or later by the Senate. The usual 'election' of the → *candidati* nominated by the Princeps created a new career model in the imperial state service. Consequently the stages of a career in high political offices change, probably already from the time of Augustus (Cass. Dio 54,26; Tac. Ann. 3,29). The *cursus honorum* then began with the vigintisexvirate (later vigintivirate), then continues via the military tribunate to the quaestorship that had already been attainable at the age of 25 and then continues on in principle according to the rules of the Republican *cursus honorum*. However, the emperors on many occasions made exemptions to the rules of the *cursus honorum* or bestowed offices and high-status positions in the Senate opportunistically. Thus the particular status enjoyed by a *candidatus principis* and direct service for the emperor, for instance as a *legatus principis*, replaced stages of the *cursus honorum*.

In late antiquity the traditional *cursus honorum* was displaced almost completely by an *ordo dignitatum*, within which the highest state offices were the highest court offices and for example the consulate essentially had only eponymous or titular honorary significance (Cod. Iust. 12,8; 12,3).

→ Magistratus; → Senatus; → Candidatus

JONES, LRE 378ff.; W. KUNKEL, Staatsordnung und Staatspraxis der röm. Republik, 1995, vol. 2, 43ff.; E. MEYER, Röm. Staat und Staatsgedanke, ⁴1975, 100f., 385ff.; MOMMSEN, Staatsrecht 1, 523ff., 536ff.; 2, 915ff., 937ff.   C.G.

Cursus publicus The term *cursus publicus*, attested from as early as the 4th cent. AD (Cod. Theod. 8,5,1), but which already appeared earlier (cf. P Panop. Beatty 2,275: 28.2.300), describes the state message and transport system of *Imperium Romanum*; in the 1st–3rd cent. AD offices, tasks and duties of the system were defined through links with *vehicula* or *vehiculatio* (CIL III 7251; RIC II 93). Augustus first established a courier service consisting of alternating messengers purely as a communications system. He extended the service into an efficient conveyance system by making transport available at certain intervals along the main routes which could be utilized alternately by users of the *cursus publicus* (Suet. Aug. 49,3–50). The *cursus publicus* was not a postal service in the modern sense as it provided neither regular conveyance nor permitted use by private individuals but just transport, the transmission of messages or transportation on behalf of public institutions (officials, military, goods).

The basis of the system was the Roman network of roads which included rest and stage way stations (*mansiones* and *mutationes*). The *cursus publicus* was for the most part financed by obliging the populace (*angaria*) to make available vehicles and animals, manage the road stations and guarantee lodging in exchange for a compensatory payment from the governor. In this way, this burden of maintenance for the *cursus publicus* rested on the people of the empire as a *munus* that at the latest in the 4th cent. was apparently no longer compensated. The office of station manager (*manceps*) appears among the compulsory obligations around this time, to whom diverse state slaves (*muliones, mulomedici, carpentarii*) were available as staff. The administrative direction of *cursus publicus* for Italy lay — probably from the time it was set up under Augustus — with the *praef. vehiculorum* [1. 89–94], assisted by subordinate offices, e.g. the *tabularius a vehiculis*, the *a commentariis vehiculorum* and the *a vehiculis* (CIL VI 8543. 8542). From the end of the 2nd cent. AD onwards, several *praefecti vehiculorum* held office simultaneously and they were obviously responsible for certain regions. In the north-western provinces they were possibly only employed if there was a special need. Normally the governors and financial procurators were responsible for the *cursus publicus* in the provinces. The latter regulated the requirements and tariffs of the means of transportation to be made available, split these costs among the individual communities (SEG 16, 754; 26, 1392) and tried to counter abuse by users. Furthermore, they looked after the station buildings. In

the 4th cent. the *curiosi* from the *schola* of *agentes in rebus* (Cod. Theod. 6, 29) were entrusted with the inspection of permit certificates (*diploma*, from the 4th cent. onwards *evectio, tractoria*) that every *cursus publicus* traveller had to show and that only the emperor (in the 4th cent. also a few high-ranking officials) could issue. These subordinates of the *magister officiorum* who represented the highest inspection authority of the *cursus publicus* after the princeps were evidently also unable to stem the frequent misuse. The *praef. praet* at that time had ultimate responsibility for the organizational management. At the latest from the beginning of the 4th cent. onwards the *cursus publicus* was divided up into the faster *cursus velox* and the slower *cursus clabularius* suitable for goods transport (Cod. Theod. 8,5,1; P. Oxy. 2675). The emperors frequently extended the circle of users by bestowing favours, for instance upon the bishops. The imperial edicts regarding the *cursus publicus* that regulated a large number of details and that were meant to stop misuse are to be found in Cod. Theod. 8,5.
→ Angaria; → Mansio

1 E.W. BLACK, C.p., The Infrastructure of Government in Roman Britain, BAR 241, 1995   2 W. ECK, Die staatliche Organisation It. in der hohen Kaiserzeit, 1979, 88–110   3 E.J. HOLMBERG, Zur Gesch. des c.p., 1933   4 JONES, LRE, 830–834   5 S. MITCHELL, Requisitioned Transport in the Roman Empire. A new Inscription from Pisidia, JRS 66, 1976, 106–131   6 H.G. PFLAUM, Essai sur le c.p. sous le Haut-Empire romain, Mémoires de l'Académie des Inscriptions et Belles Lettres 14, 1940   7 H.-CHR. SCHNEIDER, Altstraßenforsch., 1982, 90–115   8 P. STOFFEL, Über die Staatspost, die Ochsengespanne und die requirierten Ochsengespanne, 1994.   A.K.

Curtain see → Volume 4, Addenda

Curtia see → Volume 4, Addenda

Curtia Flavia Archelais Valentilla Woman of consular rank, a member of the landed gentry of Lydia [1].

1 G. PETZL, in: EA 26, 1996, 9ff.   W.E.

Curtilius
[1] T.C.Mancia. Suffect consul in AD 55 [1. 267]; governor and commander of the Upper Germanic army from 56 until at least 58 [2. 25f.]. We are uncertain whether he became proconsul of Africa (PIR² C 1605; [3. 214ff.]). Re the bequeathing of his fortune, see Domitia [II 7].

G. CAMODECA, L'archivio Puteolano dei Sulpicii I, 1992   2 ECK, Statthalter 25f.   3 VOGEL-WEIDEMANN.   W.E.

Curtisius
T.C. Former praetorian who in AD 24 instigated an uprising of the slaves in Brundisium that was soon put down (Tac. Ann. 4,27).   D.K.

Curtius Roman surname (SCHULZE 78; ThlL, Onom. 2,765–770). The fictive early republican relatives of Curtius[I 1–3] are said to be the explanation for the name *Lacus Curtius* [1. 75ff.].
I. REPUBLICAN PERIOD   II. IMPERIAL PERIOD

I. REPUBLICAN PERIOD
[I 1] C., M. Hero of Roman legend. When a crevice opened on the forum in 362 BC and an oracle announced that it would not close up until Rome's greatest possessions were sacrificed to guarantee the eternity of Rome, Curtius interpreted this as a sign of military bravery and jumped in full armour with his horse into the crevice that closed up again (Varro, Ling. 5,148). It is said that on this spot a lake, the → *Lacus Curtius* arose.

In the early imperial period the lake was emptied (Ov. Fast. 6,403f.); nonetheless, it was used by the municipal Roman populace who threw coins into it each year to wish the emperor good luck and blessings (Suet. Aug. 57,1) [2. 229f.].

1 R.M. OGILVIE, A Commentary on Livy. Books 1–5, 1965   2 L.RICHARDSON, A New Topographical Dictionary of Ancient Rome, 1992.

[I 2] C., Mettius. Sabine, fought under T. Tatius against the Romans under Romulus and escaped through a mire in the Forum (Varro, Ling. 5,149 according to C. Calpurnius [III 1] Piso; Liv. 1,12,8ff.).
[I 3] C. Chilo, C. (Name uncertain), supposedly consul in 445 BC and opponent of the *lex Canuleia* (Liv. 4,1–7; → Canuleius [1]); he is said to have consecrated the lake after a stroke of lightning (Varro, Ling. 5,150).
[I 4] C. Nicias. Grammarian and tyrant of Cos in the late republican period (→ Nicias).
[I 5] C. Peducaeanus, M. Quaestor in 61 BC, people's tribune in 57, friend of Cicero (Ad Q. fr. 1,4 etc.).

NICOLET 2, 861f.

[I 6] C. Postumus, M. (?), in 54 military tribune for Caesar (Cic. Ad Q. Fr. 2,14,3; 3,1,10); identified with the supporters of Caesar C. → Rabirius Postumus, praetor *c.* 47/6 BC.

NICOLET 2, 863; D.R. SHACKLETON BAILEY, Two Studies in Roman Nomenclature, ²1991, 21, 82.   K.-L.E.

II. IMPERIAL PERIOD
[II 1] Eques of the Augustan period (Macrob. Sat. 2,4,22); perhaps identical to the C. mentioned in a *Senatus consultum* in 19 (EOS I 517).
[II 2] C. Atticus. Roman eques who accompanied Tiberius in AD 26 to Campania and Capri; annihilated by Seia (PIR² C 1609; re identification [1. 72]).

1 R. SYME, History in Ovid, 1978.

[II 3] C.C.Iustus. Senator. His career is included in CIL III 1458 = Inscr. Daciae Romanae III 2, 91: admitted to the Senate under Hadrian; after a lengthy praetorian career governor of Dacia superior around 148/150; *cos. suff.*, consular legate of Moesia superior around 158/159 (PIR² C 1613; Piso 58ff.).

[II 4] **C. Montanus.** Senator who committed himself in AD 70 to the commemoration of Piso Licinianus and in the process was attacked by Aquilius Regulus (PIR² C 1615).

[II 5] **C. Montanus.** Son of C. [II 4], likewise a senator; indicted in the Senate in 66 for satirical poems, but not sentenced because of his father (PIR² C 1616).

[II 6] **C. Paulinus.** Eques military tribune in Egypt in 57/58 (P Oxy. 3279; Devijver, V p. 2084). Not identical to Paulinus in Jos. BI 3,344 (Demougin, no. 532, 599).

[II 7] **Q.C.Rufus.** Of lowly birth, he succeeded in getting into the Senate through the patronage of Tiberius (Tac. Ann. 11,21); he achieved a praetorship as the *candidatus* of Tiberius. Probably *cos. suff.* in AD 44 (AE 1975, 366; [1. 18]). Legate of Germania superior between 47 and 49 where he acquired the *ornamenta triumphalia*; he died as proconsul of Africa under Nero [2; 3]. It remains uncertain whether AE 1986, 475 refers to him.

1 ECK, Statthalter   2 VOGEL-WEIDEMANN, 184ff.   3 B.E. THOMASSON, Fasti Africani, 1996, 38f.   W.E.

[II 8] **Q.C. Rufus.** Author of the only known Alexander monograph in Latin (10 bks.; gaps in B. 3, 5, 6, 10; B. 1–2 are completely missing). The work (*Historiae Alexandri Magni Macedonis*) has been preserved in more than 100 MSS of the most varied quality from the period between the 9th and 15th cent. Only in the MSS is C. mentioned as the author; neither his name nor his work is mentioned by ancient authors. It is uncertain whether he should be identified with the parvenu C.R. or the rhetor Q.C.R. known from Tac. Ann. 11,20f. and Plin. Ep. 7,27,1–3 (Suet. Rhet. 33). The work could date to any time in the first four centuries, and virtually all dates have been conjectured. The famous digression (Curt. 10,9,1–6) in which the condition of the Macedonian empire after the death of Alexander is compared with the current political situation in Rome is non-specific. The most widely supported view assigns it to the time of Claudius, but the congruence of the use of metaphor and the civil war situation of the Year of the Four Emperors (AD 68/69) makes it extremely likely that the work originated under Vespasian (69–79) [4].

What appears fictive to the modern observer are those aspects unknown from the primary sources (→ Alexander historians). It is only with the → Alexander romance that one encounters a work which would be fiction by ancient standards. C. has worked too conscientiously in accordance with the sources — basing his work on the most varied of traditions which can be traced back to → Cleitarchus — for us to speak merely of → light reading.

The literary form (speeches, individual scenes) aiming for effect is, however, an ingredient of C. The work has considerable narrative qualities schooled in the traditions of the epic (particularly that of → Virgil), Graeco-Roman historiography of all eras (especially → Livius) and Roman rhetoric as well as a moralizing tendency thoroughly in accordance with the calibre of Roman → historiography [III]. Factual inaccuracies and contradictions should not be ascribed to negligence but illustrate the literary interest of C. (neglected by scholarship) to whom the design of effective individual scenes was more important than the unity of the whole work.

Ancient references to C. are unknown; this concurs with the literary finding: nowhere can we establish with certainty that an ancient author was influenced by C. Parallels in → Tacitus are merely common topoi.

EDITIONS AND TRANSLATIONS: E.HEDICKE, 1908 (repr. 1919)   K.MÜLLER, H.SCHÖNFELD, 1954 (with a German translation)   G.JOHN, Die Gesch. Al. d. Gr. von Q.C.R. und der Al.-roman, 1987.
COMM.: J.E. ATKINSON, A comm. on Q.C.R.'s Historiae Alexandri Magni 3–4, 1980.
BIBLIOGRAPHY: 1 S.DOSSON, Étude sur Quinte-Curce, 1886   2 R.POROD, Der Literat C., 1987   3 W.RUTZ, Zur Erzählungskunst des Q.C.R., in: ANRW II.32,4, 1986, 2329–2357   4 J.STROUX, Die Zeit des C., in: Philologus 84, 1929, 233–251   5 J.FUGMANN, Zum Problem der Datier. der Historiae Alexandri Magni des C.R., in: Hermes 123, 1995, 233–243.   RO.PO.

[II 9] **C. Severus.** *Praef. equitum* in the Syrian army who suffered defeat at the hands of the Cietae (PIR² C 1620).   W.E.

[II 10] **C. Valerianus.** Latin grammarian presumably of the 5th cent. AD, after → Papirianus and before → Cassiodorus. Of his work we have only the excerpts of Cassiodorus in his *De orthographia*, where they appear under the title *ex Curtio Valeriano ista collecta sunt*. These involve several orthographic notes collected in a relatively disorderly manner and showing a strong dependence on Papirianus.

EDITION: GL 7,155–158
BIBLIOGRAPHY: SCHANZ/HOSIUS, 4,2,218.   P.G.

Curubis Town in the *Africa Proconsularis*, situated on the east coast of the Bon Peninsula, modern Korba. At the time of Caesar it was a *colonia*. Literary evidence: Plin. HN. 5,24; Ptol. 4,3,8 (Κουραβίς, Κούροβις); It. Ant. 56,7; 57,5; 493,9. Inscription.: CIL VIII 1, 977–981; Suppl. 1, 12451–12453; Suppl. 4, 24099–24102; [1. 386].
→ Cap Bon

1 Bull. Archéologique du Comité des Travaux Historiques 1930–1931.

S.LANCEL, E.LIPIŃSKI, s.v. Cap Bon, DCPP, 88f.   W.HU.

Curupedion (Κούρου or Κόρου πεδίον). Plain in Lydia north of Magnesia on the Sipylos, east of the confluence of the Hyllus [4] and the Hermos [2] (Str. 13,4,5; 13), where Lysimachus was defeated in 281 BC by Seleucus (Porphyrius FGrH 260 F 3,8), and Antiochus [5] III was defeated in 190 BC by the Romans (Liv. 37,37–39).

H.BENGTSON, Griech. Gesch., ⁵1977, 389, see n. 4, 481.

H.KA.

Curvature Modern technical term of scholarship devoted to ancient architecture; it describes the *krepidoma* observable in some Doric peripteral temples from the middle of the 6th cent. BC (e.g. temple of Apollo of → Corinth = earliest evidence; Aphaea Temple of → Aegina; → Parthenon; great temple of → Segesta) and rarely also in Ionic buildings (e.g. temple of Apollo of → Didyma) — and resulting from this — the arrangement ascending to the entablature. This phenomenon mentioned by Vitruvius (3,4,5), as well as the → inclination, the → entasis and the angle contraction of the corner bays on the Doric temple (→ Angle triglyph problem are some of the → optical refinements of Greek temple construction. The unfinished great temple of Segesta provides information about the method of

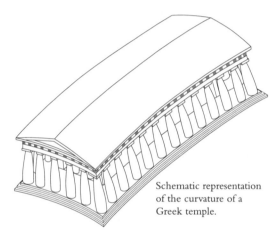

Schematic representation of the curvature of a Greek temple.

construction. Presumably by means of a slightly slack rope, the curve above the horizontal level, measured at a horizontal on the → euthynteria marked previously with a cross, was adjusted upwards; the euthynteria as the top level of the foundation was then chiselled accordingly to the segment of a large sphere and the result applied to all building levels situated above (→ Krepis; → Column; entablature) (which explains the irregularities of the craftmanship above, which could increase substantially towards the top.)

> H.BANKEL, Aegina, Aphaia-Tempel 3: Die K. des spätarcha. Tempels, in: AA 1980, 171–179; P.GRUNAUER, Der Westgiebel des Zeustempels von Olympia, in: JDAI 81, 1974, 6–8; D.MERTENS, Die Herstellung der K. am Tempel von Segesta, in: MDAI(R) 81, 1974, 107–114; Id., Der Tempel von Segesta und die dor. Tempelbaukunst des griech. Westens in klass. Zeit, 1984, 34f.; W.MÜLLER-WIENER, Griech. Bauwesen in der Ant., 1988, 217 s.v. K.; L.SCHNEIDER, CH. HÖCKER, Die Akropolis von Athen, 1990, 143–146.

C.HÖ.

Curvius Sex. C. Silvinus. Quaestor in the province of Baetica, perhaps in the Augustan period (AE 1962, 287; [1]).

> 1 W.ECK, RE Suppl. 14, 110.

Cushion (ἡ τύλη, τὸ κνέφαλλον, Lat. *cervical, pulvinus*). Cushions were used to assure comfort when sitting or lying on chairs, klines (Petron. Sat. 32), in litters (Juv. 6,353) or when lying directly on the ground. Floor cushions were also offered for comfort at the circus (Mart. 14,160). The materials used for cushions included linen, wool or leather, which were often beautifully decorated. Straw, hay, reeds, eelgrass or bulrushes (Ov. Met. 8,655) as well as flocks of wool were used as filling. For this purpose bird feathers of all kinds were popular — that is why cushions in the Roman language are also called *pluma* — among these the feathers of the white German → goose were very highly prized (Plin. HN 10,53f.); people also used feathers from partridges and also the hair of hares.

On Greek and Roman statues the shape of cushions is rectangular, sack-like or elongated and cushions are represented in the most varied of everyday and heroic scenes as padding for resting or as back support. A Roman grave relief depicts a cushion shop (Florence, UF Inv. 313, [1]), and among the 'Copt.' textiles of late antiquity fragments of cushion covers are occasionally found [2].

> 1 G.ZIMMER, Röm. Berufsdarstellungen, 1982, 124, no. 38 2 D.RENNER, Die kopt. Stoffe im Martin-von-Wagner-Museum der Universität Würzburg, 1974, 34–38, no. 16–18.
>
> H.MÖBIUS, Kissen oder Schlauch. Zur Problematik des Bostoner Throns, in: AA 1964, 294–300; M.NAPOLI, La Tomba del Tuffatore, 1970, 117–118; K.SCHAUENBURG, K. oder Ei? Zu einem unterital. Vasenornament, in: AA 1994, 393–401.

R.H.

Cuspius

[1] L.C. Camerinus. Pergamenian who entered the Senate under Nerva or Trajan; suffect consul in 126 AD [1]. Father of C. [2].

> 1 W.ECK, M.ROXAN, in: FS H. Lieb, 1995, 77ff.

[2] L.C. Pactumeius Rufinus. Son of C.[1]. *Cos. ord.* in AD 142. Often stayed in Pergamum where he also built the temple of Asclepius. A friend of Aelius Aristides (PIR² C 1637).

[3] L.C. Rufinus. Probably the grandson of C. [2]. *Cos. ord.* in AD 197 (PIR² C 1638).

W.E.

Custodia 'Guard', 'supervision'. In civil law the term mostly refers to special arrest, in criminal law *custodia* describes the supervision of a prisoner.

In the Roman law of obligations, *custodia* appeared as a technical term for the obligation of a contractual partner to exercise *custodia* in respect of a (mostly) external object, e.g. of borrowers (Gai. Inst. 3,206) and particular entrepreneurs (Gai. Inst. 3,205), of storehouse owners (Dig. 19,2,60,9), tenants (cf. Inst. Iust. 3,24,5), pledged collateral creditors (Dig. 13,7,13,1), custodians offering services (Dig. 16,3,1,35), partners (Dig. 17,2,52,3), users (Dig. 7,9,2) and vendors between the sale and the surrender of the good (Dig. 19,1,31 pr.). Within the context of the → *receptum* liability, the landlord (*caupo*), sailor (*nauta*) and storekeeper (*stabularius*) had to vouch for *custodia* (Dig. 47,5,1,4). Lawyers did not always use technical language: in this way, in Dig. 16,3,1 pr. it is said of the object to be kept in the → *depositum* that it is surrendered into *custodiendum* without implying any guard obligation in the above sense (cf. Gai. Inst. 3,207).

Where the Roman lawyers decided that someone was responsible for *custodia* (*custodiam praestare*), this meant accepting liability if the object was destroyed or if it deteriorated — which he should have been able to prevent by guarding the object. In this way, the *custodia* liability included among other things the theft of the item (Gai. Inst. 3,205 ff), as well as the escape of slaves (Dig. 13,6,5,6) and property damage by third parties (if this could have been averted through *custodia*, cf. Marcellus/Ulp. Dig. 19,2,41, otherwise Julian. Dig. 13,6,19). The person with the *custodia* obligation is (so long as he is solvent) granted *actio furti* against theft in place of the owner (Gai. Inst. 3,203 ff). He had no liability for *custodia* if the damage was caused by → *vis maior* (act of god).

How the *custodia* liability related to the liability for → *culpa* is a contentious issue: independent reason for liability or only specially pronounced liability for neglect of duty? Furthermore: objective *custodia* concept (absolute liability for theft alone) or subjective *custodia* concept (fault liability because the damage was concretely based on defective supervision by the person with the *custodia* obligation)? The objective concept presumably developed further in the Principate — at least for some of the legal experts — into the subjective concept (*custodia* as the sub-instance of *culpa*). In late antiquity it was generalized and systematized.

Custodia is also encountered in property law as the proximity of a person to an object, e.g. in the sense of the *corpus possessionis* necessary for the acquisition of property: property is acquired as the purchaser ensures supervision of the object (cf. Dig. 41,2,51). Ownership of moveable objects (with the exception of slaves) was maintained through *custodia* over them. According to Dig. 41,2,3,13, *custodia* in this connection refers to the capacity of a person to be able to establish natural ownership of an object.

In succession law, *custodela* refers to the position of the *familiae emptor* (inheritance trustee) in respect of the objects entrusted to him (Gai. Inst. 2,104).

In criminal law *custodia* means taking into custody those charged with a crime, especially in the → *carcer* (*custodia carceralis*, *custodia publica*). The *custodia libera* was a less stringent detention involving the ordering of house arrest by magistrates *coercitio*. In the case of *custodia militaris* (→ military penal law) the soldier charged with an offence was handed over to be guarded.

→ Furtum; → Commodatum; → Possessio

KASER, RPR I, 506–511; II 352 — 355; H. HONSELL, TH. MAYER-MALY, W. SELB, Röm. Recht, ⁴1987, 233–238; R. ROBAYE, L'obligation de garde, 1987; P. VOCI, 'Diligentia', 'custodia', 'culpa', in: SDHI 56, 1990, 29–143; G. MACCORMACK, Custodia and Culpa, in: ZRG 89, 1972, 149–219.

Custos Watchman, keeper, supervisor. Custos is also an epithet for Jupiter appearing on coins of the emperors from Nero to Hadrian. It is said that after the Vitellian attack Domitian built a temple to Jupiter Custos for rescuing them, in which an image was put up that shows the emperor standing under the protection of the god (Tac. Hist. 3,74). *Corporis custos* was the name for bodyguards of ancient potentates, particularly for the German bodyguard of the Julio-Claudian house (CIL VI 8803; 8804). *Custos urbis* is often found as a synonym for the *praefectus urbi*.   F.ME.

Cusus River, eastern or western border of the kingdom of Quadian Vannius founded in AD 19 *inter Marum* (March) *et Cusum* (Tac. Ann. 2,63,6), mostly identified with the *Duria*, i.e. with Hron (Gran), Ipel' (Eipel) or — archaeologically the most probable — Váh (Waag [1. 186¹⁰⁴]).

1 H.-W. BÖHME, Arch. Zeugnisse zur Gesch. der Markomannenkriege, in: JRGZ 22, 1975, 153–217.

TIR M 33,35f.; G. NEUMANN, s.v. C., RGA 5, 112f. Ipel';
                                                                    K.DI.

Cutilia Sabine town between Reate and Interocrium, founded by the local inhabitants, made famous by Varro; the *Aquae Cutiliae* and the *lacus Cutiliensis*, situated in the centre of the peninsula, considered the *umbilicus Italiae* ('navel of Italia') (Varro, Ling. 5,71; Plin. 3,109) take their name from Cutilia.

NISSEN, 2, 475.   G.U.

Cutius
[1] **T.C. Ciltus.** Suffect consul probably in AD 55 with L. Junius Gallio (AE 1960, 61f.; [1]).

1 W. ECK, RE Suppl. 14, 110.

[2] **C. Lupus.** Quaestor who had to supervise the *calles* in Lower Italy. In AD 24 he put down a slave revolt in Apulia (Tac. Ann. 4,27,2; [1]).

1 W. ECK, in: Scripta Classica Israelica 13, 1994, 60ff.
                                                                    W.E.

Cutlery Since Roman times cutlery has become increasingly important at table. The most common items were spoons, divided into two groups by shape; the *cochlearia* whose pointed handle made the eating of mussels possible, and the *ligulae* whose tip often bore a round decoration [1]. This theoretical classification was in reality undoubtedly less strict. In the course of time we observe a trend in shapes and sizes: the bow of the spoon is one of the most typical elements (in the 3rd cent. AD, for example, it assumes a characteristic pouch shape), likewise its connection with the handle was made in an increasingly complicated manner whereby the joint eventually took the shape of a disc; from the 4th cent. AD onwards often perforated, sometimes ending with the head of an animal (lion, griffin). Spoons also become larger and heavier over time; although all the materials are available (wood, bone, metal), they are often made of silver or tin-coated bronze (sometimes found in dozens together). There are also countless special shapes and combinations that on the one hand resemble a spoon and on the other hand a knife, a sieve or another small instrument. The bowl section of the spoon can bear an engraved, flattened or inlaid decoration, or bear an inscription: the name of

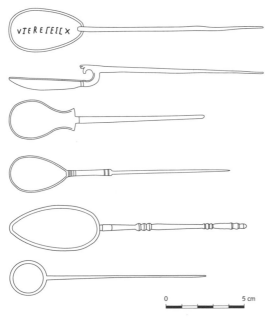

Silver spoons (*ligulae* and *cochlearia*)
from Augusta Raurica/Augst (Roman).

the owner, the wish that it be used well, or even a dedication if the spoon was offered as a votive offering [2]. The same applies to the handles, especially at the end of the Roman period and in the 6th and 7th cent. AD, on which the names of the apostles, of saints or the owner can be found, or even words from literature. Spoons were popular as gifts (Mart. 8,71), and were often placed in tombs as an offering and were thus abundant at that time and particularly in the later period. They appear, for example, very frequently in the testaments of the Merovingian period or, in the same period, in the possession of the bishops; they therefore represented an important element in the routine of the → banquets, at

the same time making them lively events (SHA Heliogab. 12) [3]. Several ancient texts (e.g. Mart. 14,120f.) and the investigation of objects (traces of wear and tear, food remnants) allow us to gain a greater understanding of their use.

Knives were undoubtedly more rarely used at table; in any case they are hardly represented in the cutlery finds. However, there are many other small utensils, the use of which increased even more at the end of antiquity; they take on the character of personal items, often combined with others in the same set, drawn onto a ring or combined into a single item with several foldable parts. The sieves to filter wine that were initially relatively large become smaller, more individual and are often worn on the finger on a ring. Many of these sets of cutlery have the character of toilet items: ear scoops and toothpicks, evidence for which is available from the 1st cent. AD (Petron. Sat. 33,1), although these were numerous from the 4th cent. onwards.

It is generally agreed that forks were not used before the Middle Ages. Several objects, however, rare in Roman times, are found in greater numbers from the 6th cent. AD onwards; these actually have the appearance of forks with two or three prongs. In finds they are often clearly combined with spoons and must have been used at table.

Some of the larger pieces were used to serve food: ladles and sieves.

→ Cochlear(e); → Table utensils

1 H. MIELSCH, Miszellen zur spätant. Toreutik, in: AA, 1992, 475–478   2 C. JOHNS, T. POTTER, The Thetford Treasure, 1983, 34–45   3 F. BARATTE, Vaisselle d'argent, souvenirs littéraires et manières de table, in: Cahiers arch. 40, 1992, 5–20.

F. BARATTE, Le trésor de la place Camille-Jouffray à Vienne (Isère), Gallia, 50. Ausg., 80–84; H. W. BÖHME, Löffelbeigabe in spätröm. Gräbern nördl. der Alpen, in: JRGZ 17, 1970, 172–200; S. R. HAUSER, Spätant. und frühbyz. Silberlöffel. Bemerkungen zur Produktion von Luxusgütern im 5. bis 7. Jh., JbAC, suppl. vol. 19, 1992; M. MARTIN, Besteck, in: H. A. CAHN, A. KAUFMANN-HEINIMANN (ed.), Der spätröm. Silberschatz von Kaiseraugst, 1984, 56–132; E. RIHA, W. B. STERN, Die röm. Löffel aus Augst und Kaiseraugst, Forsch. in Augst 5, 1982.   F. BA.

Cuttlefish see → Volume 4, Addenda

Cyane (Κυάνη). Small stream steeped in legend that has its origin about 9 km south-west of Syracusae (as the crow flies) in a source of the same name and that after about 20 km, together with the Anapus, flows through a wide swampy area into the Great Harbour of Syracusae; modern Ciani. According to Ovid (Met. 5,413ff.), the nymph C., the wife of Anapus, tried to stop Hades (Pluto) when he was deflowering Kore and dissolved in tears on the spot where he split the earth and went down into the underworld. Diodor (4,23,4; 5,4,2) attests to an annual festival for Demeter, Kore and C. established by Hercules.   Gl.F. and E.O.

Cyaneae (Κυανέαι).

[1] Two small rocky islands directly to the west of the confluence of the Bosporus and the → Pontus Euxinus, 2.3 km north of Garipçe Burnu, 100 m in front of the lighthouse of Rumelifeneri, modern İreke Taşı. In Greek myths they were identified with the dangerous → Symplegades or → Planctae (Hom. Od. 16,176; Apoll. Rhod. 2,317ff.). Here there was a shrine (Hdt. 4,85). Pompey built an altar in honour of Apollo here [1. 28f., 35–39].

> 1 R. GÜNGERICH (ed.), Gryllius, De Bosporo Thracico, 1927.   I.v.B.

[2] Town in central Lycia, in Lycian perhaps *Xbahñ* or rather *turaxssi* (TAM 1, 44a l. 54f.), to which Paus. 7, 21, 13 may have referredwhen mentioning an oracle of Apollo Thyrxeus at C. In spite of traces of older settlements (Neolithic axes, pottery from the 6th cent. BC) C. was not with the fortified castle of a dynastic ruler until the 5th cent. BC (with grave pillars). In the 4th cent. BC and after the closure of a large settlement on the nearby Avşar Tepesi, presumably involving a population movement, C. became a *pólis*, into which were integrated the other fortified castles (Korba, Trysa, Tüse, Hoyran, Büyük Avşar) and the harbour of Teimiusa as *démoi* with limited self-government [1. 67–101]. From the 2nd cent. BC onwards, C., as a member of the → Lycian League, minted coins. In the Imperial period, the centre was extended with a theatre, bouleuterion and library founded by individuals such as Jason (son of Neikostratus) in the time of Antoninus (2nd cent. AD) (IGR 704–706). Prosperity also in late antiquity and a cathedral town right through to the high Middle Ages.

The well-explored surrounding country was densely settled with numerous villages, farms, underground water tanks, oil presses etc. and it allows profound insight into the typical settlement structure of an ancient *pólis* [2; 3]: the majority of citizens lived in the country; the town was primarily a centre for services.

> 1 M. ZIMMERMANN, Unt. zur histor. Landeskunde Zentrallykiens, 1992   2 F. KOLB, Stadt und Land im ant. Kleinasien, in: J. H. M. STRUBBE (ed.), Energeia. FS H. W. Pleket, 1996, 97–112   3 Id., Lyk. Stud. 4. Feldforsch. auf dem Gebiet von K. (Asia Minor Stud. 29), 1998.   MA.ZI.

Cyanippus (Κυάνιππος, 'Black horse').

[1] King of Argus, son of Aegialeus and of Comaetho, descendant of Bias (Paus. 2,18,4; 30,10). According to Apollodor (1,103), C. is the son of → Adrastus [1] and brother of → Aegialeus [1]. Pausanias confuses his family tree: he speaks about four generations and five rulers but does not include C. among these, as the rulers cannot be called *Nēleídai* until Talaus (whose mother is a daughter of Neleus. Pausanias includes Diomedes as C.'s guardian as he assumes rule for C. who was a minor [1].

[2] Son of Phares of Thessaly, husband of Leucon. Because of his passion for hunting he neglects his wife. In her jealousy, the latter follows him and is taken by C.'s dogs to be game and torn apart. In mourning, C. burns his dogs at the stake and then dies by his own hand (Parthenius 10 MythGr 2; cf. also Sostratus (FGrH 23 F 4); → Cephalus).

> 1 K. SCHERLING, s.v. K. (1), RE 11, 2236f.   AL.FR.

Cyathus

[1] see → Pottery, shapes and types of

[2] A jug or drinking vessel that, derived from Greek κύαθος, is especially a Roman measure of capacity for dry goods and liquids of 45.6 ml. The *cyathus* amounts to $^1/_{12}$ of the *sextarius* (= 0,55 l). The number of *cyathi* drunk is counted as a multiple of *uncia*, e.g. four *cyathi* are called *trientes* (= $^1/_3$ of the sextarius) or 11 *cyathi* are called *deunx*. According to a Roman custom popular at banquets, people had to drink as many *cyathi* as the number of letters in the name of the one to be honoured. Larger goblets were also used that were a multiple of the *cyathus*.

→ Deunx; → Banquet; → Measure of volume; → Cyathus; → Sextarius; → Uncia

> F. HULTSCH, Griechische und römische Metrologie, ²1882, 117ff.; J. MARQUARDT, Das Privatleben der Römer, ²1886, 334ff.   A.M.

Cyaxares (Κυαξάρης, ancient Persian *Uvaxštra-*, etymology uncertain).

[1] Median 'king' of the 7th/6th cents. BC. In the Median *lógos* of Herodotus (Hdt. 1,73f.; 103–107) C. appears as τύραννος/*týrannos* or βασιλεύς/*basileús* of the Medes, as the son of → Phraortes, grandson of → Deioces and father of → Astyages. During his 40-year reign, he is said — after a Scythian interregnum — to have conquered the Assyrians and to have fought against Alyattes of Lydia (probably for possession of Cappadocia); in the process, a solar eclipse (probably on 28 May 585) foreseen by Thales of Miletus in his prophecy to the Ionians, is said to have induced a peace settlement between the Medes and the Lydians and brought Astyages and Aryenis, the daughter of Alyattes, to unite in marriage.

In Babylonian tradition [2nd no. 3], C. (*Umakištar*) is called 'King (*šarru*) of the Ummānmanda' or 'King of the Medes'; under his leadership the Medes are said to have unsuccessfully attacked Nineveh in 614 BC and to have captured nearby Tarbisu and ultimately even Assur. C. then entered into an alliance and pact of mutual support with the Babylonian king → Nabupolassar who had arrived in the meantime. In 612 the Babylonian and Median units met again in northern Babylonia, advanced together on Nineveh and conquered the city after laying siege to it for three months. The Medes were also apparently involved in the later capture of Harran.

If the 'Median *lógos*' of Herodotus is rightly described as a Greek invention, then much speaks in favour of the Greek historian owing the names C. and

Astyages (who incidentally only appears in his works as the son of C.) to Babylonian tradition; Herodotus may have taken the name of C.'s father, Phraortes, according to the principle of papponymy, from the insurgent of the same name who posed as a descendant of C. and opposed Darius I [4. 121 DB II 15]. In scholarship, the nature of Median rule and the political organization of Media at the time of C. (empire or only a tribal confederacy) is a particularly contentious issue.

1 I. M. DIAKONOFF, s.v. Cyaxares, Enclr 6, 1993, 478f.
2 A. K. GRAYSON, Assyrian-Babylonian Chronicles, 1975
3 P. R. HELM, Herodotus' *Medikos Logos* and Median History, in: Iran 19, 1981, 85–90 4 R. KENT, Old Persian, 1953 5 A. KUHRT, The Ancient Near East, 2, 1995, Index s.v. K. 6 O. W. MUSCARELLA, Miscellaneous Median Matters, in: AchHist 8, 1994, 57–64 7 H. SANCISI-WEERDENBURG, The Orality of Herodotus' *Medikos Logos*, in: AchHist 8, 1994, 39–55.

[2] Unhistorical last king of Media in Xenophon. J.W.

Cybele (Κυβέλη; *Kybélē*, Lat. Cybele, -a) is the goddess of fertility, city protectress (expressed in the mural crown), prophetess and healer.

A. ASIA MINOR 1. BRONZE AGE 2. THE FIRST MILLENNIUM B. GREECE C. ROME 1. INTRODUCTION TO ROME 2. THE CULT

A. ASIA MINOR
1. BRONZE AGE
The alternative form of the name Cybebe (Κυβήβη, Lat. Cybebe) allows us to equate the goddess of Asia Minor of the 1st millennium BC with the goddess Kubaba known from Hittite, Hurrian and Sumerian-Akkadian sources [1]. One of the most important centres for the worship of this goddess in the 2nd millennium was Hittite → Karkemiš/Karkamis [2] situated on the Syrian border on the Euphrates. Even before 1200 BC C. is said to have come to Pessinus. Kubela or Kubelon is either a Phrygian mountain name or epiclesis [3; 4]; a sacred stone embodied C. in → Pessinus where her priesthood reigned independently until 183 BC (Str. 12,5,3) [5]. In various places in Phrygia the goddess (once described in an inscription as *matar kubileija* [3]) is depicted in the archaic period standing *en face* in temple facades hewn out of rock.

2. THE FIRST MILLENNIUM
The Phrygians are said to have imbued the Pessinuntian cult with an ecstatic-orgiastic character through the link with Thrace and the Dionysian cult. The Greek term *gállos*/Lat. *gallus* for the priest of C. may go back to the invading Gauls who also gave their name to the river flowing through Pessinus [6]; the symbol of the rooster (Lat. *gallus*) which was found on the gravestones of several priests, likewise appears to refer to these Celts. The voluntary castration of servants of C. may be of Syrian-Semitic origin and could, if accepted as such, belong to a pre-Phrygian phase [7]. Not all priests, nor all high priests, must inevitably have been

→ eunuchs. The priests of C., particularly eunuchs, had their mythical prototype in → Attis (comparable with → Adonis); these Pessinuntian priests bore the title *Áttis*. These *mētragýrtai* ('mendicant priests of the Great Mother') are well-known in classical Greek literature and as caricatures in small works of art from the 4th cent. BC. In addition, evidence for the Lydian form of the name *kuvav-* is found in a graffito in Sardis (around 570 BC) [13]; it should be combined with the Bronze Age Kubaba of Karkemiš. Hdt. 5,102 records that the Persians destroyed the shrine of the ephichoric goddess C. in Sardis. With the Hellenization of Lydia the iconography of this goddess was adapted to the original Phrygian iconography.

B. GREECE
The Phrygian mother goddess emerges in the 6th cent. BC, particularly on the west coast of Asia Minor; she is usually called *Métēr* ('mother'), and more rarely and almost only in literature and in later inscriptions as C. The oldest evidence which comes from southern Aeolia and northern Ionia [8] consists of votive gifts in the form of a → *naiskos* [9], in front of which sits the enthroned goddess sometimes with a lion on her lap. This type of dedication, the iconography of which is hardly imaginable without the Phrygian rock depictions, also reached Samos and Miletus, the Aegean Sea and the Phocaean colonies, especially Massalia [8; 10]. The iconography on votive depictions in southern Ionia is a standing goddess in relief (similar to the depictions of Gordium and Ankara). Additional examples come from Cretan Gortyn and Chania [8]. The iconographic topos of the seated goddess with a small lion on her knees and a veil developed in the Greek colonies of Asia Minor from the 6th cent. BC onwards [11]. The goddess also reached the western and northern coast of the Black Sea (especially Cyzicus) [12] and Greece via Thrace [10] and the Aegean Islands.

We have to assume that the Phrygian goddess probably reached the Ionian coastal towns as early as the 7th cent. BC: an inscription dated to the earliest part of the 6th cent. BC from southern Italian Locri can only have followed this expansion; the form of the name (*Kubala*) proves that the Phrygian form of the name was accepted into the world of the Greek gods. In Greece C. was soon equated with → Rhea and also aligned with → Demeter; → Artemis and → Aphrodite were also comparable with aspects of C. We should not exclude the possibility that C. in her expansion westward to the Greek towns also came upon pre-existent goddesses; perhaps Rhea or Demeter concealed an ancient mother goddess of such kind who was then equated with C. [14]. This therefore applied not only to goddesses inhabiting the known, mythological and ritually known Pantheon but went another step deeper into a forgotten primary matrix, that of a nameless universal goddess ultimately merged with known goddesses. The oldest Greek literary evidence is Hipponax, fr. 121 B (around 540 BC) and Pind. Fr. 80; Euripides refers (Bacch. 78f.) to the ecstatic rites of the 'Great Mother Cybele'. The connection between the name of C. and the concept of the Great Mother is also common [15], but not every 'mother of the gods' (μήτηρ θεῶν) is necessarily the Pessinuntian C.; the literary and archaeological/topographical context is decisive. The Athenians built the Metron for C. The statue to C. created by Agoracritus of Paros for this temple determined the iconography for the entire ensuing period: C. on her throne with a tympanum (tambourine) in her hand and a lion on each side [7]. However, C. did not become part of Greek theogony and mythology: according to [7. 266] she arrived too late to still be assigned an independent role in pre-classical theogony or a general function in early Greek mythology. Only in conjunction with → Attis does a myth exist although it was certainly outside the Greek mythological cycles.

C. ROME
1. INTRODUCTION TO ROME
The founder of the Pergamene dynasty, Philetaerus, built a shrine called a Megalesion for a *Métēr Megálē* ('Great Mother') in Pergamum itself (Varro, Ling. 6,15). The idea most commonly represented in scholarship is that the sacred stone of Pessinus came to Rome by a circuitous route via Pergamum in 205/4 BC (Liv. 29,11 and 14; 36,36,3f.). Consequently the name of the Roman festival Megalesia is also derived from Pergamene Megalesion. The cult image (meteorite: Arnob. 6,11; 7,49; Prudent. Peristephanon 10,157) reached Rome on 4 April and was put up in the Temple of Victoria until the completion of the Palatine sanctuary (Liv. 29,37,2). The goddess from Asia Minor was received by a member of one of the aristocratic families, → Cornelius [I 81] Scipio Nasica. When the ship with the divine freight was stranded in the Tiber, it was an additional representative of a noble family, → Claudia [I 3] Quinta, who freed the ship from the mire and accompanied it to the gates of Rome (Ov. Fast. 291–338 [16]). In Aur. Vict. De viris illustribus 3,46,1–3, Scipio Nasica also commissioned to protect the divine stone until its actual shrine was completed.

On 10 April 191 BC it was transferred to its Palatine home; M. Junius Brutus dedicated the temple (Liv. 36,36,4–5). Remains of it have been discovered in the western part of the Palatine above the Scalae Caci [17]. This temple burned down in 111 BC and was most probably rebuilt under the supervision of Metellus Numidicus (Consul 110 BC) (Ov. Fast. 4,347–348; Val. Max. 1,8,11; Obseq. 39). After another fire Augustus had the temple rebuilt (Val. Max. 1,8,11; Ov. Fast. 4,348; R. Gest. div. Aug. 19). Elagabalus expressed the desire to transfer the divine stone to its sanctuary (SHA Heliogab. 3).

The cult was surprisingly isolated. Roman citizens were forbidden to join the Collegium of the Priests of C. (Dion. Hal. Ant. Rom. 2,1,4) and to castrate themselves (Val. Max. 7,6; Obseq. 44); the *galli* were only allowed to move around on the streets of Rome on certain days and the same applied to their begging (Dion. Hal. Ant.

Rom. 2,19,4; Diod. Sic. 36,13; Cic. Leg. 2,22,40): this meant that their cult service was practically restricted to the Palatine temple (Varro, Sat. Men. 149f.). Nevertheless, C. had been brought to Rome at the command of the Sibylinian Books (→ Sibyls) with the consent of the Senate and with the help of leading Roman families [18; 19]. In addition, the temple was in the middle of the centre of Rome inside the → Pomerium. In view of this and a) the supervisory function of *XVviri* (→ *Quindecimviri sacris faciundis*), b) the independence of the priestly state of Pessinus and its continuity after the transfer of the goddess to Rome (the question as to how that was possible without the presence of the goddess remains unanswered), c) the distance of Pessinus from the Pergamene sphere of influence where the Pessinuntian goddess was to be kept in the Pergamene Megalesion, d) the two festival cycles (March and April, whereby the introduction of the elements of the March rite falls within the imperial period), and e) the name of the goddess, Mater Deum Magna Idaea, it appears more convincing to believe that the goddess introduced in 205/4 BC was the Great Mother of Mount Ida who came to Rome with the aid of Attalus I of Troad than to ascribe to the Romans ignorance of the new goddess.

With the Roman expansion in Asia Minor, Pessinus then came into their sphere of influence and control; hence the ecstatic Phrygian C. became tangible. The nature of the two goddesses began to converse in this way.

2. THE CULT
The *ludi Megalenses* were conducted every year; from 191 BC dramatic performances were included. The festivities of the *ludi* began and ended on the original dates, 4 April (arrival) and 10 April (temple consecration). The *praetor urbanus* brought an offering to the sanctuary on 4 April (Dion. Hal. Ant. Rom. 2,19,4), and a → *lectisternium* and banquet amongst the private *sodalitates* opened the festival cycle. The *XVviri sacris faciundis* helped to wash the cult image (Luc. 1,599). This washing (*lavatio*) took place in the small river → Almo and is well known from Ov. Fast. 4,337ff. The silver statue with the meteorite was moved in a cart or litter from the shrine on the Palatine along the Via Appia to the Almo; a small sanctuary lay between the junction of the Via Appia and its confluence with the Tiber; when a wash basin was discovered in front of the Palatine temple, it was assumed that the *lavatio* also originally took place there and was not moved to the Almo until the time of Augustus [20].

It is important to make a distinction between the *ludi* in April and the ecstatic festivities of Cybele and of → Attis which are in March. The calendar of → Filocalus (→ Chronographer of AD 354) lists the following feast days for March: 15: *canna intrat* (→ *cannophori*, introduced at the time of Antoninus Pius or later [21]), 22: *arbor intrat* (→ *dendrophori*, introduced at the time of Claudius), 24: *sanguem* (*galli*, introduced at the time of Claudius), 25: *hilaria* (introduced after Antoninus Pius), 26: *requietio* (introduced after Antoninus Pius),

27: *lavatio* and *hastiferi* (introduced at the time of Claudius), 28: *initium caiani*. In *lavatio* ('washing') C. is again the focal point (Ov. Fast. 4,337–340; Luc. 1,600; Stat. Silv. 5,1,222–224; CIL VI 10098). The *dendrophori* were supervised by the *XVviri* (CIL X 3699); on 22 March they carried in the procession a pine decorated with flowers and wrapped in bandages that symbolized the dead Attis.

The word *hastiferi* may have been coined in a manner analogous to *dendrophori* [22]. These spear carriers who play a part in the *lavatio* procession are in all probability members of the → Ma/Bellona cult. → Bellona that bears the title *dea pedisequa* is part of *lavatio* since the reform of the Attis procession under Emperor Claudius. The members of the Collegium were probably in the widest sense *pedisequarii* (low-ranking officials) in public life. *Decemviri* and later the *Quindecimviri sacris faciundis* supervised worship. An *archigallus*, a *summus sacerdos* or a *sacerdos maxima* (high priest or high priestess) could be the head of a cult group; the latter were selected by town or municipal councils or by the → *XVviri*. The → Taurobolium (bull sacrifice) can be connected with their *consecratio*. *Curatores* monitored the daily cult routine and were also active in the administration. Several sanctuaries also had a special administrator (*aedituus*). *Apparatores* looked after the cult objects. Male singers (*hymnologi*), male flute players (*tibicines*), female tambourine and cymbal players (*tympanistriae* and *cymbalistriae*) were members of the cult community: however, belonging to a cult community did not necessarily mean being initiated.

The cult of C. had an initiation rite that may have given the person initiated an eschatological perspective. The form of the → mysteries is comparable with the Eleusinian rite [23]. The Frigianum (Phrygianum) in the modern Vatican was the place where the → Taurobolium and Criobolium (→ Kriobolion) took place (CIL VI 497–510 30779; ILS 4145, 4147–51, 4153). It is still unknown whether bull and goat sacrifices reached the west with the Phrygian goddess or through a link with Ma/Bellona of Asia Minor [22. 101–102]. The earliest inscription that provides evidence in Italy of a Taurobolium comes from Puteoli and dates from AD 134 (CIL X 1596). The sacrifice was, however, carried out at the command of Venus Caelestis, not of C.; possibly the two goddesses are identified here. The first evidence of a Taurobolium from Rome comes from AD 295, the last from AD 390; the detailed description in Prudent. Peristephanon 10,1006–1050 probably does not apply to a Taurobolium [23]. Votive altars in memory of a Taurobolium or Criobolium come from all the provinces, particularly though from Spain, Gaul and Africa [24. 104–105].

→ Ecstasy; → Asia Minor, Religion; → Magna Mater; → Mother goddesses; → Mysteries

1 I.M. DIAKONOFF, On Cybele and Attis in Phrygia and Lydia, in: Acta Antiqua Academiae Scientiarum Hungaricae 25, 1977, 334–340   2 E. LAROCHE, Koubaba, déesse anatolienne, et le problème des origines de Cybèle, in: Eléments orientaux dans la rel. grecque ancienne, 1960, 113–128   3 C. BRIXHE, Le nom de Cybèle, in: Sprache 25, 1979, 40–45   4 L. ZGUSTA, Weiteres zum Namen der Kybele, in: Sprache 28, 1982, 171–172   5 U. KRON, Heilige Steine, in: Kotinos, 1992, 56–70   6 E. LANE, The Name of Cybele's Priests, the Galloi, in: Id. (ed.), Cybele, Attis and Related Cults, 1996, 117–133   7 G. SANDERS, Kybele und Attis, in: Die oriental. Rel. im Römerreich, 1981, 264–297   8 F. GRAF, The Arrival of Cybele in the Greek East, in: Actes du VIIᵉ Congrès de la FIEC, 1983, 117–120   9 M. REIN, Phrygian Matar: Emergence of an Iconographic Type, in: E. LANE (ed.), Cybele, Attis and Related Cults, 1996, 223–237   10 E. SIMON, s.v. Kybele, LIMC Suppl., 745   11 E. WILL, Aspects du culte et de la légende de la Grande Mère dans le monde grec, in: Eléments orientaux dans la rel. grecque ancienne, 1960, 95–111   12 M. ALEXANDRESCU VIANU, Sur la diffusion du culte de Cybèle dans le bassin de la Mer Noire à l'époque archaïque, in: Dacia 24, 1980, 261–265   13 M.R. GUSMANI, Der lyd. Name der Kybele, in: Kadmos 8, 1968, 158–161   14 N. ROBERTSON, The Ancient Mother of the Gods, in: E. LANE (ed.), Cybele, Attis and Related Cults, 1996, 239–304   15 A. HENRICHS, Despoina Kybele: Ein Beitr. zur rel. Namenkunde, in: HSPh 80, 1976, 253–286   16 T. KÖVES, Zum Empfang der Magna Mater, in: Historia 12, 1963, 321–347   17 LTUR 1, s.v. Cybeles Tholus, 338   18 E. GRUEN, The Advent of Magna Mater, in: Id., Stud. in Greek Culture and Roman Policy, 1990, 5–33   19 S.A. TAKÁCS, Magna Deum Mater Idaea, Cybele, and Catullus' Attis, in: E. LANE (ed.), Cybele, Attis and Related Cults, 1996, 367–386   20 L. RICHARDSON, A New Topographical Dictionary of Ancient Rome, 1992, 5   21 D. FISHWICK, The Cannophori and the March Festival of Magna Mater, in: TAPhA 97, 1966, 193–202   22 Id., Hastiferi, in: JRS 57, 1967, 142–160   23 G. SFAMENI GASPARRO, Soteriology and Mystic Aspects in the Cult of Cybele and Attis, 1985   24 PH. BORGEAUD, La mère des dieux, 1996 25 M.J. VERMASEREN, Cybele and Attis, 1977.

M. BEARD, The Roman and the Foreign. The Cult of the Great Mother, in: N. THOMAS, C. HUMPHREY (ed.), Shamanism, History and the State, 1994, 164–190; I. BECHER, Der Kult der Mater Magna in augusteischer Zeit, in: Klio 73, 1991, 157–170; F. BÖHMER, Kybele in Rom, in: MDAI(R) 71, 1964, 130–151; H. GRAILLOT, Le culte de Cybèle Mère des Dieux à Rome et dans l'empire, 1912; P. LAMBRECHTS, Cybèle, divinité étrangère ou nationale, in: Bulletin de la Société Royale Belge 62, 1951, 44–60; B. METZGER, A Classified Bibliography of the Graeco-Roman Mystery Religions, in: ANRW II 17.3, 1984, 1280–1294; G. THOMAS, Magna Mater and Attis, in: ANRW II 17.3, 1984, 1500–1535.   S.TA.

Cybistra (Κύβιστρα; *Kýbistra*). Town in → Cappadocia II. It was a diocese from AD 325 and an archdiocese from *c.* 1060.

W. RUGE, s.v. Kybistra, RE Suppl. 4, 1123; HILD/RESTLE, 188–190.   K.ST.

Cychreus (Κυχρεύς; *Kychreús*). Protective hero of the island of Salamis. Son of → Poseidon and Salamis, the daughter of Asopus (Paus. 1,35,2). He liberates the

Island of → Salamis from a dreadful snake, thus making it habitable and becomes the first inhabitant and king of the island. As he has no sons, he transfers rule to → Telamon, who is fleeing from Aegina, and gives him his daughter Glauce in marriage (Apollod. 3,161; Diod. Sic. 4,72,7). C. had a shrine on the island (Plut. Solon 9) and was venerated as a protective hero that took the form of a snake (Paus. 1,36,1); in Athens he was even honoured as a god (Plut. Theseus 10). Like → Cecrops people regarded C. as having two forms (*diphyḗs*) — the upper part a human, the lower a snake and as 'earthborn' (*gḗgenḗs*) (Schol. Lycoph. 110; 451).   RA.MI.

Cyclades (Κυκλάδες νῆσοι; *Kykládes nêsoi*, Latin *Cyclades*, 'circle islands'). The modern term refers to the southern Aegean group comprising a total of more than 200 islands between the Greek mainland and the Cretan sea with the exception of the islands off the western coast of Asia Minor which essentially concurs with the original ancient concept (Hdt. 5,30). Thucydides (1,4; 2,9,4) considers that Melos and Thera belong to it, Scylax (48; 58) includes Thera, Anaphe and Astypalaea and only excludes Ios and Amorgus with Icarus. From a geological point of view, the C. are a continuation of the mountain range of Euboea and Attica and consist of the same crystalline rocks resting on top of a large undersea plateau. Only the south-eastern islands belong to a more recent fold system and consist of slate and lime. Melos, Thera and their neighbouring islands are of volcanic origin.

The usual ancient characterization of the C. as the islands 'lying in a circle (around Delos)' (Dionys. Per. 525f.) probably did not come about until late in time and is also inaccurate. Strabo (10,1,3) gives an account of the justification offered by Artemidorus who refers to the '(Ionian) islands contributing to the Delian festival '; moreover, the island list of Artemidorus is incorrect and Strabo is right to engage in polemics. The result of this statement of Artemidorus was that the Hellenistic geographers collected the islands situated more to the south under the name *Sporádes*, 'the scattered ones' that was unknown to the earlier authors; so people did not agree which islands belonged to it. Main passages: Str. 2,5,21; 10,4,1; 10,5,1–12; Dionysius Kalliphontos 130ff.; Ptol. 3,14,23f.; Plin. HN 4,22f.; Eust. in Dionys. Per. 525; 532.

The C. were of great importance to ancient shipping traffic because they were a bridge between the Greek mainland and Asia Minor and to Crete. The larger islands had been settled since the Late Stone Age. Many of the smaller ones also show traces of early settlement, such as the Neolithic settlement on the island of Salagon near Paros. In the Bronze Age the islands formed a cultural group ('Cycladic culture') that was influenced by Asia Minor, Crete and Mycenae [1. 13ff., 80ff., 134ff.; 2; 3]. After the → Doric Migration most of the C. was Ionian, the southern part was Doric, but according to Thucydides (1,8,1) and Isocrates (Or. 12,43) the older pre-Greek population was still discernible. In ancient

times Naxos had a leading role. In the 5th cent. BC the island states belonged to the → Delian League, in the 4th cent. they were initially under Spartan rule, then they were members of the 2nd → Athenian League until most of the islands left the league during the Social War (357–355). In the Hellenistic period the C. formed the 'League of *Nēsiótai*' that was alternately under Ptolemaic and Macedonian influence. Inscriptions: IG XII 5,1f. Suppl. no. 167–329; p. 212–217.

→ Aegean Koine; Minoan culture and archaeology

1 D. FIMMEN, Die kret.-myk. Kultur, 1924   2 F. SCHACHERMEYR, s.v. Prähist. Kulturen, RE XXII 2, 1398ff. 3 K. SCHOLES, The Cyclades in the Later Bronze Age, in: ABSA 51, 1956, 9–40.

O. MAULL, L. BÜRCHNER, s.v. Kyklades, RE XI 2, 2308ff.; PHILIPPSON/KIRSTEN 4, 61ff.; R.L. N. BARBER, The Cyclades in the Middle Bronze Age, in: CHR. DOUMAS, P. WARREN (ed.), Thera and the Aegean World, 1978, 367–380; CH. DOUMAS, Notes on Early Cycladic Architecture, in: AA 1972, 151–170; F.J. FROST, Here and There in the Cyclades, in: The Ancient World 4, 3/4, 1986, 97–114; W. KÖNIG, Der Bund der Nesioten, diss. Halle 1910; G. REGER, The Political History of the Kyklades. 260–200 B.C., in: Historia 43, 1994, 32–69.

E.MEY. and H.KAL.

Cycliadas (Κυκλιάδας; *Kykliádas*). *Strategos* of the Achaean League in 209 and 200 BC, as an exponent of the Macedon-friendly faction, he supported → Philippus V in 209 against Elis (Liv. 27,31,10), but adroitly rejected his offer of help against → Nabis in 200 (Liv. 31,25,3; 9f.; [1. 165–168]). Banished after the change toward Rome (Liv. 32,19,2; [2. 40f.]), C. was at the disposal of the king as an envoy to T. → Quinctius Flamininus in Nicaea (198) (Pol. 18,1,2; Liv. 32,32,10) and after the defeat of Cynoscephalae (197) (Pol. 18,34,4).

1 H. NOTTMEYER, Polybios und das Ende des Achaierbundes, 1995   2 J. DEININGER, Der politische Widerstand gegen Rom in Griechenland, 1971.   L.-M.G.

Cyclopes (Greek Κύκλωπες; *Kýklōpes*, singular Κύκλωψ; *Kýklōps*, Latin *Cyclopes*, singular *Cyclops*; etymology see below). C. is the term used to describe about 18 groups or individual figures in Greek myth who differ not just in their descent and location but also in their outward form and characteristics. As early as antiquity, Hellanicus (FGrH 4 F 88) was the first to undertake systematization and to attempt to trace them back to a single ancestor, Cyclops, son of → Uranus and/or the king of Thrace (Schol. Eur. Or. 965).

People distinguished in particular between: 1. the C. who fortified → Mycenae (Pind. Fr. 169 A 7 S.-M.; Pherecydes FGrH 3 F 12; Paus. 2,16,5f.). This mythological explanation was adopted when the technique of constructing such big fortification systems had been lost. 2. the C. who appear in literature especially as a backdrop to the individual C. → Polyphemus (→ Galatea [1])

(Hom. Od. 9,10ff.). 3. the three sons of → Uranus and → Gaia: Brontes, Steropes and Arges/Pyragmon (Apollod. 1,1ff; Hes. Theog. 139ff; Verg. Aen. 8,416–453), who were locked up by their father (or others) in the → Tartarus but were freed again by Zeus. To the latter they give lightning and thunder, to Pluto a helmet, and to Poseidon a trident (Hes. Theog. 501–506). These C. are known in later versions as armourers and assistants of → Hephaestus/Vulcanus (Orph. Fr. 179) who make, for example, the shields of → Achilleus [1] and → Aeneas [1] and live under Etna (Verg. G. 4,170ff). Callimachus was the first who explicitly placed them in the workshop of Hephaestus (Callim. H. 3,46–85). The giant C. was distinguished either by a particular round eye shape (*kýklōps*, 'round-eyed') or by a single eye on the forehead (Hes. Theog. 144–145).

→ Polyphemus

C. CALAME, La légende du Cyclope dans le folklore européen et extra-européen. Un jeu de transformations narratives, in: Études de lettres 10, 1977, 45–79; S. EITREM, s.v. Kyklopen, RE XI 2, 2328–2347; H. MONDI, The Homeric Cyclopes, in: TAPhA 113, 1983, 17–38; O. TOUCHEFEU-MEYNIER, s.v. K., LIMC 6.1, 154–159.   C.W.

Cycnus (Κύκνος; *Kýknos*, Latin *Cygnus*; 'swan'). Name of several heroes whose common element is their relationship with swans. Among these the most important are:

[1] Son of → Ares and of Pelopea (Apollod. 2,5,11: the Pyrene), king of Amphanae, husband of Themistonoe. In the grove of Apollo in Thessalonian Pagasae, C. robs pilgrims travelling to Delphi and invites them to participate in chariot races which he always wins (detailed narration [Hes.] scut. 57ff.). He kills the losers and decorates his father's temple with their skulls (Stesich. K., PMGF fr. 207). Apollo incites → Hercules to fight C. so that the pilgrims can reach Delphi unharmed. With the help of his chariot driver Iolaus and of Athene, Hercules wins and even wounds C.'s father Ares who fights with him for the corpse until Zeus separates them with a flash of lightning (Hyg. Fab. 31,3). C. is buried by his father-in-law → Ceyx but the grave is washed away by the Anaurus River upon the order of Apollo.

[2] Son of → Poseidon and of the nymph → Calyce. Fishermen find the child exposed to the elements on the beach encircled by swans. C. reigns in Colonae on Tenedus, and he marries Proclea who bears him Tennes and Hemithea (Apollod. Epit. 3,24ff.; Diod Sic. 5,83). C. is a Thracian, invulnerable ally of → Priamus who attacks → Achilles at the Greeks' landing and is strangled by him. In the process he screams like the swans in their hour of death.

[3] Son of Sthenelus, king of Liguria. C. grieves so bitterly for his friend and relative → Phaethon that Zeus turns him into a swan on the banks of the Eridanus (Ov. Met. 2,367ff.; Verg. Aen. 10,189ff.; Paus. 1,30,3: musician turned into a swan by Apollo; Hyg. Fab. 154).   C.W.

[4] see → Constellations

Cydantidae (Κυδαντίδαι; *Kydantídai*). Attic *mesogeia*(?)-deme of the phyle Aegeis, from 224/3 BC of Ptolemaïs; placed one (two) *bouleutaí*. Location unknown; Vurva [1. 173; 4. 24ff.], Kato Charvati [2], Mendeli [3 have been suggested.

1 P. SIEWERT, Die Trittyen Attikas und die Heeresreform des Kleisthenes, 1982   2 TRAILL, Attica 15f., 41, 62, 69, 111 no. 79, pl. 2, 13   3 J. S. TRAILL, Demos and Trittys, 1986, 128 with n. 17   4 E. VANDERPOOL, The Location of the Attic Deme Erchia, in: BCH 89, 1965, 21–26.
                H.LO.

Cydathenaeum (Κυδαθήναιον; *Kydathénaion*, Κυδαθηναιείς; *Kydathenaieís*). Great and only *asty*-deme of the phyle Pandionis, from 307/6 to 201 BC of Antigonis, had 11 (12) *bouleutaí*; in the centre of Athens north of the Acropolis to the Eridanus, west to the Agora. For the 5th cent. BC there is evidence of a sanctuary and *thiasotai* of Hercules on the Eridanus. The tanneries ibid. (IG II² 1556, 33ff.; 1576, 5ff.; SEG 18, 36 B9) are considered by LIND [1] to be the cause of the enmity felt by → Aristophanes [3] towards the tannery owner Cleon; both originate from C. (Aristoph. Vesp. 895 with schol. 902; Aristoph. Equ. 1023). On the *hierón* of the Heraclidae [2. 204]. Aesch. 1,114f.; two decrees on demes: Agora 16 no. 54 [2. 383].

1 H. LIND, Neues aus Kydathen, in: MH 42, 1985, 249–261   2 WHITEHEAD, Index s.v. Kydathénaion

W. JUDEICH, Die Topographie von Athen, ²1931, 172; TRAILL, Attica 8, 17, 42, 67, 111 no. 80, tab. 3, 11; J. S. TRAILL, Demos and Trittys, 1986, 31, 33, 38, 40f., 45f., 129.   H.LO.

Cydias (Κυδίας; *Kydías*).
[1] Erotic poet, quotes from Pl. Chrm. 155d, mentioned by Plut. Mor. 931e. He was obviously popular in Athens as he is depicted as a komast on a red-figured dish (Munich 2614) and on a psykter (London, BM E767) from *c.* 500 BC [1. 12–13]. He may perhaps be identical with Cydidas of Hermione referred to by Schol. Aristoph. Nub. 967 [2. 215]. Possibly (rather improbable) he is the dithyramb poet Cedeides/Cecedes mentioned by Aristoph. Nub. 985 (with schol.) [3].

1 K. FRIIS JOHANSEN, Eine Dithyrambos-Aufführung, in: Arkaeologisk Kunsthistoriske Meddelelser. Kongelige Danske Videnskabernes Selskab 4 no. 2, 1959   2 K. J. DOVER, Aristophanes Clouds, 1968   3 KROLL, s.v. Kedeides, RE IX 1, 109f.

PMG 714–715, 948; PICKARD-CAMBRIDGE/WEBSTER 30.
                E.R.

[2] Attic orator of the 4th cent. BC, known only because he is mentioned in Aristot. Rh. 1384b 32–44: he spoke against the establishment of an Attic cleruchy on Samos — probably with reference to the federal nature of the Second Delian League — and hence against a renewal of

the Athenian imperialism of the 5th cent. This probably occurred in 365 when the Athenian *strategos* Timotheus had conquered the island and the cleruchy question was debated in Athens for the first time (cf. Diod. Sic. 18,18,9).   M.W.

[3] Painter of Cythnus, worked around the mid 4th cent. BC, contemporary of → Euphranor[1]. His only work attested in literature (Plin. HN 35,130) is a picture of the Argonauts acquired at great cost by the orator Q. → Hortensius [7] Hortalus for his villa in Tusculum that was put up in a special room and that provides proof of the prestige of Greek art amongst the Roman nobility of the 1st cent. BC. Researchers consider the work to be a model for the engraved Argonaut frieze on the bronze 'Cista Ficoronica', a → Praeneste *cista* of Roman origin that was of particularly high quality. C. also developed a substitute dye for red lead made of burned ochre.

R. BLATTER, s.v. Argonautai, LIMC 2, 591ff., no. 10; K. SCHEFOLD, F. JUNG, Die Sage von den Argonauten, von Theben und Troja in der klassischen und hellenistischen Kunst, 1989, 29f.   N.H.

[4] Herophilean doctor from the Hellenistic period whose views about the Hippocratic concepts set down in a commentary or in a special lexicography were criticized by Lysimachus of Cos in 3 vols. (Erotianus, praef.; 5 NACHMANSON). C.'s interest in Hippocrates was characteristic of the school of → Herophilus.   V.N

Cydippe (Κυδίππη; *Kydíppē*, Latin Cydippe).
[1] According to Xenomedes (FGrH 442 T 2; F 1), Callimachus (fr. 67–75) tells how Acontius elicits from C., through an inscription on an apple (a quince: Aristaen. 1,10,26; on the apple-throwing motif: [1]), the vow that she will marry him. Attempts by the father Ceyx that came to nothing to marry C. to someone else lead to the Delphic oracle recommending Acontius as the son-in-law. Through the union the house of Acontiades is founded in Iulis (genealogical aition). A parallel story can be found in Nicander (→ Hermochares), allusions particularly in the Augustan poets (re Virgil [2; 3], Properz [4]), the subject is treated in Ov. Epist. 20–21 and Aristaen. 1,10.
[2] According to Anth. Pal. 3,18,2 and Dion Chrys. 64,6, Argive priestess of Hera (no name: Hdt. 1,31; Plut. Mor. 108ef and *passim*), mother of → Cleobis and Biton. For the iconography see [6].
[3] Daughter of Ochimus and Hegetoria, wife of Cercaphus (→ Heliadae), mother of the eponym of Lindus, Ialysus and Kameiros (Str. 14,2,8), also called Kyrbía (Zenon FGrH 523 F 1) or Lysíppe (Eust. 315,28). For a painting see [7].

1 J. TRUMPF, Kydonische Äpfel, in: Hermes 88, 1960, 14–22   2 E. J. KENNEY, Virgil and the Elegiac Sensibility, in: Illinois Classical Studies 8, 1983, 44–59   3 G. TISSOL, An Allusion to Callimachus' Aetia 3 in Vergil's Aeneid 11, in: HSPh 94, 1992, 263–68   4 F. CAIRNS, Propertius 1,18 and Callimachus, Acontius and Cydippe, in: CR 19, 1969, 131–34   5 H. BOPP, Inscia capta puella. Akontios und Kydippe bei Kallimachos und Ovid, diss. Münster 1966

6 P. E. ARIAS, s.v. Biton et Kleobis, LIMC 3.1, 119–20; 2, 95–96, especially fig. 6   7 A. MANTIS, s.v. Kydippe (1) I, LIMC 8.1, 766   8 H. MEYER, s.v. Kyrbia, RE XII 2, 136–37   9 G. WEICKER, s.v. Ialysos (1), RE IX I, 628–29.   T.H.

Cydnus (Κύδνος; *Kýdnos*). Aside from Pyramus and Sarus, the third large river of the Kilikia Pedias. In front of its estuary it formed the so-called Ῥῆγμα (*Rhêgma*, 'chasm'), a lagoon that served as the harbour of → Tarsus and originally flowed through Tarsus, before it was diverted, after a flood, by Justinian I eastward around the town (Procop. Aed. 5,5,17). After bathing in its cold waters (impressive waterfalls north of Tarsus) Alexander the Great fell gravely ill (Arr. Anab. 2,4,7). In the Middle Ages C. was called Nahr al-Baradān by the Arabs (like the river of Damascus); modern Tarsus Çayı (Irmağı).

H. HELLENKEMPER, F. HILD, Neue Forschungen zu Kilikien (Denkschriften des Österreichischen Akad. d. Wiss.: Philosoph.-Hist. Klasse 186) 1986 327f., 391.   F.H.

Cydonia (Κυδωνία; *Kydonía*). Town in north-western Crete, now Chania, according to Str. 10,4,7 the third biggest town on the island (cf. Flor. 1,42,4). According to legend, its establishment can be traced back to → Minos and his son Cydon (Diod. Sic. 5,78,2; Paus. 8,53,4). The town was already important in Minoan times (archaeological evidence indicates trade relationships with Thebes; settlement finds in modern Chania and mountain settlement on the summit of Debla south-west of it). Samians expelled by Polycrates settled in C. after 524 BC and were in their turn driven out by military contingents from Aegina (Hdt. 3,44; 59; Str. 8,6,16). C. that was characteristically Doric from that time, was, after internal Cretan intrigues, the object of ravages by an Athenian fleet in 429 BC (Thuc. 2,85,5f.). In 342 BC siege of C. by the condottiere Phalaecus (Diod. Sic. 16,63,2ff.; Paus. 10,2,7). In the early 3rd cent. BC there is evidence of an alliance with Aptara [1. no. 2]. Around 220 BC C. dropped out of the alliance together with other Cretan towns, Knossos and Gortyn (Pol. 4,55,4). Around 180 BC C. entered into an *isopoliteia* treaty with Apollonia that was later infringed (Pol. 28,14; Diod. Sic. 30,13). During the 2nd Mithridatic War, Mark Antony [I 8] launched a punitive campaign against C. and other Cretan towns (App. Sic. 6). In 69 BC the town was captured by Caecilius [I 23]. Because of the resistance against Antony [I 9], C. was given autonomy in 30 BC by his adversary, the future Augustus. Archaeology: there are barely any remains from the Hellenistic and Roman periods; several residential houses with mosaics from Roman times indicate private wealth.

1 A. CHANIOTIS, Die Verträge zwischen kretischen Poleis in der hellenischen Zeit, 1996. H. VAN EFFENTERRE, La Crète et le monde grec de Platon à Polybe, 1948 R. SCHEER, s.v. Chania, in: LAUFFER, Griechenland, 167f. I. F. SANDERS, Roman Crete, 1982, 169f.   H.SO.

Cylaces More correctly perhaps Gylakes (Armenian *Głak*), Armenian eunuch and 'head gentleman-in-waiting' (*Hajr mardpet*). After C. had temporarily changed over to the Persian side, he attempted from AD 368 onwards, together with the 'regent' (*hazarapet*) → Artabannes [1], to protect the interests of young king → Pap and to limit the power of the higher nobility and the Church. Around 370 Sapor II induced Pap, through secret messages, to murder his ministers and to have their heads sent to him (Amm. Marc. 27,12; 30,1,3).

J. MARKWART, Südarmenien und die Tigrisquellen, 1930, 68*–70*; 154–157.   M.SCH.

Cylinder seal see → Seal

Cyllene (Κυλλήνη; *Kylléné*).
[1] The northernmost mountain range in Arcadia in the border area stretching to Achaea, the second highest (Ziria, 2,374 m) of the Peloponnese, a limestone ridge that ends on all sides with the surrounding chain of mountains. The ancient authors considered C. to be the highest mountain range in the Peloponnese (Str. 8,8,1; Paus. 8,17,1). C. was sacred to → Hermes Cyllenius. He is said to have been born here in a cave and to have accomplished deeds like the invention of stringed musical instruments (H. Hom.3; Pind. Ol. 6,77f.). A cave with inscriptions was found under the western main summit [1], and Paus. Hom. Il. 2,602 attests to a temple on the peak, cf. also 8, 17, 1.

1 E. PIESKE, s.v. Kylene (2), RE XI 2, 2454–2458.   E.MEY. and E.O.

[2] Port on the Elian coast north-east of modern Cape Killini (formerly Glarentza) with many finds from Middle Helladic to Roman times. Mentioned as early as in Hom. Il. 15,518 as the harbour of the town of Elis. C. played a part in the Peloponnesian War; in the 3rd cent. BC C. was fortified. Evidence: Pol. 5,3,1; Str. 8,3,4; 10; Paus. 6,26,4f.; 8,5,8; Plin. HN 4,13; Ptol. 3,16,6; Tab. Peut. 7,4.

R. BALADIÉ, Le Péloponnèse de Strabon, 1980, 63f.; F. CARINCI, s.v. Elide (1), EAA², 446; J. SERVAIS, Recherches sur le port de Cyllène, in: BCH 85, 1961, 123–161.   Y.L.

Cyllenius (Κυλλήνιος; *Kyllénios*). Author of two epideictic epigrams that show thematic and stylistic affinities with the 'Garland' of Philippus, but which cannot with certainty be traced back to it. In Anth. Pal. 9,4 a wild pear tree praises in elaborate language and little-known words the one who made it fertile through a graft; in Anth. Pal. 9,33 there is a brilliant distich about a ship that was shipwrecked even before it was completed (a variant is 9,35 that Planudes attributes to the same C. whilst the P manuscript however attributes it to → Antiphilus [3]).

FGE 34–36.   M.G.A.

Cylon (Κύλων; *Kýlon*).
[1] Athenian aristocrat, son-in-law of → Theagenes of Megara, became Olympic victor in 640 BC. C. and his *hetaireía* (→ *hetairía* [2]) occupied the Acropolis in Athens around 632 in order to establish → tyrannical rule there — possibly with support from Megara. C. did not manage to mobilize the population to support him. The rebels initially were besieged by a contingent of citizens, but those left it to the senior officials to act against them with violence. C. was probably able to flee. C.'s followers who had sought protection at the altar of Athena Polias were killed when the right of asylum provided by the shrine was disregarded (Hdt. 5,70f.; Thuc. 1,126; Plut. Solon 12). Later the archon (→ *archóntes*) Megacles was held responsible for this crime — his family, the → Alcmaeonidae, was cursed for it, punished with exile and repeatedly politically persecuted right through to the time of → Pericles. The coup of C. and his bloody defeat was possibly one of the reasons for the codification of criminal law by → Dracon [2] a few years later.

A. ANDREWES, in: CAH 3.1, 368–370; RHODES, 79ff.; TRAILL, PPA 588685; K.-W. WELWEI, Athen, 1992, 133ff.   E.S.-H.

[2] Rich aristocrat from Croton who wanted to be accepted into the Pythagorean secret society but who was rejected by → Pythagoras (according to Porph. Vita Pythagorica 54 on the basis of an inspection of his face); deeply hurt, C. is said to have hatched a plot against Pythagoras which caused the latter to emigrate to Metapontum (Aristox. fr. 18 WEHRLI = Iambl. VP 248f.; cf. Aristot. Περὶ τῶν Πυθαγορείων fr. 1 ROSS = 171 GIGON; Porph. Vita Pythagorica 55f.; Diod. Sic. 10,11,1). The conspiracy should probably be differentiated from the politically motivated anti-Pythagorean uprising around 450 between 440 and 415 BC; owing to confusing tradition, this is also frequently linked with C. (→ Pythagorean School).   C.RI.

Cyme (Κύμη; *Kýmē*).
[1] C. on → Euboea. The exact location of the ancient settlement is unknown; it should be looked for near what is today the town of C., commonly Kumi, on the east coast of Euboea, possibly about 5 km north at the monastery of Sotiros (17th cent.) where there is also a Venetian fortress. Recently the remains of an Early Helladic settlement were found near Murteri south of C. whose inhabitants already traded across the Aegean. It is debatable whether C. was a secondary town of C. [3] in Asia Minor and also whether C., together with Chalcis, was the metropolis of C. [2].

H. v. GEISAU, s.v. Kyme, RE XI 2, 2474f.; F. GEYER, Topographie und Gesch. der Insel Euboia 1, 1903, 79ff.; E. FREUND, s.v. Kyme, in: LAUFFER, Griechenland, 359f.; J. G. MILNE, The Mint of Kyme in the Third Century, in: NC 20, 1940, 129–137; G. PETZL, H. W. PLEKET, Ein hell. Ehrendekret aus Kyme, in: Chiron 9, 1979, 73–81; PHILIPPSON/KIRSTEN 1, 618f.; A. SALAC et al., The Results of the Czechoslovak Expedition. K. 2, 1980; A. SAMPSON, Εὐβοϊκὴ Κύμη 1, 1981.   H.KAL.

[2] (Latin *Cumae*). Town in the → Campi Phlegraei, now north of Capo Miseno, abounding in mythological references, as according to stories passed down to us, → Lacus Avernus and Acheron [2] were placed here; the → Giants are said to have been buried here by the gods after their defeat (Timaeus FGrH 566 F 89; → Gigantomachy); place of residence of the → Sibyls of Cumae. This colony was founded in the mid 8th cent. BC by Chalcis/Euboea and Cyme/Aetolia under the *oikistaí* Megasthenes and Hippocles as a Greek outpost in trade with Etruria. C. controlled the Gulf of Naples (from Misenum to Capri). In the conflict with the Etruscans, C. gained the upper hand in 524 BC. Between the end of the 6th cent. and the beginning of the 5th cent., C. was under the tyrant → Aristodemus [5]. In 474 BC the naval battle between the Greeks and the Etruscans took place near C. With the advance of Syracuse, C. lost its traditional role of representing Greek interests in the west. In 421 BC C. was conquered by the Samnites. During the → Samnite Wars C. joined Rome; in 338 BC *civitas sine suffragio*. An intensive Romanization process began that reached its peak in the 1st cent. BC with the construction of the harbour of Misenum. From the 2nd cent. AD the decline was looming and this was intensified through a constant change of the coastline (bradyseism). In late antiquity C. continued to exist as a *castrum*.

Archaeology: excavations from the 18th cent. to 1910 exclusively as private initiatives (especially F. STEVENS in the necropoles); since that time research on the acropolis, the forum, the crypt of Mount Cuma (initially regarded as the cave of the → Sibyls) and at the 'Grotto of the Sibyls' (GABRICI and MAIURI). A city wall that can be dated to the 6th cent. BC, orthogonally laid-out settlement districts in the lower part of the town. A temple of Apollo (inscription in the Oscan language); altered in the Augustan period and later transformed into an early Christian basilica. Two temples dedicated to Jupiter: one on the acropolis (mid 5th cent. BC), another (3rd cent. BC) on the forum, in the 2nd cent. BC transformed into a capitolium. The identification of a temple with a porticus in the south of the forum (early Imperial period) remains uncertain. The Apollo oracle of the Sibyls with its links to the underworld was significant. A cult of Hera Regina attested by an inscription from the 7th cent. BC appears to provide a link with this (Phlegon of Tralleis FGrH 257 F 36). It is known that there was an Orphic School (→ Orphism) in C. in the 5th cent. BC. There is evidence of close relationships between C. and ancient Rome because of the introduction of the alphabet, the Sibylline Books and possibly the cult of Juno Regina in Rome.

H. COMFORT, s.v. Cumae, PE, 250–252; E. GABRICI, Cuma, in: Monumenti antichi, pubblicati dall'Accademia dei Lincei 22, 1913; A. MAIURI, I Campi Flegrei, ³1958; I Campi Flegrei nell'archeologia e nella storia, Atti del Convegno dei Lincei, Roma 1976, 1977; Il destino della Sibilla (Atti del convegno 1985), 1986; BTCGI 7, 7–42; G. CAMASSA, I culti delle poleis italiote, in: Storia del Mezzogiorno 1, 1991, 423–430.   A.MU.

[3] (Latin *Cyme*). Town of → Aeolis [2] on a southern secondary bay of the Elaetic Gulf (modern Çandarlı körfezi) on the site of Namurt limanı. Pre-Greek place name (? Str. 11,5,4; 12,13,21). Founded by Aeolians (Mela 1,90; Vell. Pat. 1,4,4) and Locri (Str. 13,3,3). Side was settled from Cyme (Arr. Anab. 1,24,4). Member of the Aeolian League of Eleven Cities (Hdt. 1,149). A princess of C. was the wife of Midas (Pol. 9,83). In 546 BC embroiled in the Lydian uprising under Pactyes (Hdt. 1,157–161), in 499 in the Ionian uprising (Hdt. 5,37f.; 123), in 480 BC involved in Xerxes' campaign (Hdt. 7,194), in 480/479 winter quarters of the Persian fleet (Hdt. 8,130). In 477 member of the Delian League, in 412 on the Spartan side (Diod. Sic. 13,73,3–6; Nep. Alcibiades 7) and from 400 (with interruptions) on the Persian side (Diod. Sic. 14,35,7; 15,18,2ff.; Xen. Hell. 3,4,27). In 218 it changed sides with other Aeolian and Ionian cities from Achaeus to Attalus I (Pol. 5,77,4); in 190 Seleucid (Liv. 37,11,5). In 188 exemption from tax decided by Rome (Pol. 21,46,4; Liv. 38,79,8). In 132 Aristonicus was defeated outside C. (Str. 14,1,38). In 154 Prusias II paid war reparations for the devastation caused to the C. area (Pol. 33,13,8). From 129 in the Roman province of Asia. In the 1st cent. BC presumably still affluent (fragment of high-quality statue from the late Hellenistic period). In the Byzantine period, suffragan diocese of Ephesus.

Between the two hills of the city there are the remains of a stoa, a theatre on the slope of the northern hill; here are preserved the remains of a small Ionic temple to Aphrodite (4th cent. BC) or Isis (2nd cent. AD), on the southern hill there is a stretch of city wall with a gate construction and in front of the sunken southern mole is the ruin of a medieval harbour construction.

Hesiod's father (Hes. Op. 635) and the historian → Ephorus came from C.; C. was also considered to be a 'Homeric' town (Ps.-Hdt., vita Homeri 1f.); its inhabitants who tended to be farmers rather than seafarers were joked about as simpletons (Str. 13,3,6).

H. ENGELMANN, Die Inschr. von Kyme (IK 5), 1976; F. KIECHLE, Lit.-Überblicke der griech. Numismatik, in: JNG 10, 1959/60, 148f.; G.E. BEAN, Kleinasien 1, 1969, 103–105; J. BOUZEK et al. (ed.), Kyme, 2 vols., 1974/1980; V. İDIL, Neue Ausgrabungen im aiolischen Kyme [Turkish], in: Belleten 53, 1989, 505–543; P. KNOBLAUCH, Eine neue top. Aufnahme des Stadtgebiets von Kyme, in: AA 1974, 285–291; S. LAGONA, Il porto di Kyme eolica, in: 3ª Rassegna di archeologia subaquea, Giardini/Naxos 1988, 1989, 17–23; G. PETZL, H. W. PLEKET, Ein hell. Ehrendekret aus Kyme, in: Chiron 9, 1979, 73–81; D.H. SAMUEL, Kyme and the Veracity of Ephorus, in: TAPhA 99, 1968, 375–388; J. SCHAEFER, H. SCHLÄGER, Zur Seeseite von Kyme in der Aeolis, in: AA 1962, 40–57.   H.KA.

Cymodoce (Κυμοδόκη; *Kymodóke*, Cymodoce, 'wave-receiver'). → Nereid who calms the wind and waves, in Hes. Theog. 252f., Hom. Il. 18,39, Verg. Aen. 5,826 (accordingly Verg. G. 4,338) and 10,225 (*Cymodocea*: Aeneas's ship turned into a nymph), Hyg. Fab. praef. 8, Stat. Silv. 2,2,20. Also represented on vases [1].

1 N. ICARD-GIANOLIO, s.v. Kymodoke, LIMC 6.1, 163f.

A.A.

Cynaegeirus (Κυναίγειρος; *Kynaígeiros*) from Athens, son of Euphorion, brother of Aeschylus [1], fell in battle at → Marathon (490 BC; → Persian War). Herodotus (6,114) reports that his arm was chopped off while trying to hold on to the stern of an enemy ship. This heroic act was represented in the painting of Marathon at the Stoa Poikile in Athens (Ael. NA 7,38) and was a favourite exemplum for later rhetors (Lucian.e, Iupp. Trag. 32; Luciane, Rhetorum praeceptor 18). TRAILL, PAA 588715.

E.S.-H.

Cynaetha (Κύναιθα; *Kýnaitha*). Town in northern Arcadia near modern Kalavryta, the exact location is unknown. The high valley of C. (800 m) is bordered in the north and south by low hills, in the west and southeast by the mountain ranges Erymanthus and Chelmos. In Hellenistic times it was supposedly the scene of especially brutal wars between various parties. Evidence: Pol. 4,16,11–21,9; Str. 8,8,2; Paus. 8,19,1–3; Ath. 14,626e; Steph. Byz., s.v. K.

F. CARINCI, s.v. Arcadia, EAA², 330; JOST, 51–53; J. HOPP, Kalavryta, in: LAUFFER, Griechenland, 291–293; E. MASTROKOSTAS, in: AD 17, 1961/2, Chronikon 132 (excavation report); E. MEYER, Peloponnesische Wanderungen, 1939, 107–109; Y. A. PIKOULAS, Τὸ ὀχυρὸ στὴν Κέρτεζη Καλαβρύτων, in: A. D. RIZAKIS (ed.), Achaia und Elis in der Antike (Meletemata 13), 1991, 265–268; A. SAMPSON, Προϊστορικοὶ οἰκισμοὶ στὴν περιοχὴ Καλαβρύτων, in: Peloponnesiaka, Suppl. 11, 1986, 33–39. Y.L.

Cynamolgus Pliny (HN 10,97 = Sol. 33,15) reports — taking up the work of Ps.-Aristotle (Hist. an. 9,13 p. 616a 6–13 = 8,5 of the Arabic-Latin translation of Michael Scotus) — about the cinnamon bird *cinnamolgus* (κιννάμωμον ὄρνεον; *kinnámōmon órneon*) in Arabia that builds its nest in high trees of twigs from the → cinnamon and which the inhabitants shot down with lead arrows for profit. Through Isid. Orig. 12,7,23 this fairytale went into the extended Latin → Physiologus of Ps.-Hugo of St. Victor (3,30 [1. 95], cf. [2. 103f.]) and the natural-history encyclopaedias of the 13th cent., among these Thomas of Cantimpré (5,25 [3. 188] = Albertus Magnus, Animal. 23,32 [4. 1446f.]) and Vincent of Beauvais (Spec. nat. 16,51 [5. 1186f.]), expanded with details actually related to the *kóttyphos* (κόττυφος, → blackbird; = *foccokoz* with an incorrect marginal comment *cinamolgus* in Scotus) and *kítta* (κίττα; *citita* in Scotus, 'jay'), e.g. regarding the sphere-shaped nest (Ps.-Aristot. Hist. an. 9,14 p. 616a 3–6), and the coloration and food of the → kingfisher (*alkyón*, ἀλκυών, ibid. 616a 14–15, 32).

1 Ps.-HUGO DE S. VICTORE, De bestiis aliisque rebus, PL 177, 1879 2 F. McCULLOCH, Mediaeval Latin and French Bestiaries, 1960 3 H. BOESE (ed.), Thomas Cantimpratensis, Liber de natura rerum, 1973 4 H. STADLER (ed.), Albertus Magnus, De animalibus, 2, 1920 5 VINCENTIUS BELLOVACENSIS, Speculum naturale, 1624 (repr. 1964). C.HÜ.

Cyn(n)ane (Κυν(ν)άνη; *Kyn(n)ánē*). Daughter of → Philippus II and an Illyrian, born around 357 BC. Brought up in a martial way, she is said to have participated in Philip's battles. In 338/7 C. married Amyntas [4] and bore Eurydice [3] with whom she lived in Macedonia after the death of Amyntas. In 322 C. accompanied Eurydice to Asia with an army as a bride for Arridaeus [5]. C. was murdered by Alcetas [4] and given a royal burial by → Cassander.

BERVE, no. 456. E.B.

Cynegius (Maternus Cynegius, ILS 1273). Probably born in Spain, Christian. Under → Theodosius I in AD 381 *vicarius* (?), 383 *comes sacrarum largitionum*, 383/384 *quaestor sacri palatii*. As *praefectus praetorio Orientis* 384–388, C. is said to have improved the state of the municipal *curiae* on behalf of the emperor (Lib. Or. 39,3). On two trips through the east of the empire (in 384 and 388) he intensively fought pagan religious practice (probably without explicit imperial permission) (Zos. 4,37; Chron. min. 1,244f. MOMMSEN) and in so doing he also had temples destroyed, e.g. in Edessa (Lib. Or. 30,46; Theod. Hist. eccl. 5,21,7). C. died in 388 on his return journey in the year of his consulate.

1 P. PETIT, Sur la date du 'Pro templis' de Libanius, in: Byzantion 21, 1951, 295–304 PLRE 2, 235f. K.-L.E.

Cynicism (Κυνισμός; *Kynismós*).
A. INTRODUCTION B. ANTISTHENES C. BASIC CONCEPTS OF THE ETHICS OF DIOGENES D. THE 'SHORT PATH' E. ASCETICISM F. OPPOSITION TO TRADITION G. IMPERIAL CYNICISM

A. INTRODUCTION

The philosophical protest movement of Cynicism originated in Greece in the 4th cent. BC centred on → Diogenes [14] of Sinope and his students; it existed until the 5th cent. AD. As almost none of the older literature of the Cynics is extant, our knowledge comes mainly from anecdotes and remarks — the authenticity of which is hard to test — which however mirror a coherent and uniform philosophy.

As early as antiquity the term 'Cynicism' was explained through two different etymologies. The first links the movement with the well-known Athenian gymnasium of → Cynosarges where a temple to Hercules stood and where → Antisthenes [1], a student of Socrates, taught; those who support this explanation consider Antisthenes to be the founder of the movement (Diog. Laert. 6,13). The second etymology goes back to a derisive nickname that compared the cynics with dogs (*kýnes*) because of their candid and simple but also shameless and outrageous behaviour (acts generally morally condemned, such as masturbation or sexual intercourse in public, eating in public places, sleeping in clay jars or at crossroads, were regarded by them as 'indifferent'). The description 'dog' is said to have been

The Cynic movement: the representatives of the earlier phase (4th–3rd cents. BC) according to Diogenes Laertius

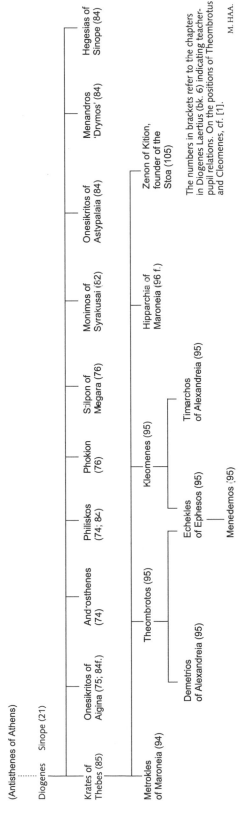

The numbers in brackets refer to the chapters in Diogenes Laertius (bk. 6) indicating teacher-pupil relations. On the positions of Theombrotus and Cleomenes, cf. [1].

M. HAA.

regarded as suitable by the Cynics and willingly adopted (Diog. Laert. 6,60).

Cynicism never developed into a 'school'. It always intentionally stayed outside the traditional institutional framework of such movements: there was no fixed place of instruction, no succession of school leaders, no instruction at all, but it manifested itself in 'shrill clamour' creating unrest in the streets, at crossings, in front of temples or if games took place, at the entrance to the stadium. Aside from Antisthenes [1], Diogenes [14] of Sinope, the philosopher in the barrel, is also mentioned as the founder of the movement. Ancient tradition favours Antisthenes, but the sources that support this view come from late antiquity (Epictetus, Dio Chrysostom, Aelianus, Diogenes Laertius, Stobaeus and the Suda). People in modern times therefore tend towards the view that several Stoics who intended to trace their movement back to Socrates had created the filiation Socrates > Antisthenes > Diogenes > Crates > Zeno; which was willingly taken up by the authors of succession literature as it facilitated their task. As the chronological details and numismatic grounds are not unambiguous, we do not know whether Diogenes of Sinope, who lived in exile, could have associated in Athens with Antisthenes.

Regardless of the significance of Antisthenes — it is obvious that he played a part, even if it was only because of his writings — there is no doubt that Cynicism as a movement was founded by Diogenes and that he determined its essential features.

The history of the movement is divided into two large periods, the older Cynicism (4th and 3rd cents. BC, see fig.) and imperial Cynicism (1st–5th cents. AD), with the movement less active in the period between these two periods. The first period is marked by the two outstanding figures of Diogenes [14] and his student → Crates [4] of Thebes. The most important students of Crates were Metrocles of Maronea (Hipparchia's brother), Monimus of Syracuse who was originally the slave of a moneychanger, and the well-known → Menippus of Gadara, likewise a slave who had a considerable influence on writers like Varro, Seneca, Petronius, Apuleius and Lucian. Other pupils of Crates were → Zeno of Citium and Cleanthes of Assus, through whom Cynicism strongly influenced Stoic philosophy (→ Stoa). In the following cent. lived two personalities atypical of Cynicism, on the one hand there was → Bion [1] of Borysthenes (c. 335 BC — 245 BC) who during his eclectic philosophical education frequented one after another the → Academy, the Cynics, the → Cyrenaics and the Peripatos, and on the other hand there was Cercidas of Megalopolis (c. 290 — after 217 BC). Aside from these ambivalent personalities, the philosophy teacher → Teles — attested to by Stobaeus — should be mentioned; he lived in Athens and Megara and addressed a circle of young people. In his *Diatribai* that represent the oldest testimony to the Cynical-Stoical → *diatribe*, he passes down to us the remarks of various philosophers of Cynicism like Diogenes, Crates, Metrocles and especially Bion whom he favoured.

In the two subsequent cents. Cynicism appears to have been less active. Worthy of mention for Greece are only → Meleager of Gadara (c. 135–50 BC) and the 'Pseudepigraphic letters' of the Cynics that partly originate in this period; amongst the Romans we only need to mention the senator M. Favonius, a relative of M. Porcius Cato of Utica, who emulated the way of life of the Cynics through his words and deeds.

From the 1st cent. AD Cynicism flourished again and even developed into *the* popular philosophy *par excellence*. It is worth emphasizing → Demetrius [24] of Corinth, a friend of Seneca and of Thrasea Paetus, → Demonax [3] of Cyprus, who represented a more moderate Cynicism, and → Peregrinus Proteus, who was a follower of both Cynicism and Christianity and directed his slander against Lucian (that contradicts the more positive testimony of Aulus Gellius). For the 2nd cent. AD we should mention → Oenomaus of Gadara whose daring views were later sharply criticized by Emperor → Julian [11] and whose work 'Against the Oracles' (other title: 'The Unmasking of the Charlatans') sharply attacked gods, fortune-tellers and oracles. In the 4th cent. AD lived → Maximus Heron of Alexandria who was initially a friend and then the most bitter of enemies of Gregorius [3] of Nazianzus and who was an adherent of both Cynicism and Christianity. In the 5th cent. AD lived the last known Cynic → Sallustius who after studying jurisprudence attended the schools of rhetoric of Alexandria, practised Cynicism in a strictly ascetic form and got a member of the circle around → Proclus off philosophy.

However the Cynicism of the imperial period was not limited to these prominent personalities. It was first and foremost a popular philosophy whose adherents, poor people and slaves, came from the underprivileged classes in the large metropoles; in addition it was a collectively practised philosophy (certainly outside any institutional framework). Groups of Cynics went around in the streets of Rome and Alexandria, begged at crossroads and made reproaches to the crowd wishing to see and hear them. Among these were also charlatans who believed that clothes made the philosopher. The criticism of Epictetus, Lucian or Julian is directed against them. Overall however Cynicism in the imperial period remained faithful to the asceticism practised by Diogenes and hence to older practice. Frequently the Cynics were compared with the strictest Christian sects like the Encratites or the Apotactites. Nonetheless it was a Cynic, Crescens [2], who in AD 165 initiated the martyrdom of Justin [6] and Church Fathers like Augustine and Sidonius Apollinaris made no secret of their aversion to the shamelessness of the Cynics and their rejection of the traditional moral values. With regard to the uniformity of Cynicism or of the philosophy of the Cynics through the cents., it can be said that this movement had neither dogmatic sources nor a philosophical system but was based on a uniform ethical teaching that was expressed in an ascetic way of life.

B. ANTISTHENES

Regardless of the influence Antisthenes personally had on Diogenes, the roots of his Cynicism can be found in the ethics of the Socratics. Antisthenes had already held the view that virtue was expressed in the actions of human beings and that people had to rid themselves drastically of social conventions; he first attacked Socratic intellectualism and associated the willpower possessed by Hercules and embodied by Socrates with the concept of virtuous action. According to Antisthenes, the wise man owes it to himself to acquire persistence, self-control and dispassionateness — all traits that were meant to play an important part for the Cynics because they made it possible for them to manage successfully the sufferings of everyday existence. Likewise the wise man must 'forget how to suffer', i.e. free his willpower from all social shackles that act as obstacles.Diogenes took up this ethics of action and radicalized it by emphasizing the necessity of practice (*áskēsis*) and the reversal of the values generally recognized (*paracháraxis toû nomísmatos*, 'counterfeiting'). Above all he was particularly successful in illustrating his ethical principles in a lively manner through his way of life.

C. BASIC CONCEPTS OF THE ETHICS OF DIOGENES

Diogenes possessed a clear consciousness of human weakness which caused him to denounce all addictions, whether they were passions, social duties, or in a wide sense, all the false values of civilized life that make human beings unhappy. These false values that promised man fame or happiness made him into a slave. As a countermeasure, Diogenes suggested an ascetic life. From his point of view the concept of the intellectual elite became meaningless: everyone could preach philosophy in public places. This widening of philosophy to the common people goes hand in hand with an enhancement of the physical. Bodies and gestures obtain the status of arguments; as Diogenes walks, he gives the best possible answer to the person who asserts that movement does not exist, and simply through his physical presence and his actions he advocates his philosophy without getting himself caught up in long discussions and arguments. In this way Cynicism appears as existentialism. Ultimately, in this philosophy that is based on a passionately supported individualism, man becomes a creator of values. These are no longer based, as in traditional ethics, on laws imposed from outside, or, as in Socratic intellectualism, on the recognition of the good, but on the will of the individual. Nevertheless Cynicism does not fall victim to relativism as it believes in the existence of universal human nature.

D. THE 'SHORT PATH'

In order to free will power from that which hinders it, Diogenes suggests a 'short-cut to virtue' (σύντομος ἐπ' ἀρετὴν ὁδός; *sýntomos' ep' aretèn hodós*). This formula comes from the Stoic → Apollodorus [12] of Seleucia (2nd cent. BC) who in the ethics section of his

'Introduction to Stoic Doctrine' (Diog. Laert. 7,121) characterizes the ethics of Cynicism in this way; perhaps the idea already existed in older Cynicism. This simple, economical path contrasts with the traditional long path of the schools of philosophy, the acquisition of knowledge and theoretical speculation. Logic, music, geometry, physics or metaphysics are regarded as 'useless and unnecessary' because they divert us from what we should concern ourselves with first and foremost, namely ourselves, and do not help us to direct our lives. For the Cynics, ethics comprises all spheres of philosophy.

The 'short-cut' also contrasts with the long way of civilization that entices man to make unnecessary efforts to obtain manual, technical or intellectual capabilities or even riches. To follow the short-cut it suffices to be poor for 'poverty is an instinctive aid to philosophy' (Stob. 4,2,32,11). Philosophy helps a person to reach true wealth that does not lie in possessions but in → *autarkeía*, the capacity to be satisfied with what you have. Animals are therefore considered to be models: they have only limited needs, are not dependent upon false values like shame or status and have an accurate perception of their environment so that in each case they bite or wag their tail for a good reason.

E. ASCETICISM

Virtue for the Cynics is not part of academic contemplation but for commerce. This explains their rejection of philosophical speeches, instruction and techniques of persuasion. Good is realized in concrete, singular action taken by the individual. Physical asceticism with an ethical goal is recommended as a method. The concept comes from the field of physical fitness, but the goal is a completely different one: you train your body in order to train your will and ultimately to affect the health of the mind.

Asceticism is understood as a preventive method to overcome future suffering and to grapple with current sorrows. The external symbol of asceticism is the official dress of the Cynics: the backpack that contains all the possessions of the philosopher, the *tríbōn* (a small folded overcoat that serves as both a blanket and an item of clothing) and the staff that accompanies the wandering orator who is constantly moving from place to place. In their uncomfortable path of asceticism the Cynics have two models: Hercules whose sorrows during the twelve tasks symbolized, in the opinion of the Cynics, the trials of man on the path to virtue, and Telephus, his son, who came to Aulis dressed in rags.

The Cynics who were inspired by the passionate desire for happiness strove for mental peace and cheerfulness (Diog. Laert. 6,38; cf. Plut. De tranquillitate animi 4,466e). By making into a source of pleasure that which is generally considered unpleasant, Diogenes succeeds in distorting the concept of pleasure; it is therefore no paradox that Cynicism is understood as hedonism and eudaemonism.

F. OPPOSITION TO TRADITION

In the various spheres of human action, the Cynic twists the traditional values and replaces them with new ones. Diogenes, who lived at the time of Alexander the Great, explained with regard to politics that he was *á-polis* ('without a home town'), *á-oikos*, without a house, and *kosmopolítēs*, a citizen of the world. This → cosmopolitanism should be understood *ex negativo*: as a citizen of the whole world the philosopher is actually a citizen of nowhere. Diogenes advocates the renunciation of all political commitment as it hinders individual freedom. He rejects the law on which the polis is founded and contrasts it with the law that controls the entire universe, in other words: the law of nature. His work *Politeía* ('Republic') caused a sensation because in it he called upon people to break all taboos and where applicable to also practice cannibalism, incest, community of women and children and complete sexual freedom. He believed that the religion of the people was based on tradition and convention and not on the laws of nature and represented a hindrance on the path to dispassionateness because of the fears in man, especially the fear of death and the punishments of hell. Diogenes rejects any anthropomorphism and criticizes the religious institutions as the happiness of man should not depend on practices that have nothing to do with his moral disposition. However, his opposition to tradition goes even further. He has no rational world view and does not believe in providence; the world was not created for human beings, and there was no world secret to be discovered.

In this way the Cynic draws his strength from his dispassionateness towards fate, not because he acknowledges its higher or secret rationality but simply on the basis of his own will to dispassionateness. His realism leads to him subjugating himself to the laws of nature and not expressing views on issues that go beyond this. He advocates agnosticism that allows him to preserve his dispassionateness and day by day to realize his happiness solely with the help of his will power.

In the field of literature the Cynics composed numerous writings despite their denial of all forms of knowledge. They used the traditional genres (dialogue, letters, tragedy, lyric poetry), as well as also inventing new ones like the → diatribe (Bion of Borysthenes), → satire (Menippus of Gadara) and → chreia (Metrocles, perhaps also already before this Diogenes); the latter is concerned with short philosophical sayings, often also with a punch-line. Characteristic of their new style, the *kynikòs trópos* (Demetrius, De elocutione 259), was the *spoudaiogéloion* in particular, a mixture of jokes and serious matters often found in the lighter lyric poetry of Monimus of Syracuse and Crates of Thebes. Although the Cynics preferred to act rather than talk, they handled language with an originality that characteristically involved humour, witty, apt remarks and puns.

With the help of his three weapons of frankness, sarcasm and provocation, the Cynic compels others to ask themselves questions and to stop being lethargic. Diogenes at the same time views himself as the bad conscience and scandal of his times. Very soon, perhaps as early as the time of the older Cynicism, the philosophy of Cynicism was attacked; at least however from the 2nd cent. BC onwards when → Hippobotus in his work 'On the Philosophical Sects' failed to treat precisely the sect of the Cynics.

G. IMPERIAL CYNICISM

In the Roman empire Cynicism flourished anew. Even if the older teachings were not developed further in late antiquity, the movement was extremely important, as it was quintessentially *the* popular philosophy. What was particularly new was that now many adherents of Cynicism were poor people or slaves. As in the case of the older Cynicism, there was no school; anyone who listened to the Cynics at crossroads or the entrance to the temple did this without formally belonging to a school. They were reproached for insulting their fellow men and leading the life of scroungers begging for their food or even demanding what they believed was their due; however, people especially criticized their shamelessness that was highly incompatible with the Roman *gravitas*. Some of the Cynics of imperial times were charlatans and the extant testimonies (in Epictetus, Julianus and Lucian that are at the same time the main sources on Cynicism) are not impartial in their judgement; nonetheless the ethics of Cynicism remained faithful to the asceticism of Diogenes. If we read the 'Pseud-epigraphic Letters' of the Cynics that represent a sort of manual of popular Cynicism during imperial times, we find that in this work the old teachings of the first Cynics are reiterated. Even if Cynicism in the imperial period lost spontaneity when its dress was now a symbol of a certain conformity and the ethical teachings to a certain extent became slogans, the Cynicism of the great moral philosophers like Demetrius, Agathobulous or Demonax was a lively philosophy.

CYNICISM

EDITIONS: M.BILLERBECK (ed., trans.), Epiktet. Vom Kynismus (Philosophia Antiqua 34), 1978; Id., Der Kyniker Demetrius. Ein Beitrag zur Gesch. der frühkaiserzeitlichen Popularphilosophie (Philosophia Antiqua 36), 1979; T.DORANDI, Filodemo. Gli Stoici (PHerc 155 e 339), in: Cronache Ercolanesi 12, 1982, 91–133 (here also testimonies of Diogenes, 'Republic' from Philod. De Stoicis); SSR II, 135–589, commentary IV, notes 21–55, pp. 195–583; J.F.KINDSTRAND, Bion of Borysthenes. A Coll. of the Fragments with Introduction and Commentary (Studia Graeca Upsaliensia 11), 1981; E.MÜSELER, Die Kynikerbriefe, 1. Die Überlieferung, 2nd. crit. ed. with a German trans. (Stud. zur Gesch. und Kultur des Altertums 6–7), 1994.
TRANSLATIONS: L.PAQUET, Les Cyniques grecs. Fragments et témoignages (Philosophica 4: Éditions de l'Université d'Ottawa), 1975; Id., (Philosophica 35), 1988 (new expanded and corrected edition); Id., Le Livre de poche. Classiques de la philosophie, 1992 (with a foreword by M.O. GOULET-CAZÉ).
BIBLIOGRAPHY: M.BILLERBECK, Die Kyniker in der modernen Forschung. Aufsätze mit Einführung und Bibliographie (Bochumer Studien zur Philosophie 15), 1991; R.BRACHT BRANHAM, M.-O. GOULET-CAZÉ (ed.), The Cynics. The Cynic Movement in Antiquity and its Legacy, 1997; A.BRANCACCI, Oikeios logos. La filosofia del linguaggio di Antistene (Elenchos 20), 1990; G.DORIVAL, Cyniques et Chrétiens au temps des pères Grecs, in: Valeurs dans le stoicisme. Du portique à nos jours. Mél. M.Spanneut, 1993, 57–88; D.R. DUDLEY, A History of Cynicism. From Diogenes to the 6th Century A.D., 1937 (repr. 1974); M.-O. GOULET-CAZÉ, L'ascèse cynique. Un commentaire de Diogène Laërce VI 70–71 (Histoire des doctrines de l'Antiquité classique 10), 1986; Id., Le cynisme à l'époque impériale, in: ANRW II 36.4, 2720–2833; Id., Le livre VI de Diogène Laërce: analyse de sa structure et réflexions méthodologiques, in: ANRW II 36.6, 3880–4048; Id., Le cynisme est-il une philosophie?, in: M.DIXSAUT (ed.), Contre Platon, 1: Le platonisme dévoilé, 1993, 273–313; Id., R.GOULET (ed.), Le cynisme ancien et ses prolongements in: Actes du colloque international du C.N.R.S. (Paris, 22–25 juillet 1991), 1993.; H.NIEHUES-PRÖBSTING, Der Kynismus des Diogenes und der Begriff des Zynismus (Humanistische Bibliothek, Reihe I: Abh. 40) 1979; P.SLOTERDIJK, Kritik der zynischen Vernunft, 1983 (French trans.: Critique de la raison cynique, 1987). M.G.-C.

FOR THE STEMMA: 1 M.O. GOULET-CAZÉ, in: Hermes 114, 1986, 247–252.

Cynics' letters see → Cynicism

Cynisca (Κυνίσκα; *Kyníska*). Rich Spartan woman, born around 442 BC, daughter of Archidamus [1] II, sister of Agesilaus [2] II. C. was the first woman to participate in chariot races at Olympia where she was twice victorious (Xen. Ages. 9,6; Plut. Agesilaus 20; Paus. 3,8,1f.; 6,1,6; SGDI 4418). K.-W.WEL.

Cynocephali (Κυνοκέφαλοι; *Kynoképhaloi*, 'dog heads') is the term for various fanciful frontier peoples; they settled in Libya (Hdt. 4,191), in Ethiopia (Aesch. fr. 603ab *Mette*; Str. 16,4,16) and in India (Ctesias, FGrH 688 F 45), and are considered to be particularly just and long-lived. The link between animal and ideal human traits typifies this utopian thought. Moreover the word also describes the baboons sacred to Egypt. → Monsters F.G.

Cynopolis, Cynopolites

[1] The Greek town called κυνῶν πόλις (*kynôn pólis*); 'town of dogs'; Str. 17,812) was at times the capital city of the 17th nomos of Upper Egypt (κυνοπολίτης; *Kynopolítēs*) and according to Ptol. 4,5,29 was situated on an island. C. (Egyptian *Ḥr-dj*) is often mentioned in texts of the New Kingdom and was the cult town of the dog-headed god → Anubis. Under Ramses XI it was destroyed in a civil war. Its exact location is unknown, presumably it was near Sheikh Fadl where a dog cemetery was also found. Plut. De Is. et Os. 72 reports on a religion-related 'war' between the inhabitants of C. and those of the neighbouring → Oxyrhynchus.

A.H. GARDINER, Ancient Egyptian Onomastica 2, 1947, 98–103; F. GOMAÀ, s.v. Hardai, LÄ 2, 962.

[2] Κυνὸς πόλις; *Kynòs pólis* (Str. 17,802). Town in Lower Egypt on the west bank of the Damiette branch of the Nile south of Abusir, modern Banā; in Christian times it was a diocese.

ST. TIMM, Das christlich-koptische Ägypten in arabischer Zeit 1, 1984, 318–24. K.J.-W.

Cynortium (Κυνόρτιον; *Kynórtion*). The mountain above the theatre of the Asclepius sanctuary of Epidaurus with the sanctuary of Apollo Maleatas (Paus. 2,27,7).

V. LAMBRINUDAKIS, Excavation and Restoration of the Sanctuary of Apollo Maleatas and Asclepius at Epidauros, in: Peloponnesiaka Suppl. 13, 1987f., 298ff. Y.L.

Cynosarges (Κυνόσαργες; *Kynósarges*). Sanctuary of Hercules first mentioned for the year 490 BC (Hdt. 6,116) with a gymnasium in the deme Diomea south of the Ilissus in front of the walls of Athens (Plut. Themistocles 1; Diog. Laert. 6,13; Steph. Byz. s.v. K.). Because of the finding-place of IG II[2] 1665 it is vaguely considered to lie near Hagios Pantelemon. The link between a dromos to Agrae (IG II[2] 2119 Z. 128) and C. is doubtful. The C. gymnasium was meant for illegitimate children (→ *nóthoi*) (Dem. Or. 23,213; Ath. 6,234E; Plut. Themistocles 1,2). At the beginning of the 4th cent. BC → Antisthenes [1] founded in C. the philosophical school of the Cynics (Diog. Laert. 6,1,6; Suda s.v. Ἀντισθένης; *Antisthénes*. In 200 BC it was destroyed by Philip V (Liv. 31,24,17), afterwards it was reconstructed. In C. there are altars to Hebe, Alcmene and Iolaus (Paus. 1,19,3).
→ Academy; → Cynicism

E. HONIGMANN, s.v. Kynosarges, RE XII 1, 33; W. JUDEICH, Die Topographie von Athen, [2]1931, 170, 422ff.; H. LIND, Neues aus Kydathen, in: MH 42, 1985, 257f.; TRAVLOS, Athen 340f., 579, fig. 379, 441, 442 (with bibliography); R.E. WYCHERLEY, The Stones of Athens, 1978, 229ff. H.LO.

Cynoscephalae (Κυνὸς Κεφαλαί; *Kynòs Kephalaí*, 'heads of dogs'). Part of the central Thessalian mountain range Chalcodonion (modern Mavrovuni, formerly Karadağ) between Pherae and Scotussa with many limestone rounded hilltops (hence the name). At C. in 364 BC the Thebans under Pelopidas defeated Alexander of Pherae (Plut. Pelopidas 32). In 197 Philip V suffered decisive defeat here against T. Quinctius Flamininus (Pol. 18,20ff.). Antiochus III had the bones of the fallen Macedonians buried in 191 (Liv. 36,8,3ff.). It seems certain that the battlefield was located between Scotussa and Thetideum.

J. CL. DECOURT, La vallée de l'Enipeus en Thessalie, 1990, 92ff., 107ff.; F. STÄHLIN, s.v. Kynos kephalai, RE XII 1, 34f. (evidence). HE.KR.

Cynossema (Κυνὸς σῆμὰ; *Kynòs sêma*, 'dog grave'). Cape on Thracian Chersonesus south of Madytus near modern Kilit Bahır where the Hellespont is at its very narrowest, well known for the sea victory of the Attic fleet over the Peloponnesians in 411 BC (Thuc. 8,104–107; Diod. Sic. 13,40,6; cf. also regarding the name 'dog grave' Eur. Hec. 1270ff.; Ov. Met. 13,569). I.v.B.

Cynosura (Κυνόσουρα; *Kynósoura*, 'dog's tail'). Name of several headlands.
[1] Promontory on the east coast of the island of Salamis, 4 km long and narrow (Hdt. 8,76,1; 77,1).

PHILIPPSON/KIRSTEN 1, 870. H.KAL.

[2] Narrow headland in the north-east of the bay of Marathon, where the Persian fleet landed in 490 BC (Paus. 1,32,3; 7), modern Cape Stomi. On C. there are walls of unknown date and function. Evidence: Ptol. 3,14,7; Hsch. s.v. K., Phot. s.v. K.; Hdn. 13,24.

1 J.R. MCCREDIE, Fortified Military Camps in Attica, Hesperia Suppl. 11, 1966, 41ff. fig. 8.

A. MILCHHOEFER, Erläuternder Text, in: E. CURTIUS, J.A. KAUPERT, Karten von Attika 3/6, 1889, 50; TRAVLOS, Attika, 223 fig. 271. H.LO.

[3] With Limnae, Pitane and Mesoa the most southerly of the four settlements from which the *pólis* → Sparta was founded (Paus. 3,16,9; IG V 1,480; 566: Lacon. Κονοουρεῖς; *Konooureîs*, situated on the hill of Psychiko that falls down to the south of where Magula and → Eurotas meet. The four original villages of Sparta are alternatively described in literature and inscriptions as *démoi* (Hdt. 3,55 for Pitane), *kômai* (schol. Thuc. 1,20 for Pitane), spots (*chória*, Str. 8,5,3 for Mesoa), *phýlai* (Hsch. s.v. K.), *póleis* (Schol. Pind. Ol. 6,46a for Pitane), parts of towns (*mérē*, Str. 8,5,3 for Mesoa), suburbs (*proásteia*, Str. 8,5,1 for Limnae) without the sources allowing for definite and objective classification.

L. PARETI, Le tribu personali e tribu locali a Sparta, in: Rendiconti della Reale Accademia dei Lincei 19, 1910, 455. Y.L. and E.O.

[4] The Megaris (→ Megara) was originally divided into five 'villages' (κῶμαι, Plut. Mor. 295b), i.e. administrative districts of which C. was one; the inhabitants of C. were called *Kynosureîs* (Κυνοσουρεῖς). People presume that C. was on the north-western promontory of the peninsula of Mitikas between Aegosthena and Pagae.

PHILIPPSON/KIRSTEN 1, 940ff. E.O.

[5] see → Constellations

Cynthus (Κύνθος; *Kýnthos*, Latin *Cynthus*). Name of a mountain 113 m high on → Delos with a sanctuary to Zeus (Cynthius) and Athena (Cynthia).

G. GRUBEN, Die Tempel der Griechen, [4]1986, 146f. H.KAL.

Cynuria (Κυνουρία; *Kynouría*, Κυνοσουρία; *Kynos-souría*).

[1] Landscape on the Gulf of Argolis on the north-eastern coast of the Parnon mountains. As a border region between Laconia and Argolis, C. was often the cause of disputes between Sparta and Argos (cf. Str. 1,4,7). The northern part, the Thyreatis, one of the most fertile plains of the Peloponnese, consisted of the valleys of Tanos and Vrasiotis. According to Herodotus (8,73,1; 3), C. was originally Ionian and was made Doric by Argos. Through the legendary battle of the 300 Argives and Spartans at Parparus ([1; 2]; Hdt. 1,82 with [3]; Str. 8,6,17) C. came into the possession of Sparta but always remained disputed territory. In 424 BC Thyrea, where the Spartans had settled exiled Aeginetans, was conquered and destroyed by the Athenians (Thuc. 4,56; Diod. Sic. 12,44,3; Plut. Nicias 6,6; Paus. 2,38,5). It is probable that Argos recaptured it in 370/369 BC (Diod. Sic. 15,64,2), and this is obviously confirmed by the arbitration of Philip II. Thuc. 5,41,2 mentions the cities of Thyrea and Anthene (cf. Lys. fr. 15 Th.), Paus. 2,38,6 the villages of A<n>thene, Neris (Stat. Theb. 4,46; Steph. Byz. s.v. Ἀνθάνα; *Anthána*) and Eua (Steph. Byz. s.v. Eâ; modern Helleniko? [4]), the definite locations of which remain a contentious issue [5; 6]. The ancient remains close to today's monastery of Luku have been identified as domains of Herodes Atticus. Inscriptions: SEG 13, 261–267; 16, 274; 30, 372; 376–380; 35, 276–302; 39, 367–369; 40, 340; 41, 280; 295; 42, 287.

1 P. PHAKLARIS, Η μάχη της Θυρέας (546 π. X.), in: Horos 5, 1987, 101–120 2 L. MORETTI, Sparta alla metà del VI secolo. II. La guerra contro Argo per la Tireatide, in: RFIC 26, 1948, 204–213 3 J. DILLERY, Reconfiguring the Past: Thyrea, Thermopylae and Narrative Patterns in Herodotus, in: AJPh 117, 1996, 217–254 4 J. CHRISTIEN, T. SPYROPOULOS, Eua et la Thyréatide, in: BCH 109, 1985, 455–466 5 J. CHRISTIEN, Promenades en Laconie, in: DHA 15, 1989, 75–80 6 PRITCHETT 3, 1980, 116–127; 4, 1982, 75–79; 6, 1989, 84–90; 7, 1991, 169–177, 209–222.

Y. C. GOESTER, The Plain of Astros, in: Pharos 1, 1993, 39–112; C. KRITZAS, Remarques sur trois inscriptions de Cynourie, in: BCH 109, 1985, 709–716; E. MEYER, s.v. Kynuria, RE Suppl. 12, 521f.; P. PHAKLARIS, Ἀρχαία Κυνουρία, 1990 (= Diss. Thessalonica 1985); K. A. RHO-MAIOS, Ἐρευνητικὴ περιοδεία εἰς Κυνουρίαν, in: Praktika 106, 1950, 234–241; I. WALKER, Kynuria, diss. Columbia, 1936.

[2] Landscape in western Arcadia north of the Lycaeum mountain range on both sides of → Alpheius with the towns of Gortys, Thisoa, Lycaea (Lykoa), Alipheira [1], included in the → synoecismus of Megalopolis [2. 311]. Evidence: Paus. 8,27,4; Stat. Theb. 4,295; Cic. Nat. D. 3,22,57 (*Cynosura*); Syll.³ 183.

1 JOST, 201–210 2 M. MOGGI, I sinecismi interstatali greci, 1976. Y.L.

Cynus (Κῦνος; *Kŷnos*). Town of Opuntian → Locris (Hom. Il. 2,531; Scyl. 60; Lycoph. Alexandra 1147; Ptol. 3,15,9; Plin. HN 4,27; Hecat. in Steph. Byz. s.v. K.; Mela 2,3,40) and ship mooring place (ἐπίνειον; *epíneion*, *emporium*) of → Opus (Paus. 10,1,2; Str. 9,4,2; Steph. Byz. loc. cit.; Liv. 28,6,12). The settlement covered the peak of the hill, known as modern Palaiopyrgos or Pyrgos after the ruins of the ancient walls and after a medieval tower that juts out over the little bay on the northern tip of the plain of Atalandi close to the modern village of Livanates. On the hill and in the surrounding area, remains of burial sites were unearthed as well as of private houses and storerooms with ceramics (Middle Helladic to the Byzantine period).

PH. DAKORONIA, Lokrika 1, in: AD 34, 1979, 56–61; Id., MH Gräber in Ost-Lokris, in: MDAI(A) 102, 1987, 55–64; J. M. FOSSEY, The Ancient Topography of Opuntian Lokris, 1990, 81–84; PRITCHETT 4, 149–151; TIB 1, 272. G.D.R.

Cypaera (Κύπαιρα; *Kýpaira*). Neighbouring town of Xyniae in south-western Achaea Phthiotis on the border with Dolopia, near modern Palaia Giannitsu (not near modern Makryrrachi, formerly Kaitsa). For 363 BC a temple donation from C. is noted in Delphi (Syll.³ 239 B 12). From the end of the 3rd cent. C. belonged to the League of the Aetolians who conquered it back in 198 BC from its short-term possession by the Macedonians (Liv. 32,13,14).

B. HELLY, Incursions chez les Dolopes, in: I. BLUM (ed.), Topographie antique et géographie historique en pays grec, 1992, 49ff.; F. STÄHLIN, s.v. Kypaira, RE XII 1, 46f. HE.KR.

Cyparissia (Κυπαρισσία; *Kyparissía*).

[1] Town on the Messenian west coast and the location of the modern town of the same name with a few remains mostly from Roman times; parts of the wall of the acropolis below a medieval castle. Aside from Pylos and Methone, the harbour of C. with its good connection to the upper Pamisus Valley was considered the only significant Messenian access to the sea. C. is already mentioned in the Pylos Tablets and is in any case identical to Κυπαρισσήεις (*Kyparissées*) in Hom. Il. 2,593. The shallow bay is named *Cyparissius sinus* after the town (Plin. HN 4,15; Mela 2,50f.). The Arcadians conquered C. in 365/4 BC (Diod. Sic. 15,77,4). After it was liberated, C. was likely to have belonged to Messenia. C. was involved in 219/8 BC in warding off the Spartan-Aetolian attack on Messenia. In the imperial period it had its own coins. Evidence: Str. 8,3,16; 22; 25; 4,1f.; 6; Paus. 4,36,7; Ptol. 3,16,7. Inscriptions: IG V 1, 1421–1424; 1559f.; V 2, 1421; SEG 11, 1025–1028a; 15, 225. Coins: HN, 433.

E. MEYER, s.v. Messenien, RE Suppl. 15, 204f.

[2] Spartan perioecic community (→ *períoikoi*) on the Laconian Gulf on the western side of the → Parnon peninsula on the isthmus that connects the peninsula of

Xyli with the Peloponnese. The position is uncertain, and is mostly regarded as being near Boza (if Asopus is modern Plitra). At the time of Pausanius, C. was in ruins. Evidence: Str. 8,5,2; Paus. 3,22,9f.; Ptol. 3,16,7.

A.J. B. WACE, South-Eastern Laconia, in: ABSA 14, 1907/8, 163f.; AD 28, 1973, 175; Archaeological Reports 25, 1978/9, 20 (excavation report).　　　　　Y.L.

Cyparissus (Κυπάρισσος; *Kypárissos*).
[1] of Ceos, beloved of → Apollo. Pained because he had accidentally killed his own favourite stag, C. begged to be allowed to mourn for ever and was turned into a cypress (Ov. Met. 10,106–142). Even though Ovid provides the earliest documentary evidence, the story itself is believed to be much older [1. 52]. In Servius' version, C. is a son of → Telephus, also hailing from Crete, also beloved of → Zephyrus or → Silvanus, but the stag was killed by Silvanus (Serv. Aen. 3,680). There was a sanctuary dedicated to C. on Cos (from the 4th cent. BC dedicated to Asclepius) [1. 49]. Whereas in Greece, C. was linked with the gods of the upper world, in Rome the → cypress was the tree of the dead. The possible link was perhaps the Orphic belief in life after death as found in lower Italy [1. 51].
→ Minyas

1 F. BÖMER, P. Ovidius Naso, Metamorphosen. Komm. zu B. X–XI, 1980, z.St.　　　　　K.SCHL.

[2] Listed amongst the Phocian *póleis* in Homer's Catalogue of Ships (Il. 2,519; Str. 9,3,13 [Hom.]; cf. Paus. 10,36,5), its location is uncertain: according to Strabo (loc. cit.) below Lycorea and in his time a 'village' (κώμη; *kṓmē*), according to Steph. Byz. located on the slopes of Mount Parnassus near Delphi. The etymology, too, is uncertain, a dendronym or an eponym (after a brother of Orchomenus: Str. loc. cit.; schol. Codex Venetianus A on Il. 2,519). Furthermore, there are alternative versions of the name having been changed by translation: from C. to *Anticyra* (Paus. loc. cit.), from an original name of *Eranos* to *Cyparissus* and subsequently to *Apollonia* (Steph. Byz. s.v. Κυπάρισσος καὶ Ἀπολλωνία; schol. Codex Ven. B on Il. 2,519). Additional evidence: Hom. Il. 2,519; Str. 9,13,3; Paus. 10,36,5; Steph. Byz.: Κυπάρισσος; Eust. ad Hom. Il. 273,15; 274,1, Κυπαρισσοῦς; Stat. Theb. 7,344.

E. PIESKE, s.v. Kyparissia (4), RE 12, 50; F. SCHOBER, Phokis, 1924, 34f.　　　　　G.D.R.

Cyphanta (Κύφαντα or Κύφας; *Kýphanta* or *Kýphas*). Spartan perioikic polis (→ *períoikoi*) on the east coast of the → Parnon peninsula with an Asclepius sanctuary, already in ruins at the time of Pausanias, located in the bay with the mod. name of Kyparissi. Documentary evidence: Pol. 4,36,5; Paus. 3,24,2; Ptol. 3,16,10; 22; Plin. HN 4,17.

PRITCHETT 7, 1991, 146–149; A.J. B. WACE, F. W. HAS-LUCK, East-Central Laconia, in: ABSA 15, 1908/9, 173.
　　　　　Y.L.

Cypress see → Volume 4, Addenda

Cypria (τὰ Κύπρια; *tà Kýpria*; also τὰ Κύπρια ἔπη; *tà Kýpria épē*, τὰ Κυπριακά; *tà Kypriaká*, αἱ Κυπριακαὶ ἱστορίαι; *hai kupriakai historíai*, its title derived from the dominance of Aphrodite = Cypris in the causality of the plot [3; cf. 9. 287]). This epic, a part of the → epic cycle, recounts in 11 bks. (according to Proclus) the history of Troy prior to the better-known *Iliad* (→ Homerus [1]). Approximately 50 hexameters in 12 [1] or respectively 10 [2] frs. are extant; in addition there are short summaries in → Proclus and → Apollodorus, as well as numerous reports and references, as well as a rich pictorial tradition (catalogue in [1. 213–215]).

The author is unknown; the early attribution to Homer was already refuted by Hdt. 2,117; later the C. is either quoted without reference to an author (Hdt., Plat., Aristot. et.al.), or attributed to a certain Stasinus (frequently), Hegesinus (or rather Hegesias) or Cyprias [6. 2394f.], or at times explicitly referred to as anonymous [1. test. 10, fr. 17]. The period in which the extant version was written, had — on the basis of linguistic indications — already been classified as late by WILAMOWITZ [4] and WACKERNAGEL ([5. 183]: 'originating from Attica not much before 500 BC'; misunderstood by RZACH [6. 2396]: '7th cent.' and BERNABÉ [1. 43]: 'saec. VII'; see also [7. 90⁶]); DAVIES [7], based on JANKO [8], dates its creation definitely at just before 500 BC — basically the same as the Alexandrian philologists earlier, e.g. Aristarchus in schol. A on Hom. Il. 1,5: the interpretation of 'Zeus' plan' as a way of decimating humanity (Cypria fr. 1,7) was seen as part of 'fantastic ideas of later generations'.

The material of the C. is largely pre-Homeric (→ Epic cycle). Contents (only a selection; even Aristotle had already criticized the overwhelming wealth of events as an artistic *faux-pas* [1. test. 5]: deliberations of Zeus and Themis on the Trojan War; marriage of Thetis to Peleus (first reference to their son Achilles; intervention by Eris); judgement of Paris; birth of Helena; abduction of Helena; the two musters of ships at Aulis (the first in conjunction with the story of Telephus, the second with the sacrifice of Iphigenia; no catalogue of ships [!]); on Scyros, Achilles begets Neoptolemus with Deidamia; the abandonment of Philoctetes on Lemnos; the landing in the Troad (Protesilaus, Cycnus); rejection of Helena's return; first combat; Achilles kills Troilus; Briseis is given to Achilles, Chryseis to Agamemnon; Zeus' decision (Διὸς βουλή; *Diòs boulé*) to decimate the Trojans by Achilles' refusal to fight; catalogue of the forces of the Trojan defenders (probably a supplement to the Trojan catalogue in the 'Iliad' on the basis of better knowledge of Asia Minor [6. 2393]).

The pictorial images of some of these topics — some of them very early — probably go back to the same fount of 'ancient myths' [6. 2378; 7. 100⁶⁴], upon which the 'Iliad' and 'Odyssey' as well as the C. also draw; within this repertoire, the C. provide an 'upward' extension of the *Iliad*.

EDITIONS: 1 PEG I 2 EpGr.
BIBLIOGRAPHY: 3 IACOB PERIZONIUS, in: KUEHN (ed.),
C. Aeliani Varia Historia etc., 2, 1780, 26 4 U. V. WIL-
AMOWITZ-MOELLENDORFF, Homer. Unt. (Der ep.
Cyclus), 1884 5 J. WACKERNAGEL, Sprachl. Unt. zu
Homer, 1916 6 A. RZACH, s.v. Kyklos, RE 11, 2347–
2435 7 M. DAVIES, The Date of the Epic Cycle, in:
Glotta 67, 1989, 89–100 8 R. JANKO, Homer, Hesiod
and the Hymns, 1982 9 R. KANNICHT, Dichtung und
Bildkunst. Die Rezeption der Troja-Epik in den früh-
griech. Sagenbildern (1979), in: Id., Paradeigmata, 1996,
45–67 (engl.: Poetry and Art, in: Classical Antiquity 1,
1982, 70–86).
FURTHER LITERATURE: see → Epic cycle. J.L.

Cyprianus

[1] C. Gallus. see → Heptateuch poet
[2] C. Thascius Caecili(an)us
A. BIOGRAPHY B. WORKS (SELECTION) C. THE-
OLOGY D. LATER RECEPTION

A. BIOGRAPHY

Caecilius Cyprianus qui et Thascius (his transmitted
name, combining his original Punic cognomen Thascius
C. with a newly adopted Christian cognomen after his
godfather Caecilianus, according to Pontius, vita 4 —
or rather Caecilius, according to Jer. Vir. ill. 67 [1. 110,
n. 1]) was the son of wealthy parents. Prior to his conversion to Christianity (after AD 240), he worked as a
rhetor, but then gave up his profession in favour of an
abstemious life and renounced most of his wealth.
Against the enduring opposition of a small faction of
presbyters, he soon became a presbyter himself and
shortly after that bishop of Carthage (248/9). At the
onset of the Decian persecutions of Christians, C. went
into hiding (as did e.g. → Dionysius of Alexandria), but
with his letters kept in constant contact with his congregation. His assets were confiscated, but he still had
money at his disposal. He may have been urged by the
Carthaginian congregation to go into hiding; however,
this action met with the most ironic and sharpest criticism of the Christian congregation in Rome, writing to
North Africa: taking this step, 'he may have done the
right thing, because he is an outstanding personality'
(Epist. 8,1). However, this difference of opinion, further complicated by internal disputes within his congregation, was soon overshadowed by the question
whether those who during the persecutions had 'lapsed'
(*i.e.* abandoned their faith; *lapsi*) should be readmitted
into the congregation: Rome rejected that notion emphatically — *i.a.* influenced by → Novatianus. The Carthaginian confessors, by contrast, took it upon themselves to issue indulgences; it was C. who acted as
mediator. In AD 251, a synod in Carthage decided that
those who had used bribery in order to obtain a certificate of sacrifice (*libellatici*) were to be readmitted immediately, but those who had actually performed a sacrifice (*sacrificati et turificati*) only after lengthy penance.

During the period of office of the Roman bishop Stephanus I (254–256), a dispute developed between Carthage and Rome on whether it was necessary to baptize
those heretics who, having been baptized before, now
sought readmission to the Church. C. together with a
North African synod (protocol: CPL 56) voted in 256
(apparently in line with African traditions) for rebap-
tism, Rome for the laying-on of hands. No definite solution to the conflict was found, but tensions seem to have
eased soon after. In the early phase of the Valerian persecutions of Christians, C. was first exiled to → Curubis
(August 257); following the execution of the Roman
bishop Sixtus (6.8.258), he was ordered to return to
Carthage and there executed on 14 September 258
(*Acta proconsularia*, CPL 53).

B. WORKS (SELECTION)

For Church history, C.'s extensive — but incomplete
— correspondence is a source of the greatest importance (CPL 50; of 81 letters, 16 are addressed to C. or
the clergy in Carthage). Soon after his conversion, reported in *Ad Donatum* (CPL 38, chs. 7 and 14 of this
treatise also contain one of the most acute contemporary descriptions of the empire in crisis, even though C.
at that time did not yet expect the Roman empire to
collapse in the short term [2]), C. compiled *Ad Quiri-
nium* (also called *Testimonia*), a collection of passages
of the scriptures indexed according to their headings
(CPL 39). Upon his return to Carthage (March 251), C.
gave a public address (*De lapsis*, CPL 42), in which he
confronted the apostates with those who had remained
steadfast and with their obligation to do penance. Of
particular importance is the treatise *De ecclesiae catho-
licae unitate* (unit., CPL 41, probably also written in
251), in which C. emphasizes the unity of the Church
under its one bishop: 'Who does not hold the Church to
be his mother, can no longer claim God as his father.'
(unit. 6; for a discussion of unit. 4 [3; 4]: a second version by the author (differently in [5]); even the probably
original reference to a *primatus*, granted to Petrus, and
thus representing one Church and one bishop's throne,
must not be read in the sense of a modern understanding of the bishop of Rome's 'primacy of jurisdiction';
labelling C. as a 'papalist' definitely misses the point).

C. THEOLOGY

Characteristic for the highly educated C.'s understanding of his role as a bishop is his statement *Christianus sum et episcopus* (Act. Cypr. 1,2). It is linked
with his understanding of the role of the Church, which
is a particular focus within his theology (leading to the
cautious question whether in C.'s view the Church had
taken the place of the state within the Roman conception of the world): monarchic bishops are linked within
a world-wide community, guaranteeing the true faith,
and thus demonstrating unity (*unitas*) within the world
Church as well as the early Church. C. sees this as a
consequence of the Church as a self-acting 'secret of
salvation'; thus he refers to the Church in his translating

the Greek *mystérion* (Eph 5) as *unitatis sacramentum* (Unit. 7; cf. Epist. 73,21: *salus extra ecclesiam non est*, 'there is no salvation outside of the Church').

D. LATER RECEPTION
First evidence of C.'s influence is a biography, written only a few months after his death by the Carthaginian deacon → Pontius (CPL 52), probably the earliest literary Lat.-Christian biography, furthermore the various Pseudo-Cyprianica (e.g. CPL 58–61, 67, 75–76, 1106, 2276); even Erasmus still wrote his *De duplici martyrio ad Fortunatum* under C.'s name. C.'s complex understanding of the Church has often been claimed more or less one-sidedly by a great variety of groupings. → Decius;　→ Dionysius of Alexandria;　→ Novatianus; → Quod idola dii non sint; → Stephanus; → Valerianus

1 H. GÜLZOW, C. und Novatian, 1975　　2 G. ALFÖLDI, Der hl. C. und die Krise des röm. Reiches, in: Id., Die Krise des röm. Reiches, 1989, 295–318　　3 M. BÉVENOT, St. C.'s De Unitate, Chap. 4 in the Light of the Mss., Rom 1934　　4 Id., The Tradition of Mss., 1961　　5 U. WICKERT, Sacramentum Unitatis (BZNW 41), 1971.

EDITIONS: Cyprian; CPL 38, 40–57; W. HARTEL, CSEL 3/1–3; R. WEBER et.al., CCL 3–3B, 1972–1994; Pontius, ed. A. A. R. BASTIAENSEN, in: CH. MOHRMANN (ed.), Vite dei Santi II, ³1989, 4–49
LITERATURE: M. BÉVENOT, s.v. C., TRE 8, 1981, 246–254; M. SAGE, C., 1975; CH. SAUMAGNE, Saint C., évêque de Carthage, 'pape' d'Afrique, 1975.　　　　　　C.M.

Cypriot
I. ANCIENT CYPRIOT　II. MODERN CYPRIOT

I. ANCIENT CYPRIOT
The sources for C. are inscriptions in → Cypriot script (most important finding places: Idalium, Golgi, Paphus, Marion; oldest Text: o-pe-le-ta-u /opʰeltau/11th/10th cents. BC), → glossography (esp. Hsch., schol. on the Iliad and the Odyssey, fr. of an anonymous grammarians: Anecd. Bekk. 3,1094) and Cypriot proper names.

C. a) corresponds particularly with → Arcadian and in parts also with → Mycenaean, and b) has its own specific features.

For a): arsis of *e, o* before a nasal sound (/in/= ἐν, /on-/un-/ = ἀνά) and of *o* (gen. sg. in /-au/< -āo, 3rd sg.-tu < -to); *ṛ > or/ro (/kateworgon/); *kʷi > tʼi (/sis/= τις, /sioi/= τίοι); noun ending in -ēs = -eus (/basilēs/ alongside /basileus/), demonstrative pronouns /honu, hone/; 3rd pl. -an (/kat-ethiyan/ alongside /kat-ethisan/); verba vocalia ending in -āmi (3rd pl. /kumernahi/< *kumernansi); /apu, ex/with dat. (= ἀπό, ἐξ with gen.), /en, in/ with acc., /pos/(= πρός), /kas/(= καί), /ptolis, ptolemos/; iterative composita (/āmati-āmati/); patronymic adjectives (/Theodokidau/).

For b): *-lị- > -il- (/ailōn/, gen. pl., Attic ἄλλων), gen. sg. *o*-stems ending in -o-ne (/aneu misthōn/'without wages'), but gen. sg. of the article always as /tō/; acc. sg. of the consonantal declension ending in -an/(/ton

īyatēran/); Inflection -ās -āwos, -is -iwos. C. retains some remarkable archaisms in its morphology (e.g. dat. sg. ending in /-ei/in /Diweiphilos/, /Diweithemis/; 3rd sg. imperfect (tense) /ēs/'he was'; 3rd sg. medial /-toi/: /keitoi/) and in its vocabulary by 1) correspondences with the epic (e.g. /aisa, aroura, autar, oiwos, posis, thalamos/) or respectively poetic (/īnis/= Attic υἱός) vocabulary and 2) rare lexemes, sometimes only evident in C. (e.g. /grasthi, ewexe/= Attic φάγε, ἤνεγκε).

Sample (Idalium, 478–470 BC): /hote tān ptolin Edalion kateworgon Mādoi ... basileus Stāsikupros kas hā ptolis Edaliēwes anōgon Onāsilon ... ton īyatēran kas to(n)s kasignēto(n)s īyasthai to(n)s a(n)thrōpo(n)s to(n)s i(n) tāi makhāi ikmameno(n)s aneu misthōn/.

Corresponding Attic: ὅτε τὴν πόλιν Ἐδάλιον κατεῖργον Μῆδοι ... βασιλεὺς Στησίκυπρος καὶ ἡ πόλις Ἐδαλιεῖς ἐκέλευον Ὀνήσιλον ... τὸν ἰατρὸν καὶ τοὺς ἀδελφοὺς ἰᾶσθαι τοὺς ἀνθρώπους τοὺς ἐν τῇ μάχῃ βαλλομένους ἄνευ μισθοῦ.

→ Eteo-Cyprian;　→ Greek dialects;　→ Arcadian; → Cypriot script

SOURCES: MASSON; T.B. MITFORD, O. MASSON, The Syllabic Inscriptions of Rantidi-Paphos (Ausgrabungen in Alt-Paphos auf Cypern 2), 1983; Id., Les inscriptions syllabiques de Kouklia-Paphos (Ausgrabungen in Alt-Paphos auf Cypern 4), 1986; T.B. MITFORD, The Inscriptions of Kourion, 1971; Id., The Nymphaeum of Kafizin. The Inscribed Pottery (Kadmos Suppl. 2), 1980; C. TRAUNEKKER, F. LE SAOUT, O. MASSON, La Chapelle d'Achôris à Karnak (Centre Franco-Egyptien d'étude des Temples de Karnak), 1981.
GLOSSES: Anecd. Bekker 3, 1094–1096 (Γλῶσσαι κατὰ πόλεις); K. HADJIOANNOU, Ἡ ἀρχαία Κύπρος εἰς τὰς Ἑλληνικὰς πηγάς. Γ' Β', 1977; O. HOFFMANN, Die k. Glossen als Quellen des k. Dial., in: BB 15, 1890, 44–100; Id., Die griech. Dial. 1, 1891, 104–124.
LITERATURE: BECHTEL, DIAL.² 1; M. EGETMEYER, WB zu den Inschr. im k. Syllabar, 1992; Id., Zur k. Bronze von Idalion, in: Glotta 71, 1993, 39–59; Id., in: Kadmos 35, 1996, 178f.; 36, 1997, 178f. (research report); A. HINTZE, A Lexicon to the Cyprian Syllabic Inscriptions (LEXOR 2), 1994; J. KARAGEORGHIS, O. MASSON (ed.), The History of the Greek Language in Cyprus. Proc. of an International Symposion Sponsored by the Pierides Foundation. Larnaca, Cyprus, 8.–13.9.1986, 1988; A. MORPURGO DAVIES, Mycenaean, Arcadian, Cyprian and some Questions of Method in Dialectology, in: J.-P. OLIVIER (ed.), Mycenaïca. Actes du IXᵉ Colloque international sur les textes mycéniens et égéens, Athènes 2–6 oct. 1990 (BCH Suppl. 25), 1992, 415–432; R. SCHMITT, Einführung in die griech. Dial., 1977, 14–16, 87–94; THUMB/SCHERER, 141–174.　　　　　　A.HI.

II. MODERN CYPRIOT
As with all → Greek dialects, one needs to look at the relationship of the present-day dialect of Modern Greek, spoken on Cyprus, to Ancient Cypriot, a very ancient language (linked with Mycenaean!), which into the Hellenistic period was still written in a syllabary. However, in contrast with → Tsaconian and Pontic, the Modern Greek of present-day Cyprus cannot be de-

scribed as descended from of Ancient C., even though certain continuations and extensions of ancient tendencies are evident in its phonology, namely its inclination — in diametrical opposition to 'mainstream dialects' — to retain or even create closed syllables, geminates, and the terminal sound –/n/ (εγούνι for ἐγώ; cf. the ancient, epigraphically evident, –μαν for –μα. The preservation of geminates is mainly familiar from the Greek dialect of lower Italy; in line with dialect-geographical insights, it must be understood as an independently preserved common archaism. In the same way, the (recent) change py/>/pk/ can be seen as the development of a tendency already evident in antiquity.

Other characteristics of the modern Cypriot dialect, such as the change from /ç/ to /š/ before/e/ and/i/ e.g.in š'er for χείϱ, can be dated at the latest to the early Middle Ages (misspellings using <σι> for <χι> in MSS), but they were much more common, e.g. also within the Greek of the Middle East, as shown in the secondary literature; for that reason, they cannot be classified as being unique to Cyprus; however because the other regions where this phonetic feature was common were lost to the Greek language community with the Arab expansion and the spread of Islam, Cyprus became geographically peripheral (also an explanation for the preservation of ancient features, particularly in the vocabulary, and later on for its unique innovations) and thus this feature was preserved. However, as Cyprus enjoyed a central geographical position at the time of the koineization processes (→ Koine), esp. in the Hellenistic period and the Roman Imperial period, a thorough koineization took place; in morphology and syntax, the C. dialect mainly displays the habitus of Modern Greek, with some archaisms in vocabulary.

J. NIEHOFF-PANAGIOTIS, Koiné und Diglossie, 1994; J. KARAGEORGHIS, O. MASSON (ed.), The History of the Greek Language in Cyprus, Proc. of an International Symposium Sponsored by the Pierides Foundation, Larnaca 8.–13.9.1986, 1988; B. NEWTON, Cypriot Greek, 1972.
V.BI.

Cypriot Archaeology see → Cyprus

Cypriot Script The Cypriot script (CS), probably a further development of the → Cypro-Minoan scripts [1; 2], is a syllabic script, related to → Linear B, with signs for vowels and open syllables. Their common origin is apparent in signs which correspond not only in form, but also in phonetic value (lo/ro, na, pa, po, se, ta/da, to, ti). In contrast with Linear B, CS is a purely syllabic script (without ideograms). There are also minor differences in the orthographic rules: in CS, t and d are not differentiated (i-ta-te = Attic ἐνθάδε), whereas r and l are (lu-sa-to-ro = Attic gen. Λυσάνδϱου); there are special signs for i- and u-diphthongs (a-ro-u-ra-i = Attic ἀϱούϱᾳ), syllable-ending consonants, including resonants and s, with the exception of a medial n (a-to-ro-po-se = Attic acc. ἀνθϱώπους) and initial consonant clusters including s (se-pe-re-ma-to-se = Attic Gen. σπέϱματος) [3. 51–57].

The oldest extant evidence of CS are the five syllables o-pe-le-ta-u on a bronze spit dating from the Cypro-Geometric period I (= CM I, 1050–950), found in 1979 in Kouklia-Skales (OldPaphos) [4. 50f.]. This text represents the link between the scripts of the 2nd and 1st millennia BC and thus proves the continuity of script on Cyprus throughout the → Dark Ages as well as the existence of a Greek Cypriot dialect (→ Cypriot) in the 11th/10th cents. The latest examples of CS — signs on seals dating from the 2nd/1st cents. BC — also originate from the area around Paphos [5; 6. 64–67].

Cypriot script
('syllabaire commun', standardized form)

	a	e	i	o	u
	✳	✳	✕	⩔	⋔
y	○			⌇	
w	⋋	ⲓ	⋋	⌂	
r	Ω	⋔	Ͽ	Ջ	)(
l	⋎	8	⊿	+	ᖽ
m	⋋	✕	⋎	⊕	⋈
n	⊤	I⌇I	⋎	⫻	⋋
p	‡	⟨	⋁	⌇	⩡
t	Ͱ	⋎	↑	F	Fᵢᵢ
k	⬆	⋋	Ⲟ	⊓	✕
s	∨	⊢	⬘	⩡	⋇
z	⋋ za?			⫝̸	
x	)(	⊢			

CS is preserved on a variety of writing materials (e.g. on stone for grave inscriptions or dedications, on coins, seals, pottery vessels, ostraca) as well as in a number of local variants, which can be divided into two groups: The most widespread is the syllabary used in the important inscription on a bronze tablet found at Idalium, with 31 lines the longest text in CS ('syllabaire commun', see illustr.); it consists of 55 signs, and with only a few exceptions is written from right to left. Different is the syllabary of Paphos: some special forms of signs and the predominance of left-to-right writing link it particularly closely to CM I [3. 57–67; 7. 71f.; 8]. The above-mentioned oldest inscription in CS shows some feature of the syllabary of Old Paphos [2. 376f.]. Two different languages were written in CS: a) the Greek Cypriot dialect, and b) the as yet uninterpreted → Eteo-Cyprian (in the 'syllabaire commun'). Alphabetic texts are sporadically found from the 6th cent. BC onwards, initially in digraphs alongside the same text in CS [9], but they only become more frequent from the 4th cent., and from then on they increasingly and finally completely replace the Cypriot dialect and syllabary.

After knowledge of texts in CS spread around the middle of the 19th cent., a number of scholars collaborated and succeeded between 1871 and 1876 in deciphering them with the help of a Phoenician-Cypriot bilingual inscription [3. 48–51].

→ Greece, systems of writing; DECIPHERMENT

1 J. CHADWICK, The Minoan Origin of the Classical Cypriote Script, in: Acts of the International Archaeological Symposium 'The Relations between Cyprus and Crete, ca. 2000–500 B.C.', 1979, 139–143　2 E. MASSON, La part du fond commun égéen dans les écritures chypro-minoennes et son apport possible pour leur déchiffrement, in: J. T. KILLEN et al. (ed.), Studies in Mycenaean and Classical Greek. FS John Chadwick, 1987, 367–381 (= Minos 20–22)　3 MASSON　4 V. KARAGEORGHIS, La nécropole de Palaipaphos-Skalès, in: Dossiers d'Archéologie 205, 1995, 48–53　5 E. UND O. MASSON, Les objets inscrits de Palaepaphos-Skales, in: V. KARAGEORGHIS (ed.), Palaepaphos-Skales. An Iron-Age Cemetry in Cyprus. 1983, Appendix IV, 411–415　6 O. MASSON, Les écritures antiques a Chypre, in: Dossiers d'Archéologie 205, 1995, 62–67　7 HEUBECK　8 E. MASSON, Le Chyprominoen I: Comparaisons possibles avec les syllabaires du Ier millénaire et l'étéochypriote, in: E. RISCH, H. MÜHLESTEIN (ed.), Colloquium Mycenaeum 1975, 1979, 397–409　9 C. CONSANI, Bilingualismo, diglossia e digrafia nella Grecia antica III: Le iscrizioni digrafe cipriote, in: Studi in memoria di Ernesto Giammarco, 1990, 63–79 (Orientamenti Linguistici 25).

O. MASSON, En marge du déchiffrement du syllabaire chypriote I et II, in: Centre d'études chypriotes, Cahier 15, 1991; 16, 1991; Id., T. B. MITFORD, The Cypriot Syllabary, in: CAH 3,3, ²1982, 72–82, 479 (bibliography).
A. HI.

Cypro-Minoan Scripts

Cypro-Minoan Scripts Term coined by Arthur EVANS to describe the late Bronze Age Cypriot linear scripts related to → Linear A [1. 69f.] (→ Cyprus). The writing system is presumed to have been syllabic, but the texts are still largely undeciphered. Differences in writing modus, form of signs, and sign inventory have led to the distinction of three variants [2. 11–17]: (a) Cypro-Minoan (= CM) 1, (b) CM 2, (c) CM 3.

On (a): From the late 16th to 11th cents. BC, texts in CM I are found all over Cyprus and also in north Syrian Ras Šamra (→ Ugarit). The signs are painted on or respectively incised into various writing materials (e.g. ceramics, metal, stone weights, seals, clay tablets and balls); most of the texts are very short. One of the oldest (c. 1500 BC) is a clay tablet from → Engomi, whose characters are referred to as 'archaic' because of their obvious similarities with Linear A [3]. Clay balls (boules d'argile) and clay cylinders showing a script with a more developed ductus date from the 13th to 11th cents. BC.

On (b): CM 2 is documented on four clay tablet fragments from Engomi (13th/12th cents.) with longer, coherent texts, possibly written by professional scribes. In its appearance, the script also bears similarities with Near Eastern cuneiform texts [4. 59; 5] (→ Cuneiform script).

On (c): Texts in CM 3 come from Ugarit. They date back to the 13th cent. and were also evidently influenced by cuneiform.

Detailed studies, especially by E. MASSON, led to the assumption that CM 2 and 3 were adaptations of CM 1. Texts in CM 1 and 2 not only represented different types of script, but also different languages. The language behind CM 2 may be → Hurrite [2. 47–53]. Attempts at deciphering CM 3 were made possible by a completely preserved clay tablet from Ugarit, found in 1956 (RS 20.25), apparently containing lists of tripartite names (of the type 'X son of Y'), some of which can be interpreted as Semitic [2. 29–46; 6]. CM 1, however, which was common across all of the island and evident for a long period of time, may represent the written encoding of the unknown → Eteo-Cyprian language of the indigenous population of the 2nd millennium [4. 60–64; 7. 79–93]. It is likely that the → Cypriot script developed from CM 1 [8].

→ Greece, systems of writing

1 A. J. EVANS, Scripta Minoa. The Written Documents of Minoan Crete 1, 1909　2 E. MASSON, Cyprominoica. Répertoires, documents de Ras Shamra, essais d'interprétation (Stud. in Mediterranean Archaeology 31, Stud. in the Cypro-Minoan Scripts 2), 1974　3 Id., La plus ancienne tablette chypro-minoenne, in: Minos 10, 1969, 64–77　4 HEUBECK　5 E. MASSON, Les syllabaires chypro-minoens: mises au point, compléments et définitions à la lumière des documents nouveaux, in: RDAC 1985, 146–154　6 P. MERIGGI, La nuova iscrizione ciprominoica di Ugarite, in: Athenaeum 50, 1972, 152–157　7 ST. HILLER, Die kypromin. Schriftsysteme, in: AfO Beih. 20, 1985　8 E. MASSON, Le Chyprominoen I: Comparaisons possibles avec les syllabaires du Ier millénaire et l'étéochypriote, in: E. RISCH, H. MÜHLESTEIN (ed.), Colloquium Mycenaeum. Actes du sixième colloque international sur les textes mycéniens et égéens tenu à Chaumont sur Neuchâtel du 7 au 13 septembre 1975, 1979, 397–409. SOURCES: J. F. DANIEL, Prolegomena to the Cypro-Minoan Script, in: AJA 45, 1941, 249–283 (finds to 1940) O. MASSON, Répertoire des inscriptions chypro-minoennes, in: Minos 5, 1957, 9–27 (all finds to 1956) ST. HILLER, Die kypromin. Schriftsysteme, in: AfO Beih. 20, 1985, 67–74, 87, 102　A. SACCONI, A proposito di un corpus delle iscrizioni ciprominoiche, in: J.-P. OLIVIER (ed.), Mycenaïca. Actes du IXe Colloque international sur les textes mycéniens et égéens, Athènes 2–6 oct. 1990 (BCH Suppl. 25), 1992, 249f. (prospectus of a corpus of Cypro-Minoan texts). LITERATURE: E. GRUMACH, Die kypr. Schriftsysteme, in: HdArch 1, 267–288　HEUBECK, 54–74, 194–196 (bibli-

ography) St. Hiller, Altägäische Schriftsysteme (außer Linear B), in: AAHG 31, 1978, 53–60 (research report) Id., in: AfO Beih. 20, 1985, 61–102 (research report) A. Morpurgo Davies, Forms of Writing in the Ancient Mediterranean World, in: G. Baumann (ed.), The Written Word. Literacy in Transition. Wolfson College Lectures 1985, 1986, 51–77 Th.G. Palaima, Cypro-Minoan Scripts: Problems of Historical Context, in: Y. Duhoux, Th.G. Palaima, J. Bennet (eds.), Problems in Decipherment, 1989, 121–187 C. Baurain, L'écriture syllabique à Chypre, in: Id., C. Bonnet, V. Krings (ed.), Phoinikeia Grammata, 1991, 389–424 O. Masson, Les écritures antiques a Chypre, in: Dossiers d'Archéologie 205, 1995, 62–67.   A.HI.

Cyprus

[1] For prehistory of Cyprus see → Kypros.
[2] (Κύπρος; *Kýpros*, Lat. *Cyprus*).
I. Geography II. History III. Exploration IV. Religion

I. Geography

With an area of 9250 km², C. is the third-largest Mediterranean island; measuring 227 km in length and 95 km in width. 65 km separate C. from the closest point in Asia Minor, Cape → Anemourion, and the distance between the eastern tip of the long and narrow Karpasia peninsula in the east and the Syrian coast is *c.* 96 km. Geologically, C. is quite a young, tertiary formation. Along its northern coast runs a narrow, steep limestone ridge, peaking in the west at 1019 m. The south-west of the island is filled by the neo-volcanic massif of the Troodos range with the highest elevation at 1953 m. In the south and south-east, limestone plateau flank to the mountains. The large plain in between, mod. Mesaoria, consists of Neocene marl with deposits of sandstone and conglomerate, at times taking the form of isolated, steep table mountains as the product of erosion. The largest river is the → Pediaeus, mod. Pedieos, which together with the Yialias flows through the Mesaoria in an easterly direction; however, it frequently runs dry. Even in antiquity, C. was notorious for its particularly hot climate (Mart. 9,90,9). Precipitation — only in winter — is at the lower end of the average for the eastern Mediterranean. But the fertility of the island was much praised by ancient authors (Aesch. Supp. 555; Str. 14,6,5; Ael. NA 5,56; Amm. Marc. 14,8,14). → Aphrodite allegedly emerged from the sea on C.'s southern shore; her most famous sanctuary in antiquity was located in → Paphos. In antiquity, the island was rich in forests (Str. loc. cit.; Amm. Marc. loc. cit.) and thus an important supplier of wood for shipbuilding (→ Wood) and the smelting of ores. → Copper in particular, found on the slopes of the Troodos and named after the island, was of great importance even as early as the 2nd millennium BC. Deposits of gold and silver are also mentioned in ancient sources (Aristot. fr. 266 Rose); in addition, C. supplied → asbestos and → salt. The most important towns along the north coast from east to west are Carpasia, Cerynea,

Lapethus, Soli, Marion, along the south coast from west to east Paphos, Curium, Amathus, Citium, Salamis, and in the centre of the island Tamessus, Idalium, Golgi. Ancient descriptions: Scyl. 103; Str. 14,6,1f.; Ptol. 5,14; Stadiasmus maris magni 297–317; Plin. HN 5,129–130.

II. History
A. History to the end of Hellenism B. Roman period C. Late antique and Byzantine period

A. History to the end of Hellenism

Neither the origin of the original population nor that of the → Cypriot language is clearly established. The oldest known settlements date back into the pre-Ceramic Neolithic (*c.* 7000/6800–6000 BC; for chronology see → Cyprus), followed by a culture with highly developed incised and painted pottery. Towards the end of the Chalcolithic, some artefacts displaying parallels with the south Anatolian culture and progress in metallurgy point to the presence of immigrants from that region; place names, too, show elements from 'Asia Minor' alongside a predominance of Greek ones. The extraction of copper, which began soon after, was important for the island, and was the foundation for its own metal tools industry [1]. Because of its geographical location and its mineral resources, C. was in close contact with its surrounding important cultural regions from the earliest period; despite these outside influences, however, it retained its own cultural identity into the Hellenistic period.

In the Oriental languages, the name of the island is → *Alashia*, Egyptian Alaša, Hebrew (after the inhabitants of the Phoenician city of → Citium) *Kittim*. Initially, there were few links to the Aegean and to Minoan Crete. For that reason, it is not clear whether the syllabic script, demonstrably from *c.* 1550 BC and similar to the Cretan (→ Linear A), was adopted from Crete (→ Cypro-Minoan scripts). Its continuation is the 'classical' Cypriot syllabic script [2], extant in inscriptions in the → Eteo-Cyprian language into the 4th cent. BC found in Amathus and other places (→ Cypriot script). The Greeks adopted this script and used it alongside the Greek one until the end of the 3rd cent. BC.

The intensification of relations with Greece is evident in the increasing import of late Mycenaean pottery from *c.* 1400 BC; however, the immigration of Greeks only began around 1200 BC in conjunction with the collapse of the → Mycenaean culture and the → Doric Migration. The mythical foundation of Cypriot cities by Greek heroes in the aftermath of the Trojan War (→ Trojan Myths) is a reflection of these events (Str. 14,6,3). Around and after 1200 BC, on C., too, a number of settlements were destroyed. The immigrants came from the Peloponnese, proven on the one hand by the dialect which is related to → Arcadian, on the other by place names such as Achaion Acte (Ἀχαιῶν ἀκτη) and Cerynea, Lacedaemon, Corone/Coronea, Asine

(Steph. Byz. s.v.), and Epidaurus (Plin. HN 5,130). Greek immigration was supplemented around 800 BC by Phoenicians concentrated in Citium, a Tyrian foundation (inscriptions: CIS 1 no. 10–96). Inscriptions from the time of Sargon II [3] and Asarhaddon [3. no. 690, 709] (8th and 7th cent. BC respectively) indicate that the island with its Assyrian name of *Jadnana* was divided into small principalities and at that time tributary to the Assyrians. Over the following cents., the hegemonic power changed [4. 9–79], but up to the annexation of C. by Ptolemy I, the individual city kingdoms endured, and from the end of the 6th cent. minted their own coins [5]. Only the lengthy inscription found at → Idalium provides unique evidence for the existence in the 5th cent. BC of democratic institutions within a monarchy [2. 235–244]. From the end of the 7th cent. BC, Egypt increasingly influenced C.'s culture and politics; military campaigns against the island were undertaken by the pharaohs Apries and Amasis, with the result that C. was conquered (Diod. Sic. 1,68,1; 6; Hdt. 2,182,2).

In the archaic epoch, the island experienced a renewed bloom; its culture was characterized by the amalgamation of influences from Greece, Asia Minor and Egypt [6]. This is not only evident in the numerous imports, but more importantly in the indigenous art and its products. Architecture in particular experienced a boom, as did sculpture with artefacts made from clay and limestone, and vase painting in an orientalizing style [7]. From the last quarter to the end of the 6th cent., C. was under the rule of the Persian empire [8]. C. provided an important naval contingent; Cypriot kings thus participated with 150 ships in → Xerxes' campaign against Greece, before which most of Ionian cities had unsuccessfully risen against the Persians in the → Ionian Revolt. Equally unsuccessful were Athens' repeated attempts at having the island join the → Delian League, as e.g. for Cimon's campaign in 450 BC. In the early 4th cent. BC, → Evagoras [1] I of Salamis tried, but failed, to extend his rule across the entire island and gain its independence from the Persian empire [9]. A renewed uprising in 350 BC was quelled by Artaxerxes III in 344. During the siege of Tyre, C. joined forces with Alexander the Great. As early as 321 BC, four Cypriot kings entered an alliance with Ptolemy I, who defended the island successfully against Antigonus [1] Monophthalmos and, after temporarily losing control over the island to → Demetrius [2] Poliorcetes in 306 BC, recaptured C. in 294.

The royal houses of C. did not survive these struggles. To the end of the Ptolemaic kingdom, the island remained continuously under its rule; for a time during the dynastic disputes of the 2nd and 1st cents., it formed a subordinate kingdom in its own right. Ptolemaic rule was assured by occupational forces within the various cities; the administration lay in the hands of a governor, initially residing in Salamis, from the 1st cent. BC in Nea-Paphos, who was also the naval commander and high priest of the island [10]. During this period, the Phoenician and Eteo-Cyprian languages vanished, along with the syllabic script. Theatres, gymnasia, and temples changed the face of cities and sanctuaries. The rulers tried to influence the increasing → Hellenization; thus three new cities bearing the name Arsinoe were founded under Ptolemy II (285–224), and cults for the ruling dynasty instituted [11].

B. ROMAN PERIOD
In 58 BC, C. was annexed by Rome, and finally in 30 BC became the Roman province of → C.   E.MEY. and R.SE.

C. LATE ANTIQUE AND BYZANTINE PERIOD
Following a number of earthquakes in the 4th cent. AD, the provincial capital was moved from → Paphos to → Salamis, and the latter renamed Constantia in honour of emperor Constans II. In the Church, C. was initially under the patriarchy → Antioch [1], but in AD 488 was declared autocephalous (and still is). From 649, C. was frequently the target of Arab attacks. A Byzantine-Arab treaty conveyed a status of neutrality to the island in 680, stipulating that the tax revenue was to be shared and that the ports should be open to either power. With the exception of a short period under Byzantine rule from 874 to 878 (?) — in spite of serious violations by both sides on numerous occasions — this status continued until the recapture of the island by Byzantium in 965. The population remained predominantly Greek, but in the south-west of the island there were some Arab settlements. C. achieved independence in 1184, but in 1191, in the course of the 3rd Crusade, it fell into the hands of the crusaders.   AL.B.

III. EXPLORATION
In the 19th cent., many sites had been unsystematically searched by travellers and amateur archaeologists, and the finds spread to museums all over the world; it was the Swedish Cyprus expedition 1927–1931 which laid the foundations for scientific exploration of C.'s ancient culture. Today, a number of international teams work on C. alongside the island's own archaeological service. For the archaeology, see → Cyprus [1] and [2].
→ Phoenician; CYPRUS

1 H. MATTHÄUS, Metallgefäße und Gefäßuntersätze der Brz., der geom. und archa. Periode auf Cypern (Prähistor. Br.-Funde, Abt. 2,8), 1985   2 MASSON   3 D.D. LUCKENBILL, Ancient Records of Assyria and Babylonia 2, 1968, Index s.v. Jadanana   4 CHR. TUPLIN, Achaemenid Studies (Historia Einzelschr. 99), 1996   5 BMC, Gr Cyprus, 1904   6 A.T. REYES, Archaic Cyprus, 1994   7 V. KARAGEORGHIS, J. DES GAGNIERS, La céramique chypriote de style figuré, 1974   8 H.J. WATKIN, The Cypriote Surrender to Persia, in: JHS 107, 1987, 154–163   9 H. SPYRIDAKIS, Euagoras I. von Salamis, 1935   10 T.B. MITFORD, Helenos, Governor of Cyprus, in: JHS 79, 1959, 94–131   11 H. VOLKMANN, Der Herrscherkult der Ptolemäer in phönikischen Inschr. und sein Beitrag zur Hellenisierung von K., in: Historia 5, 1956, 448–455.

P. BOCCI, s.v. Cipro, EAA², 628–643; H.G. BUCHHOLZ, V. KARAGEORGHIS, Altägäis und Altkypros, 1971; S. CASSON, Ancient Cyprus, Its Art and Archaeology, 1937; A. CAUBET, La religion à Chypre dans l'antiquité, 1979; Id. et.al., Art antique de Chypre au Musée du Louvre, 1992; L. PALMA DI CESNOLA, Cyprus, Its Ancient Cities, Tombs and Temples, 1877; R. P. CHARLES, Le peuplement de Chypre dans l'antiquité, 1962; R. GUNNIS, Historic Cyprus, ²1947; A. HERMARY, Musée du Louvre. Département des antiquités orientales. Cat. des antiquités de Chypre. Sculptures, 1989; G. HILL, A History of Cyprus 1, 1940; D. G. HOGARTH, Devia Cypria, 1889; V. KARAGEORGHIS, Cyprus, 1982; Id. (ed.), Archaeology in Cyprus. 1960–1985, 1985; Id. (ed.), Acts of the International Symposium: Cyprus between the Orient and Occident, Nicosia 1985, 1986; F. G. MAIER, Cypern, ²1982; MASSON; O. MASSON, M. SZNYCER, Récherches sur les Phéniciens à Chypre, 1971; J. L. MYRES, The Metropolitan Museum of Art, Handbook of the Cesnola Collections of Antiquities from Cyprus, 1914; E. OBERHUMMER, Die Insel Cypern, 1903; Id., s.v. K., RE 12, 59–117; M. OHNEFALSCH-RICHTER, K., die Bibel und Homer, 1893; M.H. OHNEFALSCH-RICHTER, Griech. Sitten und Gebräuche auf Cypern, 1913; E. PELTENBURG (ed.), Early Society in Cyprus, 1989; E. GJERSTADT et.al. (ed.), The Swedish Cyprus Expedition, 1934ff.; V. TATTON-BROWN (ed.), Cyprus B.C., 7000 Years of History, 1979; C. VERMEULE, Greek and Roman Cyprus, 1976; C. WATZINGER, K., HdArch 1, 1939, 824–848.   E.MEY. and R.SE.

BYZANTINE PERIOD: R.J.H. Jenkins, Cyprus between Byzantium and Islam A.D. 688–965, in: G. E. MYLONAS (ed.), Studies Presented to D.M. Robinson, 1953, 1006–1014; E. MALAMUT, Les Îles de l'Empire byzantin VIIIᵉ-XIIᵉ siècles, 1988; A. A. M. BRYER, G. S. GEORGHALLIDES (ed.), The Sweet Land of Cyprus, Symposium Birmingham 1991, 1993.   AL.B.

IV. RELIGION

C.'s prehistoric religion is particularly evident in female statuettes, similar to those found in the Levant and in Anatolia; earliest examples of cult shrines dating from the 4th millennium BC point to differentiated religious activities within the village settlements [1. 108–124]. The Bronze Age saw the beginning of a religious iconography, in which (as in Minoan Crete) the bull is of great symbolic importance, pointing to links with Anatolia as well as with Minoan Crete [2]. It continued into the 1st millennium in the great number of votive offerings, but also in the bull-mask wearers featuring in Ovid's tale of the Cerastae in Amathus (Ov. Met. 10,220–237), which seem to be rooted in archaic notions of bull cults [3]. Here, too, numerous examples of sanctuaries from the 3rd as well as 2nd millennium provide an insight into the cultic activities of the still predominantly village-type settlements in the interior of the island. In the course of the 2nd millennium, a process of urbanization began along the coast, which in the second half of the millennium resulted in proper temple complexes such as those of Enkomi or → Citium (with copper production within the temple precinct). During the late Bronze Age, Aegean-Mycenaean as well as Le-

vantine settlers introduced their respective traditions into the culture of the island — flourishing despite all upheavals; its complexity is evident e.g. in the discussion of the 'Horned God' of Enkomi, linked with the Babylonian-Assyrian culture as well as with the Mycenaean-Greek one [1. 127–137].

Some of these Bronze Age traditions continue into the 1st millennium BC, despite the cultural break of around 1050 and the massive immigration of Egyptian-Greek and, in the second half of the 9th cent. BC, of Phoenician settlers, as evident in the architecture of some of the local sanctuaries (particularly the → Aphrodite temple in → Paphos, built around 1200 BC and in use into the Imperial period) [4. 28–32; 5]. However, the strong Levantine influence is particularly evident in the image of → Aphrodite with its close links to → Ištar and → Astarte: the image of → Baetylia; in the sacred prostitution, linked explicitly with the Assyrians in Hdt. 1,199 (→ Hierodouloi); or in an aetiological detail in Ovid's tale (Ov. Met. 698–764) of → Iphis and Anaxarete, set in the Cypriot Salamis and indicating strong roots in the Cypriot and Oriental Aphrodite cult [5]. After 850 BC, the largest Phoenician temple of Astarte was built in the ancient temple precinct of Citium. However, alongside these urban centres, numerous rural sanctuaries experienced a blossoming particularly during the 7th/6th cents. BC. Independent Cypriot developments of the archaic period included e.g. the large terracotta and limestome votive figurines [4. 32–40].

The Hellenization of the late archaic period also involved C.'s Phoenician deities; some characteristics of their cult, however, survived and were noted by local historians. During the Hellenistic period, the Aphrodite sanctuary of Paphos rose to a supraregional centre, famous in particular for divination of sacrifices (Tac. Hist. 2,3). In the wake of Jewish diaspora, Christianity soon gained a foothold on C.; → Paulus and Barnabas visited the island and preached 'in the synagogues of the Jews' of Salamis (Acts 13,5). In commemoration of a miracle in Paphos, a cathedral was built there in the early 4th cent., and in the course of the 4th cent., ascetic monasticism spread (Hier. Vita Hilarionis 30), supported by → Epiphanius [1], the bishop of Salamis.

1 E. PELTENBURG (ed.), Early Society in Cyprus, 1989
2 M. LOULLOUPIS, The Position of the Bull in Prehistoric Religions in Crete and Cyprus, in: Acts of the International Archaeological Symposium 'The Relations Between Cyprus and Crete, ca. 2000–500 BC', 1979, 215–222
3 GRAF, 415–417   4 A. T. REYES, Archaic Cyprus, 1994
5 W. FAUTH, Aphrodite Parakyptusa, 1967.   F.G.

[3] The island was incorporated into Roman possessions in 58 BC and remained part of the province of Cilicia until 48/47 BC. It was returned to the Ptolemaic kingdom by Caesar and Antony, and came permanently into Roman possession from 30 BC. As a province in its own rights, it was initially administered by a *legatus*, then from 22 BC by the Senate through an annually appointed *procurator*; following Diocletian's reorgani-

zation of the provinces, it was placed under the administration of the *consularis* of the *dioecesis Oriens* in Antioch [1] . After the initial financial exploitation of the island in the late Republican period, many buildings in the larger towns and sanctuaries bear witness to the prosperity enjoyed later in the imperial period. Devastations were only caused by the Jewish uprising of 115/16 and several earthquakes. After having been completely destroyed by an earthquake in AD 342, Salamis was rebuilt under the name of Constantia and replaced Paphos as the administrative centre. Christian mission (as early as AD 45 by Barnabas and Paulus) led to the foundation of the autocephaly of the Cypriot Church.

> G. HILL, A History of Cyprus 1, ²1972, 226–256; T. B. MITFORD, Roman Cyprus, in: ANRW II 7.2, 1980, 1285–1384.   R.SE.

Cypsela (Κύψελα; *Kýpsela, Cypsala*). Inland Thracian town on the lower left bank of the → Hebrus at the *via Egnatia* (Str. 7,7,4), in a very marshy area (Str. 7,7,4; 6; 7a,1,9f.; 48; 57), mod. Ipsala. In the 4th cent. BC, C. was residence and mint of the → Odrysae dynasty. Because it was in Ptolemaic possession, the town was besieged by → Antiochus [3] II in 254 BC (Polyaenus, Strat. 4,16); in *c.* 200 BC, it was taken by Philip V. In 188 BC, Cn. Manlius Vulso was attacked by Thracians near C. In the Byzantine period, C. was an important military base.

> A. FOL, Trakija i Balkanite prez ranno-elinisticeskata epoha, 1975, 9of., 107.   I.v.B.

Cypselides (Κυψελίδαι; *Kypselídai*). Dynasty of the Corinthian tyrant → Cypselus [2], who followed the → Bacchiadae around the mid 7th cent. BC. The rule of the C. (Cypselus, → Periander, → Psammetichus) was limited (probably post-event) by the Delphic oracle to Cypselus and his sons, and was supposed to end with the generation of his grandchildren (Hdt. 5,92e). According to Aristotle (Pol. 1315b 11ff.), the → tyrannis of the C. was the second longest lasting in Greece (73 ¹/₂ years). He explains this long duration with

Cypselus' popularity (cf. also Nicolaus of Damascus FGrH 90 F 57–60) and his son Periander's ability as a military leader, who in other ways, however, acted like a typical tyrant. The C. continued the trade policy of the Bacchiadae and intensified trade and commerce. Colonies or trading posts were set up, i.a. Leucas (Hdt. 8,45; Thuc. 1,30,2), Anactorium (Str. 10,452), and Ambracia (Str. 7,325; 10,452), perhaps also Potidaea. Periander's friendship with Thrasybulus of Miletus and his links with Alyattes of Lydia indicate an extension of the trading area towards Miletus and the Orient (Hdt. 1,20; 3,48). The interest in marriage alliances is evident in the marriage of a daughter of Cypselus to a member of the Attic Philaidae (indirectly Hdt. 6,128) and that of Periander to Melissa, daughter of Procles of Epidaurus (Hdt. 3,50).

The C. initiated building projects in → Corinthus / Corinth and in → Delphi. According to Herodotus (1,14), the Corinthian treasury in Delphi, in which the votive offering of Midas, Gyges, and Euelthon of Salamis were displayed (Hdt. 1,14; 4,162), was built by Cypselus; it is an indication of the extensive connections of the C., also evident in the Egyptian origin of the name of the last tyrant (Psammetichus). On numerous votive offerings, the C. are named as endowers, amongst them the → Cypselus chest in the temple of Hera in Olympia (Dion. Chrys. 11,45; Paus. 5,17,5–19,10), a golden bowl, also from Olympia (Boston, MFA), and a golden statue of Zeus (Agaklytos FGrH 411 F 1; Str. 8,3,30; 6,20; Plut. Mor. 400E; Paus. 5,2,3; Apellas FGrH 266 F 5).

> H. BERVE, Die Tyrannis bei den Griechen, 1967, 24, 32f., 47f., 69, 81; L. DE LIBERO, Die archa. Tyrannis, 1996, 137ff.; J. B. SALMON, Wealthy Corinth, 1984; E. WILL, Korinthiaka, 1955, 441ff.   B.P.

Cypselus (Κύψελος; *Kýpselos*).

[1] Son of → Aepytus [2], ruler of Arcadia at the time when the Heraclids attempted to invade the Peloponnese once more. He gave his daughter Mesope in marriage to → Cresphontes, Heraclid and king of Messenia, and was thus spared the invasion (Paus. 4,3,6; 8,5,6).   AL.FR.

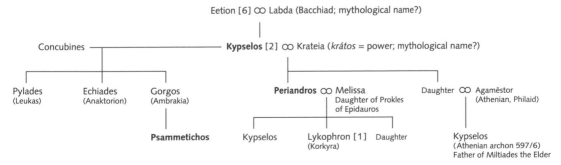

The Cypselids and their external connections.

[2] Tyrant of Corinth (probably 657–627 BC), son of Eëtion. He followed the → Bacchiadae, a group of ruling aristocrats, and established the first → tyrannis in Greece. His genealogy and the circumstances of his coming to power are distorted by legends. Through his mother Labda, he was allegedly related to the Bacchiadae. A positive oracle from Delphi predicted his assumption of power as a liberation from the ruling Bacchiadae. In an aetiological birth legend — following the pattern of the popular Ancient Oriental → exposure myth —, the child, under threat because of this oracle, was hidden in a beehive (*kypsélē*) by his mother and thus saved. A further oracle predicted that C. would be received in Delphi with royal honours and celebrated as the founder of the tyrannic dynasty of the → Cypselides (Hdt. 5,92b-e). The legends indicate a retrospective recognition of his usurpation and tyrannic dynasty as well as its support by Delphi. Later records (Nicolaus of Damascus FGrH 90 F 57 according to Ephoros) provide historical details, but they are coloured by the political terminology of the 4th cent. BC.
→ Cypselus chest

H. BERVE, Die Tyrannis bei den Griechen, 1967, 15ff., 522ff.; L. DE LIBERO, Die archa. Tyrannis, 1996, 138ff.; J. B. SALMON, Wealthy Corinth, 1984.   B.P.

Cypselus chest Container (*kypsélē, kibōtós, lárnax*) made from cedar wood decorated with ivory and gold plaques and carvings, described by Pausanias (5,17,5–

19,10) as a votive gift from → Cypselus [2] or the → Cypselides in the temple of Hera in Olympia. Legend declared the chest to be the vessel in which Cypselus [2] was saved from the Bacchiadae as a child, or rather as its replica. It was probably manufactured in the mid 6th cent. BC.

Because of the description provided by Pausanias, the Cypselus chest is an important source for the exploration of archaic imagery. Against the widespread notion of a rectangular chest, a reconstruction as a round vessel with five circular friezes is more plausible. The central register showed parading warriors. Both above and below it, mythical deeds, couples, and personifications were depicted on a metope frieze. The top and bottom registers were dedicated to heroic deeds and pairs of gods. Selection and sequence of the individual scenes were random; Trojan and Theban myths were represented, as are Theseus, Hercules, Perseus, Peleus, and Pelops. Annotations and epigrams made them easier to understand. Extant ivory plaques (→ Ivory carvings) of similar items in Delphi give some idea of the appearance of the Cypselus chest.

E. SIMON, in: EAA 4, 427–432; E. BRÜMMER, Griech. Truhenbehälter, in: JDAI 100, 1985, 85–89; L. LACROIX, Pausanias, le coffre de Kypsélos et le problème de l'exégèse mythologique, in: RA 1988, 243–261; K. SCHEFOLD, Götter- und Heldensagen der Griechen in der früh- und hocharcha. Kunst, 1993, 187–192.   R.N.

Addenda

Abacus

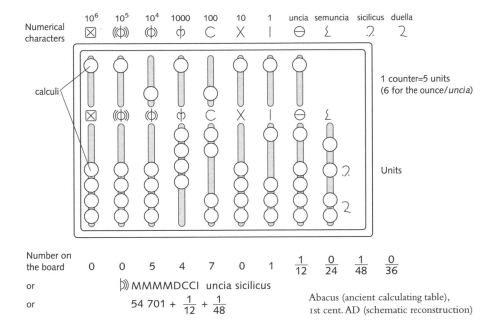

Numerical characters	10^6	10^5	10^4	1000	100	10	1	uncia	semuncia	sicilicus	duella
	⊠	(((φ)))	(φ)	φ	C	X	I	⊖	⊊	⁖	2

1 counter=5 units
(6 for the ounce/*uncia*)

Units

Number on the board	0	0	5	4	7	0	1	$\frac{1}{12}$	$\frac{0}{24}$	$\frac{1}{48}$	$\frac{0}{36}$

or   ⅅ MMMMDCCI uncia sicilicus

or $54\,701 + \frac{1}{12} + \frac{1}{48}$

Abacus (ancient calculating table),
1st cent. AD (schematic reconstruction)

Baptism
I. NON-CHRISTIAN II. EVOLUTION OF THE CHRISTIAN BAPTISM III. IMPORTANCE IN CHRISTIAN LIFE IV. BAPTISM RITUAL

I. NON-CHRISTIAN

There are analogies to the Christian baptism (βάπτισμα; *báptisma* or βαπτισμός; *baptismós*, Lat. *baptisma* or *baptismus*) in the history of other religions: rituals involving immersion in, or sprinkling with water and cleansing rituals were widespread prior to and alongside Christianity. However, these rituals followed different procedures and were interpreted differently, even though from the Christian point of view they were seen as a satanic mockery of the Christian baptism (Tert. De baptismo 5). Ritual baths were part of the Isis cult (→ Isis II. E.). It is questionable, whether the → taurobolium, evident in the cults of Cybele (→ Cybele C. 2.) and → Mithras, was indeed a kind of baptism with bull's blood, as described by the Christian author Prudentius (Prud. Peristephanon 10,1011–1050). It has to be assumed that Judaism provided the most important impulses for the development of the Christian concept of baptism; however, in this instance, it is not the ritual ablutions and baths, which for the purpose of atonement could be repeated as often as required and which are also known from → Qumran, and neither is it the Jewish baptism of → proselytes (for the admission of gentiles), of which no documentary evidence exists prior to the period of the NT. Jesus' baptism by John the Baptist provided the clearest stimulus (Mt 3,13–17); the latter belonged to the wider sphere of Palestinian-Jewish baptismal movements (→ Mandaeans). For John, baptism was a unique act, a sign of repentance and remission of sins in view of the imminence of the kingdom of heaven (Mt 3,2). Jesus took on this message (Mt 4,17), but it is unlikely that he himself performed any baptisms (cf. however Jn 3,22; 4,1 f.). At the time of the NT, John's baptism remained in competition with the Christian one.

II. EVOLUTION OF THE CHRISTIAN BAPTISM

Baptism began to be practised — obviously in an adaptation of that performed by John — immediately after the formation of the first Christian communities; here, too, it was intended as forgiveness of sins (Rom 6,7) and a preparation for the imminent Kingdom of God. However, it was seen as a baptism with the spirit, as opposed to John's mere water baptism (Mt 3,11 f.; Jn 1,33; Acts 18,24–19,7). This was justified later by attributing to Jesus the call for mission and baptism (Mt 28,19; Mk 16,15 f.); added to this was a typological derivation from the OT, e.g. the Great Flood (Epistle of Barnabas 11; Tert. De baptismo 8). Baptism leads to a new life (Rom 6,4) and also into a spiritual community 'in Christ' (Gal 3,28); it is a rebirth (Tit 3,5; 1 Petr 1,3.23). Originally, baptism was performed 'on the' or 'in the name of Jesus (Christ)' (*eis to ónoma/en tôi onómati Iēsoû (Christoû)*, Acts 8,16; 10,48). Baptism permits partaking in Jesus' death and resurrection (Rom

6,3 f.). The formula quoted in Mt 28,19 — 'in the name of the Father, and of the Son, and of the Holy Ghost' — is a later development (cf. also Didache 7,1). However, baptism was always linked to the effect of the Holy Ghost on the life of believers (1 Cor 6,11).

III. IMPORTANCE IN CHRISTIAN LIFE

Baptism was based on the decision of the individual; the baptism of children is only evident from the beginning of the 3rd cent. AD (Tert. De baptismo 18,4 f.; Traditio Apostolica 21). From the 2nd. cent. AD, the view of baptism as the singular remission of sin (Herm. Mand. 4,3,1 f.) was modified by the development of a penitential system within the Church. In the 4th cent., it was quite common to postpone baptism until death was imminent, in order to make sure that no further sins could be committed afterwards (for an early opposing view, cf. Tert. De paenitentia 6,3). Initially, baptism was preceded only by a brief instruction (Acts 2,37–40), but by the beginning of the 3rd cent. this had developed into an institutionalized course (catechumenate) of up to three years' duration (Traditio Apostolica 17). If a catechumen was martyred, this was seen as a 'baptism of blood' (*baptisma sanguinis*, Cypr. Ad Fortunatum praef. 4; Tert. De baptismo 16,1 f.; cf. Mk 10,38; → Martyrs). The immediate preparation for baptism included ascetic exercises, prayers, and repeated examination of the worthiness of the candidate. Spiritualist movements (→ Gnosis C., → Messalians) saw baptism as less important (cf. Iren. Adversus haereses 1,21), because it could not reach its full potential impact without understanding or additional spiritual experiences. In the early Christian understanding, baptism also means 'divine inspiration' (Clem. Al. Paedagogus 1,26,1 f.). Gnostics saw the use of matter (water) in baptism as problematic (Tert. De baptismo 1). From the 3rd cent., the question whether to recognize baptisms carried out by 'hereticss' became a contentious issue (→ Heresy; → Schism); this was rejected by → Cyprianus [2].

IV. BAPTISM RITUAL

For the beginning of the 3rd cent BC, the following elements of the baptismal ritual are confirmed by Tertullian and the *Traditio Apostolica*: prayer over the baptismal water, renunciation of the devil (*abrenuntiatio diaboli*), the actual baptism, anointment all over the body, laying-on of hands with prayer, first participation in the eucharist. The chrism was seen as the medium of the Holy Ghost. Baptisms were generally performed in Easter night by the bishop, who was assisted by priests and deacons. The actual act of baptism consisted of pouring water on, or (more rarely) immersing the candidate three times, each time with the question whether he believed in God the Father, the Son and the Holy Ghost. The creed (→ Baptism, symbol of) was spoken by the celebrant, the candidate replied affirmatively. Immediately before or after Easter, this was followed by 'mystagogical' catechesis (→ Cyrillus [1] of Jerusalem, → Ambrosius), instructing the candidates on the deeper mysteries of the Christian sacraments. From the 4th cent., confirmation as the anointment and laying-on of hands by the bishop became separate from the actual baptism ritual; from then on, the baptism of children became increasingly common and the preparatory catechesis shorter or abandoned altogether. Separate baptisteries apart from the main body of the church are evident from as early as the 3rd cent. (→ Dura-Europos). The Christian understanding of baptism finds its expression in cross-shaped or octagonal (symbol of eternal life) fonts (increasingly evident from the 5th cent.).

→ Sacramentum; → Sethianism; → Baptism, symbol of

A. BENOÎT, CH. MUNIER, Die Taufe in der Alten Kirche (1.–3. Jh.), 1994; G. KRETSCHMAR, Die Gesch. des Taufgottesdienstes in der Alten Kirche (Leiturgia 5), 1970; L. HARTMANN, Auf den Namen des Herrn Jesus, 1992; S. RISTOW, Frühchristl. Baptisterien (JbAC Ergbd. 27), 1998; K. RUDOLPH, Ant. Baptisten, 1981.   K. FI.

Baptism, symbol of. Symbols of baptism are the professions of faith (= creed), which were spoken during or in conjunction with a → baptism. The assumption of older scholars that NT professions of faith such as Rom 10,9 or Phil 2,11 were connected with baptisms, are not supported by any documentation apart from a single interpolation dating from the late 2nd cent. (Acts 8,37). Set formulae for the profession of faith during baptism are documented from the early 3rd cent., but originally they were not spoken by the celebrant himself. The earliest clear confirmation of the baptismal symbol (*symbolum* in this context is found first in Cyprianus [2] (†258): Epist. 75,10 f.); it consists of questions posed by the celebrant (→ Baptism IV.) regarding the profession of faith in the Trinitarian God. In the 2nd and 3rd cents., the creed was not yet a set formula, defining the contents of faith, but consisted of the *regula fidei* (κανὼν τῆς ἀληθείας/ *kanòn tês alētheías*), a didactic formula with local variations (Iren. Adversus haereses 1,22,1; Tert. Adversus Praxean 2,2,1), upon which the candidate could be bound in conjunction with his baptism (Iren. ibid. 1,9,4).

Declarational professions of faith, i.e. those professed by the candidate himself, are only evident from the 4th cent. (Cyrillus [1] of Jerusalem, Baptismal Catechesis 18,32). Augustine emphasized that the speaking of the creed was a custom originating in the city of Rome (Aug. Conf. 8,2,5), but it is also confirmed by Ambrose (Ambr. Explanatio symboli 3), as well as by Egeria (Aeth. 46): Before Easter, the creed was taught and explained to the catechumens (*traditio symboli*). They learned it by heart and recited it publicly, but before the actual baptism ritual was performed (*redditio symboli*). In the West, the ritual frequently remained nonetheless limited to the consent to the baptismal questions (Ambr. De sacramentis 2,20); only gradually it became common practice during baptism that the 'Roman creed' (*Romanum*) or respectively in the Mid-

dle Ages the 'Apostolic creed' (*Apostolicum*) was spoken. In the East, the → Nicaeno-Constantinopolitanum became the normative baptismal profession of faith.
→ Baptism

A. HAHN, Bibl. der Symbole und Glaubensregeln der Alten Kirche, 1897; J.N. D. KELLY, Early Christian Creeds, ³1989; W. KINZIG, CH. MARKSCHIES, M. VINZENT, Tauffragen und Bekenntnis, 1999; A.M. RITTER, s.v. Glaubensbekenntnis(se) V.3., TRE 13, 404–408.   K.FI.

Blessing (Hebrew *bᵉrakā*, Greek εὐλογία/*eulogía*, Latin *benedictio*); its original OT meaning refers to a 'power that engenders grace'. The passive *bārūk* ('blessed') refers to the state of possessing it, without the implication that this had to be preceded by an actual act of blessing [1.355]. *Bārūk* can also refer to the creator of a situation of grace , who could be human or God, and who is thus praised as being endowed with the power of grace (e.g. 1 Chr 29,10 and passim). For that reason, in the OT the verb *berak* not only means 'to bless', but often also 'to praise' and 'to give thanks to'. Amongst fellow men, *berak* can also simply mean 'wishing good luck'; thus a 'blessed man' is also a fortunate one. This meaning is illustrated in the story of Jacob's blessing by Isaac. It demonstrates how the final farewell between people is very much seen as a causative process: the blesser is

fortified with a meal, thus increasing his strength to turn the recipient of his blessing into someone with the power of grace (*bārūk*) (Gen 27,19). In early Judaism, blessing was increasingly understood as a sign of God's acceptance of an individual. In the Jewish-Hellenistic tale of Joseph and Aseneth (→ Novel IV.), the blessing is evidence of Aseneth's unconditional recognition by God and thus his acceptance into the Jewish community [2.40]. This also applies to the NT understanding of blessing. Εὐλογεῖν (*eulogeîn*, 'to bless') is predominantly used in conjunction with the praise of God. Blessing is the expression of being part of God's covenant with his people [3]. Blessing thus fulfils a social function, insofar as the blessed enters a union with both God and the congregation. The table grace, a praise of God over bread and wine, is greatly important for the development of the eucharistic prayer within the early Christian liturgy.

1 C.A. KELLER, G. WEHMEIER, s.v. ברך brk pi. segnen, in: E. JENNI, C. WESTERMANN (ed.), Theologisches HWB zum AT 1, 1971, 353–376   2 A. OBERMANN, An Gottes Segen ist allen gelegen, 1998   3 M. FRETTLÖH, Theologie des Segens, 1998.   LUK.KU.